For Reference

Not to be taken from this room

ENCYCLOPEDIA OF WORLD DRESS AND FASHION

Volume 1

Africa

ENCYCLOPEDIA WORLD

OF
DRESS
AND FASHION

ROGERS MEMORIAL LIBRARY

Volume 1

Africa

Edited by Joanne B. Eicher and Doran H. Ross

OXFORD
UNIVERSITY PRESS

2010

OXFORD

UNIVERSITY PRESS

Oxford University Press, Inc., publishes works that further
Oxford University's objective of excellence
in research, scholarship, and education.

Oxford   New York
Auckland   Cape Town   Dar es Salaam   Hong Kong   Karachi
Kuala Lumpur   Madrid   Melbourne   Mexico City   Nairobi
New Delhi   Shanghai   Taipei   Toronto

With offices in
Argentina   Austria   Brazil   Chile   Czech Republic   France   Greece
Guatemala   Hungary   Italy   Japan   Poland   Portugal   Singapore
South Korea   Switzerland   Thailand   Turkey   Ukraine   Vietnam

© Berg Publishers 2010

Published by Oxford University Press, Inc.
198 Madison Avenue, New York, NY 10016
http://www.oup.com/us/

Oxford is a registered trademark of Oxford University Press

Published simultaneously outside North America by Berg Publishers.

The Library of Congress Cataloging-in-Publication Data

Encyclopedia of world dress and fashion.

v. cm.

"Published simultaneously outside North America by Berg Publishers"–V. 1, t.p. verso.

"Available online as part of the Berg Fashion Library"–V. 1, t.p. verso.

Includes bibliographical references.

Contents: v. 1. Africa / editors, Joanne B. Eicher, Doran H. Ross – v. 2. Latin America and the Caribbean /
editor, Margot Blum Schevill ; consulting editor, Blenda Femenías – v. 3. The United States and Canada /
editor, Phyllis Tortora ; consultant, Joseph D. Horse Capture – v. 4. South Asia and Southeast Asia /
editor, Jasleen Dhamija – v. 5. Central and Southwest Asia / editor, Gillian Vogelsang-Eastwood –
v. 6. East Asia / editor, John Vollmer – v. 7. Australia, New Zealand, and the Pacific Islands /
editor, Margaret Maynard – v. 8. West Europe / editor, Lise Skov ; consulting editor, Valerie Cumming –
v. 9. East Europe, Russia, and the Caucasus / editor, Djurdja Bartlett ; assistant editor, Pamela Smith –
v. 10. Global perspectives / editor, Joanne B. Eicher ; assistant editor, Phyllis Tortora.

ISBN 978-0-19-537733-0 (hbk.)

1. Clothing and dress–Encyclopedias.   I. Eicher, Joanne Bubolz.   II. Oxford University Press.

GT507.E54   2010

391.003—dc22   2010008843

ISBN 978-0-19-975728-2 (vol. 1)
ISBN 978-0-19-975729-9 (vol. 2)
ISBN 978-0-19-975730-5 (vol. 3)
ISBN 978-0-19-975731-2 (vol. 4)
ISBN 978-0-19-975732-9 (vol. 5)
ISBN 978-0-19-975733-6 (vol. 6)
ISBN 978-0-19-975734-3 (vol. 7)
ISBN 978-0-19-975735-0 (vol. 8)
ISBN 978-0-19-975736-7 (vol. 9)
ISBN 978-0-19-975737-4 (vol. 10)

1 3 5 7 9 8 6 4 2

This Encyclopedia is available online as part of the Berg Fashion Library.
For further information see www.bergfashionlibrary.com.

Typeset by Apex CoVantage, Madison, WI.
Printed in the USA by Courier Companies Inc., Westford, MA.

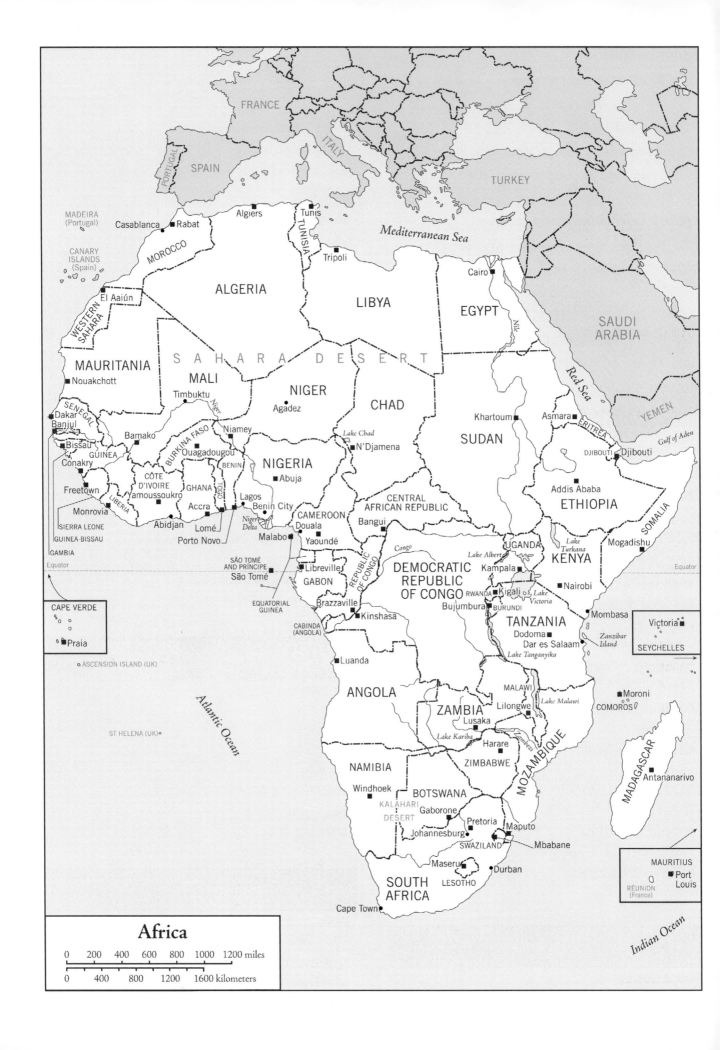

FRANCE

PORTUGAL

SPAIN

ITALY

TURKEY

Mediterranean Sea

MADEIRA
(Portugal)

Casablanca • Rabat

Algiers

Tunis

TUNISIA

Tripoli

Cairo

SAUDI
ARABIA

CANARY
ISLANDS
(Spain)

El Aaiún

MOROCCO

ALGERIA

LIBYA

EGYPT

Nile

Red Sea

WESTERN
SAHARA

S A H A R A   D E S E R T

YEMEN

MAURITANIA

MALI

NIGER

CHAD

Khartoum

Asmara

ERITREA

Gulf of Aden

Nouakchott

Timbuktu

Agadez

SUDAN

DJIBOUTI • Djibouti

Niger

SENEGAL

Dakar
Banjul

Bamako

Niamey

BURKINA FASO

Ouagadougou

BENIN

Lake Chad

N'Djamena

Addis Ababa

ETHIOPIA

Bissau

GUINEA

Conakry

CÔTE
D'IVOIRE

GHANA

NIGERIA

Abuja

CENTRAL
AFRICAN REPUBLIC

SOMALIA

Freetown

Yamoussoukro

Accra

TOGO

Lagos

Benin City

Bangui

Mogadishu

Monrovia

LIBERIA

Abidjan

Lomé

Porto Novo

*Niger
Delta*

Malabo

CAMEROON

Douala

Yaoundé

Congo

UGANDA

Lake Albert

*Lake
Turkana*

KENYA

SIERRA LEONE

GUINEA-BISSAU

GAMBIA

Equator

SÃO TOMÉ
AND PRÍNCIPE

São Tomé

Libreville

GABON

EQUATORIAL
GUINEA

REPUBLIC
OF CONGO

DEMOCRATIC
REPUBLIC
OF CONGO

Kampala

RWANDA

Kigali

BURUNDI

Bujumbura

*Lake
Victoria*

Nairobi

Mombasa

Equator

CAPE VERDE

Praia

Brazzaville

Kinshasa

TANZANIA

Dodoma

Dar es Salaam

*Zanzibar
Island*

Victoria

SEYCHELLES

ASCENSION ISLAND (UK)

CABINDA
(ANGOLA)

Luanda

Lake Tanganyika

Atlantic Ocean

ANGOLA

MALAWI

Lilongwe

Lake Malawi

Moroni

COMOROS

ST HELENA (UK)

ZAMBIA

Lusaka

Lake Kariba

Harare

Zambezi

MOZAMBIQUE

MADAGASCAR

Antananarivo

NAMIBIA

ZIMBABWE

Windhoek

KALAHARI
DESERT

BOTSWANA

Gaborone

Pretoria

Johannesburg

Maputo

SWAZILAND

Mbabane

MAURITIUS

RÉUNION
(France)

Port
Louis

Maseru

LESOTHO

Durban

SOUTH
AFRICA

Cape Town

Indian Ocean

Africa

0   200   400   600   800   1000   1200 miles

0   400   800   1200   1600 kilometers

Contents

Publishing, Editorial and Production Staff

Project Manager

Sarah Waldram

Head of Production

Ken Bruce

Publishing Assistants

Louise Butler
Helen Caunce
Augusta Dörr

E-content and Systems Managers

Helen Toone
Fanny Thépot

Production Editor

Jonathan Mazliah

Maps

Martin Lubikowski, ML Design

Managing Director

Kathryn Earle

Editorial Manager

Janet Phillips

Editorial Administrators

Angela Greenwell
Amy Laurens

Editorial Assistant

Jessica Hobbs

Freelance Editors

Andrea Belloli
Fiona Corbridge
Catherine Foley
Julene Knox
Fintan Power

Project Managers, Apex CoVantage

Emily Johnston
Julia Rosen

Consultant

Sylvia K. Miller

Picture Researcher

Sophie Basilevitch

Picture Assistants

Aisling Hanrahan
Simon Reid

Interns

Cecilia Bertilsson
Lacey Decker
Sian Jones
Kimberly Manning
Maria Sarnowska
Nina Schipper
Cathryn Steele

Freelance Proofreading Manager

Timothy DeWerff

Head of Sales and Marketing

Jennifer Howell

Contributors

Rowland Abiodun, *Amherst College, United States*

Joseph C. E. Adande, *Université d'Abomey Calavi, Benin*

Agbenyega Adedze, *Illinois State University, United States*

Heather Marie Akou, *Indiana University, United States*

E. J. Alagoa, *University of Port Harcourt, Nigeria*

Martha G. Anderson, *Alfred University, United States*

Mary Jo Arnoldi, *National Museum of Natural History, Smithsonian Institution, United States*

Lisa Aronson, *Skidmore College, United States*

Cynthia J. Becker, *Boston University, United States*

Rayda Becker, *Independent Scholar, South Africa*

Barbara W. Blackmun, *San Diego Mesa College, United States*

Elisabeth L. Cameron, *University of California, Santa Cruz, United States*

Clara Carvalho, *ISCTE (Lisbon University Institute), Portugal*

Meriem Chida, *Philadelphia University, United States*

Herbert M. Cole, *University of California, Santa Barbara, United States*

Kathy Curnow, *Cleveland State University, United States*

Patricia Davison, *Iziko Museums of Cape Town, South Africa*

LaRay Denzer, *Northwestern University, United States*

Margaret A. Deppe, *University of Minnesota, United States*

William J. Dewey, *University of Tennessee, United States*

Remi Douah, *University of Minnesota, United States*

Deborah Durham, *Sweet Briar College, United States*

Joanne B. Eicher, *University of Minnesota, United States*

Francine Farr, *Montgomery College, United States*

Christraud M. Geary, *Museum of Fine Arts, United States*

Suzanne Gott, *University of British Columbia-Okanagan, Canada*

Walter Hawthorne, *Michigan State University, United States*

Hildi Hendrickson, *Long Island University, United States*

Rachel Jean-Baptiste, *University of Chicago, United States*

Curtis A. Keim, *Moravian College, United States*

Susan M. Kenyon, *Butler University, United States*

Ruth Kerkham Simbao, *Rhodes University, South Africa*

Lombuso Khoza, *University of Maryland Eastern Shore, United States*

Michelle Kisliuk, *University of Virginia, United States*

Peri M. Klemm, *California State University, United States*

Sandra Klopper, *University of Pretoria, South Africa*

Judith Knight, *Dress Scholar, United Kingdom*

Corinne A. Kratz, *Emory University, United States*

Frederick John Lamp, *Yale University, United States*

Babatunde Lawal, *Virginia Commonwealth University, United States*

Juliette Leeb-du Toit, *University of KwaZulu-Natal, South Africa*

Kristyne Loughran, *Independent Scholar, Italy*

John Mack, *University of East Anglia, United Kingdom*

Jane Martin, *Independent Scholar, United States*

Marie-Amy Mbow, *Université Cheikh Anta Diop, Senegal*

Kimberly Miller, *Wheaton College, Massachusetts, United States*

Justin Serge Mongosso, *Independent Scholar, United States*

Hudita Nura Mustafa, *Harvard University, United States*

Venny Nakazibwe, *Makerere University, Uganda*

Sylvia Nannyonga-Tamusuza, *Makerere University, Uganda*

Rehema Nchimbi, *University of Dar es Salaam, Tanzania*

Mohamed N'Daou, *Chicago State University, United States*

Enrique Okenve, *University of the West Indies-Mona, Jamaica*

Simon Ottenberg, *University of Washington, United States*

Manuel Jordán Pérez, *Dress Scholar, United States*

Louis P. Perrois, *Institut de Récherche pour le Développement, France*

John Picton, *School of Oriental and African Studies, University of London, United Kingdom*

Philip W. Porter, *University of Minnesota, United States*

Fiona Rankin-Smith, *University of the Witwatersrand, South Africa*

Tineke Rooijakkers, *Textile Research Centre and Leiden University, the Netherlands*

Doran H. Ross, *Fowler Museum, University of California, Los Angeles, United States*

Victoria L. Rovine, *University of Florida, United States*

Christopher D. Roy, *University of Iowa, United States*

Judith Scheele, *University of Oxford, United Kingdom*

Enid Schildkrout, *Museum for African Art, United States*

Brenda Schmahmann, *Rhodes University, South Africa*

Kathleen Sheldon, *University of California, Los Angeles, United States*

Thadeus Shio, *Ardhi University, Tanzania*

Fred T. Smith, *Kent State University, United States*

Barbara Sumberg, *Museum of International Folk Arts, United States*

Gary Van Wyk, *Axis Gallery, United States*

Gillian Vogelsang-Eastwood, *Textile Research Centre and the National Museum of Ethnology, the Netherlands*

Michele D. Wagner, *Independent Scholar, United States*

Betty Wass El-Wakil, *University of Wisconsin–Madison, United States*

Norma H. Wolff, *Iowa State University, United States*

Encyclopedia Preface

The *Encyclopedia of World Dress and Fashion* covers a fundamental and universal human activity relating to personal and social identity—the vast topic of how more than six billion people dress across the globe. To accomplish this, the first nine volumes are organized geographically, and the tenth addresses global issues. The approach throughout is both cross-cultural and multidisciplinary and allows readers to appreciate the richness and complexity of dress in all its manifestations. However, even a ten-volume encyclopedia must limit itself in either time or geography in order to provide in-depth scholarship. The focus is therefore on the nineteenth to the early twenty-first centuries, although overview materials covering the long history of dress have been included to provide essential context, as is appropriate in so ambitious a scholarly undertaking.

Many disciplines have developed an interest in dress studies, underscoring the need for a major reference work with a broad scope. The range of interpretations will help readers develop a critical understanding of cultural practices. The intended audience for the *Encyclopedia* is broad and encompasses general and curious readers as well as students and teachers in the humanities and social sciences, in short, anyone interested in the full spectrum of issues relating to dress in a given time and place. More specialized researchers in anthropology, apparel design, art and cultural history, cinema, cultural studies, dance and drama, fashion, folklore, history, and sociology will also find the *Encyclopedia* an invaluable reference.

Dress, costume, and *fashion* are often used interchangeably in common parlance, but this work makes crucial distinctions between them because terminology is important. The aim of this preface is to clarify for readers the distinctions that have been drawn throughout this particular project by the editors and contributors, in order to achieve scholarly consistency across the work. Contributors were asked to define *dress* as any supplement or modification to the body, the purpose of which is either to cover or to adorn. Dress is a broad category that includes costume and fashion, with the term *costume* defined as a specific type of dress that is worn for theatrical, dance, or masquerade performances. *Costume* is frequently used by many distinguished museum curators and scholars in connection with both the historical study and the display of clothing in a general way. In contrast to dress, which ordinarily expresses a wearer's identity, costume hides or conceals it in various degrees. *Fashion* is defined as changes relating to body modifications and supplements, usually easily perceived and tracked, often within short periods of time.

While fashions may have permanent consequences with respect to an individual (as in the case of tattooing, for example), most are characterized by impermanence within the larger socioeconomic or fashion system (a complex process by which changing fashions in dress spread through formal and/or informal channels of design, manufacture, merchandising, and communication).

Supplements to the body include conventional attire such as clothing, jewelry, and items typically called *accessories,* such as hats, shoes, handbags, and canes. Modifications include cosmetics, hair care (cutting, combing, and styling), scarification, tattooing, tooth filing, piercings, and gentle molding of the human skull or binding of feet (the latter two usually done during infancy). Thus, in many cultures where people display these modifications alone, a person can be unclothed but still dressed. In addition to visually oriented practices, the definition of *dress* acknowledges that all senses may be incorporated, not just the visual. Therefore, sound (for example, rustling or jingling), odor (perfumes or incense), touch (such as tight or loose, silky or rough), and even taste when applicable (some cosmetics, breath fresheners, and tobacco products) frequently feature in discussions.

Being dressed is a normative act because human beings are taught what is right and wrong in concealing and revealing the body and keeping it clean and attractive. Contributors to this encyclopedia primarily describe dress and explain how it is worn within specific cultural contexts, although, where it is likely to be helpful, they have been encouraged to embrace and explain theoretical approaches to the interpretation of dress (for example, postmodernism, psychoanalytic theory, semiotics, and queer theory). The geographic organization provides overviews by country. An attempt has been made to focus on all countries, but in some cases, qualified authors could not be found and an entry was regretfully omitted. Readers may, however, find references to a country in the volume and section introductions and in the index. Supplementing country essays are articles on types or categories of dress along with select articles on influential or particularly well-known ethnic groups. Shorter "snapshots" on specific topics serve as sidebars to longer articles. Volume 10 addresses issues of global interest relating to the first nine volumes and is divided into five main sections: Overview of Global Perspectives; Forms of Dress Worldwide; Dress and the Arts Worldwide; Fashion Worldwide; and Dress and Fashion Resources Worldwide. Inclusion of a timeline on the development of dress and related technologies is a special feature.

At the end of each article, a list of references and suggestions for further reading has been included. Where possible, cross-references to other relevant articles in the *Encyclopedia* have also been inserted. Each volume has its own index, and readers will find a cumulative index to the entire set in volume 10. Volumes 1 to 9 also each feature a regional map.

While it is tempting when writing on the body and dress to focus on the most spectacular or visually engaging examples of dress from a given culture, authors have been asked to balance their discussions between the ordinary dress of daily life and the extraordinary dress of special occasions. In both instances this includes protective clothing of various sorts as well as general distinctions between genders, among age groups and various vocations, and within other realms of social status, as defined by religion, wealth, and political position. Along with prehistoric and historical traditions of dress, authors have been charged with addressing contemporary fashions in their own areas of interest, as well as traditional dress forms. An important aim of the *Encyclopedia* is to show the full range and transformative power of dress in cultural exchanges that occur all over the world, of which the influence of Western fashion on other parts of the world is only one example.

The editor in chief recruited scholars with particular expertise in dress, textiles, and fashion in their geographic areas and a scholarly network to edit specific volumes, develop tables of contents, draft a descriptive scope for articles requested, and contact and commission contributors. (Some experts were not available to participate in contributing articles.) The ten volumes include 854 articles written by 585 authors residing in over 60 different countries. Authors had freedom to develop their articles but always with a general reader in mind. Scholarship around the world and in different disciplines has many approaches; this presents daunting challenges for authors, who were asked to employ a relatively broad but consistent definition of dress. As a result of a rigorous review and revision process, their work has resulted in a comprehensive compilation of material not found before in a reference work of this type. Their efforts allow readers to find the excitement, variety, sensuality, and complexity of dress presented in clear descriptions, reinforced by historical and cultural context. As much as possible, entries have been written by experts from within the culture being discussed. Each was assigned a certain number of words, determined by the volume editor and editor in chief in the context of the desired depth and balance of the *Encyclopedia* as a whole, and each followed instructions and guidelines developed by the editorial board and publisher. The structure of each volume also varies according to the editor's perspective, the constraints of the historical, political, and social configuration of the geographic area, and the research known to be available.

A variety of images have been included, from museum photographs that show detail, to anthropological photographs that show dress in action and context, to fashion and artistic images that help to convey attitudes and ideals. Many of these have come from the contributors' own fieldwork. The goal is that the variety of approaches and interpretations presented within the *Encyclopedia*'s architecture combine to create a worldwide presentation of dress that is more varied, less biased, and more complete than any heretofore published. Articles are extensively illustrated with 2,300 images—many seen here for the first time.

The process of conceiving of and completing the *Encyclopedia* took place over a number of years and involved much scholarly consultation among editors, contributors, and staff. The common goal demanded a flexible approach within a set framework, and such a balancing act presented a range of challenges. Doubtless some decisions could be argued at further length, but hopefully readers will find most were sensible, bearing in mind the daunting ambitions of the work. Specific terms for items of dress vary throughout the world, and such variation often also reflects regional differences in the item of dress itself. Where possible, the editors have worked with contributors and translators to preserve the closest regional spelling of the indigenous term for the area under discussion, bearing in mind also the necessity to translate or transliterate such terms into English, the language of publication. While the *Encyclopedia* cannot be perfectly complete and consistent, the goal has been to produce a landmark achievement for its scholarly standards and impressive scope. The editorial team has endeavored to present authoritative treatments of the subject, with the particular hope that readers will find in the *Encyclopedia*'s pages a measure of the excitement, fun, and fascination that characterize dress across time and cultures. Browsing or reading in depth, volume to volume, will provide readers with many examples of what people wear, whether mundane or marvelous, uniform or unique, commonplace or rare. The encyclopedia will continue to grow as articles on recent developments, new information, and research add to knowledge on dress and fashion in the online Berg Fashion Library.

The volume editors and contributors are gratefully acknowledged and thanked for their enthusiasm for and dedication to the enormous task that has culminated in this encyclopedia. Many thanks also go to the publisher and project management team, who have valiantly seen the project to its successful completion.

Joanne B. Eicher

Preface to Africa

African dress offers a spectacular kaleidoscope of forms, materials, textures, and colors, in some instances combined on a single human armature. Depending on time and place, coiffures may be sculpted into soaring shapes or compacted into intricate, tightly braided styles. Massive gold earrings eight inches (twenty centimeters) across are found in one culture, and elegant ivory ear spools in another. Amulet-laden war shirts contrast with intricate, message-bearing silk textiles. Lavish, multilayered robes characterize parts of the continent, and sophisticated, multipatterned beadwork predominates elsewhere. In addition, throughout much of Africa, virtuosic handwoven textiles coexist with affordable machine-woven, roller-printed cloths, the latter often borrowing designs and meanings from the former. While processions of traditionally adorned warriors, chiefs, and brides may still be seen, parades of uniformed soldiers, well-dressed politicians, and fashion models on runways are creating new traditions. And while influential print media have been in existence for well over a century, films, television, cell phones, and the Internet are all serving a barrage of globalizing fashion agendas in the early twenty-first century.

Until the second half of the twentieth century, few books focused in any detail on African dress, textiles, or fashion, whether in specific countries or on the continent as a whole. This volume is the first to describe, illustrate, and analyze what Africans have worn in the past, and do wear in the early twenty-first century, across a bewildering array of often-unfamiliar cultures and peoples. The intention is to stimulate readers with a general curiosity about Africa, as well as students and researchers who are looking for information about a particular country, group, textile, garment, or type of jewelry. This volume should also attract the attention of those with more specialized interests, such as a costume designer working on a play or film, or a writer attempting to evoke definitions of identity in a given place or time.

Scholars from such diverse disciplines as art history, history, anthropology, textiles and apparel, folklore, sociology, and geography have shared their knowledge. For the 85 articles within, 64 writers have contributed approximately 377,000 words and provided information for over 300 illustrations. In addition, many contributors are of African descent or are currently living in Africa. This volume covers the 53 continental countries of Africa plus the island nation of Madagascar. European colonial history and culture link the dress practices of the African island nations of Cape Verde (in the Atlantic Ocean, near Senegal), São Tomé/Príncipe (off the coast of Gabon), and Mauritius, Seychelles, and Comoros (all three in the Indian Ocean) to those of their colonizers. Because little detailed research about or descriptions of dress appear to be available, the islands are not included in this volume. Early scholarship on Africa often linked North Africa to the Middle East by emphasizing Arab populations, thus separating North Africa from "Black Africa," often known as sub-Saharan Africa. Recent scholarship demands that the continent of Africa be viewed in its totality, for non-Arab groups were indigenous to North Africa for millennia, and Arabs and Islamic cultures migrated south of the Sahara. In addition to country-by-country essays, articles within this volume also address topics that range across the continent, such as "Headdresses and Hairdos," "Beads and Beadwork," and "Footwear."

The volume begins by covering material that pertains to the continent as a whole: political and cultural history, categories of traditional and contemporary dress, and commentary on fashion and fashion designers. An overview of textiles across the continent concludes this introductory section. The majority of the volume is divided by geographic regions and by country within each region. An alternative system of organizing by peoples was decidedly unfeasible simply due to the sheer numbers. Specific peoples, however, may be located by consulting the index. Decisions about the length of the essays on each country depended on several factors, including population size and availability of research information. Although not all countries or ethnic groups are equally represented or described in the same detail, an effort was made to provide coverage that is as balanced as possible. Contributors helped frame an article's focus and have drawn from their own fieldwork and expertise as well as other documentation, such as evidence from early histories, explorers' or missionaries' accounts, anthropological monographs, photographs, drawings, and oral histories. In addition, articles on some countries with large metropolitan cities, such as Johannesburg, Lagos, and Cairo, provide data from newspapers and periodicals about fashion and dress over time.

This volume systematically attempts to organize information about how Africans engage the world in terms of dress choices, either for everyday wear or for special events, whether within the family or in public arenas. Features of the volume include cross-references, definitions of terms within the text, and an analytical index, as well as a substantial body of previously unpublished research.

We thank the support group at Berg Publishers. In addition, we would like to thank a number of people who helped at various stages along the way. Several colleagues stepped in to suggest writers for countries where we needed assistance: Shirley Ardener, Florence Bernault, Suzanne Blier, Janice Boddy, Tamara Giles-Vernick, Karen Hansen, Walter Hawthorne, Allen Isaacman, Wendy James, Douglas Johnson, Lansine Kaba, Sandra Klopper, Alisa LaGamma, Hudita Mustafa, Elisha Renne, and Ruth M. Stone. Other colleagues providing critical support were Marla Berns, Tom Seligmann, Elizabeth Semmelhack, and Amy Staples. Our colleague Fred Smith deserves a special thank you for producing an article requested at the last minute.

As a graduate research assistant, Meriem Chida helped with the beginning stages of organizing the table of contents and valiantly pursuing contributors. Megan Wannarka and Hilary Falk, project assistants, cheerfully undertook a variety of support tasks.

Becky Yust, department chair, Design, Housing, and Apparel, College of Design, University of Minnesota, steadfastly supplied office space and computer resources in McNeal Hall. All three Eicher daughters, Cynthia, Carolyn, and Diana, along with sons-in-law Blake Johnson and Andy Zink and six grandchildren, Wiley, Spencer, Keith, Isabella, Sabina, and Violet, shared this project during summers at the Eicher family cottage in Holland, Michigan, and in Saint Paul the rest of the year. Betsy H. B. Quick provided essential research and critical review, and Diane L. Ross offered crucial support throughout. Many thanks to all.

Joanne B. Eicher
Doran H. Ross

PART 1

Overview of Dress and Fashion in Africa

Introduction: The Study of African Dress

- Traditional Dress
- Effects of Colonialism
- Rural and Urban Differences
- Globalization, Contemporary Dress, and Fashion

Samburu warrior (*moran*) applying face paint and wearing ivory earspools and a beaded bracelet in the form of a watch. 1973. Photograph by Herbert M. Cole.

For readers familiar with Africa, this volume reinforces and expands knowledge about how Africans dress in the twenty-first century as well as in the near and distant past. For readers not informed or indeed misinformed about Africa, surprises may follow. Unfortunately, perceptions of dress in Africa are subject to more stereotypes than perhaps for the rest of the world. This has been fostered by images in popular literature and film, even in the early twenty-first century, in which African dress frequently has been depicted as primitive, exotic, salacious, and even savage, when, in fact, African traditions of dress are as sophisticated, complex, and visually compelling as those anywhere in the world.

Some basic facts about Africa have obvious implications for dress and its variety. The continent covers 20 percent of the earth's land surface, second after Asia's 30 percent. Africa spreads about five thousand miles (about eight thousand kilometers) in length from the Mediterranean coastline in the north to the Cape of Good Hope in the south, and about forty-six hundred miles (roughly seven thousand four hundred kilometers) in width from the Cape Verde Islands in the Atlantic on the west to the Horn of Africa projecting into the Indian Ocean on the east. Although Africa straddles the equator and 80 percent of its surface resides within the tropics, it nevertheless includes a variety of landscapes and climates. Geographic regions span from high mountains such as Kilimanjaro, deep rain forests such as the Ituri, nearly barren deserts such as the Sahara, and numerous sunny beaches. Nevertheless, more of the continent is warm or hot rather than cool or cold. The Sahara Desert, the largest in the world and about the size of the contiguous United States, is an increasingly dominant geographical feature of the continent.

Human origins are now conclusively traced to Africa in the current countries of Tanzania, Kenya, and Ethiopia. Although evidence of dress from those early finds is nonexistent, obviously these early humans began at some point to dress themselves. From that point on, the human body increasingly became an armature for a variety of resources. Marine shell beads in Africa date back at least two hundred thousand years, and a forty-thousand-year-old ostrich eggshell bead workshop has been excavated in Kenya. Also emerging early in the history of African dress was the practice of covering the human body with local materials readily at hand, easily constructed, and that allowed the body to keep cool or warm and dry. Still, geographic factors alone do not account for how individuals dress either on a daily basis or for special occasions such as funerals or masquerade performances. Cultural traditions and knowledge of current fashions often take precedence over climate or geography as discussed in "Climatic Zones and Cultural Regions." What becomes obvious, however, is that the reliance on the local natural environment for materials is diminished as most African groups begin contact with their neighbors and as imported items are incorporated as part of dress.

Africans in more than fifteen hundred ethnic and language groups have dressed from one extreme of wearing *no* attire of the sort that covers the body or indicates modesty from a Western point of view to being garbed in voluminous layered garments with splendid, often sumptuous, accessories. Regardless, individuals within their own culture were considered to be fully dressed. Peoples in areas where clothing was historically minimal, except for beads, chalk, body paint, leaves, and/or scarification, began, under the tenets of Islam, Christianity, and various colonial administrations, to cover their bodies more fully to conform to these foreign belief systems. This is a topic discussed in virtually every article on individual countries. Increasing familiarity with many types of media across the world since the twentieth century has accelerated change. Dress traditions that honor the past, however, continue in the twenty-first century side by side with (and, on select occasions, in preference to) contemporary dress and fashions

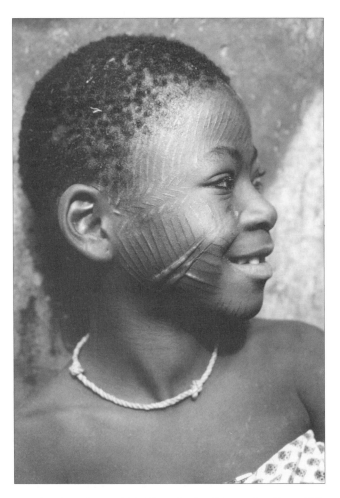

Young Nanakanse female with facial scarification. Sirigu, northern Ghana, 1972. Photograph by Herbert M. Cole.

in dressing the body in Africa as elsewhere. Africans engage in many conscious renewable acts that relate to appearance, sometimes subtly and other times dramatically: combing, cutting, and styling hair; applying oil, chalk, powders, scent, cosmetics, and paint to skin. More permanent alterations to the body include scarification, cicatrization, piercing, or tattooing.

Most people think of dress as clothing made from textiles. African textiles include a rich array of types and techniques. The development of looms and weaving was followed by dyeing and embellishing thread and cloth in various ways. In earlier times, bark cloth was produced in several countries, and, where weaving occurred, locally grown hand-spun and hand-dyed cotton initially was the primary resource. By the end of the nineteenth century, however, imported aniline dyes and machine-spun and commercially dyed thread became increasingly available. In addition, machine-made fabrics were imported for local hand-processing procedures such as the resist-dyed textiles of the Yoruba of Nigeria or the hand-stamped fabrics of the Asante of Ghana. While the textiles of Africa include such familiar materials as cotton, wool, flax, and silk, several essays in the volume address less familiar resources such as bark and raffia. Cloth in Africa is hand-woven on a wide variety of looms from the simple to the complex, and also machine woven in modern factories across the continent as outlined in many entries. Less familiar technologies include the cut and pulled thread cloths of the Kalabari in Nigeria and the ikat textiles of Madagascar.

TRADITIONAL DRESS

Discussions of dress in Africa often employ the word *tradition* to describe indigenous dress as arising from a set of practices repeated over time, often a very long time. Sometimes the word *custom* serves the same purpose. In both cases, but to the greatest degree with *tradition*, the implication is that the behaviors under consideration are monolithic and unchanging. The traditional and the customary are frequently juxtaposed with the modern when discussing African culture, which, in the past, has been emphatically defined as being traditional. But *tradition* may be among the most problematic words still used by Africanists, scholars of dress, and the general public. Tradition implies that something is bounded, confined, and limited, but these assumptions must be questioned. First of all, every tradition must begin at some point; that, in itself, requires a change from a preceding practice. In other words, traditions are built upon change. Second, all traditions are subject to change, so a bigger question is how much change is necessary to modify a tradition in order to become a new tradition? A third consideration is the fact that many traditions can be short-lived. Some exist only under the leadership of a given individual—perhaps a senior family member, religious leader, or head of state. When that individual is replaced or dies, the situation may be ripe for new traditions. Furthermore, for better or worse, the inauguration of a new tradition carries an expectation of longevity in contrast to the inauguration of a new fashion that carries an expectation of brevity. And finally, the unfortunate fact of most writing about Africa that contrasts the traditional with the modern is that tradition is often perceived to include everything that preceded substantial European or Arab contact.

These important issues arise when considering dress, because the European conception of African tradition is antithetical to the West's conception of what constitutes fashion in the

that indicate involvement in and commitment to being "modern." This is another leitmotiv running through the volume.

The broad definition of dress used for all volumes of the encyclopedia focuses on both supplementing and modifying the body. A beginning point is the "natural" human body and materials from the natural environment. Supplements in Africa include easily obtained materials such as leaves, palm fronds, hides, powder, or chalk and a wide variety of clothing types, particularly cloth used as wrappers and full-length robes. Jewelry from stone, bone, shell, ivory, seeds, coral, and amber is used extensively. In addition, copper, brass, iron, silver, gold, and even aluminum and glass have been worked through a wide variety of techniques into an array of spectacular forms. Both the clad and unclad body can be modified with complicated hairdos—braided, plaited, or sculpted with mud and decorated with various kinds of readily available shells, feathers, bones, and beads. Headwear of many styles from caps, derbies, crowns, helmets, turbans, veils, and other head ties sometimes protects the head, but more often indicates a specific status. Footwear ranges from minimal sandals to thigh-high boots. Other accessories of dress are particularly rich in Africa and include fans, fly whisks, pipes, bags, and canes. Ceremonial staffs, scepters, and especially weapons also receive considerable artistic attention. Royal umbrellas carried by an attendant date back at least one thousand years in West Africa. Sometimes overlooked as a category of dress, body modifications are equally important

Woman wearing handwoven cloth with multiple images of Amilcar Cabral, leader of the nationalist movement for the independence of Guinea-Bissau. Bissau, Guinea-Bissau, 1987. Photograph by Doran H. Ross.

was influential in formulating the final chapter of *The Arts of Ghana*, in which Herbert M. Cole and Doran H. Ross argued that for over four hundred years the Akan peoples aggressively pursued the new and unusual and rapidly incorporated both into their clothing, jewelry, and accessories. These include everything (in rough chronological order) from silk threads, locks and keys, firearms, Victorian jewelry design, European-style crowns, heraldic lions, rayon and Lurex threads, T-shirts, sneakers, and an enormous array of other influences spread throughout this history, almost as quickly as the Akan were exposed to them.

The Akan situation is probably different from most of the rest of Africa only by degree. The gold trade exposed them to a wide variety and quantity of new materials, designs, and object types, which provided a wider range of creative fashion opportunities generally not available to the same extent in other regions of the continent, with perhaps the exception of coastal North Africa. Akan trade contacts with Europeans in the south and Muslim states in the north were the first globalizing influences on their local textile design and clothing styles. In the nineteenth century, European print media began to provide an array of images that could serve as inspiration for changes in fashion, including tailored clothing. The electronic media of film, television, computers, and camera phones in the twentieth and twenty-first centuries has further accelerated opportunities to manipulate and transform what an African might wear, always creating new traditions in the process, some of which may survive for several generations, and some of which will disappear before 2020.

Beyond articulating the various types of indigenous dress, at least three important interrelated themes surface throughout the articles. Perhaps most fundamental and pervasive are the ongoing effects of colonialism on dress, a phenomenon dating back at least three thousand years in parts of Africa before the formal European takeovers in the late 1800s. Equally important is the distinction between rural and urban dress. A third theme relates to issues of globalization, contemporary fashion, and the increasingly influential role of African fashion designers on the world scene.

EFFECTS OF COLONIALISM

The history of colonization of African peoples has been long and meandering with more time depth than usually acknowledged, beginning with Phoenician, Greek, Roman, Byzantine, and Ottoman occupations in North Africa. In the late nineteenth century, however, the artificial boundaries imposed by Belgians, British, French, Portuguese, and Spanish created a configuration of countries with little concern for the locations of ethnic groups. Furthermore, colonial structures introduced and imposed their own practices on indigenous peoples in regard to dress, food, religion, and other cultural behaviors. The effect of this infiltration most often resulted in either the request or requirement that indigenous people wear more garments than their usual practice. Members of some religious groups had strong beliefs that bodies should not be naked, and Christian missionaries and Muslim clerics demanded that conversion and commitment include dressing in a new, religiously responsible way.

Colonization proceeded differently depending on the colonizers. Among those governed by the French, one result was an admiration for French culture, which often included the desire to wear French clothing, even haute couture, whether men's suits or

modern world. The distinction, however, is, in part, evidentiary. Just because no evidence exits for certain changes in traditional African dress does not mean that they did not take place. And indeed, changes in tradition differ from changes in fashion only in terms of pace of change. The latter, of course, includes deliberately planned obsolescence, almost embracing a "use by" date for particular fashions, much for Africa as for the rest of the world.

Anthropologist Simon Ottenberg wrote a seminal essay titled "Ibo Receptivity to Change" in which he addresses the active consumption of new ideas, institutions, and material culture, including dress of the Igbo people of southeastern Nigeria. His essay

Wedding party. Dar es Salaam, Tanzania, 1999. Photograph by Doran H. Ross.

women's dresses. This continued after independence, when new leaders like Habib Bourguiba, who, after being elected president of Tunisia in 1957, thought that Tunisian citizens should dress like the French to show that by wearing "modern" clothes, their country was also modern. Another result of colonization was the enforcement of dress codes on indigenous peoples by colonial administrators, which was sometimes followed without protest and other times with condescension. Although the British were effective in encouraging Western dress in offices and the military during colonial regimes, after independence in countries such as Nigeria, nationalists like Mbonu Ojike, returning from an education in the United States, urged other educated Nigerians to return to indigenous forms of dress. His exhortation and support by others influenced many artists and politicians to make changes, beginning with independence in 1960. In a contrasting example in Namibia, colonization during the 1800s brought about a shift for Herero women from leather garments to cloth dresses in Victorian styles that over time became more voluminous. Significantly, these styles have continued to be worn into the twenty-first century and are thought of as traditional. Herero men, meanwhile, adopted European-style military uniforms as their dress for some ceremonial occasions, wearing other Western garments for everyday activities.

RURAL AND URBAN DIFFERENCES

Many authors comment on the rural and urban differences found throughout the continent over time, as well as in the early twenty-first century. Closely connected to colonization is the contrast of dress between rural and urban residents, because urban populations generally have had more access to broad sweeps of change than those living in what are largely agrarian contexts. For example, in rural West Africa, the wrapper or *pagne* appears ubiquitous in remote places, but is also often a choice by both men and women for relaxing at home in urban areas. In general, city residents have more choices and often favor Western garments for government and commercial office work, in both former French and British colonies. Western and Muslim styles are found side by side in many North African cities such as Tunis and Cairo, with the tunic known as caftan and the robes known as *boubou* and *baba riga* found in West Africa as well as North Africa. Men appear to wear more Western clothing than women in most contexts, but frequently, the white wedding dress, indicating familiarity with Western wedding practices, is chosen for the wedding ceremony. Sometimes Western dress is worn by the bride for part of the ceremony while indigenous dress is worn for another part. As economic circumstances have changed in several

African countries, some textiles formerly abandoned by urban residents began to reappear as fashionable choices, such as bark cloth garments in Côte d'Ivoire and Uganda and handwoven strip textiles in western Nigeria known as *aso-oke*. Some of these are quite faithful to the original, while others are imaginative, contemporary adaptations.

GLOBALIZATION, CONTEMPORARY DRESS, AND FASHION

Since the nineteenth century, people living across the African continent have increasingly become consumers of various media, beginning with local and international newspapers and magazines, and continuing with radio, cinema, television, cell phones, and the Internet as each has developed. Both urban and rural populations are aware of a globalized world and know about current fashions in other African countries and on other continents. Similarly, some indigenous textiles such as kente from Ghana and mudcloth (*bogolanfini*) from Mali have crossed the Atlantic, particularly to the United States. Strips of kente cloth draped over the shoulders of graduation gowns or mudcloth fashioned into coats, vests, and dresses have become symbols of the ancestral past for African Americans. Wax-print textiles with motifs specifically designed for African markets also have been exported to the United Kingdom and the United States and are popularly used for apparel and home furnishings. U.S. Peace Corps workers in West Africa during the 1960s co-opted a Yoruba indigenous top garment known as the *dansiki*, taking it back to the United States as a leisure shirt, renaming it the *dashiki*. Some Africans living abroad select a traditional item from their own backgrounds to wear for special occasions, such as a professor leading the faculty at graduation who proudly allows his hand-embroidered robe to be visible under his academic gown.

African fashion designers, whether incorporating indigenous resources or creating contemporary fashions, have attracted attention beyond the continent as promoted in publications such as *The Art of African Fashion* (1998) and the 1997–1998 *Revue Noire* special fashion issue. The 2005 traveling exhibition and catalog *Mode in Afrika* promoted African fashions in Germany and beyond, and the book *Africa Is in Style* featured designers in the 2005 International Festival of African Fashion in Niamey, Niger. Contemporary fashion designers discussed in this volume include Oumou Sy of Senegal, Ozwald Boateng of Ghana, and Folashade Thomas-Fahm ("Shade") of Nigeria.

Embedded within the three broad themes discussed above, there are a number of subthemes addressed in this volume. Several of the country-specific essays develop significant ideas that apply to many states. The Tanzanian entry addresses the impact of protected game parks and the adoption of national and international animal conservation acts on local clothing practices. The discussion of Togo considers how one country's national colors permeate its political and athletic dress, a reality for virtually every nation in Africa. Some of the more nuanced behaviors involving conventional attire consider the gliding walk and flowing robes of Wolof women as a form of public seduction in Senegal and Gambia, a potential model analysis for other cultures.

The kinetic aspects of dress in performance are still understudied, but several essays have examined the role that motion plays in choices of clothing, jewelry, and other accessories, such as the creative dance attire of the BaAka peoples (so-called pygmies)

African National Congress (ANC) Youth League campaigner Nkeko Mphake in Mpileng Village, Moutse, South Africa, 2006. She wears a "Vote ANC" black T-shirt and a wrapper printed with the image of Nelson Mandela. Photograph by Chris Kirchhoff.

in the Central African Republic and dress and dance in North Africa, especially costumes worn in belly dance performances. The conceptually oriented cross-cultural essay on masquerades scrutinizes African masked theater and dance. The article on footwear considers both constraints on movement and the sonic potential of movement.

Resources for the study of African dress are both ancient and recent. Prehistoric records, such as rock art and archaeological findings, document numerous and widely varied examples of dress and testify to a time depth of thousands of years as surveyed here in "Archaeological Evidence." More recent findings derived from firsthand observations, interviews, oral histories, and historical documents are the basis of most of the country essays. Photographs began to be used for analysis in the mid-twentieth century as singled out in "Photographic and Other Visual Sources." And extant examples of African dress from as early as the seventeenth century, first collected as curiosities and then as natural history specimens, have also provided additional evidence.

Serious interest by the Western world in African dress and masquerade traditions began with the early-twentieth-century appreciation of African masks by European artists such as Picasso, Braque, Matisse, and others. Unfortunately, this indirect valorization of African art through European eyes was as much an impediment to appreciation as it was an encouragement. Among other problems, Europeans focused on the carved mask and rooted it in notions of the "primitive," ignoring the rest of the costume. Beyond the arena of European artistic exploitation, in the first half of the twentieth century, African dress typically received attention only from missionaries as evidence of the "exotic" and "pagan" practices of nonbelievers or as more "scientific" specimens of the social and cultural practices of Africa in the emerging discipline of anthropology.

Not until the 1950s and 1960s were African textiles and other items of dress appreciated as meaningful and vital aesthetic expressions in their own right. The benchmark 1972 traveling exhibition and publication *African Textiles and Decorative Arts*— curated and authored by art historian Roy Sieber and originated by the Museum of Modern Art in New York City—included numerous textiles, hats, and jewelry. Since then, such items as northern Cameroon beaded pubic aprons, Mbuti painted barkcloth loin wrappers, Mangbetu ivory hairpins, and Akan gold

Professor Rowland Abiodun's hand-embroidered robe is visible under his academic gown during a graduation ceremony at Amherst College, United States, 2007. Some Africans living abroad select a traditional item of their own to wear for special occasions. Charlie Quigg/Amherst College Public Affairs.

finger rings have become much-sought-after collectors' items to the extent that copies are created for tourists or even artificially aged for sale on the international art market. These four examples could be multiplied one hundred fold.

Academic interest has kept pace with the marketplace. As essays within this volume demonstrate, numerous exhibitions and publications have followed that only begin to reveal the artistic quality and significant meaning found in African dress. A few key resources may be useful to readers, such as the two bibliographies on African dress published in 1969 and 1985 that contain many references not ordinarily thought to refer to dress. The quarterly periodical *African Arts*, established in 1967 at the University of California, Los Angeles, has consistently covered topics of dress and masquerade. The listserv HAfrArts began in 1996 and frequently provides a useful forum for discussions on dress. The Arts Council of the African Studies Association was established in 1982 and has assumed sponsorship of a triennial symposium that was begun in 1968 at Hampton Institute. In addition, the collected bibliographies of this volume may be the most comprehensive yet compiled.

Most studies on dress must admit to something of an elite bias, because both the scholarly community and the marketplace tend to focus attention on visually compelling attire (past and present) only available to those with the means to afford it. Many populations across the planet still suffer from severe poverty, and their clothing choices are often restricted to used garments either handed down within an extended family or acquired from the secondary clothing markets supplied by numerous foreign sources. But as the "Migrant Workers Production and Fashion" essay makes clear, there are still numerous creative opportunities to be found within the choice of alteration and embellishment of used clothing. Competing with the secondary clothing market are the inexpensive new products of the extraordinarily cheap labor of China that are now ironically supplanting the few African textile and garment industries that once employed the urban poor. Future studies will hopefully address the ramifications of unemployment, poverty, and dress in a globalizing world.

References and Further Reading

Cole, Herbert M., and Doran H. Ross. *The Arts of Ghana*. Los Angeles: UCLA Museum of Cultural History, 1977.

Eicher, J. B. *African Dress: A Select and Annotated Bibliography*. East Lansing: African Studies Center, Michigan State University, 1979.

Gardi, Bernhard. *Boubou, c'est chic: Gewänder aus Mali und anderen Ländern Westafrikas*. Basel, Switzerland: C. Merian, 2000.

Geoffroy-Scneiter, Bérénice. *Africa Is in Style*. New York: Assouline, 2006.

Geurts, Kathryn. *Culture and the Senses: Bodily Ways of Knowing in an African Community*. Berkeley: University of California Press, 2002.

Luttmann, Ilsemargret. *Mode in Afrika*. Hamburg, Germany: Museum fur Volkerkunde, 2005.

Ottenberg, Simon. "Ibo Receptivity to Change." In *Continuity and Change in African Cultures*, edited by Wlliam R. Bascom and Melville J. Herskovits, 130–140. Chicago: University of Chicago Press, 1958.

Picton, John. *The Art of African Textiles: Technology, Tradition, and Lurex*. London: Barbican Art Gallery; Lund Humphries Publishers, 1995.

Picton, J., and J. Mack. *African Textiles: Looms, Weaving, and Design.* London: British Museum Publications, 1989.

Pokornowski, I. M., J. B. Eicher, M. F. Harris, and O. C. Thieme. *African Dress II: A Select and Annotated Bibliography.* Lansing: African Studies Center, Michigan State University, 1985.

Rabine, Leslie. *The Global Circulation of African Fashion.* Oxford, UK: Berg, 2002.

Revue Noire. Special Mode: African Fashion, no. 27 (1998).

Ross, Doran H., ed. *Wrapped in Pride: Ghanaian Kente and African American Identity.* Los Angeles: UCLA Fowler Museum of Cultural History, 1998.

Rovine, V. *Bogolan: Shaping Culture through Cloth in Contemporary Mali.* Washington, DC: Smithsonian Institution Press, 2001.

Sieber, Roy. *African Textiles and Decorative Arts.* New York: Museum of Modern Art, 1972.

Spring, Christopher, and Julie Hudson. *North African Textiles.* London: British Museum Press, 1995.

van der Plas, Els. *The Art of African Fashion.* Trenton, NJ: Africa World Press, 1998.

Joanne B. Eicher and Doran H. Ross

See also volume 10, Global Perspectives: Beads: Prehistory to Early Twenty First Century; Secondhand Clothing.

Climatic Zones and Cultural Regions

- Environmental Regularities
- Sources of Regional Distinctiveness in Attire
- Authenticity and Identity
- Clothing and Credibility
- Indigenous Textile Industry
- Cosmetics and Masks
- European Clothing

Africa, over three times the size of the United States, extends north–south over seventy-two degrees of latitude and east–west over sixty-nine degrees of longitude, thus encompassing a wide range of climates of the tropics, subtropics, and midlatitudes. It also has extensive highlands, thus adding to the variety and complexity of climatic types. If one draws a line northeasterly from the Gulf of Guinea (where Nigeria becomes Cameroon) to the Red Sea (around Eritrea), one divides lowland Africa to the west from highland Africa to the south.

In Africa, folk classifications of climate are made first according to rainfall and rainy and dry seasons, and then by temperature. The reason for this is the primacy of rain in determining crop seasons and livestock management. It does not reflect a concern for clothing. Midlatitude folk classifications of climate that emphasize temperature—how hot or cold a season is—and corresponding periodic changes in appropriate clothing contrast with high-latitude folk classifications of climate that focus on light and darkness and length of day. At the equator, each day has twelve hours of light and then twelve hours of darkness.

ENVIRONMENTAL REGULARITIES

Africa exhibits remarkable regularities and symmetries in the distribution of rainfall and regional variation in temperature, according to latitude and elevation. Africa includes tropical, subtropical, and midlatitude portions (southern Africa and countries fringing the Mediterranean). At the equator, one finds two rainy seasons, each six months apart, occasioned by the overhead passage of the sun (a vernal equinox on 22 March and an autumnal equinox on 23 September), with atmospheric instability and heavy tropical rains lagging some four to six weeks behind. In northeastern Tanzania, the local name for the April rains is *masika*, "greater rains," and for the October rains, *vuli*, "lesser rains"; farther north, in Kenya, they are called, respectively, the "main" rains and the "grass" rains. Both sets of rainy periods are separated by dry seasons. In Liberia, there are two rainy seasons, peaking in June and September, separated by a two-month period called the "middle dries."

As one moves toward the midlatitudes, the dates for the overhead passage of the sun approach each other so that by 21 June they unite at the tropic of Cancer, 23.5 degrees north latitude (for example, Aswan, Egypt), and by 22 December, they unite on the tropic of Capricorn, 23.5 degrees south latitude (for example,

Massinga, Mozambique). These are subtropical areas with a single short summer rainy season (the higher the latitude, the shorter the rainy period) and many months that are dry, dusty, and sometimes cold. The long dry season in West Africa is sometimes called the *harmattan*, after the dry, dust-laden air that flows south out of the Sahara. It is also called "The Doctor" because it brings such relief from hot, humid conditions. Relative humidity levels can plunge from the ninetieth to the thirtieth percentile in a matter of an hour or two.

On reaching midlatitude areas (north of the Sahara and south of the Kalahari, in Namibia and Cape Province, South Africa), one finds dry, hot summers and cool, rainy winters, which are called *Mediterranean climates* (also found in California). Southeastern South Africa has its biggest rains in summer, thus resembling the southeastern United States.

A second environmental regularity of interest involves elevation. Temperatures vary systematically with height above sea level, something called the *lapse rate*. As a general rule, one can say that the lapse rate is 6.5 degrees Celsius/1,000 meters (or about 3.6 degrees Fahrenheit/3,280 feet), although this can vary greatly. Thus, if the temperature is 30 degrees Celsius (86 degrees Fahrenheit) at sea level, at 2,500 meters (8,200 feet), it will be 17 degrees Celsius (63 degrees Fahrenheit). Not only is it cooler at higher elevations, there is a greater diurnal range in temperatures than at sea level—cool at night and warm during the day. Also, the relative humidity will be lower. If you know the latitude, elevation, and time of year of a place in Africa, you have a good basis for intuiting the sort of weather that people there are experiencing and how warmly they will be clothed. It can get cold nearly anywhere in Africa, at least in some seasons. On clear nights, outward long-wave radiation, which reflects heat into outer space, can result in significant drops in temperatures, which explains, in part, the popularity of sweaters.

One question, then: Does the clothing people wear reflect the differences in temperature and weather? The answer is yes and no, because clothing is worn for many reasons other than to cover one's body and protect it from the elements. For example, one might expect that in hot climates (lowland tropical) people would wear white or light-colored garments (which reflect rather than absorb the sun's rays), and indeed the *kanzu*—a long-sleeved, loose-fitting garment whose hem reaches to the feet—worn along the Swahili coast of East Africa is white. Yet the Tuareg of the Sahara, a hot place during daytime for much of the year (upland arid subtropical), wear black turbans and black outer garments. It gets cold at night in the Sahara in winter months, and turbans and headwraps protect against dust as well as the cold. In highland areas that experience cold seasons and cold nights, many people wear greatcoats (the legacy of some colonial encounter, as in Ethiopia [wet/dry highland subtropical], where Italian troops introduced them). In highland Lesotho (wet/dry midlatitude), which has a long, cold winter and much cool weather year round, the blanket is a sort of national symbol and worn as a garment as well as used for bedding. Indeed, in 1868, when Moshoeshoe I, king of the Sotho, persuaded Queen Victoria to declare Basutoland a British protectorate, he thanked her for permitting his people to "rest and live in the large folds of the blanket of England."

The Tuareg men of the Sahara often wear dark garments and a head covering to protect against dust and the cold nights. Sergio Pitamitz/Getty Images.

Despite accommodating to great ranges in temperatures and rainfall, nearly every African, if asked, will say he or she lives in a normal climate. The hill farmer in one place, asked about living on the plains spread out below, will reply: "No, it is too hot there." If asked about living higher up in those nearby hills, he will reply: "Oh, no, much too cold and cloudy up there."

SOURCES OF REGIONAL DISTINCTIVENESS IN ATTIRE

It is difficult to regionalize something as complex as African modes of dress and adornment. Some commonalities exist across large environmental zones, such as desert, savannas, highlands, or tropical forests. There also may be commonalities arising from the livelihoods pursued in these different environments, as, for example, livestock keeping, crop cultivation, hunting and gathering (engaged in by very few people), fishing, or, indeed, urban life and the varied occupations pursued there that may involve distinctive, even required, dress. One can invoke many contributing features—climate, topography, culture, religion, as well as livelihood—including the raw materials readily at hand for garment making: cowhide among pastoralists (for garments and footwear), cotton where it can be grown, or bark cloth where fig trees flourish.

The first thing to consider is comfort and practicability. Garments for everyday use are simple, often loose fitting, and airy.

For a woman, the norm may be a simple wrapping of the upper and lower body in a sturdy cotton cloth. For a man, a voluminous ankle-length robe or Western-style shirt and trousers may serve. The second consideration is context. Clothes are differentiated as to occasion. There are clothes for every day and clothes for special events, such as weddings, funerals, holidays, religious services, or even a visitor's request to be allowed to take a photograph of the person. So family members may dress simply for daily labors and dress up for occasions.

Keeping livestock is an important livelihood, and it has regional similarities, which may include riding horses, camels, or sometimes donkeys. There are commonalities in dress and appearance among Fulani herders (found everywhere in semiarid/subhumid subtropical West Africa from Senegal to Chad), with their leather-trimmed conical hats woven of straw, and Lesotho cattle keepers at the far southern end of the continent, with their strikingly similar Sotho conical hat, as well as the hats worn by the Wodaabe camel and cattle keepers of northern Niger. Hats protect the eyes from sun and glare and also provide ethnic identification. (Dark glasses, popular in urban areas, are a response to bright sun and glare and can also be a fashion statement.)

Religion certainly contributes greatly to regional distinctions in dress. Much of Africa—stretching from the Sahel of West Africa across the Sahara to encompass the northern part of the continent (Morocco to Egypt) and along the eastern coast (Red Sea and Indian Ocean) as far as Mozambique—is dominated by

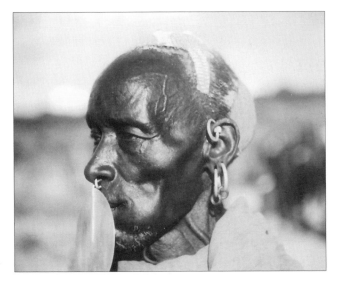

An elder Pokot man showing a *syoliup* (a skullcap made of fine mud worked into the hair) symbolizing his circumcision, which marks a young man's entry into adult life. He is a member of the *camarmar* (zebra) age set. A hammered aluminum shield hooked through his nose is intended to prevent evil spirits from entering his body, should he be injured in battle and lose consciousness. Western Kenya, 1961. Photograph by Philip W. Porter.

Islam. Islamic dress is characteristic over this vast area—the kanzu or similar long, flowing robe for men and for women and full covering of the body, including the *hijab* or head scarf. There is also the *kiniki*, a blue head scarf worn by women in mourning or during their menstrual period. In coastal Kenya, women wear the black *buibui* (spider), which covers them from head to toe. Christian groups, particularly some of the syncretic offshoots of that faith, commonly feature flowing robes with distinctive color schemes. An example is the Dini ya Msambwa sect of western Kenya and Uganda, whose men wear billowing white robes with blue trim.

If one envisions umbrellas as a colorful accoutrement for festive occasions, coastal West Africa comes to mind. In Kumasi, Ghana, the procession of the king and his royal stool is accompanied by a bobbing sea of umbrellas and parasols. So, if one closes one's eyes, one can summon up peopled landscapes everywhere in Africa and see characteristic patterns of dress: people bundled up against the cold in misty highlands in Swaziland; protected from dust and the sun's glare in Mopti, Mali, by loose-fitting robes and turban-like head scarves; or formally attired in Western suits and dresses for the wedding of a prominent couple in Nairobi, Kenya.

AUTHENTICITY AND IDENTITY

In African societies where there is little material wealth, one's young body may be about the best and most beautiful object one possesses. Grooming, adorning, and clothing this body well is important to the individual and to the community at large. Africans care about their appearance and give considerable thought to proper dress, grooming, hair arrangement, jewelry, body markings, and application of cosmetics. They may incur considerable costs to achieve the appearance they desire. Among groups where Western clothes have not been widely adopted, appearance commonly tells others something about the individual, such as age set or clan affiliation.

For example, among Pokot men in western Kenya, an adult who has been circumcised, which marks a young man's entry into adult life, wears a *syoliup*, a sort of skullcap made of a fine mud worked into the man's hair. There are two age sets that alternate in a cycle about every twenty-five years. Each man is a member of one of two color sections of a *sapana*, or age set. The color sections are established by a ceremony called *munian*, which assigns an age cohort to one of two groups within the sapana: *camarmar* (zebra) or *nyimur* (stones). The color sections change about every twelve years. One can read a Pokot man's color section (and estimate his age) from his *atoro*, the front half of the syoliup, which is painted either in reddish brown stripes on a white background (zebra) or in reddish brown dots on a white background (stones). After a time, as hair grows, the syoliup becomes cracked and unsightly and must be redone. It can cost a great deal to have a good syoliup made, and there are specialists who do such work. The syoliup has plugs and rosettes inset to accommodate decorative elements for special occasions or ceremonies. Ostrich feathers and black pom-poms may be placed in these receptacles. Clothing consists of a togalike cloth, usually black or red, fastened across the shoulder. A man typically carries a walking stick—to guard against snakes and steady himself in rough terrain—and a small, light stool that can be used in numerous ways—as a seat, pillow, arm rest, and so on. (Pastoralists have to travel lightly.) Another cloth or leather piece is wrapped around the waist. A hammered aluminum shield hooked through his nose is intended to prevent evil spirits from entering his body, in the event that he is injured on the battlefield and loses consciousness. The younger Pokot generation shows both disaffection from and interest in the old ways of life, and there are generational tensions. A recent revival of pastoral identity has taken place among youth, which manifests itself in a very strong "repokotization" of identity markers among the young men. Long black robes are very much back on market days. Many young men have again chosen to be warriors, even those with education.

Pokot women braid their hair in numerous short plaits, pierce their ears in multiple places to accommodate earrings, and, upon reaching puberty, wear an abundance of bead necklaces. The proper colors for Pokot are red and yellow. Bead strings of white and blue, on the other hand, reflect the influence of the neighboring Turkana people. Women also wear an apronlike skirt made of cowhide. Periodically, elders in Pokot communities (rather as happens in the U.S. Army) will issue an order enforcing a stricter dress code so that people will look smart and correct.

Pokot girls, before they reach puberty, may be permitted one or two strings of colored beads, but mainly they wear wooden "practice beads" and wooden plugs in their ears, in preparation for the real thing, the plastic and glass beads worn by adults. A girl's wooden necklace may be as large and nearly as heavy as the colored beads she will wear when she becomes a woman.

The Pokot are not alone in being concerned about how their hair looks. An extensive account could be written about hair care in urban settings in Africa. Barbershops usually have painted panels displayed in front of the shop, showing the many different styles of haircut the proprietor is ready to undertake. Similar facilities for women can also be found.

The Pokot occupy elevations ranging from 1,000 meters (3,500 feet) to 3,350 meters (11,000 feet), and their clothing reflects this altitudinal range. On the hot lowland plains, people are lightly clad, whereas in the highlands, people wear greatcoats

Indigo-dyeing pits with tie-dyed textiles set out to dry in Kano, Nigeria, 1978. Patterns that have been created on the cloth by stones tied with string are visible. Photograph by Philip W. Porter.

and heavy jackets when it is cold. At each elevation, in each season, people's clothing reflects how cool, hot, or humid the weather is. People in other parts of Africa respond similarly to thermal variations in weather and seasons.

Clothing choices in Africa do not respond to rain as they do to temperature and humidity. Of course, people try to avoid getting wet when it rains, either by staying under a shelter or by using an umbrella (or a handy banana leaf). Although umbrellas are ubiquitous, many people cannot afford one; thus, if it rains and they cannot avoid it, they will simply get wet and dry off later.

In addition to wearing beads and other decorative items, the Pokot (both men and women) also do extensive scarification on their bodies, especially on the back, chest, and arms. Their choice of colors (red and yellow beads, use of reddish brown and white earths) distinguishes them from neighboring cultural groups. The differences in dress and adornment between men and women and between pre- and postpubescent youngsters are striking among the Pokot. One can tell immediately by type of mud pack or beads if a young man or woman has been circumcised and initiated into adulthood. In this respect, they are typical of many other groups in Africa. Some cultures are very dramatic in their display of self—for example, the Wodaabe of Niger—and others less so, yet everywhere one finds preferences in color, scarification patterns, and use of local earths and animal products in cosmetics.

CLOTHING AND CREDIBILITY

It is well known that attitudes toward people are affected by how they are dressed. There is an ongoing conflict throughout Africa between European clothes and indigenous modes of dress. Contempt in the West toward traditional garb is embodied in a witty section of novelist Antoine de Saint-Exupéry's *The Little Prince*:

> I have serious reason to believe that the planet from which the little prince came is the asteroid B 612. This asteroid has been seen only once by telescope, in 1909, by a Turkish

astronomer. He then made a great demonstration of his discovery at an International Congress of Astronomy. But no one believed him because of his clothes. Grownups are like that. Happily for the reputation of the asteroid B 612 a Turkish dictator forced his people, under pain of death, to dress like Europeans. The astronomer redid his demonstration in 1920, in very elegant clothing. And this time everyone agreed with him.

Considering the astronomer and the disbelief or credibility attached to his lecture, it must be said that the standard male dress for the entire world—full-length trousers and long-sleeved shirt—has been widely adopted in Africa. Another more local borrowing and adaptation is the *busuti*, the national dress for women in Uganda's southern (Buganda) and eastern regions. This is an adaptation of a nineteenth-century Victorian dress (introduced by missionaries), with long sleeves and puffed shoulders, a full skirt, and commonly a colorful bow tied around the waist.

Most African politicians dress in Western business suits despite their unsuitability in hot, humid areas and the discomfort they cause. Politicians, of course, may at times adopt traditional clothing for ceremonial occasions or to make a statement about cultural authenticity. President Julius Nyerere, after a visit to India, modified the Nehru jacket by adding an open neck and pockets to meet the needs of Tanzanians. He wanted Tanzanian men to have a formal jacket that was different from the Western norm.

INDIGENOUS TEXTILE INDUSTRY

Africa has a rich tradition of garment making that involves every aspect of the process, from cotton cultivation through the making of thread and yarn, and from dyeing and weaving to sewing and tailoring. (Until recently, weaving and tailoring, like secretarial work, have generally been male occupations.) One need think only of the narrow strips of blue-and-white country cloth in West Africa, including the more colorful *kente* cloth of the

Asante, the *pelete bite* (cut and pulled threads to create designs using madras or gingham cloth) of the Kalabari people of the Niger Delta region of Nigeria, and the checkerboard cloth of the Dogon of Mali, whose "onion fields" (a wafflelike grid of tiny square plots, with raised edges) are cultivated with a strict rule that resembles the back-and-forth movement of weaving. The intricate patterns in kente cloth sometimes incorporate proverbs and sayings. There are other rich traditions as well, such as those of working hides and pounding out bark cloth from the soft inner bark of fig trees.

There has been a history of interaction between the West and indigenous crafts related to clothing. For example, the ubiquity of hand- or foot-driven Singer sewing machines is evidence of a signal innovation in clothing manufacture. One can find tailors using ancient Singer sewing machines in the remotest villages in Africa. Further evidence of interaction is reflected in the fact that, at one time, British manufacturers of cotton cloth, in order to compete with African cotton weavers, programmed their looms to leave some threads out of the cloth in the warp direction about every four inches (ten centimeters). On arrival in West Africa, the bolts of cotton cloth could be cut to resemble the strips of country cloth. These were bought by local people who sewed them together to make garments that met their aesthetic requirements.

In the 1960s, nearly every African nation of any size had its own cotton textile industry. It may have consisted of old second-hand machinery from Europe or Asia, but the cloth manufactured was sturdy and inexpensive and featured designs created by local artists. The result was colorful, colorfast fabrics that were and still are the foundation of dress, especially for women. In East Africa, typically, a woman wears two *kangas* (a colorful rectangular piece of bordered cloth worn as a wrapped garment), each measuring about 100 centimeters by 150 centimeters (three and a half feet by five feet). They are frequently sold in pairs (*doti*). The first may be wrapped tightly around her waist and the second draped across her upper body and tucked in at the breast. Frequently, one sees a baby held tightly to the back by a kanga. This close contact and the mutual movement of mother and child is good for the infant's development and leaves the mother with two hands free for work. Sometimes, a kanga or other cloth is used to cover the head.

The difference between kanga and *kitenge* (pl. *vitenge*) may be noted. The kanga is a rectangular piece of cotton cloth with a border all the way around it; it has colorful, bold designs. The kitenge, similarly colorful, has edging along only the long dimension and is of a thicker cloth than the kanga. The origins of the kanga are disputed. Some say it originated in Zanzibar; others claim it was first developed in Mombasa. In any event, Mombasa is an important center of kanga manufacture, and many kangas bear the imprint K.H.E.—Mali ya Abdulla, after a famous Mombasa trader, Kaderdina Hajee Essak, also known as Abdulla, who was active in the early decades of the twentieth century. There is no special connection between climate and whether people wear kangas or vitenge, although, because it is drier, more marginal parts of eastern Africa are also poorer, and one is less likely to encounter the more expensive, less affordable kanga.

In addition to colorful patterns, the kanga or kitenge may have Kiswahili sayings or aphorisms printed along the longer side. There are hundreds of examples, but three can serve here. *Hiari yashida utumwa*, or "It is better to volunteer than to be

Man weaving country cloth in Kano, Nigeria, 1978. Until recently, weaving and tailoring were considered to be male occupations. Photograph by Philip W. Porter.

conscripted"; *Jee umepata?* or "Well, do you get it?"; *Duniani kaa ya heshima*, or "Live in the world with pride." Kangas and vitenge are sometimes specially printed to help political candidates or to support community development projects, in much the same manner as special T-shirts are produced in the United States.

Earlier, the kanzu was described. Usually worn with the kanzu, at least by older men, is the *kofia*, a round-shaped, flat cap with intricate designs embroidered into it.

There may be regional and cultural preferences in color schemes for garments. For example, among Maasai pastoralists, an ochre red is preferred for the togalike cloth they wear. In the late 1960s, one saw in Sukumaland and Geita District in north central Tanzania women wearing different vitenge colored yellow and green. Whether this was an enduring or a passing color preference is not known, yet it contrasted with other parts of Tanzania, where red and blue or red and yellow patterns were popular. The eight terms used here to characterize clothing in eastern Africa are but a sampling, and every other region of Africa would reveal a distinctive set of clothing terms.

COSMETICS AND MASKS

African cultures use many local sources for cosmetics—earths, plants, and animal products and parts. Every culture has local names for soils, and, in many cases, the names have nothing to do with agriculture, but rather concern the earths' other uses, including for cosmetics. For example, the Sebei, who live on Mount Elgon in Uganda, have twenty-three distinct names for soils, only seven of which relate to agriculture. Sixteen of the names are related to keeping livestock, domestic needs (pot making), or cosmetics. The cosmetic earths are valued for their consistency and color—white, red, gray, or black. With regard to the Pokot syoliup discussed earlier, at least eight kinds of clay are used in the making of head packs. One widely used red clay called *pikos* is found only in one place. Circumcised girls spread the clay on their precircumcision beads, and before dances, they spread oil and then pikos on their bodies to make themselves pretty. Circumcised boys also smear pikos on their bodies for decoration.

Two Sande girls wearing masks to conceal their identity during an initiation ceremony into adulthood. Liberia, 1906. General Research and Reference Division, Schomburg Center for Research in Black Culture, The New York Public Library, Astor, Lenox and Tilden Foundations.

Masks are another form of adornment, and they figure importantly in the lives of people in West and Central Africa. In Liberia and neighboring countries are two secret societies—the Poro and the Sande—whose purpose is to prepare young boys and girls, respectively, for life as grownups. Separate secluded training camps for young people are convened when a group of boys or girls is to be initiated to instruct them in proper behavior, particularly in marriage. Ceremonies leading to initiation into adult life include circumcision. Much of the ceremony is conducted using masks, which heightens the spiritual and awesome features of the initiation and also conceals the identity of the individual behind the mask. People wearing masks also participate in national and other festive events. In a photo taken during President Tubman's birthday festivities in Monrovia, Liberia, one sees a masked figure whose entire body is covered with intricately woven grass. Grass and palm fronds are frequently used to hide the human body below the mask.

EUROPEAN CLOTHING

A key aspect of colonial occupation was the use of uniforms to indicate social distance and to distinguish those who served the colonial administration from the general public. This was fundamental to colonial control, as was the ever-present possibility of the use of force. Colonial officers wore uniforms, and instantly recognizable uniforms were devised for all others who formed part of the administrative structure, whether they were *askaris* (soldiers), police officers, waiters, or train conductors. The uniforms of the Colonial period continued in use after independence and can be seen today in many African countries.

There is a longstanding trade in used clothing coming from Europe and North America to Africa. A regular feature of weekly or periodic markets all across the continent is the early morning arrival of a truck filled with used clothing, which is then spread out on large tarpaulins or hung from racks for market goers to examine and buy. The balance between the production of clothing in Africa and imports of clothing, both new and secondhand, to the continent has changed over time. For a long period, cheap cotton goods from Asia dominated the market. In the 1960s, many countries began their own textile industries and were able to meet most of the local demand for clothing. Various charitable organizations (for example, Caritas Tanzania, a Catholic charity) began to import secondhand clothing for free distribution to poor people and refugees. Secondhand clothing, known somewhat ironically as *kafa Ulaya* (clothes formerly worn by dead Europeans), became popular among the general public, both because the variety of clothing available increased and the clothes were inexpensive. Private firms other than charities began to import used clothing in great quantities. More recently the trade has been called *mtumba*, Kiswahili for "bale" or "bundle," referring to the tightly packed fifty-kilogram (110-pound) bales in which used clothing is packed.

As the International Monetary Fund forced on various African countries structural adjustment programs that involved deregulation of currency and removal of import tariffs, indigenous textile industries (both artisan and factory-based) experienced increasingly unfavorable terms of trade and found themselves unable to compete with cheap imported secondhand clothes as well as increasingly inexpensive new clothes from Asia. The trade in used clothing in Africa quadrupled in the 1980s, and between 1990 and 1997, according to a report by the Civil Society Research and Support Collective, the value of exports of secondhand clothing from the United States more than doubled from US$174 million to US$390 million.

Although the trade in imported secondhand clothing has negative impacts on local producers all along the production chain—cotton growers, dyers, weavers, tailors, and others—it provides employment for many people in such port cities as Mombasa, Durban, Dakar, and Lagos. These are the people who sort, wash and retailor garments to meet local tastes, as well as the many retailers who transport the clothing from market to market or sell them in stalls in major cities. One report states that 50,000 people are employed in jobs relating to secondhand clothing in one market in Kampala, Uganda. Local production as a proportion of total sales of clothing has declined almost everywhere in Africa, and even the proportion of secondhand clothing sold has declined as inexpensive new clothes produced mainly in east and southeast Asia command a larger share of the market. Clearly globalization is having an effect on the clothes people in Africa buy and on the look of city streets and villages as traditional forms of apparel disappear. Makers of kangas and kitenge increasingly are trying to fill niche markets with innovative, elaborate Web sites aimed at an international market. Thus do modernization and tradition face off as, indeed, they do continually throughout Africa in every aspect of clothing and adornment.

References and Further Reading

Civil Society Research and Support Collective. "Developing a Strategic Response to the Trade in Used Clothing in Africa." http://clean clothes.org/publications/04-ig.htm (accessed December 2004).

de Saint-Exupéry, Antoine. *Le Petit Prince*. New York: Reynal & Hitchcock, 1943.

Dougherty, Carter. "Trade Theory vs. Used Clothes in Africa." http://www.nytimes.com/2004/06/03/business/trade-theory-vs-used-clothes-in-africa.html?scp=1&sq=dougherty%20trade%20theory%20used&st=cse (accessed November 2009).

Gorelick, Melissa. "The Secrets of Used Clothes: Western Cast-Offs Reveal Surprising Insights." *UN Chronicle* 43, no. 3 (Fall 2006). http://www.un.org/Pubs/chronicle/2006/issue3/0306p33.htm

Harley, George W. "Some Notes on the Poro in Liberia." *Papers of the Peabody Museum of American Archeology and Ethnology* 19, 1941.

Kinabo, Oliva D. "The Textile Industry and the Mitumba Market in Tanzania." Paper presented to the Tanzania-Network Conference on textile market and textile industry in rural and urban areas in Tanzania, 2004.

Schnee, Heinrich. *Deutsches Kolonial-Lexikon.* Leipzig, Germany: Verlag von Quelle & Meyer, 1920.

Zelinsky, Wilbur. "Globalization Reconsidered: The Historical Geography of Modern Western Male Attire." *Journal of Cultural Geography* 22, no. 1 (2004): 83–134.

Philip W. Porter

PART 2

History of Dress and Fashion in Africa

Archaeological Evidence

- Rock Art
- Northeastern Africa
- Northwestern Africa
- West Africa
- Eastern and Southern Africa

In Africa, the human body has always been a focus for creative expression. Each culture has evolved its own patterns of dress and associated symbolic system, yet cross-cultural influences and change have constantly occurred. Particular types of dress—especially those connected with rituals or celebrations—tend to change very slowly. A society's political structure and religious institutions can determine the type of dress worn. Societies with a centralized organization often have elaborate, even grandiose programs of visual culture associated with leadership. The ruler or an elite group often reserves the right to use a particular type of object or a certain material, such as gold, ivory, or bronze. Moreover, generally a noticeable discrepancy exists regarding possessions of the ruling class and the majority of the population. It is usually the possessions of the ruling elite that survive for future investigation.

The earliest written material on African dress is found in ancient Egyptian, Greek, and Roman references. However, when no or little written documentation exists, only by investigating both two- and three-dimensional artifacts does it become possible to re-create aspects of earlier types of dress. The overwhelming majority of the visual references for the archaeological material in Africa relate to ceremonial or prestige dress or both. With the exception of Egypt and Roman North Africa, archaeological work on the continent has been limited. Many finds have not been adequately excavated or investigated. Yet in terms of dress, the existence of visual images—even out of context—can provide valuable visual information. Information on the precise context of a particular item of dress or the nature of stylistic changes is relatively scanty.

ROCK ART

The rock art from the southern and northern parts of the continent is the source of our earliest information on African dress. Yet the material is difficult to decipher, because many of the images are abstract, showing a minimal concern for specificity. The engravings and paintings found south of the Zambezi River, fabricated on the walls of rock shelters by the hunting and gathering San peoples, provide valuable but incomplete records of prehistoric dress and social activities. The earliest works from this region—painted stones—have been dated back to between 26,500 and 24,300 B.C.E., making the southern African tradition much older than rock art elsewhere in Africa. Rock shelters with walls painted in red, white, and black pigment are found in many parts of southern Africa, including the interior of South Africa, the Tsodilo Hills in Botswana, the Namibian Brandberg, and the Maluti Mountains of Lesotho. These paintings range from depictions of individual figures to complex narratives involving humans and animals.

Humans are seen in a variety of postures and dress, some wearing wrist ornaments in the form of bands with stringlike attachments and what appear to be feather headdresses. Streamers flowing from the back of the neck or shoulder blades are a common occurrence. Women wear long robes, back aprons, or grass tails, while men wear penis decoration and dance rattles on their arms or legs. Some men carry fly whisks, and some wear caps with antelope ears tied back to stand upright. Others seemingly have a feather coming from the top of the head. Some individuals, probably shamans, have antelope heads or a bird atop the head. Round objects apparently attached to the head were possibly inflated gallbladders of sacrificial animals. The use of gallbladders attached to the hair of certain twentieth-century Nguni and Sotho ritual functionaries, particularly diviners, has been documented.

Some interpretations of rock art dress have been highly speculative. One example from the Drakensberg of South Africa depicting a figure wearing a robe or tunic of variable length under a sheepskin cloak—similar to ancient Sumerian dress—was interpreted by the archaeologist Abbé Breüil to be of Phoenician origin, therefore implying a connection. More recent scholars have claimed the cloaked figure is actually similar to a contemporary Basuto woman of prestige. A fairly detailed painting from Namibia, which for years was called the *White Lady of Brandberg*, is actually a man with white and red body paint and bands of bead decorating the knees, ankles, neck, and hair. Possibly these beads were made from ostrich shell, which is still used for this purpose.

Examples from Zimbabwe, many from 13,000 to 5,000 years ago, exhibit a range of differences. The heads of men have lines hanging down over the back of the neck, lines standing upright across the crown, similar lines painted in the middle of the head, large triangular or cone shapes on top of the head, or a series of tufts across the head with narrow stems and wide splayed ends. A male's penis has a line or bar across it or a sinuous line coming out of the end. Some penis sheaths culminate in a splayed or tufted shape. Males also carry a bow and arrow or a short club or stick and, in some cases, a shield. Most humans carry a small bag with a narrow neck, slung high on one shoulder by a looped handle. There is evidence of white paint on the body. Women often wear tasseled aprons over their buttocks, and some have a second apron in front. At times, the complete skin of a small animal hangs over the back as a cape. Many figures carry long sticks. The scenes from southern African rock art are usually interpreted as celebratory events. Many recent scholars on the southern African material suggest that the figures illustrate trance phenomena or reflect spiritual energy or potency.

In the mountainous areas of the central Sahara, a long tradition of rock art lasted thousands of years. By 10,000 B.C.E., hunting and gathering societies were found throughout northwestern Africa, including the Tassili-n-Ajjer mountain range in southern Algeria. The earliest examples of Saharan art, consisting of numerous engravings and some paintings, date from around 10,000 to 8,000 B.C.E. The many types of animals that inhabited the region at that time, as well as hunting activities, were commonly represented. Around 4,000 B.C.E., pastoralism replaced a hunting way of life, and painted scenes of both herding and village life became standard for the next 2,500 years. Rock art at Tassili and related sites documented masquerading, food preparation, and economic pursuits. A variety of apparel such as short loincloths and long tunics, some with linear patterns, has been found. Figures were also depicted with bands around their waist, arms, wrists, and legs, some embellished with strands. A few figures have lines on their body, and some wear bulbous hatlike headdresses.

NORTHEASTERN AFRICA

A Neolithic way of life developed in Egypt by the second half of the fifth millennium B.C.E. Because of its long history, wealth, and dry climate, a considerable amount of material culture has been preserved from ancient Egypt. Tombs provide the primary source of information for all phases of Egyptian art history. The earliest anthropomorphic figurines of the Neolithic period show evidence of possible tattoos, scarification, or cicatrization. Treasured personal items such as jewelry, cosmetics, and fine vessels were already being placed in tombs or burials. Aprons, cloaks, penis sheaths, and sandals were made of leather; sandals were also made of papyrus and palm fiber. Geometric paintings in white, black, yellow, or blue decorated leather aprons and cloaks. Ivory and bone combs, pins, and pendants embellished male and female heads. Well-preserved bodies indicate that circumcision was practiced. Amulets, which date back to predynastic times, were worn as jewelry by the living as well as the dead. Protective amulets were usually attached to a string of beads, frequently tubular or spherical in shape, made from carnelian, diorite, garnet, hematite, steatite, serpentine, quartz, agate, limestone, calcite, shells, clay, faience, or copper and infrequently gold or silver.

Funerary amulets were often placed between the various layers of a mummy to protect the body on its dangerous journey to the afterlife. Amulets in the form of a scarab (or dung beetle), which symbolized new life and resurrection, were popular. By the end of the Old Kingdom, the scarab had also become a common item of jewelry. Another prevalent predynastic form of amulet was the eye, especially the *wedjat* eye (the left eye of the god Horus, son of Osiris), which had great protective and restorative qualities. The deceased were provided with palettes of slate used to grind eye makeup throughout predynastic times. The two most common eye paints, malachite (green ore of copper) and galena or kohl (dark gray ore of lead), have been found in the raw state or prepared into a paste or powder. Red ochre was used for lip paint and rouge. Henna was used to color the hair and other parts of the body.

Much of the art of ancient Egypt relates to leadership. The basic artistic conventions and style of Egyptian art can be seen in the *Palette of Narmer* (ca. 3100 B.C.E.), which depicts Narmer, the first pharaoh of the first dynasty of a united Egypt. On the front of the *Palette of Narmer* in the upper register, Narmer, wearing a kilt and the cobra crown of Lower Egypt, is inspecting a battlefield. On the other side of the palette, the pharaoh, wearing a kilt and the white bowling-pin crown of Upper Egypt, is seen in the process of slaying an enemy with his mace. Narmer is followed by a court official carrying his sandals. The carved portraits of kings during the Old Kingdom give additional evidence for royal attire. In the seated statue of Khafre (2500 B.C.E.), the ruler wears

a linen kilt, a common item of clothing in Egypt. Linen was the standard textile used for clothing, bedcovers, and mummy wrappings. In this and other representations, the ruler is depicted with symbols of royalty consisting of a fake rectangular beard and a striped linen headdress (*nemes*) with a *uraeus* (rearing cobra) on the brow. On some works—including the famous coffins and death mask of Tutankhamen—the king is seen wearing a nemes with a vulture's head and a cobra on the brow. For most coffin lids and some statues, the pharaoh holds across his chest a shepherd's crook and the flail, emblems of the god Osiris.

As the high priest for every cult and temple, the king is depicted in wall paintings and reliefs performing major rituals for the gods. All types of dress, human and divine, appear in these scenes. For example, the use of kohl to outline the eyes in black and the wearing of wigs, sometimes very heavy and elaborate ones, are seen frequently. During the Old and Middle Kingdoms, small wooden figures and models were placed in the burials of wealthy individuals. These images provide great insight into the day-to-day tasks and daily dress that would be encountered on an ancient Egyptian estate. Men wear loincloths or kilts, a few with a shoulder strap; women are dressed in loosely fitted dresses or skirts. Many men are bald, but women have straight shoulder-length hair.

The great expansionist and imperialist period for Egypt, called the New Kingdom or Empire (1550–1069 B.C.E.), enjoyed a tremendous amount of wealth. Although grave offerings including jewelry begin in predynastic times, rich finds characterize the New Kingdom. Necklaces strung on linen cord used the same types of beads recorded in the predynastic period, but faience and gold beads became more numerous, especially for broad collars and elaborate necklaces. Linen was produced in a variety of weaves, with softer fabric used for garments such as loincloths, shirts, shifts, and tunics. A delicate, pleated linen cloth was worn as an elegant outer garment. Women's dresses became even looser in the New Kingdom and were decorated with pleats and folds. Dress associated with royal portraits exhibited less change. In all of her portraits, Queen Hatshepsut—one of the most powerful New Kingdom pharaohs—is dressed as any Egyptian ruler would have been, and, in many examples, she is even wearing a fake beard. An excellent presentation of royal dress is the facade of the mortuary temple of Pharaoh Rameses II (1279–1212 B.C.E.) at Abu Simbel, where four colossal statues of the seated pharaoh wear a linen kilt, a nemes with a uraeus, the double crown of Upper and Lower Egypt, and a fake beard.

In 30 B.C.E., Egypt became a Roman province and changes in the art occurred, including the introduction of more realistic portrait mummy masks and a new style of dress. By the mid-first century C.E., funerary masks in the form of a bust were painted on either thin wooden panels or linen burial shrouds and were placed over the face of the deceased. A few males are depicted without clothing, but most wear a white or sometimes a colored tunic and a mantle over the left shoulder. These portraits, painted in tempera, show careful observation of facial features and dress. In fact, the time period for the individual may be determined by the style of the coiffure and facial hair. A variety of beards and mustache types are found for most adult male images. Elderly individuals have gray hair, shown as black and white strokes. In one example from the late first century C.E., a light, barely visible mustache suggests that the deceased was probably in his teens. Jewelry was also meticulously rendered. Gold circular

Four statues of Pharaoh Rameses II at Abu Simbel, Egypt, thirteenth century B.C.E. The pharaoh is wearing royal dress that includes the double crown of Upper and Lower Egypt (with *uraeus*). Photograph by Fred T. Smith.

earrings and gold necklaces with crescent or circular pendants are common. Gilded wreaths, sometimes with attached images such as an ankh, are placed across the crown of the head for both males and females.

Ancient Nubia, centered on the upper Nile River, is located immediately south of Egypt. The basic cultural differences between Nubia and Egypt were recognized by both the ancient Nubians and the Egyptians. In Egyptian wall decoration, for example, the skin color, hairstyles, and clothing of Nubians were clearly different from those of the Egyptians. Items of dress, symbols of leadership, burial practices, and many of the artistic forms remained distinctive throughout history. Yet Nubia's relationship with Egypt was a reciprocal one characterized by a number of shared traits—Nubian culture both influenced Egypt and was influenced by it. During the Neolithic period (5000–3000 B.C.E.), pottery, clay figurines, slate palettes, and fine jewelry were produced and subsequently used for grave offerings. Female figurines with wide hips and usually wearing only a loincloth indicated by a series of horizontal lines date from Neolithic times to the early centuries C.E.

Jewelry was also a major product of Nubia from earliest times, and there is a strong probability that earrings were introduced into Egypt from Nubia. Clothing in Nubia was made of leather, and the loincloths, skirts, girdles, sandals, and caps that were made from tanned leather were frequently decorated with

beads. Some men wore on their heads ostrich feathers secured with beaded headbands. The wearing of leather clothing and the use of beaded decoration has continued in northeastern, eastern, and southern Africa to the present day. Kerma, first settled during the late fourth millennium B.C.E., was a major crafts center. Bronze tools and weapons (especially daggers); jewelry made of faience, gold, silver, and ivory; plus exceptionally fine pottery were some of its products. During the ninth and eighth centuries B.C.E., the powerful kingdom of Kush emerged in Upper Nubia. Major developments at this time occurred around the town of Napata. Egyptian influence on these developments was minimal. In fact, the early finds, especially tombs, reflect the strong African background of the rulers. Bodies of the deceased nobility, dressed in cowhide or tanned leather loincloths, were placed on wooden beds with ivory inlays and legs in the shape of cow hooves. Colossal statues of the Kushite pharaohs wear distinctly Nubian dress, including a caplike headdress with a double serpent. A bronze figure of a kneeling Kushite king—perhaps Taharqo (690–664 B.C.E.), who was also the greatest pharaoh of Egypt's twenty-fifth dynasty—exhibits a number of Kushitic features, including the double uraeus, or serpent, at the forehead (only one was customary in depictions of Egyptian kings). The headdress worn by this figure appears in many depictions of Kushite rulers and consists of a close-fitting skullcap with a band of cloth tied at the back and long cloth streamers. Such headgear was seemingly favored by Kushite kings, but they are also depicted wearing traditional Egyptian crowns and wigs. Another item of Kushitic royal regalia is a cordlike necklace bearing pendants in the form of rams' heads—representing Amun as worshipped at Napata. The Kushite pharaohs also wore a rich assortment of fine jewelry, especially wide armbands, bracelets, and anklets. The exceptional gold jewelry from Napata and Meroe was well known throughout the ancient world. Many of the raw materials for jewelry production came from Nubia—notably gold, semiprecious stones, and an assortment of beads, including ostrich eggshell, glass, stone, and gold. Enamel work was especially well developed, and Meroe was an important early center for this art form.

The culture that emerged at Napata and Meroe, from its beginning in the ninth century B.C.E. to its final phases in the fourth to fifth centuries C.E., exhibited a strong militaristic tendency, as suggested by the numerous depictions of rulers holding weapons and by the practice of burying weapons with the dead. At times, notably from the second century B.C.E., a queen with the title *kandake* acted as the sole ruler of the state, or shared the throne with the king. An unusual feature is that when the kandake is depicted on royal monuments, she is seen as quite heavy—covered with jewelry and wearing elaborately fringed and tasseled robes, a reference to her high status. East of Nubia and the Nile valley, Axum developed as the center of an expanding maritime kingdom from the fifth century B.C.E. to the sixth century C.E. The earliest examples of figurative sculpture display pleated dresses, ankle-length cloaks tied around the neck, multistranded necklaces with large pectorals, and hair in circular forms in low relief.

NORTHWESTERN AFRICA

In 814 B.C.E., the Phoenicians established Carthage, located in what is now Tunisia, as a permanent settlement. A widespread Punic (Carthaginian) object type—with many examples preserved in and around Carthage—is a stone stele, usually functioning as a grave marker but also as an offering at a sacred site. One side was often embellished with relief carving of a deceased person or deity. Clothing, usually some type of tunic, and gesture frequently identified the position or status of the individual. For males of higher status, a toga was worn over the tunic. Carthage was sacked by the Roman army in 146 B.C.E., and it became a Roman province called Africa Proconsularis.

The townhouse of an upper-class Roman was elaborately embellished in the interior with mosaic floors, wall painting, and sculpture. Of these art forms, the numerous mosaics beginning in the second century C.E. provide the best information on material culture. Certain types of images were common throughout the Mediterranean area, such as references to mythology in which the participants wore standard Greek or Roman modes of dress. A good fourth-century mythological scene from the house of Dionysus and Ulysses in Dougga shows Ulysses wearing a short tunic draped over his left shoulder in the manner of a toga. The sailors, carrying shields, are clad in white tunics covered by a heavier blue cloak attached at the right shoulder. Scenes of both daily life and special events in the cities were especially popular in northwestern Africa, and these scenes display a wider spectrum of attire. In banquet scenes, guests, servants, and entertainers were represented with the seated or reclining guests; they were more elaborately attired in robes and cloaks and, in some examples, they carried or wore emblems of sodalities or confraternities to which

they belonged. These emblems included ivy, reeds, five-pointed crowns, and staffs. Male workers and servants often wore plain tunics or a piece of cloth pulled between the legs and tied around the waist. Knee-length tunics decorated in some cases with short, broad bands of color were common for casual activities. Scenes of hunting and rural life involving humans and animals in outdoor settings were quite characteristic of North African mosaics. A mosaic with three registers from the late fourth century C.E. depicts a fortified villa surrounded by the Lord Julius and his wife engaged in seasonal activities. In the upper register, the lady of the estate—wearing a long, voluminous, loose-fitting tunic with her right shoulder exposed—is seated on a bench, holding a fan. In the bottom register, she is adorning herself with the help of a servant who is holding a jewelry chest and handing her a necklace. In both scenes, the woman has wavy locks of hair drawn to the side and piled upon her head. The male workers on the estate generally wear short tunics, leg wrappers, and, for some activities, capes that appear to be made of animal skin. Unadorned tunics were the basic garment for working people at this time.

WEST AFRICA

The earliest West African ceramic sculpture, named after the Nigerian village of Nok, has been conservatively dated to between 500 B.C.E. and 200 C.E. Nok possibly dates back to 900 B.C.E. The great majority of the more than fifteen hundred pieces of terra-cotta sculpture recovered represent human heads and bodies with good evidence of dress. The Nok terra-cottas were first identified and named in 1943 after being discovered in the alluvial deposits of a tin mine. Unfortunately, very few examples have been scientifically excavated. The facial features of Nok heads are stylized and usually share certain common characteristics, such as a semicircular or triangular eye with arching brow. Although a few figures have lightly scored lines on the cheeks and forehead, it is not clear whether these lines represent scarification. Most of the male figures have mustaches, normally consisting of small tufts on each side of the mouth, and beards, usually triangular in shape. All of the figures wear some kind of apparel but do not wear any type of shoe or sandal, finger or toe ring, earring, or lip plug. Both male and female pubic covering in a variety of forms is found. A waistband with a short, flat apron and a bundle of tied grass or plaited palm hung from tubular beads around the waist are two female examples. Over twenty-five types of male pubic covering, including penis sheaths, have been documented.

Variations in hairstyle and adornment are a major characteristic of Nok sculpture. Both males and females are depicted with elaborate hairstyles and in some cases also wear caps. Bernard Fagg, the first scholar on Nok, and later work by Bernard de Grunne have reported the following types of coiffures: tiers and ridges, cones, buns, pendant tresses, vertical ruffs, topknots, hair built up into crownlike coifs, braids, and spirals. The largest head yet known, over fourteen inches (36 centimeters) high, has an elaborate coiffure of five buns. Four of the buns have a hole on top, probably for the insertion of feathers or other decoration. The coiffure is separated from the forehead by three strands of beads or twisted fiber. The smallest known Nok figure, measuring only four and three-sixteenths inches (eleven centimeters), is a kneeling man with one hand up to his head, strongly illustrating the importance of beaded jewelry for Nok, because bracelets, anklets, a thick waistband, a heavy beaded collar, and many strings of beads embellish the figure. Hundreds of quartz beads and the equipment for making them have been found at Nok. Weapons are not represented, but one example shows an individual holding a stick and shield. Northwest of the Nok culture, a burial site with hundreds of clay vessels and terra-cotta figures has been excavated. The objects from this site, which are stylistically more diverse than Nok, have been categorized as Bura and date to between 200 and 1000 C.E. Freestanding and equestrian figures wear necklaces and torso decoration consisting of wide textured bands that in some examples crisscross the chest. Many of the figures are shown wearing large metal bands around the wrist, neck, and lower arm, and raised linear patterns are on the forehead between the eye and ear.

Numerous terra-cotta figurative sculptures were discovered in the inland Niger Delta region around the town of Djenne in Mali. These figures, excavated by Susan and Roderick McIntosh and dating from the ninth to the seventeenth century C.E., display a broad range of iconographic themes. Inland Delta figures may be standing, kneeling, reclining, seated, or mounted on horseback. The males on horseback have beards and wear a circular helmet with chin strap as well as a wrapper with incised decoration, especially at the hemline, and have a knife strapped onto the upper arm. Wearing a knife in this manner is still practiced in the western Sudanic area of Africa today. Other figures are adorned with fringed skirts, necklaces, anklets, and bracelets. Some examples have short vertical cicatrices at the temple. More terra-cotta figures from a tradition called *bankoni* have been found near Bamako, the capital of Mali. These date from the fourteenth or fifteenth century C.E. and are embellished with heavy disklike bangles around the wrists, strands of beads around the waist, and triangular scarification on the torso. Men, sometimes on horseback, have beards; women have coiffures that are usually crested.

Another early Nigerian tradition, largely consisting of pottery vessels and bronze sculpture, was discovered at the site of Igbo Ukwu, located in the northern Igbo area near the city of Awka and dated to the tenth to eleventh centuries. A few artifacts first appeared in 1939, but it was not until the excavations of the early 1960s that a good archaeological record was established. The richness of Igbo Ukwu art suggests a political system with a degree of social stratification. A bronze hilt or fly-whisk handle, with an equestrian figure on top, is one of the most spectacular objects from a burial chamber. In this work, the rider's face is embellished with striated bands. The scarification pattern on this piece resembles Igbo *ichi* scarification, an indicator of rank within the Ozo title association. Ivory tusks and beads were also found in the chamber. Another important Igbo Ukwu discovery, a regalia treasury, yielded a wide variety of objects. Over sixty-three thousand glass and stone beads were found in and around this repository. These items of regalia were probably stored in the treasury when not in use. One example, an openwork cylindrical bronze pot stand or altarpiece, is decorated with male and female images. A fascinating feature of this work is that the woman is embellished with facial scarification (ichi), while the man has circumnavel scarification, representing a gender reversal in the scarification patterns. Both the male and female wear ropelike belts with pubic covering. Various bronze accessories were found in the repository, such as ornate staff heads, frequently encrusted with beads of different colors strung through loops on the casting. In addition, coiled-snake staff ornaments and a number of small figurative pendants three to eight and a half inches (eight

Phoenician grave marker from Carthage (Tunisia), second century B.C.E., with a relief carving of the deceased dressed in a toga. The dress and gesture of the carved figure represents the level of status. Photograph by Fred T. Smith.

to twenty-two centimeters) long came from the repository. Igbo Ukwu is one of the richest African sites for actual accessories.

The ancient Nigerian city of Ile-Ife is a sacred place for all Yoruba people. It is possible to date the art of ancient Ife from the tenth to the fifteenth centuries C.E. From the late 1950s, systematic excavations have been undertaken. The production of glass beads appears to have been a major industry in ancient Ife. Fragments of crucibles used in the manufacturing process have been excavated in different parts of the town. Although a number of different types of art objects have been produced at Ife, the best known are the terra-cotta and cast-brass heads, which conform to a style of idealized naturalism and are often marked with overall scarification, especially the terra-cotta ones. Two specimens, however, have raised keloids instead of incised lines. Moreover, a few heads have unusual patterns of scarification such as cat's-whisker marks. These heads, functioning as royal ancestral shrine pieces, are much more numerous than the brass ones and considerably more varied in their facial features, dress, and scale. Hairstyles and headgear show a wide range of variation. Wicker caps—sometimes decorated with a few rows of beads—or beaded caps positioned on the back of the head constitute the most basic type of headwear. Some of these caps have holes for inserting additional enhancements such as feathers or are modeled with other decorative elements. One example has a circlet around the head with three bell-like ornaments jutting onto the brow. The most elaborate terra-cotta head from Ife, said to represent a queen, wears a complex five-tiered beaded crown with a crest fragment on the center of the forehead. Traces of red and white paint exist on the crown—with traces of red paint found on the necklace, possibly to indicate colored beads. A most spectacular Ife casting is a brass vessel of less than five inches (thirteen centimeters) in height depicting a queen wrapped around a pot and holding a small human-headed staff in her hand. As an indicator of her social position, the queen is wearing a four-tiered crown with crest that has been found on other works representing a royal woman.

Although almost identical in style to the terra-cotta heads, Ife brass heads are less varied in scale and detail. Some of them have overall scarification, and some have a crown cast as part of the piece. The fact that not all Ife heads have scarification is problematic, because patterns of scarification in Africa usually refer to ethnic identity, status, or a particular associational affiliation. Because these heads represent royals, usually the king, one would expect that all would be identical in terms of this trait. Possibly, the striated marks represent a temporary embellishment for a specific ritual occasion. A number of unsubstantiated reasons for this phenomenon have been suggested, such as the pieces' representing different time periods or dynasties. The life-size heads are the most numerous and do not have a crown as part of the casting but would have worn an actual crown or the appropriate headgear of a royal. These heads have holes for the attachment of the real crown.

Brass figures representing the king (*oni*) also have been found. With the full figures, the overall nature of beaded adornment for ancient Ife is more fully revealed. The regalia of the oni includes a beaded crown with vertical crest, heavy beaded collar, various strands of beads on the chest, longer strands of beads framing the torso, and beaded anklets and wristlets. King figures display a double-bow pendant on the chest, which is an emblem of royal status. The ruler wears a wrapper elaborately tied on the right side. Moreover, in his left hand, the king is holding a ram's horn, possibly filled with magical substances, and in his right hand he has a scepter or handle of a fly whisk, both power symbols.

About one thousand soapstone figures have been found near the northeastern Yoruba town of Esie, which represents the largest concentration of stone sculpture in Africa. Available evidence suggests that these carvings date from the twelfth to the fifteenth centuries C.E. Male and female figures with elaborate hairstyles and beaded ornaments are usually depicted sitting on a stool. Many Esie figures hold staffs, cutlasses, or daggers, which depict leadership regalia. Although Esie overlaps chronologically with Ife and a few formal similarities exist, the styles of these two traditions are clearly different. For Esie, coiffures, for example, are more elaborate and the scarification is more varied. An unusual bronze, found 120 miles (193 kilometers) north of Ife near the town of Tada, is a standing figure representing a warrior wearing an embroidered tunic. Around his neck, he wears a leopard-tooth necklace and a pectoral with depictions of birds and a ram's head. On his head, he wears an unusually complex helmet, topped by abstract birds and fronted by a medallion in the form of a horned human face with snakes issuing from the nostrils. The birds relate stylistically to the beaded crowns of contemporary Yoruba kings as well as to medicine staffs from the Benin kingdom to the east. In addition, a bat or snake-winged bird motif appears on the side of the figure's garment. This ancient Ife motif is a symbol of the king's supernatural power.

Although not excavated, over five hundred years of Benin artifacts were removed from the royal palace with the British conquest in 1897, including the two largest groups of shrine heads and plaques. Three chronologically distinct style periods have been proposed for Benin: Early period, from the fourteenth to the mid-sixteenth century; Middle period, from the mid-sixteenth to the late seventeenth century; and Late period, from the late seventeenth century to 1897. The brass heads provide insight into changing patterns of royal dress. A tiered coiffure or headdress, iron inlays above the eyes, and a coral bead collar around the neck are characteristic traits of the early style. The anthropologist, Paula Girshick has suggested that this type of head is not a royal ancestor but rather a trophy head because it lacks an elaborate headdress. She suggests that these heads represent vanquished enemies, in part, because the particular hairstyle and the marks above the eyes have been documented in neighboring groups. The brass heads of the Middle and Late periods became progressively heavier, less naturalistic, and more ornate. The Middle period heads, which have three raised scarification marks on the forehead above each eye, depict the *oba* (king) in full regalia wearing a lattice-work beaded crown. Strands of beads frame the face, and a high beaded collar envelops the chin. By the Late period, the head has additional ornaments, such as vertical wings projecting from the headdress. The oba today still wears the same elaborate coral-beaded headdress seen on these Late period heads.

About one thousand palace plaques were produced during the Middle period, providing an excellent document of Benin court life and dress of that time. Details of jewelry, clothing, and weapons are skillfully replicated. A few plaques portray ritual or ceremonial scenes, but most represent members of the royal establishment and important foreigners. By the sixteenth century, war chiefs and the military were increasingly influential and consequently were frequently depicted on plaques. A war chief can be identified by a leopard-tooth necklace with a pendant bell, a leopard-skin vest, and a shield or weapon. Portuguese warriors and dignitaries are depicted wearing sixteenth-century military uniforms. These plaques are fascinating because they are an early example of the representation of Europeans in African art. The two most important sword types, the *ada* and *eben*, are depicted on plaques. The longer-bladed ada—a more ancient type dating to the first dynasty—can be used only by the oba, a few high-ranking chiefs, and certain priests. The eben are associated with chiefs who receive them when they acquire their title. Chiefs either carry an eben on ceremonial occasions or have an attendant carry it for them. On a few palace plaques, the oba is shown with an eben in his right hand.

EASTERN AND SOUTHERN AFRICA

Seven hollow terra-cotta heads, found in the Transvaal site of Lyndenburg in South Africa, have been dated to the first millennium C.E. The heads are decorated with notched bands across the face and forehead, probably representing scarification, while the necks

A plaque from the Benin Kingdom, sixteenth–seventeenth century C.E. Approximately a thousand plaques were produced during this time, showing the type of clothing that was worn by members of the royal establishment and war chiefs. Gift of Joseph Hirshhorn to the Smithsonian Institution in 1979 (85-19-18). Photograph by Franko Khoury. National Museum of African Art, Smithsonian Institution.

are banded and incised with a chevron pattern depicting a beaded collar. In addition, small terra-cotta figurines of women and cattle, dated from the ninth to fourteenth centuries C.E., have been found in numerous southern African sites. On the female figures, some horizontal grooves appear on the torso, and incised lines or raised pellets of clay below the waist may indicate beaded girdles or loincloths. The Limpopo River valley of southeastern Africa was a major source for small terra-cotta figurines by the ninth century C.E. The archaeologist Peter Garland has suggested that these figurines may have been amulets, charms, or votive offerings.

After 800 C.E., several large settlements emerged in hilly locations south of the Zambezi River, including the Mapungubwe state, which achieved prominence around 1100 C.E. Around 1250 C.E., another state made up of Shona peoples north of Mapungubwe replaced the latter as the most important political entity in the region, and the hegemony of Great Zimbabwe lasted until the mid-fifteenth century. Excavations of ceramic spinning weights have revealed that the Shona also practiced weaving and spinning in the thirteenth century. Many small soapstone figurines from 1100 to 1550 C.E. have been found at Great Zimbabwe. The female figurines had bare breasts and cylindrical torsos decorated with groupings of usually three small raised lines that might represent a type of clothing. Unfortunately, very little archaeological work has been done on any of the Zimbabwean sculpture.

During the second half of the fifteenth century, new centers of power at Khami and Mutapa continued the Shona traditions that had been developed at Zimbabwe. These new states survived, in one form or another, into the middle to late nineteenth century. Based on archaeological and written documentation, it would appear that men wore long undyed cotton skirts over which they placed a wrapper of animal skin. Unmarried women wore a pubic apron; married women covered the apron with a cotton wrapper. Both men and women wore necklaces, bracelets, and anklets of copper, bronze, or gold. One of the best descriptions of local dress from this area comes from a seventeenth-century burial at a Portuguese trading post.

As cultural artifacts, the specific elements of apparel and body adornment in Africa have many aspects of meaning; they serve as vehicles for the expression of values, symbols of identity and social status, and statements of aesthetic preference. Each item of a costume has its own history and sociocultural significance and must be considered along with the total ensemble. Certain categories or types of dress are shared by a number of different cultures, yet the range of variation on the continent has been significant from early times to the present based on the archaeological record.

References and Further Reading

Adams, Barbara. *Predynastic Egypt.* Aylesbury, UK: Shire Publications, 1988.

Eyo, Ekpo, and Frank Willett. *Treasures of Ancient Nigeria.* New York: Alfred A Knopf, 1980.

Fagg, Bernard. *Nok Terracottas.* London: Ethnographica, 1990.

Garlake, Peter. *The Hunter's Vision: The Prehistoric Art of Zimbabwe.* London: British Museum Publication, 1995.

Garlake, Peter. *Early Art and Architecture of Africa.* Oxford, UK: Oxford University Press, 2002.

Grunne, Bernard, de. *The Birth of Art in Black Africa: Nok Sculpture in Nigeria.* Paris: A Biro, 1998.

Holl, Augustin F.C. *Saharan Rock Art.* Walnut Creek, CA: Altamira Press, 2004.

Hornung, Erik, and Betsy M. Bryan, eds. *The Quest for Immortality: Treasures of Ancient Egypt.* Washington, DC: National Gallery of Art, 2002.

Kendall, Timothy. *Kerma and the Kingdom of Kush 2500–1500 B.C.* Washington, DC: National Museum of African Art, 1995.

Lewis-Williams, J. D. *Discovering Southern African Rock Art.* Cape Town and Johannesburg, South Africa: David Phillip, 1990.

Ling, Roger. *Ancient Mosaics.* Princeton, NJ: Princeton University Press, 1998.

Perani, Judith, and Fred T. Smith. *Visual Arts of Africa: Gender, Power, and Life Cycle Rituals.* Upper Saddle River, NJ: Prentice Hall, 1998.

Phillipson, David W. *African Archaeology.* Cambridge, UK: Cambridge University Press, 1985.

Shaw, Thurstan. *Nigeria: Its Archaeology and Early History.* London: Thames and Hudson, 1978.

Stahl, Ann Bower, ed. *African Archaeology.* Oxford, UK: Blackwell Publishing, 2005.

Vogelsang-Eastwood, Gillian. *Pharaonic Egyptian Clothing.* Leiden, The Netherlands: Brill, 1993.

Willett, Frank. *Ife in the History of West African Sculpture.* New York: McGraw-Hill, 1967.

Fred T. Smith

Photographic and Other Visual Sources

- Early Depictions
- Missionaries, Anthropologists, and Art Historians
- Professional Photographers in the Twentieth Century
- African Photographers and African Sitters

Dress in Africa has attracted the attention of foreign observers since the earliest encounters with peoples on the continent. Whether they deemed it exotic, curious, ugly, beautiful, or comical, writers of all backgrounds often mentioned and depicted dress in their publications. From the seventeenth century onward, descriptions of Africa were published with engravings, woodcuts, and, later, lithographs, among other types of illustrations, that helped readers to envision faraway worlds and peoples and their garments, jewelry, coiffures, and body modifications.

With the advent of photography in the nineteenth century, images that showed dress became more common and began to circulate in different ways. Initially photographs were distributed in limited numbers of single images and, by the 1870s, in the form of cabinet cards. A *cabinet card* was a paper print mounted on a cardboard backing measuring four and one-fourth by six and a half inches (eleven by seventeen centimeters), which was

inscribed with the name of the photographer and studio location on its front. Smaller *cartes de visite*, photographic prints on cardboard in the size of two and one-third by three and a half inches (six by nine centimeters), became popular in the 1860s, and—as their designation indicated—were photographic portraits of their bearers to be exchanged during visits. By the 1880s, both cabinet cards and cartes de visite—which presented images of landscapes, architectural views, and foreign peoples—were produced in larger quantities and could be purchased by eager customers in African harbor towns and in Europe and the United States. Another popular medium was *stereographs*, which consist of two side-by-side cardboard-mounted pictures, paired to create the illusion of a three-dimensional image when viewed through a stereoscope. Stereographs were popular in Europe and the United States from the 1850s through the first decade of the twentieth century. They, too, brought images of distant peoples and their dress to the European and American consumer. The University of California, Riverside, California Museum of Photography has an extensive archive of these stereocards, the Keystone-Mast Collection (www.cmp.ucr.edu).

Printing technologies did not allow the cost-effective rendering of actual photographs in books and magazines until the last decade of the nineteenth century. Therefore, artists employed by publishing houses transformed photographs into engravings and other formats, often altering the originals to make them more interesting or beautiful. When cheaper techniques, such as the

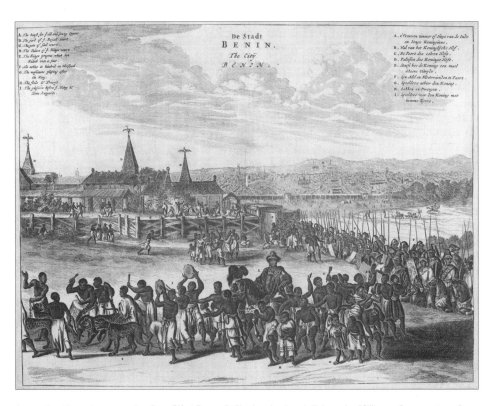

A seventeenth-century engraving from Olfert Dapper's *Naukeurige beschrijvinge der Afrikaensche gewesten*, showing a spectacle at the court of the Kingdom of Benin (present-day Nigeria). Manuscripts Archives and Rare Books Division, Schomburg Center for Research in Black Culture, The New York Public Library, Astor, Lenox and Tilden Foundations.

collotype and halftone printing processes, allowed the addition of photographic plates to books and illustrated magazines, images also began to appear in picture postcards, which, during the first two decades of the twentieth century, circulated by the millions and were the focus of a buying and collecting craze that swept the entire globe. In their initial visual coverage, these postcards were akin to newspapers and magazines. They were not only souvenirs purchased in Africa and sent home; they could also be acquired in postcard emporiums in Europe and the United States and could be exchanged among collectors. Their themes were much broader than today, when postcards depict landscapes, fauna and flora, and, of course, the inhabitants of major tourist destinations.

Initially in the mid-nineteenth century, photography was the domain of a few enterprising individuals. The profession of photographer, who operated a studio and took images of people and scenes, only developed in the second half of that century. It should be noted that many Africans entered this lucrative line of work, opening photographic businesses along the western and central African coasts, side by side with studios of European practitioners. The detailed history of African photography needs yet to be written, but we know that in 1853 the African American daguerreotypist Augustus Washington (1820/21–1875) left the United States and arrived in Liberia, where he established a studio in Monrovia. By 1857, he expanded his business to Freetown, Sierra Leone, and the Gambia, as photographic historian Ann M. Shumard described in her 2000 monograph entitled *A Durable Memento. Portraits by Augustus Washington, African American Daguerreotypist.* Washington may well have served as an inspiration for enterprising African men who took up photography as a profession. By the 1880s, Africans operated studios or worked as traveling photographers along the West African coast. In East Africa, photographers from India (mainly of Goan origin) predominated. The photographer A.C. Gomes, for example, who hailed from Goa, opened his first studio in Zanzibar in 1868, and others followed. Portraiture was one of the most common ways to make a living for all photographers, whether European or African. In reference to the study of dress, these early portraits are excellent resources to examine fashions, innovations, and transformations over time.

With the advent of handheld cameras, photography ceased to be the domain of trained specialists. By the end of the nineteenth century, handheld cameras began to replace earlier cumbersome models that required longer exposure times and tripods. Amateur photographers now took images for family albums, to exchange among friends, and to circulate in many other ways. Among these colonials and travelers in Africa a small but significant number were scholars—anthropologists and, in the second half of the twentieth century, art historians—who employed photography in documentation and research.

The twentieth century also saw the development of new photographic specializations: the documentary photographer, the news photographer, and the artist photographer. Many of these professionals photographed in Africa—some with general agendas and a few with particular emphasis on capturing African dress. Looking at the enormous number of images produced in Africa, it might not be an exaggeration to state that any portrait, any depiction of people, any family snapshot, whether taken by professional or amateur photographers, added to the huge corpus of visual documentation that can be consulted by scholars of

dress. Other significant advances included the invention of celluloid film and the later arrival of color film and 35mm slides.

The following discussion will focus on these visual materials useful as evidence in the study of dress. It differs from many other entries in this encyclopedia, which summarize an already established body of research, because it may be the first overview of this subject and thus brings together unfamiliar materials. The first part deals with prephotographic modes of documentation, such as engravings, woodcuts, and lithographs. Other sections explore the work of missionaries, anthropologists, and art historians who had special interests in visual documentation and discuss the oeuvre of several Western professional photographers whose images are particularly rich resources. Finally, the focus will be on representations authored by African photographers and their patrons, which are of unique importance not just as evidence on dress, but also as testimony to the development of photography in Africa. This contribution does not claim to be comprehensive—far from it—and there are by necessity many omissions of important photographers and relevant bodies of visual documentation (such as moving films) that are not included in this article because they are comprehensive sources in themselves. Rather,

Ein Weib der Njam=Njam (nach eigner Photographie von Richard Buchta).
Vgl. Text, Einleitung, S. 63.

A woodcut after a photograph by Richard Buchta depicting an Azande woman, from what is now northeastern Democratic Republic of Congo. Published in Friedrich Ratzel's *Völkerkunde*, vol. 1, *Die Natuvölker Afrikas*, 1887. Courtesy of Christraud M. Geary.

this short essay provides some access to and stimulates thought about visual sources and resources for the study of dress.

EARLY DEPICTIONS

From the first explorations onward, beginning in B.C.E., European authors described the lands and peoples of Africa. Writings proliferated after the sixteenth century. Some of the authors had firsthand experience, having come to the continent as travelers, traders, and missionaries, while others compiled their accounts from various earlier writings. Among the latter was the Dutch physician and writer Olfert Dapper (1635–1689), who in 1668 published *Naukeurige beschrijvinge der Afrikaensche gewesten*, an extensive description of Africa accompanied by maps and plates. Adam Jones, a historian who specializes in early sources on Africa, suggested in a 1990 article that the maps and the engravings were the work of the book's publisher, Van Meurs, who had his artists base them on maps and illustrations in earlier works. Thus, depictions of African dress, such as the attire of the courtiers in the famous engraving of Benin City, the capital of the Benin kingdom in present-day Nigeria, were mostly imagination, reflecting European ideas about African dress conventions. While useful for research on European modes of representation, the images do not help much in the reconstruction of seventeenth-century African dress.

By contrast, the renderings in another early account resulted from direct observation. In 1817, the English traveler Thomas Edward Bowdich (1790–1824) undertook a mission to Kumase, the capital of the Asante kingdom in modern Ghana, in order to facilitate the establishment of British control over the coastal areas with the support of the Asante. In his lively 1819 book of the voyage, *Mission from Cape Coast Castle to Ashantee*, he mentioned the splendid reception he received in Kumase. He was particularly impressed with the military leaders' (the "captains'") dress and described it in some detail.

> The dress of the captains … was a war cap, with gilded rams horns projecting in front, the sides extended beyond all proportions by immense plumes of eagles feathers, and fastened under the chin with bands of cowries. Their vest was of red cloth, covered with fetishes and saphies [scraps of Moorish writing, as charms against evil] in gold and silver; and embroidered cases of almost every colour, which flapped against their bodies as they moved, intermixed with small brass bells, the horns and tails of animals, shells and knives; long leopard tails hung down their backs, over a small bow covered with fetishes. They wore loose cotton trowsers, with immense boots of a dull red leather, coming half way up the thigh, and fastened by small chains to their cartouch or waist belt; these were also ornamented with bells, horses tails, strings of amulets, and innumerable shreds of leather; … their black countenances heightened the effect of this attire, and completed a figure scarcely human.

A hand-colored engraving by Bowdich himself accompanies this vivid account and turns out to be an accurate if somewhat clumsy rendering useful for scholarly research.

Some forty years later, the German explorer Heinrich Barth (1821–1865) recounted his experiences during an expedition from North Africa through the Sahara to western and central Africa in a five-volume work that appeared in an English version entitled *Travels and Discoveries in North and Central Africa: Being a Journal of an Expedition Undertaken Under the Auspices of H.B.M.'s Government in the Years 1849–1855*. Unlike Bowdich's accurate rendering of an Asante military leader in full regalia, two lithographs by J.M. Bennertz based on Barth's sketches show an idealized Musgum chief in northern Cameroon and a chief of Kanem in northern Nigeria in flowing robes and in poses that resemble conventional representations of non-Western peoples in earlier accounts, which were a testimony to Western imagination rather than visual documents on African dress. A closer analysis of the images reveals, however, that certain elements of adornment are accurately rendered, a reminder that all such illustrations need to be carefully assessed when used in the study of attire.

By the mid-nineteenth century, photographic processes that allowed the production of a permanently visible image through the action of light on a sensitive surface had become manageable enough for Europeans with an interest in new technologies to take the first pictures in Africa. At the same time, European powers were gearing up to bring most of the continent under colonial domination. Exploration reached a fever pitch, and many travelers created astonishing pictures of Africans. The Austrian explorer Richard Buchta (1845–1894), for example, journeyed up the Nile to Uganda in 1877 and published in 1881 amazing depictions of people in an album entitled *Die oberen Nil-Länder; Volkstypen und Landschaften, dargestellt in 160 Photographien* (The Upper Nile Countries: Ethnic Types and Landscapes in 160 Photographs). These acclaimed early images appeared in many magazines and books, most often in the form of engravings. Scholars of dress might consult the photographic records of other explorers, among them the British journalist and explorer Henry Morton Stanley (1849–1904), who traveled in central Africa and published many books; Paul du Chaillu (1835–1903), a French explorer and scholar who visited in Gabon; and the German Julius Falkenstein (1842–1917), a medical doctor and avid amateur photographer who participated in the German Loango expedition in central Africa. Du Chaillu's pictures, in the form of engravings, illustrated his 1861 book entitled *Explorations and Adventures in Equatorial Africa, with Accounts of the Manners and Customs of the People, and of the Chase of the Gorilla, Crocodile, and Other Animals*, while Falkenstein's images appear as engravings in his book *Afrikas Westküste* (1883).

MISSIONARIES, ANTHROPOLOGISTS, AND ART HISTORIANS

In 1884–1885, representatives of Great Britain, France, Germany, Spain, Portugal, the Belgian crown, and a few other countries assembled in Berlin to draw the colonial borders of their African possessions. Once the territories had been officially delineated, the colonial penetration began in full force. Missionaries were at the forefront of bringing the Christian faith and what they and their contemporaries perceived as civilization to African peoples. Part of this effort focused on eradicating the outward signs of perceived savagery and paganism—the civilizing of the African body by dressing and grooming it in European ways. The dress forms of new African Christians constitute an interesting arena for research, and the visual sources to do so can be found in the repositories of many missionary societies. The camera proved to be an indispensable tool for the missionaries to document their

Ndebele woman, South Africa, ca.1940. Photograph by Constance Stuart Larrabee, who opened a studio in Pretoria and took photographic portraits of the diverse groups of people in South Africa. EEPA 1998-060531. Constance Stuart Larrabee Collection, Eliot Elisofon Photographic Archives, National Museum of African Art, Smithsonian Institution.

work and, beyond the missionary endeavor, even at times to capture peoples in their cultural setting. Missionary societies have opened their doors to researchers, among them the Mission 21 (formerly known as the Basel Mission), whose Web site contains a wealth of images showing all kinds of African dress in Ghana and Cameroon in the nineteenth and twentieth centuries (see www. bmpix.org). Other missionary societies will follow suit in making

these materials accessible as they become increasingly aware of the importance of their visual holdings.

The second half of the nineteenth century—with European rule over Africa being implemented—was also the time when the discipline of anthropology (a word derived from the Greek, meaning the study of man) developed. Its practitioners pursued the examination of African peoples, including their material culture and, with it, dress and bodily practices. In 1887, the German geographer Friedrich Ratzel (1844–1904) devoted a short discussion to the importance of dress and adornment in the introductory part of his *Völkerkunde* (ethnography), which appeared in many editions and also in the English language under the title *The History of Mankind* in 1897. Unable to include photographs because cheap printing techniques had not yet developed, Ratzel added over one thousand woodcuts and thirty chromolithographs. The first volume contains many images of Africans based on photographs, recycling mostly the illustrations that had appeared in the earlier accounts, such as those of Buchta, du Chaillu, and Falkenstein mentioned earlier.

As photography made inroads and printing techniques improved, now allowing the rendering of photographs in publications, photographic documentation became a requirement for professional anthropologists and for men and women in Africa—administrators, military, merchants, and plantation owners who had scholarly aspirations and wanted to contribute to science. In 1899, Felix von Luschan (1854–1924), the director of the Berlin Museum für Völkerkunde (now the Ethnological Museum Berlin), produced a small guide for ethnographic observation and collecting for the layperson. In terse entries, he presented a to-do list. Entry 39 on page 13 states, for example: "Everything that is part of dress must be collected and exactly registered, or possibly at least fixed through sketches or photographs." Some fifty years later, in the often reprinted sixth edition (1951) of the British bible for anthropologists and amateur scholars entitled *Notes and Queries on Anthropology*, similar advice is given: "Photographs, drawings, paper-patterns and native-made models, and descriptions are necessary when the garments themselves cannot be obtained." It comes as no surprise, then, that many anthropologists created extensive photographic documentation of dress, jewelry, and bodily practices. Historians of African art, a field that developed in the second half of the twentieth century, adopted the fieldwork methods of anthropologists and also engaged in photography, activities that resulted in a huge archive of images depicting dress. Many illustrations in this encyclopedia are a testimony to these practices.

Some anthropologists and art historians produced exceptional photographs that have been frequently published, while amateurs who shared these scholarly interests were also active. A few of the most prolific and outstanding of these scholar-photographers should be mentioned here, for their work is of great importance for the study of dress. Alfred Martin Duggan-Cronin (1874–1954), a South African of Irish descent, embarked on an ambitious project to document the peoples of southern Africa visually. Among his many books containing photographs of peoples of the region is the multivolume 1928 work *The Bantu Peoples of South Africa*. While Duggan-Cronin focused over many years on one large region of the continent, the Austrian Hugo A. Bernatzik (1897–1953) conducted two relatively short expeditions, one to the then Anglo-Egyptian Sudan in 1927 and another to the Bissagos Islands off the coast of Portuguese Guinea in West Africa in 1930–1931. Bernatzik was a professionally trained documentary photographer and later in life also received a doctorate in cultural anthropology. His archive, now in the private collection of Kevin Conru in Brussels, is a treasure when it comes to analyzing dress and jewelry forms. Numerous black-and-white images depict daily activities, rituals, and ceremonies among the Bidjogo of the Bissagos Islands and the Nuba, Nuer, Shilluk, Dinka, and other

peoples on the upper Nile. The 2003 book *Bernatzik—Africa* highlights some of his most impressive photographs.

Not all scholars and amateur anthropologists were as accomplished photographers as Duggan-Cronin or Bernatzik. Yet their images have great relevance. Robert Sutherland Rattray (1881–1938) was a British anthropologist who worked in Ghana, in particular among the Asante. His photographs can be found in the Pitt Rivers Museum at Oxford as well as in his many publications, among them the 1927 book *Religion & Art in Ashanti*. The American Melville J. Herskovits (1895–1963), who taught at Northwestern University in Evanston, Illinois, was one of the founding fathers of African and African American studies in the United States. During his fieldwork, he always carried a camera and sometimes made films. His photographic documentation of the Fon peoples in Benin (formerly Dahomey) has been preserved in the Eliot Elisofon Photographic Archives (EEPA) at the National Museum of African Art, Smithsonian Institution in Washington, DC. Its Web site (http://africa.si.edu/research/archives.html) is a must when researching dress in Africa.

In a field that requires visual documentation, many art historians have made major pictorial contributions. The following discussion is by no means comprehensive, but highlights some of the more significant holdings, some still with the scholars, other accessible in visual archives or through the Web. Doran H. Ross, former director of the Fowler Museum at UCLA and one of the editors of this volume, is also among the best and most prolific photographers, having documented Ghanaian peoples as well as those in many other parts of Africa. Christopher Roy, of the University of Iowa, focuses mostly on Burkina Faso in his own extensive photographic and filmic documentation. A Web site dedicated to the University of Iowa's Art and Life in Africa Project contains a wealth of materials that can be used in the analysis of dress (www.uiowa.edu/~africart). Hans-Joachim Koloss, former curator of African ethnology at the Ethnological Museum Berlin came out of the German tradition of visual documentation of material culture, best represented by the Institut für den wissenschaftlichen Film, Wissen und Medien (Institute for Academic Film, Knowledge and Media) of Göttingen University, Germany (www.iwf.de), where he received his initial photographic training. His thousands of slides and films are a first-rate documentation on dress and masquerades in the northern parts of the Cameroon Grassfields and illustrate the catalog *Cameroon: African Art and Kings*, edited by Swiss anthropologist Lorenz Homberger in 2008.

Even less accomplished photographers but luminaries in the discipline left relevant photographic records behind, among them the American Roy Sieber (1923–2001). Christraud M. Geary, who studies the history of photography in Africa, discussed the photographs of this major figure in African art history in the United States in a 2003 article. His images are also in the EEPA. This archive also contains the work of many other scholar photographers, among them images of the Yoruba peoples in Nigeria by the art historian Henry John Drewal and the performance specialist Margaret Thompson Drewal. Their documentation of masquerades allows the analysis of dress used in these and other rituals. Their colleague Marilyn Houlberg, another Yoruba specialist and one of the first scholars to study the integration of photography into African cultural practice, also donated her images to the EEPA. The art historian Herbert M. Cole took photographs in Kenya, Ghana, and Nigeria, and the anthropologist

One of the Yoruba kings, the Alake of Abeokuta (seated), and his son, the Chief Justice of the Federation of Nigeria (supreme court), 1959, photographed by Eliot Elisofon, a photographer for *Life* magazine who traveled extensively in West and Central Africa. EEPA EECL 2016. Eliot Elisofon photographic Archives, National Museum of African Art, Smithsonian Institution.

Simon Ottenberg provided images from Sierra Leone and Nigeria with an important corpus of pictures taken during masked performances of the Afikpo Igbo peoples, now at the EEPA.

PROFESSIONAL PHOTOGRAPHERS IN THE TWENTIETH CENTURY

In the twentieth century, Africa became the destination of many professional photographers in the employment of magazines, such as *Life*, on assignment for official projects, or working independently. Their often huge photographic archives inevitably contain important images of dress and jewelry in Africa. In some instances these professionals even devoted lavish photographic books to this topic. In the early 1930s, Constance Stuart Larrabee (1914–2000), a young woman from South Africa, apprenticed with a famous woman photographer in London and then attended the Bavarian State Institute for Photography in Munich, Germany. Upon her return to South Africa—a mere twenty-one years old—she opened a studio in Pretoria and began photographing the diverse peoples around her, then an unusual pursuit considering the racist regime in her country. Her images, which she perceived as art and not ethnographic documentation, provide an unsurpassed look at the Ndebele, Zulu, Tswana, and other Africans then living in townships, or

"locations." Captivating, close-up portraits make her black-and-white photographs prime sources on dress and jewelry. A selection can be found on the Web site of the EEPA, which now holds Larrabee's extensive collections.

During the same time period, Polish photographer Casimir Zagourski (1883–1944), who lived in what was then Léopoldville (now Kinshasa) in the Belgian Congo, embarked on an ambitious documentation project. Catering mainly to a Belgian clientele, he began photographing peoples in central and eastern Africa for a series of over four hundred photographic prints and postcards, entitled *L'Afrique qui disparaît!* (Disappearing Africa). Zagourski had two goals. On the one hand, he meant to depict the various "types," now a derogatory term that refers to organizing peoples by their racial characteristics—ranging from the least evolved to the white "race" at the apex, which was a nineteenth- and early-twentieth-century practice in anthropology, now discredited. On the other hand, Zagourski created an unsurpassed visual ethnography of the region. Seen from today's perspective, the images or peoples and their rituals, which include masked performances, are a treasure trove for research on dress and jewelry as they existed in the 1930s. One should bear in mind, however, that like many other photographers Zagourski tried to capture primordial Africa, an Africa that never existed. Thus, he systematically omitted all visual allusions to change in dress over time and rarely depicted people in contemporary attire based on dress forms from Europe. Sets of his images can be found in several archives, among them the Photograph Study Collection of the Department of Arts of Africa, Oceania, and the Americas (AAOA), Metropolitan Museum of Art in New York, and in many private photographic holdings.

The mid-twentieth century was the period of new media, such as television, and saw a proliferation of illustrated books and magazines—now with color photographs. Journalist/photographers, who published photographic accounts of their voyages, were much in demand. René Gardi (1909–2000), a Swiss author and photographer captured peoples in northern Cameroon and other parts of Africa. Bernhard Gardi, his anthropologist son who lives in Basel, still owns the image collection of his father. In France, photographer Michel Huët (b. 1917) engaged in long-term photography and publishing projects, which resulted in several books, among them *The Dance, Art, and Ritual of Africa*, published in 1978. Many of his colorful images also appeared in postcards from the 1960s to the 1980, distributed by his picture agency Hoa-Qui, which to this day is based in Paris.

The American Eliot Elisofon (1911–1973) came out of a different milieu. A photographer for *Life* magazine, he discovered his passion for Africa south of the Sahara and African art when he was sent on assignment in 1947 to cover a trip of the British royal family through Kenya and South Africa. This was the first of his many voyages mainly to West and Central Africa, which resulted in a substantial photographic documentation. He left a legacy of over one hundred twenty thousand black-and-white images and 35mm color slides, many of them useful for the analysis of dress. His images are in great demand and have appeared in numerous art historical publications They can be found at the Eliot Elisofon Photographic Archives (EEPA), at the Harry Ransom Center (University of Texas at Austin), and in the extensive archives of Time-Life in New York.

Other photographers followed in Elisofon's footsteps, creating similarly extensive visual records. Chester Higgins Jr. (b. 1946), a staff photographer of the *New York Times* and author of photographic books, has dedicated much of his life to photography in Africa (see www.chesterhiggins.com), as have the American Carol Beckwith (b. 1945) and the Australian Angela Fisher (b. 1947). After Fisher published her photographic book *Africa Adorned* in 1984, which provides ample documentation of African dress and jewelry, she began to collaborate with Carol Beckwith, whose first photographic book, *Maasai*, appeared in 1980. Like *Africa Adorned*, *Maasai* contains valuable images of dress and jewelry. Their most important collaboration, the 1999 *African Ceremonies*, traces Beckwith and Fisher's travels through the continent and their personal visions of African peoples.

One of the questions to be asked of all photographers who work in the commercial and art market arenas pertains to issues of staging and adjusting the dress of their photographic subjects so that the pictures at times present traditional Africa and thus also a restricted, traditionalized view of dress and jewelry. A 1995 essay by Christraud Geary entitled "Photographic Practice in Africa and Its Implications for the Use of Historical Photographs as Contextual Evidence" clearly points to pitfalls when using such imagery as visual record for research. Some professional photographers' work has come under heavy criticism for this practice. Leni Riefenstahl (1902–2003) is one such case. While her two hugely successful photographic books about the Nuba in southern Sudan—the 1974 *The Last of the Nuba* and its 1976 sequel *The People of Kau*—present a unique resource to analyze body

A woman in evening dress, Bamako, Mali, photographed by Seydou Keita, mid-twentieth century. Keita provided his sitters with accessories and occasionally lent them different types of attire in which to be photographed. Courtesy of the Pigozzi Collection.

modification and various forms of dress and jewelry, she was also accused of manipulating the images, asking Nuba men and women to perform for her camera and don traditional dress, or, in this case, discard Western-style attire, to create a timeless African past. Rarely have photographic books raised such profound criticism; in this case, the criticism was due, in part, to the photographer's background. Riefenstahl was a propaganda filmmaker and film star in Hitler's Germany. In her essay "Fascinating Fascism," which appeared in the *New York Book Review* on 6 February 1975, critic and writer Susan Sontag chastised the first Nuba book as celebrating the primitive and promulgating a fascist aesthetic that focuses on physical prowess, courage, dominance, and control.

AFRICAN PHOTOGRAPHERS AND AFRICAN SITTERS

Travelers, missionaries, anthropologists, art historians, and documentary and art photographers may have connected with Africa and its peoples in deep and meaningful ways, but they have essentially remained outsiders looking in. Increasingly, historians of photography in Africa turn their attention to African photographers and the role of African subjects in encounters with both indigenous and foreign photographers. Published Afrocentric overviews of the history of African photography include an *Anthology of African & Indian Ocean Photography* (1999) and Tobias Wendl and Heike Behrend's 1998 *Snap Me One. Studiofotografen in Afrika*.

Recent studies of photographic portraiture in Africa focus on the close link between photography and dress in African photographic practice, for dress is critical in the representation of self in front of the camera. As publications and exhibitions of the oeuvres of African photographers proliferated in the 1990s, their images revealed the desire of the sitters to assert their modern identities, for the very act of having one's portrait taken in a studio, most often located in an urban environment, was an expression of one's aspirations to be cosmopolitan and urbane. Choices of setting and poses, particular dress, and props convey a person's sense of self. As historical evidence, these portraits are a unique and largely untapped resource for the study of dress—especially for changing dress forms and fashions in the twentieth century.

Seydou Keita (1923–2001), of Bamako in Mali, was one of the first African photographers whose work came to the attention of curators and collectors in Europe and the United States. All of his admirers, including the art historian Michelle Lamunière, pointed to the importance of dress in Keita's carefully crafted portraits. Like many of his colleagues, Keita placed his sitters in front of a backdrop mounted to a wall in his open-air studio. He provided small side tables, chairs, and flowers to stage his subject and also supplied props, such as wristwatches, jewelry, a telephone, and a radio to enhance the sitter's persona. In fact, like other photographers, he also lent different types of attire to his clients for the photographic occasion. Dress was important not only to the sitter but also to the viewers of these portraits. In a short essay introducing a 1995 French publication simply entitled *Seydou Keita*, the Malian writer Youssuf Tata Cissé recalls showing Keita portraits to several Malian women. What mattered most in the eyes of these woman viewers was the cultural and artistic value of Seydou Keita's oeuvre expressed through clothing—such as jackets, dresses, wrappers, and head-dresses—and the coiffures and jewelry. This emphasis on dress in formal studio portraits and in the perception of the viewers may well reflect the African understanding of portraiture, which in the West is mostly seen as a way to reveal the character of the sitter. In the African context, the social persona with all its decorum—the presentation of the civilized and enhanced body—takes center stage.

The interwoven nature of photography and dress has been explored by German anthropologist Kerstin Pinther in a groundbreaking 2008 essay entitled "Textiles and Photography in West Africa," which was first published in German in 1998. One of her most interesting findings pertains to the photographic profession in Ghana and Burkina Faso. While photographers in nineteenth-century Europe often began their careers as painters, many of their African counterparts moved from tailoring, a profession clearly concerned with appearances and clothing, into photography. This observation has been confirmed by anthropologist Liam Buckley in his essay "Self and Accessory in Gambian Studio Photography" (2000–2001). He stresses the close relationship of the two professions in the Gambia, where practitioners easily moved from one to the other, and tailor shops and photography studios could be found in close proximity.

Pinther draws other parallels between photography and clothing. Both textiles and photographs express general wisdom in the form of allegory, the representation of abstract ideas or principles, in this case in pictorial form. In textiles, this occurs through allusions to proverbs and through named patterns in Ghana and neighboring countries. As new textiles come on the market, women wholesalers in Lomé, Togo, link them to proverbs and give them names that may or may not relate to the actual pattern. If a pattern catches on, women wearing it silently communicate messages, such as "Precious beads do not make noise," a maxim that refers to the fact that subtlety in conversation and interaction is ideal behavior. Pinther cites another instance in which a fabric alluded to a proverb: "If marriage were a groundnut, we would open it beforehand and look inside," a reference to the unpredictability of marital relations. In photographs, the sitters, through gestures and poses, may indicate friendship, familial relationships, and certain desires—for example, the wish for children is expressed in the image of a woman who is surrounded by the children of friends and raises her arms in an expectant gesture. Viewers, who share the cultural background of the depicted, will immediately understand this subtle visual language of the image, just as they understand the messages of textiles and distinct types of dress for particular occasions. Photographs, of course, also inscribe dress and their meaningful patterns for posterity. In fact, many women in Ghana, Burkina Faso, Senegal, and other African countries create veritable photographic archives of their different dress ensembles. Whenever a tailor made a new outfit for them, they visited the photographic studio next door to have their portrait taken—often with three different views showing the new ensemble in the round.

To return to the theme of photographs as evidence on dress, it would be interesting, then, to analyze such images for scholarly projects. Where do we find them? Books devoted to the oeuvres of African photographers are one source. In some instances, scholars have been able to study private family albums and photographic holdings. Among the first was Betty M. Wass, a textiles and clothing specialist, who in 1979 analyzed Yoruba dress in five generations of a Lagos family through about one thousand family photographs of some six hundred subjects, which included family members and their friends. Wass counted all individual items in

the photographs according to Western and indigenous categories and then tabulated the principal garments of those portrayed. She also interviewed seventeen family members and found that modes of dress, whether indigenous or Western-inspired, are indicative of social roles and changing self-concepts in society. While this was an expected result, the method she chose was certainly innovative and might set a precedent for systematic work with similar bodies of visual materials.

Some twenty years later, anthropologist Hudita Mustafa examined the connection of portraiture, fashion, and comportment in Dakar, demonstrating how women—and, to an extent, men—through portraiture reinvent themselves. The parallels between dress and photography and how both operate are obvious. Dress, of which the photographic portrait is an inscription, is part of strategies of self-representation and may indicate one's desire for status advancement and gaining prestige. So are the photographs, which are accumulated in Senegalese households, displayed on the walls of living spaces, and shared with friends and family when photographic albums circulate during visits and on special occasions. Another study that relies on photographic portraiture in studios is Laura Fair's analysis of modes of dressing and social

Three elegantly dressed people in Western-style clothing, Port-Gentil, Gabon, ca. 1925. Postcard published by the Compagnie Exploitation Forestière Africaine. Courtesy of Christraud M. Geary.

mobility of women in Zanzibar in her 2001 *Pastimes and Politics: Culture, Community, and Identity in Post-Abolition Urban Zanzibar, 1890–1945.* Her study demonstrates the relevance of family portraits. In addition, she was able to study photographs in official archives in Zanzibar, which points to yet another source for such images—the national archives in some African countries.

While private family albums may be difficult to access, an unexpected wealth of visual documentation can be found in early postcards from Africa. A small but significant corpus was published by African photographers who operated successful studios in the coastal regions of the continent and took photographs of their African clients. European photographers also catered to African sitters, as did the photographers of Indian origin along the east African coastlines. The outdoors studio settings resemble those found several decades later in the images of photographers such as Seydou Keita, attesting to the long development of the conventions in the portrayal of African sitters. What is striking about the dress and accessories African patrons choose for the occasion—whether provided by themselves or the photographer—are the emblems of modernity, which give them a cosmopolitan flair. Western-style attire, with such items as boater hats, European leather shoes, fans, elegant canes, umbrellas, and wristwatches, is common; such features are found in outdoor portraits taken of men and women in the 1920s by an unidentified photographer in the then French colony Gabon.

It remains a mystery how these private images migrated into the postcards medium. One might suggest that buyers, overwhelmingly foreigners in the African colonies, were attracted by the exotic nature of the portraits or were amused by African dress that integrated modern elements. Extensive postcard collections that include many such portraits can be found in some repositories, among them the EEPA at the Smithsonian Institution and the Photograph Study Collection, AAOA, Metropolitan Museum of Art in New York. Private collectors also own large collections and often allow scholars to use them for study. Publications with and about historical postcards from Africa have proliferated and can also be consulted. Geary's and Virginia-Lee Webb's 1998 edited volume *Delivering View: Distant Cultures in Early Postcards* and Geary's essay "The Black Female Body, the Postcard, and the Archives" present examples of postcards that are excellent sources for study.

In conclusion, visual sources on dress, jewelry, and body modifications in Africa, by both African and Western image makers of various backgrounds and covering different time periods, are abundant and still awaiting discovery and further scrutiny.

References and Further Reading

Buckley, Liam. "Self and Accessory in Gambian Studio Photography." *Visual Anthropology Review* 16, no. 2 (2000–2001): 71–91.

Geary, Christraud M. "Photographic Practice in Africa and Its Implications for the Use of Historical Photographs as Contextual Evidence." In *Fotografia e storia dell' Africa*, edited by Alessandro Triulzi, 103–130. Naples, Italy: Istituto Universitario Orientale, 1995.

Geary, Christraud M. "The Incidental Photographer: Roy Sieber and His African Images." *African Arts* 36, no. 2 (2003): 66–81, 96.

Geary, Christraud M. "The Black Female Body, the Postcard, and the Archives." In *Black Womanhood. Images, Icons, and Ideologies of the African Body*, edited by Barbara Thompson, 143–160. Hanover, NH: Hood Museum of Art, Dartmouth College; Seattle: University of Washington Press, 2008.

Jones, Adam. "Decompiling Dapper: Preliminary Search for Evidence." *History in Africa* 17 (1990): 171–209.

Lamunière, Michelle. *You Look Beautiful Like That: The Portrait Photographs of Seydou Keïta and Malick Sidibé.* Cambridge, MA: Harvard University Art Museums; New Haven, CT: Yale University Press, 2001.

Luschan, Felix von. *Anleitung für ethnographische Beobachtungen und Sammlungen.* Berlin: Gebr. Unger, 1899.

Mustafa, Hudita. "Portraits of Modernity: Fashioning Selves in Dakarois Popular Photography." In *Images and Empires: Visuality in Colonial and Postcolonial Africa*, edited by Paul Landau, 172–192. Berkeley: University of California Press, 2002.

Pinther, Kerstin. "Textiles and Photography in West Africa." *Critical Interventions: Journal of African Art History and Visual Culture* 1 (2007): 106–118.

Shumard, Ann M. *A Durable Memento. Portraits by Augustus Washington, African American Daguerreotypist.* Washington, DC: National Portrait Gallery, 2000.

Wass, Betty. "Yoruba Dress in Five Generations of a Lagos Family." In *The Fabrics of Culture: The Anthropology of Clothing and Adornment*, edited by Justine M. Cordwell and Ronald A. Schwarz, 331–348. The Hague, The Netherlands: Mouton, 1979.

Christraud M. Geary

See also Gambia and Senegal; Ghana; Mali; Yoruba in Nigeria and Diaspora.

Prehistory to Colonialism

Among the earliest evidence of dress in Africa are marine shell beads excavated in Morocco dating back as far as eighty-two thousand years, and ostrich eggshell beads over forty thousand years old have been recovered from sites in central Kenya. The oldest known textiles on the African continent come from Egypt and Nubia. Neolithic objects associated with textile and clothing production (including earthenware spindles, needles, and so on) have been found. From later eras, fragments of fabric have been documented from tombs. Additional evidence is represented on the temples and funerary architecture of the ancient Egyptians. Tombs of the Old Kingdom (2700–2200 B.C.E.) provide documentation of daily activities and garb worn for both the tomb's occupant and the retinue interred with him or her to provide services in the afterlife.

In this period, men's clothing was minimal, often covering only part of the lower body; some garments were narrow enough to be termed a waistband and frequently are referred to as a girdle. Other variations were wider (eight to ten inches; twenty to twenty-four centimeters), tied at center front, and covered part of the hips. Other garments such as loin skirts (some writers call them "kilts") varied in length but usually ended above the knee. One style that appears specific to Egyptian royalty involves variations of a lower garment wrapped in such a manner that it projected a triangular shape, possibly with a framework underneath. Near the end of the Old Kingdom, loin skirts were lengthened and some were pleated. The simplicity of the garment offered many opportunities for accessories. Wigs with horizontal rows of carefully articulated curls were relatively common among the upper classes. An assortment of additional headwear often topped the wigs. Beaded broad collars or pectoral collars were worn by a wider range of society. Usually Egyptian men were shaven, but a king could wear a long and thick artificial beard.

Women's clothing of the same period was also basic and simple, usually a straight sheath gown, sometimes with a shawl. Women also wore wigs, but their natural hairline might be revealed. Jewelry was, in general, minimal. These types of men's and women's dress continued with little change during the Middle Kingdom (2100–1788 B.C.E.), although the triangular projection became minimized. New styles of wigs for women became more bulky, and jewelry, as an accessory, gained prominence. Some examples include cloisonné crowns, pectorals, armlets, and girdles using faience, gold, and semiprecious stones such as carnelian, turquoise, lapis lazuli, and agate.

During the Empire period, known as the New Kingdom (1580–1090 B.C.E.), dress of workers changed little, but variety occurred among upper-class men, such as a garment shaped like a kimono, often long and secured around the waist with a girdle. Another was the royal apron, a symbol of authority, made of narrow patterned panels in front and streamers on each side. Women's sheath dresses continued as a basic style, but upper-class women had sheer gowns, beautifully pleated. Women also wore the kimono-type garment but tied it with a narrow sash.

Cleanliness and cosmetics were important to early Egyptians. Perfumes of lotus and jasmine, kohl to emphasize the eyes, and ointments to protect the skin were applied. Fabrics were primarily woven from flax, with evidence dating to 3000 B.C.E., although in the Empire period, wool-bearing sheep were introduced. Prior to that time, wool apparently was considered unclean. Although colors were found in textiles in the Old Kingdom, white was most prevalent because flax is difficult to dye, accounting for the importance given to laundering. Hand pleating for both men's and women's garments was admired and used extensively.

Black people, whether princes or prisoners, are easily recognizable and are frequently represented wearing semicircular earrings. Lighter-skinned Nubians are portrayed in mid-length loincloths, while those of the black Africans are very short animal skins. The women are dressed in loincloths that fall to mid-ankle. The children are naked, with their heads shaved except for three tufts of hair. They are carried on the women's backs in a leather sack with a tumpline. The chiefs and princesses of Kush wear draped garments fastened with a clip, loincloths, and white linen tunics decorated with geometric motifs and gold jewelry studded with semiprecious stones (lapis lazuli, cornaline). The servants and lower classes wear short loincloths, *shenti*, that pass between the legs. Hair is either finely braided or partly shaved.

Around 716 B.C.E., Chabaka, the founder of the Twenty-Fifth dynasty of Ethiopian pharaohs, gained control over the entire Nile Valley to the delta and became the pharaoh of Egypt. In his tomb at El Kurru, sculptures and funerary statuettes are dressed in the Egyptian style, but their heads are covered in a hemispheric Ethiopian cap, more often of leather than cloth, held in place by a thick band.

EIGHTH TO FIFTEENTH CENTURIES

After the Arab conquest of Egypt and the Maghreb beginning in 640 C.E., Arabs entered into direct contact with the Sahel, and travelers published accounts of the lands of the blacks (Bilad al-Sudan). Other Arabs and Persians settled in the area between the Nile and the Indian Ocean along the coast of East Africa, where they traded with the Arab Peninsula, India, and East Asia.

Between the eleventh and fifteenth centuries, the practice of Islam spread, notably in the Sahelo-Sudanese regions, having a direct influence on people's dress, especially among the Islamic elites in the states of Bilad al-Sudan (from west to east, the kingdoms and empires of Ghana, Takrur, Gao [Kaw Kaw], Mali, Kanem, and Bornu) as well as the towns of Takkada (known for its copper mines) and Timbuktu, a great intellectual center.

Don Alvaro, King of Kongo, gives audience to the Dutch, in an engraving by Olfert Dapper, ca. 1650. Both the king and his nobles combine European clothing and boots with Kongo dress such as the *mpu* (hat worn by chiefs). The *mpu* has been slightly Orientalized. Manuscripts, Archives and Rare Books Division, Schomburg Center for Research in Black Culture, The New York Public Library, Astor, Lenox and Tilden Foundations.

Textiles arrived from Europe and Egypt by trans-Saharan commercial routes and from southern Morocco, passing through Fez, Tlemcen, Marrakesh, and Sijilmasa, where they were traded for gold, slaves, and various other products.

The wearing of sewn clothing was a sign of wealth and prestige. In eleventh-century Ghana, the king and his heir apparent were the only people allowed to wear sewn clothing. Others had to limit themselves to girded loincloths. Detailed accounts of ceremonial clothing worn in the fourteenth century by the kings of Ghana, Kaw Kaw, and Mali describe them and other upper-class Muslims as adopting styles of dress from regions involved in the trans-Saharan trade, Morocco in particular. These clothes were made of imported fabric, especially silk goods, wool, *zardkhana* (a Persian word designating a cloth made in Alexandria with animal designs or gold threads), and velvet and red woolen cloth from Europe. Cloth dyed with saffron was also exported from Bornu (west from Lake Chad) to Takkada-Tigidda (southwest Aïr) in Niger during the fourteenth century.

Various terms (*izar, kadawir, kalisa, djubba, durra'a*) have been used to describe the tunic commonly worn in the kingdoms bordering the Senegal and Niger rivers and in contact with the Maghreb. This tunic could be narrow or full, long or short, open at the front or not, and could be worn alone or over a shorter shirt. It was made of wool, linen, or imported fabric as well as of local cotton, white or dyed. Sometimes dignitaries wore a cape or coat, *ma'azir* or *burda*. The tunic was worn over a pair of baggy pants, the *sarwal* or *sarawil*, which were narrow at the leg and wide at the bottom; the width indicated the social status of the wearer, the baggiest being most pleasing to the king.

The Berbers preferred a full draping garment to a tunic, and underneath they wore the sarawil. The Berber Muslims, the Massufa of Tadamakka (Es-sūk or Essouk today in the Adrar of Ifoghas in northern Mali) veiled their faces like the Saharan Berbers. They dressed in cotton and in *hūlī*, red-dyed wool or silk goods imported from the Jerid by the Tunisian merchants who settled in the town during the ninth century. Tadamakka became an important commercial stopover during the ninth through fourteenth centuries, northeast of Gao, on the caravan route to Ghadames and Tripoli, the Ghat, the Fezzan, and Egypt.

Different ways of dressing coexisted in the caravan stopovers, depending on the commercial connections established, principally with northwestern or northeastern Africa.

A female corpse found in a tomb at the Saharan necropolis of Iwelen (northern Aïr) in Niger was wrapped in a leather shroud dating from the second half of the eighth century; she is dressed in a long flared and embroidered tunic with short red, green, and blue woolen sleeves. The tunic was edged with piping that hid the seams and framed the armholes and rectangular neck opening. At the end of each sleeve was a pom-pom. The deceased's hair was dyed with henna and covered, along with the upper body, by a cotton veil embroidered in blue wool with an anthropomorphic Berber motif. The motifs and techniques indicate northern influence or origin (Cyrénaïque, Algeria, Tunisia). Such tunics were called *jubba* in Muslim Andalusia and *jebba* in Tunisia, where they were, above all, the choice of the women of Sahel (Sousse, Sfax, Monastir).

The Berbers of Lamtūna wore the *litham* of an indigo color, while those from Sudan wore the light-colored *karziya*. The *taylassan* (a veil worn on the head by muftis, imams, or cadis) was put on by the Sudanese (blacks) on Muslim festival days. The king of Ghana was coiffed with a golden cap, around which a cotton turban was wound, during the eleventh century, and the princes of his court had braided hair mixed with gold pendants.

Everyday clothes and those of the common people were made of local cotton, undyed or colored using plant extracts such as indigo. In the fourteenth century, Ibn Battuta commented on the importance to Kano, in the north of Nigeria, of the vats and pits of indigo dyes of Kofar Mata, which, seven centuries later, are still in operation.

Along the Bandiagara escarpment in Mali, rock shelters used as burial caves have yielded several garments (tunics, pants, caps, loincloths) dating from the eleventh to the eighteenth century C.E. The cotton cloth was constructed by assembling woven bands about nine and a half inches (twenty-four centimeters) wide. The seventy-five tunics found, dating from the eleventh to sixteenth centuries, belonged to the Tellem culture. Some of the later pieces have been attributed to the first Dogon, who dominated the Tellem around 1500. The cut of these pieces is similar to that of current garments, denoting remarkable continuity. Traces of blue and red decorative striping in the weft, probably in silk or cotton threads, have been observed in several of the oldest pieces. The clothing displayed simple embroidered patterns (Kanaga mask motifs) and circular motifs obtained by tie-dying. Belts of leather or cotton and leather boots or sandals completed the men's attire. The fragments of woolen blankets recovered are similar to the blankets of the North African Berbers with geometric motifs produced in southern Morocco and imported via the trans-Saharan route of Sijilmasa since the ninth and tenth centuries.

Spindle whorls, evidence of the practice of local weaving, have been recovered from excavations at Sanga (eleventh to fourteenth centuries) as well as at other sites in Mali and at Kumbi-Saleh, the old capital of the kingdom of Ghana (eighth to fifteenth centuries), Tegdaoust (fourteenth to sixteenth centuries) in Mauritania, Ogo (tenth to twelfth centuries) in the kingdom of Takrur, on the middle valley of the Senegal River, as well as Niani (Guinea, fourteenth to sixteenth centuries), the old capital of the kingdom of Mali. Archaeological and Arab sources thus tend to prove that weaving was a well-established practice in the eleventh century in western Africa.

Cotton was the principal raw material of weaving and clothing in western Africa during medieval times, and it could be mixed with other fibers, such as extracts of the fruit of *tawrzā*

or *kapokier* (*Calotropis procera*). In East Africa, Ibn Battuta, who visited Mogadishu (Somalia) in 1331, mentioned that cotton fabric, *toob* or *futa benaadir*, was of superior quality. It was sold everywhere in Egypt and probably in the Arab villages situated along the coast. Wool is associated with the Berber populations of the southern Maghreb as well as with the Nubians and Ethiopians to the east, where its use was observed in the twelfth century. The introduction of weaving to the interior delta of the Niger in the late eighth century has been attributed to the artisanal Peul group, the Maabuube, who also introduced the use of indigo. Other materials were also used for clothing. For example, in Nigeria, at Igbo Ukwu (ninth to eleventh centuries), fragments of bark cloth and fibers much like raffia have been recovered. The wearing of clothes was not universal in the Sudan. Outside of the elites and the Muslim court, the rest of the population went largely naked, as did the slaves of the royal entourage. However, the corpses of Tellem women from caves such as those above Sanga were dressed in fiber aprons and belts of woven fibers.

Shoes were not generally worn, except perhaps by royalty, although archaeological evidence suggests that some shoes were made locally. Men's goatskin boots were found at Sanga (Tellem culture); they date from the fourteenth and fifteenth centuries and were decorated with geometric lines and pigments. Cross-strapped sandals appear on the feet of a fragment of a ceramic statuette from the necropolis of Bura-Asinda-Sikka (third through eleventh centuries) in Niger. Gobir, one of the northern Hausa states, in Nigeria, was described in 1510 to 1513 by Leo Africanus as an important leather craft center, producing sandals, bags, cushions, and saddles, which were exported in Timbuktu and Gao as well as in North Africa.

Arabic authors report among the objects of commerce small items of glassware, necklaces in cornaline and other stones, leather bracelets, and gold jewelry. The king of Ghana in the eleventh century liked to wear necklaces and bracelets. The knights of Mansa Musa of Mali also wore bracelets, necklaces, and gold ankle rings, according to rank. Terra-cotta sculptures from the great cultures of Nok (500 B.C.E. to 600 C.E.), Ile-Ife (tenth to fifteenth centuries), Bura-Asinda-Sikka (third to eleventh centuries), and Djenné-Djenno (ninth to seventeenth centuries) all depict elaborate jewelry ensembles. Beautiful gold necklaces and pectorals in the form of metal cylinders, filigree medallions on metal disks, and knitted balls found in excavations at Tegdaoust (eleventh-century Mauritania) and Rao-Nguiguelakh (Senegal, fourteenth to fifteenth centuries) attest to the skill of African goldsmiths.

Gold was not the only metal worked. The skeleton of the Lady of Iwelen was dressed in two copper ankle bracelets (one on each leg) as well as two animal horn bracelets (one on each arm). At Igbo Ukwu, the technique of bronze casting was known in the ninth to tenth centuries. In Podor, Sintiou Barra, and Ogo, sites along the Senegal River, bimetal assemblages of iron and copper from around the tenth century have been found. Twisted iron hairpins were uncovered in the grottoes of Tellem Sanga, dating from the eleventh through the twelfth century.

The Lam Lam or Dam Dam, who lived to the west of Gao or in the Niani region (south of Bamako), practiced scarification of the face and temples at initiation rituals. Ceramic statuettes and figurines from sites at Bura-Asinda-Sikka in Niger, Djenné-Djenno in Mali, and Ile-Ife in Nigeria display scarification on their faces, necks, and chests in the form of raised lines or dots.

A Wolof man of the southern Sahara wearing a wide-sleeved robe. 1884. General Research and Reference Division, Schomburg Center for Research in Black Culture, The New York Public Library, Astor, Lenox and Tilden Foundations.

FIFTEENTH TO SEVENTEENTH CENTURIES

Portuguese navigators sailed along the coastline of western Africa (1444), central Africa (1471), the Cape of Good Hope (1485), and eastern Africa (1498). They founded commercial enterprises along the coast at river outlets and established trading relationships with the river populations and those of the interior. Thanks to the intermediary networks of the merchants of Dioula and Malinké and the children of unions between African women and Portuguese men, these new trade routes were expanded year after year to the detriment of some traditional trans-Saharan business. The increase and diversification of trade, combined with the effects of Islamization, quickly affected styles of dress in the coastal regions and in certain areas of the interior. With the arrival of the Portuguese and the Dutch, imported textiles assumed an increasingly important part in intra-African trade. Political elites adopted clothing styles from trading partners: North African and Islamic-Arabic influences for the West and East African countries and European traditions for the countries of central and southern Africa. The wearing of imported fabrics of high quality was tied to power and was used by the political elites to establish their prestige and distribute privilege to their supporters. In select

locations, local production of textiles was galvanized by the demands of Portuguese and Dutch traders.

In the regions of western Africa from the Senegalese coast to the Gulf of Guinea—the area that navigators and slave traders called "Guinea"—the Portuguese chroniclers remarked on the weaving of cotton into narrow bands that were sewn together to make cloth of various widths. These activities were described on the coast of Senegal in 1455 to 1456 and in Takrūr (Tucurol), a kingdom situated in the middle valley of Senegal, in 1506 to 1507. South of Senegal, in modern-day Guinea-Bissau, weaving was also highly developed. The Kassanga, Mandingized Baïnounk, and the Mandjak were known during the fifteenth century for the quality of their weaving, as were the countries of the Gulf of Benin and the interior regions of West Africa.

Between the fifteenth and sixteenth centuries, textiles took on an increasingly important role in intra-African business. At the end of the sixteenth century, cotton goods made in Gao or Djenné (current-day Mali) and in Bornu (southwest of Lake Chad) were traded by merchants of the Guinea-Gambian regions, who were Manding Muslims. They were indistinguishable from the rest of the population except for their shaved heads under their caps and their white caftans, worn for Friday prayers. The Portuguese traded the *pagnes* (rectangular cotton garments used as loincloths and for other purposes) bought in the Kingdom of Benin for the gold of Elmina. In response to an increase in demand, they developed the cultivation of cotton in the islands of Cape Verde, where they established weaving houses with indentured hand workers taken from the interior. The textiles thus manufactured, *pano d'obra*, were sold along the African coast or exported to the Iberian Peninsula and other parts of Europe.

Despite the increasing use of textiles, the wearing of animal skins continued in the mid-fifteenth century among some parts of the population and in certain places in Senegal and Guinea, although some rulers and notables wore huge cotton shirts. Adult women were naked from the waist to the head and wore a pagne tied at the waist, which fell to mid-leg. When they left their houses, Wolof women draped themselves with another cloth that covered the lower part of the body. Both men and women went barefoot and generally wore nothing on their heads, although their hair was dressed in various ways. Further south, in the rivers of Casamance, the men of the Balanga people (currently the Balant) dressed themselves, when not receiving guests, in goatskins, which they used as pants. When they went out or received guests, they also wore a cotton shirt with short sleeves. The women wore cotton panels that covered them from the waist to mid-thigh. In Guinea, where cotton was abundant, almost all the men and women wore shirts, except the very young, whereas, in Sierra Leone, little, if any, clothing was worn apart from a belt.

Tattooing and scarification were performed on the chests, arms, and necks of women in Guinea and on the face, in particular the lips, and all over the body among certain Barbecins (Sereer) in Senegal. In the region of Cape Sagres (currently Conakry) and in Sierra Leone, men and women had their ears, noses, and lips pierced to accommodate gold rings.

In the Kingdom of Benin, fabric based on vegetable fiber (from the bark of a tree) was used to make clothing. Here individuals needed the king's permission before they could wear clothes or have long hair. The Dutch chronicler Olfert Dapper noted that most men and women braided their hair and that some wore hats made of tree bark or coconut shells or attached feathers to their heads with brass wire. Men and women wore silver rings in their ears and noses, fragments of wood, and rings of ivory and animal horn. Women also wore copper bracelets on their arms and smeared their bodies red. Occasionally the lower lip was pierced with a very large opening that allowed the tongue to pass through it.

In Nigeria, an archer in a group of bronze sculptures from sites on the Niger River islands of Jebba and Tada, dating from the fourteenth and early fifteenth centuries, was dressed in a fringed tunic, with *popo* motifs, an assemblage of white warp-faced woven strips approximately four to five inches (ten to twelve centimeters) with alternating thin (probably indigo) weft stripes, reminiscent of those weaved today by the Ibo women of Akwete in Nigeria and the Ewe weavers of Togo.

In the central African kingdom of the Kongo, the Portuguese recorded in the late fifteenth and early sixteenth centuries the use of fabrics made from raffia palms. They were astonished by the quality and fineness of the weave (*panos de palma*) and by the technical mastery required to make them. It was one of the prerogatives of the king, and those selected by him, to dress in these fabrics. Officials covered the lower part of the body with animal skins (e.g., leopards and civets) hanging at the front, as an apron. A further prerogative of the king was the wearing of a sort of mesh tunic called *zamba kya mfumua*.

The poor dressed in rough fabric loincloths obtained by soaking and beating the *aliconde ou bondo*. Women covered the lower part of the body with three cloth bands of different lengths, the shortest edged with a fringe. They covered their chests with a bodice to the waist and wore a cape over the shoulders. A decorated cloth indicated the status of women. Slaves and women of the lower classes were covered only from the waist down. Elephant tail hair was much sought after and sometimes braided with that of other animals to construct necklaces, belts, bracelets, and other ornaments.

After conversion to Christianity, the elite members of the court began to dress themselves in the style of the Portuguese, with coats, capes, scarlet cardigans, silk hats or bonnets, velvet and leather sandals, Portuguese-style boots, and large swords. The women of the court covered their heads with veils and black velvet bonnets decorated with jewels. In southern Africa during the sixteenth and seventeenth centuries, shipwrecked Dutch and Portuguese noted that at initiation ceremonies among the Cape-Nguni, the circumcised wore leaf skirts and loincloths made of animal hides. In the seventeenth century, in the Cape region, the Khoïsan peoples wore a sort of three-piece coat of sheep, rabbit, or antelope skin, with the fur side in, that reached to the thigh, with colorful markings and hanging strips of hide. The women wore the coat longer with an animal hide on the lower back. They also wore animal-skin bonnets. Men decorated their hair with little metal plates or pennies, white shells, and pieces of coral. They shaved their heads to leave tufts here and there and painted their faces with dark colors. Their shoes were made of rhinoceros hide fastened to the foot with straps. Their earrings were made of bundles of nine or ten coral branches. The rich wore brass chains around their necks, ivory bracelets, and buckles of copper or other metal. Others made necklaces out of animal entrails. Fragments of cloth found in excavated graves at Igombe Ilede, Zambia, dating to the fourteenth and fifteenth centuries, have blue and white and indigo stripes. These cloths could have been imported from neighboring countries.

Toward the end of the sixteenth century, the cultivation of cotton and the practice of weaving by the population living in lower Zambese near Sena were widely known. In the kingdom of Mono-motapa (Zimbabwe), the men are said to have worn robes of cotton embroidered with gold. Long robes were still being worn in the seventeenth century, sometimes with a sort of knee-length belted skirt. Common men were clothed only in a loincloth of calico or silk cloth. Women did not wear clothes, apart from the *cache-sexe*, until they married and had children, after which they covered their breasts and the rest of their bodies.

In East Africa and Madagascar in 1498, people living on the coast south of Sofala (Beira) wore only a loincloth of cotton, but archaeological evidence indicates that weaving dates at least back to the tenth century in Madagascar. In the beginning of the sixteenth century, they also unraveled blue and multicolored imports of Cambay (in the west of India) and used this thread to make multicolored weavings. They wore turbans of scarlet bands of silk or cotton and a dagger to the side.

Nearby, the inhabitants of the kingdom of Mozambique simply covered their genitals with a piece of blue cotton, a leaf, or a piece of tree bark and painted their bodies with various colors or

A *signare* (woman of high status, married to a European) of the southern Sahara wearing a *pagne* with a European-influenced design. Late nineteenth century. General Research and Reference Division, Schomburg Center for Research in Black Culture, The New York Public Library, Astor, Lenox and Tilden Foundations.

rubbed themselves with red earth. Some made three holes in each lip, into which they inserted ivory or bone.

The wealthy Swahili inhabitants of the kingdom of Quiloa (Kilwa) had robes of gold brocade, cotton, or silk and turbans of the same material. The women wore chains of gold and silver on their arms and legs and beautiful earrings.

Across the channel, in Madagascar, cotton loincloths were also worn by wealthy men in the late sixteenth century.

Further north, in Ethiopia, cotton was grown and used to produce fine fabric called *buckram*. In the sixteenth and seventeenth centuries, in the valleys of Gojam (Gojjam), Begameder (Begedir), and Olecâ, where cotton grew in abundance, large, solid fabrics called *bezetes* were made. In Aksum, robes (*panni*) were made of silk, wool, and cotton, which were embroidered when destined for the *presta* (the priest-king) or nobles. The wealthiest wore all sorts of silk cloth and beautiful Turkish velvets in bright colors. Their top robe was always highly decorated in gold and silver. The women dressed even more lavishly than the men.

EIGHTEENTH TO NINETEENTH CENTURIES

From the eighteenth century to the nineteenth century, increased exploration revealed other populations of the African interior, most notably those of central and southern Africa, while trade intensified and diversified with future colonial powers. The various basic forms of clothing known for century in West Africa have continued more or less unchanged until recent times. From the mid-seventeenth to the eighteenth century, the ordinary clothing in Mauritania and Senegal was made of ecru cotton from Pondicherry in India, called *guinée*, and indigo dyed locally. In southern Morocco and Mauritania, men wore a tunic of guinée, the *d'rrah*, down to the ankles with very wide sleeves that also reached to the ground. Pants made of over five yards (about five meters) of guinée covered men from the waist to the knees; over the tunic a square of fabric served as a scarf. Alternatively, a turban was wrapped around the head; rarely were sandals worn. The less-well-off simply wore an indigo-blue pull-on *coussabe* made from a large rectangle of fabric folded in two, with a hole cut in the center for the head. The women's garment, the *malafé* (or *melfa*), was a half piece of guinée wrapped in three layers. Openings were provided for head and arms. Among the Moors, children's heads were partially shaved to create designs or tufts of hair. At age twelve, a girl's hair was allowed to grow. At age eighteen, boys' heads were completely shaved. Women used bands of guinée to bind their hair; two long braids fell on their shoulders, with yellow amber occasionally attached to the ends. They rarely veiled. Toenails and fingernails were painted red with henna, and eyelids were lined with black kohl produced by the charring of certain fats and grease.

The habitual dress style of the Wolof of the south Sahara in the eighteenth and nineteenth centuries consisted of pleated pants in the Turkish style, closed at the front with a tie and a sleeveless camisole (*mboube, mbubb, or boubou*) or wide-sleeved, knee-length tunic (*coussabe*). A pagne worn as a scarf completed the ensemble. They often secured enormous amulets on a belt around their hips. Women dressed with two pagnes, the first was belted around the hips and draped down to the knees, and the second covered the bust. Some women wore a handkerchief on their heads; the wealthiest had up to six filigreed ornaments made by local silversmiths hanging from each ear. *Signares* and

mulatto women adopted European clothes, stockings, and shoes. To these they added beautiful pagnes made by local weavers, some of which they embroidered themselves, imitating designs from France.

The mode of dress of some of the other people of Senegal—Peul, Toucolour, Soninké, Manding, and Bambara—resembled that of the Wolof. Among the Sereer and the Diola, however, only married women and men wore clothes. The Diola south of Senegal, in Casamance, wore beautiful pagnes only on important occasions. Among their neighbors in Guinea-Bissau, girls and women wore only an extremely wide fringed belt made of fibers, which fell to the knee. On their arms and legs, they wore copper and tin bracelets.

In the large urban centers of Timbuktu and Djenné in Mali, men and women wore a boubou and coussabe. In Djenné, children and adults wore a coussabe made of white cloth from Sudan and flowing, belted pants that reached to the ankle. Women wore a pagne underneath. Everyone wore slippers of various colors, made of leather imported from Morocco via Timbuktu.

The Mossi people of Burkina Faso wove bands of cotton fabric sold in Dori (at Liptako in Mali) and also wove silk and embroidered. They created pagnes dyed red and yellow exclusively for the wives of traditional chiefs (*naba*). Ordinary women wore an indigo pagne knotted beneath the armpits or around the hips. The naba were distinguished by tall white hats. The women wore wide copper bracelets and anklets.

In the northern part of present-day Nigeria, Kano, the capital of the Hausa kingdom, was renowned for its embroiderers and leather tanners and was at the center of the regional clothing industry. The local notables wore pantaloons and richly embroidered boubous, on top of which were worn beautiful coats made of fabric imported from the coast by the Arabs. The outfit was completed by a turban scaled in proportion to the importance of the man. In Bornu, northeast of Kano (west of Lake Chad), some chiefs and notables of the Shaykh Ashim's court, in Koukawa, had elaborate hairstyles and sumptuous armor, with coats of chain mail and Saracen helmets. The most powerful traditional chief after the Shaykh of Bornu, the Galadima of Bakousso, was dressed in 1892 in a heavy red velvet caftan above a white silk *burnous*; he wore a crown made of a thick band of gold brocade Turkish cloth on top of a white turban.

In addition to raffia fabrics for short and long pagnes, colorful skirts were worn in the interior regions of central Africa, Lower Ogoué and Upper Congo. Fang warriors in Gabon wore skirts of red-dyed fibers, and Balanga women of the Congo wore a short skirt composed of numerous layers of plant fibers, sometimes dyed red or yellow and falling to the mid-thigh. Balanga men were dressed in a piece of fabric pulled between the legs and held up by a narrow belt around the hips. In some areas, the pelts of small mammals were attached to the pagnes.

Hairstyles were often elaborate. For example, Fang warriors braided their hair in a long plait that fell down their backs and augmented the plait with white beads, brass rings, or feathers. Beards were clipped and braided into two or three fine plaits. Young girls were given totemic coiffures called *enzogha*, which were created by cutting the hair to form tufts that were then braided. Young men had a tuft of hair at the front. Fang men were ornamented with necklaces, bracelets armlets, ankle rings, and sometimes facial chains between ears and nose. The Batéké of what is now the Democratic Republic of Congo hung cylinders or large elongated brass beads from their necks, while others wore necklaces of lions' or leopards' teeth, the claws of animals, or talons of birds of prey.

Among the Fang, the face was scarified with numerous motifs that had symbolic and aesthetic significance. Various types of scarifications existed among the river people of the Upper Congo. Among the Baputo, scarifications covered the entire face, whereas the Mongwandi had round, prominent scars, often in groupings of five, on the median line of the forehead. The filing of the front teeth to a point was also practiced among the Fang and the inhabitants of the Upper Congo, particularly the Batéké.

Sudanese Nubia and Ethiopia have been in contact with the Middle East and the Mediterranean since ancient times. Cotton cultivation and weaving were widely known. *Dammour* is the name of a rough cotton fabric used to make the *tob*. The *tob dammour* was commonly employed as a garment and as a form of currency. Another sturdy indigenous weaving product in Darfur was sewn into *teqâqi* clothes. A finer fabric, *kalkaf*, was preferred by the wealthy.

In southwestern Tanzania, the Fipa were well known for the quality of their weaving. In eastern Africa, the draped garment was more widely used, consisting simply of wrapping leather or cloth around the body. The coastal Afar wore a pagne, the *taube* or *tob* (in Arabic), of white or colored cotton around the hips. The Maasai of Kenya wore (and many still wear) a piece of cloth knotted on the shoulder. Among the Waduruma or Wa-Nyika along coastal Kenya and Tanzania, the men dressed in a simple piece of cloth knotted at the waist, occasionally placed over the shoulder. The clothing of the Vouasagara or Wasagara men of the high central Tanzanian plateaus consisted of the *shukkah*—a loincloth that is six feet (about two meters) long, passed around the waist in a single fold, drawn tight behind, and, with the fore extremities gathered up, tucked in over the stomach, where it is sometimes supported by a girdle of cord, leather, or brass wire, in dark blue or unbleached cotton. Cloth was a privilege of the rich, and the poor were restricted to a narrow covering of bark cloth and perhaps tanned goat-or sheep-skin. Chiefs were distinguished by their right to add a fez and wear a sleeveless waistcoat called a *kizbáo*.

For the numerous regions south and southwest of Ethiopia and Mozambique, textiles for clothing were nearly unknown. Most men wore only a piece of bark cloth, animal hides, or leather around their shoulders and hips. Women wore a skirt of inner bark, a hooded cape made of sedge, or cotton cords around their hips. Long cloaks were worn only in the villages or for special occasions.

At puberty, the Afar women began to wrap prepared goatskins around their waists and to wear a taube or a dark-colored shirt over the shoulders. The women of Wa Duruma had a short pleated underskirt. In general, dark cotton goods, Indian blues, and check patterns were preferred. Children were carried on the back and were supported by wide leather straps.

The simplicity of the clothing in eastern Africa contrasts sharply with the elaboration of hair and headdresses. The Issa Somali, particularly those who lived in Toudjourah, wore their hair long and frizzy, with very fine locks, and shaved them all around the ears. The hair was dyed auburn with the application of a layer of lime. Hair was almost always fixed with a pin of carved wood or combs with two or three teeth. The inhabitants of Choa combed their hair with a sharp, slender stick also worn in their hair with feathers or flowers. The Maasai braided their hair dramatically

and covered it with red ochre. Some of the Wasagara shaved their heads, while others wore the *shushah* of the Arabs, a sort of skullcap. Warriors and young men added the feathers of an ostrich, vulture, or jay to their hair arrangement. No one other than the chief wore a turban or hat.

The Afar women wore copper bracelets and rings on their ankles, several rows of necklaces of glass beads, amulets, sometimes earrings, and more often pieces of copper rolled into small cones, hanging from hair braids in front of the ear. Young women went bare-headed, but married women covered their heads with cloth. Men sometimes wore bead necklaces, but more often only amulets around their necks and bracelets of iron, copper, or ivory on their wrists or arms. Ear lobes were nearly always pierced to accommodate as large a piece of ivory as possible. A preference for glass beads was widespread among the women of Galla and Amhara. They also decorated themselves with earrings of black animal horn or silver. The Wa-Durma women wore numerous necklaces of glass beads, similar to the enormous necklaces of beads worn around the necks of their neighbors, the Wa-Taita.

Maasai women encircled their arms with numerous thick iron wires. Among the Wasagara, both men and women had their ears pierced and the hole stretched to accommodate a disc of brass, ivory, wood, or rubber. The Wasagara embellished themselves with glass beads and *kitindi*, armbands of brass wire reaching from the wrist to the elbow. A bandeau of blue and white beads encircled the head, and numerous pieces of glass or porcelain decorated their chests, arms, and ankles.

Galla females wearing elaborate beaded headwear. Ethiopia, 1845. Manuscripts, Archives and Rare Books Division, Schomburg Center for Research in Black Culture, The New York Public Library, Astor, Lenox and Tilden Foundations.

The Afar, as well as the populations of western and northern Africa, used a variety of vegetable incenses (*boechera, ouaibou, oioolo*) to perfume their bodies, clothes, and dwelling places.

Boechera leaves are usually used to perfume clothes. Ouaibou, a yellow root, releases fragrant smoke when it is burned in a small hole with ash and is used to perfume women's bodies. The woman sat on the hole, wrapped in her taube, so the smell clung to her whole person, especially after her periods. Oioolo, a red wood or bark, is burned in the same way as ouaibou, but women use it for intimate purposes as an astringent.

In Morocco, as in other part in North Africa, smoke baths, *bkhour*, were used as a protection against genies or *jnoun*, bad eyes, spells and witchcraft, or to attract good luck in a business; they were also used as a body perfume or a disinfectant in the home or bath.

Myrrh (*Commiphora myrrha*) is a resin gum that is burned in a swinging censer or added to perfumes, cosmetics, creams, or *ghassoul*, a shampoo clay for the hair. Myrrh was long traded from Somalia or Arabia to North Africa, as were other aromatic plants such as *luban* or *mastica* (*oliban, Boswellia thurifera*), *ejjawi* or benzoin (*Styrax*), and *sarghina* (*Corrigiola téléphiifolia*). Cloves, (*qronfel*), water of orange blossom (*ma-zhar*), and rose water or rosebuds (*ma-werd* or *werd*) were also used as body or cloth perfume, among other vegetal, animal (musk), and mineral products (*chebba*, or alum).

Among the Wa Duruma or Wa-Nyika, who lived in the coastal regions of Kenya and in Tanzania, the women had raised tattoos on their chests and stomachs, while the Kikuyu were unmarked by a single scar or tattoo. Linear scars between the ear and the eyebrow were characteristic of the Wasagara, and some men, particularly in the mountains, filed their teeth to a point.

In Madagascar, the weaving of *calins* cloth by the Hova weavers was mentioned in 1822. This highly esteemed cloth was always made of silk and cotton and had a blue background; along the sides, white metal flat pieces were woven into the weft artistically, and in the middle, there were many flowers strikingly embossed with tin. The clothing of the Hova consisted of two large loincloths wrapped over their bodies. The men wrapped themselves in a piece of fabric thrown over their shoulders, while another rolled piece was used as a belt. Women wore something similar but larger and wrapped differently.

The use of hides and leather was very widespread in southern Africa. The San and Khosa men of the cape wore coats of cowhide fastened at the chest. Chiefs dressed in leopard skins. Less commonly, men dressed in cloth hung from the shoulder that did not cover the arms. They generally left their heads bare and, during long treks, wore sandals of cowhide. Women had circular cowhide capes reaching to the calf to cover the body entirely. On their backs, across the shoulders, were attached entire skins of wild cats. Rows of buttons were used for decoration. By 1802, most women wore a sort of bib around their breasts, decorated with bits of colored glass. Around their hips was attached an apron made of thin leather straps. A handkerchief to cover the head or throat was considered an object of great value. Children were clothed in simple coats of antelope skin. Older girls wore bonnets.

The clothes of the Zulu, described in Natal in 1841, were very simple. Men wore on the head a leather or textile cap or a headband made of leather or glass beads; all these usually were decorated with bunches of animal hair or straws. Around the neck was a necklace made of animal teeth or stone beads. On the shoulders and around the hips and calves, they wore some bits of fur to partly cover their bodies. A cartridge belt made of animal skin and a shield and spears completed the warrior dress. When a Zulu male married for the first time, his head was shaved and coated with a sort of varnish.

Women wore a simple glass-bead belt around the hips, a necklace of glass beads, and straw or fabric bracelets and bangles around the arms. Porcupine quills were stuck in the hair. During ceremonies, women wore a black skirt and a lot of glass-bead jewels around the chest, the back, and the arms; a purple headband; and some bird feathers arranged in bunch near the ears.

Unlike the men, San women covered their heads with a cone-shaped bonnet made of antelope skin, to the top of which were attached strips of copper or iron rings that hung almost to the eyelids. Four straps secured the hat to the head. Wealthier women adorned this headpiece with strands of glass beads. Ornamentation was important to the San people. The men wore ivory armlets or strings of leopard or boar teeth. They also wore a belt strung with copper or iron rings, used as money. Both sexes had strands of coral beads and necklaces of shells called serpents' heads, which were strung on a braid of hair taken from an elephant's tail and mixed with small pieces of sweet-smelling wood. Shell bracelets and glass-ball earrings were also popular with both sexes. The poor passed a leather thong knotted at both ends through their pierced ears. The San women had their backs, arms, and chest (between their breasts) ridged with evenly spaced, parallel lines. This beauty-enhancing practice was accomplished by introducing a sharp awl, as a lancet, beneath the epidermis and tearing the skin by lifting the needle a little.

The Khoï Khoï women wore a large number of ankle rings of leather or cord that could reach to the middle of the calf and bracelets of glass or metal beads on their wrists and above the elbows. Numerous rings adorned their fingers, and copper ornaments hung from their ears.

CONCLUSION

African dress from prehistory to the beginning of the Colonial era is a highly complex topic covering a very long period of time, and therefore any survey will necessarily be highly selective. Nevertheless, the above examples include a wide array of dress options ranging from leaves and animal skins to bark cloth and woven textiles. These are supplemented by a substantial variety of footwear and headwear along with handheld accessories, such as fans, whisks, scepters, and assorted weapons. Depending on the time and place, jewelry was produced from seeds, shell, stone, and such metals as gold, silver, copper, and brass. In often spectacular configurations, those who wore little clothing still dressed their bodies with scarification and/or painting. In many parts of Africa, perfumes and cosmetics were commonly employed.

References and Further Reading

Alberti, Louis. *Philosophical and Historical Description of the Kaffirs: On the Southernmost Coast of Africa*. Eds Institute of the Eastern Languages and Civilizations Eastern, collection African Files, 1974.

Alluaud, C. "Of Mombasa to the Victoria-Nyanza." *The Turn of the World*, new series t. 13 (1907): 13–36.

Alvarez d'Almada, A. "Brief Treaty on the Rivers of Guinea of the Cap Verde, from Senegal Jusqu' with the River Holy-Anne." *New Annals of the Voyages: The Geography and History*, 4th series t. 10 (1842): 75–112, 356–379.

Batuta, Ibn, C. Defremery, B.R. Sanguinetti, and Stefanos Yerasimos. *Voyages*. Paris: F. Maspero, 1982.

Bedaux, Rogier, and Rita Bolland. "Medieval Ladies' Garments of Mali: The Fibre Mask-Sex of Tellem." In *Man Does Not Go Naked*, edited by B. Engelbrecht and Bernhard Gardi, 15–34. *Beiträge zur Ethnology* 30. Basel, Switzerland: Ethnologisches Seminar der Universität und Museum für Völkerkunde, in Kommission bei Wepf, 1989.

Bolland, Rita, Rogier Bedaux and Renée Boser-Sarivaxévanis, eds. *Tellem Textiles: Archaeological Finds from Burial Hollow in Mali's Bandiagara Cliff*. Amsterdam: Royal Tropical Institute, 1991.

Boser Sarivaxévanis, Renée. "Year Introduction to Weavers and Dyers in West Africa." In *Tellem Textiles: Archaeological Finds from Burial Hollow in Mali's Bandiagara Cliff*, edited by Rita Bolland, Rogier Bedaux, and Renée Boser-Sarivaxévanis, 37–51. Amsterdam: Royal Tropical Institute, 1991.

Burton, Richard Francis. *Voyages aux grands lacs de l'Afrique orientale*. Paris: Hachette, 1975.

Cadamosto, Alvise. *The Voyages of Cadamosto and Other Documents on Western Africa in the Second Half of the Fifteenth Century*, edited by G.R. Crone. London: Hakluyt Society, 1937.

Caillié, René, and Jacques Berque. *Voyage à Tombouctou*. Paris: François Maspero, 1979.

Chambonneau, Louis Moreau de. Publ. Carson I.A. Ritchie. "Two Texts on Senegal 1673–1677." *Bulletin IFAN*, B, t. 30, no. 1 (1968): 289–353.

Combes, Edmond, and Maurice Tamisier. *Voyage en Abyssinie, dans le pays des Galla, de Choa et d'Ifat, 1835–1837 précédé d'une excursion dans l'Arabie-heureuse: et accompagné d'une carte de ces diverses contrées*. Paris: L. Desessart, 1838.

Dappert, Olfert. *Description de l'Afrique: contenant les noms, la situation et les confins de toutes ses parties*. Amsterdam: 1686.

Fagan, B.M., D.W. Phillipson, and S.G.H. Daniels. *Iron Age Cultures in Zambia*. Vol. 2. London, 1969.

Filipowiak, Wladyslaw. *Archaeological Studies on the Medieval Capital of Mali*. Szczecin, Poland: Muzeum Narodowe, 1979.

Gardi, Bernhard. "Le boubou: c'est chic." In *Boubous of Mali and Other Countries of West Africa*. Basel, Switzerland: Christoph Merian Verlag, 2002.

Gilfoy, Peggy. *Patterns of Life: West African Strip-Weaving Traditions*. Washington, DC: Smithsonian Institution Press, 1986.

Labat, Jean Baptiste. *Nouvelle relation de l'Afrique occidentale contenant une description exacte du Senegal & des pais situés entre le Cap-Blanc & la riviere de Serrelionne: l'histoire naturelle de ces pais, les differentes nations qui y sont répandues, leurs religions & leurs moeurs: avec l'état ancien et present des compagnies qui y font le commerce*. Paris: Chez G. Cavelier, 1728.

Laburthe Tolra, Philippe, et al. *Fang. Catalogue exposure*. Eds Musée Dapper, Paris, 1991–1992.

Leclant, Jean. "Koushites and Méroïtes. The Iconography of the African Sovereigns of the Ancient High-Nile." In *The Image of the Black in Western Art*, edited by Jean Vercoutter, 89–132. Freiburg, Switzerland: Office du livre, 1976.

Monod, Théodore, A. Teixeira da Mota, and R. Mauny, eds. *Description de la Cote occidentale d'Afrique (Sénégal au Cap de Monte, Archipels), par Valentine Fernandes (1506–1510)*. Bissau, Guinea-Bissau: Centro de Estudos da Guiné Portuguesa, 1951.

Monteil, Louis-Parfait. *From Saint-Louis to Tripoli by Lake Chad: Travel through Sudan and from the Sahara, Accomplished during the Years 1890–1891–1892*. Paris: F. Alcan, 1895.

Musée national des arts d'Afrique et d'Océanie, Rijksmuseum voor Volkenkunde (Netherlands), and France. *Valleys of the Niger*. Paris: Ministère de la coopération, Commissariat général de l'exposition Vallées du Niger, 1994.

Niane, Djibril Tamsir. *History of Mandingues of the West: The Kingdom of Gabou*. Paris: Kathala, Association ARSAN, 1989.

Paris, François. *Burials of the Sahara Native of Niger of the Neolithic Era to Islamization*. Vol. 2, *Funerary Habits, Chronology, Civilisations*. Paris: ORSTOM, 1988.

Poncin de, E. "Travel to Choa, Explorations in Somal and at Danakils." *Bulletin of the Company of Geography of Paris* 7, no. 19 (1898): 432–488.

Santelli, Dr. "Travel to Choa, Explorations in Somal and at Danakils." *Bulletin of the Company of Geography of Paris* 7, nos. 1–4 (1889–1899): 479–501.

Schädler, Karl-Ferdinand. *Weaving in Africa South of the Sahara*. Munich: Panterra, 1987.

Shaw, Thurstan. *Igbo-Ukwu: An Account of Archaeological Discoveries in Eastern Nigeria*. Vols. 1 and 2. Evanston, IL: Northwestern University Press, 1970.

Vercoutter, Jean. *The Image of the Black in Western Art*. Freiburg, Switzerland: Office du livre, 1976.

Marie-Amy Mbow

Colonialism to Independence

- European Methods of Colonization
- The Benefits and Limits of Change
- A Range of Strategies Concerning Dress
- European Dress as a Mark of Civilization
- Global Influences on the Resistance to Colonization

A *colony*, also referred to as an *overseas possession* (a term used by imperial powers in the nineteenth century) or *non-self-governing territory* (a term used by the United Nations), is essentially a region governed by an external authority. From 1874 to 1957, for example, the present-day nation of Ghana was known as the Gold Coast, a colony ruled by the British Empire. On the African continent, colonies were established through settlement, commercial enterprises, treaties, or sometimes invasion. To varying degrees, all of these methods of colonization affected styles of dress on the African continent.

When historians write about the colonization of Africa, they are usually referring to European colonization, which began in the late 1800s and ended in 1994 with the fall of the apartheid government in South Africa. This period of struggle and change has profoundly impacted many aspects of life in Africa, including politics, economic systems, and religion as well as types of dress. In schools, the language of instruction is usually English, French, or Portuguese instead of an African language such as Yoruba or Wolof; children wear European-style uniforms with dresses, skirts, and pants. Many doctors, scientists, and professors earn their degrees in Europe or North America, feeling most comfortable in clothing like scrubs and three-piece suits. Aspiring fashion designers like Chris Seydou and Xuly Bet still hope to make it big in London or Paris. Some scholars refer to this continuing European influence as *neocolonialism*.

At the same time, the Colonial era must be understood in a broader, more global context. In the 1800s, there were areas in the interior where people had never seen Europeans, but Africa as a whole was not the isolated "Dark Continent" that Europeans imagined. The Tunisian city of Utica, for example, was founded by the Phoenicians in the twelfth century B.C.E. and was a busy port on the southern edge of the Mediterranean Sea. Most of North Africa was colonized by a succession of Phoenicians, Greeks, Romans, Byzantines, Arabs, and the Turkish Ottoman Empire, all of which affected dress long before the colonial powers of the 1800s—Great Britain, France, Germany, Italy, Portugal, The Netherlands, and Spain—even existed as nation-states. Much like European colonization, the spread of Islam also has affected dress in many parts of Africa. In areas like Egypt and the coastal regions of East Africa, tunics, cloaks (*abaya*), and veils (*hijab*) are just as common as dresses, T-shirts, and three-piece suits.

EUROPEAN METHODS OF COLONIZATION

The history and nuances of how colonization occurred in Africa affected choices about dress for both Africans and Europeans.

In Chad, for example, colonization was relatively brief (sixty years) and did not have a strong impact on the culture or styles of dress; the French government was primarily interested in the territory as a source of cotton. The few people in Chad who wear European-style dress include politicians, professionals, and foreign aid workers. South Africa, on the other hand, went through a very long period of European occupation that built up intense resistance to European culture and styles of dress. In 1652, the Dutch East India Company built a settlement at what is now Cape Town. Eventually, gold and diamonds were discovered, and native Africans were forced to live in "homelands" or townships, where their actions could be strictly monitored. Over the centuries, European-style dress did become widespread, but many traditional or African styles of dress were designed specifically to exclude any signs of European influence.

European exploration south of the Sahara Desert began in the fifteenth century. In 1482—ten years before Columbus sailed to the Americas—the Portuguese built a fort on the coast of present-day Ghana to trade for gold and ivory (although they quickly realized there was more money to be made in the slave trade). For the most part, Europeans stayed along the coastlines, trading cloth, muskets, brassware, and other manufactured goods for gold, salt, and slaves captured inland by other Africans. During this time, Europeans had little influence on African styles of dress; however, some of the manufactured goods were readily accepted as gifts or curiosities, especially by local chiefs and kings.

By the 1800s, a new generation of explorers was venturing into the interior. Africa was an exciting new frontier, potentially rich with raw materials such as rubber, tin, tortoiseshell, copper, and diamonds, some of which Africans were already using in their own dress. By the end of the nineteenth century, the slave trade was ending and the scramble for Africa was getting underway. In 1884, the major governments of Europe met in Berlin to establish rules for the colonization of Africa. One critical rule was the Principle of Effectivity, which stated that, in order to stake a claim, a colonial power needed to demonstrate its authority by signing treaties with the locals, flying a flag, establishing a police force, and making use of the colony economically. Otherwise, the area would be considered free and open for colonization. By 1902, over 90 percent of the African continent had been colonized by Europeans.

In practice, the colonial powers assumed and maintained control over their territories in vastly different ways. Invasion was difficult, costly, and required a large military presence; treaties, on the other hand, could be easy to sign but difficult to enforce. In some cases, particularly in southern Africa, colonies were formed by settlers (usually farmers). This was a common strategy for the Portuguese, Germans, and the French, who took it as their mission to govern by "civilizing" the local population—a practice known as *direct rule*. Changing styles of dress was an important part of this mission, because the colonizers believed that "naked" Africans could hardly be viewed as civilized. Children were viewed as being easier to change than adults. In what is now Mali, for example, the French forced children to attend school, where they could learn about French history and philosophy as well as "proper" dress and comportment. To resist this kind of intrusion, many noble

TABLE 6.1 TIME LINE

Twelfth century B.C.E.	Phoenicians establish a colony at Utica in present-day Tunisia.	1830–1834	French invasion of Algeria.
Eighth century	Beginning of Greek colonization in North Africa.	1884–1885	Berlin Conference establishes rules for colonial expansion in Africa.
Third century	Roman conquest of North Africa.	1888	William Mackinnon charters the Imperial British East Africa Company, claiming present-day Kenya for the British Empire.
Fourth century C.E.	King of the Axumite Empire (present-day Ethiopia) adopts Christianity as the kingdom's official religion.	1889	Cecil Rhodes, cofounder of the De Beers Mining Company, charters the British South Africa Company, laying claim to present-day Zambia and Zimbabwe (Northern and Southern Rhodesia).
451	Coptic Orthodox Church based in Alexandria (Egypt) separates from the Roman Catholic Church.	1896	Abyssinia (present-day Ethiopia) defeats the invasion of Italy, making it the only country ruled solely by Africans.
Seventh century	Arab soldiers cross the Red Sea into North Africa; Islam spreads through conquest as well as voluntary conversion.	1908	Facing international outrage over his brutal reign in the privately held Congo Free State, King Leopold II cedes control to Belgium.
	Merchants and religious exiles from the Arabian Peninsula, Persia, and South Asia begin to settle along the eastern edge of Africa.	1918	In the aftermath of World War I, Germany's colonies are taken over by France and Great Britain.
Late 1400s	Portuguese ships explore the coastlines; in 1482, São Jorge da Mina (later known as Elmina Castle) is built in present-day Ghana as a trading post.	1922	Egypt becomes an independent country.
1485	With permission from the king of Benin, Portuguese Franciscans establish the first Catholic church in West Africa.	1940s	After Italy's defeat in World War II, its colonies are taken over by the newly formed United Nations.
1500s	Many areas along the Mediterranean and Red Sea become part of the Ottoman Empire.	1945	League of Arab States founded in Cairo (Egypt).
1637	The Dutch seize Elmina Castle for slave trading.	1957	Ghana becomes the first country in sub-Saharan Africa to regain independence.
1652	Dutch colony established at the Cape of Good Hope in present-day South Africa by the Boers (farmers), also known as the Afrikaners.	1960s	Independence for many of the English and French-speaking colonies.
1780s	Peak of the slave trade to Europe and the Americas.	1970s	Independence for the Portuguese colonies Angola and Mozambique.
Early 1800s	Peak of the Arab slave trade in East Africa.	1980	Guerrilla war ends white control over Zimbabwe.
Late 1800s	Heavy European exploration of the African interior.	1994	End of the apartheid government in South Africa.

families sent their servants to school and kept their own children at home—a tactic that would ultimately change the culture and class structure of that country. The British, on the other hand, were more in favor of *indirect rule*. Instead of sending a mass of citizens to rule the colony and run the schools, which would have required a great deal of resources, authorities simply appointed local "big men" to administer the courts and handle most of the day-to-day tasks of government. Often, these men were given special staffs and robes to demonstrate their authority—a successful strategy that built on precolonial practices of kings investing lower chiefs with special ceremonial dress.

Commercial enterprises were also allowed to stake claims. This was enough to satisfy the Principle of Effectivity without much imperial investment—an efficient use of limited resources in a time of rapid expansion. In 1888, an entrepreneur named William

Mackinnon chartered the Imperial British East Africa Company to claim authority over present-day Kenya. A year later, Cecil Rhodes, cofounder of the De Beers Mining Company, chartered the British South Africa Company to claim present-day Zambia and Zimbabwe. Because there was little oversight, some of the most brutal practices occurred in these areas; Africans had to fight not just for their styles of dress and cultural traditions but for their very right to exist.

THE BENEFITS AND LIMITS OF CHANGE

For millennia before European colonization, Africans had been weaving and using techniques such as tie-dye and embroidery to embellish cloth. Especially in areas with a large percentage of Muslims (North Africa as well as parts of East and West Africa)

or Christians (Coptic Christianity had been established in Egypt and Ethiopia since the fourth century c.e.), cloth was considered an indispensable part of dress. Artisans were quick to make use of new materials brought by Europeans. In West Africa, for example, weavers—who were used to working primarily with cotton and wool—created intricate new patterns on textiles like kente cloth by using silk threads unraveled from imported fabrics and later rayon threads. Dyers were attracted to synthetic indigo, caustic soda, and factory-made cotton cloth because they simplified the process and allowed for new design possibilities. *Adire eleko*, a type of cloth that was invented in present-day Nigeria in the early 1900s, is made by drawing intricate patterns with cassava starch on a piece of cotton cloth and then dyeing it with indigo (the starch resists the dye, giving the cloth subtle light-blue-on-blue patterns). Even the finest hand-spun threads were too irregular for this technique; only factory cloth from Europe had the kind of smooth, even surface that was required. In addition, factory cloth was much wider and longer than most hand-woven fabrics. Eager to stimulate the textile industry back home, British traders even granted credit to adire dyers so they could buy larger quantities of cloth and synthetic dyes. In present-day Ghana, artisans adopted factory cloth for *adinkra* (cotton fabric embellished by stamping with hand-carved gourd blocks). Elaborate tie-dye designs (known as *gara* cloth in present-day Sierra Leone) were made possible by the widespread adoption of factory cloth.

In many cases, imported materials were incorporated into African dress in subtle ways that fit existing aesthetics—such as combining natural and synthetic dyes, embellishing garments with machine-made embroidery, or using candle wax and sheet metal from packing crates as stencils for resist-dyeing cloth. In

other cases, ideas about what was appropriate or beautiful to wear changed a great deal. In areas where large numbers of young people were forced to attend school and were exposed to European values on hygiene and clothing, practices like scarification, body painting, and head shaping (which the Mangbetu, for example, considered very beautiful) started to seem backward and gradually disappeared, especially in cities. In the kingdom of Benin, tattoos (called *iwu*) were highly significant, used to mark citizenship, eligibility for marriage, occupational role, pedigree, and political rank at the palace. When the kingdom was disrupted by a British invasion in 1897, tattooing lost much of its relevance. Even when the monarchy was eventually restored (to establish indirect rule by the British Empire), the practice was not viewed the same way. In the 1930s, the British-educated *Oba* (King) Akenzua II requested that tailors create a new style of dress for everyone serving the palace. Because clothing would cover any tattoos, they were no longer needed or even desired.

Mixed-race men and women born to European fathers and African mothers also had to straddle different cultures. In what is now Senegal, they sought permission to show their status by wearing European dress. Some freed slaves returning from the Americas were also eager to wear European-style clothing; it was a hard-won prize as well as a solution to not having a specific home to return to (since many had little idea from where their ancestors had been taken).

In the British colony that became Nigeria and in the Belgian Congo, some young women who were forced to attend European-run mission schools took advantage of their training in the domestic arts by learning how to make their own garments using sewing machines, knitting, and crocheting. These were practical skills—useful later as a source of income or to provide clothing for the family—but they also gave women a chance to use their creative talents. In present-day Nigeria, missionaries taught needlework in hopes of imparting Africans with Victorian middle-class values of orderliness, neatness, caution, obedience, and concentration. For many Yoruba women, however, who were already skilled at the demanding techniques of spinning, dyeing, weaving, and basket making, needlework was simply an attractive new skill—hardly the life-changing experience that missionaries thought it would be. In the 1920s and 1930s, seamstresses made more money than teachers.

African consumers were attracted to a variety of imported products, but frequently modified them to suit their own purposes. In southern Africa, for example, many tribal groups had a habit of smearing the body with a mixture of clay and some kind of oil such as shea butter, animal fat, or castor bean oil. This was thought to keep the body clean, prevent the skin from cracking, and give it a beautiful, glossy appearance. In place of oil, petroleum jelly made a good substitute. In West Africa, colonization brought chemical products used by some women (less often men) to lighten or brighten their skin. Many critics have interpreted this as a misguided effort to look white, arguing that it also destroys the skin by making it thinner and leads to cancer. For similar reasons, straightening the hair has also been controversial.

The same holds true for the adoption of European-style clothing. What are the limits of dress as creative expression versus dress as a sign of colonial domination? In the anthology *Clothing and Difference: Embodied Identities in Colonial and Post-Colonial Africa*, Deborah James has noted that "if people adopt some Western clothes, they are seen as treading a one-way path from

Port Said, Egypt, ca. 1900. A mixture of dress can be seen: Arab-style tunics, turbans, and *kufi* (caps) and one man on the far right wearing a European-style three-piece suit with a Turkish fez (an influence from the Ottoman Empire). Photographer unknown. Library of Congress, Prints and Photographs Division.

tradition to modernity. In fact, the semiotics of dress…are more complex." In the delta region of Nigeria, for example, top hats and walking sticks have become part of the rank insignia for Kalabari chiefs, gentlemen, and young men of social stature. For everyday attire, but especially for important events like funerals and masquerades, women often wear European-style blouses with wrappers—traditional garments (even though the most prestigious kinds of cloth are imported from India) that emphasize the hips and waist instead of creating a smooth vertical line. This ensemble combines both European and African aesthetics.

Starting in the 1940s in South Africa, blacks were only allowed to live near cities if they were employed; even then, their official homes were in the rural townships. Using a system of identity cards and pass laws (which came to be known as apartheid), wives and children were generally prevented from living in urban areas or moving from one district to another. Farming—even when blacks were allowed to own land in the townships—was very difficult because the best land and water sources were reserved for whites. Because of this system, it was very common for men to travel hundreds of miles from their families to work in the cities or in the diamond, gold, and copper mines. In rural areas, young women were sometimes able to seek employment as domestic workers on white-owned farms, but they were often expected to stay home once they started their own families. Being able to dress well was a sign that a husband could take care of his wife

Servants of a European household in the Congo Free State. They are wearing pants, button-down shirts, and aprons. Photograph by Emile E.O. Gorlia, ca. 1915. EEPA 1977-0001-800. Emile E.O. Gorlia Collection, Eliot Elisofon Photographic Archives, National Museum of African Art, Smithsonian Institution.

and children, even though he was not always physically present. In the northern Transvaal, proper *sesotho* dress (contrasted with *sekgowa*, or "white," dress) consisted of a long apron (usually made of leather), a sizeable cloth headwrap, bangle bracelets, and a voluminous shirt decorated with smocking and pleats. Although the women learned these techniques from Europeans, their adoption was not meant to show affinity for European culture. Instead, this style of dress was an effective marker of wealth, because smocking and pleating take a lot of cloth, time, and skill.

In a chapter for the anthology *Dress and Ethnicity*, Joanne Eicher and Tonye Erekosima have identified this kind of situation as *cultural authentication*. This process has four aspects: *selection*, where an object, idea, or technique is selected out of many possibilities presented by another culture; *characterization*, where the form is renamed or somehow translated to fit the new culture; *incorporation*, where it comes to satisfy a new need in society; and *transformation*, where the form is completely integrated and no longer seems foreign. This explains how items of dress such as blouses, shorts, khakis, and three-piece suits could originate from Europe but become part of everyday African dress—being much more than just a sign of colonial domination.

It should be noted, however, that cultural authentication requires a certain amount of freedom to experiment and voluntarily devise new meanings; the process cannot be forced from outside of the culture. In Algeria, colonial officials understood that changing women's clothing might lead to significant changes in society—getting rid of the veil would make women open (or at least vulnerable) to change, and that would surely affect how the rest of society functioned. In an essay titled "Algeria Unveiled," journalist Frantz Fanon observed in the 1950s that "the indigent and famished women were the first to be besieged. Every kilo of semolina distributed was accompanied by a dose of indignation against the veil and the cloister." Europeans and Algerians alike would have read any change in dress as a sign of abandonment. Fanon argued that "holding out against the occupier on this precise element means…keeping up the atmosphere of an armed truce." Eventually, some women did wear European dress—not because they had changed their minds, but because they found that it was useful as a kind of costume or mask. It took the French several months to realize that many Algerian women in European dress were actually freedom fighters. The change in clothing was so unexpected and astonishing that women were able to carry weapons, notes, bombs, and false identity cards in their handbags while French soldiers flirted with them and complimented them on their appearance.

A RANGE OF STRATEGIES CONCERNING DRESS

Strategies for dealing with colonization and the spread of European dress can be understood as a continuum between rejection and adoption. On one extreme would be something like the cult of Mumbo, a movement that originated in western Kenya in the early 1900s. Members tried to restore pride in their cultural traditions by performing precolonial rituals and dances, rejecting Christianity, discarding European-style clothing, letting their hair grow long, and vowing never to wash. Although elders might have been able to maintain some or all of their existing dress practices, this strategy would have been increasingly difficult for young men and women. Without memories of an earlier time, they couldn't help but be affected by colonization. Refusing to wear European-style dress might have given them the same appearance as their elders, but this must be considered a choice made in the context of colonization.

On the other end of the continuum would be the outright acceptance of European-style dress. This did sometimes occur, for instance, with new converts to Christianity. From a European standpoint, being naked was shameful, so missionaries would hand out pieces of cloth and clothing and would sometimes teach women how to sew. Again, Africans made this change thoughtfully, not just with blind acceptance. Lasting change is most likely to occur when people recognize some benefit in their lives. In addition to clothing, African Christian converts gained a new belief system and the conviction to resist cultural norms in their own communities. (Whether this was a good thing depended on the eye of the beholder.)

Another strategy on the part of Europeans to change African styles of dress was to have soldiers, laborers, and servants wear uniforms. In many of the British territories (under indirect rule), native Africans could serve in the lower levels of the police force and military. Members of the Nigeria Regiment were issued a khaki shirt and shorts, a red cummerbund, a red fez, and a short jacket. British troops stationed in the area also wore khakis and some of the same insignia, but the jacket, shorts, fez, and lack of shoes or boots was designed to show the Nigerians' subordinate rank. Although the British argued that Africans were used to going without shoes, to Nigerians this was seen as humiliating. Sandals were not included in the military uniform until the 1930s, and boots were only issued during World War II. Long pants were not allowed until Nigeria regained its independence from Britain in 1960.

In many areas, Africans who wore European-style dress—easing the visual gap between employer and employee—could also improve their chances of being hired as a farm laborer, construction worker, or domestic servant. A good portion of their wages might be reinvested in clothing because it enhanced their employability. When they returned home, this new clothing also conveyed their wealth and experience to the outside world (which was often attractive to other young people). Household servants were in a particularly good position to obtain clothes from their employers in the form of hand-me-downs and to intimately observe how Europeans dressed and cared for their clothing. This was especially common in areas where there were large numbers of white settlers. In present-day Zambia, merchants eager to sell clothes to African migrant workers noted that, after acquiring a basic shirt and shorts, a man would often build up his wardrobe with fancy shirts, a hat, shoes, socks, a belt, and possibly a suit. In southern Africa, since blacks were generally not allowed to own land or a house, clothing became the primary means of accumulating and displaying wealth.

EUROPEAN DRESS AS A MARK OF CIVILIZATION

Understanding the strategies of wearing European dress could also be a source of pride. Having servants who dressed well and spoke proper French or English reflected well on their European employers. For African servants, being able to dress well or "move with fashion" was a chance to impress their peers. By the 1920s, men in the colonial city of Brazzaville (in the present-day Republic of Congo) were listening to Cuban music and jazz and dressing in European-style suits, complete with accessories like walking

sticks, monocles, gloves, and pocket watches. During the 1940s, an informal group of young men in the Congo became known as *sapeurs*, an acronym for *Société des Ambianceurs et Personnes Elégantes* (people who set the ambience and elegant people). Going to clubs and bars in fashionable, expensive European clothing was thought to show a man's superiority, be aesthetically pleasing, and make him sexually attractive to young women. This could be seen as an example of mimicry; as the postcolonial thinker Home Bhabba has observed, "a difference that is almost the same, but not quite." Sapeurs were not trying to look white, but they were trying to master the language of European dress.

Although many Europeans were eager for Africans to wear clothes, going beyond basic needs—showing any kind of taste or initiative—was another matter. If Africans could dress like Europeans, but Europeans could not control what they wore, then mimicry could be seen as a threat or even an insult. In their diaries and official reports, some complained that Africans in European dress were not dignified because it took away from their native character or that Africans would wear any combination of gaudy things no matter how ridiculous it seemed. To keep servants in their place, employers would make gestures like giving them substandard clothing (garments that were no longer good enough for the employer), forcing them to wear shorts instead of pants, or calling male servants houseboys. In British East Africa, settlers were influenced by styles of dress they saw in Nairobi or Mombasa before heading to their plantations further inland. Servants would be required to wear native garments like the *kanzu* (a long white tunic) with a fez or a turban. These were actually Arabstyle garments, but to European employers, it gave their servants something to wear while ensuring that their dress would always be sufficiently exotic or different from theirs.

In Angola in the 1940s and 1950s, many young people were attracted to the fashions worn by Brazilian and U.S. film stars. By looking beyond Portugal, they were able to appear "civilized" without exactly taking on the dress of their colonizers. Students who wanted to attend the university had little choice; African dress was not considered appropriate attire. To ride the public buses, a woman had to wear shoes and European-style dress; wearing a wrapper (*pano*) was not permitted. Often, however, a woman who worked in the city would carry a wrapper with her and tie it over her clothing as soon as she returned home, changing back and forth between cultures as the situation demanded. As traditional dress started to disappear in the cities, some Africans romanticized the "pure" lifestyles of men and women in rural areas. Some educated Nigerians complained that young women in the cities were not learning anything important and were far too preoccupied with fashion. Influenced by returning slaves and pan-Africanism, many debated whether it was appropriate to have a Christian name or dress like a European.

For most Europeans, however, "going native" by wearing African dress would have been unthinkable. No matter how ill-suited their clothing was for the climate, Europeans took it as a sign of citizenship, civilization, and good breeding to maintain their appearance. For European soldiers and missionaries (especially Catholic nuns), any change in dress was slow because it had to be approved from outside the colony. The Yoruba thought that European men were suffocating themselves by not letting air circulate around the body—a ridiculous and dangerous practice. Even doing field work in Botswana and Namibia in the late 1980s, Hildi Hendrickson (1994) found that people were astonished to see a white woman in native dress. Children and non-Herero would laugh at her appearance, but Herero men told her she looked like a "real" woman.

GLOBAL INFLUENCES ON THE RESISTANCE TO COLONIZATION

Although Africans had many strategies for resisting colonization and the spread of European dress (as should be apparent from the preceding discussion), other global influences—particularly Islam, pan-Africanism, and Christianity—also played a role. These ideologies helped many groups to recognize the threat of colonization, come up with solutions, and form alliances outside the sphere of European influence.

In East Africa, for example, the Sudanese, Somali, and Swahili had a long history of interaction and intermarriage with Arabs and had often adopted their styles of clothing. Europeans could hardly label them as naked savages like some other groups in Africa, where body modifications (tattoos, scarifications, body painting, and so on) were the primary form of dress. Because many parts of North Africa and the Middle East—such as Algeria, Egypt, and present-day Yemen—were colonized by Europeans before sub-Saharan Africa, ideas about how colonization could be resisted were already circulating in the Islamic world. Being geographically close to the Arabian Peninsula made it possible for some in East Africa to make the hajj (pilgrimage) to Mecca and to interact directly with Muslims from other parts of the world. The same was true for Coptic Christians in Egypt and Ethiopia, who already had a unified church and saw no reason to accept European missionaries in areas that were already Christian.

In the Islamic world, one major train of thought was that Muslims should try to purify the religion of foreign influences by paying close attention to the Qur'an and trying to live as much as possible according to the example set by the prophet Mohammed (who died in 632 C.E.). The strict monotheism of Islam was also clearly different from Christianity. Another idea was to fight for the establishment of a new Islamic caliphate (empire) where Muslims could live under Islamic law (*shari'a*) instead of colonial or European-style laws. This gave rise to movements such as the Muslim Brotherhood (in Egypt), Mahdism (in present-day Sudan), and Wahabbism (a puritanical version of Islam that still influences present-day Saudi Arabia). In British Somaliland, Mohammed Abdulle Hassan—whom the British derisively called the "Mad Mullah"—was inspired by his time in Mecca to return home and lead an armed rebellion against colonial forces in the early 1900s. Soldiers in Sudan and Somalia both wore uniforms that were modeled on the clothing worn by pilgrims undertaking the hajj—a piece of white cloth to wrap around the lower body, another piece to drape over the upper body (or wear as a turban), and a strand of Islamic prayers beads (*tusbah*).

In areas such as present-day Sierra Leone, Liberia, Ghana, and Nigeria—where there were large numbers of Creoles (mixed-race Africans) and Saros (the descendents of slaves from Europe and the Americas who returned to West Africa after liberation)—pan-Africanism presented another strong alternative to colonization. In Sierra Leone as early as the 1880s, nationalists tried to restore African dress because they saw it as the first step to gaining independence from Europe. Having been stripped of their identities as slaves, many were eager to stimulate greater respect for African history, languages, and cultures.

A photograph entitled "Sudanese Warrior," early twentieth century, taken by Frank George Carpenter (1880–1923). The man wears two wrapped, white pieces of cloth and a strand of prayer beads (*tusbah*) around his neck. This is a style based on the clothing worn by male pilgrims making the hajj to Mecca. Library of Congress, Prints and Photographs Division.

In the city of Lagos in present-day Nigeria, issues regarding teaching Yoruba in the schools (instead of English), the education of women, the role of Christianity, and whether polygamy was still appropriate in Yoruba society were openly debated. Some took the movement personally by changing their names to be more African. Many women switched from wearing European clothing to Yoruba dress, consisting of an *iro* (wrapper), *buba* (loose-fitting blouse), and *gele* (headwrap). Adire cloth was especially popular because it was modern, being made of European textiles, but still traditional because it was dyed with indigo. Africans in the cities often romanticized rural life, but there was little interest in truly rural practices such as going barefoot or bare-chested.

In the 1940s, political activist Funmilayo Ransome-Kuti (founder of the Abeokuta Women's Union) adopted the iro, buba, and gele both to protest colonization and to show her solidarity with ordinary Yoruba women, even though her own family's background was Saro. From that time on, she was never photographed in European clothing. Much like Gandhi, she wore this native (but carefully constructed) style of dress at home as well as abroad to meet with socialists and feminists. Although she was well educated and spoke English, when she met with colonial authorities, she always spoke in Yoruba, forcing them to translate. To shame an *alake*, a Yoruba king under British authority, members of the

Women's Union demonstrated their defiance by standing outside his palace and stripping off their clothes—an act that was so shocking it clearly showed how little respect the women had for his rule.

Kwame Nkrumah, the first president of Ghana, spent ten years in the United States and was strongly influenced by the writings of W.E.B. DuBois and Marcus Garvey (Jamaican leader of the Back to Africa movement). When he returned to present-day Ghana in 1947, he deliberately adopted traditional dress for formal occasions—kente cloth (worn as a togalike garment by the Asante people) and the *fugu* (a smock from northern Ghana)—even though his own family was from a different region of the country. For informal occasions, however, he continued wearing European dress in an effort to show there was room for both influences to coexist. As president of the first sub-Saharan nation to regain its independence from Europe, Nkrumah's dress and political legacy have inspired many others both inside and outside of Africa.

References and Further Reading

Allman, Jean, ed. *Fashioning Africa: Power and the Politics of Dress.* Bloomington: Indiana University Press, 2004.

Bhabba, Homi. *The Location of Culture*, 2nd ed. New York: Routledge, 1994.

Burke, Timothy. *Lifebuoy Men, Lux Women: Commodification, Consumption, and Cleanliness in Modern Zimbabwe.* Durham, NC: Duke University Press, 1996.

Byfield, Judith. *The Bluest Hands: A Social and Economic History of Women Dyers in Abeokuta (Nigeria), 1890–1940.* Portsmouth, NH: Heinemann, 2002.

Eicher, Joanne B., and Tonye V. Erekosima. "Why Do They Call It Kalabari? Cultural Authentication and the Demarcation of Ethnic Identity." In *Dress and Ethnicity: Change across Space and Time*, edited by Joanne B. Eicher, 139–164. Oxford, UK: Berg, 1995.

Fanon, Frantz. *Studies in a Dying Colonialism.* English translation by Haakon Chevalier. London: Earthscan Publications, 1989. (Originally published in France, 1959.)

Gondola, Charles Didier. "Dream and Drama: The Search for Elegance among Congolese Youth." *African Studies Review* 42, no. 1 (1999): 23–48.

Hansen, Karen Tranberg, ed. *African Encounters with Domesticity.* New Brunswick, NJ: Rutgers University Press, 1992.

Hansen, Karen Tranberg. *Salaula: The World of Secondhand Clothing and Zambia.* Chicago: University of Chicago Press, 2000.

Hendrickson, Hildi. "The 'Long' Dress and the Construction of Herero Identities in Southern Africa." *African Studies* 53, no. 2 (1994): 25–54.

Hendrickson, Hildi, ed. *Clothing and Difference: Embodied Identities in Colonial and Post-Colonial Africa.* Durham, NC: Duke University Press, 1996.

James, Deborah. "'I Dress in This Fashion': Transformations in Sotho Dress and Women's Lives in a Sekhukhuneland Village, South Africa." In *Clothing and Difference: Embodied Identities in Colonial and Post-Colonial Africa*, edited by Hildi Hendrickson, 34–65. Durham, NC: Duke University Press, 1996.

Johnson, Marion. "Cotton Imperialism in West Africa." *African Affairs* 82 (1974): 178–187.

Kriger, Colleen E. *Cloth in West African History.* Lanham, MD: AltaMira Press, 2006.

Nevadomsky, Joseph, and Exhaguosa Aisien. "The Clothing of Political Identity: Costume and Scarification in the Benin Kingdom." *African Arts* 28, no. 1 (1995): 62–73.

Picton, John. *The Art of African Textiles: Technology, Tradition and Lurex.* London: Barbican Art Gallery, 1995.

Ross, Doran H. *Wrapped in Pride: Ghanaian Kenta and African American Identity.* Los Angeles: UCLA Fowler Museum of Cultural History, 1998.

Von Ehrenfels, U. R. "Clothing and Power Abuse." In *The Fabrics of Culture*, edited by Justine Cordwell and Ronald Schwarz, 399–403. The Hague, The Netherlands: Mouton, 1979.

Heather Marie Akou

Independence to Present

- Dress, Ethnicity, and Nation Building
- Nation Building and Dress Censorship
- Dress and Authority
- Late-Twentieth-Century Transnationalism and Globalization
- Dressing Well in a Period of Economic Decline

The achievement of independence in sub-Saharan Africa, beginning with Ghana in 1957, continuing up to the end of South African apartheid in the early 1990s, brought new appreciation for indigenous African styles and an elevation of certain ethnic ensembles to the status of national dress. During the late twentieth and early twenty-first centuries, transnationalism, globalization, and worsening economies have had a significant impact on African dress practices. Western-style dress, both new and secondhand, which Joanne Eicher and Barbara Sumberg argue is more appropriately termed *cosmopolitan* or *world fashion*, has become an increasingly widespread mode of African dress. Yet ethnic dress has maintained its relevance and vitality even in this period of increasing globalization and economic hardship.

DRESS, ETHNICITY, AND NATION BUILDING

Ethnic dress connecting a group to a shared cultural heritage continues to play a fundamental role in ritual and ceremonial events. Everyday dress of Morocco's Ait Khabbash Imazighen (Berbers) changed substantially during their twentieth-century transition from a nomadic to sedentary lifestyle. Yet customary wedding dress rituals maintain community unity and ethnic identity, with particular attention directed toward the bride, whose ritually dressed body symbolizes both past and future.

The dressing of the bride takes place in a tent, now rarely used, which is emblematic of their nomadic past. The bride is adorned with the silver jewelry once worn on a daily basis, and women sing songs of their mothers and grandmothers while decorating the bride's hands and feet with henna, a time-honored divine blessing. The bride's hair, its thickness and length indicative of her fertility, is bound and braided, and her head is encased in a headdress of striped red cloth layered with ties, sashes, and silver, symbolizing the containment of female sexuality and fertility necessary for ensuring future Ait Khaddash identity.

Ethnic dress, which provided an important means of displaying pride and identity during Africa's independence movements, continued to play a significant role in nation-building efforts of the postindependence period. Dress ensembles, textiles, headdresses, and hairstyles provided leaders and citizens of emerging African states with distinctive, visually compelling ways of proclaiming and celebrating new national and political identities.

Following the independence of Sierra Leone in 1961, the print dress—a shorter, updated version of the nineteenth- to mid-twentieth-century *kaba sloht*, Krio women's long-sleeved, ankle-length yoked dress—was among the styles proposed for national dress. The print dress became a popular ensemble style for displaying Krio identity on special occasions such as wakes, postwedding festivities, and other events like church meetings and parties.

Nationalist affirmations of indigenous identities stimulated educated African elites to reintroduce ethnic styles into wardrobes that had largely featured Western-style ensembles during the pre-Colonial and early Colonial periods. In the years leading up to Nigerian independence in 1960, Nigerian men wore substantially more indigenous dress; however, in the years following independence, the modern West African "conductor's suit" gained particular popularity with elite businessmen. However, women of Nigeria's educated elite continued preindependence practices of wearing more indigenous dress, with certain modifications. The women's second wrapper, which increased body girth in a matronly manner, became unfashionable. In the 1970s, Nigerian women of all ages increasingly abandoned their straightened, Western hairstyles for indigenous braided styles, which they wore with both indigenous and Western-style ensembles.

African independence day celebrations also featured women's and men's attire fashioned from special commemorative factory-cloth designs that proclaimed and celebrated their countries' new independence. Commemorative cloths displaying images of national leaders, national colors, and emblems reinforced national unity in countries with strong ethnic divisions and promoted new government policies and development projects. Commemorative cloths with printed slogans such as "One Nigeria" and "Keep Nigeria One" (names also attached to popular hairstyles) were worn during Nigeria's (Biafran) civil war. Yet the postindependence marginalization of Nigeria's Igbo people was expressed by designating men's *agbada* ensemble, combining dress elements of Nigeria's dominant ethnic groups, the Hausa and Yoruba, as men's national dress.

Ensembles made from commemorative cloth could also be worn for more critical commentary by repositioning the pattern, as when women wore their wrapper so that a leader's portrait was upside down or sat upon. In Kenya toward the end of Jomo Kenyatta's presidency, men's commemorative cloth shirts were tailored so that Kenyatta's face was cut in two. Images of Ghana's first president, Kwame Nkrumah, whose name and image were proscribed by succeeding regimes, became rehabilitated over time and, by 2007, were included in cloth designs commemorating the fiftieth anniversary of Ghanaian independence.

With the end of apartheid in South Africa, beginning with the 1990 lifting of the ban on political organizations and especially following South Africa's first democratic elections in 1994, dress was used to establish a postapartheid identity. South Africans not only expressed pride in South African identity but also used dress to express a new sense of Africanness and connection to the larger African continent. South Africans incorporated dress elements associated with African, as well as South African, ethnic identities into what had previously been largely Western-style wardrobes.

In 1992, the Dutch company Vlisco, which has a long history of producing prestigious African factory prints for the West and Central African markets, began marketing textiles in South

Professional models dressed in the indigo dress and amber beads of Soninke women for a fashion show by Malian designer Kandioura Coulibaly during the Farafina Tigne Independence Day Celebration. Mopti, Mali, 2002. Photograph by Janet Goldner.

Africa. In 1995, Vlisco began producing African prints by South African designer Peter Soldatos based on South African cultural motifs such as Ndebele house paintings. Various hybrid styles were created incorporating elements of contemporary and historic African cultures, including clothing embellished with strips of Ghanaian kente cloth or headgear combining ancient Egyptian headdresses with those worn by married Zulu women.

Pride in ethnic and South African identity is displayed by beaded accessories or clothing inspired by Zulu and Ndebele beadwork. Victorian-inspired dress and headwraps of South Africa's Xhosa peoples, developed following nineteenth-century contact with European settlers, have become particularly popular for expressing ethnic pride and South African identity.

South African ethnic dress has also been enlisted for new purposes, as in the traditional drag adopted during the 1990s for Johannesburg's gay and lesbian pride parade. The inclusion of sexual orientation in the antidiscrimination protections of the postapartheid South African constitution stimulated new activism in South Africa's gay and lesbian communities. One strategy to counter the denigration of homosexuality as un-African and a colonial, European import was adoption of traditional African women's attire as gay drag. In Johannesburg pride parades, gay men dress in customary styles of Xhosa, Zulu, and Herero women (ethnic dress whose new status as symbols of postapartheid pride and nationalism lend support to the authenticity of gay African identities).

The issue of dress and nationalism has also acquired new significance for Africans far from their homeland, like the great numbers of Somali refugees forced to flee following the national government's 1991 collapse. Dress, particularly of Somali women, has assumed particular importance for refugees seeking to maintain a sense of national identity while dispersed in immigrant communities throughout the world. The conceptualization of Somali national dress changed as a result of political developments during the 1970s and 1980s, incorporating more concealing, Middle Eastern–inspired styles of Islamic dress. Since the early 1990s, various forms of Somali national dress have emerged in immigrant communities such as Minneapolis–St. Paul, with refugees dressing in clothing expressing this greater religiosity as a means of maintaining a distinctive Somali national and Islamic identity.

In the mid-1970s, dress expressed grassroots Islamic activism in countries such as Egypt, where an increasing number of young urban women and men replaced modern secular clothing with al-ziyy al-Islami (Islamic dress). More austere, pious modes of dress, including the hijab (from hajaba, to veil, seclude, form a separation), were in keeping with activists' efforts to create a new state of permanent religiousness. This new Islamic dress, with its emphasis on concealing the human body, displayed apparent continuities with the modesty garments of earlier Egyptian dress. Activists embraced this contemporary revival of pious Islamic dress as an expression of Islamic morality and identity and a rejection of Western values and modern exhibitionism.

The Egyptian government's initial tolerance of the Islamic dress movement was replaced with policies discouraging such attire by the late 1980s, following escalation of armed conflict with militant Islamist groups. By the mid-1990s, government efforts to curb extremist Islamic dress, combined with urban women's desire for lighter, less cumbersome dress, prompted a growing number of women to wear less conservative and less concealing forms of Islamic dress. The early twenty-first century has seen the increasing popularity of new stylish modes of Islamic dress—or "Islamic chic"—among contemporary urban Egyptian women.

NATION BUILDING AND DRESS CENSORSHIP

Following independence, the importance of dress as a visible expression of national identities brought new levels of scrutiny and control concerning both indigenous and foreign dress practices. In certain instances, government campaigns called for a particular ethnic group's abandonment of dress practices equated with nudity and social backwardness.

Tanzania's Operation Dress-Up, a campaign instituted during the late 1960s, pressured Maasai pastoralists to abandon traditional dress in favor of more modern Western-style clothing. From the late 1960s through the mid-1970s, this campaign directed persuasion and coercion at Maasai men to abandon the customary practice of adorning their bodies with red ochre. Men were also pressured to replace their wrapper, or lubega, which failed to cover their "nakedness," with "proper dress" in the form of Western-style trousers. Maasai students wearing lubega were banned from schools, and men who persisted in wearing red ochre or the lubega were threatened with denial of medical care at government facilities.

The government campaign against Maasai customary dress was cast as part of a larger effort to improve the health and welfare of its citizens. Maasai dress practices like the wearing of red ochre, it was argued, were unhygienic, and Maasai were said to smell because of a failure to wash regularly. Maasai women were refused treatment at medical facilities because their bead jewelry was classified as unhygienic. Finally, the special appeal of Maasai dress to European and American tourists was characterized as being a continuation of colonial romanticism.

In the first decade of Ghanaian independence, from 1957 to 1966, governmental and nongovernmental campaigns were directed at eliminating the "nudity" of ethnic dress, especially that of women, among Ghana's northern peoples. The customary dress of these peoples—including the Dagara, Tallensi, Bulsa, and Nankanfe—consisted of skins, waist beads, and leaves covering the genital areas of adult men and women. Yet Ghana's new leaders, largely mission-educated Akan men and women from the south with extensive textile and regalia traditions, perceived northerners' dress of skins and leaves as nakedness. Such dress practices, they argued, were outmoded and not in conformity to Ghanaian culture.

Two women wearing miniskirts in Kumesi, Ghana in 1971. Miniskirts were a popular and controversial trend among young urban women in several African states. Photograph by Suzanne Gott.

As president of modern sub-Saharan Africa's first independent nation and a prominent advocate of pan-African liberation, Nkrumah wanted to correct any perceptions of regional backwardness that might damage Ghana's international reputation. For women activists, the "nudity problem" of the north represented the social and economic subordination of northern women. Antinudity campaigns, directed primarily toward women, included economic development projects as well as distribution of free secondhand clothing from Europe and America.

Nation-building concerns of newly independent African states during the 1960s and 1970s also focused on the impropriety of certain Western-influenced dress styles popular among their country's youth. Several eastern and central African countries instituted dress censorship targeting women's dress in particular. In newspaper reports, miniskirts were blamed for rioting in Ethiopia that resulted in injury, destruction of property, and school closings. In Kenya, Uganda, Malawi, and Zambia, women wearing miniskirts were physically assaulted and stripped of their clothing.

Fashions such as miniskirts, hot pants, cosmetics, and skin-lightening creams were also condemned as holdovers of colonialism and expressions of Western decadence. Afro wigs and hairstyles were criticized for appearing wild and unkempt, while beauty contests were seen as degrading. Following Zanzibar's successful 1964 union with Tanganyika as Tanzania, dress became a major site of contention between national leaders and urban youth. Government leaders considered foreign, international youth culture fashions like bell-bottom trousers and miniskirts as an unacceptable challenge to government efforts at building a nationalist revolutionary society based on socialist and Islamic ideals. Zanzabari youth wearing miniskirts and bell-bottoms, it was argued, were not recognizably African, socialist, or Muslim. Such fashions, inspired by Western cinema, represented a decadent capitalism opposed to postindependence policies promoting a national culture of austerity and self-sacrifice.

Although miniskirts were not officially banned in postindependence Zambia, there was strong opposition to what was seen as sexually provocative clothing (against the tradition of customary Zambian dress). In fact, Zambia had no viable form of national dress, since Western-style clothing had largely replaced indigenous dress by the 1950s. During the 1970s, in response to the perceived impropriety of miniskirts and their association with the more independent professional woman, the Zambian Women's League promoted the invention of a new form of traditional women's dress. This ensemble, more in keeping with Zambian women's "proper" roles as wives and mothers, was the *chitenge*, based on popular West African women's attire of an African factory-print skirt or wrapper, blouse, and head scarf.

The reappearance of the miniskirt in Zambia during the 1990s, including skirts no shorter than two inches (five centimeters) above the knee, was met with greater levels of hostility, as well as physical violence, including public stripping and rape. Such violence, it was argued, was provoked by miniskirts' equation with loose morals and an attempt to arouse men's sexual desires. In this region, where women have historically been subject to the control of men and elders, male censorship of female dress assumed a greater significance in terms of women's rights. In the capital of Lusaka, the January 2002 stripping of dozens of women in "slut wear" brought protests from women's groups and human rights organizations, and public demonstrations by

Zambian women resulted in the arrest of twenty-five young men and the Zambian president's condemnation of such denials of women's freedom of dress.

DRESS AND AUTHORITY

The Egyptian government's promotion of Western dress, instituted as part of President Nasser's modernization efforts during the 1950s and 1960s, has had limited impact on the overall dress habits of its citizens. Although Western-style ensembles (usually business suits for men and skirts and blouses for women) are the requisite attire for workers in government offices, schools, and clinics, local clothing styles remain an important form of daily wear, particularly for those living outside of such urban centers as Cairo. Although male residents of Cairo often dress in Western clothing both in and outside the workplace, Western dress has limited use and value for men living in rural areas and in Egypt's southern region, where the *jallabiyya* ("garb" or "robe") remains an important signifier of masculine identity and power.

Male adulthood and respectability are expressed by wearing the jallabiyya. To avoid ridicule, schoolboys often conceal Western school uniforms under a jallabiyya until reaching school. In southern Egypt, a man may go to work wearing the jallabiyya, only donning Western attire after reaching the office and changing back into the jallabiyya before returning home. Such men will, however, strategically change into Western clothing when going to the city or dealing with government officials.

In 1980s Nigeria, elite young Igbo women and men appropriated dress forms associated with powerful senior men. It became fashionable, and somewhat controversial, for elite young women to commission the *alhaji* ensemble associated with wealthy and influential senior northern Hausa men who had successfully completed the costly hajj (the pilgrimage to Mecca). The male alhaji ensemble, the most prestigious form of Hausa attire, consists of a shirt, drawstring trousers, and voluminous overtunic of costly cotton Guinea brocade embellished with elaborate embroidery worn with a colorful, tall, brimless hat. During the 1970s oil boom, the alhaji ensemble, combined with expensive shoes, briefcase, and designer sunglasses, became emblematic of Nigeria's high-living entrepreneurial elite. During the late 1980s, young women commissioned this prestigious male ensemble, which they wore with high-heeled shoes or (feminine) flats and a matching handbag. They completed this ensemble with sunglasses, gold jewelry, heavy makeup, perfume, and a Western hairstyle or braided hair extensions, becoming feminized versions of an unattainable persona, the powerful senior northern man. The more daring young women also wore a men's alhaji hat perched at a rakish angle.

Also during the late 1980s, a young male Igbo designer developed a modern streamlined version of the alhaji or *agbada* power-dress ensemble for young male entrepreneurs. He broke with convention by using luxurious brocades in the customary mourning colors of black and dark blue in order to combine Nigerian men's styles with the darker tones of Western suits—a combination that Igbo elders found unsettling. The addition of costly imported accessories such as expensive watches, gold chains, and Italian shoes—prestige objects conventionally associated with senior Igbo men in positions of authority—intensified the subversive potential of this youthful dress style. Senior authority holders found one young man's addition of a velvet or felt cap, headgear reserved for Igbo chiefs, to be an unacceptable violation

of their customary power structure. Male lineage elders fined the youthful offender and confiscated his cap. Yet Igbo elders did tolerate young men's addition of a locally produced walking stick (similar to a senior man's staff) to Western-style suits whose foreign status sufficiently reduced the perceived threat to established authority.

In the Democratic Republic of Congo and the Republic of Congo, impoverished young urban men known as *sapeurs* engage in the cult of the *griffe* (expensive designer labels) centering on the appropriation of European designer clothing to create an alternative to the harsh realities faced by many late-twentieth- and early-twenty-first-century Congolese youth. The roots of this practice date to the early-twentieth-century appropriation of Western clothing by Congolese employed by French colonial officials. Men's fashion-focused social clubs were established during the 1920s and in the early 1940s, and social clubs in the cities of

Congolese *sapeur* displaying designer-label elegance, wearing a two-piece suit with green plaid waistcoat and crocodile-leather derby shoes. The cigar and bottle of beer are intended to convey a sense of ease and opulence, at odds with the poverty actually experienced by many young Congolese in the late twentieth and early twenty-first centuries. Brazzaville, Republic of Congo, 2001. Photograph by Agnès Rodier.

Brazzaville and Kinshasa provided the stage for public displays of men's prestigious Western fashions.

During the economic decline of the 1960s following independence, Congolese youth sought a better life in Western European cities, meeting racial discrimination and economic difficulties with the elegant resistance of the sapeur lifestyle. Early-twenty-first-century sapeurs represent the fourth or fifth generation of Congolese dandyism. They continue to live on the edge of poverty, seeking to fulfill their dreams and ambitions by dressing in designer-label elegance ideally acquired abroad by migrating (often illegally) to such European cities as Paris and Brussels. Once there, sapeurs live in impoverished conditions, working as manual laborers and spending as much as a month's salary on a pair of designer shoes.

The rigorous demand for designer-label elegance extends to every element of sapeur attire: suits, shirts, and pants by Dior, Gaultier, Yves Saint-Laurent, and Giorgio Armani; designer-label shoes and underwear; and accessories such as Cartier watches, Valentino belts, Armani sunglasses, and Yves Saint-Laurent perfume. The sapeur's successful return from his transcontinental quest for the griffes, having overcome its challenges and deprivations, is one means by which Congolese urban youth on the margins of the formal economy achieves a new identity that blurs Congolese as well as European distinctions of class and social status.

Sapeurs have described their lifestyle as a political response to the colonial past as well as to over two decades of Mobutu Sese Seko's dictatorship and enforced policy of *authenticité*. The 1974 legislation prohibiting Western dress in favor of a more authentically African mode of dress required women to abandon Western-style dresses, skirts, and trousers for *maputu* (wrappers) of African factory-print cloth. Men had to replace their business suits, shirts, and ties with the *abacost* jacket designed by the president himself and modeled on the Maoist jacket. Those sapeurs refusing to abandon their Western-styled elegance were routinely harassed and barred from public spaces during the early 1980s. Following the 1997 overthrow of the Mobutu government and into the beginning years of the twenty-first century, sapeurs experienced greater freedom and an elevation in status.

LATE-TWENTIETH-CENTURY TRANSNATIONALISM AND GLOBALIZATION

African dress of the late twentieth and early twenty-first centuries is a complex mixture of the local, transnational, and global that is a phenomenon of Africa's rapidly growing urban populations. In the Senegalese capital of Dakar, young male tailors situate their shops in the heart of the city to keep abreast of the latest fashion trends and find inspiration in Dakar's deteriorating but dynamic visual environment. Tailors also seek inspiration for new clothing designs by watching satellite television programs (especially such popular soap operas as the Mexican *Marimar*) and music videos from Africa, Europe, and the United States featuring fashions of hip-hop and rap culture.

In a continent where the focus has historically been directed toward adulthood and the authority of elders, the late-twentieth- and early-twenty-first-century development of a globally oriented urban youth culture is new. African urban youth have embraced those forms of world fashion that connect them to a globalized youth culture portrayed in music videos from the United States, Europe, and Africa. These fashions have also been popularized via satellite television programs from abroad and African versions of youth-oriented reality television programs. Growing access to the Internet and increased rates of migration and travel abroad, much of it economically driven, also keep African youth apprised of the latest fashion trends.

But for the vast majority of African urban youth, the influx of relatively inexpensive secondhand clothing from America and Europe has enabled them to satisfy desires to become connected to global youth culture and its seemingly affluent world. In Ghana, young urban women try to stay trim rather than develop the rounded figures that were once the feminine ideal in order to fit into the smaller secondhand youth fashions from abroad. In Ghanaian cities, fitness clubs have become popular for style-conscious youth as well as more health-minded adults.

African youth have adopted the fashions of African American youth culture's hip-hop and rap styles in varying degrees. In the early 1990s, young male Zambian street vendors began to adopt the big look of American hip-hop and rap fashions by dressing in looser, bigger clothing with shirt tails hanging out that had previously been worn tucked in. After 1994, Johannesburg's postapartheid generation adopted and recast African American styles to express their distinctively South African urban mixture of township and city youth cultures. The head cloths and shoes worn by married women working as domestic servants during the apartheid era have been reclaimed and transformed into postapartheid youth fashions. The image and name of martyred antiapartheid activist Stephen Biko was featured in brilliant red in a recent line of low-cut, tight-fitting T-shirts.

Although Senegalese youth find Western-style imported clothing appealing—including new and used T-shirts, jeans, shirts, pants, and sports attire—others regard such clothing as only suitable for the young or those who cannot afford the custom-made Senegalese ensembles produced by tailors and seamstresses. The preferred mode of women's attire, in keeping with Islamic ideals of modesty, remains the *boubou* (a loose robe with a neck opening), the voluminous, long dress called *ndoket* with its multitiered sleeves, and the West African blouse and skirt or *pagne* ensemble Senegalese call *taille basse*.

Leslie Rabine's investigation and analysis of the global circulation of African fashion linking Dakar, Nairobi, and Los Angeles has revealed the late-twentieth-century transnationalism and globalization of African fashion. The distinctive localized meanings of transnational and globalized modes of African dress are exemplified by differing local perceptions of the West African boubou. While Senegalese value the boubou because it is traditional, Kenyans value recently acquired West African fashions popularized via the mass media and African American community for their modernity.

In Kenya, the African dress worn by middle-class Nairobi women as special-occasion attire beginning in the late 1970s has been based on the borrowing and blending of West African styles and fabrics. During colonialism, Western dress imposed upon Kenya's Kikuyu peoples by colonial officials and missionaries largely supplanted indigenous dress forms. Following Kenyan independence in 1963, Western-style clothing remained the primary mode of everyday dress, especially in such urban centers as Nairobi. The popularity of these recently adopted, modern styles from Senegal, Mali, and Côte d'Ivoire increased during the 1990s, in part due to Kenyans seeing African American versions of these styles in U.S. television programs and fashion catalogs.

In researching Dakar's dynamic visual environment, scholar Joanna Grabski documented how young tailors situate their workshops in the heart of the city for creative inspiration and to keep abreast of the latest fashion trends. Dakar, Senegal, 2002. Photograph by Joanna Grabski.

Historically and into the early twenty-first century, the West African boubou is one of the most widely adopted forms of African dress both within Africa and abroad. Another widely worn style of African dress is the two- or three-piece women's ensemble, usually of African factory-print cloth, that originated in West Africa. This ensemble, consisting of a sewn blouse, sewn or wrapped skirt, and unsewn cloth for a second wrapper or stylish headgear, was developed by the incorporation of a European-inspired sewn blouse into West African women's one- or two-piece indigenous wrapped styles. This process of cultural authentication occurred over centuries of coastal trade and cross-cultural interaction. During the Independence and post-Independence periods, this ensemble was invested with new significance as an expression of African identity and nationalist pride, not only in West Africa but by the citizens of certain newly independent southeast African nations as well. In Ghana, this ensemble is called the *kaba*, a term probably derived from the West African English word for cover. In Côte d'Ivoire, it is the *complet trois pagne*, *pagnes* being a widely used French term for women's wrappers as well as for the African factory-print textiles commonly used for these ensembles. In Senegal, it is known as the *taille basse*. In southern and eastern Africa, a region without the widespread textile traditions of West Africa, this ensemble has been adopted as a popular mode of African dress by nations whose own indigenous dress traditions were supplanted by the Western-style dress introduced or imposed during colonialism. In Zambia and Kenya, respectively, the African-print ensemble is called the chitenge or *kitenge*. In postindependence Zambia, this West African ensemble has become an established national

dress tradition that has continued to incorporate stylistic innovations from West and Central Africa.

By the latter decades of the twentieth century, dress in most regions of Africa was a combination of local ethnic or national styles and more globalized world fashion. Increasing urbanization, emigration abroad, and mass media in the form of fashion magazines (both local and global), radio, films and videos, global television networks, and the Internet have intensified Africa's connections to the wider world. Although connections beyond the local via Africa's regional, long-distance, and transcontinental trade networks have been a fundamental feature of Africa's history, the scope of this cosmopolitanism has expanded, and its pace has accelerated.

Despite the seemingly homogeneous nature of world fashion items such as T-shirts and jeans, the selection and manner of incorporation of more globalized fashions are specific to each sociocultural context and locality. In Ghana's Ashanti region, where the Asante pride themselves on their adherence to customary funeral practices, the ongoing dynamism of this time-honored custom is evidenced by such late-twentieth-century innovations as the incorporation of T-shirts in mourning colors of red and black into men's and women's funerary dress that display locally silk-screened photographic images of the deceased.

In Mali, handwoven and hand-dyed Bamana *bogolanfini*, once obligatory for life transitions and customary rites, were, by the late 1980s, being fashioned into Western-style dresses, blouses, skirts, and purses and were now popularly referred to as Malian rather than exclusively Bamana. Fashion-conscious youth combine bogolan vests, baseball caps, and other accessories with

Western-style garments such as T-shirts or denim skirts to create a Malian version of world fashion that expresses a renewed awareness and pride in their country's cultural heritage.

DRESSING WELL IN A PERIOD OF ECONOMIC DECLINE

The worsening economic conditions and crises that have afflicted most of sub-Saharan Africa during the late twentieth and early twenty-first centuries have substantially affected African dress practices. Secondhand clothing from the United States and Europe has become an increasingly significant mode of dress as a relatively affordable form of clothing that has enabled many Africans to continue dressing well during this period of economic crisis and decline. Karen Tranberg Hansen, whose research and publications have stimulated a new recognition and understanding of African secondhand clothing, has emphasized the role of secondhand clothing as a valued resource that meets the needs of Africa's financially strapped citizenry and provides an increasingly available means of meeting desires to be fashionable and engaged in Western modernity. Tranberg Hansen has also emphasized the importance of *clothing competence*, involving the processes of careful selection and combining of secondhand garments to create a new, fashionable, well-coordinated look.

In the postindependence years, many African countries restricted or banned the importation of used as well as new Western-style clothing as part of economic austerity programs. The exponential growth of Africa's already existing secondhand trade began in the mid-1980s, following the liberalization of trade and deregulation of African economies imposed by World Bank and International Monetary Fund structural adjustment programs. Despite rising concerns during the 1990s that cheaper secondhand clothing was adversely affecting local textile industries, especially in western Africa, secondhand imports met the needs of a growing percentage of the African population for stylish, affordable clothing.

The late-twentieth- and early-twenty-first-century expansion of the secondhand clothing market has largely taken place in sub-Saharan Africa rather than in North African Muslim countries. By 1998, sub-Saharan Africa was receiving one-third of total world exports, becoming the world's largest importer of secondhand clothing. In Africa, secondhand clothing is known by different names in different localities: in Ghana it is *buroni waawu* (white person who has died); in Senegal it is *fuug jaay* (shake and sell); and in East Africa it is *mitumba* (bale). In Zambia, where Tranberg Hansen has focused her research, it is known as *salaula* (to select from a bale in the manner of rummaging).

The largest source of secondhand clothing originated as donations to major charitable organizations in the United States and Europe, who sell their excess clothing (approximately 40 to 60 percent) to textile recycling companies, where the clothing is sorted, baled, and shipped to Africa. In Africa, local wholesalers open the bales for sale to retail vendors. In Zambia, clothing from a newly opened bale is valued by retailers for being fresh and new. When displaying their clothing for prospective customers, Zambian retailers stopped their earlier practice of laundering and ironing the clothing after finding that clothing hung up fresh from the bale, with wrinkles and folds, is more appealing to customers. It is also evidence that the garment is genuine and not "thirdhand"—that it, is secondhand clothing from abroad and not clothing previously owned and worn by Zambians.

Secondhand clothing is sold in open-air market stalls and carried by street vendors along city thoroughfares. In Nigeria and Ghana, it is commonly displayed in heaps on sidewalks, earning the popular name of "bend-down boutiques." In Ghana, used clothing is sorted into first, second, and third grades. Some vendors sell the highest-quality first-grade clothing—also known as *selection*—by taking it around to offices of government and business employees. The cheaper grades are generally sold in rural

Shopping for secondhand clothing at Kamwala market, Lusaka, Zambia, 1992. Photograph by Karen Tranberg Hansen.

areas or as work clothing. In certain locations, such as Senegal and Zambia, tailors and dressmakers may custom-fit, alter, or completely transform secondhand garments for a customer.

In addition to its affordability, secondhand clothing is worn and valued for a variety of reasons, depending on the region and sector of the local population. In those parts of southeastern Africa without an indigenous textile-based dress tradition and with well-established twentieth-century practices of wearing Western-style dress, good-quality imported secondhand clothing has wide appeal throughout the general population. In Zambia, second-hand clothing is particularly attractive because of its distinctive and exclusive styles. However, in western Africa, a region with a long history of indigenous textile production and imported textile consumption, the appeal of secondhand and Western-style clothing depends on age, gender, and income.

During the 1960s and 1970s, many newly independent, financially strapped African governments implemented economic austerity programs that restricted or banned the importation of textiles and Western-style clothing, policies that also supported nationalist cultural objectives. In West Africa, with its rich textile traditions, these restrictions stimulated a renewed interest in wearing local clothing in ethnic clothing styles.

Structural adjustment programs imposed by the World Bank and International Monetary Fund in many African nations beginning in the 1980s have had a devastating effect on the incomes and quality of life of increasing numbers of Africa's citizens. This deregulation and liberalization of the economy has adversely affected the formal economies and job markets of many African nations, forcing middle-class civil servants and professionals into informal economy professions. One of the results was rapid growth in small-scale informal tailoring and textile production workshops, where dire economic necessity stimulated creativity and design innovation.

During the Nigerian oil boom of the mid-1960s to late 1970, Yoruba elite dressed in European haute couture such as Christian Dior, Nina Ricci, and Gucci, with the most prestigious forms of local dress fashioned from imported textiles such as the cotton/synthetic cloth with eyelet embroidery known as lace. However, the Nigerian government's 1978 ban on prestigious imported clothing and textiles, followed by the 1980s devaluations of the Nigerian currency, increased the patronage of more local forms of prestige dress.

In the 1980s, locally hand-dyed *adire* and prestigious hand-woven *aso-oke* strip-cloth textiles became increasingly popular with the Yoruba elite. New techniques and modern imported materials were employed to create fashionable, contemporary versions of indigenous Yoruba dress. For aso-oke, which became the most prestigious dress form, this was accomplished primarily by replacing cotton thread with an increasing percentage of shiny metallic plastic Lurex thread, culminating in *shain-shain* (shine-shine), aso-oke cloth composed primarily of shiny Japanese-manufactured Lurex thread. During the mid-1990s, Yoruba dress was fashioned from Super-Q, a densely woven aso-oke combining Senegalese and Ghanaian strip-cloth designs and techniques; it was produced by migrant Ghanaian Ewe weavers.

In the 1960s and 1970s, Senegal's first president, Léopold Senghor, banned *tenue traditionnelle* (traditional dress) for official audiences in favor of Western-style suits and gowns. During that time, Senegalese dress styles were not considered fashionable and were worn largely by older Senegalese and devout

Mrs. Monica Boadu modeling a new *kaba* ensemble of Chinese-manufactured African-print cloth, Kumase, Ghana, July 2007. Photograph by Suzanne Gott.

Muslims. But following Senghor's 1980 resignation amid a severe economic crisis and the increasing impoverishment and urban decline caused by policies instituted by structural adjustment programs, middle-class Senegalese turned to more affordable Senegalese styles and African fabrics. The collapsing economy also brought thousands of unemployed middle-class men and women into Senegal's informal economy as tailors, seamstresses, and fabric dyers.

In the capital of Dakar, despite a worsening economy and the resulting urban decline, the acquisition and display of elegant dress remained a priority during the 1980s and 1990s. For Senegalese women in particular, stylish beauty continued to be equated with cultural ideals of honor. Middle-class women rather than the elite have fueled Dakar's fashion explosion, facilitated by the availability of cheaper East Asian and Nigerian imitations of prized European damasks, African prints, and other luxury textiles—a contemporary continuation of Senegal's long history as a center of long-distance and intercontinental trade. Women also employ financial strategies such as savings groups, gifts, and loans to fund their dress consumption.

In Ghana, the structural adjustment policies implemented in 1987 initially increased the availability of imported European and West African factory-print textiles. During the late 1980s and early 1990s, Ghanaian women invested significant percentages of their income in costly Dutch wax-print textiles and more affordable factory-prints from Ghana, Nigeria, and Côte d'Ivoire. By the late 1990s, the worsening economy began limiting women's acquisition of African-print cloth, but money or cloth sent by family members living abroad provided one means of continuing to dress well. New, cheaper versions of African-print cloth manufactured in China have become increasingly popular, enabling Ghanaian women to continue wearing fashionable African-print kaba ensembles. At the same time, world fashions, especially imported secondhand clothing, have become increasingly popular not only with Ghanaian men and youth, but with a growing percentage of middle-aged women who now largely reserve their African-print ensembles for church, funerals, and special occasions.

In the period from independence to the early twenty-first century, African dress has been an important means of expressing ethnic, national, and transnational African pride and identity. The increasing urbanization and globalization during this time has created new and expanded social contexts and identities.

References and Further Reading

Allman, Jean, ed. *Fashioning Africa: Power and the Politics of Dress.* Bloomington: Indiana University Press, 2004.

Burgess, Thomas. "Cinema, Bell Bottoms, and Miniskirts: Struggles over Youth and Citizenship in Revolutionary Zanzibar." *International Journal of African Historical Studies* 35, no. 2–3 (2002): 287–313.

Eicher, Joanne B., ed. *Dress and Ethnicity: Change across Space and Time.* Oxford, UK: Berg, 1995.

Eicher, Joanne B., and Barbara Sumberg. "World Fashion, Ethnic, and National Dress." In *Dress and Ethnicity: Change across Space and Time*, edited by Joanne B. Eicher, 295–306. Oxford, UK: Berg, 1995.

Grabski, Joanna, "Visual Experience and Fashion in Dakar." In *Mode in Afrika*, edited by Ilsemargret Luttmann. Hamburg: Museum für Völkerkunde, 2005, pp. 52–60.

Fandy, Mamoun. "Political Science without Clothes: The Politics of Dress; or, Contesting the Spatiality of the State in Egypt." In *Beyond the Exotic: Women's Histories in Islamic Societies*, edited by Amira el-Azhary Sonbol, 381–398, 456–457. Syracuse, NY: Syracuse University Press, 2005.

Gondola, Ch. Didier. "Dream and Drama: The Search for Elegance among Congolese Youth." *African Studies Review* 42, no. 1 (1999): 23–48.

Hansen, Karen Tranberg. *Salaula: The World of Secondhand Clothing and Zambia.* Chicago: University of Chicago Press, 2000.

Hendrickson, Hildi, ed. *Clothing and Difference: Embodied Identities in Colonial and Post-Colonial Africa.* Durham, NC: Duke University Press, 1996.

Klopper, Sandra, "Re-Dressing the Past: The Africanisation of Sartorial Style in Contemporary South Africa." In *Hybridity and Its Discontents: Politics, Science, Culture*, edited by Avtar Brah and Annie E. Coombes, 216–231. Oxford, UK: Routledge, 2000.

Maynard, Margaret. *Dress and Globalisation.* Manchester, UK: Manchester University Press, 2004.

Mazrui, Ali A. "The Robes of Rebellion, Sex, Dress, and Politics in Africa." *Encounter* 34 (1970): 19–30.

Nuttall, Sarah. "Stylizing the Self: The Y Generation in Rosebank, Johannesburg." *Public Culture* 16, no. 3 (2004): 430–452.

Perani, Judith, and Norma H. Wolff. *Cloth, Dress, and Art Patronage in Africa.* Oxford, UK: Berg, 1999.

Rabine, Leslie W. *The Global Circulation of African Fashion.* Oxford, UK: Berg, 2002.

Schneider, Leander. "The Maasai's New Clothes: A Developmentalist Modernity and Its Exclusions." *Africa Today* 53, no. 1 (2006): 101–131.

Spruill, Jennifer. "Ad/Dressing the Nation: Drag and Authenticity in Post-Apartheid South Africa." *Journal of Homosexuality* 46, no. 3/4 (2004): 91–111.

Van der Plas, E., and M. Willemsen, eds. *The Art of African Fashion.* Trenton, NJ: Africa World Press, 1998.

Wipper, Audrey. "African Women, Fashion, and Scapegoating." *Canadian Journal of African Studies* 6, no. 2 (1972): 329–349.

Suzanne Gott

See also Colonialism to Independence; Fashion in African Dress; African Fashion Designers.

Snapshot: Heads of State and Dress

The modes of dress worn by African heads of state since independence have served as highly visible expressions of political philosophies and programs during different periods of national leadership. African leaders have also developed memorable trademark ensembles for projecting political personas.

NATIONALISM, PAN-AFRICANISM, AND ETHNIC DRESS

During Ghana's struggle for independence, Kwame Nkrumah and other leaders of the Convention People's Party adopted the *fugu* (northern men's smock) historically worn by Ghanaian chiefs when going into battle. For the vigil held on the eve of independence in Black Star Square, they donned war smocks to signify their fight for freedom from colonial rule. On Independence Day, 6 March 1957, President Nkrumah and members of the new government wore togalike robes of handwoven kente, Ghana's most prestigious cloth (and male attire). This southern Ghanaian ensemble of kingship and chieftaincy was a regal evocation of Ghana's proud heritage signifying continuities with precolonial systems of political authority. Such a proud, victorious display of ethnic dress by leaders of sub-Saharan Africa's first independent nation expressed Nkrumah's political philosophy of the "African personality" and his pan-Africanist vision of an independent, unified Africa.

During the 1950s and 1960s, Egyptian president Gamal Abdel Nasser spearheaded a secular pan-Arabic movement, popularly known as "Nasserism," combining socialism and revolutionary Arab nationalism. Nasserism advocated modernization, industrialization, and the abolition of traditional society. The Egyptian president wore business suits, and modern Western attire was required for workers in government offices, schools, and state institutions. In contrast, Nasser's successor, Anwar Al Sadat, appeared in *jallabiyya* robes of Egypt's rural peasantry during the 1970s, signaling a movement away from secular socialism toward a new rural populism and Islamism. Libyan head of state Muammar al-Qaddafi, whose political philosophy combines Nasser's pan-Arabism with a pan-Islamic socialism, wears traditional Bedouin robes over formal and informal Western dress, often receiving visitors in a Bedouin tent.

CIVILIAN AND MILITARY DRESS

Elisha Renne examines relationships between dress and Nigeria's cycle of changing leadership, where shifts between civilian and military governments are popularly known as movements between *agbada* (robe) and khaki (military uniform). Civilian leaders have worn Nigerian robes of chieftaincy, the flowing embroidered dress known as *agbada* in Yoruba or *babban riga* in Hausa, as time-honored expressions of nationalism and political authority. Military leaders wear khaki uniforms based on colonial military dress.

Following Nigerian independence in 1960, Sir Abubakar Tafawa Balewa, president of Nigeria's First Republic, dressed in nationalist attire of flowing white babban riga until being shot during an attempted 1966 military coup. General Obasanjo, who headed Nigeria's military government from 1975 to 1979, dressed in khaki, while his civilian successor, President Shehu Shagari of Nigeria's Second Republic (1979–1983), wore a new mode of nationalist dress featuring a white robe, a shirt with green embroidery, and a tall embroidered cap that became known as the "Shagari-style" ensemble until his 1983 overthrow by a military regime.

Khaki-green military uniforms, worn with dark sunglasses, became the signature style of General Sani Abacha, who took control in a 1993 bloodless coup. When international pressures forced a transition from military to civilian rule, Abacha

Kwame Nkrumah, president of Ghana, with Daniel Chapman Nyaho in 1958, wearing togalike robes of handwoven kente, Ghana's most prestigious cloth (and male attire). Time & Life Pictures/Getty Images.

entered the 1997 presidential campaign, replacing khaki with civilian attire of a modestly embroidered caftan also adopted by his supporters, which became known as *tazarce* ("continue" or "carry on").

SUITS AND AFRICAN LEADERSHIP

Although leaders of several newly independent African nations wore ethnic dress or elements of ethnic dress, other heads of state dressed in business suits as the modern, internationally recognized attire of executive authority and political leadership. Senegal's first president, Léopold Senghor, whose nationalist philosophy of négritude emphasized a modern African identity, wore suits and banned *tenue traditionnelle* (traditional dress) for all official functions. During the 1960s and 1970s, suits became the requisite attire for Senegal's male political and business elite. Following Senghor's 1980 resignation as a result of economic crises, his successor, Abdou Diouf, reinstated Senegalese traditional dress. Muslim men's boubou ensembles of trousers, tunic, and voluminous overtunic of richly embroidered luxury textiles were designed by renowned Senegalese couturiers, becoming the prestigious political dress of President Diouf and government officials.

Mobutu Sese Seko, Zaire's head of state from 1960 independence until his 1997 overthrow, instituted a policy of *authenticité,* enacting 1974 legislation banning Western-style dress. To replace business suits, Mobutu developed the *abacost* (from *bas le costume,* "down with the costume"—that is, down with the European man's suit), which featured a Maoist-inspired jacket. President Mobutu's trademark attire was the abacost worn with a spotted ascot and leopard-skin hat. This hat, called *glengarry style* in the British army, combined the form of a European military hat similar to those worn by West African troops in the French colonial army during the 1950s with the leopard-skin regalia of central African kingship and chieftaincy.

A NEW POPULIST INFORMALITY

In postapartheid South Africa, political dress was transformed by a new informality introduced by Nelson Mandela. Following the 1990 lifting of the ban on political organizations, including the African National Congress headed by Mandela, dark business suits remained the appropriate attire. Yet in 1993, after visiting Indonesia, Mandela began to wear loose-fitting, colorfully patterned shirts. These long-sleeved cotton or silk shirts, worn outside the trousers and buttoned up at the collar, were reportedly inspired by Indonesian president Suharto's batik shirts.

Following Mandela's 1994 inauguration, this informal mode of dress became the signature style of his presidency and South Africa's new African leadership. President Mandela's shirts, popularly known as *Madiba,* the name of his family clan, provoked controversy in the South African press and media. A 1995 interview, in which Archbishop Desmond Tutu voiced disapproval of Mandela's shirts and his preference for Mandela's dignified elegance in suits, drew strong support for Mandela's relaxed informality, which supporters, as well as Mandela himself, ascribed to a desire for freedom after the years in prison uniforms. Mandela's shirts, widely believed to be African inspired, projected an image of the president as a man of the people and of a new South African government committed to the welfare of ordinary citizens.

REFERENCES AND FURTHER READING

Klopper, Sandra. "Re-dressing the Past: The Africanisation of Sartorial Style in Contemporary South Africa." In *Hybridity and Its Discontents: Politics, Science, Culture*, edited by Avtar Brah and Annie E. Coombes, 216–231. Oxford, UK: Routledge, 2000.

Maynard, Margaret. *Dress and Globalisation*. Manchester, UK: Manchester University Press, 2004.

Renne, Elisha P. "From Khaki to Agbada: Dress and Political Transition in Nigeria." In *Fashioning Africa: Power and the Politics of Dress*, edited by Jean Allman, 125–143. Bloomington: Indiana University Press, 2004.

Suzanne Gott

See also Colonialism to Independence.

Fashion in African Dress

Africa is a continent rich in fashion and tradition, where styles of dress provide insights into both ancient cultures and the latest global fashion trends. Flowing robes with richly embroidered patterns, cloth dyed or printed in brilliant colors, towering head ties and turbans, profusions of beaded bracelets and necklaces—these and many other elements of African dress are associated with traditional cultures, yet an exploration of such dress practices as fashion elucidates African history and creativity. Fashion, the domain of dress that is defined by change, provides a wide range of insights into cultures and histories, containing information about cultural exchange, aesthetic systems, and the innovations of creative individuals. The multiple manifestations of fashion in African dress encompass both past and present dress practice, as well as the work of African designers who participate in national and international markets.

A consideration of African dress as fashion requires an expansion of prevailing definitions of fashion, which generally take modern Western fashion markets as their standard. African attire is rarely associated with fashion, yet the importance of changing sartorial styles is clearly evident in Africa. Like people everywhere, Africans both follow trends and set themselves apart through personal inventiveness. Through such creative efforts, garments may be transformed into fashion, for change is the crucial element that sets fashion apart from clothing practices more broadly. This change may take many forms, including transformations in the style of garments, the materials and techniques used to make them, and the way they are worn.

Popular conceptions of fashion focus on the speed of change and often on the close association of fashion with Western cultures, as demonstrated by a definition from fashion writer Charlotte Seeling, reflecting on fashion in the twentieth century: "Fashion comes from Paris, and one of its greatest characteristics is that it changes. No sooner is something 'in fashion' than it is 'out of fashion' again." The seasonal trends of Western high fashion, marked by style arbiters who declare garments that were recently in to be out, are the epitome of fashion's chronology. Africa's fashion economies have not, until recent decades, featured this type of trend marketing. In cultures where clothing styles do not change in this self-conscious cycle of trends, the existence of fashion may be less obvious. Such cultures, which in popular imagination are often generalized to include all non-Western parts of the world, are essentially absent from discussions of world fashion. Yet closer examination, and fewer preconceptions about African and other non-Western dress, reveals that many African dress practices should be considered fashion.

FASHION IN AFRICAN DRESS: IMPLICATIONS

All explorations of fashion, whatever part of the world they take as their focus, must address the movement of styles and media between regions and across cultures. The changing styles that are the defining feature of fashion are often inspired by forms and ideas that have been introduced through contact between cultures. Fashion everywhere is, directly or indirectly, part of global networks. Yet African dress has long been conceived of as distinct from this world of changing styles, its clothing practices excluded from the category *fashion*. This exclusion is part of a larger series of barriers to international recognition of Africa's participation in contemporary global culture; fashion provides insights into this powerful set of preconceptions about African and other non-Western cultures. African cultures have long been incorrectly associated solely with tradition, stasis, and conservatism—traits that seem to preclude the production of fashion.

In fact, the modern Western model of professional designers, industrial manufacture, and mass marketing is not applicable to a great deal of the fashion produced in Africa. In many parts of Africa, changing styles of dress are designed, produced, and consumed in local markets. Although global markets and international clothing styles have long influenced changing styles of dress in Africa, much African clothing remains distinctly local, an important element of regional and ethnic identities.

Beneath much of the cultural activity surrounding dress practices in Africa is the distinction, often vague, between traditional and modern styles of dress. This dichotomy has a long history, and it continues to shape perceptions of African attire, as innovations are often compared to styles of dress associated with indigenous cultures. African dress styles are too often broadly conceptualized as either traditional or modern; the former has come to represent indigenous culture, the latter Westernization. Although they are often treated as wholly separate, these categories are more accurately conceived of as points on a continuum, for Africans have long adapted Western forms to local practices, and African styles of dress have long influenced clothing styles in other parts of the world.

The classification of African dress has broad implications, for it offers insights into many commonly accepted preconceptions about both Africa and fashion, bringing together two categories that have long been held separate. Temporality is central to these preconceptions, epitomized by the all-too-prevalent location of African and other non-Western dress in a timeless present as opposed to the perpetual future associated with Western fashion's rush to the next season. The role of dress as a tool for representing, and often misrepresenting, African identities is inseparable from the larger politics of the colonial and postcolonial relationship between Africa and the West. Dress was frequently used by Western observers to justify the classification of African cultures as primitive, a notion that reflected the Eurocentrism of the Colonial era. One example, from a 1923 U.S. magazine titled *Lace and Embroidery Review*, coalesces the presumed distinction between African and Western dress. The anonymous writer, using the racist language of the day, compares Central African and American dress, sharply distinguishing the creative, aesthetic motivations

King Njoya in an adapted version of European military uniform. Foumban, Bamum Kingdom, Cameroon, ca. 1905. King Njoya presided over dress innovations that offered him a means of visually declaring his power to both local audiences and Western visitors. Copyright: Museum für Völkerkunde Hamburg.

for Western dress from the supposedly simple practicality of African dress: "When one thinks of the wearing apparel of the savage a mind picture is created of only sufficient clothing to defend the body against the elements, or perhaps to preserve what we are taught is a sense of modesty. The American woman looks to her clothing as a necessary essential to improving her beauty."

While the racialized language of the past has largely disappeared, African dress is still associated with unchanging tradition in popular imagination. For example, *New York Times* reporter Mark Lacey, writing in 2003 about European talent scouts seeking potential fashion models in rural Kenya, noted that Orma women's dress never changes: "Their fashion is the same every season: colorful robes that billow with the breeze and shield virtually every bit of flesh." Analysis of African dress practices as fashion gives the lie to such misconceptions about African cultures, revealing the long history of African innovation and creativity in the realm of dress.

FINDING FASHION IN AFRICA'S PAST

An investigation of past African dress as fashion provides an important foundation for reassessing Africa's role in contemporary global fashion production, emphasizing the distinctly African character of this realm of artistic creativity. Firm information about African attire in centuries past is scarce, making assessments of the precise chronology of change—a crucial element in the definition of fashion—difficult. Yet we have no reason to believe that sartorial innovation in Africa is a modern phenomenon. African dress has never been sealed into static ethnic or regional styles; garments and other forms of personal adornment have always changed in response to new media, new styles, and new ideas about beauty and power.

The study of fashion in Africa's past presents numerous challenges, largely due to the dearth of documentation of African attire in historical perspective. Because fashion is defined by change over time, incomplete information about the chronology of styles in a particular region or community limits the potential for analysis of past dress practices as fashion. Beginning in the seventeenth century, trade and travel accounts by Western observers offer an important source of historical information about many aspects of African life, including dress. Although it is possible to glean valuable information from these accounts, they are distorted by the perspective of early observers, many of whom viewed the clothing styles they encountered as if they had remained unchanged for generations, as one aspect of these presumably static traditional cultures. Yet a variety of sources provide tantalizing glimpses of past dress styles in Africa. The information we can extract from archaeological sites, from the written accounts of early visitors to African communities, and from trade records indicates that the preferences of African consumers for imported textiles, beads, and other products used in personal adornment were varied and mobile, no more bound by tradition than was European dress of the day. The vibrancy and diversity of contemporary African dress should be viewed as the continuation of this long history of creativity and change.

Although garments are unlikely to survive in archaeological contexts, for they are generally made of ephemeral materials, the textiles and garments that have been discovered in African archaeological sites hint at the complexity of past dress practices and the possibility that styles changed in a fashion cycle. Because archaeological preservation of garments is rare—and rarer still in Africa, where relatively little archaeological research has been conducted—these discoveries represent isolated snapshots rather than sustained surveys of historical dress in a particular society or period of time. Yet these ancient garments contain valuable information about textiles and clothing, and it may be possible to draw out information about the existence of diverse and changing styles of dress—markers of fashion in Africa's distant past.

The textiles and garments preserved in the caves of the Bandiagara Escarpment in Mali have been studied extensively by African textile specialist Rita Bolland and offer an extraordinarily broad survey of ancient garments in chronological depth. The sites, which range from the eleventh to the seventeenth century, are associated with the Tellem, a population that predates the current inhabitants of the region, the Dogon. One of the excavated sites, known as Cave C, contained a particularly wide variety of garment styles that is suggestive of, or at least indicates the potential for, a fashion system in Tellem society. The cave was used as a cemetery from the eleventh to the thirteenth century. It contained the remains of approximately three thousand people, many of whom wore garments that survived in the dry, undisturbed environment.

The large number of garments in Cave C permitted researchers to document a range of approaches to the construction of a single garment type. This variety is exemplified by the many strip-woven cotton tunics and fragments of tunics found in the cave. In some cases, the differences between tunics are substantial, while other tunics share general styles yet have subtle distinctions. In particular, Cave C tunics have a wide range of neck opening styles, which incorporate cuts and folds in varied shapes, some with decorative embroidery. The diversity in this single aspect of clothing construction is significant, for the variations point to the possibility that these garment styles and decorative elements reflect changing clothing trends in Tellem society rather than slow change over the course of centuries. Although very little is known about Tellem culture, the wide range of clothing styles indicates that a great deal of creativity and skill was devoted to clothing production—a prerequisite for the existence of fashion in this ancient West African culture.

Along with archaeological material, written accounts, primarily by non-Africans, may provide information about past dress practices in Africa. Styles of dress were—and still are—a subject of great fascination for visitors to Africa. Although written records may offer important documentation of historical dress practices in Africa, they generally provide only indirect information about the style changes that characterize fashion, for the observers rarely made note of shifting tastes and styles, instead describing what they encountered at a single historical moment. In addition, many of the historical accounts that might be mined for information about dress practices were written by Europeans who were predisposed to view African attire as inferior to their own.

The collision of Western and African cultures, largely during the late nineteenth and early twentieth centuries, inspired numerous critical commentaries on African dress by Western observers. Perhaps ironically, many of these critiques provide insights into the creativity Africans devoted to their changing styles of dress. One example of African sartorial creativity that raised the ire of colonial authorities can be found in early-twentieth-century Brazzaville, in what is today the Republic of the Congo. The historian Phyllis Martin has quoted a 1914 letter from one European official who noted his frustration at the "misuse" of Western attire: "I tried several times to get my boys to dress like you and me with the shirt tucked inside the trousers, but they said that is for whites and continued to do it their own way." Such protestations indicate that African consumers of Western-style dress were creating new styles, adjusting and recombining new and existing forms to suit changing tastes. Although European observers of the day did not credit such adaptations as fashion, they can be seen in hindsight as innovative adaptations under circumstances that offered limited opportunity for self-expression through clothing.

Occasionally, the accounts of pre-Colonial and Colonial-era visitors to Africa provide insights into the role of specific individuals in the production of changing styles of dress. One fascinating and vividly documented example of innovation in early-twentieth-century dress illustrates the importance of personal style as an expression of power and has been researched in detail by anthropologist Christraud Geary. King Njoya, ruler of the

Bamum Kingdom in Cameroon between the mid-1880s and 1933, posed for the cameras of several German visitors to his kingdom, and he took pictures himself using a camera acquired from these visitors to his domain. In all of these photographs, Njoya's dress indicates that he presented himself with care, clearly aware, like many successful rulers, of the effectiveness of clothing as a tool for communicating—and enhancing—one's status. Njoya presided over dress innovations that offered him a new means of visually declaring his power to both local audiences and Western visitors.

In most of the photographs, Njoya wears long, flowing, richly embroidered robes—clothing that, to the eyes of nonlocal observers, appears to epitomize traditional African dress. In fact, a closer examination of this style of dress reveals that its appearance in Bamum was the result of specific historical circumstances. This attire—a voluminous, untailored robe adorned with embroidered motifs, drawstring pants, and an elaborately wrapped turban—is the dress of local high status. The robes are local adaptations of attire from regions to the north of Bamum, home to traders from the Hausa ethnic group. When the nobles of Bamum and neighboring kingdoms adopted them, the Hausa-style robes were effectively transformed into local dress. Thus, these "traditional" Bamum robes are rooted in imported styles; they were absorbed into local practice through decades of use, modified to suit local tastes and techniques.

In other photographs, Njoya wears a different form of high-prestige attire. To Western eyes, this style of dress is immediately recognizable as imported: a European-style military dress uniform, tightly tailored with buttons and ornamental braids. European military uniforms are today nearly universal symbols of power. In Njoya's day, this style of dress was associated with the growing power of European residents and visitors at the dawn of the Colonial era. Rather than wholesale borrowing, the Bamum version of a German uniform has been subtly adapted to the new context. Njoya's garments were made by local tailors, and, significantly, they incorporated beads in place of the braided ornamentation of the German uniforms. Because beads are the medium most closely associated with the royal arts of Bamum, Njoya's transformation of braiding into beads is particularly meaningful in this cultural context, for beadwork was an important symbol of royal power in Bamum and neighboring kingdoms. Rather than copying the German uniform, Njoya and his collaborators have subtly transformed it to suit their own visual language of power. Although this innovation did not take hold in Bamum—Njoya and the members of his court suddenly ceased wearing the uniforms in 1909, likely the result of political shifts—this adaptation of an imported style is part of a history of innovations, as attested to by the Hausa-style robes that were earlier adaptations from outside Bamum culture.

Historical records contain other, less well-documented instances of individual African fashion innovators. The observations of a mid-nineteenth-century British missionary in southern Africa include a description of an extraordinary tailored man's suit worn by the Tswana Chief Sechele, as anthropologist Jean Comaroff has cited. Unfortunately, there are no images of this ensemble, which the missionary described as being made of tiger skin, likely actually leopard pelt. This innovation brought together local style—the wearing of leopard skin was, and is, associated with high status in the region—with garments whose prestige was likely based on their association with the European

Wodaabe men wearing conical hats with ostrich feathers, Ingal, Niger, early twenty-first century. What is deemed fashionable among the Wodaabe is quick to change, and different styles come and go. Photograph by Philippe Bourseiller.

foreigners whose wealth and power impressed and threatened local leaders. One can imagine the impact of the leopard-skin suit, which would have communicated the chief's power to local audiences just as it made an impression on a European visitor.

Most information about past sartorial creativity in Africa is not associated with specific, named individuals but rather appears as an element of general observations by visitors to African communities. Some of the observers who made note of the speed with which clothing trends changed in African communities drew comparisons to the fashions of their homelands. For example, scholar George Brooks has found through his research that, in 1789, a French visitor to the Senegalese city Saint Louis, long a major center for transatlantic trade, commented on the dress of *signares*, local women of high social status whose marriages to European men enhanced their access to business opportunities. Signares were famed for their beauty and their elegant attire. Describing how they make use of the gold they accumulated as successful businesswomen, this visitor noted: "The women have some of this gold made into jewelry, and the rest is used to purchase clothing, because they adore, as do women everywhere else, fashionable clothing."

Similarly, local trends in bead shapes and colors inspired one mid-nineteenth-century European visitor to the Natal region of South Africa to compare consumers there to the British market for women's hats, which epitomized fashion's unpredictability.

J. W. Colenso, a British visitor, wrote in 1855: "the Natives…are as capricious in their taste for beads, as any English lady in the choice of her bonnet. The same pattern will suit them for only a season or two; and they are at all times difficult to please." In coastal East Africa, as elsewhere, the chief fashion trend was in cloth. Writing of Zanzibar's young women and the speed with which fashions in printed cloth wrappers, called *kangas*, changed, one colonial official noted in a report on trade and commerce on the islands of Zanzibar and Pemba that Zanzibar is the Paris of East Africa with regard to its attitude to fashion and the frequent purchasing of new kangas to keep up with emerging trends. For the European merchants who sought to do business in Africa, these fashion trends in beads, textiles, and other personal adornments were worthy of note because they presented a challenge. Fortunately, their comments also provide a record of the long history of clothing trends in Africa.

AFRICAN DRESS IN THE EARLY TWENTY-FIRST CENTURY: A CONTINUUM OF STYLES

Fashion in Africa today emerges out of the continent's long history of creativity and participation in global networks, and it continues to provide a window onto political, economic, and broad social changes. All over the continent, dress has been affected to varied degrees by the influence of Western-dominated fashion systems.

Many modern and contemporary dress practices in Africa are familiar to non-Africans, for they emerge out of the same global markets. Many people in Africa wear the same styles and brands of clothing that are worn in the United States, Europe, or in many other parts of the world within the orbit of Western cultures—business suits, blue jeans, and baseball caps are common elements of daily dress in many African communities. These styles of dress have been thoroughly absorbed into long-standing local aesthetics.

Many other Africans wear distinctively local clothing, which has itself changed over time to reflect shifting tastes. These styles of dress may include locally woven and dyed cloth, garments created by neighborhood tailors, and other elements of dress that are locally produced. Usually, however, clothing styles are not cleanly separated into distinct categories. A single garment may combine local and international influences in varied proportions, these elements sometimes losing their original associations to take on new meanings in changing contexts. In addition, many African people routinely move between styles and categories of dress. Clothing that emerges out of indigenous styles may be required on special occasions, while Western-style dress might be worn every day. Thus, categories and dichotomies melt into ambiguities; African and Western styles are points on a continuum rather than discreet categories.

That the terms *African* and *Western* are more abstract than literal in their points of reference, reflecting conventions rather than realities, is dramatically illustrated in contemporary contexts by the internationalized realms of clothing manufacture, distribution, and marketing. The suits, T-shirts, and blue jeans associated with modern Western style may be designed, manufactured, and sold without ever entering a Western market. Wherever they are made, many such Western garments have been transformed into local styles. Dress and textile scholars Joanne Eicher and Barbara Sumberg have offered the terms *world fashion* and *cosmopolitan fashion* as alternatives to *Western*, noting that, "although a wide variety of tailored garments, as well as certain haircuts, cosmetics, and accessories, are often referred to as Western, many people in both Eastern and Western hemispheres wear such items of apparel. Designating items as Western for people who wear them in other areas of the world, such as Asia and Africa, is inaccurate." In the exchanges between African and non-African cultures, clothing exemplifies the ways in which identities of objects and styles can shift as consumers in new markets transform them to create local fashions.

Despite its integration into international networks of manufacture, promotion, and inspiration, African fashion may be a powerful force for reinvention or revival of indigenous dress practices—the styles and media associated with tradition. In some instances, fashion and tradition intersect in ongoing practices, so that the very forms of dress that are most closely associated with tradition are subject to the swift changes in style that characterize fashion. Fashion and tradition also merge in the many instances of revivals of forms that are no longer in use, adapting them to new contexts in order to create a distinct dress practice. In these instances, it is often the association with traditional culture that leads to the revival or transformation of a style of dress—tradition and fashion are more than coincident; they are interdependent.

Wodaabe dress offers a vivid illustration of the first category of fashion in indigenous African dress, as has been documented by anthropologist Mette Bovin. The Wodaabe, a subgroup of the large Fulani ethnic group, are a nomadic people who live in Niger, Nigeria, Chad, and Cameroon, moving along with their herds of cattle, sheep, and other animals to find grazing pastures. The Wodaabe, primarily Wodaabe men, have been a subject of fascination for Western observers, largely due to the attire of young men at the periodic dances that are central to Wodaabe social life. Each participant creates his own ensemble, devoting great attention to clothing, hairstyle, jewelry, and other elements of visual appearance. Although the event and the basic ingredients of Wodaabe dress are deeply rooted in local tradition, fashion is central to the performance of the dances and, more importantly, to being a respected member of Wodaabe society. At dances and other public social interactions, young Wodaabe men and women strive to adorn themselves in the latest styles, keeping abreast of constantly changing fads. For example, the hats worn by young men have been the subjects of much fashion attention. In the 1960s, young men wore conical straw hats adorned only with a ring of ostrich feathers. In the 1970s and 1980s, young men began to adorn their hats in progressively more elaborate styles, with patterned fabrics, leather and metal ornaments, plastic, mirrors, and other embellishments. This trend reached its peak in 1988; then the trend shifted so that, by 2000, the more minimalist style was back in vogue: a conical hat adorned with ostrich feathers. The Wodaabe term *kessum-kessum* (new-new) refers to this premium on change in dress styles, a distinctively local fashion market.

That fashions change in indigenous styles of dress is likely obvious to any visitor to West Africa who has shopped for cloth in the region's many weekly and daily markets. Here, mechanically printed textiles in bold colors and patterns (known as *wax*, *Dutch wax*, *imi-wax*, and *fancy print*, depending on their quality and the markets in which they are sold) are produced in great variety, for they are ubiquitous elements of dress throughout the region. The cloth is used to create garments that are associated with long-standing dress practices, such as women's wrappers and flowing robes worn by both men and women, as well as clothing in contemporary, international styles, such as short skirts and tailored business suits. These textiles are the subjects of swiftly changing fashion trends, as patterns appear and disappear with great speed. While a handful of patterns have remained popular for

Wax prints in a shop in Mopti, Mali, 2006. Factory-printed cotton cloth is a primary element of dress practices in many parts of Africa. Colors and patterns change frequently, as do the garment styles into which the cloth is tailored. Photograph by Victoria L. Rovine.

generations, many are fashionable only for a season. In the mid-1990s, one Nigerian textile company, Afprint, was producing fifteen to twenty new patterns per month, while also continuing to produce at least fifty of its popular patterns. Thus, factory print cloth is central to local fashion systems in many parts of Africa, part of a long history of change in indigenous dress practices.

In addition to the fashion cycles that are integrated into indigenous, traditional dress practices in Africa, distinctively African fashion is also created through revivals or readaptations of dress forms associated with indigenous cultures. These fashions may emerge out of political or broad cultural movements, for indigenous dress styles may be effective statements of affiliation with indigenous culture, often in opposition to Western-style dress. Such fashions may arise out of political movements, exemplified by the many indigenous styles of dress that became fashionable in the wake of independence in Nigeria, Kenya, Swaziland, and Ghana. The end of apartheid in South Africa offers a more recent example. In all of these instances, forms of dress that had been suppressed or marginalized by nonindigenous styles experienced resurgence, moving from the realm of ethnic dress into the world of fashion.

References and Further Reading

Allman, Jean, ed. *Fashioning Africa: Power and the Politics of Dress.* Bloomington: Indiana University Press, 2004.

Bolland, Rita. "Clothing from Burial Caves in Mali, 11th–18th Century." In *History, Design, and Craft in West African Strip-Woven Cloth,* 53–82. Washington, DC: Smithsonian Institution, 1992.

Bovin, Mette. *Nomads Who Cultivate Beauty: Wodaabe Dances and Visual Arts in Niger.* Uppsala, Sweden: Nordiska Afrikainstituet, 2001.

Brooks, George. "The Signares of Saint-Louis and Gorée: Women Entrepreneurs in Eighteenth Century Senegal." In *Women in Africa: Studies in Social and Economic Change,* edited by Nancy J. Hafkin and Edna C. Bay, 19–44. Stanford, CA: Stanford University Press, 1976.

Colenso, J. W. *Ten Weeks in Natal.* Cambridge, UK: Macmillan, 1855. Quoted in Sandra Klopper, "From Adornment to Artefact to Art: Historical Perspectives on South-East African Beadwork." In *South-East African Beadwork 1850–1910: From Adornment to Artefact to Art,* edited by Michael Stevenson and Michael Graham-Stewart, 9–43. Vlaeburg, South Africa: Fernwood Press, 2000.

Comaroff, Jean. "The Empire's Old Clothes: Fashioning the Colonial Subject." In *Cross-Cultural Consumption: Global Markets, Local Realities,* edited by David Howes, 19–38. New York: Routledge, 1996.

Eicher, Joanne B., and Barbara Sumberg. "World Fashion, Ethnic, and National Dress," In *Dress and Ethnicity: Change across Space and Time,* edited by Joanne B. Eicher, 293–306. Washington, DC: Berg, 1995.

Geary, Christraud M. *Images from Bamum: German Colonial Photography at the Court of King Njoya.* Washington, DC: National Museum of African Art, 1988.

Geary, Christraud. *Patterns from Without, Meaning from Within: European-Style Military Dress and German Colonial Politics in the Bamum Kingdom (Cameroon).* Boston: African Studies Center, Boston University, 1989.

Hay, Margaret Jean. *Fashioning a Modern Identity in Colonial Western Kenya: Struggles over Clothing in the Interwar Period.* Boston: African Studies Center, Boston University, 2002.

Hendrickson, Hildi, ed. *Clothing and Difference: Embodied Identities in Colonial and Post-Colonial Africa.* Durham, NC: Duke University Press, 1996.

Klopper, Sandra. "Re-dressing the Past: The Africanisation of Sartorial Style in Contemporary South Africa." In *Hybridity and Its Discontents,* edited by Avtar Brah and Annie E. Coombes, 216–232. New York: Routledge, 2000.

Kuper, Hilda. "Costume and Identity." *Comparative Studies in Society and History* 15, no. 3 (1973): 348–367.

Lacey, Mark. "In Remotest Kenya, a Supermodel Is Hard to Find." *New York Times* (22 April 2003): A3.

Martin, Phyllis M. "Contesting Clothes in Colonial Brazzaville." *Journal of African History* 25 (1994): 401–426.

Oyelola, Pat. "Textile Markets in Nigeria: A Diary." In *The Art of African Textiles: Technology, Tradition, and Lurex,* edited by John Picton, 41. London: Barbican Art Gallery, 1995.

Rabine, Leslie W. *The Global Circulation of African Fashion.* New York: Berg, 2002.

Renne, Elisha P. "From Khadki to Agbada: Dress and Political Transition in Nigeria." In *Fashioning Africa: Power and the Politics of Dress,* edited by Jean Allman, 125–143. Bloomington: Indiana University Press, 2004.

Ross, Doran H., ed. *Wrapped in Pride: Ghanaian Kente and African American Identity.* Los Angeles: UCLA Fowler Museum of Cultural History, 1998.

Seeling, Charlotte, ed. *Fashion: The Century of the Designer (1900–1999).* Cologne, Germany: Könemann, 1999.

"Textile Designs from Primitive Sources." *Lace and Embroidery Review and Dress Essentials* (May 1923).

Victoria L. Rovine

African Fashion Designers

F ashion design is an increasingly visible realm of African creative expression. Fashion designers throughout Africa, most of them based in large cities, produce clothing in a vast range of styles. This small but growing industry has produced a handful of internationally successful designers and many more designers who have achieved prominence in local or regional markets. African fashion design provides insights into complexities of contemporary national and ethnic identities in Africa. It vividly illustrates the impact of global networks of imagery and products as well as the continued relevance and popularity of indigenous styles of dress, often associated with traditional cultures.

Although the use of clothing as a medium for creative expression and aesthetic innovation has a long history in Africa, past clothing innovations were not part of a self-conscious fashion market. Fashion design as a formal profession has a relatively short history in Africa, gaining prominence in the 1970s. Particularly vibrant fashion markets have emerged in several West African countries, including Senegal, Ghana, and Côte d'Ivoire, producing designers who have international reputations. South Africa, too, has a burgeoning market for fashion design. While other regions have produced important designers, this survey of the field of African fashion reflects the greater relative influence and visibility of West African designers.

The distinction between clothing innovations as a broad category and innovations that are classified as fashion design is often unclear, and the distinction does not always lie in the garments themselves. Fashion design is fueled by the deliberate obsolescence of clothing styles, dependent upon a market that places a premium on constantly changing styles of dress. Professional fashion designers in Africa are also generally trained in design techniques that are Western in origin, including the use of sketches, patterns, and a vocabulary of shapes and seams by which garments are shaped to the body. Such training formerly required aspiring designers to study outside Africa, though growing numbers of fashion programs and institutes in Africa have enabled many young designers to train in Africa. In addition, fashion design is distinguished from other forms of dress innovation through the branding and marketing structure by which its practitioners seek to promote their work—successful designers' names appear on labels, and their clothing is presented at fashion shows and in fashion magazines.

The styles of clothing created by African fashion designers are as varied as those produced by designers elsewhere; there is no intrinsically African style that unites designers of diverse backgrounds, making sweeping generalizations about their work impossible. Yet common themes and concerns traverse the work of many African designers. The work of many designers reflects the connections, and in some cases the tensions, between indigenous styles of dress and the styles of dress that dominate the international fashion industry. It is useful to consider the strategies used by a number of African designers to negotiate the relationship between distinctively African styles of dress and the international sartorial styles that dominate the global mass media.

To address fashion design across a wide range of countries and styles, this survey describes the work and careers of several African designers in terms of two broad thematic approaches to sartorial innovation. The first, which represents the largest number of African professional designers, centers on bringing together distinctively indigenous African forms with garments that are associated with Western dress. Some incorporate local materials and styles to enhance garments that are clearly nonlocal in conception, such as a man's suit with lapels made of cloth produced locally or a woman's miniskirt adorned with beadwork in a style associated with indigenous dress. Other designs are based on indigenous garments, modified or transformed by the use of new fabrics, shapes, and styles of adornment. Just as a three-piece suit can be recreated in infinite styles, so too are well-established African garments subject to creative reinvention.

The second category consists of designers who do not make use of media or imagery that is associated with traditional African cultures but whose work is still influenced by African cultures and histories. Their references are conceptual rather than literal, making no direct visual reference to forms and materials that are associated with African cultures. This approach might be characterized as conceptual African fashion; these are designers who draw inspiration from African approaches rather than African forms. Of course, many African fashion designers do not fit neatly into a single category; these classifications provide a framework for exploring this broad subject rather than absolute distinctions.

INDIGENOUS FORMS IN GLOBAL FASHION

One of these two approaches elucidates the work of the first generation of professional fashion designers in Africa. They were not the earliest African fashion innovators, but their combination of Western-based training and African-centered identities makes them pioneers in the creation of distinctively African fashion design. These designers came of age as the struggle for African independence from colonial rule was culminating, when pride in national identity was a prominent element of political and cultural life in many African communities. After decades of colonial rule, accompanied by powerful Western influence in every realm of culture, including dress, fashion became a medium for the visible expression of pride in African identity. While wearing indigenous styles of dress was once the norm, in the post-Colonial era, such styles could become a statement of national or regional pride, because they represented an alternative to the business suits, tailored dresses, T-shirts, and other nonlocal forms that have become so prevalent in much of urban Africa. In many African countries, political leaders and other influential members of society championed local styles of dress.

Not surprisingly, much of the work of African fashion designers whose sensibilities were informed by the political mood of this period reflects a desire to bring African styles to global fashion markets. Most studied and worked in Europe or the United States, bringing the techniques and styles of international fashion to their work in Africa. All of the designers in this category explored the adaptability of local textiles and other elements of indigenous African dress to the techniques of European fashion design. Several, including Ly Dumas and Mickaël Kra, have collaborated with development projects to preserve and promote indigenous weaving, dyeing, and other technologies.

Several designers who have been credited with establishing contemporary African fashion design are part of this first generation. Chris Seydou, Alphadi, Kofi Ansah, and Mickaël Kra were all instrumental in the creation of an African fashion design movement, through both their own success as designers and entrepreneurs and their efforts to champion African design abroad. Led by Chris Seydou, they were among the group of designers who created the Fédération Africaine des Créateurs in 1993, the first transnational organization of African fashion designers. The organization has provided a platform for fashion shows and other promotional events aimed at raising the visibility of African fashion design both in Africa and abroad. Seydou passed away in 1994; the others all continue to work as fashion designers and promoters of Africa's fashion industry. Other designers who have used indigenous forms as their points of departure include Oumou Sy, a prominent Senegalese fashion designer and cultural activist, and Beninoise designer Pépita Djoffon, whose brand Pépita D. is best known for garments that incorporate indigenous weaving and appliqué of Benin and neighboring Togo.

CHRIS SEYDOU

Chris Seydou is a revered figure in African fashion circles, and his name is evoked often among the cultural figures in his home country, Mali. Because he was central to the development of the contemporary field of fashion design in Africa, and because his career emblematizes the challenges and opportunities that continue to characterize fashion design in Africa, Seydou bears examination in some detail. Seydou's career also encapsulates the tension between Western and African influences as well as the creative potential at their intersection. Seydou's high-profile combination of an indigenous Malian textile and European tailoring allowed him to operate successfully in two markets, each of which was drawn to nonlocal styles. His work appealed to African women who sought *la mode occidentale* (Western fashion) and to Western women who were drawn to the "exoticism" of his designs. Even Seydou's name itself brings together Mali and France, his two primary sources of influence, for he changed his name from Seydou Doumbia to Chris Seydou in homage to Christian Dior.

Seydou's earliest interest in fashion emerged out of this intersection of local sartorial practices and global fashion media. Born in 1949 in Kati, a small town north of Mali's capital, Seydou was exposed to clothing production at a young age. His mother was a seamstress who, like many tailors and designers in Africa, kept European fashion magazines in her workshop as a source of inspiration for herself and her clients. Spending time there, Seydou had access to the practical realities of small-scale clothing production in Mali as well as global images of fashion and the mass media that surrounds it. He apprenticed with a tailor—a profession that lies close to fashion design—before continuing his training in neighboring Burkina Faso and in Abidjan, the famously cosmopolitan capital of Côte d'Ivoire. He worked and studied in Paris until 1981, when he returned to Africa to establish a studio in Abidjan. After great success there, building an international reputation, Seydou returned to Mali in 1991 to be closer to Malian weavers and dyers, his chief sources of inspiration.

The textiles and garment styles of Mali were the sources of the innovation that is most closely associated with Seydou's

A model wearing a creation by Franco-Ivoirian designer Mickaël Kra during the Ethical Fashion Show, Paris, 2007. Kra creates jewelry made from metal, glass, stone, and shell based on indigenous styles. Pierre Andrieu/AFP/Getty Images.

career: his adaptation of a distinctively Malian textile, *bogolan* (or mudcloth), to European-style tailored garments. The strip-woven cotton cloth is dyed by women using a labor-intensive technique to create bold geometric patterns in white on a deep brown ground. Bogolan has powerful associations with indigenous Malian cultures, because it is believed to provide protection at crucial moments of physical and spiritual danger. Girls wear bogolan wrappers immediately following their initiations, and hunters wear bogolan tunics for protection from wild animals and dangerous spirits. Seydou's earliest use of bogolan, in the mid-1970s, was revolutionary because it demonstrated that a textile with deep roots in traditional culture could be transformed into international fashion.

Adapting bogolan to tailored garments such as miniskirts and blazers required stylistic as well as psychological adaptations. Seydou described having to overcome his reluctance to cut this cloth, which had such power in its original contexts. He also needed to adapt it to his Western-based techniques, which centered on cutting and tailoring cloth. Bogolan's geometric patterns posed a stylistic challenge, for the diversity of motifs in a single cloth was not conducive to the need for symmetry along both seams of a tailored garment. Seydou solved both challenges by commissioning bogolan specifically for his use, aimed at preserving the handmade quality of the cloth yet separating it from the ritual functions that gave it special power. Going a step further, in 1991 he collaborated with a Malian textile factory (called ITEMA) to design a factory-printed bogolan cloth. Although this took the cloth's production out of the hands of rural women, the ITEMA cloth was part of Seydou's efforts to promote bogolan and ensure that its distinctive patterns would retain their associations with Mali (an effort in which he was unsuccessful, for bogolan-patterned cloth is now made in factories all over the world). Although he employed numerous other types of textiles throughout his career, Seydou continued to incorporate both handmade and factory-printed bogolan into his designs until his death in 1994. Bogolan was central to his efforts to bring Africa into global fashion, bridging the distance between these realms that were long held separate.

ALPHADI

Alphadi, like Chris Seydou, is identified with the use of local textile forms to create garments in the precisely tailored style of classical Western fashion, including form-fitting women's gowns and sharply pleated men's suits. Like Seydou and many other designers of his generation, Alphadi studied in Paris, presenting his first collection there in 1985. He is based in Niamey, capital of his home country Niger, as well as in Paris. He has created dresses and coats using the brightly colored cotton strip-woven blankets associated with the Fulani of Mali and Niger, tunics and dresses cut from bogolan, and tightly fitted bustiers adorned with the elaborately detailed embroidery associated with Timbuktu, in Mali. He has also focused a great deal of attention on the business and promotion of fashion; he is the only African designer to have diversified his brand to encompass ready-to-wear, sportswear, and accessories. In 2001, Alphadi moved beyond clothing to launch his perfume, Aïr, named for a region in northern Niger that is associated with the Tuareg, his own ethnic group.

In addition to his clothing and related products, Alphadi is known for his promotion of African fashion through large

The back of an "Ori" man's coat by Yoruba designer Adebayo Agbelekale, ca. 2001. Agbelekale's studio is in Santa Cruz, California, and his designs are influenced mainly by Nigerian techniques and styles. Courtesy of I.B. Bayo. http://www.ibbayo.com/

biannual fashion shows, called FIMA or Festival International de la Mode Africaine, the first of which was held in 1998. These events, like the periodic African Mosaïque fashion shows organized by Ethiopian former model Anna Getaneh, bring together African fashion designers from throughout the continent and beyond. Because few African designers have access to the network of European fashion shows that dominate international fashion marketing, FIMA, African Mosaïque, and a growing number of other events and competitions provide many of the designers discussed here with valuable international platforms. Through FIMA and its associated traveling fashion show Caravane, Alphadi has become the most visible international advocate for African fashion designers.

LY DUMAS

Ly Dumas is one of a small number of women fashion designers from Africa to have built an international career. Beginning in 1990, this Cameroonian designer has been among the most visible European-based African designers, working from Paris and Geneva. In Africa as elsewhere, fashion design is a male-dominated profession—a paradoxical circumstance in a field whose primary consumers are women. Few women have access to the funds and infrastructure necessary to produce and promote clothing. Dumas's success is even more exceptional, because she is one of the few high-profile African designers who had no professional training.

Dumas has a long-standing interest in African textiles and the preservation of indigenous weaving and dyeing practices throughout Africa; her projects have combined fashion design with support for weavers and other textile artists. Although her designs incorporate a wide range of textiles, from bogolan to embroidered raffia cloth from central Africa, Cameroonian textiles have appeared most prominently in her work. Her designs include miniskirt-length versions of men's long embroidered robes—a dramatic transformation of these garments from their associations with men's power to daringly revealing women's wear. In addition to distinctively Cameroonian embroidery, Dumas has made extensive use of the indigo resist-dyed cloth known as *ndop*, associated with royalty in the Grassfields region of western Cameroon. As Seydou did with bogolan, Dumas makes use of the strip-woven ndop cloth as well as factory-printed versions made in a variety of colors beyond the indigo blue of the original cloth. For Dumas, as for many of the other designers who seek to make an African contribution to global fashion, traditional forms and styles are not static; they inform and inspire changing dress styles.

MIKAËL KRA

Franco-Ivoirian jewelry designer Mickaël Kra also participated in the development of a transnational network of African fashion designers who were creating new forms based in indigenous styles. Working in the media of jewelry—using metal, glass, stone, shell, and other materials—rather than textiles, Kra achieved prominence through his collaborations with others, including Chris Seydou, Alphadi, and Guinean designer Katoucha.

Kra studied design in the United States during the late 1980s. He first achieved success while still in New York with his line of jewelry based on the lost-wax cast goldwork of the Baule ethnic group of Côte d'Ivoire and Ghana. Beginning in 1991, Kra's reinterpretations, in gold-plated metal, were sold under the brand name Reine Pokou, a legendary Baule queen. He designed jewelry for the runway shows of African fashion designers, beginning with Chris Seydou. He also designed for major European designers, including Pierre Balmain. His influences are varied—from Baule gold beads and Tuareg crosses to Maasai beaded collars and Zulu beadwork of South Africa.

Since 2000, Kra has focused on a collaborative project in Namibia and Botswana, working with San women to create a line of jewelry made of ostrich eggshell beads. The Pearls of the Kalahari project, facilitated by a German development organization, employs an art form with deep roots in San culture to produce jewelry for international markets.

KOFI ANSAH

Ghanaian designer Kofi Ansah was an early promoter of indigenous African forms in the international fashion arena. Ansah trained in London and was based there for many years before returning to Accra in 1992, where he created a design studio and has worked to promote Ghana's fashion industry. Ansah was among the founders of the Fédération Africaine des Créateurs and is Ghana's most prominent designer. While he might have relied on kente cloth, Ghana's—and arguably Africa's—most famous textile, he instead works largely with resist-dyed indigo cloths and brightly colored factory-printed textiles, including patterns of his own design commissioned from Ghana's textile factories. He has created clothing in a wide range of styles, from tight-fitted gowns for women to minimally tailored men's attire, all in distinctively local fabrics. His line of ready-to-wear garments is sold under his brand name ArtDress.

Ansah has also designed textiles for one of Ghana's two leading textile manufacturers, GTP (Ghana Textile Printing). He recently designed a commemorative cloth in honor of the fiftieth anniversary of the country's independence. As the country's leading designer, he hosts design competitions and represents Ghana's fashion industry in numerous international venues.

ADEBAYO AGBELEKALE OF I. B. BAYO

Nigerian designer Adebayo Agbelekale, who is based in the United States, creates elaborately worked appliquéd and quilted garments that are each made entirely by hand, largely on commission. His jackets, vests, and shirts incorporate batiks and other resist-dyed textiles as well as mass-produced cloth in a wide range of styles. The interplay of the exteriors and linings of his garments is an important aspect of his work; paired sets of vividly contrasting colors and patterns lend his garments a sense of drama, because unexpected interiors are revealed as the wearer moves.

I. B. Bayo garments are based on Nigerian, and broadly African, technical and stylistic precedents, and the designer's Nigerian identity figures prominently in the marketing of his work. Agbelekale was born and raised in Osogbo, a city in southwestern Nigeria famed for its artistic production. He participated in textile production from a young age, because his family's occupation for generations has been weaving. Along with his family-based education, Agbelekale studied textile production, dyeing, and appliqué techniques at an arts center founded by renowned batik artist Nike Davies, who has long worked to preserve and promote the textile arts of the Yoruba ethnic group. There he learned the reverse appliqué techniques that would become the most distinctive aspect of his work. In the United States, Agbelekale worked with an American designer to further hone his skills and to shape his work to suit the tastes and trends of the U.S. market. He consistently maintains the distinctively African identity of his garments, using African textiles and iconography, such as appliqué elements in the shape of the African continent. In North American markets, the bold colors, patterns, and symbols of Africa find a ready audience.

CONCEPTUAL AFRICAN FASHION

While some designers aim to create garments that are distinctively African, others do not make use of recognizably African forms. Some, in fact, are rarely identified with Africa. Yet designers' work emerges out of their experiences and identities, regardless of whether these elements appear explicitly. Thus, analysis of the careers and work of the designers in this category as African elucidates their work and provides a fuller picture of the continent's diverse contributions to global fashion markets. The designers presented here are all members of the second generation of professional African fashion designers. Their chronological distance from the political and cultural milieu of the immediate pre- and postcolonial moments may well have influenced their design approaches. In the case of South Africa's flourishing fashion industry, political liberation came much more recently, with the end of apartheid in 1990. Still, many of the country's young designers have taken a conceptual approach, using indirect references to their ethnic and national identities rather than borrowing directly from indigenous forms.

The work and careers of several leading designers is presented here: Ozwald Boateng, Stoned Cherrie, Lamine Kouyaté, and Joël Andrianomearisoa. Many others could be added to this list, including the South African design team Strangelove (Carlo Gibson and Ziemek Pater), who use performance and sculptural garments to comment on their country's history, and the New York–based Nigerian designer Moshood, whose minimalist clothing incorporates stereotypical images of Africans, transformed into icons of African pride.

OZWALD BOATENG

Ozwald Boateng, an Anglo-Ghanaian menswear designer based in London, has a very high profile in international fashion markets. He has received numerous awards, and in 2003, he was named creative director of Givenchy's menswear division—a prominent position for any designer, making him by far the most visible African designer at work today. In 2006, he became the subject of a U.S. reality television show called *House of Boateng*, which followed his efforts to break into the U.S. fashion market. From his exclusive menswear shop on Savile Row in London, Boateng has worked to revive the British tradition of bespoke tailoring, in which clothing is made for each individual client without using a pattern.

The fact that he is African—both of his parents are Ghanaian—rarely appears in the press coverage and promotional materials that accompany his work. His designs are classically British in their conception, featuring suits with sharp lapels and sleekly fitted pants made with intricate seams in solid-colored wools. His collections have included frock coats, jodhpurs, morning coats, and other garments that evoke British country estates rather than Britain's former African colonies, which include Ghana. Yet Boateng's work does have African elements, demonstrating that not all African fashion design incorporates explicit stylistic references to indigenous African forms.

Had he emphasized his African identity early in his career, Boateng likely would have been expected to create recognizably African clothing. While Boateng has not made his African identity a central element of his work, he has clearly acknowledged that his fashion sensibility may in part reflect that identity. The color combinations and fabric textures he applies to his thoroughly British garment styles have been interpreted as one manifestation of this sensibility—mustard yellow coats worn with bright green shirts, purple velvet and magenta plaid suits. Even garments in more standard hues of black, brown, and gray have brightly colored linings. Timothy Hagy, the Paris editor of *Fashionlines* who interviewed Boateng, described how his 2004 menswear vividly illustrates these unexpected conjunctions of color: "Saffron jackets were inlaid with hot pink stripes, while split sleeves in otherwise classic Bond Street pinstripe suits revealed a flash of hot fuchsia lining.…Chocolate and lime green glazed leather blazers were inlaid with lemon stripes, while ebony tailcoats were tapered to perfection." Thus, reading Africa into Boateng's work requires attention to the implications of color combinations in a three-piece suit and tie. In some of his designs, however, the African connections are more clearly evident.

In 2001, Boateng created his first explicitly African collection, entitled Tribal Traditionalism. Soon after presenting the collection, Boateng commented to Hagy on the pressure an African designer may feel as international markets expect distinctly African fashions: "Last season I produced a collection called 'Tribal Traditionalism.'…For the first time in my life, I felt ready to express my cultural and ancestral spirituality in a collection. I allowed the spirit and colours of Africa to flow through everything that I created. At long last I felt the confidence to do this without feeling stereotyped." Boateng's Tribal Traditionalism line bears little overt resemblance to the clothing one might associate with Africa's traditional cultures. Instead of the Africa of Western imagination, Boateng's work embodies the Africa of his own imagination—urbane, international, neither African nor Western yet adaptable to both worlds.

STONED CHERRIE: SOUTH AFRICAN DESIGN

In the decade since the nation's much celebrated transition from apartheid to nonracial democracy, South Africa's arts scene has flourished, with many artists using their media to work through the physical and psychological violence of the apartheid era and to express pride in the identities they can now claim. Fashion is no exception, and South Africa's fashion industry is among the continent's most vibrant. The country's professional designers represent a significant portion of the fashion markets; their clothes are sold in department stores and megamalls as well as exclusive boutiques. Fashion magazines, trade shows, and fashion competitions raise the visibility of the industry both in South Africa and beyond.

Stoned Cherrie is one of the country's most prominent brands, and it offers a different set of insights into African fashion design that does not look to indigenous forms. Its distinctive clothing makes reference to South Africa's unique history without adapting the styles associated with the country's traditional cultures. Like Ozwald Boateng, Stoned Cherrie's founder, Nkhensani Manganyi Nkosi, has focused on creating clothing with an African sensibility rather than explicitly African forms. The company is a design collective founded in 2000 that consists of Manganyi Nkosi and a staff of designers, including Habani Mavundla and Palesa Mokubung, who create jewelry and eyeglasses as well as clothing. The promotional materials that accompany its products emphasize the brand's expression of "afro-urban culture," bringing together past and present.

Stoned Cherrie is best known for its influential Sophiatown styles, named for a community outside Johannesburg where urban black culture flourished in the 1940s and 1950s. Beginning in the mid-1950s, the population was forcibly removed by the apartheid government and buildings razed. The culture of Sophiatown was international—the clothing associated with the community owed as much to Harlem as it did to Johannesburg. Although distinctly South African, Sophiatown was not traditional. Stoned Cherrie's Sophiatown-inspired clothing includes 1940s-style dresses and hats, worn with T-shirts emblazoned with *Drum Magazine* covers (a popular black news and culture magazine that was an important force in the struggle against apartheid). Thus, the designs are deeply rooted in local history without making reference to traditional forms; the beadwork that is the hallmark of much indigenous South African dress does not appear in these designers' work. In a 2003 interview, Manganyi

Models wearing Stoned Cherrie creations at Cape Town Fashion Week, 2007. Stoned Cherrie is one of South Africa's most prominent brands. Gianluigi Guercia/AFP/Getty Images.

Nkosi told South African journalist Lin Sampsom that she deliberately avoids creating clothing that suits consumers' expectations of African design: "What I like about my clothes is that they are not obviously African. People have a very stereotypical idea of African clothes." Yet the clothes do reflect the country's specific history; in the same interview, Manganyi Nkosi made that link explicit: "I would like most people to learn about the history of their country from my clothes."

LAMINE KOUYATÉ OF XULY BËT

Another leading designer whose work illustrates this conceptual approach to African fashion is the Paris-based Malian-Senegalese designer Lamine Kouyaté. His work has been featured in fashion shows and magazines throughout Africa and Europe, generally presented not as African fashion but rather as part of a global movement that emerges out of the gritty, urban aesthetic associated with grunge music (he is a musician). He gained recognition in the mid-1990s, and since then has been best known for his recycled clothing. Using clothing purchased in flea markets and charity shops, he creates entirely new garments by cutting seams, stitching together elements of separate garments, and often silk screening slogans and logos onto the resulting shirts, dresses, pants, and other garments. Instead of concealing the garments' origins, Kouyaté emphasizes their histories by using bright red thread to stitch new seams on the outsides of his creations and by leaving old labels in even as he adds his new one.

These clothes, sold under the brand name Xuly Bët (a slang term in the Senegalese language Wolof, meaning "watch me"), are not marketed as African, nor does Kouyaté's African identity figure prominently in the reception of his work. Yet these garments do provide insights into contemporary Africa, where recycling clothing is a practical adaptation to economic challenges as well as a form of creativity. All over Africa, people purchase used clothing, most of it imported from Western countries. As they are adapted to their new context, the clothes may be transformed—pants made into shorts, sleeves removed or shortened, garments dyed to disguise stains or suit new tastes. In Senegal, where Kouyaté spent the latter part of his youth (after moving from Mali, where he was born), recycled clothing is particularly associated with the Baye Fall, a subgroup of the Mouride sect, an important West African Muslim brotherhood whose history is rooted in resistance to French colonialism. The Baye Fall reject all worldly things, living outside the monetary economy so that they can devote themselves to religious worship—a stance that implicitly challenged the French colonial authorities in the early years of Mouride practice. This rejection is visible in their clothing, which is made of scraps given to them as charity.

Kouyaté's recycled clothing may be viewed as a conceptual reshaping of Baye Fall garments, subverting the global fashion economy just as the Baye Fall subverted the colonial economy. His reworked used clothing may be viewed as a commentary on the history of Africa's interactions with the West. Africa was long excluded from the Western-dominated realm of international fashion production, its cultures treated as outposts of unchanging tradition. Kouyaté's purchase of garments that have been discarded by their original owners, transforming them from refuse into fashion, allows him to resell them—at much higher prices—back into the system that discarded them. Although the garments bear no stylistic resemblance to African precedents, the process by which they are made does elucidate important aspects of Senegalese—and African—history.

JOËL ANDRIANOMEARISOA

Malagasy designer Joël Andrianomearisoa has received attention as a conceptual artist as well as a fashion designer. Like Kouyaté, he works across artistic media, designing sets for theater and television and performance pieces for his fashion shows, and creating photographs both to document his designs and as works of art in their own right. He studied fashion in Madagascar, gaining attention as a young student for his experimental approach to clothing design. Many of his garments are based in the notion of wrapping, using lengths of cloth to envelop the body in layers. His interest in wrapped forms is made explicit in several performance pieces, some of which double as fashion shows. Here the clothes are constructed, or deconstructed, as performers encircle each other with lengths of cloth, wrapping bodies in a ritualistic manner.

While these garments, many made of black cotton sheeting, bear no overt resemblance to any Malagasy—or African—dress practices, Andrianomearisoa's work is richly elucidated by a comparison to funerary practices among numerous Malagasy cultures. Wrapping the body in locally woven silk shrouds is a crucial element of preparing the deceased for the journey into the realm of ancestors. These shrouds, preferably long cloths that can be wrapped many times around the body, are an important symbol of community and continuity. Although Andrianomearisoa does not make explicit reference to this practice, the concept of wrapping is key to appreciating his work as African fashion. Like Ozwald Boateng, Stoned Cherrie, Lamine Kouyaté and many other African designers, Andrianomearisoa demonstrates that fashion design need not look African in order to be African.

References and Further Reading

Braune, Annette, Francine Vormese, et al. *Mickaël Kra: Jewellery between Paris Glamour and African Tradition.* Stuttgart, Germany: Arnold-sche, 2006.

Dadson, Nanabanyin. "Ozwald Boateng: Exclusive Interview." *Agoo* 1, no. 2 (April–June 2002): 32–39.

Geoffroy-Schneiter, Bérénice. *L'Afrique est a la mode.* Paris: Éditions Assouline, 2005.

Hagy, Timothy. "Ozwald Boateng: Out of Africa." *Fashion Windows*, 1 July 2003. http://www.fashionwindows.com/runway_shows/ozwald_boateng/MS041.asp (accessed 20 September 2007).

Hendrickson, Hildi, ed. *Clothing and Difference: Embodied Identities in Colonial and Post-Colonial Africa.* Durham, NC: Duke University Press, 1986.

Mendy-Ongoundou, Renée. *Elégances africaines: Tissus traditionnels et mode contemporaine.* Paris: Éditions Alternatives, 2002.

Mustafa, Hudita Nura. "Oumou Sy: The African Place, Dakar, Senegal." *Nka* 15 (Fall/Winter 2002): 44–46.

Rabine, Leslie W. *The Global Circulation of African Fashion.* New York: Berg, 2002.

Revue Noire. Special Mode: African Fashion, no. 27 (1997–1998).

Rovine, Victoria L. *Bogolan: Shaping Culture through Cloth in Contemporary Mali.* Washington, DC: Smithsonian Institution Press, 2001.

Rovine, Victoria L. "Working the Edge: XULY. Bët's Recycled Clothing." In *Old Clothes, New Looks: Second-hand Fashion*, edited by Alexandra Palmer and Hazel Clark, 215–227. Oxford, UK: Berg, 2004.

Sampsom, Lin. "Cherrie on Top." *Sunday Times* (South Africa), 20 May 2003, 4.

Tischhauser, Anthony, ed. *10 X SA Fashion Week: Voices and Images from Ten Years of South African Fashion Week.* Johannesburg, South Africa: Channel F Publishing, 2006.

Van der Plas, Els, and Marlous Willemsen, eds. *The Art of African Fashion.* Trenton, NJ, and The Hague, The Netherlands: Africa World Press and Prince Claus Fund, 1998.

Victoria L. Rovine

PART 3

Types of Dress in Africa

Body and Beauty

As many scholars have pointed out, the body is much more than flesh, bones, and blood. Apart from defining an individual, it is socially constructed in different ways by different cultures, relating an individual to his or her habitus. As anthropologist Jean Comaroff has put it:

> The relationship between the human body and the social collectivity is a critical dimension of consciousness in all societies. Indeed, it is a truism that the body is the tangible form of selfhood in individual and collective experience, providing a constellation of physical signs with the potential for signifying the relations of persons to their contexts. The body mediates all actions upon the world and simultaneously constitutes both the self and the universe of social and natural relations of which it is a part.

Hence a well-shaped body is a cultural asset because it attracts attention, facilitating social mobility. Admittedly, European colonization and Western popular culture have made a significant impact on Africa. Yet many indigenous concepts of beauty remain intact despite the use of new materials to reinforce them.

BODY, BEAUTY, AND GOODNESS

It is important to note at the outset that not much has been published on the relationship between body and beauty in Africa; thus, interpretations are based on the limited data available, collected from a number of cultures scattered across the continent. According to art historian Robert Farris Thompson, who has done extensive fieldwork in different parts of sub-Saharan Africa, a review of the notions of beauty in different parts of the continent reveals a kind of "unity in diversity," that is, an emphasis on a midpoint between two extremes. In other words, an individual must not be too dark nor too light; not too short and not too tall, not too beautiful and not too ugly but, at the same time, well proportioned and pleasing in appearance. For example, African folktales often associate the unusually ugly with the demonic. No wonder that some cultures use masks with grotesque features in ritual dances aimed at repelling evil forces. That appearances can be deceptive is evident in didactic tales of irresistibly beautiful women who later turn out to be evil spirits in disguise. The emphasis on a midpoint between

two extremes in African aesthetics has been documented by the anthropologist Karl Laman for the Kongo of equatorial Africa, most of whom are dark-skinned:

> A very darkly pigmented skin is not considered beautiful, nor is a fair complexion. But a person with a shining brown complexion, like the fish *ngola zanga*, is pleasant to look upon. If the skin is too dark, it is likened to the sooty *mfilu*-trees, where a prairie fire has passed. If a person has too fair a complexion, the mother is considered to have come into contact, for example when bathing, with *nkisi Funza* or *simbi* spirits.

A similar concept is found among the Wodaabe Fulani, whose skin is relatively lighter than that of most of their West African neighbors. To be considered beautiful, a Wodaabe must be red-skinned or light brown rather than pale or too black.

It suffices to say that the criteria for beauty in terms of height, skin color, and appearance vary from one culture to another. Almost everywhere, members of the opposite sex admire one another's bodies for a variety of reasons. Young women are often

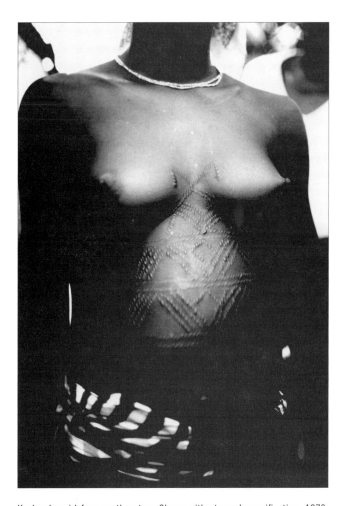

Konkomba girl from northeastern Ghana with stomach scarification, 1973. Photograph by Herbert M. Cole.

attracted to men with fine features, good looks, height, broad shoulders, and athletic build. So it is that the Yoruba of Nigeria and Republic of Benin expect the ideal man to be tall and well built (*sìgbonlè*). Yoruba women admiringly tease such men with nicknames like *Agúnléjiká* (the square-shouldered one) and *Agùn t'ásoólò* (tall enough to display the robe to full advantage). Although it must be moderate, a protruding belly signifies wealth among the Yoruba. Hence, corpulent rich men are given appellations such as *Arówóyokùn* (rich enough to have a belly) and *Aríkùnjobè* (the one with a stomach big enough to accommodate plenty of food). Similar notions resonate in the square shoulders and prominent torsos of statues dedicated to deceased ancestors in many parts of sub-Saharan Africa as well as in the idealized portraits (*ndop*) of Kuba kings. According to historian Jan Vansina, MboMboosh, one of the Kuba kings who reigned in the eighteenth century, is fondly remembered "as a beautiful man—very dark skin and very heavy set."

On the other hand, most of the criteria for female beauty are predicated on the degree of their curvaceousness as manifested in their face, breasts, hips, thighs, and buttocks. Many female representations in African art stress these features. According to Sylvia Boone, the Mende (of Sierra Leone) judge the female buttocks (*ngoto*) "by their size, shape and movement. Even if the girl is otherwise slim, she must have bulging buttocks, of relatively greater mass." Terms such as *potroo* (plump) and *afefedee* (beautiful) sum up the reaction of the Akan of Ghana to the body rhythm of such a lady, especially when she walks or dances. Among the Igbo, Efik, Ibibio, and Ijo of southeastern Nigeria, the relatively plump woman epitomizes the feminine and fertile. Hence, in the past, girls getting ready for marriage were secluded for a given period of time and fed lavishly to increase their weight or roundness. The *D'mba* emblematizes the nexus between roundness and female beauty among the Baga of Guinea. A massive wooden headdress in the form of a female bust with large breasts, the D'mba is worn with a costume of raffia and cloth and, as art historian Frederick Lamp has pointed out in his book *Art of the Baga*, it is danced to signify the quintessential female, "an abstraction of an ideal female role in society…the universal mother…to be honored because she had borne many children, and had nursed them to productive adulthood…the vision of a woman at her zenith of power, beauty, and affective presence."

The capacity of the beautiful to command attention is often likened to a feast for the eyes or what the Yoruba of Nigeria call *onje oju* (food for the eye). Thus, the Wodaabe Fulani of Niger Republic use the terms *nyirre* (edible) for a likable person and *nyiddudo* (inedible or sour) for the ugly. Correspondingly, the Asante of Ghana perceive an ugly man as one whose "body is unappetizing to women" (*wo ho enye maa akonno*), while the Zulu of South Africa describe a pretty girl as *semomonthane* (delectable).

However, since natural beauty is a given, dress not only complements one's natural endowment, it may also be used to make up for a biological defect over which an individual has no physical control. Moreover, it can be used to convey a variety of messages regarding taste, prestige, social worth, and political or spiritual power. This explains why dress constitutes part of a culture's system of visual metaphors, reflecting environmental influences, its worldview, social structure, occupation, and gender roles. In the process, jewelry, tattoo, scarifications, body painting, hairdos, and such accessories as footwear, headwear, fly whisks, staffs, and canes are loaded with meanings that may have aesthetic, political, or spiritual import. In effect, the dressed body combines personal and group values, initiating a visual dialogue between the self and others whose anticipated evaluation or reaction often determines choice of materials and their configuration. Nonetheless, as Harry Memel-Fote has pointed out, the African notion of ideal beauty goes beyond the physical self; it has ethical elements as well—elements that constitute a major ingredient for the reception, taste or "edibility" of that self. Thus, terms such as *nyande* (among the Mende of Sierra Leone) and *busoga* (among the Lega of the Democratic Republic of Congo) equate beauty with goodness. Or, as a Zulu proverb puts it: "You see a beautiful person through her deeds" (*Motho ea motle re mo bona ka diketso tsa hae*). Moreover, the public image of an individual also may be affected by other factors such as ancestral background, professional skills or reputation in a given field, wisdom, intelligence, and/or potentials for success in life. Any discourse on body and beauty in Africa must be cognizant of these factors.

THE BODY: LOCATION, CLIMATE, AND LIFESTYLES

The dress traditions of a given culture depend as much on geographical conditions as on its belief system and lifestyles. That is why relatively warm clothing is the norm in the colder and windy regions of northern, eastern, and southern Africa, and less substantial clothing is preferred in tropical western central and equatorial Africa. A review of the prehistoric rock and ancient arts of Africa—ranging from the rock engravings and paintings of South Africa and the Sahara to the stone and terra-cotta sculptures of Ancient Egypt, Nubia, and Nok—shows many human figures wearing skirts and wrappers apparently made of fiber and animal skin, thus suggesting that these were the most common dress materials in ancient times before the invention of textiles.

Most of the inhabitants of modern-day northern Africa are light-skinned, reflecting centuries of interaction between the local populations (primarily Berber or Imazighen) and immigrants such as the Phoenicians, Greeks, Romans, Arabs, and Europeans. Here, the climate is seasonally hot and cold, compelling both men and women to dress accordingly. In the hot and dry months, they wear light clothing consisting of long tunics, flowing robes, and long trousers frequently adorned with arabesque patterns or embroidery. Some, especially women, decorate their body with henna dye, tattoo, and assorted jewelry. Head scarves and turbans are common, being worn differently to reflect gender and individual tastes in addition to serving as a veil (called *tagelmust* or *cheche* by the Tuaregs) to shield the face from the sun and the strong winds from the Mediterranean Sea or Sahara desert. To keep warm in the cold season, men and women wear thick blankets over their dresses. Regardless of weather conditions, some married Muslim women wear special veils (*burga*, burqa, burkah, afar, ajar) that conceal their bodies, revealing only the outline. And since men and women are covered from head to toe, when it is cold or windy, height, gait, elaborate jewelry, and colorful head covering (worn by women) and sheathed swords (*takuba*) and leather pouches (carried by the men) become the only means of differentiating the sexes.

on short and long waistcloths and wrappers. There is a general tendency here to leave the upper part of the body bare, thus turning it into a canvas for displaying elaborate body painting, tattoo, and scarification as well as jewelry in assorted forms and materials. Women sometimes wear a loose blouse or robe (called *boubou* in Senegambia and Mali) on top of their wrappers, while the men may wear tunics and bigger robes with or without embroidery (called *bobani* by the Mende of Sierra Leone, *riga* by the Hausa/Fulani of the West African savanna, and *agbada* by the Yoruba of Nigeria and Benin), long-sleeve shirts (*buba*) or sleeveless smocks (*danshiki* or *batakari*) over a waistcloth or pair of trousers. It has been suggested that the Berbers/Tuaregs from North Africa might have introduced some of these robes and trousers to western and central Africa in the course of the trans-Saharan trade that started before the Christian era and lasted until the late nineteenth century. Some of the earliest evidence of the flowing robe in sub-Saharan Africa comes from a ninth-century C.E. burial site excavated at Igbo-Ukwu in eastern Nigeria. A painting based on the archaeological data indicates that the corpse was dressed in elaborate regalia and then positioned upright inside a spacious burial chamber holding a staff of office and surrounded by ceremonial objects reflecting high status.

GLORIFYING THE HEAD

The head dominates the body in much of African figural sculpture essentially because of its physiological, social, and spiritual importance. Physiologically, it is the locus of important organs in the body such as the brain (seat of wisdom and reason), the eyes (the organ for sight), the nose (for smell and breath), the mouth (for eating and communicating), and the ears (for listening)—all enabling an individual to navigate his or her way through the labyrinth of life. Socially, the head is the crown that identifies the self in relation to other members of a given community, facilitating individual and collective aspirations. Its spiritual import derives from a strong belief that it is the seat of the soul, without which an individual cannot exist. Thus, as in sculpture, there is an emphasis on the head in African dress.

In some cultures, mothers and midwives massage the head of a newborn baby to make it as round as possible and to correct any birth defect that might embarrass an individual in the future. In view of their association of a high forehead with beauty and intelligence, the Akan of Ghana and Côte d'Ivoire mold an infant's soft cranial bones accordingly. On the other hand, members of the upper class among the Mangbetu of the Republic of Congo once practiced skull elongation (*lipombo*), augmented with intricate hairdos and a variety of accessories to differentiate themselves from commoners. In recognition of its biological, cultural, and spiritual functions, both men and women pay special attention to their hair. Apart from the Tuareg and Wodaabe Fulani, who naturally grow long hair and often braid it, a good majority of the men in sub-Saharan Africa sport a clean-shaven head or cut their hair short. They may also wear wigs and hats of different shapes and colors for aesthetic reasons and to protect the head from the elements. In the past, women normally wore their hair long, frequently plaiting, tying, or fashioning it into a variety of designs, accentuated with wigs and beaded, ivory, silver, and gold ornaments. However, it is customary for women to wear their

Titled Igbo leaders, with the male displaying semipermanent *uli/uri* indigo body paint. Agwa village group, Nigeria, 1983. Photograph by Herbert M. Cole.

People living near the coast or oases (in the Sahara) often lead a sedentary life, depending on arts and crafts, agriculture, fishing, hunting, and trade with neighbors and foreigners. Because the inhabitants of the hinterland (especially the semidesert and desert regions) move from place to place in search of water and greener pastures for themselves and their cattle, they find it necessary to wear most of their body adornments most of the time. These consist mainly of jewelry fabricated from found objects (coins, glass beads, precious stones, shells, gold, silver, and other metals). To protect their eyes from the glare of the desert sun and sandstorms, Saharan dwellers (Tuareg) often adjust their headgears and turbans to cover much of the face, leaving only a small opening to see through. This manner of wearing the veil can also be observed in the grassland and semidesert areas of western and eastern Sudan as well as the East African (Swahili) coast, where contact with North Africa and the Middle East dates back several centuries.

As one moves inland from present-day Republic of Sudan into sub-Saharan Africa, where it is relatively warm all year round, one observes different dress traditions with an emphasis

Turkana man from northern Kenya wearing a clay-packed hairdo with ostrich feathers and an ivory ball under his lower lip, 1973. Photograph by Herbert M. Cole.

A headdress with a lion's mane identifies a Maasai warrior (*moran*) who has single-handedly killed a lion, while a beaded hat adorned with horns and colorful beads (*misango mapende*) proclaims the role of a Pende chief as the head of a village. A king's headgear or crown is usually the most distinguished or spectacular in a given town and may be adorned with gold (as among the Asante), beads (as among the Yoruba and Benin), and feathers (as among the Tikar, Bamum, and Babanki of Cameroon) or made of leopard skin (as among the Ganda of Uganda)—to hint at the physical and metaphysical powers associated with divine kingship. In areas where Islam predominates (as in some parts of Mali, Burkina Faso, Ghana, Nigeria, Cameroon, Sudan, and eastern Africa), a big turban may identify the ruler in public. Yet traces of divine kingship survive not only in the awe that these Muslim rulers inspire in their subjects but also in some of their royal symbols, particularly the sculptured and consecrated thrones of Bamum monarchs.

THE FACE AS A FAÇADE AND MASK OF COOLNESS

Given the importance of the face as a site of identity, perception, and social interaction, it may be painted, tattooed, or scarified not only to underscore its significance as a façade, demarcating the outer from the inner self, but also to relate an individual to a given lineage/extended family, to protect against disease, to attract good luck, or simply for aesthetic purposes. In the past, some individuals filed or chipped their teeth to empower their smiles.

All over the continent, women wear assorted earrings, ear pins, nose pendants, and ivory lip plugs or plates (especially among the Nuba and Kichepo of southern Sudan) to further enhance the face and increase its visual impact. Regarded in many parts of Africa as a mask, the face manifests the state of mind or the inner beauty of an individual. As a result, the extent to which an individual is able to control his or her emotions or visual expressions may influence the amount of respect he or she receives. And because a calm, cool face facilitates dialogue and social interaction, kings and chiefs are obliged to look composed in public to reinforce their image as well as their capacity to lead. This is particularly the case among the Yaka of the Democratic Republic of Congo, where an elder should not express raw emotions of anger and weakness in public. The scholar Rene Devisch has indicated that tradition requires elders to "display a stable mood and gravitas (*zitu*, literally, 'weight rest') in movement, gestures and facial expression, especially of the eyes." The Yaka word *luzitu* (worthy of respect) hints at the beauty or affective power of such a bearing. In some cultures (for example the Kuba), the king must maintain a facial composure to accord with his symbolic role as a living embodiment of the divine ancestor Woot.

ADORNING THE NECK

Because it elevates the head, an appreciably long neck is one of the hallmarks of beauty in different parts of Africa. Hence the epithet for a pretty Wodaabe Fulani woman is *Nyallo Silliide* (the one with a straight neck and good poise), an attribute also

hair short among East African pastoralists such as the Maasai, Turkana, Pokot, and Samburu (among others) to facilitate the display of beaded ornaments. In other African cultures, women may put on colorful scarves to further stress the apical position of the head. In short, elaborate hairdos and headgears usually proclaim taste, high status, political authority, or spiritual power, in addition to marking life-cycle transition, marital status, age group, lineage, and occupation.

valued in men and articulated in the Yoruba phrase *Egun gaga niyi orun* (longishness is the beauty of the neck). All the same, the length of an ideal neck varies from one culture to another. To the Baule of Côte d'Ivoire, for example, the ideal neck should not be long like that of a camel nor too short like that of a cricket. Instead, as anthropologist Philip Ravenhill has observed in his book *Dreams and Reverie*, it should be "longer than average and, if possible, with the highly desirable features of beauty lines (*komin nglelie*). These lines or rings around the neck are not folds of fat but rather slight creases horizontally aligned; such natural striation is recognized within the culture as inherently beautiful, a natural endowment complementing a neck already pleasing by its correct dimension." The same is true of the Mende of Sierra Leone, who identify the ringed neck (*mbolo genye*) as "physical beauty incarnate." In fact, the long and ringed-neck motifs abound in figure sculptures from different parts of Africa, especially among the Dan, Asante, Yoruba, Igbo, and Bamileke of West Africa and the Hemba, Luba, Lulua, Ndengese, and Songye of equatorial Africa, to name only a few.

One of the advantages of a long neck is that it provides ample space for displaying jewelry that further accentuates the apical position of the head. This enables many unmarried women among the pastoralists of East Africa—such as the Samburu, for example—to bury their neck in a pile of beads given to them by admirers and to assemble enough that marriage proposals result. Among the Ndebele of South Africa, women may sometimes wear copper or brass coils (*tzila*) and beaded or unbeaded hoops (*golwani*) around the neck to make it appear longer, thus making their faces more distinct.

It suffices to say that materials for necklaces vary from one culture to another, ranging from coral beads and cowry shells to bones, ivory, copper, silver, and gold. Moreover, the higher the status of an individual, the more expensive the materials as well as the quantity used. Consequently, kings and chiefs are the most richly adorned.

THE BODY AS ARMATURE FOR DRESS

As mentioned earlier, much of sub-Saharan Africa lies within the tropics, so there is a tendency to bare the upper part of the body. Both sexes wear skirts and wrappers. Yet, as Judith Perani and Norma Wolff have observed: "Gender dictates basic male and female clothing styles. The structure of the garments, the parts of the body covered, the accessories thought necessary, and sometimes the type of cloth, differ according to gender. These gender-specific clothing styles provide a base on which variations tied to activities, life stage, and status are built." In the past, most infants, regardless of sex, wore only diapers and waist beads, the quantity of which depended on the status of their parents. This tradition survives in some villages, though children in urban areas now wear short pants and trousers. As they approached adolescence, girls put on small wrappers tied round the waist or above the breasts like their mothers, adding blouses on special or ceremonial occasions. Similarly, young boys wore (and some still do) a loincloth or a wrapper like a toga or tied around the neck. As an individual advances in age, the nature, type, and elaborateness of dress and accessories would normally reflect changes in the life cycle, taste, status, and, sometimes,

occupation. Leather sandals or slippers were once common footwear but have been replaced by rubber and plastic sandals, though modern shoes are also worn.

Women usually wear more jewelry than men, with some (especially among the Mende, Akan, Yoruba, Edo, Igbo, Efik, Ibibio, and Ijo) putting on waist beads of various sizes to heighten the sensuousness of their buttocks, while, at the same time, alluding to the general belief that women with big hips are more fertile and deliver babies more easily than those with smaller hips. Although some men endeavor to impress women by wearing the latest fashion and looking well groomed, others focus on the attainment of fame, wealth, or power, hoping that celebrity status or material success will endear them to beautiful women. Groups such as the Fulani of West Africa, the Nuba of southern Sudan, and the Surma of Ethiopia may organize competitions of dance, wrestling, stick fights, swimming, fishing, hunting, harvesting, physical endurance, and men's beauty contests that result in spinsters falling in love with winners. Among the Senufo of Côte d'Ivoire, there is an annual hoeing contest after which the winners are presented with champion cultivator staffs (*tefaliptiya*), in addition to having the opportunity to marry some of the most beautiful women in a given village.

Leadership attire in sub-Saharan Africa is spectacular partly because of its elaborateness. Besides, it frequently incorporates certain motifs (such as leopard and snake skins, elephant tusks, and eagle feathers), thus implying that a leader is in a unique position to metaphorically harness the physical and metaphysical powers of these creatures to bolster his or her authority and for the social and spiritual well-being of the community. The emphasis on bigness in the ceremonial regalia of some African kings is significant. That of the *oba* (king) of Benin, for example, consists of a crown, assorted necklaces and collars that cover his chin and neck, a vest, and a voluminous skirt—all made of coral beads. He often wears ivory wristlets and a belt of ivory symbols, which contrast vividly with the reddish costume. Almost always flanked by two male attendants who hold his arms as if bracing him up against the weight of the regalia, the oba moves slowly, evoking the abundance and prosperity that his subjects expect during his reign. The Kuba king (*nyim*) cuts a similar image. His massive regalia consists of an elaborately embroidered skirt and an assemblage of leopard skins, numerous strips of raffia cloth adorned with beads, cowries, and ivory objects, all weighing about 170 pounds (77 kilograms) or more. Concealing his head and exposing only his face, the nyim's headdress is surmounted by assorted feathers, which, when related to the leopard skins and cowry shells on his regalia, hint at the convergence in his persona of celestial, terrestrial, and aquatic forces, which endow him with an architectonic and authoritative presence.

Among the Yoruba, the oba wears a beaded robe and a beaded crown (*ade*) with a veil that often conceals his face. Most Yoruba crowns have a stylized face in front that serves as the official visage of the monarch when appearing in public, depersonalizing and converting him into a symbol of the living dead. This stylized face (or a similar one, should a new king decide to replace an old crown) identified his predecessors in public and will do the same for his successors. Commonly identified with the mythical ancestor Oduduwa (the progenitor of the Yoruba), the face makes the king appear like a masked figure—a liminal being and an icon radiating the splendor of divine kingship, functioning as

Kuba *nyim* (king) Kota a Mobweeky III in a state dress with royal drums at Mushenge, Zaire. Photograph by Eliot Elisofon, 1971. EEPA EECL 2139. Eliot Elisofon Photographic Archives, National Museum of African Art, Smithsonian Institution.

a paradigm of the oneness of the king and his subjects, on the one hand, and of the reigning king and the royal dead, on the other.

The fact that some African kings appear uncomfortable in their bulky regalia clearly shows that they are compelled to wear them by social and political expectations and to reflect an aesthetic ideal. The Asante of Ghana dramatize the apical position of leadership during important festivals by carrying their king and paramount chiefs in palanquins surrounded by musicians and gorgeously dressed attendants. As a result, these leaders, lavishly adorned with gold ornaments and colorful beads, tower above the masses, looking majestic and larger than life in their paraphernalia of office, exemplifying the Asante vision of the beautiful and desirable. All told, the interconnectedness of ethics, aesthetics, politics, and metaphysics in many African cultures clearly shows that their concepts of the beautiful transcend the materiality of the body to emphasize the goodness inherent in the visible and invisible self.

References and Further Reading

Arnoldi, Mary Jo, and Christine Mullen Kreamer. *Crowning Achievements: African Arts of Dressing the Head*. Los Angeles: Fowler Museum of Cultural History, 1995.

Biebuyck, Daniel. *Lega Culture: Art, Initiation, and Moral Philosophy among a Central African People*. Berkeley and London: University of California Press, 1973.

Boone, Sylvia Ardyn. *Radiance from the Waters: Ideals of Feminine Beauty in Mende Art*. New Haven, CT, and London: Yale University Press, 1986.

Bowin, Mette. *Nomads Who Cultivate Beauty: Wodaabe Dance and Visual Arts in Niger*. Uppsala: Sweden: Nordiska Africainstitutet, 2001.

Cole, Herbert M. "Vital Arts in Northern Kenya." *African Arts* 7, no. 2 (1974): 12–23, 82.

Cole, Herbert M., and Doran Ross. *The Arts of Ghana*. Los Angeles: Museum of Cultural History, University of California, Los Angeles, 1977.

Comaroff, Jean. *The Body of Power, Spirit Resistance: History of a South African People*. Chicago and London: University of Chicago Press, 1985.

Courtney-Clarke, Margaret. *Ndebele*. New York: Rizzoli International Publications, 1986.

Devisch, René. "The Human Body as a Vehicle for Emotions among the Yaka of Zaire." In *Personhood and Agency: The Experience of Self and Other in African Cultures*, edited by M. Jackson and Ivan Karp, 115–135. Washington, DC: Smithsonian Institution Press, 1990.

Glaze, Anita. *Art and Death in a Senufo Village*. Bloomington: Indiana University Press, 1981.

Hallen, Barry. *The Good, the Bad and the Beautiful: Discourse about Values in Yoruba Culture*. Bloomington: Indiana University Press, 2003.

Laman, Karl. *The Kongo*. Uppsala, Sweden: Studia Ethnographica Upsaliensia, 1953.

Lamp, Frederick. *Art of the Baga: A Drama of Cultural Reinvention*. New York and Munich: Museum for African Art and Prestel Verlag, 1996.

Lawal, Babatunde. "Some Aspects of Yoruba Aesthetics." *British Journal of Aesthetics* 15, no. 3 (1974): 239–249.

Lawal, Babatunde. *The Gelede Spectacle: Art, Gender, and Social Harmony in an African Culture*. Seattle and London: University of Washington Press, 1996.

Memel-Fote, Harris. "The Perception of Beauty in Negro African Culture." *Colloquium on Negro Art: 1st World Festival of Negro Arts*. 45–65. Paris: Presence Africaine, 1968.

Northern, Tamara. *The Art of Cameroon*. Washington, DC: National Museum of Natural History, Smithsonian Institution, 1984.

Palmenaer, Els De. "Mangbetu Hairstyles and the Art of Seduction: Lipombo." In *Hair in African Art and Culture*, edited by Roy Sieber and Frank Herreman, 117–123. New York and Munich: Museum for African Art and Prestel, 2000.

Perani, Judith, and Norma H. Wolff. *Cloth, Dress, and Art Patronage*. Oxford, UK: Berg, 1999.

Powell, I. *Ndebele: A People and Their Art*. New York: Cross Rivers Press, 1995.

Ravenhill, Philip L. *Dreams and Reverie: Images of Otherworldly Mates among the Baule of West Africa*. Washington, DC, and London: Smithsonian Institution Press, 1996.

Ribane, Nakedi. *Beauty: A Black Perspective*. Durban, South Africa: University of KwaZulu-Natal Press, 2006.

Schildkrout, Enid, and Curtis Keim. *African Reflections: Art from Northeastern Zaire*. Seattle: University of Washington Press, 1990.

Shaw, Thurstan. *Igbo-Ukwu: An Account of Archaeological Discoveries in Eastern Nigeria*. 2 vols. Evanston, IL: Northwestern University Press, 1970.

Thompson, Robert F. "The Sign of the Divine King: Yoruba Bead-Embroidered Crowns with Veil and Bird Decorations." In *African Art and Leadership*, edited by Douglas Fraser and Herbert M. Cole, 227–260. Madison: University of Wisconsin Press, 1972.

Thompson, Robert F. *African Art in Motion: Icon and Act*. Los Angeles: University of California Press, 1974.

Vansina, Jan. *The Children of Woot: A History of the Kuba Peoples*. Madison: University of Wisconsin Press, 1978.

Warren, Dennis M., ed. *Akan Arts and Aesthetics: Elements of Change in a Ghanaian Indigenous Knowledge System*. Ames: Iowa State University Research Foundation, 1990.

Babatunde Lawal

See also Body Modification and Body Art; Jewelry; Headdresses and Hairdos; Footwear; Nigeria Overview; Yoruba in Nigeria and Diaspora; Mangbetu Dress.

Body Modification and Body Art

- Permanent Body Marks
- Body Painting and Dyeing
- Shaping the Body
- Hair
- African Body Arts and Change

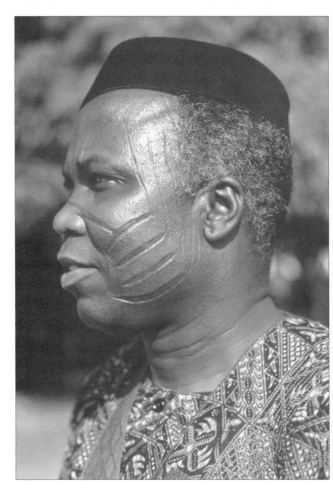

Chief Samuel Ladoke Akintola, premier of the Western Region in Nigeria in the 1960s, wears facial marks that identify him as coming from the Ogbomosho region of Yorubaland. Marks from this region typically combine two designs: *keke*, a V-shaped mark on the cheek and forehead, and *baamum*, a line across the bridge of the nose. The latter mark is also applied to sickly children (*àbíkú*) from any Yoruba region to scare off the spirit companions that would otherwise take their life at an early age. Photograph by Eliot Elisofon, 1959. EEPA EECL 1953. Eliot Elisofon Photographic Archives, National Museum of African Art, Smithsonian Institution.

The U.S. anthropologist Enid Schildkrout characterizes the body as a "site where culture is inscribed (and) a place where the individual is defined and inserted into the cultural landscape." Cultures throughout the African continent use the transformed body as means for expressing identities, norms, values, and aesthetic principles through a wide range of body art media, including everything from scarification, tattooing, painting, and oiling the skin to styling the hair and reshaping designated areas of the body. Some of these arts are temporary in nature (e.g., body painting and hairdos), while others are permanent (e.g., scarification, tattoos, and reshaping the body). The former tend to mark momentary identities or liminal states in one's social development, and the latter signal an achieved status or an enduring canon of beauty. Schildkrout and historian and political scientist Curtis Keim have argued that the ephemeral and transportable nature of the body makes its artistic embellishments forever subject to change. Perhaps the most dramatic changes resulted from the pressures of colonialism, which imposed its own canons of beauty and attitudes about the body to the detriment of certain African body art traditions. Yet other African ones have persisted, and even evolved in interesting and modernizing ways.

African artists often carved their figurative sculpture, much of it spirit related, with the very same marks that their own people once wore. This tendency not only attests to the primacy of the decorated body that Africans should so readily honor their spirits with it but also provides useful tools for reconstructing the history of Africa's body art practices. The earliest evidence of African body decoration comes from ancient Egypt, beginning circa 3100 to 2950 B.C.E. in the Predynastic period. Like Egyptian art in general, much of the body adornment of this time was done for the purposes of aiding the dead in their journey to the hereafter. The famous *Book of the Dead* describes how Egyptians painted divine imagery such as the Eye of Horus on the body to give it the necessary vigor for its successful journey to the land of the dead.

Some of that body imagery came in the form of tattoos, a permanent form of body decoration Egyptians often used in the context of burials. Egyptians would create these indelible marks by injecting a bluish-black pigment of soot and oil into the cut skin with the aid of a hollow, pointed metal instrument. Archaeologist Robert Bianchi notes that Egyptians were tattooing bodies as early as the Predynastic period, as evidenced by a series of small, abstract female figurines whose bodies are adorned with geometric, colorful tattoolike patterns. Bianchi, in Arnold Rubin's *Marks of Civilization*, suggests that these tattooed, female figurines were deliberately placed in graves to link their "physical procreation with loftier aspirations of a resurrection in the Hereafter." The link between tattooing, femaleness, and the afterlife continues well beyond this early period, though in different forms. By 2100 B.C.E. (Middle Kingdom), tattoos came to be associated with Hathor, a goddess of sexuality and lascivious behavior. This is illustrated in a mummy of a priestess of Hathor named Amunet whose body was covered with a series of abstract tattoos in the form of dots and dashes. By then, such marks were firmly linked to Hathor, which suggests a continued connection between tattooing and fertility. By the New Kingdom (1550 to 1070 B.C.E.), abstract tattooed designs of dots and dashes give way to figurative representations of a tutelary household deity known as Bes. Although less religious in nature, Bes was still associated with revelry and sexuality.

Ancient Egyptians were also fond of applying oils and cosmetics to their bodies, some for therapeutic reasons and others for the sake of beauty. They rubbed their bodies with oil for protection from the hot, dry climate and added fatty matter to their eye makeup to prevent eye disease. But most cosmetics were used as beautifying agents. Egyptians rubbed their feet, hands, and cheeks with henna to give these areas a reddish hue, a practice fairly ubiquitous throughout Africa (see discussion of henna and ochre later in this essay). They also liked adding color and definition to their eyes. Kohl, the most popular form of eye makeup, was made from galena, with a gray-black metallic hue, or malachite, with its rich green hue. The oil-based pigments made from these minerals were stored in personalized tube-shaped containers equipped with a small application stick. A thick line of black

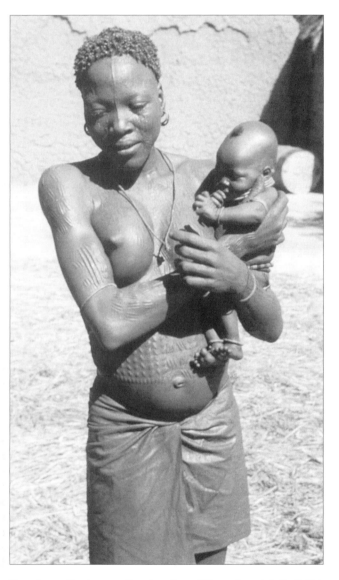

Nkwapinsu, a Margi woman (from the village of Kirngu, formerly in the British Northern Cameroons but now Jalingo, Nigeria), photographed in 1974. She is freshly covered in red camwood paste (*yinsidu*) on the day that she first publicly displayed her newborn daughter. This female custom of wearing red to mark celebratory occasions has earned Margi and other Mandara women the title "the red women of Nigeria." Photograph by James Vaughn.

or green was drawn along the upper and lower edges of the eye and from the eye's outer corner to the side of the face. So important were such cosmetics and other body-adorning agents that people were buried with them. Some were even depicted accompanied by their mirror and makeup, and appropriately adorned, in their journey to the afterlife.

Ancient Egyptians were also very attentive to their hair. In its various manipulations, it served as a significant aspect of beauty, a social marker, or a way to provide spiritual protection. Egyptians cut their hair, braided it, dyed it, added extensions to it, threaded gold tubes on each tress, and covered their heads with elaborately constructed wigs. Because of the perpetual problems of lice and stifling heat in the Nile region, Egyptians often shaved their heads. Priests were the only ones obliged to keep it that way for religious reasons, and they are the only ones depicted as such in art. All others covered their heads with wigs, making the construction and sale of wigs a vibrant and lucrative market. The lower classes wore wigs made from vegetable fiber, and those worn by the elite were made from finely and tightly plaited human hair that was attached to a foundation cap with beeswax and resin. Some of the human hair wigs were padded with vegetable fiber to give it the sense of fullness often depicted in Egyptian tomb art. Women also used hair extensions to elongate or elaborate their own hair or to fill it out when it became thin. In their obsession with youthfulness, women would cover their gray hair with henna to minimize the signs of aging.

Elsewhere, fifth-century B.C.E. rock paintings at Tassili N'Ajjer in Tanzoumaitak feature images of female nomads—possible ancestors of the Fulani (Peul)—bearing elaborate hairdos and tattooed marks. The so-called Tattooed Negress is adorned with an elaborate array of marks consisting of three or four rows of dots running vertically along her arms, torso, and thighs. More recent finds at three different archaeological sites in Nigeria point to historical roots of traditions that were still very much in practice by the early twentieth century. These include elegant bun-shaped coiffures on terra-cotta heads uncovered at Nok (500 B.C.E. to 200 C.E.) and striated facial marks on a series of sculptures from the Igbo site of Igbo-Ukwu (900 C.E.) and the Yoruba site at Ife (eleventh to fifteenth centuries C.E.).

PERMANENT BODY MARKS

The most striking and permanent of body arts is the cutting and scarring of skin. This practice was fairly widespread throughout Africa before colonial influences discouraged or outlawed it. What Africans saw as a means for beautifying the body and inscribing it with markers of social status and identity Europeans viewed as barbaric and savage. Even the Western-imposed term *scarification* has negative connotations, causing some Africans to reject it in favor of descriptors more in keeping with their own terminology such as *body marks*.

Whatever the name, this once common skin-cutting and embellishing technique took many forms. In some instances, a small cut was made in the skin to create a single, thin scar. At other times, rows of small cuts were applied to the skin in quick succession to create overall designs of varying lines and shapes. When the cuts were rubbed with materials such as soot, they became raised scars or keloids, a process sometimes referred to as cicatrization. In some cases, dark pigment was rubbed into a shallow cut in the skin to form skin pigmentation or tattoos.

Even more varied than the technologies were the reasons Africans applied such marks to their bodies. Some African peoples still practice cutting the skin as a way to provide physical or spiritual protection for the individual. The Baule of Côte d'Ivoire make small incisions at the middle of a person's chest, upper arm, wrist, or corners of the mouth and then infuse them with medicinal substances to protect the body from illness. Likewise, the Yoruba of Nigeria rub powerful herbal substances into the cut areas of an initiate's head as a way to enhance his or her spiritual power (*ashe*). In the 1960s, the Khoisan, a cattle-herding culture of southern Africa, were still rubbing charred meat and fat, turned to magic by the "Ceremony of the First Kill," into incisions on a boy's face, arms, back, and chest to give him the will to hunt, good sight, and accurate aim.

Because of the pain and permanency of scarification, it was an integral feature of many transition rites to mark one's maturation in a society at particular stages in the life cycle. The accumulated and irreversible markings of a lifetime would attest to the important events in a person's life and to the personal growth of the individual.

In general, women received more marks than men, particularly in agrarian societies. According to anthropologist James Vaughan, Margi women of northeastern Nigeria once received marks over much of their body in stages over several years before reaching puberty. Art historian Marla Berns has noted a similar tradition among the neighboring Ga'anda, whose women's bodies were heavily scarified to celebrate womanhood and the years leading to it. The daughters of families who could afford it would receive their marks (*hleeta*) over an eight-year period beginning at age six and ending at puberty, with each application drawing attention to different parts of the body (navel, head, arms, thighs, torso) at the appropriate stages in her maturation. She would receive her first marks (*hleexwira*, or scarification of the stomach) around the navel area to draw attention to the young girl's womb and reproductive abilities. Subsequent ones would be applied closer to the more erotic areas of her body such as her buttocks and upper thighs. By age fourteen, she would have received the final and most arduous series of marks (*hleenguy*, or scarification all over), paving the way for marriage and the bearing of children. So powerful were these bodily symbols of fertility and nurturing that hleeta-inspired designs were often painted on the walls of granaries and etched into the surfaces of ceramic pots in which the souls of the departed or spiritual beings would be housed.

Manhood could also be celebrated through scarification. According to British anthropologist Edward Evans-Pritchard, cattle-raising Nuer men in the Sudan and Ethiopia typically received six lines along the brow, each applied at a different stage, to gradually wean them from maternal ties and to prepare them for cattle herding. The first of the six marks would bear the name *woc dohl*, meaning "the wiping out of boyhood," and the second (*guec man diviel*) implied that the man could no longer plead to his mother for food but must sit quietly and endure the pain of hunger. Only after receiving all six marks were the young men able to participate with others in the hunt, own cattle, and assume the general responsibilities associated with adulthood.

In more hierarchical cultures, scarification had less to do with individual rites of passage than with lineage connections. Art historian Babatunde Lawal has argued that, for the Yoruba, a monarchical society, facial marks called *ila oju* were intended as indicators of clan identity. Even sculptures honoring locally

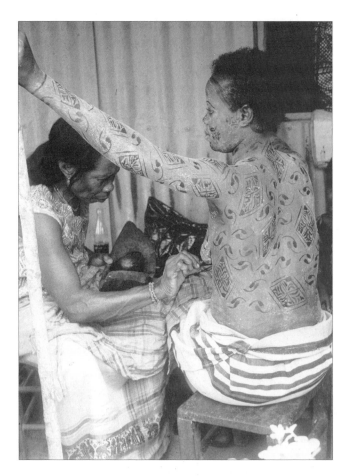

Ibani Ijo artist from Finima, Nigeria, paints *buruma* designs of the crab on the body of a woman at the end of her week of ritual seclusion during her coming of age (*iria*) ceremony in 1990. The camwood foundation will be washed off, leaving her with indigo patterns that will last for a week or longer. Photograph by Lisa Aronson.

worshipped deities would bear specific marks as a reminder of the loyalty that a clan member had to that deity. Yoruba facial marks were made up of several types: *gombo*, a quick succession of stitchlike marks; *keke*, a long, deeply cut V-shaped mark on the cheek and forehead; and *baamun*, a line that crosses the bridge of the nose. The gombo and baamun patterns are also used to identify regional origins as seen on the face of the late Chief Samuel Ladoke Akintola, whose marks identify him as coming from Ogbomosho in Oyo State. Like most Yoruba, he would have received his marks in early childhood to identify him as early as possible as coming from a particular region, thus protecting him from being kidnapped and taken elsewhere.

Africans also marked the body to make an individual visually attractive and to associate him or her with deeply held values and beliefs. The Baule once decorated an individual's forehead, neck, and abdomen with raised marks in the form of lines and dots. These are the same marks that Baule carvers would apply to spirit-related sculptures along with a host of other conventions of beauty, including frontal and erect posture, elaborate hairdos, and formidable thighs. Art historian Susan Vogel has argued in Rubin's *Marks of Civilization* that these aesthetic conventions impose on spiritual beings the same ideals and proper modes of behavior upheld by humans in a society "where correct rules are observed, where people are productive, and share a respect for traditional conventions of belief and behavior."

BODY PAINTING AND DYEING

Although Africans have now largely abandoned scarification, they continue to paint and dye their bodies to assert identities and mark ritual and celebratory occasions. Camwood, a reddish powder from a small African tree (African sandalwood), is one of several sources for red body paint. When mixed with water, the camwood powder turns into a reddish orange paste that can be applied on the body at critical junctures in people's lives. Nkwapinsu, the Margi woman described earlier, had been freshly covered with camwood (*yinsidu*) on the day that she first publicly showed her newborn daughter, a custom that has earned Margi women the title "the red women of Nigeria."

The use of ochre, another source of red pigment, seems to have few cultural boundaries and a long history in Africa. Traces of red ochre have been found at numerous archaeological sites throughout eastern and southern Africa, demonstrating that ochre was vital for daily and ritual use for at least twenty thousand years. Certain African groups from this broad geographic region continue to use ochre to paint their bodies red. The Himba, a pastoralist culture from Namibia, are still called "ochre people" because they continue to use it to cover their bodies. Young Maasai men of southern Kenya and northern Tanzania have earned a similar label because of the extensive use of ochre as body paint during the coming-of-age ceremony during which they achieve warrior status. Prior to this ritual transition, the young men cover their entire bodies, including uncut hair, with ochre. During the critical warrior-shaving ceremony (*eunoto*), the young man's mother shaves off his long lock of hair as a symbolic break from childhood, leaving him with a smooth, ochre-covered head (and body) that reminds people of his newly acquired status.

Henna dye has an appeal that goes well beyond Africa's borders. Derived from the Arabic word *hina*, it is commonly used by women in Islamized countries throughout the world. In Africa, henna body art is found throughout much of the northern half of the continent as well as in pockets along the Swahili coast and southern Africa. This dye or stain comes from a red pigment extracted from a tropical flowering plant of the *Lawsonia* family. Because of its particular molecular structure, it easily adheres to protein, making it an effective color on human skin, with the hands and feet being the areas most often decorated with it.

Although the resulting patterns vary from culture to culture, the stencil-like technique for applying them is about the same everywhere. It involves laboriously adhering cut pieces of adhesive tape to the skin surface, and then applying henna ink to the exposed spaces. Henna stains last up to a month, making it a visible reminder of the celebratory occasions that initially prompted its application, such as weddings, childbirth, and important Muslim holidays like Tabaski. So linked is henna to life-affirming events that the Berber of Morocco regard it as a symbol of the life cycle and fertility. They even use the four colors inherent in the henna application—green for the henna leaves and paste, black for the color when it is first applied, and red and yellow-orange as the stain fades—as the basis for a woman's elaborate wedding attire.

One of the most well-known body painting traditions is *uli* among the Igbo of Nigeria and its derivative, *buruma*, found among their southern neighbors the Ibani and Kalabari Ijo. The terms *uli* and *buruma* refer both to the painting tradition itself and to the plants and shrubs from which the required pigments are derived. Both traditions adorn a woman's body with blue designs during her rite of passage ceremony as a way to accentuate her curving shape and plump contours and to highlight her spiritual and social well-being.

Among the Ibani, Okrika, and Kalabari Ijo, the full-bodied woman is indeed highly cultivated. Young women undergoing their rite of passage (*iria*) must spend a designated period (at one time a year or more, but now just a week) in ritual seclusion during which she is fed large quantities of starchy, heavily oiled, and otherwise rich foods to fatten her so that her body mimics the fecund and well-fed water spirits who live in the surrounding ocean floor environment. The water-related image extends to the buruma designs, many of which are sea-related (for example, fish and crabs). British roller-printed textiles may have been the partial inspiration for the overall aesthetic of buruma, with its repetition of a single pattern covering the entire body.

Igbo uli has a rather different aesthetic and is more broadly based in its use. Uli places a greater emphasis on abstraction and on a play of large negative spaces. Moreover, the designs refer to items meaningful in Igbo culture, such as the wooden bowls that the Igbo use to serve kola nuts. And uli goes well beyond just adorning the bodies of women during their coming-of-age ceremony. It is also painted on the bodies of men and women who

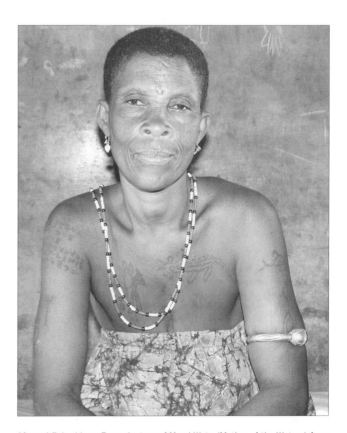

Aframsi Fukeshi, an Ewe priestess of Mami Wata (Mother of the Waters) from the town of Hatukope, Ghana, in 2005, wearing tattooed designs. These include a snake and a crocodile, thought to speak to the Vodun spirits, including the water deity to whom she is devoted. The words on her right upper arm remind her students that if they obey their Vodun spirits, good things will come. Photograph by Lisa Aronson.

have received titled status, on the walls of shrines and people's houses during celebratory occasions, and on the surfaces of Igbo sculpture and masks—all in an effort to bring the deeply rooted values associated with uli to these spirit-related entities.

One of the least permanent of body paints is a pigment derived from a white claylike mineral known as kaolin. Because of its association with the spirit realm, the white paint is frequently applied to the body to evoke or communicate with the spirits. The Mende of Sierre Leone use this white pigment, which they call *wuji*, to paint the faces and bodies of young girls at strategic moments during their initiation into the Sande society. Sande is a women's association found among many cultures of Côte d'Ivoire, Liberia, Sierra Leone, and Guinea that prepares and educates young girls about the expectations of female adulthood. It guides them on issues concerning sexuality, oversees the excision procedures that they must undergo, and teaches them the practical skills necessary for becoming good wives and mothers. It also provides knowledge about the world of spirits, whom, it is believed, Sande initiates ritually marry during their time in seclusion. The white claylike paint suggests the young girl's continued tie to the spirits as she transitions from seclusion to the village. As those ties are severed, the white paint is washed away and replaced with oil to make her skin glisten and to bring attention to her supple and curvaceous body as she prepares for marriage.

White clay is also the appropriate body paint for diviners to draw the attention of the spirits and assert their spiritual identity. A Kalabari Ijo diviner from the town of Buguma, Nigeria, paints areas of her body with white checkerboard designs evocative of powerful land spirit helpers known as *oru*. In ceremony, the tattooed Ewe priestess of Mami Wata (Mother of the Waters), Aframsi Fukeshi, covered her body with white paint and white cloth for the benefit of the Vodun spirits and their gaze. Vodun devotees regard the body as a receptacle through which the spirits are brought forth and honored. To avoid such visual codes would disrespect the spirits and severely compromise the Ewe's ability to serve them.

SHAPING THE BODY

Some African cultures have taken to shaping (or reshaping) areas of the body to achieve a certain ideal of beauty. Some of that shaping involves piercing certain areas with decorative motifs. In the past, young Senufo and Dogon girls would have their ear and chin areas pierced to be able to accommodate the wearing of decorative ornaments as they got older. Some Senufo women elders can still be seen wearing a small wooden lip plug, or *labret*. In the Dogon area, this plug would be several inches long, often causing viewers to misinterpret it as being a man's beard when depicted in sculptural form.

In many areas, the pliable earlobe is also pierced to accommodate large earringlike objects called *earplugs*. The earlobe is usually, but not always, pierced on young women as a marker of gender. Frank Jolles has noted that the Zulu of South Africa once performed a ceremony known as *qhumbuza* to mark the official piercing of the young woman's ears. Once the hole was sufficiently widened, they would insert disk-shaped ear spools. In the nineteenth century, the spools were made of stone or wood; by the 1920s, the Zulu began overlaying the wood spools with house paint, plastics, or linoleum that would bear colors and

patterns resembling glass beadwork also worn during a coming-of-age ceremony. In aggregate, these strikingly patterned elements would not only serve as markers of her social status and ethnic identity but, perhaps most importantly, aid in attracting male suitors.

The head received the most aesthetic attention throughout Africa because of its visibility combined with its symbolic importance. Art historians Mary Jo Arnoldi and Christine Mullin Kraemer have noted that most Africans regard the head as "the determinant of one's personal destiny, the seat of one's intelligence and spiritual power, and the marker of one's social identity," making it one of the primary areas of the body deserving aesthetic attention. Almost as soon as a Mende girl emerges from the womb, her mother begins rubbing her still-soft forehead to elongate and accentuate it. As the hair grows, it is appropriately shaved or tightly wound into braids to reveal the contours of the forehead. The enlarged forehead becomes an important focal point of beauty on Mende *sowei* masks that the young women witness as the exit from seclusion during their coming-of-age (*sande*) ceremonies.

During the early Colonial period, women of status among the Mangbetu of present-day Democratic Republic of the Congo shaped and elongated their heads and styled their hair accordingly to achieve an elongated aesthetic once considered by the Mangbetu to be the height of chic. Infants' foreheads would be bound by their mothers with braided strips of raffia to begin the shaping process. By young adulthood, girls would have the hair pulled back and tied into a bun, with the head then wrapped tightly with black string. To accentuate the shape even further, a round basketry halolike disk was attached to the top of the hairdo. Even while admiring the beauty and elegance of this transformation, the Belgian colonial government outlawed it for being barbaric and primitive, leaving only photographs and sculptures in which it is depicted as visual evidence that it was once practiced.

HAIR

As an extension of the head, hair is an important aesthetic medium and a social marker that Africans from ancient Egyptian times to the present have used to identify one's gender, age, social status, and profession. Hair can be one of the most visible of bodily arts, and the texture of most black African hair lends itself to braiding, sculpting, and shaving into desirable forms, making it a convenient medium to manipulate aesthetically. As a rule, many African children have their hair closely cropped until reaching young adulthood, leaving little more than pierced ears to differentiate girls from boys. As children mature, their hair is allowed to grow, and a young woman's hair, in particular, may be elaborately coiffed to celebrate her marriageable and childbearing status. Many of these elaborate hairdos are recorded in photographs and survive on sculpture, although often in an idealized way, sometimes long after the particular hairstyle has gone out of style. Women's hairdos are styled through any number of means, including elaborate braiding and sculpting with natural or fabricated materials. Women of many cultures—the Mende and Fante as two examples—donned elaborately structured wigs. Some cultures, such as the Yoruba, Igbo, and Ekoi, tended to emphasize height, whereas others such as the Luba, Baule, and Senufo placed more emphasis on extensions from the neck

This young Igbo woman in 1977 identified her hairdo, with its spiral-shaped projections, as *esam*, the Igbo word for "periwinkle," a small, spiral-shaped shell common to the delta region from whence she comes. At the same time, urbanized Yoruba were referring to it as the "sex act." Akwete, Nigeria. Photograph by Lisa Aronson.

and/or forehead. Either way, hair art has always been one of the most visually striking ways Africans used to transform and beautify women as they reach young adulthood.

Whereas elaborately coiffed hairdos evoke order and acculturation, disheveled and uncut hair suggests disorder and alienation from cultural norms. Spiritual diviners are known to let their hair grow into long locks as outward extensions of the spirits to which they are closely connected. The Yoruba believe that children born with thick and curly hair have close ties to the spirit realm and privileged powers to evoke them. The Ijebu Yoruba, in particular, believe that these curly hair projections resemble seashells of the type found in the surrounding rivers that dominate the Ijebu landscape, where the spirits are believed to reside.

Although hairdos change over time, they are always a vehicle for expressing cultural values and ideas, including prevailing social issues. Like printed textiles, hairdos function as a nonwritten symbolic system that individuals draw on to communicate popular themes. The Yoruba seem to have always viewed hairstyles as a potential means of communication, with various named styles triggering socially acceptable, or unacceptable, ideas. In the 1970s, men wore hairstyles bearing names associated with popular rock stars such as Chubby Checker or James Brown. Women's hairdos have commemorated important events, such as the end of the Biafran War or the construction of the Eko bridge that connected Lagos Island to the mainland. A study of hairstyles cross-culturally serves as a reminder that hairdos, like any body

art, take on localized meanings. For example, Yoruba women referred to hairdos with corkscrew projections popular in the 1970s as the "sex act." The same hairdo worn by Igbo women living near the Niger Delta was called *esam*, an Igbo name for an edible marine snail with a spiral-shaped shell.

AFRICAN BODY ARTS AND CHANGE

Just as the styles and meanings of body arts can vary from region to region, they forever evolve and change over time. Colonialism and the influence of Western values significantly compromised African body art practices. Europeans tended to regard certain African body arts as bizarre, if not a sign of their "primitive" nature. The documented and fairly common practice of filing or chipping teeth to a sharp point was viewed as supporting evidence by some that Africans were cannibals. Teeth were also filed flat or removed in some cultures. Europeans were critical of the nude, or partially nude, body and were quick to introduce textiles as a way to cover it. Essentially, the introduction of Western dress during the Colonial period subverted many forms of indigenous body art.

Significantly, it is through textile imports and European-inspired fashion shows that Africans have come to respond to the negative effects that the West has had on their traditional body arts. One man from the Bini culture of Nigeria used cloth as a way to revive tattoo traditions. Up to the period of colonialism, men and women tattooed their torso areas with vertical, blade-shaped lines (*iwu*) as a way to assert affiliation and respect for royalty. An individual without iwu was, in Edo terms, a savage individual. Neither men nor women could enter the palace of the king (*oba*), and men could not marry if they did not have the proper marks. Although iwu did not survive the Colonial period due to legislation, its designs were resurrected at a 1986 fashion show hosted in the king's palace, where a man showcased men's loose-fitting shirts appliquéd with iwu-like patterns. In essence, he used a Western-introduced form of attire—that is, the tailored garment—as a modernized and more acceptable form for preserving iwu.

Textiles and fashion shows also provided a venue for countering the modern African women's increasing preference for a thin body, an aesthetic that goes very much counter to that of their elders. One particular printed textile from the Côte d'Ivoire featuring traditional women's hairdos tells an interesting story about the effects of such diverging canons of beauty. The name of this cloth is "Hair of Aoulaba." The Baule word *aoulaba*—meaning "beautiful, large, full-figured woman"—was the name of a beauty pageant organized by Madame Thérèse Houphouët-Boigny, wife of the former president of Côte d'Ivoire, herself a large woman. She had organized the Aoulaba pageant to counter the recent Miss Côte d'Ivoire one, which extolled the slim, svelte body so popularized in Western media. In celebration of Madame Thérèse's call for more traditional standards of beauty, cloth manufacturers came up with a cloth called "Aoulaba," featuring abstract, curving designs suggestive of the traditional body aesthetic, with its more curvaceous shape. Soon to follow would be a cloth called "Hair of Aoulaba," featuring curving lines combined with rows of traditional women's hairdos. Examples such as these are testimony to the deeply engrained cultural values associated with certain body art traditions such that they would resurface in these new and modernized ways.

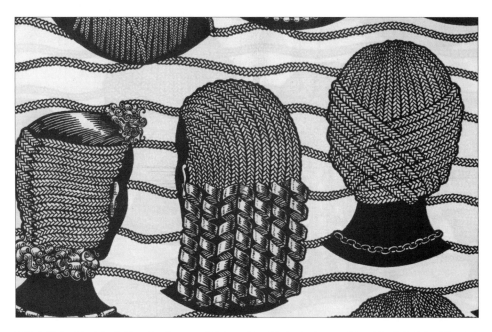

Called "Hair of Aoulaba," this printed cotton cloth from Côte d'Ivoire depicts traditional Baule hairdos. The cloth was intended to accompany another cloth titled "Aoulaba," meaning "full, curvy woman," created in response to the call by Madame Thérèse Houphouët-Boigny, first lady from 1960 to 1993, to celebrate a more traditional body-type aesthetic. Private collection. Photograph by David Seiler.

References and Further Reading

Arnoldi, Mary Jo, and Christine Mullin Kreamer. *Crowning Achievements: African Arts of Dressing the Head.* Los Angeles: UCLA Fowler Museum of Cultural History, 1995.

Barham, I.S. "Systematic Pigment Use in the Middle Pleistocene of South-Central Africa." *Current Anthropology* 31 (2002): 181–190.

Becker, Cynthia. "Amazigh Textiles and Dress in Morocco." *African Arts* 39 (Autumn 2006): 42–55, 95.

Evans-Pritchard, Edward Evan. "The Nuer: Age Sets." *Sudan Notes and Records* 19 (1936): 233–269.

Houlberg, Marilyn. "Social Hair: Tradition and Change in Yoruba Hairstyles in South-western Nigeria." In *Fabrics of Culture: The Anthropology of Clothing and Adornment*, edited by Justine M. Cordwell and Ronald A. Schwarz, 349–397. The Hague, The Netherlands: Mouton, 1979.

Jolles, Frank. "Zulu Earplugs: A Study in Transformation." *African Arts* 30, no. 2 (Spring 1997): 46–59, 94–95.

Lawal, Babatunde. *The Gelede Spectacle: Art, Gender, and Social Harmony in an African Culture.* Seattle: University of Washington Press, 1996.

Marshall, Lorne. "Marriage among !Kong Bushmen." *Africa* 29 (1959): 335–364.

Nevadomsky, Joseph, and Ekhaguosa Aisien. "The Clothing of Political Identity: Costume and Scarification in the Benin Kingdom." *African Arts* 28, no. 1 (Winter 1995): 62–73, 100.

Phillips, Ruth. "Masking in Mende Sande Society Initiation Rituals." *Africa* 48, no. 3 (1978): 265–277.

Rubin, Arnold, ed. *Marks of Civilization: Artistic Transformations of the Human Body.* Los Angeles: UCLA Museum of Cultural History, 1988.

Schildkrout, Enid. "Inscribing the Body." *Annual Review of Anthropology* 33 (October 2004): 319–344.

Schildkrout, Enid, and Curtis A. Keim. "The Art of Adornment." In *African Reflections: Art from Northeastern Zaire*, edited by Enid Schildkrout and Curtis A. Keim, 122–141. Seattle: University of Washington Press; New York: American Museum of Natural History, 1990.

Sieber, Roy, and Frank Herreman, eds. *Hair in African Art and Culture.* New York: The Museum for African Art, 2000.

Van Rippen, Bene. "Practices and Customs of the African Natives Involving Dental Procedure." *American Anthropologist* 20, no. 4 (October–December 1918): 461–463.

Willis, Liz. "Uli Painting and the Igbo World View." *African Arts* 23, no. 1 (November 1989): 62–67, 104.

Lisa Aronson

See also Archaeological Evidence; Headdresses and Hairdos; Egypt: Historical Dress; Morocco; Côte d'Ivoire; Yoruba in Nigeria and Diaspora; Igbo in Nigeria and Diaspora; Sierra Leone; Mangbetu Dress; Fang of Equatorial Guinea and Gabon.

Jewelry

The jewelry of the African continent is diverse, ornate, and creative. Part of dress practices, adorning the person is a holistic endeavor. Jewelry is not solely worn for the purpose of adornment; it is an important social marker and carries multivalent and complex meanings within each group. Jewelry is a commodity, a visible sign of wealth, and also reflects cultural attitudes toward dress systems. It reveals both aesthetic criteria and values and cultural norms and ideals, and it exhibits the innovative resourcefulness of the artisans, artists, and jewelers who manufacture it.

The more noteworthy jewelry traditions stand out for specific characteristics, which become emblematic of the group. They are also visually compelling. For example, North African Berber jewelry is known for flamboyant color and bulk. Equatorial necklaces and anklets emphasize large and heavy forms, often cast in single pieces. South and East African traditions, though vastly different, are significant for their profuse use of beads and intricate beadwork.

Men and women wear head ornaments, earrings, nose rings and plugs, labrets, necklaces, armlets, bracelets, rings, belts, anklets, and various accoutrements such as fibulae for their clothing. African jewelry is singular for the process of grouping items that coordinate with each other and for the assemblage and accumulation of different materials and objects chosen for color, motif, design, and volume. In Kenya, for example, Maasai women coordinate colorful beaded earflaps with a profusion of neck collars. Africans rarely put emphasis on a singular type or piece of jewelry.

Jewelry items are small and are easily carried across geographical and political boundaries. Contact and trade have had a decisive impact on African adornment. Indigenous African jewelers have manipulated and perpetuated Mediterranean, Asian, and Arabic aesthetic traditions for centuries, thus giving rise to new styles and designs across the continent. The ornate gold diadems decorated with precious stones and manufactured in Fez, Morocco, in the late nineteenth century are surely derived from a Byzantine or Andalusian tradition. With the exception of items such as these, however, the use of precious gems such as emeralds or diamonds is not widespread in Africa, except in contemporary designs.

In the twenty-first century, African jewelry is known and appreciated in the West, where it has acquired new meanings. The allure of the exotic renders it desirable and therefore valuable. African jewelers are espousing new ideas and seek to produce items that accommodate new fashions, a changing clientele, and the globalized world. For example, Hermès, the famous leather goods store in Paris, uses a workshop in Agadez, Niger, to produce exquisite, modern Tuareg jewelry for Hermès stores worldwide.

READING AFRICAN JEWELRY

Jewelry serves many functions in African societies. With respect to the human body, it emphasizes and complements culturally learned ideals of beauty. It accents, extends, and enhances gestures and movements of all sorts, especially on the arms, hands, and ankles. For example, young Wodaabe women display heavy brass anklets known as *jabo*, which make their hips swing when they walk. Jewelry makes noise, thus announcing a person's presence and punctuating his or her movements. During Baule dance contests in Côte d'Ivoire, members of youth associations wear ankle bells to create rhythm. Adornment has a tactile quality that is enhanced by use. Jewelry empowers individuals and defines their self-image. It embodies personal and private aspects of individuals' lives as well, such as love tokens and mementoes, and is frequently a precious heirloom passed down from one generation to another. In the Egyptian oasis of Siwa, for example, a woman's jewelry is her personal possession and is inherited by her daughters.

On special occasions, jewelry is a sign of prestige: individuals utilize it to indicate importance and social rank. Among the Asante, chiefs wear velvet headbands decorated with gold studs representing flowers and other motifs. These often allude to proverbs and symbolize power. They also place rings on every finger and wear beaded and cast bracelets, necklaces, and amulets. The *oba* (king) of Benin's regalia worn on formal occasions is equally striking. He is known to wear a crown, a coral shirt, and jewelry made of coral beads or *eshugu*. These represent the king's supreme authority and rank and symbolize his duty to protect the fertility of the land. Coral bead regalia is handed down from one generation to another. In Côte d'Ivoire, among the Lagoons cultures, important village dignitaries show their personal wealth and family heirlooms by displaying their gold ornaments during village festivals. Refined beads and pendants depicting animals and human heads display the artistry of the gold casters. Women sometimes wear the pendants in their hair, above the forehead and ears.

Jewelry also carries religious and magical symbolism and is used as a protection against evil. It is a repository of traditional knowledge as well. For example, among the Fali in Cameroon,

Enya *mokota*, or chief, wearing a leopard-tooth necklace, chains with medal pendants, beaded armlets, and a leopard-skin hat decorated with beads and feathers symbolizing his social office. Democratic Republic of Congo. Photograph by Eliot Elisofon, 1951. EEPA EECL 2134. Eliot Elisofon Photographic Archives, National Museum of African Art, Smithsonian Institution.

women wear lip plugs symbolizing the image of the frog—thought to have taught their female ancestors "the things" of women. Adornment often highlights parts of the body that have special meanings within the group. Among the Tuareg, the head is considered the place of knowledge and intelligence, and men take pride in arranging their indigo face veils, which they decorate with silver amulets.

Jewelry acts as a visual emblem through which individuals indicate their social status. Among the Tuareg, for example, the jewelry worn by a young girl, a married, a divorced, and an elderly woman differs and symbolizes specific life stages. Young girls wear lightweight necklaces with little pendants. When they marry, they wear heavier necklaces, bracelets, earrings, and rings. In the case of divorce, they wear no jewelry. As women age, they bestow their prized pieces on their daughters. Among stratified groups, men and women from different strata also favor and wear distinct kinds of jewelry forms. Words that name jewelry pieces, or the metals they are made of, also have cultural significance. The *Al Hamsa* (also known as the Hand of Fatima) refers to a pendant worn in North Africa and other areas, that symbolizes the number five and the hand, both considered to offer protection against the evil eye. Gold symbolizes power and wealth throughout Africa, but is also thought to incite greed and jealousy. Among North African Berbers, silver is thought to bear light and symbolizes purity and divine blessings.

When jewelry is traded from one place to another, its meanings and associations often change. In addition, to conform to cultural tastes and norms, jewelers also manipulate jewelry designs and forms. This explains, in part, why many similar items appear in different cultures. Nomadic cultures, whose art must be portable, are known to create very intricate and ornate jewelry items—a form of portable wealth. Thus, the intricate bracelets and headdresses worn by Berbers in Morocco and Algeria might mirror those worn by the Raishaida in Eritrea, but they will have different symbolic meanings and uses.

MATERIALS

Traditional materials used in the manufacture of African jewelry forms are not only the precious metals (gold and silver) and stones (stony coral) one associates with jewelry in the West but also include organic materials such as fibers, seeds, bark, roots, and animal products such as shells (seashells, eggshells, coconut shells, and land snail shells), coral, skin, bone, teeth, ivory, and horn. Minerals include precious and semiprecious stones, beads, and glass. Other metals such as nickel and tin and copper alloys such as brass and bronze are used.

Iron-bearing minerals have been found and used throughout Africa for centuries, though smelting is rare now because ready-made iron is available. Copper was mined in the Republic of the Congo, Zambia, northern areas of South Africa, and Niger. Copper is also imported from Europe and can be combined with tin, zinc, lead, and antimony. Gold is found in South Africa, Zimbabwe, Ghana, and other countries. Aluminum is found in Ghana, and tin is mined in Nigeria, the Democratic Republic of Congo, and South Africa. Finally, African metal casters often use scrap metal (usually nickel or aluminum) procured from old tools and car parts.

Silver, favored by the Tuareg and Ethiopians of the Highlands, is not found in Africa. Early sources of silver were foreign coins, brought in through trade networks. Merchants in the Gulf of Guinea introduced the Maria Theresa thaler in Africa in the nineteenth century. Since the coin was so popular, the English and the Italians continued to mint it for use in Africa, where it was in circulation until the 1960s. In the past twenty years, sterling silver has become more popular because tourists and foreigners prefer it when they buy silver jewelry. It is usually imported from Europe, where it is much less expensive than on the African markets.

Trade has had an important impact on jewelry materials and on techniques. For example, the important glass bead-making centers in Egypt used aesthetic systems originating in earlier Mediterranean cultural traditions. In the seventh century C.E., Arabs began to trade in brass, cloth, stone, and Baltic amber in exchange for coral, gold, ivory, spices, and slaves. In the fifteenth century, West African trade began with European explorers. They brought Venetian glass beads and Bohemian glass to exchange for incense, ivory, timber, and other items. These foreign items were incorporated into many African jewelry forms. The value attached to beads and other materials also turns jewelry into a commodity.

Bozo woman near Mopti, Mali, ca. 1970. The women favor these four-lobed gold earrings known as *kwotene lange*, which are inherited from their mothers or received as gifts from their husbands. Photograph by Eliot Elisofon, 1970. EEPA EECL 2584. Eliot Elisofon Photographic Archives, National Museum of African Art, Smithsonian Institution.

Beads have always been an important element in the manufacture of jewelry. Glass and agate beads were traded directly from India to East and South Africa at an early date through Arab merchants. These beads were known as monsoon beads, because ships following the monsoon trade winds in both directions brought them. In the 1900s, the trade of agate stones came into the hands of the gem industry at Idar-Oberstein, Germany. The industry used artificially dyed gray agates from Brazil, which quickly rendered the trade with India uncompetitive. Red, triangular *mekkawi* stones (the name probably refers to Mecca, and they are decorated with star and crescent moon designs) are still popular items among pilgrims returning from the hajj. In addition, various shells (cowries), ostrich eggshell beads, Venetian millefiore beads, Bodom (Krobo) beads from Ghana, blue aggrey beads, chevron beads, and copal are also used. Today's bead market includes colored glass beads, which imitate semiprecious stones such as jade and coral, and beads made from bottles.

NOTEWORTHY JEWELRY TRADITIONS

Early pieces illustrate the importance and the consistent presence of adornment in African cultures. Rock engravings and paintings from the first millennium B.C.E. in the Sahara desert regions of Algeria, Libya, and Niger depict individuals dressed and adorned in ritual attire.

The Nile Valley tombs in Luxor, Egypt, have yielded beautiful jewelry and exquisite reliefs portraying individuals wearing all types of adornment and ceremonial dress. Ancient Egyptian jewelry such as headdresses, collars, girdles, belts, and bracelets were manufactured in gold, silver, copper, semi precious stones (such as carnelian, amethyst, peridot, turquoise, and lapis lazuli), and organic and animal materials. Egyptians put more emphasis on color, which held symbolic virtues (for example, green referred to fertility and lapis to joy and delight), and amuletic powers than on the actual value of the metals or stones.

Nok heads from Nigeria dated from approximately 800 B.C.E. to 200 C.E. are adorned with elegant hairstyles, braids, and forehead pendants. Cast brass heads from the kingdom of Benin from the fifteenth to sixteenth centuries represent the Queen Mother wearing an elongated conical headdress made of coral beads, earrings, and necklaces symbolizing her rank and prestige. The bust of Oni Lafogido from Ife, Nigeria, dated between the thirteenth and fifteenth centuries, wears a beaded crown embellished with a frontal crest and elaborate necklaces, collars, and bracelets.

North African Berber women's jewelry is generally characterized by flamboyant bulk and vivid enameled colors such as blue, yellow, and green set off by coral beads and pendants. The pieces are accumulative constructions made of silver and gold. Their typology spans from diadems to rings, necklaces, armlets, and fibulae. The presence of geometric form and decorations and floral designs renders this aesthetic similar to Islamic jewelry forms.

Saharan nomads such as the Tuareg are known for their proud demeanor and for their lavish use of intricate and elaborate silver jewelry styles. Women don their finest pieces for weddings and ceremonies. These are primarily geometric forms with finely engraved motifs that accentuate the head, the arms, and the hands. Men among the pastoral Wodaabe attach great importance to physical beauty and emphasize this with their complex and innovative jewelry ensembles. They cover their braids with rounded brass plaques and cowry shells; wear glass bead necklaces and

amulets in their headdresses; and decorate their embroidered shirts with items such as mirrors, suitcase locks, and brass pendants and whistles.

Equatorial and West African jewelry traditions are enriched by the use of organic materials such as fiber, horn, and leather and by heavy and beautifully cast ornaments made of brass and more precious metals such as silver and gold. Mangbetu elders in the Democratic Republic of the Congo wear necklaces of leopard teeth to indicate their rank. The Benin, Yoruba, Asante, and Cameroon kingdoms are known for their intricate beaded necklaces produced by specialized craftsmen. The oba of Benin supported a bronze caster's guild and encouraged specialists to produce objects of great delicacy and sophistication.

The Akan, Baule, Fulani, and Wolof peoples of West Africa have produced gold jewelry that is distinguished for its superior craftsmanship and beauty. Fulani women in southern Mali favor very large twisted gold earrings and biconal pendants. Wolof women in Senegal consider their jewelry a sign of wealth and prestige. They wear necklaces, earrings, throat ornaments, brooches, pendants, and chains. The jewelry is distinguished by the use of filigree, and forms often imitate European ones such as butterflies. Women also wear clusters of pear-shaped head ornaments decorated with granulation. Akan gold jewelry is worn for

A woman of the Ouled-Naïls people, Algeria, wearing an embroidered dress, coin necklaces, bracelets, a diadem, and temple ornaments, ca. 1905. EEPA Postcard Collection, EEPA AE 1995-0020-54. Eliot Elisofon Photographic Archives, National Museum of African Art, Smithsonian Institution.

festivals and ceremonial functions and includes rings, necklaces, bracelets, and pectorals. Baule jewelry from Côte d'Ivoire displays the sophistication of lost-wax techniques. Pendant forms and especially beads are a dominant form. Pendants are rectangles, tubes, disks, or biconal shapes.

Ethiopian jewelry styles from the Highlands are distinguished by a predominant use of silver. Regional styles vary—the more simple being in the central and southern areas and the more ornate items (decorated with silver wire and beads) in the north. Ethiopian silver crosses (like their Tuareg counterparts) are often named after the regions they come from. Early designs were similar to Greek or Roman examples, and more recent crosses display openwork motifs. The addition of hinges to the hanging loops is thought to be influenced by nineteenth-century European examples.

Like jewelry everywhere, East and South African jewelry forms emphasize and complement the human body. Among Samburu and Turkana women, the neck is emphasized with multiple monochrome bead necklaces. The Zulu and Ndebele groups in Southern Africa make ample use of beads to create beautiful aprons, waist belts, and bracelets embellished with geometric designs. The designs and colors convey messages. Xhosa and Zulu beaded necklaces include small rectangular beaded panels considered love letters, and encoded messages are transmitted through color. White, for example, symbolizes the purity of love.

AFRICAN JEWELRY FORMS

As mentioned earlier, one of the most distinctive characteristics of African jewelry is the process of ensembling—mixing and matching and creating eclectic assemblages of pieces to fashion a visually striking whole. Classical ensembles worn by women typically include earrings, a necklace, bracelets, and rings. These items do not necessarily match in form and design but are meant to be worn together. Men usually wear bracelets and rings and talismans around their necks or on their arms. As individuals pass through different life stages, they earn the rights to use certain pieces. As they grow older, they divest themselves of their objects and pass them on to daughters and sons.

On a daily basis, women adorn themselves with earrings and a necklace or ring, and they tend to use less adornment on a daily basis than for profuse displays during coming-of-age ceremonies, weddings, ritual celebrations, and festivals. It is at such events that men, women, and children wear all of their finest pieces, thus offering a stunning visual image. These practices of public display often confer unity and pride upon individuals and a sense of ethnic identity.

HEADDRESSES AND HAIR ORNAMENTS

Headdresses and hair ornaments emphasize the head. These ornaments can be a simple leather headband made of ostrich eggshell worn by women in Namibia, or they can be the complicated metal constructions displayed by young Berber women in Algeria at wedding ceremonies. These frame the head and are attached into the hair. Ornaments are sometimes added to hairstyles. Songhay women in Timbuktu and Gao, Mali, don the *zoumbo*, a wool disk at the front of their hairdos, recalling the customary hairstyles displayed by members of the imperial court. Unmarried Fulani women in Mali first wear skullcaps made of

amber or copal beads. Once married, they often decorate their hair with large copal beads that run along the center of the head and down each side. The Tukulor (sedentary Fulani) and Wolof in Senegal prize massive pear-shaped ornaments, or *khoulalat*, arranged in clusters of two or three above their ears. During ceremonies, young Maasai warriors in Kenya put on ostrich-feather headdresses, which surround their faces to communicate that they have yet to kill a lion. Generally, Berber headdresses from North Africa are distinguished by the accumulative quality of the pieces: some are made with silver coins joined with chains, others are made with elaborate triangular and rectangular elements decorated with enameled designs and coral beads, which represent life and blood. Because they frame the face and are hooked into the hair above the ears, the headdresses follow the wearer's body movements. Drawa women in the Draa Valley of Morocco decorate and cover their two front braids with large silver and stone rings, and young Bella women in Niger braid glass ornaments known as *talhakimt* into their hairstyles. In the Democratic Republic of Congo, Mangbetu men and women sport exquisitely carved ivory hairpins with elongated stems decorated with circles, triangles, and other decorative shapes reminiscent of finials.

EARRINGS

Earrings are worn by both women and men in the African continent and often symbolize age, grade, or political rank. Married Maasai women in Kenya use long, beaded earflaps to announce their marital status, and Maasai men display earplugs. Fulani women in Mali wear massive twisted gold earrings, or *kwotene lange*, made by Fulani goldsmiths. These are either inherited from their mothers or are gifts from husbands. The earrings typically have four lobes, and the ends of the hoops are wrapped in red thread to protect the ears and to create a color contrast with the gold. Straw examples reproducing these earrings were already recorded in the 1900s, and in the 1980s, yellow wire copies were being manufactured in Bamako, Mali. Berber women in Tiznit, Morocco, prize their heavy hoops decorated with enameled designs and dangles, which are attached to the hair because of their weight. Equally heavy are the forged earrings, or *tizabaten*, preferred by Tuareg women in Niger. These are part of their dowry and are decorated with stamped polyhedral ends. Bilena women of all ages in Keren, Eritrea, use very thin and flattened gold hoops with engraved geometric designs. Swahili women on Lamu Island adorn their ears with gold or silver spools decorated with exquisite geometric and appliqué decorations. Gold ear clips, shaped like an earlobe and having up to twelve little hoops, are worn by the Sarakole women in Senegal. In other areas, such as Lamu Island, Kenya, women wear small hoops in their earlobes.

NOSE AND LIP ORNAMENTS

Nose ornaments such as simple rings or small pendants are common among the Wodaabe in Niger and the Pokot in Kenya. Dogon women wear lip rings symbolizing the shuttle and bobbin used in the mythical weaving of speech. Large lip plates or labrets worn by the Sara women in the Republic of Chad symbolize beauty, though it has been reported they were also used as a foil, to avoid slave traders. The Kirdi women in Cameroon use smaller lip plugs to protect themselves from danger and supernatural forces. Among the Kichepo peoples of southeast Sudan,

A Turkana woman in Wamba, Kenya, 1973. She wears earrings, a coiled arm-let, and beaded necklaces that emphasize the neck. Among these East African nomads, jewelry is considered moveable wealth. Photograph by Herbert M. Cole, 1973. EEPA 2000-080229. Herbert M. Cole Collection, Eliot Elisofon Photographic Archives, National Museum of African Art, Smithsonian Institution.

triangular-shaped lip plates are put on in the presence of hus-bands and are a sign of beauty. Surma women, in the Omo Valley in Ethiopia, display terra-cotta lip plugs before they marry. The diameter of the plug indicates the amount of cattle necessary for the dowry.

NECKLACES

Necklaces are made from an assemblage of different elements such as chains and central pendants, amulet cases, and an as-sortment of beads. Some necklaces are named after their central pendants such as the *khomessa* worn by Tuareg women in Niger. Shamans in South Africa don striking assemblage necklaces that include vertebrae, tortoiseshell, teeth, little beaded amulets, seeds, and pieces of shell—all tools of their trade and items that enable them to face the natural elements. Wodaabe brides in Niger also use long necklaces made of small leather pouches and beads as a form of protection. In East Africa, where aesthetic emphasis is put on the neck because it separates the head from the heart, young Samburu women in Kenya place one beaded necklace over another, from their shoulders up to their chins, to communicate

their marriageable status. Maasai women in Kenya shave their heads to emphasize their colorful beaded necklaces. Among East African nomads such as the Maasai, Turkana, and Samburu, where portability governs all aspects of their lives, beaded jewelry represents moveable wealth.

In Angola, Chokwe chiefs sport necklaces, or *cimba*, made with a central cone shell pendant that symbolizes the moon. Among the Bamun in Cameroon, the Bateke in Gabon, and the Teke in the Democratic Republic of Congo, heavy cast-brass col-lars or neck rings decorated with geometric designs are associated with wealth and prestige. Once emblems of chiefs, they became a form of currency when women wore them. In Harer, Soma-lia, great prestige and wealth is associated with amber and copal beads, which are thought to have healing powers and are part of a woman's dowry. These large and heavy necklaces may be deco-rated with delicately repoussé centerpieces of gold or silver—often amulet cases and, in some instances, large ornate pectoral pendants augmented with chains and bells.

Amber and copal necklaces are also found among the Fulani in Mali and Berber groups in Morocco and Algeria, where they are embellished with silver baubles and pendants. Beads made with ambergris, musk, and rose petals are prepared by young Berber brides in Morocco and interspersed with other beads to create scented necklaces. Berber women from Tiznit, Morocco, favor necklaces made of disk pendants engraved with spiral decorations symbolizing eternity. The simplicity of woven grass necklaces made by the Kikuyu in Kenya is countered by the brilliance of Tukulor, Akan, and Baule gold. In Ghana, dancers wear gold breastplate ornaments at funerals. The Baule create intricate pendants and masks that are strung together to create necklaces. Tukulor women in Mali prize their heirloom biconi-cal bead pendants, or *corval*, as centerpieces on gold chain neck-laces. In Namibia, it is customary for married Himba women to don iron and shell dorsal weights as well as ostrich eggshell buttons.

PENDANTS AND PECTORAL ORNAMENTS

Pendants and pectoral ornaments can be viewed separately from necklaces. Pectoral ornaments are distinguished by their large size, which confers visual impact. One of the most famous items to have been recovered from a gravesite near Saint Louis, Sen-egal, is the Rao Pectoral. Thought to have been manufactured as early as the fourteenth century C.E., it is a large disk mea-suring eighteen centimeters (seven inches) in diameter, made of twenty-two-karat gold, displaying exquisite filigree, repoussé, and granulation designs and techniques. In Angola and parts of Namibia, Cuanhama brides are presented with ivory button-shaped pendants that they sometimes attach to their clothing or to belts. Owning many of these pendants confers respect in the eyes of beholders. Among the Baule in Côte d'Ivoire, finely cast round or rectangular gold pendants were the purview of dignitaries. The rectangular pendants, or *srala*, symbolize the chief. The Baule also manufactured little bronze mask pen-dants, intended to depict enemies killed in battle. Some pen-dants represent a person's valor, and elected Maasai warriors in Kenya adorn themselves with coiled-brass chest pendants that symbolize their character. In the oasis of Siwa, in the western Egyptian desert, young women of marriageable age wear very large silver "virginity disks" decorated with incised geometric

A sixteenth-century ivory armlet such as was worn by the Yoruba peoples, Owo region, Nigeria. This elaborate armlet highlights the virtuosity of Owo-Yoruba ivory carvers. It displays kneeling hunchbacks, monkeys, crocodiles, and mudfish. Gift of Walt Disney World Co., a subsidiary of The Walt Disney Company. 2005-6-8. Photograph by Franko Khoury. National Museum of African Art, Smithsonian Institution.

motifs. Among the Lobi in Burkina Faso, high-ranking men use an elongated ivory pendant known as the "elephant flute" to proclaim their status.

One of the more widespread and recognized pendant styles is the cross. West African jewelers manufacture the graceful *Croix du Sud*, which are cast and elaborated with intricate filigree decorations. The Coptic crosses manufactured in the Ethiopian Highlands refer to specific churches such as Lalibella, Gonder, and Aksum. In addition, their elegant openwork designs allow individuals to recognize the origins of the crosses. Crosses made by the Tuareg in Niger, Algeria, Mali, and other neighboring countries are cast and engraved with geometric patterns. As a result of colonial expansion, crosses were given place names such as Agadez, Ingall, or Tahoua—all cities in Niger. Crosses continue to have wide cross-cultural appeal both in Africa and beyond.

AMULETS

Some jewelry functions primarily in apotropaic fashion. For example, the Merina aristocracy in Madagascar use a charm case called *mohara*, which contains objects such as nails, coins, and bones and whose bottom section displays prongs thought to represent crocodile teeth. These charms are said to have protective qualities and are used to perform magic. African amulets range from ornate and intricately decorated amulet cases made of silver and other metals and leather to silver pendant charms such as the Hand of Fatima to stones and animal horns strung on leather cords.

BRACELETS AND ARMLETS

Bracelets enhance the hands, fingers, wrists, and upper arms. They also can be used as weapons. Wrist knives worn by Toposa men in the Sudan are oval plates lined with leather around the central opening. Two blades, which project upward, are the knife section. The Aït Atta Berber women in Morocco wear cast bracelets surrounded by long pointed spikes. Less lethal in appearance are the stone bracelets once sported by Algerian Tuareg men on their upper arms, thought to ward off enemy blows. Rare today, these bracelets were presented to young men by their fathers when they came of age. Bracelets are either cast, forged, or carved and are made of various metals, leather, or ivory. In Kenya, Samburu men and women don coiled brass armbands on their forearms and upper arms. The Dinka people of the Sudan wear ivory bracelets decorated with little circles. When broken, they are repaired with wire or metal pins because they are highly valued. The ivory bracelets manufactured by the Songhay of the Democratic Republic of Congo are decorated with metal studs or small dots and can be quite large (fourteen and a half centimeters [six inches] in diameter). These were used during religious ceremonies to beget male heirs.

Brass bracelets from Owo in Nigeria are decorated with animals and human figures and are used by the Yoruba during ritual meetings of the Ogboni cult. Ivory cylindrical bracelets from the same area display highly refined carvings depicting figures on horseback and are a sign of power and wealth. Dogon priests in Mali wear twisted iron bracelets during rituals. The Senufo of

Côte d'Ivoire have a long tradition of bronze jewelry. Their brace-lets are often decorated with representations of stylized pythons, believed to be a medium between diviners and the spiritual world. Oromo bracelets in the Ethiopian Highlands are long silver cylin-ders decorated with linear designs and pin closures and are often worn in pairs. Their decorative designs vary from one region to another. Large wooden archer's bracelets, or *igitembe*, donned by Tutsi noblemen in Burundi are often decorated with metal inlay designs. The Fayoum area and other Egyptian oases such as Siwa display distinctive jewelry traditions. Bracelets are usually forged out of solid silver and decorated with floral and geometric de-signs. In northern Ghana, Kasena women consider their elon-gated ivory armlets, made from lateral sections of elephant tusks, a sign of prosperity. Silver bracelets decorated with wooden inlay, silver ball studs, and engraved motifs exhibit refined techniques mastered by Mauritanian jewelers.

RINGS

Women and men wear rings in myriad shapes and forms. Mostly these are cast or forged in silver, brass, or gold. Among the Senufo and the Lobi in Côte d'Ivoire and among the Bobo in Burkina Faso, there is a predilection for rings depicting animals. Bobo rings often display tickbirds, valued for their protective relation-ship with cattle. Senufo rings often represent the chameleon, snake, turtle, crocodile, and hornbill, considered primordial ani-mals. The Tiv in Nigeria have created ingenious snuff rings that have a flat top portion, thus enabling the wearer to offer snuff to another person. The Tuareg, the Moors, and other groups in the savanna don heavy forged silver rings. These are decorated with incised geometric motifs, and some have open-cut designs. Tuareg women wear rattle rings, which are domed constructions that hold seeds and make noise when women dance. Dinka men in the Sudan indicate their status with beautiful ivory rings that resemble bull's horns.

ANKLETS

Often part of a dowry and symbols of status, anklets are heavy and sometimes cast in solid metal—generally brass or silver. Dan anklets are large with rounded shapes and may be decorated with pierced circle designs. The heaviest anklets (some weigh up to six kilograms [thirteen pounds]) are those worn by Kru women in Liberia. These are rounded bell shapes and symbolize status. An-klets donned by Fang women in Gabon are made to resemble a stepladder and are striking because of their sculptural and three-dimensional qualities. Igbo women in Nigeria adorn themselves with *ogba* anklets. These have earned some popularity in the literature because of their very large diameter (they resemble a large plate with a central cylinder) and because women roll their hips and alter their gait when wearing them. Among the Bobo in Burkina Faso, anklets incorporate representations of ancestor heads in an effort to communicate with them and receive their protection. Mauritanian anklets are forged and include a central rectangular plaque decorated with ball studs and engraved mo-tifs. The Rashaida in Eritrea prize heavily decorated anklets, in keeping with Arab and Indian influences, a result of centuries of trade.

CLOTHING ACCOUTREMENTS

Women in Morocco, Algeria, and Tunisia use pins and fibulae to se-cure their cloaks. Moroccan examples are massive, often decorated with enameled motifs, and their triangular shape represents the female shape. Among Tuareg nomads, women use counterweights to secure their veils. These are heavy and intricately decorated with pierced and engraved motifs and copper additions. These weights are a larger version of the keys women use to close leather bags.

FOREIGN ELEMENTS IN AFRICAN JEWELRY

Over centuries, jewelry that came from European, Middle Eastern, and Asian countries was readapted for use among African ethnic groups. For example, Akan gold necklaces with central pendants depicting delicate filigree birds and hearts were inspired by Vic-torian jewelry from England. Others items are signet rings, ball-tip bracelets and bracelets with love knots, hair combs, teething rattles, and watches. The assemblage so typical of African jewelry forms has encouraged jewelers to create necklaces mixing classical African elements (amulets, for example) with Western items. But-tons, coins, zippers, and other eclectic elements are popular addi-tions when creating new designs. The Wodaabe, for example, use mirrors, whistles, chains, safety pins, and keys to decorate their shirts, head dresses, and necklaces. The Baule of Côte d'Ivoire cre-ated gold spectacles with thin wire mesh instead of lenses, which were very popular in West African countries in the 1970s.

AFRICAN JEWELRY IN THE TWENTY-FIRST CENTURY

Classical African jewelry forms have evolved in diverse ways in the twenty-first century. In African countries, many traditional

An anklet made of copper alloy, worn by the Ekonda peoples, Democratic Re-public of the Congo, nineteenth–twentieth centuries. Anklets such as these were not only used as jewelry but also represented wealth. Gift of Tom Joyce and museum purchase with funds donated by Carl Jennings. 2002-10-41. Photograph by Franko Khoury. National Museum of African Art, Smithsonian Institution.

pieces of adornment are still manufactured; individuals want to own them because they represent their cultural identity. Jewelers are also accommodating changing tastes and fashions. Among the Tuareg, for example, women who once preferred silver now commission modern gold jewelry. It is fashionable and is a stable form of investment. In parallel, this has also encouraged some Tuareg jewelers—once principally silver specialists—to work with gold.

Materials have changed as well. Contemporary jewelry findings include clasps, earring clips, catches, joints and pin stems for brooches, spring rings, and round jump rings for necklaces and metal or plastic wire. These, as well as the small zip-lock bags used to store finished items, are all imported from Europe.

The innovation and creativity of African jewelry designers has earned them lucrative businesses in their countries and a margin of success in international arenas. Many individuals strive to create innovative pieces, and some—such as Tuareg jeweler Moussa Albaka—have won recognition at international jewelry competitions. These pieces retain traditional decorative motifs, yet incorporate new materials, techniques, and approaches to form. Jewelers also travel abroad, where they are receptive to different ideas and designs, which they then adapt to fit their own cultural aesthetic. Today, many jewelers enjoy the renown and reputations accorded to emerging artists and are no longer anonymous creators.

In the twenty-first century, a growing number of African jewelry designers are coming to the fore. Senegalese fashion designer Oumou Sy creates dramatic jewelry for her collections. One ensemble included adornment in the form of CDs. In 2000, she designed a halter dress decorated with enlarged Tuareg cross elements. The Cameroon designer Anggy Haif exhibited striking bracelets made of calabashes in the 2003 FIMA (Festival International de la Mode Africaine) festival held near Niamey in Niger. Aya Konan, from Côte d'Ivoire, has created a line of jewelry called Makeda, inspired by Akan and Asante forms. Her necklaces are composite constructions made of round pendants. The Nigerian fashion designer Alphadi has also commissioned Tuareg smiths in Niamey, Niger, to create striking engraved breastplates for his evening dresses. Malagasy jewelry designers such as Silvia Andrianaivo and A-Ni-Ra both create rings, necklaces, and bracelets with local materials such as seeds, horn, wood, metals and semi-precious stones. Their sculpted creations reflect their attachment to Malagasy culture and traditions.

Mickaël Kra is an Ivorian jewelry designer who was born in France and raised in Abidjan before attending Parsons School of Design in New York City. Kra's work is characterized by flowing bead necklaces, waist belts, and sophisticated headdresses. His jewelry has a sculptural quality, and he blends precious metals with semiprecious stones. He uses Baule beads and motifs and Tuareg crosses to create necklaces that enhance clothing. He has designed items for African fashion designers such as Katouchka and Alphadi and for French designers such as Paco Rabanne and Louis Féraud. Kra participated in a development project entitled Pearls of the Kalahari with San bead makers, who create necklaces, belts, and bracelets with ostrich eggshells. Kra blends his African aesthetics and heritage with European marketing systems.

African jewelers continue to produce exquisite pieces of jewelry for African patrons and lovely pieces for a foreign clientele while remaining true to their cultural aesthetic codes. They have added new materials to their repertoire and continue to be extraordinarily creative and inventive. Considering the beauty of African jewelry forms and the originality of their creators, new internationally recognized African designers will doubtless be recognized in the years to come.

References and Further Reading

Andrews, Carol. *Ancient Egyptian Jewelry*. New York: Harry N. Abrams, 1997.

Becker, Cynthia, and France Borel. *The Splendor of Ethnic Jewelry*. New York: Harry N. Abrams, 1994.

Braun, Annette, Esther Kamatari, Adam Levon, Sandra Tjitendero, and Francine Vormese. *Mickaël Kra. Jewellery between Paris Glamour and African Tradition*. Stuttgart, Germany: Arnoldsche Art Publishers, 2006.

Brincard, Marie Thérèse, ed. *Beauty by Design: The Aesthetics of African Adornment*. New York: African American Institute, 1984.

Dubin, Lois Sherr. *The History of Beads*. New York: Harry N. Abrams, 1987.

Fisher, Angela. *Africa Adorned*. New York: Harry N. Abrams, 1984.

Garrard, Timothy. *Gold of Africa. Jewellery and Ornaments from Ghana, Côte d'Ivoire, Mali and Senegal in the Collection of the Barbier-Mueller Museum*. Geneva, Switzerland: Barbier-Mueller Museum; Munich: Prestel, 1989.

Herbert, Eugenia. *Red Gold of Africa*. Madison: University of Wisconsin Press, 1984.

Linden Museum. *Schmuck aus Nord Afrika*. Stuttgart, Germany: Linden Museum fur Volkerkunde, 1976.

Mack, John, ed. *Ethnic Jewelry*. New York: Harry N. Abrams, 1988.

"Mickaël Kra, Sylvia Andrianaivo and A-Ni-Ra." *Revue Noire. Special Mode: African Fashion*, no. 27 (December 1997): 96–103.

Rabaté, Jacques, and Marie-Rose Rabate. *Bijoux du Maroc*. Aix-en-Provence, France: Edisud, 1996.

Ross, Doran, ed. *Elephant. The Animal and Its Ivory in African Culture*. Los Angeles: Fowler Museum of Cultural History, University of California, Los Angeles, 1992.

Ross, Doran. *Gold of the Akan from the Glassell Collection*. Houston, TX: Museum of Fine Arts, 2002.

Sieber, Roy. *African Textiles and Decorative Arts*. New York: Museum of Modern Art, 1972.

Silverman, Raymond A., ed. *Ethiopia Traditions of Creativity*. East Lansing: Michigan State University Museum; Seattle: University of Washington Press, 1999.

Kristyne Loughran

See also Headdresses and Hairdos; Beads and Beadwork; Footwear; Morocco; Ghana; Niger; Kenya; Nguni, Zulu, and Xhosa Dress and Beadwork.

Headdresses and Hairdos

- The Head in the African Imagination
- Hats and Hairstyles: More Than a Matter of Taste
- African Headwear: A Communication System

African headwear has been an important feature of everyday attire and ceremonial display in Africa from ancient times to the present. Hats and hairstyles can mark or celebrate changes in the life cycle; denote a person's status in the community; signal membership in a religious or initiation society; designate key participants at rituals and festivals; or identify political and religious leaders and occupational specialists such as warriors, hunters, priests, and musicians. Within the same society, people often share similar notions of social propriety, custom, and beauty, and these shared notions dictate a variety of acceptable modes of decorating the head.

Headwear can be modest and formally restrained, encircling the head and emphasizing its shape. Hats designed for daily wear speak to pragmatic solutions to the problem of physical comfort. They are designed to protect the wearer from the elements, providing shade and serving as effective rain gear when needed. Besides their practical functions, everyday headwear serves to satisfy the community's notion of decorum and modesty. It can also stand as a statement of ethnic or religious affiliation. The choice of everyday hat or hairstyle, while modest, may also serve as a vehicle through which a man or woman expresses a personal aesthetic or ideas about fashion and modernity. For example, among the Lesotho in southern Africa, farmers wear modest woven conical fiber hats to protect them from the sun and rain. At the 1984 Olympic Games in Los Angeles, however, the Lesotho team wore the farmer's hat as part of their national costume in the Parade of Athletes. In this global context, the everyday farmer's hat was transformed into a symbol of national identity.

Hats and hairstyles can also be complex and voluminous, dramatically calling attention to the head, visually altering its shape, and extending it vertically and laterally into the surrounding space. Ceremonial hats and the materials that are used to fashion them are usually rich in cultural symbolism. Many ceremonial hats and hairstyles are the prerogative of particular groups or specific offices. Hunters and traditional healers throughout much of West Africa often wear distinctive cloth or leather caps on which they attach multiple amulets, including leather pouches, animal horns, and animal skins. The amulets are material signs of their chosen professions, and they function to protect these specialists from potentially harmful physical and spiritual forces.

THE HEAD IN THE AFRICAN IMAGINATION

Throughout Africa, people devote a great deal of thought and attention to the human body. High and center, the head has always been an ideal site for aesthetic and symbolic elaboration. In the thought and moral imagination of many African societies, the head plays a central role in beliefs about the person. Among the Yoruba of Nigeria, the head is the site of *ori*, personal destiny. The physical head, visible to the world, surrounds the "inner head," and the physical head becomes the focus of elaboration through ritual. Among the Kaguru of Tanzania, the head connects persons both to birth and ultimately to the land of the dead. Among the Kalabari Ijaw of Nigeria, the head—and specifically the forehead—is the locus for *teme*, the spirit that controls a person's behavior. For the Tabwa of the Democratic Republic of Congo, the center of the forehead is regarded as the seat of wisdom, prophecy, and dreams. African men and women regularly use headwear and hairstyles to express deeply held cultural beliefs and values. Dressing the head transforms the head and, by extension, the natural body into a wholly cultural entity.

HATS AND HAIRSTYLES: MORE THAN A MATTER OF TASTE

African hats and hairstyles are compelling artistic forms. More than fashion statements, they serve as significant cultural indices. Headwear can mark the wearer's ethnic identity and social status. For example, among Tuareg nobles, a man's turban and veil are the dominant symbols of his male identity and his position in society. Fashioned from lengths of cotton cloth, either white or dyed a deep indigo, Tuareg men wear their turban and face veil as part of their everyday attire. Throughout the day, a man wraps and rewraps his turban and adjusts his face veil depending on the social context in which he finds himself. In formal contexts, among strangers, or in the presence of his in-laws, a man will pull his face veil tighter and higher across his face, leaving only his eyes exposed. When relaxing among his friends, he generally chooses to loosen the veil and more fully reveal his face. When a man adjusts his face veil differently depending on the social context, he is articulating and responding to the shifting moods and behavioral expectations of others. Adjusting his veil actualizes the deeply held Tuareg cultural values of respect and reserve that contribute to a noble's self-definition. How a man wears his turban and veil in any particular social context shapes how others define, judge, and relate to him. When a man veils his face, he hides his personal sentiments. The veil reminds the wearer of the need for caution and self-control in his relationships with others. When Tuareg men travel abroad for school or business, they often choose not to wear the face veil, although they often wear their turbans on formal occasions to assert their ethnicity. Abandoning the face veil when traveling abroad might be seen as a man's declaration of his modernity in the global context, but perhaps it also reflects the fact that his social interactions abroad generally do not involve encounters with other Tuareg elders or with his in-laws, which are the occasions at home that demand that he demonstrate the highest degree of reserve.

Throughout the Cameroon Grassfields, a man's headgear and other forms of dress convert material wealth into symbolic capital within the context of male prestige. In the marketplace or in other public venues when a man wears his distinctive burled crocheted raffia cap or a multicolored knit cotton cap, his headwear evokes a complex set of meanings. His hat asserts the wearer's ethnic identity within a multiethnic environment; it alludes to

Kwilu Pende chief wearing a beaded hat, near Gungu, Democratic Republic of Congo. Photograph by Eliot Elisofon, 1970. EEPA EECL 2257. Eliot Elisofon Photographic Archives, National Museum of African Art, Smithsonian Institution.

local history and to shared cultural values about decorum; and it underscores a man's social status and his sphere of influence within his community.

Distinctive forms of hairstyles and headwear often figure prominently in rituals for major life passages such as initiation, title taking, marriage, motherhood, and funerals. Throughout much of Africa, most children's hair is kept short or is periodically shaved. Children's hairstyles are, for the most part, simple and unadorned. However, there are exceptions. For example, in both urban and rural communities in Mali, young girls wear modest versions of the elaborately braided styles of their older sisters. Among the Igbo of Nigeria, children's heads are often shaved in bold asymmetrical patterns; in Namibia, Himba boys' heads are shaved into decorative patterns, and line drawings are created in the shaved areas.

Many coming-of-age rituals in Africa involve special practices associated with the head. Among the Okiet of Kenya, girls' heads are shaved to mark the beginning of their initiation into adulthood. During this one-day ceremony, which may precede the final initiation rites by many years, the child's and the mother's heads are shaved in the morning, and later in the evening the child is given a new name to signal her impending new status. When Temne and Kuba boys in Sierra Leone and the Democratic Republic of Congo enter a period of seclusion during their initiation into adulthood, their heads are shaved to remind them of

their current status as children. Later, when they are symbolically reborn as adults in a public ceremony, the initiates don special headwear (a cloth hat and a fiber cap, respectively) that signals to their communities their new status as young adult men.

In East Africa among several groups—including the Pokot, Karamojong, Turkana, Maasai, and Samburu—after young men are initiated into the warrior age grade, they begin to grow out their hair and to invest hours in grooming and creating elaborate hairstyles. A young warrior's coiffure is a sign of his masculinity, courage, and strength. Karamojong and Pokot warriors create similar elaborate mud-pack hairdos that they wear on a daily basis. Among the Karamojong, the front of the hair that forms the plate is mudded over with gray ochre. When dry, this base is divided into six or eight squares, each of a different color forming a border between the two squares. The whole is then stippled with a tooth comb. Ostrich feathers and other decorative items are inserted into the crown of the mudpack, adding height and drama to the hairstyle. Young men maintain and repair these elaborate coiffures for weeks. However, when their hair begins to grow out, they chip away the mud, clean their hair, and create new coiffures. Maasai and Samburu warriors twist their hair into hundreds of small braids, which they saturate with fat and red ochre. They then pull the braids forward and backward and secure them with wooden pendants or wrap them to form a larger braid. On ceremonial occasions, Maasai warriors wear a distinctive leather and feather face ruff. An oval leather band frames the face and draws attention to it. Ostrich feathers, some left natural and some dyed red, are sewn around the rim of the leather frame and extend the ruff vertically and horizontally in space. A similar style of ceremonial face ruff is also worn by warriors among the Kikuyu and other groups, who are neighbors of the Maasai. During the Colonial period, this face ruff became an iconic symbol of the Mau Mau rebellion against the British colonial authority. Later, when a Maasai warrior marries, he abandons his preoccupation with creating elaborate coiffures and cuts his hair short, signaling to the community his shift to elder status.

Among the Bidjogo of Guinea-Bissau, new initiates into the men's association appear in public ceremonies wearing elaborate headwear to mark their movement from childhood to manhood. Hats fashioned for these new initiates use natural materials and symbols drawn from benign marine creatures and domesticated animals such as the blowfish and cattle. As men move up within the age association, their ceremonial headwear changes. Older men's hats include natural materials and symbols of powerful wild animals such as the bush bull, the hippopotamus, and the swordfish that speak to their growing capacity, authority, and power within the community.

The Lega, who live in the Democratic Republic of Congo, are well known for their spectacular headwear. Lega woven fiber and wild animal skin hats are important insignia of rank within the Bwame association. This association, which once played a central role in Lega communities, was open to all adult men and their wives. Upon initiation, a man received a small woven fiber skullcap that he wore daily and that embodied the very philosophy and spirit of Bwame. As a man moved up within the Bwame structure, he acquired the right to wear more elaborate ceremonial headwear, but he always wore the small skullcap underneath his other hats. The central place that this modest skullcap played in the larger repertoire of Lega headwear was made clear during funeral rites for a Bwame member. A man was buried wearing his Bwame skullcap. During his funeral, his other hats and insignia of the rank he had achieved were placed on top of his grave. Moreover, if a man died away from home, his small skullcap became his substitute body and was returned to the community for a formal burial.

Among the Kuba of the Democratic Republic of Congo, all young boys undergo initiation. As new initiates, they receive a small raffia skullcap that marks their transition from boys to men. Although men may eventually take additional titles and acquire the right to wear more elaborate headwear, it is their small raffia skullcap that marks their ethnic affiliation and that signals their attainment of adult status. The care that some Kuba men take with these small caps and their other hats, the type of embellishment they choose to add to them, and their attention to personal grooming go well beyond just marking titles taken but also serve as the expression of a man's personal style and his sense of self-esteem.

For many African women, distinctive hairstyles or headdresses mark their status as wives and mothers. In many areas, these practices have undergone change over the past century and are not as prevalent in the twenty-first century. For example, among the Zulu of South Africa in the early nineteenth century, married women wore a special hairstyle. To create the hairstyle, a woman first shaved her head, leaving a small oval or circular patch on the crown, which she then greased and colored with a mixture of animal fat and red ochre. This tuft of hair was then worked into a topknot that resembled a small truncated cone. Sometime

Maasai man whose face is framed by blue glass beads on a leather structure outlined with cowry shells and surrounded by dyed ostrich feathers, worn on ceremonial occasions, ca. 2000. Photograph by Joseph Van Os.

in the mid-nineteenth century, this small topknot was artificially lengthened through the addition of extensions made of grasses bound with fiber. In addition to her distinctive hairstyle, a married woman also wore a decorative band across her forehead. Hairstyle and headband were the material symbols of a woman's respect for her husband and his family. Beginning in the early decades of the twentieth century, Zulu women's distinctive hairstyle began to be replaced by a fiber hat that was worn on a daily basis. Depending on the area, these fiber hats were constructed in a conical or flared form. The hat's form was either covered with human hair or wrapped in string that was dyed with a mixture of fat and red ochre. During this period, women also began to attach decorative headbands to the crown of these hats. By the late 1970s, however, these distinctive Zulu hats were no longer part of a woman's everyday attire. They are still donned for special occasions such as weddings, regional fairs, and national festivals as a mark of Zulu ethnicity in this multiethnic nation.

Among the Ndebele of South Africa, brides wear elaborately beaded back veils as part of their marriage ensembles. The geometric beaded designs that are woven into these veils echo similar designs that married women traditionally paint on their houses. In the latter half of the twentieth century, figurative motifs such as airplanes have made an appearance on these veils, speaking eloquently to both the timelessness of marriage and to a bride's place in the modern world. When an Ndebele bride dons her marriage ensemble, she announces her intention to move from one social state to another. This ritual not only transforms the bride, but her new identity as a married woman profoundly alters and shapes her future relationships with others in her community and, in turn, their future relationships with her.

Among the Herero and Himba of Namibia, who are cattle keepers, women once wore elaborate leather headdresses every day to mark their status as wives. Not surprisingly, cattle symbolism played a prominent role in these hats. The headdress consisted of a curved leather cap that fit snugly on the back of the head. Three tall, flat projections called horns were sewn onto the top of the cap, a symbol of cow's horns. A triangular-shaped skin veil was attached to the front of the cap. When worn every day and on most ceremonial occasions, a woman wore her hat with the skin veil rolled back off her face, and its ends trailed downward in two tails to sit on her shoulders. A leather band with decorative patterns of locally made iron beads, which were symbols of wealth, was worn on the front of the cap. The body of the cap and the horns were decorated with lines of ornamental stitching, and rows of iron beads ran vertically down the back of the cap. During two rituals, a woman wore the veil unrolled: when a new bride was escorted to her husband's home and when a widow returned to her natal home. During the rituals of marriage and widowhood, the women symbolically became cattle by covering their faces with the leather veil and walking bent from the waist and swaying gracefully from side to side. These ritual performances were an especially potent reminder of the central role played by the exchange of women for cattle at marriage among these groups. Although this exchange may be minor in economic terms, it is important symbolically as a token of good faith on the part of the groom's family and as a pledge of security for the new bride. Beginning in the late nineteenth century, Herero women, who converted to Christianity, abandoned the traditional leather caps for cloth headwraps. However, they adapted the headwrap to their cultural needs by adding two stuffed cloth projections, which they called cattle horns, to the top of the wrap, thus preserving the important cattle symbolism of their traditional cap. In postcolonial Namibia, this same styled cloth headwrap with its cloth cattle horns and the Victorian-style cotton dress worn with it remain the national costume for Herero women and an important marker of their ethnic identity.

Special hairstyles and hats can also mark a woman's status as a mother. Among Kuba-affiliated groups in the Democratic Republic of Congo, special hairstyles and headdresses were once reserved for first-time mothers. Among the Shoowa, expectant mothers added a mixture of camwood and palm oil to their hair to create a sculptural horseshoe-like extension. Among the Kalabari Ijaw of Nigeria, a new mother appeared in a public ceremony of thanksgiving after the birth of her child wearing a small cloth hat, either elaborately embroidered or covered with beads and other decorative materials sewn onto the cloth base. Among the Bura of Nigeria, a calabash sun hat is part of a baby's layette. For the first year or so of a child's life, the mother carries her baby on her back. The gourd sun hat, secured by a leather strap under the baby's chin, protects the child from the elements. Besides being highly functional, these intricately pyro-engraved hats, which draw upon the repertoire of traditional gourd designs, serve as

a marker of the ethnicity of mother and child and an object of aesthetic display. Highly valued by women, gourd baby hats are often kept within families and passed down for use with each new child born into the family.

Yoruba women's head ties, *gele*, are some of the most elaborate and sculptural of women's headwear worn in Africa. The head tie is an important cultural marker of a Yoruba woman's married status and her adherence to social norms about propriety and decorum. Among the Yoruba, wrapping one's head also honors a person's spiritual capacity, because the Yoruba believe a person's destiny lies within one's inner head. In addition to their cultural symbolism, head ties are also the material expression of a woman's sense of style, artistry, and individuality. The head tie is made from about a two-meter (seven-foot) length of fabric. A woman folds and wraps the fabric around her head and tucks and pleats it to create a beguiling sculptural form. Locally woven cottons, as well as luxurious imported fabrics such as damask, silk, and velvet, are all used to create head ties. At each wearing, a woman rewraps her head tie anew with variations. This refashioning allows a woman to demonstrate her artistic skills, keep up with the latest styles, and rearrange her head tie to complement her attire. The wearing of head ties is not restricted to specific ritual or ceremonial occasions, but women regularly don them whenever they are in public.

Some of the most spectacular hats in Africa are, not surprisingly, associated with political and spiritual leadership. Hat forms and the materials from which they are fashioned embody key cultural, historical, and symbolic meanings. Among the Ekonda and neighboring groups in the Democratic Republic of Congo, ritual chiefs wear distinctive woven raffia or cane hats to mark their office. The hats are tall cylinders accented with woven horizontal bands along the top that project out from the surface of the hat. A large brass disk, a symbol of wealth, is generally sewn onto the front of the hat, and other brass disks or safety pins may be sewn to the top or back of the hat as expressions of a man's personal taste. The chief's hat serves as the material symbol of the office and of his authority and power.

Silver and brass crowns are worn by Ethiopian Christian priests and deacons during important religious rites and have been part of the ecclesiastical vestments of the church for centuries. The crowns are generally fashioned from beaten metal sheets cut out and engraved with intricate designs and attached to a brow band, a central band, and an apex plate. Bells and chains may be added as fringe to the base of the crown. A colorful cloth turban is worn under the crown to match the priest's elaborately embroidered vestments.

Among the Yoruba of Nigeria, the *oba* (divine king) derives his authority from a mythological-religious charter. The king's crown is a tall conical form that is covered with elaborate beadwork. When placed on the king's head, the crown unites his inner head with all past Yoruba kings. In formal audiences, the king appears with his face masked by a beaded veil. By veiling his face, the king's humanity is concealed and his divinity revealed. The act of wearing the crown and the veil intensifies the king's performative powers and accords him a heightened spirituality.

Emirs in northern Nigeria also derive their authority from a historical/religious charter that links them directly to Sheikh Usman dan Fodio, the founder of the Sokoto Caliphate, a powerful early-nineteenth-century theocracy. While the contemporary Nigerian state invests emirs with secular power, their spiritual authority derives its force from their direct descent from the founder. When an emir appears in public, he wears an ample turban that is fashioned from meters of white or indigo-dyed cloth. His formal ensemble also includes richly embroidered caliphate robes. An emir's turban and his robe are potent material symbols of his legitimacy both as a political leader and religious authority.

Among the Kongo living in Angola and the Democratic Republic of Congo, a chief's exceptional powers come from the ancestors of his matrilineal descent group, in whose name he rules. At his investiture, a chief received a tall woven raffia hat, a symbol of his office. The chief was also anointed with many of the same medicines that are used by diviners and healers to constitute power objects. Most of the tall caps were woven in a spiral form, working from the center of the crown out to the edge of the hat border. Intricate geometric patterns were woven into the entire surface of these hats.

Kalabari Ijaw men wear spectacular hats for ceremonial occasions that are made by professional hat makers. The hat is crescent-shaped, and its form echoes the historical headwear of British naval officers. The hat is worn vertically from front to back on the head and has three critical components: a ram's beard, feathers, and appliqués of concentric circles. Other elements such as plastic items and foil papers are added to the hat for aesthetic

Zulu woman in a wedding headdress, recalling an ancestral hairstyle, Gauteng Province, South Africa, 1996. Hats like these are now worn on a variety of special ceremonial occasions. Photograph by Carol Beckwith/Angela Fisher.

effect. A chief wears such a hat at his installation and may also wear it during other important events. At the funeral of an esteemed elder, the hat is worn by the primary male mourners to celebrate the achievements of the lineage. This ceremonial hat is part of a formal ensemble that includes luxury silks and embroidered velvets. Historically, Kalabari sumptuary laws limited access to imported goods to chiefs, and these restrictions included the ownership of hats and luxury textiles. Although these sumptuary laws are no longer in effect in the twenty-first century, these items remain powerful symbols of wealth and prestige in Kalabari communities. A man's formal ensemble of velvet gown and spectacular hat constitutes a category of appropriate dress for wealthy and powerful men among the Kalabari, and it expresses local views about correct comportment and appearance.

Initiation into religious cults and curing rituals often involve creating special hairstyles or donning special headwear. During initiation into a Yoruba *orisa* cult, a new member's head is prepared to receive the god by first shaving the hair and then anointing and painting the head with spiritually potent substances and symbolic colors. During the curing rituals for spirit possession, a Tuareg woman dons a man's turban and face veil and performs the *asul*, the head dance, in time to drumming and choral singing. This dance, performed while in trance, is said to be directed by the occupying spirit. During this dance, the woman enacts behaviors that vacillate between the reserved and the flamboyant, thus expressing basic contradictions in Tuareg social life. Assuming the man's turban and face veil protects the woman's inner self in this period of spiritual and psychological crisis and transition.

Funerals are important occasions for which people modify their heads as part of mourning rituals. Among the Merina of Madagascar, for example, a widow unbraids her hair and leaves it uncombed throughout the period of mourning. Among the Samburu of Kenya, young men who are closely related to the deceased shave off their hair to ward off misfortune. Following the death of the king in Benin in Nigeria, all of his subjects shave their heads as part of collective mourning rituals. During funerals for important chiefs among the Akuropon of Ghana, townspeople wrap their heads with leaves, and some gather beehives from the forest and wear them on their heads. This practice is a fundamental statement about the state of disorder in the community following the death of a chief. Through this practice, participants bring the natural and cultural worlds together. By donning untransformed natural materials, they draw attention to powers located in the natural realm.

In the 1930s as part of a revolt against the Belgian colonial authority in the Congo, Pende men reintroduced the *mukotte*, a type of traditional wig that had fallen out of use by the beginning of the twentieth century. They reinvested this wig with a new meaning as a symbol of the popular resistance. The wig is fashioned as a cap that sits on the back of the head. A graceful crest extends from the center back of the wig forward, curving over the forehead and ending at the eyebrows. Fiber braids are sewn in parallel lines along the side of the cap and on its side edges to frame the face. Copper and brass tacks are inserted along the length of the center crest and are arranged in parallel lines and triangular designs.

Between 1946 and 1964, Jomo Kenyatta, a leader of the nationalist movement in Kenya and later its first postcolonial president, regularly appeared in public wearing a tall colobus monkey fur hat. His choice of this type of hat, along with other items of local chiefly regalia, was certainly a conscious act. This chief's hat is associated with power, spirit mediumship, and political authority. The symbolism of Kenyatta's chosen headwear was widely understood, and it was an object around which people could unite in their common struggle against the British.

Other postcolonial politicians and leaders have also regularly exploited traditional forms of headwear to legitimate their rule. In the Congo, renamed Zaire under the Mobutu regime, President Mobutu regularly appeared in public wearing a leopard-skin cap. Although the form of the hat derives from a military cap, his choice of leopard skin was calculated to exploit the powerful association of the leopard with leadership, which is a symbol that has a long history in many societies in this zone. The Mobutu-style hat was later adopted by local rulers in the country, including the Kuba king, who redesigned the hat by overlaying it with elaborate beadwork designs drawn from the local Kuba repertoire of prestige forms.

AFRICAN HEADWEAR: A COMMUNICATION SYSTEM

African hat makers create imaginative art works from a wide variety of local and imported materials. Materials are selected according to local criteria. Some may be chosen for their rarity or for such qualities as sheen, color, or pliancy. An incredible variety of local flora and fauna enter into the manufacture of headgear throughout Africa, where bark, cotton, palm fiber, animal manes, wool, hides and skins, as well as minerals such as clays, stones, and metal have been exploited in creative ways by various societies in the process of elaborating the head. Many communities have also incorporated into headdresses a rich variety of imported textiles, glass beads, and other materials such as tacks, buttons, and safety pins. Techniques that African artists use for fabricating headwear are as varied as the materials they choose. Some artists make hats using basketry techniques such as plaiting and twining; others shape and sew cloth or animal skins. Many people decorate their hats by painting, pyro-engraving, incising, dyeing, appliquéing, or embroidering the base materials.

For centuries, Africans have actively engaged in long-distance trade both within the continent and with the Middle East, Asia, and Europe. Many headdresses, in form or decoration, are creative expressions of this fluidity of goods and ideas. Many Islamic and European forms have been widely adopted or reproduced in local materials. In the nineteenth century, during the Islamic reforms that swept West Africa, Islamic-style headwear was often adopted to proclaim the owner's adherence to the faith and served to set him or her apart from non-Muslim neighbors. The use of Islamic amulets and design motifs is also widespread in Africa. Although their adoption symbolically associated a person with the power of Islam, it did not oblige the individual to embrace the religion. Materials such as European brocades, velvets, and other textiles along with items like beads, buttons, glass mirrors, and brass tacks were imported from outside the continent and circulated through networks of intracontinental trade routes. Imported forms and materials are often combined with those manufactured or found locally, and the hat or headdress is invested with local value and symbolism that ultimately transcend any single element in its creation.

Some borrowed hat forms were quickly domesticated through the creative reworking of various elements to conform to local

A Kalabari Ijo man's ceremonial hat (*ajibulu*), largely restricted to chiefs and "chief mourners," at a funeral. Buguma, Nigeria, 1988. Photograph by Joanne Eicher.

sensibilities and aesthetics. For example, in the early nineteenth century, repatriated African slaves from the United States, who called themselves *Americo-Liberians*, settled on the West African coast and founded the country of Liberia. This new urban society was animated by nineteenth-century Christian values of the U.S. South, and these settlers reproduced many features of southern American culture, including formal apparel. Americo-Liberian men wore top hats to all public functions. Rural chiefs in this larger region soon began adopting the top hat as part of their own ritual and ceremonial attire. They, however, often reworked the basic form of the top hat by adding a number of decorative objects to it that were part of the local symbolic repertoire of wealth and prestige. Cowry shells used as local currency, ostrich feathers traded into the region from the north, and wool fabrics from the coastal trade with Europeans were favorite materials added to chiefs' top hats.

Hausa men in Nigeria wear elaborately embroidered hats in the form of a small pillbox shape as part of their formal attire. These hats serve both as a mark of their ethnicity and their Islamic identity. The popular multicolored hats were originally inspired by hats brought back by pilgrims from Mecca in the 1950s. Local production of these hats began soon after their introduction, and Hausa hat makers created elaborate embroidery designs. They gave their designs local names that encoded references to local historical personages and to current events in northern Nigeria. Since the late twentieth century, these Hausa-style hats have been adopted in many areas in Nigeria and have been exported to many parts of West Africa, where they are purchased by Muslims and non-Muslims alike. Embroidered Hausa-style hats have also become fashionable among young African Americans in the United States as part of an Afrocentric fashion statement.

In Africa, hats and hairstyles that are imported from abroad tend to undergo the most rapid transformations, responding to the global and local dynamics of fashion and taste. Baseball caps have become ubiquitous among young African men, and some of them have adopted the African American hip-hop style and wear baseball caps with the brim facing to the back or to the side. Hairstyles for both men and women are also part of the ever-changing fashion field. Most of the intricately tressed and braided women's hairstyles and the sculpted and shaped men's styles worn in cities throughout the continent are created by professional hairstylists and barbers. Women's popular hairstyles are often labor intensive and require a substantial investment of time and money by the client. Human and synthetic hairpieces and hair extenders and a multitude of hair products including hair dyes, hair relaxers, and so on constitute a growing business. Professional hairstylists and barbers often advertise the latest hair fashions by posting photographs or printed posters or by commissioning hand-painted tableaus. The hand-painted barber signs have been part of visual urban culture in Africa for at least half a century. Many commercial barbershop signs are painted by self-trained artists; others are created by academically trained commercial artists. Many of the imported hairstyles that appear on the signs are given names that relate them to local contemporary events or highlight local notions of modernity.

The sheer variety of headwear made on the continent provides a window into the dynamic cultural history, social processes, symbolism, aesthetics, and technologies of diverse African societies. Dressing the head in Africa has always been more than a matter of taste. A single hat or hairstyle, when worn alone or as part of a larger costume ensemble, can be a multivocal symbol with layers of associations and meanings. Headwear and hairstyles enhance and beautify the body and communicate personal and cultural knowledge. Headwear can recall founding myths or historical episodes, celebrate individual achievements, or glorify an office. Hats and hairstyles can signal the wearer's endorsement or commitment to a particular role, status, or course of action. Headwear also can communicate the wearer's personal aesthetic, or it can convey mood. Imported forms and materials used in the fashioning of headwear serve as material testaments to the history of active trading networks that have linked African societies to one another on the continent and have linked Africa to the Middle East, Asia, and Europe for thousands of years.

Hats and hairstyles can be put on, and taken off, manipulated, and invested with an aggregate of meanings depending on how and in what contexts they are put into play. African headgear and hairstyles are never passive reflections of culture, but through the mediation of human action, they are technologies that people use to construct social identities and to produce, reproduce, and transform their relationships and situations through time. Whether hats and hairstyles are reserved for ceremonial and ritual purposes or are more generally popular, they communicate important messages about modes of life and the attitudes, values, and beliefs that shape the human experience.

References and Further Reading

Arens, William, and Ivan Karp, eds. *Creativity of Power: Cosmology and Action in African Societies*. Washington, DC: Smithsonian Institution Press, 1989.

Arnoldi, Mary Jo, and Christine Mullen Kreamer, eds. *Crowning Achievements: African Arts of Dressing the Head*. Los Angeles: UCLA Fowler Museum of Cultural History, 1995.

Berns, Marla, and Barbara Rubin Hudson. *The Essential Gourd: Art and History in Northeastern Nigeria*. Los Angeles: UCLA Museum of Cultural History, 1986.

Biebuyck, Daniel. *Lega Culture: Art, Initiation, and Moral Philosophy among a Central African People*. Berkeley: University of California Press, 1973.

Biebuyck, Daniel, and Nelly Van den Abbeele. *The Power of Headdresses: A Cross-Cultural Study of Form and Function*. Ghent, Belgium: Snoeck-Ducaju en Xoon; Brussels, Belgium: Tendi, S. A., 1984.

Brown, H. D. "The Nkumu of the Tumba: Ritual Chieftainship on the Middle Congo." *Africa* 14, no. 8 (1944): 431–447.

Cole, Herbert M. "Vital Arts in Northern Kenya." *African Arts* 7, no. 2 (1974): 12–23, 82.

Conner, Michael, and Diane Pelrine. *The Geometric Vision: Arts of the Zulu*. West Lafayette, IN: Purdue University Department of Creative Arts, 1983.

Drewal, Henry John, John Pemberton III, and Rowland Abiodun. "Yoruba: Nine Centuries of African Art and Thought." *African Arts* 23, no. 1 (1989): 68–77, 104.

Duquette, Danielle Gallois. "Woman Power and Initiation in the Bissagos Islands." *African Arts* 12, no. 3 (1979): 31–35, 93.

Eicher, Joanne, and Tonye Victor Erekosima. "Kalabari Funerals: Celebration and Display." *African Arts* 21, no. 1 (1987): 38–45, 87–88.

Gibson, Gordon. "Bridewealth and Forms of Exchange among the Herero." In *Markets in Africa*, edited by Paul Bohannan and George Dalton, 617–639. Evanston, IL: Northwestern University Press, 1962.

Gibson, Gordon, and Cecilia McGurk. "High Status Caps of the Kongo and Mbundu Peoples." *Textile Museum Journal* 4, no. 4 (1977): 71–96.

Gilbert, Michelle. "Sources of Power in Akuropon-Akuapem: Ambiguity in Classification." In *Creativity of Power: Cosmology and Action in African Societies*, edited by William Arens and Ivan Karp, 59–90. Washington, DC: Smithsonian Institution Press, 1989.

Gulliver, Pamela, and P. H. Gulliver. *The Central Hilo-Hamites*. Ethnographic Survey of Africa, Part 7. London: International African Institute, 1953.

Lamp, Frederick. "Frogs into Princes: The Temne Rabal Initiation." *African Arts* 11, no. 2 (1978): 38–49, 94–95.

Seligman, Thomas K., and Kristyne Loughran, eds. *Art of Being Tuareg: Sahara Nomads in a Modern World*. Los Angeles: UCLA Fowler Museum of Cultural History, 2006.

Sieber, Roy, and Frank Herreman. *Hair in African Art and Culture*. New York: New York Museum for African Art, 2000.

Spencer, Paul. *The Samburu: A Study of Gerontocracy in a Nomadic Tribe*. Berkeley and Los Angeles: University of California Press, 1965.

Mary Jo Arnoldi

See also Ghana; Yoruba in Nigeria and Diaspora; Hausa in Nigeria and Diaspora; Republic of Congo and Democratic Republic of Congo; Kenya; Namibia.

Beads and Beadwork

Although today most African communities purchase locally manufactured and imported glass beads for daily and ritual use, indigenous communities originally relied on locally available materials such as seeds and ostrich eggshells or marine shells to adorn themselves and their leather garments. Recent discoveries in Morocco indicate that deliberately perforated *Nassarius* marine shells, some still smeared with red ochre, were manufactured eighty-two thousand years ago. Because some of these marine shells show microscopic wear patterns, it seems likely that they were strung into necklaces or bracelets. This evidence suggests that symbolic material culture, including the use of beads, probably first emerged in Africa and related Near Eastern sites rather than Europe, as was previously assumed. The same species of marine shell has also been found at other African sites, notably Blombos Cave in South Africa. In contrast to later Upper Paleolithic sites in Europe, where single cultural groupings used more than one hundred fifty bead types, the evidence at these sites indicates that concerns with personal adornment were underpinned by reciprocal exchange networks similar to those found among more recent hunter-gatherer communities.

The earliest record of ostrich-eggshell beads, which were manufactured more than forty thousand years ago, comes from the central Rift Valley in Kenya. Later Stone Age sites in eastern and southern Africa contain large quantities of ostrich-eggshell beads that were manufactured in one of two ways: either by drilling a hole in an irregular fragment of shell, which was then rounded off to the required circular shape, or by first making disks, which were drilled once they had been ground to the required shape. In both cases, the beads were subsequently strung and polished to a uniform size.

Like seashells, obsidian and ostrich eggshells were strung together and worn in a variety of ways by prehistoric peoples and attest to the existence of early alliance networks between neighboring as well as more distant communities. These materials moved from source to destination through exchange (gift or trade) from person to person since they were rarely sourced directly through long-distance travel. Among Stone Age hunter-gatherers in southern Africa, ostrich-eggshell beads formed part of elaborate gift exchange networks. Termed *hxaro*, this practice is still followed by some contemporary San communities, who exchange ostrich-eggshell beadwork with spouses and blood relatives, thereby creating ties of friendship and a sense of community between individuals and families. Importantly, this circulation of beads and other commodities had the effect of distributing goods equally in San society. By far the majority of seashells found at inland Stone Age sites in southern Africa were turned into beads or pendants. Like the recent finds in Morocco, some of this marine-shell jewelry was further modified through ochre-staining. Once farming communities became established, hunter-gatherers commonly exchanged shell beads like these with settled agropastoralists, in some cases making comparatively large ostrich-eggshell beads for use by these communities. In Namibia, some Ovambo women still wear heavy ostrich-eggshell skirts on special occasions. Although these women make their own ostrich-eggshell beads, the techniques they use to produce beads of this kind were originally acquired from the San.

Predynastic Egyptian burials also frequently reveal small, disk-shaped, ostrich-eggshell beads. Some of the most sumptuous and best documented traditions of African beadwork have been revealed by archaeologists in Egypt. Imported carnelian and lapis lazuli beads in a variety of shapes from West Asia have been recovered from Egyptian cemeteries dating back to before 3000 B.C.E. The small size and durability of most beads allow for easy portability, and beads were certainly among the earliest of trade items. In addition to the semiprecious carnelian and lapis lazuli stones, obsidian, quartz, agate, electrum, turquoise, steatite, and amazonite (feldspar) also served as bead materials to be shaped in a wide variety of forms and strung in various combinations for use across classes in ancient Egypt. In addition, locally produced glass beads became increasingly prevalent after about 1500 B.C.E. Gold ("the flesh of the gods") and gilt copper beads were widespread among the elite. Although elaborate beaded jewelry was extensively worn by the wealthy and privileged, a substantial amount of jewelry was expressly manufactured to dress the dead in the afterlife.

The most common bead type in ancient Egypt was made from faience (sometimes called "Egyptian paste"), a synthetic material that is fundamentally a siliceous self-glazing ceramic. Considered the ancestor of glass, but invariably opaque, faience was produced in a variety of colors, with a range of blues, greens, and blacks particularly prevalent. These are also the so-called mummy beads of ancient Egypt that were often strung by the thousands to form lavish bead net mummy coverings. These beaded funerary garments were commonly topped by a broad collar or pectoral collar (*wesekh*), the favored item of adornment for gods, royalty, and commoners throughout much of ancient Egyptian history. Typically consisting of multiple rows of cylindrical faience beads strung radially, the form might be embellished with stone beads or cast gold ornaments. A widespread phenomenon in ancient Egypt was the incorporation of prophylactic amulets as bead elements shaped from a variety of materials, especially faience, often as centerpieces in both simple and complex necklaces or collars. These might include representations of lotus buds, cornflowers, bulls, lions, falcons, scepters, and, most famously, scarabs. Amulets were created in an array of colors, with each material, form, and hue evoking its own symbolic meaning.

THE PRESTIGE VALUE OF STONE BEADS IN IRON AGE COMMUNITIES

In stark contrast to the role indigenously manufactured beads played in cementing egalitarianism in these Stone Age communities across Africa, elite groups in later sub-Saharan Iron Age communities used comparatively rare stone beads to reinforce hierarchical relations of power and authority. At Ile-Ife, in present-day Nigeria, the production of highly valued cylindrical red beads (okun) made from jasper and carnelian (red chalcedony) stones appears to have been brought under royal control in the thirteenth century C.E. Grooved or dimpled stones used for grinding and polishing these stone beads have been excavated not only at Ile-Ife but also at Old Oyo. Initially, Ile-Ife effectively controlled the regional distribution of these stone beads, especially to its rain forest–belt neighbors, but between the thirteenth and fifteenth centuries, Old Oyo gradually came to dominate the export trade in jasper and chalcedony beads. The importance these prestige commodities played in shaping African societies is evidenced in the fact that Old Oyo became politically centralized most probably because of its role in linking the rain forest belt with the Middle Niger in what is now Mali.

Indigenously crafted stone beads are also commonly found in other parts of Africa. Thus, for example, although the production of bauxite beads has declined in present-day Ghana, these stone beads once formed part of a thriving industry southeast of Kumase as late as the 1940s. At that time, bauxite beads were traded throughout Ghana and Côte d'Ivoire, and the profits that could be expected from producing beads of this kind were so high that large numbers of producers—both men and women—made bauxite beads either on a full-time basis or as a lucrative part-time hobby. The Yoruba city of Ilorin, in today's Nigeria, also produced red lantana beads made from stone obtained from Hausa traders who brought it down the Niger River from quarries located to the north of Ilorin, in what is now the Niger Republic. The manufacturing processes used in the production of these beads were long and very demanding, but, like the bauxite producers in Ghana, the men formerly involved in cutting lantana beads made huge profits from selling their stone beads throughout the region.

THE INTRODUCTION OF IMPORTED GLASS BEADS

Imported glass beads from India first reached the African continent through Arab traders using trans-Saharan caravan routes via Mecca or Bagdad and Cairo, as early as the fourth century C.E. By the ninth century, trans-Saharan trade was conducted by a number of West African communities, but recent excavations at Goa in Mali suggest that long-established assumptions regarding the African trade in glass beads need to be revised. The Goan sites, located on the Niger River, date to the eleventh and twelfth centuries and have yielded Egyptian glass beads that are very similar to those found at Igbo-Ukwu in present-day Nigeria. Although the carbon dating of material from Igbo Ukwu remains uncertain, it seems likely that the beads found at an Igbo-Ukwu burial site were acquired through Goa in exchange for ivory. This burial pit for a highly respected officeholder or person of unusual wealth or ritual importance included the remains of tusks and representations of elephants in bronze. The trade route between Goa and Igbo-Ukwu was probably controlled, in stages, along the

Niger River. Other trade routes between West Africa and Egypt also appear to have passed through Goa.

While Igbo-Ukwu is probably the best-known African funerary site pointing to the prestige value African communities attached to imported beads before the second millennium C.E., the discovery in 1996 of graves dating to the fifth to seventh centuries C.E. near Mare de Kissi in northeast Burkina Faso affords evidence that wealthier members of that community also had access to imported glass beads and other exotic goods. But, as the content of these graves confirms, locally manufactured stone beads were also highly valued. Beadwork items from the Mare de Kissi site include ones made from quartz, jasper, and carnelian.

It would appear that the social and ideological value communities began to attach to imported beads and other objects of long-distance trade before the second millennium C.E. transformed these commodities into loaded symbols of political and economic power. At Ile-Ife, for example, it seems likely that this trade was a catalyst for major change in the Yoruba-Edo region. The development of an elite material culture that differentiated rulers from their subjects seems to have been the most concrete outcome of these long-distance trade relations. Although, initially, imported beads were acquired through the trans-Saharan trade via the Middle Niger, they presumably originated in Europe and the East.

The social distinction, power, and political capital ascribed to imported beads stemmed directly from the fact that they were both rare and expensive. In the Yoruba region, where beads were used to sanction monarchical systems of government, kings had beaded crowns, caps, and other regalia that were made by male embroiderers who worked secretly in the king's palace or in their own homes. These kings and other important dignitaries also wore heavily beaded necklaces, anklets, and wristbands. Bronze figures of the oni, or king, of Ife depict him dressed in richly beaded garments believed to have been introduced to Ife by Olokun, the female divinity of the sea and of wealth. According to Yoruba oral tradition, Olokun acquired her wealth by producing beads.

In southern Africa in the Shasha-Limpopo region, where local elites controlled long-distance trade routes from citadels like Mapungubwe and, later, Great Zimbabwe, glass beads from South or Southeast Asia first appeared in the late ninth or early tenth century C.E. Threaded into simple strands or onto coiled wire, these trade beads appear to have been worn by both adults and children as earrings, necklaces, armbands, and around the pelvis. Archaeological evidence also suggests that beads may have been sewn into the hair of infants. Although these imported beads were therefore used as forms of adornment, they served above all to reinforce hierarchical social relations and to secure political alliances, in many cases by creating obligations that could never be repaid. Some of the beads found in other East African contexts may have been manufactured in China. Compared to the drawn beads—that is, beads made from molten glass pulled to form a tube before being cut—found at southern African sites, these east coast assemblages contain a significant number of wound beads, which are made by winding a filament of molten glass around a rotating wire.

LOCALLY MANUFACTURED GLASS AND METAL BEADS

Although it is generally assumed that all glass beads used by African communities were imported from Egypt, West and South

Asia, and later, from Europe, evidence suggests that at least some of these beads were refashioned by African communities long before they established large-scale contact with Asian and European traders. At Ile-Ife, imported glass beads appear to have been reheated, melted, and possibly remixed some time between the ninth and eleventh centuries C.E. Activities associated with this indigenous production of glass beads seem to have taken place at a site now known as Olokun Grove. A glass-smelting crucible containing beads was also found at the Ita Yemoo site. It is not clear how these refashioned beads were made, but it appears that existing glass was ground to a powder before being mixed with water, rolled out, and pierced with a thin piece of iron. Thereafter, these refashioned beads were probably placed on an iron sheet before being baked in a clay oven.

This powder-glass technology is also found in Ghana among Krobo glass bead makers; they use molds made from clay into which they pour the glass powder. A stick is placed in the mold to provide a hole for the bead. Since the furnaces used to bake these molds are not very hot, the glass particles never melt, but do eventually stick together. In the twenty-first century, the glass used in the production of these beads varies considerably. Some are made from old bottles, while others are made from glass obtained from new, imported beads, especially if a particular color is not available locally. Ceramic dyes have also become fashionable in the production of nontranslucent beads. Demand for these beads increases during the celebrations of the Krobo Dipo festival, which is held annually in April or May. At this rite of passage, the beads worn by pubescent girls are supplied by their relatives.

In the past, the royal regalia of some West and Southeast African leaders also included beads made from locally panned gold. A Venetian map dating to about 1489 described the Ahanta state in present-day Ghana as containing a very productive gold mine, while a seventeenth-century visitor mentioned the fact that gold mining and smithing were practiced on the Ghanaian coast. Nine gold beads were recovered from seventeenth-century contexts at Elmina Old Town. Measuring less than one millimeter (four hundredths of an inch) in diameter, they are believed to have been made by cold hammering. Other techniques used by goldsmiths from this coastal region included drawing, bending, folding, cutting, and stamping, but over time, these techniques were gradually supplanted by casting technologies. Tubular cast gold beads with facets have been found at Elmina Old Town site, while the discovery of two crucibles in nineteenth-century contexts points to the production in Ghana over several centuries of gold beads by casting. Beads and bangles from graves on Mapungubwe Hill indicate that some members of this Southeast African community also adorned themselves with gold jewelry. These ornaments probably belonged to senior members of the royal family.

To this day, some African communities manufacture iron and copper beads. Iron beads, apparently strung on leather thongs, have been found in funerary contexts in Burkina Faso, while metal beads are still worn by Himba women in Namibia. In East Africa, Turkana leather skirts (*adwel*) with metal bead trimmings—associated with ceremonies related to marriage, birth, and mourning—were reserved for mothers. Similar antelope skin aprons, worn by pregnant women, may be found to this day among Zulu-speaking communities from the Thukela-Ferry region of KwaZulu-Natal. The brass beads attached to the aprons are now bought rather than manufactured by local metalsmiths and play an essential role in protecting the wearer's unborn child.

THE TRANSATLANTIC BEAD TRADE

In West Africa, the trans-Saharan trade had been supplemented by coastal commerce with Dutch and Portuguese beginning in the late fifteenth century. Trade opportunities with Portuguese merchants, who were the first Europeans to establish close relations with African communities, stimulated greater commercial activity and population buildup in coastal areas, notably Benin. Cowry shells, already known to the Yoruba-Edo region through the trans-Saharan trade, became one of the most important imports. The first shipment of these shells arrived from Lisbon in 1515. By the end of the nineteenth century, at least thirty billion cowries had been offloaded at the Bight of Benin. Although they were used primarily as a form of currency in different parts of Africa, cowry shells have long been accorded ceremonial or ritual significance in adornment practices among both West and East African communities. In West Africa, their association with the commercial life and activities of these communities encouraged a widespread tendency to ascribe to them a symbolic status as harbingers of prosperity and wealth. Here, necklaces and other items of adornment fashioned from cowries are still believed to improve the economic prospects of the wearer. In East African communities, cowries are often used as protective amulets, especially for young children. Their association with fertility is also common among communities such as the Hammar of southern Ethiopia.

Coral beads also became increasingly popular following the advent of European trade relations. Although it is not clear when these beads first entered West Africa, it is possible that coral was imported via the Sahara before the sixteenth century. In the mid-nineteenth century, the king of Oyo wore a strand of large coral beads around his neck as well as a coral crown whenever he appeared in public. Much earlier, in the Nigerian coastal city of Benin, coral also formed a significant part of the Edo king's costume and regalia. When the *oba* or king of Benin surrendered to the British in 1897, he was covered in strings of coral beads. His coral headdress was so heavy that his attendant repeatedly removed it for short intervals from his head. His lower arms and ankles were draped in coral beads, while his neck and chest were completely hidden by the beads.

Ewuare the Great, who ruled Benin from 1440 to 1473, is credited with having introduced coral beads and scarlet cloth to the kingdom. Although, traditionally, Ewuare is supposed to have found coral in the rivers around Benin and is said to have stolen coral beads from Olokun—in Yoruba tradition, the goddess of the sea—it is clear from the historical evidence that control over imported coral played a major role in the management of title systems and of hierarchical relations of power in the kingdom. Following the death of a titled officeholder, the coral beads given to him by the king were always returned, because owning them without the permission of the oba was punishable by death.

Because European trade with West African communities went through periodic phases of decline, the coral used by the oba and his titleholders appears at times to have included locally manufactured stone beads, like the lantana beads from Ilorin, which were originally made in Old Oyo. This regalia also may have included beads made from locally available agate or jasper.

These Edo women wear imported coral beads as anklets, bracelets, necklaces, and hair ornaments. As chiefs' wives, they are canvases that display his wealth. The expense of coral means that imitations in glass and plastic are common. Benin City, Nigeria, 1994. Photograph by Kathy Curnow.

Although in the nineteenth century it was commonly believed that the oba's treasury contained large quantities of coral, hardly any coral of real value was found when Benin was sacked by the British in 1897. In the early twentieth century, the beads used in Benin's annual Festival of Corals were definitely from Ilorin.

When European glass beads were first introduced to West Africa, they were exchanged for gold, slaves, ivory, various oils, and other raw materials. Initially, these beads came from Murano, one of the Venetian islands off the Adriatic coast of Italy. A large variety of bead types and designs were made by the glassmakers working on this island, including millefiori (thousand flower) beads in an endless array of colors; chevron beads made of alternating layers of glass, usually red, blue, and white; bicone beads, which in Ghana appear to have been traded for their own weight in gold; and hand-decorated fancy beads. In the course of its history, the Murano manufacturing center probably produced between two hundred thousand and three hundred thousand different wound beads.

In the sixteenth century, Italian glassmakers also began to make beads in the Netherlands. Working in Amsterdam, they manufactured plain round or oval beads in a variety of colors, from white to blue and black. Now known as *dogons* because of their popularity among the Dogon communities living in present-day Mali, they have been copied by African glassmakers. Italian glassmakers also settled in Bohemia, where they specialized in the production of molded beads. This included so-called Vaseline beads, which acquired their name from their transparent, milky appearance, and snake-bone beads, which resemble the vertebrae of serpents.

CHANGING VALUES

By the seventeenth century, traders selling glass beads to West African communities had to satisfy an increasing market for novelty.

Surviving records indicate that there was stiff competition among the different European traders supplying this market. Unable to compete with the comparatively low price of beads supplied by other traders, the Dutch were forced to abandon their foothold in West Africa. In the course of the twentieth century, they nevertheless managed to regain control of this market through the well-known Amsterdam-based bead exporter J. F. Sick and Co. Using price controls and its skills in sourcing and buying beads from various European manufacturers, J. F. Sick and Co. eventually managed to establish a virtual monopoly over the West African bead trade after World War II.

As elites gradually lost control over the consumption of imported beads, their prestige value as signifiers of wealth and power was replaced by more inclusive social and ritual values. But as late as the nineteenth century, the role ascribed to beads in sustaining hierarchical relations of power varied considerably from one area to another. Thus, for example, when a missionary visited the royal homestead of the second Zulu king, Dingane, in the 1830s, the twenty-one posts supporting the king's reception chamber were covered from top to bottom with beads of various colors. Dingane was an ardent aesthete who took great pride in displaying his beadwork garments to foreign visitors. He also expressed a fervent desire to find someone who could teach the art of bead making to his subjects. More than ten years later, when the artist-traveler George Angas visited the royal homestead of the third Zulu king, Mpande, in 1847, he reported that on festive occasions, the beaded garments worn by the king's women were so heavy that they found it difficult to dance in them.

To this day, beads are often used well beyond the period in which they were first manufactured or traded. Some of the beads currently available on the Ghanaian market come from archaeological contexts, while others have become part of heirloom collections. Strung and restrung over time, beads usually have a very long use-life. This includes amber beads made from fossilized pinesap that originally came from the Balkans region of eastern Europe and that are now very expensive. In contemporary Morocco, as well as other parts of West Africa, lack of access to amber has led to the introduction of various substitutes. Among Berber communities, these substitutes include copal, a semifossilized amber; ambroid, formed by melting amber pebbles and pressing them together into larger pieces; and modern, industrially manufactured composites such as Bakelite.

Although originally the widespread practice of salvaging beads or bead pieces from older garments was probably motivated by the cost of beads, symbolic—rather than economic—considerations now tend to inform this tendency to reuse beads. In some African communities, old beads are believed to contain vital energies transmitted to them through contact with the original owner, while in others they are said to mediate relations between the living and the dead. This explains the widespread tendency to attach strings of beads to the bodies of infants in the belief that they protect newborn babies against disease and other metaphysically inspired negative forces.

The conviction in some African communities that beads either embody or mediate powerful spiritual forces also underpins the contemporary association of beads with ritual contexts and rites of passage. Color often plays a significant role in the symbolic value attached to these beads. Thus, for example, among diviners from the present-day KwaZulu-Natal region of South Africa, it is customary to place a white charm (*ikhubalo*) in the thatch above the diviner's doorway. In some cases, this charm is the vertebrae of a ritually slaughtered animal, but it may also be a single white bead or a cluster of white beads. In most situations, it is also common for these diviners to attach white beads like these—which are associated with both the ancestors and notions of purity—to the large black cloths they wear during their consultations with clients. In outlying rural areas, white beads are still scattered around the wounds inflicted on ritually slaughtered animals consumed at weddings. Elsewhere in South Africa, among some Xhosa-speaking communities from the eastern Cape, the beaded garments worn by diviners tend to be made predominantly from white beads. To ensure that their offerings reach both the ancestors and the water spirits, these diviners often pour tobacco and white beads into the whirlpools of rivers.

The use of beadwork in rites of passage, such as the puberty rituals signaling the transition to adulthood of African girls and boys, is so widespread that it can be described as a pan-African tradition. Likewise, elaborately beaded headdresses, necklaces, bracelets, and anklets are commonly worn by women during their marriage ceremonies. To this day, Maasai brides from Kenya wear multiple circular beaded disks (*imankeek*) around their necks, while Ndebele brides from present-day Mpumalanga province in South Africa once wore elaborately beaded capes and veils.

THE IMPACT OF CHRISTIANITY ON THE USE OF BEADS IN AFRICA

Throughout Africa, the use of beadwork has been condemned as un-Christian by new or recent Christian converts. In the past, communities often destroyed their beadwork garments under pressure from missionaries. This is not, however, to suggest that Christianity has always been in conflict with African tradition. Historically, African communities living in the vicinity of Catholic missions experienced greater tolerance toward indigenous forms of dress and adornment than those who came in contact with Protestant missionaries. Moreover, although the Protestants invariably claimed that the habit of wearing beadwork was barbaric, in practice many of them were forced to become involved in the bead trade, because the European missionary societies responsible for their well-being did not always provide adequate funds for their survival.

In the course of the twentieth century, religious groups that seek to integrate Christian and African values and beliefs, such as the Ibandla lamaNazaretha in present-day KwaZulu-Natal, have spearheaded a renaissance in the production of beadwork garments. The beaded garments made by women belonging to this church are worn in acknowledgment of the powers not only of the ancestors but also of God. Beadwork patterns developed by these women include elaborately designed multicolored crosses set against a background of white beads.

CONTEMPORARY BEADWORK

Despite the obvious symbolic significance of Ibandla lamaNazaretha beadwork pieces inscribed with crosses, in recent years women belonging to this church have developed new styles and colors. These pieces appear to have been inspired by the fact that at least some of them have participated in self-help and commercial beadwork projects that favor the use of new, often synthetic, bead colors with a view to exporting beadwork aimed at, or commissioned by, the European fashion industry. Likewise, it has become increasingly common for some African communities to use large plastic beads. Contemporary aprons worn in the rites of passage of young Lovedu girls from Mpumalanga Province in South Africa include not only plastic beads and small plastic toys but also discarded watches, bird mirrors, and medicine spoons. The plastic bead marriage capes worn by Zulu-speaking women from the Valley of a Thousand Hills near Durban are another example of this trend, which can be ascribed to a number of interrelated factors, including aesthetic choices, the fact that fewer women are in a position to dedicate their lives to producing beadwork garments from small seed beads, and the prohibitive cost of beads in a country where the exchange rate has become increasingly unfavorable in recent years.

Although the production of beads and beadwork garments remains fairly common in rural communities throughout Africa, indications suggest that it is unlikely that these art forms will survive into the foreseeable future. Changing local values, the growth of urbanization, the impact of globalization, and a lack of interest in tradition—especially among younger people—all mitigate against a continued commitment to supporting these industries. West African traders still move between different countries in the region, selling beads from one area to another, and, following the founding of the Ghana Bead Society in 1994, members of that society now have access to information regarding the names of beads and where they are manufactured. But throughout Africa, there is growing evidence of a decline of interest in what has arguably been the continent's greatest art form over many millennia.

References and Further Reading

Bascom, William. *The Yoruba of Southwestern Nigeria*. New York: Holt, Rinehart and Winston, 1969.

Beck, Roger B. "Bibles and Beads: Missionaries as Traders in Southern Africa in the Early Nineteenth Century." *Journal of African History* 30 (1989): 211–225.

Becker, Cynthia. *Amazigh Arts in Morocco. Women Shaping Berber Identity*. Austin: University of Texas Press, 2006.

DeCorse, Christopher, Francois Richard, and Ibrahima Thiaw. "Towards a Systematic Bead Description System: A View from the Lower Falemme, Senegal." *Journal of African Archaeology* 1, no. 1 (2003): 77–110.

Drewal, Henry, John Pemberton III, with Rowland Abiodun. *Yoruba: Nine Centuries of African Art and Thought*. New York: Center for African Art, 1989.

Fage, John D. "Some Remarks on Beads and Trade in Lower Guinea in the Sixteenth and Seventeenth Centuries." *Journal of African History* 3, no. 2 (1962): 343–347.

Insoll, Timothy, and Thurstan Shaw. "Goa and Igbo-Ukwu: Beads, Interregional Trade, and Beyond." *African Archaeological Review* 14, no. 1 (1997): 9–23.

Klopper, Sandra. "From Adornment to Artefact to Art: Historical Perspectives on South-East African Beadwork." In *South East African Beadwork, 1850–1910*, edited by Michael Stevenson and Michael Graham-Stewart, 9–43. Cape Town, South Africa: Fernwood Press, 2000.

Klopper, Sandra. "The Postmodern Context of Rural Craft Production in Contemporary South Africa." *The Future Is Handmade: The Survival and Innovation of Crafts. Prince Claus Fund Journal* 10a (2003): 184–99.

Labelle, Marie-Louise. *Beads of Life. Eastern and Southern African Beadwork from Canadian Collections*. Quebec: Canadian Museum of Civilization Corporation, 2005.

Liu, Robert K. *Collectible Beads*. Vista, CA: Ornament, 1995.

Maagnavita, Sonja. "The Beads of Kissi, Burkina Faso." *Journal of African Archaeology* 1, no. 1 (2003): 127–138.

Mitchell, Peter J. "Prehistoric Exchange and Interaction in Southeastern Africa: Marine Shell and Ostrich Eggshell." *African Archaeological Review* 13, no. 1 (March 1996): 35–76.

Ogundiran, Akinwumi. "Chronology, Material Culture, and Pathways to the Cultural History of the Yoruba-Edo Region, 500 B.C.–A.D. 1800." In *Sources and Methods in African History: Spoken, Written, Unearthed*, edited by T. Falola and C. Jennings, 33–79. Rochester, NY: University of Rochester Press, 2004.

O'Hear, Ann. "Ilorin Lantana Beads." *African Arts* 19, no. 4 (1986): 36–39.

Roth, H. Ling. *Great Benin, Its Customs, Art and Horrors*. London: Routledge and Kegan Paul, 1968.

Ryder, A.F.C. *Benin and the Europeans 1485–1897*. New York: Humanities Press, 1969.

Wilson, Alexandra, ed. *The Bead Is Constant*. Accra: Ghana University Press, 2003.

Sandra Klopper

See also Egypt: Historical Dress; Dress in Egypt in the Twentieth Century; Morocco; Benin; Ghana; Mali; Nigeria Overview; Yoruba in Nigeria and Diaspora; Tanzania; South Africa Overview; volume 10, Beads: Prehistory to Present.

In discussions of dress in Africa, soled footwear is generally considered only as an afterthought, and the barefoot stereotype still pervades popular thinking about Africa. Feet, however, are conceptually dressed and framed in many of the same ways as hands and head. And much like the adornment of other parts of the body in Africa, elaborate forms of footwear were and are generally reserved for wealthier segments of society, although distinctions based on gender, age, vocation, and religion are also factors. In addition to sandals, shoes, and boots, the term *footwear* includes anklets in a wide variety of techniques and materials, and the painting and tattooing of feet, footrests, and stilts. While the head is obviously the locus of thought and most of the senses, and hands are potentially the most dramatically expressive part of the human body, feet are literally the foundation of human mobility and are as essential for most work and play as are the hands and sometimes even the head. Emphasizing this fact in many cultures, feet are a frequent proverbial metaphor for various paths through life that address issues such as progress, direction, and stability. In their most fundamental senses, soled footwear obviously serve physically and materially protective functions, but many of the various forms of footwear discussed here also serve as protective amulets and charms. Some of these function under the tenets of Islam, where images of the sandals of the Prophet Mohammed are a recurring design motif in jewelry, leatherwork, and even carved wood doors.

ANKLETS

In many cultures, related forms and styles of dress are employed to encircle wrists and ankles and as such may carry related messages. There is some evidence that bead production in Africa dates back two hundred thousand years, although there is no evidence to suggest how these beads were used. It is tempting to speculate whether beads were first employed on necklaces, bracelets, anklets, or threaded onto the hair, but the answers remain unknown. Still, the first anklets were probably not beaded, but rather were hide or plant fiber ties, because sinew or fiber threading was a prerequisite for the beading process. Indeed, both hide and fiber may have been twined or plaited before they were used as threading. And considering the continuing role of anklets as idiophones in African ritual and dance, it is possible that naturally occurring lengths of various dried seed pods also figured early in the history of ankle ornaments.

Speculation aside, the range of materials, techniques, and designs employed in anklets is enormous and is clearly seen in some of the early archaeological evidence. Ancient Egypt offers numerous examples of multiple strands of beads made from lapis lazuli, carnelian, and gold encircling the ankle. The terra-cotta figures from the two-thousand-year-old Nok culture of Nigeria and those of medieval Djenné in Mali, as well as the twelfth- to fifteenth-century bronze and terra-cotta figures from the sacred Yoruba city of Ife, all reveal elaborate stacks of beaded anklets rising up the lower leg from just above the foot.

Nearly as widespread are coiled copper, brass, and aluminum wire anklets that also often wind from the top of the foot to just below the knee. These range from the Kassari of Guinea to the Maasai of Kenya and Tanzania and the Ndebele of South Africa, to cite just three examples. Married Ndebele women might wear the coils with fully beaded ankle and leg rings in solid colors that may be from six to ten centimeters (two to four inches) thick.

Anklets in silver, nickel, and aluminum have a fairly wide distribution across North Africa and the Sahel and into Somalia and Ethiopia. Primarily worn by women, at one time they were the prerogative of ruling classes, although in most areas they eventually became available to anyone who could afford them. Many examples simply slip around the ankle, while others are hinged. Some Mauritanian anklets are embellished with square plaques of finely worked repoussé sheet gold. In the western Sahara, silver anklets called *khal khal* were thought to protect against snakebite or other foot injuries. In Somalia, hinged cast-silver anklets called *hujuul* were ringed with repoussé bells worked from a silver alloy to improve their sound. These anklets were especially favored at weddings.

Cast-metal anklets more sculptural in form are found elsewhere in Africa. Among the Bwa and related peoples of Burkina Faso, women wear cast-brass and aluminum anklets that curve upward on both front and back, depicting leaf mask imagery at each end. Art historian Christopher Roy notes that these are worn by women whose families perform the masquerade in honor of Do, the son of the creator god. They are also commissioned to cure illness or to promote fertility in women struggling to conceive.

The Igbo peoples of southeastern Nigeria once wore some of the most substantial and spectacular anklets in all of Africa. According to art historian Herbert M. Cole, large cumbersome platelike brass anklets (*ogba*), thirty to thirty-five centimeters (twelve to fourteen inches) in diameter, were worn until the 1920s by girls and women well into middle age. They were also worn by "maiden spirit" masqueraders. These anklets were wrought rather than cast, and the upper surfaces of the plates were stamped and incised with geometric and occasionally figurative designs. In addition, senior women leaders among the Igbo were entitled to wear heavy sections of ivory tusks that stretched from the top of each foot to just below the knees. For both forms, Cole observed that "practicality and comfort...are supplanted by the display of privilege and prestige," and quoted one of his titled female colleagues as saying, "You can sacrifice for beauty."

Massive and heavy anklets have been documented among many peoples of West and Central Africa in a variety of contexts, but almost always worn by women. Anthropologists Eberhard Fischer and Hans Himmelheber have recorded anklets worn by Dan women in Liberia weighing up to six and a half kilograms (fourteen pounds) on each ankle. These were worn by wealthy

Senior Igbo woman wearing ivory anklets and bracelets. Ugbene, Nigeria, 1983. Photograph by Herbert M. Cole.

high-status women who had many servants, and the anklets were "the mark of a woman too distinguished to know the sweat and rush of work." They were publicly presented to the women by their husbands during a prominent festival and were pounded closed around the ankles to be worn for the rest of their lives. These anklets also served as a form of currency. Large metal anklets cast or wrought in an array of shapes, almost all worn by women, are especially well known from the Baule of Côte d'Ivoire; the Fang of Gabon; the Fulani of Niger; and the Mbole, Ekonda, and Mangbetu of the Democratic Republic of Congo. In almost all instances, the anklets also served as currencies.

An important dimension of ankle wear in much of Africa concerns its potential sound-producing properties. Many anklets serve as idiophones that are activated by movement, especially dance. Dried seed pods are naturally occurring rattles and are employed in several parts of the continent as anklets. Strings of shells, glass or metal beads, bells, and even bottle caps produce a distinctive range of sounds from the subtle to the bold when activated by the movement of feet. More complex anklets, especially cast-brass examples, maximize the aural potential of the genre. A frequently seen form across the Sahel of West Africa features three, four, or five crotal or pellet bells integrally cast into a single anklet, such as those found among the Frafra of northern Ghana. Wrought iron examples are also known. Some cultures, however, take this basic idea and multiply it by stacking the ankle rattles. The Gio of Liberia cast as many as five layers of five bells each as one substantial piece producing both a visually stunning anklet and, when worn in pairs, an impressive acoustic experience. At the other end of the spectrum, a single pellet bell in many cultures is often attached to the ankle of a child after she or he begins to walk, so the caregiver can be alerted to the child's movements.

Extreme examples of cumbersome and constraining anklets raise issues of volition. Most notions of African dress are associated with voluntary decisions about asserting identity within a given culture. While there are certainly social, political, and religious pressures influencing those decisions in the name of custom or tradition, participants in the decisions are generally viewed as willing. Nevertheless, the appearance of an individual may be deliberately altered for punitive reasons. In some cultures, scarring or the removal of toes or fingers, or even feet or hands, is both punishment and stigma. In the same vein, shackles or leg irons in much of Africa are associated with both criminals and slaves. The history of the slave trade in Africa marks shackles as among the most dehumanizing and loathsome items ever imposed on the human body, but they are a reality of both indigenous and foreign practices that remain major symbols of oppression.

TATTOOS AND HENNA

Until the second half of the twentieth century, the tattooing of Amazigh or Berber girls of Morocco and other parts of North Africa marked the transition to womanhood. Considered an essential part of the rites of passage, a girl's forehead, hands, and feet would be tattooed with symmetrical geometric motifs named after forms in the natural environment that they resembled. In addition to these rites, tattoos were also applied for prophylactic reasons or to cure a disease once it occurred, such as a neck tattoo to alleviate goiter. Tattoos were also thought to help ward off the evil eye. Tattooing has largely disappeared under the pressures of Islam, because the Prophet Mohammed proscribed it and it is considered to hinder the effects of ritual ablutions.

The Arab introduction of the temporary dye called *henna*, applied to both hands and feet, was embraced by women across North Africa and down much of the coast of East Africa. The Prophet was thought to have dyed his beard with henna, so its use has religious sanctions. Henna is applied at key life events such as weddings or childbirth, and, in addition to being highly decorative, henna designs, like those of tattoo, are considered to serve prophylactic functions. The use of henna is particularly well documented in Morocco, where, as art historian Cynthia Becker, a specialist on Berber culture, has noted, "henna is believed to protect and purify the body during rites of passage ceremonies due to its association with 'divine blessing' (*baraka*). The *baraka* of henna further protects the bride against the danger of the evil eye and the *jnoun* that prey on people as they pass through crucial moments in the life cycle." One of the overall intentions is to create a sense of well-being. Although the use of henna in life-cycle events is ritually charged, it is also employed during more secular social occasions. The process of applying the henna to both hands and feet may take from six to eight hours, and the designs are primarily geometric and floral, although the potential symbolism of individual motifs is not as important as the process of application and the overall effect.

SANDALS, SHOES, AND BOOTS

Across most of Africa and for most of its many peoples, sandals, shoes, and boots were very much the exception rather than the norm until after the middle of the twentieth century. In terms of the actual physical protection of the foot, sandals certainly preceded more encasing footwear. The best evidence for early sandal use in Africa comes from ancient Egypt. Most of the substantial numbers of sandals that survive from that time have soles made from coiled grasses, papyrus, or palm leaves. Leather and wood were only occasionally employed in the production of the soles. Multiple pairs of sandals were recovered from the tomb of Tutankhamen (1336–1327 B.C.E.), ranging from the humble to the truly majestic. His mummy was adorned with strapped sandals with sheet gold soles that were clearly never intended to be worn, but rather to accompany the deceased king in the afterlife. A number of similar examples have been recovered with evidence that they were molded to the foot of the obviously elite deceased.

One pair of sandals found in Tutankhamen's tomb was fashioned from wood, leather, gold foil, and pigment. Depicted on the insoles are two bound but well-dressed prisoners, one clearly Nubian and the other West Asian. The symbolic idea, of course, is that the leaders of Egypt are literally standing on their enemies and indeed obliterating them. Reinforcing the idea of Egyptian superiority are representations of eight bows, four above and four below each pair of prisoners, further emblems of ancient Egypt's suzerainty over its traditional enemies. Beginning after about 1500 B.C.E., select Egyptian rulers, including Tutankhamen, were also buried with individual toe stalls placed over each toe after mummification. Fashioned from gold ("the flesh of the gods"), each stall typically features a carefully rendered nail and toe ring.

Although largely a luxury, sandals in various materials and configurations, through time and across Africa, have been the most affordable and favored form of soled footwear. These typically feature a hold between the first and second toe and lateral

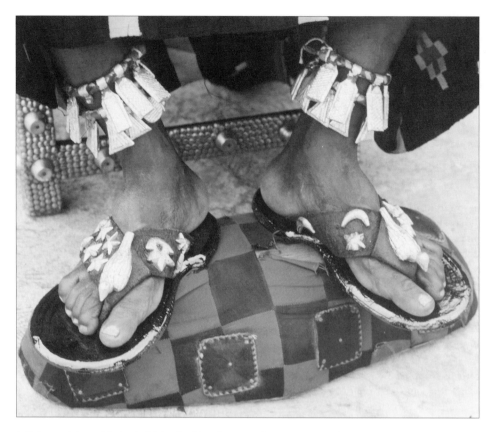

Anklets, sandals, and footrest of Odeneho Oduro Numapau II, paramount chief of the Asante state of Asumegya. Ghana 1976. Photograph by Doran H. Ross.

straps secured on each side toward the back. Other common types are constructed with a single wide strap across the foot with no toe hold, or crossed straps over the top of the foot. Subtle and nuanced differences exist in traditional sandal construction and decoration from culture to culture. Outside of ancient Egypt and Nubia, some of the earliest sandals in West Africa were discovered through excavations at burial caves in the Bandiagara escarpment above Dogon villages in what is now Mali. Dating from the eleventh to the fourteenth centuries, fifteen individual leather sandals (no pairs) were uncovered. They featured slightly tanned and oiled cow-or buffalo hide soles with individual ankle and toe straps embellished with incised lines and dots. Some of the sandals had decorated rectangular ankle guards attached on the outside. Like many sandal forms in Africa, these could not be identified by gender based on burial associations.

Among the best documented of African sandal traditions are those of the Tuareg, an Amazigh/Berber group that spans much of the Sahel and has crossed the Sahara Desert along ancient trade routes for many centuries. Tuareg specialist Henri Lhote has suggested that their leather sandals can be divided into three types associated with three different environments—desert, mountain, and steppe—but Danish anthropologists Johannes and Ida Nicolaisen have cautioned against any rigid environmental determinism in their distribution. As might be imagined for nomadic and pastoral peoples such as the Tuareg, their sandal traditions share an as-yet-unraveled history with their trading partners and far-ranging neighbors, including the Berbers of Morocco, the Mande peoples of Mali and adjacent states, and the Hausa/Fulani groups of northern Nigeria and beyond.

The paramount chiefs of the Akan peoples of southern Ghana, the former Gold Coast of West Africa, have some of the most elaborately ornamented sandals on the continent, and they are considered the single most important items of regalia in wardrobes that are among the most extensive and sumptuous in Africa. Sandals (*mpaboa*) are worn with gold covered anklets that began in many northern Akan states as a string of matched Muslim amulets. Contemporary examples are primarily ornamental. Although the general construction of the leather sandals is similar to most West African types, the straps are covered with representational motifs cast in gold or carved in wood and then gold leafed. A slightly larger focal ornament is positioned where the straps meet above the toe hold. In addition to being an obvious statement of wealth and status, the ornaments typically illustrate traditional proverbs that celebrate the power, wisdom, and leadership of the chief. The clever trickster spider Ananse, the source of the famous spider stories of the Akan, is a common image on sandals. It is often associated with the maxim "No one goes to the house of Ananse to teach him wisdom" because Ananse (and the chief) is thought to be keenly intelligent in the first place. Some Akan sandals are completely covered in gold, except for the outsoles, and other sandals have soles shaped as silhouettes of animals seen as powerful, such as the eagle, crocodile, and scorpion. These, too, represent proverbs proclaiming various attributes of the chief—for example, "The sting of the scorpion is as slow to subside as a fire is to cool." An important chief may have as many as ten or twenty pairs of gold-ornamented sandals. The most important examples are carried in front of him in festival processions. When a man is installed as chief, the critical ritual act is the placement of designated sandals on his feet. If a chief does not live up to his duties, the removal of his sandals indicates that he has been removed from office.

Sandal makers in Africa, like most of the rest of the world, attempt to balance the stiffness and durability of the sole with the pliability and comfort of the straps and toe hold. Nevertheless, some African sandal types are fully rigid. A familiar form in East Africa and parts of North Africa are all-wood clogs with a short cylindrical vertical toe hold but no straps. The sole may be flat, have a low heel, or rest on a platform heel in back and a support of a similar height under the front. These wood sandals are usually worn in domestic situations (they are often called *bath sandals*), especially among the Swahili of Somalia, Kenya, and Tanzania. High-status versions have been documented with ivory toe holds, and exceptional examples are encased in silver and are worn by bridegrooms at weddings.

Perhaps the most extreme forms of rigid sandals are the cast-brass examples worn by Kran chiefs in Liberia. Cast as one piece by the lost-wax process, the resulting product is an inflexible monolithic sandal with solid brass sole and straps. The upper perimeters of the sole are sometimes fully edged with integrally cast scalloped motifs, and the straps are cast as skeuomorphs of braided fibers.

The informal-sector production of sandals made from discarded rubber tires was a near-worldwide phenomenon and began at least as early as 1950 in Africa. Tires provide an inexpensive and durable resource for the soles and straps of sandals, although one significant variation employs inner tubes for straps. Upon their initial introduction to rural Africa, these sandals had a certain modest prestige. Unfortunately, in fashion-conscious urban Africa, the wearing of tire sandals often stamps one as poor, rural, and uneducated—with all three collectively implied by seeming identification as a farmer. While many discussions of dress and fashion in Africa focus on what is popular and what is not at any given point in time, very few scholars have addressed the criteria and language used in these evaluations. Anthropologist Dennis Warren and his colleague Kweku Andrews documented a number of disparaging comments used to discredit tire sandals in urban Ghana, including, "You will weed or farm until you die" and "They stick to your feet even if you fall." The sandals are also called *katapila*, after the steel tracks of Caterpillar bulldozers. With the increasing importation of cheap molded rubber and plastic sandals throughout Africa, tire sandals became even more unpopular from the 1980s on. Nevertheless, in the early twenty-first century, they seem to be making a comeback. Confronted by expanding mounds of abandoned tires and growing media attention promoting ecological awareness, more formal commercial initiatives in Kenya, South Africa, and elsewhere have renewed production of tire sandals for both local consumption and export.

From the beginnings of European and West Asian contact, foreign footwear began to exert an assortment of influences on African practices. Greco-Roman intrusions probably introduced shoes to Egypt, and the Arab sweep across North Africa in the seventh century led to the leather *babouche*, still one of the most distinctive forms of African soled footwear. Often identified with Morocco and Tunisia, the babouche is actually found in several forms throughout the Mahgreb and Egypt as well as in many parts of Muslim West Africa and in coastal areas of East Africa. Typically, the soles consist of several layers of leather, and the uppers are continuous and not split. The rear quarters may be upright, folded down on the insole, or entirely absent. The leather is frequently dyed red or less commonly yellow or green. Early examples had an upturned toe, but this has largely disappeared. High-status babouches have decorative welts, pinked edges, and finely braided throat rims and are heavily embroidered with silk and/or metallic threads.

A Libyan variation of the babouche has been documented by British Museum curators Chris Spring and Julie Hudson as part of a bride's trousseau from the Ghadamis Oasis. The leather uppers are dyed red and intricately embroidered in multicolored silk with bold curvilinear motifs. Rising above the ankle is the tongue of the shoe in the form of the Hand of Fatima. Fatima was the mother of Mohammed, and the upraised hand motif with an open palm is widely associated with her in the Muslim world. The motif is considered to be an effective means to ward off the evil eye. In addition, the five fingers are said to recall the five obligations or pillars of faith of Islam. The reflective silver bosses carefully positioned at junctures of the embroidered designs are also thought to deflect the evil eye, an especially important concern at key events such as weddings.

Traditional African leaders have long been identified with distinctive footwear. Among the most unusual are the raffia shoes (*mateemy manneemy*) worn by the kings of the Kuba and Kete of the Democratic Republic of Congo as part of some of the most extravagant ensembles of royal dress anywhere in Africa. They are also worn by titled chiefs, the mother of the king, and by the two masqueraders who represent royal initiatives among these groups. Rare in African royal footwear (the Hausa occasionally feature this on boots), each toe is individually encased in its own sleeve, and the top of the footwear is often adorned with lines of

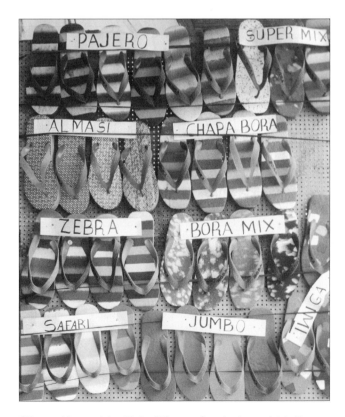

Chinese rubber sandals with Swahili names for sale at a market in Mwanza, Tanzania, 1999. Photograph by Doran H. Ross.

cowry shells and blue and white beads, often in a distinctive guilloche pattern. In addition, carefully rendered toenails cut from cowry shells (or alternatively whole cowries) are positioned on the outside tips of the toe sleeves. These shoes are worn below a dense stack of ankle ware that includes, from the top down, copper anklets, circlets of glass beads, multiple strands of cowries, and ankle rattles. Befitting their importance, the shoes are required funerary attire for deceased kings.

Some of the most influential and famous sandal, shoe, and boot forms in West Africa are a product of leather workers centered in the Hausa city-states that began to flourish in the fifteenth century in what is now northern Nigeria and Niger. The sandals and shoes catered to wealthy traders and to the Muslim leaders of these states, and the boots were produced for the cavalries that helped sustain and expand the states. The more elaborate examples of all three types of footwear feature leathers dyed red, green, and black and combined in appliqué and reverse appliqué techniques. They may be further embellished with stamped, painted, and embroidered designs. On sandals, the juncture of the straps might be decorated with a fringed leather circlet or an ostrich feather rosette. The leather boots generally rise to just below the knee and have leather extensions that continue up the front of the thighs, the whole providing a larger canvas for decorative elaboration, especially with appliqué cutwork in the form of divided squares, diamonds, and circles.

The royal shoes and boots of Yoruba leaders living to the south of the Hausa may have been derived from the construction of Hausa examples, or perhaps from those of Europeans visiting the coast with whom the Yoruba traded since the sixteenth century. Regardless, the lavish beadwork that covers all exposed surfaces of Yoruba chiefly footwear distinguishes their shoes and boots (and their crowns) from the rest of Africa. Until the early twentieth century, sumptuous footwear was considered the exclusive prerogative of chiefs and designates. In celebratory praise of chiefs, the Yoruba say, "May the crown rest long on your head, may shoes remain long on your feet." A common motif near the tip of the uppers is a human head with prominent eyes that, according to scholars Henry Drewal and John Mason, are "ever watching for impending trouble, guiding the steps of the [chief] on his journey through a life of momentous rites." Intertwined guilloche designs are common to both Yoruba crowns and footwear and suggest the "interlace of life and reincarnation." European-style crowns are another common beaded motif on shoes and boots, an example of Yoruba chiefs embracing foreign symbols of royalty.

Among several leadership traditions of Africa, a footrest is a critical component of royal regalia for a seated chief. Although footrests might be categorized as furniture, they are also an essential accessory of dress to the same extent as handheld swords or scepters. Yoruba chiefs rest their feet on thick circular cushions fully beaded on the sides and tops with the same styles and motifs that are found on chiefs' beaded shoes and boots. Many leaders in the Cameroon Grassfields rest their feet on an elephant tusk, sometimes carved in relief with royal symbols. In at least one example, the chief has a small floor of elephant tusks in front of his throne. Alternatively, a chief might rest each foot on the base of a tusk, with both tusks projecting symmetrically forward as if they were positioned on a living elephant. The Asante of Ghana once used amulet-laden leather footrests containing the heads of defeated enemies. Other Akan chiefs have carved wood footrests with elephants or leopards as favored royal emblems. Kuba and

Kete leaders from the Democratic Republic of Congo often rest their feet on leopard skins when seated in state.

Due to international media attention and to the political and musical associations of the genre, gumboots or Wellington (Welly) boots—the most common rubber workboots across the continent—may be among the best known of all African footwear. They gained both fame and notoriety as the waterproof black boots worn by migrant workers in the gold mines of South Africa. According to local oral traditions, a system of coded communication based on slapping the black rubber boots and rattling the constraining chains of work gangs developed into a series of performance behaviors that took the place of prohibited verbal exchanges. It subsequently expanded into more elaborate dances for leisure entertainment in the all-male miners' hostels. The slapping and stomping of the boots produced distinctive percussive sounds that amplified the dance and added new, more positive dimensions to an enforced regime of dress. Topical songs and chants were composed to accompany the dances. At some point, metal bottle caps were threaded on short rods and attached to the boots, adding another sonic dimension to the performance. The bottle caps are thought to recall the chains worn by early workers forced into the mines. This history inspired a 1985 Paul Simon song on the *Graceland* album and the 1999 South African musical *Gumboots*, which became a major international theatrical event. It toured through most of the first decade of the twenty-first century, and a filmed version of the performance along with a documentary was released on DVD in 2000.

Contemporary sandals and shoes in Africa follow globalizing phenomena. Molded rubber and plastic sandals, especially from Chinese sources, remain the norm for a large majority of Africa's populations. The expanding used-clothing enterprises that permeate much of Africa, including remote village markets held every four or five days, offer an assortment of tennis shoes, sneakers, and similar casual wear in an array of labels, both counterfeit and authentic. Used leather shoes with full uppers and quarters are also available. For wealthier segments of many nations, most of the international offerings of footwear are available in major cities or through extended family connections and international travel.

STILTS

The most substantial and dramatic forms of footwear are the stilts worn by a wide range of masquerade societies in West and Central Africa. As dress is defined in the encyclopedia, stilts fall into the category of costume elements. Nevertheless, similar to the ideas leading to platform shoes, high heels, and even footrests, the most obvious intention behind stilts is heightened elevation. The typical stilt consists of a single vertical shaft, the upper portion of which is secured to the calf below the knee with a footrest appropriately placed farther down the shaft. The length of the stilt below the footrest varies anywhere from a couple of feet (two-thirds of a meter) to eight feet (two and a half meters) or more depending on local traditions. Although some stilts are ornamented on their wood structures, the appearance of the stilts themselves is generally not important, because the structures are typically covered by other costume elements that create the illusion of an exceptionally long-legged being. Although various stylized manners of stilt walking are certainly part of the masked performances, it is the often acrobatic stilt dancing that captures the attention of the audience. The overall effect may be

Igbo stilt masquerade called *ekeleke*, Agwa, Nigeria, 1983. Photograph by Herbert M. Cole.

simultaneously entertaining and supernatural. Stilts are clearly employed not for the ordinary, but for the extraordinary.

Dance ethnologist and art historian Robert Farris Thompson begins his evocative discussion of the love of stilt dancing by the Dan peoples of Liberia with, "In a world of tested balance and inner calm the stilt dancer is exquisitely appreciated." Although the Dan call stilt maskers *gle gbee*, or "long spirits," they apparently have no religious significance. Nevertheless, some accounts suggest that stilt dancers were originally spirits that emerged from the water. Thompson's 1974 description of stilt dancing among the Dan could apply to several other parts of Africa:

> The dancer crosses his stilts before his body. He relaxes his elbows, waist, and knees and sits down on thin air, posterior brought perilously below the level of his knees. He rises and walks with giant steps. He stands, staring down, at the admiring populace ten feet below. He jumps backwards seven times. He twists his body at the waist and swings his enormous legs, literally dancing.

Thompson concludes his provocative discussion thus: "Finally, the stilt-dancer, incarnating directional strengths transcending conventional stability, furthers the lessons of composure under fire. He works against the pull of the earth and the play of the witches. Moving within the richness of his heroism, his motions take on the irreversibility of a sacred act." This description could have been prompted only by a dancer wearing stilts.

Another masquerade on stilts called *ekeleke* is Igbo in origin and is described by Herbert M. Cole as "a very pretty, finely choreographed group display and drama…with an imposing and stately character." It is performed in support of a water spirit, but is considered a "lighthearted spectacle" without "strong ritual underpinnings." The masquerade is spread over a number of days and is notable for its carefully tuned unison dancing with as many as ten maskers performing at once. It is also known for its virtuosic solo performances with a competitive component encouraging vigorous and fast-paced movements that are visually heightened by the fact that they are performed on stilts.

These accounts could be multiplied with examples from the Dogon of Mali, Fante of Ghana, Punu of Gabon, and Yao of Mozambique, among many others, performed in contexts ranging from funerals and initiations to carnival-like festivals and contemporary cultural displays. African-descended populations in the Caribbean are also renowned for stilt-dancing traditions.

Footwear in performance, however, is not limited to the theatrical movements of stilt dancers. Some of the most demonstrative acts illustrating the role of sandals and shoes in a given society have to do with when and where they are removed. For Muslims in Africa, the removal of sandals and shoes for ritual ablutions before entering a mosque is a religious requirement. Among the Akan of Ghana, chiefs and their attendants remove their sandals before entering the sacred ancestral stool rooms. Similar deferential and reverential acts of removing footwear are repeated in a broad cross-section of African cultures. As with many dress practices and clothing types, what is not worn is often as telling as what is worn, and sometimes a person is only properly dressed when a key item of clothing is publicly removed or omitted in the first place.

References and Further Reading

Becker, Cynthia J. *Amazigh Arts in Morocco: Women Shaping Berber Identity*. Austin: University of Texas Press, 2006.

Bravmann, René A., and Raymond A. Silverman. "Painted Incantations: The Closeness of Allah and Kings in 19th-Century Asante." In *The Golden Stool: Studies of the Asante Center and Periphery*, edited by Enid Schildkrout, 93–108. New York: American Museum of Natural History, 1987.

Cole, Herbert M., and Chike Aniakor. *Igbo Arts: Community and Cosmos*. Los Angeles: UCLA Museum of Cultural History, 1984.

Cornet, Joseph. *Art Royal Kuba*. Milan, Italy: Edizioni Sipiel Milano, 1982.

Drewal, Henry John, and John Mason. *Beads, Body, and Soul: Art and Light in the Yoruba Universe*. Los Angeles: UCLA Fowler Museum of Cultural History, 1998.

Fischer, Eberhard, and Hans Himmelheber. *The Arts of the Dan in West Africa*. Zurich, Switzerland: Museum Rietberg, 1984.

Frank, Barbara. *Mande Potters & Leather-Workers: Art and Heritage in West Africa*. Washington, DC: Smithsonian Institution Press, 1998.

Lhote, Henri. "Les sandales." *Memoires de l'I. F. A. N.* 10 (1950): 512–533.

Loughran, Katheryne S., John L. Loughran, John William Johnson, and Saidsheikh Samatar, eds. *Somalia in Word and Image*. Bloomington: Indiana University Press, 1986.

Nicolaisen, Johannes, and Ida Nicolaisen. *The Pastoral Tuareg: Ecology, Culture, and Society*. London: Thames and Hudson, 1997.

Ross, Doran H. *Gold of the Akan from the Glassell Collection*. Houston, TX: Museum of Fine Arts, Houston, 2002.

Roy, Christopher. *Art of the Upper Volta Rivers*. Paris: Alain et Françoise Chaffin, 1987.

Spring, Chris, and Julie Hudson. *Silk in Africa*. Seattle: University of Washington Press, 2002.

Thompson, Robert Farris. *African Art in Motion*. Los Angeles: University of California Press, 1974.

Vogelsang-Eastwood, G.M. *Tutankhamun's Wardrobe*. Rotterdam, The Netherlands: Barjestch van Waalwijk van Doorn, 1999.

Warren, Dennis M., and J. Kweku Andrews. *An Ethnoscientific Approach to Akan Arts and Aesthetics*. Philadelphia: Institute for the Study of Human Issues, 1977.

Doran H. Ross

See also Egypt: Historical Dress; Dress in Egypt in the Twentieth Century; Morocco; Ghana; Yoruba in Nigeria and Diaspora; Hausa in Nigeria and Diaspora; Kenya.

Masquerade, Theater, Dance Costumes

African masquerades, perhaps the continent's premier art form, play grandly with illusion, ambivalence, and paradox. Masks and masquerades are both more, and less, than what they appear to be. Their illusionist play can be comic and lighthearted, or deeply serious, but always it is creative and imaginative, art and artifice. Never is it ordinary, and usually it is deeply meaningful and sometimes powerfully instrumental. Masquerades both create and help organize values and knowledge, and they are thus anything but trivial—a word that characterizes many Western ideas about masks. Masking is a powerful, pervasive aesthetic component in many African cultures.

Masquerade dress components are many and varied, but they all begin with the active human body as armature or model, although in their most imaginative extensions into the otherworldly, they appear to depart the human realm entirely to enter fantasy or pure invention, so non- or metahuman do they become. And even if the masked character mirrors a human being, it embodies transformation as a defining characteristic; the wearer is not himself, and, simultaneously, he is not *not* himself. It is rare for a masker to wear clothing seen in a village, just as his face is never seen except as a mask. Dress components show the same creative artifice as heads: unusual combinations of materials, gloves, stockings, rattling anklets, and other elements not seen among the general populace, at least in those combinations.

Donning a mask creates for its wearer a liminal experience from which he can literally act out, experiment with, and violate normal constraints and behaviors. Masking transforms him into an other. His observers, too, face a paradox: a persona that is and is not real. Very often masking helps create a liminal, ritual period for the community, as, for example, during the two most important rites of passage in Africa—the initiation of youths to adults and the funeral (or second burial)—as well as during times of crisis when extraordinary measures are required to restore health and balance to a community. What both players and audience members choose to wear helps to define the event.

Masking has been so prevalent on the continent—albeit mostly among settled agriculturalists and thus mostly in the vast areas drained by the great Niger and Congo Rivers—that there are many tens of thousands of masks, or rather headpieces, in existence today both in Africa and in collections elsewhere, mostly in Europe and America. Usually just the head has been collected without the full body costume, and this limits understanding by outsiders. A face or head covering alone—especially as fixed on a wall or in a case in a museum or home—is but a fragmentary afterlife of the vibrant character or spirit, the being moving actively, often with other maskers, in space and time. Yet the face itself is very important as the primary carrier of identity. As the focus of most masquerade personas, the invented face by itself is often a captivating, expressive work of art. These faces—masks and headpieces—exist in bewildering variety, from miniatures an inch or two long (two to five centimeters) to those thirty feet tall (nine meters) or others weighing two hundred pounds (ninety-one kilograms).

Many, but by no means all, maskers honor or embody supernatural beings and are locally called spirits, which is, of course, part of the illusion, for always there is human agency and human intention as well as meanings that reverberate in the human community. In fact, the extent to which a masker *is* a spirit whose powers are believed in or only *represents* a spirit, a player, is a contested issue. In either case, they are all invented beings, even those that look convincingly like real women or men.

Masquerade components, properly understood, must include time and space as well as physical materials such as body suits, anklets, rattles or bells, head coverings, whips, porcupine quills, and palm fronds. In this essay, the word *mask* usually refers to the entire masked character, the fully dressed masker with his implements (spear, fly whisk, knife, animal horn). The field of the masquerade—usually with multiple characters—as a unified event, its context, is the village square or pathways (and these days, the town or city), daytime or at night, always with designers and mask makers behind the scene, often attendants to the players, always an audience, and the reason for the masquerade outing: funeral, festival, agricultural or other rite. The masker is one of the characters, yet there may be a hundred or more in a single masquerade event, such as the Dogon Dama in Mali (a second burial rite, an initiation, a festival, a purification, and a rite of renewal, among other things). A large Dama assembles as many as sixty or more distinct mask characters, each different from the next in name and appearance and action. Illustrations of Dogon masking show eight, ten, or more characters. Some represent

A woman wearing an Igbo Adamma mask at a festival in a soccer stadium, Engug, Nigeria, 1993. She also wears a red, green, and yellow miniskirt; white gloves; and chromed-plastic bead stockings that rattle. Photograph by Benjamin Hufbauer.

birds or Fulani girls; the Fulani are cattle herders who live among the Dogon and whose young women are admired for their beauty. They wear false breasts of baobab fruit attached to a fiber bra. Their headpieces are dyed black with and woven of wild plant fibers to simulate elaborate hairdos and are often embellished with cowry shells (formerly a form of currency and thus signifiers of wealth). Most of the maskers wear bright red hibiscus fiber armlets, wristlets, and skirts that are deeply important Dogon symbols of water spirits, menstrual blood (with which they are said to be dyed), female energy and potentiality, and the concealing putative sexual organs (whose moisture they seek to preserve for childbearing). The fibers, as essential complements to male maskers, make the masked spirits androgynous.

Thus head coverings (masks) are sometimes small but vital components of entire characters with headdress or flowing layered costume—often with symbolic elements, with leg rattles, mirrors, the whip or fly whisk held in the hand, with the sounds emitted by the characters or their attendants, their hand and dance gestures, and their interactions with other maskers and members of the audience. Among the Dan of Liberia and Côte d'Ivoire, the elaborate multimedia headdress that extends sometimes eighteen

inches (forty-six centimeters) backward from the top of the mask may be more relevant in portraying the specific character being invoked than the face mask itself; and that head extension participates too in that masker's vocabulary of gestures.

Spatial components may include temporary structures for entrances or exits, cleared ground, the edges of the audience, and the built environment. Temporal dimensions, often marked by drums, gongs, and other music, include entrances from the netherworld (or the wilderness); stories, songs, or skits (i.e., scripts); chasing or acrobatics; the climax; and the departure. The physical components are neither fixed nor unchanging; they are affected by light levels and all the activity of the varied masking personnel and the environment (dust, the sun, firelight), with multiple and ever-changing points of view, over many hours in some cases, and occasionally over several days. As the Nigerian proverb from the Igbo has it: "You must not stand in one place to watch a masquerade." Implied here, of course, is all that one misses if the mask and masquerade are seen as fixed or static or seen only from one vantage point. The best recording medium for masquerades is film or video; still pictures do not do justice to the time and space factors that so affect the physical components and the meanings of most masquerades. The proverb also alludes to points of view. Any masquerade necessarily embraces many points of view, those of the masker, the old men who know the ropes, uninitiated boys, women who try to recognize their men, strangers, leaders praised by the dances, and others.

Masks may be classified or modeled in many different ways according to disparate paradigms: by the nature of the masked characters, whether human, animal, and/or spirit; by gender; by use, purpose, and function; by materials employed in their construction and costuming; by size and shape; by the nature of the plays or dramas in which they appear; by their roles in embodying beliefs, legends or myths, and worldviews; by their degree of power and sacredness or, alternatively, their secular or purely dramatic character—that is, by examining their place on the continuum between ritual and play; by the distribution of types by ethnic group, region, or geography (e.g., eco-zone); by the inclusion or exclusion of females as mask carriers or members of masking organizations; by the nature of masks' liminality and their role in mediation (e.g., between forest and village, men and women, health and disease, life and death, leaders and the people, etc.); by the changes in and history of masks generally, including ancient or pre-Contact examples, or of those in a specific area, among others. Most of these are at least touched upon here, although space does not permit a thorough analysis of masking types, ideas, materials, models, history, and meanings.

DEPICTIONS OF EARLY MASKING IN ROCK ART

There is no way to know when masking began on the African continent, but it has been both so widespread and so important in the past few centuries that it is likely very ancient indeed. The presence of both masks and masked dancers in rock paintings and engravings—though these are notoriously hard to date accurately—takes us back at least three to five millennia. While the continent boasts thousands of rock art sites, the two main concentrations of them are in the Tassili region of the now-dry Sahara and in San regions of southern Africa. Animal heads and skins worn by humans suggest that these masked beings might have been early hunters in the Drakensberg Mountains in South Africa. Large-eared masks, as well as drawings of people wearing these with what appear to be netted costumes, closely resemble twentieth-century examples. And there are numerous other hard-to-interpret rock art images of people who might (or might not) be wearing masks. What is, however, clear is the fact that the true origins of African masking are lost in the mists of prehistory.

GENDER IN MASKING

The gender of masking institutions, mask characters, and mask carriers reveals some important and widespread traits of African masking. While many unrelated African peoples in different regions (e.g., Kuba, Dogon, Mende, Senufo, Igbo, and Baule) ascribe the discovery or invention of masks and masking and their rituals to women, as recounted in sacred history (also called mythology), these stories also recount a misadventure by the female founders that ended in men taking over masks, their rites, and their institutions and barring women from future involvement. Thus, apart from a few relatively small areas (among Mende and related peoples of Sierra Leone and Liberia, some Igbo groups, and a few others), men control masking. Men make, wear, and dance perhaps 98 percent of all known masks on the continent. In several cultures, on the other hand, select women are honorary or actual members of male masking associations, sometimes playing vital ritual roles, but pointedly not inside a mask.

At the same time, thousands of varied masks, though danced by men, portray women of virtually all known ages, types, and pursuits: youthful beauties, married mothers, old crones, harridans and prostitutes, market women, foreigners, and ancestors. Yet usually there are details of costuming that women ordinarily do not wear. A general characteristic of most female masks is their association, in the minds of local people, with the order and peacefulness of village life, features often symbolized by the use of textiles—everywhere seen as valuable and symbolic of civilized human life—as part or most of their costumes. Probably the most widespread of all female characters, known from virtually every ethnic group that embraces masking, is the maiden, the beautiful unmarried girl. Because youthful beauty is universally admired, the headpieces that evoke these varied female maskers across Africa represent a fine catalog of varying aesthetic ideas of the good, the pure, and the beautiful, traits that are often considered synonymous. The melding of these ideas in African thought also reveals that Africans rarely separate purely aesthetic concerns about dress and personal decoration from moral and utilitarian ones. Most of these headpieces show refined facial features, including scars or tattoo, and are carefully finished. Equally, the garments the maiden wears are normally well tailored, even if the whole character is a slight caricature of what women really look like. Not surprisingly, in masking activity the pretty girl is often pursued by a rather aggressive and frequently older (and sometimes quite deliberately ugly) man—again, of course, a masker. This gendered interaction is played out in a thousand different ways, sometimes with mothers, sisters, a controlling father, a buffoon brother, or other characters as part of the play.

Many of these same headpieces show a wide range of facial markings—raised keloidal scars and tattoos—as well as lip labrets, earrings, and other attached forms of jewelry once fashionable among varied ethnic groups. The well-known maiden and other female face masks of Chokwe of Angola and related peoples,

for example, display an especially rich array of facial markings (many with esoteric cosmological references), jewelry, headbands, and hairstyles, most of which no longer survive among the people. Filed teeth, common on most Chokwe masks made and danced late in the twentieth century, were rarely seen after 1910 or 1920. Makonde helmet masks from Mozambique and southern Tanzania, similarly, catalog hundreds of facial marking patterns as well as styles of hair dressing that were imperative for many Makonde people in the early twentieth century (and earlier) but were abandoned by about 1950–1960. Thus, a careful survey of headpieces or masks collected around 1900 or earlier might reveal modes of personal decoration not otherwise known. Such readings, however, must be cautious, because among the Igbo, for example, much fancier and elaborate hairstyles are featured on masks than were ever affected in life—the result, apparently, of competition (better, new, different!) among both carvers and masking organizations.

Where masks figure in the initiatory passage of boys into young men, as is widespread on the continent, gender play by maskers serves as part of the novices' education. Male–female interaction is often explicitly sexual, a form of instruction seen as an essential part of the socialization process. Mask headpieces among the Yaka of the Democratic Republic of Congo are occasionally graphically sexual, but much more common is sexual dancing—whether or not part of initiation—gestures unmistakable even when the masker's face is fixed, stoic, and unemotional, as it virtually always is. Among the Bamana of Mali, in dances by the Chi Wara initiatory association, for example, the male and female maskers may not be separated while dancing, sometimes

Two Bwa men at a funeral wearing leaf masks that represent Do, the god of the wilderness. Boni, Burkina Faso, 2006. Photograph by Christopher Roy.

with explicitly human sexual miming. They wear not human headpieces, but rather, small carved male and female antelopes lashed to basketry caps and long, flowing hibiscus fiber costumes. The legendary founder of this men's initiation society, Chi Wara, was an antelope or hybrid animal, but one with human traits, as revealed by the sexuality of the dance and by the baby antelope on the back of its mother, a position found among humans but not among antelopes. Other male–female interactions involve miming with a huge phallus, even if the gendered play is not overtly sexual. Across the continent, few human situations are not held up for examination in masked theater.

PORTRAIT MASKS

Virtually all portrait masks represent or commemorate women and are of the fine-featured and refined, well-finished type. According to reports, Dan, Baule (Côte d'Ivoire), and Northern Edo Okpella (Nigeria) examples (and there are surely others) are less accurate imitative likenesses than they are portraits by name, context, and costuming—and sometimes by scarification and hairstyle on headpieces (even if Dan artists insist that their portraits really resemble their subjects). Such portraits by designation work well in face-to-face communities where most people know one another. Commemoration rather than verisimilitude seems to prevail, for the women so honored were usually famous for their beauty, dancing skill, or other accomplishments. The dancing of portrait masks affords the honored person, sometimes after her death, public recognition, the admiration provided by the collective memory of the community. Such masks normally appear in the company of their namesakes or perhaps a close relative if the woman is too old or infirm. Among the Baule, when the portrait mask subject dies, a daughter or granddaughter also known for her dancing skill is chosen as her successor, and the mask then takes her name. Deceased mothers are similarly commemorated among the Okpella, but only if they have achieved fame, wealth, or high title. In some cases, the older woman herself commissions the portrait mask; in others, members of her family do so. What is important is that the mask continues to be danced out of respect for the woman and her achievements. Yet again, these masks are danced by men.

A UNIQUE ANCIENT MASK

The Obalufon mask, cast in almost pure copper and dated to between the twelfth and fifteenth centuries, is said to have been kept in the palace of the *oni*, or king, of Ile-Ife, the ancient and current spiritual capital of the Yoruba peoples in southwestern Nigeria. Remarkable for its sensitive, fleshy naturalism, the mask is said to represent Obalufon II, the third ruler of ancient Ile-Ife. It may be a near-mimetic portrait, but, if so, like other Ife works, it is idealized. It has no blemishes, no indication of age apart from generalized adulthood. Obalufon is said to have introduced copper alloy casting to the Yoruba people of Ile-Ife, where a series of cast heads, also in a style of idealized naturalism, were discovered in the early twentieth century. Most were revealed in archaeological excavations. The Obalufon mask may have been used in funerary rites for Ife kings, with facial hair, beaded veils, or costume elements attached to the rows of holes. A second ancient Ife mask, made of terra-cotta, is probably from the same period, but its use is uncertain.

A metaphorical model underlies many masks that depict women and men, touched upon in the earlier discussion of gendered opposition. The model is a series of binary opposites:

Women	Men
Village	Bush/wilderness
Day, light colors, white	Night, dark colors, black
Beauty	Ugliness
Clarity, order	Obscurity, mystery, chaos
Cloth	Raffia and other natural materials
Culture	Nature

These opposing structural categories are especially evident in Igbo Okoroshi masking and in the Goli masking sequence of the Baule and Wan (Côte d'Ivoire), yet they are implicit in most gendered masking as well—as in the Bamana concepts of *badenya*, "motherchildness" (gentle, passive, submissive behavior associated with home), and *fadenya*, "fatherchildness" (aggressive, competitive activity associated with venturing out). The Bamana hold that every individual has components of each, yet one or the other may be dominant in different people or at different times in any life. These complementary notions, then, comprise systems of thought about both the world and social life, albeit in reductionist, black and white terms, and what the activity of masking does is mediate these oppositions to better reflect the actual complexity—the many shades of gray—of both the world and human life.

In southern Nigeria, several cultures—the Edo, Igbo, Idoma, Ibibio, Ogoni, Igala, and others—exemplify this light-dark structural opposition in their masking even though each of these peoples tends to have its own styles of both light (usually white) female and dark male masks. For most of these peoples, the white clay of female masks symbolizes goodness, abundance, health, and beauty, whereas black (or dark colors) is associated with warfare, amorality, evil, sometimes disease, and ugliness. Among the Ibibio, dark masks, usually with black raffia costumes, appear only at night and portray ancestral souls sentenced to perpetual wandering and ghosthood. Light-colored Ibibio maskers, who invariably wear nice cloth wrappers or garments, portray benign ancestors with slow and graceful dancing; they embody the souls of people who led productive and morally upright lives. The inflections of meaning, like the styles, vary somewhat among these often-contiguous peoples, but the essential oppositions prevail.

A marvelous example of quite recent adaptation and changing materials in masking garments is an Igbo maiden mask from the 1990s called *Adamma*. She wears a long black synthetic wig hung with multicolored plastic beads that frame her naturalistic tan mask face, with bright red lipstick, eyes emphasized with heavy black eyeliner, at least four types of modern factory-made cloth—one metallic and multicolored, another sewn with sequins, yet another gauzy, and, fourth, a ruffled red, green, and yellow miniskirt—plus white polyester gloves, rattling chromed-plastic bead stockings, and a sculptural yellow chiffon head tie. Her dances are flirtatious, even licentious, her poses coquettish; yet her character had three varied aspects: virtuous daughter, wife, and mother; glamorous pop star; and flashy, rather disreputable vamp. She was one of many maskers at the 1993 Enugu State Mmanwu Festival in Nigeria, a competition held in a stadium, but perhaps the most modern of masked characters in appearance and behavior. Two male maskers who danced opposite Adamma were a palm wine tapper and a leopard, both of whom wore factory-printed bodysuits with deliberately rough, if not precisely ugly, wood masks. The tapper carried a plastic jug and a wooden rifle.

MASKING BY WOMEN

The main area where women dance masks (or at least did before the warfare of the late twentieth century), in parts of Liberia and Sierra Leone (a tiny segment of African geography), is an exception to the male-as-maskers rule. Several contiguous peoples, the best known of which are the Mende (yet including as well the Vai, Gola, Temne, and other nearby peoples), have inclusive women's associations, Sande, that dance shiny black helmet masks with black dyed fiber attached to their bases, and with all-concealing body costumes, again usually black raffia. The helmets display an abundance of good/beautiful female traits (with associated values): finely dressed hair (high status, wealth, orderliness); downcast or nearly closed eyes beneath a long forehead (the mysteriousness of the spirit); a closed mouth (demure silence and seriousness); a neck that shows creases or rings of flesh (good health and probably fertility); and a glistening, oily or wet-looking black surface (refers to the oiled bodies of girls emerging from initiation or to the mask as a wet river spirit). The well-dressed girls, however, still wear the white chalk that signifies their spirit status during the liminal period of their initiation. Called *Nowo* or *Ndoli Jowei*, the masks dance at key events in the initiations of young girls becoming women as well as at the installations of chiefs and at other important events in the community calendar.

MASKING MATERIALS

Masking materials are meaningful. Cloth is associated with village order and safety, and raffia represents the danger, mystery, and often the sacred character of the forest wilderness. A masker's physical components usually are chosen with motion in mind: for example, the staccato athletic rhythms of much Burkinabe masking in Burkina Faso, with swirling and jerking fibers never still; the waving feathers of Kalabari Ijo water spirits; and the twirling, floating layers of rich cloth in Yoruba Egungun. Depending on its specific nature, of course, motion conveys meanings. And so do the rest of the materials that comprise the character. Although the word *costume* is perhaps inappropriate from the point of view of African peoples themselves—who usually see in masks the bodies of spirits—it may be acceptable for this explanatory context, in part because such ensembles are consciously constructed of many different materials, each of which adds meaning. Natural materials include skins of leopards, other cats, or many other animals; leaves, raffia, hibiscus, or baobab fiber netted or flowing; feathers; and palm fronds. One of the more spectacular natural spirit bodies is the Bwa leaf, fiber, and feather ensemble of the Do masquerade in Burkina Faso. With varied names and compositions, these spirits are born in the wilderness as young Do initiates collect karate tree leaves (which are symbols of fertility) and wrap the performer in fresh green-leafed vines from head to toe, as Do. This spirit represents the dependence of humankind on the forces and products of nature, as well as growth and renewal. It dances in compounds and in agricultural fields, and at the end of the day returns to the bush, where the leaves and vines are burned. The symbolic birth and death of this spirit, of course, signifies the cycle of life.

SKIN-COVERED MASKS AND HEADDRESSES

Another kind of natural material employed in mask manufacture is the skin of animals, stretched tautly over carved wood heads and masks, oiled and polished, and given finishing cosmetic touches to appear quite realistic. These are found among several contiguous peoples living along the Cross River in eastern Nigeria and western Cameroon (Ejagham, Efik, Ibibio, Boki, Igbo, Akbarabong, Anyang, Widekum, and others). Many are complete heads on necks lashed to basketry caps or disks that are in turn tied atop a masker's head. Some heads are doubled or tripled, lashed to a board also tied to the masker's head. Several of these look very much like trophy heads and thus are likely to be later versions of actual heads once taken in warfare. Head-hunting was still practiced in this region in the late nineteenth century, and a few surviving headdresses are comprised of actual human skulls.

Female headdresses often feature two, three, four, or five ribbed spiraling horns recalling fancy hairstyles; many of these were danced by members of the Ikem society among several of the above-mentioned peoples. These versions, apparently not derived from trophy heads, rather stemmed from "fatting house" practices of several Cross River peoples. Nubile girls were secluded, sometimes for many months; given high-calorie food; and instructed in deportment, dance, song, sexual technique, cooking, and other female pursuits needed in marriage. They also rubbed their bodies with camwood, oiled and painted them, and affected elaborate and time-consuming hairstyles. Dressed in finery, with cosmetics, jewelry (beads at the neck, waist, and arms, brass rods spiraled around legs), and finely dressed hair, the girls were presented to society. After their coming out from seclusion, the girls were then ready for marriage. These masks are replicas of the fancy coiffures affected by marriageable girls of several Cross River peoples, and their costumes echoed some of their dress and accessories.

Other female headdresses are helmet masks with one, two, three, or four faces, the dark one usually male, the light ones female. Many have realistic-looking pegged-in teeth, open eyes with pupils, as well as scarifications and tattoos. Among the tattoos are many ideograms known as *nsibidi*, a form of writing among several Cross River peoples and linked especially with local leopard societies such as Ngbe, which served many governmental functions in pre-Colonial times, occasionally using skin-covered and other masks as agents of social control.

THREE-PART COMPOSITE MASKS

Other examples of intensely powerful meanings accorded masking materials come from the Bamana Komo societies in Mali and from other parts of West Africa, where analogous three-part composite headpieces are made and ritually danced. The three parts are snout, head, and horns. *Composite* refers to the usual merging of (parts of) several usually wild animals in the masks' compositions: crocodile, antelope, warthog, hyena, bird, buffalo, and human. Among the Bamana, Komo headpieces are deliberately horrific amalgams of the spirit powers and actual organic parts of many such creatures (claws, beaks, shells, fur, teeth), with an emphasis on spiky menacing horns. They are anointed with repeated blood and other sacrifices. They are meant to be terrifyingly ugly and appear when deputized and consecrated by leaders to help rid their communities of crime, disease, malevolent forces, and other negative phenomena, all toward making life more healthy and prosperous for the people. Some Senufo examples in Côte d'Ivoire and southern Mali of these three-part headpieces have animal horns, grasses, and other "power" materials added to their wood armatures, and others are danced with suits made of sacred *flafanni* or *fila* cloth. This locally woven cotton-strip cloth, dyed in esoteric indelible patterns with iron-bearing mud mixed with high-tannin-content vegetal decoctions, is accorded protective power associated with wilderness spirits and was given by them to humans in legendary primordial times.

Analogous three-part composite mask headpieces are found among more than forty other peoples across West Africa (including the Toma/Loma, Baule, Senufo, Baga, Malinke, and several Burkinabe and Nigerian groups, plus Duala and other Cameroon peoples), each with a somewhat different style, costume, and combination of animals. Virtually all costumes emphasize wilderness materials, often having medicinal properties. Because most of these have similar sociopolitical functions (the rooting out of evil from their communities), the strong implication is that this type of mask has origins so deep in history that many centuries have passed since they were first conceived—time enough for them to differentiate from one another in style and somewhat in function and meaning. Undoubtedly, most of these three-part masks are related to one another, and their uses are of critical local importance. Nevertheless, they can be divided into two classes: horrific antiaesthetic versions, such as Komo and some Senufo and Toma versions, and others that are less messy and deliberately unattractive with added materials.

Other examples of medicinal and power materials added to mask headpieces and costumes abound on the continent, from the Dan/Kran, We/Ngere, and Toma/Loma of Liberia to Yoruba, Igbo, and several other Nigerian peoples to the Chokwe, Kuba, Pende Yaka, and Songye of the Congo. Can we imagine that the cartridge cases, animal horns, bones, and bells attached to We/Ngere masks are there only for decoration? Can it be that

the esoteric medicines that turn Dan/Kran headpieces into power objects so strong that they may no longer be danced, but rather are consulted as oracles, are comprised of neutral or innocuous materials? Is it possible that the expensive beads, metal appliqué, shells, imported upholstery tacks, locks, keys, and bells that transform the looks and shapes of mask headpieces from several areas are without meaning? Rhetorical as these questions are, we may not in all cases know the diverse and layered local meanings of all the added materials of which so many headpieces are comprised, yet we can usually be fairly certain that these accumulations are about layered and intensified spiritual power, and sometimes political power as well, for the strongest masks in Africa are usually in the hands of leaders or those deputized by them.

MASKS OF EPHEMERAL MATERIALS

Imaginative, fanciful, and deliberately nonhumanoid masking constructions of raffia and other plant fibers—another mask type, and a varied one—are known from many peoples of West and Central Africa, yet these are not featured in the masking literature because they are not collectible masks that can be hung on the walls of museums and private homes. In their careful workmanship, their dramatic sculptural shapes, and in motion, however, many of them are nevertheless substantial works of art. Small northern Edo ethnic groups in Nigeria such as the Otuo, for example, make some of the more spectacular of these full-body fiber masks, with layered skirts and aprons of different colors and textures, and huge heads—either a domical, bowler-hat-like cut raffia construction (called an "umbrella") or a flatter oval nimbus of stiff, radiating, concentric rings of varicolored fibers, all precisely cut. Both have sprays of raffia at the ankles that dramatize complex dance steps. Neither of these display masks has obvious human features. The latter, for example, has a tassel in place of a nose and no discernable eyes on its head. These maskers each

Otuoyema age-group masqueraders in Olu fiber costumes at Igugu Festival, Otuo, Nigeria, 1973. Photograph by Jean Borgatti.

carry a coiled rope cracked at the end of the performance as a whip might be; they are said to be village purifiers, while the others are admired for their dancing skills. Danced by fairly senior age-grade members, these masks, while their symbolism is esoteric, do not appear to be especially strong spirits.

Mende and nearby peoples of Sierra Leone used to dance several carefully constructed masks of mostly fiber, but with basketry, leather, mirrors, colored thread, and some cloth used to articulate their nonhuman headpieces. Some maskers, such as Gbini, are powerful spirits associated with paramount and lesser chiefs, while others, still considered spirits, are more oriented to entertainment in spectacular displays of dancing and acrobatics. Their bodies are either enlarged humanoid shapes with huge legs and arms and a broad and large shoulder cape that can be manipulated, all of raffia (Yavi), or they are large conical raffia haystacks (Jobai). The heads of both these examples are carefully fashioned rectangular constructions (basketry, cloth, mirrors, yarn, pompoms) without human features (one is based on the shape of a European crown), and their dances are varied and dramatic. The fluid motions of the Jobai haystack undulate rhythmically in a wide circle, its huge shape gliding and enveloping objects (even small children), making them seem to disappear. Yavi, with its enlarged limbs, has more abrupt, broken movements that depend more on fancy footwork and the bending of knees and elbows. The deliberately nonhuman shapes and spectacular movements of many such fiber masks emphasize the otherworldly nature of these spirits at the same time that they are wonderfully entertaining. The Bamana of Mali also dance several fiber masks, made mostly of grasses, that are equally abstract (i.e., nonhuman) yet more amorphous in shape than those of the Mende and that portray generic bush animals as well as hyenas and porcupines, even though they do not resemble these animals.

The Chewa of Zambia and Malawi also dance a series of basketry, grass, and cornhusk constructions created by the Nyau masking and initiation society. Danced primarily at funerals, these large, carefully detailed, communally made constructions, although they portray several wild animals in a stylized manner, are also said to embody spirits of the human dead. (The fact that boys are initiated as an adjunct to funerary rites suggests that the newly inducted men replace those lost to death.) At least seven different creatures are made: eland, tortoise, impala, cow, lion, hyena, and fingers (a conical mask representing the fingers of a sorcerer who digs up its victims' graves). Their presence in the community recalls the primordial era during which, according to legend, animals and humans lived together harmoniously, when animals simply died for humans when they became hungry. But humans became jealous of one another, so God separated them from animals. Both humans and animals then hunted one another. During a funeral, when a deceased person returns to God, the animals return—as maskers—to cry at his departure, while helping to effect it. The transformation of men into masked spirits parallels the transformation of the deceased into an ancestor and, in turn, that of boys into men.

CLOTH IN MASKING

Contrasting with the foregoing examples of strong natural materials are mask bodies made from an array of manufactured textiles that range from rough country cloth of local manufacture across much of West Africa to the fine ikats of Baule and Guro

(Côte d'Ivoire) mask costume ensembles to the rich and expensive imported brocades, tapestries, and appliqués of the sort common in Yoruba Egungun costumes. Wherever sumptuous and costly fabrics (either locally made or imported) are incorporated into masking costumes, as they are in many parts of West Africa and the Congo, at least two things are being expressed: first, the wealth and high stature of the sponsoring association and, second, the dignity, affluence, and power of the spirit or being so embodied. In Baule, the sumptuous cloth worn with a portrait mask honors the woman commemorated by the mask. Even though the mask is very naturalistic, only the scars on its cheeks are the portrait elements. Egungun maskers—with layers and layers of both locally made and imported appliqué and embroidered cloths—are ancestors whose influence from their world, it is hoped, will benefit people living in this world. The more cloth worn by the masker, the deeper and older is the lineage. The formula is: the more affluent and high status is the ancestor, the greater the benefits he or she can bestow on the living. Thus, ancestral spirits are usually embodied by expensive and elegant clothing, and sometimes by lots and lots of it (as among some Yoruba subgroups). This is seen, with variations, in the masquerades of the Cameroon Grassfields and among the Kuba and related peoples of Congo.

A dramatic cloth mask probably originated by the Nupe of Nigeria but now danced by Yoruba, Igbo, and a few others is an undulating, writhing, expanding, and telescoping cloth tube whose actions seem to be truly miraculous. Called *Ndako Gboya* by the Nupe, this tube, at its greatest extent, is about ten or twelve feet tall (three or four meters). It evokes the power and mystery of the ancestors it commemorates in a thoroughly abstract way, because there is no head, body, or limbs, simply a mobile and enigmatic cloth tube.

ROYAL MASKS

Many masquerades in the many kingdoms of Cameroon are owned by the king or operate with his blessing and exist primarily to support kingship and the royal court. Many such organizations are populated by nobles and titled men whose stature is signaled by layered costumes of a royal textile called *ndop* or *niesia*, resist-dyed indigo and white cloth, gathered around the waist and worn with many different masks or headdresses. These heads generally reflect their royal associations in either being appliquéd with expensive and exclusive copper alloy sheeting or with beads (sometimes both). In addition, some of these maskers, particularly those of Bamileke Elephant Societies, wear beaded vests, wide beaded belts, and, on their backs, a leopard pelt. The royal cloth was sometimes edged with the fur of rare colobus monkeys. Originally, ndop, a royal cloth of raffia tie-dyed indigo and white, was imported from Wukari in northern Nigeria, involving travel over hundreds of miles, but the tie-dying technique was brought from Wukari to Fumban, the Bamum capital, sometime during the reign of King Njoya (r. ca. 1885–1933), who was a great patron of the arts, especially the arts of dress.

At least three types of Cameroon royal elephant masks are known: the first is a relatively naturalistic carved wood elephant head about four feet (one and a quarter meters) long; the second, a smaller wood head covered with beads; and the third, a quite stylized beaded cloth, hoodlike mask with a pendant rectangular beaded cloth (earlier, bark cloth, raffia, or hibiscus fiber) panel representing the trunk and circular beaded ears, all trimmed with prestigious red trade cloth. Combining elephant and leopard in a single masker, plus expensive beads, at least doubles the symbolism of power, affluence, and royalty. In fact, the entire costume is a study in royal opulence: lengths of indigo and white cloth; thousands of beads sewn to cloth panels fringed with imported red cloth; and sometimes flaring, conical headdresses of red-tipped black feathers. Large rattling seedpod anklets and beaded horsetail fly whisks, plus walking sticks, complete the costume. The name given these costumes among the Bangwa is hardly surprising: "thing of money." Elephant maskers danced at annual festivals and the funerals of chiefs and society members.

The three best-known Kuba masked beings in Democratic Republic of Congo are also danced with elaborate costumes bespeaking the legendary royal persons signified by the threesome. The heads of each are multimedia accumulations, sewn or attached in orderly patterns: beads, shells, raffia, cloth, small metal charms, leather, sometimes leopard skin or civet fur, animal teeth, and sheet copper and sometimes topped with feathers of parrots, eagles, and other birds associated with rank and privilege. These are all costly prestige goods bespeaking the wealth and power of the ranking of mythical royals embodied by the masks. Costumes are rich with layers of embroidered or meticulously painted cloths, beaded bandoliers and belts, while fly whisks or other prestige implements are carried. The female member of the trio, Ngaddy Mwaash, represents (paradoxically) both the wife and mother of the king, who is represented in another masker, who competes with a third for Ngaddy's affection. The same masks are also featured at boys' initiations.

MASKS AND LEADERSHIP

The foregoing examples speak of close relationships between African leaders and masking, which is apparent wherever masks are danced. The mysteries and ambiguities of masking are largely controlled by leaders both to reinforce their authority and to exorcise perceived evils and threats to the orderly progress of community life. Especially trenchant examples are the masking societies of the Songye of the Democratic Republic of Congo, which enforced obedience to rulers through Bifwebe masks, especially by the aggressive and malevolent actions of numerous male masks. Covered from head to toe, maskers were seen as alien supernatural beings from the wilderness. The costume consists of netted raffia leggings, goatskins covering the hips, and long raffia from the mask down as far as the knees. While female masks had the benign role of detecting the hidden, males induced fear though their miraculous, sometimes savage, feats: breathing fire or spewing snakes or bees. Their mystique was so complete that people believed they could fly or cut themselves in half. While male masks could inflict destruction or even death (anonymously, but directed by leaders), females represented the source and continuity of life, the fertility of humans and the fields. The coded symbolism of male masks (and costumes) was a composite of mostly threatening animal parts and powers: crocodile snout, a beard (for an elder mask, raffia down to the waist) called "lion's mane" or "locusts," the stripes of zebra and antelope, nasal hair sharp like porcupine quills, a bird beak, the crest of a cock, elephant feet, and costume cords called "snakes." A horn projecting from the back of the mask symbolized elders' wisdom. The dramatic, exaggerated, and thrusting facial feature of Bifwebe headpieces—neither very human nor those of a specific animal—backed by the dread of powerful sorcery, apparently induced sufficient awe in the people at large that social order was maintained.

ANIMAL MASKS

The elephant and three-part composite masks discussed above are among the many masks on the continent that derive from

Otuoyema age-group masqueraders wearing Ugbokpa raffia velvet headdress at Igugu Festival, Otuo, Nigeria, 1973. Photograph by Jean Borgatti.

animals of almost every conceivable sort, from the crabs and fishes of the Niger Delta Ijo peoples to the sharks, sawfish, and bulls of the Bidjogo of Guinea-Bissau. Varied antelope and buffalo incarnations or variations are found among diverse peoples across the span of West Africa and extending south from Cameroon into Gabon and into the Congo, then into Angola and Zambia, and across to Malawi. Some such masks are fairly naturalistic renderings, while most are stylized, some to the point of fanciful abstraction, such as the antelopes among the Kwele of Gabon. Among the peoples of Burkina Faso (mainly Bwa, Nunuma, and Nuna), the following animal masks have danced during the mid- to late twentieth century: warthog, python, crocodile, scorpion, butterfly, hawk, roan antelope, duiker antelope, hippopotamus, rooster, duck, hornbill, ram, monkey, fish, buffalo, hyena, chameleon, and baboon. In keeping with their habitats in the natural world, many of these masks have costumes of raffia or other fibers that are usually said to represent the wilderness origins of these animals and their associated spirits.

LARGE ANIMAL MASKS

Some animal masks are so large that more than one man is required to manipulate them. Two West African examples are the cloth animal masks of the Senufo and the huge fantastic multi-horned animals with cloth bodies that are used as stages for puppet theater among the Bozo and Bamana along the upper Niger River in Mali. Masks with cloth bodies and carved wood heads, called *Nosolo* or *Kagba*, appear in third-level Poro initiation rites of the Senufo. *Kagba*, meaning "house of the village," is a large tentlike construction with a slender-necked three-part composite wood mask as its head. *Nosolo*, which means "buffalo-elephant," is a buffalo the size of an elephant; it is about ten feet (three meters) long and is carried by two men. The Igbo have a recently invented cloth elephant mask with plastic pipe for a trunk that is danced by four men, one in each leg. Bozo and Bamana mobile stages (for rod and string puppets) are huge rectangular body structures of locally woven and imported cloth with a many-horned wood head. Young male members of a youth association animate this gigantic beast, while young female members and others in the community sing and dance around it. Some of these great creatures are called antelopes, others buffalo, but none are in any way naturalistic by virtue of their overly long necks in some cases and multiple horns (on which small puppets sometimes perch) in others. These entertainments are substantially secular, although they hold up social relationships and cultural values for scrutiny and review.

OTHER LARGE MASKS

Other oversized masks are the tall, slender planks of the Bwa, Nunuma, Mossi, and Dogon (Burkina Faso and Mali). These are contiguous, related peoples, so it can be assumed that some of their masks had a single place of origin and later diffused among nearby groups. The first two of these peoples carve snake masks about fifteen feet (four and a half meters) tall as well as shorter, more abstract plank masks painted in black, white, and red geometric patterns. The Mossi and Dogon, respectively, carve abstract masks with openwork planks from six feet (two meters) to nearly twenty feet (six meters) in height. The Dogon example, *Sirige*, which is danced in Dama funerary rites, is the smaller and

more public version of one of West Africa's most powerful masks, the so-called Great Mask or *Sigi*, which is the ritual centerpiece of Dogon masking and the rich mythology that explains it. Renewed (by being recarved) every sixty years in each Dogon village, Sigi is so tall, heavy, and powerful that it cannot be worn or performed. Rather, it is carried out for rituals, and other masks are brought to its cave home, touching it so as to be energized by its power. Sirige, the smaller version that can and does dance, is comprised of alternating openwork and solid rectangles stacked up; the openwork slots resemble the facades of *ginna*, houses occupied by senior village elders. Thus Sirige is also called *ginna* as well as "ladder to heaven," a reference to its great height, and it is a surrogate for the still taller great mask that it resembles.

Probably unrelated to Dogon or Burkina masks are less slender but also very large and heavy ones called *Bedu* of the Nafana, Kulango, and Degha peoples of the Ghana–Côte d'Ivoire border region. Ranging in size from about five feet (one and a half meters) to over eight feet (two and a half meters), Bedu, wearing bulky, full-length raffia skirts, are danced in male-female pairs. Simple faces (at least eyes and a mouth) are cut into the lower, usually triangular, portion that is connected to an upper part consisting of horns (for males) or a large disk (for females) with cutout holes or crescents, and sometimes notches around the perimeter. After being ritually awakened, washed, fed, and dressed, Bedu masks come out annually to bless and purify the community and to honor ancestors.

MUKANDA CIRCUMCISION AND INITIATION RITES

Yaka/Suku, Pende, Chokwe, Lunda, Luvale/Luena, Mbunda, Kuba, and other Congolese peoples share a mask-using initiatory institution, with local inflections, that indicates a commonality and shared history among these Bantu-speaking peoples. In an initiatory schooling period that once lasted from one to three years (today six months or less), seven- to eleven-year-old boy novices are (sometimes forcibly and by maskers) removed from their mothers and taken to a restricted camp in the forest. There they endure ordeals, including circumcision, and learn skills needed in the adult world as well as ethical and spiritual principles. They are introduced to the secrets of masking—its legends, dancing skills, and manufacture—which they must forever keep from women and uninitiated children. This ritual is *Mukanda*. The initiates' preceptors are sometimes masked ancestral beings, *makishi*, who act as teachers and mediators between the village and the camp, between ignorance and knowledge, between boys and the men they must become. Mukanda instills knowledge and values, in large measure by means of makishi, who represent, as one scholar puts it, the "spiritual backbone" of Mukanda and thus of society at large.

Often undergoing a symbolic death at the beginning of the Mukanda process, the novices emerge, reborn, at the graduation ceremonies presided over by makishi. Thus, their symbolic death, liminality inside the camp, and their birth as adults all take place accompanied by masked beings of several types (of course, with countless variations in the style of masks and the institution itself from one ethnic group to another and from one year or decade to the next). Some maskers wear mask/charms, a term that refers to the spiritual and protective powers embodied in their dress ensembles. Makishi have specific roles in or outside the camp;

they traffic between the camp and the village and appear in numbers at graduation dances. Makishi help inculcate the social, economic, and other cultural values central in the lives of the people. The spirits embodied in these masks are, appropriately for their important roles, those of famous people: hunters, chiefs, those with many children, or those who are otherwise wealthy. These ancestral spirits are said to rise from the dead to help the living. Importantly, too, these mask characters are in a more or less constant state of flux, adapting to new values and conditions, adding characters such as airplanes, and responding to the presence of AIDS and other facts of contemporary life.

Mask categories and hierarchies exist, and approximately one hundred different characters have been identified among the Chokwe and related peoples. Although all the characters are said to be ancestors, one scholar sees three classes: sacred—a powerful royal mask only owned by high-ranking chiefs; circumcision—those active in the initiatory process; and dance masks, which are substantially secular and primarily entertainers.

MASKS THAT ARE NOT DANCED

Clearly, masks are often symbols of critical import, so much so that they appear in countless situations as emblems of authority or spiritual power, but are either too large or too small to be danced. Indeed, dance was never intended. Thus, there is the Great Mask Sigi among the Dogon, which is too powerful to be worn, and Dan/Kran masks that have accumulated so much experience over several generations that they are retired from dancing to become oracles or power objects so strong that they are rarely seen, sometimes not even by the priests who consult them. Among Congolese peoples are numerous charm-masks owned or manipulated by priest-rulers and kept in their treasure houses, as among the Pende, to heal or otherwise deal with social and political problems.

There are also miniature masks carried by initiates as charms among some West African peoples (Dan, Kran, Bassa, and others) and in the Congo (Pende, Kuba, and others). Leaders in several areas wear masks too small to be face covers on their hats (Baule), at their waists (Benin), or in series around their necks (Cameroon kingdoms). The Lega of eastern Democratic Republic of Congo have a wide variety of ivory and wood masks, most too small to be worn over faces, which are owned by high-ranking members of the men's initiatory society, Bwame. The masks represent a series of proverbs and precepts about leadership, wisdom, peacemaking and other ideas associated with their leader-owners. Some Lega masks are placed on fences or carried in the hands or worn on the arm, shoulder, or forehead (but not concealing the face), when, as in other contexts, they are emblems of rank, authority, and experience. Many are heirlooms handed down through the generations. Unlike most masks, those of the Lega are handled by women, who use them in their own initiation rituals.

THE AESTHETIC AND COMMUNICATIVE VALUES OF MASKING

While it is possible to explain aspects of masks and masking in words and to verbally tease out some of their meanings and values and their relationships to worldviews, there comes a point where words fail, and they should. This is true despite the fact that many masquerades contain song texts or other verbal interchange, that masking action may derive from myths or legends (as in the Dogon Dama and Sigi), and that often narratives can be easily discerned in masked play. Yet no one claims that music and dance can be translated into words. So it is with an understanding or appreciation of masking, which depends crucially on music and dance along with myriad material forms and surprising, enigmatic, or puzzling substances, plus colors and textures. Surely some of the power of masking, for both local Africans and outsider observers, derives from ineffable qualities in their display, movement, timing, and context. Surprise, invention, terror, humor, sudden death, and other odd or puzzling acts, traits, exclamations, or contexts are situations that may involve masking. A further difficulty is the cultural and linguistic difference between African masquerades that outsiders observe and outsiders' cultural predispositions. Does what we say about masking ring true for the masker? Not often has this question been asked—or answered. Are we and African maskers speaking the same language about the transcendent and the metaphysical nature of masks?

For locals experiencing their own masquerade, the power of belief, the compelling necessity for masking, and its not infrequent ability to change lives must color and partly control their response, just as its differences from our own relatively trivial masking and its exoticism (for us) shades our own understanding. It is valuable to reassert the conjunctions among physical beauty (or, in the case of Bamana Komo and analogous antiaesthetic masks, ugliness), utility or effectiveness, and moral goodness (or terror) in masking, for therein lie essential differences between mere play and instrumentality: that is, ritual or sociopolitical purpose and effect. Mere play is rarely applicable here, because masking is too deeply embedded in the African cultural fabric. As entertaining and lovely as masking can be, it is almost always more—at least it used to be until the mid- to late twentieth century. The something more cannot easily be translated, because it operates in murky, largely inaccessible emotional and psychological realms, and, like good art of other kinds, it feeds a not-easily-explained need. The fact that masking often attends and helps effect changes of state (in initiations, funerals, ruler installations, harvest rites, etc.) provides clues to its affects and effects as well. Quite often, masking moves people because the paradoxes of human existence are confronted by the paradoxes of the created beings embodied in masks. Masking does not explain the changes brought on by birth (or rebirth, as in initiation) and death, but in providing experiential paradox and ambiguity, it seems to help people deal with those changes, thus to assimilate and live with the inexplicable. In a funeral (as among the Senufo, Chewa, and many other peoples), it is often a masked ancestor or nature spirit who presides over the body/soul of the deceased, helping to effect its transfer to the invisible ancestral and spirit realm, and the same is true of countless initiations.

Much of the masking described above is now history, even if some of the masks are still made and danced. Many of them, on the other hand, are being made for sale to tourists, and some are being deliberately faked—that is, they are bruised and given false patinas that suggest long use and great age so they can be sold to unsuspecting people for high prices. The strong, decisive roles masks once played in social control are pretty much gone today, and the powerful local polytheistic and pantheistic beliefs that sustained much masking in the past have given way, perhaps 90 percent or more, to Christianity or Islam. Thus, most masquerades performed these days are largely secular even if their roots run deep in the history and values of their sponsoring cultures. Their settings too have changed. Masking festivals are now held as secular public displays and even competitions in urban streets or soccer stadia; an Igbo Ijele mask is commissioned by a politician and danced so as to draw large crowds for speech-making and propaganda. Dogon Dama dances by a hundred or more maskers that once lasted six days are truncated to a twenty-minute display by a dozen maskers for tourists in Sangha, and masking troupes are brought in trucks from villages to perform briefly at expensive city hotels in many African nations today.

On a brighter note, however, the dynamic characteristic of mask costuming through the twentieth century continues with vigor in the twenty-first. New synthetic materials and flashy new colors are seen, along with new characters, one of which, inevitably, is the White Man with a video camera. As far back as the 1970s, Jolly and Ode-lay Societies in Freetown, Sierra Leone, created masks collaged of many different old and strikingly new materials—from raffia, porcupine quills, and a calabash head to plastic beads, Christmas balls and tinsel, foam rubber, and mirrors. One Ode-lay mask is its maker's idea of a robot, as inspired by a science fiction film. Global ideas, new media, and new materials find their way into masks in the early twenty-first century even if change has long been part of the masking ethic.

References and Further Reading

Arnoldi, Mary Jo. *Playing with Time: Art and Performance in Central Mali.* Bloomington: Indiana University Press, 1995.

Borgatti, Jean. "Age Grades, Masquerades, and Leadership among the Northern Edo." *African Arts* 16, no. 1 (1982): 36–51, 96.

Bravmann, Rene. *Islam and Tribal Art in West Africa.* London: Cambridge University Press, 1974.

Cole, Herbert M. *I Am Not Myself: The Art of African Masquerade.* Los Angeles: UCLA Museum of Cultural History, 1985.

Colleyn, Jean-Paul. *Bamana: The Art of Existence in Mali.* New York: The Museum for African Art, 2001.

DeMott, Barbara. *Dogon Masks: A Structural Study of Form and Meaning.* Ann Arbor, MI: UMI Research Press, 1979.

Drewal, Henry John, and John Pemberton III. *Yoruba: Nine Centuries of African Art and Thought.* New York: Harry N. Abrams, 1989.

Glaze, Anita J. *Art and Death in a Senufo Village.* Bloomington: Indiana University Press, 1981.

Hersak, Dunja. *Songye Masks and Figure Sculpture.* London: Ethnographica, 1986.

Hufbauer, Benjamin, and Bess Reed. "Adamma: A Contemporary Igbo Maiden Spirit." *African Arts* 36, no. 3 (2003): 56–65, 94, 95.

Jordan, Manuel. *Makishi: Mask Characters of Zambia.* Los Angeles: UCLA Fowler Museum of Cultural History, 2006.

Kasfir, Sidney. *West African Masks and Cultural Systems.* Tervuren, Belgium: Musée Royal de l'Afrique Noire, 1899.

Lamp, Frederick John. *See the Music; See the Dance: Rethinking African Art in the Baltimore Museum of Art.* Munich and New York: Prestel, 2004.

Napier, A. David. *Masks, Transformations, and Paradox.* Berkeley: University of California Press, 1986.

Nicklin, Keith. "Nigerian Skin-Covered Masks." *African Arts* 7, no. 3 (1974): 8–15, 67–68, 92.

Nunley, John. *Moving with the Face of the Devil: Art and Politics in Urban West Africa.* Chicago: University of Illinois Press, 1987.

Phillips, Ruth. *Representing Women: Sande Masquerades of the Mende of Sierra Leone.* Los Angeles: UCLA Fowler Museum of Cultural History, 1995.

Roberts, Allen. "Tabwa Masks: An Old Trick of the Human Race." *African Arts* 23, no. 2 (1990): 37–47, 101–103.

Ross, Doran H. *Elephant: The Animal and Its Ivory in African Culture.* Los Angeles: UCLA Fowler Museum of Cultural History, 1992.

Roy, Christopher. *Art of the Upper Volta Rivers.* Paris: Chaffin, 1987.

Rubin, Arnold. *African Accumulative Sculpture.* New York: Pace Gallery, 1974.

Vogel, Susan M. *Baule: Africa Art, Western Eyes.* New Haven, CT: Yale University Press, 1997.

Yoshida, Kenji. "Masks and Secrecy among the Chewa." *African Arts* 26, no. 2 (1993): 34–45, 92.

Herbert M. Cole

Children's Masquerade Costumes

Children's masquerades in Africa south of the Sahara most often occur in the western and central areas—the major regions of adult masquerading—although some are found in southern Africa. Most performances are by boys; while girls' masquerades are rarer, they have not been as well reported in the past due to gender bias. In children's masquerades, as in adult ones, the performers' dress and mask are generally considered as a whole and have one name. Child masqueraders may play musical instruments and hold whipping sticks, horsetail or feather whisks, and other items; these are also aspects of the whole.

There are two basic children's masquerade forms: young children's masquerades for those not yet initiated, ranging in age from four to adolescence, and initiating masquerades, associated with adolescent rites of passage. The classification has become compounded as children initiate at younger ages, so that overlap occurs between the two masquerading forms. In general, dress, mask, and behavior of initiating masqueraders are prescribed by adults, while in young children's masquerades, there is greater freedom to create their own appearance and actions. In some African societies, there are taboos against young children using masks and dress materials similar to those used in adult masquerades. In some African societies, children's masquerading has been strongly discouraged and even punished; for example, in Liberia children are told to wait until they are initiated. In other African cultures, dressing and masking is allowed and even encouraged by parents, older siblings, and other adults.

Young children's masquerades can be grouped roughly into three categories, although there is no similar categorization for initiating masquerades. A rare form of young children's performances is where they are explicitly integrated with adult masquerading or ritual. Here the young masquerader is under the supervision of adults, who generally prescribe mask and dress. This is the case with the children's *sagiri* masquerades among the Dogon, where boys dress in a full head and body costume of a certain leaf, carry a stick, and frolic about, shaking their rustling leafy dress as if they were bushes in motion, while attempting to scare and catch younger children, especially girls. This humorous masquerade, however, has a serious aspect, as adults require it to be performed before the major rites of the Dogon year can commence.

In a more common form of children's performance, youngsters dress and mask in emulation of adult masquerades—as among the Kuba of the Democratic Republic of Congo and the Afikpo Igbo of southeastern Nigeria—although without being as fine in appearance and as sophisticated in movement as in adult masking forms. At Afikpo, boys prepare fresh raffia, then dress in raffia strands that go from shoulders to feet, and wear masks they have created that emulate forms of the *logholo*, or men's secret society masquerades. Instead of well-carved wooden adult masks, the cruder boys' face coverings are of coconut shell, coconut tree-trunk fiber, cloth, or cardboard. Once dressed, a group of logholo prance around the village square, their loose raffia costumes shuffling about as they wave a stick in one or both hands while chasing younger boys who try to throw them. Among the Yoruba of southwestern Nigeria, boy performers in the Egungun masquerade also emulate adult forms—for example, in the *alabala Egungun*, where the boy's dress consists of a number of full, voluminous cloths, rich in colors, that cover the entire head and the body, except the feet. The boy masquerader manipulates the cloths in an acrobatic manner without revealing his body, moving through a range of extreme positions to the beat of an unmasked adult drummer or two. The masker appears as a wondrous, even mysterious, cloth in motion. Several boys may masquerade together, and they may be joined by one or more adults in larger cloths who carry out similar movements.

A third young children's masquerade form occurs in modern urban areas, where adult masquerade forms may be rare or absent, and there may be no initiating masquerades. Examples have been reported from Ougadougou, Burkina Faso, Bissau in Guinea-Bissau, and Bo in Sierra Leone. In Bissau, boys and also girls, sometimes with adult assistance, prepare grotesque papier-mâché masks of strange-looking animal or human-face forms, the lightweight masks sometimes being much larger than the head of the wearer. These maskers join other youthful and adult masqueraders, musicians, and floats in a long parade down the main streets of Bissau. This is an unusual form of masquerading because it occurs outside of a central square or place, although the judges' stands provide an ultimate focus. Although colorful, the child's body dress of a variety of commercial dress materials seems secondary to the striking masks.

Also employing papier-mâché masks along with wire screen examples are the fancy dress groups of southern Ghana. They perform primarily at Easter, Christmas, and New Years, but they may turn out for any important festival occasion. In 2004, the Cape Coast Anchors Youngsters Masqueraders Club had forty-eight members from eight years old to twenty-two. Four of the older members were masked stilt dancers. Depending on location, fancy dress masks might feature such characters as fetish priests, gorillas, police officers, or even Native Americans. Although the masquerade societies are named after British costume balls, they have been heavily influenced by West Indian traditions of carnival.

For both dress and mask, children in the urban scene often draw on images from commercial films, movie posters, videos,

Young boys wearing papier-mâché masks and local handwoven cloth at Carnaval in Bissau, Guinea-Bissau, 1987. Photograph by Doran H. Ross.

magazine and newspaper cartoons, kung fu images, and Disney figures, drawing little from tradition.

Considerable variation exists within and across cultures in dress and mask forms in both young children's and initiating masquerades. As noted, the outfit may completely cover the body and head, or the child's arms, legs, feet, and may be visible. Body and head coverings may be of vegetation—frequently raffia or leaves—occasionally of indigenous cloth, though more often of factory-made materials or a combination of these. For some young children's masquerades, the dress is a bricolage of discarded cloths patched together, but initiating dress is generally finer. Raffia, leaves, and loose body cloth flow as the masquerader twirls about; movement is essential to display body dress and head covering well, as with the Bwa child dancers of Burkina Faso, who also carry sticks.

When young children masquerade, they often prepare their own dress and masks, sometimes with help from older relatives. Masks may be made of wood, gourd, cloth, string, coconut shell, plastic, cardboard, metal, papier-mâché, or other materials. Young maskers sometimes chase unmasked children, swing a stick, or just move about energetically. Musical instruments are likewise often made by young children out of tin, wood, or plastic, or they are made from discarded adult instruments handed down by adults or older children. In young boys' performances, unmasked boy or girl singers or instrumentalists may take part in the event, wearing different outfits from the maskers. A troupe may have only a single masker, though more than one is common. Young children's troupes are generally of age peers, and a community may have a number of these of different ages, each also carrying out other activities, such as an occasional feast based on gifts received through performances. In both young children's and initiating masquerades, the players hope for rewards in food, cloth, money, and other items. Children know who has wealth in their community and try to dress well and perform with skill in front of their homes in expectation of generous gifts.

Initiating children's masks are often made by adults, sometimes of differing materials from young children's masks. Adults also may dress the child for his social transformation and guide the child through the rites.

Young children's performances often occur at Christmas, when persons return for the holidays, and, in some Muslim African regions, at Ramadan. Child masking also may be seen before, during, or between adult masquerades and other adult rites, sometimes at the fringe of the main event. Initiating masquerades are generally held in the months following the harvest, when sufficient food is available, for the rites often involve feasting and gifting by numerous individuals and groups.

Some young children become quite skilled at preparing dress and masks and in performing in them, doing so for up to ten years before initiating, the level of skills clearly increasing as they mature. They become well versed in handling masks and dress by the time of their own initiation and later on can readily partake in adult masquerades. Children's experience with dress, masks, and music in the company of other children teaches them aspects of their culture's aesthetics and how to act in cooperating groups, as they perform in lively, spontaneous, and creative ways, sometimes humorous and satiric in nature, sometimes mirroring the adult world.

Young children also learn nonverbal communication as they project animal, human, and spiritual forms of dress and mask

Young Fante boys wearing wire screen masks and patchwork costumes sewn from mill-woven cloth during fancy dress performances at Fetu Afahye, Cape Coast, Ghana, 2001. Photograph by Doran H. Ross.

onto viewers and acquire skills in controlling their own bodies. They learn to play at secrecy, which will hold them in good stead as adults, for secrecy is fairly common in adult African cultures. The dress, mask, and whole body may be believed to be secret, even when viewers know who the child performers are; it is a pretend secrecy. Animal forms are popular in young children's masquerades. This is consistent with the prevalence of animals in African tales and in metaphors in the speeches of elders. Large beasts such as elephants or crocodiles may involve several children in a single costume. At other times, dress and mask do not indicate any particular identity.

Young children's masquerades are not generally religious in nature unless they are occasionally linked to an adult masquerade or rite. Older children's initiating rituals often have religious elements to them that are associated with major spiritual forces. Initiating masqueraders are considered to be spirits in whom sacred qualities are embedded in the whole figure, but young children's masquerades are generally viewed as secular play by adults. Rivalry for masquerade leadership roles among young children is common; older boys like to exhibit their dressing and performance skills to attract the attention of girls, while younger masqueraders may seek adulation from parents or older siblings.

Young children's masquerades are not usually political in nature, although anthropologist and sociologist Nicolas Argenti has recorded Cameroon masquerades with political motifs explored through dress, masks, and action. In Ouagadougou (Burkina Faso), the government annually sponsors a children's public masquerade, suggesting new and more and more elaborate images and dress to the performers. In Guinea-Bissau, the government, at various at times, has had child masqueraders depict health and development issues during the annual city festival. Initiating masquerades always have a political side, because the rites turn immature individuals into full citizens, even though they may not become directly involved in political matters for some years.

As noted, some masquerading girls take part in preparing papier-mâché masks and in wearing them with boys in the annual Bissau festival. Children of both genders masquerade together among the Chewa in the region where Zambia, Malawi, and Mozambique meet, the girls with a loincloth face covering. In Senegambia, girls formerly masqueraded in full cloth representing various animals, and the Kpenigbai girls' masquerade of the Loma of Guinea-Conakry features performers who wear a conelike cloth headpiece, raffia body hangings, and shorts and hold a large stick. In Sierra Leone and Liberia, where, in the past, women's masquerading has been endemic, girls' masquerading has not been reported.

References and Further Reading

Argenti, Nicolas. "Kseum-Body and the Places of the Gods: The Politics of Children's Masking and Second-World Realities in Oku (Cameroon)." *Man: Journal of the Royal Anthropological Institute* 7, no. 1 (2001): 67–94.

Ottenberg, Simon. *Boyhood Rituals in an African Society: An Interpretation.* Seattle: University of Washington Press, 1989.

Ottenberg, Simon. "Initiations." In *Handbook of Psychological Anthropology*, edited by Philip K. Bock, 351–377. Westport, CT: Greenwood Press, 1994.

Ottenberg, Simon, and David A. Binkley, eds. *Playful Performers: African Children's Masquerades.* New Brunswick, NJ: Transaction Publishers, 2006.

Simon Ottenberg

See also Masquerade, Theater, Dance Costumes; Igbo in Nigeria and Diaspora.

PART 4

African Textiles

North Africa

North Africa consists of Egypt in the east and the lands to the west, or *Maghreb* (the Arabic term for "the place of sunset"). Because of a rich archaeological record, a substantial amount of information exists on ancient Egyptian textiles. In ancient Egypt, loincloths and linen kilts with a belt were common items of male clothing, while women wore tight-fitting dresses or skirts. Women's dresses became looser in the New Kingdom and were decorated with pleats and folds. Both sexes wore woolen cloaks and wigs. The dress of the ruler, however, included symbols of royalty consisting of an artificial rectangular beard and a striped linen headdress (*nemes*) with a *uraeus* (rearing cobra) on the front. Robes with embroidered and needlework decoration were also associated with the pharaoh. Although Egypt has had a long tradition of contact with other ancient Mediterranean cultures, it was not until Hellenistic and Roman times that non-Egyptian types of clothing predominated.

The earliest information on the existence of textiles in the Maghreb can be derived from rock paintings located in the mountainous areas of the central Sahara, especially the Tassili-n-Ajjer range in southern Algeria. Around 4000 B.C.E., when painted scenes of herding and village life occur, humans are seen in a variety of postures and dress. They are depicted wearing an assortment of apparel such as long tunics (some with linear patterns), short loincloths, and bands around their waist, arms, wrists, and legs. Some of these bands were embellished with fiber or hide fringes. A few figures have lines on their bodies, possibly indicating body paint or scarification, and some wore bulbous hatlike headdresses.

Sometime after 3000 B.C.E., towns and small kingdoms began to develop along the Mediterranean Sea and the Nile River. For the next five thousand years, Berbers (Imazighen), the indigenous societies of North Africa west of the Nile Valley, experienced significant outside influence with the influx of Phoenicians, Romans, Byzantines, Arabs, Andalusians, Jews, Ottoman Turks, French, and British. Although foreign influences have helped form the cultures of North Africa, internal patterns of adaptation and authentication have refined and modified these external influences to create distinct types of textiles and clothing. A varied topography and climate also characterize North Africa, a region of coastal plains, high mountain ranges, river valleys, vast deserts, and oases.

The connections between the Maghreb (defined today as the western part of Libya, Tunisia, Algeria, and Morocco) and the ancient Mediterranean world began around 1000 to 900 B.C.E.

with the arrival of the Phoenicians, a seafaring people from what is now Syria. *Punic* is the name commonly applied to this culture that developed in and around Carthage. Punic clothing consisted of a tunic and, for men of high status, a toga worn over the tunic. With Roman control in the second century B.C.E., Roman dress became standard. The most common item of clothing for men was a loose-fitting tunic tied at the waist with a belt. A toga could be worn over the tunic only by citizens. The toga remained the dress of state among the patricians and rulers in North Africa until the end of Roman control. The color of a toga indicated the rank or office of the wearer and the occasion for which it was worn. Cloaks with *fibulae* (brooches used for fastening clothing) were added during colder weather. A married woman wore a long ankle-length tunic with a shawl. Roman textiles were normally made from wool or flax; cotton was restricted to the wealthy.

TEXTILE PRODUCTION

In general, handwoven textiles are produced by Berber women in towns and villages and by Arab men in major cities. Gender distinctions determine loom type. Women usually weave on single-heddle ground looms and fixed-frame vertical looms. The primary Berber loom is the vertically mounted, single-heddle loom, characterized by heddles (short lengths of wire or flat steel strips) that are used to deflect the warp to either side of the main sheet of fabric. The structure of this loom allows it to be set up in a tent easily, where it is attached to the poles supporting the tent. In more permanent structures, the loom is placed in front of a wall. For Berber women, rituals accompanied every stage in the preparation of the yarn and loom to ensure success and ward off evil. Wool, sometimes combined with goat or camel hair, is the basic material used by Berber women for apparel and home furnishing textiles. In addition, Bedouin women in the Nile Delta make use of a small rectangular metal frame with no heddle to create woolen rugs. Some nomadic women in Tunisia use a horizontal loom to produce long strips of woven wool or goat hair that is then made into tents, blankets, and cushions.

Arab men use both wool and cotton to weave on some variant of the more complex horizontal heddle loom. The typical North African men's loom produces a wider band in contrast to the narrow-band loom used by men in sub-Saharan Africa. However, in southern Egypt, men also use a smaller horizontal loom to make narrow strips of cloth to serve as decorative borders for larger textiles. A horizontal loom with a number of supplementary heddles has been used in Fez for centuries to create intricately patterned silk textiles and belts. Men in urban areas employ imported silk for textile production, especially for more affluent patrons. By the mid-twentieth century, rayon and, to a lesser degree, Lurex were being used instead of silk.

Yarn was traditionally dyed by professionals in cities and by individual weavers in rural areas. Mauve, soft blue, green, and golden yellow were the primary traditional colors. Aniline dyes introduced in the mid-nineteenth century had supplanted natural dyes in the rural areas by the twentieth century. Tie-dyed cloth, widespread south of the Sahara, is found in several parts of North Africa, where it is used for diverse items of dress. Berber women in southern Morocco produce tie-dyed cloth with circular patterns for head ties and belts, while women in southern Tunisia use the technique for head ties and for small wool shawls that cover married women's shoulders. These shawls are more than just decorative, because they function to prevent excess oil that has been applied to the hair from damaging clothing. Henna has a long history in North Africa, dating back to predynastic Egypt, but as a dye or paint for textiles, henna is particularly popular in parts of southern Morocco.

ARAB, ANDALUSIAN, AND OTTOMAN INFLUENCES

New textile technologies, decorative features, and, to some extent, types of attire were introduced into North Africa as the result of the Arab/Muslim invasion of the late seventh century. Men continued to wear ankle-length, flowing tunics with or without sleeves, now over loose-fitting trousers and under long robes with hoods. The Arabs introduced new types of head coverings such as caps and turbans. White, associated in Islam with purity, brightness, and loyalty, became the most fitting color for clothing. White is also the color for the hajj pilgrimage to Mecca and for burial attire. The Arabs also introduced the horizontal loom used by men as well as the ground loom used by women to weave heavy blankets and household textiles, both of which have been discussed. After sweeping across North Africa, the Arabs established a number of dynasties that ruled, one after the other, until the Ottoman conquest in the late sixteenth century. From the seventh through the sixteenth centuries, a series of royal textile workshops were set up in palaces to produce textiles for the royal household and to be given as gifts to supporters. During the rule of the Fatimids over Egypt and Tunisia (tenth to twelfth

centuries), elaborate costumes with tiraz (embroidered, brocaded, or woven inscriptions) conveyed political messages that supported the ruling caliphs. In the centuries that followed, tiraz became more widespread among the elite residing in cities and large towns. Although the Qur'an discourages the wearing of silk, Arab rulers and the upper classes used silk garments by the tenth century. Tunis (Tunisia) and Fez (Morocco) became major centers of production by the twelfth and thirteenth centuries.

In the late fifteenth and early sixteenth centuries, many Muslim and Jewish refugees from Andalusian Spain brought new ideas and new techniques to North Africa. Bicolored tunics, for example, were introduced by the Andalusians and became popular across the Maghreb. Similar tunics are still worn today. In addition, embroidery, especially in silk, was strongly influenced by Andalusian styles, including the character of such motifs as stars, diamonds, herringbones, birds, trees, and geometrized plant forms. The Ottomans—who effectively controlled North Africa, except for Morocco, from the sixteenth to the eighteenth centuries—did not impose uniformity on the various parts of their empire but provided a political framework that enabled the different groups to live together peacefully, each retaining to some degree its own beliefs and customs. Ottoman control and influence on clothing styles in Egypt lasted until the early twentieth century. The Ottomans introduced into North Africa lavishly embroidered jackets, trousers, and robes and used more tailoring in the production of clothing. They also used clothing (especially headgear) to distinguish different political functionaries. The principal Ottoman garment of high political status was the silk caftan (a long robe, opening at the front, with long sleeves). Most complex were the large patterned robes and belts often embellished with gold. Young wealthy women used silk to embroider

Two Berber women at a market near Zaghouan (eastern Tunisia, 2004) wearing Berber dress consisting of a loose-fitting shirt, a cloth draped over the shoulder attached with fibulae, and a head scarf. Despite the influences of European-style dress from the twentieth century onwards, traditional styles of Berber female dress have remained common. Photograph by Fred T. Smith.

elaborate floral designs onto wall hangings, curtains, and other items of personal use for their hope chests. The long tradition of embroidery executed primarily by women became especially elaborate and ornate in urban North Africa during the Ottoman period. Most motifs consisted of nonfigurative and stylized plant forms, often grouped together into harmonious patterns enhanced by color contrasts. Although Morocco was never under the rule of the Ottoman Empire, its artisans were influenced by Turkish design. Embroiderers from Fez and Rabat in Morocco borrowed patterns and motifs that included volutes, tulips, roses, pomegranates, and bouquets of flowers. As another aspect of trade and outside contact, woven textiles from North Africa, especially those for household embellishment, were popular export items to other parts of the Ottoman Empire.

The distinctive and colorful embroidered designs of North African textiles and garments are still important today, especially for life course ceremonies. Newborn children and human corpses are covered in cloth embroidered with protective motifs such as the upraised hand. Embroideries in the rural areas also employ motifs that represent popular symbols of luck such as stars, birds, fish, and crescents as well as those that emphasize fertility or protection against the evil eye, such as fish, celestial forms, or the open palm with five fingers. This upraised hand motif, often referred to as the Hand of Fatima (the daughter of Mohammed), is called in Arabic *khamsa*, referring to the number five, a significant and auspicious number in Islam. It represents the five pillars of faith or required areas of action for Muslims as well as the obligation to pray five times a day. Five is also an auspicious number in the Jewish faith, and the upright hand as an amulet was popular in Moroccan and Tunisian Jewish communities, which were quite sizable until the mid-twentieth century. In North Africa and other parts of the Mediterranean, the human eye is believed to reflect the soul and to have magical powers. Certain geometric shapes used in textile decoration, such as diamonds, triangles, or a dot in the center of a pattern, are able to protect against the evil eye. Charms and amulets have been worn or attached to clothing in both urban and rural areas by men and women to ward off both the evil eye and malevolent spirits.

URBAN AND RURAL TEXTILES

Although common patterns of attire and textile design exist for North Africa, there are definite ethnic and regional differences, in part based on diverse historical forces. By the thirteenth century (if not before), the majority of the population in the urban centers and along both the Mediterranean and Atlantic coasts were of Arab origin, while the mountainous areas and southern oases were occupied by the indigenous Berbers, who are divided into sedentary populations and the nomadic pastoralists. Berbers constitute a larger percentage of the population in Morocco and Algeria than they do in Tunisia. In general, the types of clothing in the urban areas were similar to those in the rural areas, being differentiated basically by the materials and the way a garment was worn or decorated. Textiles have long played an important role in the economic and social life of North Africa, where they indicated status, were bestowed as gifts, and were displayed prominently at important life cycle ceremonies. In both rural and urban areas, girls, upon reaching puberty, began to dress more modestly, usually in full-length smocks with long sleeves, loose trousers, and head scarves and shawls. Both the *burqa*, a draped

garment that completely covers a woman, and the face veil are rarely seen in the Maghreb. Even head scarves are discouraged by some of the more Westernized middle and upper classes in the early twenty-first century.

In the past, the traditional clothing for urban women consisted of wrapper, robe, shawl, and head cover. First, a cotton wrapper was draped around the body and gathered at the waist with a sash. A loose-fitting robe or caftan with seams on either side and long sleeves covered the wrapper. These robes, usually of cotton but sometimes silk or cotton and silk, were light in color, frequently white. In early-twentieth-century Morocco, fashionable rayon caftans were embellished with metallic thread and colorful brocaded geometric or floral patterns repeated over the surface. These patterns were usually light red, green, or yellow. Less ornate caftans were typically worn as indoor dress. When women wore tunics or robes, they frequently added very wide, billowing ankle-length trousers. The large trousers had drawstrings at the end that were tied under the knee, causing a mass of material to fall to the ankles. For everyday activities, women wore less elaborate attire. For example, a large rectangular piece of cloth wrapped around a woman's waist was worn with a blouse and another lighter-colored rectangular piece of cloth draped over the head and onto the back. These cotton wrappers were frequently decorated with a warp-faced stripe. Other women might wear an ankle-length white or blue robe with a large plain or patterned scarf covering the head and shoulders when going outdoors. Another option was an ankle-length skirt with a loose-fitting, full-sleeved blouse tailored from commercially printed cotton textiles.

When leaving the house, a woman covered her head with a type of cloth cap for ceremonies or, more traditionally, with a cotton scarf that draped onto the neck and shoulders. Several scarves folded or twisted together and embellished with some form of jewelry has been a common headdress in North Africa. These head scarves were usually white or black, either plain or with a small amount of embroidered decoration. For marriage ceremonies, head scarves were more colorful. In northwestern Egypt, a black base cloth was embroidered with small red, yellow, or orange patterns associated with fertility or protection. In Tunisia, supplementary heddles were employed to create complex patterns organized into three different styles of longitudinal stripes. The widest, most complex, and most densely patterned stripe alternated motifs such as the khamsa (hand of Fatima) and the eight-pointed star. In general, the greatest range of headgear was encountered during festive occasions. For many events, rectangular shawls of various sizes were draped over the upper part of the body. These were often embellished with broad stripes or intricately patterned with a variety of geometric motifs depending on the geographic area and the occasion. Generally, a woman donned a long shawl when leaving the house. In some areas, such as southern Tunisia, the color of a shawl indicated a women's status: white for unmarried women, red for women of childbearing age, and blue or black for older women. In early-twentieth-century Algeria, narrow cotton shawls elaborately embellished with needlework were worn by wealthy women while at home. These were worked with purple, green, yellow, and pale red silk to create foliage and floral motifs. In urban areas, belts made of gold-embroidered fabric, often silk, were an important element of dress until the twentieth century. These belts with warp fringes at each end were large, measuring about thirty to forty centimeters (twelve to sixteen inches) wide and at least two meters (six and a half feet) long. Two to four different designs were repeated on each belt. The most frequent motifs were the upright hand, assorted geometric forms, floral patterns, and eight-pointed stars. For older examples, the two horizontal sections that make up a single belt had different background colors. In addition, each half might have different designs and employ different techniques. Fez was an important center of production for these belts. The belts were worn folded in half and wrapped a number of times around the caftan or robe. In addition, women and girls in Fez and other Moroccan cities densely embroidered geometric motifs with silk thread on the borders of rectangular pieces of cotton fabrics for wall hangings, curtains, and cushion or mattress covers. The edges were hemmed in blanket stitch in a color matching the horizontal border.

From ancient times to the twentieth century, tunics and robes have been distinctive items of male clothing in both urban and rural areas. The *djellaba* (*jellaba*), a short-sleeved outer garment with a hood, made in a variety of colors, sometimes striped, has been widespread male attire in most of North Africa. In rural areas, the djellaba made of unbleached wool was typically used during the winter months. The caftan—probably introduced from the Middle East, although some evidence indicates a Spanish origin—was popular with the urban elite, becoming especially significant under Ottoman control. Many caftans were made of brightly colored silk and brocades. Metallic threads were featured in urban areas to enhance a variety of garments, including the caftan. Copper wire was introduced later in the nineteenth century. A short sleeveless outer coat or vest, popular among men in Egypt, was introduced into Libya and Tunisia during the eighteenth century and, by the late nineteenth century, was worn by Moroccan men. More affluent individuals would cover themselves with a number of elegant and ornate garments, one atop the other, to display their wealth and good taste. Similar ideas occur among Islamic populations in the western and central Sudanic areas of West Africa. Finally, a hooded semicircular, sleeveless cloak (*selham*), normally made from wool and serving as an over garment, was commonly worn during the winter months. The hood of the selham was sometimes decorated with silk pompoms. For centuries, wide trousers that narrowed at the calf and a long white shirt were popular male undergarments. Many types of male headgear were characteristic of North Africa. Skullcaps, small felt hats (generally red), close-fitting knitted caps, loosely wrapped white turbans, and flat-brim straw hats were the predominant types.

In the rural areas of North Africa, especially those inhabited by Berber-speaking peoples, tunics, robes, caftans, draped garments, shawls, loose-fitting shirts, vests, hooded jackets, head coverings, and belts were common items of clothing. A greater use of wool, the shape and size of the garments, and the favored motifs differentiated these rural examples from similar types of clothing in the urban areas. Many of the rural people, especially those in the mountainous areas are Berber. In general, Berber textiles were less affected by outside influences and can be seen as more indigenous to the region. Berber women wove all of the clothing and other textiles needed for daily living. Men wore shirts and trousers covered with a locally produced djellaba or selham. Most Berber djellabas were loose fitting, had large hoods and wide sleeves, and were beige or brown. Details varied from one Berber group to another, especially in the nature and meaning of

their decorative designs. For example, diamond patterns found on some Moroccan djellabas refer to the importance of individual households. Djellabas from the Rif mountains of northern Morocco were usually knee length and had short sleeves. Men also wore swathed turbans and caps or dome-shaped hats with small brims, sometimes decorated with silk tassels and mirrors.

Most women in the rural areas of the Maghreb covered their bodies with draped garments. The most common type consisted of a rectangular piece of woolen cloth draped over the shoulders and fastened above the breasts with fibulae. In some areas an additional textile or woolen shawl decorated with narrow transverse stripes would be added. Belts were used to gather the garment at the waist. Different styles of wool or silk belts were used; a simple red type was the most common. Braided cords in wool or wool and silk as well as silk belts with woven designs were also worn around the waist. A head cover, usually a scarf, completed the outfit. Scarves ranged from simple square or rectangular pieces of cloth to larger pieces decorated with tassels. Women also covered their heads with a woolen shawl that fell onto the shoulders and across the back. Sometimes a cap was worn as well. Berber motifs reflect the concerns and beliefs of local areas. Within every community, basic geometric, but sometimes floral, motifs were combined to produce distinctive elements. The cross, lozenge, step motif, triangle, diamond, and star as well as cross-hatching were also frequently used. A common pattern was the arrangement of the diamond or chevron motif along horizontal registers. Distinctive color combinations were also important. The harmonious balance of recurring elements unified the final product. Some motifs took on specific meaning, such as the diamond that was viewed as symbol of protection and security. Other nonfigurative motifs might reference a lion's paw, gazelle horns, or a human eye. It is not possible to assign a definite meaning to a specific motif, because the meanings of geometric symbols vary from region to region. Some of the meanings connect to early cultures such as Phoenician, Roman, Arab, and Andalusian.

In addition to weaving strips of cloth for tents, Berber women produced flat woven textiles of various sizes and colors on the vertical loom for household purposes. Household textiles were usually decorated with transverse stripes or bands of geometric motifs, but some had a band of repeated geometric forms along the border and a central field with another larger pattern. The most common motifs are triangles, diamonds, linear forms, rectangles, zigzags, comblike designs, chevrons, and dots. Red, white, and black were the most popular colors, along with blue, yellow, and green. These flat textiles were used as rugs, prayer rugs, blankets, pillow and cushion covers, or wall hangings. As a sign of hospitality and a demonstration of a family's success, the reception area of a house or tent was embellished with rectangular, often embroidered, pillows that were arranged on colorful rugs. These were especially evident during festive occasions such as weddings or religious ceremonies.

THE SAHARA

The Berber-speaking Tuareg, a noncentralized, nomadic people, live in an extensive area of northern Africa that includes the Algerian, Libyan, and Malian Sahara as well as parts of Niger and Burkina Faso in West Africa. The ancestors of the Tuareg were Berbers from eastern Algeria and western Libya who migrated

Traditional Berber wedding at the Tataouine Oasis, Tunisia. Such elaborate traditional headdresses have continued to be worn at weddings into the twenty-first century. Photograph by Bruno Barbier.

south more than a thousand years ago. Tuareg clothing styles and types of fabrics have traditionally indicated gender, age, class, and regional identity. Unlike other Islamic societies, it is the men and not the women who wear veils. Face veiling for men consists of wrapping the head—leaving a slit for the eyes—with a shiny indigo cloth (*aleshu*) produced by the Hausa of Nigeria. This distinctive head wrap of the Tuareg that leaves a slit for the eyes is called *tagulmust* and is a characteristic trait of Tuareg men, especially those of noble birth. A young man will first wear a tagulmust after his initiation to adult status in his late teens. Men also wear a long dark blue or white cotton robe over baggy trousers. Because the Tuareg do not weave, all cloth had to be imported, usually from the western Sudan. However, leather caftans and dresses have been documented from southern Algeria in the nineteenth century.

Tuareg women have fewer restrictions and a greater freedom of behavior and dress than the Arab women of North Africa. They wear elaborately folded head scarves, often of indigo-dyed cloth, for festive occasions. For everyday activities, women usually adorn themselves with a simple head scarf that also wraps around the neck. Adolescent girls will begin to cover their head in this way when they reach marriageable age. Tuareg women regularly dress in black or blue indigo cloth. In some cases, a woman will wrap a piece of cloth around her lower body or wear a large, flowing skirt combined with a loose blouse, often embroidered

with red, green, or yellow bands. Some of the embroidery motifs on women's clothing depict natural features with symbolic meaning, such as stars, sun, moon, plants, and flowers. Another option is the wearing of a long voluminous robe that wraps around both the body and the head. Loose, baggy clothing is considered by the Tuareg to be aesthetically appealing and highly functional. A more recent development is the use of commercially manufactured wax print cloth for wrappers.

CEREMONIAL DRESS

Ceremonies, festivals, and other rituals provide structures for individuals or groups to reaffirm social values and ties. They tend to be public events, seen as different from everyday life. Especially important are rites of passage involving a transition from one status or condition to another. Although often based on ordinary types of clothing, the costumes worn at these times are frequently special to the occasion as well as being dramatically symbolic. Different stages or events characterize some celebrations, requiring many changes of costume or dress. In North Africa, weddings are major events that not only unite two individuals but provide a permanent linkage between families and kin groups. A concern with fertility and status is another important component of the ritual. Ethnic identification and historical factors also influence the style of ceremonial dress. In parts of Tunisia, Libya, and

Egypt, brides wear loose, uncomplicated cotton tunics reminiscent of Roman types that are elaborately decorated and reflect the standing of the bride in the community. Until the mid-twentieth century, embroidered Jewish wedding dresses were used in the urban areas of Morocco and Tunisia. These styles were based on types developed in Spain and brought to North Africa in the late fifteenth and early sixteenth centuries.

In North Africa, marriages represent a significant change of status and require significant expense and attention; wedding ceremonies last for several days, and most people of the village will turn out. A popular component of the Tunisian wedding ceremony is the display of the bride's personal clothing. Tunisian wedding garments are decorated with sequins, elaborate embroidery with gold and silver threads, and coral beads (associated with fertility). There is a greater emphasis on goldwork in urban areas. The metal-thread embroidery motifs include flowers, birds, fish, concentric squares, and circles. Women wear a variety of tunic styles with different types of decoration at distinct ceremonial stages of the wedding ritual. An important part of a Tunisian wedding ceremony is for a bride to be displayed formally to the groom, her relatives, and the relatives of the groom. At these times, she is dressed in several different tunics that she removes one by one until the last one, the richest of all, is revealed. A good example of an Arab wedding tunic (in the British Museum collection) from the northern Tunisian village of Raf-Raf was worn as an outer garment on the third day of the wedding ceremony. It is a type called *suriya mwashma*, or tattooed tunic, because its embroidered motifs are identical to henna tattoos found on women's hands. The primary design for the tunic is a series of squares created by red and orange bands; an embroidered star motif occupies the square. The sleeves and bodice are embellished with stylized flowers and good luck symbols such as fish, peacocks, and various moon and star designs. The bottom band is decorated with three pyramid forms supporting a floral arrangement representing the tree of life. Richly decorated tunics reflect the well-being of the bride and her family. A considerable amount of money and time are spent on the production of these wedding ensembles. The wedding apparel, which has become increasingly expensive, may be borrowed from neighboring families or rented from a woman specialist who helps plan wedding ceremonies.

Although Berber weddings in southern Tunisia and Morocco include ritual events similar to those of urban areas, variations in dress do exist. Clothing in general is characterized by the layering of loose-fitting forms. The wearing of veils, elaborate wedding headdresses, and shawls during ceremonies is more pronounced in Berber areas. Large wool and cotton shawls with detailed decoration featuring linear patterns are reserved for ceremonial occasions. Red and white woolen belts are worn in southern Tunisia at the completion of a wedding festival to reference the link that a bride maintains with her own female relatives. Elaborate silk belts with tassels and mirrors are used during weddings in the Middle Atlas Mountains of Morocco. Certain colors such as blue, yellow, and red; embroidered triangular or khamsa motifs; and added materials such as metallic thread and sequins are used on textiles worn by the bride to emphasize concerns with fertility. Indigo-dyed motifs are common in the Anti-Atlas Mountains of southern Morocco and among the Tuareg of the Sahara. For Berber men, the wearing of turbans, woolen gowns, and cloaks at a wedding connects them with the importance that Islam assigns

to modesty, privacy, and morality. A white or indigo blue tagulmust (turban and veil) is the appropriate head cover for a Tuareg man. Tuareg women, on the other hand, wear indigo headwraps, a body wrapper, a voluminous embroidered blouse, and abundant jewelry.

TEXTILES AND DRESS IN THE EARLY TWENTY-FIRST CENTURY

By the early twentieth century, various styles and types of European clothing began to influence the attire of North African men and women. Today, many North Africans, particularly those in urban centers, wear commercially manufactured Western dress. Young men and women are seen in blue jeans, khaki trousers, shirts, sweaters, skirts, and blouses. Men now wear suits and ties or uniforms to work. For more casual occasions or during summer months, they may wear safari suits. Many North Africans alternate between European and local garments depending on the situation. Various modifications in older patterns of dress occurred over the course of the twentieth century. Beginning in the 1930s, some women in Morocco began wearing a djellaba over other garments. In parts of Morocco, men now wear a djellaba over Western trousers and shirts. Throughout North Africa today, many older women wear locally produced long cotton dresses with floral or geometric decoration along with a plain or patterned scarf that covers the head and falls in diverse ways about the neck and shoulders. Many North African women wear ankle-length skirts or pants and long-sleeved blouses along with head scarves. In response to a growing demand, both Morocco and Tunisia have developed a significant contemporary textile and apparel industry. The continued importance of traditional ceremonies and local festivals as well as tourism have, to some extent, encouraged the survival of older forms of clothing.

In both urban and rural areas, items of Western attire are often combined with those of local origin. For example, one Berber woman from Matmata, a mountainous region in southern Tunisia, wears a draped cloth secured by a fibula along with sweat pants and Adidas socks. Ironically, the Berbers who live in Matmata have a long history of trying to avoid the impact of outside influence. Yet the nature and type of clothing in both rural and urban North Africa has never been static. New materials, styles, and decoration have always been filtered through the desire to use apparel as a way of expressing individual and cultural identity.

References and Further Reading

Becker, Cynthia. *Amazigh Arts in Morocco: Women Shaping Berber Identity.* Austin: University of Texas Press, 2006.

Becker, Cynthia. "Amazigh Textiles and Dress in Morocco." *African Arts* 39, no. 3 (2006): 42–55, 96.

Besancenot, Jean. *Costumes of Morocco.* London and New York: Kegan Paul, 1990.

Brend, Barbara. *Islamic Art.* London: British Museum Press, 1991.

Jereb, James F. *Arts and Crafts of Morocco.* London: Thames and Hudson, 1995.

Paydar, Niloo Imami, and Ivo Grammet, eds. *The Fabric of Moroccan Life.* Indianapolis, IN: Indianapolis Museum of Art, 2002.

Reswick, Irmtraud. *Traditional Textiles of Tunisia and Related North African Weavings.* Los Angeles: Craft and Folk Art Museum, 1985.

Scarce, Jennifer. *Women's Costume of the Near and Middle East*. London: Unwin Hyman, 1987.

Seligman, Thomas K., and Kristine Loughran, eds. *Art of Being Tuareg*. Los Angeles: UCLA Fowler Museum of Cultural History, 2006.

Spring, Christopher, and Julie Hudson. *North African Textiles*. London: British Museum Press, 1995.

Spring, Christopher, and Julie Hudson. *Silk in Africa*. London: British Museum Press, 2002.

Stone, Caroline. *The Embroideries of North Africa*. London: Longman, 1985.

Fred T. Smith

See also Algeria; Egypt: Historical Dress; Dress in Egypt in the Twentieth Century; Snapshot: Libya; Morocco; Tunisia; Niger.

West Africa

- Aesthetics of West African Woven Textiles
- Cloth as Protection
- Symbolism in Handcrafted West African Textiles
- Factory-Printed Textiles
- Dyeing Techniques

West African markets are well known for their tightly packed displays of textiles in rich arrays of colors and patterns, and tailors on their sewing machines can be heard everywhere sewing visually striking garments that seldom go unnoticed when worn in public. So vital and richly varied are textiles in West Africa that even prominent contemporary artists such as El Anatsui from Ghana and Nigeria and Yinka Shonibare from Nigeria are inspired by them as powerful mediums for discourse on historical, social, and economic aspects of West African life.

In West Africa, woven textile construction almost always involves piecing together woven strips or panels to make what is the most basic element of attire, a rectangular-shaped cloth. The so-called wrapper in English, or *pagne* in French, is commonly woven on one of two types of looms. The first, and by far the most ubiquitous, is the horizontal foot-treadle loom on which long, narrow strips are woven, cut into desired lengths, and selvage-sewn together to make the full cloth. The latter requires anywhere from twelve and twenty-four strips depending on its desired size. Considerable variation in its designs exists from region to region, everything from simple plain-woven stripes to elaborate weft-float designs, and often a combination of the two. A similar range of patterns is created on the second type of loom. Found mainly in Nigeria, this type features a vertical fixed frame with a continuous warp. Because its cloths are considerably wider than those done on the narrow-strip loom, they can be left single for use as a baby tie or shoulder cloth or combined with one to three others to create a full wrapper.

Suggestive of its English name, the rectangular cloth is traditionally wrapped and draped around the body. Women tend to wear two small pieces of equal size, one layered over the other, with an additional one used as a baby carrier, shoulder cloth, blouse, or head tie. Men generally drape one cloth on their body, though differently depending on the region. For example, in the Ewe, Asante, and Baule areas, men wear large cloths toga-style, with a substantial portion covering the left shoulder and placed under the right arm. In contrast, men from the Edo-, Igbo-, Ijo-, and Ibibios-speaking areas of southeastern Nigeria wrap a smaller cloth around the lower half of their body, with the upper corners tied or tucked in at the waist. In Muslim areas, where covering the entire body is essential, the wrapper has given way to loose-fitting, tailored robes (see later discussion of Hausa dress).

Some of the earliest evidence of strip-woven West African textiles was uncovered at burial sites in the Bandiagara region of Mali. Dating between the eleventh and fifteenth centuries C.E.,

these textile remains may well have provided the foundation for subsequent weaving and dyeing in Mali and elsewhere in West Africa. The Bandiagara sites reveal a variety of bodily coverings, some woven on narrow-strip looms, and all presumably made by the non-Muslim Tellem people encountered by the Dogon when they arrived in the area in the sixteenth century. The findings at these important sites included leather sandals, simple skirts made of suspended vegetal fibers, and the remains of men's shirts tailored from narrow strips of cloth in a manner similar to the way shirts continue to be made today in the region. Indigo dyeing was evident in many of the textile fragments, some of which had warp strips or checks made from a combination of natural and indigo-dyed threads and others resist-dyed with indigo using the tie-dye technique.

The archaeological remains of the Tellem offer a unique window into early textile production in the western savanna region of West Africa. Seen more broadly and in more recent years, West African textiles have come to include every technique imaginable, from numerous varieties of weaving and cloth dyeing to painting, writing, stamping, embroidery, and other additive forms of embellishment, providing a rich and varied range of textiles for use predominantly as dress. European and Asian imports have become an essential part of that mix. From the time Europeans arrived in the fifteenth century, they were bartering their cloths and clothing in exchange for African commodities, making imported damasks, silks, woolens, and cottons as common today as anything locally manufactured. Whatever the source of the cloth, textile artists throughout West Africa are firmly rooted in their own regional histories, and responding to localized needs, aesthetic preferences, and the ongoing impact of trade and globalization.

AESTHETICS OF WEST AFRICAN WOVEN TEXTILES

Aesthetically speaking, the warp-faced stripe is the most basic design element in woven textiles. A classic example of this can be found among the Mende of Sierra Leone and Liberia. Mende textiles, known as *kondi-gulei*, or simply "country cloths" in English, consist mainly of plain-woven, warp-faced striped cloth in contrasting muted tones of natural, indigo, and kola nut–dyed cotton, either hand-spun or imported. When the anthropologist T. J. Alldridge was working among the Mende between 1871 and 1908, he expressed both admiration for indigenous country cloth and concern that the importation of European-manufactured textiles would cause the demise of the traditional. Yet, as late as the 1970s, the Mende still believed native yarn to be more powerful than English yarn, and hand-spun, hand-dyed cotton kondi-gulei, with its pervasive warp stripes, to be the most honored gift one could bestow on someone, if not the most ideal form of attire for Mende individuals of rank.

In most other areas where narrow-strip weaving is done, the simple warp stripe is the mere backdrop to a rich palette of color and design introduced through weft-floats and other forms of embellishment. Examples of such weaving include the well-known Yoruba *aso-oke*, Asante and Ewe kente, and, as described here, the lesser-known Baule strip weaving, with its distinctive

Vendors selling factory prints in the Kejetia market at Kumase, Ghana, 2005. Photograph by Lisa Aronson.

color palette of dark blue and white. Baule weavers from the towns of Bomizombo and Tuenzuebo, located just outside of Bouake, like to combine the basic blue and white warp strips with geometrically shaped weft-float designs of referential or proverbial meaning, resulting in a cloth that is both richly textured and culturally significant. The weavers may add resist-dyed designs by tightly wrapping and dyeing either select areas of the warp threads before they are woven or the entire cloth after it has been removed from the loom. At important ceremonies, high-ranking Baule chiefs and elders typically display their power and status by wearing these richly patterned blue and white textiles toga-style, with an emphasis on volume and bulk, and always accompanied by an abundance of gold regalia in the form of crowns, necklaces, armlets, sandals, and staffs. The conscious attention to volume, accumulation, and complex patterning typifies how Africans throughout the continent choose to communicate notions of wealth and status through dress.

Similarly, Yoruba textiles from Ijebu-Ode, Nigeria, made for members of the Oshugbo Society, convey a sense of power and authority through their multifaceted designs and the volumetric way in which the cloths are worn. Both men and women members of the Oshugbo Society, an ancient and powerful governing institution, wrap themselves in opulent and visually striking attire to mark their affiliation with the organization. Woven by women on the vertical, fixed-frame loom, the Oshugbo cloth ensemble consists of a large body wrapper (*iborun*, meaning "large, ceremonial cloth") made from four individual panels that are sewn together along with a single-panel shoulder cloth (*itagbe*). Oshugbo textiles are known for their rich panoply of designs and textures, including rows of shag interspersed with rows of weft-float woven designs of animals and other symbols of power and decorative fringes along the edge. The shag motif (*shaki*) refers to the inner lining of the cow's stomach, suggesting notions of interiority and, by association, the clairvoyant powers of the Oshugbo members. Weft-float patterns of animals include the crocodile (*onile*), who is the omnipresent and clairvoyant spirit present at Oshugbo shrines. The Oshugbo member sometimes wraps his or her head in a single panel of cloth, with the tightly bound fringes hanging downward to evoke the spiritual power (*ashe*) believed to emanate from one's head. Everything about Oshugbo textiles—their striking imagery, potent symbols, textures, and the accumulative style in which they are worn—conveys power and agency for its privileged members.

The aesthetic of abundance and accumulation in dress is also ever-present among the many Islamic cultures that span the continent. The demand for bodily coverings imposed by Islam

Kobbi Klutse wearing kente in the style typical of his Ewe culture, Anlo, Southern Ewe region, Ghana, 2005. Photograph by Lisa Aronson.

with Islamic script. Without question, Islamic-inscribed cloth was the inspiration for the Hausa art of embellishing men's robes, pants, and caps with embroidered designs. The meanings of these designs derive from Qur'anic magical configurations, described by some as *hatumere*. Consisting of squares, grids, and figure-eights, these geometric designs, in their combination and in the rich and colorful ways in which they are articulated for Muslims who wear them, reflect the geometric order of their cosmos, with Allah at the center of that universe. Associated with the words of Allah himself, these geometric designs provide wearers with spiritual protection and honor.

CLOTH AS PROTECTION

Hausa garments, with their Islamic-inspired motifs, are just one of a number of examples of West African textiles whose richly textured surface designs enhance and give spiritual protection to the wearer. Some of those textile traditions may have their roots in Islamic-inscribed cloth. One example would be Asante *adinkra*, a traditional funerary cloth whose geometric stamped designs of proverbial meaning evoke the aesthetic of Islamic-inscribed cloths. Most certainly, Islamic inscription plays into the construction of the so-called hunter's shirt, a man's garment found throughout the savanna regions of Mali, Burkina Faso, Côte d'Ivoire, and Ghana, including Mande-speaking ones. Generally, it is a smock-style shirt made from narrow strips or, more recently, imported muslin that is infused with a reddish (probably camwood) color, and then decorated with powerful substances. The latter includes animal horns, claws, teeth, hair, mirrors, and leather amulets containing pieces of paper on which magical words, including Qur'anic passages, have been written. Viewed as spiritual armor, such decoration serves to protect the hunter from both real and spirit forces. These shirts have historical implications as well. When one Dyula male elder was asked to recount the historic, southward migration of his people from Mali, he brought out his father's hunter's shirt, noting that it had been brought from Mali as testimony and proof of the southward migration of his father's clan.

The Senufo of Côte d'Ivoire, Mali, and Burkina Faso have their own protective clothing, known as *fila*. The foundation of fila is a narrow-strip-woven cloth made from undyed, hand-spun cotton. Left plain, the cloth is often used as a burial shroud. To make it into fila, the cloth artist paints straight or zigzag lines on it using a pigment made from vegetal, mud, and mineral substances. A key design element on fila cloth is the zigzag design referring to the python, which gives the cloth its special prophylactic powers. When needed, the Senufo must wear fila cloth (in the form of a tunic for men and a wrapper for women) on designated days of the week and accompanied by certain food restrictions to ward off angered spirits who the diviner determines to be at the root of their illness or infertility.

Although fila continues to be used for such reasons in rural areas of Côte d'Ivoire, it has also evolved into something considerably more pictorial. Known by the name Korhogo cloth, for the northern Côte d'Ivoire city where much of it is sold, the cloth is now popular among tourists and urbanized Ivoirians for use as wall hangings rather than as prophylactic attire.

By contrast, *bogolanfini* (Bamana for "mudcloth") from the neighboring country of Mali, a cloth also once worn as protection, has followed a very different modernizing trajectory that

may even have prompted the spread of narrow-strip weaving and other forms of cloth production throughout much of West Africa, including areas of northern Nigeria, home to the Hausa, Fulani, and Nupe. The Muslim emirates that eventually took power in this area of West Africa introduced a style of male dress consisting of flowing, elaborately embroidered robes and huge baggy trousers adapted for horseback riding. Initially, these robes and trousers were made from hand-spun cotton or locally manufactured silk woven on narrow-strip looms and more recently from imported cottons or synthetic materials. Whatever the source of cloth, the manner in which they are then tailored and worn emphasizes volume and bulk to again communicate the wearer's power and wealth.

Islamic West Africans also wear the words of Allah on their body as protection, either in the form of leather amulets containing Islamic-inscribed pieces of paper or undergarments covered

Yoruba man from Ijebu-Ife, Nigeria, wearing an *iborun* ensemble that identifies his membership in the Oshugbo Society. Nigeria, 1978. Photograph by Lisa Aronson.

retains its function as dress. Traditionally, this painted mudcloth was worn by women in the context of circumcision, marriage, and childbirth. In recent decades, it too has become a popular tourist commodity, but is still used primarily as dress in the form of vests and jackets. It has even entered the modern, globalized world of fashion, with Malian couturiers based in both Paris and Bamako using bogolanfini materials in their designs. The Bamana cloth has become a popular source for dress among African Americans for whom it serves as a symbol of their African roots.

SYMBOLISM IN HANDCRAFTED WEST AFRICAN TEXTILES

For West Africans, the symbolic meaning of textiles tends to be based on their patterns and what are the most basic colors in West African symbolic systems of thought: white, blue (black), and red. Such is the case among the Bunu Yoruba of Nigeria, for whom these three colors are key in bringing a sense of social and spiritual order to their lives, and, in turn, in influencing the categorizations of textiles within their weaving repertoire. Two of the colors, white (*funfun*) and blue (*dudu*), largely correspond with the female-related sphere. For example, the Bunu associate the color white with nature spirits, including spirits of the water (*ejinuwon*), which are often female. The Bunu also link the white color to moist, and often fertile, substances such as milk, rain, mucus, tears, urine, and semen. One chooses to wear white in an effort to solve a host of spirit-related problems and to provide the path through which humans and spirits can travel between each other's worlds as needed.

For the Bunu, blue (black), and cloths of that color, represent life fully lived. Thus their reference to the most humanly productive act in which women can engage: the bearing of children and marriage rituals leading up to it. A particularly special blue cloth called *adofi* is believed to evoke both spiritual and real women of the past believed to have taught women the art of weaving. Because adofi is so powerful, it is the one cloth Bunu women continue to weave today.

In contrast to white and blue cloth, red (*pupa*) cloth of a particular type referred to as *aso ipo*, meaning "funerary cloth," is predominantly male in its association with chieftaincy for the Bunu, and the ancestors over whom male authority is in firm control. Aso ipo serves largely as funerary attire for chiefs and kings, and is used to construct the Egungun costume performed by men to honor the ancestors and to bring them back to the living when needed.

Color (and pattern), and the underlying beliefs they evoke, also dictated the types of cloths Africans were willing to accept through trade. This was very much the case among the Ijo-speaking groups (Nembe, Kalabari, Okrika, Ibani, and Opobo) of the coastal eastern Niger Delta region of present-day Nigeria. Because there is little history of weaving in this area, the Ijo have a long history of receiving textiles traded from elsewhere in Africa, Europe, and India. However, it was only cloths of particular colors and patterns that they were willing to accept. As quickly as they received them, the eastern Ijo were assigning them local meanings drawn from their beliefs in spirits from the water (*owu*) and from the land (*oru*). For example, the carapace-like designs of a range of blue and white cloth imports, one from the Ijebu Yoruba area and another from India by way of England, evoked the trickster tortoise (*ikaki*) spirit, prompting the Ijo to assign them meaning associated with the tortoise. A familiar inhabitant of the delta environment, the tortoise's wise, cunning, and trick-sterish behavior has long made him a fitting role model in governance and the tortoise cloth (*ikakibite*) a favored form of attire for royalty. These and other cloth imports of preferred colors and patterns became the official attire of their water-spirit masquer-ades and of women during their coming-of-age ceremonies (*iria*). It is only after women have successfully completed iria that they are allowed to wear such cloths in public.

One of the many imports the eastern Ijo took in and made their own was cloth woven in the neighboring Igbo town of Ak-wete, located fifty miles (eighty kilometers) north of the delta. The history of Akwete weaving is traced back to a woman named Dada Nwakwata, an astonishing weaver active in the late nine-teenth century, when palm oil trading was at a peak. Using

Dyula man from the village of Sazaso, Ivory Coast, in 1985, wearing the hunter's shirt his father had brought with him when he migrated from Mali. Photograph by Lisa Aronson.

brightly colored imported cottons, Dada Nwakwata began weaving textiles in patterns and dimensions resembling the cloth imports that her eastern Ijo partners in trade had come to value. The Akwete weaver's repertoire of patterns, numbering well over fifty in the twenty-first century, hints at cloth imports as a source, though with variations and twists that make the cloths quintessentially Akwete. The Ijo continue to commission Akwete cloths of particular designs when needed as prescribed attire for their coming-of-age ceremonies, coronations, and other important life markers.

By the mid-nineteenth century, the Asante and Ewe of the then Gold Coast (now Ghana) were acquiring vast quantities of silk fabrics, which they unraveled and rewove using a bevy of rich and

vibrant colors. The impact of this cloth trade on kente production among both the Ewe and Asante was profound, leading to a wider array of warp-striped patterns and their associated names. One highly valued kente cloth, *sika futuro*, meaning "gold dust," gets its name from its prevailing gold background or field of color. Sika futuro is one of the few Asante kente cloths whose name is based on the color alone. Other colorful versions of kente are more proverbial in meaning. A cloth with a predominantly yellow-striped warp bears the proverb, "If you climb a good tree, you get a push"—the meaning of which has nothing to do with the color of the cloth per se and everything to do with its underlying message: that a good deed gets good results, if not help from others. A kente cloth bearing a black-and-white-striped warp bears the name *kyeretwie*, meaning the "lion or leopard catcher." Said to symbolize courage and bravery, this particular kente was designed by a nineteenth-century Asante king who encouraged warriors working under his leadership to catch leopards as proof of their valor and bravery. The black-and-white stripes are said to evoke the leopard's black-and-white spots. Kyeretwie is one of hundreds of kente designs woven from factory-manufactured threads, whose referential meaning extols qualities of leadership and power.

FACTORY-PRINTED TEXTILES

Today, machine-printed textiles are the most common types of cloths sold in West African markets and the primary source that Africans turn to for dress. The history of their production and marketing in West Africa dates to the early nineteenth century, when the Dutch and English began perfecting printed cotton production and experimenting with designs to better appeal to their growing African market. These patterns included replicas of Asian imports that the Dutch and English had been marketing to West Africa in previous centuries.

Such was the trajectory of the Dutch cloth trade to West Africa. By 1700, they found West Africa to be a receptive market for hand-painted Indonesian batiks with their rich colors, curvilinear floral patterns, and crackle backgrounds resulting from the wax resist. When the Dutch East Indies trade came to a standstill in 1800, the Dutch invented mechanized roller printing techniques—using resin instead of wax as the resist—to imitate the Asian batiks. They even crushed the resin-infused cloth prior to the printing process to create the much-desired crackled background. Today, Dutch wax, as it has come to be called, is the most highly cherished of textiles among West Africans, who readily name them, assign them proverbial meanings, and tailor them into African fashions to make the Indonesian-inspired imports their own.

Although the Netherlands still has its own Dutch wax industry, other countries, including many African ones, and even China, have come up with their own imitations of the cloth, making it imperative for Dutch manufacturers such as Vlisco to print labels that state, "Guaranteed Real Dutch Super Wax from Holland" along the border of their cloths to affirm that it is the real thing. Even so, there is ongoing debate among West Africans as to the identity of the true Dutch wax.

The British were equally zealous in their desire to tap the West African cloth markets of the nineteenth century by inventing their own state-of-the-art looms and roller printers to maximize production and developing a rich array of aniline dyes to

Kalabari Ijo King Amachree (upper right) and his wife and brothers wearing traditional Kalabari Ijo formal attire. His wife is wearing a version of tortoise cloth (*ikakibite*) traded from India. Buguma, Nigeria, 1978. Photograph by Lisa Aronson.

Mande woman from Bouake, Côte d'Ivoire, wearing a boubou and headtie that her husband, to her right, dyed using a cassava paste–resist technique. 1985. Photograph by Lisa Aronson.

make the cloths all the more attractive to their African consumers. Like their Dutch competitors, the British were also replicating cloth imports once brought from Asia, in their case, chintz and calicos from India. By the end of the century, the British were also manufacturing for export a wide range of roller prints featuring geometric or figurative designs scattered over a solid field of color. Both they and the Indian imitations continue today to be very popular in certain areas of West Africa.

Another popular import was the British commemorative handkerchief. These small, handheld cottons with printed images of people and places were commonly used in England for commemorating events of a political or social nature, such as the coronation of Queen Victoria. Such cloths became the foundation for the so-called commemoratives, which today are extremely popular in West Africa as a form of dress. Like the British prototypes, they combine printed words and images that celebrate individuals running for office or important political events. But unlike them, African commemoratives are the size of a cloth wrapper so that the West African consumer can wear it as such. Groups of African supporters will typically commission commemoratives honoring their preferred candidate or political cause and then wear them en masse at political rallies to affirm their loyalties. Because of the timely nature of politics, commemoratives may be worn on only one or two official occasions, sometimes giving

them a particularly short shelf life compared to other factory-printed cloths.

During one Ewe woman's coming-out ceremony marking her initiation as a member of the Yeve, a Vodun cult centered around the thunder god Heviesso, she appeared to dance in public wearing a commemorative that declared her allegiance to Emmanuel Bob-Akitani, the candidate who lost to Faure Eyadema in the 2005 presidential election in Togo. Although the ceremony was taking place in her home village in southeastern Ghana, the commemorative she wore during it affirmed her political loyalties in her current place of residence in Togo.

Other factory-printed cloths can serve social needs on a more daily basis. The Agni of Ivory Coast read their printed designs as proverbial messages intended for others to decipher. The cloths, with their bright colors and either representational or abstract designs, can function as a silent, yet powerful, and often moralizing language through which Agni women may communicate to others. One Agni man who had divorced his first wife later had a lover who frequently wore a cloth with a wild spider motif. He assumed that she was thinking about the proverb "What one does to *cendaa* [a small harmless spider], one does not do to *bokohulu* [a large spider, considered dangerous]," warning him not to mistreat her as she assumed he mistreated his first wife (represented as the harmless spider). Such an axiom quickly reminds him of the importance of being as loyal to his current wife as he was to his former one. A cloth featuring large brown circular shapes evokes the proverb, "Co-wifery is like cow-dung"—that is, hard on the outside but sticky on the inside. A woman will deliberately wear this cloth to remind her cowives and her husband of the potential conflicts and unpleasantries that one can experience in a polygamous household. In general, Agni women choose the cloth they will wear based less on aesthetics and more on the proverbial messages it is able to communicate.

DYEING TECHNIQUES

Increasing imports of cloth and dyes brought about through heightened commercialism in the late nineteenth century greatly stimulated local cloth industries throughout West Africa, with women in charge of much of its production. A good example is the indigo dyeing of imported damask (*bazin*) that Malinke- and Peul- (Fulani-) speaking women of Guinea do to make women's clothing. Referred to as *gudha ngara*, or "indigo cloths" in Guinean languages, the cloth may have had its start in Guinea's Futa Jalon region but eventually spread eastward through the migration of Mande- and Peul-speaking peoples. Besides in Guinea itself, there are major centers of this production today in Soninke-dominated regions of Nioro du Sahel and Kayes, in Mali, and in Malinke-speaking districts of the city of Bouake in Côte d'Ivoire.

Throughout this broad region of West Africa, the indigo-dyed cloths are used for making wrappers (pagnes) and flowing, loose-fitting dresses (boubous) for mainly female consumption. The cloths are often given as gifts for important social occasions (marriage and childbirth) and to reinforce friendship and familial ties. In Guinea, they have become an important national emblem of identity.

Although some of the cloths are made from indigenously manufactured blue- and white-striped strip weave, the majority are made from bazin. To the foundational cloth, the women tightly whip-stitch threads where they want the indigo to resist. The resulting patterns of *xs*, dots, lines, and other shapes move in a linear and often warp-oriented direction across the cloth, as though to be imitating the aesthetic of the men's strip weave, the foundation cloth of gudha ngara before the importation of damask. One of the designs, *kolo*, meaning "bones," is a reference to the warp-faced stripes. Another design, *wara*, consisting of an undulating pattern of white and indigo, refers to a panther or leopard, a fitting symbol of power and agency for a cloth used predominantly to mark a woman's married and childbearing status.

Yoruba women in Nigeria have perfected an indigo tradition of their own, called *adire* (meaning "resist"), that taps an even wider range of resist techniques than the Mande/Peul one. Adire artists use everything from tie-dye (*adire oniko*) and sew-dye (*adire alabere*) to cassava paste—resist dye (*adire eleko*), with the paste either painted directly on the cloth or brushed over a tin stencil. Adire had its roots in the late nineteenth century, when Yoruba indigo dyers responded to British imports of cheap white muslin. Using these cloths as their canvas, Yoruba dyers applied an array of imagery derived from their local environment, such as shrine wall paintings, architectural door reliefs, and building facades. The Ibadan adire draws on the pillared facade of Mapo Hall, a massive structure that the British built in Ibadan in 1927. Other patterns draw on everything from the indigenous, such

as scarification designs, to European-introduced material culture (such as keys, combs, records, and scissors). In the 1930s, adire artists created their own commemorative titled "coronation" (*olaba*), a cassava-resist design featuring a central medallion image of English royalty. In its original form, it was a copy of a portrait produced in England for the 1935 Royal Jubilee, but it was reworked for the 1936 crowning of King Edward VIII. Yoruba religious and mythological figures complete the overall design. Adire is very woman-specific, with only women making and selling it and mostly women wearing it.

Research on adire indicates that its production has experienced highs and lows since its inception in the late nineteenth century. The tradition had seriously waned by the end of the Depression years but then reached a high point by the time of Nigeria's independence in the 1960s. It would have again disappeared by the 1980s were it not for enterprising and creative individuals such as the textile artist known as Nike, who brought adire production to new heights. Initially inspired by Ulli Beier and his art center at Oshugbo, Nike has successfully created workshops in three Yoruba towns (Oshugbo, Ogidi, and Abuja), where women actively engage in the production of both traditional adire and its wax batik derivatives. An up-to-date Web site has greatly expanded Nike's reputation as a textile artist, making her adire clothing visible to an international audience.

Nike's textile work is one of many resist-dye textile industries now prospering in mainly urban areas of West Africa. Done mostly, though not entirely, by women, these urban-based dyeing industries draw on a variety of techniques—everything from stamp wax or cassava paste resist to tie-dye or sew-dye. Although some of the dyes are made from indigenous materials such as kola nuts, most are factory produced, bringing a vibrant sense of color to the cloths. Initially, these urban dyeing traditions may have been inspired by the patterns on imported factory-printed cloths, but they have since moved in many new and exciting directions, producing some of the most creative and strikingly beautiful hand-dyed textiles both for everyday and ceremonial dress in West Africa today.

References and Further Reading

Aronson, Lisa. "Ijebu Yoruba Aso Olona." *African Arts* 25, no. 3 (1992): 52–63, 101.

Aronson, Lisa. "Tricks of the Trade: Ikakibite (Cloth of the Tortoise) among the Eastern Ijo." In *Ways of the River: Art and Environment in the Niger Delta*, edited by Martha Anderson and Phil Peek, 250–267, 354. Los Angeles: UCLA Fowler Museum of Cultural History, 2002.

Bolland, Rita. *Tellem Textiles: Archeological Finds from Burial Caves in Mali's Bandiagara Cliff*. Amsterdam: Royal Tropical Institute, 1991.

Byfield, Judith. *The Bluest Hands: A Social and Economic History of Women Dyers in Abeokuta (Nigeria), 1890–1940*. Portsmouth, NH: Heinemann, 2002.

Domowitz, Susan. "Wearing Proverbs: Anyi Names for Printed Factory Cloth." *African Arts* 25, no. 3 (1992): 82–87, 204.

Kriger, Colleen. *Cloth in West African History*. African Archaeology Series. Lanham, MD: AltaMira Press, 2006.

McNaughton, Patrick. "The Shirts That Mande Hunters Wear." *African Arts* 15, no. 3 (1982): 54–58, 91.

Pemberton, John, III, with contributions by Rowland O. Abiodun and Ulli Beier. *Cloth Only Wears to Shreds: Yoruba Textiles and Photographs from the Beier Collection.* Amherst, MA: Mead Art Museum, Amherst College, 2004.

Picton, John. *Technology, Tradition and Lurex: The Art of Textiles in Africa.* London: Barbican Art Gallery; Lund Humphries Publishers, 1995.

Prussin, Labelle. *Hatumere: Islamic Design in West Africa.* Berkeley: University of California Press, 1986.

Renne, Elisha. *Cloth That Does Not Die: The Meaning of Cloth in Bunu Social Life.* Seattle: University of Washington Press, 1995.

Ross, Doran. *Wrapped in Pride: Ghanaian Kente and African American Identity.* Los Angeles: UCLA Fowler Museum of Cultural History, 1998.

Rovine, Victoria. *Bogolan: Shaping Culture through Cloth in Contemporary Mali.* Washington, DC: Smithsonian Institution Press, 2001.

Sieber, Roy. *African Textiles and Decorative Arts.* New York: Museum of Modern Art, 1972.

Torntore, Susan, ed. *Cloth Is the Center of the World—Nigerian Textiles, Global Perspectives.* St. Paul, MN: Goldstein Museum of Design, Department of Design, Housing, and Apparel, University of Minnesota, 2002.

Vaz, Kim Marie. *The Woman with the Artistic Brush: A Life History of Yoruba Batik Artist Nike Davies.* Armonk, NY: M.E. Sharpe, 1995.

Lisa Aronson

East Africa

- Mainland Traders and Vendors
- Imported versus Locally Produced Cloth
- The Social Roles of Kanga and Vitenge
- Building a Nation through Cloth
- Cloth in East Africa since the 1990s

The production of textiles in East Africa has a long and varied history. In countries like Tanzania, Kenya, Uganda, Rwanda, and Burundi, which now form part of the East African Community, cotton garments were comparatively uncommon prior to the introduction of imported cloth in the course of the nineteenth century. Although cotton weaving techniques were probably first introduced to this region by Persian invaders who settled on the East African coast in 975 C.E. to form the Zeji Empire, centered at Kilwa, it took several centuries before Arab traders began to produce good quality cotton cloth around Sofola. In the period of mercantile capital, from about 1500 C.E., when the East African coast was controlled by the Portuguese, some port towns, like Kilwa, were sacked, leading to a rapid decline in local trade relations. But as the interest of the Portuguese shifted to India, these centers gradually managed to regain their former prosperity. By the early eighteenth century, Kilwa had established strong trade links with the interior, importing textiles from India, along with arms and ammunition and salt.

Among East African communities living in the Sudan and in Ethiopia and Somalia—the region that today is known as the Horn of Africa—locally woven cotton predates trade relations with Muslim Arabs by several centuries. The earliest evidence of cotton cultivation in the Sudan and possibly also Ethiopia was recorded in the mid-fourth century C.E. In Ethiopia, where the habit of wearing skin garments appears to have been abandoned by religious authorities and the upper classes almost a thousand years ago, raw cotton seems to have been imported by Arab traders by the Middle Ages, while the looms used in the production of cotton textiles appear originally to have come from India or China. To this day, weavers from this region use pit-style looms, or ground looms, named for the hole men dig in the ground to accommodate their feet while they sit at the loom.

Elsewhere in East and Central Africa, bark cloth made by stripping, scraping, and beating the inner bark of certain trees, most commonly the *Ficus* species, was widely used long before Arab traders introduced weaving to the region. Historically, this cloth was employed for a variety of mundane purposes; but among the Baganda of Uganda, where it is still used in healing ceremonies as shrouds and during the investiture of the heir to the throne, it attained spiritual significance. Although the production of this cloth was once very widespread, it declined rapidly in the course of the nineteenth century, when imported cloth began to dominate the East African market.

Already in the fourteenth century, weavers from present-day Somalia were exporting cloth to Egypt and elsewhere. By the mid-nineteenth century, Somali cloth was being sold mainly in southern Ethiopia, but some of the textiles from this region were also exported through coastal ports as far south as Mombasa. It was only after they became independent in the 1960s that other countries on the East African coastline, such as Kenya and Tanzania, began to manufacture cloth for large-scale local consumption. Before the nineteenth century, woven cloth was produced in small quantities on the island of Zanzibar and in the Nyamwezi area, but imported cotton remained a luxury item exchanged by wealthy coastal elites for slaves and for local commodities such as ivory, rubber, and beeswax.

In the nineteenth century, imported cloth from India, Europe, and the United States became more freely available to other sectors of the community. This was a direct spin-off of the Industrial Revolution, which witnessed both a massive increase in cloth production due to the mechanization of the textile industry and a significant increase in ivory prices because of the growing need for knife handles, billiard balls, and piano keys in the West. On the island of Zanzibar, where ivory prices doubled between 1820 and 1850, and then tripled between 1850 and 1890, the importation of cloth expanded rapidly, first among the local elite, then, more gradually, among slave communities. The comparatively cheap cloth acquired by these slaves, which originally was known as *leso* after the Portuguese word for "handkerchief," first appeared on the island of Zanzibar in the mid-1870s, where strips of handkerchief material were sewn together to form large wraps. More affordable than any of the other imported cloth that had until then been available on the local market, these leso gradually replaced the *merikani*—literally, "American"—cloth that slave women continued to wear until the abolition of slavery in Zanzibar in 1897.

In the late nineteenth century, leso were dyed with indigo by local slave women. This initiative appears to have encouraged Asian merchants to produce block-printed designs that became known as *kanga za mera*, the precursors of modern *kanga*, which are paired rectangular pieces of cloth decorated with interlacing ornamental patterns along their borders, with additional motifs printed in the center of the rectangle. Worn as wraps, they are draped and knotted in a variety of ways to form skirts, under-arm dresses, tops, and head coverings. By the early twentieth century, these kanga had become an important symbol of freedom as former Zanzibari slaves abandoned the cheaper, undecorated cloths that had signaled both their poverty and servile status.

The term *kanga*, which derives from the Swahili word for "guinea fowl," appears to have been inspired by the fact that the earliest of these designs included white spots on a dark background. The subsequent expansion of the market for kanga in postabolition Zanzibar encouraged British and other manufacturers to produce pairs of brightly colored cloth for the entire East African market. Unable to impose fashion trends on the women consumers of these kanga, the European textile factories that came to dominate this market at the turn of the twentieth century regularly sent local merchants samples of potential designs for approval or modification. Guided by local women, Asian merchants also produced designs that they sent to these textile manufacturers. It appears to have been at the suggestion of these women consumers that kangas first began to include proverbs and aphorisms, known as names (*majina*), some time in the second decade of the twentieth century.

MAINLAND TRADERS AND VENDORS

On the Tanzanian mainland, where textile and clothing imports accounted for 52 percent of total imports by the end of the nineteenth century, the market for imported kanga was initially controlled by street vendors and the owners of small shops, who bought this cloth from coastal trade vessels before selling it to individual consumers, mostly women. These street vendors were like mobile shops walking around with items displayed on their shoulders, heads, and arms. In the early years of this expanding market, most of these vendors were descendants of Asian traders, who, because they struggled to pronounce Swahili words like *nguo*, meaning "cloth" or "garment," became known as the *guo guo*. The descendants of these street vendors now tend to run small businesses in downtown Nairobi, Dar es Salaam, and Zanzibar. But in Tanzania they also have modern counterparts called *machingas*. Originally, these Tanzanian youths came from the Machinga hills region of Lindi and Mtwara in southern Tanzania, but today young men from other rural areas also sell goods on the streets, not only in Dar es Salaam but in other towns and cities throughout East Africa as well.

While, to this day, traders like these continue to dominate the East African cloth market, by the 1890s, women in Dar es Salaam began to buy cloth directly from a vessel that docked twice a year at the local harbor. Nicknamed *Meli ya fundi*, this vessel was always laden with kanga. At that time, competition for this imported cloth was so fierce that women began to seek new forms of employment in the expanding urban economy of Dar es Salaam to support their purchase of kanga. Most became petty traders, who in the early twenty-first century are still known as *Mama Ntilie*—literally, "Mother, serve me food." Working in open markets, these women benefited from regular opportunities to cross-check different kanga designs and other fashion items that might still be missing from their collection of clothes and accessories. Their location in these markets thus made it easier for them to source particular items, which gave them a competitive edge over women who were financially less independent and socially less mobile. Women who had access to disposable income could also be more selective in their purchases than other women, who were less able to afford either new kanga or limited-edition Dutch designs, which were considerably more expensive than the mass-produced English prints.

Although the choice of cloth available to women who waited for the biannual arrival of the trade vessel was fairly limited, they regularly named these cloths. Thus, for example, a cloth called *Meli ya Fundi ya Bamvua ya kwanza mwaka jana* referred to a consignment brought during the first high tide the year before. Other names included allusions to the women's immediate environment, such as plants, and the activities they performed in their daily lives. *Mpunga wa kichele* alluded to rice, while others were ascribed names that invoked the idea of a woman's feelings for both her husband and her children.

IMPORTED VERSUS LOCALLY PRODUCED CLOTH

Numerous factories were established for the production of cloth in post-Independence Kenya and Tanzania. In Tanzania, a number of textile plants were established between 1961 and 1968; these included the Friendship, Mwanza, Musoma, Sun-Flag, and Kilimanjaro textile companies. Some of these belonged to local Indian entrepreneurs, who were former textile importers, and the first two factories in Dar es Salaam were built with capital brought in from Kenya. But others were established through co-operative agreements with the Chinese and with Swedish and British firms. During a trip to Africa in 1964, Zhou Enlai, the premier of the Peoples' Republic of China, proclaimed eight principles on Foreign Economic and Technical Aid that guided relations between the Chinese and African countries like Tanzania for several decades. These included a commitment to supporting and promoting Africa's liberation movements, in part through noninterference in the internal affairs of independent states but also by helping local industries, including the textile sector, to become completely self-reliant.

Following the Arusha Declaration of 1967, efforts were made to boost the production of Tanzania's newly established factories by banning the purchase of imported cloth. But attractive kanga from India, China, and Malaysia could still be obtained thereafter through Tanzanian traders of Indian descent. This cloth reached Dar es Salaam through the islands of Pemba and Unguja, where it was comparatively difficult to control the movements of trade vessels, which were often disguised as fishing boats. Imported kanga with words, kanga maneno, were especially valued because they contained Swahili proverbs and aphorisms free from Islamic censorship, many of which included messages of condolence, appreciation, thanks, or the idea of reconciliation between individuals. Others expressed feelings associated with negative emotions such as anger and fear. But even today, some of these imported kanga do not have any aphorisms printed on them. In Tanzania these are called *bubu*—literally, "dumb kanga."

In the post-Independence period, it also became fairly common for Kenyan consumers to buy better quality Tanzanian kanga and for Tanzanian consumers to acquire Kenyan kanga because of their tendency to focus on personal rather than political issues. For a time, the kanga produced in Tanzania by Mutex (Musoma textiles) were closely linked to those made in Kenya. These kanga were much thicker than the ones made on the outskirts of Dar es Salaam at the Urafiki Friendship Textile Company (originally, the Friendship Textile Mills Ltd.). Although the Swahili texts used on Kenyan kanga were not as refined as those produced in Tanzania, where Swahili is spoken more widely, this did not detract from their popularity among Tanzanian consumers. Among Muslim communities, the private sayings found on many Kenyan, and some Tanzanian, kanga renegotiated culturally entrenched notions of power, affording women opportunities to voice concerns that they were prevented from speaking openly, usually because of hierarchical boundaries of gender, age, and status. Especially in Kenya, the term *mafumbo* (veiled speech) is used to this day to signal the idea of rebelling against patriarchal norms while at the same time avoiding direct engagement or confrontation. In non-Muslim Tanzania communities, where speech prohibitions are not upheld, social communication through kanga has always been more open. Here, men also buy kanga for wives to express or convey their feelings.

Because transgression of import restrictions was very widespread in post-Independence Tanzania, the state repeatedly tried to encourage women to support local industry. Thus, for example, during the 1965 conference of the Union of the Tanzanian

Women, conference delegates discussed at length the importance of national dress and how it should be worn, especially during celebrations and conferences. Some delegates went so far as to call for a total ban of aphorisms on kanga because of the abusive words sometimes included—such as *mtaa wa pili mtanikoma*, Swahili for "you people on the next street, watch out [beware]," an aggressive challenge, and *sanamu ya michelini*, which means, "You are a statue of a Michelin tire," a derogatory comment about women. At the end of this conference, the delegates voted to inform the Ministry of Commerce of their deliberations and called for the production of larger and heavier kanga that would preserve a woman's modesty.

THE SOCIAL ROLES OF KANGA AND VITENGE

Historically, some comparatively thin kanga, which potentially compromised female modesty, were reserved for the private domain, a practice that still survives to this day. When a man got married, he sent his future wife a gift of *sanduku*—a suitcase—which contained the bride's attire, ranging from outer garments to delicate lingerie as well as gold ornaments. The larger the number of paired kanga included in the sanduku, the better. Many of these kanga contained messages with sexual allusions, such as *karibu wangu muhibu*—literally, "Welcome, my darling." Because, under Islamic law, a man is required to provide his wife with new clothes on a regular basis, Muslim women could also expect regular gifts of kanga after marriage. At the turn of the twentieth century, fashion-conscious Zanzibari women commonly owned as many as twenty or thirty sets of kanga. Because they form part of a woman's wealth, these kanga could be pawned in times of need.

After independence, when kanga first began to be manufactured locally in East Africa, their popularity grew so rapidly that the Tanzanian government issued a directive to all textile mills in 1977 to print only one design (albeit in a number of different colors) every three months in an effort to balance supply and demand. Because imports were banned and local production was insufficient to cope with the demand for kanga, most new designs were sold out before they could reach outlying rural areas, leading to an undersupply among village consumers. This decree was upheld until the early 1980s, when the demand and supply equilibrium was restored partly through an increase in local factories, partly because a gradual relaxation of trade regulations fueled the then growing market for European and secondhand clothing.

As early as the 1960s, in Tanzania's coastal regions and among women attending state functions, it had become common for some kanga to be worn in public. In many cases, those chosen for official functions commemorated particular political personalities. To this day, these kanga designs incorporate photographic portraits of prominent figures and words carrying particular messages. The images and words found on these kanga were, and still are, used as didactic tools in emancipation and propaganda campaigns. The designs on many of these kanga were initially inspired by example of African leaders such as Kwame Nkrumah from Ghana and others from Nigeria and Ethiopia who traveled to East Africa to support local efforts to achieve political transformation and who signaled the newly won political sovereignty of their own countries by wearing African forms of dress to the United Nations and elsewhere in the West.

Tanzania's president, Julius Nyerere, who insisted that he should be treated like any other Tanzanian, refused to allow his face to appear on commemorative kanga while he was still in office. Also for this reason, he rejected efforts to have sculptures of himself erected in public. In 1985, one of the designer-artists who worked at Urafiki in the 1970s, Nokanoga—he went on to teach in the School of Drama, Fine Arts and Music at the University of Dar es Salaam—completed a bust of Nyerere in collaboration with Swedish sculptor Stanislous Lux and another local artist, Festo Kijo, which has never been displayed. But this did not stop the designers at the Urafiki mill from producing commemorative cloths of other dignitaries or from making cloths of this kind on commission for foreign patrons. Thus, for example, in the late 1970s, it designed a commemorative kanga that included the face of Sultan Kabuz of Oman, which relied on Congolese *vitenge* with faces as a source of inspiration.

In Tanzania, long dresses made of vitenge—that is, cloths without words or text—became more or less the uniform for women who held political and high government posts in the 1970s. These modest garments came to symbolize the idea of power, perfect motherhood, and nationalism. Headwraps knotted in various styles also became increasingly popular among these women politicians and other office bearers, not only at work but also when attending social gatherings. Except in the coastal regions and among Muslim women, the use of headwraps had until then been confined to the private domain, regardless of the social status of the wearer. It is not clear why the use of headwraps became more frequent in public at this time, but it is possible that they were inspired by the growing links between East and West Africa, where headwraps were fairly common. As symbols of power and political authority, these wraps underlined the newly acquired status of women seeking public office.

Although, from the mid-1980s onward, women politicians began to adopt Euro-American clothing styles, in the early twenty-first century the management of TV Tanzania was forced by the state to demand that its women employees wear dresses made from locally manufactured cloths—that is, vitenge—to promote the idea of a Tanzanian identity and cultural pride. Likewise, women university students learning subjects such as social work and education, which require them to engage the community, tend to wear vitenge dresses to signal their respect for more traditional modes of dress.

Paired kanga nevertheless remain popular to this day, partly because they are so versatile. They can be used in the privacy of the home as sleepwear or as comfortable wraps before and after taking a bath. On these occasions, women normally wear a single wrap because they do not experience any sense of compromise to their privacy in their own homes. But kanga are also worn in pairs to political rallies and at weddings. At these celebratory events, the feeling of festive solidarity is often reinforced by the fact that women guests tend to wear the same kanga designs. More recently, this practice has also become common at funerals, where women mourners now tend to express their common sense of grief by wearing identical kanga. It is probably significant to this development that, in contrast to the black wraps women wore at funerals in the past, these kanga can be reused.

In Tanzania, kanga are also commonly exchanged as gifts to mark girls' entry into adolescence. In this context, they signal the fact that the recipient is on the brink of womanhood. As adults, women invariably carry kanga for emergency personal needs or to assist someone else who might need one unexpectedly. In the latter and other similar cases, the recipient is never expected to return the kanga. In this sense, a kanga is never lost but is simply passed on. Exchanges like these cement social relations between women, regardless of their age or their status in the community. The central role kanga play in preserving people's dignity in day-to-day social relations is further underlined by the fact that they are commonly used to cover the bodies of those killed on the road.

BUILDING A NATION THROUGH CLOTH

Most of Tanzania's textile mills were established in cotton-growing regions across the country after independence. Notable among these were Mutex (Musoma textiles) and Mwatex in Mwanza, which used a range of modern and automated technologies imported from Europe. The largest and most important among these textile mills was the Urafiki Friendship Textile Mill, which operated with Chinese equipment, some of which had been designed in the 1930s. Despite the use of this outdated technology, Urafiki initially ran a far more profitable establishment than some of the better-equipped factories set up in cotton-growing areas. Established in 1968, it was initially situated beyond Dar es Salaam's urban sprawl. An intentionally labor-intensive operation with a capacity for thirty-five million square meters (roughly thirty-eight million square yards) of cloth per annum, it was the largest single employer in Tanzania in the early 1970s. Since virtually every Tanzanian had a link to the factory, it rapidly became a symbol of national pride, achievement, and belonging, which was reinforced by the fact that it produced cloth for the Tanzanian army and even had its own band, the Urafiki Jazz Band, led by Juma Mrisho. Like other members of the band, he had belonged to another group before seeking employment at the mill. Formed in the late 1960s for marketing purposes by the management of Urafiki, the band played regularly in urban as well as rural areas until the early 1980s, when some of its members passed away. Always dressed in Urafiki cloth, the band sang songs that praised and marketed the products of the mill, thereby actively fostering patriotism and contributing to the Tanzanian government's nation-building efforts.

Although in the twenty-first century Urafiki is under Sino-African management, initially Chinese technicians were involved in only three departments: spinning, weaving, and processing. In the design department, each technician was tasked with training nine Tanzanians. Because most of the local trainees had virtually no prior design experience, they had to be taught on the job. But Tanzania's initially very successful post-Independence centralized employment policy meant that they could also rely on the input of a number of Tanzanians who had obtained fine art degrees from the University of Makarere in Uganda. The Tanzanian Ministry of Manpower, which at that time kept records of people who were potentially useful to the promotion of local industrial development, regularly redeployed these graduates to support the country's efforts to achieve greater economic independence. Nokanoga, who now works in the fine arts department at the University of Dar es Salaam, was one of the Makarere graduates employed at the Urafiki mill from 1974 to 1979. While there, he painted a large mural of the mill in the factory's social hall, which served as a backdrop for many of the performances of the Urafiki Jazz Band.

In keeping with Tanzania's post-Independence commitment to nation building, the Urafiki factory established various facilities for its workers, including two dispensaries, a cafeteria that provided them with cheap meals, affordable housing for them and their families, and transportation. The Ministry of Trade and Industries also encouraged designers who worked at the mill to travel to trade fairs in neighboring countries such as Mozambique, Botswana, and Zambia to learn more about regional developments in the cloth industry. Likewise, to research their potential markets, these designers visited Asian merchants in Kenya, who alerted them to recent trends in the Kenyan preference for Swahili proverbs and color schemes. They also traveled regularly to Tanzania's Regional Trading Corporations, where wholesalers proved to be an invaluable source of information on local market trends. Thus, for example, in Sumbawamga, where red was associated with witchcraft, merchants repeatedly advised against the use of this color, whereas in the coastal region, these designers were encouraged to produce kanga with large areas of white as a background. In contrast to this coastal preference, communities in the interior tended to reject predominantly white designs because they revealed dirt from the dark local soils too readily.

When the Urafiki Friendship Textile Mill first opened, it established a cooperative shop for its workers, which was subsequently opened to the public. This shop survived the breakup of the East African Community in 1977, the liberalization of trade relations in the 1980s, and the growth of the secondhand clothing industry, but it finally closed down some time after 2000. In the early years, both ordinary people and small traders queued to secure some of the new designs printed by the factory after learning, through the word-of-mouth descriptions of people working at Urafiki, what it was planning to issue.

Despite this fierce interest in fashionable new designs, certain kanga patterns and names that were first introduced in the 1930s or 1940s have remained in vogue to this day. Included among these is a kanga known as *kisutu*, which originated in Zanzibar during an epidemic that required the intervention of the Red Cross. Superstition surrounds cloths like this one, which, although popular in most regions, are not worn by some communities in the belief that they will become ill if they do so. Another example that has been repeatedly printed over several decades, known as *mpunga wa kisele*, has a very small motif that looks like a rice field. Consumers originally named this cloth after Kisele, a well-known rice-growing area. Other popular kanga include one called *penye ubhia tia rupia*—literally, "solving the problem with money," which is a very gentle way of saying that money can oil the way—and another called *Je iko namna?*—literally, "Is there a problem?" Consumers also continue to favor old proverbs: for example, *Ukipenda boga panda na ua lake*—literally, "If you love pumpkin, you should also love the leaves the pumpkin lies on," advice that is often given to married couples as regards their extended families. In some cases, literal translations from Swahili do not suffice. Thus, for example, *Mbona kununua chakula dukani ukiwa nyumbani?*—literally, "Why go shopping for food when you have meat at home?"—asks, "Why sleep with a prostitute when you have a wife at home?"

In recent years, the practice of commissioning kanga has become increasingly common, even among private institutions and religious groups. In Tanzania, Christian references are especially common, as in *Moyo wa Yesu ni kitulizo chca matatizo yangu*, meaning "The heart of Jesus is the consolation of my problems";

Ushinde na utawale—moyo safi wa Bikira Maria, meaning "You conquer and you reign—Immaculate heart of the Blessed Virgin Mary"; and *WAWATA (Wanawake Wakatoliki Tanzania)— Kwa Upendo wa Kristu Tutumikie*, meaning "Catholic Women of Tanzania—For the Love of Christ, Let Us Serve."

After former President Nyrere's death in 1999, numerous commemorative cloths were also dedicated to his memory, some with photographic portrait images. Among these were cloths with slogans like *Watanzania tumuenzi Baba wa Taifa*—"Tanzanians, let us honor the Father of the Nation"—and *Baba wa Taifa, MKombozi wa Afrika: 1922–1999. Pumzika kwa amani*—"Father of the Nation, Savior of Africa: 1992–1999. Rest in Peace."

CLOTH IN EAST AFRICA SINCE THE 1990s

Since the 1990s, the East African cloth industry has embraced the fashion for West African styles, with some factories producing vitenge inspired by West African designs. Increasingly, cloth from West and Central Africa has also entered the East African market through border trade. Although in Tanzania, illegally imported wax-printed textiles called "real waxes" (in contrast to less-expensive textiles or "false waxes," also known as "roller prints" in the industry as a result of the technology used) initially came from the Congo via the Kigoma region as early as the 1970s, in recent years, it has become difficult to determine the origins of waxes or easily to tell the difference between real and false waxes. Before the liberalization period of the 1980s, when the trade in Congolese and some West African textiles was still secret, it was controlled by men working in the border areas. In urban areas, however, the real waxes were handled by women working from the privacy, and therefore relative protection, of their homes. Although Chinese imports have since had a far-reaching impact on this market, many consumers still value densely woven cottons obtained from long-established African suppliers.

In Kenya, where the use of locally printed and imported West African textiles is much less common than in Tanzania, dresses made from African print fabric are generally reserved for special occasions like weddings. Here, the coastal market for kanga broke down rapidly in the course of the 1990s, a far cry from earlier days when consumers eagerly awaited the arrival on the market twice a year of between two and four new designs. Even in Tanzania, where many women, including young women, continue to wear kanga and vitenge on a daily basis, there are signs that the popularity of indigenous forms of dress is waning. Reflecting on this shift, Zanzibari fashion designer Farouque Abdellah noted recently that although kanga attained the status of a national costume in Tanzania in the course of the twentieth century, the popularity of these paired clothes is increasingly threatened by the growing market for imported, secondhand clothing.

References and Further Reading

Beck, Rose Marie. "Aesthetics of Communication: Texts on Textiles (Leso) from the East African Coast (Swahili)." *Research in African Literatures* 31, no. 4 (Winter 2000): 104–124.

Beck, Rose Marie. "Texts on Textiles: Proverbiality as Characterisic of Equivocal Communication at the East African Coast (Swahili)." *Journal of African Cultural Studies* 17, no. 2 (December 2005): 131–160.

Fair, Laura. *Pastimes and Politics. Culture, Community and Identity in Post-Abolition Urban Zanzibar 1890–1945*. Athens: Ohio University Press, 2001.

Gevers, M. "Cotton and Cotton Weaving in Meroitic Nubia and Medieval Ethiopia." *Textile History* 21, no. 1 (Spring 1990): 13–30.

Hanby, Jeannette, and David Bygott. *Kangas: 101 Uses*. Dar es Salaam, Tanzania: Tanzania Printers, 1992.

Linnebuhr, Elisabeth. "Kanga: Popular Cloths with Messages." In *Sokomoto. Popular Culture in East Africa*, edited by Werner Graebner. Amsterdam: Rdopi, 1992: 81–90.

Nicholson, G. Edward. "The Production, History, Uses and Relationships of Cotton (Gossypium spp.) in Ethiopia." *Economic Botany* 14, no. 1 (January 1960): 3–36.

Rabine, Leslie. *The Global Circulation of African Fashion*. Oxford, UK: Berg, 2002.

Sandra Klopper and Rehema Nchimbi

See also Tanzania; Uganda.

Southern Africa

- Isishweshwe
- BaSotho Blankets: New Variants and Uses
- The AmaQaba: Xhosa and Tembu Dress
- The Development of Popular Diviner's Cloth
- African Independent Church (AIC) Cloth Preferences
- Mblasela
- Domestic Workers' Wear and Power
- Cross-Cultural Dress

Moshoeshoe Day celebrations, Maeru, Lesotho, 2005. Printed blue (or sometimes brown, red, or green) cloth is known as *isishweshwe*, traditionally associated with the nineteenth-century BaSotho leader, Moshoeshoe. Photograph by Juliette Leeb-du Toit.

The designation *southern Africa* marks a region shaped by cultural distinctiveness coupled with early settler and colonial boundaries that are the result of economic and legislative control. This resulted in the demarcation of specific countries inflected by European and British settler influence and occupancy—namely, South Africa, Botswana, Namibia, Lesotho, and Swaziland. However, these boundaries belie cultural and economic exchange that transcended such artificial geographic boundaries. Migrant labor and waves of refugees from elsewhere in Africa to this region have also shaped the rapid spread of textiles into and from regions beyond the southern African constituency.

Beadwork has been regarded as the dominant marker of differentiation among black peoples in southern Africa, but textiles have become equally distinctive in their usage and association. Textiles currently used result from a centuries-old crossing of Eastern and Western cultural and geographical boundaries that are the result of trade between the East, Africa, and Europe. Accounts by voyagers recall the presence of hides but also of woven cloth of cellulose fibers (some have suggested strip-bark weaving), with looms discovered in the Limpopo (Transvaal) province, further indicating that weaving existed in pre-Colonial times. Balls of indigo dyestuff recovered at archaeological sites in central Botswana suggest that some textiles may have been dyed blue.

The discontinuance of such cloth production was prompted by the increased presence of Arab trade along the east coast of Africa from as early as 1200 and may have been preceded by Chinese trade much earlier. By the fifteenth century, Portuguese voyagers cornered the textile trade, to be followed by the Dutch East India Company, which established a key entrepôt at the Cape of Good Hope in 1652 to monopolize trade with the East. European-based dress that entered the Cape was invested with implicit class association, reinforcing cultural superiority. From the outset, cloth at the Cape was augmented by materials imported from the East, and, by 1659, company stores stocked Ireland and Guinea linen, English sheets, striped cloth, calico, serge, bafta, negros cloth, chintz, *salempore*, and gingham—both for trade and local use. Slaves entered the Cape from 1654 hailing from Madagascar, Bengal, Cormandel, Surat, Guinea, and East Africa, female seamstresses among them being highly regarded. Male slaves wore blue *cursaij* (kersey) jackets, blue shirts, and neck cloths (handkerchiefs); female slaves wore patterned skirts,

often blue and white. Further, many Indian and Indonesian political prisoners exiled to the Cape were identifiable by their long indigo robes and woven hats.

Poorer white and other working classes wore dark plain serviceable cotton and woolen fabrics, while Free Burghers' wives wore serviceable dresses in cotton or linen, white hooded caps (kappies) typical of Dutch and German peasantry and Indian shawls. By 1834, this dress code was adopted by dissident Voortrekkers, a group who elected to leave the Cape rather than be subject to British rule and associated legislation. This dress form was adopted by the mixed-race community and some Africans in the eastern Cape, at times located in secondhand garments from abroad. Such dress subsequently came to be worn by Afrikaners as South African national dress from the 1930s, associated primarily with the Voortrekker cultural movement, but it has since receded in prevalence.

ISISHWESHWE

One of the earliest cloth forms that originated both in slaves' and farmers' wear and in imported cloth from the East is *isishweshwe* (Afrikaans, *bloudruk*), a recent appellation for indigo blue or brown discharge-printed cloth. Indigo-patterned cloth was initially sourced by local traders in India, the Netherlands, France, Switzerland, Germany (where it was termed *blaudruck*), Hungary (where it was known as *kékfésto*), and the United States. Starting in the late nineteenth century, patterned indigo cloth destined for southern Africa emanated largely from Manchester,

England. Its production is now centered in South Africa. A German Moravian mission founded at Genadendal (for the Khoi-San) in 1772–1773, followed by ongoing German mission activity and immigration throughout the nineteenth century, seems to have established this precedent for blaudruck. Not surprisingly, many groups acknowledge a German source for this cloth, the Pedi referring to it as *motoishi* (from *Duits* or *Deutsch*), the Xhosa as *amajamani*, *ujamani*, or *jelmani*.

Oral tradition has it that in the mid-nineteenth century, Moshoeshoe, the first BaSotho leader, was given blueprint cloth and blankets by members of the Paris Evangelical Missionary. By the late nineteenth century, both children and matrons wore blueprint/isishweshwe and woolen blankets, associating the wearer with conversion to Christianity and education, and later becoming an intrinsic manifestation of national dress. Most southern Africans refer to printed indigo cloth as *isishweshwe*, clearly sourced in Moshoeshoe's name and BaSotho association.

Cultural distinctiveness in isishweshwe is predominantly the domain of men in the kingdom of Swaziland, where it is worn and termed a *sidwashi*, mostly consisting of red, maroon, and brown (rarely blue) isishweshwe cloth, often a combination of two or three variants, allegedly to prevent transparency. While worn for ceremonial and cultural display, this cloth is designated dress for the *amabutho*, the male traditional military force that dedicate their lives to the protection of the king (*ingwenyama*, or lion) and in honor of the authority of the Queen Mother (*inhlopukathi*, or she elephant). Mature women in Swaziland also elect to wear Western-designed isishweshwe dresses as their counterparts do in South Africa and with similar age-grade associations. Wearers in contemporary KwaZulu-Natal reinforce the BaSotho origin of isishweshwe, its usage here preceded by early accounts of preferences for plain blue salempore cloth. Women widely associate the wearing of isishweshwe with marriage, maturity, and childbearing; bolts of isishweshwe are regarded as central to the marriage gift. Isishweshwe has also come to be regarded as national dress in Botswana and among the maHerero population who live there and in Namibia. However, in Namibia, preferred dress textiles are largely synthetic. Isishweshwe has become one of the most popular cloths in a burgeoning contemporary South African fashion arena while simultaneously functioning as a marker of national consciousness, evoking a colonial history of exchange and serving as a marker of contemporary South African identity.

BASOTHO BLANKETS: NEW VARIANTS AND USES

Heavy woven cloth and blankets constitute a significant part of the textiles used in southern Africa, with sheeting among the Xhosa, Mfengu, and Mpondomise and cloth and blankets among the BaSotho. Two distinctive types of commercially made blankets occur in Lesotho. The first, in two main color fields, has organic, geometric, or other pictorial motifs, often with one or more centrally situated red stripes. Images associated with the British monarchy and military insignia became popular. Frasers established a network of trading outlets across Lesotho to market these, but by the 1960s, Waverleys became the main local producer. The blankets initially served a functional purpose, supplanting more costly hide covering, but by the mid-twentieth century, the blanket had acquired national significance as traditional dress for both men and women.

More recently, a second, cheaper, commercially produced gray blanket has been identified. With or without a line or two

The *amabutho* (Swazi male regiment) wearing traditional *sidwashi* cloth at King Mswati's birthday celebrations, Swaziland, 2005. Photograph by Juliette Leeb-du Toit.

of lighter gray or beige and white or red near the borders, these garments have been heavily embroidered by young herders, having been taught sewing at their initiation schools. The motifs on these blankets vary; some include biblically sourced images, some contain images associated with the late-1990s skirmishes into Lesotho by the South African Defence Force, and others display adages such as, "May my enemies live a long life so that they may see my success."

Blankets have also become the dominant textile of the Ndebele. Also of northern Nguni origin, the Ndebele gravitated to areas in Gauteng and the North West Province after being dispersed as a result of the Mfecane, a period of political disruption and population migration in southern Africa that occurred during the 1820s and 1830s. The Ndebele developed distinctive design preferences in blankets; beadwork strips are sewn on or above the colored striped area on the lower register of the blanket. An example of this type of blanket is the *irari* multicolored beaded blanket worn by mature married women.

THE AMAQABA: XHOSA AND TEMBU DRESS

Tembu, Xhosa, and Mpondo occupy the eastern Cape, between the Bashee and Umtata rivers in a region previously divided into the Transkei and Ciskei under the Bantustan and Homelands policy of the former nationalist government. The well-documented textile use in the region accrued over two centuries, increasing rapidly after the 1830s, when restrictions on border trade were lifted. After the disastrous Cattle Killing of 1856–1857, inspired by the prophetess Nonqawuse, the use of blankets and other textiles steadily increased; missionaries and traders contributed to the use of cloth with their zealous enforcement of prescriptive covering or merely catering to emergent local preferences.

For the Tembu and Xhosa, the wearing of cotton pile sheeting has been central in both male and female dress since the late nineteenth century. Brushed cotton sheeting, variously known as "k-sheeting" (formerly "kaffir" sheeting), became the preferred fabric. It is left its original creamy white, rendered a whitish blue through the use of *blousel* (a whitening agent) or darkened red or ochre through being kneaded with red clay or as a result of being washed in red oxide or yellow ochre. Ochre from Grahamstown is widely marketed in the interior. The process of reddening or yellowing the sheeting is associated with the verb *qaba*, "to redden"; hence, the Tembu are often referred to as *amaQaba*, "the red people."

Red has deep religious significance to the Tembu; it is associated with the blood of the earth and is beloved by the ancestors. Those who wear red are ritually cleansed and lead a normal tribal life, while those who are affected by the supernatural or a disruptive event such as childbirth or breast-feeding replace the red with a white garment, indicating the need to renew access with the ancestors. The young *umkwetha* (initiate) undergoing circumcision whitens his blanket and body to indicate his status.

Worn as a loose wraparound skirt (*umbhaco*) with or without a cloak (*ibhayi*), k-sheeting has become synonymous with Tembu, Xhosa, Mfengu, and Mpondo cultural dress. Other variants in this cloth include beaded cloth waistcoats and head scarves.

For her trousseau later in life, the young girl will have two sets of dress—one white and the other red ochre. Unlike the northern Nguni, the Xhosa diviner wears white, indicative of his or her proximity to the ancestors and other spirits.

While the wearing of k-sheeting is located in traditional practice, it has become associated with resistance to Western conquest, values, and restrictions and with deepening cultural conservatism by the amaQaba as opposed to the educated elite. Further, the wearing of Tembu dress by Nelson Mandela at his trial reinforced associations of defiance. Currently, Xhosa dress and cloth is embraced in widespread contemporary fashion by designers such as Sun Goddess.

Besides isishweshwe, salempore is one of the most widely used trade cloths in southern Africa, identified as a loosely woven blue or black cotton cloth that may have multicolored stripes in green, white, red, and light blue. Originating in Madras (now Chennai), India, salempore was later replicated by the British and more recently by the Portuguese. It was among the first trade cloths identified as significant to Portuguese traders and by the Dutch East India Company. It is currently used predominantly by the Vhavenda, Zulu, Tsonga-Shangana, and some diviners. Besides its use at the Cape as a trade cloth, early evidence indicates that plain dark blue salempore was worn in the nineteenth century as an *ibhaye* (shoulder wrap) by women of the royal *isigodlo* (female enclave) under Zulu king Cetewayo.

By the 1920s, the Vhavenda hide cloak worn by women and slung over one shoulder had been replaced by the *rimenda/nwenda* made of dark blue–striped salempore and was also worn as a wraparound skirt. Salempore is untainted by associations with conversion, and the Vhavenda wearing of salempore is associated with nubility and maturity. As Venda gained relative autonomy in 1979 and became a homeland under the apartheid government, the Vhavenda were subject to ethnic separation. This was marked by the refining of their ethnicity in dress as groups marked their transition to quasi independence and a degree of autonomy by emphasizing their difference in dress. The manufacture of salempore, formerly in England and India, was transferred to South Africa in the late 1970s. The woven salempore was replaced by a more durable tight-weave printed cotton, and the colors were heightened and intensified. An Indian trader from the Transvaal

Pedi dress and associated cloth: cotton *salempore* and braid. *Salempore* is a plain blue cloth, sometimes with colored stripes. With colonial origins, it is one of the most widely used trade cloths in twenty-first-century southern Africa. Photograph by Juliette Leeb-du Toit.

town of Louis Trichardt (now Makhado), wishing to escape the economic sanctions and the rising cost of the imported cloth, developed a local variant typified by a wider range of color schemes in both ground and stripes, with radiant blue, black, red, orange, yellow, pink, green, brown, and gray background colors. This cloth is now made by Da Gama textiles in King Williams Town. Vhavenda women wear four yards—two for a cape draped over the right shoulder (*nwenda*) and two for a back apron (*mukhasi*) and front apron (*tshiluvhelo*)—onto which rickrack, bias binding, and cloth strips are sewn at right angles, creating a complex geometric pattern. More recently, Vhavenda attire has been popularized under the Funduzi label, named after the sacred lake in the area. In the early twenty-first century, clothing sourced in this fabric is applied to contemporary Westernized dress variants.

The use of salempore is also central to the dress of the Tsonga-Shangana (formerly known as the Magwamba), who hail from the eastern Mpumalanga (formerly Gazankulu), separated as they were from Mozambique by the Kruger National Park. Early references indicate that peoples from the eastern coast made a bark cloth from the ficus tree, and there is a suggestion that cotton weaving was known among the BaVenda and the Tsonga. Trade cloth emanating from India and Europe supplanted indigenous cloth with salempore (known as *mashikambe*) and plain blue cotton cloth (*kapulane*) as well as a plaid cloth.

Blue- and red-ground salempore—usually purchased by men as a gesture of protection and for women to cover themselves—is made up into a gathered skirt, a *xibelani* (or *xitlhekutana*), consisting of eighteen yards (sixteen and a half meters) of salempore, a third of which is folded over along the length and tied with a rope belt (*xisuti*). While originally regarded as the dress of the mature married woman, it has come to be associated with distinctive Tsonga cultural identity. The two tiers move in opposite directions when worn, eliciting admired sensual movements. The xibelani has been replaced by skirts of wool or strips of cloth similarly knotted and strung, over which the *minceka* appear, prompted by the rising cost of the preferred salempore.

More recently, women wear a skipper or T-shirt covered with one or two brightly colored commercial minceka, each a meter and a half (five feet) in length and each tied and draped over a shoulder (that is if two are used simultaneously). These are worn intentionally unmatched, in bright, almost neon, cerise and pink. Patterned head scarves are added to complete the attire.

Since about the 1950s, a variant of minceka is embroidered and modified by the addition of mirrors and brass safety pins. Many of these embellished minceka have become valuable as South African collectors and galleries increasingly recognize the exceptional creativity of the Tsonga-Shangana. Embroidery also decorates white cotton cloth, white recycled cotton flour bags, and *makhwata*, a dark royal blue or maroon cloth with a black floral design at the perimeters and in the center.

Skills in embroidery originated both in terms of mission and state schooling expectations and projects, but many Tsonga-Shangana women are self-taught. Tsonga-Shangana men are also accomplished embroiderers; miners, in particular, are known for the exceptional embroidery on their bedclothes, curtains, and vests onto which images of cattle, birds, aircraft, and other motifs were sewn. Minceka embroidered motifs are locally derived or are from preferred patterns located in commercial cloth, such as the peacock. Some motifs derive from current events and political themes. Found on minceka are images of F. W. de Klerk

Variants of the *sangoma*'s (diviner's) *ibhaye* (wrap or head scarf). Swaziland, 2005. Photograph by Juliette Leeb-du Toit.

and Winnie and Nelson Mandela. Scenes of the 1994 voting procedures have appeared on women's embroidered minceka, prompted in part by wide-scale collecting by galleries both nationally and internationally. The Xihoko workshop, initiated by Jane Arthur, Daina Mabunda, and Reckson Mabunda, developed a commercial outlet for local embroiderers who have extended their production to making bedclothes and other items as well as the traditional minceka.

THE DEVELOPMENT OF POPULAR DIVINER'S CLOTH

The distinctive identity of the *sangoma* (Zulu healer or diviner) in many urban centers and regions of South Africa has recently become expressed in the use of commercial cloth that has acquired localized significance, names, and associations. While the cloth combinations vary, depending on the region or school where the *uthwasa* (neophyte or trainee sangoma) trained, consistencies in color and their implications are especially noticeable among Nguni peoples (Zulu, Swazi).

Said to have first appeared in the 1960s, one particular cloth is referred to as an *ibhaye*, a term commonly used for any shoulder wrap worn by a matron as a sign of respect associated with the *ukuhlonipha* tradition (respect for males and ancestors), but also worn as a wrap skirt. Characterized by the colors black, red, and white—more rarely with maroon or royal blue variants—the cloth is further identified by a central motif of animals, birds, or royalty (e.g., Mangosuthu Buthelezi or King Goodwill Zwelethini), with a decorative motif at the border. Images of lions, leopards, crocodiles, ostriches, peacocks, or Zulu shields betoken enlightenment and access to the ancestral spirits (*idlozi*). Symptomatic of a calling by the shades, the potential diviner becomes ill and, dreaming constantly of wild animals or serpents, he or she expects to kill or snare one of these. The ibhaye is usually worn as a skirt wrap (*indwango*), on the shoulder (*emahlombe*), or both; if it is tied above the breasts and is open at the front, it is an *ibhubesi*. It is worn over a black (or red) cotton or synthetic skirt to emulate the black pleated leather skirt worn by married Zulu women, *isidwaba*; black is also the color associated with the ancestors. The colors red, white, and black have profound religious and prophylactic significance for diviners, and certain medicines are associated with certain colors: black (*imithi emnyama*), red (*imithi ebomovu*), and white (*imithi emhlope*). Healing occurs by establishing a balance in the body from black to red and ultimately to white.

In addition, the sangoma uses various amounts of *ingwe* (imitation leopard-pelt cotton corduroy on color grounds of red, blue, white, and turquoise) to be worn as an ibhaye, wrap, head scarf, or in a synthetic skipper.

While essentially resembling the ibhaye in color and manufacturing source (India and South Africa), a similar cloth type has come to be identified among Swazi men and women as central to the cultural dress of the male amabutho and Swazi matrons. Such is the extent of its usage in the early twenty-first century that specific cloth designs have been designated *Swazi* by traders and differ considerably from those used by sangomas. This more recent imagery is of the Swazi monarchy.

Red or maroon, white, and black also appear in a distinctive loosely woven cloth featuring a crisscross trellis grid, known as *injeti* (*ingethi/injiti*), which is said to have originated in India. It may be worn as a wrap or over the shoulders when performing a ritual sacrifice, in which case it is termed an *indawo*. A white cloth sold as "Pondo sheeting" has also acquired significance, as has *palo* cloth, a loosely woven, light blue and white cotton plaid cloth with red stripes at one side. An elderly Swazi man from Nelspruit claimed that he was buying a meter (approximately three feet) of the cloth to place under his pillow, because the palo was thought to be allied to his male ancestors, whose power and blessing he hoped to invoke. At the same time, he purchased a piece of injeti, representing potential access to his female ancestors, both for invocation and protection.

AFRICAN INDEPENDENT CHURCH (AIC) CLOTH PREFERENCES

Plain colored cotton cloth has become one of the fabric types that marks a variety of cultural and religious dress preferences. The emergence of numerous breakaway churches created by local Africans resulted from dissatisfaction with an intellectualized and institutionalized Western Christianity. Marked by a syncretism that embraces Christianity, Old Testament teachings, and central aspects of indigenous belief systems, over six thousand African Independent Churches have been identified in South Africa. They encourage speaking in tongues, healing, baptism, and ancestral invocation, and dogma is not expressed in text but in hymns, prayers, sermons, and symbols. Color-coded dress is supernaturally revealed to the leader/founder, marking group distinctiveness. For men, a white surplice or coatlike outer garment is worn over ordinary Western clothing. Women wear the same or a tunic/blouse and skirts of various colors and designs. These are enhanced by corded or cloth belts or sashes (girdles) in various colors or color combinations. In addition, the white cloth may be embellished with crosses, stars, or moons sewn onto the garment.

Most color symbolism is prophylactic and can promote well-being, provide protection from illness, and reinstate the vital force as expressed biblically in Luke 8:44. Red is rarely used because it refers to blood (including menstrual blood) and passion and can signify death, infertility, and suffering. However, the women of the Amabediya community wear a red dress and ibhaye with a green or red head scarf. Blue (faithfulness) and green (spirituality), both associated with water and its healing powers, are commonly worn.

Possibly the best-known Zionist movement (a syncretic tradition that encompasses African and Judeo-Christian beliefs) is the Zionist Christian Church, which meets annually every Easter at Moria in Mpumalanga. The men followers wear distinctive khaki pants and shirts, and the women wear khaki shirts and skirts. Sourced in Western military dress precedents, these garments are marked by a black badge, bottle-green patches of cloth, a silver (chrome) brooch, and the letters ZCC at the center. The letters also appear on the military caps and green berets worn by members.

Another prominent Zionist church is the *Ibandla lama Nazaretha* (popularly known as the *Shembe*, which refers to both the followers and the church itself), which has its centers at Ebuhleni and Ekuphakameni in KwaZulu-Natal. The founder, prophet Isaiah Shembe, envisioned a church that restored the authority of Zulu cultural practice and ritual, and he had dreams and

Uthwasa (*sangoma*, or diviner, neophytes) wear distinctive patterns and colors to mark their spirituality. Red, white, and black have religious significance. Pietermaritzburg, KwaZulu-Natal, southern Africa, 2006. Photograph by Juliette Leeb-du Toit.

visions regarding appropriate dress. Many of the garments worn by members of this church are made from commercial textiles. Neophytes and those about to be baptized or who cannot yet afford correct regalia wear a white smock not unlike a liturgical surplice. Mature women wear a black leather isisdawba or a black cloth skirt resembling the latter and a black ibhaye festooned with bright blue and pink embroidered circles or pom-poms. Young women wear short red skirts. Men wear traditional pelt-based garments, and boys wear short black skirts, white shirts, and green bowties or a white shirt with a red and white plaid skirt. Mature men wear a variant of Zulu male attire with leopard or genet pelts, but, more recently, a range of variants of the latter appear in commercial cloth or reedbuck or springbuck (gazelle) skin with artificially painted leopard spots.

MBLASELA

The cloth embellishment of men's pants and waistcoats, initially in beads, is a unique form of decorative recycling that has appeared since at least the 1940s and that straddles both traditionalist and Western influences. Known as *mblasela*, the practice consists of affixing triangular patches of plain-colored fabric bordered by braid to areas of commercially bought pants or waistcoats. The origins of mblasela are directly linked to migrant labor policy that coerced rural inhabitants to urban centers and particularly to the mines. Having originated in the patchwork repairs done on Zulu migrant workers' pants by their wives, such repairs were perpetuated in the hostels and were precedents for sewing by males noted earlier. Because most migrants hailed from traditional areas, and still do, the appliquéd motifs resemble beadwork, carved or painted patterns such as Zulu *amabhaxa* (mat racks), and designs on *izinkhamba* (clay, Zulu beer-drinking vessels). The wearing of mblasela conveys a distinctive Zulu ethnicity when worn in competitive dance and singing groups at

the mines. Mblasela has acquired national status as one of the many pan-African dress forms.

DOMESTIC WORKERS' WEAR AND POWER

For at least a hundred years, black South African domestic workers and laborers have been obliged to wear distinctive clothing that marked the nature of their employment and their implicit subservience. Manufacturers such as Johnson Brothers cornered the market for workers' wear. The black woman in domestic employ wore a dark blue or green overall with a white apron and cap (later supplanted by a head scarf) or a pinafore over her Western clothing. "Garden boys" or "house boys" wore a white or navy blue denim suit edged in red bias binding, manufactured specifically for this purpose. The garden or kitchen suit, first created at the turn of the twentieth century for a twelve-year-old Zulu boy named Pendula, was based loosely on a Victorian boy's tunic and knickers. But by the mid 1960s, this suit became a demeaning insignia for Zulu males in all spheres of domestic employment. Deconstructing its erstwhile associations, this garment has recently been worn by political figures, musicians, and the youth as a countercolonial insignia that challenges former prescriptive associations.

For female domestic workers, dress conventions have persisted in the present with few exceptions other than that the garments are more stylish and fabrics are located in national preference (e.g., isishweshwe). The domestic pinafore has become central to dress in the rural areas, as it is protective and reflects desirable domesticity.

CROSS-CULTURAL DRESS

In contemporary southern Africa, cross-cultural dress is central to a burgeoning fashion market. Such cross-culturalism originated in

Printed cloth in southern African designs. Since the 1960s, such designs have had nationalist and political associations. Photograph by Juliette Leeb-du Toit.

the 1940s and was linked to emergent nationalisms and the associated embrace of indigeneity. As opposition to the apartheid state grew in the 1960s, many black and white women formed allegiances across cultural divides; local black clothing traditions embraced by white women reflected a clear partisanship and challenge to mainstream dress, culture, and oppression. Cross-cultural dress and textile use became even more politicized when political prisoners such as Nelson Mandela wore Tembu dress in the 1960s as a gesture of defiance toward state oppression. Dress functioned as a salient marker of emergent pan-Africanism and as prelude to independence in many former colonies or protectorates such as Botswana, Namibia, Swaziland, and Lesotho. The 1960s saw a widespread diaspora of South Africans to other parts of the world, many electing to express their self-representation in terms of their particular ethnic distinctiveness. By the late 1980s, well-established cloth usage was challenged by the Dutch textile maker Vlisco, which aggressively marketed cloth with overt African National Congress color symbolism to an emergent market in South Africa.

In the 1960s, Rorke's Drift (the Evangelical Lutheran Church Arts and Crafts Centre) saw the emergence of a highly popular, screen-printed cloth that earned widespread local and international acclaim and became popular among a white elite. Drawing on the expertise of teachers trained at Konstfack (a world-renowned art school, founded in 1844) to lead courses in printmaking and design, Zulu women draw their inspiration from local material culture but also rely on Swedish and Finnish counterparts such as Marimekko cloth, which was simultaneously widely marketed in South Africa at the time, for process and aesthetics.

Further, the province of KwaZulu-Natal has one of the largest Indian populations outside of India. This and several other areas in southern Africa are peopled by culturally distinctive Indians who wear imported textiles and dress from their homeland. Indian textile traders and manufacturers have been at the forefront as culture brokers in maintaining a supply of distinctive textiles to African communities that still constitute one of their largest clientele bases. This interaction has shaped and maintained local cloth preferences for over a century.

References and Further Reading

Beck, R. "The Legalization and Development of Trade on the Cape Frontier, 1817–1830." Ph.D. dissertation, Indiana University, 1987.

Berglund, A-I. *Zulu Thought-Patterns and Symbolism.* London: Hurst and Co.; Cape Town and Johannesburg, South Africa: David Philip, 1976.

Broster, J. A. *Red Blanket Valley.* Cape Town, South Africa: Hugh Keartland, 1967.

Hendrickson, H. "Bodies and Flags: The Representation of Herero Identity in Colonial Namibia." In *Clothing and Difference. Embodied Identities in Colonial and Post Colonial Africa*, 213–244. Durham, NC: Duke University Press, 1996.

Klopper, S. "Mobilizing Cultural Symbols in Twentieth Century Zululand." Paper presented at the Centre for African Studies, University of Cape Town, 24 May 1989.

Klopper, S. "The Art of Zulu-Speakers in Northern Natal-Zululand—An Investigation of the History of Beadwork, Carving and Dress from Shaka to Inkatha." Ph.D. dissertation, University of the Witwatersrand, 1992.

Leeb-du Toit, J.C. "Cloth Usage by Popular Sangomas in KwaZulu-Natal." Paper presented at the South African Association of Art Historians, University of Pretoria, 1998.

Leeb-du Toit, J.C. "White Women in Black Clothing." Paper presented at the South African Art Historians Society Conference, Natal University, 2004.

Leeb-du Toit, J.C. "Indigo in Southern Africa: The History of Isishweshwe." Paper presented at the Dress in Southern Africa Conference, Centre for Visual Art, University of KwaZulu-Natal, Pietermaritzburg, August 2005.

Mchunu, M. "The Paradox of the 'Kitchen Suit': A Demeaning Uniform Which Was Worn with and without Pride by Zulu Male Servants." *Proceedings of the Dress in Southern Africa Conference, Centre for Visual Art*, University of KwaZulu-Natal, Pietermaritzburg, 2005.

Nieser, K. "'German Wear' in Southern Africa—European Sources of Indigo Dress." Paper delivered at the Dress in Southern Africa Conference, Centre for Visual Arts, University of KwaZulu-Natal, Pietermaritzburg, August 2005.

Phophi, N. "Venda Traditional Female Dress: Use and Significance." Unpublished Magister Tecnologiae: Fashion, Tshwane University of Technology, 2005.

Schulze, M. "The Interplay of Attire and the Evolution of Identity as Exemplified in Women's Attire of the Vhavenda Culture during the Past 150 Years." Paper presented at the Dress in Southern Africa Conference, Centre for Visual Art, University of KwaZulu-Natal, Pietermaritzburg, August 2005.

Shaw, M., and N.J. van Warmelo. "The Material Culture of the Cape Nguni. Part 4. Personal and General." *Annals of the South African Museum* 58, no. 4 (1988): 1–101.

Strutt, D.H. *Fashion in South Africa 1652–1900. An Illustrated History of Styles and Materials for Men, Women and Children, with Notes on Footwear, Hairdressing, Accessories and Jewels.* Rotterdam, The Netherlands: A.A. Balkema, 1975.

Tyrrell, B. *Suspicion Is My Name.* Cape Town, South Africa: T.V. Bulpin, 1971.

Winters, Y. *More than a "Postcard Zulu"—Contemporary Traditional Dress and Crafts from the Valley of a Thousand Hills (Inanda/Ndwedwe) in Jabulisa: The Art of KwaZulu-Natal.* Durban, S. Africa: Durban Art Gallery, 1996.

Juliette Leeb-du Toit

See also Botswana; Namibia; South Africa Overview; Swaziland.

PART 5

North Africa

Algeria

Algeria, situated at the crossroads of several civilizations and large intercontinental trade routes, has participated in all the major cultural developments of the Mediterranean and the Middle East. Since the early twentieth century, its large emigrant community provides close links with both. Historically, Algeria can be divided into several large cultural areas, all distinguished by their vestimentary tradition: eastern Algeria, centered on the city of Constantine, close to Tunisia and its Middle Eastern influence; the region of Algiers, where Ottoman and other outside influence was more strongly felt than elsewhere; western Algeria around Oran and Tlemcen, culturally close to the cities of Morocco; predominantly Berber-speaking areas such as Kabylia, the Aurès, and the Mzab; and the Algerian south, largely desert and bordering on West Africa. In the past, in addition to regional differences, dress also marked distinctions of occupation, status, age, wealth, and religious affiliation. Colonization and, more importantly, nationalism, created its own, more unified dress; until today, dress remains central to the expression of political and other kinds of allegiances. Such allegiances often exceed national boundaries, such as support for political Islam or cultural affinity with the West. Fashion thus reflects the questions and divisions at the heart of Algerian society as well as its overreaching unity.

THE EAST

The city of Constantine, situated halfway between Algiers and Tunis, is the intellectual, social, political, and economic center of the Algerian East. Its fashion has had a lasting influence on the surrounding countryside. Fashion in Constantine is generally epitomized by the female parade dress, *djoubba* or *djebba*. Dating from the fourteenth or fifteenth century and based on models and materials imported by Andalusian Muslims and Jews after their expulsion from southern Spain, the dress was a long sleeveless silk tunic characterized by a heavily embroidered front and held together by a thin silk belt around the waist. It was worn over a light long-sleeved shirt and with a pointed *chechia* (woven cap) covered by a light veil. The embroidery on the front, often repeated at the bottom of the dress and on the shoulders, was made of gold thread; its density and quality were a direct reflection of the wearer's economic status. Similar embroideries were repeated on smaller veils, handkerchiefs, and other accessories and were

the most distinctive feature of Constantine dress. Its designs were varied but mainly consisted of geometric forms or floral shapes, which, as the nineteenth century progressed, were increasingly filled in. Since the twentieth century, synthetic materials have replaced the gold thread.

Everyday female dress was much simpler. It copied in form the djoubba, but it was made without the embroidered front and was made out of cheaper material—locally produced wool and increasingly also European calicoes. Outside the house, women used to wear a large veil, or *haïk*, loosely wrapped around the body from head to toe and held together in front of the face. Legend recounts that after the French occupation of the city in 1837, the formerly white haïk was dyed black as a sign of collective mourning; this color is still used. With French influence, the shape of the djoubba was slightly modified: from a straight tunic, it was made to widen out toward the hem in imitation of the shape of French dresses. The djoubba continues to be reserved for formal occasions such as weddings and tends to be made of machine-produced velvet.

Male dress was less distinctive and resembled that of most Algerian coastal towns: a long shirt, or *gandoura*, worn over wide drawstring trousers and a red skullcap covered by a turban, underneath a woolen *burnous* (hooded cloak) in winter. The Algerian East was famous for producing fine white woolen burnouses that were exported throughout North Africa and the Arab world, while Constantine long served as the central market for clothes imported from Tunisia.

THE CENTER

Algiers is the most cosmopolitan city of Algeria and has long been so. Regional origins and professions were generally revealed by the way people dressed. Algiers has been open to a large variety of outside cultural influences for a long time. Fashion trends and materials changed rapidly, setting the pace for the hinterland. Several features remained nevertheless characteristic, especially of women's dresses: a *caraco*, or embroidered silk short jacket; a *ghila*, of similar shape and material, out of velvet, sporting a low oval décolleté; the embroidered flat chechia; and an open caftan. Wide trousers, or *seroual*, unlike dress elsewhere in Algeria, remained visible under knee-length shirts that were worn under the various jackets. Outside the house, the whole was covered by a white haïk worn with a small face veil. Jewish women did not veil their faces and wore a pointed chechia; slave women did not veil and wore less costly and more colorful clothes.

Male dress was equally varied, depending on origin, occupation, status, and wealth. According to a nineteenth-century description by French Orientalist, writer, and painter Eugène Fromentin, the city-dwelling Moors, including a wide variety of tradesmen, wore broad trousers resembling skirts, tight waistcoats, and belts. The commercial middle classes of nearby towns were dressed in a sober burnous with methodically folded turbans, closed waistcoats, plain woolen socks pulled up to the calves, and slippers. The religious elites, scribes, and judges were recognizable by their headgear (large turbans) and long silk robes covering their trousers, both in sober colors of white, gray, and black. Manual laborers wore short tunics made out of coarse wool. Mzabi merchants from southern Algeria wore striped gandouras; shepherds from the surrounding countryside on errands to the city wore short coats attached at their waists, skullcaps made of braided felt, and sheepskin sandals held by straps. Kabyles, very numerous in the capital, were recognized by their coarse burnouses, shaven heads, and simple headdresses. Children were dressed according to regional origin, profession, and status of their parents, although their outfits were often simplified and, for boys, reduced to a pair of ample trousers, open waistcoats, and small red chechias worn on their shaven heads. French conquest introduced varieties of new cheap materials and impoverished the city considerably; cotton calicoes made their first appearances, and fashion became more unified.

THE WEST

The region west of Algiers—in the past centered on the ancient cities of Tlemcen and Mascara and, since the nineteenth century, Oran—is culturally close to Morocco. Tlemcen used to be the capital of a powerful kingdom and the terminus of the trans-Sahara gold trade; Oran had long been a Spanish colony, and, under French colonial rule, it became the Algerian city where the direct impact of European settlers, many of whom were originally from Spain, was most marked. Western Algeria is thus generally known for two ensembles: the traditional female dress of Tlemcen, which combines Berber items of clothing with an abundance of gold jewelry; and the *blouza* from Oran, a hybrid dress combining various local and Arab elements with styles taken from European dress. For special occasions, Tlemcen female dress was composed of a silk, pastel-colored *melhafa*, a large piece of cloth attached at the shoulders with brooches, and a *fouta*, a colorful piece of cloth tied around the waist, vertically striped. The melhafa covered a long caftan or *abaya*, resembling the Constantine djoubba in everything but its embroidery, a long shirt with sleeves, and a seroual that remained covered; it was worn with a pointed chechia, similar to that of Constantine, but often encrusted in gold. The most remarkable items of the Tlemcen outfit included an abundance of jewelry: golden chains, pearls, amulets, earrings, and diadems, a display that still characterizes contemporary wedding dresses. Outside the house, a white haïk used to cover the whole face, leaving only one eye visible. The Tlemcen haïk was famous for the quality of its cloth and was of great value and prestige. The blouza, originally from Oran but by now widespread throughout Algeria, is a cross between a simple tunic resembling a djoubba and a European dress. Its widening out toward the hemline, its short billowing sleeves, and its adjusted waistline are of European origin, whereas the rigid embroidered front echoes Eastern and Andalusian traditions. In the late nineteenth century, the silk belt that used to hold it together around the waist was gradually replaced by one made out of fake gold coins, a fashion that rapidly spread throughout Algeria. Today the blouza or related hybrid dresses tend to be worn by most women of the older and middle generations, at least within the home, in the Oranais and beyond. Men's fashion differs little from urban dress in Constantine.

KABYLIA AND THE AURÈS

Outside the cities and towns, dress was less varied and rich, and materials were more often produced locally: wool was more common than silk, and silver more common than gold. Berber-speaking

Depiction of various forms of dress worn in Algiers in the nineteenth century, including Jewish, Turkish, urban, desert, Berber, black, slave woman's, child's, and free woman's dress. After a painting by F. Philippoteaux, reproduced in *L'Algérie historique* by A. Berbrugger, 1843. Courtesy of Judith Scheele.

areas developed their own style of dress, although urban influence was never entirely absent. In the early nineteenth century, the basic female dress in Kabylia—a Berber-speaking mountainous area between Algiers and Constantine—was the *akhellal* or *lhaf*, in form similar to the melhafa from Tlemcen but generally held together at the waist by a belt made out of homespun and woven wool and held at the shoulders by two silver brooches. Alongside simple decorations, these brooches constituted the principal ornament. They were often linked by a chain from which amulets and mirrors were suspended. Kabyle jewelry, in silver and decorated with coral or colorful enamel, is famous throughout the country, and, according to late-nineteenth-century studies, jewelry often represented more than three-quarters of the value of a woman's wardrobe. The akhellal was covered from the waist down by a fouta. From the mid-nineteenth century onward, the akhellal was first used with, and then was gradually supplanted by, the *taqendourth* (from the Arabic *gandoura*), a sewn woolen, cotton, or calico tunic with a square piece of material sewn on over the shoulders. Most Kabyle women did not veil but merely covered their hair with a colorful scarf. Men generally adopted a simplified version of Arab apparel: a long linen gandoura shirt with two sleeves (in winter this was covered by an additional gandoura made of wool); a pair of wide linen drawstring trousers made from up to six meters (twenty feet) of cloth; one or two woolen burnouses; a red woolen chechia surrounded by a linen turban; leather shoes; goatskin gaiters (to work in thorny bushes); and, at harvest time, a very large straw hat.

In the Aurès, a mountainous region south of Constantine inhabited in the past by seminomadic pastoralists, dress was strikingly similar. The *elhaf*, similar to the Kabyle akhellal and the Tlemcen melhafa but increasingly over time made of black cotton with colorful geometric embroidery, was worn over a long cotton shirt with sleeves and one or several tunics (*tijbibin*) that derived their form and name from the djoubba from Constantine. As a trace of urban influence, the tijbibin were also a sign of prestige and wealth and constituted an important part of Auresian wedding garb, where many of them were worn simultaneously. From the mid-nineteenth century, in everyday life, the elhaf gradually disappeared in favor of the *tejbibt*, promoted from inner to outer garment. Here, as in Kabylia, most attention was paid to jewelry, exclusively made out of silver. Men dressed in the same way as their Arab counterparts.

THE SOUTH

The Algerian Sahara is inhabited by a large variety of people, nomadic and sedentary, Arabic- and Berber-speaking. Yet certain patterns of dress used to be common to all, with the exception of the southern Tuaregs. The most distinctive feature of female desert dress, which generally followed the Auresian model, was an elaborate headdress composed of fake braids made of wool, a large turban, a veil, and a large silver tiara, leaving visible large earrings and a loose chin strap. This emphasis on rich headdresses was found throughout the Saharan Atlas and in the Berber cities of the Mzab. These headdresses could reach extraordinary heights, especially at weddings. In everyday life, nomadic Arab women wore a large cotton dress, a red embroidered woolen belt, a large veil, a cotton turban, silver anklets and bracelets, and velvet slippers embroidered with golden thread. Nomadic Arab men wore long shirts made of cotton or wool, a silken veil or haïk, a cotton or woolen gandoura, a burnous made of cotton in summer and wool in winter, a white or red skullcap, slippers, red morocco riding leggings, and a leather belt. Male slaves and children were dressed in similar fashion.

Tuareg female dress was composed of a long sewn dress covered by a large veil draped around the shoulders but left open in front and held in place under the chin by a large heavy silver pendant engraved with geometrical designs. Most garments were made out of uniformly dark material, glazed until they became shiny, and imported from West Africa. Ceremonial dress was further distinguished by a large silver breastplate (*teraout*) composed of a large triangle held by a leather cord from which another three or five triangles were suspended and whose bottom side was decorated with smaller pendants. Jewelry was central to an ensemble.

Male Tuareg dress also bears traces of sub-Saharan influence and materials. It consisted of three long tailored shirts with sleeves up to two meters (six and a half feet) wide, one worn over the other, and all made out of narrow strips of West African cotton sewn together. A large embroidered pocket was on the left breast, and the right shoulder blade was embroidered with silk thread. Under the shirts, men wore narrow-cut drawstring trousers, dark blue with light blue stripes, whose lower edge was embroidered with blue silk. The headdress consisted of a red skullcap imported from Tunis surrounded by a long blue cotton turban whose ends fell over the shoulder after wrapping around the neck and the lower part of the face. As a general rule, dress in the oases on trans-Saharan routes combined materials and styles from the Middle East, the Mediterranean, and sub-Saharan Africa. Until today, inhabitants of the southern oases like to sport long white shorts and *chechs* (tight skullcaps) rather than Western-style shirts and trousers, especially in their free time.

THE IMPACT OF FRENCH COLONIAL RULE

The French, fascinated by Algerian fashion, aimed to preserve it and adapt it to their own use, at least in the political sphere. In the mid-nineteenth century, Paris fell under the spell of "Oriental" fashion, as if to capture a romanticism that had disappeared with the French Revolution. Oriental dress was worn by many artists and even at Napoleon III's court. Algeria allowed French romantics, army officers, and, to a lesser degree, civilians to indulge in splendor, heroic displays, and social hierarchies that had disappeared at home. From the first years of colonial rule onward, the French developed uniforms and clothes that would mirror the colorful splendor of the Orient, as they saw it, and maintain its hierarchical structure. Algerian troops were dressed in wide trousers, short waistcoats, and hats in bright colors; investiture of indigenous high-ranking administrators and local rulers was symbolized by the bestowal of elaborate dress; and the official burnous, always in bright colors expressing rank, came to represent the administrative office as such. Outside the ranks of the colonial administration, dress adapted to economic hardship and European imports, as indicated above. Most outfits, apart from those of the very poor, displayed a mixture of both traditional and European elements; up to then, regional origin, status, and occupation had been expressed by difference in dress, but the functional distinction now became degrees of occidentalization. Despite their passion for Oriental dress, the French saw the adoption of European dress as an infallible sign of assimilation, education, and, ultimately, success. Nevertheless, oral poetry ridiculed locals who were all too keen to adopt ill-fitting narrow trousers, French shirts, jackets, and hats. For the wealthier classes, especially merchants, the dress adopted depended less on who they were than on where they were. Dress worn by a Kabyle merchant on business in Algiers would differ from dress worn by the same merchant back in the village. At the same time, the coast was increasingly peopled by European settlers who brought with them their own, often very simple, dress. A large percentage of the poorer settlers came from Spain, and the simple southern European cotton dress had a strong impact on female fashion throughout the country, changing the shape of the djoubba in Constantine, replacing historical dresses in the hinterland of Oran, and supplanting the akhellal in Kabylia. Yet the settlers and the indigenous population always remained distinctive, and fashion played an important part in maintaining these distinctions, thereby often overriding practical considerations.

Given the importance of dress as an indicator of origin, socioeconomic status, and assimilation, it is not surprising that early nationalism in Algeria developed its own dress code. From the 1920s onward, the Turkish fez, worn with European-style dress by men, became the sign of young, dynamic nationalists influenced by the Young Turk movement. Although some of the leading advocates of the more popular nationalism that was to emerge in the following decades opted for a more traditional style, the conscious mixture between modern—that is, European—styles and some token reference to cultural difference was always maintained. Similarly, Islamic Reformism, which became popular from the 1930s onward, not only fostered a search for religious renewal based on a return to the original scripture, but also launched its specific dress code that made reference to a tradition by thoroughly transforming it and adapting it to contemporary circumstances. Leading reformists would thus wear simplified religious dress—less extravagant and stripped of past hierarchical markers. Most of their followers wore suits with a token sign of their allegiance. Henceforth, dress did not so much convey social status or origin (although these factors obviously still played a part) as political allegiance, education, and general cultural orientation.

CHANGES IN FASHION SINCE INDEPENDENCE

Although in popular imagery the stereotypical nationalist fighter in the war of independence (1954–1962) tends to be depicted in a coarse peasant's burnous, the local elite who governed Algeria at independence followed worldwide fashion and wore European-style suits, setting the example for most Algerians. Access to modern clothes became a status symbol and was used in this sense by the Algerian government. Large clothes factories were set up to kick-start industrial development, mainly producing European-style clothes or cotton material. Women who had partly gained access to the public sphere dressed in similar ways to their French counterparts, although most women maintained a more traditional style or developed a compromise between styles—sometimes also inspired by Egyptian influence, as seen on television. Traditional dress—in everyday life now often a variety of the blouza—was increasingly associated with the house or was reserved for special occasions, especially weddings. Fashion became more unified, although, in the 1990s, rural immigrants to the cities could still be identified by their local dress. The capacity to procure foreign clothes identifiable as such rapidly became an indicator of socioeconomic success; with economic liberalization

in the 1980s, imported blue jeans and trainers (sneakers) became the foremost symbol of wealth among the younger generation and set successful emigrants apart from their poorer Algerian cousins. In 1988, when riots broke out in Algiers, large numbers of such items were publicly burned as a sign of protest against socioeconomic inequality.

By then, a new, more easily accessible style of fashion had started to appear in the sprawling suburbs of Algiers and included a simple, ankle-length shirt, or *djelleba*, made out of Chinese synthetics, cheap sneakers, a skullcap, and a beard; this look was identified with the supporters of political Islam from London to Afghanistan. Women adopted the *hijab*, a small head scarf tied under the chin and covering the neck, throat, and ears with either a long simple robe or jeans and a knee-length shirt. Much better adapted to modern life than traditional female dress, the hijab, and its male counterpart the djellaba, allowed the younger generation of Algerians to become part of modern city life while demonstrating a critical attitude toward their elders and toward excessive Western influence and the socioeconomic inequality and other kinds of immorality they associate with it. Once more, Algerian fashion spilled over to France (or had it come the other way, this time?) when second-generation immigrants from North Africa started to wear the same outfit in France, much to the displeasure of the French government. As in earlier times, fashion made a clear statement of belonging and

Elaborate headdresses worn by Ouled Nail Berbers in southern Algeria, late nineteenth century. Library of Congress, Prints and Photographs Division, LC-DIG-ppmsca-04758.

difference; and it is telling that, throughout Algeria, people tend to refer to partisans of the Islamic cause mainly as the "bearded ones," or *hijabistes*.

At the same time, a heightened consciousness of a separate Berber identity made headway in Berber-speaking areas, in particular in Kabylia. The taqendourth, described previously, became one of the foremost signs of allegiance to this movement, and it was sometimes seen as the declared opposition to Islamist dress defined as foreign to the region. Female students at the regional universities now openly wore these dresses that had for a long time been relegated to the home. At weddings, it almost became obligatory to wear at least one Kabyle dress, in addition to the by-now customary white wedding dress, and then to change into (or simply display) up to seven different dresses adopting various Arab styles. At the same time, the Kabyle taqendourth became more unified throughout the region. The sociopolitical importance of Islamist and Berber dress is but one instance of a more general way in which dress is used to renegotiate gender roles and such central categories as the public and the private. Throughout Algeria, "suitable" and "unsuitable" dress codes—and the ideal female proportions that best accompany them and the kind of diet and activities that allow women to maintain such proportions—provide daily stuff for debates on all levels; these debates reflect both the divisions and the shared concerns that run through contemporary Algerian society and through attempts to define its place in the wider world.

FASHION DESIGNERS AND THE ALGERIAN DIASPORA

Several young designers such as Nassila, Yasmina, Akli Boudrene, and many others have recently made names for themselves by adapting traditional regional dress to new materials and modified styles. They have thereby furthered national homogeneity and led a cultural revival of the Algerian heritage among second-generation emigrants in France. Indeed, most designers run shops and fashion shows in both Algeria and France, and numerous French Web sites with a large second-generation immigrant audience promote and discuss their products. Because so many of these designers work in both Algeria and France, boundaries between French and Algerian design are not always easy to establish, and North African fashion has found many admirers among young Frenchwomen. At the same time, contact among second-generation emigrants from various North African countries has led to a homogenization of North African dress as young Moroccans, Tunisians, and Algerians exchange ideas and designs. The former variety of materials and their high cost and quality—so striking in Algerian nineteenth-century dress—have disappeared to make way for synthetic imitations, thereby rendering dresses formerly reserved for the wealthy accessible to all. Web sites, local fashion magazines, photos, wedding videos, and the widespread sewing workshops help to spread these models throughout Algeria. Although most of the designers' creations and imitations are reserved for special occasions, they are widely admired and eagerly copied, because no wedding would be complete without the display of at least one regionally traditional dress. This, however, is mainly true for female dress; men only rarely display more traditional outfits. Whether the dresses are original or homemade, worn by Algerians or second-generation emigrants in France, they remain central to the expression of cultural and socioeconomic identity, local creativity, and cultural change.

References and Further Reading

Belkaïd, Leyla. *Algéroises—Histoire d'un costume méditerranéen*. Aix-en-Provence, France: Edisud, 1998.

Belkaïd, Leyla. *Costumes d'Algérie*. Editions du Layeur, 2003.

Boulifa, Saïd Ameur. *Recueil de poésies kabyles*. Algiers, Algeria: Jourdan, 1904.

Carette, Antoine-Ernest-Hippolyte. *Recherches sur la géographie et le commerce de l'Algérie méridionale*. Paris: Imprimerie Royale, 1848.

Darasse, Vincent. "Paysans en communauté et colporteurs émigrants de Tabou-Douchd-el-Baar (Grande Kabylie)." *Les Ouvriers des deux mondes* 5 (1885): 459–532.

Fromentin, Eugène. *Une année dans le Sahel*. Paris: Plon, 1858.

Geoffroy, Auguste. "Arabes Pasteurs Nomades de la tribu des Larbas." *Les Ouvriers des deux mondes* 1, no. 8 (1887): 409–464.

Khadda, N., and Monique Gadant. "Mots et gestes de la révolte." *Peuples méditerranéens* 52–53 (1990): 19–24.

Martinez, Luis. *La guerre civile en Algérie*. Paris: Karthala, 1998.

Judith Scheele

See also North Africa.

Egypt: Historical Dress

The history of dress in Egypt is long and complicated and highly influenced by the country's geographical location at the crossroads of Asia, Africa, and Europe. For centuries, various groups have fought for control of Egypt because of its strategic economic and political position. Each group has left its mark on Egyptian culture, including the dress worn by its inhabitants. The study of dress in Egypt is facilitated by the hot, dry climate that has preserved organic artifacts such as textiles, garments, and accessories including jewelry, makeup, and footwear. These preserved artifacts have enabled scholars to reconstruct dress worn in Egypt over a period of about five thousand years and to gain insights into how social, cultural, political, and religious developments have affected the way in which Egyptian men and women clothed themselves.

Flax was the most common fiber used for textiles and garments during the prehistoric and Pharaonic periods. Wool was sometimes used, but it was not common. With the coming of the Ptolemaic Greeks in 332 B.C.E., this situation changed and wool became widely used for a range of men's and women's dress. Other changes took place in the first century B.C.E., when silk from China and cotton from India became available. Again, these fibers were quickly assimilated into clothing, especially women's dress. A major factor in this development was the opening of trade links by both land and sea with these countries.

By the medieval era, a wider range of fibers was used throughout Egypt, including flax, cotton, wool, silk, and camel and goat hair. The first four fibers listed were employed in most garments—notably, pants, dresses, gowns, and light cloaks. Camel and goat hair were normally reserved for outer garments such as coats and cloaks. The use of these fibers continued into the twentieth century, when they were superseded by modern artificial and synthetic fibers.

Because flax is difficult to dye, ancient Egyptian linen clothing normally remained white. If dyed, it was usually colored red with madder or blue with indigotin (probably woad). In contrast, wool and silk are relatively easy to dye. The love of color is a feature of clothing from the Greco-Roman period onward.

During the Pharaonic period, simple looms were used, and thus only two weave types generally were used for textiles: plain and warp-faced plain weaves. Greeks and Romans introduced new loom technologies, allowing a wider range of weaves, including twills, tapestry, compound weaves, damasks, and brocades. These textiles embraced a variety of colors and decorative forms, from simple stripes and checks to complicated geometric and naturalistic designs. Such textiles have been found at various archaeological sites. As a result of these changes in fibers, dyes, and weave types, clothing in the Roman era is much more colorful and varied than the garments worn during previous periods. Embroidery was not widely used among the ancient Egyptians. Examples survived in the tomb of the Egyptian pharaoh Tutankhamen, where embroidery had been used to decorate his clothing. Similarly, it was little used during the Greco-Roman period. By the Islamic period, however, embroidery was widely used to embellish clothing.

Egyptians have worn jewelry since prehistoric times. Until the Greco-Roman period, men and women wore head and hair decorations, earrings and ear studs, many types of necklaces, armbands, bracelets, rings, and anklets. Jewelry items were made from faience, glass, semiprecious stones (such as carnelian, turquoise, and garnet), gold, and silver. Both men's and women's jewelry was often decorated with intricate designs based on characters and even

A reconstruction of a linen and beaded tunic from the Egyptian pharaoh Tutankhamen's tomb (ca. 1333–1323 B.C.E.), made by Jolanda Bos, Textile Research Centre, Leiden, for the Textile Museum, Boras, Sweden. Length: thirty-one inches (about eighty centimeters); width: twenty inches (about fifty centimeters). Photograph by Gillian Vogelsang-Eastwood.

from mythology. Attitudes changed during the Greco-Roman period, and men tended to wear only a seal ring (usually made of gold for someone of the aristocracy, silver for those of equestrian rank, and iron for ordinary citizens). The types of jewelry worn by women remained the same, although their appearance changed as they were influenced by court fashions and the origins of the wearer. The introduction of Islam continued this pattern, because men were forbidden to wear gold or jewelry apart from silver seal rings. Again, there was little change in the range of jewelry worn by women. This pattern continues to the present day.

During the Pharaonic period, men and women shaved their heads to wear wigs of human hair (these were cooler and prevented lice). Wigs were made and worn in a variety of forms, although women's wigs tended to be longer. Wig styles varied by context and current fashions. Throughout the Pharaonic period, men shaved their facial hair as well as their heads. In contrast, the Greeks regarded hair and beards as signs of being cultured. Men again shaved their facial hair during the succeeding Republican Roman period, but beards started to become more common in the Roman Empire. The situation changed during the Byzantine period, and clean-shaven appearance again became more fashionable. Religious Christians, however, tended to grow long beards. Following the arrival of Islam, men adopted the Islamic practice of growing a beard to confirm their religious beliefs. During the medieval period and later, a wide range of styles of mustaches and beards developed. The situation changed in the late nineteenth century with the introduction of European styles. By the twentieth century, there were various discussions about whether it is better to be clean-shaven or to have a beard. This discussion has become a feature of contemporary life in Egypt that reflects political, economic, and religious opinions.

Both men and women wore perfumes in ancient Egypt that were made from a variety of substances, including almonds, cardamom, cinnamon, crocus, honey, jasmine, juniper berries, linseed, myrrh, roses, safflower, sesame, unripe olives, wine, and water lilies. The berries, seeds, and leaves were dried, ground, and then mixed with fat, oil, or beeswax to make a salve. There were seven basic perfumes, which the Egyptians called by various names depending on what they were made of or when they were used. These names are: festival, praise (for religious ceremonies), Syrian balsam, *nechenem* salve (unknown type), salve oils (unknown type), cedar oil, and Libyan oil.

Cosmetics were worn from the prehistoric period onward. Eye paint was the most common form and was used to shield the eyes from the sun. Eye paints were made of green copper oxide (malachite) and black lead galena (kohl). These were ground and then mixed with water or fat and applied with a small stick. Lipstick and a form of rouge were also occasionally used. The use of these types of perfumes and makeup continued until the twentieth century, when most were replaced by Western versions.

EARLY CLOTHING PRACTICES

Because no garments have survived from the prehistoric period, it is necessary to rely on visual representations of what people were wearing. It would appear that both men and women wore simple loincloths, possibly animal skins, and simple wrap-around garments such as dresses, skirts and hip-wraps. Sometimes women are depicted with a series of dots around the pubic region. Some authors say these indicate pubic hair, in which case the women are naked, others say the women have on some form of decorative underwear. The former seems the more likely.

The Pharaonic period is loosely defined and ranges from about 3000 B.C.E. to 332 B.C.E. This time is subdivided by modern Egyptologists according to the reigns of the various pharaohs and rulers. Information about ancient Egyptian dress survives in garments and accessories, tomb paintings showing people of all social levels, and in written accounts such as temple records and wills.

Some ancient Egyptian garments were unisex, while others were gender specific. The oldest form of unisex garment is the triangular *loincloth*, which was worn from the Old Kingdom onward. The other important unisex garment was the tunic, introduced into Egypt around 1600 B.C.E. The *tunic* is a rectangle of cloth folded in half and sewn down the sides leaving holes at the top for the arms with a slit or a circle for the head. Some tunics have sewn-on sleeves. The length of the tunic varied depending on one's gender and status. Women normally wore long tunics, while men wore versions that varied from knee to ankle length; the higher the status, the longer and wider the tunic. The men's tunic was often worn with a sash and hip wrap of varying sizes and shapes depending on the wearer's rank. The decoration of the tunic also varied according to the wearer's status and wealth. Lower-class versions were white, and higher-class tunics had narrow red and blue stripes down the selvages and along the lower hem. The tunics worn by a pharaoh were often highly decorated in a variety of techniques, such as multicolored tapestry weave, embroidery, beading, and gold applications (usually circular)—or, indeed, a combination of several of these techniques.

Cloaks of linen draped over the shoulder were worn by men and women in the cold of a desert evening and night and, of course, throughout winter. A tailored form, adopted by male priests and high-ranking officials, was fastened with ties at the left shoulder.

Sometimes leather loincloths were worn over linen versions. The leather ones were worn by soldiers, sailors, farmers, and

A selection of glass beads found in Egyptian pharaoh Tutankhamen's tomb, used on his clothing (ca. 1333–1323 B.C.E.), Egyptian Museum, Cairo. Photograph by Gillian Vogelsang-Eastwood.

An illustration depicting the nineteenth-century dress of Egyptian men of the middle and upper classes (from Edward Lane, *An Account of the Manners and Customs of the Modern Egyptians: Written in Egypt During the Years 1833–1835*; London, 1836). Men wore a striped, ankle-length caftan of silk and cotton, with a girdle made from a colored shawl or long piece of white figured muslin, wrapped around the waist. The outer robe was a long cloth coat. Often a piece of white muslin or a Kashmir shawl was wrapped around the head-covering in the form of a turban. Courtesy of Gillian Vogelsang-Eastwood.

around the waist and a wide sash draped diagonally from the left shoulder to the right hip. The introduction of the tunic added a new layer of social nuance: high-ranking officials wore long, hip-covering versions with a very wide sash, and lower-ranking officials wore shorter tunics with narrower sashes. Artisans also wore tunics, while men of the lowest rank normally did not.

Women wrapped lengths of linen around the body in a number of ways. Again, higher-status women utilized more material. Some women wore wraparound dresses (the so-called *sheath dress*), sometimes reaching to the ankles. More elaborate sheath dresses were knotted at one shoulder (either right or left). During the Old Kingdom, some women wore tight-fitting, long-sleeved dresses decorated with horizontal pleats. Another type of dress was made from beads. Some dresses were beaded, while others were made of a net of beads that was placed over the wrap.

The long-sleeved dress vanished following the introduction of tunics during the New Kingdom, while beaded dresses were only rarely depicted. By then most women were represented in either a wraparound dress or a tunic. Wraparound dresses gradually became elaborate creations that were wrapped, draped, tucked, knotted in complex and elegant ways, and often worn over tunics, giving a wider range of expressive dress. Throughout the Pharaonic period, servants and lower-class women wore shorter versions of the wraparound dress or simply a skirt, often leaving the upper half of the body bare. Footwear for men and women during the Pharaonic period consisted of sandals made out of palm, grasses, and occasionally leather.

THE CLOTHING OF TUTANKHAMEN

Finds from the tomb of the ancient Egyptian pharaoh Tutankhamen (ca. 1333–1323 B.C.E.) provide a rare opportunity to see the range of textiles and garments worn by a pharaoh. Tutankhamen was an obscure pharaoh whose tomb was found intact and well preserved in 1922. The textiles and clothing from the tomb present a fascinating insight into how a variety of garments were adapted to the sacred role played by the pharaoh. All garments were constructed from linen and include loincloths, hip wraps, sashes, tunics, head coverings (the simple semicircular *khat* and the royal blue and white *nemes*), as well as royal and religious items such as pairs of linen falcon and vulture wings and leopard skins (real and linen), indicating Tutankhamen's secular and spiritual duties, both as a god in his own right and as a high priest to the other gods.

The color range of the king's wardrobe was limited to reds, blues, and whites. Decorative techniques include woven stripes, inlaid designs (especially birds), tapestry, and embroidery (chain, running, and stab stitches). Sewn onto the outer garments were vast numbers of beads (mainly gold or faience), as well as gold disks, stars, and amulets. Tutankhamen's tomb contained a number of simple sandals made from palm or grass and sometimes decorated with gold. More elaborate ceremonial sandals were made from either palm or leather and decorated with beads and plaques of gold, carnelian, turquoise, and glass.

GRECO-ROMAN DRESS

The Greco-Roman period dates from about 332 B.C.E. to 640 C.E. and is normally divided into the Ptolemaic, Roman, and Byzantine periods. Around 640 C.E., Egypt was absorbed into the

some officials. The better-quality loincloths were fashioned from fine gazelle skin with intricate patterns cut into the skin. In the absence of a leather loincloth, a skirt or hip wrap was worn over the linen loincloth. A sash was used to keep the loincloth and hip wrap in place. Priests wore a short hip wrap with a narrow sash new Islamic Empire (Dar al-Islam). The Greco-Roman period is marked by numerous foreign influences and saw significant changes in Egyptians' dress. Unfortunately, from the Ptolemaic and the early Roman periods (ca. first and second centuries C.E.), very few textiles have been preserved, because the dead were not buried clothed. Still, mummy portraits fashionable in the early Roman period provide abundant sources of information on the Romanized elite at the time. With the introduction of Christianity, the clothed corpse once more became popular, and many textiles can be dated to the late Roman (ca. third and fourth centuries C.E.) and Byzantine periods. Evidence of these textiles, however, often comes from looted tombs and badly recorded excavations and has been highly compromised because the ornamented elements were frequently removed by dealers and collectors and the rest of the garment was discarded. Archaeological textiles surviving from the late Roman, Byzantine, and early Islamic periods are often incorrectly labeled *Coptic*, after the main Christian church in Egypt.

Clothing for this period consisted mainly of a tunic or *chiton* (sometimes with an undertunic) first made up of a rectangle of cloth, folded over and sewn along the sides, leaving an opening for the arms. In late Roman times, a sleeved tunic, the *dalmaticus*, was introduced with either wide or narrow sleeves. The wide-sleeved tunic disappeared in the Byzantine period in favor of the narrow-sleeved version. Men usually wore short tunics reaching between the mid-thigh to halfway down the calf; women's tunics reached to the ankles or feet. The tunic could be worn either loose or belted. For women, the belt was positioned underneath the breasts, and, for men, the tunic would be belted at the waist. The elite usually combined the tunic with a mantle (himation, pallium, or *palla*), which consisted of a rectangular piece of cloth occasionally with L- or H-shaped decoration on it. It could be draped around the body in various manners.

Elite men in the early Roman period donned white garments with purple *clavi* (two vertical bands running down the front and back). Women, on the other hand, wore clothing in various colors, also with clavi. By the late Roman period, garments were increasingly decorated with borders, roundels (round, rectangular, or star-shaped ornaments) and short clavi. During the Byzantine period that followed, the detail within the roundels and clavi became more ornate and colorful, including floral, animal, and human depictions and showing mythological (often Dionysian) scenes.

Cloaks include the *sagum* or *chlamys*, a thick, rectangular, military cloak, dark in color, and held at the left shoulder by a fibula (mantle pin or brooch). In the fourth century C.E., the rectangular cloak became increasingly popular and largely replaced the *toga*, a large, semicircular garment that was used by the Romans to indicate male rank. Other types of capes and hooded cloaks were worn as protection from the weather but are rarely depicted. Leather sandals increased in use during the Greco-Roman period and later. Leather shoes, boots, and palm sandals were also used to protect the feet.

Headgear was not common at this time, although separate hoods and cone-shaped felt caps have been found at some Egyptian sites. Women generally wore a small veil or mantle over their hair when in public. Most elite women are depicted with elaborate hairdos, which could include bands, ribbons, and jewelry. It seems that it was also quite common to cover the hair with a sprang hairnet, since numerous examples have been found in

An illustration depicting nineteenth-century dress for upper-class women in Egypt, worn in private, including a robe, a shawl worn around the waist as a girdle, and a headdress (from Edward Lane, *An Account of the Manners and Customs of the Modern Egyptians: Written in Egypt During the Years 1833–1835*; London, 1836). Courtesy of Dr. Gillian Vogelsang-Eastwood.

burials. These colorful, decorative nets were probably a Hellenistic introduction.

Other garments popular in the late Roman Empire were trousers or leggings. Whereas in the early Roman period, only wraps were used to protect the shins, there is increasing evidence for the use of trousers and leggings (some with integrated feet) in the late Roman period. Hellenistic and Roman styles of clothing were relatively easily adopted in Egypt, because they corresponded with local clothing systems. Both Pharaonic and Greco-Roman garments are centered on a few tailored items, such as the tunic, and on various types of clothing that are draped and wrapped around the body. The most dramatic difference from the Pharaonic period is the choice of fiber and the use of color in the Greco-Roman clothing.

Roman mummy portraits provide clear evidence of the elite adopting the clothing style of the court, but it is not certain whether the rest of the population adopted new types of clothing. Certainly in earlier periods, most ordinary Egyptians were likely to have continued to wear Pharaonic-style clothing. For example, in the early Ptolemaic tomb of Petosiris, an interesting amalgam of clothing traditions appeared; both Pharaonic- and Greek-style garments were worn by commoners and the upper class. Pharaonic-style clothing in linen also persisted for religious and ceremonial rituals and events. Wraparound dresses closely associated with the popular Isis cult were an example of this survival, as seen in early Roman depictions of the goddess and her female followers wearing this type of garment.

Moreover, foreign fashions were not slavishly adopted but rather reinterpreted to fit the Egyptian context. For example, a colorful Roman tunic could be worn underneath a Pharaonic wraparound dress. Clavi were not commonly worn on clothing by Roman women but were consistently worn among the Egyptian female elite. In contrast, typical Roman clothing such as the toga (worn on official occasions by male Roman citizens) and the *stola* (a long dress worn over a tunic; it was the female equivalent of the toga and a marker of the Roman matron) were seldom used by the Egyptians.

EARLY ISLAMIC DRESS

Around 640 C.E., Egypt became part of the rapidly spreading Islamic empire that eventually stretched from Spain to Central Asia. The attire of the early Muslim court was influenced by Arab as well as Persian and Byzantine fashions. Significant changes occurred in the appearance of Arab clothing under the Ummayads and the Abbasids, including the development of the so-called Islamic vestimentary system. Arab Muslim attire typically consisted of layers of loose, flowing garments with little tailoring. The basic outfit for both men and women included an undergarment, either an *izar* (wrapped hip cloth) or *sirwal* (underpants); a *qamis* (undershirt); a *thawb* (long gown or tunic), an overgarment such as a mantle or coat; shoes, sandals (*na'l*), or boots (*khuff*); and a head covering such as a *qalansuwa* (cap), *'imama* (turban) or sometimes a *burnus* (hood). Like their Greek and Roman counterparts, Muslim women were expected to draw their mantle (*jilbab*) around them when in public. Most women also wore a shawl or cloth over their head and hair, and covered their faces with a veil of some kind, such as the *mandil* (a short length of cloth that covers the nose and lower face), *burqa* (a two-piece face veil that covers the entire face except the eyes), or *niqab* (a single length of cloth that covered the complete face with holes or a slit for the eyes).

This sequence of clothing is similar to the Greco-Roman tradition: undertunic, overtunic, and a cloak. The main differences are the use of underpants, coats, and a wider range of headgear. The Islamic vestimentary system is also noted for its austerity toward male attire with respect to color and materials. According to the Qur'an, believers would be rewarded with clothing of silk in paradise, but in this world, it is "the garment of piety…that is best," as noted in Sura 7:26. Nevertheless, colorful silk clothing was widely used by both men and women.

Surviving textiles from this period show some links with Greco-Roman traditions but also many changes. There is a tendency toward stylization of the tapestry decoration on garments. Still, the earlier tradition of showing human figures remained very popular, and these decorative themes included dancing and mythological figures as well as biblical scenes such as the story of Joseph and the Nativity. In general, however, tapestry ornamentation was in decline. Clavi gradually vanished toward the end of this period. Braids and brocaded or embroidered bands placed around the tunic's neck, cuffs, and hem replaced tapestry decoration. Embroidery became a more popular technique, and the sewing of garments received more attention, often employing two or three colors of thread. Patterned textiles also increased in popularity.

An important Islamic initiative was *tiraz*, a woven or embroidered Arabic inscription on a textile or garment. At first, tiraz was restricted by the ruler and distributed as a sign of honor, but later it became an important part of Islamic attire and was worn by many.

Nineteenth-century Egyptian women and children of the lower classes tended to wear a blue cotton *thawb* with a large scarf (*tarha*) to cover the head (from Edward Lane, *An Account of the Manners and Customs of the Modern Egyptians: Written in Egypt During the Years 1833–1835*; London, 1836). Courtesy of Dr. Gillian Vogelsang-Eastwood.

Construction of the tunic also evolved under Islam. At the beginning of the Islamic period, tunics were very wide with narrow sleeves. The tunic remained straight, but tailored features such as round necklines, tapered sleeves, vents under armpits, and side slits were increasingly incorporated. From the eighth century C.E., cut and tailored garments were fashioned with gores, sleeves, and a round neckline with a buttoned slit, all due to Persian influences.

During the early Islamic and medieval periods, there were attempts to differentiate clothing for Muslims and certain non-Muslims, or *dhimmi* (Christians, Jews, and Zoroastrians). In the Islamic world, dhimmi life, property, and religious beliefs were protected as long as non-Muslims acknowledged and showed humility to their Muslim rulers. The Pact or Covenant of 'Umar is the first known legal document where clothing differentiation is described. It is named after the second caliph, 'Umar b. al-Khattab (r. 634–644), although the first mention of this law does not come until the second half of the eighth century C.E. It states that dhimmi were prohibited from imitating Muslims in their appearance. Various official laws based on this pact were passed from the ninth century C.E. onward, although none seems to have been enforced for long periods of time. They usually state that some garments had to be worn, while others were forbidden. Obligatory garments included a thick cord (*zunnar*) around the waist, color coding (blue for Christians, yellow for Jews) of garments or patches on garments, and branding or tattooing. Although dress rules were usually not enforced for long, in the eleventh and twelfth centuries, attitudes toward the dhimmi hardened again due to external pressure.

MEDIEVAL DRESS

More information on dress is available for the later medieval period (1250–1517 C.E.). These data come from archaeological finds (notably Quseir al Qadim, Qasr Ibrim, and Fustat); administrative records (such as the *Cairo Geniza*); and other accounts. Mamluk-illustrated stories and fables; illustrated travelogues by Western merchants and pilgrims; and paintings, especially by Italian artists, provide information about the garments worn by various groups in different settings. In general, Egyptian society had become very stratified under the Mamluk sultanate of the thirteenth to sixteenth centuries. A man (and his family) belonged to a well-established group: the military caste, the bureaucracy, men of religion, nobles, Sufis, various associations or guilds, or the masses. Each group had its outfits or distinguishing items of clothing (often headgear) that indicated social status.

As a generalization, wealthy men and women wore many layers of clothing, sometimes with more than one garment of the same type. Some fashions changed over time, such as the length of underwear, the size and quantity of material used for the sleeves, and so forth. Changes were usually related to the introduction of new materials and modes of decoration rather than the cut of the garments. In general, however, more garments were tailored than in the preceding period.

The principal male garments of the medieval period continued to follow the basic form of the early Islamic period: long underpants (*sirwal*); long shirt (*qamis*); long outer gown (*thawb*, usually with very wide sleeves); and sometimes a long coat (*jubba*). Men's headdresses included a skullcap (*taqiyya*), a tall cap (*qalansuwa*), and a winding cloth (*takhfifa*) or a full turban ('*imama*). In cold weather, a sleeveless outer garment (*aba*) made from wool and open in the front was often worn. Footwear consisted of flat slippers (*ni'l*) with curled toes and sandals. The lower one's social position, the less clothing and the poorer the quality of material. Lower-class men might wear only a short, close-fitting tunic and a cap. While working in a field, a man might wear only a pair of *tubban* (knee-length trousers); a beggar might only have an izar wrapped around the waist and hips.

Women's ensembles consisted of either a *mi'zar* (knee-length underpants) or sirwal (longer underpants). The latter could be very elaborate and made from brocaded cloth, decorated with embroidery, or even studded with jewels. These were kept in place using a drawstring called a *tikka*, which could be equally ornate. The underpants were covered by either a short chemise or longer chemise (*qamis*), and a long outer gown (*thawb*). Types of headgear included caps and winding scarves. The caps could be very ornate and were often worn with a long rectangular head covering kept in place with a headband ('*isaba*). Footwear included a range of shoes and slippers. When in public, a women's dress consisted of a colorful outer wrap, also called izar, with a face veil such as the mandil or a burqa. As with the men, the lower the woman's status, the fewer garments worn and the poorer the quality of cloth.

During the Islamic period, a wide range of footwear included slippers, sandals, shoes, and boots made out of a wide variety of decorated materials. Many slippers, for example, were made of colored leather and decorated with quilted designs, embroidery, luminescent insect wings, beads, metal threads, and so forth.

OTTOMAN DRESS

The arrival of the Turkish Ottomans in 1517 had a considerable impact on dress in urban centers such as Cairo and Alexandria. Ottoman Turks and Egyptians employed by them, as well as those wishing to emulate the new social elite, wore Ottoman dress. Lower-status men and women continued to wear the Mamluk style described previously.

Ottoman attire continued well into the nineteenth century and changed according to the fashions of the court at Istanbul. British chronicler Edward Lane (1801–1875) lived in Egypt in the 1820s and 1830s and itemized Ottoman-Egyptian dress for men as including a pair of knee-length linen or cotton underpants (sirwal) secured with a string or band (tikka). Over this was worn a long striped shirt (qamis) of linen, cotton, muslin, silk, or a mixture with very full wrist-length sleeves. In winter, men normally wore a *safari*, or waistcoat, over the shirt. A striped ankle-length caftan of silk and cotton was designed with a front opening, diagonal in cut and fastened, with long sleeves extending beyond the wrist. The extra length allowed the covering of hands in the presence of a superior. A girdle made from a colored shawl or long piece of white figured muslin was wrapped around the waist. The ordinary outer robe was a long cloth coat (Turkish: *jubbeh*; Arab: *gibbeh*) of any color with sleeves that reached to just above the wrist. Alternatively, in cold weather, a black woolen aba or cloak was worn. The headdress could be a small, close-fitting cap (taqiyya) or a *tarbush*, a red felted cap with a tassel of dark blue silk. Often a long piece of white muslin or a Kashmir shawl was wrapped around the tarbush in the form of a turban. A descendant (*sharif*) of the Prophet would wear a green tarbush. Footwear consisted of stockings (in the winter) and shoes of thick, red morocco leather with pointed and turned-up toes.

Male servants to higher-class families tended to wear Ottoman-style clothing when serving the family and friends and when in public. Some Europeans also wore this style while in Egypt. The outfit worn by Lane, now in the Ashmolean Museum, Oxford, is Turkish. It consists of underpants, a knee-length shirt, baggy overtrousers, a cummerbund in fine wool, a jacket, and a skullcap. There probably also were a waistcoat, a large tarbush, and some form of turban, all now lost.

Lower-status men continued to wear Arab/Mamluk dress: a pair of loose, knee-length undertrousers (tubban), a waistcoat (sudari), and a long, full shirt or gown of blue linen, blue cotton, or brown wool, occasionally with a white or red woolen sash. A tarbush and a wrapped length of cloth covered the head. Only the poor wore a cap without a turban. In cold weather, a coarse, sleeveless aba was worn. Footwear consisted of red or yellow leather slippers. Colored turbans distinguished various religious groups. Jews and Copts (Egyptian Christians) wore black, blue, gray, or light brown turbans with dull-colored outfits, while Muslims had no such restrictions.

There are greater variations in Ottoman-Egyptian dress for women than for men. In general, elite and higher-class women wore Turkish-style clothing, while middle- and lower-class women wore what is regarded as Arab-Egyptian attire. After the Ottoman conquest, elite women's clothes changed from the wider Arab-style garments to more closely fitted garments. According to Lane, the basic indoor clothing worn by elite and middle-class women began with an undershirt reaching to the knees made from linen, cotton, muslin, silk, or a mixture of cotton and silk. This was worn with voluminous knee-length trousers (shintiyan) of striped silk and cotton or white muslin. The shintiyan, a very wide garment, could be fastened around the waist or the hips with a drawstring (tikka) set in the waistband. Over these garments was worn the Egyptian yelek, a long robe with trailing skirts slit at the sides up to the hips. It had long, deeply slit sleeves revealing the sleeves of the undershirt. Over the yelek was worn a short jacket (anteri). A square shawl or embroidered kerchief was folded diagonally and then loosely wrapped around the waist in the form of a girdle. Sometimes women would also wear a short coat (salteh) in deep green or blue that was elaborately embroidered with gold thread or, alternatively, a longer coat (gibbeh, qibeh).

The headdress (rabtah) consisted of a close-fitting cotton cap (taqiyya) and a larger cap (tarbush) wrapped with numerous scarves (farodeya). Hairstyles were based on variations of numerous long, braided plaits hanging down the back and threaded with black silk cords with little gold ornaments (safa). Often a rectangular white scarf of cotton (tarha) embroidered at each end was thrown over the headdress. This was an Egyptian rather than Ottoman fashion. The outfit was finished with flat slippers (mezz) in red or yellow leather, sometimes decorated with gold embroidery.

Although the above descriptions pertain to women's attire in the 1830s, depictions of women wearing this range of clothing can also be seen in late-nineteenth-century paintings. Changes occurred in styles of decoration and range of materials, but the basic cut remained. The outdoor dress (tezyera) of elite women continued in the Mamluk style with a large, loose pink or purple silk gown (thawb, sebleh) with sleeves nearly equal in width to the length of the garment. A long white muslin face veil (burqa) draped nearly to the ground. The ensemble was then covered by

A studio portrait of an Egyptian woman, ca. 1900. She wears a *burqa* (face veil) decorated with metal ornaments and a *tarbush* (tasseled cap). Library of Congress, Prints and Photographs Division, LC-USZ62-87593.

a large glossy silk sheet (habara), which was black for married women and white for unmarried women. Outdoor footwear featured yellow leather short socks (khuff) with slippers (babug) of yellow leather with high, pointed toes. In contrast, lower-middle-class Egyptian women wore undertrousers (shintiyan style but of a plain material) with a long blue linen or cotton gown (thawb) and a muslin or linen head scarf (tarha). Additional headwear included either a small kerchief (asba) folded diagonally in half and bound around the head or a tarbush with another scarf (farudeya). Outdoor wear demanded a large cotton outerwrap (milaya) with small blue and white checks or stripes and a burqa of coarse black crepe decorated with small flat ornaments of metal (bark) or beads. The lowest classes tended to wear a blue cotton thawb with a large scarf (tarha) to cover the head. Throughout Egypt, urban women covered their faces with either a special face veil (burqa), part of their head scarf (tarha), or the milaya.

LATE-NINETEENTH-CENTURY DRESS

The clothing styles noted in the preceding section continued well into the nineteenth century. At that time, some major changes took place. As Western (especially English and French) influence became stronger, more of the elite adopted Western clothing. Emmeline Lott, a governess to Ibrahim Pasha, son of the Khedive

Ismail in the 1860s, noted that eastern Mediterranean, as well as English and French, women could be seen in Alexandria wearing European styles. It appears that, by the 1860s, the influence of Western styles was well underway. Shortly afterward, Ellen Chennells, another governess employed by Khedive Ismail, documented Princess Zeyneb wearing a black velvet dress in the latest Parisian fashion. Much of Princess Zeyneb's wardrobe was apparently French in origin. Once the elite women started to wear European styles, upper-middle-class women followed suit.

In urban regions, lower-status men and women continued to wear Turkish- or Egyptian-style garments. With the end of the Ottoman Empire (officially in 1918), Turkish-style garments virtually vanished from the Egyptian clothing repertoire, except among groups such as water carriers, who continued to wear them well into the late twentieth century. This was done more as a tourist attraction rather than as a statement of occupation and social standing. Egyptian peasant farmers (*fellaheen*) and lower-class women in general continued to wear Arab-style dress with various Egyptian and regional variations.

References and Further Reading

Chennells, Ellen. *Recollections of an Egyptian Princess by Her English Governess*. Edinburgh and London: Blackwood, 1893.

Croom, Alexandra T. *Roman Clothing and Fashion*. Charleston, SC: Tempus Publishing, 2000.

de Moor, Antoine. *Coptic Textiles: From Flemish Private Collections*. Zottegem, Belgium: Provinciaal Archeologisch Museum van Zuid-Oost Vlaanderen, 1992.

Driel-Murray, Carol van. "Leatherwork and Skin Products." In *Ancient Egyptian Materials and Technology*, edited by Paul Nicholson and Ian Shaw, 299–319. Cambridge, UK: Cambridge University Press, 2000.

Fletcher, Joanne. "Hair." In *Ancient Egyptian Materials and Technology*, edited by Paul Nicholson and Ian Shaw, 495–504. Cambridge, UK: Cambridge University Press, 2000.

Lane, Edward W. *Manners and Customs of the Modern Egyptians*. London: Macmillan, 1895.

Lott, Emmeline. *The Governess in Egypt, Harem Life in Egypt and Constantinople*. London: Chapman and Hall, 1893.

Nicholson, Paul, and Ian Shaw. *Ancient Egyptian Materials and Technology*. Cambridge, UK: Cambridge University Press, 2000.

Pritchard, Frances. *Clothing Culture: Dress in Egypt in the First Millennium AD*. Manchester, UK: Whitworth Art Gallery, 2006.

Sebesta, Judith Lynn, and Larissa Bonfante. *The World of Roman Costume*. Madison: University of Wisconsin Press, 1994.

Stillman, Yedida Kalfon. *Arab Dress: A Short History from the Dawn of Islam to Modern Times*. Leiden, The Netherlands: Brill, 2000.

Vogelsang-Eastwood, Gillian. *Pharaonic Egyptian Clothing*. Leiden, The Netherlands: Brill, 1993.

Vogelsang-Eastwood, Gillian. *Tutankhamun's Wardrobe: Garments from the Tomb of Tutankhamun*. Rotterdam, The Netherlands: Barjesteh van Waalwijk van Door, 1999.

Vogelsang-Eastwood, Gillian. "Textiles." In *Ancient Egyptian Materials and Technology*, edited by Paul Nicholson and Ian Shaw, 268–298. Cambridge, UK: Cambridge University Press, 2000.

Walker, Susan, and Morris Bierbier. *Ancient Faces: Mummy Portraits from Roman Egypt*. London: Trustees of the British Museum, 1997.

Wild, John Peter. *Textile Manufacture in the Northern Roman Provinces*. Cambridge, UK: Cambridge University Press, 1970.

Gillian Vogelsang-Eastwood
and Tineke Rooijakkers

See also Dress in Egypt the Twentieth Century; volume 5, Central and Southwest Asia: Ottoman Dress; Christian, Secular, Monastic, and Liturgical Dress; Laws of Differentiation; Khil'a: Clothing to Honor a Person or Situation; Tiraz: Textiles and Dress with Inscriptions; Face Veils in Central and Southwest Asia; volume 8, West Europe: Greek Dress; volume 9, East Europe, Russia, and the Caucusus: Roman Dress.

Dress in Egypt in the Twentieth Century

- Urban Dress
- Coptic Christians
- The Delta and Nile Valley
- Nubia
- The Oases
- The Sinai and the Deserts

E gypt has been ruled by foreign powers seeking to control its resources for much of the country's history. The governing powers throughout history represented the elite, who served as a major influence on styles and fashions in clothing and dress. From the late eighteenth century onward, the French and the British had been attempting to displace the Turkish Ottoman rulers (1517–1798) and gain control over Egypt. The French under Napoleon invaded and occupied Egypt from 1798 to 1805. The Ottoman sultan sought to retain control by establishing Muhammad Ali, a soldier who fought for the Ottomans, as viceroy in Egypt in 1805. Descendants of Muhammad Ali held positions as *khedives* (kings) in Egypt until 1952. Khedive Ismail (1863–1879) particularly strove to modernize Egypt, but, as a result of his efforts, huge financial deficits were incurred that made Egypt indebted to European powers. Egypt was under British control from 1882 to 1952. As well as traditional forms of dress, Ottoman, French, and British styles were all influential.

In the beginning of the twentieth century, there was a considerable difference between the garments worn by urban, village, oasis, and Bedouin women. Wealthier urban women tended to wear European forms, while village and rural women had styles identified with their areas. The oasis and Bedouin dresses were characterized by embroidery that reflected cultural and economic differences. By the end of the twentieth century, however, Western styles were predominant in many regions. Village styles were being adopted in the oases and by Bedouins. In the 1980s and 1990s, when traditional embroidered dresses had nearly disappeared from the areas where they had originated, women of the wealthier educated classes in Cairo and Alexandria began to admire these dresses and made it fashionable to wear such garments to social events. All of the dresses, whether they came from the oases or the deserts, were called Bedouin.

Throughout Egypt, a woman's jewelry indicated her family's financial status. In villages where there were no banks and women were secluded, a wife could comfortably wear the family's assets, and it was customary to wear all of one's jewelry at the same time. Jewelry was also a woman's personal property, which provided security for the future should she need it. A personal collection might include earrings, bracelets, necklaces, rings, a nosering, ankle bracelets, and hair ornaments (usually made of silver or base metals, because gold was expensive). Superstitions were strong, and particular designs or features on jewelry—as in clothing—persisted to divert the evil eye.

Late-twentieth-century Egyptian man's vest called a *sudeyree*, which is worn under a *gallebeyya* (robe). The front section, which would be visible, is made of fine silk and cotton fabric called *shahee*. Textile Research Centre, Leiden (TRC 2008.0487). Photograph by Betty Wass El-Wakil.

A range of cosmetics are used by women of all social classes. In particular, both urban and rural women outline the edge of the eyelids with kohl (black eyeliner). This custom has prevailed since the days of the pharaohs.

Sandals, slippers, or plastic scuffs with no socks or stockings are usual footwear throughout the country for village, oasis, and Bedouin women. Urban women normally follow Western styles of footwear.

Tattooing was common in the 1800s, and tattoos of delicate blue or green designs applied to the chin, hands, arms, feet, middle of bosom, or lips were still sometimes seen on older women throughout the twentieth century, but now they are rare.

URBAN DRESS

Approximately one-quarter of the population of Egypt lives in Cairo (the capital) and Alexandria (the main seaport). In 1900 the middle and upper classes in these cities were generally wearing European styles, but vestiges of earlier dress remained. Men replaced the Ottoman robes with Western-style suits but retained the *tarbush*, a tasseled felt cap that was the base for the turban. In 1952, young military officers led a revolution that brought Egyptians long-desired power. The tarbush became a symbol of foreign oppression, and it vanished quickly.

Similarly, the dress of middle- and upper-class women followed European styles, with the addition of veiling in public, which was universal in cities in 1900. A *melaya* (dark, cloaklike outer garment) covered the entire body. In addition, a *burqa* (face veil) was used to cover the face below the eyes.

During the late nineteenth century, Egyptian intellectuals began to encourage participation of upper-class women in public life. This culminated in a public protest in 1919, when hundreds of veiled women rallied against the British government and British-owned businesses. The veil was interpreted as a symbol of female oppression, and, in 1925, Hoda Shaarawi, daughter of a pasha, came back from a women's conference in Rome and symbolically shed her veil in a widely publicized act of protest about women's status. The fashion spread rapidly, and, in the 1950s, some observers said that the veil was almost extinct in Egypt. At this time, chic shops offering European imports lined the commercial centers of Cairo and Alexandria, and Egyptian factories produced ordinary ready-to-wear. Unfortunate economic strategies implemented by the Egyptian government plus the 1967 and 1973 wars with Israel left Egypt in dire economic straits. Factories become nationalized and Europeans left. As the country failed to achieve nationalistic goals (jobs were scarce and individual futures seemed bleak), the veil began to appear again. Coverings for women called *higab* were interpreted as a mandate of Islam in the Qur'an. The incidence of veiling increased gradually from 1970 onward and experienced a groundswell of popularity after 2001. In 2007, roughly 90 percent of Muslim women in public wore higab, but these veiled women rarely covered their faces. Around 2003, several attractive young actresses added status to the movement by adopting higab, wearing chic draped styles closely fitted and covering all but the face, hands, and feet. Other stylish young women covered their hair with tightly wrapped silk scarves coordinated with long-sleeved tops and trousers or long skirts, all in bright colors.

As long as Egypt was under foreign domination, the country was seen as a source for raw materials, and very little manufacturing was fostered. After independence in the 1960s and 1970s, stringent economic conditions continued to make fashion goods scarce. The small percentage of Egyptians who comprise the wealthy upper class traveled to Europe—or later to Lebanon or Dubai—to buy their clothing. A large majority depended on local dressmakers and tailors or on utilitarian garments produced in government-owned factories. Dressmakers and tailors can be creative, but clothing designers need the support of a fashion industry. Economic liberalization in the 1980s and 1990s began to encourage foreign investment and restimulate manufacturing. Knits and sportswear such as sweatpants and shirts were among the first ready-to-wear goods made in Egypt at this time. Shopping venues were also changing as the first mall opened in 1989; by 2005, there were thirty malls in Cairo. Protectionist policies intended to aid the nascent Egyptian industry kept foreign ready-to-wear out of the country until 2003, when laws were eased. Since then, several multinational retailers have established businesses in Egypt, and, while stimulating excitement about fashion, they also contribute to standardizing the goods available throughout the world.

Egypt had no widely known designers until after 2000. Three Egyptian designers who are recognized for expressing their Eastern heritage in high fashion in the early years of the twenty-first century are Hani El-Beheiry, Talaat Sharkas, and Mohamed Nahas. In the area of jewelry, Azza Fahmy is an internationally

Detail showing coins and stitches on the bodice of a well-worn dress from the Dakhla oasis in the Western Desert, Egypt. Traditional embroidered oaseis dresses started to be considered old-fashioned only in the 1960s. Textile Research Centre, Leiden. (TRC 2008.0495)

acclaimed contemporary designer whose career spans nearly forty years. To further enhance the individual in contemporary times, Cairo and other urban areas have a large number of accomplished hairstylists, makeup artists, nail artists, and specialists in hair transplants, cosmetic surgery, and surgical implants.

The population of Cairo, the largest city in Africa, increased from about one million in 1920 to well over sixteen million in 2000. The vast majority of people are not middle or upper class. Most are from the lower classes and moved from towns or villages when the land or jobs were too scarce to sustain them and they hoped to find work in the city. Their dress tends to reflect the dress of the areas from where they came. The women from poorer classes generally wear black outer garments in public that cover the hair and body. The garments may conceal dresses considered economically inferior and thus equalize statuses among peers.

COPTIC CHRISTIANS

Throughout the twentieth century, Coptic Christians have made up about 10 percent of the population of Egypt. There is little difference in Coptic and Muslim dress except in periods when many Muslim women veil in public, while Copts may be identified by their lack of veiling. Religious leaders among both Copts and Muslims wear special dress that indicates position and status.

THE DELTA AND NILE VALLEY

Agriculture is the backbone of the Egyptian economy, yet only around 4 percent of the land of Egypt is agriculturally productive; the rest is desert. All agriculture is dependent on water from the Nile River. Until the Aswan High Dam was completed in 1963, the Nile flooded annually, leaving a narrow strip of fertile silt at the river's edge from the border with Sudan to Cairo. North of Cairo, the river fans out into tributaries connected by canals that form a rich agricultural area known as the Delta. South of Cairo the area is known as Upper Egypt, and the people are sometimes called *Saeedi*. The agricultural workers live along the Nile or in the Delta. Whether day laborers, sharecroppers, or small land-owners, they are called *fellaheen* (m: *fellah*; f: *fellaha*), an Arabic word meaning tiller of the soil, peasant, or farmer.

The quintessential garment of the fellah is a loose long-sleeved gown called a *gallebeyya*, which slips over the head and extends to the ankles. The garment is tapered, giving the hem fullness that allows one to walk and move easily. A summer gallebeyya is made of striped or solid cotton material, usually blue or white; for winter, a man may have a wool gallebeyya in darker colors. The round neckline has an opening slit to the chest. As an undergarment, the fellah wears a *sudeyree* (sleeveless vest), a garment retained from the Turkish era that is typically striped and made from a silk and cotton fabric called *shahee*. The vest, with edges trimmed with braid and many tiny close-set buttons, peeks out from under the front opening of the gallebeyya. *Sirwal* (large baggy drawers) fastened by a drawstring at the waist extend to the knees. The gallebeyya is worn by rural men, whether rich or poor, Christian or Muslim, and is worn by lower classes in cities as well. Toward the end of the twentieth century, a gallebeyya resembling a Western-style shirt with a collar, neckband, and front opening became popular among younger men.

Headgear for the Delta fellah is a skullcap in knitted wool or white cotton. Typical Saeedi headgear is a brimless cap made of brownish felt. As an alternative, a man may wrap a narrow scarf casually around the cap and tuck in the ends to form a simple turban. Fellaheen leave their head coverings on for all occasions, formal or informal, and are clean-shaven but may sport a mustache.

The fellaha wears a modest dress with long sleeves. It usually comes to the ankles. She typically gets one or two new dresses a year, so she may own only two or three dresses in total. The dress will be sewn by the woman herself or by a local dressmaker from either a print or a solid-colored cotton. In the 1980s, a Delta town of 50,000 had approximately two hundred dressmakers, and each one would contribute to fashion change by doing distinctive work while staying within community dictates.

Social anthropologist Andrea Rugh described styles that typified each of the five governates in the Delta. Decorative details on the yokes provided the main distinguishing elements that varied through the use of different braid, latticework, velvet, and other trims. A governate near Alexandria, for example, has a high-waisted style called *embire* based on the French Empire style from the early nineteenth century.

Rugh followed the Nile River southward and found the mode alternating between dresses with fitted waistlines and yoked dresses with no waistline seaming. Dresses fitted to the body at the yoke have fullness in the lower section. The silhouette obscures the figure and allows the garment to be worn through pregnancy or weight gain, practical concerns for the person with a very limited wardrobe.

The fellaha normally covers her hair with a *mandil irruss* (head scarf) with edges that may be decorated with crochet, beading, or tassels. It is folded into a triangle, placed on the head with the points wrapped around the back and tied on top in a knot. She

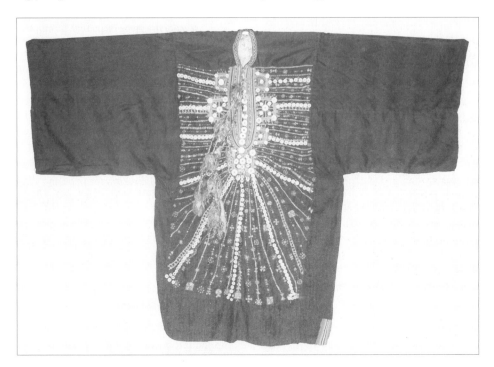

Wedding dress from Siwa oasis, Egypt, with buttons and embroidery that may represent rays of the sun. Traditionally, and into the twenty-first century, Siwa oasis brides may wear several different dresses in the course of their marriage celebrations. Photograph by Betty Wass El-Wakil.

may wear a *tarha* (black rectangular cloth) over the scarf. Two to four yards (almost two to about three and a half meters) long, the tarha is wrapped around the head a few times, leaving the ends to hang over her shoulders to the back. Her jewelry consists of a single strand of beads, small bracelets, and earrings.

A black outer garment is worn over her colored dress when a woman appears in public. Up to the mid-twentieth century, a fashionable outer garment for fellaha was the *melaya liff*, a plain black sheet deftly wrapped to provide total covering. It was replaced by a long black outer dress with a round yoke, a round collar, and a front opening.

The dress of the Saeedi fellaha is similar to her northern counterpart, but tends to have waistline seaming and may be cut a bit lower at the neckline. It is also loosely fitted, allowing for figure changes, and does not have as much decorative detailing on the bodice. An opening that buttons down the bodice front is common. It is also common in Upper Egypt to wear a *shaal* (shawl), a square cloth measuring about two yards, placed either over the head or across the shoulders and over a scarf tied Delta-fashion and a tarha.

As one goes south from Cairo, the overdress of the women becomes less constructed or fitted, is more of a wrapper, and gains some color. In the area of Minya and Assyut, a *hubbara* or *shugga* (large black cloak) that requires six or seven yards (up to six and a half meters) of material is worn. Further south, in Sohag, a *birda* (rectangular shawl) measuring four yards (three and a half meters) has brown and black stripes. Still further south, yardage similar in size to a tablecloth is plaid with red and white lines on a black background. Near Luxor, a typical overwrap is made of yellow, white, and black plaid.

The Saeedi fellaha wears colorful bead necklaces, silver, gold, glass, or plastic bracelets, earrings, and distinctive *khul khaal* (silver ankle bracelets) that make a ringing sound when the wearer walks. The large inflexible ankle bracelets, forming about two-thirds of a circle with a knob at each open end, indicate that a woman is married, and the bracelets may be removed only if the woman is widowed.

NUBIA

As one goes southward, skin tones darken and the Nubians, being the farthest south, are the darkest Egyptians. Numerous small villages bordering the Nile River and extending from Aswan to the border with Sudan comprised their homeland. The population of Nubia in 1900 was around seventy thousand. The area, however, was flooded in 1903 with the opening of the first Aswan Dam. Further rises in the dam's water level in 1933 caused serious flooding of Nubian lands. As a result, migration to the cities to find work became common. In 1964, the Aswan High Dam was constructed, which flooded even more land and left the area uninhabitable. A massive resettlement was undertaken by the Egyptian government, and the Nubians were moved to a new location at Kom Ombo.

European travelers in Nubia during the nineteenth century said the men, women, and children wore very little clothing. After the 1850s, many Europeans came to work in commerce and government in Egypt, and tourism on the Nile brought more Europeans to the area. As a result, Nubian modes of dress gradually changed.

The Nubian culture has two major groups: the Kenuz from northern Nubia and the Fedija from the south. Nubian men from

both groups are known for wearing a white turban and a white or somber-colored gallebeyya. A more prosperous man may have an extra large white turban. Boys wear gallebeyyas made of striped cotton similar to that used for Western pajamas. Boys do not wear head coverings.

Village Nubian women normally wear cotton dresses made from brightly colored prints. The form and cut of these dresses changes over time. Kenuzi women in their villages do not wear a garment covering the dress, but they drape a brightly colored tarha over their head, hair, and shoulders. The tarha among the Fedija is usually black. Fedija women also have a fashion called the *jirjara*, which is a black, long-sleeved overdress with a short train. It is made from sheer material with a woven floral design. The effect of this overdress is one of shades of light and dark as the colors of the underdress are visible.

Nubian women often plait their hair into numerous tiny braids. Girls up to about twelve years old wear a variety of inexpensive garments in Western styles. Many Nubian women, especially in cities, choose conservative dress consisting of a heavy black overdress and a black tarha. Others may dress in lightweight wrapped ensembles in pastel colors. Dresses worn underneath are usually ankle length and long-sleeved made from vividly colored prints.

Nubians are conservative Muslims, but they express themselves aesthetically with realistic human, plant, and animal designs. A woman's black tarha may be embroidered with geometric and floral patterns and enhanced with tassels and beads. Traditionally, a young woman might embroider a bright skullcap or a pair of wide trousers with fanciful designs such as flowers, birds, and good wishes for her future husband.

When a young woman marries, her mother and family and friends of her mother will present the bride-to-be with gold or silver jewelry as part of the wedding preparations. In addition, the groom will give jewelry. A bride might be adorned with ankle bracelets, pendants, necklaces, hair ornaments, a nose disk, multiple earrings (three hoops per ear), and more. Gold coins may be

A woman's slippers worn with a wedding ensemble from Siwa oasis, twentieth century. Textile Research Centre, Leiden (TRC 2008.0491a-b). Photograph by Betty Wass El-Wakil.

fastened into the hair at the center of the forehead and spaced to frame the face. Distinctive Nubian jewelry includes a cucumber-shaped amulet that is worn as a pendant and other silver pendants in crescent or disk shapes engraved with designs of flowers, birds, and small houses. In the early twenty-first century, the Nubian bride is more likely to wear a white wedding dress and jewelry similar to that worn by Western brides.

Some older Nubians may still be seen with three vertical or diagonal lines scarring each cheek, a marker of tribal affiliation. Similarly, some women may have blue tattooed lips or a small tattoo in the center of the forehead.

THE OASES

In general, the Western Desert is a desolate mass of arid land; however, a few depressions in the desert are at or near sea level. These depressions are the sites of springs that allow agriculture. The five main oases are Kharga, Dakhla, Bahriyah, Farafara, and Siwa. Each oasis contains a number of small villages. Some of the areas were inhabited as early as the Paleolithic era, but, until the twentieth century, the only means of transport in the area was by camel caravan. Roads were paved between 1960 and 1980, reducing travel time to the oases from many days to a few hours. Although less than 1 percent of the population of Egypt lives in these desert areas, their distinctive dress warrants attention. In general, men's dress mirrored the dress of the working classes throughout Egypt. Men in positions of authority adopt Western dress, while the farmers wear the traditional gallebeyya and turban. Most women during the first half of the twentieth century wore embroidered dresses that identified them with a specific oasis. The second half of the century saw considerable changes. The tastes of those who could afford it shifted to gold jewelry and mirrored the tastes of other Egyptian women. The embroidered dresses began to disappear around 1960, when younger women saw them as old-fashioned and began to adopt Nile Valley village styles.

The basic traditional dress of women in the oases of Kharga, Dakhla, Bahriya, and Farafara is a black shift cut with straight panels in the front and the back and tapering panels on each side in the shape of the gallebeyya. Women in a family make their dresses as part of a dowry or for other special occasions. Almost no material is wasted in cutting or construction.

Oasis dresses are beautifully embroidered utilizing a wide range of colors and a variety of stitches. Orange is used most frequently, but in small amounts. The dominant color is usually a shade of red with accents of other colors. In addition to embroidery, coins are a popular decoration. In the late 1800s, old gold and silver coins from Egypt and Constantinople were in circulation but becoming scarce because women were collecting them to attach to their clothing. Base metal replicas of coins were still used on clothing in the mid-twentieth century. Coins are attached in various configurations on the bodices of dresses from all of the oases except Siwa, where they are not used.

Kharga is the largest oasis and was probably the scene of more foreign intervention than the other oases during the twentieth century. The embroidery on the Kharga dresses is not as dense as that on dresses from Bahriya and Dakhla. Each seam is concealed by a line of embroidery wide enough to form a stripe. Vertical lines of embroidery interspersed with motifs decorate the front, but large spaces are left undecorated between the lines.

A favorite Dakhla style is more densely embroidered and contains more coins than that of Kharga. Vertical and horizontal lines of embroidery cover the front bodice area, ending about ten inches (twenty-five centimeters) down from the shoulder. At that point, the width of the decorated area is reduced from about twelve inches (thirty centimeters) to eight inches (twenty centimeters) and continues down the front panel, ending in a triangular point around eighteen inches (forty-six centimeters) from the neckline. Vertical stripes of embroidery placed one to two inches (two and a half to five centimeters) apart cover the side panels and sleeves. The area from the hip to the hem on the back panel is embroidered in harmonizing patterns.

A typical Bahriya dress is solidly embroidered with double herringbone and other stitches in blocks of about six inches (fifteen centimeters) square on each side of the neck opening. The embroidery continues centered below the opening and extends down the front panel in another indented block similar to the Dakhla dress, but it is finished straight at the bottom rather than in a point. Wide patterned stripes executed in closed Cretan stitch cover the side panels, the lower section of the back panel, and the sleeves. Fringes formed by tassels at the bottom of the bodice panel and on the shoulders are a distinctive feature of a Bahriyan dress.

Compared to the other oases, Farafara had the fewest inhabitants and the least resources, and this is reflected in the clothing. The Farafara dress has a yoke with a back opening. A few coins

Detail of stitches on Bedouin dress from Sinai, twentieth century. Textile Research Centre, Leiden (TRC 2008.0488). Photograph by Betty Wass El-Wakil.

are sewn onto the bottom of the yoke, but fewer than the number sewn on other oasis dresses. The lower part of a Farafara dress is gently gathered or pleated over the bosom, where it is attached to the yoke. The lower edge of the dress may have a short ruffle, a feature common to both oasis and fellaheen dresses.

Women going out from their homes in Kharga, Dakhla, Bahriya, and Farafara either drape a tarha over their hair and shoulders, or, if they are working in gardens or fields, they wear a head scarf with the ends brought around the head and tied in a knot on top.

Siwa is the westernmost oasis in Egypt, near the border with Libya. The population was around five thousand in the mid-twentieth century. The area has been inhabited since ancient times, but its isolation allowed Siwa to develop a culture and beliefs that are different from the rest of Egypt. It was not until 1980 that a paved road came to Siwa. In general, Siwa women rarely leave their homes. When a woman journeys from her house to visit friends or relatives, she will be wrapped in a *derfudit*, a large rectangle of blue and white plaid cloth that leaves only one eye exposed.

The wedding dresses of Siwa are unique. A bride will be married at about age fourteen and may have as many as seven different tunic-type dresses to take her through a week of celebration. Two special dresses, one white and one black, are elaborately embroidered following a traditional design. The bride wears white at first and then dons the black dress when her mother visits her after seven days of marriage. She will continue to wear the black dress as an outer garment for special occasions for years to come. The dresses are decorated with bright colors: orange, red, yellow, green, and black. Rows of solid chain stitches encase the neckline, and straight lines executed with variations of running stitch and cross stitch radiate from the front like rays of the sun. Many small designs depict positive features in their environment such as palm trees, leaves, dates, and water. Also decorating the dresses are conch shells, suspended multicolored braided cords that move with bright-colored tassels, and one or two dissonant green or blue buttons, all intended to confuse the evil eye. The wedding dresses are worn over wide pants that are drawn in by a drawstring at the waist and shoes or boots, often embroidered with fishbone stitch and tasseled.

A Siwan woman may wear six to ten pounds (three to four and a half kilograms) of high-quality silver jewelry. Several pieces of traditional jewelry are unique, including a headpiece that falls over the ears. Two crescent-shaped disks are attached to leather straps that are decorated with buttons and amulets and assembled to fit the head. Nine double chains, each measuring twelve inches (thirty centimeters), are attached to the disks with round bells completing the ends of the chains. The hair is arranged in numerous small braids and may be topped with a tarha embroidered in characteristic Siwan designs.

In all of the oases, a woman's jewelry indicated her family's financial status. The range of jewelry worn includes earrings, bracelets, necklaces, rings, a nosering, ankle bracelets, and hair ornaments. These are normally made of silver or base metals because gold was too expensive. Superstitions were strong, and particular designs or features on jewelry, as in clothing, persisted to divert the evil eye. A woman from Farafara may have only simple silver hoop earrings, but more elaborate styles are worn in the other areas. One Bahriyan earring has a circular center that is built up in layers to form a cone. One small tulip-shaped disk representing a hand dangles from the center of the cone, and six identical "hands" are suspended from the lower half of the cone.

Until the mid-twentieth century, gold noserings worn in one pierced nostril were common. The size varies but the design is consistent; a round hoop is divided in half, and the lower half is decorated with filigree. This ring may be large enough to reach to the mouth.

Domlug (three-inch-wide bracelets), worn in pairs with one on each arm, are characteristic in the oases and the Nile Valley. They are embossed with designs such as fish, birds, and the sun. Married women may wear khul-khaal identical to those worn by the Saeedi women. Necklaces of glass or plastic beads are common.

THE SINAI AND THE DESERTS

The Bedouin people are known as inhabitants of the desert. Numbering around five hundred thousand in Egypt, they make up less than 1 percent of the population, but their culture has figured prominently in descriptions of Egypt. In the early twentieth century, all Bedouin groups depended on camels, sheep, and goats for their living and moved according to the availability of water and grass. In recent times, Egypt's quest for urban development to accommodate a burgeoning population has been paired with resettlement schemes for the Bedouin and has changed the lifestyle of the desert people drastically.

The headgear is the distinctive dress of the Bedouin man. A *kefiyya* (square cloth) is folded into a triangle and anchored on the head with *'aqal* (decorative ropes). The kefiyya covers the head and neck, providing protection from the hot sun and blowing sand, and can be wrapped around to shelter the face if needed. Beards and long hair are considered manly. The basic male garments are the *thob* (long cotton tunic or gown or gallebeyya) and a variety of cloaks, jackets, or coats. One outer cloak called *abayeh* was made from lengths of handwoven wool fabric, navy blue in northern Sinai and brown in the south. A corded tie fastened the front. In addition to providing protection from the weather, the abayeh could serve as a blanket at night or a wrapper for carrying goods. Personal necessities were tucked into a sash or a belt. Boys often went barefoot, and men wore sandals, shoes, or boots. Men had no jewelry except possibly signet rings and, in recent times, watches.

Bedouin dresses for women from the Sinai are similar to oasis dresses in that they are heavily embroidered on firm black or dark blue cotton fabric and there is no waistline fitting. However, Bedouin dresses are densely embroidered in only one stitch: a fine cross stitch on the bodice, sleeves, and skirt. The hem is finished in a slanting satin stitch. Red is the designated color for married women; blue is for the unmarried, widowed, or divorced. When red predominates, eight or nine other colors are usually included in the patterning. The designs are highly stylized and geometric but have names such as "cypress tree" or "tree with lions." Superstitions abound, and some designs may be left unfinished or a distracting color will be used to divert the evil eye. A belt or sash is worn over the dress and goes around the waist. It may be woven or plaited into multicolored bands of wool with tassels at the ends and worn over a wider band of black goat hair. Women also cover their hair with a tarha that falls over the shoulders.

In Bedouin society, a girl must begin to dress modestly at age ten or twelve. She must cover her arms, wear an ankle-length dress, and learn acceptable behavior. When she marries, she begins to wear a face veil of some kind. In the late 1800s, the Bedouin veil was red or white, fringed with silver coins, and extended barely to the chin. A hundred years later, some Sinai Bedouins wear a burqa with strings of coins and beads suspended from it. The coins are centered draping over the nose and are attached to chains below the ears so that the mouth is covered.

A woman may choose not to wear the full black overdress in public, but she will cover her shoulders with a black shawl when she leaves her home. A woman learns complex rules for manipulating the veil according to social relationships with individuals or groups. In essence, Bedouin women veil, which may mean covering the face or simply pulling the head cover over the lower part of the face, in front of men who have authority over them. Women do not cover for those considered lower in their social hierarchy. A woman may veil in front of her father, but she may walk unveiled in big cities, where she is seeing no one to whom she must defer as she would in her tribal milieu.

At times, it was fashionable for a Bedouin woman to have lines of tattooing on her chin or to wear a gold nosering. Jewelry would include items of silver or brass: bracelets, necklaces with many chain links, dangling pendants and coins, hair ornaments, and rings. Jewelry also includes beads of materials such as amber, coral, bone, cowry shells, glass, plastic, and other materials.

The Egyptian government began to promote the Sinai and the northern coastal area as tourist destinations in the latter part of the twentieth century. In an effort to integrate the Bedouin population into Egyptian society, sedentary lifestyles have been encouraged. Dress reflects the uneasy integration. Some Bedouin men adopted garments similar to those of the villagers, and women started to wear long-sleeved ankle-length dresses made from inexpensive prints or flowered fabrics. But elements of their dress (men's headwear, women's sashes and veils) are still used to indicate their cultural and ethnic origins.

References and Further Reading

Abu-Lughod, Lila. *Veiled Sentiments*. Cairo: American University in Cairo Press, 1987.

Ammoun, Denise. *Crafts of Egypt*. Cairo: American University in Cairo Press, 1991.

Atiya, Nayra. *Khul-Khaal*. Syracuse, NY: Syracuse University Press, 1982.

Fakhry, Ahmed. *The Oases of Egypt*. Vol. 1, *Siwa Oasis*. Cairo: American University in Cairo Press, 1973.

Fakhry, Ahmed. *The Oases of Egypt*. Vol. 2, *Bahriyah and Farafra Oases*. Cairo: American University in Cairo Press, 1974.

Fernea, Robert A. *Nubians in Egypt*. Austin: University of Texas Press, 1973.

Geiser, Peter. *The Egyptian Nubian: A Study in Social Symbiosis*. Cairo: American University of Cairo Press, 1986.

Gordon, Lady Duff. *Letters from Egypt (1862–1869)*. London: Routledge & Kegan Paul, 1969.

Lane, E.W., *Manners and Customs of the Modern Egyptians*. London: East-West Publications, 1978. (Originally published in 1836.)

Leopoldo, Bettina. *Egypt: The Oasis of Amun Siwa*. Zamalek, Egypt: Akhnaton Gallery, 1987.

Rodenbeck, Max. *Cairo: The City Victorious*. Cairo: American University in Cairo Press, 1999.

Rugh, Andrea B. *Reveal and Conceal*. Syracuse, NY: Syracuse University Press, 1986.

Spring, Christopher, and Julie Hudson. *North African Textiles*. Washington, DC: Smithsonian Institution Press, 1995.

Vivian, Cassandra. *Islands of the Blest: A Guide to the Oases and Western Desert of Egypt*. Monessen, PA: Trade Routes Enterprises, 1990.

Weir, Sheliagh. *The Bedouin*. London: Museum of Mankind, 1976.

Whately, M.L. *Among the Huts in Egypt*. London: Seeley, Jackson, & Halliday, 1872.

Betty Wass El-Wakil

See also Egypt: Historical Dress; volume 5, Central and Southwest Asia: Face Veils in Central and Southwest Asia.

Snapshot: Dance Costumes

The category of dance costume is a specialized type of dress usually reserved for performances and masquerade. In North Africa as elsewhere, dance costumes are worn for performances at special events and in entertainment venues. Three general categories of dance in North Africa are *raks shaabi* (popular dance), *raks beledi* (country dance), and *raks sharqi* (eastern dance).

RAKS SHAABI

Raks shaabi is a social form of dance engaged in by men and women among family members and peers in private situations. Men and women do not typically dance with one another, though they may share the social space in gender-segregated groups. In such mixed-gender situations, women may wear the same outer modesty wrap over their party clothes that they would wear when on the street. Festive dress, but no special costume, is worn for celebrations where dance is a part of the social proceedings, such as weddings. When dancing among friends at home, girls or young women may tie a scarf around their hips over everyday clothing to accentuate movements.

RAKS BELEDI

Raks beledi is usually performed by professional dancers at the occasions of festivals and weddings in homes, hotel ballrooms, tents, or on the street in villages or rural areas. Dancers wear costumes inspired by local ethnic clothing styles that are called *beledi* (country) dress. Local and regional variations of dance are often closely related to the style of dress in that certain movements are dictated by or emphasized by clothing elements.

In southern Egypt, male dancers often wear a cap with a wrapped head cloth and the *gallebeyya*, a bell-shaped wool tunic with long, full sleeves. Men's dances typically involve a stick or staff, incorporating movements that imitate the training of horses or demonstrate martial ability. Female Egyptian dancers often mimic this style using a smaller stick or cane, wearing a head scarf and a gallebeyya made of simple cotton fabric or a straight-cut dress. These may be ornamented with sequins or beaded fringe, especially for tourist shows. Women may also wear a scarf at the hip to highlight practiced movements. Dancers of both genders must capably manage the full sleeves to avoid interfering with movements of the stick or staff. When these types of dances are performed in nontraditional costumes, as when beledi dances are incorporated into urban nightclub shows, stylized postures and arm movements specifically relating to the management of the sleeves are often retained, even if the costume worn is sleeveless.

In Tunisia, female beledi dancers wear a long dress with a long wrapped modesty garment called *melia* (sheet) as the outermost layer. The melia is a length of fabric of five to eleven meters (sixteen to thirty-six feet), which is first wrapped across the front and around the back of the body and then pinned at the shoulders with ornate silver fibulae. First one end is wrapped around the body and pinned, then the remaining length is folded in half the long way and draped over the yarn belt and then gathered by hand across the back, leaving a pouf of fabric when the yarn belt is tied. When the fabric is longer, more gathering takes place. The top half (above the belt) of the gathered fabric dangles down over the belt and swishes when walking or dancing. (If the melia is worn for everyday, the top half can be used as modesty covering or veil over the shoulders and face.) The fasteners are often connected by long chains to which coins, pendants, and hand-shaped talismans called *khamsa* (five) are attached for good luck. The melia is finally tied at the hip with a two-meter (six-and-half-foot) wool yarn belt, with the excess fabric gathered over the belt across the back for fullness. This fullness amplifies the dancer's hip movements, which are characterized by horizontal twisting motions that make the fabric and ends of the yarn belt sway vigorously.

Moroccan weddings typically include performances by *sheikhatt* (wise women), who entertain the guests with song and dance. For special occasions, both women guests and dancers customarily wear a two-layer dress ensemble called *takshita*, which is cinched at the waist with an ornate belt. The dances include vigorous pelvic movements highlighted by the belt as it visually separates the upper torso from the pelvis, drawing attention to movement below the waist. Dancers may also tie a spangled scarf around the hips for further emphasis.

Women dancers throughout North Africa typically don a head scarf with spangled fringe over the hair. In Egypt, a scarf sometimes features brightly colored tufts of yarn representing flowers. Nubian dancers in the south of Egypt usually wear a semicircular veil that extends to the hips, held at the corners by the fingertips and moved in and out so the fabric ripples around the body.

North African women's jewelry includes silver or gold necklaces, bracelets, and especially *khul khaal*, which are heavy anklets that make a jingling noise as a woman moves. Lyrics often mention khul khaal, and dancers accentuate the movements and sounds of their anklets accordingly. Earrings are common, although heavy pendants may be stitched to a head scarf to simulate very large earrings. The noisy, glittering spectacle of the dancer's jewelry symbolically displays female personal wealth, especially at wedding performances, as brides use dowry money to purchase gold or silver jewelry.

In Morocco, the men's beledi costume is a simple white tunic and pants. This is often augmented with bandolier-style belts worn at the waist and diagonally across the body over the shoulder; these are made of leather or woven bands and accentuated with brightly colored yarn fringe and spangles. A felt hat, crocheted cap, or wrapped head cloth may top off the costume depending on the region and venue.

Cosmetics highlight women's facial features, especially the eyes, which are considered to be particularly beautiful and are celebrated in many song lyrics. Female beledi dancers may

A. Margaret Deppe, a *beledi* dancer in the United States, posing in an Abla theater *beledi* dress with stylized *tulle bi telli* (metallic net) motifs. Modest costumes worn for Egyptian dance shows in the twenty-first century often include theatrical interpretations of *beledi* dress, a type of costume inspired by local ethnic clothing styles in Egypt. Photograph by Peter Ellison.

apply fake tattoos to the face and hands when performing styles of dance inspired by rural or nomadic dances. This represents earlier times, when many rural girls had facial tattoos indicating family or clan ties. Tattooing is no longer fashionable in most areas, but dancers may still apply fake tattoos, recalling rural origins. Male dancers do not typically wear cosmetics, although they will wear stage makeup for theater performances.

Because raks beledi may be performed indoors or outdoors, on rough wooden stages or gravel streets, dancers usually wear sandals or shoes for protection. Wearing shoes may also be an indicator of social or economic status for dancers in very poor areas, where some villagers cannot afford shoes.

RAKS SHARQI

Raks sharqi is the best known form of dance outside Egypt and is called *oryantal dansi* (Oriental dance) in Turkey. Elsewhere in the world, raks sharqi is often called *belly dance* because dance movements of raks sharqi are centered in the torso. In

many regions, there is a particular emphasis on movements of the hips. *Belly dance* has become a generic term for theatrical women's solo dances of North Africa, Turkey, and the Middle East, including raks sharqi and occasionally raks beledi. Fusion and interpretive styles loosely based on a wide variety of ethnic dances from other countries are also included in this category. Consequently, the costume for raks sharqi is recognized globally as the principal type of belly dance costume.

In North Africa, costuming for raks sharqi varies greatly with context and the role of the professional dancer. Performance venues include nightclubs, theaters, and tourist shows as well as extravagant weddings and other private celebrations, usually formal-dress occasions. The distinctive style of dress for professional dancers is a performance costume called *bedlah* (suit), designating it as specifically professional attire. This costume evolved from Orientalist fantasy interpretations of Middle Eastern women's dress that began to appear in stage shows and movies in Europe and the United States, especially Hollywood, during the first decade of the twentieth century. Egyptian costume designers emulated and modified theatrical and cinematic styles, and, by the 1930s, dancers in Egyptian films were wearing the now characteristic two-piece bedlah costume.

Bedlah is a two-piece ensemble made of a stylized bra top worn with a long skirt that is closely fitted at the hips. The whole costume is intricately embellished with sequins, beads, and rhinestones. Hip ornamentation may be worked directly onto the skirt or onto an ornamental belt worn over a long, full skirt. The costume typically includes matching accessories such as cuffs and sleeves, a stylized wrap or stiffened fabric headpiece resembling a crown, and sometimes anklets.

Egyptian dancers often make an entrance with a floor-length cape or veil made from lightweight fabric that is later cast aside. Similarly, many dancers begin their show wearing high-heeled shoes, which are conspicuously removed during the first set. The act of discarding coordinating elements of the costume demonstrates that, while they are important parts of the ensemble, they are unnecessary for the whole performance. The doffing of shoes is also a social gesture that indicates that the dancer is relaxed, and many Egyptians feel that dancing in high heels is contrary to the grounded nature of raks sharqi. In Turkey, high heels are typically worn for the entire show.

Fabrics used for bedlah costumes range from flowing crepe chiffon to sheer mesh to stretch fabrics such as panné velvet or satin spandex. In some North African countries, laws regarding modest dress dictate whether certain areas of the body, such as the torso or upper thigh, must be covered. For example, in Morocco, dancers typically perform with a bare midriff, whereas in Egypt the midriff is usually covered with a mesh body stocking. Floor-length beaded evening gowns are popular performance costumes in venues where the dancer's torso must be fully covered. Modest costumes worn for Egyptian dance shows often include theatrical interpretations of beledi dress, which may incorporate *tulle bi telli* (metallic net), a cotton mesh fabric ornamented with metal in geometric designs originally made in the region of Assuit, or dresses worked in beads and sequins in those same motifs. These costumes evoke a rural essence while conforming to the glamorous look of the theater stage.

Whether performing in theater venues under bright lights or in dim restaurants by candlelight, dancers must wear dramatic stage makeup. Dancers performing at weddings and parties may also wear heavy perfume.

Raks sharqi is performed in nightclubs and theaters by professional dancers, some of whom achieve celebrity status. Although Turkey and Lebanon have many talented dancers, most of the best known dancers are Egyptian. Through their performances in movies and other media, Cairo has become the world capital for raks sharqi and thus for belly dance costume designers as well.

CAIRO COSTUME DESIGNERS

Following World War II, Egyptian films often featured dancers. With the expansion of the movie industry and the global distribution of Egyptian television, music, and video via media industries, Egyptian dancers became known worldwide, and belly dancers in other countries sought Egyptian dance costumes. By the 1980s, Cairo became a fashion center for belly dance costumes for a growing international dance community.

Until her death in 2006, Madame Abla was Egypt's premier costume designer. Abla created both bedlah and theatrical beledi-style costumes for celebrities, including Nagwa Fouad, Mona Said, and Fifi Abdou. Belly dancers from around the world traveled to Cairo to visit Abla's salon, and her designs set the supreme standard for professional costumes for decades.

The growing demand for Egyptian dance costumes has provided global business opportunities. Pharonics of Egypt, by designer Amira Kattan, was one of the earliest labels recognized inside and outside of Egypt. Many designers started their careers as exclusive costumers for celebrity dancers. Sahar Okasha originally worked for star dancer Dina; by 2005, Sahar had her own atelier in Cairo, and her designs are among the most highly coveted by belly dancers worldwide.

As with other clothing fashions, bedlah and stylized beledi costumes are constantly changing. Many Egyptian designers, such as Eman Zaki, look to the runways of Europe for inspiration, keeping bedlah styles current with fashion trends. The influence of costume designers outside of Egypt also steers fashion preferences among dancers worldwide. For example, lavish rhinestones and daring cutouts are often-imitated elements of bedlah designs by Bella of Turkey. The diversity of costume styles available demonstrates the ability of Cairo designers to continuously build on the rich heritage of Egyptian raks sharqi and dominate the costume design industry in the international community of belly dancers.

REFERENCES AND FURTHER READING

Shay, Anthony, and Barbara Sellers-Young, eds. *Belly Dance: Orientalism, Transnationalism, and Harem Fantasy.* Costa Mesa, CA: Mazda Publishers, 2005.

van Nieuwkerk, Karin. *"A Trade Like Any Other"—Female Singers and Dancers in Egypt.* Austin: University of Texas Press, 1995.

Vogelsang-Eastwood, Gillian. *For Modesty's Sake?* Rotterdam, The Netherlands: Barjesteh, Meeuwes & Company/Syntax Publishing, 1996.

Zuhur, Sherifa. *Images of Enchantment: Visual and Performing Arts of the Middle East.* Cairo: American University in Cairo Press, 1998.

Zuhur, Sherifa, ed. *Colors of Enchantment: Theater, Dance, Music, and the Visual Arts of the Middle East.* Cairo: American University in Cairo Press, 2001.

Margaret A. Deppe

Snapshot: Libya

Libya is located on the North African coast, surrounded clockwise by Egypt, Sudan, Chad, Niger, Algeria, and Tunisia. In the north, Libya has shared a long history of dress with its Mediterranean neighbors Egypt, Algeria, and Tunisia, but, unfortunately, research on issues of dress has been hindered by Libya's political isolation from the rest of the world since the rule of Muammar al-Qaddafi beginning in 1969.

THE NORTH

Like its Mediterranean neighbors, most of what is now coastal Libya was ruled by a succession of foreign powers, initially the Phoenicians, Greeks, and Romans. Indeed, the Libyan-born Septimius Severus became Roman emperor (r. 193–211 C.E.), and Leptis Magna, just outside modern Tripoli, became a commercial and cultural entrepôt, second only to Rome, with all the trappings of leadership and elite dress that characterized the capital. Shortly before their sack of Rome in 455 C.E., the Vandals gained control of Libya, followed by the Byzantines in 533. Each of these early powers brought their own traditions of dress, which were to exert some temporary influence on privileged local peoples, but it was not until the Muslim Arab invasions from the east, which led to control of the coast and interior by 663, that more pervasive and enduring practices were introduced.

Muslim dress protocols were sustained by a series of Islamic dynasties that maintained at least nominal control of Libya until the twentieth century and have been identified with a series of distinct contributions to dress in the area. For example, under the Fatimid dynasty (909–1171), silk weaving was introduced to Libya and indeed across North Africa. The Mamluk Sultanate in Egypt (1250–1517) is identified with the introduction of distinctive striped silk and cotton garments. The Turkish Ottoman Empire occupied Tripoli in 1551 and held at least indirect power until 1912 and was especially well known for its silk brocades and thick silk velvets.

Running throughout much of the preceding history is a Jewish presence that also impacted dress. Jewish populations in Libya date back as early as the third century B.C.E. Jews experienced serious conflicts with the Romans, but Jews in Tripoli coexisted with Muslim peoples until the rise of Qaddafi in 1969. Jewish businessmen and artisans were instrumental in the trade and manufacture of gold jewelry and were also heavily involved in silk products.

Twentieth-century women's dress outside of the urban centers is noted for the silk *trabelsi* (meaning "from Tripoli") wrapper with distinctive stripes of dark maroon or black on yellow or blue. The wrapper is worn over a velvet *gilet* and a chemisette and is tied on the left shoulder. In some instances, it is fastened with a silver fibula instead of tied. The wrapper may hang loose on the body or may be gathered at the waist with a large wool sash. The choice of silk to produce this dress as well as the way it is fastened on the shoulder is reminiscent of the dress worn by some women on the island of Jerba south of Tunis in Tunisia, where it is also called *trabelsi*. Women's dress is completed with silver jewelry including chest ornaments, bracelets,

and earrings. Head scarves are generally worn in styles typical of Amazigh (Berber) women, tied in front of the head or sometimes worn with a larger scarf over it tied at the back.

Among the most famous items of Libyan dress are the silk embroidered slippers from the oasis and caravan town of Ghadamis. The production of this distinctive variation on the North African *babouche* is frequently identified with the extended Ben Yeddar family, but they are actually produced by a much larger group of artisans. Dyed in an assortment of bright colors, but most frequently red, these shoes feature a tongue cut in the shape of the Hand of Fatima, named after the mother of Mohammed. This motif is thought to serve a number of prophylactic functions and especially as protection against the evil eye. The five fingers are also thought to represent the five obligations, or pillars of faith, of Islam. Although worn in a variety of festive contexts, these slippers are considered essential items of wedding dress.

In the nineteenth century, tattoos were not uncommon among Berber women, although this practice largely disappeared by the end of the twentieth century. The application of henna on the hands and feet of women, however, has remained an enduring practice, especially at weddings, where it is thought to provide protection against harmful forces, especially the evil eye. In some places, small, embroidered woolen wrappers are used to protect freshly applied henna from staining other clothing. Typically dyed red, these cloths are also thought to promote fertility.

Men in northern Libya wear a plain cotton or velvet jacket embroidered at the sleeves, a fashion extending back to Ottoman Empire days, along with baggy pants known as *salwar*. Men in Libya wear a pillbox-style hat in black; however, it is larger than the red one usually worn in Tunisia, where it is known as *chechia*.

The most typical item of dress identifying its wearer as a Libyan man is the Berber *burnous*, a floor-length outer garment woven of wool or camel hair (or a mixture of both), usually in solid white, brown, or beige. The cloth is a rectangle ranging from five to six feet (about one and a half to two meters) in width and eighteen to twenty feet (about five and half to six meters) in length, depending on the height and weight of the wearer. Men purchase this garment in a market (*souk*), essentially custom-ordering it, for it cannot be found in retail stores. The burnous may or may not have a hood. Generally, the embroiderer uses a technique known both in Libya and Tunisia as *kobbita* to decorate the edges and sometimes body using either the same color as the burnous or accents of different colors, depending on the wearer's aesthetic taste. If the wearer orders a hood, then embroidery stitches are used to attach it. North African men wear the burnous in several ways, but typically Libyan men place the burnous under the right arm and over the left shoulder, without the hood covering their heads, allowing freedom of movement.

Since rising to power, Qaddafi has chosen to wear the burnous on select occasions to highlight being Libyan. The garment is said to be symbolic for many Libyan men, being associated with bravery and courage. Past anticolonial leaders have worn it, such as Omar Mokhtar, a famous revolutionary who led the Libyans against the Italians. Habib Bourguiba, before becoming president of Tunisia, escaped detection when fleeing the French by wearing the burnous Libyan-style while crossing the Tunisian border into Libya.

THE SOUTH

The earliest evidence for dress practices in the Libyan portion of the Sahara desert is found in the rock art of the Fezzan in the southwest, especially the Jebel Acacus. Depending on the site, an assortment of loincloths and belts were worn, and hair was fixed in a variety of configurations. On some rock faces, men are depicted with horned headdresses and masks representing jackals. In some areas, there is evidence that individuals wore body paint. Males are regularly represented carrying a bow and arrow or a shield and spear. Dating of these sites, however, remains tenuous, with some sites representing dress practices probably going back six or seven thousand years.

The best-known population in southern Libya, especially around the caravan town of Ghat, is the Berber-speaking Tuareg, who are even more numerous in Niger and Mali. This formerly nomadic and pastoral camel-riding and -herding group (now largely sedentary) was once responsible for much of the trans-Saharan trade. They are most readily identified by the substantial indigo-dyed turban/veil (*tagelmust*) worn exclusively by men, earning them the oft-cited appellation "the men who wear the veil." The tagelmust is a five-meter- (sixteen-foot) long piece of shiny, dark blue cloth that is folded, wrapped, tucked, and draped in a variety of configurations and is typically worn with either long white or dark robes over baggy pants, sometimes trimmed with embroidery at the ankles. The men usually wear leather sandals except when riding camels, when they go barefoot. On ceremonial occasions, men carry distinctive knives and swords.

At one time, corpulence was an admired trait among Tuareg women, but much less so toward the end of the twentieth century. Women generally wear a long robe embroidered on top and featuring somewhat billowy sleeves or a separate overblouse with a wrapped skirt. Bright red embroidery on dark blue cloth is a preferred color combination. A head scarf drapes to the side and back but does not veil the face. The Tuareg are internationally renowned for their silver jewelry worn by both men and women and extensively marketed to tourists. Jewelry includes a wide assortment of stamped and incised cast bracelets, rings, and necklaces as well as a rich variety of amulets. Most famous are the so-called crosses often assigned to specific regional origins but now produced in all their variety throughout the Tuareg orbit.

AFTER INDEPENDENCE

Following a short period of Italian rule from 1911 to 1943 and an even shorter period as a post–World War II British protectorate, Libya regained its independence in 1951 under King Idris I, the emir of Cyrenaica. The monarchy was deposed

Libyan leader Muammar al-Qaddafi in custom-designed military dress. Tripoli, 1999. Marwan Naamani/AFP/Getty Images.

in a 1969 coup led by Muammar al-Qaddafi, who was still in power as of 2009. Over this period of forty years, Qaddafi may have established himself as the most fashion conscious of all world leaders in the second half of the twentieth century. His dress is certainly among the most flamboyant, eclectic, and eccentric on the international political scene. Depending on the occasion, he has been photographed in Western coat and tie, Arab robes, military uniforms, and an assortment of wrappers, smocks, and leisure suits, all custom designed and tailored to his taste. He frequently wears a red fez, the emblem of a Muslim administrator, or a pillbox variation in embroidered satin or silk. In the past, at official events, he has even mimicked Michael Jackson wearing one white glove, loafers, sequined socks, and sunglasses. Although he has not been observed wearing one himself, watches with his photograph on the face are widely marketed in Tripoli.

One high-profile reflection of Qaddafi's rule and his fashion sensibilities is the formation in the early 1980s of his all-female body guard, popularly referred to in the foreign press as the Green Nuns, Revolutionary Nuns, or the Amazon Guard. Numbering about five hundred, these reputedly highly trained guards (all said to be virgins) have served as his personal protection both locally and, famously, during international travel. Most of these women could easily qualify as beauty contestants, and although they are dressed in uniforms, they are allowed the freedom to choose their own eyeliner, lipstick, and nail polish among other makeup decisions. Individual choices in jewelry are also allowed. The military gear ranges from stylish camouflage fatigues with pleated pants to khaki uniforms with fringed epaulettes and gold braids. Headgear may include a bright red beret, a glengarry, or a head scarf, but apparently never a veil. They typically wear fashionable black boots, but some have been photographed in red stilettos while in uniform. The number of uniform designs would appear to be substantial, with a color shift in fatigues from green to blue sometime around 2000. AK47s are the primary accessory, and it is frequently said that "they carry their Kalashnikovs like Gucci bags." In 2006, the group was satirized by the British band Asian Dub Foundation in *Gaddafi: A Living Myth*, created for the English National Opera.

The isolation of Libya began to end in 2003, when Qaddafi yielded to international pressure and renounced its weapons development programs and terrorist associations. This helped open new fashion opportunities for both consumers and local designers. Trained in Rome, Rabia Ben Barka is probably the most widely recognized contemporary fashion designer in Libya and has designed clothing for Qaddafi and his daughter Aisha. Ironically, Barka's father once owned several textiles mills in Tripoli that were nationalized by Qaddafi when he seized power. Barka's creations have been described as a fusion of Western and North African designs. She is known for her brightly colored gowns and robes, often with bold stripes and embroidery in silver and gold thread. Her more Western-style men's suits are also characterized by embroidery on the sleeves, chest, and waist.

REFERENCES AND FURTHER READING

Mori, Fabricio. "The Earliest Saharan Rock Engravings." *Antiquity* 48 (1972): 87–92.

Prussin, Labelle. "Judaic Threads in the West African Tapestry: No More Forever?" *Art Bulletin* 88, no. 2 (2006): 328–353.

Seligman, Thomas K., and Kristyne Loughran, eds. *Art of Being Tuareg: Sahara Nomads in a Modern World*. Los Angeles: UCLA Fowler Museum of Cultural History, 2006.

Spring, Christopher, and Julie Hudson. *North African Textiles*. London: British Museum Press, 1995.

Spring, Christopher, and Julie Hudson. *Silk in Africa*. London: British Museum Press, 2002.

Doran H. Ross

See also Tunisia; Niger; Chad.

Morocco

A well-known Moroccan proverb, "Eat according to your own taste but dress with the taste of others," demonstrates the important public role dress plays in this northwestern corner of Africa. The country of Morocco has long been a crossroads between Europe, the Middle East, and sub-Saharan Africa, and dress reflects the richness of its history as well as its geographic and cultural diversity. Morocco's geographic distance from the Middle East, its former conquest of Spain, its historical involvement in the trans-Saharan trade, and its ability to withstand Ottoman invasion distinguish it from other North African countries. In addition, 40 to 60 percent of the Moroccan population is Berber (also called *Imazighen*, meaning "the free people"), and many have retained the indigenous Berber language called Tamazight.

After the Phoenicians and then the Romans settled in Morocco and encountered the Berbers, Arabs moved into Morocco in the seventh century C.E., founding the city of Fes and gradually converting Berbers to Islam. Both Arab and Berber Muslim dynasties ruled Morocco during different time periods. The Moroccan cities of Fes, Rabat, Salé, Tetouan, and Marrakech as well as Seville and Granada in Islamic Spain became centers of learning and the arts, where textile and embroidery workshops flourished. However, until the early twentieth century, Morocco had a distinct rural character; approximately 85 percent of Moroccans lived in rural areas, where women wove from wool the majority of textiles needed for clothing and adorned themselves with tattoos and elaborate silver and amber jewelry. Berber weaving especially flourished in the mountainous regions of the country. While an ancient Jewish population lived in Morocco, the number of Jews increased after the fifteenth-century Catholic reconquest and the Inquisition forced both Muslims and Jews to flee Spain for Morocco, bringing weaving and jewelry-making techniques with them.

Despite ethnic and regional diversity, Moroccan dress in both rural and urban areas consisted of various styles of loose tunics and outer wraps created from handwoven fabrics and gold and silver jewelry primarily made by Jewish metalsmiths. In 1912, when Morocco became a French protectorate, handwoven cloth began to be associated with poverty, and imported cotton and other fabrics began to dominate dress in most regions of Morocco. In contemporary Morocco, dress allows people to express their religious beliefs, cultural heritage, and economic status, as older forms of dress exist side by side with Western-style shirts, trousers, suits, dresses, and sportswear.

CHILDREN'S DRESS

Women, especially in rural areas, dress their children to protect them from the evil eye. The *evil eye* can be described as a glance or look accompanied by a compliment that is connected with envy and covetousness. The evil eye can cause bad luck, illness, and even death. Because the first glance of a person is considered the most dangerous, children may wear pendants that represent animals considered repulsive, such as scorpions and snakes, to attract a negative first glance and prevent the person from being harmed. Children wear beaded necklaces made by their mothers that incorporate substances venerated for their protective powers, including amber, cowry shells, silver coins, and amulets. Amulets might be leather packets decorated with five cowry shells in a formation often referred to as a *khamsa*, meaning "five" in Arabic. The khamsa symbolizes the human hand, and the hand has the ability to deflect the negative energy of the evil eye. Five is also an important number because there are five obligations of Islam, and Muslims pray five times a day.

Children also wear amulets around their necks, wrists, and ankles filled with herbs and writing from the Qur'an to protect against the jinn. The *jinn* are capricious beings prone to mischief who live in passageways such as drains, wells, and doorways and

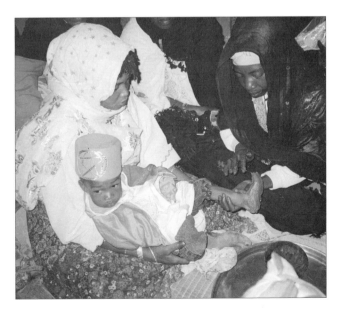

A young boy in Khamlia, southeastern Morocco, 1997, wears a green fez and cape and has his hands and feet adorned with henna in preparation for his circumcision. Photograph by Cynthia J. Becker.

prey on people passing through one phase in the life cycle to the next. Circumcision and marriage are two examples of a metaphorical passage.

An important moment in the life cycle for young boys is circumcision, and, for the occasion, boys wear ceremonial clothing and amulets believed to be protective. A boy is typically dressed in a white gown, a green cape, and a green fez, and women apply henna to his hands and feet the night before the ceremony. Moroccans associate the color green with Islam, and henna is believed to have *baraka*, or divine blessing. The henna is absorbed through the skin to infuse the body with positive healing energy, counteract pollution associated with bloodshed, and provide protection against the evil eye and the jinn.

Arab and Berber children in the rural south once commonly had their hair cut to mark gender difference. Boys and girls had their hair shaved except for a thin, vertical band of hair running from the front or center of the head to the nape of the neck. Boys sometimes wore a single lock that was braided, while girls also grew bangs.

FROM THE HAIK TO THE JELLABA

The *haik* (also called the *ksa*) is a draped outer garment once commonly worn by both men and women made from a large rectangle of white wool that was sometimes striped with silk. It is five to six meters (sixteen to twenty feet) long and almost two meters (six and a half feet) wide. The haik would be wrapped around the body and head and thrown over one shoulder so it enveloped the arms. Some scholars stress the antiquity of this garment and trace its origins to ancient Greece or Rome.

A man often wore the haik draped over his jellaba. A *jellaba* consists of a short- or long-sleeved outer garment with a hood and slits at the front, bottom, and sides. The antiquity of this garment is unknown, but the jellaba of the nineteenth and early twentieth centuries had wider sleeves and a larger hood than the contemporary version. Considerable regional variation is demonstrated by the various fabrics and forms of the men's jellaba. In rural areas, women formerly wove jellaba for their husbands and sons, commonly using black, brown, or beige wool and sometimes adding hints of bright colors to create a solid-colored or striped jellaba. In the Rif Mountains, Berber men wore a knee-length jellaba with short sleeves. In southeastern Morocco, the jellaba worn by Berber men was sometimes slit up the front so that it resembled a cape. The side panels could be flipped over the shoulders so that a man did not have to put his arms through the sleeves and had more freedom of movement. Tailors have been making the jellaba from imported fabrics since the beginning of the twentieth century, but in Fes, some workshops continue to weave jellaba fabric from imported silk and wool with the addition of locally spun wool thread sometimes called *hubub* (meaning "grains") or *couscous* because its rough irregular texture resembles the grains of this national dish.

Until the 1950s, the outerwear of urban women consisted of wrapping themselves in a haik and covering the bottom half of their faces with a piece of fine, translucent cloth called *litham*. In most rural areas, Berber and Arab women did not drape themselves with layers of cloth when leaving their homes, because the heavy work loads and manual labor performed by rural women made this cumbersome and impractical.

In the 1950s, women began to make the transition from the haik to the jellaba, modifying the men's jellaba for themselves but using brighter colors and synthetic fabrics with the addition of

A woman in urban Essaouira visits the market wearing a *jellaba* (Morocco, 2000). The adoption of the *jellaba* coincided with the increased public mobility of women and became a symbol of modernity. Photograph by Cynthia J. Becker.

colorful embroidery and a tassel at the end of the hood. Women sometimes wore the jellaba hood draped over their heads and covered their faces with litham. The adoption of the jellaba by women coincided with the increased public mobility of women and became a symbol of modernity. Today the jellaba has been elevated to a symbol of national dress for both men and women, but women wear it more frequently than men.

Although the women's haik has almost disappeared, different versions continue to be worn in Essaouira, Taroudant, and the Tafilalet oasis. For example, Arab women in the Tafilalet oasis wear dark-colored fabric (considered to be more modest than white), draping the fabric to cover their entire bodies and exposing only one eye. This conservative style of covering is due to the large numbers of *shurfa*, people who trace their ancestry to the Prophet Mohammed. These women pride themselves in their strict style of covering, which they believe reflects the practices of the Prophet Mohammed and inspires a high level of respect. Berbers in the region adopted their own version of the Arab head covering but "Berberized" it with the addition of colorful embroidery and silver-colored sequins.

SELHAM AND OTHER MEN'S GARMENTS

The *selham* is an outer garment worn by men that can be described as a full, sleeveless cloak with a hood often decorated with a large silk tassel at its end. The front is open, but a small sewn band about fifteen centimeters (six inches) long closes the cape over the breastbone. In urban areas, the selham would be made from finely woven white or dark-colored wool, while in rural areas, men often wore coarser brown wool. In the Siroua Mountains, Berber and Jewish men wore a type of selham called an *akhnif*. The akhnif was made from dark brown or black wool decorated with a long elliptical design woven with red or yellow wool interpreted as a protective eye motif. While Muslim Berber men wore the striking eyelike decoration facing the exterior, Jewish men wore theirs inside as a sign of their difference.

Urban men, especially merchants, also wore a suit called a *keswa del mahsour* made of baggy trousers (*serwal*), two waistcoats, and a jacket often decorated with embroidery. The serwal were very wide at the waist and tight at the calves, with a seat hanging very low behind and drawn in at the waist with a cord. Men in urban areas wore fez hats with a pointed or flat top made of red wool with a black tassel attached to the crown. Berber men living in the Rif and Middle Atlas Mountains wore a wide rectangular garment with slits for the arms and a rounded neckline (*gandora*) made from handwoven wool over their serwal while working. Until the mid-twentieth century, Zemmour Berber men in the Middle Atlas region of Morocco commonly wore wide hats (*taraza*) woven from reed or esparto grass and lavishly decorated with wool embroidery, mirrors, sequins, and multicolored tassels. Men in the deep south near Goulmime, the gateway to the Sahara, and the Draa Valley wear clothing similar to Mauritanians that includes large flowing tunics made of white or blue cotton cloth with massive turbans, baggy serwal, and leather amulets around their necks. Throughout Morocco, men commonly wore yellow leather shoes with pointed toes and the back of the heel folded forward into the shoe where the heel of the foot rests.

The turban (*rezza* in Arabic and *arezziy* in Tamazight) has a long history in Morocco and is historically associated with Berbers. Men from the Almoravid dynasty, a Muslim Berber dynasty that ruled Morocco and Spain in the eleventh and twelfth centuries, were known for their turbans that covered the lower halves of their faces. In southern regions of Morocco, both Berber and Arab men wear turbans made from long, thin pieces of white or blue fabric. A man winds his turban around the crown of his head several times, sometimes wrapping one fold across the entire face, leaving a narrow slit for the eyes. Turbans carry important social meanings, symbolizing honor, dignity, and respect. If a man has been dishonored, people will say that his turban has fallen. Although fewer and fewer men wear the turban on a daily basis, it continues to be worn during important ceremonial occasions, such as weddings.

In the early twentieth century, men living in both urban and rural areas carried daggers. Daggers were contained in engraved silver or metal cases that were often embedded with decorative stones such as amber. A man wore his dagger on a silk cord draped across his chest so he could easily reach it. Three different types of daggers existed in the different regions of Morocco: the *sboula* with a straight blade, the *khanjer* with a heavy curved blade, and the *koummiya* with a long curved blade. Daggers are no longer part of a man's daily dress, but Arab and Berber grooms often wear daggers as part of their ceremonial dress. Men also wore leather satchels (*shkara* in Arabic and *akrab* in Tamazight), typically decorated with embroidery, draped diagonally across the body on a cord.

WOMEN'S WOOL SHAWLS

Berber women throughout Morocco once commonly wore flat-woven wool shawls (called *handira* in Arabic and *taghnast* in Tamazight) draped over their shoulders that measured approximately two and a half meters (eight feet) wide by one and a half meters (five feet) long. Shawl styles varied from region to region but typically featured vertical bands of solid-colored wool that was sometimes interspersed with bands of intricate geometric patterns, tufts of wool, and silver-colored sequins. In some areas of the Middle Atlas Mountains, women owned both simple everyday shawls and elaborate ceremonial shawls with complicated woven patterns that often required two years to complete. A woman first wore her ceremonial shawl during her wedding ceremony, when she rode a mule from her birth home to her husband's home. She guarded her shawl during her lifetime and often used it as a bed covering for honored guests; her shawl was draped over her body after her death.

Berber women in the south and the High Atlas Mountains wore finely woven wool shawls that were simply decorated with alternating red, blue, black, or white vertical stripes enlivened with small touches of green and yellow. Beni Ouarain Berber women often wore thick two-sided shawls with tightly woven patterned bands on one side and five- to seven-centimeter- (two- to three-inch) long wool loops on the other side to form bands of shag. Women considered this the more attractive side of the shawl and usually wore it shag side out, but the shag side worn inside during wet or cold weather provided much-needed insulation.

Berber women continue to weave shawls for the tourist market, and, in some areas, such as among the Ait Haddidou Berbers of the High Atlas, the shawl continues to be worn on a daily basis. Women prepare, spin, and weave local wool and once used natural materials to dye it, such as cochineal, madder, indigo, and henna. Around 1900, natural dyes were replaced by chemical ones. The dense geometric motifs that adorned women's shawls in some regions resembled those woven into Berber rugs, saddle coverings, and other textiles. Textile motifs do not have a specific representational value. Women name them after plants and animals present in the natural environment that not only resemble the geometric textile patterns but also suggest fertility and protection. For example, some motifs suggest fertility, such as a palm tree, a stalk of wheat, and bird tracks. Women named other patterns after sharp objects and animals considered dangerous and repulsive, such as the lion's paw, serpent, saw, tarantula, and sickle. These motifs protected against the evil eye.

THE CAFTAN AND ITS ACCESSORIES

A *caftan* can be best described as a long gown with wide sleeves and no collar. The origin of the caftan is unknown, but some scholars suggest a Turkish origin, and some evidence suggests that it was worn in Andalusian Spain prior to the rise of Ottoman power in the Mediterranean. Until the early twentieth century, male scholars and high-ranking male officials living in urban Morocco wore the caftan. Urban women once wore the caftan on a daily basis over wide ankle-length serwal; however, since the end of the twentieth century, both urban and rural women primarily wear the caftan during ceremonial occasions.

A woman hires a tailor to create her caftan from expensive brightly colored silk, velvet, or brocade fabric decorated with gold embroidery and braided trim. A row of small round handmade buttons typically lines the entire front of the garment. In the nineteenth century, women purchased fabric from weavers in Lyon, France. These French weavers originally made brocade fabrics for use as Christian religious vestments, and, when the market died in Europe, they specifically targeted the Moroccan market. Some families in Fes also weave slightly modified versions of French brocade patterns on draw looms; Fes is one of the few cities of the world where the draw loom remains viable.

Gold and silver embroidery, a specialty of Fes and Tetouan, is often used to decorate caftans and backless velvet shoes (typically flat with a pointed toe) called *cherbil*. Women who are commissioned by male tailors do embroidery work in their homes and tend to specialize in embroidered caftans, vests, and belts.

Rear view of a Berber woman's embroidered headcovering from southeastern Morocco, 2004. The traditional *haik* headcovering has been adapted by Berbers in some regions to include sequins and colorful embroidery. Photograph by Addi Ouadderrou.

Men embroider leather bags and shoes. Women place patterns made from paper cutouts under dark-colored fabric and use small stitches to couch the gold thread to create scrolling floral patterns. Jewish men locally manufactured gold and silver thread but today it has been replaced by imported thread.

In the early twentieth century, urban women also wore a garment over their caftan made from sheer white fabric that mimicked the cut of the caftan called a *mensoria* or a *dfina*. The elaborate caftan underneath showed through the front and side slits of the overgarment. Until the mid-twentieth century, the caftan was not only ceremonial garb but was also worn by urban women on a daily basis. They would pull back the wide sleeves and sheer mensoria with a sleeve holder called a *tahmal*, which was made of a long, thick cord decorated with trimmings of gold thread. Women looped the cord into a figure eight and placed their arms through it.

Women belted their caftans at the waist. Belts came in various shapes and sizes, but the most prestigious belts were the stiff brocaded silk and metallic thread belts from Fes made on the draw loom. The Fes belt, rarely worn today, was around three to four meters (ten to thirteen feet) long and forty centimeters (sixteen inches) wide. Belts had at least two identical designs woven in contrasting colors, allowing the belt to be worn several different ways depending on how it was wrapped and tied. Designs were inspired by Islamic architectural forms, medieval Spanish decorative arts, heraldic motifs, paisley and floral designs, and Japanese- and Chinese-inspired patterns. Eight-pointed stars and khamsa on the edges of Fes belts may have been apotropaic.

WOMEN'S DRAPED GARMENTS

Until the mid-twentieth century, most rural Berber and Arab women wore draped garments called *izour* or *lizour* (singular, *izar* or *lizar*) on a daily basis that scholars often compare to ancient Greek or Roman dress. The izar is made from a piece of fabric measuring three meters by one and a half meters (ten by five feet). Women wrap it around their bodies and hold it together at the shoulders with two silver pins or fibulae and a belt around the waist. Today fibulae are rare, and women knot the fabric at their shoulders. Until the 1960s, women also attached a piece of tie-dyed, embroidered, or appliquéd cloth over their backs and shoulders to protect their izour from henna or other perfumed herbs worn in the hair.

In the Middle Atlas region, Berber women wore elaborate belts made from silk and wool called *taggoust*. Women decorated the belt with mirrors, silver coins, and cowry shells plus a long fringe that ended with red tassels. In the Siroua Mountains, Berber women wore long belts with tapestry-woven designs and long knotted fringe. In the Rif Mountains until the end of the nineteenth century, Berber women wrapped tie-dyed belts (*kourzia*) around their white wool izour. Today a Berber woman from the Rif wears two pieces of red and white fabric (one over the skirts of her dresses and another over her shoulders to be used as a carrying cloth), a tie-dyed belt, and a wide-brimmed straw hat.

The method of draping the izar and the type of fabric used varied from region to region. Berber women typically wore izour made from plain handwoven white wool, except for Ida ou Nadif Berber women in the central Anti-Atlas Mountains, who wore white wool garments (*afaggou*) whose edges and corners were embellished with brightly colored woven and hand-embroidered geometric motifs enhanced with painted henna patterns. They then draped their heads with white wool head scarves (*adrar*) embellished with intricate designs on three sides, painted henna patterns, and large pom-poms at the corners. In the southern slopes of the Anti-Atlas and in the deep south, women preferred indigo-dyed fabric. Indigo gave the skin a bluish tinge that, in addition to its pleasant smell, conditioned the skin and improved the complexion.

By the beginning of the twentieth century, imported cotton, rather than wool, was used to create the izar. Until the 1960s, most Berber women did not wear garments under the izour, often exposing their bare bodies underneath. Berber women in the mountainous regions of Morocco wore wool leggings knitted by men. They also wore leather sandals to protect them from the region's cold winter temperatures; the sandals were colorfully decorated with embroidered designs and had high or low heels. Berber men and women also wore sandals made of a dried hide sole held to the foot through cords made of palm fronds.

Arab women in the southern oases wore long-sleeved, ankle-length polyester dresses and long cotton fabric pants with elastic waistbands (serwal) modeled after urban Moroccan fashions under their izour. By the mid-twentieth century, Berber women began to wear similar garments under their izour, and, by the end of the century, the izar fell out of fashion and was only worn during ceremonial occasions.

WOMEN'S JEWELRY AND HAIRSTYLES

Jews dominated the metal-working industry in Morocco, probably due to the Islamic prohibition of usury and the popular belief that working with fire exposed one to the wrath of the jinn. In addition to the jewelry given to them by their husbands during their weddings, Berber women often saved up silver coins and older pieces of silver jewelry that would be melted down by jewelers to create new jewelry for themselves and their unmarried daughters. This jewelry served as a woman's portable bank account and could be sold in times of financial duress.

Women from the cities of Fes, Tetouan, and Meknes preferred gold to silver and wore gold jewelry embellished with diamonds, rubies, emeralds, and seed pearls. In mid-twentieth-century Fes, for example, women typically wore gold filigree jewelry that included a circular pendant on the forehead (twelve centimeters [five inches] long) with a guilloche interlace pattern embellished with diamonds and hanging pendants, long oval-shaped dangling earrings, necklaces made from small gold coins, and a necklace with a large khamsa pendant to deflect the evil eye.

Women throughout Morocco pinned their izour at the shoulders with two fibulae linked by a chain called *tiseghnas*. The fibulae consisted of a pin with a ring decorated with coins or triangular pendants. In the Anti-Atlas Mountains, Berber women wore enormous triangular fibulae that could be as long as thirty centimeters (twelve inches). The fibulae were attached to a chain that ended with a silver egg (*tagmout*) or an amulet in the form of a square box. The entire grouping was decorated with yellow and green enamel work.

Arab and Berber women created voluminous hairstyles that they covered with scarves, fabric cords, and silver and bead pendants. In the rural south and the High Atlas Mountains, the length and thickness of a woman's hair was associated with fertility. Both Arab and Berber women wrapped their hair around balls of wool thread and applied henna and aged butter to structurally reinforce their hairstyles. Ait Morghad Berber women living in the High Atlas braided their hair and wrapped their braids around wool pads, turning the braids back and upwards to symmetrically frame their faces. The hairstyle was then topped with a silk scarf and ornaments that included a pendant made from silver chains (*isensirn*) and two convex silver disks or other pendants arranged on top of each of the braids near the temple. On special occasions, women applied a perfumed paste made from pounded myrtle leaves to their hairstyles and decorated their hair with orange and yellow smudges made from ground saffron and dried pomegranate skins.

Berber women in the Anti-Atlas region wore diadems consisting of a band of silver or leather to which they attached enameled and niello silver pendants, amber and coral beads, and silver coins. Women also wore earrings made from large hollow silver rings decorated with glass beads, circular niello plaques, silver coins, coral and amber beads, and cowry shells. Due to their heavy weight, women usually did not insert the earrings into their earlobes but attached them to their diadems with leather cords or hooked to them to their hair; they covered the entire ensemble with a piece of cloth draped over their heads.

Women also wore necklaces whose designs varied from region to region. In the Anti-Atlas, Berber women's massive necklaces consisted of large amber, coral and glass beads, pieces of silver money, cowry shells, conus shell whorls, and a large ball of silver or an enameled amulet. Married Berber women of the southeast wore necklaces made from massive beads of amber (from the Balkans) or less expensive copal, ambroid, Bakelite, or casein (*tazra n lluban*) and heavy silver bracelets called *izbian n iqerroin*, meaning "bracelets of animal horns." These consisted of a series of twelve triangular points that radiate from a central band. A woman wore two of these (one on each arm) with another wide silver bracelet and a thin circle of leather between them to prevent her skin from being pinched.

Women living in the Saharan areas near Goulmime and the Draa Valley dress in a style similar to Mauritanian women. Women style their hair into a series of long thin braids (horsehair may be added to increase their length) to which they attach beads and shell pendants. Women also create a headpiece from leather, canvas, or horsehair adorned with amber, carnelian, glass, silver, and shell beads that they attach to their heads with a wire framework. This time-consuming hairstyle is worn for almost two months before it is redone. When women perform the *guedra* dance, they show off their hairstyles and swing their long braids back and forth. Saharan women also wear a long strand of wooden beads inlaid with silver, necklaces with silver cross pendants, silver fibulae attached to indigo-dyed or light blue izar, silver bracelets ornamented with small studs around their diameter, and engraved silver anklets.

TATTOOS

Tattoos thrived primarily in rural areas, and, until the mid-twentieth century, when a girl reached puberty, her mother, aunts, or family friends would tattoo her face, forearms, hands, ankles, and lower legs. Today most people believe that tattoos permanently alter the body, and Islamic tradition prohibits anything that permanently changes God's perfect creation. Furthermore,

An Ait Atta bride has her face painted with saffron and wears a headdress with hornlike projections on the final day of the wedding ceremony in a nomadic camp on the outskirts of Merzouga, Morocco, 1997. Photograph by Cynthia J. Becker.

people believe tattoos stop water from penetrating into the skin; hence they render ineffective the ritual ablutions proscribed before daily prayer.

Nonetheless, tattooing was an important art form practiced by Moroccan women for centuries. As described by various writers, the techniques used appear to have been basically the same all over Morocco. Women would draw the tattoo design on the skin with charcoal or pot-black, the soot that is deposited on the bottom of a cooking pot, then prick the design onto the skin with a pointed object and apply alfalfa or another material to give the design a greenish color. Berber tattoos from the Middle Atlas

region of Morocco were among the most intricate. Always sym metrical, tattoos rose up in rows from the ankle to the lower le and from the top of the hand to the forearm. Small boys and girl were sometimes tattooed on the tip of their noses or their cheek to cure them of illness.

Women of the same generation and living in the same regio often had similar tattoos. Tattoo, textile, and ceramic motifs re sembled each other, demonstrating that tattoos were gendere symbols of women's creative powers. In recent years, henna ha replaced tattoos as a method of decorating the female body an celebrating womanhood.

A Gnawa man in Essaouira, Morocco, 2003, plays metal cymbals and wears a black sash and wool headdress adorned with cowry shells during possession-trance ceremonies. His blue robe indicates his affiliation with the spirit Sidi Moussa, who is associated with the ocean. Photograph by Cynthia J. Becker.

HENNA AND NATURAL MAKEUP

Cultivated in southern Morocco, the use of henna is widespread. Women pound dried green henna leaves, mix them with water, and apply the resulting paste to their skin. Henna stains the skin a color that ranges from deep orange to almost black. Women typically mix henna with sweet-smelling herbs or orange blossom water to mask henna's earthy, pungent scent. People especially appreciate the cool, soothing quality of henna and enjoy applying it to their hair during hot summer months. In fact, the use of henna brings so much pleasure that women refrain from using it during Ramadan. Women and men also value henna's healing properties, and, because people believe that it strengthens their bones and teeth, they apply it to sprained ankles and wrists. Henna also protects and heals the skin, and men use it to heal their chapped hands. Besides its practical applications, henna's association with baraka (divine blessing) means that it is used during ceremonial occasions and rites of passage to guard against danger and impurity. Until the mid-twentieth century, Berber women in the central Anti-Atlas also enhanced the decoration of their white wool izour and head scarves with henna patterns.

The application of henna has become one of the central features of almost all Moroccan wedding ceremonies. In many areas, henna is applied by a professional *neggafa*, or makeup artist, who may spend as many as eight hours decorating the bride's hands and feet with intricate lacelike designs inspired by Indian henna patterns and Moroccan textile, jewelry, and tattoo motifs. To create decorative lacelike patterns, henna is mixed with water and placed into a syringe. Women break the tip of the needle to create thin lines on the surface of the skin. After application of henna to the hands and feet, they are placed over hot coals to harden the henna. Sugar water is then applied to hold the henna in place, and the designs are further protected by wrapping the hands and feet in cotton or another cloth to keep the henna from flaking off and ensuring that it dyes the skin well.

In rural areas of southern Morocco, henna plays a less central role in the bride's adornment; a woman uses her index finger to quickly smear henna on the bride's palms and soles; for them, the auspicious nature of henna is more important than the patterns themselves.

In addition to henna, women throughout Morocco outline their eyes and sometimes their eyebrows with kohl, a silvery gray powder made from antimony sulfide. Kohl not only gives the impression of dark black eyes and eyelashes but also cleanses the eyes of impurities. Men also outline their eyes with kohl to protect them from the glare of the sun. During ceremonial occasions, women once commonly outlined their faces with orange-colored ground saffron and painted small geometric patterns on their foreheads, cheeks, and eyes with handmade black paint called *harqus*. Women also chewed on bitter morsels of walnut root to brighten and dye their gums a bright orange color, and they perfumed their clothes with the smoke of incense, activating the senses of taste and smell.

WOMEN'S WEDDING DRESS

Wedding dress in Morocco signifies a change in status from adolescent to adult. Women dominate wedding ceremonies, and each bride has a unique style of dress that varies from region to region. Wedding dress for the elite of Fes includes numerous layers of expensive handwoven brocade fabric. The bride also wears necklaces of seed pearls, jade, and gold and has bunches of pearls hanging from the side of her head and face. Her face is painted with small red and white dots, and she wears a very heavy gold diadem on her head. The bride sits on a mass of pillows and in front of gold-embroidered wall decorations. Red and gold brocade fabric, positioned to resemble sleeves, is pinned to the decorations behind her so that her entire form, except for her face, is hidden, and she is transformed into a splendid display of wealth and opulence.

In the rural south, Ait Atta Berber brides wear silver and amber jewelry given to them by their husbands that, until the mid-twentieth century, they wore on a daily basis to mark their marital status. In case of divorce, a woman returns the jewelry to her husband, and if money is needed, jewelry is sold to provide for the family. The Ait Atta bride also wears a red cloth over her face with two hornlike projections at the top (*aâbroq*) during the four-day wedding ceremony, only revealing her face painted with ground saffron and harqus on the final day of the wedding. A woman brushes the bride's hair with sweet-smelling myrtle (*rihan*) and ties small packages of perfumed herbs and cloves into her white izar to please her husband and to pacify the jinn, protecting her during this rite of passage.

Throughout Morocco, contemporary brides dress in seven to ten different exquisite outfits during their three- to four-day wedding ceremonies that draw from many ethnicities and social groups. The bride hires a neggafa to organize and manage the entire wedding, performing a role that would have been done by the bride's female relatives in the past. The neggafa typically rents the elaborate Fes wedding costume to the bride, even if the bride is not from Fes. The neggafa also dresses the bride in numerous finely made caftans, a stereotypical Berber wedding outfit, an Indian sari, and a Western-style wedding dress. As gender roles change and more Moroccan women enter the workforce, the non-elite bride's ability to purchase these expensive outfits and hire female professionals indicates her earning power. The bride becomes a commodity and consumer on display rather than a gift in a marriage transaction hidden beneath layers of cloth.

JEWISH WOMEN'S DRESS

Much of Jewish daily dress resembled Muslim dress, as men wore dark blue and black jellaba and the akhnif. As early as the 1930s, Jewish women living in the urban areas of Morocco wore ready-made European style dresses. Jewish brides, however, guarded their own particular style of ceremonial dress called *keswa el-kbira*, meaning "great costume." Originating in Spain, the garment was carried by Jews who settled in northern Moroccan cities in the fifteenth century. Although each town had its own particular cut, embroidery style, and color, this velvet outfit was basically the same from city to city. Given to a bride by her father, it consisted of a floor-length wraparound skirt with gold embroidery, a lavishly decorated low-cut jacket, detachable long wide sleeves, and an embroidered frontispiece with a wide belt. Embroidery often featured large spiral designs thought to represent the sun or infinity and belief in the afterlife. Women wore this dress after their weddings for religious festivals and special occasions. The bride's hair was covered with a wig made of cloth, thread, or horsehair and topped with a pearl and precious stone–encrusted diadem and fringed silk scarf. According to the Talmud, Jewish women were forbidden from showing their hair after marriage, but, in early-twentieth-century Morocco, urban Jewish women only followed this proscription during weddings. The keswa el-kbira captured the imagination of European painters, such as Eugène Delacroix and Alfred Dehodencq, who painted Jewish women wearing this outfit. Until the mid-twentieth century, married Jewish women also wore their keswa el-kbira on ceremonial occasions.

While women in urban Morocco only wore wigs during ceremonial occasions, married Jewish women in the south wore wigs on a daily basis that they made of cow hair, ostrich feathers, or wool adorned with silk scarves and silver and gold pendants. Jewish dress in southern Morocco shared many aspects of dress with rural-dwelling Berbers and Arabs, but one of the most interesting hairstyles existed in Erfoud, where women wore hairstyles called *grun*, meaning "horns." A woman created this hairstyle by placing two pieces of wool on either side of her head that she covered with several bands of brocaded and silk cloth to create the impression of two projecting horns. This headdress was possibly linked to the talisman of the horn as protection against the evil eye. It also resembled the hornlike headdress worn by Berber brides in the region, demonstrating how dress mixed across ethnic and religious boundaries.

Most Jewish people in Morocco immigrated to Israel after independence from French colonialism in 1956. Today approximately sixty-five hundred Jews remain in Morocco, and dress such as the keswa el-kbira has disappeared.

GNAWA CEREMONIAL DRESS

The Gnawa are descendents of enslaved Sudanic Africans in Morocco who cure illnesses through possession by spiritual entities they call *mlouk*. Gnawa hold possession-trance ceremonies where they evoke the spirits through specific forms of dress, color symbolism, dance, incense, and rhythms played on musical instruments of Sudanic origin. Each spirit is represented by a particular color and style of clothing that is worn by a follower of the spirit during possession. For example, people possessed by the spirit of Sidi Hamou, the spirit associated with blood and animal sacrifice, wear red tunics and dance with knives in their hands under trance. In urban areas, Gnawa male musicians who perform for possession-trance ceremonies often wear wool headdresses decorated with long wool fringe, cowry shells, and beads. These headdresses stylistically resemble hats worn by those with special spiritual status in Sudanic Africa, such as Bamana hunters or those initiated to certain Fulani spirits during Hausa possession-trance ceremonies called *bori*. Gnawa men may also wear red fez-style hats and black sashes across their waists adorned with cowries inspired by the military dress worn by *Tirailleurs Sénégalais*, French colonial foot soldiers recruited from West and Central Africa. Gnawa urban ceremonial dress demonstrates the rich cross-fertilization and interweaving between religions and philosophies that occurred across the Sahara.

TWENTIETH-CENTURY INNOVATIONS

Although it is common to see men in their fifties and sixties proudly wearing the jellaba, since the mid-twentieth century, young men began to abandon this style of dress, first in urban and then in rural areas, for European-inspired pants and shirts. Increased educational opportunities for both men and women are reflected in their styles of dress, especially female dress. Women who wish to show their devotion to Islam often wear the loose-fitting jellaba or the *hijab*, a general term given to Islamic women's clothing that covers the shape of the female body. The hijab commonly includes a head scarf, a large long-sleeved shirt, and a long skirt or pants. Although daily dress continues to change for Moroccan women, the caftan remains the preferred garment for ceremonial occasions such as weddings, and most women will buy one new caftan each year. In the 1960s and 1970s, the sleeves of the caftan became more narrow, probably due to the influence of European-style clothing, but this style changed in the 1980s, when young female designers such as Tami Tazi and Fadilah Berrada began to experiment with traditional dress and combine it with their training in Western fashion. Tazi, for example, replaces the voluminous shape of the caftan that was designed to mask a woman's body for one that emphasizes the female silhouette, and she revived interest in centuries-old embroidery and bell-shaped sleeves of the past. Some designers such as Nourreddine Amire, reject imported fabrics completely for locally made ones. These designers have established a Moroccan haute couture that caters to the Moroccan elite. In the mid-1990s, women's fashion magazines, such as *Femme du Maroc*, firs appeared and began featuring the haute couture caftan, influencing the fashion trends of the general public. The materials, cuts, colors, and styles of the caftan now change with each season, and Moroccan designers hope that their garments will inspire fashion outside of the country.

References and Further Reading

Alaoui, Rachida. "The Caftan Revival." *Revue Noire* 33/34 (1999): 28–33.

Becker, Cynthia. *Amazigh Arts in Morocco: Women Shaping Berber Identity*. Austin: University of Texas Press, 2006.

Besancenot, Jean. *Costumes of Morocco*. London: Kegan Paul International Limited, 1990.

Bynon, James. "Berber Women's Pottery: Is the Decoration Motivated?" In *Colloquies on Art & Archaeology in Asia No. 12*, edited by J. Picton, 136–161. London: University of London, 1984.

Combs-Schilling, M. Elaine. *Sacred Performances: Islam, Sexuality and Sacrifice*. New York: Columbia University Press, 1989.

Forelli, Sally, and Jeanette Harries. "Traditional Berber Weaving in Central Morocco." *Textile Museum Journal* 4, no. 4 (1977): 41–60.

Jereb, James. *Arts and Crafts of Morocco*. London: Thames and Hudson, 1995.

Kapchan, Deborah A. "Moroccan Women's Body Signs." In *Bodylore*, edited by Katharine Young, 3–34. Knoxville: University of Tennessee Press, 1993.

Kapchan, Deborah A. *Gender on the Market: Moroccan Women and the Revoicing of Tradition*. Philadelphia: University of Pennsylvania Press, 1996.

Korolnik-Andersch, Annette, and Marcel Korolnik. *The Color of Henna: Painted Textiles from Southern Morocco*. Stuttgart, Germany: Arnoldsche Art Publishers, 2002.

Liu, Robert K., and Liza Wataghani. "Moroccan Folk Jewelry." *African Arts* 8, no. 2 (1975): 28–35, 80.

Mann, Vivian B., ed. *Morocco: Jews and Art in a Muslim Land*. New York: Merrell, in association with the Jewish Museum, 2000.

Morin-Barde, Mireille. *Coiffures féminines du Maroc*. Aix-en-Provence, France: Édisud, 1990.

Paydar, Niloo Imami, and Ivo Grammet. *The Fabric of Moroccan Life*. Indianapolis, IN: Indianapolis Museum of Art, 2002.

Spring, Christopher, and Julie Hudson. *North African Textiles*. London: British Museum Press, 1995.

Stack, Lotus. "A Wedding at Fez: Textiles in Transition." *Saudi Aramco World* 44, no. 3 (May/June 1993): 28–33.

Stillman, Yedida Kalfon. *Themes in Islamic Studies*. Vol. 2, *Arab Dress: A Short History from the Dawn of Islam to Modern Times*, edited by Norman A. Stillman. Leiden, The Netherlands: Brill, 2000.

Stone, Caroline. *The Embroideries of North Africa*. Burnt Mill, Harlow, Essex, UK: Longman, 1985.

Cynthia J. Becker

Tunisia

Tunisia has a population of ten million, lies on the Mediterranean Sea, and is bordered by Libya and Algeria. The earliest inhabitants were the Imazighen, who spoke Berber languages; predated the Phoenicians who founded Carthage; and were followed by the Romans, Vandals, Byzantines, and Arabs. In 1576, the Muslim Ottoman Empire annexed Tunisia, but in 1881, the area fell to the French, who maintained control until independence in 1956. All of these shifts in Tunisia's social, economic, and political environment had a dramatic impact on traditions of dress.

HISTORY

Earlier evidence concerning dress of the Imazighen provides skimpy data from sparse archaeological discoveries or scattered passages by writers such as the Greek historian Herodotus (ca. 484–425 B.C.E.) describing Imazighen life. Links to Greece are indicated in Jerba, southern Tunisia, where Imazighen women wear a dress like that on a statue found in Tanagra, Greece, from the classical Greek era (fourth century B.C.E.) along with a pointed straw hat, found in the Moroccan Atlas Mountains as well as commonly worn by Imazighen women in Jerba, southern Tunisia. Until the early seventh century C.E., Imazighen women wore a draped dress like the Greek chiton and the Roman toga fastened with silver fibulae and a woolen or leather sash wrapped around the waist.

In the midst of all these successive occupations, the Imazighen, wanting to regain control of their land, made a strategy of allying with the enemy of their enemy—for example, with the Carthaginians against Rome or vice versa. By the end of the third and last Punic War, Carthage was annexed to Rome, thus creating the province of Africa (or Ifrykia, the name later given to the continent by the Arabs). The Arabs brought Islam to Tunisia and influenced local dress and life. Islam carried notions of equality, justice, and modesty, and dress reflected this. Modesty dictated that men avoid gold, silk, and velvet and required that both inner garments and loose-fitting outer ones cover the body. The Arabs also introduced royal embroidery schools called *tiraz*, where elaborate stitched patterns from the Arabian peninsula were taught. For centuries, these embroideries gave Tunisian and North African clothing a distinctive look.

These embroideries were enriched with the influence of other empires that conquered Tunisia. The Ottomans conquered all of North Africa, interspersed with fierce Berber outbursts and even Ottomans fighting among themselves. Finally, the Ottomans gained control for more than three hundred years, until the French took over in the early eighteenth century. In general, the various subregions of North Africa share a common history related to dress from the prehistoric era until the period of Ottoman domination. An important influence on dress occurred during the sixteenth century, when Muslims and Jews fled Spain during the Spanish Inquisition. Textile and clothing production became Tunisia's second-largest industry after agriculture during the late nineteenth century. Both men and women produced clothing—men, for commercial sale, and women, for domestic use (usually a wife clothed her family, and a bride-to-be prepared her own trousseau, embroidering wrappers and blankets). Most textiles and garments were locally consumed, but some

A man wearing a traditional Tunisian hat known as a *chechia*, worn throughout Tunisia from before the 1800s into the twenty-first century. Manufacture of *chechias*, largely for export, continues into the twenty-first century. Photograph by Mary Eastman.

were exported. By the end of the nineteenth century, Imazighen, Turks, Arabs, Moors from Spain, and Europeans dressed distinctively but borrowed designs and techniques from each other. Rural women made wool garments for household use, beginning with carding wool to spinning, dyeing, weaving, and sewing. An exception was in the production of *chechia*, a headdress for men produced for sale in other northern African countries and Europe. Another exception was that urban women excelled at making fine embroidery on both silk and cotton using a technique called *chebka*, which was in great demand in Europe. Urban men wove and sold silk and cotton textiles and sold wool products.

MALE DRESS

Scholars have paid very little attention to the dress of Tunisian men, focusing on women's wedding dress because of its richness and diversity. Young boys, young men, and older men all dressed alike based on their cultural heritage. A male ensemble consisted of head cover, outer and inner garments, and shoes. The chechia, a hat for men made of fine red wool and usually featuring a black tassel, was produced locally or imported from Spain. It was dyed red with cochineal and kermes. Usually the tassel, falling to the shoulders, was of deep blue or black silk. Tunisian production of this item greatly increased with the arrival of Muslims from Spain and the Turkish rulers' encouragement of production and export to enhance the economy. In 1865, exports of chechia were second after olive oil, with wool and cotton third. Markets in Europe and Asia looked for the Tunisian trademark as a sign of quality. In fact, many "Turkish" fezzes were produced in Tunis and sold in Constantinople and were called "Tunsy" to distinguish them from those produced in Turkey or southern France (where cheap knockoffs were mass-produced). Islamic and Jewish traditions decreed that men's heads be covered, and Tunisian men followed the practice , which varied only in the different styles of wearing the chechia: Muslims centered it on the head, and the Jews tilted it back. Both urban and rural Muslims wrapped a turban around it as a sign of religious piety, imitating the style popular among religious leaders or educators. Another head cover, the *arrakya*, is smaller, crocheted of white cotton, and worn for prayer inside the house or under the chechia in winter when in public. In summer, men wear an arrakya made of woven cotton, similar in size to the chechia.

The *mdhalla*, a straw hat, also differs in shape depending on geographical area and tribal affiliation. In the west and on the island of Jerba, they are often round and simple. Oversized examples decorated with short woolen tassels of different colors are worn by men in cities bordering Libya to the south and Algeria to the west. Short tassels are hallmarks of Imazighen dress for both men and women. Farmers only remove their mdhalla when going inside. As a symbol of hard work, the mdhalla was placed by farmers on top of their chechia or arrakya. In general, this head covering was synonymous throughout the country with the word *fellah* (farmer), a term later used by French settlers to suggest ignorance and backwardness.

Outer garments included the *barnous*, a cloak made of fine wool, camel hair, or a mixture of both. The finest wool ensures easy movement. The Tunisian scholar Ibn Kalhdoun, (1332–1406 C.E.), contrasted the *Baranis* ("wearers of the barnous") with the *Butr* ("wearers of short dress"), who showed their legs. To make a

An Imazighen woman wearing a separate head shawl, a *houli* (the red undergarment covering from the shoulders to midcalf, secured with two silver fibulae), and a *fouta* (a smaller cotton cloth) tied at the front over her *houli*. Southeastern coast, Tunisia, 1970s. Photograph by Mary Eastman.

barnous, a rectangular hood is fashioned from two woven pieces, and the body of the garment shaped in a semicircle to allow draping. The sides are loose and are either kept simple or are accentuated with subtle, intricate embroideries indicating social status or the cultural heritage of the wearer. Known for centuries as a typical North African Imazighen item of dress, the barnous is usually light beige or dark brown and falls from both shoulders or drapes across one shoulder to cover the body fully. Wrapping it under the left arm and over the right shoulder means that the wearer is of Libyan descent, often the case of Tunisians living near the southern border. Another outer garment is the *kashabya*, worn exclusively during cold, snowy winters and mostly in western cities. Made of heavy, dark (usually brown) wool, this sleeved and hooded garment has eyelets or a zipper in the front for easy wear. It is decorated with short, round, black woolen tassels along the gathering.

The *jebba* is a shorter version of the African boubou sewn from silk, cotton, or linen, depending on the season and social occasion. The front opening is embroidered using silk thread, and only by men. The design and extent of the embroideries define the cost of this item. If it is made of linen, the jebba is called *kamraya*; if a mixture of silk and linen, it is called *sekrouta*. Both types were seen at formal social ceremonies; otherwise, men wore a wool and silk jebba in winter or a cotton jebba for everyday wear. Predominant colors were white in summer and dark beige or dark maroon in winter. From the capital, this fashionable item traveled to the interior of Tunisia and became a status symbol because of the workmanship (and thus cost) involved. However, nomadic men from the furthest south did not wear the jebba because it was not convenient for riding horses.

Reserved for working men, the *kadrun* is worn over other clothes for protection from dirt; it is easily categorized as work clothes. Constructed from cotton or wool, usually gray, it has either buttons or a zipper on the front. It originated in the cities of the Sahel and the south and became prevalent in the northern and western cities when rural southerners migrated there for work. Because of distinctive cultural meanings carried through dress, in the city of Tunis and in the west, a kadrun wearer would usually be referred to as *Jerbi* or *Sahli*—that is, a Tunisian from Jerba or Cap Bon. As a garment underneath the jebba, Muslim men both in cities and rural areas wore the Arab *sarwaal*, a white pantaloon of cotton cloth with extra room between the legs, allowing not only for everyday comfort but also an easy fit for horse riding. The tailor adjusts garment ease by increasing or decreasing the number of pleats in the pants, which are finished at the calf with subtly embroidered eyelets. Men fastened the sarwaal with a belt about three centimeters (slightly less than one inch) wide that they wrapped around the waist. The belt was made of the same fabric and was usually covered with a beautiful, thick silk sash about half a meter (twenty inches) wide and at least two meters (six and a half feet) long. This silk sash usually shows when men are in public, when they lift their jebba to get ready for prayer or when lifting their barnous. Once in the house, men normally remove the jebba and remain in the sarwaal. Other urban men of European and Turkish descent wore Western-style pants. Tunisian Jews in the capital also strayed from Tunisian ethnic dress and adopted European-style clothing, except for the southern Jews, who kept their ethnic dress.

The *fermla* is a vestlike garment, usually of silk or cotton, embroidered with silk filaments and with eyelets down the front, that is worn for everyday use or special occasions. The back can also be embroidered when the farmla is meant for a groom or the father of the bride at a wedding or for a young boy at his circumcision. It is worn on top of a long-sleeved linen shirt underneath the jebba. Young boys also imitate men's dress, especially during formal religious and social ceremonies. Men's dress was never embroidered using gold or silver; instead they preferred silk in the same color as their garment to ornament it, due to religious modesty. In winter, men would wear a farmla and over it a *sadrya* (a long-sleeved, waist-length jacket with embroidered eyelets on the front).

Bolgha are flat leather slip-on shoes with no back that complete a man's outfit; they are typically worn by both urban and rural men from North Africa to the Middle East. Leather work was so prominent in Tunisia that each market had an area dedicated to selling bolgha. Southern Imazighen men as well as rich western land owners wore knee-high leather boots called *sabbat* that had intricate embroidery on the sides and/or the front and were fastened around the leg by securing side hooks onto the gaiter (spats). This footwear was reserved for adults as a symbol of membership in the cavalry. Shorter ankle boots and moccasins (made from a single leather piece) were for men's everyday wear and for boys.

As previously mentioned, Islamic law encourages modesty in dress in general and discourages men from accessorizing to the point of attracting attention. For this reason, Muslim men wear a silver (not gold) wedding ring and a silver watch. Similarly, they use amber and floral essences rather than strong perfumes, which are reserved for women. Some southern men use kohl to line their eyes, mostly as protection from the harsh Saharan weather. Also in the south, men wore leather belts that sat high on the chest and the back; these were originally brought to Tunis with the coming of Islam but then filtered into the rest of the country. The leather work resembles that of the sabbat. Horsemen place their swords and knives in the front side pockets for easy retrieval.

An Imazighen woman wearing a bridal wrapper and headcover of synthetic fibers. Tunisia, 1970s. Photograph by Mary Eastman.

URBAN FEMALE DRESS

Before the Treaty of Bardo was signed in 1881, giving the French full control over the Tunisian economy and government, women were seemingly worlds apart from men. Urban women and young girls, regardless of their religious affiliation, were not expected to work and had to be accompanied on those rare occasions when in public by men or by another (usually older) woman. Muslim women in Tunis generally came from two cultural backgrounds: they were either descendants of Andalusian refugees who had fled the Spanish Inquisition or were of Turkish origin and had resided in the capital since Tunisia's annexation to the Ottoman Empire in 1575. Customarily, urban women did not leave the house except to go to the public baths, to visit relatives for mourning, or to visit cemeteries early on Friday mornings. Clothing differences between these urban women and their Imazighen counterparts were obvious, given that Imazighen women did not veil. They also worked side by side with their husbands on the land, dyeing fibers or warping heavy looms, often located outdoors, for weaving. Europeans and Tunisians lived in the same cities, but the women from these groups did not socialize. When European women went to the market, however, they interacted with Tunisian men, and they could interact with upper- and middle-class Tunisian families when hired as tutors for their daughters. Dress for women during the late nineteenth century distinguished women into the categories of Imazighen and non-Imazighen.

There is little distinction between urban Muslim and Jewish women's dress, except that Jewish women were expected not to mix animal fibers with vegetable fibers. These groups of women shared clothing practices before fleeing the Inquisition in the twelfth and thirteenth centuries. When in public, urban women were covered from head to foot in a silk garment called *safsari*, either white or beige for Muslims or with yellow or maroon stripes for Jews, that is believed to be of Spanish origin. Social status was displayed by the type of fabric from which the safsari was made. The safsari and *a'ajar* (a face cover that obscured the face completely) worn by wealthy women was made of silk; middle-class women wore a woolen safsari and a black face covering (*tchertches*) that left only the eyes showing. Religious distinctions were exhibited when Muslim women covered their faces with the safsari or used an additional rectangular piece of silk called *ajaar* embroidered with motifs that resembled those found in both Turkey and Andalusia. Jewish women wore a conical hat under the safsari.

In general, most urban women wore some type of a head cover. Jewish women wore the *duka*, a pointed skullcap finished with a rectangular panel about half a meter (twenty inches) wide that was folded and used to fasten the duka to the head. Muslim women, on the other hand, used a different style of hat called *kufya*. These varied from jewelry crowns fitted to the skull to somewhat rectangular embroidered fabric hats. Women's hats had back panels called *k'fa* (literally "the back") embroidered with designs using silk, gold and silver, tassels, fringes, and sequins. Fabrics varied but were usually of silk, satin, or velvet. The kufya is believed to have originated in Syria and traveled to Spain, where Christians, Muslims, and Jews all wore it but with each group displaying distinctive designs carefully chosen to proclaim their particular religious affiliation.

Muslim and Jewish women dressed somewhat similarly. Both women wore the Arab sarwaal, whose amplitude increased with the woman's wealth. While doing housework, women wore a *fouta*, a rectangular piece of cotton cloth wrapped to protect their sarwaal and usually tied in front—similar to a twenty-first-century apron. When not wearing the sarwaal, women wore different types of pants for ease. These house pants were more close-fitting and made of cotton knit, similar to twenty-first-century leggings. Customarily, women covered their heads while doing housework by folding a scarf in a triangle and tying it at the front of the head. This style was called *takrita* (tie) or *takrita asfour* (a bird-style tie), because the front knot mimics the wings of a bird.

With the fouta, women wore either a cotton sweater or a chemisette. The sweater, called *maryoul fadhila*, came in different colors and had distinctive vertical black stripes. Its colors ranged from white to violet, yellow, and green. It had long sleeves, a round collar, and three flat buttons in front. The chemisette (*surya*), made of silk or linen, was hand-embroidered and had long, wide, transparent sleeves. It was worn underneath a bralike vest called *hassara*, which was embroidered with gold and/or silver.

Women adopted slip-on shoes of wood, fabric, leather, or a combination and of different heel heights. At home, women wore elevated wooden sandals (*kobkab*) that were equally high in the front and back, as if having a heel on each end. When dressing to go out, women would wear either *beshmak* (slip-on shoes with closed toes made of embroidered satin) or a *tmag* (a slip-on with a wooden base and a leather upper).

IMAZIGHEN FEMALE DRESS

In the nineteenth century, Imazighen women continued to wear wrappers, but no longer were they made of linen. The wrappers changed from Matmata in the south to El Kef in the west, not just in color but also in style and material. Differences correlated with the type of fiber used, the season, and the region. Usually wrappers were made of a cotton and wool mixture in winter, cotton in summer, and silk for special occasions. The garment was formed by wrapping a piece of fabric (four to five meters [thirteen to sixteen feet]) long fastened by two silver fibulae on the shoulders and a woolen sash at the waist that created a Greek chiton effect. Colors varied from deep blue, using indigo dye, to deep maroon, using pomegranate skins. The wrapped dress differed from one region to another by its distinctive embroideries made either by women (in the south) or by men (in Mahdia and Jerba).

Inner garments changed more than outer, but regional and cultural differences persisted in embroidery. The inner garments consisted of the shirt worn by urban women, with maryoul fadhila underneath their wrapper.

Imazighen women also covered their heads but never their faces. Their distinctive style ordinarily included two to three scarves. One square scarf was folded in a triangle and tied on the head, while the other one, usually a rectangle, was folded around the head turban style, tying it in the front over the first scarf. Alternatively, a shawl (the head and shoulder veil) was woven by women using cotton or wool and embroidered by men. It is believed that women wore their veil the way the Punic goddess Tanit and the Egyptian goddess Isis were depicted as having worn theirs, as a symbol of femininity and fecundity. These shawls were white for young girls, red for young women, and black for older women. Embroidery was in white, green, yellow, and red. Some shawls were decorated using a technique called *Berber batik*. When visiting cities for trade or looking for work, Imazighen women adopted the urban fashion of adorning the safsari but wore it Imazighen style, folded in half and worn on the head and the shoulders, more to stay true to the Imazighen way of life than to follow urban fashion.

The most striking trademark for Imazighen women was their tattoos. Even though Islamic law forbids body marking, Imazighen women kept the practice, believing that tattoos protect from evil and black magic and ensure longevity and good health. Women chose designs of different sizes and for different places on the body. Some women tattooed entire arms; some, only their ankles; and others, their faces.

A woman from southern Tunisia wearing an Imazighen embroidered wrapper, ca. 1970. There is evidence to suggest that Imazighen women wore a wrapped style of dress from as early as the first few centuries B.C.E. In the nineteenth century, the style of Imazighen women's wrappers changed to incorporate new fabrics and colors. Photograph by Mary Eastman.

WEDDING DRESS

Tunisian wedding ceremonies typically lasted seven days and seven nights, and brides wore a different ensemble for each day; in the early twenty-first century, most families no longer do week-long weddings. Women's wedding dress varied by city and cultural group but was similar in that all variants involved layering several items of different types of fabric together. For instance, several cities adopted the inner wedding garment called *kmijja*. This garment was made of silk, linen, or both and featured embroideries selected by the bride; it was typically ankle length or calf length and A-shaped. Both the bottom of the kmijja and the edges of its sleeves were embroidered in point lace. Typically, the front of this garment was also embroidered with gold thread, depending on regional fashion, to protect the bride from the evil eye. Some of the frontal embroideries had designs with talismanic significance that dated as far back as Phoenician times—including fish, hands, and horns—while other motifs came from the Islamic era—such as flowers and animals. Most important, this garment, and any other item of dress the bride would wear during those seven days, was to never be tied with a belt, because tying was believed to magically hinder her ability to bear a child. In addition, all wedding garments were oversized in order to fall loosely on the bride and cover her body entirely.

The country's heritage in wedding dress is as rich as the history of the country itself. In El Kef, once the Roman trade capital, the bride wears one wrapper over another, a style called the *peplum*, which dates back to the fifth century B.C.E. The outer wrapper, which is wider and blue, is worn on top of the inner tunic, which is often red or yellow. In El Kef, the bride wears this double wrapper on the seventh day of the celebration. On this day, the outer wrapper typically is green, and the inner one, red or orange. At times, a third wrapper that is narrower and usually yellow is worn. Under the wrapper, the bride wears the kmijja and a pair of pants finished with needlepoint embroideries. Jewelry, vests, and shoes complement the ensemble.

Women of the capital display their cultural and religious backgrounds through subtle differences in wedding attire. The Turkish bride's oversized sarwaal, gathered at the ankle, has gold embroidery on black or deep maroon velvet with a bolero-style vest, or fermla, also embroidered with gold. The ensemble is complemented with a kufya on her head and a silver-plated pair of tmaq on her feet. A Jewish woman wears a duka on her head, gold and silver embroidered bolero or fermla, satin tmaq on her feet, and gold and silver embroidered silk pants with heavier embroideries on the fitted calves. These are called "pants with legs" and emphasize the shape of the leg rather than hiding it under fabric as with Turkish pants. These two groups of brides are similar in their wearing of a chemisette of finely embroidered silk with wide sleeves finished with point lace underneath their bolero. In cities, there are more shared traditions than differences. For instance, on the day the bride appears in public unveiled for the first time and shows her henna and makeup for an audience of women, she wears a shorter version of the kmijja. In other Tunisian cities, she would have a longer, loose, untied kmijja, on top of which she would wear either a short bolero with wings on the shoulders or a longer, fully embroidered, oversized stiff chemise. Both groups also shared similarity in adorning their dresses with gold jewelry.

The wedding week is a revelation of sexual life for the young woman. Her body is bathed, waxed, and treated with *baruq*, a soothing mix of chalklike powder mixed with rose water; her teeth are bleached with walnut stain; and her hair is treated with oils of olive, almond, and walnut and colored with henna, thought to have protective properties. Henna also decorates her hands and feet. Because the prophet Mohammed dyed his beard with henna, its use implies his blessing and is always found on a bride, applied over three days. On the first day, her hands are dyed in designs that indicate both cultural affiliation and current fashion. Because her hands are tied while the henna is drying, the bride is fed by the woman who beautifies her, called *hannena* (she who applies henna) or *mashaata* (she who brushes her hair, or hairdresser). The second day, after applying a second layer on the hands to obtain a darker, blackish color, henna is applied to the feet. The third day, after returning from the hammam (Turkish-style bath), the henna is then decorated with a black, scented dye obtained via a chemical process involving acorns, cloves, and copper sulfate. The black mixture is applied around the henna using a needle. Brides' faces are also decorated with this mixture by drawing a straight line across their forehead and a vertical line on their chin, directing attention away from their beauty to protect them from envious eyes, which are believed to transmit evil. To finish the facial makeup, the bride decorates her eyes with kohl. Women attending the ceremony wear their ceremonial dress

A young Tunisian girl dressed in a bridal *fouta-ou-blouza*, ca. 1970. This wedding dress is composed of a wide *sarwaal* and a bralike bodice. Traditionally, both are heavily embroidered with sequins, gold or silver filaments, or a mixture of both. Her hat shows Turkish influence. Photograph by Mary Eastman.

(wedding dress) and also display all their jewelry. Similarly, they dye their hair with henna or by using a homemade mixture called *mardouma*, which colors the hair black. In preparing their faces, women cleanse with essence of rose.

Beyond issues of fashion, jewelry in Tunisia throughout the centuries has served at least two main functions: economic display and protection. The relative prosperity of the groom and his family is demonstrated by the jewelry offered by the in-laws to the bride on an ongoing basis until the wedding day. Gold was as highly regarded in urban areas as silver was for the Imazighen; however, among the latter, silver was plated with gold for urban families of limited income. On her wedding day, the bride was expected to wear her entire jewelry collection, and creativity was essential to putting together an aesthetically pleasing ensemble. Some items were worn as received, and others were altered to suit her style. Unaltered items included round jewelry such as earrings, bracelets, anklets, and fibulae for the draped dress. The bride would, however, create her own design for necklaces, tiaras, and jewelry for the temples and chest. Brides also added coral, pearls, and glass beads of white, red, or dark blue. Jewelry stays with the woman her entire life and is her savings account, her wealth. She continues to buy more jewelry as she can, to display and possibly to redeem for money during difficult economic times for the family or in case of divorce or widowhood. But jewelry also wards off bad luck or misfortune. A woman always wears her circular jewelry; bracelets, fibulae, and anklets are never left behind, no matter what her social status. This tradition may date as far back as the Punic era. Although Islam prohibits belief in the power of spirits, for there is no power but that of God, for many Imazighen, the belief in spirits known as *jnun* (plural of *jinn*) continued.

Silver was highly regarded in Imazighen culture, with some geographical differences. For instance, women in Jerba preferred gold and gold-plated silver, but most others preferred silver, such as in two large fibulae to fasten wrappers that were attached to a necklace (sometimes made of more than two chains) that covered the chest. Bracelets, earrings, and anklets were also important jewelry. The latter were wide and weighed up to half a kilogram (one pound) if solid. As a symbol of wealth, the anklet was given by the husband to his bride.

TUNISIAN DRESS AND FASHION UNDER FRENCH RULE

In 1881, the Treaty of Bardo was signed, which gave France total control of the Tunisian government and full managerial rights over the country's economy. In short, this agreement guaranteed France advantages such as low import taxes for French settlers while also securing low export taxes on goods produced by French settlers for the French market. On the other hand, the treaty limited exports of handicrafts produced by Tunisians by increasing the taxes on their exports. Just before French colonization, cheap imitations of Tunisian items of dress and textiles flooded the market.

The loss in revenue from exports could not be replaced locally because the displacement of farmers, in conjunction with the increase in population, intensified poverty and deprived buyers of cash needed to purchase locally produced garments and textiles. Local production also diminished due to the lack of purchasing power of the increasingly poor population. Producers of handmade garments and cloth slowly disappeared and with them the distinctiveness of Tunisian fashion. The native ethnic clothing that remained was too ragged to carry any meaning except that of poverty. Few rich families continued to wear traditional dress, and most Tunisian men slowly adopted European pants and jackets. Women stayed at home and dressed in ethnic apparel made from cheap synthetic fibers (such as the wrapped dress of the Imazighen). Others incorporated European fashions along with everyday Tunisian styles. New terms appeared such as *banouar*, a cut and sewn dress of jersey knit worn a few inches below the knees with long or short sleeves.

Tunisian handicraft was controlled by rich French settlers who opened technical schools designed to produce laborers for all export-led industries. Some schools trained men to be machinery workers, and schools for females focused on handicraft skills. These schools were established in each region of Tunisia according to the regional specialty. They varied in focus or emphasis from embroideries of fine lingerie (handkerchief, chemisette, chemise) to embroideries of gold and silver and to the weaving of carpets and blankets. Outside of these schools, local handicraft industries waned, and sartorial differences started to diminish, except for subtle differences between Muslim Tunisians and French settlers.

FROM COLONIZATION TO INDEPENDENCE

With poverty, unemployment, and civil unrest at their highest point ever during the 1930s, the French government was eager to settle problems by inviting Tunisians to assimilate French culture—theoretically, of course, and without social benefits, given that they were not considered full citizens and that all administrative jobs were taken by French and European settlers. In addition, the French saw a great value in encouraging Tunisian women in the cities to remove the safsari and in rural areas, the wrapper, as they saw that garment as symbolizing backwardness and ignorance. To suggest that Tunisians were emancipated and fully civilized, the French wanted women and men to dress like them, Western style.

By the mid-1930s, Tunisian dress had changed dramatically. Older men and women wore Tunisian dress in cheaper versions using cloth that was industrially produced in France or Tunisia and that imitated local handmade goods. Younger women donned a gown called *bannoir* along with the safsari in public. The ajaar that was worn in the late nineteenth century as a face covering was replaced by a rectangular black piece of cloth covering the face from the nose down. This new face veiling, the *lahfa mesri* (an Egyptian oval-shaped drape or wrap in black silk, also called *tchartchef*) appeared around this time. As guardians of culture, women were still expected to cover themselves in public. Tunisian Jews had moved out of their Arab quarters and into French areas, where they adopted Western styles to the fullest, except for those living in the south, who continued to wear Tunisian ethnic dress. Younger boys dressed in Western styles and wore chechias. Educated older men who returned from Cairo or France wore suits—some with the Turkish fez and others with the chechia, declaring themselves the generation of Habib Bourguiba, the resistance leader and first president of Tunisia (from 1957).

CHANGES IN MEANING

Teaching French values to women was seen as a way to transform Tunisian society in the 1930s, but these French initiatives were countered by Bourguiba, who, like other educated nationalists, found himself in a country governed by political descendants of the revolutionaries of 1789 who preached freedom for France but practiced otherwise in his own country. Downtown Tunis was segregated to a point that on Avenue Jules Ferry, Café Lorraine had printed on its windows, "Dogs and Arabs are not allowed." The resistance came through Bourguiba, who used both religion and culture to define Tunisian identity and protect it from being supplanted by French culture. Bourguiba saw women's emancipation no longer as a question of equal access to education but more as a matter of safeguarding Tunisian identity and asserting Tunisian sovereignty. Between 1929 and 1933, Tunisian dress became part of the rhetoric of the independence movement. Definitions of identity were set, and violating them attacked the well-being of the nation. This link between protecting Tunisian identity and preserving Tunisian dress traditions pervaded Bourguiba's career as a resistor. Dress, in his view, was a symbol of the country's ideals and customs, good or bad. It did not matter whether Tunisians agreed with the customs; what mattered was the fact that, for the time being, given that Tunisian identity was on the verge of disappearance, ethnic dress suddenly was very important.

In light of the civil unrest, Tunisian ethnic dress grew in importance and more than ever carried political and religious significance. According to Bourguiba, sociocultural values could not be borrowed from outside and inculcated by force on a group of people who shared a different set of values. He mocked the French, who believed that by changing Tunisian dress (a symbol of backwardness and savagery), Tunisians would ascend to the status of a civilized people.

POSTCOLONIAL TUNISIA AND TUNISIAN DRESS, 1956 TO 1987

Tunisia was declared self-governing in 1954, after guaranteeing to France that the trade agreement signed in 1881 with the Ottoman Empire binding Tunisia to France economically was left in force. Full independence was granted in 1956, and Bourguiba assumed power of the new republic in 1957. His most ambitious policy was the passage of the Code of Personal Status, which gave women full social, economic, and political rights that were unheard of in the Arab world. The state of the country was deplorable, the poverty rate was at its highest ever, and the literacy rate was extremely low. The country had no skilled labor to manage administrative positions, because most of the Tunisian labor force worked in the agricultural sector, with only a small percentage in manufacturing and mining.

Bourguiba feared that resurgent Arab nationalism in Tunisia's neighboring countries due to the problems in the Middle East would split Tunisia apart. All his speeches after 1956 mentioned women, equal access to education, and, most important, modernizing his country and its people. He needed to find a strategy to overcome the differences between Tunisia and its neighbors and unite Tunisians behind their government. One way of doing that was by modernizing dress throughout the country—a reversal of his prior position. He wanted every Tunisian to have access to modern, presentable clothes. And to implement that policy, thousands of bales of used clothes from the United States entered the country, killing what was left of the local garment industry.

century wore Western-style clothing, except for wedding dress. In addition, a few Imazighen women, mostly in the south, kept their wrappers and became such an attraction when seen in public places that tourists photographed them. Women with tattoos became an embarrassment to the point that, in some Tunisian weddings at the eve of the twenty-first century, brides or grooms of urban cities did not want to be photographed with an in-law wearing an Imazighen dress and displaying body tattoos. Slowly, the many Tunisian dress styles, with their symbols, meanings, and shared values, vanished, making room for Western fashion.

THE TWENTY-FIRST CENTURY

Twenty-first-century Tunisians dress like many citizens in major cities around the world, and clothing no longer portrays regional identities. Even the white wedding dress has become common in Tunisia. Although ethnic dress continues during some or all days of the wedding ceremony, the bride may not have internalized its significance. She adopts such a style because of fashion dictates, aesthetic appeal, or family pressures. Similarly, ethnic dress items from different parts of the world have become highly fashionable in wedding ceremonies. For instance, Indian saris have been sold or rented at a high premium. When bought as cloth, the sari can be cut and sewn in a fouta and blouza style (sarwaal and short bolero) and not necessarily worn as a sari per se.

After the coup in 1987 and the election of the second president, Zin El Abidin Ben Ali, in 1989, traditional dress started to regain value. Embroidery schools were reopened, studios were subsidized to produce handmade items of dress, and the Office National de L'Artisanat gained full legal power to control production of such items and to authenticate them. Similarly, the new president and first lady always dressed in Tunisian ethnic dress on formal cultural and religious ceremonies. Re-instilling pride in ethnic dress has encouraged new waves of creativity in young fashion designers. Samya ben Khlifa, for instance, has designed fashionable wedding dress with influences from Tunisian cultural heritage. Other fashion designers have won international acclaim, primarily designing world fashion rather than drawing on ethnic styles. Some remained in Europe and worked for couture houses, while others developed their own brands, such as Azzedine Alaya, known worldwide for his knit designs.

Similarly, by the late twentieth century, the country had a strong cadre of graduates from renowned schools in textile engineering and fashion garment production. Along with Western-style apparel exports supported by foreign investment, Tunisia started developing its own fashion trademark, primarily for local consumption and not yet reaching export status. Fabric availability is also being addressed, as Tunisia has maintained its rank as the fourth-largest supplier of textiles and textile by-products to Europe since 1997. Tunisian fashion faces stiff competition from international brands such as Max Mara, Coach, and Armani, but nevertheless, the Tunisian dress industry has its own famous designs, such as Mabrouk and Blue Mountain. The Tunisian government is even beginning to sponsor pan-African fashion competitions to increase world awareness for young Tunisian and African designers.

A Tunisian woman wearing an evening dress in a two-part *fouta* and *blouza* style of hand-embroidered silk with a crocheted shawl, ca. 1970. Photograph by Mary Eastman.

This newly elected African president believed in mind over matter and had a vision that all Tunisians would have access to free education, a health care system, and a stake in the economy. It was his view that, in order to achieve such a goal, a new identity needed to be shaped—one that would speak of modernity. In doing so, he established a dress code for Tunisians. Gaining respect and restoring dignity, in his view, went hand in hand with appearance, and reforming dress customs was thus the first means of crafting a new Tunisian identity. For him, Tunisians were poorly dressed because of penury and traditions that, in his mind, needed to be fought. Bourguiba was very driven, and no doubt he loved his country and its people (whom he referred to as his children). To him, dressing the part was a matter of national advancement, and therefore the government had to clothe its citizens.

He fought ethnic dress and strongly believed in the correlation between European styles and evolution toward a modern culture. He argued that ethnic dress was undignified and not conducive to hard work, because it carried meanings of old traditions and old ways of thinking, that could hinder economic and social advancement.

As a result, people strayed away from ethnic dress for fear of its symbolism. Almost all Tunisians by the end of the twentieth

References and Further Reading

Bakalti, S. *La femme tunisienne au temps de la colonisation (1881–1956).* Paris: Edition L'harmattan, 1996.

Bertholon, L., and Chantre, E. *Recherches anthropologiques: berberie orientale.* Lyon, France: A Ray Imprimeur Editeur, 1913.

Brett, M.a.E.F. *The Berbers (The People of Africa).* Malden, MA: Blackwell Publishing, 2003.

Cayci, A. *La question tunisienne et la politique ottomane (1181–1913). Conseil supreme d'Atataurk pour la culture, langue et histoire.* Ankara, Turkey: Société Turque d'Histoire, 1992.

Courtney-Clark, M. *The Vanishing Tradition of Berber Women.* New York: Clarkson Potter Publisher, 1996.

Fontaine, J., and Gresser, P. *Tunisie carrefour des civilisations.* Courbevoie, France: Acre, 2000.

Gabous, A. *La Tunisie des photographes.* 2nd ed. Tunis, Tunisia: Ceres Editions, 2005.

Gargouri, S. *Les bijoux de Tunisie.* Tunis, Tunisia: Dunes Editions, 2005.

Institut National du Patrimoine. *L'Art de la coiffure traditionnelle: Musée National du Bardo.* Tunis, Tunisia: Institut Nationale du Patrimoine, 2000.

Kraiëm, M. *La Tunisie précoloniale. Tome I and Tome II: Etat, gouvernement, administration.* Tunis, Tunisia: Société Tunisienne de Diffusion S.T.D., 1973.

Le Centre des Arts et Traditions Populaires. *Les costumes traditionels feminins de Tunisie.* Tunis, Tunisia: Le Concours du Ministère des Affaires Culturelles, 1985.

Lee, M. "Constru(ct)ing Gender in the Feminine Greek Peplos." In *The Clothed Body in the Ancient World*, edited by L. Cleland, M. Harlow, and L. Llewellyn-Jones, 55–64. Oxford, UK: Oxbow Books, 2005.

Perkins, K. *A History of Modern Tunisia.* Bloomington: Indiana University Press, 2004.

"Revue du Centre des Arts et Traditions Populaires." *Centres des Arts e Traditions Populaires* 7, no. 9 (1968): 187–188.

Robichez, J. *Maroc centrale: cent-vingt-trois photographies commentée (1937–39).* Grenoble, France: B. Arthaud, 1946.

Salem, N. *Habib Bourguiba, Islam and the Creation of Tunisia.* Sydney Australia: Croom Helm, 1984.

Spring, C., and Hudson, J. *North African Textiles.* London: British Museum Press, 1995.

Stillman, Y.K. *Arab Dress: From the Dawn of Islam to Modern Times, Short History.* Koninklijke, The Netherlands: Brill, 2000.

Sugier, C. "Survivances d'une civilisation de la laine chez les Jebalia d Sud Tunisien." *Cahier des Arts et Traditions Populaires de Tunisie* (1971): 35–48.

Tanfons, A. "Noces Tissées Noces Brodées: parures et costumes féminin de Tunisie." In *Musée des Arts d'Afrique et d'Océanie*, edited by Bernard Dupaigne and Jean Hubert Martin. France: Joël Cuénot, 1995.

Temimi, A. *Habib Bourguiba & l'établissement de l'état national: approche scientifiques du bourguibisme.* FTERSI Série 6: Monde Arabe, Turqui et Afrique L'Epoque Contemporaine, 10. Zaghouane, Tunisia: Fonda tion Temimi pour la Recherche Scientifique et l'Information, 2000.

Meriem Chid

See also North Africa; Snapshot: Libya.

Mauritania and Western Sahara

- Female Dress
- Beads, Coiffure, and Jewelry
- External Influences on Dress

Mauritania and Western Sahara/Sahrawi Arab Democratic Republic occupy a large region in northwest Africa on the edge of the Sahara Desert, bordering the Atlantic Ocean and the Sahel. For centuries, trade, migration, slavery, and intermarriage have created economic and cultural exchange across this desert region, bridging Arab and black Africa and their traditions of dress. Across the Senegal River, the famed Senegalese city of St. Louis long served as a host for Mauritanian merchants and migrants. Until their sudden expulsion in 1989 after a border dispute and riots in Dakar, Mauritanian merchants had been part of the social fabric of Senegal's major cities since the post–World War II era.

Arabic (Hassaniya) and Wolof are Mauritania's official languages, although French is common in urban areas because the country was a French colony from 1904 to 1960. Since independence in 1960, Mauritania has had long periods of authoritarian rule, and average incomes of the populace remain low. The economy still relies on nomadic livelihoods, livestock, and agriculture. Throughout the region, the droughts of the 1970s and 1980s led to rapid urbanization and further urban poverty. Offshore oil is a resource that remains untapped, and the once-rich fishing grounds of the Atlantic coast have been exploited by foreign interests. In the north, the former Spanish Sahara, now Western Sahara/Sahrawi Arab Democratic Republic is disputed territory. In 1975, Spain ceded the territory to Mauritania and Morocco.

Mauritanian women wearing *malafas*, ca. 2000. The *malafa* is a lightweight cotton cloth, about thirteen by five feet (four by one and a half meters), worn wrapped around the body, tied at the shoulder, then draped again around the shoulder and head. Photograph by Joseph Hill.

However, the Polisario movement for Sahrawi independence sought national independence. Mauritania withdrew its claims in 1978, but a guerrilla war with the Moroccan military ensued until 1991. The United Nations–led peace process is still unfinished. Camps in Algeria hold around 100,000 refugees. Although studies on the inhabitants of Western Sahara are sparse, available evidence suggests that their clothing practices share more with Moroccan, especially Imazighen examples, while Mauritanian dress has more in common with that of the Senegambia.

Mauritanian society is multiethnic, highly stratified, and dominated by Maurs (Moors), an Arab cultural group. Traditionally, divisions of labor defined rigid status groups. There were high-status warriors and religious specialists and low-status artisan groups including musicians and blacksmiths. These status groups are part of the larger Arab-descent Moorish community called *bidan*. Communities of black Africans, called locally *harratine*, include farmers of freed slave origin and slave groups of earlier times who did domestic work and aided in caravan trips. The population (about three million) is almost entirely Muslim, mostly Sunni. In such a situation of long-term ethnic mixing and inequality, population figures are contested. Generally, population figures assign one-third each to Maur, mixed, and black African categories. Although slavery was banned in 1981, many reports allege that forms of bondage continue through historical familial ties.

The medieval kingdom of Ghana (not to be confused with the modern nation) has long been thought to be sited within the boundaries of Mauritania. With its putative capitol at Kumbi Saleh in the southeast, ancient Ghana was known to Arab geographers as early as the eighth century C.E. The most detailed published account dates to 1068 and is based on interviews with trans-Saharan traders by the Arab chronicler al-Bakri, who was a resident of Córdoba, Spain, and never visited the kingdom. Nevertheless, his account of the court provides some convincing and provocative details: "None of those who belong to the imperial religion may wear tailored garments except the king himself and the heir-presumptive, his sister's son. The rest of the people wear wrappers of cotton, silk or brocade according to their means. Most of the men shave their beards and the women their heads. The king adorns himself with female ornaments around the neck and arms, on his head he wears gold-embroidered caps covered with turbans of finest cotton."

FEMALE DRESS

A millennium later, dress asserts sociopolitical power and personal identity amid both rigid hierarchies and rapid change. Despite significant population shifts from pastoral to urban lifestyles since about 1970, lineage remains the core of social life and loyalties. In this context, concepts of femininity represent a social order organized around lineage, rigid status groups, ethnicity, religion, and gender. As in many societies, both religious and patriarchal ideologies construct feminine sexuality as potentially disruptive to the social order. Ideals of noble, feminine beauty emphasize corpulence, coverage of the body, and carefully selected adornment. Stylized etiquettes of courtship and seduction regulate sexuality. The *malafa*, a lightweight cotton cloth about four by one and a half meters (thirteen by five feet), is wrapped around the body, tied at the shoulder, then draped again around the shoulder and head. In this hot desert climate, draped swathes of cloth protect from severe heat, sun, and wind. The wraps are selected from many kinds and qualities of cloth, although they were traditionally made from cotton dyed a dark blue indigo. Malafas may be longer than the body length, and so when a woman walks in a malafa, she seems constrained and slow. Gestures of coquetry include adjustment of veils over heads, lifting of the cloth off the floor to facilitate walking, fluttering eyelids, and the use of fans. In private, a sense of protected, leisurely womanhood is conveyed by lounging postures, and the use of refreshing chewing sticks and, again, fans. Coverage, of course, allows for the playful revealing and concealing flow of fabric and for adjustments to allure and capture attention. For instance, in walking, an ankle may be exposed out of the left side of the malafa, so the left foot may be adorned with a more costly bangle than the right, in silver rather than copper. Women especially enjoy the bright colors of factory-made Indian and Chinese cottons for malafas. In the north, women of all ages, incomes, and ethnicities strive to conform to these ideals of feminine grace in the use of the malafas. Outside urban centers, and in the more West African–influenced south, women are freer to wear their own robes, called boubous, and head scarves.

The highly decorative Moorish ideal of feminine dress includes coordinated jewelry and coiffure based on codes of age and marital status. Forty-day-old babies are adorned with protective amulets, ankle bracelets, and, for girls, tiny gold earrings. Throughout the region, from birth to death, amulets with Qur'anic inscriptions protect from evil spirits and the evil eye of humans. Materials are functional. Copper bracelets, for example, are medicinal, and glass beads deflect the evil eye. Ideally, earrings match necklaces. The latter feature large metal or painted leather pendants that sometimes hang to the waist.

BEADS, COIFFURE, AND JEWELRY

Among the most admired products of African tradition are the powdered glass beads called *kiffa*, after the Mauritanian city where they were first documented. These distinctive polychrome

Mauritanian man in plain boubou. This form of dress has continued to be popular throughout West Africa into the twenty-first century. Photograph by Joseph Hill.

beads were thought to have protective powers and were also employed for medicinal purposes and to promote fertility. They were worn as hair ornaments and were assembled often in prescribed combinations on necklaces and bracelets.

Traditional coiffure involves numerous intricate braids arranged in ornate styles that frame the face and adorn the head. For unmarried women, a front roll of hair rises from the forehead, and other rolls hang on the sides. Married women wear three horizontal braids and three braids down the back of the head. Beads, shells, and jewelry in silver, gold, and copper ornament the hair and add to the weight and value. Women of black African descent with shorter hair may wear wigs with these braids and shapes. Women of artisan families specialized in hairdressing, women's health needs (including midwifery), and wedding procedures.

The aesthetic ideal of beauty, wealth, and fertility expressed through corpulence until recently was held to an extreme among noble groups. Through force-feeding (*gavage*, from the French word for force-feeding ducks to produce foie gras), girls of noble families, from ages five to fifteen, were forced to drink fat rich camel's and cow's milk. The aim was to fatten them and stimulate sexual and reproductive maturation for marriage. The immobility of these women reflects the wealth and status of their fathers and husbands, for they are exempt from work and enjoy the domestic service of low-status women. As with other ideals of beauty in all societies, corpulence both restrains and enables women's social power. It is not merely a sign of fertility, status, and male wealth. In fattening themselves and younger females, women cultivate and socialize critical forces of sexuality and desire. They do so through embodying aesthetic and moral values of sexual and bodily enclosure, endogamy, and community integrity. In recent years, the government, medical establishment, social conventions, and women themselves have rejected this extreme body weight ideal. Women, commonly over 200 pounds before, now pursue lighter bodies and healthier lifestyles. Nevertheless, in cities throughout the Sahel and Mauritania, some adult women still take pills to gain weight.

A nomadic heritage often means that female wealth is concentrated in heavy jewelry and other ornaments worn on the body, displayed on coiffure, and attached to flowing veils. Necklaces feature silver pendants and beads on cotton or leather strands. Bracelets of silver, wood, or horn and silver finger rings and earrings complement the ensemble. Older women wear more because they have accumulated jewelry as property over a lifetime. Intricate braided hairstyles called *dafra* (Arabic) frame the face, and beads, shells, and pearls accentuate the coiffure. Influenced by Berber heritage, cosmetics were made from medicinal plants. Heavy black kohl highlighted the eyes. Henna was used to paint the hands and feet in intricate floral designs. As in other parts of the Sahel, scent was and is critical to allure. *Afida*, a sachet of fragrant plants, may be attached to the inside of a garment. Camels with their own finery were also important signs of status for families.

EXTERNAL INFLUENCES ON DRESS

The boubou, a flowing Muslim robe, is worn by men of all groups. In the north, formal wear requires a three-piece outfit in which the boubou covers loose shirts, caftans, or pants. Turbans and shawls complete the outfit. Men favor traditional white or hand-dyed blue fabrics with gold embroidery for most formal wear. Cloth is imported from Europe as well as India in various qualities. In cities, younger men, and some women, may wear Western clothes, especially in office settings.

The nomadic Arab communities that comprise the population of Western Sahara/Sahrawi Arab Democratic Republic share much culturally with the Moors of Mauritania. They also wear boubous and malafas. Notably, in their political struggle for an independent nation, dress has become a marker of cultural pride. It helps assert national identity in the absence of autonomy. Sahrawis wear distinctive local dress in occupied areas to show Moroccan military and government representatives that, even though Sahrawis are poor and disenfranchised, they will maintain their own identity and practices. In the dangerous refugee camps, young girls are required by the community to wear a thoroughly draped malafa as protection. This example shows that even a simple dress form like the malafa can have a major social impact for the people who wear it as well as those who observe it. Both positive and conflictual encounters such as trade and war spread goods and styles. At the turn of the twenty-first century, Moroccan troops have taken gifts of malafa back to women kin in Morocco, where, despite the national conflicts, this dress style has become fashionable.

References and Further Reading

du Puigaudeau, Odette. "La Vie matérielle." *Hespéris Tamuda, Rabat* 9 (1968): 329–427.

du Puigaudeau, Odette. "Costumes féminins." *Hespéris Tamuda, Rabat* 11 (1970): 5–48.

Gabus, Jean. *Sahara: Bijoux et Techniques*. Neuchâtel, Switzerland: Editions de la Baconnière, 1982.

Popenow, Rebecca. *Feeding Desire: Fatness, Beauty, and Sexuality among a Saharan People*. London: Routledge, 2004.

Simac, E. "Traditional Mauritanian Powder-Glass Kiffa Beads." *Ornament* 29, no. 3 (2006): 50–54.

Simac, E. "Mauritanian Powder-Glass Beads: Decline, Revival, Imitations." *Ornament* 29, no. 5 (2006): 60–63.

Tauzin, Aline. *Figures du Feminin dans la Société Maure*. Paris: Karthala, 2001.

Trimingham, J. Spencer. *A History of Islam in West Africa*. London: Oxford University Press, 1975.

Hudita Nura Mustafa

See also Jewelry; Morocco; Gambia and Senegal.

PART 6

West Africa

Benin

The Republic of Benin (formerly called Dahomey and not to be confused with the Kingdom of Benin in Nigeria) is bounded on the south by the Atlantic Ocean, on the west by Togo, on the north by Burkina Faso and Niger, and on the east by the Federal Republic of Nigeria. It naturally shares both history and culture with the peoples of these neighboring countries. In Benin, clothing, regardless of definition, is as complex and varied as its numerous linguistic groups. The history of this country as elsewhere in Africa has been shaped by the migrations and encounters of peoples, particularly through the Dahomey Gap, in which the savanna extends almost to the sea. This has facilitated the melding of different influences in an ecological zone where the circulation of people and ideas has been fluid over time.

A number of kingdoms (such as Savi, Allada, and Abomey) were vying for power and resources, some from the fourteenth century on—almost as early as the Yoruba kingdoms to the east. By the middle of the seventeenth century, the Fon peoples of Abomey prevailed. Although the Fon and the Yoruba were in competition, the Fon also admired and borrowed Yoruba clothing habits and other cultural expressions, including the pantheon of Yoruba divinities. Although not in direct competition with the Akan, especially the Asante in modern Ghana, the Fon also admired and assimilated Akan practices, such as their royal stools. In addition, the trade in slaves was important in the history of the Danhome, Akan, and Yoruba kingdoms. The enslaved peoples taken from neighboring cultures to Danhome have contributed to its artistic wealth and traditions of dress.

In contrast to the south, the people of northern Benin developed a rather loose political organization without kings as leaders. Their roots are broadly to be found in the history of the Gurma and Mande peoples, and it is known that they settled in their mountain environment largely to avoid slave raids. Whether north or south, clothing is diverse and is used to assert local values and stress identity. Somewhat paradoxically, it is also clear that dress serves to stress the importance of the nude body.

Southern Benin popular wisdom assumes that humans are born naked and will be buried likewise. If culture illustrates how false this primary assumption is, it nevertheless remains true that, upon birth, humans are obviously already clad with a skin—some might say the best clothing one can ever own because no one can remove it from you. Body arts, however, deal with how to adorn or disguise the skin for the sake of the gods, personal beauty, or the interest of the community.

DRESSING TO PLEASE THE GODS

In the Benin Republic, Vodun adepts and masquerade performers dress first to please their gods and offer them the appropriate manifestation in human life. Vodun training teaches not only how to make ointments but how to adorn the devotee's body with keloids. These small round tumescences of the skin, organized in different patterns to cover mainly the upper part of the body, identify a devotee as an initiate related to a specific deity. Both men and women can bear keloids, but they are more frequently found on women's torsos. Individuals who choose to bear them dispense with any cloth that might hide this privilege and "divine signature" from public eyes. Keloids are also expensive signs of beauty. To avoid health problems or even death, they require medication and constant attention from the priest who makes them. This explains why popular wisdom forbids poor people to marry a Vodun devotee bearing keloids. Overall, keloids are transcultural signs, a common expression unifying all devotees of the same deity without consideration of ethnic origin. The keloids also suggest mastery of climatic conditions, because the adept is not supposed to wear any cloth to cover them, whatever the weather.

Scarification and tattooing are two other ways of embellishing the skin. These processes either cut the skin to produce scars when the skin heals or embed pigment in the skin. These practices do not seem to have a direct link to local religions. Some scholars argue that scarification was originally intended as a marker of tribal identity and also suggest that it was an invention related to the slave trade. While the scarified patterns would have been useful to prevent the disappearance of people from their communities, more likely they served as beauty marks for the face and other parts of the body. Each area and people had its own aesthetic program. Some of these are rather well known, such as the "two-by-five" configuration of marks of the python temple keepers of the Adjovi family from Ouidah. They are from the *hueda* ethnic group, and their scars can be found on anyone from this group. Also well known are the scars of the Shabe population. The most common scarification pattern is three vertical lines.

In the northwest, Batamalibe peoples produce scarification patterns that cover the whole face with such tiny lines that they tend to disappear as the skin sags or wrinkles with age. Since 1960, the popularity of these marks has increased because the first president of the country originated from this area. The beauty of these scars has been so much admired in southern Benin that they are still imitated on oranges sold by retailers along the streets.

Tattoos are known and used all over the country as a major way to embellish the body in nonsacred situations. Young, mainly illiterate, girls use them to inscribe their own name or the name of their lover on visible parts of the body such as the arms and the belly or more rarely on the thighs. Tattoos are typically blue. Tattoos often go together with teeth carved in striking points. In the 21st century, laws prohibit such permanent modifications to the body, making scars and tattoos much less common and unfashionable. Thus, they tend to disappear from the aesthetic programs for dressing the body.

CLOTHING TYPES

Different types of clothing can be used to complement keloids during festive or important Vodun ritual ceremonies throughout the country. For those occasions, expressions of beauty along with performance of sacrifices are seen as necessary to restore harmony to the community. Clothing made from natural fibers assists in this process of restoration. Vodun tradition specifies basic types of clothing to provide effective communication between humans and the universe. Today, the most striking garments are made from plant fibers such as raffia. In this case, the fibers are not woven but kept in fiber form and thickly packed, creating the appearance of a mobile and soft sponge. These skirts are sometimes dyed in different colors, and the upper body is smeared with a mixture of oil and flour or different imported powders. The Kokou devotees, whose divinities originate from Ewe country in Togo or Ghana, apply perfumes or white powder to complement this apparel. Body painting can also enhance different parts of the face to alter its human aspect. In southern Benin, garments made of fresh palm fronds, banana leaves, and products from other trees are also compulsory when priests and devotees engage the whole community in a public protest for social justice or a collective curse called *oman*.

Since at least the eighteenth century, the substantial imports of industrial fabrics coupled with the generosity of the kings have prompted most Vodun devotees to appear in colored cloth skirts made of separate panels. When they dance and turn in circles and when they make acrobatic movements, their skirts combine the colors of their panels to display the hues of the rainbow. This is thought to be a manifestation of another god, Dan Ayidohwedo, the snake god, who provides wealth and offers the ability to seduce the profane. Wealth offered by Dan is generally seen as coming from abroad and, for the Fon people, takes the form of clothing, iron, and money in the form of cowries. From the eighteenth century on, Vodun costumes have become increasingly complex. Its priests never displayed keloids but wore the best cloth produced locally or brought in by Western trade, sponsored by the kings who were their allies. The priests would not appear in public without gold, silver, or brass bracelets and armbands and would wear necklaces made of the most expensive beads. Imported hats were and still are a distinctive part of the regalia, and the Dagbo Hounon, the supreme chief of the Vodun hierarchy in Whydah, wears them mainly for public ceremonies. In the same manner, the king of Nikki, although not a Muslim, wears long robes and turbans common to Islamic traditions adopted by most of his citizens since the eighteenth century. Other imported religions have their own gowns, most of them preferring white. Gods do help humanity to dress up.

MASQUERADES

The Yoruba *gelede* and *egungun* masquerades and initiation masks from the northwestern part of the country are shared by many communities in southern Benin. These rituals remind human communities of their beliefs and the need for their feelings to be translated through appropriate means of display. Different masquerade traditions, from south to north, offer an array of costumes for actors expected to embody, for a certain time, deities acting for the benefit of humans. Under these circumstances, dress no longer attempts to transform the skin, but instead effects a comprehensive change in the appearance of performers so that they are no longer clearly identified by the community as individuals. Wooden masks combined with various fiber or cotton materials are an essential part of such costumes. A masquerade is not headwear alone, nor just the simple garment. The power comes from the total ensemble.

Gelede male performers dress to honor the "mothers," those women of secret power to be soothed for the benefit of the community. They balance their presence and performance between night and day so that it covers an entire cycle encompassing darkness and light. They also drape from their masks cloths normally worn by women to express both their wealth and beauty. It has never been an easy task for a man to resemble a woman. Most African women are expected to have well-rounded buttocks, and this is an essential beauty criteria. Thus, gelede performers build up the roundness and the beautiful strength of the lower torso by wearing layers of cloth around their hips. They also may attach a carved frontal piece with prominent breasts. The mask resembles a Yoruba woman, often with elaborate coiffure and sometimes facial scars. The gelede spectacle emphasizes the admiration women have for their own bodies and the way they are dressed. For the mothers to be soothed, they need their own image to be imitated by men.

The egungun masquerade is one of the most important in Yoruba culture. It reenacts the presence of the ancestors. Luxurious appliqué cloth panels often include beads, corals, and golden threads, all glittering in the sun. Masquerade configurations are specific enough to have precise names for classifying them. African gods and ancestors love beautiful clothing and are attracted to this luxury. They are expensive to invite to the community, and individuals who desire their presence have to pay for it.

DRESSING FOR WAR

Activities such as war require special dress to frighten and impress the enemy and to protect the fighter against deadly attack. Military cultures have always paid great attention to the way their warriors dress. In the nineteenth century, while the Fon kingdom was at the height of its prosperity, there was a professional army in Danhome. Both men and women soldiers (the latter, the famous Amazons) were clad in smocks allowing easy gestures and great mobility. Shields were not used. The preferred technique was close combat with weapons such as cutlasses. Later, guns were employed, said more to frighten than to kill. Indeed, the Amazon warriors swore that they could eliminate their enemies with a hand or a hoe. Some mud reliefs on the royal palaces of Ghezo and Glele recall this. Men and women soldiers wore trousers called *tchahunka*, which were tied at the waist, cuffed under the knees, and loose and baggy between the waist and the knees, allowing easy movement. Sewn from woven cotton strips, tchahunka resembles the pants worn by horsemen across the Sahel, where the garment probably originated. The tchahunka was worn with a smock, known as *akonmèwu*, which was loose at the upper torso, tapered slightly, and flared at the bottom. Sometimes a cotton belt secured it to the body. This uniform was incomplete without a round hat adorned with the blazon of the company. The smock has become such a part of the Fon warrior's identity that it is reproduced in one of the most famous African metal sculptures from the nineteenth century—the Gu figure created by the enslaved Yoruba smith Akati Akpele Kendo and now in the Louvre. The numerous imitations of this same sculpture maintain the war dress.

ROYAL DRESS

Leaders are the first to afford sumptuous clothing. Their public appearances were made to impress, and even when the material was not cut and sewn but worn as a wrapper, it was of good quality and multicolored. In the eighteenth and nineteenth centuries, most of the weavers were linked to the monarchy and were settled by the king next to his palace or in a special section of the town, Djegbe. According to oral sources, King Agonglo (1789–1818) is said to have contributed to the consolidation of the weaving traditions of the Fon kingdom. A closer look at what remains of the dress for the court shows that the ministers and most dignitaries were wearing Yoruba-style clothing, made of locally woven cotton adorned with embroideries, while the king would appear with a dress and a large piece of cloth, either locally woven or imported from the West, hanging from his left shoulder or tied around his waist. He can wear a hat called *abeti*, which sounds like the Yoruba *abo eti*, that covers the ears. Distinctive Fon *recados* (scepters) complete this ensemble. The recado most of the time recalls a "strong name" of a leader and hangs from the top of the left shoulder, ready to be used as a weapon or a dance staff. The need for distinction can push the king to adopt specific items, such as the silver dust filter that covers the Fon king's nose. Nevertheless, leaders acquired their clothing by any means (local industry, foreign trade, purchase, or diplomatic gift) to ensure required quality and quantity. Cloth among the Fon and other southern leaders is not solely intended to protect the body but expresses wealth and, in its sheer abundance, is allowed to drag on the ground. It is fairly common, however, to see leaders and kings clad in Western clothing.

EVERYDAY DRESS IN THE EARLY TWENTY-FIRST CENTURY

For the majority of the population in Benin, the elaboration of handwoven or machine-produced material resulted in different styles of garments, all adapted to tropical conditions. Familiar forms such as the *buba*, *agbada*, and *danshiki*, borrowed from neighboring Yoruba and related cultures since the fourteenth century at least, are still in fashion throughout the country. Loose garments keep the body cool. Contemporary fashion consists of a male ensemble of three pieces for the torso—danshiki (short tunic), trousers, and a robe known as agbada, plus a hat that should not be removed in public. Possibly this is an imitation of the French *costume trois pieces*. Contemporary women dress in multiple styles, but they have come to prefer the *gen* or *mina* style, where the fabric is cut to hug the body and enhance it. Wax prints are the main material used in the gen style, and women give the patterns names and use them as a language describing felicitous or conflictual social situations. Yoruba women are also attracted to much more expensive handwoven *asho oke* strip cloth that is made into wrappers and machine-woven laces (generally, eyelet fabrics). In recent years, a cotton brocade manufactured in Germany called *bazin* is highly appreciated by both men and women.

Female hairdos and coiffures following Yoruba traditions are seemingly infinite in style. They complete the female appearance and are supposed to change often. Stylish dressing is an expensive and time-consuming affair for women. An elaborate hairdo can take more than eight hours to complete.

Western clothing is currently seen across Benin. However, contact with Europe since the fifteenth century has provided ongoing familiarity with European styles. The introduction of tailoring has led to fundamental changes in the traditional way of dressing. Closer contact with Westerners, mainly in the nineteenth and twentieth centuries, has accelerated the adoption of Western-inspired clothing. This is the case of the *abacoste* in Zaire (Democratic Republic of the Congo), which spread quickly as far as West Africa as a substitute for the Western jacket and a means of affirmative action for authenticity and independence.

DRESSING: A MENTAL CONSTRUCT

This article has focused mainly on dress and clothing as visual and religious phenomena. It has stressed its importance in different circumstances of life. However, Yoruba and Fon people, at least, have another perception of cloth and dress that is deeply embedded in the culture, linked with life itself, and its transmission is considered a privilege. Yoruba culture of southwest Nigeria, with which the neighboring Benin Republic people have had a long historical and cultural interaction, has a saying, *Omo l'Asho, omo l'ere aiye*—"Children are the cloth, the means for you to dress, a benefit from life." In these cultures as well as in others, children are expected to provide for their aging parents. However, the proverb goes further in looking at children as a projection of one's own image as "clothing you and dressing you up." Children's presence and strength make an individual beautiful, and their absence leaves an individual not only alone but also unclothed and unable to dress up. Everybody in your surroundings knows how much "cloth" of this nature that you possess. This "clothing" (sons, families, relatives, and friends as an ultimate homage) goes as far as an individual's funeral, where the body is also dressed up in a beautiful white funerary garb provided by family and friends.

References and Further Reading

Abiodun, Rowland, Ulli Beier, and John Pemberton. *Cloth Only Wear to Shreds*. Amherst, MA: Mead Art Museum Amherst College, 2004.

Adande, C.E.J., and S. Tornay. *Au revoir Dieu Gu*. Paris: Le Musé de l'Homme, 1997.

Blier, S. P. "King Glele of Danhome: Divination Portraits of a Lion King and Man of Iron." *African Arts* 23, no. 4 (1990): 42–53, 93.

Blier, S. P. "King Glele of Danhome: Part 2: Dynasty and Destiny." *African Arts* 24, no. 1 (1991): 44–55, 101–103.

Drewal, H.J., and M. T. Drewal. *Gelede: Art and Female Power among the Yoruba*. Bloomington: Indiana University Press, 1983.

Forbes, Frederick E., *Dahomey and the Dahomans*. London: Longman, Brown, Green and Longmans, 1851.

Hendrickson, Hildi, ed. *Clothing and Difference*. Durham, NC: Duke University Press, 1996.

Herskovits, M.J. *Dahomey: An Ancient West African Kingdom*. Evanston, IL: Northwestern University Press, 1967.

Kriger, Colleen E. *Cloth in West African History*. Lanham, MD: Altamira Press, 2006.

Lawal, Babatunde. *The Gelede Spectacle: Art, Gender and Social Harmony in an African Culture*. Seattle: University of Washington Press, 1996.

Joseph C. E. Adande

See also Masquerade, Theater, Dance Costumes; Yoruba in Nigeria and Diaspora.

Burkina Faso

- Mossi Men
- Mossi Women
- Secondhand Clothing
- Bwa/Marka
- Lobi
- Fulani

Burkina Faso is located at the crossroads of several important trade routes that cross West Africa from the Sahara (Niger) to the old Gold Coast (Ghana) and from the inland delta of the Niger River (Mali) to the former Slave Coast (Benin). The peoples of Burkina have always participated actively in the long-distance trade in salt, kola nuts, cotton cloth, and gold. The Mossi and other people in central Burkina speak Voltaic languages that are very closely related to the languages of northern Ghana, while the Bobo and other peoples in western Burkina speak Mande languages and are culturally related to the Bamana and Malinke. These intersections of cultural areas are mirrored by the clothing people wear: The clothing of Voltaic peoples is very similar to that of Dagomba and Mamprussi to the south, while the clothing of Mande peoples is similar to that of the Bamana to the west.

MOSSI MEN

The Mossi people are the largest group in Burkina Faso, comprising over half the country's population. They are the only people in the country with an ancient tradition of centralized political authority, so one can speak of royal dress and regalia as well as the dress of commoners. They are also very heterogeneous, so it is important to understand that people who are descended from the ancient farmers who first occupied the land may dress quite differently than the chiefs who are descended from the horsemen who invaded the region in 1500 C.E. Based on personal experience from 1970, and on illustrations in books and journals published in the late nineteenth and early twentieth centuries, it is possible to draw a word picture of Mossi dress or clothing before independence in 1960. By far the best early source is *Le Noir du Yatenga*, based on research in northern Mossi country from 1912 to 1913 by the French ethnographer Louis Tauxier. In 2005, the national museum in Ouagadougou published *La tenue traditionnelle au Burkina Faso*, by Sidi Traore and Margriet Renders, providing comprehensive information about dress.

The Mossi have been weavers of cotton for centuries. A particular group among the Mossi called the Yarse specialize in weaving long, narrow cotton strips that could be cut into shorter bands and sewn together selvage to selvage to form a whole piece of cloth. To create a piece of clothing, a buyer could go to the market and pick out the strips he or she liked, in patterns and colors of one's choosing. The merchant measured the strips against the wearer's body—a certain number for the body, a certain number for the back, another group for the sleeves. The customer then

The Mossi artist Raogo Sawadogo, from the village of Kirsi, east of Yako, Burkina Faso, 1976. He is carving an antelope mask and wearing very ancient Mossi-style clothing consisting of a cotton smock and hat. Photograph by Christopher D. Roy.

took these to a tailor, who sewed the strips together to form a shirt, trousers, wrapper, or any other garment. The long strips were also wound up into very large rolls (seventy-five centimeters to one meter [two and a half to three feet] in diameter), hundreds of thicknesses in diameter but only one band wide, which Yarse merchants then carried south into the forest of Ghana and sold to the Akan-speaking peoples who could not grow cotton in the forest.

Mossi men wore a pair of loose-fitting short trousers called *kourouga* that fell to just below the knees or midcalf. The waist was enormous, much larger than the man's real measurements, and was drawn up tight with a leather belt or a drawstring. There was often an excess of material between the legs that bunched up and left a great deal of freedom of movement. Shorter trousers that came to the knees and were worn when farming or hunting were called *kurukwega*. The trousers could be blue or white or might be warp-striped, but plain white was the most common. Men wore shirts called *fugu* that were sewn from narrow bands into the large, roomy shirts that are also common in northern Ghana in Dagomba and elsewhere. These shirts have numerous gussets around the waist that allow them to flow or flare outward when the wearer spins in place in a dance or rotates from side to side. Many of these were sleeveless, but the most elegant and costly had sleeves and pockets and were sewn of expensive warp-striped cloth. Shirts of this type have become very popular again in the past ten or twenty years. Mossi men also wore (and continue to wear) long robes called *kolokore* that reach to the ankles; they are sewn of strips of warp-striped cloth with a keyhole opening for the head and neck. These were often embroidered by hand in the past, by machine now.

All men wore hats, either of basketry or of woven cotton strips. The most common type, called *pugulugmaka*, rarely seen now, consisted of two rectangles of thick cloth sewn together along two adjacent sides and worn as a peaked cap, with one corner pointing straight up and two opposite corners turned up above the ears. They may be dyed brown or black or even warp-striped. Hats of this type were also worn by other Voltaic people, especially the Dogon, who live to the northwest of the Mossi. They are quite unique and picturesque. The second important type of hat, which is still ubiquitous in Mossi country, consists of various large round or circular pointed hats made of grass and decorated with red, black, and brown leather (*piriga*). Many men still wear them, especially in the countryside, and lots of tourists buy them and carry them home on the airplane. There are several centers of production, but the most famous is the large village of Sapone, southwest of Ouagadougou. Because they are twined like baskets and worn on the head, they are called Sapone head baskets or *Sapon zug peogo*. These are often worn by Mossi men

over a close-fitting skullcap of the type that is common all over West Africa, especially among Muslims. They may also be worn as extra protection over a light cotton head cloth or turban, so the hat rides on top of the turban. This is truly the mark of a man from a remote rural area, especially herders such as the Fulani.

Mossi men used to carry goatskin sacks called *wowsé*. These were fabricated of whole skins that had been stripped from the goat's carcass without cutting them, so they formed a secure container with only one opening, where the neck had been. Some of these were tanned so well that they were as soft and supple as the finest leather gloves. They are now rather hard to find.

Finally, Mossi men once wore numerous armlets and bracelets made of leather, brass, stone, or silver. These were intended to protect the wearer from accidents, evil magic, and disease and to make the wearer successful in love and attractive to the opposite sex. The most unusual of these were smooth stone bracelets worn above the elbow. The marbled stone from which they were carved comes from Hombori, in Mali northeast of Bandiagara. The Mossi call Hombori *Manogo*, and so the armlets are referred to as *manogokaka* or sometimes *kugukaka* (*kugri* means stone). They were expensive, so for many years the glassmakers of the Nigerian city of Bida made glass facsimiles that were sold by merchants to Mossi men.

The structure of Mossi society is based on two poles: the chief, or *naba*, holds all secular power and is a descendant of the horsemen from Dagomba who invaded the region in 1500 C.E. The earth priest, or *tengsoba*, holds all spiritual power and is a descendant of the farming peoples who had occupied the land for centuries before the invasion of the chiefly class. The dress of the tengsobadamba is distinctive. Like many such religious leaders,

Professional Mossi dance troupe at a regional fair in the city of Koudougou, 1970. The dancers are wearing the gusseted cotton smocks that are common in central and southern Burkina. Photograph by Christopher D. Roy.

the earth priest of the village of Ziniare in 1976 wore a black and white checked cotton blanket pinned over one shoulder; a broad, round, pointed straw hat; a large leather bag decorated in red, white, and black; and his sacred staff, called a *rayaka*, which has a fork at the upper end and which he uses to catch the thunderclouds and draw down lightning on his enemies, the chiefs.

For many centuries, all Mossi chiefs have worn colorful pillbox caps or bonnets (*pugulugwili*), which mark them as rulers, chiefs, and members of the *nakomse* class of political elite. These hats are round, brimless, with vertical sides and a flat top, and are crocheted of fine yarn. Each one has four crosses of equal arms at each of the cardinal points (one over the nose, one over each ear, one at the back). These crosses have nothing to do with Christianity and predate the arrival of Christian missionaries by centuries. In 1488, King John II of Portugal heard of these hats and, assuming incorrectly that the wearers were Christians, wrote a letter to the Mossi emperor asking if it were possible he were the legendary missionary priest named Prester John.

The power of Mossi chiefs comes from their position as descendants of the horsemen who invaded the region five hundred years ago. The horse is so important to the ruling class that it is a symbol of their power. A horse is kept tethered outside the home of most Mossi chiefs. The bridles, bits, saddles, and stirrups are among the important royal art forms of the Mossi. Leather and cast brass have been central to royal art for centuries, and many Mossi men, especially chiefs, commission leather sacks, brass staffs and fly whisks, and other objects made by the same craftsmen who create tack for their horses.

Mossi chiefs also wear voluminous and costly robes of the type that are common from Senegal to Lake Chad and that, in style, originate among the Hausa kingdoms of northern Nigeria. In the old days, these robes were woven of cotton cloth or wild silk and were hand embroidered in the same patterns used by the artists of the Nupe and Hausa in Nigeria. Now they are sewn of expensive damask or other imported textiles and most often embroidered by machine.

In several Mossi villages, chiefs wear very distinctive textiles that have been imported from the Akan to the south. In 1976 to 1977, the *tansoba* or war chief in Yako wore a large, yellow *adinkra* cloth stamped with black Ashanti patterns. The Yako chief used a sacred stool in the concave pattern that is well known among the Ashanti. It was kept off the ground by a goatskin laid on the ground. The Mossi and Ashanti were military allies in much of the nineteenth century, and Akan regalia influenced Mossi royal regalia rather heavily.

During the Colonial period, governed by the idea that to be civilized one must be French, French clothing design dominated the apparel of all government officials and businessmen. In the period from 1960 to the 1980s, men who worked in offices wore tailored suits called *fonctionnaire* suits. These consisted of tailored Western-style trousers and shirt jackets with collars, a row of buttons up the front, and a high breast pocket. In the late 1970s and through the 1980s and 1990s, this neocolonial style gave way to much more relaxed and appropriately traditional local dress as a symbol of growing national identity and pride in traditional culture. In the early twenty-first century, most government ministers, many businessmen, and all teachers wear so-called national dress. In Burkina Faso, the favored men's style is again the very loose flaring shirts with numerous broad gussets that are well known in northern Ghana. Men make a point of having these elegant shirts

A senior Bwa hunter wearing his hunter's hat and shirt and carrying a powder horn and musket in the village of Bagassi, Burkina Faso, 1983. Photograph by Christopher D. Roy.

tailored using expensive, high-quality, handwoven cotton strips. Loose-fitting, voluminous trousers are made to match. At official receptions, government ministers and ambassadors wear large, flowing, beautifully embroidered robes on the Hausa pattern.

MOSSI WOMEN

In the decades that led to independence in 1960, Mossi women in rural areas wore a woven cloth wrapper around the hips and legs. The wrapper was carefully tucked in at one side to hold it in place, and it was quite common to see women pause to unwrap and adjust it. Beneath this they wore a lighter cotton wrapper. The wrapper was designed to cover the legs almost as far as the ankles, for among the Mossi and many other neighboring peoples, the thighs were the focus of sexual interest and were kept carefully covered out of a sense of modesty. In addition, women wore a white cotton shawl carefully folded over the left shoulder. This could be worn over the head or shoulders or as an extra cloth over a baby carried on the back. Tauxier wrote in 1912 that wealthy women wore the distinctive blue- and white-striped cloths made by the Marka and other peoples to the west, which the Mossi women called *torofugu*. Today these are worn by women in central Burkina, but not by the Mossi.

Before the arrival of the French in the 1890s, most women did not wear blouses, and their breasts were uncovered. The Mossi did not associate women's breasts with sexuality. Breasts were instead associated with motherhood and childbearing, and modesty did not require that they be hidden. In fact, it was considered bad form for a woman to conceal her breasts, especially in the presence of the chief. All of that changed when the French arrived in 1897. They imposed their sense of modesty on the Mossi and made it an offens to be seen in Ouagadougou bare breasted. All women wore blouses like those worn by women all over Africa during the Colonial period and ever since. Because it was offensive to the Mossi to bare the legs, they passed laws in the late 1960s against the wearing of miniskirts, and the first time the French

ambassador's wife descended from an airliner in 1968 wearing a short skirt, she was arrested. To this day, only midcalf skirts are acceptable in Burkina Faso, and white women often wear long wrappers over shorter skirts or shorts when in public.

Decades ago, women wore a distinctive hairstyle called *gyonfo*, in which the hair was carefully braided up into a high crest that ran from the forehead to the back of the head. There was a small pigtail at the back if the woman was married (Tauxier said this looked like a scorpion's tail) and small braids over each ear. Silver or brass combs or coins were sometimes incorporated into the hairstyle, as Fulani women continue to do to this day. This crested or sagittal hairstyle may be seen frequently in Mossi figurative sculpture. The hairstyle has long since gone out of fashion, to be replaced by a thousand different elegant styles of the type seen all over black Africa.

Until the late 1970s, all wives of chiefs wore on their left wrists distinctive brass bracelets called *kobre*. These bracelets were spherical, with an opening to allow them to be put on the wrist and a broad sharp ring at the equator like the rings of Saturn. In the old days, commoners were not permitted to speak to the wife of the chief, and these women were identified by the distinctive bracelets intended to warn off commoner men. Mossi chiefs' wives also once wore heavy cylindrical anklets called *fodo* that covered from ten to twenty centimeters (four to eight inches) of the lower leg.

A century ago, most people in Burkina wore bracelets, rings, anklets, and pendants cast of brass or carved from stone. These objects were intended to provide protection against disease and misfortune of all kinds. Many of them were nonfigurative, but a significant number incorporated images of the spiritual beings that were to provide protection to the wearer. Most Burkinabes stopped wearing such objects in the early 1960s, and now it is very unusual to see any being worn in rural villages or in the city. In the 1970s, tons of old brass bracelets were gathered up by scrap metal dealers and sold by the kilogram to brass casters in Ouagadougou, who turned them into ashtrays and chess pieces for tourists.

Mossi brass casters used to cast a wide variety of shapes and types, including *kambanga*, small bracelets worn above the elbow; *kalembanga*, made of copper and iron twisted together and worn on the wrist to prevent eye diseases; *zouwêra*, twisted bracelets of solid silver or copper; *karzouri*, massive round bracelets that are fitted to the wrist with a great hammer and are almost impossible to remove; and *zusokadaga*, which have a section that separates to permit the bracelet to be removed from the arm.

There are dozens of intricate and attractive bracelet and anklet shapes that were once made in various places all over Burkina Faso. While many were intended to provide some form of protection to their owners (the way some Americans wear copper or iron bracelets), fashion plays an important role, so many others are worn simply because they look attractive. A style originated by a Mossi caster may become fashionable among Fulani or Bwa women, and hundreds of them may be worn only by women in those groups. They come to be called Fulani bracelets regardless of whether they were the work of a Fulani artist. Such bracelets are still very common in many parts of Burkina Faso and are proudly worn by very beautiful and elegant women. Although few people wear bracelets for spiritual protection these days, many people still wear them to enhance their appearance.

Burkinabe men who belong to families that use wood masks once wore cast brass rings that bore tiny models of their masks to

The head war chief (*tansoba*), of the (then) village of Yako, in the Tansobongo neighborhood, Burkina Faso, 1976. The *tansoba* is wearing an Asante *adinkra* cloth tailored and embroidered as a Mossi-style robe. Mossi and Asante have traded in textiles for centuries and are closely tied economically and politically. Photograph by Christopher D. Roy.

A senior Nuna *griotte* (female musician) in the village of Tisse, central Burkina Faso, 2001, sings praises and greetings for guests to the village. She wears a factory-printed head tie and blouse. Photograph by Christopher D. Roy.

secure the protection of the spirit represented by the mask. Similarly, Nunuma, Winiama, and Nuna men wore cast brass rings bearing tiny masks. These serve the same purpose as women's cast brass crescent pendants—to secure the blessings of the mask spirit. Casters in Nunuma villages make rings with masks, which they place along the wood stems of long tobacco pipes. Some old pipes in Nunuma villages had up to fifteen small masks. In the past two or three decades, casters have made large numbers of these pipes to sell to tourists.

Since the 1950s, the large number of mopeds made by Peugeot or Motobecane have been the most important means of transportation. These motorbikes have engine blocks cast in a white metal that looks like aluminum, although it is an aluminum alloy. Casters have been very adept at casting jewelry from this light alloy. Bwa women wear anklets made of aluminum or brass that are cast for them by Dafing smiths. These anklets are curved upward at the front and back and bear on the front a representation of the leaf mask that represents Dwo and an elaborate plaque sometimes decorated with feather shapes at the back. Bwa women whose families wear leaf masks also wear these anklets for spiritual protection. When a woman becomes ill or cannot conceive a child, her brothers commission such an anklet to provide her

with the blessings of Dwo. The same protection is provided or aluminum bracelets and pipe bowls.

Many Bwa and Gurunsi wear pendant brass crescents on the chest. These protect the wearers from disease, and very simple small examples were still worn in the mid-1980s in large number by children. The most elaborate examples, frequently bearing miniature models of wood masks, are worn by Gurunsi women especially in the north among the Nunuma. These are named *tchienê lui ni benê*, "crescent shape with a figure," and, again, like Bwa anklets, represent the mask owned by the wearer's family. A woman who is suffering from a reproductive disease may consult a diviner, who instructs her to seek the help of her family's protective spirit. She then returns to her father's home, where her brothers commission a crescent bearing the family mask. It is her brothers who commission these amulets for her, because they are responsible for the family masks. The mask spirit cures the woman after she returns to her husband's home. Similar brass crescents are worn by the Senufo, Lobi, Bobo, and other peoples in southern Burkina Faso.

All of the elegant women in cities such as Ouagadougou, Bobo Dioulasso, Koudougou, and Ouahigouya wear expensive, carefully tailored, high-fashion couture of the type that is ubiquitous

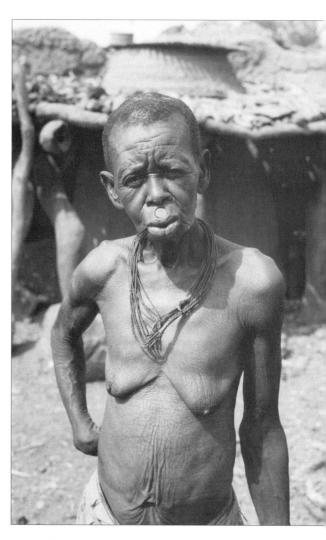

Elderly Lobi woman, Mrs. Hien, wearing an ivory lip labret, Kampti, Burkina Faso, 1984. Photograph by Christopher D. Roy.

everywhere in Africa. Tailor shops for men and women are everywhere in the cities, and women search the markets for the most unusual and beautiful textiles. Tailors travel from city to city and country to country to see the latest fashions and to bring the ideas they have collected home to their clients. The best designers fly to Paris to show their work in fashion salons.

SECONDHAND CLOTHING

Not all Burkinabe men and women wear only traditional, handwoven, African-style clothing. In fact, secondhand clothing that is imported in enormous bales from the United States and Europe is ubiquitous in Burkina. Thirty years ago, only a few people wore white people's cast-offs, but now it is rare to see rural farmers who wear homespun cloth. American T-shirts and soccer shirts are sold in all rural markets for a fraction of what traditional clothing costs, and, because these imported secondhand items are generally in good condition, people appear to be well dressed. In Ghana, people call these clothes "dead white men's clothing," but the term is not used in Burkina. Although people who may once have worn rags can afford to be better dressed now, used clothing has had a detrimental impact on the manufacture of homespun and dyed African styles.

From about 1970 until the late 1980s, there was a very large, modern, efficient cotton textile mill called Voltex in Koudougou, in the center of the country. The factory turned out huge quantities of fairly inexpensive cotton cloth that was printed with bright, colorful patterns of the styles known as Dutch wax. Shops were full of these textiles, and people wore colorful shirts, blouses, and skirts sewn from them. The factory was fed by the large cotton plantations in the center of the country. In the late 1980s, the factory was nationalized, high-ranking officials sold all the assets, including machinery, to feed their bank accounts, and the factory went bankrupt and shut down. Now printed cotton cloth is again imported from Côte d'Ivoire and Europe, to the detriment of the Burkinabe economy.

BWA/MARKA

The Marka or Marka-Dafing live in north-central Burkina around Safane and farther north. They play an important role in the economic life of the country, because they are merchants, weavers, and dyers. Dafing women dye cotton and local silk yarns blue with indigo, and Dafing men weave the blue yarns into narrow strips on horizontal double-heddle looms. There are never any weft patterns, but the warp stripes alternate several shades of dark, medium, light blue, and white. Women associate each of the warp-striped patterns with aphorisms about the course of life and human relationships, as is common among peoples all over Africa. The very beautiful blue-striped cloths, two by one meters (seventy-nine by thirty-nine inches) in dimension, are marketed by Dafing merchants all over central Burkina, and they are avidly collected by the women of many different cultures. The cloths are rather expensive, ranging from 2,000 CFA (US$8) for the cheapest, coarsest cotton, to well over 10,000 CFA (US$40 in 1985) for the finest silk textiles. Bwa women avidly collect them, store their collections carefully in wooden boxes in their bedrooms, and wear them on important occasions, especially religious celebrations. On such days, every woman in a large village might be wearing the beautiful blue-striped Dafing cloth as wrappers

with the stripes arranged horizontally. The effect is impressive and pleasing. The Dafing area is one of the few in Burkina where indigo dying is still an important industry. So little indigo is worn elsewhere that most dyers have given up their trade.

LOBI

The Lobi are by far the most independent and picturesque people in Burkina. The Mossi and other Burkinabes describe them as obstreperous and difficult. They refuse to recognize any authority other than that of their village diviners and have battled first the French and later the government of Burkina for their independence. Although there is a significant amount of literature from the Colonial and post-Colonial periods about the Lobi, there have been few photographs published of them, and far fewer of them that show their bodies below the waist. This is because, until the 1970s, Lobi dress was rather minimal and offended French sensibilities. Decades ago, Lobi men wore only a thin cord around their waists, into which they inserted the head of the penis, allowing the testicles to hang free. They wore their hair long, to the jaw line, and dressed it with clay and fat, forming tight thin locks that stuck out all over. They wore numerous leather and brass amulets on their wrists and around the neck that provided magical protection of the *wathil*, the spirits of the wilderness. That was all they wore. Women dressed in a similar way but wore two small bundles of fresh green leaves tied to their belts in front and back for the sake of modesty. Of course, like almost everything else in Africa, all of this has changed, and nowadays Lobi men and women dress much as do men and women in any other area of rural Burkina: in secondhand American T-shirts and shorts or wrappers. The Lobi were also famous for the quantities of ivory jewelry they once wore. (Burkina still has the largest herds of wild elephants in all of West Africa.) Like the Gurunsi to the east, they wore large armlets above the elbow cut lengthwise from the elephant tusk. Lobi men wore pendants carved in the shape of whistles on their chests called *thungbubiel*. All Lobi women wore ivory lip plugs, or labrets. These were usually small, no more than the size of a silver dollar, but they were, nevertheless, rather striking to see.

All such objects have been collected years ago and are now in public or private collections outside Burkina Faso. In about 1980, the renowned art dealer Merton Simpson displayed in New York thirty or so of the thungbubiel whistle-shaped pendants, patinated in colors from white to orange to red to black. As late as the 1980s, people in Nuna villages showed me nose ornaments in ivory, but by that time hardly anyone wore them.

FULANI

There are large numbers of Fulani in northern Burkina Faso. They comprise the second-largest group of people in the country after the Mossi. The Fulani are very important across West Africa, from Senegal to Lake Chad, and are very numerous in Guinea, Mali, Niger, and Nigeria. Ever since the first European explorers trekked across the savanna grasslands of Senegal and Nigeria in the early nineteenth century, they have described the great physical beauty of Fulani women and their wonderful sense of style in dress. The Fulani are very heterogeneous. There are many different Fulani peoples, including the Wodaabe in Niger; the Udalan and Liptako in Burkina; settled town Fulani; nomadic cattle

A young Fulani mother with an infant in the market, wearing a fashionable Jelgobe women's dress. Dori, Burkina Faso, twentieth century. Photograph by Christopher D. Roy.

Fulani; and the famous Fulani of Mali, who specialize in weaving elaborate wool and cotton blankets with weft patterns in brick red, black, white, and yellow.

The Fulani women in northern Burkina are as fashion conscious as Fulani women everywhere. Pastoral Fulani women wear very bright shawls and scarves of imported rayon and wear their hair in elaborate coiffures—of which the most common is the sagittal crest from the front of the head to the back, heavily decorated with rows and rows of silver coins and other silver ornaments and amber beads. In the 1970s and 1980s, the favored cotton wrapper was of blue or black warp stripes worn with a colorful machine-printed cotton blouse and lots of amber and silver jewelry. Settled town or village Fulani women near the town of Dori wear very intricate and beautifully tailored blouses and skirts of colorful imported printed cotton cloth. These are sewn into elaborate gussets, frills, collars, layers, wide puffy sleeves, and other intricate combinations of cloth in bright colors by tailors in the Dori market who cater especially to Fulani clientele. The women also tattoo their lips and chins and paint black dots on their foreheads and cheeks. The overall impression is of great elegance, a powerful sense of individual style, and stunning beauty.

Fulani men also pride themselves in their personal beauty, but their clothing is very much more plain and darker than that of their wives. The Fulani herders around Barsalogho, Djibo, Aribinda, and Dori wear unique cotton shirts sewn of narrow strips dyed brown or black and covered with row upon row of white plastic buttons. The sleeves are very large, almost like wings, and are not sewn along the inside seam, so they fly and flap free of the arms if a wind comes up. It is quite usual to see a young Fulani herder with his cattle and goats wearing one of these spectacular shirts covered with buttons, along with baggy trousers bunched around the waist, purple or white plastic lace-up shoes, and a large, disk-shaped basketry hat. Fulani herders always carry a long, heavy stick with a large round boss at the end that they use to encourage their cows to move in the desired direction.

In the past twenty years, the economic and political elite of Burkina have shown a strong interest in African fashion, and several skilled and talented couturiers have established businesses in the capital. The most prominent are Martine Some and Ba-zemsé, who showed their work on March 2, 2007, at a *défilé de mode* at the president's palace in Ouagadougou during the week of FESPACO (Festival Pan-Africain du Cinema). Women's dress in Burkina features bare shoulders, high, stiff bustiers, and skirts that reach to the ankles. Into the twenty-first century, modern couture follows ancient local tradition, and short skirts are never shown. The two Burkinabe designers showed their work in company with Michael Gamor of Ghana and Eloi Sessou and Gilles Toure of Côte d'Ivoire. The high point of the evening was the work of the tremendously talented and original couturier Oumou Sy, from Senegal. Fashion shows are held regularly in Ouagadougou and several other cities and towns in Burkina, and are often sponsored by Madame Chantal Campaore, the wife of the chief of state. These *défilés* are attended by the very small, affluent economic elite of the country.

References and Further Reading

Barth, Heinrich. *Travels and Discoveries in North and Central Africa: Being a Journal of an Expedition Undertaken under the Auspices of H.B.M.'s Government in the Years 1849–1855*. New York: Harper and Brothers, 1857.

Capron, Jean. *Communautés villageoises bwa: Mali Haute-Volta*. Paris: Institut d'Ethnologie, 1973.

Cardinall, Allan W. *The Natives of the Northern Territories of the Gold Coast*. London: George Routledge, 1920.

Delobsom, A. A. Dim. "Le Mogho Naba et son cour." *Bulletin du comité des études historiques et scientifiques de l'A.O.F* 11, no. 3 (1928): 386–421.

Delobsom, A. A. Dim. "Les Nioniosse de Goupana (Ouagadougou)." *Outre-Mer, Revue generale de colonisation* 1, no. 4 (1929): 419–446.

Duperray, Anne-Marie. *Les Gourounsi de Haute-Volta*. Stuttgart, Germany: Franz Steiner, 1984.

Hammond, Peter. *Yatenga*. New York: Free Press, 1966.

Haselberger, Herta. "Bemerkungen zum Kunsthandwerk in der Republik Haute-Volta: Gurunsi und Altvolker des aussersten Sudwestens." *Zeitschrift fur Ethnologie* 94, no. 2 (1969): 171–246.

Izard, Michel. *Gens du pouvoir, gens de la terre*. Paris: Cambridge University Press, Editions de la Maison des sciences de l'homme, 1985.

Izard, Michel. *Le Yatenga precolonial: un ancien royaume du Burkina*. Paris: Editions Karthala, 1985.

Labouret, Henri. *Les tribus du rameau lobi*. Paris: Institut d'Ethnologie, 1931.

Lambert, G. E. (Capitaine). *Le Pays mossi et sa population. Etude historique, economique et géographique suivie d'un essai d'ethnographie comparée*. Ouagadougou, Burkina Faso: Centre National des Recherches Scientifique et Technologique, 1907.

Le Moal, Guy. *Les Bobo: nature et fonction des masques*. Paris: Organization des Recherches Scientifique et Technologique d'Outre Mer, 1981.

Mangin, Eugène. *Les Mossi: essai sur les usages et coutumes du peuple mossi au Soudan occidental*. Paris: Augustin Challamel, 1921. (Reprint of the 1914–1916 Anthropos publication.)

Marc, Lucien. *Le Pays mossi*. Paris: Larose, 1909.

Pageard, Robert. "Recherches sur les Nioniossé." *Etudes voltaiques* 4 (1963).

Roy, Christopher D. "Mossi Weaving." *African Arts* 15, no. 3 (1982): 48–59, 91–92.

Roy, Christopher D. *The Land of Flying Masks*. Munich: Prestel, 2007.

Ruelle, E. "Notes anthropologiques, ethnographiques, et sociologiques sur quelques populations noires du deuxieme territoire militaire de l'A.O.F." *L'Anthropologie* 15 (1904): 520–561, 657–703.

Tauxier, Louis. *Le noir du Soudan*. Paris: Larose, 1912.

Tauxier, Louis. *Le noir du Yatenga*. Paris: Larose, 1917.

Tauxier, Louis. *Nouvelles notes sur le Mossi et le Gourounsi*. Paris: Larose, 1924.

Traore, Sidi, and Margriet Renders. *La tenue traditionnelle au Burkina Faso*. Ouagadougou, Burkina Faso: Ministère de la Culture, 2005.

Christopher D. Roy

Senegal and Gambia

The location of Senegambia between the Sahara Desert, Atlantic Ocean, and West African savannas makes it a prime spot for cross-cultural exchange. The region consists of two nation-states—Senegal (a French colony 1890 to 1960) and Gambia (a British colony 1888 to 1965)—marked by millennia of shared history, culture, and geography. The area is in turn part of the larger subregion of the Sahel, formed from medieval African empires and formerly (mostly) French, Portuguese, and British colonial states. Portuguese explorers reached the peninsula of Cap Vert, the westernmost tip of Africa, in the fifteenth century, and, by the seventeenth century, this coast was an urban, trading, and then administrative and cultural center. European, African, and Arab/Islamic societies came into contact here, all influencing local dress codes and styles in their own ways. The main ethnic groups are the Wolof (44 percent), whose kingdoms collapsed during the eighteenth century, and the Peul/Toucouleur (24 percent, part of the broader Fulani grouping), with smaller populations of Serer, Jola, Mandinka, Soninke, French, and Lebanese (the latter two in Dakar). Urban culture is heavily influenced by the Wolof, the dominant group along the coast, and, for the most part, the region is characterized by a high level of religious and ethnic tolerance. Dakar, former colonial capital and national capital since 1960, hosts one-fourth of the national population of twelve million. Despite being a low-income country, Senegalese cultural producers—from the poet statesman Léopold Senghor to Ousmane Sembene, grandfather of African cinema, to the numerous tailors—are international leaders. Dakar is a creative center of fashion production, consumption, exchange, and display for a loyal local market and numerous regional and transnational markets.

COASTAL COSMOPOLITANISM

Contemporary Senegambian fashion processes are shaped by the economy and culture of the cosmopolitan, urban Atlantic coast. The African love of pageantry, adornment, and ceremony, along with newer forms of trade, artisanal labor, social networks, media, and public spaces combine to create *la mode Dakaroise* (Dakar fashion). Dakar fashion, in turn, is the major influence on contemporary regional dress. Senegambians have a thriving culture that combines modern cosmopolitanism and traditional values in this gateway region for Islamic, African, and European interaction. As in many West African societies, cloth and fashion are embedded in deep local heritages of artisanal production and gift exchange. Cloth was a form of currency until the turn of the twentieth century, as was gold during medieval times, and both are still prized forms of personal property. Yet while in the modern West haute couture and mass production have tended to centralize clothes production, Senegambian fashion processes are characterized by significant tensions between the centralizing dynamics of urban centers and the cultural dominance of the urban elite and the decentralizing effects of artisanal production and local creativity.

The history of dress shows how cultural creolization and Western civilizing processes have long been interconnected. Portuguese, British, French, and Dutch enclaves on the coast, at Gorée Island and St. Louis, developed rival imperial trades in cloth, gold, slaves, and gum. Eventually, the handicraft production of cloth by persons of caste—low-status, hereditary artisanal groups—was replaced by European factory-made cloth. West Africa became an important market for European industrial growth. French trading houses dominated the market and sold products primarily from the French textile industry—cotton prints in floral, striped, and geometric motifs. French tailors staffed colonial institutions and trained Africans.

Since the 1980s, the globalization of the textile trade has eliminated French and Lebanese control of the market. With the aid of Senegalese traders, Hong Kong producers have imitated luxurious German, Austrian, and Swiss *bazin* (damask), jacquards, and voiles, as well as wax cotton prints, the sheer cotton Khartoum, and various accessories. The colors and motifs of the European fashion season are rapidly copied. Since 2000, Senegalese traders have been traveling to India for synthetic brocades and beaded voiles. Chinese competition for low-end consumption has captured the local market, and the national textile firms are being closed. Chinese industry also supplies fashion accessories and counterfeit goods in synthetic materials, such as shoes, bags, jewelry, and scarves in bright colors.

Banjul, Gambia's capital, was an entry port for informal trade routes in the 1980s that led from Jeddah, Las Palmas, Hong Kong, and Europe to Senegalese markets via the towns of Kaolack and Touba, the Mouride holy city. Dakar's major marketplaces, Sandaga, Tilene, and HLM 5, the major cloth market, are centers of regional trade. Sufi Islamic religious brotherhoods have created a new commercial middle class in Dakar and throughout the world, including the United States, Europe, Saudi Arabia, South Africa, and Japan. This commercial diaspora is at the heart of the survival of Dakar's informal economy, which supplies consumers and producers with global goods.

Dakar has become a nexus for global goods, artisanal production, and creativity. Traders from throughout the Sahel and West

Two Senegambian men in traditional-style white boubous, one with cap, and a boy in Western-style clothing. The boubou became the national dress of Senegal in the 1980s. Photograph by Joseph Hill.

Africa purchase here, and Senegalese travel around the world. With its porous border, Gambia is central to this globalized trade. Its consumers follow Senegalese fashion. Incomes are lower and secondhand clothing is used more than in Dakar. Among young women in interior towns and villages, especially in the south, color preferences generally become more muted and styles more modest. As goods spread, the creativity of Dakarois keeps traders coming back to Dakar for style ideas.

URBANIZATION AND FASHION

As the French colonial state consolidated its control, the trading enclaves became the four communes (Gorée, St. Louis, Dakar, and Rufisque), and their African residents became "black Frenchmen." They had the political rights of French citizens and were "civilized" through francophone skill, education, employment in colonial institutions, political representation, manners, and, importantly, elegance. Men were subject to punitive measures that made Western dress obligatory in official contexts, such as in schools and offices, and also served as a stylish sign of civilized modernity. Taking their assimilated status seriously, these suit-wearing, rights-bearing men were among the first, in an African context, to voice anticolonial sentiments.

The history of trade and imperialism on the cosmopolitan coast is crystallized in the legacy of the seventeenth- and eighteenth-century Signares, who remain a reference point in the coastal cultural life and imagination. These mixed-race traders created a culture of Creole feminine elegance in the form of the *dirriankhe* (see below under Senses and Memory) that influenced cuisine, dress, and comportment in St. Louis and Dakar. Increasingly, clothing came to represent not just family honor but also individual women's courage, wealth, and autonomy. Women of all ages and incomes endeavor to dress with civility, propriety, and fashion. Feminine coquetry in dress, charm, and gestures is considered common in urban Senegal, and this has inspired popular critiques of female narcissism, consumption, rivalry, and sexual laxity.

Two powerful trends have shaped the extraordinary growth of contemporary fashion at the turn of the twenty-first century. First, there has been a reorientation away from the colonial dimension toward a global outlook. Second, this shift coincided with the emergence of a Mouride commercial urban class. However, in the 1980s, the foundations of this urban elite and middle class were eroded in the wake of economic reforms and a decline in educational institutions and employment, as the state and companies downsized. Urban middle-class women entered tailoring as entrepreneurs. They hired *nawkat* (male tailors), relied on their social networks for financial support and a clientele, and publicized their work through their own dress. Thanks to the trade in used sewing machines from Europe (the price of such machines fell to as low as US$50 by the 1990s), in 2007, medium-range embroidery could be ordered for the equivalent of US$20, a reasonable sum for a small trader. However, while persons of caste origin no longer dominate in these fields, manual or service work is still considered low status. Tailors and women entrepreneurs, few of whom are skilled, generally call themselves designers.

The expansion of global trade and local production and the blossoming of social life enabled the acceleration and broadening of fashion. The collaborative design process enabled tailors and clients to modify, invent, and recombine cloth and styles in their own way and according to local lexicons. They may wear African boubous for Friday prayers, slinky black Lycra attire for a Saturday evening ball, and jogging suits when selling goods in the marketplace. Inspired by Senegalese music videos, Brazilian soap operas, Parisian fashion magazines, and Dakar street life, garment designs are recorded in journals created with the help of tailors. Locally produced, often homemade, visual, musical, and performance cultures spread styles rapidly across a broad spectrum of social income and status groups.

There are four consumption cycles that shape fashion seasons and styles. First, darker, heavier cloth is worn during the cool/dry season in the first part of the year and lighter/brighter colors during the wet/hot part. Second, the monthly cycle of cash circulation is that the first ten days of the month are for settlement of wages, debts, and purchases. The peaks of consumption are the two Muslim Eid celebrations of Korite and Tabaski, one month apart, which are times of sacrifice and renewal. Finally, each family network has its own cycle of celebrations such as weddings, naming ceremonies, and funerals.

While building upon enduring forms and values, dress also possesses a fertile capacity to evolve. For example, billowing boubous, robes of six meters (twenty feet), simply cut and often richly embroidered around the neck, are recognized the world over as traditionally West African. Yet the boubou is not a static symbol of origin but an object of dynamic dialogue between tradition and modernity, hybridity and authenticity. It was further spread by Islamicization in the nineteenth century and, while the basic form stays constant, it has its own fashions. Another example is the brightly colored cotton floral or geometric print known as African cloth or wax cloth. This is actually an imitation of Indonesian batiks manufactured, in consultation with African traders, since the nineteenth century in Dutch factories for the African market.

The naming of styles exemplifies a hybridity based on the mixing of material, visual, and musical cultures. For instance, Alexis, the infamous character from *Dynasty*, the U.S. television series, is used as a name for the long, slit skirt also popular in Europe. In 1993, "Yow lele," the title of a Youssou N'Dour song, was used to name a woman's skirt suit and a revival of a Peul hair braiding style. At the same time, a long, straight hair wig was named

Muslim Senegambian men in boubous, shawls, caps, and sunglasses, ca. 2000. Photograph by Joseph Hill.

cheveux indiens after the black supermodel Naomi Campbell. This wig was worn with an Indian sari borrowed from a Hindi film. Televised images of political rallies, mosque visits during holiday prayers, the evening news, and music videos publicize the work of the elite designers who dress celebrities. These spread fashion ideas and inspire their naming. In the anticolonial period of the 1950s, there were hairstyles and dresses named after Lamine Gueye and his political party, Parti Bloc, for example. Today, printed cloth for pagnes and T-shirts are produced for political rallies with imprints of politicians' photos or political party logos.

Since the 1980s, a small group of elite designers has emerged. Many of them have converted the *pagne rabbal*, handwoven cloth, into cloth for haute couture and interior design. Costume designer Oumou Sy works with film, fashion, and museum shows. An industrial park in Dakar, SODIDA, also hosts a small number of firms that make uniforms, elite dress, and garments for export.

CLOTHING AND VALUES

Fashion thrives largely because human beauty is valued; the body has long been the principal canvas of cultural expression in this region. *Sañse*, from the French *changer* (to change), means

"to transform oneself." This refers to the deep cultural ideal of continual self-cultivation as respect for self and others. The spectacular garments worn by the individuals who populate contemporary Dakar's public spaces illustrate the vital importance of appearance, dress, and beauty there. However, Dakarois are well aware of the contradiction between their financial hardship and their obsession with fashion.

In urban heterogeneous contexts, everyday markets, streets, and visiting are competitive sites for dress. Yet deep cultural values of *tar*, *teraanga*, *jom*, and *kersa* (Wolof terms that relate to pan-regional values, respectively: generosity, dignity, discretion) still find expression in the use of cloth and clothing as gifts and garments. More recent values such as being *civilisé* (civilized, clean, fashionable) reflect the impact of French colonialism and of status in a global context. Women are responsible for maintaining dignity through dress, especially when the family is impoverished. They sacrifice financially, borrow, and rely on cheaper qualities of cloth and clothing. Cloth and clothing have always been important gifts and expressions of self, hierarchy, and community. Therefore, celebrations of religious holidays and *xew* (family ceremonies)—weddings, baby naming days, and, increasingly, funerals—are central times of display and gift giving. Bazin, *pagne rabbal*, money, and gold are prized gifts. Savings groups, afternoon visiting, *sabar* (young women's dances), and religious singing events are important to social networking in the unstable economy. Ceremonies regroup extended kin from across the country and are organized by and for women. Cloth gifts are also given to older kin at important holidays or in gratitude for support.

As garments age, they move from ceremonial wear to everyday life, such as less important social events than afternoon visiting or commercial work. They are part of patronage networks and so are passed down to younger, poorer, or rural relatives. When young people return to regional towns and villages, they must show their clothing as a sign of urban success. In practice, many families and women go into severe debt to kin or merchants and default on credit payments in order to finance dress and ceremonies. Today clothing is not only a marker of sophistication but also a mask that conceals unstable status and wealth.

Wrapping, layering, and tying are at the heart of the practical, moral, and aesthetic aspects of African dress. Two simple practices show how, in birth and in death, families care for the bodies of their members. Babies, from birth, are wrapped in cotton and handwoven pagnes and then strapped to the back of their caregivers. Baby massages elongate the nose and neck, while girls' hips are shaped to protrude and boys' hips are straightened. At the end of life, corpses are carefully washed and wrapped in cheap white cotton percale according to religious prescription.

While wrapping conforms to religious and cultural norms of modesty, it also allows for revealing and concealing. Playful manipulation of garments with falling necklines, shawls, and billowing arms produces continual reminders of the power of cloth as well as gestures of flirtation. Wrapping also creates hierarchy and solidarity. It creates symbiosis as well as silhouettes of power expressed through volume and density and so distinctions of wealth and status. Some garments are large (six to ten meters [twenty to thirty-three feet] long) and require minimum stitching. In the hot, sandy climates of the Sahel, great swathes of cloth, shawls, and head covers envelop the body and so protect from sun, wind, and sand. Coverage of the body, especially the female one, expresses values of modesty and propriety, or, indeed, social control. Concealing becomes more important as women reach adulthood, marriage, and motherhood. Still, while legs, hips, and breasts should be covered, their shape is often alluded to in the drapes and the sway of hips under the cloth. Far more than propriety, dress creates multisensorial impressions of movement, texture, and color.

Attitudes toward undress, the absence of clothing or only the underlayer, reveal much about a society's attitudes toward dress as symbols of proper personhood and social belonging. In Senegambia, a common comment on an improperly dressed person is that "he [or she] is wearing whatever, she [or he] is a crazy person." The prototype of the crazy person is the quasi-nude man with dreadlocks, tattered rags, and skin blackened with accumulated dirt and dust, talking and gesturing wildly. This image is the polar opposite of the civilized person, who is clean, proper, and restrained in conduct. Mentally challenged persons under family care are dressed at minimal cost and inadvertently serve as spectacles of disorder at social events. In earlier times, pagnes were used as undergarments. Along with other objects of modernity and civilization, such as sewing machines and watches, underwear and bras were included from the 1940s in the gifts offered by grooms to brides. They are now a normal part of clothing.

STYLES AND SOCIAL CONTEXTS

Modern urban fashion provides a telling cultural expression of the social dynamics of both inequality and mobility. The strict hierarchies of Senegambian societies are organized by longstanding patriarchal inequalities of gender and age and precolonial status systems of caste and slavery. They are also shaped by modern processes of class and ethnic differentiation. Instability and new commercial classes make dignity and dress even more important. While precolonial sartorial splendor was an expression of masculine political and religious power, modern dress highlights female elegance in urban cosmopolitanism. The ascendancy of the boubou and *n'dockette* owes much to the intensification of ceremonial and commercial life and the rise of new commercial classes.

Esquisses sénégalaises (1853), by the Catholic priest Pierre Boilat, provides a lavish catalog of precolonial dress traditions. Royalty and elite groups of aristocrats, warriors, and religious men are shown wearing multiple layers of cloth, necklaces, wigs, and scarves. Hand-dyed and handwoven indigo pagnes are layered around torso, waist, or legs. Most wear head scarves or caps. Before the introduction of sewing machines in the late nineteenth century, boubous and outfits were made by sewing bands of strip cloth together using large iron needles made by blacksmiths. The few images of lower-status persons show them also in draped garments of woven cloth.

Although the basic categories of dress are traditional/African and modern/European, the diversity of styles transcends this opposition. These categories are symbolized in the French suit, the attire of the civilized black Frenchman, and the embroidered boubou, the attire of the traditional Muslim man. The embroidered boubou is, and has always been, the pinnacle of prestige. African dress is associated with religious and traditional ceremonial events, domestic space, and modesty. Western dress is appropriate for public spaces such as offices and schools. The categories imply cultural origin and values related to modesty, ornamentation, and cultural (in)authenticity. In general, form-fitting Western clothes are less modest and simpler, while African clothes are more modest, more ornamental, and appropriate for gift exchange.

Most *tenues européenes/toubab* (European-style outfits) are custom-made by tailors originally trained by the French in colonial institutions in the 1950s. Ready-made garments represent only a small new niche in the garment market. The *costume* (European men's suit) was a charged symbol of colonial authority. Despite its discomfort in the warm climate, it was required wear, under threat of punishment, for schoolboys in the Colonial and early Independence era. It was promoted as official dress by Léopold Senghor, the first president of Senegal. Yet, even in the Colonial period, 1950s studio photographs of urban middle classes and elites show that men wore a range of styles including caftans, boubous (some embroidered), and suits. A captivating photo shows a young man wearing what resembles the standard black wool pinstripe suit. The blazer, however, is accompanied by a red fez and baggy Wolof *tchaya* pants in pinstripe wool. These baggy pants fall low to the knees and are full and gathered between the legs, contrasting with the neat look of trousers.

In the 1980s, the second president, Abdou Diouf, replaced the suit with the boubou as national dress. It was prescribed for official events, which were increasingly televised, and for Friday prayers. With the decline of the educated elite and the rise of the commercial elite, the boubou has superseded the suit as the standard dress of modern urban identity. The boubou is not only formal dress but everyday wear. It is made in virtually all materials for both genders and all ages, income levels, and contexts. It has become popularized and feminized, some would say degraded. Once made of sober colors such as white and light blue, it is now made in bright greens and pinks with multicolor threads. Damask is the cloth of choice for men's robes, but luxurious lighter materials such as voile, jacquard, linen, and their cheap Chinese imitations are now available and popular. For men, everyday wear is a caftan or boubou with pants. Full formal wear is a three-piece outfit of caftan, loose trousers or tchaya pants, all covered by an embroidered grand boubou. The Toucouleur, generally more conservative people, prefer the largest boubous of hand-dyed cloth. For religious events, or as they age, men add shawls and caps. The latter may be white skullcaps, often embroidered, pillbox caps, or red or brown fezzes. Few men, other than marabouts, now wear turbans. For shoes, they prefer handmade leather babouches or slippers. Heavy silver rings and bracelets, prayer beads, and leather pouches or amulets hanging on the chest complete the proper outfit.

For women, the boubou is worn over a *ser*, a two-meter (six-and-a-half-foot) skirt wrapper. It is accompanied by a *musoor*, head scarf, and a shawl worn on one shoulder or both in cooler wet seasons. For domestic work, women may tie a wrapper around their waist to constrain the boubou. Traditionally, women wore several (up to ten) wrappers to show their wealth. Cottons were covered in heavy, handwoven pagnes laced with gold thread. Like the boubou, the n'dockette became very popular in the 1990s for both formal and everyday wear. Other styles such as *taille bas*, dresses, and skirt suits tend to be limited to specific, less formal contexts such as shopping, visiting, school, or young women's social events. For formal wear, elaborate hairstyles and jewelry complete the full outfit.

A major impact on the balance of power of Western and Dakarois forms is the changing importance of the social contexts with which they correlate. In recent decades, Westernized institutions have become unsustainable and traditional familial and religious ceremonial networks more important. This is because investing in the social and religious-based economic networks of the informal economy is the only option for most people's survival. Given the massive unemployment, small businesses, savings associations, ceremonial exchanges, loans, and mutual aid form the basis of the fragile family economy. African dress is required for matters such as transacting deals in marketplaces, seeking aid from religious figures, or attending neighborhood women's savings groups.

PAGEANTRY AND MODERN ELEGANCE

As the sources of socioeconomic power diversify, modern elegance, of both men and women, is replacing the pageantry of charisma as the expression of symbolic power. Furthermore, the ideal of sartorial splendor is exemplified now by women rather than men. Traditionally, the value of garments was judged by the quality and amount of cloth. In modern fashion, distinction is achieved through balancing several forms of value—financial, aesthetic, and social/moral. The quality and exotic origin of cloth, the workmanship, and the originality of design convey this complex value.

Embroidery, *diamina*, is the epitome of value and beauty in dress. In the pre-Colonial era, elaborate dress displayed masculine religious or political power and charisma. The embroidered boubou was the dress of "princes and marabouts," with its ten meters (eleven yards) of handwoven cotton cloth strips worn over large caftans and trousers or very baggy Wolofchaya pants. Motifs such as *netti palme*, three hands, were hand embroidered in gold silk thread that covered the entire length and width of the front of the garment. Until the 1950s, boubous were handmade by Dianankhe Peul craftsmen. An elaborate motif took a month to complete (and cost the equivalent of a modern bureaucrat's monthly salary). Since then, Cornely sewing machines in the 1950s, Berninas in the 1970s, and Pakistani tailors in the 1990s have mechanized and popularized this formerly elite form.

The diversity of styles, qualities, and raw materials for ornamentation exploded with the expansion of tailoring and global trade in the 1980s. Qualities of cloth are ranked numerically from one to four based on appearance (rich/real, false) and origin of production. High-quality cloth offers sheen, weight, and durability, while lower-quality Chinese cloth loses weight and color over time with washing. In this context of diverse values of cloth, ornamentation adds financial, aesthetic, and social/moral value. Ironically, in order to valorize cheap cloth, clients and tailors may spend more money and time on the ornamentation than on the cloth. Lace trim, appliqué, painting, and embroidery are used on materials, including those that can barely sustain the weight of decoration such as Khartoum or percale. The use of percale, a funerary white cotton, for embroidered boubous is a sign to many of the degradation of the value of dress. Embroidery is now worn by all ages, genders, and social groups for both special and everyday wear. In fact, embroidered boubous are mass produced in Dakar markets as ready to wear. Small lines of trim even adorn dresses worn for housework. In the context of this spread of decoration, a traditional form of prestigious cloth has been revived. Soninke and Bamana women specialize in hand-dyed cloth called *tub*. Prized colors continue to be sky blue, white (associated with piety), indigo navy, and rust brown. Innovative designs range from repeated geometrics to big tie-dyed circles.

HYBRIDITY AND FEMININITY

In contemporary Senegal, women's fashion (*cutur femme*) and the embroidery associated with it are in a constant state of change. Conditions of economic crisis have been vehicles for economic innovation and for a design culture that has brought a broad array of producers and consumers into fashion and design. At the same time, both these areas of style are revitalizations of tradition. The most creative and competitive sector, women's fashion, has revived Euro-African styles, the n'dockette and taille bas, that can be traced as far back as the mid-nineteenth century through

In early-twenty-first-century Gambia and Senegal, Western secondhand clothing, *fuug jaay*, is bought mainly for children. Photograph by Joseph Hill.

visual historical records. The n'dockette is a loose gown with elbow-length, loose sleeves. Its necklines, sleeves, and even the body of the dress are decorated with trim such as satin ribbons, eyelet lace, or embroidery. The base form of earlier versions of the n'dockette in photographs from the 1950s was the camisole, a full, long dress with loose, elbow-length sleeves and an open neck. It resembles garments in nineteenth-century drawings of Signares. From the postwar period, modifications include looseness of the garment, seams at the waist, puffy sleeves, and the length of sleeves.

The taille bas is a modification of the skirt suit with straight skirt and fitted top. These garments were made of imported French cotton prints bought from the French trading firms that monopolized the textile trade until the 1970s. The top has elaborate styling around the hipline, neckline, and sleeves. These decorations may be layers of cloth, flounces, trims, appliquéd motifs, embroidery, or various creative cuts. Sleeves are often puffy. The architectural look of the taille bas combines the most rigorous of European tailored cuts—the straight skirt and the blazer—and the decorative, kinetic features of an African garment. Other outfits borrow from other West African styles such as a tunic with pants, the Beninois two wrappers (long and hip length), and the *abaya*, a large hip-length tunic with wrapper.

The ser/pagne is a two-meter (six-and-a-half-foot) cloth that is the staple of women's dress and of feminine propriety; it is worn wrapped around the waist and tucked or tied on the left side. By age three, girls learn how to wrap and wear pagnes. Fancy pagnes of heavy cloth such as embroidered satin or handwoven cloth may be worn under fancy boubous or n'dockettes. Elderly women prefer the old-fashioned style of layered wrappers and wear two or three at a time for ceremonies with the prestigious woven wrapper on top. Controversially, young women now may tuck or tie it at the middle of the back instead of the side, which calls attention to the hips. Since the 1990s, n'dockettes or loose dresses without pagne or tunic-pants sets have become fashionable. Pagnes are often cut from the standard six- to eight-meter (six-and-a-half- to nine-yard) length of cloth. Fancy pagnes, synthetics made in Hong Kong, are imported from Jeddah and worn under n'dockettes. As the decoration of n'dockettes has become costly, a new style is the "worked pagne," which decorates the wrapper extensively and leaves the dress simple.

If older women express a cosmopolitan culture, young women may indulge in masquerades and dress à l'Indienne, à la Japonaise, à l'Arabe, and so on. The popular styles of the 1990s and 2000s, such as the *sharee*, a sari made with a drape and a stitched rather than wrapped skirt; the Mauritanian *mulf*, a six-meter (twentyfoot) length wrapped around the body and the head; and the *hijab*, a head scarf wrapped around the face and worn with a Muslim long robe, are all wrapped, layered garments borrowed from female dress in India, Mauritania, and the Middle East; they show that the irrepressible cosmopolitanism of Dakarois fashion defies the oppositional logic of African–European or traditional–modern.

RELIGION AND DRESS

In Senegambia, piety is not generally opposed to worldly engagement with culture, global flows, or commerce. Therefore, African/Muslim/traditional dress, such as boubous, caftans, and n'dockettes, undergoes creative modifications. As across the Muslim world, the two Eids (Korite and especially Tabaski) are the

major moments for urban production, consumption, and fashion creativity. For these holidays, new clothes, sacrifices and gifts of lamb, a clean house, and visiting are prescribed. Various celebratory events, including singing, maraboutic visits, and pilgrimages to Mecca and regional sacred sites are reasons for feasts and display. The pilgrimage to Mecca is an opportunity to enjoy the Gulf shopping zones in Jeddah and Dubai. Pilgrims and traders alike return with new goods and gifts for relatives. The streets come alive as people parade their new clothes. As with the pageantry of Catholic bishops, marabouts wear the most extravagant, embroidered gowns. The latter, with their many wives, benefit from constant gifts of cloth and boubous from their followers.

Adherents of Islamic reformism follow principles of modesty but still enjoy fashion. Young men wear fuller caftans and caps. Young women wear a high-necked loose robe over pants or

A Senegambian follower of the resurgent Baye Fall movement, in patchwork and dreadlocks. This style symbolizes Sufi renunciation of the world, implying lack of time and money to spend on dress. By the 1990s, increased demand for patchwork meant that tailors, rather than using leftover cloth, were buying up material for the specific purpose of cutting it into squares. Photograph by Joseph Hill.

pagnes, socks, and sometimes gloves. Head scarves are wrapped and pinned around the face, chin, and neck. They cover the body fully and avoid sheer fabrics but follow fashionable colors and cuts and use ornamentation such as embroidery, beading, and trimming. Accessories are color coordinated like those of any Dakaroise young woman. Veiling is a highly symbolic and controversial dress statement and until recently was seen as an un-African, Arab practice. It is practiced by some educated urban girls, including university students, who can face family protest or peer ridicule for their choice.

Images of the Mouride and Tijiane prophets Cheikh Ahmadou Bamba and El Hajj Malick Sy are found on wall murals, vans, calendars, and television, and protective portraits are kept in wallets, neck purses, and on van dashboards. Sy is depicted wearing a boubou, but Bamba is especially striking with his flowing white gown and covered head. Unlike most men, marabouts wear turbans and shawls and are publicly seen and photographed with large tinted sunglasses. Tijianes live throughout West Africa and share regional influences, from the Moroccan fez and turban to the heavier threads of Nigerian-style embroidery.

The recent history of *jaxass*, Baye Fall patchwork, shows the mobility of fashion. The followers of their mid-nineteenth-century founder, Cheikh Ibra Fall, dress in a patchwork of brightly colored ends of cloth, and their hair is in dreadlocks. This eye-catching, unconventional jaxass look is presented as a renunciation of the world and symbolizes the Mouride ethic of devotion to work as prayer and the absence of time or money to dress. By the 1990s, tailors bought cloth and cut it into squares to be resewn as patchwork for caftans, n'dockettes, and trousers. Sotiba, the national textile firm, has manufactured a cotton print that looks like patchwork.

YOUTH FASHION

Youth fashion centers around blue jeans worn with heavy sneakers, T-shirts, Lycra leggings, spandex midriff tops, and baseball caps. The boy *disco/thiouf* and *diskette*, the hip young man and woman, frequent discos and seek to buy Italian leather shoes or fancy jeans. Mouride market traders or suitcase traders import jeans, Lycra garments, T-shirts, bags, sneakers, and shoes from New York and increasingly China (Hong Kong). *Friperie* or *fuug jaay* (French: old clothes; Wolof: dust off and sell), low-status Western secondhand clothing, is sold in marketplaces (especially Colobane in Dakar) and street markets. It is seen as dirty, undignified, and a sign of poverty and is bought mostly for children and by many youths and poor adult men. A small number of tailors specialize in transforming fuug jaay into fashionable clothing with cuts, restyling, and the addition of decorations.

JEWELRY

The hair, head, and neck areas are extensively modified and adorned with ornate hairstyles, cosmetics, and jewelry. Jewelry originated as protective leather chains of multiple amulets that contained written verses of the Qur'an that had been washed. These were worn around the neck, waist, or arm. Berber-influenced heavy silver jewelry has long been prominent in the north. There is a long Sudanic tradition of trade in gold dating back to the eleventh century. This trans-Saharan trade brought Arab/Berber influences to the region, followed later by Mediterranean and European influences. In the nineteenth century, French colonial officers took artisans to colonial expositions, which introduced a French influence on techniques and styles. Gold mining, trading, and smithing were also central to the Mali kingdom of the thirteenth to seventeenth centuries.

Like woven cloth, gold is a highly prized gift, adornment, and personal property. Until the eighteenth-century spread of Islam, both men and women wore gold. Since then, it became a wedding gift for and property of women. Today's wealthy women traders show their success and independence with their own gold purchases. Most women dream of a cache of a half kilo (one pound); these women distinguish themselves with gold ornaments bought in Saudi Arabia that reach down to their waist, accompanying bangles and earrings—more than a half kilo no doubt.

Throughout the region, from the Atlantic Ocean to Lake Chad, a mixture of styles demonstrates that goldsmiths, objects, and materials traveled far and wide. Artisanal hereditary groups of goldsmiths once made gold for royal families. Influences on the hybrid Wolof style include North African/Berber styles, Portuguese, French, and regional influences from Toucouleur and other Sahelian societies. Drawn wire, iron, or steel plates show Moorish influence. Wolof goldsmiths are renowned for their skill and incorporation of foreign influence. As early as the 1590s, they bought and reworked silver coins from Portuguese explorers. In the nineteenth century, Wolof goldsmiths traveled to France for colonial exhibitions, where they were both lauded and trained in European techniques.

Major skills in this craft include filigree, granulation, repoussé, and hammering. Wolof styles emphasize air, light, and ornateness through filigree and incorporate international styles. The heavier Toucouleur work adorns flat surfaces with decoration or enamel in bright red or yellow. Florals, half-domes, beads, cones, coins, and coiled rings are common. Classic Toucouleur forms include the corval, a conical bead, or twisted earrings wrapped with red thread, four lobed rings, or beads in sizes as small as a small dime to as big as a hand. Until the 1950s, large, sculptural coiffures were accentuated with adornments of multiple pieces of pear-shaped beads, coins, or coils that protruded from large, loosely tied head scarves. Gold beads of various sizes are worn on the forehead, earrings, and neck collars on short or long chains. Throat ornaments, especially a four-pronged lion's claw, are popular throughout the region as far as Ghana. Pieces are hollow, and less-costly imitations may be gold-plated or made from clay, silk, wax, or straw. The traditional classic Wolof *kostine* form is inspired by French flower motifs and accentuates the delicacy of flowers with ornate filigree. A central frame includes a pendant of a basket of flowers composed of two or three repeated motifs. It is framed by a series of pear-shaped wire, conical shapes, raised beads, and hanging twisted wires. Two smaller pendant baskets hang on either side. This creates a polyphonic, highly textured image with several overlapping but centered frames.

From the tiny earrings of a child to the light chain of a young woman to the prized marriage gift of a betrothed woman, gold marks the beauty, value, and property of a woman. A photograph from the 1970s depicts a young nomadic Peulh woman with coins in fine hair braids, a band of cloth with gold coils half covered in red thread framing her face, and three twisted earrings piercing the ear. Two collars circle her neck with a series of small gold-filigree spheres, and a long chain of a bicone bead larger than her hand hangs down to her waist over a gold-embroidered grand boubou.

Unlike tailoring, which has flourished with global trade and influence, goldsmithing has been dying out since the 1960s. Since the 1990s, the suitcase trade in gold from Turkey, Saudi Arabia, and now Dubai and India has come to dominate the market. Many women have melted down their older artisanal pieces and had them remade as copies of foreign styles. Many Senegalese smiths now travel to New York to work for Pakistani jewelers.

COIFFURE

Head scarves have always been the proper form of dress for both men and women. Tying styles (height, tilts, layering, knotting) vary among ethnic groups and regions and depend on the context of use. Dakar women of all ethnicities may wear tall, layered pieces for an important event, a closer-to-the-head wrapping for everyday outings, or a simple cloth wrapping at home. Even if covered, hair is cared for and shaped. Before the wide availability of Western hair care products (some now made locally), hair was treated with animal butters, shea butters, and other local materials. Sisal, wool yarn, and twigs lent structure. In the past, children's ages were marked by hairstyles, shavings, or braids. The shaving of newborn babies' heads for their seventh-day naming ceremony marks entry into social life. In St. Louis, families announced that girls were ready for betrothal by adorning them with a coiled style.

Women from St. Louis developed elaborate hairstyles that expressed their age and family origin as well commented on current affairs. Until the 1950s, they wore multiple puffs or heavy braided wigs adorned with jewelry, coins, or beads and a large head scarf that exposed the bottom half of the hairdo and framed the chin. The fine braiding styles of the Toucoleur have been revived more recently. In the 1990s, women invested in hair salons. Using hair extensions, they revived some intricate braiding styles, and European-style wigs became more widely available. Like jewelry, sculpted chignons have multiple ornate attachments, curls, and swirls, and they may shine with gel. The most ornate styles are worn for special events and can be costly. False hair, *meche*, is made in Korea or Dakar factories owned by Koreans. It adds texture, length, width, and durability.

THE TOILETTE

Elaborate self-care prepares the canvas of the body for *sañse*, its adornment and display for the eyes of others. Cosmetics were traditionally based on medicinal plants, roots, and animal fats that protected the eyes and skin from the harsh winds, dust, and sun of the arid and desert climates. Tattooing of the lips, gums, and face was cosmetic as well as medicinal. In urbanized areas, fairly costly factory-made soaps, lotions, and perfumes are now preferred. Henna, a red or black stain, is still used on hands and feet with floral or geometric designs, especially for weddings. The emphasis on beauty is seen in the traditions of nomadic groups, such as the Berbers, who used antimony powder for both medicinal and decorative purposes. The admired, light-brown-skinned Toucoleur nomadic women traditionally traced the eyes with black liner, drew a dark blue or black line down their long noses, and stained their tattooed lips blue. In other parts of the Sahel, young Toucoleur men are also elaborate beauticians of the self. As with cloth, there are varied qualities of cosmetics. Dark, traditional hues of blue, black, and red are replaced, especially by younger urban women, with lighter or brighter tones of blues and reds, emphasizing texture and moistness, and giving definition to eyes, lips, and gums. Styles have included painted-on eyebrows, heavy white face powder, and outlined lips, which give an impression of a painted face. Heavy makeup and elaborate coiffure are used to create a stylized look that lends dramatic flair to ceremonial appearances and the portrait photography that is central to an event's success.

Although they do not follow elaborate facial care regimes as in the West, Senegalese women pay great attention to skin care by using lotions to impart softness, smoothness, and sheen. The best come from the United States and France, and cheaper versions from Nigeria. *Karite*, shea butter, is the traditional skin care, hair care, and massage remedy that has recently gained international prominence in high-end skin-care products. In Senegal, it is still also used for newborn baby massage.

Xeesal, a controversial but widespread practice of chemical skin lightening, is the most extreme example of the distortion of ideals of beauty in the modern context. Xeesal uses chemical creams, many with a hydroquinone formula, to block melanin production. Those who can use injections. More commonly, mixtures combine body lotions, or even household detergents and bleach, with the chemical. Creams are imported from Nigeria or the United States. After two decades of use and despite medical, social, and religious efforts to denounce it, the practice continues to be popular. Women say that it is fashionable, brightens tone, and that men prefer lighter-complexioned women. Many women use Xeesal to lighten and brighten to a dark brown tone, but others bleach to a pinkish shell color, especially for ceremonial events. The consequences can be severe, with women suffering skin problems ranging from cancer to severe sloughing. It is extremely harmful to babies in utero as well.

Whitening agents aside, women's culture of dress cultivates sensuous care for the self and each other. In elaborate preparations for dress, they loan garments, tie each other's head scarves and necklaces, adjust robes, do makeup together, and generally admire each other in the course of sañse. Young women live in close quarters and share clothing and style ideas. They also rely on the financial help and advice of older female kin.

SENSES AND MEMORY IN DRESS

All fancy dress seeks to arrest with a visual image, but pageantry is mobilized, along with the other senses. Scent more than anything signals cleanliness and sensual allure. Just before venturing out, a woman may spray herself with perfume and, most importantly, stand over a pot of burning incense so that her clothes will absorb the alluring scent. Good posture is considered important. Swathed in boubou robes and wearing a tall head scarf and gold chains and *jangjulli* (beads) around the waist, a dirriankhe walks with her head held high, a distant facial expression, and a slow gait with lightly swaying hips. Cloth, walk, and scent all combine to announce a woman's elegance and allure. As they reach their thirties, women, married or not, cultivate demeanors of reserve and gravity. Even at ceremonies, adult women dance with restraint and only for short periods, leaving the women of caste to perform for the event. Younger women have more freedom to openly express the joy of sociality and dress. They organize *sabar* dances or ceremonies involving sharp leg and arm movements and more exuberance.

No detail is left untouched in the public and private arts of seduction. The ideal of *jekk*, "elegance," is a mode of public seduction. The dirriankhe, with cloth flowing, scents lingering, and waist beads clicking, brings beauty and fashion into public life. *Mokk pocc* is a set of practices of self-preparation, self-presentation, and seduction that uses objects, scents, and care to arouse conjugal eroticism. It is essential to be thoroughly clean, soft-skinned, and fragranced. Special wrappers, incense, massage, charming gestures, and trinkets arouse both partners. Short wrappers (*beco*) cover just the upper thigh area and are vital to the erotic arts. They may be embroidered with motifs ranging from simple geometric shapes to humorous or erotic figures of genitalia. Delicate fringes, lattices, and small beads both decorate and accent the hips and thighs.

Through dress, people create personal and family memories. Photographs, videos, and life narratives recall the ceremonies, gifts, and fashion styles that mark an individual's progress through life. From their teens, many women keep portraits taken by amateur itinerant photographers at social events. These serve as reminders of gifts of cloth and clothing and of social relationships, past trends, and changes in lifestyles.

References and Further Reading

Andrewes, Janet. *Bodywork: Dress as Cultural Tool*. Leiden, The Netherlands: Brill, 2005.

Biaya, T. K. "Hair Statements in Urban Africa: The Beauty, the Mystic and the Madman." In *The Art of African Fashion*, edited by Marlous Willemsen and Els Van Der Plas, 75–99. The Hague, The Netherlands: Prince Claus Fund for Culture and Development, and Africa World Press, 1998.

Boilat, Pierre. *Esquisses sénégalaises*. Paris: Eds. Karthala, 1853.

Brooks, George. "The Signares of Saint-Louis and Gorée: Women Entrepreneurs in Eighteenth-Century Senegal." In *Women in Africa: Studies in Social and Economic Change*, edited by Nancy Hafkin and Edna Bay, 19–44. Stanford, CA: Stanford University Press, 1976.

Fall, Sokhna. *Seduire*. Paris: Editions Alternatives, 1998.

Garrard, Timothy F. *Gold of Africa*. Munich: Prestel, 1988.

Heath, Deborah. "Fashion, Anti-fashion and Heteroglossia in Urban Senegal." *American Ethnologist* 19, no. 1 (1992): 19–33.

Johnson, Marion. "Gold Jewelry of the Wolof and Tukulor of Senegal." *African Arts* 27, no. 1 (1976): 36–49.

Mustafa, Hudita Nura. "Sartorial Ecumenes: African Styles in a Social and Economic Context." In *The Art of African Fashion*, edited by Marlous Willemsen and Els Van Der Plas, 13–45. The Hague, The Netherlands: Prince Claus Fund for Culture and Development, and Africa World Press, 1998.

Niang, Fatou Niang Siga. *Reflets de mode et traditions saint-louisiennes*. Dakar, Senegal: Editions Khoudia, 1990.

Rabine, Leslie. *The Global Circulation of African Fashion*. Oxford, UK: Berg, 2002.

Hudita Nura Mustafa

Snapshot: Designer Oumou Sy

Oumou Sy was born in Podor, Senegal, in 1952. Working at the intersection of art, spectacle, and social space, Sy's multifaceted work in historical, art, and couture garments expresses the cosmopolitan creativity of the Senegambian region. Rather than elaborations of a design concept, her works are historical tableaux. In this region, cloth densely symbolizes wealth and power, dignity and beauty, history and tradition. Sy's work and life valorize the arts of cloth, clothing, and body adornment to parity with the fine arts, literature, and cinema, in all of which the Senegalese excel.

Dakar's status as a centuries-old center of transregional trade, French colonial capital, and current national capital has bred a fertile cultural terrain. As a creator, entrepreneur, teacher, and administrator, Sy builds institutions that bridge popular and elite worlds of Dakar in the Medina and Plateau districts, respectively, the African and French quarters of the former colonial city. Since the 1980s, she has collaborated with artists in cinema (seventeen films), theater (thirteen productions), and music (Baaba Maal and Youssou N'Dour). In the mid-1990s, with late husband and business manager Michel Mavros, she founded schools of tailoring (Leydi) and modeling (Macsy), an international African fashion week (SIMOD), a street carnival and Metissacana cultural center, internet café, and Web site in Dakar. When Sy arrives in her colonial officer's helmet and says she has come to colonize, or decolonize, perhaps, she means it.

Sy's spectacular fashion shows are visual and sensory feasts that mine the past and present to produce a future that is in constant dialogue with origins. As with the most innovative of designers, Sy's materials extend beyond cloth and stitching and evoke multiple senses, images, textures, light, and shapes. In her *Femmes* series, a pantheon of reckless goddesses delight in female beauty as they commemorate Afro-European encounters (mid-1990s). Icons of African tradition and Western modernity such as CDs, calabashes, kora instruments, perfumes, and peacock feathers anoint Cyberfemme and her consorts, each named after her object. These surplus objects, both city garbage and ornament, decorate luxurious gowns by valorizing neck and chest, as does Muslim embroidery cascading from heads. A heterodox woman herself, Sy's postmodern goddesses mock femininity as they subvert Europe's civilizing mission in Africa.

Dakar's postcolonial public spaces, even more than art or fashion shows, magnify these spectacles. They are photographed in the decaying cityscape amid broken pavements, garbage, wrecked cars, minivans, cracked walls, and crowds of curious children. Pageantry crystallizes political, aesthetic, and social values and hierarchies. Sy's photographs, shows, and parades are pageants that fleetingly transform city ruins into spectacles. Paraded and shot in the Medina, Cyberfemme is a utopian figure of light, speed, and beauty—a kind of cyber angel.

The Sahel Opera (2006) culminates a body of work inspired by regional cultural history. This includes the film *Hyenas* (1991), the *Kings and Queens* series, and *Desert Envelope* (mid-1990s). The opera is a multinational, multidisciplinary

Robe Calebasse (Calabash dress) designed by Oumou Sy, Dakar, Senegal, 1997. Sy's materials extend beyond cloth and stitching to include icons of African tradition and evoke a commentary on the Afro-European encounter. Photograph by Mamadou Touré Behan.

project bringing the Western operatic format to the continuing odyssey of Africa in the context of global inequality. In this story, a young mother-to-be, like many youth, takes a dangerous journey across Morocco to Spain in search of a better life for herself and her baby. One hundred fifty costumes were made over the course of a month in Dakar at a cost of US$30,000. The cast of eighty-five came from throughout the Sahel region of West Africa. Sponsored by the Prince Claus Fund for Culture and Development (The Netherlands), the opera retains cultural difference, because each performer uses his or her own ethnic heritage of music, language, art, and costume in a universal story of personal hope amid injustice. The garments include blue jeans, elaborate robes, and neutral garments that fuse with the desert scenery to create visual effects of severity.

Garment forms throughout Sy's work—costume, couture, and prêt-à-porter—are characterized by simple stitching of long swathes of cloth that are layered, wrapped, and often voluminous. Like all African designers, Sy innovates cloth traditions: first, by using African cloth with Western styles; second, by using newer European and Asian industrial cloth including synthetics, jerseys, taffeta, and smooth silks; and, finally, by working with master artisans to innovate (broad-loom) weaving styles with mixtures of thread (such as silk, cotton, raffia, or linen) as well as broadening strips from two to four feet (two-thirds to one and one-fifth meter). She also experiments with hand-dying of colors and motifs, though still favoring traditional dark hues. Tunics, stoles, heavy amber jewelry, hair jewelry, woolen wigs, and makeup complete the ornate adornment.

Gendered struggles shape Sy's life and work narratives. Sy was raised in a conservative, religious family in the old coastal city of St. Louis, then was a single mother and artist in Medina. Kalidou Sy, head of the Fine Arts Academy, introduced her to the art world. Authentic and bold in both artistic work and personality, Sy has won numerous prizes from the Prince Claus Fund for Culture and Development (1998), the City of Rome (2003), Woman of the Millennium (Guinea, 2003), and several film festivals. She won the Radio France International Net Africa Prize (2001) for Metissacana, Senegal's first cyber café. She has shown her work in major European museums and for the French Revolution bicentennial events in Dakar.

Despite Sy's elaborate aesthetic imagination and labors on the body surface, she reiterates traditional Senegambian beliefs, found reproduced in a Web site:

Beauty, it is an interior matter. Bodily beauty is not very important. All bodies are beautiful. But true beauty, the true value of beauty, it's in the interior that one must search. It is there that there is true value and it's there that is rare. That's the answer to your question. Interior beauty should be the goal of us all.

In sum, the broad scope of Sy's creative and institutional interventions in Senegalese culture demonstrates not only her individual genius but also the dense embeddedness of cloth and fashion in Senegalese society. In effect, Sy's oeuvre places the rich, cherished Senegambian heritage of artisanship and body adornment into dialogue with the transnational terrain of the contemporary arts.

REFERENCES AND FURTHER READING

Mustafa, Hudita Nura. "Sartorial Ecumenes: African Styles in Social and Economic Context." In *The Art of African Fashion: Cosmopolitan Identity in the 21st Century*, edited by Els van der Plas and Marlous Willemsen, 13–45. The Hague, The Netherlands: Prince Claus Fund for Culture and Development, 1998.

Mustafa, Hudita Nura. "Ruins and Spectacles: Fashion and City Life in Contemporary Senegal." *Nka: A Journal of Contemporary African Art* 15 (2002): 47–53.

Hudita Nura Mustafa

Ghana

M odern Ghana (to be distinguished from the medieval kingdom of Ghana in Mali) is centered on the Atlantic coast of West Africa and is firmly within the tropics with its shoreline about five degrees north of the equator. The country is bordered by Togo on the east, Burkina Faso on the north, and Côte d'Ivoire on the west, and, like all countries in Africa, it shares a history of dress with its neighbors. The contemporary peoples of Ghana may be conveniently divided between the largely Muslim north in predominantly savanna regions and the mostly Christian south in tropical forest areas and coastal plains. This simplification, however, should not obscure past and continuing interchanges among peoples and the very fluid traditions of clothing and adornment between the two areas.

Evidence of dress practices prior to European contact beginning with the Portuguese in 1471 is rather sparse throughout Ghana. Surviving rock paintings and engravings provide scant information, but the archaeological record reveals a rich assortment of bead types made from shell, coral, stone, bone, ivory, pottery, and gold, and, following Contact, glass and cuprous metals. These may have been threaded into the hair or strung together to encircle any combination of head, neck, arm, wrist, finger, waist, leg, ankle, or toe. In addition, monoxylous armlets in ivory, bone, and stone have been recovered in a number of pre-Contact sites throughout Ghana. Evidence of cast brass jewelry became increasingly common in archaeological contexts with the acceleration of trans-Saharan and European trade in metal basins, which were often melted down and recast in local genres of dress.

NORTHERN GHANA

The peoples of what is now northern Ghana may be divided between the less hierarchical groups (e.g., LoDagaa and Tallensi) that typically followed a local custodian of the earth, called a *tendana*, and the generally larger Islamic states (e.g., Mamprussi and Dagomba) headed by a paramount chief and a structure of lesser chiefs with roots in the Hausa of northern Nigeria. For the Koma-Bulsa peoples in the former category, there is an archaeological record of iron (and, to a lesser extent, copper) armlets,

LoDagaa (Lobi) elder wearing distinctive Hausa-influenced, Bolgatanga-made leather work including hat, bag, boots, and cane, along with strip-woven smock (*fugu*). Birifu, 1976. Photograph by Doran H. Ross.

bracelets, and anklets and of funerary terra-cottas dating from about 1400 to 1800 that provide substantial evidence of dress traditions, many of which continued well into the twentieth century. The widely admired sculptures excavated and studied by Ghanaian archaeologist James Anquandah depict a rich variety of bangles, an assortment of beadwork configurations, and sometimes dramatic hairstyles—all of which point to well-developed personal arts over a long period of time. Although male figures were often carefully depicted with beards, only modest evidence exists for scarification in sculptures of either gender. Enduring dress practices seen in the terra-cottas include cowry-adorned gourd helmets, identified with tendanas and hunters, and crescent-shaped iron or brass pendants said to be associated with the souls of their wearers. In addition, a number of other amulets suspended from necklaces coincide with current practices.

As revealed by the careful studies of British social anthropologists Esther and Jack Goody in northern Ghana, important distinctions can be made between indigenous notions of being fully dressed and the actual wearing of coverings (whether animal hide, bark cloth, or woven fabric). For example, in precolonial times, a man among the LoDagaa (Lobi) and several other northern groups was only considered dressed if he was wearing a skin penis sheath, while a younger boy would simply tuck his uncovered penis under a cord tied low around the waist. A young girl would typically wear only waist beads until approaching puberty, when she would assume a fiber waistband with the ends suspended in front covering the pubic area. A married woman would adopt a more elaborate belt, sometimes of goatskin, with freshly cut leaves tucked in front and back. To these basic configurations were added more optional items such as bracelets, necklaces, and anklets as status and wealth would allow. Hair was generally closely cropped for both sexes. Senior men would often grow beards, although in several areas a beard was not permitted as long as a man's father was living. In addition to changeable forms of dress, such permanent modifications of the body as circumcision, female excision, scarification, tattooing, teeth filing, lip plugging, and ear piercing were practiced in various combinations by a wide variety of non-Muslim northern groups. In some areas, transgressions within a community were punished by the removal of a finger or ear or by adding a distinctive scar.

The best documented and most visually dramatic of these practices are the rich assortment of cicatrization patterns found on the torsos and faces of both females and males. Patterns rarely distinguished genders and were applied at a young age—three to seven years in many areas and at infancy in some. Captain Cecil Armitage, once the British Commissioner of the Northern Territories, compiled a substantial inventory of northern tribal markings, especially well-developed among the Gurensi, Tallensi, and Nabdam (sometimes collectively called Frafra). The most widespread scarification mark was a deeply cut diagonal on one or both cheeks running down and out from the bridge of the nose. More numerous and subtle cuts in multiple parallel lines framing the eyes, nose, and mouth were added to the prominent diagonal sometimes in a herringbone pattern on the forehead. Radial marks from the corners of the mouth were also common, as were similar patterns around the navel. The motivations for these programs of scarification range from an indication of ethnicity or locality to the identification of slaves, clans, or members of the royal family. Some marks were applied for purely medicinal purposes, others primarily to beautify.

The dress of the earth priests and diviners in the north was generally more elaborate than that described above. The custodians of the earth frequently wore basketry or gourd hats and an animal skin (sheep, cattle, or antelope) tied over one shoulder and a second tied around the waist. A leather bag was generally a required accessory. The hats were not restricted to these leaders, and, for mature men, a bow and quiver with arrows were also considered essential.

The foundation of Islamic states in the north often resulted in the de facto incorporation of less populous peoples into their jurisdictions, leading to the gradual imposition of regimes of dress that argued for covering the human body. This led to a strip-woven and sewn smock (*fugu*) and drawstring pants for men and lower and upper wrappers for women. Over time, men's dress became conventionalized into smocks with no sleeves, short sleeves, or full sleeves. On important public occasions, these smocks (frequently worn in multiples) cover the tops of very wide and baggy pants, elaborately embroidered like the smocks. The pants had their origins with the cavalry of the Hausa-influenced Islamic states but were also independent statements of status and wealth. The ensemble was completed with tall leather boots also based on Hausa models. When dyed brown and covered with arrays of leather-encased Qur'anic amulets, the smocks served as the dress of hunters and warriors and are still seen in the early twenty-first century on leaders identified as war chiefs.

The most elaborate men's garments were and are the long and wide embroidered strip-woven gowns that reach to the ground with side extensions rolled up over each shoulder. This is the pan–West African boubou that originated in Islamic North Africa but came to northern Ghana via the Hausa *baba riga* from northern Nigeria. Leaders of the four major Islamic states—Dagomba, Mamprussi, Gonja, and Wala—typically adopt this garb with clusters of amulets sewn onto hats, worn around the neck, and/or handheld. An amulet and metal-clad staff is usually carried on state occasions. A number of northern chiefs still wear silver medallions depicting George V given to designated rulers under the British policy of indirect rule during the Colonial period, or even earlier silver pendants of a mudfish, crocodile, or a mudfish in the mouth of a crocodile, given to leaders recognized by the Asante after their conquest of several northern states in the eighteenth century.

The covering of women generally lagged behind that of men and did not become widespread until the ready availability of machine-manufactured cotton cloth. Ghanaian independence in 1957 led to the legislation of dress codes for those tribal areas not meeting standards of decency as perceived by the mostly Akan ruling population. This was reinforced by both Islamic and Christian ideas of modesty.

Certain northern groups employed distinctive male headwear for festival occasions. These include cowry-covered basketry hats with two projecting antelope or cow horns worn by the Frafra and other groups, especially during funeral events. Another characteristic form is a variation of the gourd hat worn by some tendanas but anthropomorphized with leather appliqué, creating a human face on the front—an idea attributed to the Mossi. Less localized and often in daily use is a conical fiber hat typically covered with loose flaps of leather dyed red with black geometric accents. The red fez, originally an Islamic administrator's emblem, became a more generalized badge of leadership to the extent that even Catholic priests were documented wearing them. Another commonplace form found across the north and into the south, and indeed commercially sold outside of Ghana, is the fully brimmed "elephant grass" hat with dyed bands of varying colors set off against the pale yellow of the undyed grass on the cylindrical crown. Popularly called the Bolga hat, based on its locus of production around the city of Bolgatanga, it is sold with other accessories of dress in the same technique, including carrying baskets and fans.

Stone armlets displayed above the elbow were found across the north, as were ivory armlets cut from the cross-section of an elephant's tusk. Also worn above the elbow, but less common and more prestigious, were lateral sections of ivory tusks with arm holes cut in their centers. The less wealthy adopted leather and

Mamprussi divisional chief wearing amulet-laden war shirt and hat along with embroidered pants. Nalerigu, 1976. Photograph by Doran H. Ross.

plaited straw armlets and bracelets, the latter often exchanged by couples during courtship regardless of their social standing. Northern Ghana is especially well known for the diversity of its cast metal armlets, anklets, and pendants. British archaeologist and historian Timothy Garrard has meticulously identified an enormous range of brass bangle forms, from the rare to the commonplace, produced by the Frafra peoples. These include the so-called mother-in-law bracelet that was a required gift from a man to his wife's mother. Many bangles were considered to have individually accumulated a certain amount of spiritual power and when not worn were often stored in their own ceramic pots, where they periodically received sacrifices and libations. Other bangles from a deceased elder might be embedded in the large phallic-shaped ancestor shrines made of earth, usually found buttressing granaries. Bangle shrines were at one time a widespread phenomenon in northern Ghana, and they speak to the significance that a single item of dress may have within a culture.

COASTAL GHANA AND THE FANTE PEOPLES

Nearly half of Ghana's population is from one of several Akan-speaking groups that populate most of the southern half of Ghana (excluding the Ga-Dangme and Ewe peoples in the southeast). Gold has been a defining feature of Akan history for at least six hundred years. Indeed, for much of the area's history prior to regaining independence in 1957, the region was called the Gold Coast. Ghana is still the second-largest producer of gold in Africa.

Initially drawn by the lure of the gold trade, numerous European interests visited the coast, established forts and trading posts, and provided provocative descriptions of coastal dress in what are still among the most comprehensive set of early records of sub-Saharan expressive culture. The Dutch chronicler Pieter de Marees sailed to the Gold Coast several times before publishing his frequently quoted observations (many of which were made in Elmina, "the mine") in 1602, where he paid particular attention to details of the appearance of local residents, mostly Fante peoples. Among other customs, he noted the gentle modeling or flattening of a young infant's head, a practice that continued into the twentieth century as important for both health and beauty. For the dress of women, he documented modest patterns of scarification, which today are understood as medicinal, since cicatrization as either a form of tribal identification or beautification is foreign to and discouraged by the Akan. He also wrote about a fairly lavish program of body painting. Hair was enhanced with oil, as it often is today, and was dressed with a small two-tine comb inserted into the finished coiffure.

In addition, de Marees recorded the wrapping of cloth by women "below their Breasts or Navel down to their knees," another practice widespread well into the middle of the twentieth century. He also documented both bark cloth and strip-woven cloth. In one, perhaps curious, observation he writes that, "Although they may not have many Chests or Trunks, they nevertheless hang many keys around their bodies, because it looks nice." Far from an erroneous or isolated description, miniature cast gold keys are still, in the early twenty-first century, frequently strung on necklaces, and one or more designated court officials among the Akan are still identified by and parade with substantial bunches of ancient keys as symbols of a chief's power and access.

De Marees was particularly attentive to Fante men's hairstyles. "Firstly, they are very proud of the way in which they cut their hair, each in his own fashion and competing in style, one in the form of a Crescent, another in the shape of [a] crown, a third with three or four Horns on his head…so that among fifty men one would not find two or three with the same haircut (or shaved after the same fashion)." He also recorded Venetian glass beads, in whole or part, hung from or threaded into hair. In addition, they wore glass bead necklaces and strings of gold and glass beads just below their knees. A fairly substantial cloth passed between the legs and was tied around the waist so that the excess hung down both front and back.

The descriptions of de Marees provide a detailed benchmark of late-sixteenth-century dress in a sub-Saharan context, observations largely substantiated by later writers visiting the Gold Coast. Among the most telling of these early records, either published or archival, are the inventories of the impressive quantity and variety of European textiles traded to Africans for gold, ivory, and slaves. In addition to unworked cloth in cotton, wool, flax, and silk, everything from ribbons and veils to rugs and tapestries was sold on the coast at one time or another. These exchanges subsequently influenced local textile production in terms of raw materials, color, design, and, much later, tailoring. Several accounts record that some imported fabrics, especially those in silk, were unraveled for their shiny threads and unusual colors and then rewoven on local narrow-strip horizontal treadle looms with the silk primarily used for weft-faced designs. Beyond the extensive commerce in English, Dutch, and other fabrics, European traders were involved in the lively exchange of locally produced textiles from across the coast of West Africa, with some cloths introduced to the Gold Coast from as far away as Cape Verde. Indian and Indonesian textiles were also imported in substantial quantities.

Some forms of Akan gold jewelry were likewise inspired by foreign prototypes. In particular, nineteenth-century Fante jewelry production was heavily influenced by Victorian forms circulated through retail samples, official gifts, and illustrations on trade cards printed by British commercial interests. A number of foreign observers commented on the local goldsmiths' ability to copy models of such images as butterflies, hearts, hands grasping roses, and baskets of forget-me-nots. Queen Victoria's betrothal ring featuring a serpent seems to have been especially influential. Signet rings, Masonic symbols, and signs of the zodiac also became popular at this time. Victorian influence on gold jewelry styles and motifs was so pervasive that it spread throughout most of southern Ghana, and many designs persist into the twenty-first century.

Victorian designs still flourish in the array of gold pins inserted into the wigs Fante women adopt on festival occasions. They have long been recognized for their elaborate hairstyles created either from their own hair or that of others. A famous 1874 page from *The Illustrated London News* depicts over thirty-five different Fante coiffures and head ties, both of which have substantial sculptural qualities—although distinguishing between actual coiffed hair and wigs is difficult. Contemporary Fante wigs generally have the appearance of a series of as many as twelve stacked rings of hair tapering toward the top. Bands of gold and up to twenty gold pins hold the rings together.

These wigs with their ornaments are regularly displayed by the women leaders of the traditional Fante warrior groups called *asafo*. Although their military functions were usurped first by the British colonial administration and then by Ghanaian police and army units, the asafo still flourish today as social and ritual organizations with both men and women members and age groups that often include children as young as five. There may be as many as fourteen different asafo companies in a given Fante state, and at least three Fante cities have seven companies. Each company has it own sets of colors and motifs that constitute exclusive prerogatives. Rivalries between companies were and are often intense. In many of the larger towns, up until about 1990, each asafo group would annually create a new set of fanciful uniforms, often different outfits for each subgroup, all in company colors. In the past, some companies mimicked the uniforms of the Ghanaian police, army, or boy scouts, and at least two groups influenced by global media have paraded in their own interpretations of the dress of Native Americans, complete with feathered headdresses and bows and arrows.

Beginning in the early 1990s, the men and women of a number of asafo companies abandoned custom-made ensembles and started appearing in T-shirts consistent with company colors. These were typically silk-screened with the name and number of the company and almost inevitably with the logo of a sponsoring commercial interest, most frequently a brewery or distillery. The commercialization of festive dress is lamented by many Fante and indeed other Ghanaians, but it is a trend that appears to be accelerating in the twenty-first century.

Paramount chief of the Mamprussi, Adam Badimsogoro, in embroidered gown with Asante-made silver crocodile pendant around his neck. Nalerigu, 1976. Photograph by Doran H. Ross.

With a few exceptions, masquerade traditions in Ghana are modest, and those that are found are better represented by examples more fully entrenched outside Ghanaian borders. Perhaps the strong centralized powers of chieftaincy discouraged competing institutions like masking societies that often tried to exert their own agendas of social control. One important exception serves primarily entertainment functions. In many of the larger coastal towns like Elmina, Cape Coast, and Winneba, masquerade groups typically appear during local festivals and during Christmas and New Year's celebrations. Called "fancy dress" after British costume balls, the mask forms, worn almost exclusively by boys and young men, are primarily made from papier-mâché or wire screen mesh. Masked characters include ship's captains white men, devils, the water spirit Mammy Wata, and animals such as goats, roosters, and monkeys. Most groups have one or more stilt dancers. Locally produced masks appear alongside imported masks originating from an assortment of foreign traditions (Halloween, Carnaval, and so on). The full body costumes worn with the masks are constructed from multicolored, heavily fringed patchwork, producing an overall harlequin effect.

CENTRAL GHANA AND THE ASANTE EMPIRE

Although de Marees's encounters were restricted to the coastal Fante, their economic and cultural rivals for most of the past three hundred years have been the inland Asante (Ashanti) peoples, the most famous of the Akan subgroups and the most influential in terms of traditional dress. The Asante kingdom, founded around 1700 with its capital at Kumase, continues to thrive in the early twenty-first century with significant political and ritual power and with festival displays of some of the most spectacular elite dress in all of Africa. Asante and other Akan royal dress is characterized by visually striking handwoven cloth (kente) and the lavish use of gold in the adornment of chiefs and queen mothers and in the accessories of leadership employed by the court officials that surround them. An important chief may wear thirty or more cast gold or gold-leafed items. A crown, coronet, or royal fillet invariably adorns the head. One or more chains are worn diagonally over the exposed right shoulder and under the left and largely covered by the chief's cloth. A long necklace with a prominent pendant may be accompanied by two or three other necklaces. Up to five clusters of amulets appear above the right elbow with multiple bracelets below, one often in the form of a solid (obviously nonfunctional) cast-gold watch. A single massive bracelet is typically found on the left arm. Rings may dress all ten digits. Gold anklets and gold ornamented sandals complete the ensemble, with some chiefs wearing clusters of ornaments tied below the knee. The right hand would usually carry a short sword and the left a horsetail fly whisk.

In addition to the gold and to the sumptuous and almost total envelopment of the human body, the traditional formal dress of Akan chiefs is distinguished by the ubiquitous references to Akan oral literature. Among many conceptual frames for the definition of dress is the frequently cited assertion that it is a nonverbal means of communication. For the Akan, there is a decidedly verbal component. The vast majority of motifs depicted on crowns, necklaces, rings, sandals, and so on represent proverbs or other conventionalized verbal forms such as praise names, boasts, insults, and riddles or even more extended constructs such as folktales and historical narratives. Thus, the chief is not only adorned with both wealth and visual splendor but also with a wide array of recognizable ideas that might variously proclaim the powers of the chief, assert the importance of his state, or define the responsibilities of citizenship, among other possible themes. A particularly well-ornamented chief might have as many as twenty-five different messages embedded in his overall dress, not counting those encoded in the cloth he might be wearing. These verbal forms are conveyed by a wide variety of images drawn from the material culture of the Akan or from the flora and fauna of their environment. Finger rings may include such volatile animals as lions, crocodiles, and scorpions or such seemingly docile creatures as mudfish, tortoises, and frogs, each with its own proverbial saying. For example, a chief's coronet might display repeated gold-leafed

Nana Sefa Ababio, bearer of one of the king of Asante's principal swords of state, wearing an eagle-feather headdress and gold gongs around his neck. Kumase, 2004. Photograph by Doran H. Ross.

images of a star and crescent moon. On the surface, this might appear to be a reference to Islam, but, in most instances, the Akan would provide the proverb, "Although the moon is brighter, a star is more constant." Here the images liken the chief to the star as a predictable and reliable source of leadership.

Although crowns and related headwear are the defining dress of European monarchs, and indeed of many African kings, among the Akan, the royal sandals are the most important and definitive elements of chiefly dress. The placing of designated sandals from the state treasury onto the feet of a chief-to-be during the installation rites is often considered a critical step in the process. The reverse is also true. When a chief is removed from office, the first act is to remove his sandals. When citizens of a state come before their chief, they are expected to remove their sandals. The only time a chief is expected to remove his sandals in front of an audience is when he is in the presence of his own ancestors inside the sacred stool rooms. When an important chief is either walking or being carried in a palanquin during festival occasions, additional pairs of sandals are carried by designated court officials in front of the chief. Miniature cast gold sandals may appear on finger rings, bracelets, and pendants or on the earrings of queen mothers. The traditional cosmetic containers of chiefs and queen mothers were also adorned with images of sandals.

Many Akan court officials have a single distinctive item of regalia that identifies their position. The principal counselors of a chief carry a carved wood and gold-leafed staff with a figural finial that conveys a telling maxim relating to the successful functioning of the state. The court heralds wear a colobus monkey–skin headdress with a large gold-covered rectangular blazon on the front. The varied categories of former slaves of the Akan were typically identified by a cast, repoussé, or gold-leafed disk worn as a pectoral. The abandonment of slavery has led to the transfer of these disks to the sword bearers. The latter are further identified by the named sword they carry in procession, often with a cast gold ornament tied to the sheath or with an elaborately carved gold-covered grip. Antelope-skin skullcaps with gold leaf or cast gold ornaments also distinguish the sword bearers.

In many states, one of the most extravagantly dressed members of the court is the bearer of the principal sword of state. He typically dons a visually complex headdress with an array of eagle feathers spread across the back and with gold ram's horns

Queen mother of Akuapem, Nana Dokua, at the fortieth anniversary of her reign. Akuropon, 2006. Photograph by Doran H. Ross.

and gold bird nests symmetrically arranged on the front. Again a proverb explains the ram's horns: "A ram fights with its heart not its horns." In Kumase, the bearer of the Mponponsuo sword, the name of which means "responsibility," wears an ensemble of gold gongs and amulets suspended from the neck. The sword has a large cast gold ornament of a python with a hornbill bird in its mouth, representing an involved story about the virtues of patience. The gun bearers or body guards of the paramount chief also wear more involved regalia that include a cartridge belt with powder horn ornamented by gold seashells and miniature human mandibles. They also display a similarly ornamented bandolier across their chest. The seashell casting is often repeated on the stocks of their muskets and on their skullcaps.

AKAN TEXTILES

The most famous of all the Asante arts of dress and adornment are the textiles now commonly called kente. Originally woven in long strips roughly three inches (eight centimeters) wide (today five inches [thirteen centimeters] is more common), the strips were cut and sewn together selvage to selvage to form large men's cloths about two meters by four meters (six and a half feet by thirteen feet). These were wrapped around the body toga style over the left shoulder and under the right arm. This characterization, however, is a rather simplified description of the draping of the cloth on the body, because there are numerous nuanced variations, each with their own name, such as "braveman," "humility," and "hide it," some of which position the cloth on both shoulders or expose the lower legs. There is a recognized skill to the stylish wearing of kente, and some chiefs in procession have an attendant whose single responsibility is to help maintain the majestic positioning of the cloth.

Women's cloths were much smaller, about one by two meters (three by six and a half feet), and originally a single cloth was worn as a skirt wrapped around the body under the breasts. In the late nineteenth century, a matching upper wrapper was added to be worn over the breasts, but under the arms. Later in the twentieth century, a third matching piece was added to the ensemble and worn as a shawl draped over the left shoulder. The wearing of kente as described above was (and is) typically reserved for formal occasions when high-status festive dress was required. Kente was originally the exclusive prerogative of paramount chiefs and queen mothers and was worn by other chiefs only with the permission of the head of the traditional state.

Each kente cloth has a distinctive name associated with its warp stripe pattern. A number of cloths are named after esteemed leaders of the past, including warrior chiefs and influential queen mothers. One of the most popular warp configurations features red, green, and gold stripes and is named *Oyokoman* after the lineage of the Asante king. And much like the gold jewelry, some names refer to telling proverbs. One kente pattern, a rare plaid, is called, "Kindness does not travel far." The basic idea is that if you behave badly, the news will spread, but if you perform good deeds, they never receive the recognition they deserve. Another pattern with red, green, and blue stripes on a predominantly yellow warp is named, "If you climb a good tree you get a push"— that is, if your intentions are good, people will help you.

One prestigious, highly valued, and especially elaborate cloth foregoes blocks of plain weave and instead covers virtually the whole surface of the cloth with weft-faced designs. Called *adweneasa,* its name is conventionally translated as either, "my skill is exhausted" or "my ideas are finished," suggesting that the weaver put his best efforts into the cloth. Kente was originally woven from cotton; then unraveled silk threads entered the picture early on, followed by rayon in the early twentieth century and Lurex threads in the last third of the century. All four are still woven in the early twenty-first century.

The second most famous Asante textile tradition is *adinkra,* whose patterns are created by a large inventory of designs carved from gourds and stamped with a black dye in a dense grid. Designs were originally applied on strip-woven cloth, possibly accounting for the grid work. Since the mid-nineteenth century, adinkra has been made from machine-woven fabric. Men's and women's cloths are sized and worn as kente. Adinkra is typically characterized as the mourning cloths of the Asante when produced in red, dark brown, or black; the red is worn by close members of the deceased's family. Nevertheless, adinkra may be produced on white cloth or any of a wide variety of solid colors and even on tie-dyed and multicolored fabrics. Categorized as "Sunday adinkra," these may be worn on virtually any festive occasion. Because adinkra is quickly produced, it is less expensive than equivalent sizes of kente, and has always been more accessible to a broader range of society.

Like the proverbs conveyed by the gold jewelry of chiefs, individual adinkra designs convey considerable meaning, and, indeed, the conceptual agenda for both seems to be the same—that is, to surround the wearer with conventional wisdom. One of the most popular motifs on adinkra is typically translated as "except God" or "only God." Another common image is that of a ladder, referencing adinkra's funerary functions and the proverb, "The ladder of death is not climbed by one man alone"—that is, death is inevitable. The complete inventory of designs numbers well over five hundred, with new creations occurring on a somewhat regular basis. In addition to representational motifs such as birds, crocodiles, stools, and swords, there are a variety of more abstract curvilinear and geometric motifs. Rather than using a discrete symbol to reference a proverb, one recent trend is to literally spell out the proverb in the Asante language and carve this into the stamp. Beginning about 1990, silk-screened versions of adinkra began appearing alongside stamped examples.

Also composed on a grid and featuring proverbial images, some shared with adinkra and royal jewelry, is the cloth called *akunitan,* usually translated as "cloth of the great," and again worn as a wrapper toga style. Here the motifs are much larger and are arranged in four to six horizontal rows with four to eight images in each row. These cloths come in two versions. The more common consists of an imported British wool blanket in black, dark purple, or brown that is machine-embroidered with red, green, and gold-colored rayon thread, the same colors as both the Asante kente called Oyokoman and the national flag of Ghana. The second version has a more expansive multicolored palette and is assembled by appliqué from cotton cloth or felt. Akunitan are generally reserved for chiefs and designated members of their courts. In addition, a wide variety of damasks, brocades, chintzes, velvets, and other imported materials may be worn by royals on festive occasions and have been for three hundred years.

An archaic material still found in a few ritual contexts is bark cloth. The inner bark of a specific tree was softened in water and its fibers pounded and compressed much like felt. In the past, Asante slaves, poor farmers, and hunters wore bark cloth, persisting for

Asante paramount chief of Edweso, Nana Diko Pim III, wrapped in *adweneasa* kente cloth and wearing multiple items of gold regalia. Edweso, 1976. Photograph by Doran H. Ross.

the latter two until the early twentieth century. During earlier festivals celebrating the new yam harvest, an Asante king would remove his kente and dress in bark cloth at a key point in the ritual program.

One of the most frequently seen items of dress in southern Ghana is the baby carrier. Usually a piece of machine-made cloth, often mismatched with the rest of the ensemble, it is used to support the baby on the caregiver's back and is wrapped around and tucked or tied in the front. This is often the mother, but sometimes a sister as young as four or five years. On special occasions, the mother may choose a matching baby carrier, even one made of kente. Related to this practice, one of Ghana's most famous art forms, called *Akua'ba* (Akua's child), was once a visible component of Akan dress. When a woman was struggling to conceive, she would often go to a local priest, who would typically prescribe the carving of a wood figure (misleadingly called a doll in the West) and instruct the woman to carry it on her back with its head exposed and to care for it as a real child. This practice was widely believed to result in the birth of a healthy and beautiful baby. The carving in the Asante version inevitably had a flat round face and a high forehead, both considered important attributes of female beauty among the Akan. One of the most distinctive and ritually important items of Asante and other Akan royal dress is the amulet-laden *batakari* or war shirt, which was borrowed from northern Islamic states. Muslim clerics were influential at the Kumase court for much of the eighteenth and nineteenth centuries, perhaps reaching a peak during the reign of Asantehene Osei Bonsu (r. 1804–1823). The foundation of the garb is fundamentally the short-sleeved, strip-woven, and sewn smock (fugu) discussed earlier but dyed a dark brown or black like the northern hunter's shirt. Its surface is covered with tanned leather, animal skin, silver, and/or gold-encased amulets of various shapes containing Qur'anic passages and medicinal and magical formulas, sometimes obscuring the entire smock. It was typically worn with a hat also laden with amulets. The batakari was not only thought to provide both real and spiritual protection during battle but was also thought to cure gunshot wounds, prevent illness, ensure prosperity, and promote fertility, among other benefits. Because of its efficacious properties, it was often prescribed dress for Akan leaders during liminal events such as the installations and funerals of chiefs. In a few states, including that of the Asantehene, fully inscribed men's cloths, with Qur'anic and other Islamic texts, still serve key ritual roles. Although the vast majority of Akan chiefs are now Christians, the batakari persists as ritual dress in contemporary versions minus the Islamic contents of the amulets.

BEADS IN AKAN SOCIETY

While kente cloths and batakari are among the most high-profile elements of Asante/Akan dress, the least visible but most provocative items are women's waist beads. American art historian Suzanne Gott is one of the few people to study this fairly widespread practice in West Africa, and she emphasizes the erotic nature of these beads among the Akan. One to six strands were traditionally worn under a woman's clothing and were thus hidden from view—although for a period during the 1980s, there was a trend in Kumase to wear oversized beads so that their existence would be evident under the cloth. Their presence was further emphasized by an affected walk that caused the beads to audibly rub or bounce against each other. On the one hand, the strands served a practical function in that a woman's undergarment was tucked under then over the strands in front and back. On the other hand, the beads were considered sensual and had strong sexual associations. One of Gott's Asante colleagues confessed that, "When I put them on, my husband counts them like a rosary." A popular name for the beads in the late 1990s was "high-tension wire."

The use of beads for all varieties of dress in Ghana is extensive, with both locally made and imported examples employed in large numbers in virtually every imaginable material, including pottery, stone, seed, wood, gold, brass, plastic, with glass beads being the most prevalent. Shell beads were made from seashells, coconut shells, and from the shells of large land snails. Early observers on the Gold Coast frequently commented on the spiritual powers that the local populations associated with gold beads in particular, leading to the disparaging phrase, "fetish gold." Nevertheless, these beads were clearly thought to have efficacious properties that extended their importance well beyond the display of wealth and the enhancement of beauty.

Two glass bead types stand out as being especially coveted and financially valued, *aggrey* (*akori*) and *bodom*, and both have achieved a kind of mythical, if not mystical, status. Large examples of each, when available, are used as centerpieces on necklaces with other glass beads or alone as a singular pendant. Some are individually named and are considered vital heirlooms. Various spiritual powers are attached to them that relate to health, fertility, prosperity, and other aspects of well-being. There is also considerable confusion and misinformation about both bead types. The origin of aggrey is unclear, although they are considered to be very old and are popularly thought by the Akan as having come from the ground. Aggrey is rather simplistically identified as a blue glass bead, but it has considerable refractive properties that turn the blue into gold or green under different types of light. Powder glass bodom beads are perhaps better understood and, according to many scholars, are produced by the Dangme-speaking

Asante divisional chief in silk-screened *adinkra* cloth. Kumase, 2004. Photograph by Doran H. Ross.

Krobo peoples, close neighbors of several Akan states. These yellow beads often have cruciform surface designs in black, blue, red, and green. Small amounts of gold dust are said to be mixed into their cores.

Also bridging most of northern and southern Ghana across ethnic groups and spanning most of the region's documented history is the use of shea butter as a cosmetic, medicinal pomade, and hair-care product. In exploiting this vegetal fat, the precolonial inhabitants of West Africa preceded the rest of the world by perhaps a thousand years. This oil/fat was extracted by boiling the seeds of the shea tree, found widely in the savanna of West Africa, with the processed shea butter traded extensively to the south. Shea butter was so important to the Akan that, to hold the fat, they fabricated elaborate repoussé brass containers made from imported sheet metal. Asante and other Akan groups customarily apply shea butter mixed with gold dust on the exposed skin of royals for festival occasions and on the faces and hands of deceased chiefs, queen mothers, and other elite members of society before they were laid in state for final viewing. The fat was also mixed with either ochre or soot for mourning rituals.

SOUTHEASTERN GHANA AND THE GA-DANGME AND EWE PEOPLES

After the royal dress of the Akan, perhaps the most famous program of personal adornment in Ghana is that employed by young women in the nubility rites (*dipo*) of the Krobo, one of the seven subgroups of the Dangme that have been studied in considerable and respectful detail by Hugo Huber. During the span of the ritual, initiates follow a nuanced set of steps marked by repeated changes in the forms and materials of dress. To cite just a few examples, at the very beginning, the initiate's glass waist beads are replaced by a cord made from pineapple leaves strung with a single red bead. She is also given a large shiny red loincloth that hangs to the ground in front and back. The young woman's head is then shaved and an array of raffia fiber is tied around her neck. Many such steps are symbolically related to an adolescent girl being transformed into an adult Krobo woman.

At the climactic dipo, each initiate is adorned as if she were nobility, in some areas complete with crown and sandals and in all cases with sumptuous—often precious—strands of glass beads. According to the Dutch cultural anthropologist Marijke Steegstra, this last phase of the ritual is called "dressing up," and lyrics sung to celebrate the young women frequently conclude with the phrase "beautifully adorned girl." Subtle cicatrization in the form of twelve small cuts on the back of the initiates' hands and other configurations elsewhere on the body traditionally marked completion of dipo. This practice, however, and indeed the whole ritual, is increasingly being attacked by Christian adherents who find the exposure of bare breasts to be un-Christian.

The Ewe peoples weave their own versions of kente that vary from that of their Asante rivals in a number of significant ways. Perhaps most noticeable is the subdued palette with more pastel hues than the Asante, who favor primary reds, greens, blues, and yellows. The Ewe design their cloths without borders, so the strong vertical element created by the border seen on the proper left of an Asante man's cloth when worn does not appear in Ewe dress. The Ewe also wind two contrasting thread colors onto the weft shuttle, creating a mottled effect for select bands of weft designs. In addition, Ewe weavers hand-pick representational motifs into their cloths that include an assortment of animals, human figures, items of regalia such as swords, umbrellas, and stools, and even lettering in either their own language or English. The combined effect of all of these elements gives Ewe kente an appearance quite distinct from Asante weavings, although both groups have been borrowing from each other for well over one hundred years.

Except for paring down the walls of ivory trumpets, the Akan did not generally carve ivory. On the other hand, ivory is a significant material in the regalia of Ga-Dangme and Ewe chiefs, including counselor's staffs with a variety of figurative finials, trumpets with substantial relief carving, and crowns with multiple representational motifs. These are probably a series of arts with considerable time depth, which may have origins among the Yoruba of Nigeria, their distant relatives to the east.

BRITISH COLONIZATION

Great Britain gained exclusive control of the Gold Coast in 1872 when the Dutch, the last of the other remaining European powers, "transferred the flag" of their forts and posts to the British. Although British hegemony was at this point still largely limited to coastal regions, the sacking of the Asante capital of Kumase in 1874 began the process of controlling the hinterlands. The first systematic introductions of European clothing practices to the Gold Coast were found in the military uniforms assigned to African forces attached to the European forts, which continued with colonial forces that served many police functions within the Gold Coast Colony and substantial military roles in both world wars. Paralleling Victorian jewelry designs, the images found on military decorations and insignia filtered into the regimen of gold jewelry worn by chiefs.

These were just the first of a series of Western-style uniforms to be imposed on local populations that included prescribed dress for domestic help and school uniforms—shirt and shorts or blouse and skirt in both cases. Christian churches brought their own rules for the robes of clerics and choirs and defined conventions of dress for their congregations. This, of course, was on top of considerable pressure on segments of society to be acceptably covered when appearing in public, especially in urban situations.

The early mission stations, in particular those of the Swiss Presbyterian Basel Mission (founded in Ghana in 1834), specified what constituted proper dress, especially for female converts. Needlework classes, especially sewing, provided both domestic and vocational training to reinforce the concept. The roots of the enduring three-piece women's ensemble called the *kaba* (a local pronunciation of the English "cover") date to this period. Blending indigenous ideas of dress with European ones, the kaba features a tailored short-sleeved blouse with either a wrapped or fitted skirt and a third cloth used as a shawl, head tie, or sometimes a baby carrier, all sewn from industrially manufactured cloth.

The European development of roller-printed designs on machine-woven textiles (called fancy prints) in the middle of the eighteenth century and of resin resist designs for machine-woven textiles (called wax prints) in the middle of the nineteenth century provided relatively inexpensive cloth for local consumption. Over time, kente and adinkra, either hand-crafted or machine-printed, were also employed in these ensembles. Of course, the pattern of the cloth and the style of the blouse were and are very important choices, but cloths had distinctive names assigned to them (e.g.,

"Good Husband," "Tree of Life," "Men Are Not Grateful") that prompted consideration as well. Both individual paper maquettes and mass-produced paper posters with multiple images feature sample blouse styles, which place a premium on the sculptural qualities of the sleeves and bodice.

Hairstyles generally followed precolonial practices, and, indeed, many of these continue into the twenty-first century. For the most part, men wore and still wear their hair closely cropped. On the other hand, women's hairstyles followed a long-standing tradition of innovation and change. Hair straighteners were introduced in the 1920s and 1930s and are still in use by some. Hair extensions became popular beginning in the 1970s. All but the very elderly of both sexes dye their hair to maintain a deep black color.

POSTINDEPENDENCE AND CONTEMPORARY GHANA

Although handwoven kente began as a royal prerogative, the history of Ghana's signature item of apparel is largely one of increasing democratization. This process began in the late nineteenth century, continued through the Colonial period, and accelerated with independence, when more egalitarian impulses began to penetrate Ghanaian politics and culture. The widespread introduction of inexpensive machine-woven, roller-printed kente fabrics during the second half of the twentieth century was part of this process of democratization. Today, kente—either hand-crafted or industrially produced—can be worn in virtually any pattern by anyone who can afford it. Nevertheless, to show up at a major event wearing a cloth in the same pattern as the host paramount chief is considered an affront. Forward-thinking chiefs largely avert this possibility by commissioning new cloths in innovative patterns and colors for the most important occasions, with a commitment from the weaver not to copy it until after the event, when requests for replication are considered a compliment.

Many practices of the post-Independence era have continued into the early twenty-first century, especially on royal or national holidays. Despite the fact that younger Ghanaians disparagingly refer to most wrapped clothing as "bed sheets," it remains de rigueur for chiefs, queen mothers, and their attendants on festive public occasions, although many women will opt for tailored blouses. The Asante president of Ghana, John Agyekum Kufuor, and his wife, Theresa, both wore distinctive kente at his first inauguration in 2001, which were rapidly copied in handwoven and machine-printed versions called "President" and "First Lady." On the other hand, Kufuor was widely criticized when he appeared in a Western suit and tie in lieu of kente at the official celebration of the fiftieth anniversary of Ghanaian independence in Black Star Square on 6 March 2007.

On a periodic basis as elections approach, mass-produced "photo cloths" featuring the colors and logos of political parties and images of their candidates become a part of the visual culture. They are tailored into shirts for men and blouses for women, who also wear the cloth as wrapped or fitted skirts. Commemorative photo cloths also regularly appear, often at five-year intervals, to celebrate significant anniversaries of the reigns of both chiefs and queen mothers. It is common to see hundreds of people dressed in the same specially commissioned textile, although in some cases, photo transfer, silk-screened white or light yellow T-shirts are seen as sufficient commemoration for both sexes.

Two fundamental realities of twenty-first-century African dress also dominate clothing practices in Ghana. Estimates suggest that up to 90 percent of all Ghanaians have bought at least a few items of secondhand clothing during their lifetime. Its popularity is such that retailers and their consumers look forward to new bales of clothes and appreciate those that retain the wrinkles from the baling process as potential evidence of more current fashion trends. The secondhand clothing market includes the full range of apparel types, including footwear, especially sneakers, from a variety of labels and knockoffs of almost all labels. The Ga peoples from the Accra area collectively refer to these secondhand garments as "dead white men."

A second pervasive trend for the average Ghanaian consumer is the accelerating presence of imported Chinese fabrics and garments, the former copying popular African fabrics and the latter fashioned in both Afrocentric and conventional Western styles. Among the "African fabrics" are a large number of designs replicating the most popular current releases of the Ghanaian textile industry in violation of Ghanaian copyright. Whether raw cloth or garment, the Chinese imports undercut prices for locally made products by a significant percentage.

Another telling fashion phenomenon related to both of the preceding trends is the country's version of American "casual Fridays." Called "national Friday-wear" in Ghana, businesses in the urban centers are encouraged to relax dress codes that typically call for Western attire and promote dress fashioned in local styles from local fabrics—that is, made in Ghana—that more accurately reflect the nation's cultural heritage. While national pride is part of the motivation, issues of comfort in Ghana's hot climate are certainly a consideration as well. An even larger part of the agenda is the attempt to address and promote the failing textile industries of Ghana, which have lost jobs and market share to cheap and inferior Chinese imports of both fabric and ready-to-wear clothes. The success of national Friday-wear has been mixed. Although it encourages heritage-based clothing, it also provides license to secondhand clothing in the workplace. Chinese imports of African-style patterns make African-style garments affordable, but like secondhand clothing, they undercut initiatives to promote Ghanaian-produced textiles and locally sewn apparel.

A much more controversial practice, especially in urban areas, is the widespread use of skin-lightening creams. Skin bleaching has a long history worldwide, and, for some in Ghana, lighter skins are associated with beauty, status, and both career and marriage opportunities. Estimates of 25 to 35 percent of southern Ghanaian women and 5 to 10 percent of Ghanaian men have tried skin bleaching for at least a short period of time. Perhaps inspired by Michael Jackson, such popular Ghanaian musicians as Daddy Lumba and Nana Acheampon have progressively lightened their skin over the years. Although creams, lotions, and soaps with high concentrations of certain potentially harmful ingredients have been banned in a number of African countries (including Kenya, Uganda, Tanzania, and Ghana), these bans have been largely ineffective, and bleaching products with dangerous chemicals are still widely available. What would appear to be convincing arguments related to issues of health and to racial and national pride and integrity do not seem to be discouraging the practice in any measurable way.

Although the Ghanaian textile manufacturing industry is struggling, it is still producing new designs for local markets. In 2005, Ghana Textile Printing, a subsidiary of the Dutch firm Vlisco, released a series of "real wax designs" with environmentally friendly patterns and names such as "Plants Are for Life," "Recycling Is Wise," "Exhaust Fumes Pollute," and "Deforestation Is Bad " Another pattern that repeats circular forms borrows from a forty-year-old adinkra motif somewhat ironically called "The Steering Wheel Kills the Driver."

Although the average Ghanaian must increasingly rely on secondhand clothing and Chinese imports, there is a growing market for high fashion among the elite. Ghanaian designers living both within the country and abroad are establishing substantial reputations for innovative apparel. Celebrations of the fiftieth anniversary of Ghanaian independence in 2007 prompted a number of fashion shows—both locally and abroad in England, Italy, Germany, and the United States—showcasing Ghanaian designers.

Inside Ghana, Kofi Ansah, a 1977 Chelsea School of Art (London) graduate, has built a solid reputation for kente-inspired designs for everything from bath robes to sportswear. He employs an array of locally printed textiles in his clothing lines and has created fabric designs for Ghana Textile Printing, most notably the wax print collections "Ahenfie" and "Sika Print." In addition, Ansah works with batik, tie-dye, and splash resist textiles in fashions that have been described as embracing the realms of fantasy and the avant-garde.

Outside of Ghana, the designer Francis Selorm has been working in Copenhagen since 1992. His designs, manufactured in Denmark, rely heavily on the inspiration of Asante kente cloth and include hats and kente-accented jackets as well as ready-to-wear dresses in kente prints, which he presents at shows with names like "The Kente Revolution" and "Kente and Gold." Selorm also borrows clothing details from the inventory of adinkra designs (especially the "except God" stamp) and others more typically associated with northern Ghanaian embroidery.

The London-born Ozwald Boateng is perhaps the most famous Ghanaian fashion designer. Creating clothing almost exclusively for men, Boateng frequently reaches into his family's Asante origins for inspiration, as with his spring 2004 collection "Ashanti Hip Hop," which incorporated strands of gold beads and "tribal headbands" among other touches in work that is widely admired for its elegance. His London Savile Row flagship, Bespoke Couture, has attracted an international celebrity clientele, and in 2003, he was appointed creative director of menswear at Givenchy in Paris.

THE AFRICAN AMERICAN DIASPORA

Kwame Nkrumah's leadership role in establishing Ghana as the first sub-Saharan African country to regain its independence in 1957 and the enormous importance of this historical benchmark had a profound and high-profile impact on the descendents of African peoples in the Americas and especially the United States. Independence celebrations attracted numerous African American dignitaries, including Reverend Martin Luther King Jr., Coretta Scott King, Mrs. Louis Armstrong, Ralph J. Bunche, and Congressmen Adam Clayton Powell and Charles Diggs, among others. All were consistently impressed with the ensembles of traditional dress that they encountered at both public and private events. Many returned with kente cloths of varying sizes as commemoration of this momentous occasion.

Nkrumah's two highly publicized visits to the United States in 1958 and 1960 included numerous photographs of his substantial entourage wearing kente, most memorably in *Life* magazine with President Dwight D. Eisenhower and Vice President Richard M. Nixon at a state dinner. The writings of such African American luminaries as Richard Wright, John Biggers, and Maya Angelou also singled out kente and helped increase the awareness of this distinctive cloth in the United States. The civil rights and black pride movements of the 1960s served as additional catalysts for embracing Afrocentric modes of dress, and kente was at the forefront. During this diaspora period, kente was tailored into blouses, skirts, and dresses for women and shirts, vests, and hats for men. In smaller, two- to four-strip cloths, it was worn as a scarf or shawl by women and as a single strip, conventionally called a stole, by both sexes. Kente and kente-inspired garments began appearing in such television programs as the *Bill Cosby Show* and in the films of African American directors such as Spike Lee. Both Lee and Michael Jackson were on covers of the black-oriented magazine *Ebony* wearing kente. From the mid-1960s to about 1990, kente was frequently fashioned into wedding dresses and into formal wear for bridegrooms. It was not unusual for other members of the wedding party to wear kente accents as part of their wedding apparel as well. Kente was the African textile of choice for Afrocentric attire until the mid 1990s, when machine-printed cloth with designs based on Kuba raffia textiles from the Democratic Republic of Congo and on Bamana mudcloth from Mali began to replace kente in popularity.

Nevertheless, kente seems to have found a relatively permanent place in at least three important contexts. In the 1960s, kente began playing liturgical roles in black Christian churches, dressing pulpits and adorning the pastoral robes of church leaders and the robes of their choirs. Although this practice has diminished somewhat in the early twenty-first century, kente is still prevalent during services falling within the February celebration of African American History Month.

At the end of the academic year, kente is ubiquitous at high school and college graduations, where it is worn as a stole by many African Americans. Black fraternities and sororities at colleges and universities are especially committed to wearing a kente stole on this and other important occasions. Because of this interest, Ghanaian weavers produce on an annual basis custommade strips featuring the individual colors of each organization, their identifying Greek letters, and the date of graduation. For non-Greek graduates, strips are also made with school colors, the name of the university, and the year. This practice has become so entrenched that non–African American graduates at predominately black institutions are commissioning strips from Ghanaian weavers that feature the flag colors of their own cultural or national heritage.

Another important context for wearing either handwoven or machine-manufactured kente are the annual observances of Kwanzaa. This festival, inaugurated by the scholar and activist Maulana Karenga in 1966 and recognized by millions of African Americans in the United States and elsewhere, occupies the seven days following Christmas on 25 December and is based on African rites of first fruits and thanksgiving and celebrates African American heritage and achievements. In addition to the use of kente on Kwanzaa altars, kente stoles, hats, and other apparel are worn regularly throughout the seven days and are also popular gift items for the occasion.

Tourism remains one of Ghana's major industries in the early twenty-first century, and, given the country's history in both the slave trade and the independence movements of Africa, it is a

Graduates at the nineteenth annual All African Peoples' Graduation Celebration, University of California, Los Angeles, 1998. Photograph by Betsy Quick, courtesy of the Fowler Museum at UCLA, Los Angeles.

pilgrimage site for African American travelers. In addition to the work of contemporary fashion designers, Ghanaian weavers and other artists produce an enormous array of dress items incorporating kente for visitors to their country. Especially popular are hats in various configurations, especially baseball caps, Muslim-inspired skullcaps similar to the red fez in shape, a variety of fully brimmed types, and even tam-o'-shanter and glengarry styles. There are also vests, ties, sandals, and shoes. Handwoven kente-

covered jewelry includes earrings, pins, necklaces, and bracelets, and men's formal wear is served by packages with bow ties, cummerbunds, and cufflinks. Purses and backpacks are sewn from both hand- and machine-woven versions of the cloth. The large number of Ghanaians living in urban centers of the United States help maintain and foster the role of kente as a focal element in Afrocentric dress. The future of kente as an iconic African textile is probably assured.

Snapshot: Asantehene Nana Osei Bonsu (r. 1804–1823)

One of the most observant and detailed precolonial accounts of an African leader's dress was recorded by the British envoy Thomas Bowdich in Kumase in 1817. His remarkable description of the seventh *asantehene* (king) Nana Osei Bonsu at the then-annual Odwira festival was published in 1819:

His deportment first excited my attention; native dignity in princes we are pleased to call barbarous was a

curious spectacle; his manners were majestic, yet courteous: and he did not allow his surprise [at seeing his visitors] to beguile him for a moment of the composure of the monarch; he appeared to be about thirty-eight years of age, inclined to corpulence, and of a benevolent countenance; he wore a fillet of aggry beads [rare blue glass beads considered to have spiritual powers] round his temples, a necklace of gold cockspur shells strung by their largest ends, and over his right shoulder

Asante celebrants at the fifth anniversary of the reign of Asantehene Osei Tutu II, dressed in *kaba* ensembles tailored from handwoven kente cloth. Kumase, 2004. Photograph by Doran H. Ross.

a red silk cord, suspending three saphies [amulets] cased in gold; his bracelets were the richest mixtures of beads and gold, and his fingers covered with rings; his cloth was of a dark green silk; a pointed diadem was elegantly painted in white on his forehead; also a pattern resembling an epaulette on each shoulder, and an ornament like a full blown rose, one leaf rising above another until it covered his whole breast; his knee-bands were of aggry beads, and his ancle strings of gold ornaments of the most delicate workmanship, small drums, sankos [harp lutes], stools, swords, guns, and birds, clustered together; his sandals, of a soft white leather, were embossed across the instep band with small gold and silver cases of saphies; he was seated in a low chair, richly ornamented with gold; he wore a pair of gold castanets on his finger and thumb, which he clapped to enforce silence.

This account is consistent with twenty-first-century practices and could be used in large part to itemize the dress of the sixteenth asantehene, Nana Osei Tutu II, at the fifth anniversary of his reign in 2004, and to a lesser extent many other Akan paramount chiefs on prominent state occasions.

References and Further Reading

Adler, Peter, and Nicholas Barnard. *African Majesty: The Textile Arts of the Ashanti and Ewe*. London: Thames and Hudson, 1992.

Anquandah, James. *Koma-Bulsa: Its Art and Archaeology*. Rome: Istituto Italiano per l'Africa e l'Oriente, 1998.

Armitage, Cecil H. *The Tribal Markings and Marks of Adornment of the Natives of the Northern Territories of the Gold Coast Colony*. London: Royal Anthropological Institute of Great Britain and Ireland, 1924.

Bowdich, Thomas Edward. *Mission from Cape Coast Castle to Ashantee*. London: John Murray, 1819.

Cole, Herbert M., and Doran H. Ross. *The Arts of Ghana*. Los Angeles: UCLA Museum of Cultural History, 1977.

de Marees, Pieter. *Description and Historical Account of the Gold Kingdom of Guinea (1602)*. English translation by Albert van Dantzig and Adam Jones. Oxford, UK: Oxford University Press, 1987.

Garrard, Timothy F. "Brass-Casting among the Frafra of Northern Ghana." Ph.D. dissertation, University of California, Los Angeles, 1986.

Garrard, Timothy F. *Gold of Africa*. Munich: Prestel, 1989.

Goody, Esther, and Jack Goody, "The Naked and the Clothed." In *The Cloth of Many Colored Silks: Papers on History and Society Ghanaian and Islamic in Honor of Ivor Wilks*, edited by John Hunwick and Nancy Lawler, 67–89. Evanston, IL: Northwestern University Press, 1996.

Gott, Suzanne. "Golden Emblems of Maternal Benevolence: Transformations of Form and Meaning in Akan Regalia." *African Arts* 36, no. 1 (2003): 66–81.

Gott, Suzanne. "The Power of Touch: Women's Waist Beads in Ghana." In *Dress Sense: Emotional and Sensory Experiences of the Body and Clothes*, edited by Donald Clay Johnson and Helen Bradley Foster, 85–95. Oxford, UK: Berg, 2007.

Gott, Suzanne. "Asante Hightimers and the Fashionable Display of Women's Wealth in Contemporary Ghana." *Fashion Theory* 13, No. 2 (2009): 141–176.

Huber, Hugo. *The Krobo: Traditional Social and Religious Life of a West African People*. St. Augustin, Germany: Anthropos Institute 1963.

Kyerematen, A.A.Y. *The Panoply of Ghana*. New York: Frederick A. Praeger, 1964.

Lamb, Venice. *West African Weaving*. London: Duckworth, 1975.

McLeod, Malcolm. *Asante*. London: British Museum Publications, 1981

Rattray, Robert Sutherland. *Religion and Art in Ashanti*. Oxford, UK Clarendon Press, 1927.

Rattray, Robert Sutherland. *The Tribes of the Ashanti Hinterland*. 2 vols. Oxford, UK: Clarendon Press, 1932.

Ross, Doran H., ed. *Wrapped in Pride: Ghanaian Kente and African American Identity*. Los Angeles: UCLA Fowler Museum of Cultural History, 1998.

Ross, Doran H. *Gold of the Akan from the Glassell Collection*. Houston TX: Museum of Fine Arts, Houston, 2002.

Ross, Doran H. "Misplaced Souls: Reflections on Gold, Chiefs, Slaves and Death among the Akan." *Bulletin of the Detroit Institute of Arts* 76 no. 1/2 (2002): 22–39.

Smith, Fred T. "Frafra Dress." *African Arts* 15, no. 3 (1982): 36–42.

Steegstra, Marijke. *Dipo and the Politics of Culture in Ghana*. Accra Ghana: Woeli, 2005.

Willis, W. Bruce. *The Adinkra Dictionary: A Visual Primer on the Language of Adinkra*. Washington DC: Pyramid Complex, 1998.

Yankah, Kwesi. *Speaking for the Chief: Okyeame and the Politics of Akan Royal Oratory*. Bloomington: Indiana University Press, 1995.

Doran H. Ross

See also Independence to Present; African Fashion Designers; Headdresses and Hairdos; Footwear; West Africa; Burkina Faso; Côte d'Ivoire.

Guinea

- Nineteenth-Century Animist Dress
- Nineteenth-Century Muslim Dress
- Twentieth-Century Dress
- Twenty-First-Century Dress

Guinea is a country surrounded by Guinea-Bissau, Senegal, Mali, Côte d'Ivoire, Liberia, and Sierra-Leone; it shares history with each of these countries that has influenced Guinean modes of dress up to the present day. From the eleventh century to the late nineteenth century, Guinea was an ensemble of separate animist and Islamic precolonial kingdoms, each of them diverse ethnic groups that the French colonizers transformed into a colonial nation called French Guinea from 1895 to 1958, after which it became independent. From 1958 to 1984, Guinea was radically restructured into a revolutionary nation called Popular Revolutionary Republic of Guinea led by Ahmed Sékou Touré until his death in 1984. He was followed by General Lansana Conté, who seized power through a military coup and initiated social changes based on liberal and democratic principles.

In each historical period, dress was determined by the Guinean elite, who created sociopolitical, cultural, and economic environments for clothing practices. According to the changing historical contexts, individuals and social groups, on the one hand, have used dress—that is, any modification of the body or items of clothing—to embody their images of themselves and their social groups; on the other hand, dress has also formed their images of their social boundaries with outsiders. These images may be projected on the body itself or on the clothes covering the body. The principal types of dress used by animist and Muslim Guineans include body painting, tattoos, jewelry, clothing, hairdressing, amulets, and masks. As embodied texts, clothed, tattooed, painted, and scarified bodies mirror the desires and ideological perceptions of the animist, Muslim, and modern Guineans.

Two case studies for the history of dress and social change in the precolonial animist societies are the Baga and Coniagui people. Two groups using an Islamic dress style are the Fulani of Futa Jallon and Dialonka of Solimana. In the late nineteenth century, in order to emphasize its animist culture against the Fulanis' political and cultural expansionist ambition, Solimana modified but did not abandon the Islamic dress style that it had already borrowed from the Fulani and Mandingo.

NINETEENTH-CENTURY ANIMIST DRESS

In the southern part of the Bagataye, women wore a strip of cloth about three feet (one meter) wide around the body and another cloth, generally of a different color, thrown over the shoulder. The ornaments are beads and shells hung around the neck, wrists, and ankles and plaited strings of beads worn around the pelvis, weighing nearly three or four pounds (one and a half or two kilograms). The Susu name of the narrow strip of cloth is *tuntungee*. It was used in the wedding ritual, with beautiful plaited strings of beads wound round the pelvis. In the northern part of the Bagataye, inhabited by the Baga Sitemu, this strip of cloth was called *yikda*. The Baga, like their Susu neighbors, manufactured the cotton cloth and partly traded it in exchange for tobacco, powder, muskets, and beads. The Baga women's hair was braided in rows. Two scarification marks under the eyes of the woman clearly served as marks of Baga ethnicity.

In the southern part of the Bagataye, men's dress generally consisted of a shirt and trousers, but Muslims in the area usually wore the Mandingo gown and trousers. The Mandingo gown, a full-length, ample and flowing robe, is called *boubou* in French and *domma bélé-bélé* in Susu. Trousers are *wantanyi* in Susu, but when they are short trousers ending at the knees, they are known as *monti*.

In the northern part of the Bagataye, women wore a nose ring and had a series of carefully chosen objects such as keys, snap clasps, cadenzas, and other hardware items hanging around their waist. Their heads were shaved to leave only clumps of hair geometrically shaped into diamond forms. In addition, tattoos embellished women's backs. Six to seven holes were pierced in women's ears, through which straws of rice, shaped into small yellow cylinders, were used as earrings. The yellow color looked like white gold against the dark skin. Baga Sitemu women had their upper teeth shaped into points. They also tied small beads around their waist attached to an embroidered square cloth. In the late nineteenth century, both Baga and Susu women of the Rio Nunez used the French five-franc silver coin with an image of Hercules and two young females as an ornament.

Especially important in conceptualizing the Baga image of themselves is the D'Mba mask, the Baga goddess of fertility and symbol of womanhood. The Baga projected through their masks their physical and ideal qualities of the clothed body. The images of the D'Mba Baga female identity are materialized through the large and heavy head and the big breasts of the mask. A D'Mba mask may be as tall as four and a half feet (one and a quarter meters) and two feet (three-quarter meter) deep. This massive wood shoulder mask may weight up to eighty pounds (thirty-six kilograms). The dominant image of the D'Mba is further emphasized through its clothed head, with its hair intricately braided in parallel rows and a high crest down the center, her face and neck decorated with linear patterns. Adding impact to the image is the mask's clothed flat and pendant breasts, which are decorated in linear patterns. Comparatively, the raffia-fiber dress, which covers the full length of the body of the mask, only suggests the divine nature of the D'Mba. D'Mba's cloth shawl is made of cotton of varying colors: dark indigo or black and tie-dye. In the twentieth century, the Baga used European printed cloth for the D'Mba's costume. Symbolically, the Baga identified with the visibly most important sculpted head and breasts, the "spirit of the D'Mba." The raffia-fiber dress, the "body of the D'Mba," is an embodiment of the spirit. Similar to the painstaking effort to make the wooden sculpted headdress of the D'Mba, the Baga women took much time and energy to braid their hair and put on their ornaments. Clearly, the physical form of the D'Mba is a text—a well-structured system of symbols that the Baga instrumentally used as a means of self-representation and self-identification.

NINETEENTH-CENTURY MUSLIM DRESS

In middle and upper Guinea, a three-piece ensemble consisting of a long-sleeved white shirt, a full-length flowing robe called *dôlôkè* in Fulani, and a pair of pants constituted the typical dress of Muslim men. Here, it was mostly the cloth but not the body that bore the meanings that Muslims projected about themselves, their societies, and their neighbors. Even though the Fulani borrowed their dress style from the Arab Muslims, they added original features that allow one to recognize authentic Fulani dress. Those features are the cotton cloth; the indigo dye; long-sleeved, loose-hanging, and cloaklike robes; and the geometric patterns of the embroidery. The first decades after the founding of the Theocratic Empire of Futa Jallon in 1725 were characterized by the antagonistic conflict between animists and Muslims. During this time, Islamic clothes mostly differentiated the Muslims from their external animist enemies instead of emphasizing the internal social differentiations among Muslims. Based in the rural areas, with headquarters in Fitaba, Bousra, and Gomba, the dissident movements implemented their version of Islam, which emphasized a work ethic, a politics of mass education, a jihad of the mouth and the heart, and a more liberal dress code, only requiring decency. Pictures taken of Fulani women during a beauty contest show their naked breasts, elaborate braided hair, and their wrappers wound around their waists; these photos reveal the existence of a secular life beyond the religious façade.

The Solima also redefined their adopted Muslim dress code to both reject the Fulani leaders' Islamic dogmas and oppose their attempt to dominate them. In addition to the military form of struggle, they used cultural and political forms of resistance against the Fulani: they founded Falaba as a center of resistance, ended public prayers, opposed the building of mosques in Falaba, used Dialonka animist names and hairstyles, and redesigned the Muslim dress. As a result, the Solima dress became similar to the Muslim Mandenka's, even though it was dyed either black using oxide metal or yellow using the bark of the néta tree. A traveler could recognize the Solima anti-Islamic culture through the female dancers, whose hairstyles and ornaments were unique. Their hair was divided and arranged into small bushy tufts and was decorated with glass beads, cowry shells, and pieces of red cloth. The spaces between the tufts were filled with a thumb of fresh shea butter. The dancers also wore beaded bracelets on their wrists and ankles that were made of glass in varying colors, and they wore heart-shaped earrings. They wore dresses in silk or taffetas, with a shawl hanging over their shoulders held by their arms. The musicians were elegantly ornamented with feathers, little bells, and multicolored clothes.

The fundamentalist Fulani saw the Solima dancers' display of their naked breasts, their body movement, and the overall charm that they evoked in the audience as indecent. The Solima saw the same cultural elements as creative means for reviving their animist traditions. Solima women further contributed to the revival by wearing earrings made of gold, but only on the left ear, where they could place two or even three, to demonstrate that it was not because of poverty that they wore them on only one ear, but simply to distinguish themselves from the women of Futa Jallon.

The ornate spurs and the military uniform of the *keleh mansa* (military commander) were impressive. To project the animist warrior image of the Solima, the military uniform included a hat, a large short-sleeved shirt, short trousers, four protective thick guards for the wrists and upper legs, a spear, and amulets sewn on the shirt or worn like necklaces. The hat, shirt, trousers, and

Keleh mansa (military commander) wearing a uniform consisting of short pants, a large short-sleeved shirt, protective guards for the arms and legs, and amulets worn around the neck. From *Travels in the Timannee, Kooranko, and Soolima Countries in Western Africa*, by Alexander Gordon Laing, 1826. Manuscripts, Archives and Rare Books Division, Schomburg Center for Research in Black Culture, The New York Public Library, Astor, Lenox and Tilden Foundations.

guards were all made out of cotton cloth. They symbolized the powers of the second-ranking authority of the Solima government. The Solima perceived the *mansa* (king) and the keleh mansa as the legitimate rulers of Solima, with strictly defined powers. Keleh mansa exercised his powers during wartime and exclusively on the battlefield. After the war, to enter the gated city of Falaba, he was obliged to ask for permission and wait to be allowed in. Inside Falaba, the keleh mansa lost both his title and his powers; he became an ordinary citizen, subordinate to the mansa, and simply called by his name. Here, the keleh mansa's identity disappeared, to be replaced by that of the servant of the king. The transformation of the keleh mansa into servant is visibly accomplished by the means of changing clothing and embarking on ordinary, peacetime social activities. During peacetime, both the mansa and keleh mansa wore full-length flowing robes not very different from those of the Muslim Fulani and Mandingo.

TWENTIETH-CENTURY DRESS

Conakry, the cosmopolitan capital of French Guinea, was the embodiment of French colonial politics and culture. It became a place of cultural encounters between the Guineans and Europeans on the one hand, and the Guinean animists and Muslims on the other hand. At first, the French used both the Islamic and the animist traditions along with Christianity and French culture as a means of ideological control. Until the 1930s, the animists (Coniagui, Susu, and Baga of lower Guinea; Toma, Guerze, and Kpele of upper forest Guinea) and the Muslims (Fulani and Mandingo) were still known to be very attached to their traditional dress styles. Coniagui girls continued to wear several strands of glass beads, and their bodies were marked with decorative scarification. The young men wore tasseled skirts with fanciful headdresses and numerous necklaces.

The long-sleeved, loose-hanging gowns that drape the bodies of Fulani men were also kept. Generally, these cloaklike robes are heavily embroidered in geometric patterns. In 1935, young Fulani and Fulakounda girls creatively adopted the French and British silver coins as supplements to their traditional ornaments. They combined the traditional and modern ornaments, to reinvent themselves. After 1930, when Western education had already made some impact through the creation of an elite class consisting of teachers, clerks, returned servicemen from World Wars I and II, and modern wives and mothers, European clothing styles were adopted by a few educated Guineans. In addition to their customary clothing, they appropriated the European dress style to embody their new identities. The returned military servicemen were the first political activists that greatly impacted the precolonial Guinean societies. The military uniform became the symbol of their new spirit of resistance to exploitation and oppression. It consisted of trousers, a shirt, and a red hat as well as a heavy pair of shoes. Medals were added to this military uniform on special occasions to individually distinguish the servicemen. The trousers and short-sleeved shirt were made out of European khaki cotton cloth. The uniform could also be blue for the advanced divisions.

Some educated Guineans became teachers in elementary and secondary schools after they had graduated from their regional and urban schools and from the specialization programs of the secondary high schools of Rufisque, Saint-Louis, and Gorée in Senegal. Later on, the graduates of these elementary and high schools became the union organizers and leaders of the political parties that spearheaded the anticolonialist struggle for independence. They were influenced by the new ideology of self-determination for the colonized Africans. These educated few appropriated the European dress style as their means of self-representation. As auxiliary functionaries of the colonial administration, the men wore a suit, a long-sleeved shirt with a tie, and a pair of dress shoes every day. Even in the rural areas, teachers dressed the same way. In the vocational schools, the dress was adapted to the work conditions. The dress clothes (*tenues de sortie* in French) that the directors and teachers of these schools generally wore during weddings, naming ceremonies, dance parties, and official meetings were not very different from those of the Guinean auxiliary administrators. Generally, the leaders of the struggle for independence kept the European dress style, until the end of the Colonial period. They used their dress style to project their modernist spirit. For example, Ahmed Sékou Touré was always dressed with the latest fashion wool (*drap*) clothes imported from France. Because of his elegant European wool clothes, he was nicknamed Sékou Drap.

Ahmed Sékou Touré was a self-made man, who combined his skills as a union organizer and a political activist to mobilize the Guineans against the French colonizers and their system of domination, which he defined as the cause of the underdevelopment of Guinea. He believed that only a multifaceted social revolution could transform French Guinea into a modern society that would rehabilitate the history and culture of the Guinean people. The Guinean traditional dress style was reinvented to serve as a means of revolutionary self-representation. Ahmed Sékou Touré served as the model of the revolutionary. All of the Revolutionary Teaching Centers were training places for the new lifestyle. In government meetings, political rallies, popular meetings, as well as the Friday prayer time, everyone was encouraged to wear authentic African clothing, be it traditional or reinvented—that is, a dress combining traditional features with newly imagined and/or borrowed modern African elements. Specially, during the Friday prayer time, a Muslim wearing a European dress was frowned upon and maybe criticized as counterrevolutionary. At any time and at any public place, it was mandatory to clothe the body. It did not matter which type of everyday clothes one wished to wear at a wedding, naming ceremony, dance party, or workplace. Thus, not surprisingly, as modernizers, the leaders of the struggle for independence used violent means to force the Baga, Coniagui, Bassari, and other animist groups—perceived as undressed—to adopt "civilized dress styles"—that of the Muslims or Christians.

After Sékou Touré's landslide political victory of 28 September 1958, and Guinean independence, he started to wear exclusively a white three-piece African ensemble (a pair of pants, long-sleeved shirt, and full-length flowing robe) combined with a hat and white, flat, pointed shoes called *mouké* in Susu. These symbolize his African-rooted modernist vision of his political enterprise. This attire has become a fashion called *tenue Ahmed* (Ahmed fashion). A typical dress of the revolutionary women of the Parti Democratique de Guinée (PDG; Democratic Party of Guinea) consisted of a large wrapper, a short-sleeved blouse, and a scarf that was worn on top of beautifully braided hair, *à l'Africaine*.

Male and female students of each of the levels of the hierarchical educational system wore a mandatory revolutionary school uniform that readily represented them as members of that particular level of education and distinguished them from other groups of students. These revolutionary uniforms were means of a collective ideological self-definition, based on the PDG's revolutionary perspective but not on the students' personal economic, political, and cultural backgrounds. For instance, elementary high school students wore a blue pair of pants and a short-sleeved white shirt, while secondary high school students wore a khaki pair of pants and a three-pocket, round-neck khaki shirt, nicknamed *col Mao* (Mao collar). The students of the Institut Gamal Abdel Nasser of Conakry and Julius Nyérérê of Kankan wore a military-type uniform consisting of a khaki pair of pants and a short-sleeved khaki shirt with military insignia, symbolizing the military discipline and the revolutionary spirit that these two universities were supposed to cultivate. Gamal Abdel Nasser was the nationalist Egyptian revolutionary president of the 1960s, well known for his successful nationalization of the Suez Canal. Julius Nyérérê was the nationalist revolutionary leader who organized the struggle for independence in Tanzania (East Africa) against the British colonizers and implemented the socialist-based policy of economic, social, and cultural development known as *Ujaama*.

Ahmed Sékou Touré's main political base consisted of women and youths. He worked for the emancipation of these two groups and never lost their support until the women's uprising of 27 August 1977 that protested against postcolonial Guinea's growing social and economic injustices. Women were organized through the PDG's women's associations at all levels, from the village (rural areas) and urban quarter to the PDG national women's organization. Their white dress, which consisted of a large blouse (*gouba* in Susu and Mandenka), a scarf, and a wrap skirt symbolized the revolutionary spirit and loyalty to Ahmed Sékou Touré and the PDG. This traditional or reinvented traditional cotton dress was sometimes replaced with imported fabrics bearing the PDG's ideological symbols (such as an elephant, a picture of Ahmed Sékou Touré, or other historical figures). As members of their own organized *Sêrê* (female age groups in Mandenka), women could wear clothes that reflected their own independent activities. A *Sêrê* symbolically projects itself through the dress that the members selected because of its effectiveness as a vehicle of meanings and for its aesthetic value.

Traditional dress was still worn but was associated with the meaning of authenticity—that is, African traditional values as opposed to European dress styles and alien culture. The traditional dress helped to foster the PDG's nationalist values. All of the ethnic groups continued to wear traditional attire. The exception was the animist attire that the PDG eliminated violently in the name of modernization through demystification and invention of a new clothing tradition. The animist Baga, Coniagui and others of forest Guinea were all constrained to modernize by converting to either Islam or Christianity or by adapting their traditions to the Guinean modern lifestyle. The Baga people were forced to change their clothing mainly by appropriating the dress style of the supposedly most advanced Muslims and Christians.

TWENTY-FIRST-CENTURY DRESS

The postcolonial clothing traditions have not yet changed under the current postsocialist government (1984 to present) of Ahmed Sékou Touré's successor, General Lansana Conté. However, due to the intense competition over the hearts and minds of Guineans stimulated by the liberal orientation of the new government, the youth deeply feel external cultural influence. A group of young people called the *branchés* ("plugged-in youths" in French) is accused of having abandoned African traditions in favor of European alien traditions. Supposedly, this group informs itself about and irresistibly adopts every fashion invented in the West. Lately the branché have started to wear sexy clothes (*sexi dugi* in Susu), which both Muslims and Christians condemn as immoral and anti-African. Generally, fundamentalist Islamic groups manifest their opposition to the branchés by physically abusing them. For instance, in May 2007, during widespread antigovernment demonstrations in the neighborhood of Bambeto, in Conakry, radical Islamic groups undressed and raped many girls who were wearing the so-called sexy clothes.

The animist groups are also reviving their cultural traditions to ward off the external influence that is coming from either the government-controlled cultural institutions and the Islamic and Christian organizations or the Western media. For instance, from 18 to 23 May 2007, all of the ethnic groups of the administrative region of Boké organized a festival that celebrated their cultural traditions through the exhibition of sacred masks, traditional clothing, and dance performances.

As a new trend, liberal professional activities have started to grow in the major cities of Guinea in general and in the capital, Conakry, in particular. In the area concerning dress and the aesthetic representation of the body, the growing professional businesses are tailoring shops, hair-braiding salons, and schools. Without any discrimination based on sex, age, and ethnicity, young people are the targeted population of these economic

Ahmed Sékou Touré wearing a white African embroidered robe, October 1958. After his landslide presidential victory, he exclusively wore this type of clothing, symbolizing his African roots and Guinean independence. AFP/Getty Images.

enterprises run by entrepreneurs who are still caught in the webs of the surviving dominant traditional and socialist cultures. The liberal economy is growing and will soon give life to its own liberal culture and help create corporate groups of professional men and women. After having effectively differentiated itself through its own modes of thinking and working, this growing social class of well-to-do professionals will certainly create its own modern clothing tradition and participate in the transformation of the social institutions of the present postsocialist state.

The history of dress in Guinea certainly reflects the history of Guinean society. Here, the body has constantly reflected the changing ideas and images that individuals and social groups have constructed about themselves and their society during different changing historical circumstances. The current struggle between traditionalists and modernists, old and new generations, and men and women is reflected through the clothes that Guineans have invented, reinvented, or appropriated as their symbolic representations of themselves and their relationships with others.

References and Further Reading

Camara, Abraham. "L'Art Baga." *Mémoire de diplôme de fin d'études supérieures.* Conakry, Guinea: Institut Polytechnique Gamal Abdel Nasser, 1975.

Coffinières de Nordeck, André. "Voyage au pays des Bagas et du Rio Nunez (1884–1885)." *Le Tour du Monde, 1er semester* (1886): 273–304.

De Chételat, Eleanor. "My Domestic Life in French Guinea." *National Geographic Magazine* 67 (May 1935): 695–727.

Eicher, Joanne B., and Barbara Sumberg. "World Fashion, Ethnic, and National Dress." In *Dress and Ethnicity*, edited by Joanne B. Eicher, 295–306. Oxford, UK: Berg, 1995.

Keita, Sidikhi Kobélé. *Ahmed SéKou Touré. L'homme et son combat anti-colonial (1922–1958).* Conakry, Guinea: Editions Sidikhi Kobélé Keita, 2005.

Laing, Alexander Gordon. *Voyage dans le Timanni, le Kouranko et le Soulimana, Contrées de L'Afrique Occidentale, Fait en 1822 par le major Gordon Laing.* Paris: Dela-Forest, 1826.

Lamp, Frederick. *Art of the Baga: A Drama of the Cultural Reinvention.* New York: Museum for African Art; Munich: Prestel, 1996.

Marty, Paul. *L'Islam en Guinée.* Fouta-Djallon, Guinea; Paris: Editions Ernest Leroux, 1921.

McLachlan, Peter. *Travels into the Baga, and Soosoo Countries.* Freetown, Sierra Leone: J. Mitton Company, 1821.

Saint-Père, M. "Petit historique des Sossoe du Rio-Pongo." *Bulletin du Comité d'Etudes Historiques et Scientifiques d'AOF* 13, no. 1 (January/March 1830): 26–47.

Mohamed N'Daou

Guinea-Bissau

Guinea-Bissau, northwest of Guinea and south of Senegal, is located on the Atlantic coast, with many estuaries and swamps that extend into the countryside. The region has long been home to dozens of relatively small-scale, politically decentralized societies. Since long before the arrival of Europeans, people from these societies traveled far and wide, trading goods down the coast in canoes to Sierra Leone. From as early as the fourteenth century, they also hosted merchants, particularly Muslims from the interior, in thriving coastal marketplaces. Strong economic and cultural links between the Guinea-Bissau coast and Muslim interior have continued through today. In the mid-fifteenth century, Portuguese sailors first set foot in the region, and very quickly whites began settling permanently in coastal entrepôts and establishing what were often very intimate relationships with local people. Of course, the nature of the relationship between Guineans and outsiders changed over time. This was particularly true in the early twentieth century, when Portuguese and mercenary soldiers began a process of carving out a colony they would call Portuguese Guinea. In 1974, after a protracted war for national liberation, Guineans claimed political independence. In the postcolonial world, Guinean engagement with the world through radio, television, cinema, commerce, and travel has continued.

This is not to imply that foreigners ever established cultural, political, or economic hegemony over the Guinea-Bissau region. To the contrary, rural communities and their locally controlled institutions have long dominated Guinean life and have proved an impediment to foreign control. Given this, it should not be surprising that locality is central to an understanding of Guinean fashion. Because of their long history of engagement with the broader world, Guineans have adopted elements of clothing styles that originated elsewhere, mixing them, in some cases, with their own styles. However, Guineans have actively constructed the meaning of Western- or Muslim-style dress within local fields of power. In so doing, they have transformed the meanings of particular items of clothing that have moved across space and time.

FIFTEENTH THROUGH NINETEENTH CENTURIES

Since before the arrival of the Portuguese on Guinea-Bissau's shores, people dressed themselves with items they manufactured from both local and imported materials. The earliest Portuguese visitors to the region noted clothing made from skins as well as cotton and silk cloth and jewelry made from gold. Silk cloth was quite rare and, therefore, valuable. It was traded south across the Sahara Desert and then taken west to the Guinea-Bissau region by Muslim trade networks. Powerful Guineans likely used it as a show of wealth. The earliest Portuguese visitors also noted that people from the ethnic group Biafada on Rio Grande purchased gold from seafaring African canoe men who traveled to and from Sierra Leone. "And all these people," one observer wrote, "have their ears pierced with holes all around in which they wear a number of small gold rings, one behind the other, and further, they have their nose pierced at the bottom, in the middle, in which hole they wear them." The same merchants brought blue dye, which was used in Guinea-Bissau in cloth manufacture.

In Guinea-Bissau, imported cloth and accessories assumed a place beside local manufactures. Locally a variety of peoples wove colorful *panos di banda*, strips of cloth that could be sewn together to produce larger cloths that were worn by both men and women as shawls or wraps. Pano production was especially important in the Casamance River state known as Casa or Kasa. The name of the state reveals a great deal about how peoples in the Guinea-Bissau region incorporated foreign notions of fashion with their own. The word *kasa* is Arabic for "garment" and was adopted by interior Mande people, who for centuries engaged in desert-side trade with Arab and other Muslim merchants. Over time, most Mande embraced Islam as well as many Arab articles of dress, such as the long smock (*bubu*) and turban. In the thirteenth century, Mande merchants expanded westward and established long-standing contacts with Guinea-Bissau region communities, especially along the Casamance River in the place they dubbed Kasa because of its vibrant textile industry. Throughout the Guinea-Bissau region, some who had long-standing relationships with Mande embraced Islam. Others did not convert but did recognize the power of Mande trade networks and, therefore, attempted to identify themselves with them through their fashion. Hence, Mande-influenced smocks, hats, headwraps, and amulets have long been central to a Guinean sense of style.

Recognizing the centrality of cloth in coastal cultures, Portuguese merchants sought to market cotton and eventually cloth. In the early 1500s, they directed slaves to grow cotton on the Portuguese-controlled Cape Verde Islands, exporting cotton fiber to the coast. Later, Portuguese established spinning and weaving facilities on Cape Verde, exporting panos di banda that were made by African slaves. Accounts from the period indicate that Cape Verdean cloth was highly prized by coastal peoples.

Cloth from the interior, Kasa Mansa, Cape Verde, and elsewhere circulated widely in the Guinea-Bissau region and was an integral part of local expressions of fashion. Everywhere fashion was, as it is today, an indicator of ethnic origin and class standing, a symbol of local notions of masculinity and femininity, and an expression unique to each generation. In the late sixteenth century, Portuguese visitors described people from the ethnic group Brame wearing "long smocks and wrap-around cloths, and underneath the cloths, they wear a garment made out of an animal skin." Among the Brame, women wore cloths "which go down to their knees, with all the rest bare," while young girls wore "only a strip of cloth in front, a hand-span long," coving their "shameful parts." Once married, they received the longer cloths of more mature women. Powerful Brame leaders wore the rarest and, therefore, most expensive cloth that had been purchased from Atlantic sailing vessels or Muslim merchants from the interior. Similarly, Papel elites wore "dyed cotton cloths, called *barafulas,* which the whites sell them." Across the region, powerful men fashioned imported cloth into what the Portuguese called "Moorish smocks." *Moorish* signified Muslim—or, in this case, Muslim-influenced—smocks.

But imported items of dress were not the exclusive domain of elites. "No black considers himself a man of standing," André Álvares de Almada noted, "unless he had snatched hats from our people." Whereas elites demonstrated wealth by dressing themselves with items purchased from foreigners, commoners demonstrated bravery by snatching items from foreign visitors, proudly displaying these indicators of masculinity in their communities. Further, it should be emphasized that elites never completely turned their backs on local fashion sensibilities. Although they frequently appealed to outsiders donning expensive imported cloth, they just as often appealed to their followers by dressing in garb that had symbolic power at the most local levels. Almada wrote that "kings" wore fine imported clothing when Portuguese merchants visited but when "the call is over, they immediately resume their goatskins." In the seventeenth century, Manuel Álvares also noted elites wearing imported cloth at times and small locally crafted straw coverings at other times, concluding that the latter "form of dress is so ancient that all the kings…own such pieces."

Cloth was not, then, an essential element in fashion in all social settings. Indeed, many people walked naked or wore goatskins or palm leaves in the form of loincloths or skirts. This was especially common on the Bijagos Islands where observers noted men rarely wearing clothes. Bijago women, on the other hand,

dressed as they often do today: bare from the waist up and in a skirt made from palm leaves that hangs to the knee. In Papel territories, commoners were said to wear goatskins wrapped around their waists.

A considerable number of Portuguese and African Christians, or Luso-Africans (people of both Portuguese and African heritage), also lived in the Guinea-Bissau region. As traders who negotiated commercial links between local communities and Atlantic merchants, they often looked to the broader Atlantic world for their fashion sensibilities. In the sixteenth century, Almada said they imported "ready-made clothing, shirts, doublets, footwear, and all other kinds of clothing." Portuguese and Luso-African styles were also adopted by other coastal dwellers seeking opportunities in Atlantic trading communities. This was particularly true in coastal trade entrepôts. On Bissau, for example, people from the Papel ethnic group were said to sometimes dress like Portuguese. Further, Almada noted, "Among the blacks there are many who can speak our Portuguese language. They dress as we do, as do many black women of the advanced kind known as *tangomas,* because they serve the adventurers who go to those parts." But, as coastal dwellers, Portuguese and Luso-Africans also adopted coastal fashions. Indeed, Luso-African women and men more frequently than not draped panos over European clothing. Further, when away from coastal entrepôts, Portuguese and Luso-Africans were said to "go naked…in order to get along better with the heathen of the land where they trade by appearing like them."

TWENTIETH CENTURY

The relationship between Portugal and Africa changed dramatically at the start of the twentieth century, when Portugal waged aggressive "wars of pacification" aimed at spreading control over a wide area. Having carved out a colony, Portugal then set out to impose new administrative structures, collect taxes, develop small urban centers, and increase the inflow of Cape Verdeans, who worked as clerks, administrative personnel, traders, and rural entrepreneurs on plantations. Despite this, Guinea-Bissau remained relatively weak, lacking large amounts of direct economic support. After World War II, the Portuguese government stepped up investment to defend itself from international criticism of colonialism. Between 1946 and 1947, the colonial administration was expanded; urban centers were redesigned; and roads, bridges, health centers, and administrative offices were built all over the colony.

The broad economic, political, and social changes that were forced on Guineans influenced the Guinean sense of style. Most noticeable was the embrace of European fashions by African elites. In the last period of colonization, elite social life became more distinctive in the colonial capital, Bissau, where dressing in such a manner emerged as the norm. As in other colonial systems, dressing in European style was in part mimicry, but it had another significance for Guineans. In Portuguese colonies, colonial law differentiated two groups of Africans. Most were classified as *indigenous,* which, to the Portuguese, meant *backward.* But Guineans could claim the status of *assimilated* or *civilized* if they could prove able to live "in a European way," including dressing as Europeans and reading and writing. The assimilated had rights similar to the Portuguese. Unlike the indigenous, they were exempt from compulsory work in public services and could travel freely inside the territory without an official pass.

This portrait of the son of a ruler (center back row) with his wives and children shows how they have adopted Western dress. The women wear floral dresses combined with a headwrap; the man is dressed in white. Guinea-Bissau, ca. 1950. Courtesy of National Archives, Guinea-Bissau.

Male elites and urban traders who wanted to be classified legally as civilized were compelled, therefore, to adopt European clothing styles. Women generally did not gain the status, because they were most often illiterate. Nonetheless, elite women often wore European-style dresses. Until today, Western styles are called *branku* in rural settings. This word derives from *branco*, the Portuguese word for white. Ironically, elite Guineans who adopted the branku style derived most of their fashion sense not from white Europeans but from brown Cape Verdean migrants. In pictures from the 1950s onward, a distinct urban fashion consisting of a Western suit for men and a floral dress with scarf wrapped from behind the head for women is evident. Guinean women, both urban and rural, were also influenced by Christian missionaries, who introduced the brassiere and other elements of Western dress.

In the countryside, local rulers (*régulos*) also felt considerable pressure to adopt European styles. Régulos were considered part of the Portuguese colonial administrative order, receiving a small salary and a uniform consisting of a white jacket, trousers, and cap. After the wars of pacification, Portuguese administrators selected the régulos who would work for them. Some régulos were chosen from the ranks of the traditional chiefs and would use the traditional symbols to buttress their claims to authority at the local level. In the coastal regions, many of these men wore traditional outfits and regalia consisting of a pano di banda and particular headdresses. In Muslim-dominated regions, régulos wore bubus. However, other régulos had had no previous chiefly duties, having been put in place by the Portuguese administration. These men's claims to authority could never be rooted to tradition. Hence, the white uniform—expressive of their relation with colonial administration—was particularly important. It was their only sign of distinction. For some local rulers, dressing African style was an outward symbol of resistance to the colonial order, while, for others, the white uniform was a sign of their support of it.

INDEPENDENCE PERIOD

Guinea-Bissau achieved independence in 1974 after a prolonged nationalist war. Because the population of the region was ethnically, religiously, and linguistically diverse, the war became the principal marker of a new national identity. The war defined what it meant to be a Guinean, and symbols of the period of the nationalist struggle acquired a great value. Most important among the leaders of the war was Amilcar Cabral. In photos taken during the war, he is seen in a Western-style shirt and a woven wool cap, which was of Muslim origin, although he was not Muslim. In independence, this same image of Cabral became the symbol of the new Guinea—a country that was rooted in tradition and seeking its own form of modernity.

After 1974, Guineans looked both inward to ethnically rooted traditions and outward to the world for other styles of dress that would mark their independence from Portugal. Influenced by pan-Africanism, the flag of an independent Guinea-Bissau was red, yellow, and green, and these colors were adopted in printed cloth and woven pano di banda. Further, in official portraits, national dignitaries chose dress that was expressive of their ideological options. The first president, Luis Cabral, fancied a suit with an open shirt, like other leaders of nonaligned countries. He was followed by Nino Vieira, president from 1980 until 1998 and

again after 2005; Vieira introduced the military uniform to official events. He later adopted ethnic outfits, such as the Pepel-style pano di banda and Muslim bubu. Dressing ethnically was a way for him to portray his Guinean origins and to distinguish himself from some in the opposition, who were of Cape Verdean descent. After the implementation of political and economic liberalization in the late 1980s, Vieira's official portrait shows him dressed with a complete dark suit, in Western globalized fashion.

Economic liberalism opened Guinea-Bissau's markets to international and African fashion. The oldest fashion professionals in Guinea-Bissau are the *alfaiate* or tailors, a male occupation of Mande origin. Tailors dress both men and women, quickly reproducing any clothing style. Hence, from the late 1980s onward, a wide array of styles were adopted across Guinea-Bissau as people latched onto fashions about which they learned from foreign visitors, television, magazines, and movies. The most common style for women was and is called *senegalese* (from neighboring Senegal); it consists of a large smock covering the body to the feet with a matching headdress. A variation of this style is a large tuniclike suit with matching trousers and headdress—an outfit worn by both men and young women and known as *grand bubu*. This style is costly, because it requires large amounts of expensive fabric, mostly *basang*, or damask, that can be purchased in different colors and is often embroidered after being tailored. For everyday use, women wear a kind of basang called *basang-ris*, which is an inexpensive damask tie-dyed in indigo. It is tailored into a long wrap that is worn around the waist and a large top that falls down a shoulder.

Also fashionable are dresses made of *legos*, a machine-printed cotton cloth with colored designs that gets its name from the town of Lagos, Nigeria, but is currently exported from Senegal and Gambia. Legos is less expensive and is, therefore, used for everyday clothing. Its malleability allows a great variation of tailored models, the most fashionable being the same as basang-ris, a long wraparound skirt completed with a blouse that can be distinctively tailored in a kind of bolero. Basang in the grand bubu style has become popular among men, losing its ancient connotation with Muslims and being developed into outfits often used during formal ceremonies.

Local markets also sell factory-made clothes. Many of these are secondhand items that are donated by Western countries, circulated by nongovernmental organizations, and then sold in urban centers by local traders. Although factory-made secondhand clothes are inexpensive, people prefer new factory-mades, which come mainly from neighboring Senegal but also from Brazil through Cape Verde. The market in these imports is controlled by *bideira*, women who work through transnational networks created by emigration. Bideira-supplied cloths give young people new choices in their quest for modern and global styles. Hence jeans—and especially baggy jeans—miniskirts, and large printed T-shirts for men or tight ones for young women have become commonplace in youth fashion across Guinea-Bissau. Accessories such as sunglasses, fake brand watches, high-heeled sandals, brand-name tennis shoes, and backpacks are also prized in the youth market.

Economic liberalization also encouraged the social display of fashion through formal spectacles that became important urban events. Indeed, in the 1990s, fashion shows featuring catwalks were the main elite social events in Bissau. Until a 1998 coup, the capital was a cosmopolitan city in which the national bourgeoisie

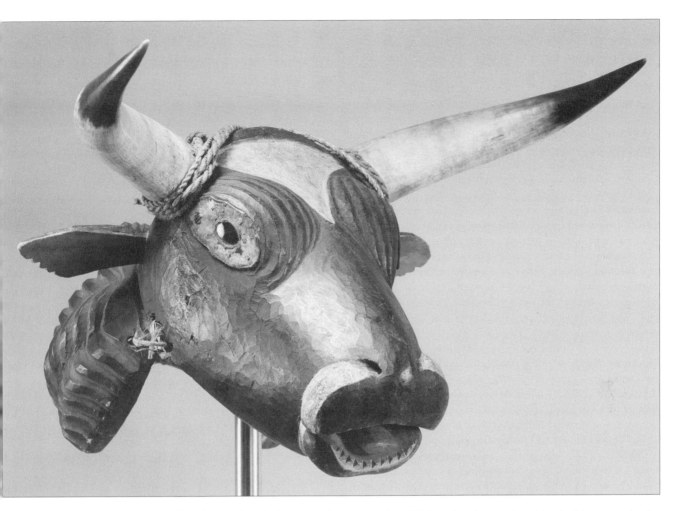

Bijago bull mask (Bijagos Islands, Guinea-Bissau), made of wood, pigment, cow horns, and cordage. This type of mask is worn by *nalo* for ritual dress when dancing and feasting. It is still in use in the twenty-first century. Typically, the mask is isolated in museums without the complete costume, which would in this case most likely be a raffia skirt with armbands and leg bands also in raffia. Getty Images.

lived. With wealth derived from international connections, elites had the capacity to spend considerable sums to acquire the latest fashions. When attending marriage celebrations or most any party, and even when having drinks at any of the capital's few cafes, dressing in styles seen on the most recent catwalk became a social expectation for the rich. After the 1998 coup, part of the country's elite and middle class left Bissau, and most of the international organizations moved to neighboring Senegal. The capital, then, lost its high-end fashion market, but the fashion shows continued, revealing their resilience as social events.

ETHNIC DRESS: THE BIJAGO

If Guinean fashion has responded to the forces of globalization, it has also remained rooted in ethnic traditions. Space does not allow for an exploration of the traditional garb of the country's twenty-plus ethnic groups, so we will only touch on the traditions of three of the largest groups—the Bijago, Manjaco, and Balanta.

The Bijago inhabit an archipelago and are well known for clothing styles that have been subject to a folklorization process in the last decades. Bijago have a gerontocratic system of age grades, and each grade has its own ritual dress. Over the course of their

lives, males pass through different grades that correspond to their ages—*nañoka* until adolescence, *nalo* until adulthood, and *nabidu* and later *asuka* in old age. If they die before passing through all of the grades, women, who carry their spirits, replace them. Nalo adorn themselves for dancing and feasting with painted grass and wood masks representing animals or objects such as the shark, bull, and hippopotamus. Nabidu wear outfits that represent their war capacities, including small grass shields, bags crossed over their chests, headdresses made of cloth, and, sometimes, Muslim wool-weaved caps. Women wear large grass skirts made in several layers and cover their heads with colorful scarves and printed cloths during ceremonies. The vibrant Bijago ceremonial outfits and effusive dances have become the main symbol of Guinea traditional cultural creation, being folklorized by the national ballet and by the tourist market, which has become a mainstay of the Bijago economy.

ETHNIC DRESS: THE MANJACO, PEPEL, AND BRAME

Manjaco, Pepel, and Brame are closely related populations whose traditional homeland is the coastal regions of northern Guinea-Bissau. People from each of these groups were among the first to trade with Europeans and to carry out seasonal migrations over long distances for work. Indeed, these migrations have been ongoing since the eighteenth century. Young male migrants have, for many generations, spent a considerable portion of their earnings on garments they have acquired while away from their homelands, and this collective cosmopolitan experience has been incorporated in local ritual outfits and regalia. For instance, Western-style clothing has long been considered customary wear in emigrant burial services. Moreover, the ritual dress of régulos displays a mix of both local and foreign elements that are linked to seasonal and life-long migrations. Régulo dress includes both a goatskin loincloth and a long, laced white smock, which is used by traditional healers, especially women, in Atlantic communities in Bissau, Benin, and Brazil, among other places. Over this, régulos wear a couple of panos di banda, one wrapped around the waist and another crossing over the shoulder. They cover their heads in a red scarf over which they wear a tall hat from Gambia. Their regalia includes a ring, a bracelet imported from the Mande, an earring, a small grass fly whisk or cow's tail, and an iron bell.

ETHNIC DRESS: THE BALANTA

Balanta society is at once gerontocratic and democratic. At the village level, a council of elder males (*balante bndang*) reached decisions affecting the whole by consensus. Before becoming a balante bndang, youths (*blufos*) pass through a number of grades that correspond with their ages. Those belonging to specific age grades frequently wear dress that distinguishes them from those in other grades. Youths in some grades may walk almost naked, while youths in another grade sometimes dress like women. Blu-fos are encouraged to demonstrate their bravery by stealing cattle, and, in some regions, they receive a thick braided bracelet for each cow obtained. The easiest group to identify is the blante bndang, who often wear red caps and a red piece of cloth draped over one shoulder and covering their bodies. Historically, the caps might have been manufactured locally or imported from Europe. Hats have long been a major trade item into Guinea-Bissau. They may also have been associated with red sailors' hats, often donned by white seafarers in the era of Atlantic slavery. Today, the caps are typically made of polyester or cotton and have a red ball on the end. In the West, they would be identified as ski caps, and they may well be marketed as such in many parts of the world, because they are manufactured in Asia and shipped to vendors far and wide. However, in Guinea-Bissau, the red cap is clearly associated with male authority. Before the 2000 presidential election, Balanta candidate Kumba Yala campaigned in a Western-style suit and tie and a red cap. He also wore the cap for the photo that appeared on the national ballot. If the suit symbolized authority at a global or national level, the hat symbolized authority at another. It was an outward demonstration of the rural as opposed to urban, of manhood in a specific cultural context, and of a uniquely Guinean form of democracy by consensus that was rooted in traditional local politics.

CONCLUSION

Kumba Yala's choice of how to adorn himself is best understood in light of the history of the place in which he lives. The Guinea-Bissau region has witnessed the comings and goings of foreigners for many centuries. These outsiders have certainly influenced

A *régulo* in Pecixe, Guinea-Bissau, twentieth century. Régulo attire includes a *panos di banda* and a tall hat from Gambia. Regalia consists of a ring, a bracelet imported from the Mande, an earring, a small grass fly whisk, and an iron bell. Courtesy of National Archives, Guinea-Bissau.

the Guinean sense of style, but rural communities and their locally controlled institutions influenced how people view what is fashionable and what is not. That is, Guineans have, for centuries, actively constructed the meaning of Western- or Muslim-style dress within local fields of power and, in the process, have transformed the meanings of particular items of clothing that have moved through space and time.

References and Further Reading

Almada, André Álvares de. *Tratado Breve dos Rios de Guiné.* Translated by P.E.H. Hair. Issued personally for the use of scholars, Department of History, University of Liverpool, 1984.

Álvares, Manuel. *Ethiopia Minor and a Geographical Account of the Province of Sierra Leone.* Translated by P.E.H. Hair. Department of History, University of Liverpool, 30 September 1990.

Boletim Cultural da Guiné Portuguesa. Bissau, Guinea-Bissau: Centro de Estudos da Guiné Portuguesa, 1946–1973.

Brooks, George E. *Landlords and Strangers: Ecology, Society, and Trade in Western Africa, 1000–1630*. Boulder, CO: Westview Press, 1993.

Brooks, George E. *Eurafricans in Western Africa: Commerce, Social Status, Gender, and Religious Observance from the Sixteenth to the Eighteenth Century*. Athens: Ohio University Press, 2003.

Carreira, António. *Panaria Cabo-Verdiano-Guineense: Aspectos Históricos e Sócio-economicos*. Lisbon, Portugal: Junta de Investigações do Ultramar, 1968.

Carvalho, Clara. "Ambiguous Representations: Power and Mimesis in Colonial Guinea." *Ethnográfica* 6, no. 1 (2002): 93–111.

Coelho, Francisco de Lemos. *Description of the Coast of Guinea (1684)*. Translated by P.E.H. Hair. Issued for circulation from the Department of History, University of Liverpool, 1985.

Forrest, Joshua B. *Lineages of State Fragility: Rural Civil Society in Guinea-Bissau*. Athens: Ohio University Press, 2003.

Gable, Eric. "The Funeral and Modernity in Manjaco." *Cultural Anthropology* 21, no. 3 (2006): 385–415.

Hair, P.E.H., and Avelino Teixeira da Mota, eds. *Jesuit Documents on the Guinea of Cape Verde and the Cape Verde Islands, 1585–1617*. Issued for the use of scholars by the Department of History, University of Liverpool, 1989.

Hawthorne, Walter. *Planting Rice and Harvesting Slaves: Transformations along the Guinea-Bissau Coast, 1450–1850*. Portsmouth, NH: Heinemann, 2003.

Henry, Christine. *Les îles où dansent les enfants défunts. Âge, sexe et pouvoir chez les Bijago de Guinée-Bissau*. Paris: CNRS Éditions et Éditions de la Maison des Sciences de l'Homme, 1994.

Loureiro, João. *Postais Antigos da Guiné*. Lisbon, Portugal: João Loureiro e Associados, 2000.

Mark, Peter. *"Portuguese" Style and Luso-African Identity: Precolonial Senegambia, Sixteenth–Nineteenth Centuries*. Bloomington: Indiana University Press, 2002.

Walter Hawthorne and Clara Carvalho

See also Children's Masquerade Costumes.

Côte d'Ivoire

Côte d'Ivoire, on the Gulf of Guinea, has neighbors in Ghana to the east, Burkina Faso and Mali to the north, and Guinea and Liberia to the west. More than 60 ethnic groups make up the approximate population of seventeen million. The geography ranges from humid equatorial forest in the south to dry and sparsely treed savanna in the north and has influenced the development of cloth production and dress. The lack of tsetse flies in the north allows livestock breeding, including wool-producing sheep—an impossibility in the south. Trade between these zones was an important aspect of the economy in Côte d'Ivoire in precolonial times. The area where these zones meet, called the arboreal or wooded savanna, was a logical place for the gathering of traders and transport and for the exchange of ideas and technology.

HISTORICAL OVERVIEW

Côte d'Ivoire was at the nexus of successive waves of migration from the north, west, and east from the first millennium C.E. Indigenous peoples already living in the country were probably absorbed through marriage into the new social structures brought by the migrants. Mandé invaders brought Islam into the northern part of the country by the eleventh century. Earlier migrants, resisting conversion to Islam, moved east (Senufo groups) and south (southern Mandé) into the middle of the country. Cotton spinning and weaving, which was a well-developed art in the Sudanic empires, came with these migrants. In the east, Akan and related groups from present day Ghana, fleeing the expansion of the Asante Empire in the eighteenth and nineteenth centuries, settled the area around Bondoukou in the northeast and the city of Bouaké in the center of the country and spread south to the coast, where they mixed with the Lagoon groups. They are also recognized as longtime weavers of cotton. Trading of brass basins from the north provided cuprous materials that were melted down and cast into bangles. Further south, gold casting was practiced by the Baule and the Lagoon peoples.

The oldest inhabitants of the territory seem to be the Krou speakers of the tropical forest of western Côte d'Ivoire such as the Bété, Dida, and Wé. They are closely related to groups living in Liberia, and there is still frequent migration across the border. Cotton does not grow in this region, but fibers gathered and processed from plants and trees provided materials for clothing and household needs. Woven cotton cloth was obtained through trade with people living north of the forest zone.

Although the first Europeans to land in Côte d'Ivoire were the French in 1687, contact was limited. Lack of a good harbor

Gouro man wearing a handwoven cotton-wrapped garment and hat in the town of Mamanagui, Côte d'Ivoire, 1998. Photograph © Barbara Sumberg.

along the entire coast meant that the slave trade was never as big a disruption or influence in the area as it was in other places along the West African coast. The middle of the nineteenth century brought further involvement by the French in an uneven pattern. The final decade of the 1800s saw serious exploration and dominance by the French, who were asserting their control over their "share" of the newly partitioned territory of Africa. With colonial rule came attempts to force the cultivation of cotton in the north to feed the French textile industry for the African market. Although the selling of raw cotton and woven strips of cotton was strictly controlled by the French, Africans still managed to circumvent these controls. Raw cotton was held back from market and spun and woven at home to meet family clothing needs. Illicit cross-border trade in cotton strips provided a more lucrative market than the state-dictated price for fiber into the 1950s. Still, styles of dress and materials changed in response to these new opportunities and pressures.

Côte d'Ivoire gained its independence from France in 1960 as a participant in the modern world, albeit with many different levels of development, wealth, and opportunity spread across the landscape. The textile industry, begun in 1921 by M. Gonfreville with a spinning factory located in Bouaké, had achieved a certain level of sophistication with spinning, weaving, and printing factories operating in Bouaké and Abidjan. Uniwax, a company that produces high-quality wax-print cloth was started in Abidjan in the late 1960s and continues to produce fabrics for the domestic and export markets to the present.

MATERIALS AND PROCESSES

With its widely varied growing conditions and climate, different fibers were used for dress and textile production across the country. Cotton is indigenous to the north and has been processed, spun, and woven into cloth for centuries. Cotton was grown as part of the household economy; both women and men had roles to play in cultivation. Once the cotton was harvested, women cleaned the raw fiber and spun the yarn to give to a male family member to weave into narrow strips that were then edge-sewn to make garments and domestic textiles. Perennial varieties of both white and naturally brown cotton still grow in Côte d'Ivoire. Wild indigo was gathered to dye the yarn or the finished cloth various shades of blue. Kola nuts from the forest produced a red-brown color. Dyed yarn was combined with undyed to weave striped and plaid patterns. Decorative motifs were woven in with a supplementary weft on a white or indigo blue ground. Plain white strips were dyed various shades of blue or were tie-dyed to produce patterns either before they were sewn into cloths or after. Baulé weavers and weavers from Kong produced *ikat*.

Strips and finished cloth were major trade items from the transitional zone north to the Sahara and south to the forest. Cloth, both locally produced and coming into Côte d'Ivoire from the north, was traded for kola nuts from the forest. The kola was then sent north, where it was a valued necessity for marriage and other rituals.

In the forest and transitional zones, the bark of certain fig trees was stripped from the tree, soaked, and beaten to obtain cloth. The resulting cloth was used as mats, blankets, and clothing. In the center of the country, bark cloth formerly played an important role in funerals, but its use was subsumed by cotton cloth. The leaf of the raffia palm produces fiber that was plaited into hats, mats, garments, and bags. In the southern part of the country, the Dida and some Lagoon groups produced complex-looking textiles of raffia on a fixed loom. These tubular pieces were plaited, tie-dyed, and used as loincloths, hats, cloaks, wrappers, and, in the mid-twentieth century, cut and sewn into garments of current style.

Other materials were and still are used to dress the body. Animal products such as teeth and claws were obtained through hunting and were worn as necklaces and attached to clothing as well. Mandé hunters in northern Côte d'Ivoire, similar to those in Burkina Faso, Ghana, and Mali, wear shirts with leather amulets and animal teeth and claws attached for protection during the dangerous time of hunting. Animal pelts were incorporated into garments and also used to make amulet packets. Prestige hats might include the pelt of a lion or leopard.

Iron, brass, and gold are used for jewelry. Glass beads, imported from Europe and from other places in West Africa, decorate the body as waist beads, armlets, and necklaces. Paint made

Man in a tunic, trousers, and hat tailored from wax-print cloth. Yamoussoukro, Côte d'Ivoire, 1998. Photograph © Barbara Sumberg.

from chalk and mineral pigments is applied to on the faces of young Boo or Guéré girls in the final stages of initiation in the western part of the country. Other ethnic groups also apply chalk or paint to young women's bodies during coming-of-age ceremonies. Chalk is applied to the face and body of a newborn and its mother for medicinal and decorative purposes, while ash or mud might be smeared on the face and hair of women in mourning. Chalk is also worn by Baulé spirit mediums, often around the eyes and mouth. Women oiled their skin with shea butter and other emollients to make themselves shine.

Scarification—deliberate cuts on the skin that leave either a raised welt or a depression—was practiced by various groups in Côte d'Ivoire. Patterns on the face or torso were made to beautify the body. They could be medicinal or protective as well. Scarification marks were displayed on both men and women. Although certain designs were favored by different groups, they were not necessarily conceived of as tribal identifiers. This practice mostly vanished in the late twentieth century. The scarification seen on statues and masks reflects actual scarification patterns on people, but the relative height of the relief is exaggerated.

FORMS OF DRESS

In the late nineteenth century, men in Côte d'Ivoire chose from four basic garments. A narrow length of cloth sewn from a few strips was worn around the waist and tucked between the legs to cover the genital area. This was everyday wear, especially practical for working in the fields. A garment with a similar use was a small triangle of cloth with strings to tie around the waist. A larger cloth of several strips was worn over the shoulders as a shawl and provided a means of carrying things as well as warmth. Men also wore an even larger rectangular cloth wrapped around the torso with one end draped over the left shoulder, leaving the right bare. Men dressed this way for important occasions. Strips could also be cut and sewn into a large robe called a boubou in French-speaking West Africa. A boubou would be made from cloth with weft-faced motifs woven in or from differently striped strips. This cloth took more time and skill to weave and thus contributed to the prestige of the garment and the wearer. Whether the weaving was plain and simple or ornately patterned depended on the kind of garment. A loincloth worn for working in the fields would be plain, perhaps starting out white and then dyed blue as it became stained and worn. Men also wore various types of hats.

Women's garments were even simpler than men's. For working in the fields, women would also wear a strip or two of cloth tied between their legs or simply passed between the legs and held up by a string tied around the waist. When more cloth was called for, it was a rectangular *pagne* wrapped around the waist. Another cloth could be thrown over the shoulders for warmth. Upper garments covering the breasts were not often worn; occasionally, a second wrapper would be wrapped under the arms. Lobi women in the northeast wore braided grass belts around their waists, sometimes with leaves attached. For special occasions, they would attach cowry shells and wires that hung both in front and behind. No other garments were worn.

Young children often were minimally dressed in a string of beads around the waist. Beads and amulets were given to babies to protect them from harm during the vulnerable stage of infancy and usually were worn for a number of years. As children grew, they might wear a strip of cloth around the waist as well. A girl would be given a piece of cloth, possibly part of a worn women wrapper, to tie around her waist as she got older. At puberty, girl would assume the dress of an adult woman. Sometimes special hairstyles distinguished different ages of children.

Jewelry serves many purposes among the people of Côte d'Ivoire. It can add an erotic dimension, as in a woman's waist beads hidden under her clothes, whose presence is known only by her husband or lover; it can have protective functions such a amulets worn around the neck that contain Qur'anic verses; i can be worn in ritual contexts by the Akan-related peoples of the lagoon and southeastern regions; and it can be purely decorative. Most jewelry combines several of these functions, and it can be difficult to distinguish between what is functional and what i ornamental.

The earliest jewelry was natural objects of bone, teeth, stone and seed beads worn around the neck. Glass beads, possibly coming across the Sahara or from other West African sources, were traded along the coast. When the Dutch arrived by ship, the took advantage of this trade and local preferences for beads b providing Venetian glass beads.

Cast brass bracelets, anklets, and rings were made by Senufo casters in the north. Brass jewelry is associated with divination and with the belief in the power of bush spirits. Certain motifs are worn by particular people—for instance, the principal insignia of the Nöökaariga healer is the bush cow. A ring surmounted by the head of a bush cow is worn during healing rituals and sometimes placed between the lips of an initiate during the funeral of a healer. Bracelets in the shape of a python are worn both by Sando diviners and their clients, attesting to the importance given to this creature and its power to mediate between the worlds of spirits and people. The python is considered the chief messenger of the spirits. Children wear brass bracelets that express the pride and love of the parents. Multiple bracelets create a rhythmic sound that amuses children. Children also wear small brass amulets called *yawiige* as protective medicine. These take many forms such as miniature anklets and miniature bracelets, both of which may have animal imagery. Among the Lobi, jewelry also performs spiritual functions as well as adding to the wearer's beauty. Amulets and bracelets depicting chameleons, snakes, and birds are cast or forged and worn to symbolize the spiritual powers of good spirits known as *kontee-bouo*. Women also wore a plug or labret of ivory or wood in their upper lip.

The brass used in Côte d'Ivoire was usually an imprecise mixture of metals. Copper was not mined in the area and was thus obtained as sheet metal vessels from Europe. European pewter and brass were traded in the northern part of the country from the Gold Coast through Bondoukou and Kong. Brass was cast by the lost-wax technique, indigenous to much of West Africa. Gold was mined and worked in the southeast among the Akan and Akan-related groups. Baulé and Lagoon goldsmiths cast beads and pendants, primarily used for personal adornment that were stylistically similar to but not the same as Akan gold work in Ghana. Beads took the form of rectangles, disks, tubes and bicones from large to small. Within this limited number of shapes, great variation was achieved with the wax-thread method of modeling. Beads were worn as necklaces by women and children. Pendants in the shape of a human head, ram's horns, and various animals were worn suspended on a necklace, as hair ornaments, and attached to hats. In the twentieth century, the French colonial administration established district chieftaincies in the

Mwan/Wan hairstyle. Special jewelry (rings wrapped in yellow and red thread and cast-metal beads) and a cowry-shell hairstyle mark the girls who were excised and became women. Kounahiri, Côte d'Ivoire, 1998. Photograph © Barbara Sumberg.

a skullcap composed of hand-woven strips, embroidered by hand or machine or crocheted. A special hat is conferred upon the best cultivator during a hoeing competition among the Senufo. Headgear is also a fashion item, and forms originating with one group are adopted and worn by other groups if they are found attractive or useful. For women, covering the head with a head tie or piece of cloth can be a religious observance, a means of protection from the sun, or a fashion statement.

With the arrival of European traders came new kinds of textiles as well as imported garments. On the coast, where the most direct contact between Africans and Europeans occurred, men of style and substance wore tailored garments such as coats and trousers and brimmed hats. Mill-woven cloth was introduced in the mid-nineteenth century. Only a small proportion of the population had access to these goods since trading was not easy without a good harbor.

Changes in dress accelerated during the Colonial period from 1902 to 1960. The two most important factors were the change from direct trade to a money economy and the forced cultivation and sale of cotton. Colonial governments liked to collect taxes to pay their administrative costs. Paper bills and coins were required, so the whole population of a colony was forced to buy and sell with hard currency. This, in turn, facilitated their ability to pay taxes. Once this transformation was effective, Africans had money to buy imported cloth, which was lighter weight, more comfortable, and easier to clean than handwoven material. Inexpensive cotton prints allowed for a larger and more varied wardrobe, while more expensive wax prints and other imports demonstrated the wearer's wealth and modernity. Old techniques of decorating cloth such as tie-dye were used on commercially woven fabrics to produce vivid patterns.

Although the use of handwoven cloth for everyday wear—incorporating a wider spectrum of colors with commercially produced yarn—persisted among some people into the 1960s, it was effectively replaced by domestic and imported factory-woven cloth. New styles of fitted tops and slim skirts for women replaced upper and lower wrappers. Details of sleeve size, peplum, and skirt length as well as styles of head wraps varied widely, changed rapidly, and indicated the level of a woman's fashion sense. At the same time, men abandoned handwoven cloth except for very special occasions and began wearing trousers, shorts, shirts, T-shirts, and other garments imported from Europe, Asia, and North America. Printed cloth became a vehicle for expressing unspoken sentiments when particular designs were named, often with an abbreviation of a proverb. The ability to accumulate both classic and new designs of printed cloth for use in clothing is an indicator of a woman's status.

In the twenty-first century, men, women, and children in Côte d'Ivoire have many choices in their wardrobes. An urban professional woman might wear a wax *complet*, an outfit consisting of a tailored blouse, two wrappers or a long, slim skirt, and a head tie for work; fashionable jeans to go out; and a soft, faded wrapper or tie-dyed boubou at home. A Muslim woman in the north of the country might wear a loose ankle-length dress embellished with ruffles and lace over a wrapper for her female association dance; a print wrapper and T-shirt for chores at home; and a length of cloth over her head when she steps out to the market. Secondhand clothing is widely available and often furnishes a child's wardrobe, along with a tailor-made outfit for ceremonies and a school uniform. Small children wear a length of print fabric taken

southeast. Although these offices were not traditional, they survived and, over the years, the use of gold and gold-leaf regalia by these appointed chiefs grew. Handheld objects such as fly whisks, staffs, sandals, bracelets, and rings are made in Côte d'Ivoire or are imported from Ghana to supply the demand.

In the true Akan kingdoms of the Abron near Bondoukou and the Anyi close to the Ghanaian border, kings and chiefs use a plethora of gold and gold-leaf regalia. Once produced locally, it is now mostly purchased in Kumasi, Ghana. With the scarcity and rise in price of gold, gold casting has been replaced by electroplated brass and gold leafing by paper foil. Iron was mined and forged in the north by the Senufo and Lobi and in the west by the Gouro of Oumé. Although the bulk of production was in agricultural tools and weapons, bracelets and anklets were made. Iron was also imported as manilas (ringlets) and in other forms and then reworked into implements and jewelry.

Leather packets with Qur'anic inscriptions inside were worn around the neck by Muslims, sewn into hats and garments, and applied to hunter's and war shirts for protection. With over sixty ethnic groups in the country with various forms of social organization, there was significant variation in some aspects of these basic forms of dress.

Long and helmet-shaped cloth hats were worn by senior Gouro men in the center of the country. How the hat was worn, with the top folded over to the left or the right or straight back, communicated something about the wearer. Among the Baulé, an Akan-related group of the southeast, some chiefs wear pillbox-type hats decorated with gold or gold-leaf ornaments along with a variety of other types. Many Muslim men, regardless of ethnicity, wear

Mwan/Wan girls wear a distinctive hairstyle with a "necklace" safety-pinned to the hair for initiation ceremonies. Kounahiri, Côte d'Ivoire, 1998. Photograph © Barbara Sumberg.

under the arms and tied around the neck to make a kind of dress. In the north around the city of Korhogo and west around Man, handwoven strips made into loose dresses for women and tunics for men have found a market among visitors and among young Ivoirians from all over the country. The short-sleeved dress shirt made by a tailor from a length of wax print is stylish casual apparel for men of all ages and ethnicities. Men also wear trousers and tunics tailored from wax print, often with a matching hat.

Dress in Côte d'Ivoire can have ethnic and religious connotations, but there are seemingly few rules about dress. A garment primarily worn by Muslim men, a long robe that reaches the feet, is worn by Christian men as well. Finely tailored wax print ensembles are considered defining dress by Baulé women but are worn by all women who can afford the cloth and tailoring. Women's head ties cross all ethnic boundaries. Some types of cloth are used locally and are not known outside the region where they are produced. The Gouro of Oumé make and use a tie-dyed cloth that is woven by men and worn primarily by women and is virtually unknown in the rest of the country. Baulé weavers are well known for material purchased and used by all groups. Kentelike cloths called *kita* are woven on the coast and used by people in the center of the country for funeral gifts, replacing their own handwoven fabrics.

A common use of dress across West Africa shows group solidarity. An association, whether government sponsored or volun-

tary, will pick a pattern and order enough cloth for the members to dress alike during an official function or especially during funeral celebrations. In the latter case, whenever the garment is subsequently worn, the wearer will remember the circumstances of its purchase and recall sentiments for the deceased. Dressing in a common fabric pattern by members of a group is unofficially known as a uniform.

SPECIAL OCCASION AND MASQUERADE DRESS

Along with funeral and association uniforms, dress is important during special occasions, both personal and social. Religious holidays present an opportunity for new clothing, especially for children. Muslim families celebrate Eid al Fitr with gifts of clothing. Small boys wearing matching trousers and tunics of shiny polyester fabric with machine embroidery at the neck are a common sight on the streets of cities and towns during Eid. At Christmas, young girls in flounced and ruffled dresses and matching bows in their hair attend church with their parents. Weddings are also a time for dressing up.

Initiation into secret societies and other rites of passage into adulthood often call for distinctive dress that marks the candidates participating in a "time out of time." Guéré girls, as mentioned above, dance and have their faces painted on the day of emergence from seclusion as women. Special jewelry and a cowry-shell hairstyle also mark the girls who were excised and became women. In a village near Kounahiri in the center of the country, Wan girls dancing in an initiation ceremony wear a distinctive hairstyle with decorative elements associated with other ethnic groups, such as cast metal ornaments from the Baulé and wrapped earrings similar to Fulani earrings. Senufo boys initiated into the Poro society wear a white hoodlike hat and loincloth while they are in the bush for three months.

Masquerades usually call for specific dress, rightfully called costume, because it is generally intended to disguise the wearer. Along with a mask that covers or sits on the head, a masked dancer (depending on the masquerade) may wear handwoven cloth, factory-made cloth, or specially constructed garments—perhaps knitted, knotted, or even made entirely from palm fronds. Senufo painted cloth, now produced primarily for sale to tourists, was originally made for use in masquerade dress, by hunters, and by initiates to Poro. The lively patterns and figures of animals, birds, and masked figures are painted on handwoven cotton strips in a two-step process. The designs, now purely decorative, were considered protective and brought good luck. Some objects that are worn as jewelry also function as musical instruments during masked performance. Cast brass anklets with bells attached, fiber or cloth strips with nut shells attached, and forged iron anklets all create rhythmic sound when danced.

CONTEMPORARY FASHION IN CÔTE D'IVOIRE

Abidjan has been a center of the West African fashion industry. Home to many designers who studied in Europe, it is also the headquarters of the Fédération Africaine des Créateurs (FAC) established in 1993 and in Abidjan since 1996. A number of designers have been working there for several decades. Angy Bell, born in Benin, has been in the fashion business since 1976, combining techniques such as batik with commercially made fabrics

Zauli masquerader wearing a knitted costume with raffia skirt and anklets with metal leg rattles, shaped like nutshells. The musicians behind him wear shirts made from Baulé strip-woven cloth. Maminigui, Côte d'Ivoire, 1998. Photograph © Barbara Sumberg.

and, above all, raffia. She is one of the founding members of FAC and has been working in fashion longer than anyone else in the Abidjan scene. Gilles Touré, born just a few years before Bell started her career, spent two years training in Paris and returned to his hometown of Abidjan. After ten years in business, he was made a knight in the Ivoirian Order of Merit for his success in promoting fashion in Côte d'Ivoire.

Pathé Ouédraogo, known as Pathé'O, was born in Burkina Faso but has been living in Abidjan since 1969. Trained as a tailor in the city, he opened his own shop in 1977 and created a niche for himself as designer when he saw how African fabrics were shunned by African designers at the time. He won the first Ciseaux d'Or (golden scissors) competition sponsored by Uniwax in 1987. Since then, he has pioneered the use of African textiles in fashion and opened boutiques all over West Africa. Nelson Mandela, former president of South Africa, wore Pathé'O creations during his presidency. The two men finally met in 1997.

The presence of a developed textile sector in Côte d'Ivoire has promoted the growth of the fashion industry. Uniwax, a wax printing company that sponsors many fashion shows, created the Ciseaux d'Or competition to recognize the most talented designers. In 1985, another textile manufacturer, CFCI-Textiles (Compagnie francaise de Côte d'Ivoire) launched WOODIN, a line of print fabric targeting a younger, fashion-forward clientele t spectacular success. WOODIN introduced a prêt-a-porter co lection in 1999 using African prints and again targeting a youn, urban audience.

The use of handwoven or handmade cloth in the fashio context has recently blossomed in an unexpected form. Bar cloth, made from the bark of certain trees and considered t be the most archaic type of cloth in Côte d'Ivoire, has entere the marketplace in a fashionable new form (see Snapshot). Th use of handwoven cloth, particularly that made by Baulé weaver outside of Bouake, in fashionable ensembles worn to concer and cultural events in Abidjan appeared at least as early as th late 1990s. But the overwhelming majority of fashion designer use wax or print cloth, alone or with other fabrics, to produc African couture.

Snapshot: Miss Zahui and Tapa

In recent years, because of civil strife and economic stress, bark cloth known as *écorces battue* and *tapa* (a word the French have borrowed from the Polynesians) has become part of the Ivoirian lexicon, especially when it comes to fashion, thanks to Miss Zahui, a fashion designer who specializes in using tapa in all aspects of her design process. "Tapa means *taper*—to beat in French. It alludes to the process through which the tapa cloth is made," says Zahui. "It is made of the bark of a tree that grows in the central part of Côte d'Ivoire, Bouake and, more specifically, in N'Zikro in the department of M'bayakro."

The tapa cloth is extracted from the bark of the tapa tree, usually a type of ficus. Farmers cut a thin layer of the bark of the tree in sections based on its use. The raw product is then beaten with a stick to soften it. It is then washed and dried and eventually dyed according to its intended use. "One does not really have to cut down the whole tree to get the tapa. If that was the case, the ministry of the environment will complain about long term effect of deforestation. We must plant more trees to preserve the tapa," says Zahui.

She continues, "The good news is that Côte d'Ivoire is not the only place where one can find the tapa. In almost every African country you find it. In central Africa in my family in-law, you find tapa; the pigmy still wear tapa today. It is found in Gabon, Congo, Zaire, and Guinea as well."

Zahui has been in the fashion industry in Côte d'Ivoire since 1986, after working as a secretary for an Ivoirian firm for fourteen years. She entered that world because of her passion for making clothes. "I was established since 1986. I entered the world of fashion because it was my ambition for making dress. I bought a sewing machine then; I absolutely wanted to create a fashion design school. I wanted to sew, but more important, I wanted to do art in motion 'l'art en movement,'" says Zahui.

Her passion led her to seek out several Ivoirian designers who, unfortunately, told her that it was impossible to do such a thing as art in motion. She took that as a challenge. Indeed, the challenge led her to explore other avenues in different regions of the country. "I went to Korhogo, in the north of the country and worked with cloth from that region. It went well. I did raffia and it went well. I had a successful business with both cloths. But what really motivated me was the tapa."

She was exposed to tapa by accident when one of her friends suggested she examine a special cloth made in the M'bayakro region. "I came across it by accident. I was doing a TV show in Bouaké when a friend of mine told me that in Bouaké there was tree that produced cloth or one could make cloth out of. She brought me a sample of that cloth. I made a vest for my first trial for a journalist who was hosting a show I was invited to. At the end of the show the host told me that we had to go to a village, N'zikro, in the department of M'bayakro to learn more about tapa."

Examining the process of making tapa with the local people changed her life in a way that she did not expect. "I spent a day there [M'bayakro] and observed the whole process of making tapa. I was mesmerized and inspired by it. Today, tapa is my life, my passion. Thanks to tapa I was able to impose a new way of looking at fabric and clothing in Côte d'Ivoire. I was able to meet various presidents and dignitaries around the world [including] the Queen of Spain."

It is important to note that tapa is a very expensive cloth. It is sold to people with means, such as heads of state and celebrities. There has been a trend to help the masses enjoy tapa. The alternative of renting tapa dress for special occasions has allowed anyone to enjoy its beauty.

Zahui continues, "Today, I am devoting my time to conducting research on tapa. With respect to interior design, one can use tapa to make lamps, table cloth, et cetera. It is easy to wash tapa by hand or in a washing machine; you can even steam-iron it. You can do everything with it. If you are trapped in the rain and it gets wet, you can just let it dry in the sun." She is the only one in Côte d'Ivoire who works with tapa to make fashionable dress and items for interior design.

Zahui sees her work in a larger context of African and Ivoirian politics. Tapa, according to her, is a vehicle through which Africans should rally to get African designers the place they deserve in the international arena. She has a plan to make it happen.

In 1993, Zahui opened a fashion design school in Abidjan named Cours Figaro-Couture. Students graduate after three years of intensive training. This says a lot about Zahui's desire to create an outlet for African youth to express and nurture its creative artistic talents. She notes, "Tapa is more than a fabric; it is a product of combat. It must help us to put Africa on the global map. I make a plea to the ministers of the environment to plant and preserve the tapa trees across Africa. We need to fight together to have Africa get the spot it deserves in the global arena. I want to organize and help all fashion designers not only in Côte d'Ivoire but throughout the continent. We must promote more TV shows on fashion because fashion and peace go together. When you see any creative work, it brings a sense of calm and peace that is truly needed in times of crisis that the country [Côte d'Ivoire] and other African countries are going through now."

Her enthusiasm can affect the thought process and work of both local and African designers in general. One might instead think in terms of "dress without borders," as designers from all corners of Africa gather on a regular basis to share, learn, and promote new ideas and new techniques.

What is remarkable about Zahui is that, unlike most of her predecessors who studied in the West in prestigious schools, she is a self-made fashion designer. Like her predecessors, she made use of the raw materials that Africa has to offer, but she exploited the natural resources in a way that no one ever thought possible and with unparalleled success. The same can be said about her nongovernmental organization, the YEHE. "It is an exclamation that alludes to something marvelous, magnificent, beautiful, brilliant," says one of Zahui's close associates. YEHE has gained wide success. It organizes a salon of fashion whereby designers from across the continent gather in several countries across Africa to showcase their work. YEHE has been endorsed by heads of state in Africa who have hosted and welcomed African designers in their countries. It is no longer an Ivoirian phenomenon; it has become an African cultural event that has been given credence by world designers as well.

References and Further Reading

Adams, Monni. "Dida Woven Raffia Cloth from Côte d'Ivoire." *African Arts* 25, no. 3 (1992): 42–51, 100.

Barbier, Jean Paul, ed. *Art of Côte d'Ivoire from the Collections of the Barbier-Mueller Museum.* 2 vols. Geneva, Switzerland: Barbier-Mueller Museum, 1993.

Bickford, Kathleen. "Knowing the Value of Pagne: Factory-Printed Textiles in Côte d'Ivoire." Ph.D. dissertation, Indiana University, 1995.

Bosc, Julien. *Lobi Art and Culture.* http://www.africanart.net/pages/etlob3.htm (accessed 10 April 2009).

Domowitz, Susan. "Wearing Proverbs: Anyi Names for Printed Factory Cloth." *African Arts* 25, no. 3 (1992): 82–87, 104.

Forester, Till. "Senufo Masking and the Art of the Poro." *African Arts* 26, no. 1 (1993): 30–41, 101.

Garrard, Timothy F. *Gold of Africa.* Munich: Prestel, 1989.

Glaze, Anita. "Senufo Ornament and Decorative Arts." *African Arts* 12, no. 1 (1979): 63–71, 107.

Picton, John, and John Mack. *African Textiles.* London: Icon, 1989.

Revue Noire. Special Mode: African Fashion, no. 27 (1997–1998).

Sumberg, Bobbie. "Panther Skins and Loaves of Bread: The Tie Dye Cloths of Oumé." *Hali* 124 (November–December 2002): 88–93.

Vogel, Susan. "Baulé Scarification: The Mark of Civilization." In *Marks of Civilization,* edited by Arnold Rubin, 97–106. Los Angeles: UCLA, Museum of Cultural History, 1988.

Vogel, Susan. *Baulé: African Art Western Eyes.* New Haven, CT: Yale University Press, 1997.

Barbara Sumberg and Remi Douah

See also West Africa.

Liberia

Glebo men in Harper, Maryland County, Liberia, 2006. Glebo men traditionally wear *lappas* using country cloth made of strips of woven cotton. They often tie the *lappas* in front with a great knot, known as a "big belly button." Photograph by John Sanders.

Liberia is bounded by the Atlantic Ocean, Sierra Leone, Guinea, and Côte d'Ivoire. It has a population of approximately three million people with at least sixteen different ethnic affiliations as well as immigrant descendants. From 1989 to 2003, Liberia went through a series of civil wars that resulted in vast numbers of deaths and the destruction of towns and homes. Many citizens became refugees in neighboring countries or were displaced within Liberia itself. At the beginning of the twenty-first century, many people returned to start life anew.

The greatest influence on Liberian fashion over the last two centuries has been the dress of the African Americans who first came to Liberia in 1822 under the auspices of the American Colonization Society and continued to immigrate to Liberia, especially during the next fifty years. Liberia declared independence in 1847, and the country maintained its independence through the nineteenth and twentieth centuries, when other areas of Africa were dominated by European powers.

The settlers and their descendants established a government based on that of the United States, and their religious and social institutions as well as their attire were reminiscent of what they had known in the antebellum South. Photographs of families and school and church groups in the late nineteenth century illustrate the formality of the dress. For their portraits, men wore white shirts with stiffened collars and bow ties, waistcoats, and frock coats. On the most formal occasions such as presidential inaugurations, men wore tails and top hats. Women, even in informal settings, wore long dresses, sometimes buttoned to the neck, with long sleeves and ruffs.

The emigrants met Africans who wore clothing suited to a tropical climate. Men may have worn loincloths, and bare-breasted women may have worn locally made raffia wrappers as skirts. As early as 1838, the Colonial Legislative Council decreed that all African residents within the bounds of the several counties were required to wear clothes and would be fined if they violated the law. Various societies sought to clothe the converted. Missionaries, a dominant presence in Liberia, also encouraged "proper" dress.

The colonists' style of dress spread among the different peoples of Liberia through the relationships between local indigenous communities and the settlers. Women became "country wives" of immigrant men as these interactions grew. They were not legally married. A system of wardship also developed. Settler families took young people into their homes. Wards were more than servants, although they often could be recognized by their plain clothes, bare feet, and brooms or pails. However, it was expected that a ward would be schooled, and, over the generations, some of these family members might become professionals, government officials, and leaders in churches, schools, and other institutions with attachments and commitments to their birth families and their urban patrons. Mission schools also gave young people opportunities for recognition and positions.

In time, the terms *kwi* and *country* came to identify an individual's status in society. Kwi means civilized, schooled, and salaried; country people are those from different ethnic groups without Western schooling or big jobs. Yet people were primarily identified as kwi or country by what they wore. For men, kwi meant long trousers, a white shirt, a suit coat, closed shoes, and perhaps a briefcase; while women with Western dresses, hose, gloves, hats, and high heels were recognized as kwi. Country often meant long country cloth gowns or country cloth shirts with short pants and sandals for men. Country cloth was made of woven strips using native cotton sometimes first dyed with indigo or other natural dyes. Instead of dresses, country women wore untailored tops and lappas. A *lappa* is a wrapper made from a two-yard (almost two-meter) piece of cloth wide enough to reach from waist to ankle; it was tied around the waist, above the breasts, or over the shoulders and could be used for carrying a baby or food stuffs.

DRESS AND FASHION TRADITIONS OF INTERIOR LIBERIA

Some traditions that originated in the interior continue to affect both rural and urban styles today. Few people today are acquainted with bast or raffia cloth—once made in western and eastern interior areas and wrapped around the body—but everyone knows the raffia fiber costumes of masqueraders who dance at the 26 July Independence Day or on other special occasions. The masqueraders wear a variety of headdresses that carry special names and traditions. The masquerader's movements within the raffia—sometimes appearing like a dancing bundle of hay—give these entertainers an otherworldly quality, as if they came straight from the forest.

Weaving was introduced to peoples of the western regions of Liberia by Mende weavers from the west and Mandingo traders and migrants from the north. The weavers produce long white cotton strips with some variegated designs using threads dyed indigo, brown, and black. The strips were sewn together to make large attractive cloths used as blankets or made into chief's gowns, too expensive for an ordinary man, who had to be content with shorts and a singlet. The gowns are wide and long with wide openings for sleeves, a large opening for the head, a well-tailored large pocket in front, and often with embroidered designs. Pants and shirts or other tops are worn beneath the robe.

Travelers commented on the different fashions among women upcountry in the early twentieth century. A woman might tie her lappa like a shawl around her hips or wind it tightly several times around the body and arrange the waist using a string so that she could pull up material in loops and folds. Traditionally, throughout the country, being bare breasted was natural, but it was considered inappropriate and vulgar for a mature woman to show her thighs.

Other prestige garments in the western interior of Liberia were the hunter and warrior gowns. Special amulets—perhaps containing writings from the Qur'an—and animal substances such as horns, talons, and leopard skin were added to a country cloth base. Pieces of red cloth might also be added. Red is a powerful color—the color of the leaders of the traditional bush schools. There is no traditional red dye, and the red cloth was often obtained from the belts of French military officers stationed in Guinea.

In eastern Liberia—in the interior and along the coast—weaving was not practiced, and lappas of factory-made cloth were worn by both men and women, although there were different traditions about how they should be worn. During the nineteenth and early twentieth centuries, these lengths of cloth were received as pay or were purchased down the coast by the many Glebo and Kru men of eastern Liberia who worked on ships as well as on the shore in African towns like Accra, Lagos, and Calabar. The cloth—called *fanti cloth*—was manufactured in The Netherlands and England but now is made in many Asian and

A girl of the Mende ethnic group, near the Liberia–Sierra Leone border, wearing silver ornaments including bracelets, pendant, and decorated animal horn. Late nineteenth or early twentieth century. Courtesy of Jane Martin.

African countries. Glebo men still tie their lappas around their waists sometimes with a great knot (called the "big belly button") in front. With this, they often wear a long-sleeved shirt, perhaps a tie, a suit coat, and maybe a bowler hat. The most prestigious cloths for men in eastern Liberia have been the kente cloths that men brought back from Ghana.

In the nineteenth and twentieth centuries, Liberians along the coast and in the interior often mixed Western and traditional clothing in ways that are unusual to Western eyes. At one meeting in 1931, an American representative noted that one chief wore a tall silk hat, another was clothed in a footman's great coat, and others wore frock coats over their skirts and bare feet. In an interior town, two of Chief Towei's four favorite wives were photographed in 1927 wearing country cloth lappas, leopard-teeth necklaces, and top hats. To the American, George Schwab, who took the picture, the hats looked "utterly incongruous," but in retrospect they appear quite stylish.

TRADITIONS OF JEWELRY AND ADORNMENT

Eastern and western Liberia had different traditions in jewelry as in clothing during the past. Brass jewelry was popular among the Dan and Kran peoples in the interior. Silver ornaments were made by Bandi and probably Vai craftsmen in western Liberia. Neither type of jewelry is found today, but pieces in museums and private collections illustrate the creativity and talents of these earlier artisans.

The few brass casters among the Dan and Kran were respected members of the community, responsible for making tools and weapons as well as jewelry. They used the lost-wax method to produce a wide variety of castings, including figurines, bracelets, anklets, knee rings, and neck rings. Sometimes three or four anklets strewn with bells were cast together as a single piece. Large anklet bracelets for the head wives of a distinguished chief signaled wealth and power but made walking difficult—recognition of the fact that such women need not toil. All this jewelry was prestigious, confirming the wealth and status of the wearer and the giver. It was also dazzling. As George Schwab wrote, "The Goo (Dan) are aglitter from head to foot. Theirs seems to be an exuberant spirit, bursting forth in tinkling bells and clanging brass."

The silver jewelry of the Bandi was equally unusual. The work was done by blacksmiths who may have learned the craft from Mende or Mandingo neighbors. Since no silver is mined in Liberia, French francs from Guinea and U.S. silver coins provided raw material for the craftsmen. A wide variety of pieces were made: twisted bracelets often with incised designs and small knobs at the ends, square box pendants with silver wire decorations, ear hoops, long silver chains, and silver neck wires. The jewelry was often worn by girls who were completing their training in the Sande secret society bush schools, where young women in western Liberia were prepared for adulthood.

Vai silversmiths may have been the makers of cow and ivory horns, incised and decorated with silver and silver chains. These could be worn as necklaces and used for amulets or holding snuff. Some of these horns were worn by Kru women who lived along Liberia's east coast.

CHANGING STYLES IN LIBERIA IN THE 1960s AND 1970s

Until the mid-twentieth century, Liberians maintained the styles of clothing that had characterized kwi and country labels. However, in the 1960s and early 1970s, kwi women began to wear boubous and lappa skirts—usually with a blouse of the same material and a second lappa tied around the waist in a variety of ways.

The following anecdotes indicate the changing mood of the time. A family visited Ghana after independence and began to wear lappa dresses when they returned. A female college student admired Mandingo women and their boubous and asked them to make her similar dresses. A distinguished faculty member at the University of Liberia adopted a "nativistic style of dress" during what she called the "nativistic revolution" in the 1960s. Another began to wear boubous and lappas in the early 1970s and has never worn Western dress since the day she made the change.

A key event dramatized the changing attitudes toward dress. When President Tubman died in 1971, his vice president, William Tolbert, was summoned immediately to Monrovia from his upcountry farm to take the presidential oath of office. Usually inaugurations involved top hats and tails, but Tolbert was wearing a "relaxation" or "leisure" suit. It became known as a "swearing-in suit." The style consists of matching pants and a tailored shirt with buttons and an open lapel in conservative colors. The suit was

Three women wearing *lappa* suits in Monrovia, Liberia, ca. 2000. The outfit includes a *lappa* skirt tailored with a waistband, zipper, and perhaps pleats and tucks. The blouse or *buba* may be fitted or loose, and there are a great variety of possible sleeves, bodices, and embroidery. Photograph by Jane Martin.

quickly adopted by many professionals in Liberia. At the same time, men representing counties in the House of Representatives felt freer to wear their traditional large gowns (with a slender gown underneath) to sessions.

In the 1970s, there were other innovations in dress. *Tipoteh* sandals made from old rubber tires, said to be first worn by an activist university professor, Togba Nah Tipoteh, were copied throughout the country. The *Sweet Mother suit*—a tie-dyed T-shirt and short flared wraparound skirt named for the very popular song by Nigerian High Life composer Prince Nico Mbarga—was worn by Liberian students as well as Peace Corps volunteers.

WOMEN'S FASHIONS IN THE EARLY TWENTY-FIRST CENTURY

Modern Liberian dress is, in many ways, part of the wider West African fashion scene. Lappa suits for women are popular throughout the region, and the billowing caftan/boubou and its variations are also admired and worn in many countries.

A woman's lappa suit in Liberia usually has four pieces, all made of the same material. Such an ensemble includes a lappa skirt tailored with a waistband, zipper, and perhaps pleats and tucks. The blouse or buba may be fitted or loose, and there are a great variety of possible sleeves, bodices, and embroidery. The popular harlequin style has a *buba* with a high waist and a flared skirt.

Another part of a lappa suit is the head tie, which has increased in variety—and size—over the years. Head ties are daily wear, worn by women who "tie" lappa as well as women of education and wealth. Many women do not feel dressed without a head tie, but, in the twenty-first century, some are comfortable bareheaded. Often the tie is wound around the head and covers the ears. Some tie the cloth around the head above the ears and across the forehead. Styles have become more elaborate. Skill is required to fashion the bows and knots that secure the cloth.

The fourth part of a lappa suit is a cloth that originally would be used to tie a baby on the wearer's back. Now this piece (called *ashoka* in Liberia) has been transformed into part of the outfit and is folded and worn over one shoulder.

Women also wear boubous—long one-piece dresses, sometimes slimmed and sometimes ample, often made of damask cloth manufactured with designs embedded in the cloth, which is then dyed in indigo, camwood, or German dyes. Various types of lace are used. Such dress may also be worn with a headdress and an ashoka. President Ellen Johnson Sirleaf wore one of these ensembles at her inauguration in January 2006.

MEN'S FASHIONS AT THE BEGINNING OF THE TWENTY-FIRST CENTURY

The swearing-in suit continues to be worn in Liberia, although men also wear Western dress. A popular men's outfit is long pants with a Vai shirt. The shirt—worn as early as the seventeenth century—falls straight to the hips. It can have short or long sleeves. Vai shirts are collarless with a slit in front that, like the neck opening, is often embroidered and decorated. Materials range from plain or designed damask cloth, tie-dyes, strip-woven pieces, or any factory lappa that is sometimes overdyed. It is said that the Vai shirt will serve you all your life. No matter how you grow—sideways or up—it will always fit.

Nigerian suits with full pants and a flowing long top (sometimes made of lace) are worn, but the more popular outfits for men's formal attire are of damask embroidered at the neck and hemline and perhaps at the sleeves as well.

CLOTH AND THE MAKING OF CLOTHES

Cloth itself, before it is tailored as a dress or gown, is an important commodity in Liberia, pleasing for its own sake. Cloth is wealth, often accumulated and used as a gift symbolizing kinship and friendship. Country cloth was a major item of trade before the twentieth century, and cloth might be part of a fine for settling a dispute or paying a debt. Today, cloth may confirm marital arrangements as part of bride price or enhance loving relationships between a man and a woman. In one case, cloth and clothes given to a woman as part of a marriage agreement were later claimed by her to be only a gift when she sought to break off the relationship. A compromise was reached.

A tradition among the Glebo people shows another use of cloth: a woman's death is an occasion to display all the cloth that she acquired over the years from husbands, lovers, brothers, and sons. The cloth from her trunk "dresses the room" where the body is laid out—it is draped on walls, ceilings, and furniture to show and celebrate her life.

Although some individuals make their own outfits, most Liberians turn to the many tailors found in Monrovia and local towns. In earlier times, there were seamstresses among the Liberian American communities. Now most people go to the small shops of local male tailors. The tailors are often Vai or Mandingo from Liberia, but there are also Fulani tailors, Guineans, Sierra Leoneans, Ivoirians, and Nigerians. No one uses patterns; each tailor is a designer. Many have materials from which one can choose and suggestions for styles. Tailors embroider as well as fashion the outfits to suit the customer. Many customers consult African and U.S. fashion magazines for styles that they want to wear. Often they select African materials to be made into Western-style dresses. Country cloth can be made into an A-line skirt with a modern jacket, and a factory print might be made into a halter style called "dig my back."

Special commemorative factory-made lappas are especially appealing for outfits as well as for one's cloth collection. Outfits of this cloth may be worn by all members of an organization. This is called *pumping*, derived from the term *peplum*. A cloth made to celebrate President Tolbert's coming to office displayed his picture with the words "Congratulations Mr. President" and "Liberian Marketing Association." Such commemorative cloths were produced when President Ellen Johnson Sirleaf was inaugurated in January 2006, and lappas, bubas, and shirts were worn in celebration. The cloth quickly went out of stock.

MOURNING AND PRAYING: CLOTHING IN BLACK AND WHITE

Wakes and funerals are very significant events in Liberia, not only for solidarity in sharing grief, but also for marking the social attachments that have been broken and the ties that bind. Whether in traditional communities or urban church settings, black clothes are proper, as is the lack of adornment. Formerly black veils and gloves were expected in urban settings, but requirements are more flexible now. One is likely to see purple as well as black garments, and the choir may wear white.

Mourning, like grief, lasts a long time. In Liberia, family members may mourn for a departed loved one for six months, a year, or a year and a half. Members will wear black during the first mourning period and black, purple, or black and white checks during a second mourning period, as the family decides.

White garments—the sign of a pure heart, purity, and peace—have been worn by women members of prayer bands in traditional as well as independent churches. Often members pray on city streets or at the homes of individuals who are facing struggles. In March and April 2003, in the midst of civil war, about one thousand women, members of the Women in Peace-Building Network (WIPNET), walked the streets of Monrovia with banners and sat in at the airfield and in front of the executive mansion. The women wore white WIPNET shirts with their regular lappas and white turban head ties to protest the failure of the government to work for peace. Their action had a powerful effect. President Charles Taylor agreed to go to Accra for the peace meetings, at which a final peace was made.

"DOKA FLEH": USED CLOTHES

The used clothing markets in Liberia have been referred to as "dead body clothes" or "bend down boutiques," but the modern appellation is *doka fleh* (or *doga fleh*). The phrase may be derived from an expression from Mende languages farther north, *donka fleh*, meaning roughly "try it on! Voilà!"

Importing used clothing was against the law through the 1960s. The trade restrictions were abolished in the 1970s, and now doka fleh markets are found in every part of Liberia, and used clothes are hawked on the streets from wheelbarrows or the heads of the sellers. Visitors from the United States may see T-shirts or jackets from their own high schools or hometowns worn by people on the streets of Monrovia or on clotheslines and stalls upcountry.

Liberians of all walks of life patronize these markets. Women farmers and market women often pick up T-shirts and other blouses to wear with a lappa. Men have been seen wearing women's blouses that are in line with their flashy preferences. Mothers search for children's clothes that they can turn into the required school uniforms. Baseball caps, used sneakers, rain gear, and overcoats—appreciated in the chills of a long rainy season—are part of a person's fashion statement. University women and men have a wide choice of jeans. Elite men and women may search for—and find—Western dresses and suits.

GOLD JEWELRY

In Liberia, gold has always been the precious metal of choice among those who could afford it. Gold and diamonds are mined upcountry in western and central Liberia, and eighteen- to twenty-four-karat gold jewelry can be purchased from Lebanese jewelers in air-conditioned shops or from Mandingo and Vai jewelers crowded into other parts of central Monrovia. Customers need to be wary; some seemingly reasonably priced gold in the shops is actually brass that has been sprayed with gold and a clear coat.

One of the most distinctive pieces of Liberian gold jewelry is the V ring, which was inspired by Winston Churchill's hand sign for victory at the end of the Second World War. The V ring identifies Liberians and Liberian friends in the United States as well as other West African countries. Filigree V rings have been used as wedding rings, as was the handshake ring with two clasped hands. Pendants featuring the Liberian seal, the palm tree, Cleopatra's head, African masks, and African maps remain popular, as do gold chains.

Gold has not only been valued and worn by urban dwellers. In the 1980s and perhaps today, young women graduating from the traditional Sande society secluded bush schools in western Liberia were expected to have some gold in their coming-out outfit and in their elaborate hairstyles.

HAIRSTYLES AND BODY MARKINGS

In general, Liberian men wear their hair closely cropped, although there is some indication that men in western Liberia may have shaved geometric patterns into their hair long ago.

In earlier times, kwi women ironed and waved their hair. Now many women have their hair tied or braided, or they tie it themselves and use extensions or wigs. For many occasions and especially for church and social events, women follow settler traditions and wear hats.

Many young women from western Liberia attend the secluded Sande bush school during vacation break from government or mission schools. One part of the training includes having one's hair tied. The hairstyles are elaborate and can be seen on the Bundu/Sowei masks worn by the *zoes*—the women leaders of the Sande Society—and danced at the "breaking of the bush."

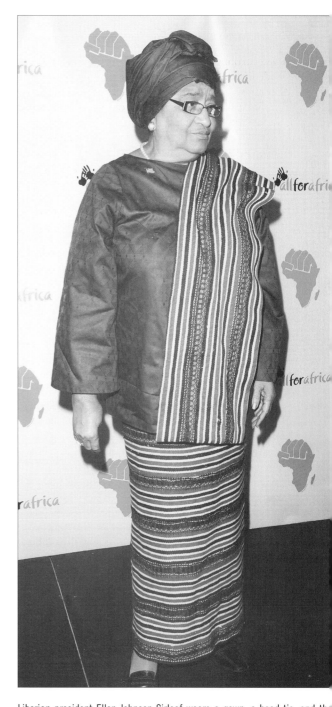

Liberian president Ellen Johnson Sirleaf wears a gown, a head tie, and the cloth that Liberians call *ashoka* worn over her left shoulder. She also wears a single strand of pearls. 2008. Joe Corrigan/Getty Images.

One style consists of a series of high ridges going from the front to the back of the head; another involves several lobes or buns arranged around the crown. The braids are tiny and detailed and the patterns are intricate. The braiding may take two days, and the young girl has to lie across the lap of her mentor so she can braid properly. In the course of the experience, the girl and her mentor develop a close relationship. The new hair style becomes a symbol of a young girl's transformation from childhood to womanhood as well as of her membership in the Sande society.

In former times, young women who joined the Sande and young men who became members of Poro (the secret society for men) received markings on their bodies. The scarification patterns are made with a small knife that is used to lift a small piece of skin. Substances such as charcoal and dried plantain leaves are inserted. Some scarification patterns can be seen in statues carved in the late nineteenth or early twentieth century.

There are thousands of Liberians in the United States and in other countries in West Africa and Europe who remain attached to their homeland. Many continue to wear Liberian dress, especially at weddings and church services. There are Liberian tailors in places like Philadelphia and Brooklyn. When relatives come to visit from Liberia, they often fill up their suitcases with outfits. Clothes from Liberia bring memories of home, pride in dress, and a sense of the continuity of life.

References and Further Reading

Givhan, Robin. "A New Leader's True Colors." *Washington Post*, 24 March 2006.

Johnston, Sir Harry. *Liberia*. Vols. 1 and 2. New York: Negro Universities Press, 1969. (Originally published in 1906.)

Moran, Mary H. "Clothing Differences: Commodities and Consumption in South Eastern Liberia." In *The Gender of Globalization: Women Navigating Cultural and Economic Marginalities*, edited by Nandani Gunewardena and Ann Kingsolver. Santa Fe, NM: School of American Research Press, 2008: 84–102.

O'Connell, Patricia. "Bandi Silver Jewelry." *African Arts* 12, no. 1 (Fall 1978): 49–51.

Schwab, George. *Tribes of the Liberian Hinterland*. Cambridge, MA: Peabody Museum of American Archaeology and Ethnology, Harvard University, 1947.

Siegmann, William. *Rock of the Ancestors: namoa kuni*. Suacoco, Liberia: Cuttington University College, 1977.

Siegmann, William. "Women's Hair and Sowei Masks in Southern Sierra Leone and Western Liberia." In *Hair*, edited by Roy Sieber and Frank Herreman. New York: Prestel, 2000: 71–77.

Jane Martin

Mali

Mali in West Africa is landlocked and borders seven countries. Although the country has experienced rapid urbanization since the mid-twentieth century, most Malians still live in rural communities. There are over fourteen ethnic groups in Mali. In the arid northern zones, the largest groups are the Tuareg, who are primarily nomadic herders, and the Sonräi, who are settled in the towns and villages along the Niger River and work as farmers, traders, and fishermen. The majority of Malians live in the central and southern regions, where the land is more arable. Ninety percent of Malians identify as Muslims. Approximately ten percent of the population continue to follow local African religions or Christianity.

EARLY EVIDENCE OF DRESS FROM THE ELEVENTH THROUGH THE EIGHTEENTH CENTURIES

The earliest body of evidence for Malian dress comes from three sources: clothing recovered from burial caves in the Bandiagara escarpment that date from the eleventh to the eighteenth centuries; inland Niger Delta terra-cotta figures dating from the twelfth to the sixteenth centuries; and journals by foreign travelers to Mali.

In the 1960s, archeologists excavated a series of caves used as repositories for the dead. The deceased, dressed and wrapped in blankets, were laid out on the floor. These eleventh- to fifteenth-century remains are associated with the Tellem, a non-Islamic group. Those dating from the sixteenth to the eighteenth centuries are associated with the Dogon, who migrated in the fifteenth century and are the current principal ethnic group in this area. Clothing consisted of cotton tunics and caps, vegetable fiber skirts and belts, loinskins, loincloths, girdles, leather sandals, and boots. Personal ornaments included plaited leather bracelets, forged iron rings and bracelets, iron hairpins, faceted carnelian and glass beads, and quartz lip plugs. Other grave goods included leather sacks, wooden headrests, iron blade hoes, arrows, quivers, and leather knife sheaths.

During the eleventh and twelfth centuries, Tellem women wore fiber skirts and belts, and men wore loinskins, but these garments began to disappear by the thirteenth century. The quartz lip plugs and faceted carnelian beads, as well as plaited leather bracelets and certain styles of iron hairpins and bracelets, were no longer in evidence by the thirteenth century. Men's handwoven cotton tunics and caps, leather sandals, knife sheaths, and leather sacks were found in all time periods. Cotton knee-length trousers with a wide leg and leather boots painted with elaborate geometric designs were found in Tellem caves dating from the fifteenth century.

Tellem and Dogon men's garments are similar in weaving techniques, cut, and decoration. The cotton tunics are fashioned from

A Dogon man wearing a handwoven cotton tunic, drawstring pants, and cotton cap, typical of Malian dress. 2005. Photograph by Craig A. Subler.

cotton strips measuring from twenty to twenty-six centimeters (eight to ten inches) wide. The body of the garment was folded in half, and a neck opening—either round or slashed—was cut into the textile. Sleeves were inset, and some of the tunics had patch pockets sewn onto the center front of the garment just below the neck opening. The shapes of tunics are both flared and straight, and all of the fabrics are a balanced plain weave with threads either left a natural color or dyed with indigo. Indigo and white checked fabrics used to fashion tunics are also in evidence. Tunics extended to the knee, and the sleeves fell just below the elbow. Necklines are sometimes finished with a braid sewn along the opening, and several of the tunics are embellished with embroidery motifs along the neckline or down the back of the garment.

Men's skullcaps and hats were also found in the caves. The hats with chin ties were fashioned from two or four layers of rectangular pieces that are sewn together to form the body and finished along the opening with a long narrow piece of fabric that ends in two strings for securing it. Most were made of undyed or indigo-dyed cotton fabric, although a complete skullcap in a checked blue and white fabric and a hat fashioned from a blue and white tie-dyed textile were also excavated.

In one Dogon cave dating from the seventeenth century where the skeletal remains were primarily female, no caps or tunics were found. There was, however, an abundance of textile fragments probably used as loincloths and as shawls. Some have weft float decorations, and many are finished with a twisted fringe. The abundance of cotton garments and cotton and wool blanket shrouds found in these caves points to a robust domestic weaving complex.

The inland Niger Delta figurative terra-cottas, associated with non-Islamic groups, depict men and women whose dress mirrors the style of garments and personal ornaments excavated from the Tellem burial caves. Males and females are depicted wearing loinskins or loincloths and leather or fiber girdles as their principal items of clothing. Most wear upper arm, wrist, and ankle bracelets of leather or metal. Some also wear torques and necklaces. Several of the male figures are shown with leather sandals and sheathed knives attached to their upper arms. Figures on horseback, which date primarily from the fifteenth century and later, wear leather boots and helmets of either basketry or leather and carry quivers on their backs that are attached to the body by leather straps that cross over the chest. Clothing representations on terra-cottas, taken together with the archaeological garments and accessories recovered from the Bandiagara caves, suggest that, over several centuries, the groups living throughout this zone shared similar types of dress and personal adornment.

Ibn Battuta, a Moroccan geographer who traveled in Mali between 1352 and 1353, visited the Muslim court of Mansa Sulayman, the king of the Malian empire. The king appeared wearing a tunic fashioned from a velvety red textile that was imported from either southern Europe or Byzantium, and he wore a gold crown in the form of a skullcap. Court musicians wore red woolen tunics and white skullcaps. Men and women courtiers donned robes made from luxurious textiles, and the women wore gold and silver ornaments in their hair. For public prayers, every man wore white garments. Ibn Battuta was scandalized, however, by the everyday dress of women servants and even highborn young girls, who wore little or no clothing.

Little is known about modes of dress in Mali between the fourteenth and eighteenth centuries. In 1790, Mungo Park, an Englishman, traveled through Mali and described people's everyday dress. Men wore locally manufactured handwoven cotton tunics, knee-length trousers, and white cotton caps—similar to the garments found in burial caves from Bandiagara, suggesting continuity in men's dress over a long period. Adult women wrapped a rectangular piece of cloth around the lower body and tied it at the waist, with a second cloth thrown casually around the upper body. Both wrappers were about six feet (two meters) long and three feet (one meter) wide. In some areas, the women dyed the cloth with indigo to a luxurious purple-blue glossy color. The wrapper and shawl as a common mode of women's dress may well indicate the growing influence of Islamic notions of modesty and propriety throughout Mali over several centuries.

Itinerant leather workers produced sandals, quivers, knife sheaths, belts, and other ornaments that were dyed red or yellow. Women of means wore heavy gold earrings supported by a red leather band passed over the crown of the head from ear to ear and elaborate necklaces of gold plates and beads. For public prayers, both Muslim men and women dressed entirely in white garments as a mark of their religious affiliation.

NINETEENTH AND TWENTIETH CENTURIES

From the mid-nineteenth century, there are abundant records of local dress published in travelers' journals and ethnographies and available through engravings and photographs. The basic everyday dress for men and women described by Park remained popular in rural communities in south central Mali well into the mid-twentieth century. Ethnic variations exist but are more often based on preferences for certain fabrics, patterning, or surface embellishment than on differences in garment types. For example, the Fulani are the only wool weavers in Mali, and men wear long wool sleeveless tunics when herding. Fulani men generally wear leather or molded plastic sandals and often wear a wide-brimmed conical coiled basketry hat of local manufacture with leather reinforcements sewn on the brim and crown. Leather straps tied under the chin secure the hat. Until the early twentieth century, Fulani women wore wool wrappers with decorative stitching and embroidery, although cotton fabrics now generally replace wool.

Indigo textiles are associated primarily with the Dogon, Soninke, and Maraka in south central Mali. Indigo garments were already present in the eleventh century. Dogon men and women continue to wear similar styles for both everyday dress and ritual occasions like funerals.

In the mid-nineteenth century, the commercial production of indigo-dyed textiles reached its zenith in Muslim Soninke and Maraka communities, and large quantities were exported. Within local communities, men and women wore indigo and undyed cotton garments, although the former were considered more valuable. Maraka women, who were the dyers, generally provided their husbands with a present of indigo garments each year. These also played a ritual role; during initiation, young girls wore indigo wrappers and shawls to differentiate them from their non-Muslim neighbors. Textiles, whether solid indigo or dyed with elaborate stitch-resist patterns, were considered valuable commodities. Soninke women, the preeminent dyers in western Mali, created the most luxurious and costly stitch-resist textiles, which were sewn into both men's tunics and women's tunics and wrappers. The finest of these continue to be in high demand, especially among urban women.

A Fulani herder wearing an embroidered wool tunic. Mali, 1980. Photograph by Bernhard Gardi. Museum der Kulturen. Basel.

Bamana and Malinke farmers and Boso and Somono fishermen wear the same basic types of garments as their neighbors, but they generally prefer undyed handwoven cotton fabrics or cloths dyed ochre or a deep red-brown color. Among the Malinke and Bamana, certain occupational specialists including warriors, hunters, and praise singers wear variations on the basic men's tunic and drawstring trousers. During the nineteenth century, Malinke warriors' tunics were dyed ochre or reddish brown, while Bamana warriors often had tunics fashioned from *bogolanfini*, a mud-dyed cloth with geometric designs. The warrior tunic was shorter than the everyday work tunic, and it just brushed the hips. Like the common tunics, the warrior tunics were sleeveless or had elbow-length inset sleeves but were cinched at the waist with a leather belt. These were adorned with amulets made from knotted lengths of cotton threads, strips of leather, and leather packets that were sewn on the shirt in a symmetrical pattern. The amulets were believed to render the wearer invulnerable to injury or death. The tunics could only be used at war, or for warrior's dances and related ceremonies.

Hunters' tunics are dyed the same colors as warrior shirts but are longer and fall below the hips. Sleeves are wrist length and sewn closed from the elbow to the wrist and left open from the elbow to the armpit. The shirt usually has four pockets for

carrying gunpowder, shot, and various amulets. Two loops sewn on the front of the tunic hold a small knife and a whistle. The tunic is worn with a leather belt on which is hung a large hunting knife, amulets, and occasionally a fly whisk. The shirt derives its protective power from the dye steeping, when incantations are spoken over the garment, as well as from the amulets in the pocket. Hunters sew few amulets on their tunics, because this would impede their movements through the brush. A hunter's shirt is never washed with soap because washing would destroy the protective power of the dye and diminish the smell of the dye that masks human scent from the prey. A hunter normally wears his shirt only when hunting or participating in hunters' ceremonies; for daily wear, he might choose an identical style of red-brown tunic. With no special protective properties, this tunic can be washed with soap when soiled.

Hunters adopt specialized trousers and distinctive hats. Unlike the knee-length drawstring trousers commonly worn, hunters' trousers are loose fitting to the knees and then close fitting from the knee to the ankle. The knees are reinforced with two or three layers of cloth. The trousers facilitate movement through the brush and protect the hunter from thorns and biting insects. Hunters have several hat options. One is a soft cap that is constructed of three cotton triangles—worn with one triangle over each ear and one on the forehead. Attached to each point are small cotton pom-poms that function as protective amulets. Additional amulets might also be attached to the inside of the cap. Dogon men also have indigo versions. A second type of hunter's hat is a cotton skullcap reinforced with a leather sweatband around the edge. Many have additional whip-stitched stuffing applied in concentric circles to the base. These provide heft and texture to the cap and may serve a protective function. Amulets made from leather packets, animal claws, and bits of bone are sometimes attached to the cap just above the leather sweatband, and a short fringe of leather can be attached to the back of the hat to protect the neck.

Hunters' praise singers wear tunics identical in cut to the hunters' tunics when they perform at hunter's ceremonies and other festivities. They differ from them by being covered with all manner of protective amulets, including leather packets, cotton and leather cords, animal horns, teeth and claws, as well as mirrors to ward off the evil eye. Many praise singers sew cowries, a precolonial currency, to their shirts in decorative patterns. Praise singers' hats and trousers are similar to those of the hunters', although they may add mirrors to the front of their hats.

Throughout south-central Mali, the wrapper remains the principal item of a woman's everyday dress. Wrappers are garb for working in the field and home. When going to the market, visiting friends, and so on, most women now wear loose-fitting tunics over their wrappers and cover their hair with a head tie to mark their status as married women and as an expression of fundamental Islamic notions of modesty and decorum.

Late-nineteenth- and early-twentieth-century photographs of south-central Mali consistently show women with handwoven striped cotton wrappers in different widths and combinations of indigo, black, ochre, brown, and natural-colored stripes. The influx of imported industrial cotton threads in a variety of new colors had, by the mid-twentieth century, opened up the palette, although striped fabrics remained the primary pattern and were sometimes sewn into loose tunics that fell below the hips and over a matching fabric. The wrapper's stripes were oriented horizontally and the tunic's, vertically.

A postcard of the wife of a trader taken in Nioro, Mali, ca. 1910. The woman is wearing a wrapper and head tie of indigo resist-dyed cloth and a tunic made from handwoven cotton-strip cloth. Museum der Kulturen. Basel.

The most famous textile tradition of Mali is *bogolanfini*, the mud-dyed cloth with geometric designs created by Bamana women. In some communities, men wore bogolanfini tunics and trousers and women wore bogolanfini wrappers as everyday dress well into the twentieth century. Warriors and hunters wore tunics fashioned from bogolanfini, and the named designs chosen for these garments had protective properties. Women during initiation, marriage, and following childbirth also wore bogolanfini wrappers with specific named patterns considered to have protective properties. As Bamana communities converted to Islam throughout the twentieth century, bogolanfini textiles became less desirable and fell out of use. Bamako artists and designers fueled a revival of the cloth in the 1990s. Hand-painted bogolanfini textiles and factory cloth printed with bogolanfini designs were fashioned into tailored jackets, vests, blouses, miniskirts, and classic men's and women's tunics. Youth, both Bamana and non-Bamana, first embraced these contemporary garments in the capital city, and, soon after, they were sought by young people throughout the country. They consider these garments to be both chic and a shared statement of a postcolonial Malian identity.

Tuareg men's dress remains one of the most distinctive styles in Mali. Men wear long, voluminous blue or white cotton robes over billowing ankle-length trousers. The defining feature of a man's ensemble is the *tagulmust*, a long piece of generally blue or white cotton cloth that serves as veil and turban. The veil is the dominant symbol of Tuareg male identity and honor. A young man's first wearing of the veil is a family ritual and marks his change of status to adult.

The tagulmust is created in three parts by a series of winding motions. The first turn covers the mouth; the second covers the face and falls onto the chest; the final draping goes around the head several times to create a low turban that covers the forehead. When a man pulls his veil high and tight over the nose, there is only a narrow slit revealing the eyes. Men sleep, eat, and live in their veils. Throughout the day a man adjusts his veil, pulling it higher and tighter or relaxing and lowering it in response to changing social situations. Men from noble clans follow the strictest protocols when veiled. A noble maintains full veiling to communicate reserve and distance in the presence of strangers and as a gesture of respect in the presence of chiefs and elders and especially after marriage in the presence of his parents-in-law. He may assume a more relaxed veiling in the company of his trusted friends and family. Men from lesser clans, blacksmiths, and former slaves are generally more lax with their veiling practices.

Because the Tuareg do not weave, they imported cotton cloth from across the Sahara and from cloth producers to the south. Most cotton cloth currently used among the Tuareg is imported or milled in Malian textile factories. A special hand-dyed indigo cloth made in Kura in northern Nigeria is the most prestigious and expensive. Used for both tunics and the tagulmust, the cloth is heavily dyed and acquires its distinctive shimmering effect during the finishing process, when indigo powder or mica is beaten into the fabric.

THE BOUBOU ENSEMBLE: A SHARED MODE OF FORMAL ATTIRE

Islam and exchanges with the Maghreb between the eleventh and sixteenth centuries influenced Malian dress. By at least the mid-nineteenth century, Muslim functionaries, chiefs, and other male elites began wearing long, flowing, amply proportioned ankle-length robes, known generically as the boubou. The robe is worn over a shirt and drawstring ankle-length trousers in a matching fabric. By the late twentieth century, this mode of men's dress became the national dress of Mali.

Religious leaders and other notables, especially in clerical-commercial towns like Djenne and Timbuktu, wear white boubous and a white shawl over their shoulders and often wear cloth turbans as a mark of their Muslim identity. Versions of the boubou are worn across Muslim West Africa from Senegal to Nigeria. In Mali, it was probably first adopted by Muslim clerics and Soninke and Sonräi elites as a sign of their Muslim identity. Later chiefs and other wealthy men from neighboring groups adopted the boubou as a mode of prestige dress. Leather sandals are part of men's formal ensemble, differentiating them from religious functionaries and elites, who typically wear *babouches*, Moroccan open-backed leather slippers.

A boubou can be fashioned from handwoven strip cloth, imported cotton damask, or industrial roller-print textiles. The robe requires about ten meters (eleven yards) of cloth and is constructed in three parts: a central section that serves as the body of the garment and two side panels sewn to the central section. These side panels are the same length as the body of the garment and serve as the sleeves. The voluminous sleeves may extend to the hand and are often rolled up onto the shoulders. Classic boubous have slashed necklines and triangular or rectangular pockets attached to the front of the robes just below the neck opening. The most prestigious and expensive robes are made from the highest-quality imported cotton damask or finely woven cotton strip cloth and are heavily embroidered with the same color or contrasting colors of thread. Rosettes, circles, squares, and swirls are embroidered around the neck opening, on the pocket, on the upper right side of the body of the garment, and on the upper back of the robe. Less expensive boubous are made from lower-quality cotton broadcloth or from patterned industrial cloth and are minimally embroidered or not embroidered at all.

The *tilbi* and *lomasa* are two classic styles of men's luxury boubous worn through the 1950s in Mali. The tilbi is primarily associated with the towns of Djenne and Timbuktu. It is a white cotton robe that is heavily hand embroidered on the front and back with imported white silk thread. Wealthy families commissioned a tilbi for a marriage or as a gift for a local ruler or visiting dignitaries. The lomasa, primarily associated with Soninke chiefs and notables, is an indigo-dyed boubou heavily hand embroidered on both the front and back with multicolored imported silk threads.

By the end of the nineteenth century, many women, especially those in Muslim commercial towns in north and central Mali, had already adopted a variation of the men's boubou. Women's robes were less voluminous than the male version. They were made from handwoven textiles or imported cotton damasks and worn over wrappers in a matching or complementary fabric. The earliest versions have slashed necklines, although round necklines are now more common. The ensemble was completed by a head tie. The boubou remains a staple in women's wardrobes up to the present and is worn on formal occasions. Women who make the pilgrimage to Mecca often dress in all-white boubous and wear long white shawls over their head ties as symbols of piety and status.

Imported manufactured garments still claim only a small part of the clothing market, and small-scale tailor shops—an important segment of Bamako's economy—continue to produce most garments for local consumption. Beginning in the early twentieth century, the availability of industrial cotton cloth, including wax prints and the more reasonably priced roller prints, allowed for easy tailoring of garments. Throughout the century, tailors consistently fused elements from Western styles and from classic Malian dress to create garments that would appeal to local tastes.

Women's fashions have undergone dramatic changes over the past century. Elements from Western garments such as fitted bodices with peplums (short full flounces) and cap and puff sleeves are creatively combined with elements from more classical garments. The cut and shape of necklines and sleeves and the style of embroidery, cut work, and appliqué are always in flux. Tailors who specialize in women's garments regularly hang finished garments in their shops to advertise new styles, and many keep photographic books of their creations for their women clients to consult.

In the 1990s, professional designers began to set up ateliers in Bamako, and they often looked to older styles of garments and local textiles for inspiration. Fashion shows are now regular events in the city, and tailors rapidly assimilate haute couture fashions, making them available to the average consumer. Bamako's cosmopolitan style has always been a creative synthesis of local and international influences. The vitality of this synthesis continues to depend on the active collaboration between tailors and their clients.

References and Further Reading

Aradeon, Susan. "West African Textiles and Dress." In *Traditional Folk Textiles and Dress*, edited by Barbara Norquist, E. Jean Mettam, and Kathy Jansen, 14–30. Dubuque, IA: Kendall Hunt, 1986.

Battuta, Ibn. *Travels in Asia and Africa, 1325–1354*. Translated and selected by H.A.R. Gibb, with an introduction and notes. London: G. Routledge, 1929.

Bolland, Rita. *Tellem Textiles: Archeological Finds from Burial Caves in Mali's Bandiagara Cliff*. Amsterdam: Tropenmuseum/Royal Tropical Institute, 1991.

Brett-Smith, Sarah. "Symbolic Blood: Cloths for Excised Women." *RES* 3 (1982): 15–31.

Cashion, Gerald. "Hunters of the Mande: A Behavioral Code and Worldview Derived from a Study of Their Folklore." Ph.D. dissertation, Indiana University, 1984.

Gardi, Bernhard. *Le Boubou—c'est chic: Les boubous du Mali et d'autres pays de l'Afrique de l'Ouest*. Basel, Switzerland: Editions Christoph Merian, 2000.

McNaughton, Patrick. "The Shirts That Mande Hunters Wear." *African Arts* 15, no. 3 (1982): 54–58, 91.

Park, Mungo. *Travels into the Interior of Africa*, with a new preface by Jeremy Swift. London: Eland, 1983.

Rovine, Victoria. *Bogolan: Shaping Culture through Cloth in Contemporary Mali*. Washington, DC: Smithsonian Institution Press, 2001.

Seligman, Thomas K., and Kristyne Loughran, eds. *Art of Being Tuareg: Sahara Nomads in a Modern World*. Los Angeles: Iris and B. Gerald Cantor Center for Visual Arts at Stanford University and the UCLA Fowler Museum of Cultural History, 2006.

Mary Jo Arnoldi

A Bamana woman wearing a roller-print cotton-cloth ensemble, typical of that found in Bamana communities in Mali. 2006. Photograph by Craig A. Subler.

URBAN DRESS IN THE TWENTIETH CENTURY

Bamako has always played a unique role in the country, first as the colonial capital and later as the national capital. By the end of the twentieth century, the city's population was estimated to be over one million residents. Malians have always regarded Bamako as the site of modernity and the sartorial capital of the country.

Niger

Niger is a vast landlocked West African country named after the Niger River. The capital, Niamey, is a cosmopolitan city with both permanent and part-time inhabitants. Other major towns in Niger are Zinder (the capital of the country until 1926), known for its leather workers and dyers; Maradi, near the Nigerian border; Tahoua, known for its livestock market; and Agadez on the edge of the Sahara Desert. The two principal regions in Niger are the northern zone and the Sahelian, both characterized by different climatic conditions that affect Nigerien dress customs.

The population is divided into five principal groups with historical ties to the great Songhay Empire, the Hausa states, and the Aïr Sultanate. The Hausa (56 percent) and the Zarma-Songhay (22 percent) share similar dress practices, inhabit the southern central and the southwestern regions, and are sedentary farmers and traders. The Kanuri (4.3 percent) are in the southeastern areas, and the Tuareg (8 percent) are seminomadic pastoralists who inhabit the northern and western areas. The pastoral Fulani (8.5 percent), including the Wodaabe or Bororo, are found in most areas. Both the Wodaabe and the Tuareg are famous for their distinctive attire and the attention they devote to their appearance.

French is the official language in Niger, though the majority of the population speaks Hausa. Ninety-five percent of the population in Niger is Islamic, and the remainder are Christians and animists. While Islamic tenets are respected and are a fundamental factor in individuals' attitudes toward dress, older cosmologies and belief systems are tolerated and incorporated into daily life and religious practices.

DRESS PRACTICES IN NIGER

Clothing styles worn by men and women in Niger are well suited to the country's geography and climate and to its religious beliefs. The hot, arid climate in the Sahara Desert encourages the use of layered clothing ensembles, which offer thermal protection against high daytime temperatures and cold nights. Loose flowing robes worn in the hot Sahelian zone are both comfortable and practical. Among the Wodaabe, the cult of beauty and beliefs in nature spirits have resulted in particular ceremonial attire and attitudes toward the presentation of self.

With few exceptions (such as the Wodaabe), Islam has been a unifying factor in dress customs in Niger. Following Islamic tenets, both women's and men's garments are modest and neat. Social and cultural values emphasize reserved and dignified comportment in social situations: speech is often indirect; eyes are averted out of respect for adults and elders and among some groups (the Tuareg, for example); and the mouth is covered by the face veil. Bodily distance is also maintained, although it is not uncommon to see young girls walking arm in arm.

Many Nigerien (not to be confused with Nigerian populations living in Nigeria, to the south) ethnic groups belong to stratified societies, and sumptuary laws once governed dress codes. In the twenty-first century, however, these have become negotiable as a result of economic and social change, and external signs are often inaccurate measures of status. For example, among the Tuareg, silver jewelry once reserved for the noble classes is worn by vassal groups as well.

Physical attributes and ideals of beauty emphasize the learned cultural values of pride and reserve. Male stances impart dignity and status, and women's behavior expresses both poise and decorum. Corpulence is appreciated among women as a sign of well-being and wealth. Their hands should be soft, with long fingers used to make graceful gestures. Well-groomed feet are often embellished with henna motifs, and women use kohl for their eyes and scented creams, incenses, and perfumes. Individuals move slowly and gracefully, and their garments rustle when they walk. Clothing is voluminous, layered, and always being rearranged: sleeves are pulled up over a shoulder, and head scarves and face veils or shawls are redraped, folded, or twisted. These ample garments also protect people from the high daytime temperatures, windstorms, and the cool night air. Women and men both wear a plethora of leather and metal amulets, and women's silver and gold jewelry in particular emphasizes the head, neck, arms, and fingers and glitters and tinkles when they move. The amount of clothing and adornment individuals adopt represents an aesthetic of abundance.

Young Nigerien boys wear shorts and shirts and start wearing trousers when they reach adulthood. Men from all groups dress in long trousers with a large matching shirt, sometimes covered with a boubou. The word *boubou* comes from the Wolof word *mbubb* and designates a garment that can be slipped on over the head. A traditional boubou is an ample tunic with open sleeves and a triangular or rectangular breast pocket. Men and women are robed in these garments throughout West Africa.

For feasts and festivals, men don formal and richly embroidered boubou ensembles. The ensemble includes the boubou, a shirt, and a pair of trousers made of the same fabric; damask is the preferred choice, but imported cotton and homespun cotton are also used. The gown's styles range from narrower models with long sleeves to the voluminous models described above. Hausa boubous in particular are striking for the huge assortment of types and for the richly embroidered patterns, which are done by machine on the front and back panels and around the neckline.

Men also wrap turbans and face veils, or put on embroidered caps that are woven in bright-colored narrow strip cloth called *fulan* in Hausa. Their embroidered designs and motifs often symbolize historical and local events, and groups have individual wearing styles. The Zarma create a central depression on the top of the hat. It is not unusual to see these caps in the markets stretched on wooden forms, which give them their shape. Traditionally men wear sandals made by Hausa leather workers, Western-style safari jackets of British officials in the colonies. These were popular in warm climates because they are lightweight, have four bellows pockets, and the color khaki is practical. Younger men, on the other hand, favor casual trousers and blue jeans worn with button-down shirts or T-shirts and sneakers.

Little girls are clad in wrapped skirts and blouses or Western-style dresses, and women wear wraparound skirts with matching blouses and head scarves. The piece of cloth used as a skirt is often referred to as a *pagne*. A pagne is a two-yard (almost two-meter) length of cloth (usually made of wax print fabric) that has multiple purposes: it is used as a skirt, overskirt, head scarf, shawl, and to carry children on the back. The pagne does not replace the skirts fashioned by seamstresses. Women often commission elegant ensembles consisting of a straight ankle-length skirt, a matching blouse, and a head wrap. The blouses are trimmed with eyelet lace and buttons and have fanciful sleeves. Women consider their cloth and their ensembles a prestigious sign of wealth and start collecting them early on to prepare their dowries.

Women in Niamey also wear Western-style midcalf skirts and jackets to work. They are not seen in trousers or blue jeans because these are frowned upon; if younger women were to do so, they would be severely admonished. Women also favor boubou-style dresses, and, in keeping with Islamic practices, they cover their heads in public. At official functions, women are clothed in the grand boubou, worn over a blouse and a pagne with a head scarf in the same cloth. Boubous are adorned with intricate embroidery patterns around the neckline and have long sleeves. These designs in Niger are often called "Mali fashion," referring to the important role Mali has played in the dissemination of boubou styles throughout West Africa.

Women are attentive to hairstyles, and hairdressing is a lengthy process. When girls are little, mothers dress their hair, and, as they grow, young women do it for their friends. It is always an occasion for friendly gatherings. Hairstyles vary from group to group, and fashionable styles change very quickly. Songhay women decorate their hairstyles with large resin beads and pendants, as do Bella women from the Tuareg group. Women braid their hair into stylish patterns; they use extensions, and sometimes wear wigs. Head wraps and scarves are individualistic and are mostly fashioned in the same cloth as the skirt. Among the Kanuri, one style is made by wrapping head scarves very close to the scalp to create a thick rolled border. The two remaining end pieces of cloth are either tucked into the border or hang at each temple with long beaded temple ornaments. Women wear sandals, Western-style pumps, and flip-flops. Accessories such as jewelry and purses often complete a woman's ensemble.

Conventional ensembles are usually reserved for important occasions such as weddings, child-naming ceremonies, festivals, and official functions. The specific elements distinguishing one ethnic group from another are highly visible at these occasions. For example, bodyguards from the sultan's retinue in Agadez display distinctive red turbans over elegant red, white, and blue boubou ensembles. The Tuareg and the Wodaabe are noteworthy because of their attitudes toward clothing and adornment and the image they project as a group.

THE TUAREG

The Tuareg owe much of their renown in the West to their nomadic lifestyles in one of the earth's harshest environments (the

A woman in Agadez, Niger, 2004. Women wear long, dark, tunic-style gowns or blue wrap skirts with white or black bolero blouses with square necklines, adorned with red, yellow, or green embroidered motifs. The latter are typical of the northern Aïr region. Photograph by Thomas K. Seligman.

lace-up shoes and moccasins, or plastic flip-flops. Other adornment includes leather or silver amulets, silver rings, and bracelets.

In addition to their conventional attire, professionals in urban centers also adopt European-style suits, or saharienne jackets over trousers. *Saharienne* is a French word that refers to the khaki

Tuareg man and woman, Agadez, Niger, 1988. The man wears long baggy trousers and a matching shirt along with the *tagulmust*, which is used as both a face veil and turban. The woman wears a head scarf and a traditional clothing ensemble made of navy blue, black, or white cloth. Photograph by Thomas K. Seligman.

the sobriquet of "blue men." On a daily basis, men wear turbans and face veils made of ordinary imported cotton.

Men's turbans and face veils and women's head scarves symbolize social reserve, respect, and adulthood. Men assume the veil at all times, because it is shameful and undignified to show the mouth. Women, who do not veil their faces, cover their mouths in the presence of in-laws. The veil is thought to protect individuals from harm caused by evil spirits or *djinns*.

Young girls' garment choices include European-style dresses or wrap skirts and blouses; women's choices are long, dark, tunic-style gowns or blue wrap skirts with white or black bolero blouses with square necklines, adorned with red, yellow, or green embroidered motifs. The latter are typical of the northern Aïr region. When girls reach marriageable age, they adopt the *ekerkey* (head scarf) to cover the nape of the neck. Women's clothing emphasizes layers and width, because corpulence signifies well-being. Although canons of beauty dictated that young women be fattened up, these practices are rare now that women perform the work once carried out by servants. Women as well as men wear leather sandals that have a large rounded sole and a top portion that is embellished with embroidered motifs.

Hairdressing, as among other groups, is important. Little boys have shaven heads with a tuft of hair on top. Both men and women have their hair braided by members of the smith classes. Men's plaits are either at the back or the top of the head and symbolize virility. Women's hair is either braided into four large plaits that fall to the sides or into small plaits that are knotted at the nape of the neck. Some women have a single braid over the forehead. Men and women also use kohl around their eyes, and women sometimes blacken their gums and lips with indigo or kohl. They make lavish use of perfumes and incenses, thought to keep evil spirits at bay.

For feasts and festivals, men select boubou ensembles that include a striking array of turban styles. The latter combine both white and shiny aleshu cloths, creating crisp visual contrasts. Some are very high and enhanced by pleated crests at the back; others are decorated with amulets. They may also wear silver amulets and carry swords and use leather wallets decorated with fringes and tassels suspended from the neck. Women's bolero shirts and skirts are decorated with embroidered motifs on the sides. Married women use aleshu cloth overskirts and head scarves along with gleaming silver and gold jewelry.

Dark colors and sobriety were once the staple of the noble classes, whereas vassal classes wore more colorful cotton ensembles. In the twenty-first century, these parameters are shifting. Male nobles display colorful damask boubou ensembles, and it is not unusual to see women in wax print fashions or boubou dresses. Tuareg women also substitute gold jewelry forms for their traditional silver pieces. The response to recent political unrest has engendered new stances on cultural identity and new dress codes as well. Green face veils and camouflage uniforms on Tuareg rebels and embroidery motifs on women's blouses are considered emblems of Tuareg cultural identity.

THE WODAABE

The nomadic Wodaabe are Fulani cattle herders and traders. Unlike sedentary Fulani groups, they are nominal Muslims and have maintained their pre-Islamic belief systems, which are strongly tied to magic and the supernatural world. The Wodaabe are tall

Sahara Desert), to the freedom accorded Tuareg women, and to their elegant and stately appearance. Dress among the Tuareg symbolizes social identity, class, age, and gender. Comportment and self-image are essential attributes of dress, and the Tuareg have precise ideas about how they should look. Men's garments emphasize physical height; they flow and billow when they walk, giving them great dignity and allure. Women's clothing, especially their shirts and head cloths, are frequently being rearranged. Women move slowly and gracefully and have a reputation for being attractive and elegant. Traditional clothing ensembles are usually sober: predominantly made of navy blue, black, or white cloth. The aesthetic of dress among the Tuareg is based on a delicate balance between sobriety for daily wear and opulence and conspicuous display for feasts and festivals.

Tuareg boys wear short trousers until they come of age. When they become men, their choice is long baggy trousers and a matching shirt along with the *tagulmust* (which is used as both a face veil and turban). Traditionally, the tagulmust was made of *aleshu* cloth, a shiny indigo fabric manufactured in Nigeria and sold by Hausa traders. This cloth rubs off on the skin, giving the Tuareg

Tuareg women attending a wedding in Agadez, Niger, 1988. Traditional clothing ensembles are usually sober, predominantly made of navy blue, black, or white cloth. For feasts and festivals, married women use *aleshu* cloth overskirts and head scarves along with gleaming silver and gold jewelry. Photograph by Thomas K. Seligman.

and slender people known for their extraordinary makeup and for their distinctive attire and jewelry. The cult of beauty is central to the Wodaabe worldview. Anthropologist Marion Van Offelen has said that mothers press small children's noses to lengthen them and their heads to give them a perfect rounded shape. Ideals of beauty among the Wodaabe call for slender bodies and limbs representing strength, long graceful hands, high foreheads, large eyes, a long thin nose, thin lips, even teeth, a long neck, and straight hair. Skin is supposed to be light, and white teeth and white eyeballs are highly valued. Men are experts in makeup and adornment, which they use to enhance their features and attract women.

After birth, infants are given scars at the sides of the mouth in a fanlike pattern. As they grow older, additional scarification patterns are added on the forehead, temples, nose, cheeks, and chin. After the child-naming ceremony, mothers shave infants' heads and only leave a small tuft on the top. Girls are given earrings between the ages of two and four, and boys display one earring in the left ear because it represents the male side. Young children don wrap skirts.

When girls reach marriageable age, they begin to wear dark-colored sleeveless bolero-style blouses. The vivid embroidery patterns symbolize the natural world and camp life. Once they marry, they discard the blouse and make other choices of short tops, shawls over their shoulders, or, in the twenty-first century, even T-shirts. They adorn themselves with large brass hoop earrings decorated with small glass dangles, colorful beaded bracelets on their arms and forearms, and necklaces. Young women wear tall brass anklets with a pronounced center ridge decorated with geometric patterns. Women's wrap skirts are knee length and made of hand-spun navy cotton, held by a leather cord belt. They use head scarves—a long piece of cloth folded in fourths perched on top of their heads. For feasts and ceremonies, they

favor shiny, brightly colored head scarves. They also wear colorful wax print shawls. Hairdressing is primarily the reserve of women. They soften hair with butter and then divide it with little metal picks. Women braid the front part of the head in a large plait, and then twist it into a knot at the forehead. The sides are braided into thick plaits and left free at the ears. A fourth plait is made at the nape of the neck.

Men wear a sheepskin skirt around their hips and a dark colored tunic or baggy trousers and a sleeveless tunic. They also don large straw conical hats decorated with leather strips and tassels. Sometimes they also wear turbans against the wind, dust, and heat. Men's hair is dressed in two large plaits at each side of the face and fifteen thin plaits at the nape of the neck. The top of the forehead is often shaved to lengthen it. Hairstyles are decorated with colorful leather pouches containing herbs and talismans to ward off evil spirits and to increase beauty.

Before the *worso* (the annual lineage celebration) and the *geerewol* (the reunion of two lineage groups), men and women prepare their clothing ensembles and polish their jewelry. Men use ochre to lighten their skin and draw a long line down the ridge of the nose. They blacken the lower edge of their eyelids with kohl, and their lips with charcoal. They wrap their heads in white turbans, which they secure with blue cloth strips decorated with amulets. When men dance, they roll their eyes to show off the whites, and they show their teeth. Young women don elaborately embroidered wrap skirts, bolero shirts, and head scarves.

The highlights of the geerewol are dances and the male beauty contest. Men wear knee-length bolero-style shirts embellished with embroidered patterns and an infinite variety of decorations ranging from whistles to keys to safety pins. Women's wrap skirts are fastened at the knees, obliging them to take very short steps. Their turbans are decorated with talismans and beads and with long brass pendants that frame the face. For the last dance, men cross white bead necklaces over their torsos and don white bead aprons. Their belts are decorated with cowries and brass rings. Their headbands are adorned with ostrich feathers. Great honor and prestige is bestowed on the winner of the festival.

FASHION IN NIGER

The combination of conventional dress with Western-style apparel for both men and women has resulted in a cosmopolitan style that blends cultural acumen with change. Despite the exodus toward towns and cities in the past twenty years, Niger remains a largely rural country. The differences between rural and urban clothing styles do not represent the classical opposition between modern and traditional; rather, they reveal the flexibility with which individuals negotiate new social values in ingenious and creative ways.

What distinguishes fashionable ensembles from conventional ones are designs with novel cuts and styles and the new fabrics produced each year. Women are attentive to these innovations and do not want to be seen in last year's clothes. The fashionable are principally in the hands of seamstresses and tailors, who display their creations and drawings in their workshops. They often proclaim *haute couture* on their signboards to attract clients. The term refers to clothing that is commissioned, handmade, beautiful, and a step up from the *tout cousu* (ready-to-wear). Women patrons also play an important role in setting trends, and they influence the formidable array and diversity of cuts for sleeves, necklines, bodices, hemlines, and the decorative elements such as lace, beads, and buttons that change with every season. Women also look to television, catalogs, and fashion magazines to see the latest fashion trends. The Sonitextile Company in Niamey develops new patterns every year, but the favored fabrics remain the shiny damask and the Vlisco wax prints from Holland. Vlisco

produces new collections every season and is also available on the Internet. Women use cloth designs to date the clothing they sew and own.

In addition to the seamstresses and tailors, many fashionable trends come from Dakar, Accra, Abidjan, and other African capitals. Seidnaly Sidahmed Alphadi, Niger's leading fashion designer, has gained notoriety and fame in international fashion circles since the mid-1990s. Known as the "prince of the desert," Alphadi designed his first collection at the age of eleven. In the early 1980s, he studied tourism in Paris while taking design classes in the evenings at the Atelier Chardon Savard. He turned to fashion full-time in 1983 and created his first haute couture line in 1985. Among his many awards, Alphadi received the Best African Stylist Award from the French Haute Couture Federation in 1987, the Prince Claus Foundation Prize in 1998, and the prestigious *Chevalier de l'Ordre du Mérite de la France* in 2001. Alphadi creates beautiful clothes that blend traditional African textiles and designs with Western cuts. His conceptual approach and designs reflect the cultural diversity of his Nigerien heritage and his rigorous training. He is mature and not given to short-lived trendiness, and, although he does design jackets, shirts, and trousers for men, he is primarily a women's designer.

Alphadi designs range from formal evening attire to daywear to casual outfits. He mixes classical African materials (handwoven cotton textiles, wax, damask, raffia, linen) and accessories (made of leather, bronze, silver, and gold) with Lycra and Chinese silks to produce a multilayered effect.

His couture dresses have long flowing skirts and bodices, which are heavily embroidered with silk threads and inspired by Wodaabe and Hausa designs. His sportswear line, Alphadi bis, created in 1999, accentuates a young urban style: flowing tunics are worn with lace-up boots. Alphadi makes prolific use of modern African jewelry forms, and, in 2001, he created

Woman wearing a *chatchat* necklace at the Cure Salée Festival, Niger, 1990. Photograph by Kristyne Loughran.

the first perfume to be marketed by an African couturier: l'Aïr d'Alphadi.

Since 1997, Alphadi has been the president of the International African Fashion Festival (*Festival International de la Mode Africaine*, or FIMA, in French), an organization that promotes African fashion designers on an international scale and organizes fashion shows in various African nations. Alphadi also created the "Caravans" fashion collections to act as a bridge between each FIMA event and to showcase young African fashion designers. The festivals are media events, and programs include fashion shows, theatrical performances, and concerts. They attract European fashion designers such as Yves Saint Laurent, Kenzo, Gaultier, and their African counterparts: Katouchka, Oumou Sy, and Ly Dumas.

The underlying purpose of FIMA is to establish varied marketing systems to create infrastructures that will support local entrepreneurship in the textile, fashion, and accessories industries in African countries. The festivals host conferences and workshops addressing these issues. FIMA's aim is to demonstrate that fashion is an intrinsic factor in economic development. Alphadi also has a well-designed Web site, which he uses as a powerful communications tool to promote his collections and the Caravans and FIMA events.

Dress and fashion in Niger are related to religious beliefs, sociocultural values, politics, climate, and the economy. These sartorial practices exemplify individuals' bonds with cultural codes and conventions. The blend of the traditional with the fashionable, as illustrated by Alphadi's work, has produced a rich fashion acumen and leaves an open window on innovation.

References and Further Reading

Gardi, Bernhard. *Le Boubou c'est chic. Les Boubous du Mali et d'autres pays de l'Afrique de l'Ouest*. Basel, Switzerland: Christoph-Merian-Verlag, 2000.

Perani, Judith, and Norma H. Wolff. *Cloth, Dress and Art Patronage in Africa*. Oxford, UK: Berg, 1999.

Picton, John. *The Art of African Textiles. Technology, Tradition and Lurex*. London: Barbican Art Gallery and Lund Humphries Publishers, 1995.

Rasmussen, Susan. "Dress, Identity and Gender in Tuareg Culture and Society." In *Art of Being Tuareg: Sahara Nomads in a Modern World*, edited by Thomas K. Seligman and Kristyne Loughran, 139–157. Los Angeles: Iris and B. Gerald Cantor Center for Visual Arts at Stanford University and the UCLA Fowler Museum of Cultural History, 2006.

Review Noire. Special Mode: African Fashion, no. 27 (1998).

U.S. Department of State. *Background Note: Niger*. Washington, DC: U.S. Department of State, 2007.

Van Offelen, Marion. *Nomads of Niger*. New York: Abrams, 1983.

Kristyne Loughran

See also African Fashion Designers; Nigeria Overview; Hausa in Nigeria and Diaspora.

Nigeria Overview

Cloth worn over the left southern shoulder is commonplace dress for a man in the region from southern Nigeria to southern Côte d'Ivoire. In this photograph, taken in 1967, the cloth has been woven on the women's broadloom in imitation of Yoruba narrow-strip *aso oke*. The wearer has plaited hair over the place where magical medicine has been inserted under his skin. Photograph by John Picton. Reproduced by permission of the National Commission for Museums and Monuments, Nigeria.

A broad if highly oversimplistic view of dress and dress history in Nigeria would probably begin with a contrast between textiles wrapped around the body—a complex of traditions of the forests and southern savannas—and textiles cut and sewn to make garments—practices loosely associated with, but, historically, not wholly dependent on, the advent of Islam in the Sahel and savanna regions. Thereafter, however, the account becomes endlessly complicated because of (a) the interpenetration of the two sets of practices and traditions—an interpenetration that is material, geographical, and gendered; (b) regional variations in textile design; and (c) the advent of dress traditions, and fabrics and yarns, from Europe since the late fifteenth century, but most especially since the mid-nineteenth century, and the relationships between these and the indigenous traditions.

Following from this there are many questions about the relationship between dress and a complex of identities: gendered, ethnic, national, occupational, ritual, and so forth, as well as the social and political effects of conspicuous consumption. There is, moreover, a related yet quite different set of questions about the relationships between textile design (woven, dyed, embroidered, factory-printed) and dress, given that textile design and manufacture and dress forms comprise two separate sets of histories. However, there is far more to dress than the clothes a person might wear, because, apart from the social, aesthetic, and other implications of clothing, there are the clothes of masked performers as well as, in given circumstances, of houses and shrines. Moreover, even in regard to the human person, if we consider dress as the material and visual elements that transform the biological into the social person, there is a broad range of practices—some permanent, some ephemeral—that may stand prior to the question of what cloth or dress to put on; and these practices have generally been subject to greater pressures toward change than clothing, at least in the period since around the 1850s, which is generally perceived as a period of rapid change toward the modernities of the early twenty-first century.

This is also, among other things, the period in which Nigeria comes into existence, achieving independence from colonial rule in 1960. Dress clearly had its place in the politics of resistance to colonial rule, and the idea of national dress is clearly of the greatest importance to present-day Nigerians. However, it is important to realize that the period since the 1850s is equally the era of the formation of the modern ethnicities that now characterize the country; and in dress, as in all other aspects of Nigeria, the relationship between ethnic and national identities is complex. Finally, because we are writing about practices with histories that can often be traced back to a time before the emergence of the modern nation state, and also because of mercantile networks within West Africa flourishing both before and within the modern period, Nigeria is not an entirely sui generis category of cultural production.

THE EARLIEST EVIDENCE: THE NOK CULTURE

The earliest visual evidence for dress in the region now covered by Nigeria is provided by the pottery sculptures of the Nok culture and dated to a period from around 300 B.C.E. to 300 C.E. The corpus is now huge but mostly and tragically the result of

Illegal and unscientific excavation, with the result that much of the dating and discussion of these works is worthless. Nok culture deposits are found across a wide region of the central and northern Nigerian savannas and represent a material culture in the process of moving from a stone-tool to an iron-working technology; and these deposits include beads of cast tin and polished quartz as well the ceramic sculpture already mentioned. These show mostly male, though sometimes female, human figures arrayed in a variety of often elaborate coiffures and plaited fiber constructions. These latter include pubic aprons and waistbands, collars and capes, and wrist and ankle ornaments, and some of these suggest the inclusion of beadwork in their construction. Some of the male figures are shown wearing a codpiece, which might have been made of animal horn or basketry. Nok culture material, however, presents no evidence for the weaving of cloth, the earliest evidence of which is provided by the later material excavated at Igbo-Ukwu.

THE ARTS OF THE BODY

Much of what can be seen on Nok culture figures—the elaborate coiffures, the plaited fiber and beadwork, the pubic aprons and codpieces—resembles practices still extant across the same region in the late nineteenth and early twentieth centuries, among the yet-to-be-converted communities (whether to Islam or Christianity), when British colonial personnel began documenting and classifying the diverse peoples under their authority. Perhaps the most visually spectacular example from that recent past was the use of long curving antelope horns as codpieces by the men of certain peoples along the southern escarpment of the Jos Plateau. Even as late as the 1960s, in that region, it was still possible to encounter women wearing little more than bunches of leaves to shield the buttocks and pubic area. Neither of these examples from the recent past is obvious in Nok sculpture, however, which means that this corpus cannot be taken as anything more than general evidence for the arts of the body at an early date in the history of Nigeria. Moreover, there are other practices that are, perhaps surprisingly, not documented in the corpus of Nok sculpture, though nonetheless both widespread and extant in the early Colonial period in the Nok culture area and throughout the country. Such practices effect a permanent transformation from the biological to the social person and include cicatrization, tattooing, and circumcision.

Male circumcision is a commonplace element of naming traditions throughout the Nigerian region and is habitually carried out within a few days of birth regardless of whether the family is Muslim, Christian, or the adherent of local ritual tradition. In the environment of the village, the elder of the house would perform the operation; and whenever this had not been done, a man's age mates would see to the removal of his foreskin prior to marriage. There may well have been regions, especially among the peoples of the southern escarpments of the Jos Plateau, where circumcision was linked to the onset of puberty, but whether such traditions remain is unclear. Female genital modification is a more complex matter and clear data are hard to come by. In the 1960s, among the southern Edo-speaking peoples, in the Niger Delta, and the Cross River regions, some form of excision was still entailed in the practices of the so-called fatting house prior to a woman's first marriage. Fatting house practices of training for marriage, eating rich food, and

display and dancing certainly persist, but whether circumcision remains a part of the ritual is unclear. Elsewhere in Nigeria, as, for example, among some (but not all) parts of the Yoruba-speaking region, female genital modification continues to be done, as with male circumcision, in infancy. Elsewhere the data remain unclear, not least because of the adverse international criticism of the practices of female excision. (At least the removal of the foreskin now appears to provide a man with a measure of protection against HIV/AIDS.)

Cicatrization has been subject to a rather different range of significations and pressures. While circumcision and excision have a role in the social definition of gender, they were not part of the overt visual environment: the public display of genitalia was, for an adult, a mark of insanity. Cicatrization, in contrast, was intended to be more obviously visible, and thus for public consumption. By preventing the healing of a deliberately cut scar or by encouraging the development of a raised weal, the contours and textures of the body could be dramatically reshaped. Nevertheless, practices recorded in the 1950s, no matter how "traditional" they might then have seemed, have generally lapsed, often without adequate documentation. Almost the only case study from that period is an account of the Tiv of the middle Benue valley region, where the cutting of marks on a man's face and a woman's abdomen and calves was undertaken for reasons of a local aesthetic. It was considered worth enduring pain for the benefits of a more pleasing visual and social environment. A face could be reshaped, for example; and there were changing generational fashions. Even when a given design was figurative, there was no hidden meaning: it was rather that some things allowed for making a visually interesting pattern.

By the 1950s, the practice of chipping a person's incisors had already lapsed; and in the period since then, so too has cicatrization. One should not be surprised at this, given the pain of the practices and their irrelevance in the ongoing context of Tiv dress history. In the 1950s, a wraparound skirt for women and a cloth around the body and over the left shoulder for men were the commonplace Tiv norm. This is no longer the case. For women, the "up-and-down" (a simple blouse with a wraparound skirt) and, for men, the wide-sleeved gown or European-derived clothing became the Tiv dress of the late twentieth century, as it has become for most Nigerians whatever their dress histories might have been.

Among the Ebira people of the Niger-Benue confluence, whose twentieth-century dress history is similar to the Tiv, both men and women born in the late nineteenth century had a series of parallel lines cut into and covering their faces, and the outer corners of each upper and lower incisor were chipped to create a series of pegs. It was said that if this were not done, one's child would not talk. By the 1960s, Ebira facial marks had been reduced to a single vertical line on each cheek cut in infancy, but even this had become abandoned by 1965, when young men and women again had themselves marked so that they would not be mistaken for Igbos in the context of the anti-Igbo riots that led to civil war.

Elsewhere in Nigeria, cicatrization might be linked to lineage affiliation or to an age-grade system, but an aesthetic purpose was at least as widespread. Tattooing is closely related to cicatrization and involves rubbing color, invariably a dark blue-black, into a series of cuts that imparts both texture and color to the skin; these techniques continue to flourish perhaps because they

Two women spinning cotton, each wearing a wraparound skirt and a simple blouse and head tie. The woman at right is wearing an indigo resist-dyed *adire eleko* textile from the Yoruba city of Ibadan. Akoko-Edo, Nigeria, 1969. Photograph by Sue Picton. Reproduced by permission of the National Commission for Museums and Monuments, Nigeria.

are entirely a matter of personal choice. So, too, is the piercing of ear lobes for the attachment of metal or beaded ornaments.

Other forms of bodily modification were more ephemeral, such as the use of color to indicate wealth, age, ritual status, and so forth. Among the better-known examples would be the body painting among many of the Igbo-speaking peoples in which as yet unmarried girls painted each other's nubile bodies, otherwise naked apart from some beads at the waist, in dark flowing lines and patterns across the whole body. After a time, the painting would wear away, to be redone as and when desired. As with cicatrization, with the advent of dress forms that covered most of the body, this tradition became irrelevant, although it has enjoyed an afterlife in the work of certain modern artists who saw in body marking evidence for the simple fact that here were the practices of drawing, painting, and engraving that were indigenous, and not the product of a European education.

The dressing of the hair, in contrast to cicatrization and body painting, has retained its visibility and thereby its continuing relevance, especially for women. The binding and plaiting of a woman's hair has continued to develop and to provide an imagery that draws upon current topical events, while retaining older examples such as the hairstyle worn by a new bride, also worn as a mark of cult affiliation to a deity. Elsewhere, a combination of plaiting and shaving was used to provide a wide variety of patterning, sometimes related to marital or ritual status.

FORMS OF WOMEN'S DRESS

For women throughout West Africa, as far as we can tell from historical and ethnographic sources, a length of cloth worn as a wraparound skirt was all but universal, except in parts of and around the Jos Plateau (including the Nok culture area, as discussed), where pubic aprons, sometimes no more than a bunch of leaves, had been commonplace well into the mid-twentieth century. However, where the wraparound skirt was the norm, it was sometimes worn together with another length of cloth draped around the upper parts of the body, also serving as a veil as needed and always with a cloth worn around the head. These practices remain in place but with some changes, especially in regard to underwear and also the torso. An underskirt had been the norm, with the habitual use of bra and underpants developing only during the twentieth century; and simple forms of blouse had been introduced by Christian missionaries during the nineteenth century. These developments led to perhaps the most popular form of modern West African women's dress, comprising blouse, wrapper, and head tie—sometimes known as up-and-down. The type of cloth used for the wraparound skirt varied from place to place, as well as depending on the social requirements of particular occasions. Given the widespread fashion for expecting everyone to dress in the same pattern of cloth at celebratory events, women habitually acquire substantial quantities of cloth, some of which will inevitably find its way into the secondhand market.

FORMS OF MEN'S DRESS

For men engaged in farming or other manual labor, it is clear from historical and ethnographic sources that a triangular apron of cloth or leather was commonplace, though now it has been largely replaced by shorts. (The most obvious exception to this would be the Nok culture region, in which a codpiece was the main item of dress well into the early twentieth century; but, as with pubic aprons and bunches of leaves, with the progress of education, Islam, and Christianity, such habits have disappeared and the wearing of cloth is now habitual.) The apron or shorts are worn with a simple tunic or untailored covering cloth and a textile cap or a usually wide-brimmed basketry hat. A simple tunic, when the property of a hunter (and hunters, in the past, essentially comprised an on-call local militia), would invariably be adorned with magical medicines intended to protect its wearer. For formal attire, there was a fairly clear regional distribution of dress forms. In the largely once-forested region of the lower Niger, from the Benin Kingdom eastward to Cameroon, a substantial textile worn around the waist was usual. With access to European clothing, nightshirts, dressing gowns, and top hats were adapted into the tradition. Westward, from the Yoruba-speaking region and its immediate (non-Benin Kingdom) neighbors, to Côte d'Ivoire, a large cloth was worn around the body, under the right shoulder and over the left. However, in the Yoruba-speaking region from the late nineteenth century onward, it is evident that the tailored wide-sleeved gown had become the elite norm and was increasingly the commonplace dress of most men. However, the cloth over the shoulder is retained in certain ritual and chiefly circumstances in southern Yoruba and as informal attire when resting at home.

Tailored garments thus provided the third dress form for men. The full set continues to include the wide-sleeved gown worn with an undertunic, trousers (often very baggy), and a cap sometimes worn with a turban around it. The pieces may or may not be made as a matching set; and particular yarns and colors had well-established connotations of prestige, especially indigo-dyed cotton, locally spun wild silk in a range of shades from off-white to beige, and the magenta silk imported across the Sahara. Sometimes a man might wear two or more gowns of contrasting colors, one over the other, as an indication of wealth. These garments may well have their origins in Tuareg camel-riding dress, and their history and distribution in West Africa is related to those of Islam in ways that transcend ethnicity. However, in the evolution of the various forms of national dress within the politics of independence from colonial rule, the tailored forms have taken on a history and significance that also transcends religious affiliation and, by the early twentieth century, had lost their once taken-for-granted status as markers of an Islamic affiliation. Thus, Christians from all parts of the country (other than the region to the east of the lower Niger) have comfortably taken to wearing the tailored garments; indeed, the wide-sleeved gown has proved adaptable in the context of Christian vestments. The gowns and

Ebira man in Nigeria, 1967, wearing a wide-sleeved gown, with matching tunic and pants, all of plain white cotton cloth. The red cap denotes the status of elder, while the feathers of the standard-winged nightjar and the magic buffalo tail in his hand identify the wearer as a titled man within his lineage. The masked figure is the reembodied elder responsible for his initiation into titled status. Photograph by John Picton. Reproduced by permission of the National Commission for Museums and Monuments, Nigeria.

trousers were often embroidered, originally by hand but today more often by sewing machine, the patterns developing from the need to strengthen the garment at its obvious weak points. Embroidery was done by men, often by teachers of the Qur'an as a sideline. In the late nineteenth and early twentieth centuries, the finest embroiderers were said to be Nupe.

AN AESTHETIC OF DRESS

It hardly needs to be emphasized that there is an aesthetic of textile usage to be seen most especially in dress but also visible in masquerade and the other forms of public display. Daily and celebratory events, buying and selling in the market, visiting friends, attending mosque or church, the new baby's naming, all the events and stages of modern forms of marriage, the funerary and postburial celebration of a life well lived: all these events and circumstances are marked by an intense attachment to textile and dress forms of indigenous and local derivation, and they all make maximum use of the cloth available, thereby allowing the well-built man or woman to move and to dance with an elegance created by the very movement of the cloth as it develops from the movement of the body of its wearer. Of course, many forms of dress of European origin are now so commonplace and domesticated as to have become indigenous to the region, but referred to here are the ways movement is enhanced by dress forms that make use of extensive lengths of fabric, as can be seen as much in the wraparound skirt of a woman as in the wide-sleeved gown or the cloth thrown over one's left shoulder.

There is always much more to cloth than one might think. The processes of patterning a cloth manifest in a thousand different ways a West African delight in breaking up an otherwise plain surface, and this can be seen not only in handwoven cloth and in the techniques of resist-dyeing or, indeed, in body painting and cicatrization, but also in the printed fabrics that emerged since the late nineteenth century. Yet the naming of particular designs, while often visualizing proverbs or commemorating historical and topical events, also allows for interpretations based on one's personal circumstances. Textiles thereby can become the traces of histories that are, variously, mercantile and technical, aesthetic and social, communal and personal.

The point is that cloth never completely wears out. In the Ebira-speaking region of Nigeria, well known for the cloth woven by women, there is a proverb: "olden times, modern times; bottom knows the story of cloth." The inheritance of the past has been tested as to its value for the modern world just as the strength of a piece of cloth is tested by part of the body that sits on it. The fact that textiles can be repositories of ideas, memories, traditions, histories, and identities constitutes another key issue about dress in Nigeria, as throughout West Africa, and remains an area for further research.

TEXTILE DESIGN

For more than a thousand years, the region has been one of the world's great cotton-, indigo-, and textile-producing parts of the world. Moreover, West Africa, and the region now known as Nigeria, has always been a complex and eclectic mix. Textiles have been traded around the region, back and forth across the Sahara, and around the coast from the very beginnings of these trading networks. It could thus only be expected that the traditions of a given locality have developed through the engagement between forms and fabrics from elsewhere with those of that locality, sometimes through several centuries, adding to the rich variety of still flourishing arts, which, because of the complexity of these trade networks, continue to defy the commonplace ethnic designations taken for granted during the Colonial era. The wide-sleeved gown is a case in point, having become associated in the nineteenth century (despite its likely Saharan origin) with the new Fulani aristocracies throughout the Hausa-speaking region and beyond; yet the weavers of the silk and indigo-dyed cotton yarns used in their manufacture were ethnic Nupe, while Nupe weavers themselves claim ancestry from the empire of Oyo, which also provided the basis for the development of a modern Yoruba ethnicity. Moreover, if one adds in the possible identities of the spinners, dyers, tailors, and embroiderers, the narrative becomes ever more complex. So is the wide-sleeved gown Fulani, Hausa, Nupe, or Yoruba? The answer is that this is the wrong question, for here is a garment with a history for which factors other than ethnicity are relevant—factors such trans-Saharan trade, Islam,

national identity, and a local sense of modernity (such that these gowns have been worn by at least one member of the British parliament of Caribbean origin).

Nevertheless, there is an identifiable aesthetic of design, a delight in breaking up an otherwise unpatterned surface even though this is closely related to the particularities of the available technical means and their respective histories; and it is in those particularities that the "Africanness" of this aesthetic subsists. In woven cloth, for example, pattern arises from the manner in which the warps are mounted on the loom, and thence how they are interlaced with the wefts. Hand-loom weaving flourishes in many parts of Nigeria, as throughout West Africa, alongside an extraordinary range of older and newer traditions in textiles

A handwoven wrapper, commonplace dress for a man in the area from the lower Niger region eastwards. It also has many more elaborate forms, as in the dress worn by the king of Benin on state occasions. Akoko-Edo, Nigeria, 1969. Photograph by Sue Picton. Reproduced by permission of the National Commission for Museums and Monuments, Nigeria.

and other media, including resist-dyeing, masquerade, chiefly ceremonial, photography, video, easel painting, printmaking, and public sculpture.

In Nigeria, it is still both normal and commonplace for cloth to be woven in a long narrow strip often no more than about four inches (ten centimeters) wide. When the desired length is complete, it will be cut into pieces and sewn together edge-to-edge. It is only then that the visual effects intended by the weaver can be seen, manifesting a specific arithmetic in the precise counting of warps and wefts and geometry in the layout of pattern that weavers must learn and learn how to develop if a given tradition is to flourish. Resist-dyeing provides another means of inscribing pattern across the face of a textile—for example, by tying or stitching the cloth or by pasting starch (and now candle wax) over it, each medium serving to prevent the penetration of the dye, thereby creating pattern. The western Yoruba city of Abeokuta, founded in the 1830s, was one site for the elaborations of these techniques using indigo and known as *adire*. The use of indigo continues to be widespread throughout many parts of Nigeria, although the industrially manufactured dye is now largely preferred to the local version; and many other colors are available, whether locally or industrially produced. Long-running trade and family contacts between Lagos and Freetown may also have provided the route whereby a new set of resist-dyeing techniques making use of all the newly available colors arrived in and quickly spread throughout Nigeria in the late 1960s. These soon became known as *kampala*, a topical allusion to Idi Amin's offer of that city in Uganda as the location for a peace conference to settle the feuding in Northern Ireland. Although not taken up by the British government, the offer was widely reported in the Nigerian media.

We can see this same design aesthetic in the bright, almost blatant, African-print fabrics now so ubiquitous throughout Africa. In the course of the nineteenth century, Dutch textile manufacturers wanted to find a way of replicating the Indonesian wax batik process to produce the textiles at a cheaper price, thereby undercutting Indonesian production. This was not a success, but the cloths so produced sold well on the colonial Gold Coast and quickly spread to the markets of early twentieth-century Nigeria. Once the designers in The Netherlands began working to an African patronage, the designs expanded from an Indonesian exotic to include the visualization of local proverbs, emblems of chiefly ceremonial, modern education, and, in due course, the commemoration of topical events and people. These patterns and techniques were soon copied by textile factories in Britain and elsewhere, and at the time of independence, factories were established in West Africa, with the result that only one factory in The Netherlands and one in Britain are still active in the production of African-print cloth. This is best understood as merely the latest chapter in a narrative of trade and technological development, the origins of which remain lost in a still little-understood prehistory.

RELATIONSHIPS BETWEEN TEXTILE DESIGN AND DRESS FORM

When cloth is wrapped or draped around the body, the full effects of its design are at best obscured; yet the pattern-making repertoires of weavers, dyers, and factory-based designers have continued to evolve within particular traditions of textile and

dress design, distinctively from one center to another, especially with the use of new fibers, textures, and colors. Perhaps the fact that the cloth one wears is patterned and multitextured with contrasting colors is more significant than precisely what the patterns, colors, and textures are in any given case; and perhaps the frequency with which a person wears dress and textile forms that are known by his or her community to be costly is as important as anything else. This, of course, reinforces the earlier point about the delight in breaking up an otherwise plain surface: the cloth does not need to be seen in full for its pattern, texture, color, or quality to remain visible. In this context, the aesthetic

A young woman from the Niger Delta region of Nigeria in her best (machine-embroidered) clothes. Lagos, Nigeria, 1995. Photograph by John Picton.

of the patterned surface leads to the aesthetic of the draped fabric, which has now come into play with the wearing of the cloth. Moreover, the fact that the design is never fully visible may provide for another allusive property with particular regard to the fact that some kinds of knowledge are hidden, only to be learned and passed on through a long and successful life. It may be that the dazzle effect of a cloth (especially the laminated plastic fiber known as Lurex) has an apotropaic effect, with the capacity to turn away the malign influence of a witch or sorcerer. On the other hand, even those patterns that signify or visualize particular events, ideas, or proverbs do not work as precise "statements" but as the reiteration of an inheritance of ideas and a memory of past events—an inheritance and a memory that are, of course, very specific to a given location.

Finally, it is worth noting that in those relatively rare occasions when a specific form or color is called for, the frame of reference may be entirely local and sometimes the privy knowledge of just a few individuals, as when a woman in Ebira is told to wear a white cloth by a diviner. White cloth is commonplace: raw cotton is mostly white, although there is a less frequently seen brown variety. Yet one of the remedies for the healing of a woman suffering from an affliction diagnosed as caused by a witch is to wear a white cloth, white here denoting suffering (from the white scale that develops on the skin caused by dry harmattan winds). The intention is, in effect, a prayer to the afflicting witch: "I've suffered enough—please leave me alone." For much the same reason, a man might be told to wear a black gown for the night. Night is the time when witches do their work, so a gown woven of indigo-dyed yarn is thus a representation of the witch afflicting him—the point being: "I wear this gown in your honor—please cease your affliction." These uses do not exhaust the range of significances of these fabrics, however. A gown woven of indigo-dyed yard is a costly item, in contrast to the white wraparound skirt, which is a commonplace thing denoting no particular status. In Ebira, if a white warp is woven with an indigo weft, the resulting cloth can only be used either as a shroud or as the clothing of a masked performer. It can be said that the aesthetics of textile design and of dress and fashion, and the relationships between them, now taking in the modern fashion industry, will remain an area of continuing research interest for those concerned with Nigerian cultural production for some time to come.

References and Further Reading

Abiodun, Rowland. "Fabric of Immortality: In Praise of Yoruba Gods and Cloth." In *Cloth Only Wears to Shreds: Yoruba Textiles and Photographs from the Beier Collection*, edited by John Pemberton III, 39–58. Amherst, MA: Mead Art Museum, Amherst College, 2004.

Byfield, Judith. *The Bluest Hands: A Social and Economic History of Women Dyers in Abeokuta*. Oxford, UK: James Currey, 2002.

Clarke, Duncan. "Aso Oke: The Evolving Tradition of Hand-Woven Design among the Yoruba." Ph.D. dissertation, University of London, 1998.

Gardi, Bernhard. *Le Boubou—c'est chic*. Basel, Switzerland: Museum der Kulturen, 2000.

Kriger, Colleen. *Cloth in West African History*. Oxford, UK: AltaMira Press, 2006.

National Museum of African Art. *History, Design and Craft in West African Strip-Woven Cloth*. Washington, DC: Smithsonian Institution Press, 1992.

Picton, John, ed. *The Art of African Textiles: Technology, Tradition and Lurex*. London: Lund Humphries, 1995.

Picton, John, and John Mack. *African Textiles*. 2nd ed. London: British Museum, 1989.

Prince Claus Fund. *The Art of African Fashion*. The Hague, The Netherlands: Prince Claus Fund; Asmara, Ethiopia, and Trenton, NJ: Africa World Press, 1998.

Rabine, Leslie. *The Global Circulation of African Fashion*. Oxford, UK: Berg, 2002.

Renne, Elisha P. *Cloth That Does Not Die: The Meaning of Cloth in Bunu Social Life*. Seattle: University of Washington Press, 1995.

Renne, Elisha P., and Babatunde Agbaje-Williams, eds. *Yoruba Religious Textiles: Essays in Honour of Cornelius Adepegba*. Ibadan, Nigeria: Bookbuilders, 2005.

Revue Noire. Special Mode: African Fashion, no. 27 (1998).

Rubin, Arnold, ed. *Marks of Civilization*. Los Angeles: UCLA Museum of Cultural History, 1988.

John Picton

See also Masquerade, Theater, Dance Costumes; Yoruba in Nigeria and Diaspora; Hausa in Nigeria and Diaspora; Igbo in Nigeria and Diaspora; The Kingdom of Benin; Lower Niger Delta Peoples and Diaspora; Snapshot: Kalabari Peoples of Nigeria; The Nigerian Fashion Scene.

Yoruba in Nigeria and Diaspora

- Beads: The Ultimate in Self-Beautifying
- The Power of Cloth
- Yoruba Dress in the Diaspora

The Yoruba people number well over thirty million from about sixteen ancient kingdoms. They spread all over southwestern Nigeria and extend well into the neighboring countries of Benin and Togo. The Yoruba have been urbanized since the first millennium C.E. and are well known for their fine artistic achievements, especially the naturalistic life-size bronze heads and terra-cotta sculptures of Ile-Ife. In addition to being among the most accomplished carvers in wood and ivory in Africa, the Yoruba are also famous for their fine bead and textile work. Through the slave trade, Yoruba descendants have had a considerable impact on the cultures of Latin America, the Caribbean, and North America.

BEADS: THE ULTIMATE IN SELF-BEAUTIFYING

The demand for beaded attire and ornament and the extent to which they have been incorporated into Yoruba social, religious, and political life are unsurpassed in Africa. Yet there is not much archaeological evidence that beads were actually manufactured by the Yoruba until the second millennium C.E. From Ile-Ife, the ancestral home of the Yoruba, comes the most concrete evidence of clearly defined codes of highly developed dress and fashion for royalty, chieftains, religious leaders, and the aristocracy in the eleventh to sixteenth centuries. The traditions associated with such dress codes, however, must be considerably more ancient than the excavated artifacts, beads, beaded regalia, the art of making beaded dress, crowns, hats, bracelets, and anklets.

Among the Yoruba, beads have always transformed—and, to this day, still transform—the appearance of their wearers while also projecting the society's most highly prized object of adornment. On state and important ritual occasions, most Yoruba oba (sovereigns) wear beaded jewelry in addition to their beaded crown, veil, horsetail fly whisk, and staff—and, in Ijebuland, bead-covered boots as well. Of immediate relevance here is how the Yoruba formally address their oba. At all times, they must begin with the sentence: Ki ade pe lori, ki bata o pe lese—literally, "May you wear your crown and shoes forever!" Idiomatically, this means, "May your reign be long." Clearly, the oba's crown and shoes are integral to his status as an orisa, a divinity whose face and feet must always be covered.

So highly valued is the beaded costume that it is believed to be a more prestigious form of bodily attire than conventional fabric. This assumption is supported by the saying, "A person who adorns himself or herself with beads has done the ultimate in self-beautifying." Beads define a person's identity, status, and religious affiliation and have become the most durable visual symbols of leadership, power, and success. In the broader context of Yoruba aesthetics in which iwa—defined as character, being, or existence—is a prerequisite for ewa (beauty), beads are crucial in achieving the perfect notion of lasting beauty. Yoruba children inherit beads from their parents to preserve both the identity and the historical continuity of their lineage. Most importantly, however, beads connote affluence, which makes them appropriate for inclusion in the regalia of the oba, for no citizen surpasses the king in wealth.

A fourteenth-century zinc brass statue of a standing male figure, about eighteen and a half inches (forty-seven centimeters) tall, excavated from Ita Yemoo, Ile-Ife, the ancestral home of the Yoruba, typifies the use of beads in traditional Yoruba chiefly regalia. This figure wears a kind of beaded headgear or coronet, several rows of stringed bead necklaces, beaded wristlets and anklets, and what looks like a toe ring on the left foot. Apart from the loincloth around the waist, all the beaded jewelry is worn directly on the torso, arms, legs, and feet. The left hand holds a ram's horn, probably filled with oogun, a potent medicinal substance, to beam an affective ase, or life force, at a targeted person or thing. And, with the right hand, he holds what appears to be the bottom part of a horsetail fly whisk, which is traditionally used to acknowledge greeters at special public occasions. Because of the elaborate regalia and symbols associated with power, many scholars have found it irresistible to claim that this is a statue of an ooni of Ife, a divine king and the descendant of Oduduwa, who is the progenitor of the Yoruba people.

The most obvious outward visible sign of their divine kingship is the conical beaded crown with a beaded fringed veil. Such crowns have been documented by scholars who have worked in the Yoruba cities of Idowa in Ijebuland, Ila Orangun, Okuku, Oyo, and Idanre. Without exception, they all stress the indispensability of the beaded crown known as ade and iboju, the beaded fringed veil for the Yoruba oba. The ade and iboju should not, therefore, be confused with ori-ko-gbe-ofo, beaded coronets that are colorful, complicated, and textured but do not exude the awesomeness of a divine king. A partial or total concealment of the Yoruba king's face with the beaded veil is a critical component of the mysterious and impenetrable image of the oba. The Yoruba believe that the oba protects himself from malicious ase life force from without, and he protects other people from his own ase.

The conical form of the divine king's crown with the veil is patterned after ile-ori, the container or the metaphorical house of ibori, which is also conical in shape and is the symbol of the inner spiritual head, ori-inu, who won the first and only leadership contest among the 201 orisa when he successfully split the kola nut of authority, obi-ase, and subsequently became the head of all the orisa. Similarly, the oba is more than a secular leader; he is an orisa with aselike ori. His face is hidden from the public throughout his life, and it would be unthinkable to preserve its naturalistic detail for posterity. It was not until the nineteenth century with British colonization and the introduction of photography that Yoruba oba began to have portraits that revealed their faces. These photographs were framed and displayed in their reception rooms.

It would appear that the lineage of Oduduwa introduced the concept of divine kingship to distinguish himself from the Elu-Meje (Seven Elus) and Ife-Mefa (Six Ifes) who were, and still are, the traditional administrators of the original quarters of Ile-Ife.

Orangun of Ila wearing a conical beaded crown with a beaded fringed veil. Ila-Orangun, Nigeria, 1971. Photograph by John Pemberton III.

dress of the female brass figure seems to convey gender equality for the female regalia is not in any way inferior to that of her male counterpart.

Nowhere in Yoruba culture is the equality of the genders more pronounced and taken more seriously than in the *Ogboni* (council of elders with judicial function). This equality is quite evident in the *edan* Ogboni pair (linked brass staffs) usually worn on the neck by Ogboni elders to indicate their membership and status in the Ogboni society. The male figure in the bronze pair has his forefingers locked around each other in a gesture that further suggests a pact of secrecy—a code of ethics that must be followed by all Ogboni members. The legs of the male and female figures are intertwined, giving a visual impression of three instead of four legs—a reminder of the interdependency of the male and female qualities in Ogboni society. Indeed, the Ogboni have a principle that binds them, namely, "two Ogboni equals three" (where the third is the earth); it is very much in evidence here.

After obas, Ifa divination priests (*babalawo*) are the next most important users of beaded materials. Ifa divination literature mentions babalawo using beaded crowns, necklaces, armbands, wristlets, shoulder pieces, storage bags, and horsetail fly whisks. Most valuable to Ifa priests' list is *segi*, the name given to a variety of valuable beads, especially blue tubular ones. The next in rank are *iyun*, coral beads, while *akun*, a kind of bead made from the shells of palm-kernel nuts, are the least desirable. An Ifa divination verse from *Iwori-meji* opens with the line, "As a person presents himself, so that person is greeted." In the same divination verse, Orunmila, the patron divinity of Ifa, is reported to wrap himself in *odun* cloth; wear beads, a pair of brass sandals, and a brass crown; and carry an *osun* staff made of brass.

THE POWER OF CLOTH

The Yoruba word for cloth or clothing is *aso*, a noun formed by adding the prefix *a* to *so* (meaning to bud or to regenerate). Aso can therefore be interpreted as the act of regenerating and giving the human body the respect that it would not otherwise have if it were unclothed. So important is aso that the Yoruba say, "It is the aso we should greet before greeting the wearer."

What one wears is a reflection of one's design consciousness, *oju-ona*—literally, "eye for design." It reveals one's familiarity with the wide range of types of cloth that one might wear and the insight to wear them appropriately. Such persons are respected and highly regarded for their artistic skills in transforming and beautifying themselves and overriding whatever physical shortcomings they may have. For an adult to be seen in public without clothes is considered not only bizarre but an indication of either a mental illness or the effect of an irreversible curse, an example of which is to be "stripped naked" by enormously powerful and vengeful ancestors. This means that one would be abandoned and unwanted by one's relatives, friends, and colleagues—one's social fabric and metaphorical cloth.

Although not as grave as being without clothes, dressing inappropriately is highly offensive to Yoruba aesthetic and life-affirming sensibilities, one major requirement of which is the need to possess *imoju-mora*, which means "sensitivity to the need of the moment." The following Yoruba proverb cautions, "Lack of regard for anyone, lack of regard for people makes the bush dweller enter the town in a loincloth." Here, the bush dweller lacks such sensitivity in his choice to wear a loincloth (an inappropriate dress,

They wielded much political power but were certainly not divine, because they were not direct descendants of Oduduwa. These thirteen powerful quarter-chiefs could, however, don the most impressive aristocratic costume available, which makes them a likely subject for the single, freestanding bronze figure mentioned above.

There is another pair of bronze figures from Ita Yemoo, Ile-Ife, whose proportions are more or less the same as the single freestanding statue. Both figures in this pair wear beaded necklaces, wristlets, and anklets and crownlike hats with no beaded fringes. The wrapper cloth on the female figure is tied high enough on her torso to partially cover her breasts, which is comparable to the way Yoruba women still wear their wrapper over the *buba* (blouse). Her beaded shoulder sash hangs diagonally across the torso, with the tied end resting on the left hip. The woman's diagonal shoulder sash is, presumably, a mark of her status and possibly her cult or societal affiliation. This assumption makes sense when this sash is compared with the attire of an all-female association called Yeye Olorisa in Owo, 100 miles (161 kilometers) east of Ile-Ife. Here, the society members wear a bright red diagonal sash across their chest. In the pair of bronze figures, the

Yoruba man wearing an *agbada* made from indigo-dyed, handwoven *etu* cloth and a brocade *abetiaja* cap. Ila-Orangun, Nigeria, 1984. Photograph by John Pemberton III.

for elders; *aran tii pari aso*, velvet—the epitome of good taste in cloth; *mosaaji aso oba tii tanna yanranyanranyanran*, damask—the royal gold-threaded cloth that has a strong metallic sheen in sunlight; *ologinniginni aso Arada*, an ancient and extremely expensive cloth with elaborate appliqué from Arada (Alada); and *adire*, patterned, indigo, resist-dyed, imported greige cloth.

On adire cloth, art historian John Picton has written: "There are two types of *adire*. In one, the resisting agent is raffia, *iko*, and tying and stitching patterns. These cloths are called *adire oniko*. In the other category, the resisting agent is starch, *eko*, which is either painted or stenciled onto the cloth before dying. These are called *adire eleko*." Then there is *aso-oke*, which is strip-woven cloth made on a double-heddle loom with the warp elements tied at intervals to create a pattern of small holes or containing repeated weft-float-weave motifs.

A more contemporary version of aso-oke is a combination of hand- and machine-spun fibers of cotton, rayon, and Lurex called *UP NEPA* (a reference to the unreliable performance of the Nigerian Electric Power Authority, recently renamed the Nigerian Power Holding Authority). Among the relatively recent additions to the ever-growing repertoires of Yoruba textiles are the imported wax-print cotton versions of adire, embroidered eyelet, and organdy.

A Yoruba woman's attire is made up of essentially four parts: buba, a T-shaped top; iro, a waist wrapper; *gele*, a head tie; and *iborun*, a shoulder shawl. While her attire is never as voluminous or embroidered as a man's, it is nonetheless equally important that a woman demonstrate abundant use of cloth in order to be substantial and elegant. The quality and size of a woman's iro, the cloth wrapped around the lower part of the body and that often covers the buba, indicates her status in society. It should never be too short or skimpy lest people think that she is too poor to afford a good-sized iro. Ideally, the iro should be long and full. The buba, usually white or light in color and simple in construction, enhances the more expensive iro, gele, and iborun, while it shows off the woman's necklace(s). In contemporary usage, this same shoulder shawl carried on the left lower arm becomes *ipele*. It is not uncommon for women to tie the shawl around their waist, in which case it would be called *oja*, baby-carrying sash. This practice of layering cloth makes a woman appear bigger.

The head tie, gele, must not only fit the wearer but also be sculpted to make a statement about politics, her mood, or a particular situation. For example, head ties have names such as *Gowon* (head of the federal military government of Nigeria, 1966 to 1975); *Onilegogoro* (skyscraper); *Mawobe* ("It's so beautiful, don't dare look at it"); *Gbotoko* ("Listen to your husband"); *Kilo'ko ose?* ("What can a husband do?"); *Ki elenu so enu* ("Mind your gossiping"); *Ko eyin si orogun* ("Turn your back on your co-wife"); and many more. The gele must match the iborun in color and design and be appropriate to the occasion. The tying of gele is an art that puts to test every woman's oju-ona design consciousness. There is constant innovation in the art of gele tying, and having oju-ona distinguishes the creative woman from the non-creative one. Critics often invoke the proverb, "*Gele o dun bi ka moo we, ka moo we o dun bi ko yeni*" ("Head tie is no good if one does not know how to tie it; knowing how to tie it is no use if it does not look good on one").

Even though the Yoruba use imported fabrics and the design of their large garments has been inspired by the Hausa in the Islamic north, it is the way that they have modified and adapted

to the town and his failure to show consideration for others in the society.

Ideally, an elder would have the *ofi*, a superior locally woven cloth, made into *dandogo*, an elaborately embroidered and expensive garment that has ample sleeves about a foot (thirty centimeters) longer than the arms of the wearer. This type of expense is well beyond what an impecunious elder can afford. Even if he is very unhappy with *kijipa*, a rougher and cheaper locally woven cloth, there is very little he can do to change the situation, because "dandogo is not something to make in a huff." It could take over a year to make a fabric and almost another year to sew and embroider it by hand. For an elderly person who does not earn a lot of money, it could take a long time to pay off the cost of dandogo.

At social gatherings and especially at weddings, naming ceremonies, and burials, comparing the relative artistry of people's cloth is always a major focus of animated conversation. The weave, texture, color, and design must be perfectly appropriate to the person who wears it, as well as to its specific function. Cloths greatly admired by the Yoruba include: *sanyan*, cloth made of native silk created by anaphe caterpillars; *alaari baba aso*, a rich reddish handwoven cloth called "the father of all cloths"; *etu aso agba*, loom-woven cloth with threads of black and white their designs that is most significant. Adult male attire may be made up of *sokoto* (trousers); *dansiki* (short-sleeved gown with wide arm holes that reaches to the hip or knees); *agbada* (a large ankle-length gown that may be embroidered at the neck and chest and is open at the sides); buba (T-shaped shirt with a round neck and wrist-length sleeves, traditionally worn under the agbada but now worn fashionably as a shirt alone among university-educated men); and a cap to match.

There are basically three types of caps to choose from, depending on one's age, means, and status in society. The first is a cylindrically constructed cap from aso-oke or etu called *fila ikori*. It is soft enough to be pulled in and styled to meet the wearer's aesthetic taste. While many men may wear the aso-oke cap, etu is the choice of elders. The second cap is called *fila abetiaja* ("cap with doglike ears"). It is made from silk or cotton cloth, dyed or left natural. Wearers of fila abetiaja may turn the ear flaps up or down depending on the occasion.

The third kind of cap is *fila onide* ("cap with brasslike sheen"). Worn by chiefs and very wealthy men, it is a round, brimless hat with straight sides and a soft flat top. Artist and scholar Eve de Negri has written, "Special families trained in methods of making and embroidering these caps, guarded their secrets well. Velvet was the favorite cloth used, and this was laid over stiffened lining and then embroidered with metallic threads of silver and gold, in the form of trails of leaves." The ambition to rise on the sociopolitical ladder, to become a leader or king in one's community, begins with what one wears. "The head that wears a cloth cap, *etu*, strives to wear a velvet cap; the one that wears a velvet cap strives to become a king."

Large and voluminous gowns like the agbada evoke the Yoruba concepts of success, power, and influence. Other types of gowns that impart the same qualities on the wearer include the *gbariye*, a gown with pleats designed for performing Yoruba classical dance, and dandogo, which are sewn from expensive and luxurious materials like sanyan, silk cloth, alaari (reddish handwoven cloth), aso-oke, and etu. These robes enhance the wearer, affirming an authoritative presence and a substantial space that hints at the divinity in every Yoruba person. The Yoruba gbariye is an important component in the performance of dance. The choreographic possibilities with gbariye are countless. Baba Lebe, the renowned Yoruba percussionist and dancer, creates movements and forms that enable viewers to see the construction of gbariye.

Among the various styles of gbariye are *gbariye alapa adan* (gbariye with bat-wing sleeves), *gbariye dansiki* (gbariye made in a smaller dansiki size), *gbariye onigba-awe* (gbariye with two hundred gussets).

Dressing appropriately according to one's age, status, affiliation to an orisa, church, or society is favored. For example, when Owo men drape their body with *ugbero* cloth like a toga during the *ero* ceremony, it indicates that they are over sixty years of age and that they are respected elders in the community. Ugbero cloth is much larger than a woman's wrapper. Woven by women on a vertical loom, ugbero is predominantly indigo blue broken up by parallel lighter shades of indigo and accentuated by relatively thin white stripes.

The very powerful indigenous elders society of the Ijebu Yoruba called Osugbo (equivalent to the Ogboni) are charged mainly with judicial functions and are easily recognized in the community by their dress. Art historian Aderonke Adesanya has written that the dress of members of the Osugbo includes the *itagbe*, a patterned or richly decorated and textured shoulder piece cloth by which members are conspicuously singled out.

Baba Lebe wearing a *gbariye onigba-awe* to dance for the *oba* of Erin-Osun. The pleated gown is designed for performing Yoruba classical dance. Erin-Osun, Osun State, Nigeria, 1994. Photograph by Ulli Beier.

dan, gender-sensitive brass figures; *isan*, a wrapper usually made with white cloth or woven strips tied around the waist or draped on the body and tied into a knot on the left shoulder; *iyun*, beads; and *shaki*, shag.

In Owo, a ceremonial gown, *orufanran*, distinguishes men with outstanding military records. The orufanran consists of three pieces: jacket, skirt, and hat. The jacket has wide three-quarter sleeves. They are made of an inexpensive cotton material on which have been sewn scale-shaped pieces of red wool flannel. The hat is a tall miterlike headdress with two long ivory pieces on the sides, each carved to look like a feather. The overall impression of the surface of the garment is of the scaly skin of a pangolin. The orufanran alludes to the power and invincibility of its wearer through its form, its material, and its iconography.

Being anthropomorphic, Yoruba orisa are also clothed literally and metaphorically. Their cloth must reflect their identity, character, and office. Priests and devotees, as embodiments of the orisa, don the cloths or costumes of their respective orisa—displaying the orisa's favorite clothing and preferred colors. The costumes of Sango priests are predominantly red and white; those of Obatala priests are white; and Esu are red and black. The characteristic emblems or items alluding to the power and presence of an orisa are also crucial to the concretization of its iwa (character, being, and existence) and therefore its ewa (beauty).

A mural painting on the shrine of Orisa-Popo in the town of Ogbomoso exemplifies the concept of cloth as that which covers and beautifies. Moyo Okediji, an art historian, has reported that the women artist-devotees executing this kind of mural for Orisa-Ikire in Ile-Ife describe their work as "making new clothes for the orisa." This remark also applies to Orisa-Popo shrine painting because Orisa-Ikire and Orisa-Popo are both *orisa-funfun*, the term used for all the orisa that are related to Orisanla or those that are simply local forms of Orisanla or Obatala.

The overall design of the mural on the Orisa-Popo shrine recalls the format and design of an adire cloth. Significantly, adire dyeing and designing as well as orisa shrine painting are both women's art. It can be hypothesized that the art of orisa shrine paintings such as one finds at Orisa-Popo's are considerably older than the introduction of adire cloth at the end of the nineteenth and the beginning of the twentieth centuries. In all probability, therefore, shrine paintings might have served as the model for the earliest adire cloth designs. In particular, one is struck by how much the motifs from this shrine have inspired contemporary textiles. The similarity in design and style provides evidence for calling the shrine mural "cloth for the orisa." This "cloth" is a powerful, visual *oriki* (praise poem) to Orisa-Popo.

Just as it would not be acceptable for the Orisa-Popo shrine to be without its metaphorical cloth, the mural, the Yoruba people equally value their metaphorical cloth—their *ebi*, family or association. This notion is rooted in the Yoruba proverb, "People are my cloth." Indeed, most noticeable at burial ceremonies, child-naming ceremonies, weddings, housewarmings, and other important occasions are one's ebi, among them immediate and distant relatives, associates, and age mates, all wearing *aso-ebi*, the same fabric and color. This assures the celebrants that they are not only beautiful but that they will be given a fitting burial when they die because they have human "cloth."

Because cloth survives its owner and not the reverse, the Yoruba believe that, when humans return as ancestors, they will once again be covered completely with cloth even as the

Ojomo man of Ijebu-Owo wearing an *orufanran* in Owo, Nigeria, 1975. This ceremonial war gown is made to resemble the scaly skin of a pangolin, symbolizing power and invincibility with carefully carved ivory attachments and a cora-beaded crown. Photograph by Rowland Abiodun.

Egungun, ancestral masquerade, is also covered with cloth. In Yoruba thought, the deathlessness of cloth is comparable only to that of Olodumare, the supreme and self-existent being and creator-in-chief. The socioreligious and aesthetic significance of cloth in Yoruba belief far outweighs its destructibility as a material object. Egungun maskers always make their annual visits to the land of the living covered with old and new, plain and colored, local and imported strips and panels of cloth, and with medicinal attachments, *oogun*, which can take the form of amulets, gourds, animal skulls, old and new coins, and cowries for empowerment.

The design of the masquerade costume must have integrity, character, style, and color. The costume must also accommodate the needs of the moment. In Yoruba thought, tradition and change are not antithetical. Thus, the costume of the masquerade adapts and changes in order to be relevant to the living. Because the purpose of the Egungun's visit is to bless relatives and the community, it must appear substantially better endowed than the recipients of his blessings in order to be credible. This makes sense to the Yoruba, who believe that, "if a person offers to lend you a dress, you should consider what he or she has on." In other words, there has to be verifiable evidence that the Egungun itself possesses enough to be able to give abundantly and sufficiently to those on earth.

It is not unusual, therefore, for an Egungun costume to layer expensive and contemporary fabrics from overseas on top of highly regarded traditional Yoruba cloths. Such a huge display of cloth is linked to the Egungun's need to invoke ase (power, life force) associated with the chameleon (alagemo), which, with its ase, is able to appropriate the designs and colors of any cloth it chooses and to protect itself and neutralize all evil machinations directed at it. Similarly, an Egungun, with its multilayered cloth can do the same with its costume of many colors.

The line from Ifa literature, "Cloth only wears to shreds," is recalled by the free-moving panels of their costumes made of strips of cloth and/or mariwo, fresh yellowish green palm fronds also called aso-oku, "cloth of the dead." Together, shredded cloth and palm fronds become the visual metaphors for the transformation of the whole cloth to its immortal form—the human to the ancestor through Egungun performance. Egungun's visit from orun, the abode of ancestors (also called "home"), to aye, "this world" (also called "the marketplace"), celebrates the season of renewal of relationships between the ancestors and humans on earth. The Egungun receives gifts and replenishes his wardrobe with the help of relatives and the community who have been blessed in many ways by his visit. Although the cloths on the Egungun might have been made locally, in Germany, Indonesia, or the United States, the ancestral presence is, nevertheless, revered and welcomed as a guest from the "other world"—the abode of spirits, deities, and ancestors. Thus, Egungun cloths not only transform the masker socially and aesthetically, they also make him the bridge between this world and that of the dead.

The different members of one's blood relation or social unit are "shreds" of a metaphorical cloth symbolized by aso-ebi, which people wear at burials and equally important social gatherings. The underlying aesthetic of shreds is one of infinite multiplicity, the effect of which becomes apparent when the Egungun dances and spins. Visually, the strips and panels blend together and the colors fade into one another until nearly all details disappear and the costume becomes part of everything and is immortal, like Olodumare.

Cloth thus becomes a tangible point of contact with the orisa and the ancestors. When imbued with life force, the cloth of the orisa and those of his or her priests radiate with the power and presence of the orisa. Cloth conveys the awesome powers of the ancestors into the world of the living and exemplifies immortality, the perfect existence. In the end, the Yoruba forgo precious stones and metals, supposedly the most durable and expensive items of adornment, in favor of cloth.

YORUBA DRESS IN THE DIASPORA

For the diasporic Yoruba, knowing that their survival and prosperity depended on their orisa, it must have been a priority to identify, energize, beautify, and immortalize their orisa by clothing them literally and metaphorically in the New World. Thus, the practice of lavishly using expensive and colorful fabric documented in Brazil, Cuba, Trinidad, and the United States on Yoruba-derived shrines could have begun in the early years of the slave trade. Anthropologist Robert Farris Thompson illustrates several such shrines to Yoruba orisa from Bahia, Brazil, and Ibadan, Nigeria, in Face of the Gods. His photograph of an altar to Ogum (Ogun) and to the hunter gods Logunede and Oxoosi prepared by Mai Jocelinha, Cosme de Farias, Bahia, Brazil, is a stunning and sumptuous celebration of cloth—red, white, blue, and honey-colored embroidered fabrics to clothe Ogun, Logunede, and Oxoosi. Ivor Miller's photo of "The Anniversary Trono Altar to Yemaya" by the late Juan Bauzo, Brooklyn, New York, is a symphony in

fabric dedicated to Yemaya. And, to this day, the practice of tyi[ng] a white cloth or sash around the iroko tree to charge its spirit wit[h] power continues in both Nigeria and the Yoruba diaspora. Eve[n] in the Yorubaland and the diaspora, the bata drum is given exqu[i]sitely bead-decorated cloth called bante (cloth to wrap around th[e] waist) to honor Ayan, the orisa of Yoruba drumming.

In the Yoruba diaspora, it is presumed that as slaves we[re] gradually initiated into the particular orisa and became devotee[s] they adopted the distinctive personality traits, food preference[s] and the dress and color preferences of their orisa, even if that e[n]tailed some creative substitution. Imoju-mora, sensitivity to th[e] needs of the moment, is not only a crucial factor in the adoptio[n] of new styles, techniques, and materials—despite the seeming[ly] unchanging traditions of Yoruba art—but also a means whereb[y] the culture has managed to survive in new environments and th[e] difficult conditions of the New World since the slave trade.

The Sisterhood of Our Lady of Good Death in Cachoeira (Sa[l]vador, Brazil), founded in the first quarter of the nineteenth cen[]tury by freed African women slaves, may give an idea of the earlie[st] ceremonial dress worn by women in the Yoruba diaspora. At the[ir] annual festival in August, the sisterhood don their white blouse[s] large black skirts, red shoulder shawls, white scarves, and row[s] of beaded necklaces, metallic wristlets, and white slippers. Com[]prised entirely of women of African descent, their dress, color, an[d] substantial presence remind one of Yoruba women's dresses. Th[e] black voluminous skirt could easily be a substitute for an indig[o] dyed cotton wrapper; the white blouse, a buba; the head tie, [a] gele; and the red shoulder shawl, an iborun. That the sisterhoo[d] color preference here echoes the traditional Yoruba color palett[e] of red, black, and white is probably no accident. The sisterhoo[d] beautify themselves to honor the saints, offering their bodies [as] an altar—the manifestation of beauty, dignity, and power of th[e] Yoruba orisa that they could not openly worship.

In 1993, Carybé, an exceptionally gifted watercolorist, pr[o]duced a profusely illustrated book, African Gods in the Candom[]blé of Bahia—a book that, more than any other, presents n[ot] only an intimate view of the orisa and their devotees but als[o] the crucial role of fabric and color in Bahia's Candomblé. Me[n] and women wear elegant, huge, and full skirts in assorted color[s.] The design and vastness of most of these skirts remind one [of] a similar skirt called abolukun worn by the king and high chie[fs] during their most important and ancient Igogo festival in Ow[o] in western Nigeria. During this festival, male chiefs includin[g] the olowo (the king of Owo) plait their hair to respect and ac[]knowledge the authority of the goddess Oronsen. Dependin[g] on the status of a chief, one, two, or three red parrot feathers ar[e] inserted into the hair with or without a brass comb. The olow[o] in addition, wears two long egret feathers to distinguish himse[lf] as the ruler.

The top, usually in the form of pakato, a pair of beaded band[s] across the torso, and abolukun, the big skirt worn during th[e] festival, are feminine. In the context of performance, the abolu[]kun radiates feelings of majesty, power, affluence, and increas[e] mainly through its arresting white color and overwhelming siz[e.] On this occasion, the olowo is indeed regarded as the source an[d] sustainer of the community's peace and prosperity. He assert[s] this role ritually, dramatically, and choreographically durin[g] the Igogo festival. Combining the dignity and white color [of] the elaborate abolukun costume with penetrating metal-gon[g] music and graceful wavelike movements, the olowo effective[ly] moves the hearts and bodies of his subjects. And, in response to the movement and the size of the abolukun, the crowd greets the olowo thus: "The mighty, expansive ocean; The great wide umbrella-like protector of Owo; The prolific banana tree that bears much fruit."

In the Candomblé, the orisa and their priests and priestesses are recognized by what they wear. Exu (Esu), the lord of paths and crossroads, dons a red and black cap; a red top; a black, red, and yellow striped skirt; and a bead necklace, while about half a dozen medicinal gourds hang down from his neck. In contrast, Ogum (Ogun) of Opo Afonja wears a light blue top; indigo blue baggy trousers; and a cylindrical, decorated cap. This figure also brandishes a sword with his right hand as he covers most of his chest and abdomen with mariwo, the most important ritual cloth of Ogun in Yorubaland. The presence of Oxum (Osun), the divinity of the Osun River, is invoked through her coquetry, bright yellowish copper dress, extraordinarily long shawl, jewelry, and a mirror that doubles as a fan. Her loose baby-carrying sash ending in a tied bow is an allusion to her power to give children to the childless. She wears a headdress with a beaded fringe. As the sovereign, she is the fringe that at once repels negative ase and protects observers from the power of the orisa's axe.

In Cuba, the altars of the orisa are dressed with colorful, sacred cloths, as is evident in a photograph of the altar to Oya with Feast for the Dead, in Havana, Cuba, taken in 1992 by Christopher Munnelly. Robert Farris Thompson has written, "Oya's banner has nine colors, one for each of her children." Oya's nine children are her immediate ebi social unit, her metaphorical cloth (recalling the strips and panels on the Egungun costume), explained in Yoruba culture as *Eniyan lasoo mi*, "People are my cloth." As already mentioned, one is survived by his or her ebi, just as cloth survives the wearer. Oya's children protect and beautify

their mother as cloth does and hint at their mother's immortality. Thus, for Oya to be without her children is to be abandoned by them and unclothed. Oya's devotees and especially newly initiated priests and priestesses may wear simple white dresses with a head covering, but the maroon, red, or brown that they wear identifies them and their status within the orisa community.

In a shrine created by Elbida Deaneya Cancino-Ochoto Rena for orisa Yewa in Cuba, the entire ceiling was covered with a large cloth that devotees call *iro* (wrapper), an indispensable item of women's dress. At Yewa's shrine, visitors must greet this iro before greeting Yewa. The iro's canopylike installation suggests the movement of a wave as its patterns seem to float—transforming an ordinary space into a sacred one for Yewa.

The presence in an eighteenth-century American watercolor titled *The Old Plantation* of a baby-carrying sash, which could also be used as a head tie or shoulder sash points to a possible Yoruba dress origin. It is not known, however, how long Yoruba-type dress continued to be worn or used in the United States. It is plausible that with conversion to Christianity and Western-style dresses, Yoruba or African-type dress gradually disappeared. In the 1960s' revival of interest in Africa, it is significant that Efuntola Oseijiman Adefunmi, formerly Walter Eugene King, founder of Oyotunji Village in South Carolina, began his religious and cultural movement with an African clothing store in Harlem. With more and more Yoruba students and professionals coming to the United States, there are a growing number of occasions such as child-naming, housewarming, and many more that make the use of Yoruba clothes more public and part of contemporary American dress fashion.

More than superficial embellishment, Yoruba dress is the expression of religious and sociopolitical realities that sustain and validate the peoples' traditions. Yoruba dress and fashion are not static. Textile artists have engaged novel yarns like Lurex, and new imported colors have given birth to new forms and textures, leading to the formation of new identities in the twentieth and twenty-first centuries. Now the issue is not the decline and fall of once-pristine traditions, nor even their persistence as such, but rather the range of Yoruba responses to the demands upon textiles as a medium of art.

References and Further Reading

Abiodun, R. "Woman in Yoruba Religious Images." *African Languages and Cultures* 2, no. 1 (1989): 1–18.

Abiodun, R. "Understanding Art and Aesthetics: The Concept of Ase." *African Arts* 27, no. 3 (1994): 68–78, 102–103.

Abiodun, R. John Pemberton III, and Ulli Beier. *Cloth Only Wears to Shreds: Yoruba Textiles and Photographs from the Beier Collection.* Amherst, MA: Mead Art Museum, Amherst College, 2004.

Beier, Ulli. *Owe Yoruba Beaded Crowns: Sacred Regalia of the Olukuku of Okuku.* London: Ethnographica, 1971.

Carybé. *African Gods in the Candomblé of Bahia.* Salvador, Brazil: Impresso no Brasil, 1993.

Drewal, H. J., and John Mason. *Beads, Body and Soul: Art and Light in the Yoruba Universe.* Los Angeles: UCLA Fowler Museum of Cultural History, 1997.

Eyo, Ekpo, and Frank Willett. *Treasures of Ancient Nigeria.* New York: Alfred A. Knopf, 1980.

Fagg, William. *Yoruba Beadwork: Art of Nigeria.* New York: Rizzoli, 1980.

Yoruba men wearing *aso-ebi*, Ila-Orangun, Nigeria 1986. This cloth, made to be the same fabric and color for all participants, is worn on special occasions and important social gatherings, in this case for the installation of Chief Obajoko of Ila-Orangun. Photograph by John Pemberton III.

Falola, Toyin, and Matt D. Childs. *The Yoruba Diaspora in the Atlantic World*. Bloomington: Indiana University Press, 2004.

Fraser, D., and Herbert M. Cole. *African Art and Leadership*. Madison: University of Wisconsin Press, 1972.

Ogunba, Oyin. "Crowns and 'Okute' at Idowa." *Nigeria Magazine* 83 (December 1964): 249–261.

Owomoyela, Oyekan. *Yoruba Proverbs*. Lincoln: University of Nebraska Press, 2005.

Picton, J., and J. Mack. *African Textiles: Looms, Weaving and Design*. London: Trustees of the British Museum, 1979.

Renne, Elisha P., and Babatunde Agbaje-Williams. *Yoruba Religious Textiles: Essays in Honor of Cornelius Adepegba*. Ibadan, Nigeria: Book-Builders, 2005.

Thompson, Robert Farris. *Face of the Gods: Art and Altars of Africa and the African Americas*. New York: Museum for African Art, 1993.

Willett, Frank. *Ife in the History of West African Sculpture*. London: Thames and Hudson, 1967.

Rowland Abiodun

Hausa in Nigeria and Diaspora

- Hausa History
- Hausa Men's Dress
- Hausa Women's Dress
- Hausa Children's Dress
- The Baba Riga
- The Hausa Diaspora

The Hausa are spread across West Africa but are concentrated in the arid savanna regions of northwestern Nigeria and adjoining Niger, an area referred to as Hausaland. The Hausa language, spoken as a native tongue by an estimated twenty-two million people, is the most widely spoken language in sub-Saharan Africa and is a lingua franca to over fifty million. While basically an agricultural society, the Hausa are best known for their control over long-distance trade networks of West Africa. Because of their early involvement in long-distance trade and Islamic culture, the Hausa played a definitive role in spreading dress styles throughout West Africa.

HAUSA HISTORY

Between the eleventh and thirteenth centuries, Hausa city states emerged in the area of northwestern Nigeria. Surrounded by farms, the walled cities were centers of governance and commerce and the home of craftsmen creating commodities for the local market. With time, the cities became centers of long-distance trade. Hausa traders moved into networks that crossed the Sahara to North Africa, west to the Akan kingdoms of Ghana, and south to the Nupe and northern Yoruba kingdoms. Textiles and clothing, as well as leather accessories and footwear, were important trade commodities throughout Hausa history.

Under the impulse of trade, the agrarian society produced cotton and wild silk for cloth production, and craft specialization expanded to meet the demands for trade commodities. Participation in long-distance trade also led to religious change. Islam followed the trade routes. The Hausa ruling class and traders, in part as a strategy to reinforce trade relations, were the first to accept Islam, and, by the fifteenth century, Islam was strongly established in Hausaland. These early converts adopted tailored Islamic-style clothing as a sign of affiliation and high status and invited Qur'anic scholars and teachers to settle. However, it was not until the beginning of the nineteenth century that the Islamization of the Hausa people was completed as the result of an Islamic jihad (holy war) waged by militant Muslim Fulani who lived in close proximity to the Hausa.

The resulting theocratic Sokoto caliphate (1804–1903) developed into a political and economic unit that united the Hausa with peoples of the surrounding region. As an emirate of the caliphate, the Hausa extended their dominance over West African trade. There was a boom in textile and clothing production in Hausaland and the neighboring Nupe and Ilorin Yoruba

Hausa men wearing a variety of dress styles in Dutse, Jigawa State, northern Nigeria, 2008. The man having his nails trimmed is wearing a lightweight, indigo-dyed cotton *riga*, while the barber is wearing Mecca-style pants and top. The flat-crowned embroidered caps (*hula*) are the most common contemporary headgear for men. The man on the left has a turban-wrap over his cap to indicate his pilgrimage to Mecca. Pius Utomi Ekpei/AFP/Getty Images.

emirates that united the three groups into a shared dress tradition. Fulani aristocrats, who settled as overlords of the caliphate emirates, adhered more strictly to Islamic principles, including definitions of modesty and sumptuary laws. The Hausa-Fulani leaders used dress to signal class distinctions between rulers and the ruled—a practice that has continued into the twenty-first century.

HAUSA MEN'S DRESS

Hausa men in the twenty-first century choose from three traditions: centuries-old Islamic robe ensembles; twentieth-century Mecca-type clothing; and European styles associated with the modern sector. The Islamic tailored robe ensembles were developed from Near Eastern models introduced into West Africa as early as the eleventh century. Today, similar square-cut robe ensembles are worn by men across West Africa regardless of class or religion, largely as a result of nineteenth-century Hausa long-distance trade. Although the original form was derived from the Arab world, the Hausa made the robe ensembles uniquely their own through the use of local handwoven narrow strip cloth and the application of distinctive embroidery patterns.

Hausa robe ensembles are layered. Despite the hot climate, layering clothing is the norm in adult dress. A triangular loincloth is worn under trousers (*wando*) that can take many forms, from voluminous wide-waisted pants to those with very tight legs. A short, loosely fitted tunic or shirt is worn under a "great robe" (*baba riga*). This robe, which is wider than a man's outstretched arms, is worn bunched in multiple folds over the shoulders, enhancing the layered look. A hooded cloak (*alkyabba*) of Near Eastern style is added by aristocrats. A cap (*hula*) or turban (*rawani*) for the head and sandals or slippers complete the basic ensemble. A man is expected to wear a full ensemble for formal occasions. In nonformal contexts, working or relaxing, men may wear a tunic or shirt with European-cut shorts or traditional loincloth. When a top is worn with trousers, it is expected that a cap will be worn.

The baba riga is the best known of Hausa garments. Rigas vary in size but all are square cut with large open sleeves. The body of the robe is made from a large rectangle, with huge sleeves folded back over the wearer's shoulder to avoid being dragged on the ground. The gown is embroidered with distinctive patterns, with the most elaborate work done on a huge front pocket that reaches from shoulders to knees. A variation of the basic riga is the *girke* robe that is tailored with gussets that cause the lower hem to flare so that the gown stands out from the body to further increase its bulk.

Rigas are the most expensive menswear. While any man can wear a baba riga in the twenty-first century, the textiles used and the quality and amount of embroidery signal differences in social status. Depending on means and taste, the common man can choose a riga tailored from plain-weave cotton or synthetic blend factory cloth or from the more prestigious damask and lace. The robe will always be embellished with machine embroidery of varying extent and quality. The older riga styles made from handwoven strip cloth with extensive thick hand embroidery are still the province of the aristocracy. Aristocrats and their retainers also wear rigas of prestige factory cloth distinguished by the highest quality of hand or machine embroidery.

An alternative to great robes for formal and informal wear is a more contemporary style of Islamic dress described by artist David Heathcote, who has written extensively about Hausa clothing and embroidery, as "Mecca-type" dress. Heathcote has noted that, beginning in the 1950s, Islamic styles brought back from Egypt and Saudi Arabia by hajj pilgrims became increasingly popular in urban Hausaland. Younger nonaristocratic men of the modern sector liked the lighter-weight comfortable garments made from imported and locally produced factory cloth. This led to a second tradition of Hausa embroidery. Male practitioners use braid and metallic or shiny thread, attached by hand or by machine, to duplicate the Near Eastern arabesque and geometric-patterned embroidery used on garments brought back from pilgrimage but have also developed their own motifs. A popular Mecca-type garment is the caftan (*kaftani*). The caftan is basically a long, narrow shirt reaching to the midcalf or ankles with long sleeves. It is worn with narrow matching or European trousers, embroidered cap, and sandals or slippers. Caftans are made from plain cloth in subdued hues. Embroidered decoration is usually limited to the neckline opening, a small pocket, and the bottom trouser hem.

Finally, a secular style of men's dress comes from Western influences. By the end of the nineteenth century and the imposition of British colonial rule, imported European styles of informal and formal menswear signaled connections to the new society. Today, for everyday and work clothing, imported new and used clothes and locally made Western styles are readily available. Men working in the modern sector may choose the European-style business or leisure suit, but in more ceremonial contexts, the riga ensemble is still preferred over European suits.

A man's wardrobe may contain garments of all three styles depending on rank, occupation, education, and means. The most extensive wardrobes belong to aristocrats, who stockpile the finest of rigas for wear and for gifts. A farmer, craftsman, or laborer may choose between basic Hausa or European garments that are often worn to rags over time; for public events, he will have robe ensembles or Mecca-type dress. A middle-class businessman or government bureaucrat in the modern sector chooses among all three styles for work and other public contexts. One category of garment found in every man's wardrobe is a robe or Mecca-style ensemble of white clothing that is characterized as "proper" dress for Muslims because of its association with Islamic piety. White ensembles are worn for everyday dress by some and in ceremonial contexts by most. When life ends, one's last garment is a white shroud.

Dressing the head is essential to the Hausa man as an indicator of both rank and Islamic modesty. Men keep their hair closely cut or shaved, but, in public, the head is always covered. Most headgear favored by Hausa men is of the Mecca type. These include the densely embroidered brimless flat-crowned cap or hula, the Muslim skullcap favored by Qur'anic scholars, the turban, and the fez (often worn under turbans). More rarely seen are indigenous styles similar to skullcaps but with taller floppy crowns and earflaps or the sun-shade work hat with a wide circular brim woven from split palm leaves.

The flat-crowned hula, introduced in the mid-twentieth century, is the most common and distinctive item of everyday headgear for contemporary Hausa men. There is a high demand for the relatively inexpensive hand-embroidered caps. They are cheap because cap embroidery is a part-time activity for boys, young men, and women that entails a small capital outlay for materials and limited time outlay. A typical embroidered design is composed of a series of rectangles of contrasting color with repeated motifs running around the cap. Designs are particularly prone to fashion changes, with new motifs continually emerging depicting such things as airplanes, cars, and buildings.

The turban is a symbol of the pilgrimage to Mecca, a journey expected of all Muslims in their lifetimes. A typical turban is fashioned from a long cloth strip that is wound around the head over a small cap or fez. It is the preferred headgear for aristocrats, their retainers, and some wealthy men as a marker of rank and prestige. White turbans, as an indicator of Muslim piety, are worn for religious events, and a turban of colored cloth is appropriate for important secular events. Today, turbans are often made from imported prestige cloth, but one sees turbans of white and deeply dyed and glazed indigo strip-cloth in leadership display contexts.

Footwear is chosen from locally made or imported sandals or slippers made from leather, plastic, and rubber; leather shoes (with and without backs); and Western-style factory-made shoes, manufactured locally and imported. A distinctive form of Hausa sandal is decorated with narrow multicolored leather strips of red, green, black, and white sewn into the sole and straps.

Hausa men wear little or no jewelry. Necklaces and beads are not considered fitting to Islamic piety, although most men carry prayer beads. In addition, some men carry or wear decorated leather amulets that contain written passages from the Qur'an. Silver rings, bracelets, and armlets that have a protective function were more common in the past. Bags, portfolios, and wallets of cow, goat, or reptile leather are often carried on the shoulder or under the arm. Finally, heavy-scented perfumes brought from the Near East are popular with men.

HAUSA WOMEN'S DRESS

Women's dress is not as varied or as distinctively Hausa as that of men. A woman's complete ensemble includes a loin undergarment, wrapper, short- or long-sleeved blouse, head tie, and a shawl to cover the head and body as an overgarment. The ubiquitous African wrapper is the most basic garment. Traditionally, married women wore wrappers that tightly covered the body from above the breasts to the ankles, while young girls wore the wrapper with bared breasts. Today, in the privacy of the family compound, a woman may wear only a wrapper around her hips when working, sometimes with a second wrapper to cover the breasts, and a head kerchief. Outside the women's area, Islamic modesty dictates a full dress ensemble. Women are more adventuresome than men in their choice of textiles. Wrappers made from handwoven cloth can still be purchased in the markets, but factory cloth is the overwhelming choice for women's clothing. Colorful

wax prints and locally tie-dyed textiles are the most popular for informal wear, and damasks, brocades, and lace ensembles are preferred for formal occasions. Embroidery is used sparingly on women's dress. While Heathcote found a few examples of heavily embroidered women's wrappers, there is no evidence of a continuing tradition of Hausa women's embroidered dress. This may be due to perceptions of women's subordinate position and the importance of embroidered dress as a male status symbol in Hausa society.

As in many African societies, Hausa women have their hair plaited and arranged into elaborate hairstyles. However, the styled hair is usually covered by a head tie or kerchief. The head tie can be of cotton or synthetic cloth that matches a woman's wrapper and blouse or of a contrasting material. More formal contexts call for prestigious textiles such as heavy brocades, shiny silks, or rayons. Women who have completed the pilgrimage wear a turban over a cap and under a draped shawl. Like men, women can choose between a variety of locally made or imported sandals and slippers.

Women like to accessorize with beads and earrings. Beads and pendants of glass, stone, and plastic are worn as necklaces and as waist beads. Gold and silver earrings are made locally or imported from the Near East and the West. Locally made brass earrings were sold in the twentieth century but are seldom seen today. Cosmetic ointments and powders are used on the face and body. Henna is also used on the hands. The eyes are a focal point and may be lined with kohl, a black powdered mineral (antimony sulfide); this practice is also found in the Near East. Cut, tattooed, or painted face and body marking done in the past is seldom seen today.

A Hausa woman spends much of her life in the seclusion of her family compound, an indicator of adherence to Islamic principles. Under the stricter rules of Islam introduced in the nineteenth century, *purdah* (the seclusion of women from public observation) was instituted. From the age of marriage (usually between eleven and fourteen years old) to menopause, women are isolated in the female quarters of family walled compounds. Women can leave the compounds only for short visits to neighbors and families, ceremonial events held in the women's courtyards, and medical emergencies.

Seclusion does not preclude the expansion of a woman's wardrobe. It is continually augmented, as husbands are expected, as a socioreligious obligation, to give their wives cloth, clothing, and accessories on occasions such as Islamic celebrations. In this Islamic society where a man can have up to four wives, a husband is expected to treat his wives equally, so often identical cloth is given to all. This encourages group dressing, where all appear together wearing the same textile to display unity, a custom shared with other non-Muslim African peoples. With the accumulation of new outfits and accessories for each special occasion, a woman is free to wear, save, sell, or give items of her wardrobe away.

In the contemporary scene, educated Hausa women who participate in the modern sector in business and government choose between styles. A woman may choose European styles, Mecca-type loosely fitting caftans with some embroidery, or fashionable wrapper ensembles made by local fashion designers. Another expression of modernity is the fact that in the palaces of the Hausa-Fulani leaders, women, despite seclusion, can wear the latest in Saudi Arabian Islamic fashions.

Two young women in Zaranda market near Jos, northern Nigeria, 1959. They wear typical cotton factory-cloth wrappers with short-sleeved blouses and head coverings. The woman on the left wears a matching wrapper and blouse with a head kerchief, while the other wears a wax-print wrapper, contrasting blouse, and head tie. Both have accessorized with jewelry and have enhanced their appearance with face powder, lipstick, and powdered kohl to emphasize their brows and eyes. Photograph by Eliot Elisofon, 1959. EEPA EECL 2629. Eliot Elisofon Photographic Archives, National Museum of African Art, Smithsonian Institution.

A variety of *riga* types are worn by participants in a morning greeting ceremony held by the emir of Katsina (seated in chair), Nigeria, 1959. The emir can be identified by the royal cloak over his *riga* and turban with veil covering his lower face. In the front center, a man is wearing an embroidered *riga* of the old type, made of hand-woven strip cloth and an indigo-dyed strip-cloth turban. Religious leaders are identified by their white *rigas*, and palace guards by their red and green garments. Photograph by Eliot Elisofon, 1959. EEPA EECL 1383. Eliot Elisofon Photographic Archives, National Museum of African Art, Smithsonian Institution.

HAUSA CHILDREN'S DRESS

Hausa children's clothing is not distinctive. Traditionally, small children were often naked but might have a string of beads around the hips, while older boys wore loincloths. In the hot, dry season, young children at home still wear little or nothing, except for leather waist cords with protective Islamic amulets. For older boys, European-style shorts or a shirt that hangs below the hips have replaced more traditional loincloths; girls wear wrappers and blouses. If not in school uniforms, the girls put on wrappers and blouses with head ties, while boys commonly adopt Mecca-type clothing with a small amount of machine-sewn embroidery around the neck opening. Clothing worn by children in more formal contexts usually mimics adult clothing.

THE BABA RIGA

Of all the items of Hausa dress, the baba riga is historically and culturally the most important. The densely embroidered robe epitomizes the highest artistic achievement in Hausa dress and the unique qualities of this tradition. The riga was made and worn by Hausa from the earliest days of contact with Islamic traders and clerics in West Africa and produced in Hausaland as a major

long-distance trade commodity for at least five hundred years. Rigas destined for trade tend to be simple and have only a small amount of embroidery. The importance of great robes as commodities explains the complex chain of regional specialists involved in their manufacture. As already noted, production and trade of cloth and clothing in the Hausa area greatly increased in the nineteenth century Sokoto caliphate. In a desire to control the production and to increase quantity and quality, Hausa traders settled craftsmen into enclaves of spinners, weavers, strip-cloth sewers, embroiders, tailors, and cloth beaters around the great trade centers like Kano in northern Nigeria. A similar movement occurred in the Nupe and Ilorin Yoruba areas. These clusters of localized specialists are still producing similar cloth and garments in the twenty-first century, so that the older riga styles of handwoven cloth worn by the Hausa, Nupe, and Yoruba today are strikingly similar.

The finest baba rigas are embellished with dense embroidery and have been worn traditionally as markers of wealth and high status. In the twenty-first century, the most prized forms of great robes worn by the Hausa, Nupe, and Yoruba duplicate the magnificence of the nineteenth-century prestige forms. In the twenty-first century, trade linkages continue with Hausa aristocrats still recognizing the skill of Nupe embroiders and commissioning them to make some of their finest robes. The traditionally sanctioned

A member of the Hausa nobility in Katsina, northern Nigeria, 1996, at the Eid-el-Fitr Sallah celebration that marks the end of the annual Muslim fasting period, Ramadan. Riding on a highly decorated horse with elaborately embroidered trappings, the aristocrat's layered robes and turban, with a royal cloak of expensive imported fabric embellished with embroidery, project the Hausa "aesthetic of bigness" that emphasizes his high social status and political authority. Photograph by Carol Beckwith/Angela Fisher.

riga-style robes are constructed from indigenous cotton and/or silk narrow strip cloth produced on the horizontal double-heddle loom by male weavers in the region of the old Sokoto caliphate. The strips, averaging three and a half inches (nine centimeters) wide, are colorful and heavy, with two color and material choices favored and used in the construction of robes: (1) *saki* strips of indigo-dyed blue cotton minutely checked or striped with white; and (2) *barage* strips of red silk with white cotton stripes. The long strips are sold in bundles to sewers who cut them to the proper length and edge-stitch the pieces together to make the cloth suitable for tailoring. Embroiderers, who are usually Islamic clerics working on a part-time basis, embellish the cloth with distinctive patterns of geometric and curved shapes before the final tailoring is done. Heathcote has suggested that this tradition developed over the past five hundred years in the Hausa area. New motifs continually appear, but change is slow. Some motif clusters such as "two knives" and "eight knives" observed two centuries ago in West Africa are still used and play an important role in legitimizing rank. A second tradition sprang up in the 1920s, when sewing machines were introduced into Nigeria by European merchants. Male machine embroiderers are full-time specialists working for the market and on commission. While most of the patterns are not complex, and some duplicate the older motifs, the embroiderers also work with patrons to create new designs.

The cultural importance of the baba riga ensemble is most clearly shown in leadership dress, which involves the use of out-of-the-ordinary materials, embellishments, and accessories to visually express the powers of office. In the courts of Hausa-Fulani emirs, the great robes gain their fullest meaning as historical icons and symbols of wealth and power. For important secular and religious events, inside and outside the palace, emirs and their attendants appear in the finest embroidered robes to project public images of the highest social status, political authority, and religious piety. Wearing the great robes is part of an "aesthetic of bigness" in leadership dress that the Hausa share with many other African societies. In Hausa display contexts, the bulkiness of the dress amplifies the leader's actual size to generate a larger-than-life presence. The impression of bigness is further enhanced through wearing more than one great robe simultaneously so that heavy textiles increase the projected size of the body. Through layering the heavy fabric gowns and the use of accessories and regalia, the dress ensemble adds to the impression of richness, strength, and authority displayed by a leader. The densely embroidered patterns that cover Hausa prestige gowns add to the effect.

During equestrian processions, such as religious holidays that mark the beginning and end of the Muslim month of fasting, aristocrats are mounted on horses dressed as carefully as their riders. An emir wears several layered, multicolored baba rigas and a flowing cloak embellished with shining arabesque designs over voluminous embroidered trousers and a shiny *turkudi* turban of indigo-glazed cloth and carries a sword or staff of authority. Multiple colorful saddle blankets of different materials and patterns and appliqué leather and silver horse trappings provide a complex image of pattern, color, and reflected light. Surrounded by attendants on foot and horseback who are also dressed for display, the emir on his moving equestrian throne is a powerful icon of political presence, power, and authority. The impact on the spectator is one of aesthetic overload and awe.

As leadership regalia, the classic gowns worn by aristocrats and palace retainers, regarded as "robes of honor," belong to the state and are kept in the palace treasury. New robes are continually commissioned because the supply diminishes due to the practice of gifting. As a sign of favor, an emir may present the finest robes, some of which he has worn, to favored palace personnel, government officers, and honored guests. The presentation of robes of honor is a political act that can be recognition of mutual respect, alliance, superior-subordinate relationships, acknowledgement of services rendered, and a pledge of support and protection. There is evidence that robes of honor were being used in this way in West Africa as early as the eleventh century, and even earlier in the Islamic states of the Near East.

THE HAUSA DIASPORA

While dictionary definitions of *diaspora* focus on the scattering and resettlement of people, here the definition is broadened to include the diaspora of dress across geographical space. In this expanded sense, it is possible to identify two Hausa diasporas. The first began centuries ago with the movement and resettlement of Hausa traders and craft artisans along the long-distance trade networks of West Africa and the routes followed by Muslim pilgrims to Mecca. This diaspora of people and culture reached its height in the nineteenth-century Sokoto caliphate. The second, more recent Hausa diaspora is a result of globalization. For example, Hausa traders are part of the twenty-first-century New York City milieu, and the Hausa-style riga, largely in the form of the Yoruba *agbada*, is a staple on Internet sites that appeal to African Americans.

References and Further Reading

Adamu, Mahdi. *The Hausa Factor in West African History*. Zaria and Ibadan, Nigeria: Ahmadu Bello University Press and Oxford University Press Nigeria, 1978.

Heathcote, David. "Hausa Embroidered Dress." *African Arts* 5, no. 2 (1972): 201–216.

Heathcote, David. "Aspects of Embroidery in Nigeria." In *The Art of African Textiles: Technology, Tradition and Lurex*, edited by John Picton, 39–40. London: Lund Humphries Publishers, 1995.

Kriger, Colleen E. "Robes of the Sokoto Caliphate." *African Arts*, 21, no. 3 (1988): 52–57, 78–79.

Kriger, Colleen E. *Cloth in West African History*. Lanham, MD: Altamira Press, 2006.

Perani, Judith A. "The Cloth Connection: Patrons and Producers of Hausa and Nupe Prestige Strip-weave." In *History, Design and Craft in West African Strip-woven Cloth*, 95–112. Washington, DC: National Museum of African Art, 1992.

Perani, Judith A., and Norma H. Wolff. *Cloth, Dress and Art Patronage in Africa*. Oxford, UK: Berg, 1992.

Perani, Judith A., and Norma H. Wolff. "Embroidered Gown and Equestrian Ensembles of the Kano Aristocracy." *African Arts* 25, no. 3 (1992): 70–81.

Pokrant, R.J. "Tailors of Kano City." In *From Craft to Industry*, edited by Esther Goody. Cambridge, UK: Cambridge University Press, 1982.

Norma H. Wolff

See also West Africa; Ghana; Niger.

Igbo in Nigeria and Diaspora

- Igbo Ukwu
- The Twentieth-Century Igbo
- Temporary Body Arts
- Title Arts and Chieftaincy
- Masks, Costumes, and Masking

One of the largest populations of West African peoples at over twenty million, the Igbo have a history of dress and personal decoration lasting over one thousand years. The archaeological sites of Igbo Ukwu, dating from the ninth and tenth centuries C.E., begin this record in the heart of Igbo country, twenty-five miles (forty kilometers) east of the Niger River and about one hundred miles (one hundred sixty-one kilometers) north of the Atlantic Ocean. Although the documentation is largely blank in the centuries between the flowering of Igbo Ukwu and the late nineteenth and early twentieth centuries, when modern historical records begin, there can be no question that the Igbo today are firmly connected with their ancient forebears. This is seen in the material culture of dress and ornamentation, as well as their expressive uses and meanings.

At least three types of transformation occur with personal arts and dress: first, a male or female body is altered and enhanced according to local aesthetic values; second, these ensembles are expressive and meaningful statements about gender, status, wealth, and sometimes spiritual and/or political office; and, third, in masquerades, a new persona is created by virtue of what the masker wears, carries, and how he (maskers are overwhelmingly male here, as in most of Africa) behaves. There are everyday and permanent forms of adornment, but the more visually arresting are those that are worn occasionally: for coming-of-age rites, meetings of titled people, and festivals (including second burial celebrations).

IGBO UKWU

Discovered in 1938 but not scientifically excavated until 1959 to 1960, the extraordinary objects of the Igbo Ukwu (Great Igbo) were found within one compound—that of the Anozie family—in three closely spaced pits. These were (1) an undisturbed burial chamber containing the remains of an important dignitary, (2) an undisturbed shrine or storehouse for valuable ritual objects and regalia, and (3) a disposal pit. Comprised of copper and (mostly) leaded bronze castings, ceramics, ivory, and imported beads, the objects were undoubtedly the ritual apparatus and regalia associated with a wealthy priest or king and the clan and institution that he led and that held sway over several hundred square miles (about a thousand square kilometers). That clan and institution survive to this day as a title-conferring and medicine-making priesthood headed by a man given the title of *EzeNri*, (king of the Nri people), Umunri being the clan name—literally, the children of Nri.

The careful reconstruction drawing made of the burial, based on archaeologist Thurstan Shaw's meticulous excavation of that site and its finds, shows a seated, apparently wealthy dignitary with elaborate personal adornment: a bronze corona, a robe with beaded decorations, multiple pectoral elements including bronze work and beads, bronze armlets and anklets, beaded leglets, and still other copper and bronze regalia. Over 100,000 stone and glass beads were found in this one chamber, many imported from as far away as India; these and the other regalia indicate a person of substantial wealth and a culture engaged in long-distance trade. Many other ornaments of distinctive style and meticulous workmanship were found in the three excavations, most probably worn by clan members, particularly its leaders, on the body (the pendants, wristlets, and anklets) or held regalia, items such as staffs, weapons, fans, or fly whisks.

The pendants and other ornaments feature human, elephant, leopard, and ram heads, as well as snakes, mudfish, and birds, all in styles not duplicated elsewhere in Nigeria or West Africa. The human head pendants as well as the face of a small equestrian figure feature overall facial scarification known in modern times as *ichi* (forehead scars). Such scars have long been the prerogative of certain titles within the Ozo title system over which the Nri clan still presides. The buried dignitary was almost certainly the head of this clan over a thousand years ago, and the many items of regalia and personal adornment, while not identical in style to those still worn by title holders, are similar in purpose and meaning.

In Igbo Ukwu, then, there was a sumptuous program of personal adornment firmly dated to the ninth and tenth centuries C.E., surely among the earliest of analogous leadership complexes known from West Africa. Further, the metal castings of these ornaments (and the vessels and other ritual equipment found) are often intricate works of art, lost-wax (or possibly latex) castings in a confident and mature style that is consistent across the hundreds of excavated pieces.

THE TWENTIETH-CENTURY IGBO

Ozo and related title systems among twentieth- and early-twenty-first-century Igbo peoples remain the most prominent sites of fine dress and personal ornamentation (apart from the few instances of chiefs' regalia among peoples who had few chiefs or kings) even if varied temporary and permanent kinds of body decoration are far more democratic and widely distributed, beginning for girls at quite young ages. Scarification and tattoo were widely practiced during the first half of the twentieth century (and surely long before as well), but, by the year 2000, these practices had largely been abandoned. They are currently best documented in statuary and masks made early in the last century or before. Such permanent body marks varied regionally (the Igbo were never a unified people within a centralized political system), but typically, in most areas, scarification involved a panel of three or more lines from high on the chest to the navel or below, called *mbubu* (torso scars).

Sometimes these keloid patterns were supplemented with lines radiating outward from the navel, while in other instances (or areas), the chest had a pattern of intersecting diamond-shaped lines, again formed by keloids. Arms and legs were rarely scarred or tattooed, and faces were scarred only if an individual was involved in title taking, although tattoos adorned many women (and a few men) who had not taken titles. Such tattooing, most elaborate in the northeast (Izzi, Ezza, and Ikwo peoples) and still visible on older people in the 1980s, is best seen today in masks from these regions, which often show a diagonal tattoo from just below the eye near the nose to the outer part of the jaw, as well as temple markings (circles or squares) and a vertical tattoo line upward from the tip of the nose and bisecting the forehead, again with pigment imbedded beneath the top layers of skin. In young women, both keloidal scars and tattoos were usually applied by specialists during their seclusion prior to marriage; men, too, were scarred before marriage, usually during age-grade initiations.

TEMPORARY BODY ARTS

Body painting and other forms of temporary adornment, including fancy hairstyling, were once widespread, especially in younger women, although these arts are rare today. Girls, especially, were elaborately adorned for their coming-out ceremonies from fattening houses. During the months of seclusion, little clothing was worn by these young adolescent women, nor was it needed for protection against cold weather, and girls' bodies were often rubbed all over with orange or yellow camwood powder. Sometimes these pigments had stamped or painted patterns, and sometimes the color was plain. When they were reincorporated into the community and on display as marriageable women, the young women invoked more elaborate decorations: meticulously sculptured and plaited hair, indigo patterns *uli/uri* (body paint) painted on the body, limbs, and face and sometimes the wearing of heavy brass coils on the legs or heavy, flat, round, platelike brass anklets embellished with punched and incised patterns.

One prevalent hairstyle (among many forms) was a semicircular crest, front to back, built up with mud (and sometimes palm oil) mixed with charcoal, known best from "maiden masks" of the north and central regions. Carvers of such masks often dramatically embellished these crests, sometimes with three of them front to back, and usually in openwork. Indeed, the hair crests on many masks are more baroque and complex than any actual girls' coiffures ever recorded. Shaped hair was often further enhanced by the addition of combs, hairpins, buttons, brass (and, later, aluminum) circlets, and jewelry. Still other hairstyles involved the separation of hair into thin strands, twirling them, and plastering the hair down, as well as pulling it into pigtails or patterned plaits. In lieu of dressing hair, girls in some areas wore tall, hollow ceramic cones, flared at the top and bottom, with geometric patterns in relief. Fiber wigs mimicking meticulously detailed plaited hairstyles were also worn. Children often had their short hair shaved in pleasing curvilinear patterns to mark special events. Waist beads—earlier locally made beads, then Venetian and other European versions, then thin plastic circular beads—and cloths were common, as were necklaces of leopard teeth and ivory bracelets borrowed for the occasion.

Uli/uri constitute designs, motifs, and patterns painted by women with the juices of several indigo plants to beautify the body (and, with other local pigments, to embellish wall surfaces). For festive occasions, both men and women had uli painted, but it was more common among women. Artist Liz Willis and art

Ozo titled man with *uli* body painting, red bead necklace, and two caps. Mgbala Agwa, 1983. Photograph by Herbert M. Cole.

historian Sarah Adams have independently recorded well over two hundred named uli designs and patterns and plumb the depths of this painting form—its many styles, uses, and meanings. Uli is also a form that has been revived by contemporary painters and graphic artists. Although many types or styles of uli exist (regional and individual), most are characterized by fine lines that swell, taper, and turn back on themselves by delicate curves and hooks and sometimes dense patterns of parallel curves, almost all painting being asymmetrical. Few recognizable objects are drawn because uli is substantially abstract; yet the names of motifs mostly refer to real objects or processes such as kola nuts, leaves, baskets, mortar, the walk of a deer, a snake's movement, a snail, flies' eyes, a star, waist beads, and many other things and notions in the Igbo world. Most scholars, however, do not believe that many uli artists had a consciously developed and meaningful program or narrative in mind when painting a body other than to beautify it by enhancing its good features, minimizing the less good ones, and—also implied by overall beautification—rendering the person morally clean and good.

If uli is the Igbo body art par excellence, it is by no means the only kind of body painting. A wash of white clay or yellow camwood is sometimes applied to the dark skin of bodies prior to uli painting so the patterns will show up well, and both these

pigments have favorable ascribed moral and medicinal properties that may sometimes motivate their use (with or without uli).
A subtle form of body art that was still practiced occasionally
in the 1960s results from painting tight circular designs of an ir-
ritating plant decoction—mainly cocoyam (*ede*)—called *edeala*,
that, when washed away, leaves low-relief patterns lasting a few
days. Indigo patterns, on the other hand, lasted a week or more
and were very widely distributed in many different styles that varied with time and space. Bodies were also patterned with stamps
or pattern blocks. Early in the twentieth century (and doubtless earlier), teeth were filed, and children's hair was shaved into
curvilinear patterns to celebrate events such as recovery from a
debilitating sickness.

TITLE ARTS AND CHIEFTAINCY

The ornate material culture of Igbo Ukwu and its regalia of title-
granting Nri peoples and their leaders are paralleled by many
forms of personal decoration affected by Ozo titled individuals
as recorded during the twentieth century. Most of the specific
modern forms are different, and frankly less impressive, as works
of art than their ninth- and tenth-century antecedents, but the
forms and their placement on the body are largely the same: hats
(with fish eagle feathers), beaded necklaces (formerly carnelian,
more recently red glass), anklets (along with bracelets, sometimes
of ivory), staffs, leather fans, fly whisks, elephant tusk trumpets,
and stools (the last not positively identified in Igbo Ukwu). Ichi
facial scarification identical to that on Igbo Ukwu works was still
being practiced in the early twentieth century, and it was still a
prerogative of titles in the Ozo system within a few miles of Nri
village groups where the ancient pieces were excavated. Special
cloth is also usually worn; these days, the cloth is often imported
(such as embroidered Hausa gowns, *riga*, or *tokare*), but earlier
it was locally woven. While string anklets are worn every day by
Ozo title holders—by which they are recognized as such—the
men reserve most of their title regalia for special meetings and
festivities.

Members of Ekpe, the men's society in Cross River Igbo areas
(Ohafia, Abiriba, Arochukwu), have long worn a dramatic tie-
dyed cloth called *ukara*. These indigo cloths are decorated with
precise white motifs and patterns (which were tied off or sewn
with raffia before the cloth was dyed indigo), including *nsibidi*
(ideographic writing) and other Ekpe signs. Ekpe or Ngbe (meaning "leopard" in the Efik language) is the graded men's society
shared among several Cross River groups, and the symbolism
of ukara—its checkerboard and other small-unit blue and white
patterns—suggests that a man wearing such a fabric is clothed in
leopard skin. While many of the motifs and patterns on ukara
remain secret, it is clear that they have important meanings; each
grade of Ekpe has its own graphic, spoken, and gestured nsibidi
signs apparently used as passwords and tests of a man's achievements and the knowledge associated with his Ekpe grade. Thus,
ukara cloth embodies a rich and deep symbolic system, a system
of knowledge still carefully guarded by its custodians.

Women also take titles in some Igbo areas. In Onitsha and
other northern Igbo regions, huge circlets of elephant tusk ivory
were worn as anklets and on the lower arms. Various beads encircled the neck, sometimes a very large single coral bead on a strand
of elephant tail hair; expensive, often imported, cloths were also
part of titled women's wardrobes.

In precolonial times, titled men and societies such as Ekpe
served as the governments of most Igbo village groups, along
with councils of elders; yet a few communities east of the Niger
have long been headed by men known locally as kings. These
are places where influence from the Edo culture of the Benin
kingdom is acknowledged—although the regalia does not much
resemble that of the Benin court. Nevertheless, it differs from
most Igbo title regalia. (Note that Igbo Ukwu and Nri show no
evident Benin influence.) Onitsha kings and lesser chiefs, for example, wear crowns that in the mid- and late twentieth century
were studded with feathers (egret or fish eagle) and imported ostrich plumes—many of them white, others dyed a rainbow of
color—surrounding a central pillar that emerges from a mound-
like shape, the whole crown then resembling a tree with branches.
Surrounding the base are, first, a coiled decoration resembling
a snake; then, dangles of small animals (such as lizards), tiny
mirrors, iron tools, and other valuables. This chiefly crown is a
miniature version of *ijele*, the spectacularly huge masks—clearly
cosmic symbols—constructed and danced in Onitsha and in the
Anambra River valley that display many key symbols of leadership and the sacred realm.

Both title arts and everyday dress in late-twentieth-century
Igboland are somewhat different from the foregoing account.
There are chieftaincy shops in many towns and cities today, and
booths in markets, that sell all manner of imported cloth that is
embroidered on the spot and fancy new caps of beads and feathers to replace the red fez worn by titled men for the decades surrounding 1950. Some colorful printed cloths with lions' or dogs'
heads are printed with the words *title* or *chief* as if to announce
the status of the wearer. There are fans of vinyl and fancy cow-tail
fly whisks on newly carved (or even plastic) handles of a sort not
seen seventy-five years ago.

Everyday dress for professional Igbo men and women is similar to urban fashions (suits for men and pantsuits, slacks, and
blouses or dresses for women) seen in European or U.S. cities.
Many such ensembles are locally made. Rural dress remains informal. Children or poorer people often wear secondhand clothes
imported from abroad; men in the large middle class wear casual
shorts or trousers with short-sleeved shirts, and women wear wax-
print wrappers with blouses. Work clothes are often T-shirts for
both genders with shorts for men and ankle-length wrappers for
women. There does not appear to be any accepted Igbo national
dress in the early twenty-first century, although, from independence in 1960 until the late 1970s and early 1980s, both genders
affected outfits of colorful wax prints (first imported, then locally
manufactured): pants and shirts for men, wrappers with plain-
colored, often eyelet, blouses for women. In fact, though, at any
market these days, one will see a tremendous variety of clothing,
much of it quite colorful.

In the 1970s and 1980s, many affluent (or aspiring) Igbo men
adopted the voluminous *agbada*, a Yoruba word for a dress ensemble of Hausa origin (in northern Nigeria) consisting of
drawstring pantaloons and a very large tunic with extensive embroidery around the neck and often at the borders of both top
and bottom garments. Such garments were worn by businessmen and government employees, especially, and the style was
often seen by outsiders as a national Nigerian dress. They were
made from varied fabrics, but usually colorful wax prints, locally
woven strip-cloth, or more expensive and sumptuous brocades.
Anthropologist Misty Bastian has said that some young women

in Onitsha in the late 1980s adopted this usually male costume, which became known as "alhaji style" from its association with Muslim men who had made the hajj—the journey to Mecca. Igbo women commissioned and wore this "power garment," often employing rich brocade—albeit with less cloth yardage than most men and with other modifications—along with gold necklaces, bracelets, and earrings, as well as perfume and women's shoes, thus feminizing somewhat an essentially male style. A mixed reception greeted this style choice by women; older men were especially critical. Some women felt the young women who adopted it effaced their femininity, suppressing their breasts, for example. Others accepted it as a satirical comment on the despised northerners. The alhaji style is symptomatic of extensive experimentation and variation in both male and female Igbo dress throughout its known history.

MASKS, COSTUMES, AND MASKING

The ensembles worn by masqueraders provide a bewildering variety of natural and man-made materials and objects that embody multiple effects, symbols, and allusions in their work of creating the characters and personalities seen in masquerade performances. Indeed, masquerades are the quintessential Igbo art form, for virtually every village group has several named masking institutions; nearly all males are involved with them and the sometimes hundreds of specifically named maskers they sponsor.

The mask or headdress itself, which in the Igbo language is called *ishi mmuo*, "head (of a) spirit," while important and perhaps focal, is but one of many material forms marshaled to create a particular persona. Auditory and olfactory elements may be involved as well. Many maskers wear rattles (seed pods, quills, even spoons) or bells (sometimes considered the voice of the spirit), while others speak unintelligibly through voice disguisers or make an audible "whoosh" as they brush against audience members. Some very powerful spirits deliberately exude a stench as an aspect of their power, at times the result of blood, liquor, and other sacrifices made to wake up, enliven, or embolden the spirit. But the main effects in creating a costume are various visual, material objects—leaves, raffia, fiber netting, knitted yarn, and cloth of many sorts.

Because there are literally thousands of types of Igbo mask-costume combinations—or, better, "embodied spirits"—what follows can only be an impressionistic sampling. Igbo masking in the last hundred years has become progressively more secular and less instrumental. Where many masks once had powerful governmental and judicial roles, most today appear primarily for entertainment.

The "naturalistic" masker is well exemplified by characters in the *Njenji* parade among the Afikpo Igbo, as reported by anthropologist Simon Ottenberg. This relatively secular display involves as many as one hundred and fifty masked/costumed players who walk through the community, starting and ending in their home village. Several men wear married adult women's (European-style) dresses or skirts with blouses, while others wear adult men's suits, a jacket with shorts, or Hausa gowns—and generically portray such people in Afikpo life. Some of these maskers walk arm-in-arm as couples. Many masks are quite naturalistically carved, although the faces are red, pink, or yellow (occasionally white) and project forward from the face, so

it is clear that these are maskers rather than real people. These "local" types, including teachers and students, are supplemented by players dressed as Yoruba people or a white Catholic priest among many others.

Such "real" people maskers, however, are overshadowed by the unmarried *agbogho mma* (girl spirits), whose masks are feminine with a seated "child" at its top, and with a large false hairpiece at the back decorated with yarn and feathers; the costumes consist of shawls and strands of yarn over the shoulders and many colored scarves (borrowed from wives or girlfriends) tucked into strands of plastic waist beads and hanging almost to the ground. The costume is feminine and elegant, yet a kind of humorous parody of what girls once wore. It does not attempt to copy what women actually wore.

The best known of all Igbo masking ensembles is the *agbogho mmuo* (maiden spirit) of the north-central region (the Afikpo agbogho mma is a variant). The bodies of these are close-fitting appliqué suits with multicolored geometric patterns, danced with a white-faced, fine-featured mask with a more or less elaborate superstructure. Around 1900, these single-crested masks had a skeletal aspect that stressed their role as ancestral ghosts returning for a brief sojourn to the living community. Through the century, this emphasis shifted toward more elaborate hairstyles featuring three openwork crests, sometimes with pigtails and combs.

Huge naturalistic animal masks, such as elephants and birds (and probably others), were also constructed and danced in the 1980s; perhaps such masks were known earlier, but none have been recorded. Regardless, we are reminded that intervillage competition means that new mask forms are being invented yearly to this day—which helps to account for the inventive and varied forms seen at any one time and the hundreds or thousands of masks in existence. One of the two elephants of the 1980s was danced by two men; the other was danced by four men, one inside each huge leg of the cloth animal, which had a plastic hose-pipe as its trunk—another reminder of the continuing innovation characteristic of Igbo masking.

Moving away from naturalistic maskers to netted or knitted body suits, those of Ekpe and Okonkwo societies danced by Ohafia, Abiriba, Afikpo, and Arochukwu Igbo peoples are characteristic. Body suits, however, are widely distributed in Igboland and beyond. While these tend to fit the body closely and allow vigorous and athletic dancing, their featureless faces and either bright multicolored or monochromatic bodies signal a lack of human appearance, thus reinforcing their spirit designation.

Another type of mask/costume that departs from the human model is the type known especially from Ekpeye Igbo areas influenced by Niger Delta cultures and their water-spirit masquerades called Owu; these feature elaborate tableau superstructures in the form of a boat, fish, multiple small carvings of people, or a composite abstraction. Sharks, crocodiles, and hippos, usually with some human features, are found, as are Mamy Wata tableaux, or multiheaded ensembles resembling earlier Bende Igbo and Cross River headdresses. Some water spirits from Ahoada (Ekpeye) are inventive semiabstract composites pieced together from many separate pieces of wood; animal snouts and fish fins are sometimes recognizable, but these are overlain with many curved, conical, and hornlike devices, so the results appear quite abstract. Some of these are danced with costumes of imported *george* cloth (India madras), while others have richly layered multicolored cloth ensembles. In many cases, there seem to be efforts to show the spirits—and their sponsoring men's groups—as wealthy and able to afford the most sumptuous of spirit clothing.

Still other spirit ensembles are huge cones of cloth (many single pieces sewn together) out of the top of which projects a fairly naturalistic carved wood head. Such conical bodies are severely nonhuman despite being topped by a human head, and again these are widely distributed across Igbo territory.

Large, fierce male masks, usually with bared, snaggled teeth and a multihorned superstructure (often with blades and hooks), have as a class been labeled *mgbedike* (time of the brave) from one of their more widespread and celebrated types. Mystery, stubbornness, aggression, bravado, destruction, fearlessness, and medicinal power associated with the wilds characterize these spirits—notions expressed in their dress ensembles. Their large, dark, and bulky costumes are hung with seeds or quills, animal skins, skulls, bones, or snail shells, and their dances are so unruly and aggressive that they must be restrained by attendants. Like many powerful maskers, they wear young green palm leaves, *omu*, to signal the sacred and danger, and they are likely to wield a machete. Conceptually, these maskers celebrate the beauty of (male) power, whereas maidens stress the power of (female) beauty. Like large Okoroshi Ojo masks from a hundred miles (one hundred sixty-one kilometers) further south, these masks once had political and judicial powers.

The most spectacular of Igbo masks and probably the largest mask in West Africa—seventeen to eighteen feet (five meters) high by eight or nine feet (two and half meters) in diameter—is ijele, mentioned above as relating to (and probably deriving from) Onitsha chiefs' crowns. Constructed of appliqué panels of imported cloth hanging from a wooden disk that rests on the carrier's head, an ijele has a towering superstructure of intersecting rainbowlike arches. From the disk's center springs a "tree trunk" with branches and flowers that rise out of a conical cloth mound (representing a termite hill). A python surrounds the disk, along with dozens of tassels. Thirty or more straw- or foam-stuffed models of other maskers, genre scenes, mirrors, and animals such as elephants, leopards, and eagles are spread among the branches. The entire structure is anthropomorphized by the presence of a face on one of the hanging panels and two large arms in the superstructure; it thus becomes an ancestral spirit, created to welcome the soul of the deceased man whose life is celebrated by the ijele's outing. Ijele, the world renewed, is thoroughly nonhuman despite its face and hands. It is the earth, the sacred anthill, a house, and the tree of life and abundance under which chiefs gather their advisors. It displays many vital and highly expressive root symbols of Igbo life and thought, both traditional and modern, as a poetic statement activated by human agency to honor a great man now joining the ancestors. Its great size and weight and complexity reflect the depth and breadth of its cultural symbolism.

References and Further Reading

Adams, Sarah. "Hand to Hand: Uli Body and Wall Painting and Artistic Identity in Southeastern Nigeria." Ph.D. dissertation, Yale University, 2000.

Bastian, Misty L. "Female 'Alhajis' and Entrepreneurial Fashions: Flexible Identities in Southeastern Nigerian Clothing Practice." In *Clothing and Difference*, edited by Hildi Hendrikson, 97–132. Durham, NC: Duke University Press, 1996.

Bentor, Eli. "Spatial Continuities: Masks and Cultural Interactions between the Delta and Southeastern Nigeria." *African Arts* 35, no. 1 (2002): 26–41, 93.

Cole, Herbert M. "The Igbo: Prestige Ivory and Elephant Spirit Power." In *Elephant: The Animal and Its Ivory in African Culture*, edited by Doran H. Ross, 210–225. Los Angeles: UCLA Fowler Museum of Cultural History, 1992.

Cole, Herbert M., and Chike C. Aniakor. *Igbo Arts: Community and Cosmos*. Los Angeles: UCLA Museum of Cultural History, 1984.

Henderson, Richard N., and Ifekandu Umunna. "Leadership Symbolism in Onitsha Igbo Crowns and Ijele." *African Arts* 21, no. 2 (1988): 28–37, 94–96.

Ottenberg, Simon. *Masked Rituals of Afikpo: The Context of an African Art*. Seattle: University of Washington Press, 1975.

Picton, John. "Ekpeye Masks and Masking." *African Arts* 21, no. 1 (1988): 46–53, 94.

Reed, Bess. "Spirits Incarnate: Cultural Revitalization in a Nigerian Masquerade Festival." *African Arts* 38, no. 1 (2005): 50–59, 94.

Shaw, Thurstan. *Igbo Ukwu: An Account of Archaeological Discoveries in Eastern Nigeria*. 2 vols. Evanston, IL: Northwestern University Press, 1970.

Willis, Liz. "Uli Painting and the Igbo World View." *African Arts* 23, no. 1 (1989): 62–67, 104.

Herbert M. Cole

See also Independence to Present; West Africa; Nigeria Overview; Yoruba in Nigeria and Diaspora; The Kingdom of Benin.

The Kingdom of Benin

The Kingdom of Benin, a historically important traditional state, is located in southern Nigeria just north of the Niger River Delta. For centuries, its Edo people have looked to Benin City as their cultural center. The seat of a hereditary kingship, it is also a university town and state capital. The *oba*, its semi-divine monarch, still exerts considerable influence even though the modern nation has usurped most of his political privileges. About two hundred chiefs assist him and form the aristocracy of this extremely hierarchical polity. Benin's traditions are still quite visible, but Christian conversions throughout the twentieth century have affected custom and dress, as did British colonialism, which lasted from an 1897 invasion until Nigeria's independence in 1960. The most formal clothing is usually seen in the palace context, but even courtiers are masters of code switching and may wear Nigerian contemporary dress or Western business suits as situations vary.

HISTORIC DRESS

Our knowledge of Benin clothing practices is extensive, because artworks depicting dress have survived from the late fifteenth century. European contact began with the Portuguese in the 1480s and provided written observations. Benin was a trade center, producing cotton cloths traded west to the Gold Coast, as well as importing from their Ijebu Yoruba neighbors. The Portuguese quickly discovered the benefits of textile commerce; with access to European, Indian, and Asian fabrics, their varied inventory expanded Benin tastes, as did successive trade with the Dutch, French, and English. Oral history recounts that the late-fifteenth-century ruler Oba Ewuare wrested coral beads and *ododo*, a felted red wool still the privilege of those of high rank, from Olokun, deity of the sea and wealth. Both were Portuguese trade items that became emblematic of power and luxury, and the myth symbolically alludes to Benin's port, where seagoing vessels brought the items.

Early travelers' accounts speak of both infant circumcision and excision, as well as the bladelike torso tattoos of both men and women, which were badges of citizenry. Although written information about early dress is not detailed, a series of over nine hundred sixteenth-century bronze palace plaques conveys extensive visual information regarding court costume. The oba, chiefs, soldiers, musicians, priests, and pages appear, their attire indicating distinctions of rank and profession as well as clothing appropriate for specific occasions. The oba and a few high-ranking chiefs wore beaded shirts and an occasional long-sleeved tunic, but most men were bare-chested, with plain and patterned wrappers tucked and tied into place at the left hip. Prominent chiefs placed a cast-brass ornament there; examples of human, crocodile, and ram's heads survive. In some cases, fringed sashes or belts helped secure the wrapper. High extensions frequently rose from the left hip, probably indicating cloth placed over a fiber framework. Some wealthy individuals wore several wrappers of differing textiles, the upper ones drawn up festoonlike to reveal the lower in an exuberant display.

Barefoot courtiers most commonly arranged their hair in a series of short, tiered ringlets, probably fixed in place by clay and sometimes supplemented by a few long, bead-capped braids on either side. Dreadlocked men seem to have been ritual specialists. Other individuals—probably priests—also wore distinctive styles with partially shaven sections of hair or a single spiraled braid.

Warriors usually had short goatees, unlike other men. The upper ranks wore leopard-tooth necklaces with either actual leopard pelts or appliquéd cloth versions on their chests. These were hung with a series of clappered bells that would have sounded as they swung; a single pyramidal bell was suspended at midtorso. Headgear varied according to echelon. The highest-ranking soldiers' helmets had horse tails descending from the back and an eagle feather or two tucked into the band; other helmets were made of leather decorated with cowry shells or of crocodile hide, alluding to supernatural protection as well as acting as physical armor. War leaders' hip pendants took the form of a brass leopard's head. This animal symbolizes the ruler through its beauty, power, and deadliness; when worn by a chief, it indicated the oba had extended to him his right to take life. Pendants usually bore a profusion of small hanging crotal bells, which would have added to the jangling; bells of various sizes were also suspended from sword scabbard straps. The noise, elaborate dress, and coral beads suggest that many of the plaques depict warriors dressed for Isiokuo, the festival to Ogun, god of war, rather than actual battle attire.

Children, whether palace pages or royals, were nude. Adulthood meant both marriage and cloth, signs of a responsible person. Some plaques show boys with ornately decorated bodies, segmented by geometrically patterned bands. Foreign observers noted this was chalk ornamentation marking the transition to adulthood, the young man receiving visitors while sitting in state.

Unfortunately, the plaques supply no information regarding female attire, because they solely portray men. A few other contemporaneous bronze pieces do show the *iyoba*, the ruler's mother, but her dress was and is highly specific. The only woman in Benin who bears a chiefly title, her hair alone was dressed to a high peak curved toward the front, a unique style called "parrot's beak" (*ukpe-okhue*), covered with beaded netting. Ordinary women, according to a late-seventeenth-century travelers' account, created a profusion of plaited hairstyles and applied an oily substance that dyed their hair a greenish yellow. They tied wrappers of locally woven checked cotton and displayed jewelry that included copper and iron bracelets, rings, and, for aristocrats, coral.

TRADITIONAL DRESS

Until the early twentieth century, Benin girls did not wear clothing before marriage. At that time, an ankle-length wrapper tied above the breasts covered the waist beads stacked on their hips. Textiles were usually cotton, both locally woven and imported. Women did not wear head ties.

Edo men all formerly wore wrappers tied around their waist, with greater fullness than seen in the delta area to the south. The Indian madras cloth called *george* that was so popular along the coast never really caught on in Benin, nor did European hats or local shirts based on foreign models. Although warriors and senior chiefs owned leather, basketry, or cloth headgear, most men were bare-headed.

RITUAL DRESS

Benin still includes many men and women who are ritual specialists. Some are priests, priestesses, or initiates of particular deities; others create supernatural medicines. They are easily distinguishable by their dress, which is quite different from daily dress and is known as *adaigho*, or ritual attire. Footwear is removed when serving the gods.

Priestesses and initiates associated with the most popular Edo deity—Olokun, god of the sea and riches—wear white garments. This is the color of peace and prosperity, identified with ritual chalk (*orhue*, actually kaolin) and the cowry shells that were precolonial currency. Women dress in a tiered wrap skirt with blouse, both covered with cowry shells, small coral beads, brass crotal bells, and Colonial-era pierced coins—all signs of

In Nigeria, older forms of Edo men's dress such as these cotton wrappers prevail at palace occasions, even though on a daily basis men wear trousers and shirts, caftans, or embroidered robes. These three courtiers in Benin City (1997) have each tied their wrappers in different draped styles. Photograph by Kathy Curnow.

wealth. Initiates have a three-lobed hairstyle. Their distinctive cowry-and-bead pendant symbolizes Olokun's wisdom. Branch coral, not used elsewhere, at times decorates their hair. Small round leather fans are dance accessories, as are fly whisks.

Esango, a borrowed Yoruba deity, frequently inducts female initiates who are considered hot-tempered. Red dominates their dress, which is similar in silhouette and attached ornamentation to that of Olokun's followers.

Color associations are significant. White is overwhelmingly positive in its associations, red is identified with blood and power, and black with death. Ritual powders made from chalk, camwood, and charcoal are often used by priests and specialists. Chalk is applied to "clear the eye" or rubbed on the face to share joy or calm the spirit-possessed, for example. On ritual occasions, particolored facial and chest makeup refers to the union of various life states. A red tail feather of the African gray parrot—associated with prophecy in Benin and a frequent element in masquerade headdresses—is tucked into the hair of priests, emphasizing their prophetic insights.

Medicinal specialists imaginatively combine costume elements to underscore a sense of supernatural mastery. They "cook" their cloth in medicines and never subsequently wash it; its color ranges from a tan to a deep black. Amulet-laden hats, leather charms, metal pendants, and small gourds full of magical substances cover their bodies. Specialists are meant to purify themselves by abstaining from sex, certain foods, and bathing and are expected to look somewhat bizarre. Elderly chiefs regularly complain that experts' efficacy has been compromised when they are well groomed, bathed, and attired in expensive cloth like an aristocrat. Many citizens who are not specialists also wear "medicines." These range from schoolboy "love rings" to leather packets concealed in the pocket or worn on cords as belts under the clothing.

CHIEFLY DRESS

At home, chiefs frequently wear generic Nigerian dress, consisting of informal wax-print trousers and a pullover shirt or a formal set of trousers, shirt, and robe of more prestigious cloth. When they attend the oba, their costume is typically consistent with that of an earlier age, reinforcing the conservative nature of the local political sphere. Old-fashioned dress consists of a full, usually white, wrapper descending to the ankles, at times consisting of ten yards (nine meters) of cloth. Worn over underwear—a knee-length skirt (beluku)—it sometimes drapes naturally, and sometimes juts out from the waist, supported by a hidden cane framework. Several styles of wrapping and tucking the cloth are popular; one dubbed "ram's head" is folded so that a curved drape tops the main cloth.

Two new forms of chiefly wear emerged in the twentieth century. One, a long-sleeved, ankle-length robe with attached capelet, derives from Catholic ecclesiastical dress and began in the 1930s. The second, a short-sleeved shirt with embroidered versions of the torso tattoos once worn by all, was introduced in 1986 at a palace press conference. While all citizens are encouraged to own it, its popularity is really limited to palace contexts, and its visual statement of loyalty to the monarch extends to royal functionaries and cultural group performers. In 1997, the British ambassador and his wife wore these shirts and matching wrappers to a Benin public function commemorating the 1897 invasion. The crowd interpreted their wearing of this gift as an apology and

demonstration of fealty to the oba, albeit an unconscious gesture on their part.

On most ceremonial occasions, white dominates. Chiefs often wear laces, brocades, damask, and other patterned textiles. A second, much shorter white wrapper can be tied over colored cloth. The most privileged wear ododo; this prestige red cloth is difficult to find today, and other red cloths may substitute. It is an amulet in and of itself, and proverbs refer to its power: "Ododo goes to the ceremony and comes back safely." The ododo is cut in scallops to imitate the scales of a pangolin, an anteater that becomes invulnerable when curled up to protect its underbelly. This style of dress, known as ikpakpa-ekhui, symbolizes supernatural invincibility. It appeared on the plaques, and those who wore it in the past were predominantly generals; today, they function as political strategists. Their rank is additionally reinforced by sheet brass ornaments sewn to the dress and its matching peaked hat. These include representations of ceremonial swords, the sun, moon, and other forms. Thin brass "feathers" top the hat and flex as the chiefs move. Each wrist displays brass armlets, along with corals.

At ceremonies, chiefs' accessories and jewelry are more in evidence. Many wear two pairs of cloth and brass-covered leather

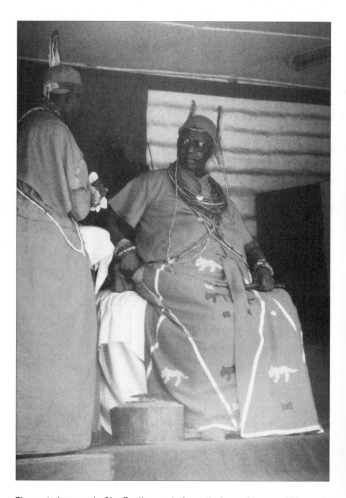

The seated monarch, Oba Erediauwa, is formally dressed in one of his coral-beaded crowns. His wrapper and shirt are made of *ododo*, an imported red cloth intended only for aristocrats. Appliquéd motifs include leopard references, an allusion to the king's beauty and power. Benin City, Nigeria, 1997. Photograph by Kathy Curnow.

ornaments at the hip. One set, *abuwa*, falls from the waist in the shape of two abstract hands, symbolizing achievement; the other, *ovbie-ovu*, stands upright in a doubled fanlike projection. The privileges of various chiefly ranks, as well as appropriateness for a given cloth or wrapping style, govern accessory choice. Chiefs sometimes wear a handwoven fringed brocade square at the hip (*egbele*). This is made by the royal Onwina n'Ido guild; chiefly examples are decorated with brocaded motifs such as the oba, Olokun, or a human face, while royal examples depict animals, weapons, or deities.

Depending on his rank, a chief's hats vary. Tall hourglass-shaped examples strapped under the chin and covered with ododo are common. Other types are restricted. The Iyase, leader of the influential counselors, owns a hat with an inverted, short-stemmed tulip shape that includes strips of leopard skin. The pelt demonstrates the oba's confidence and approbation, for he is identified with this animal's beauty and deadly power. Two priests to the oba's personal deities, Chiefs Osa and Osuan, wear ododo-covered funnel-like headgear with a tall, projecting *oro* cylinder. Oro also appear on the monarch's most formal crowns, probably tying them to the oba's own priestly duties.

Ornament is controlled by sumptuary laws, the oba granting new chiefs the privilege to wear particular jewelry. In Benin, "coral" (*ivie*) refers to two materials, only one of which is marine: Ivie-egbo ("forest beads," known by the Yoruba as *lantana*) are an opaque dark brownish red agate or jasper (both varieties of chalcedony) quarried in Niger and worked in the Ilorin area, while true Mediterranean coral (*ivie-ebo*) was imported from Europe. The latter's color fit preexisting tastes. Larger corals are no longer available and have spawned glass, clay, and plastic imitations, scorned by the nobility.

All chiefs own *ikele*, the circlet also worn by palace functionaries and minor title holders; in the past, its loss or theft was punishable by death. Most possess coral bracelets (*ivie-obo*), simple anklets (*ivie-awe*), and the *udahae*, a beaded headband worn alone or with headgear. It originated in the fifteenth century, when the short-lived Oba Ezoti was shot in the forehead by a poisoned arrow. This occurred at his installation, and the mortal wound was quickly bandaged and disguised with beads. The udahae's one long side strand—sometimes held in the mouth when chiefs dance—represents dripping blood. An eagle feather, indicative of an elder's wisdom, frequently is inserted to one side. Its usage recalls the neighboring Igbo, who associate these feathers with valor and achievement.

Higher-ranking chiefs are entitled to the full or half *odigba*, a stacked beaded collar tied at the back, and *eguen*, tied banded anklets. Baldrics, single or crossed, are made from agate (*ekan*) rather than coral. Few individuals own dress anything like the oba's, though some of the seven Uzama, descendents of early kingmakers, do possess beaded caps. One—the Ezomo—additionally possesses a netted shirt, an extraordinary privilege accorded his eighteenth-century predecessor by Oba Akenzua I. Such imitative garments are not, however, worn to the palace.

Chiefs typically cut their hair so the front is higher, forming a low transverse crest (*ugwakpata*). This allows them to be instantly identifiable, no matter their dress. Their attire at the palace or at home always includes sandals or sockless shoes. On hot days, they are fanned by retainers waving large circular fans, their leather surfaces adorned with ododo.

All chiefs, as well as the oba, royal dukes (*enigie*), and numerous priests own *eben*, a leaf-shaped sword. Danced with at ceremonial occasions, it is twirled, tossed in the air, and tipped to the ground. The eben is one of two state ceremonial weapons; the other is the *ada*, a curved blade symbolically associated with execution, whose privilege the oba restricts.

CHIEFS' WIVES

At a chief's installation, the oba grants him numerous privileges that vary according to rank. One such honor is his wives' right to wear the queens' beehive hairstyle, or *okuku*. Normally this style is only visible at their husbands' installation thanksgiving or at his ceremonies, for it is time-consuming to construct, requiring specialized hairdressers. Wigs make occasional use more practical; young female members of cultural groups often wear them as well. Wealthy chiefs gift coral necklaces and bracelets to family members.

ROYAL DRESS

Once the crown prince takes the throne, he will never wear Western clothes again. On an ordinary day, the oba dresses in a plain white wrapper (albeit of fine quality cloth) and a short-sleeved shirt or a long-sleeved white tailored gown with closed shoes. His

High-ranking Edo chiefs wear palace dress cut to look like pangolin scales. Here the chief wears a coral necklace and bracelet, and at his hip are stylized ornaments representing hands gathering riches, as well as brass face pendants said to represent conquered enemies. Benin City, Nigeria, 1997. Photograph by Kathy Curnow.

head is never bare; he wears either a white or red cloth cap, sewn with a transverse crest in imitation of the chiefly hairstyle, or a coral mesh cap. His hair is arranged in three short plaits at the back, like that of several chiefs whose titles are associated with his body. Daily adornment always includes some beaded ikele circlets, coral bracelets, and necklaces, and he is the only Edo aristocrat who wears belled coral anklets (*igheghan*), perhaps so courtiers are always alert.

On festival occasions, his costume is far more complex. Layered and heavy, it creates a silhouette that praise names compare to a termite hill. The permutations of his wardrobe are extensive, and a specialized group of palace dressers, the *enisen*, are in charge of caring for his jewelry and clothing and dressing him in the attire appropriate for a given occasion. This might include large wrappers of colored or patterned fabrics, such as imported damasks, brocades, or tapestrylike cloth, or examples locally woven by the royal weavers' guild. Although this guild has not been particularly active since the mid-twentieth century, its male weavers create royal wrappers from bark fiber woven on an upright loom; these are still worn at some formal events and decorated with motifs of leopards' heads, fans, suns, and moons.

Coral-beaded mesh is the oba's special material; he has shirts, wrappers, and full gowns made from it, as well as bead-covered shoes. At significant ceremonies, the oba also chooses from one of several coral-beaded crowns, or *ede*. Many have the oro projection; others incorporate the flanking featherlike uprights introduced in the early nineteenth century. Coral-covered medicine belts, meant to alleviate hunger and enhance other powers, cross his chest. At the annual ceremony of Ugie Ivie, a cow is sacrificed over the royal beads and representative samples of his chiefs' corals, recharging their protective energy.

The oba's queens adhere to the palace's traditionalist standards, their fashionable cloths tied above their breasts without a blouse. Coral beads adorn their necks, wrists, and ankles, but contemporary shoes, regularly high heels, complete their attire. Like the chiefs' wives who imitate them (and the oba himself), they usually carry a white handkerchief to shield their mouths in public. Their daily coiffure is a beehive (*okuku*); its dome— once supplemented by ram's hair padding, now by synthetic attachments—includes a variety of coral-ornamented braids and tufts that arch from the hairline toward the crown.

The various provincial enigie, or dukes, whose titles predominantly derive from royal brothers, dress similarly to chiefs. Many royal family members wear decorative coral, but the oba's two eldest daughters are singled out at marriage by special regalia that includes anklets, ikele, and udahae. The oba's mother possesses unusually distinguished dress. The only female chief in Benin, in earlier centuries, she wore a coral, bead-netted shirt, odigba, udahae, and a high, netted hairstyle. Although recent iyobas have abandoned the hairstyle, the odigba and unfeathered udahae, as well as a male chiefly wrapper, remain key wardrobe items.

Only members of the royal family are permitted to wear ivory bracelets. This sumptuary law has not changed; if chiefs purchase such items, they are forbidden to wear them to the palace.

CHANGES IN DRESS

The small scarifications over each brow (three for men, four for women) shown on early artworks apparently vanished some time in the nineteenth century. Facial mark usage became the choice of individual families; when they do occur, they consist of tiny shallow vertical marks on each cheek. Formerly, torso tattoos (*iwu*) were seen on every citizen, differing in number and position according to gender and bloodline. Relatively few tattoos are visible today, their use having been generally abandoned in the first half of the twentieth century. While circumcision continues to be universal, Edo State banned excision in 1999; the practice has slowed but has not ceased entirely.

What was traditional wear well into the twentieth century— a male wrapper with bare chest, a female wrapper tied above the breasts—has devolved (outside of ritual contexts) into a kind of early-morning or late-night undress. Christianity's aversion to exposed flesh was partially responsible for this shift, but the desire to be modern was the major factor. On a daily basis, most adult women wear either blouses with wrappers or "English wear"—Western-style dresses or skirts and blouses. The former are the norm for housewives and market women. Tailored blouse styles—with their rapidly shifting sleeve types, necklines, and silhouettes—quickly date the wearer's wardrobe. So-called English wear is more commonly worn by office workers or students. Adult men commonly wear Western-style shirts and trousers, suits, or drawstring pants with a matching pullover shirt in a wax print or cotton brocade. Like many Nigerians, Edo families, friends, or club members frequently purchase and sew the same cloth in varied styles for group occasions as a solidarity statement.

On more formal occasions, both sexes wear Nigerian attire derived from their Yoruba and Hausa neighbors—scoop-necked top and wrapper with head tie for women; trousers, shirt, and matching robe with cap for men. Both sexes favor imported laces (similar to eyelet or Venetian lace), though men often also wear cotton brocades ("guinea brocade"); stiff, crackly damask goes in and out of style. Women commonly accessorize with matching Yoruba handwoven *aso-oke* shoulder or waist cloths and head ties. Shoes (usually closed high heels) and a matching bag with earrings and chain complete their fashionable appearance. Eighteen-karat (or higher) gold, usually imported from Italy or the Middle East, is de rigueur in Benin.

Royal wives dress in fashionable imported "laces" in an archaic style, their wrappers tied over their chest without a blouse. Their husband grants the privilege of wearing similar domed, beehive hairstyles to the wives of chiefs he favors. Benin City, Nigeria, 1990s. Photograph by Kathy Curnow.

Wedding attire varies. For a traditional marriage or betrothal, the groom usually wears a contemporary Nigerian *agbada*, but the bride adorns herself in a blouseless wrapper tied high on the chest. If she is friendly with a chief's wife, she may borrow coral and dress her hair in the royal okuku style for what may be the only time in her life. Traditional weddings frequently adopt the Yoruba custom of disguising several of the brides' friends by covering their heads with a cloth to see if the groom can recognize his fiancée. At church weddings—and many couples marry traditionally, in church and at the registry—the groom and his attendants wear Western-style suits with white gloves, while the bride dons a white dress and veil, her attendants in bridesmaids' gowns.

Most Benin women, whether young or mature, chemically straighten their hair. Only women long past childbearing age, those in outlying villages, and schoolgirls wear their hair naturally and close-cropped. Imported extensions of both human and synthetic hair allow for a wide variety of styles. Fashionable wealthy women may have their hair woven into a brimmed hat or another whimsical shape, as fashion dictates. Colors such as maroon, gold, and blue are incorporated regularly into coiffures.

Men tend to have close-cut hair, and many younger men shave their heads, emulating U.S. hip-hop singers. Older men frequently dye their hair for a more youthful appearance. Most men are clean-shaven or have a small moustache.

DRESS OF YOUNG PEOPLE

Young people in Benin are extremely conscious of popular Western styles and designers, because of both friends and relatives who live overseas and the availability foreign videos, DVDs, and television shows. Universities are showplaces for fashion. Both sexes commonly wear jeans and English wear, although contemporary Nigerian dress commonly is chosen for weddings, funerals, or church. Both men and women favor imported cologne, and combined barbershop/beer parlors and beauty salons are ubiquitous.

During the Christmas holidays, many Benin expatriates return home from Europe and the United States with the latest overseas wear. In 2004, one such returnee generated much excitement as the first Edo to sport a "grille," a gold or platinum hip-hop accessory that fits over the teeth, hitherto only seen in music videos.

Rarely do men—other than athletes—wear shorts, for they are still the required schoolboy uniform. Even the strong influence of U.S. fashion has not mitigated this, though loose shorts of local prints with matching shirts sometimes constitute casual student dress.

References and Further Reading

Ben-Amos, Paula. "Owina N'Ido: Royal Weavers of Benin. " *African Arts* 11, no. 4 (1978): 48–53, 95–96.

Ben-Amos, Paula. "Who Is the Man in the Bowler Hat?: Emblems of Identity in Benin Royal Art." *Baessler-Archiv*, n. f. 31, no. 1 (1983): 161–183.

Ben-Amos, Paula. "The Promise of Greatness: Women and Power in an Edo Spirit Possession Cult." In *Religions of Africa*, edited by Thomas D. Blakely, Walter E. A. van Beek, Dennis L. Thomson, et al., 118–134. London: James Currey, 1994.

Ben-Amos, Paula. *The Art of Benin*, 2nd ed. Washington, DC: Smithsonian Institution Press, 1995.

Blackmun, Barbara Winston. "Obas' Portraits in Benin." *African Arts* 23, no. 3 (1990): 61–69, 102–104.

Curnow, Kathy. "The Art of Fasting: Benin's Ague Ceremony." *African Arts* 30, no. 4 (1997): 46–53, 93–94.

Curnow, Kathy. "Prestige and the Gentleman: Benin's Ideal Man." *Art Journal* 56, no. 2 (1997): 75–81.

Dark, Philip J.C. *An Introduction to Benin Art and Technology*. Oxford, UK: Clarendon, 1973.

De Marees, Pieter. *Description and Historical Account of the Gold Kingdom of Guinea* [1602]. Oxford, UK: British Academy, 1987.

De Negri, Eve. "The King's Beads." *Nigeria Magazine*, no. 82 (September 1964): 210–216.

De Negri, Eve. *Nigerian Body Adornment*. Lagos, Nigeria: Nigeria Magazine, 1976.

Egharevba, Jacob U. *Benin Law and Custom*. Benin City, Nigeria: Jacob Egharevba, 1949.

Egharevba, Jacob U. *A Short History of Benin*, 3rd ed. Ibadan, Nigeria: Ibadan University Press, 1960.

Eweka, Ena Basimi. *Evolution of Benin Chieftaincy Titles*. Benin City, Nigeria: Uniben Press, 1992.

Ezra, Kate. *Royal Art of Benin: The Perls Collection in the Metropolitan Museum of Art*. New York: Metropolitan Museum of Art, 1992.

Galembo, Phyllis. *Divine Inspirations: From Benin to Bahia*. Albuquerque: University of New Mexico Press, 1993.

Galembo, Phyllis. *Aso-ebi: Cloth of the Family*. n.p., 1997.

Hodgkin, Thomas Lionel. *Nigerian Perspectives*. London: Oxford University Press, 1960.

Jones, Adam. "Andreas Josua Ulsheimer's Voyage of 1603–4." In *German Sources for West African History, 1599–1669*, edited by Adam Jones, 18–43. Wiesbaden, Germany. Franz Steiner Verlag, 1983.

Kaplan, Flora Edouwaye S. "Fragile Legacy: Photographs as Documents in Recovering Political and Cultural History at the Royal Court of Benin." *History in Africa* 18 (1991): 205–237.

Kaplan, Flora Edouwaye S. "Images of the Queen Mother in Benin Court Art." *African Arts* 26, no. 3 (1993): 54–63, 86–88.

Luschan, Felix von. *Die Altertümer von Benin* [1919]. New York: Hacker, 1968.

Nevadomsky, Joseph. "Kingship Succession Rituals in Benin. 2: The Big Things." *African Arts* 17, no. 2 (1984): 41–47, 90–91.

Nevadomsky, Joseph. "Kingship Succession Rituals in Benin. 3: The Coronation of the Oba." *African Arts* 17, no. 3 (1984): 48–57, 91–92.

Nevadomsky, Joseph. "The Benin Bronze Horseman as the Ata of Idah." *African Arts* 19, no. 4 (1986): 40–47, 85.

Nevadomsky, Joseph. "The Costume and Weapons of the Benin Brass Horseman." *Baessler-Archiv*, n. f. 41, no. 1 (1993): 207–230.

Nevadomsky, Joseph, and Ekhaguosa Aisien. "The Clothing of Political Identity: Costume and Scarification in the Benin Kingdom." *African Arts* 28, no. 1 (1995): 62–73, 100.

Nevadomsky, Joseph, and Daniel E. Inneh. "Kingship Succession Rituals in Benin. 1: Becoming a Crown Prince." *African Arts* 17, no. 1 (1983): 47–54, 87.

Nevadomsky, Joseph, and Norma Rosen. "The Initiation of a Priestess: Performance and Imagery in Olokun Ritual." *The Drama Review* 32, no. 2 (1988): 186–207.

O'Hear, Ann. "Ilorin Lantana Beads." *African Arts* 19, no. 4 (1986): 36–39, 87–88.

Plankensteiner, Barbara, ed. *Benin Kings and Rituals: Court Arts from Nigeria*. Vienna: Kunsthistorisches Museum mit MVK und ÖTM, 2007.

Roth, H. Ling. "Personal Ornaments from Benin." *Bulletin of the Free Museum of Science and Art, University of Pennsylvania*, no. 2 (January 1899): 28–35.

Roth, H. Ling. *Great Benin; Its Customs, Art and Horrors* [1903]. London: Routledge and Kegan Paul, 1968.

Ryder, A.F.C. *Benin and the Europeans, 1485–1897*. New York: Humanities Press, 1969.

Kathy Curnow

Lower Niger Delta Peoples and Diaspora

Geographers define the Niger Delta as the watery terrain that lies between the Forcados and Imo Rivers, but Nigerians typically extend the term to encompass an area that stretches from the Cross River in the east nearly to Lagos in the west. The inhabitants of this region speak dozens of languages and represent nine different language groups. Populations range in size from the Ijo, a diverse group of about two million who live in communities spread throughout the delta region, to the Defaka, who number only about two hundred and occupy a single village. Larger groups include the Urhobo, Isoko, Itsekiri, Ikwerre, Ekpeye, Ogoni, and Obolo (or Andoni). Most delta groups have maintained their own languages and distinct identities, but they have long been connected through trade; consequently, they share many comparable customs and art forms, ranging from warrior societies and water-spirit masquerades to modes of dress.

Delta residents take great pride in the roles they played in overseas trade. Heirloom items of clothing and styles reminiscent of bygone days serve as visual reminders of a glorious past when the region flourished. For those who served as middlemen, garments and accessories can honor trading relationships that faded centuries ago. The Itsekiri, for example, trace their delicate silver and gold filigree jewelry back to the Portuguese, who dominated trade during the sixteenth century, and they continue to treasure bicorne hats from the Napoleonic era. For those in the delta's heartland, who had little direct contact with Europeans until the Colonial era, top hats dusted off for ceremonial occasions conjure up memories of a time when the world's demand for palm oil brought unprecedented prosperity.

Centuries of economic and cultural exchanges have resulted in an inventive and often fanciful mélange of indigenous and imported elements that Nigerians identify as distinctively "delta" or "rivers" dress. Peoples living within the delta, however, can often distinguish a Nembe Ijo man from his Kalabari and Okrika cousins by noting subtle differences in their attire. More affluent groups often pride themselves on their elegant sense of fashion, and some view flagrant violations of an implicit dress code as affronts on their unique identities. For example, even though Western fashions have inspired their own attire, the Itsekiri complain that the Urhobo have shamelessly appropriated their waistcoats and are brazenly wearing *george* (Indian madras), a cloth that should properly be worn only by those with a long history of European contact.

DELTA WOMEN

Although modern women in the Niger Delta region may choose to wear Western-style fashions for work, leisure, and certain events like their weddings, many prefer to tie two lengths of cloth around their waists in a style known throughout West Africa as an "up-and-down." By accentuating their girth, the folded and wrapped textiles help women achieve the well-rounded figures that West Africans typically admire. Preferred fabrics vary from one group to another but include imported madras, wax prints, velvets, damasks, brocades, eyelets, and laces; those who cannot afford such luxuries make do with less expensive Nigerian or Chinese versions. Blouses of lace and other luxurious fabrics, colorful, outsized head ties, vinyl handbags and shoes, coral beads, gold necklaces, and a variety of other ornaments typically complete the ensembles.

Although the outfits worn by delta women may look similar to outsiders, the choice of cloth and accessories can distinguish a member of one ethnic group from another. For example, Itskeiri women may wear unique, small head ties made of knotted handkerchiefs that date back to the Portuguese era. Kalabari Ijo women wear wrappers made of *pelete bite*, a distinctive, blue-and-white Indian madras that local artisans have transformed into a culturally significant cloth by cutting threads to create new patterns. Women seldom wear wax prints in the Kalabari area, where dress is strictly regulated; their neighbors to the west—the Nembe and the central and western Ijo—show a preference for wax prints and tend to conform to loosely established patterns instead of following formal dress codes.

The most distinctive female fashions appear during rites of passage, when lavish jewelry, elaborate costumes, and colorful cosmetics transform young delta women into symbols of power, wealth, and fertility. Rites may be performed for young girls to mark their availability for marriage or *iriabo*, the Kalabari term for young mothers signifying their motherhood status. The initiates' bodies are often adorned with coral beads and rubbed with camwood, a substance derived from the African sandalwood tree that is credited with medicinal and apotropaic properties and also used as a cosmetic. The reddish orange color these materials share connotes mystical and potentially dangerous powers, signifying that initiates demand the same respect as spirits and kings. Like the other expensive and imported items the girls wear, coral beads also display the families' wealth. In addition, the initiates' dress frequently accentuates their womanly bodies, which may have been rounded out by a special diet of rich foods to display their maturity, health, and potential fertility. At ceremonies that mark the end of their confinement, initiates dance in a sensual manner to show off their voluptuous bodies. Those who lack sufficient curves may compensate by adding additional layers of cloth. As the Kalabari Ijo say: "The *iriabo* who does not fatten her buttocks is plenty of cloth."

Gleaming with camwood pigment and wearing a camwood-dyed wrapper, a newly excised Urhobo initiate would hold an umbrella in her right hand and drape a folded cloth over her left shoulder. Her accessories might include paired necklaces, like those worn by kings and other important people, as well as strands of silver coins and strings of beads around her chest, upper arms, and legs below the knees. Depending on the occasion, she might embellish her head tie with a coral bead or ornament her distinctive hairstyle with silver hairpins, scented leaves, and a regal

Five Kalabari Ijo women showing ranked systems of dress in use in the lower Niger Delta, twenty-first century. *Bite pakiri iwan* (on the far left), the bead stage, is worn by little girls and is followed by *ikuta de*, half a length of cloth (wrapper). *Konju fina* is "waist-tying stage," and *bite sara* is full wrapper stage. The final stage, *iriabo*, is special dress for celebration after bearing a child. Drawing by Sylvia Rudd.

crown formed of silver animals and abstract shapes (*iria*). While sitting in state, she would hold an etched silver ornament in her mouth. This unusual adornment not only makes the words she speaks more important, but also emphasizes the self-containment and remoteness that accompany her newly attained status. Young mothers, their skin reddened to indicate that they have given birth to their first child, would join the initiates in a parade.

Most of the Eastern Ijo groups, including the Okrika, Ibani (comprising Bonny and Opobo), and Kalabari, confined initiates in "fatting houses," where they pampered and fed them to round out their bodies and keep their skin from darkening. Although this practice has now been abbreviated or abandoned, cloth still symbolizes status and indicates wealth in Eastern Ijo societies, and cloth tying continues to play an important role in women's coming-out ceremonies, when they make their first appearance as adults or new mothers.

Like other children in the region, Okrika Ijo girls ordinarily dress in school uniforms and Western-style clothing, so the special clothing and accessories they wear while undergoing initiation underscore its significance. During their confinement, the initiates (*iriabo*) have heavy anklets of winding copper rings (*impala*) fitted on their lower legs. The heavy ornaments restrict their movements, perhaps to safeguard their chastity, and provide a pleasing, rhythmic accompaniment when they walk. The camwood-dyed wrappers initiates once wore for public presentations have been replaced by hoop skirts made by folding and wrapping as many as two dozen lengths of imported textiles around their waists. The resulting wheels of cloth, which may measure more than three feet (one meter) in diameter, suggest affluence and portend pregnancy. Accessories include coral beads and other costly jewelry, as well as hats that glitter with mirrors, metallic fringe, and bright, shiny Christmas ornaments. Some initiates have intricate patterns drawn on their bodies in blue dye on a camwood undercoat. The designs, known as *burumo*, honor the water spirits; moreover, they transform the girls' bodies to reflect their transitional state and render them ready for marriage and childbearing.

Fattening, body painting, and displays of wealth also play an important role in Ibani (Bonny and Opobo) Ijo rites. Until the 1960s, an Ibani woman could not marry until she had performed her iria. Initiation involved several stages, beginning with *kala-egberbite*, or the "small tying of cloth," which was held during preparations for iria. *Opu-egerebite*, or "big tying of the cloth," took place at the coming-out ceremony, when the iriabo publicly wore two wrappers for the first time, signaling her literal and figurative transformation from a naked girl to a fully clothed adult. Periodic changes of wrappers made of progressively more valuable textiles indicated the wealth of the initiate's sponsor, who was often her fiancé. For example, she might begin wearing a handwoven Igbo Akwete cloth or *popo* (a strip-woven textile version of Ewe kente cloth that is produced in the eastern delta), then change to *plangidi* (*blangidi* in Kalabari and Nembe, a blanketlike type of flannel manufactured in England), and finally to *loogho-bite*, an imported damask. Accessories complemented the cloth: plangidi was tied with popo and worn with coral beads (*kilari*); loogho-bite required gold accessories. After completing iria, the egerebite, which was originally made of raffia and named for the rustling sound it made, would be worn as an underlayer. *Bibite*, a rite that was held during middle age, marked a woman's right to tie george, an expensive type of cloth imported from India that signified her wealth and status.

Modern Ibani women often have husbands, children, and salaried jobs before becoming iriabo; instead of performing the big-tying ceremony to signal their availability for marriage, they do it to affirm their ethnic identity, show off their families' prosperity, and assert their right to wear Ibani fashions. Cloth tying remains so important that Ibani women cannot be buried without performing it.

The Kalabari Ijo once used characteristic forms of dress to mark five transitions in the female life cycle, beginning with late childhood and culminating with motherhood. Although these can still be seen at important celebrations, only the last two, *bite sara*, which signifies maturity, and *iriabo*, which marks the birth of a child (ordinarily), usually appear. In addition to dressing as "birth iriabo," Kalabari girls and women don variations of the ensemble for special occasions like funerary ceremonies, chieftaincy installations, and centenary celebrations, where they represent the wealth and well-being of their lineages.

The ankle-length up-and-down wrappers of the bite sara ensemble, tied by a common technique the Kalabari call *sengi*, identify the wearer as an adult Kalabari woman. Iriabo ensembles require another wrapping technique called *ebre*, which involves hand gathering, pleating, and rolling layers of short wrappers and underwrappers. Preferred cloths include prized fabrics like george that the Kalabari call *injiri* (handwoven Indian madras), *loko* (a light, striped silk or silky cloth said to be made in India), and *india* (a luxurious Indian velvet embroidered by hand with metallic thread). The iriabo's upper body may be bare, covered with a cloth, or dressed in a lace, beaded, or sequined blouse. Depending on the type of fabric worn, the occasion, and even the time of day, she may wear coral, gold, or glass jewelry and a hat. The latter can include imported headgear such as bowlers and derbies; distinctive local types are often embellished with coral beads or trimmed with a multitude of tassels, mirrors, and other gaudy baubles. Walking sticks, white saucers and handkerchiefs, folded cloths, handbags, and elephant tusks often complete the outfit. Various shaved and plaited hairstyles can also signify iriabo status.

The Ogoni share the fatting-house tradition, but now generally lavish food, beautiful clothing, cosmetics, and attention only on women who have given birth to a first child. Consequently, they refer to this period as "maternity leave." The new mother's front teeth are separated to produce the gap that is characteristic of Ogoni women, and reddish dye (made from herbs) and yellowish pigment (made from the roots of a calla lily) are rubbed onto her body. If her husband violates rules against visiting her, he risks being ridiculed, because the color will rub off on him. At the conclusion of her confinement, the woman will have small, schematic patterns painted on her body, and her husband will buy her jewelry and fine cloth for the child's public presentation. If the mother is Christian, she will take her baby to church, where people will sing songs of praise and dance in a procession.

MEN'S DRESS

In contrast with women's styles, which feature a double wrapper to stress fecundity, the ensembles worn by delta men emphasize social standing and power. Traditional male dress typically consists of a long, loose shirt worn over a single wrapper, often made of Indian madras. Cloth, styles, and accessories differ according to age, wealth, status, and occasion, as well as ethnic identity. Cloth-tying methods can vary according to gender (men, for example, may tie their cloth on the right, women on the left), occasion (wrestling demands a secure knot), or the meaning one wishes to convey. The Kalabari, who have raised cloth tying to an art, compare the intricate *inturu* method of tying cloth to a Mercedes Benz. By "inadvertently" allowing a breeze to expose his immaculate, white, knee-length underpants, the wearer of an inturu wrapper shows off the extent of his good grooming, while simultaneously demonstrating his modesty, subtlety, and sophistication.

Wealthy men of the Niger Delta region have been known to wear embroidered Hausa gowns both for novelty and to signify far-flung connections, but many items of dress clearly originated

through European trade. Although shirt styles vary, most derive from Western prototypes; those with pleated and tucked bodices resemble Victorian nightshirts. Typical accessories include coral beads, canes, elephant tusks, umbrellas, and handkerchiefs, as well as an enormous variety of headgear, including crowns, top hats, derbies, straw boaters, bowlers, and distinctive local types like the spectacular Kalabari *ajibulu*. Men, like women, typically wear Western-style shoes or sandals, but may often choose to dance barefoot in order to feel the earth.

The incorporation of elements from other African cultures, as well as Western ones, makes Itsekiri dress unique. Netted coral garments and coral collars confirm influence from the Benin kingdom, and crowns trimmed with egret feathers show affinities with those worn by Yoruba rulers. However, the Itsekiri take special pride in their early and sustained contact with European traders and missionaries. Their word for waistcoat, *culete*, derives from the Portuguese *colete*, and numerous other elements of male dress—including shirts with pleated bibs and fedoras—commemorate later eras of trade. The Itsekiri sometimes claim to have introduced the delta style of dress.

The kings of the Itsekiri kingdom wore coral-beaded crowns of the Benin type as their official headgear until the seventeenth century, even though the Benin neither controlled the kingdom nor confirmed its rulers. Since that time, they have appropriated European crowns to assert the kingdom's status as the first Christian monarchy in Nigeria. The brocade coronation cape and sashed chasuble worn by the *olu*, or king, in recent years were clearly inspired by Portuguese ecclesiastical attire. On state occasions, his regalia reflects a mixture of local and imported items: he wears strings of coral and stone bead circlets as well as necklaces made of rosaries; imported, kingly cloth inserted into the top of his European-style metal crown protects his head from public view, in keeping with southern Nigerian practices.

Like the king's coronation ensemble, the long, caped garments Itsekiri chiefs wore in the early twentieth century played on styles worn by Catholic priests. However, after the Urhobo appropriated this attire, the Itsekiri substituted long-sleeved white shirts and white wrappers tied with sashes made of imported red cloth. They also resent the Urhobo for copying their distinctive chokers (*oronwu*). The chokers, which feature two large coral beads flanking a central one covered with seed beads, are paired with a necklace that incorporates stone circlets of Benin origin and a large coral bead on a seed-bead strand. Oronwu carry associations of priestly authority; other Itsekiri men could wear them but only to worship their ancestors in private.

The Kalabari, who have the most complex and prescribed dress codes of all delta groups, distinguish between five hierarchical categories of male dress. The upper garments that form the basis for these ensembles typically recall European shirts and nightgowns of centuries past. A young man wears a madras wrapper with an *etibo*. The etibo is a straight, knee-length, collarless shirt typically made of white or light-colored cotton that closes with one stud and is worn with its long sleeves folded back. Befitting his higher rank, a "gentleman of substance" sports a *woko*, a plain gabardine or serge upper garment that has three gold or silver studs, depending on the color of the fabric. Trousers or a wrapper, a cap or a straw hat, and a cane or an umbrella complete the outfit. The woko's looser fit accommodates the vigorous movements the wearer makes during dance displays. A chief or a distinguished elder layers a more elaborate gown called a *doni* over a shirt and a wrapper so that the folded cuffs of the shirt and a bit of the madras wrapper peek out. Its name may derive from the English word *down*, indicating that it reaches the ankles. Made of colorful woolens or silk, the doni typically has four studs. Accessories might include an ivory tusk and a staff or a fan as well as a top hat and ivory bracelets. Only a king or a paramount chief can wear a V-necked gown called *ebu*; its square collar may have been inspired by a sailor's uniform. Both gown and wrapper are usually made of *injiri*, a handwoven Indian madras that the Kalabari particularly esteem.

Attigra, the voluminous gowns made of embroidered Indian velvet that elite Kalabari men don on ceremonial occasions, appear to stem from African, rather than European sources. Legend points to the Igala kingdom, located on the Niger River to the north, as the source of the style; if so, the Kalabari have characteristically refashioned it—ironically using embroidered velvet imported from India—to make it distinctively their own. The dazzling ensemble includes leopard-tooth and coral necklaces, multiple gold rings, and a fantastic hat known as *ajibulu*, an elaborately decorated bicorne hat worn by principal male mourners at funerals, as well as by chiefs and other elite men. The ajibulu plays on the shape of headgear worn by European admirals in times gone by, but the addition of a ram's beard, feathers, concentric circles (a Kalabari symbol), mirrors, plastic baubles, fringe, and foil transforms the hat into something that is quintessentially Ijo. The lavish ornaments, accessories, and yards of luxurious fabrics used to fashion an attigra ensemble make it an elaborate and highly prestigious Kalabari status symbol. By manipulating the garments' billowing forms while dancing, wearers could create the impression that they were larger than life.

Delta men from other Ijo and non-Ijo groups wear similar styles but make fewer distinctions and enforce hierarchies less rigidly. The Nembe Ijo, for example, have only three categories of male clothing to the Kalabari's five: the Nembe *opu* (big) shirt corresponds with etibo, and the *angapu* with woko; the Nembe use the same term as the Kalabari, doni, for chiefly attire. The Nembe have also adopted European power emblems. In ancient times, Nembe kings wore tall raffia crowns similar to the ones still worn by the chief priest in the idu (creator) festival of Okpoama and represented in the terra-cotta figurine recovered from the excavation at Onyoma near Nembe, and dated to about 1500 C.E. In recent times, however, Nembe kings have worn feather crowns made by local craftsmen, and the last two have substituted gold crowns imported from Britain.

Unlike their relatives to the east and the Itsekiri to the west, the central and western Ijo had little direct contact with Europeans until the Colonial era, but they eagerly adopted imported fashions as they became available. English shirts had become so commonplace by the 1850s that they were even worn while fishing, and top hats, monkey jackets, and military apparel were in great demand as trade goods. Nevertheless, as late as 1890, visitors describe the standard dress as a knee-length cotton wrapper. Although groups living in the delta's heartland did not recognize leaders at the clan, or even the village level before the Colonial period, the styles that originated along the coast have spread throughout the region, and chiefs and others who can afford to do so may loosely appropriate elements of eastern Ijo chieftaincy attire; however, most men wear variations on the doni or woko for important social and ceremonial occasions. Dress codes tend to be very informal.

In the past, delta men who had earned titles in warrior societies were entitled to wear special ensembles. Among the Okrika (or Wakirike), kings, priests, and warriors all had distinctive ensembles that included two types of headgear: *ibulu*, flat hats with tufts of ram fur attached to the front and back, and *sengi*, patterned fiber caps that terminated in a knot in the back. Kings wore either type; priests wore a variation of sengi with leopards' claws; warriors added eagle feathers to ibulu to signify their valor. Some sported seven or more feathers, indicating the number of victims they had claimed for their war god.

Some Urhobo, Isoko, and central and western Ijo groups have continued the practice of honoring warriors, although the status may be inherited rather than earned. Among the central and western Ijo, clan war gods award the *peri* title to those who have killed other men or leopards; title holders wear special costumes when performing the "peri play" at festivals for their war gods or funerals for other peri warriors. In Olodiama clan, peri warriors wear red jackets and matching hats decorated with eagle feathers; elsewhere, white or navy blue wrappers and eagle-feather headgear can signify warrior status. Title holders typically string medicine gourds around their bodies and decorate themselves with white native chalk. Chalk, like camwood and other pigments, is believed to be imbued with supernatural properties and to have the ability to protect, purify, transform, and heal. The chalk marks warriors and priests wear around their eyes and along and around their arms and legs indicate shrine membership and signal supernatural protection and support.

For warfare, ceremonial occasions, and festivals, an Isoko war leader (*iletu*) holds a spear and machete, marks his right arm (and sometimes his leg) with chalk, ties medicine bundles around his body, wears a short skirt made of striped or solid cloth, and sports a huge feathered headdress. In former times, like his Okrika counterparts, he would have added a feather to his bonnet for every man he had killed. An Isoko *ovie* or "priest-chief" has two different ensembles, reflecting his dual roles as a divine king. His normal or secular dress consists of a white or plaid wrapper and a pointed red cap or crown that has a red tail feather from a gray parrot tucked into its base at the forehead. His ceremonial attire resembles that of an iletu: it includes a striped skirt, a chalked right arm, and many medicine bundles; his regalia includes a spear or staff in his right hand, a drinking horn or other kingly regalia in his left hand, and a royal cap atop his head.

BODY MODIFICATION

In former times, most men and women of the Niger Delta region bore scarification marks. Some still have faint cuts at the corners of their mouth and on their foreheads, hands, and feet that they acquired during infancy for medicinal reasons, such as preventing convulsions. When they grew older, central Ijo boys formerly had three sets of three scars applied to their chest by their uncles to provide immunity in war. The number three is auspicious, and three times three exponentially so; purportedly, these marks could signal when danger threatened or something good was about to happen. More prominent scars on the forehead and cheeks served as marks of ethnic identity. A young Isoko girl betrothed to a central Ijo man would be given Ijo markings to note her newly assumed identity. The central Ijo typically had a single scar (*andiungbowei*) down the center of their foreheads, and

Five Kalabari men (lower Niger Delta) showing ranked systems of dress still used in the twenty-first century. The man on the far left is wearing an *etibo*, a special shirt, as an upper garment, and the second man is wearing *woko*, a more formal upper garment worn by "gentlemen of substance." The third man is wearing the gown called *doni*, worn by chiefs, and the fourth is wearing a gown and wrapper called *ebu*, worn by the king. The final garment, *attigra*, worn by the man on the far right, forms part of a ceremonial ensemble worn on special occasions. Drawing by Sylvia Rudd.

many also had curving lines (*itakpa*) that began at their noses and ran along the lower edge of their cheekbones.

In addition to ethnic and medicinal marks, many Ijo women formerly decorated their bodies with delicate linear tattoos, and some continue to do so. Motifs placed sparingly on the breasts, torso, arms, and hands with little regard to symmetry create eccentric yet pleasing compositions. Although most of the designs appear to be abstract, Nembe women identify some motifs as human figures; objects from the environment such as leaves, flowers, trees, and plants; heavenly bodies like stars and the moon; and objects such as manilas, crotals, and chairs. Other more enigmatic motifs include concentric circles, tallies, and elliptical forms with hooks.

Numerous Delta residents also practiced dental modification, including the Ogoni women mentioned above. Central Ijo men and women had six of their front teeth carved, three on top and three on the bottom; although this was considered aesthetically pleasing, it also served a practical purpose by keeping meat from becoming caught in the teeth. Until the 1980s and perhaps even later, ceremonial tooth carving was conducted on a corpse if it had not been done before death.

CONCLUSION

Delta people have continued to favor imported items and adapted European styles as emblems of wealth, worldliness, and power. Cowboy hats, which nod to the delta's role in petroleum production, have become acceptable headgear for traditional ensembles, and the latter coexist with business suits, bridal dresses, and

T-shirts. Department stores carry less expensive versions of the prestigious ajibulu headgear, and India produces a less expensive version of pelete bite cloth. Nevertheless, residents continue to respect local customs, and some still enforce strict rules about dress. Even in the 1990s, an Ibani Ijo woman who wore a double wrapper without performing her coming-of-age rites risked having them ripped off by outraged onlookers. If she were to die before she had completed her iria, her female relatives and friends would ritually change her wrappers three times so that she could enter the world as an adult.

By the early twenty-first century, delta styles had spread well beyond the region's boundaries. Women throughout southern Nigeria have adopted the stiffened silk head ties that the Itsekiri claim to have introduced, and men from the Cross River area sometimes copy delta styles. Oil production has recently spread to that area, and delta peoples tease them for affecting "OPEC" styles..For women and men from the delta area who work in offices or professional jobs, their everyday dress consists of Western-type garb of blouses and skirts or dresses. Men in such jobs wear trousers and shirts, suits, or matching pants and shirts that have a variety of names, such as conductor suit, similar to what was called a leisure suit in the United States for a period of time. Children in school most often wear school uniforms on a daily basis.

References and Further Reading

Anderson, Martha G., and Philip M. Peek, eds. *Ways of the Rivers: Arts and Environment of the Niger Delta*. Los Angeles: UCLA Fowler

Museum of Cultural History; Seattle: University of Washington Press, 2002.

Daly, M. Catherine. "Iriabo Appearance at Kalabari Funerals." *African Arts* 12 no. 1 (1997): 58–61, 86.

Daly, M. Catherine, Joanne B. Eicher, and Tonye V. Erekosima. "Male and Female Artistry in Kalabari Dress." *African Arts* 19 no. 3 (1986): 48–51, 83.

Eicher, Joanne B. "Dress, Gender and the Public Display of Skin." In *Body Dressing*, edited by Joanne Entwhistle and Elizabeth Wilson, 233–252. Oxford, UK: Berg, 2001.

Eicher, Joanne B., and Tonye V. Erekosima. "Why Do They Call It Kalabari? Cultural Authentication and the Demarcation of Ethnic Identity." In *Dress and Ethnicity: Change across Space and Time*, edited by Joanne B. Eicher, 139–164. Oxford, UK: Berg, 1995.

Erekosima, Tonye V., and Joanne B. Eicher. "The Aesthetics of Men's Dress of the Kalabari of Nigeria." In *The Visible Self: Global Perspectives on Dress, Culture and Society*, 3rd ed., edited by Joanne B. Eicher, Sandra Lee Evenson, and Hazel V. Lutz, 402–414. New York: Fairchild Publications, 2008.

Foss, Susan Moore. "She Who Sits as King: Celebrations for Young Urhobo Women." *African Arts* 12, no. 2 (1979): 44–50, 90–91.

Gleason, Judith, and Chief Allison Ibuluya. "We Heard Ourselves Singing: Dawn Songs of Girls Becoming Women in Ogbogbo, Okrika, Rivers State, Nigeria, January 1990." *Research in African Literatur* no. 3 (1991): 138–148.

Michelman, Susan O., and Tonye V. Erekosima. "Kalabari Dress in N ria: Visual Analysis and Gender Implications." In *Dress and Ethn Change across Space and Time*, edited by Joanne B. Eicher, 164 Oxford, UK: Berg, 1995.

Negri, Eve de. "Itsekiri Costume." *Nigeria Magazine* 97 (19 101–110.

Opuogulaya, Chief E.D.W. *The Cultural Heritage of the Wakirike Okrika People*). Port Harcourt, Nigeria: Rivers State Counci Arts and Culture, 1975.

Sumberg, Barbara. "Dress and Ethnic Differentiation in the N Delta." In *Dress and Ethnicity: Change across Space and Time*, e by Joanne B. Eicher, 165–181. Oxford, UK: Berg, 1995.

Talbot, P. Amaury. *The Peoples of Southern Nigeria*. 4 vols. Lon Oxford University Press, 1926.

Martha G. Anderson and E. J. Ala

See also Igbo in Nigeria and Diaspora; Snapshot: Kalabari] ples of Nigeria.

Snapshot: Kalabari Peoples of Nigeria

The Kalabari Ijo have a long history as traders of cloth and apparel items in the Niger Delta. They traded with the world beyond their immediate boundaries of thirty-two islands found among mangrove swamps of the Niger River tributaries near the Atlantic Ocean. Their trading provided access to imported goods, particularly textiles, which they used and continue to use in creative ways. Rather than just borrow the textiles, they make them identifiable as uniquely Kalabari, a process that has been called cultural authentication. Several culturally authenticated items relate to dressing for important events in Kalabari life. One significant example is a textile called *pelete bite* (translated as "cut-thread" cloth) made from Indian madras (*injiri*), which is a plaid or checked cotton textile handwoven in India and imported into the Niger Delta for perhaps more than two hundred years. Ordinarily women or girls, but sometimes men, make pelete bite from various patterns of madras. The Kalabari have names for preferred textile patterns, such as *amasiri* (meaning tiger's paws), *ikaki mgbe* (tortoise shell), and *kieni* (cane). The color palette is limited: background colors of indigo, red, and burgundy (sometimes dark green) offset with white, yellow, and black. After choosing a textile, the maker uses a needle to pick up an individual thread, then, with a penknife or razor blade, cuts it on two ends and pulls out the thread, continuing to do this over the whole cloth. Various shapes result from the openings in the original plaid or checked fabric, depending on the maker's imagination or decision to repeat motifs that she has made or seen before. Many motifs are named that relate to obvious shapes that result from removing the threads, such as cross, bow tie, or fish gill. The lighter and brighter threads are the ones removed so that the process of cutting and pulling threads leaves a subtle and shadowy type of design by subtraction, making the cloth feel light and airy when worn. The origin for the process of cutting is not known. The cloths are treasured and popular, and many are historical. One extant example was made by a wife of a Kalabari chief, John Bull (1810–1893), possibly as early as the 1830s.

These specially designed cloths are used for and given at special occasions. A father is expected to give one to his infant child at the time of the baby's naming ceremony. Men and women wear pelete bite wrappers for dress-up occasions, particularly if they want to identify themselves as Kalabari, and specific families lay claim to particular cloths that have names. Men wear a single wrapper tied at the waist. Women wear a double set, also tied at the waist, the bottom one ankle-length and the top layered over it, usually ending at the knee. These are to be worn by all members of the family as wrappers for family occasions, such as following the corpse from the mortuary to the family compound on the day the body will lie in state before burial. Pelete bite is also used to cover the face of a masquerader, because the fabric allows the masquerader to see and breathe easily but disguises the facial features of the masquerade dancer from the onlookers. To celebrate the life of an elderly woman at the time of her funeral, family members may choose to borrow many cut-thread wrappers from the extended family to arrange on the funeral bed. They fold them in fancy shapes to display during the week following the burial when community members call to pay respects to the deceased and the family.

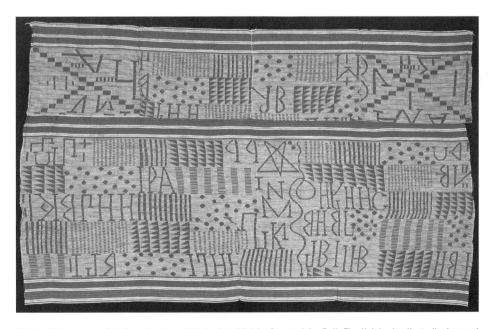

Kalabari Ijo wrapper. Cut-thread cotton cloth (*pelete bite*) by Osonta John Bull. The Kalabari collect, display, and wear many types of textiles, including those from Asia and Europe. Cut ca. 1830s in Buguma, Nigeria. 49 x 80 inches (124 x 203 cm). Fowler Museum at UCLA X84.600. Photograph by Don Cole.

A Christian family of Kalabari mourners walking to the Sunday "Thanksgiving" church service as the final funeral event. The woman in front, as chief mourner, wears a velvet wrapper and fringed hat from India, coral from Italy, and imported blouse fabric from Europe. Buguma, Nigeria, 1988. Photograph by Joanne B. Eicher.

Other examples of culturally authenticated fashions that stem from Kalabari trade history include a special occasion men's gown called *attigra* and some men's and women's hats worn for ceremonial purposes. The most common attigra seen in the twenty-first century is a large gown made from embroidered velvet that is imported from India. The embroidery threads were initially wound with silver and gold but, in the twenty-first century, may be gold- and silver-colored on a gown that is usually burgundy, red, or brown. The shape of the gown apparently originates from earlier examples of domestically woven and embroidered cloth imported from northern Nigeria and the Igalla people. The name is an elision from the words *attah of Igalla,* the title of the Igalla ruler who wore the gown. At some point, imported velvets began to replace the earlier types. Along with this gown will be worn a ceremonial men's hat called *ajibulu* that is fashioned from a bicorne

shape and must always have a ram's beard on it, along with a bull's-eye design and feathers in addition to other items that the hat maker fancies. Men wear this hat when being installed as a chief or for ceremonial use at funerals. Elaborate and large coral necklaces and a fan, perhaps also of velvet, usually complete his ensemble. Men may wear shoes or, if dancing, choose to go barefoot in order to feel the earth as they dance and to show off their footsteps.

Women also wear embroidered Indian velvets as wrappers for ceremonial occasions, when parading to end the sequestering period after giving birth, or participating as a chief mourner at a funeral. The women's hat worn with these wrappers is called *sun* and is a boat shape decorated with branch coral or made of fabric trimmed with many different objects, such as ribbons, beads, fringe, and sequins. Women use other imported fabrics for wrappers such as Indian madras; Indian soft silk of muted pink, rose, and blue stripes; and handwoven textiles by women in the Igbo town of Akwete, north of the Kalabari islands, or by Yoruba men in the west of Nigeria. The wearing of velvet wrappers with a lace blouse, a hat, and a large coral necklace, however, indicates an important occasion. Women usually wear shoes with their ensembles except when showing off their dance steps or parading as an *iriabo,* a woman celebrating the birth of her child. These examples of Kalabari ceremonial dress describe what they wear for special occasions in the twenty-first century, not for everyday, whether the event is held in Nigeria or in the United States, in celebration of a mother's safe delivery of a child, or at periodic meetings of the Kalabari National Association held in large cities in the United States such as Washington, DC, Houston, and Los Angeles.

REFERENCES AND FURTHER READING

Eicher, Joanne B. "Kalabari Identity and Indian Textiles in the Niger Delta." In *Indian Trade Textiles*, edited by Rosemary Crill, 153–171. New Delhi: Seagull, 2005.

Eicher, Joanne B., and Tonye V. Erekosima. "Why Do They Call It Kalabari? Cultural Authentication and the Demarcation of Ethnic Identity." In *Dress and Ethnicity: Change across space and Time,* edited by Joanne B. Eicher, 139–164. Oxford, UK: Berg, 1995.

Erekosima, Tonye V., and Joanne B. Eicher. "Kalabari Cut Thread Cloth: An Example of Cultural Authentication." *African Arts* 14, no. 2 (February 1981): 48–51.

Joanne B. Eicher

See also Headdresses and Hairdos; West Africa; Lower Niger Delta Peoples and Diaspora.

The Nigerian Fashion Scene

Since the advent of daily newspapers in the late 1920s, the print media have been an important source of information on fashion and style, especially the *Daily Times of Nigeria* (founded 1926) and the *West African Pilot* (founded 1937). Both newspapers regularly featured women's columns, often including photographs of contemporary European fashion, sometimes with pattern instructions for various styles. This was particularly useful for local dressmakers and tailors who sewed to order as well as for women who sewed for themselves. Until the 1950s, the fashion column of the *Daily Times* was usually written by freelance European women journalists who had accompanied their husbands to Nigeria; their target audience was clearly colonial wives interested in creating a diverse social life under trying conditions. Elite urban Nigerian women also took their lead from these columns. According to "Petite Parissienne," the pseudonym for the author of "Our Feminine Corner" (*Daily Times*), writing on 18 May 1931, "Dress in Africa is very different from dress in England, but every bit as exciting. One can get four or five ravishing dresses in West Africa [for the same price] as one well-made by a tailor in England. Dresses don't last as long so one does not get sick of them. If you get fed up with a dress, you can always swap it for some Bida brass with the next Hausaman who comes to your door."

Before independence in 1960, indigenous dress rarely appeared as a subject in these columns, although, in the early 1940s, they did criticize the important traditional custom of *aso-ebi*, whereby a group of family members, friends, or *egbe* (association) members wore the same type of cloth as an expression of solidarity at ceremonial occasions. Such attacks suggested a robust dress tradition in which various types of textiles and their design and quality were not only socially important but also subject to changing fashion dictates.

THE FASHION SCENE AFTER INDEPENDENCE

Increased public awareness of the importance of national dress and textiles was part of nationalist politics in the 1950s, which led to independence in 1960. In part, Nigeria was following the trend that had earlier emerged in the Gold Coast (now Ghana) among nationalists and ordinary citizens who donned kente cloth and other indigenous dress as an expression of their national identity. For example, the *West African Pilot* of 2 May 1947 carried the headline "Civil Servants Report for Work in Their African Attires: Ladies Take Accra Way." At home and abroad, Nigerian politicians wore traditional attire: Yoruba, Hausa, and Rivers styles, which, with their rich handwoven textiles and beads, embroidery, and flowing garments, made especially powerful visual statements

in newspaper and magazine photographs, cinema newsreels, and public appearances in local campaigns, international conferences, and even at the Ascot race track. Party supporters, wearing uniforms in the party colors and featuring party symbols and often photographs of political leaders, combined traditional and modern styles made in inexpensive cotton prints and emphasized the new national identity.

During the 1950s, *West Africa* and *West African Review*, the two most popular news and general interest regional periodicals, carried a number of photo essays dealing with tropical fashion and West Africans in the United Kingdom who were training as dress designers or performing as models in the United Kingdom. A December 1955 article in *West African Review* observed that the new political climate gave rise to "an entirely new attitude towards dress," noting that West African travelers, especially politicians, were "more conscious and proud of their national dress," while at the same time adopting and adapting Western styles. The sense of an eclectic national fashion identity with a distinct sense of what was appropriate dress for work and life ceremonies permeated these commentaries. A month before independence, the

Cover of *Dressense Fashion Catalogue*, vol. 4, ca. 1987–1988: A lavishly produced Nigerian fashion catalog aimed at the upscale market. A series of catalogs and magazines were produced by fashion designers in Nigeria in the late twentieth century. Courtesy of LaRay Denzer.

September 1960 issue of *West African Review* carried Eve de Negri's article "Nigeria's National Dress," which explored the question: would traditional dress "survive the impact of modern life?" She highlighted the impracticality of much of traditional dress and emphasized the West African love of innovative styles. She also noted the historical incorporation of Western-style elements in traditional dress (especially in the southeast) and the rich textile traditions throughout Nigeria and concluded that national dress would be reserved for "leisured moments, for ceremonies, and celebrations, for times of pleasure and relaxation."

The emergence of Shade Thomas (later Thomas-Fahm) as Nigeria's first widely recognized fashion designer in the 1960s reflected evolving syncretic ideas concerning dress that were picked by the media. Local newspapers and a variety of new Nigerian periodicals popularized her designs in their fashion pages. Among them was the Nigerian edition of the popular magazine *Drum* (first published in South Africa), which was launched in Lagos in 1958 and did much to popularize images of the "new" Nigerians.

Media interest in the Nigerian dress culture declined with the overthrow of the democratic civilian government in 1966 and the imposition of the first series of military governments, which remained in power until 1979, when civilian democratic rule was restored in the Second Republic, only to be again overturned four years later by the military. During the second period of military government (1983 to 1999), however, media interest in fashion and popular culture revived. Several reasons accounted for this revival. First, there was the development of mass-based popular institutions. Second, the 1986 Structural Adjustment Program (SAP) opened surprising new opportunities for indigenous entrepreneurs. Third, for the first time, a personality cult developed around the wife of the head of state, Maryam Babangida, who always wore beautiful traditional fashions. She and her husband, President Ibrahim Babangida, patronized local designers, whose careers flourished as a result.

Design for couples as featured in the Nigerian *Dressense Fashion Catalogue* vol. 4, ca. 1987–1988. This catalog featured designs that could easily be copied or simplified by seamstresses. Courtesy of LaRay Denzer.

THE RISE OF PRINT MEDIA AND FASHION

After 1983, the national print media took on new energy, beginning with the foundation of *The Guardian*, a new daily modeled on elite international newspapers like its namesake in Manchester and the *Times* of London. From then until the 1992 fuel crisis, the Nigerian media sector launched a wide variety of publications in English and indigenous languages. Most failed within a short time, for they lacked sufficient starting capital and efficient editorial management.

Magazines targeting women readers came and went. They included glossy magazines such as *Society*, *Metro*, *Chanelle*, and *Chic*—aimed at the elite market of women executives and professionals. Others such as *Quality*, *She*, *New Spear*, *Eko*, *Classique*, *The Sunday Magazine*, and *Climax* appealed to a more general public. For a brief time, there was even a women's newspaper, *Everywoman*. One of the most successful of these periodicals is *Poise*, a weekly that replaced the longest running women's magazine in Nigeria, the popular monthly *Woman's World*, published by the Daily Times group from 1964 to 1990. To a large extent, the vitality of women's publications reflected the new drive for women's empowerment and organization that began toward the end of the United Nation's Women's Decade (1975 to 1985).

They also demonstrated a keen interest in projecting national culture and fashion. Yet none of them survived the major fuel shortage of 1994, despite a few half-hearted attempts to revive some titles. Nonetheless, for the period 1986 to 1994, such periodicals form a major source of information about fashion trends and fashion designers.

Also after 1983, during the second military government, newspapers paid more attention to women's matters. Stimulated by the increased global interest in covering women's issues, Nigerian newspapers gave new prominence to their "woman's page" and usually included a weekly feature on fashion. This focus became more noticeable after the implementation of SAP in 1986. One feature of the SAP budget was a prohibition on importing ready-to-wear clothing, new or used. This ban galvanized the local garment industry; local dressmakers and tailors enjoyed unprecedented patronage as new customers flocked to their shops to have clothes made to order. Established designers in Lagos, many of whom had professional credentials in fashion design, reacted to SAP by Nigerianizing their fashion collections, simultaneously seeking to create a new Nigerian (or African) identity based on a fashion culture that utilized local fabrics while also intent on establishing a sustainable high-profit business. The situation allowed a group of young fashion designers to emerge as the new culture heroes of the 1990s with a defined agenda to create a Nigerian fashion identity.

NIGERIAN FASHION HOUSES

A number of fashion houses emerged as trendsetters, especially the houses of Labanella, founded by Princess Abah Adesanya; Nikky Africana, founded by Nike Okeowo; and Supreme Stitches (now Rose of Sharon), founded by Folorunso Alakija. Their collections featured in the most important dailies, and their proprietors became the subjects of numerous extensive interviews and profiles highlighting their success in Lagos society. The term glitterati was applied to the rich business elite, traditional rulers, the political class, high government bureaucrats, and other celebrities. The Nigerian public showed an avid interest in their life histories and their personal style. Successful fashion designers, however, provided extra spice and dash, verve and style. From the mid-1980s, the flamboyant acumen of fashion designers as entrepreneurs, coupled with their natural flair for glamour, projected them as the new culture heroes of SAP. The fact that some of them also had previous experience in public relations no doubt helped. In the 1980s, Woman's World featured a "Designer of the Month" page, and its successor, Poise, regularly celebrated the achievements of designers. Although most newspapers ran a weekly fashion page, some of them also had other popular features devoted to style and women achievers: "Women in Business" and "Elegance Is" in the Sunday Vanguard, "Style" in the Guardian, and "Meet a Designer" in the Nigerian Tribune.

FASHION FOCUS AND FASHION CATALOGS

In response to the fanfare heralding designers and the growing popularity of fashion shows, some interest groups in the industry, seemingly oblivious to the fashion history of the nationalist period (1945 to 1966) trumpeted the creation of a national fashion culture. In August 1987, Alhaji Wale Adeiye, an engineer by profession and executive chairman of Progress Publishing Company, launched Fashion Focus with the subtitle "An International Magazine for African Fashion." The central aim of the new magazine was to promote "fashion consciousness among our people by making use of available locally woven materials." At the launching, Opral Benson (the Iya-Oge of Lagos), a prominent businesswoman and patron of the fashion industry, addressed the assembly on the current state of the Lagos fashion world. She stressed that the industry in Nigeria had "overnight become a highly competitive area, for many, a lucrative business" characterized by innovation. Not only did it provide employment, she observed, it also simultaneously served as a source and an outlet for artistic talent, self-reliance, and nationalism.

Unfortunately, Fashion Focus folded after three issues. Somewhat more successful publishing ventures were fashion catalogs. Before SAP, the major source of clothing designs derived from foreign style catalogs, published by the major international dress pattern companies, such as Simplicity, Butterick, and Vogue. Currency devaluation made the cost of these so prohibitive that, by the mid-1990s, it was rare to find any but the most tattered copy of a foreign catalog in a fashion designer's or tailor's shop. Another popular source of designs were the back pages of popular comic magazines, especially Ikebe Super and Super Story, which

typically featured ten or twelve new designs per issue. Ikebe Super also published an annual calendar presenting an array of new styles designed to appeal to the general public. About the same time as the debut of Fashion Focus, some fashion designers issued a series of Nigerian fashion catalogs meant to appeal to sophisticated elite women (and men). Of these, the most interesting and beautifully produced was Dressense Fashion Catalogue, with lavish and innovative styles for the upscale market. Although few seamstresses or fashion designers could afford to buy it, the designs were easily copied or simplified. For the average seamstress or tailor, however, cheap posters sold in the markets and motor parks were a much more important source of designs. Typically, these featured between forty and sixty (occasionally fewer) drawings or photographs of garment styles, each featuring a particular type of garment (blouses, iro and buba, gowns, children's wear, caftans, and so on). Attractively priced, every garment maker could afford to buy them to mount on the walls of their shops both as decorations and as advertisements of the type of the styles they could produce.

Publishers and designers are still attempting to find a winning vehicle to project Nigeria's fashion image. Some have published autobiographical compendiums that feature not only their career histories but also photographs and sketches of their styles. New lifestyle magazines with foreign correspondents and sometimes published overseas seek a wider readership that includes Nigerians and other Africans in the diaspora. These include Empress and Genevieve (launched in 2003 by Betty Irabor), but perhaps the most successful of these is the London-based Ovation International Magazine, with elaborate color spreads showing the Nigerian elite and celebrities at work and play decked out in the latest fashion, both traditional and Western.

Surprisingly, Nigerian designers and fashion journalists have rarely exploited the potential offered by the Internet. Neither Shade Thomas-Fahm nor Folorunsho Alakija maintains a Web site. Although Nike Davies-Okundayo's Nike Centre for Art and Culture of Osogbo and Lagos does, she highlights tourist programs, cultural events, and art for sale but not her clothing designs. Some designers like Deola Sagoe and Jimi King seem to be toying with the idea of Web sites, but Sagoe's only posting is dated 2001, and King's site is under construction. Nor is it easy to follow Nigerian fashion journalism, for the popular African newspaper Web site, allafrica.com, which covers most countries and many topics, does not designate fashion or style for regular coverage. Some online newspaper sites, however, do include fashion and lifestyle articles, particularly the Guardian and Vanguard, both published in Lagos. The lifestyle magazines Ovation International and Genevieve mentioned earlier also have sites, but these operate mainly to solicit subscriptions.

The changing fashion world of Lagos can be illustrated by juxtaposing the careers of Shade Thomas-Fahm, regarded as Nigeria's first modern fashion designer, and Folorunso Alakija, one of the most celebrated of the new designers of the 1990s. Thomas-Fahm defied the conventions of her social class in the 1960s when she enrolled to study fashion design after abandoning training as a nurse. Upon returning to Nigeria, she set up a boutique at the Federal Palace Hotel and established a garment factory at the Yaba Industrial Estate. By 1964, her business was valued at about £10,000 (Nigerian). Her simple elegant fashions quickly attracted a clientele at home and abroad, making her Nigeria's best known designer throughout the mid-1960s and 1970s. In addition to her outlet in Lagos, she exported clothes to the United States and participated in many international fashion shows in Germany, Britain, and The Netherlands. From the beginning, she specialized in the innovative use of locally woven and locally dyed textiles, making her the first Nigerian designer to deliberately cultivate a national clothing culture and identity. In 2007, her boutique and factory were still operating, and she is regarded as the doyen of fashion designers. During the SAP years, she was one of the founders of the Fashion Designers' Association of Nigeria (FADAN), which still seeks to set professional standards for the fashion industry.

In contrast to Thomas-Fahm's simplicity and quiet dignity, the flamboyant entrance of Folorunso Alakija (née Ogbara) into the Lagos fashion scene reflected the mood of the period. In the early 1990s, she epitomized the successful fashion designer and enjoyed celebrity status in Lagos society. Fashion design, however, had not been her first choice of career. She began as a secretary, first employed by Oba Olubuse II, Okunade Sijuade, the *oni* of Ife, spiritual leader of the Yoruba and a very powerful traditional ruler. Then she transferred to the Lagos branch of the First National Bank of Chicago (later known as the International Merchant Bank). While at the bank, she demonstrated a flair for banking and rose to become the head of the corporate affairs department. Twelve years later, she decided to leave banking and establish herself in the fashion industry. After a careful assessment of the professional requirements and investment needs of a fashion enterprise, she went to London for training in fashion design at both the American College and the Central School of Fashion as well as doing an internship with a milliner. After her return to Lagos, her meteoric rise in the fashion world obscured how carefully she had planned her venture, Supreme Stitches (later renamed Rose of Sharon). Her links with influential figures like the oni, coupled with her expertise in public relations in a prestigious financial institution, ensured the right connections in Lagos society. Three months after her return in 1986, she opened her high-profile boutique and shortly thereafter received the prestigious Time Leisure Services award as Best Designer of the Year. Within two years, she expanded her enterprise into a three-story building at 156 Awolowo Road, Ikoyi. In addition, she operated two factories.

Alakija's career was not the only success story. During the early years of SAP, the fashion industry become so lucrative that a significant number of elite women decided to abandon their original professions in favor of establishing fashion houses or boutiques. Published profiles reveal that doctors, lawyers, nurses, university lecturers, teachers, bankers, and others opted for careers in the garment industry. Rarely did their training in the production of garments go beyond home sewing, perhaps learned while living with relatives engaged in dressmaking or as an interest in maintaining a chic personal wardrobe at a reasonable price. They built up their establishments on the basis of hired expertise: managers, journeymen, tailors, and seamstresses. Gladys Nwobodo, proprietor of House of 27 Gladyns (Victoria Island), boasted that

Cover of the *FADAN Annual Journal*, 1992–1993. The Fashion Designer Association of Nigeria seeks to establish professional standards for th fashion industry. Courtesy of LaRay Denzer.

"she [had] no training but she [had] ideas, a strong sense of ad venture and a background of sewing gleaned from her seamstres mother." For much the same reasons, Ore Williams (Afprin Designer of the Year in 1988–1989), managing director of Sad Fashions but formerly a lawyer, decided to leave law and estab lish a clothing industry. Chioma Ugorji, an accountant, decide to become a fashion designer because of "the state of the econom and the lack of employment." Occasionally, husbands and friend perceived an aptitude for fashion in their wives or colleagues an advised them to take up training in fashion, as was the case wit Alaba Okoye, a former nurse who is now the manager of Chinm Fashions (Kaduna), owned by her sister-in-law. Other wome went into the fashion industry after they retired from successf careers in different fields, investing their savings and gratuities i a fashion establishment. For example, Justina Ekanem set up shop in her home in Festac Town (Lagos) after twenty-one year in nursing, falling back on the training she received in a Singe sewing course as a young bride.

Snapshot: Shade Thomas-Fahm (b. 1933)

From the 1960s, Nigeria's iconic cultural nationalist Folashade (known as "Shade") Thomas-Fahm has transformed the country's fashion industry by modernizing traditional designs and popularizing the use of *aso oke* (Yoruba handwoven textiles), *adire* (Yoruba hand-dyed fabrics), *akwete* (Igbo handwoven textiles), and the new made-in-Nigeria cotton prints in creating Western styles. Not only did her clothing and accessories appeal to the urban elite and expatriates throughout southern Nigeria but it also attracted an international clientele interested in the "Africa look."

Thomas-Fahm was born in 1933 into a polygamous Yoruba family who migrated from Oyo, political capital of the Old Oyo Empire, to Lagos when she was a small child. Both parents were Christian converts who built a moderately prosperous trade in stockfish. They encouraged their children to obtain an education but also inculcated a love of traditional culture, especially through the adept use of proverbs. Both parents became community and church leaders among other Oyo migrants in Lagos.

After Thomas-Fahm completed her education in Lagos, she obtained British Council sponsorship for nurses' training in England in 1953, a career choice then popular among young Nigerian women because of its humanitarian qualities and the fact that training hospitals paid students a small allowance. Early in her training at St. Mary's Hospital in London, she

became so enamored by window displays and current fashion in Oxford Street and other high streets that she decided to leave nursing for an eighteen-month course in design at Barrett Technical College, followed by more intensive training in fashion at St. Martin's College of Arts of London University. In her autobiography, she recalls that "as a child I was often fascinated at how plain fabrics could be transformed into a beautiful ensemble."

During her student years, Thomas-Fahm's extroverted personality and stylish looks, combined with her determination to succeed, enabled her to get a place at Stenoff and Sons Furrier, a couture house on Old Bond Street, where she worked her way up, starting as a tea girl. Once she completed her St. Martin's course, she became a successful full-time model for Export Advertising Company, which held the Lux Beauty Soap account. Her image as a Lux girl graced one of the advertisements that appeared widely in African periodicals and newspapers. Meanwhile, her work enabled her to build a network in the fashion worlds of London, Paris, and Milan.

Like many educated young Nigerians overseas during the nationalist era (1945 to 1966), Thomas-Fahm was eager to return home and participate in the exciting work of nation building, and, on 7 July 1960, she returned to Lagos, just three months before independence celebrations. She arrived with plans to establish her own fashion house and with enough equipment, accessories, and sewing materials to start her enterprise and sustain it for three or four years. Her first objective was to secure a place in the new Yaba industrial estate where she opened Maison Shade, a boutique, and a factory. Two years later, she moved her boutique to a more lucrative location in the new Federal Palace Hotel, which served Western and local businessmen, high government officials, and tourists. Some time later, she made another strategic move to Falomo Shopping Center, where her shop was still located in 2007. Her factory remained in the Yaba location. By 1969, her staff consisted of close to thirty tailors and other employees.

Looking back on her role in the national fashion industry in 2004, she described the fashion climate at the time of independence: "The fashion environment I met when I returned from abroad was not decent. It was not better than how I left it. The elites were still going for imported things and looking down on what we had." She was determined to encourage an appreciation of indigenous textiles by demonstrating how beautiful aso oke, adire, and akwete were in creating the simple elegant styles that she introduced in her first independent fashion show at the Young Women's Christian Association in August 1960. Previously, aso oke and akwete had been worn mostly for traditional celebrations, and adire was regarded as only suitable for domestic servants or market women, but almost immediately her new line of styles became popular among Nigerian elite and expatriate women. She eschewed the flamboyant Western styles of the time and focused on the A-line

Designs for women's clothing by Shade Thomas-Fahm. She became known as Nigeria's first fashion designer in the late 1960s. Courtesy of LaRay Denzer.

dress, the shift, the mini and the midi, culottes, and simple blouses and skirts made with local handcrafted fabrics or the new cotton prints manufactured by local textile factories. Further, she adapted traditional wear by introducing a sewn *gele* (head tie), many new sleeve styles for the *buba* (Yoruba blouse), and a less voluminous woman's version of the *agbada*, the caftan, and the boubou. Some of these styles have endured until the present. She worked with local weavers to add more colors to their range and make lighter fabrics that were more easily incorporated into a wider variety of styles. She also used machine embroidery in her designs, made on special expensive Singer machines.

By the late 1960s, Thomas-Fahm's position as Nigeria's first fashion designer was well recognized. The populist politician Tunji Braithwaite commissioned her to design a simple outfit for both his personal wear and his followers. Early in his career, Nobel laureate Wole Soyinka asked her to design the costumes for the first performance of his play *Dark Forest*. Elite parents were pleased to allow their daughters to model in her popular fashion shows. Among her early models were Franca Afegbua, who became a senator in the Second Republic (1979–1983), Doyin Aboaba (third wife of politician Moshood Kashimawo Abiola), and Deronke Ademola (daughter of Lady Kofoworola Ademola).

Meanwhile, Thomas-Fahm acquired international recognition through participation in fashion shows abroad. In 1967, she took part in the Singer World Designers Collection in New York and was the first African designer to appear in a world collection; she won first place for the African Zone. At that time, some American designers were experimenting with an African look using handwoven and tie-dyed materials from the continent. In 1968, she was appointed as Nigeria's representative at Commonwealth Fashion Exhibition that marked the opening of the Heads of States conference. Princess Elizabeth of Toro, the popular Ugandan model who later became minister of foreign affairs in the government of notorious dictator General Idi Amin, modeled her clothes—one of the high points of the event. As a result of such international competition, Thomas-Fahm realized how important fashion was in creating a national identity and made her aware of her role as a cultural ambassador.

At home, her business expanded. The major European department stores—Kingsway, Leventis, and Paterson-Zuchonis—

marketed her lines while some American entrepreneurs—A. Marshall and S. Gitelman—went into partnership with her to import her clothes to the United States. Unfortunately, this latter enterprise ran into difficulty in 1976 with the enactment of the Indigenization Decree that required Nigerians to hold majority control in any business. The government briefly closed her boutique and factory, charging that she operated as a front for her American partners, until she showed incontrovertible proof of her total ownership.

In the 1980s, coverage of local designers declined in the popular press, but it revived in the early 1990s with the resurgence of the Nigerian fashion industry that occurred after the promulgation of the Structural Adjustment Program in 1985. Fashion designers, following in the earlier steps of Thomas-Fahm, emerged as the new cultural heroes and recreated a Nigerian fashion identity that again celebrated the use of traditional textiles and Nigerian-made fabrics. In 1989, she joined other fashion designers in setting up the Fashion Designers Association of Nigeria (FADAN) to promote further development of the fashion industry and upgrade standards of production. While new, younger designers led FADAN activities, they paid homage to her contribution to Nigeria's modern cultural history, and the press rediscovered her.

REFERENCES AND FURTHER READING

"Boutique Is Mine 100%." *Daily Times* (Lagos), 27 August 1976, 32.

Ekkunkunbor, Jemi. "Fashion of the 60s Was Greatly Influenced by Colonialism—Mrs Sade Thomas-Fahm." *Vanguard* (Lagos), 3 October 2004. http://www.vanguardngr.com/articles/2002/features/fe503102004.html (accessed 12 December 2005).

"Nigeria's No. 1 Dressmaker." *Sketch* (Ibadan), 6 April 1964.

Olisa, Joy. "FADAN: Aiming High." *Weekend Vanguard* (Lagos), 13 July 1996, 6.

"The Success Story." *Daily Times* (Lagos), 4 May 1969, 7, 11.

Thomas-Fahm, Shade. *Faces of She*. Lagos, Nigeria: Tegali Communications, 2004.

References and Further Reading

Alakija, Folorunso. *Fashion: The African Connection: The Spirit, Soul, and Body of African Fashion*. Lagos, Nigeria: Mrs. Folorunso Alakija, 2001.

Brady, Michael. "Sartorial Sidelights on West Africa." *West African Review*, December 1955, 1120–1124.

"Catholics Launch a Crusade against 'Aso-Ebi' Craze." *West African Pilot*, 11 November 1940, 1, 8.

Denzer, LaRay. "High Fashion and Fluctuating Fortunes: The Nigerian Garment Industry under Structural Adjustment." In *Money Struggles and City Life: Devaluation in Ibadan and Other Urban Centers in Southern Nigeria, 1986–1996*, edited by Jane I. Guyer, LaRay Denzer and Adigun Agbaje, 93–114. Westport, CT: Heinemann. 2002.

"New Fashions for Ascot?" *West Africa*, 5 July 1952, 621.

Thomas-Fahm, Shade. *Faces of She*. Lagos, Nigeria: Tegali Communications, 2004.

LaRay Denzer

See also Fashion in African Dress; African Fashion Designers; Nigeria Overview; Yoruba in Nigeria and Diaspora; Hausa in Nigeria and Diaspora.

Sierra Leone

Dress in Sierra Leone and the surrounding region differs according to whether it is worn in everyday life or on celebratory occasions and whether it is worn among special classes of people, such as chiefs, hunters, and various ethnocultural groups. Dress that has emerged from indigenous design is most distinctive, whether worn by adults or, in miniature version, by children. Sierra Leoneans also wear Western-style clothes. Traditionally, nudity was common.

THE TEXTILE AND CULTURAL HERITAGE

The countries of Guinea and Liberia plus the Atlantic Ocean comprise the boundaries of Sierra Leone. Weaving cultures are found in the southern and eastern areas of Sierra Leone, while historically nonweavers characterize the western coast and the entire northwest, vaguely following the lines of the Mande- and the Mel-speaking peoples, respectively. The most elaborate weaving comes from the southern half of Sierra Leone among the Mende and Vai peoples, suggesting that perhaps the great heritage of weaving in this region can be traced to the influx of their Mande-speaking ancestors over the centuries (and especially around the middle of the sixteenth century). Weaving experts Venice and Alastair Lamb report weavers among the Temne and Bullom peoples (southern and northern groups, including the Sherbro), but it is seen as an imported technology. While Mende and Vai weaving is extremely rich and distinctive, all gown styles in Sierra Leone derive from the Manding, the northern group of Mande speakers found mostly in Guinea, Senegal, and Mali and including the Kuranko and Kono in northeastern Sierra Leone.

Mende cloth is woven on a small tripod loom in narrow strips usually about twenty to thirty centimeters (eight to twelve inches) wide and in narrower strips of approximately ten centimeters (four inches), and these strips are sewn together lengthwise to form a panel. For women, the cloth is usually wrapped around the waist with the strips horizontal, but it may also be used as a longer wrap with the strips vertical and wrapped around the upper chest over the breasts. The narrow-strip cloth, *kondi gula*, generally is used to make floor-length gowns worn mainly by men, while the wide-strip cloth, *kpokpo*, is used more for display and to wrap as a blanket but also occasionally for chief's gowns, considered extremely luxurious.

The quality and status of men's gowns is determined by the style of tailoring as well as the style of cloth and its weight. Among the narrow-strip kondi gula are several subtypes of pattern. *Kula gulei* is a simple, natural-colored cloth, sometimes with subtle, alternating white and beige stripes, used for common garments as well as for burial shrouds. *Ndulu gula nyei* cloth has more distinct patterns of brown and white. *Kula nyei* cloth uses more elaborate colors, including light and dark blue, green, and brown. And *kula hina* (male cloth) is a dense weave and is even more elaborate, with indigo and pale blue on a white ground.

These patterns can appear in a number of weights and sizes. *Gri gulei* is a light weave of fine cotton thread. *Pee gula* (cover cloth), with fourteen to seventeen strips across, is a heavier-weight cloth used for blankets. Kula hina designates not only the pattern but also a heavy weight with a required seventeen strips and a length of at least three and a half meters (four yards). The largest cloth is *gbali*, with at least twenty-three strips and measuring at least five meters (five and a half yards) in length.

THE MAN'S GOWN

From northern Sierra Leone and Guinea, a ubiquitous style of man's gown called *kusaibi* has spread from the Manding and is tailored for local use by the adjacent Yalunka, Susu, Temne, and Limba to their south. Documented as early as 1830 by René Caillié, it is an extra wide gown of extremely simple tailoring, completely open on the sides, the excess of which the wearer continually needs to throw up over his shoulders on either side in an overt example of ostentatious display. Islam has dominated central Manding society since the thirteenth century, and the word *kusaibi* may derive from the Arabic *kasab* (a type of linen garment) and ultimately from ancient Egyptian.

This pattern begins simply with a huge vertical rectangular panel folded in half across the strips so that when the completed garment is spread out, it is a large horizontal rectangle with the strips hanging vertically. A tailor completes the garment by sewing a few centimeters together at the bottom and cutting and hemming a long, rectangular, vertical hole for the neck on the front panel so that the fold runs along the top of the neck opening and across the shoulders. Below the neck hole, the tailor sews a large pocket, usually trapezoidal, often of two separate pieces on a bias, with the shorter left side aligned with the left edge of the neck hole (as the viewer sees it) and the right side enlarging across the gown, with the lower right corner pointing downward. This off-center position enables the wearer to reach his right hand through the pocket toward his left chest conveniently. Sometimes elaborate embroidery covers the front and back of a gown. Patterns of embroidery may include square interlacing blocks resembling the magic squares—*hatumere*—of cabalistic writing and also variations of the swastika, zigzag lines, and chevrons and sometimes representational forms such as birds, snakes, and humans.

The kusaibi gown has been adopted by most of the groups in Sierra Leone and is worn by men of all classes, but especially by chiefs and "big men." Although it may originate with the Manding, it is among the Mende, called *bobani*, that it achieves its most glorious decorative elaboration, especially if it is made for a chief and given the special status of *ndoma hina*, always made of the heavier kula hini strip cloth. This and other gowns are usually worn with a cap, *kpini bolo*, made of the same strip-woven cloth,

Paramount Mende chief Kai Lundu of Luawa wearing his embroidered *kusaibi* gown. Sierra Leone, 1891. Courtesy of Frederick John Lamp.

usually a sort of high pillbox in which the top collapses into or over the sides. It can be folded and placed into the large pocket on the front of the gown when the costume is stored.

The simplest type of gown for men is a straight cylinder of cloth, a slender sleeveless shift of vertical strips, called *tolo* in southern Sierra Leone (the word for any Muslim gown), probably based on a common Muslim man's floor-length loose sheath. It is approximately twelve narrow strips in width, or about sixty centimeters (twenty-four inches), and sewn up both sides from the bottom to the waist. A very slight flaring from the thighs to the bottom is achieved by inserting narrow triangular shims of cloth between the strips, permitting greater movement of the legs. This garment is

usually worn with some kind of shirt and pants underneath and is considered informal but well dressed.

Of more complex tailoring is the *duriki ba* ("large shirt" in Manding), a gown worn by men everywhere, especially chiefs. The gown probably derives from the Egyptian *tawb*. This garment is a combination of a narrow, open, vertical-strip panel to which is attached full-length open wings of horizontal-strip cloth sewn together only at the bottom. The contrasting side panels are for display only, and, because of the horizontal-strip construction, they pile in a huge heap over the shoulders. As with the kusaibi, a large trapezoidal pocket is sewn to the front. Some of these garments made of plain-colored cloth are heavily embroidered. The bulky duriki ba is the ultimate luxury of excess.

There is a half-length version of a similar cut called *tànkfòl* by the Temne, or *hu-ronko* by the Limba, used especially throughout northern and eastern Sierra Leone. When the pattern is laid out before folding and sewing, it somewhat resembles a thick Teutonic cross. The completed garment, when opened out flat, is in a truncated T shape. The wings form the sleeves, which are open along the bottom. When wearing this garment, the man does not attempt to throw the sleeves up over the shoulder but allows them to hang gracefully so that the whole garment resembles a broad cape. This is especially favored by young men but is worn by men of all ages as informal wear, sometimes with shorts, even though it is quite a magnificent garment when it is made from heavy, decorative strip-woven cloth by the Temne.

Among the Limba and Yalunka people, especially hunters, the hu-ronko is usually made of a lighter, plain strip-woven cotton. It is dyed with a reddish brown color that may come from a number of woods, roots, and barks, such as *ku-wòlò*, *kubara*, *kyordo* (mahogany), and *ekuwere*. A more yellow color is obtained by using only the roots of the mahogany, especially used by the Yalunka who probably originated this garment. After the dying, when the garment has dried, black designs are stamped onto it using a mixture of leaves from the *bumalange*, *budoneye*, and *buyaya*. There seems to be no limit to the repertoire of designs, which included the rising sun motif of the reigning All People's Congress political party of Sierra Leone documented in 1980, certainly a wise choice for anyone seeking protection at the time.

HEAD DRESSING

Headgear is extremely varied. Caps are commonly made of strip-woven cloth. The type of cap worn throughout Sierra Leone with the large strip-woven gowns described in the previous section is usually made of the same strip-woven cloth with the strips running diagonally. Sometimes the top is ornamented with a pom-pom that can fall over the side of the cap.

A particular kind of high cap worn by the Limba and Kuranko, probably of Manding origin, when laid flat, is in the shape of a long oval with a point at the bottom. When worn, it appears as a transverse crest at the top and opens at the bottom with the two points extending over the wearer's forehead in front and the nape of the neck in back. This style of cap is called *bambada* (mouth of the crocodile) because of the way the opening grips the head. It is made of strip-woven, plain-colored cloth and is often decorated with either stamped designs or (sometimes elaborate) embroidery, often bearing the design of the Islamic-Judaic magic squares or hatumere.

Three-cornered hats, called *kokon dangba*, are worn by Limba and Temne hunters. Each corner ends with a sort of pom-pom.

not be the only point of comparison between ancient Egyptian pharaohs and Temne kings, including the sixteenth-century title *faran* or *faram* and their depiction riding leopards.) It also vaguely resembles a British judge's wig, but the points of dissimilarity are too many, and the wig would have been very well known to the colonial Temne, enough to have been copied precisely, if that were the source. It is not clear which Temne kings wore this headdress, but versions have been documented from Port Loko in the far west to Yele in the East.

WOMEN'S DRESS

Women's attire also owes much to the Manding north, using the same strip-woven cloth but also using much more imported cloth of lighter weight. Long gowns are worn by women sewn from either prints made in Europe or white cotton tie-dyed and resist-dyed in bright colors in sometimes extremely complex patterns (known as *gara* throughout Sierra Leone). These are constructed on the same pattern as the kusaibi of the men, but, unlike the kusaibi, there is no pocket to interrupt the liquid quality. For Manding women, the style is distinctly in keeping with their movement in dance, which involves a sweeping, circular, movement of the arms outstretched horizontally, carrying the wings of the gown, billowing with air with the motion. Temne women's dance, however, is completely different, with no such large, sweeping movements; rather, it is much more restrictive and vertical, pushing down to the earth, somewhat antithetical to the dress they have adopted from the Manding. The style was adopted in the 1970s by the U.S. designer Halston, who showed his first African collection, all in tie-dyed polyester worn by slender American models, at the Museum of African Art in Washington, DC.

The normal Sierra Leonean woman's dress, with some slight variation here and there, is in two parts. A wrapper (called *lappa* in Krio) is tucked at the waist and hangs to the ankles as a sheath, and often there are several layers of wrappers. Above is an upper garment in the shape of a high-bodice, short-sleeved or sleeveless dress that falls to the thighs. It is sometimes shorter, falling only to the loins, and tailored more tightly around the waist, creating a ruffled bottom. Another version is not gathered but hangs loosely to the hips or lower. An imported sleeveless top instead of the tailored upper garment is seen more and more, often tucked into the lappa.

The head tie is ubiquitous for women in Sierra Leone and the surrounding region. It begins as a large square scarf, usually plaid, folded in half diagonally, often bound around the forehead first at its center, then wrapped around the back of the head, and around again to the front, where it is tied in a knot at the forehead, with the excess fabric on top of the head occasionally tufted to give height. Most women keep it fairly simple and close to the head, but more flamboyant styles using stiff fabric and sometimes multiple fabrics show the influence of the Manding north as well as contact through the Yoruba (Aku) Krio with the styles of Nigeria.

In Freetown, since its beginnings in 1787 as a province for freed English slaves and then as a colony for former American and Caribbean slaves arriving from 1792 to 1800, both men and women largely disdained indigenous dress, preferring European styles. With the repatriation to Freetown of African captives liberated from slave ships intercepted by the British after their abolition of the slave trade in 1807, a cultural and linguistic

Temne woman Ai Kanu spinning cotton and wearing her imported-print gown. Yele, Sierra Leone, 1980. Photograph by Frederick John Lamp.

extending to both sides of the wearer's face and to the rear; the rear corner may be thrown up over the front. The two side corners represent the horns of an animal, in an identification of the hunter with his prey.

Some of the most elaborate and intriguing headgear was worn by the paramount chiefs or kings (*ò-kande*) among the Temne of northern Sierra Leone in the early part of the twentieth century; they are rarely seen today. They are probably derived from similar Kuranko pillbox-shaped crowns made of leather or copper alloy and decorated with talismans in leather or metal containing cabalistic Arabic script. The Kuranko hegemony throughout eastern Temne land hundreds of years ago has resulted in the extensive Mandingization of especially royal custom.

A most intriguing headdress worn only by Temne paramount chiefs is a cloth drape that wraps around the forehead and is tucked behind the head, with long flaps left to fall on either side of the head down across the upper chest. The ends of the flaps may be decorated with triangles. It very closely resembles the ancient Egyptian pharaoh's cloth headdress, the *nemes*, with the exception that the *nemes* usually bore horizontal stripes. (This would

Krio woman wearing a *kaba sloht*, with accessories, as it would have been worn in the 1920s. Freetown, Sierra Leone, 1977. Photograph by Betty Wass.

century, distinguishing them from indigenous women, although elite Krio women would wear nothing but the finest English fashions of bonnets, corsets, stockings, and silk dresses, just as the men would wear top hats, ties, tails, and gloves in the blistering heat.

The kaba sloht was a large, one-piece, loose-fitting, long-sleeved dress made of cotton that fell to the ankles, and it sometimes sported a broad gathered fringe at the bottom. This rather plain, shapeless frock, by the beginning of the twentieth century, had become quite decorative and distinctively Krio. In pattern, two identical shapes of cloth, forming the front and back of the dress, were sewn together to produce the garment. Two box pleats were made at the waist, fore and aft, to provide fullness for the skirt. Characteristically, a cloth yoke from front to back was sewn onto the dress around the wide collar and sometimes adorned with small embroidered tucks and trimmed with an edging of triangular points called *yohnitit* (ants' teeth).

In the mid-twentieth century, Krio women redesigned the dress to make it slightly shorter, lighter, with less gathering of the skirt, and with short sleeves or sleeveless. The yoke became extremely decorative, appliquéd with cloth designs stitched in rows and zigzags to a paper backing that made it stiff, and trimmed in bias strips of colorful prints. This became everyday public attire but could also be worn at traditional events such as social meetings, wakes, and marriage festivities. By the 1970s, this variation on the kaba sloht had retained its popularity, especially among older women but even among young women and the elite for special occasions.

HISTORICAL DOCUMENTATION OF DRESS

Some early European documentation of the area of Sierra Leone describes styles of dress already in use that derived from peoples located further inland. The most powerful kingdom with extensive hegemony in this area had been the Kingdom of Mali, dominated by the Manding. But the Fulbe of the Fouta Djallon highlands in Guinea were influential also, continuing through the period of European contact. André Álvares de Almada reported in 1594 that the Susu along the coast of Guinea and northern Sierra Leone regularly traded salt to the Fulbe for cotton clothing and dyes (probably indigo), which they traded in turn with the Sapi (the ancestors of the Temne, Bullom, and Baga). The men were said to wear a kind of loose gown and trousers of cotton, probably made on the Fulbe pattern that can be seen today, especially worn by traditional performers. Álvares de Almada said of the Temne, "They have tailors among them who work in their own style." He mentioned breeches with many pleats (suggesting the Fulbe style) worn by the men over a narrow loincloth (worn alone by children), "Moorish shirts," string caps made of a fiber called *nacome* and other fibers, and sandals. Both men and women wore elaborate ornaments of glass, crystal, and coral, with brass rings on their fingers.

The attire of kings and chiefs, as one might expect, seems often to have differed vastly from common dress, at least after a critical political juncture. In the sixteenth and seventeenth centuries, much was written about the influx of a foreign people from the East known as Mani or Mane (ancestors of the Mande), who had probably been filtering into the area in small bands for several hundred years but seem to have become increasingly assertive as European traders arrived. They were generally described

mélange emerged that eventually took the name Krio, resulting in some modification of European dress. Apparently, the new liberated captives, according to Wass and Broderick, particularly the women, unaccustomed to Western dress as the established residents were, first refused to wear the mandated government-issue garments and would tear them up to make small bags, but the British administrators insisted in no uncertain terms: "Cover, slut" (that is, an unkempt woman). This led to the Krio term for the standard women's dress, *kaba sloht*. The kaba sloht became the cultural marker for Krio women until the mid-twentieth s the missionary André Donelha did in 1625: "courageous and valiant.... They are well dressed…and look splendid; at feasts and for wars the…king dresses himself in all his silks." Álvares de Almada in 1594 mentioned the Mani warriors' "little coats or cassocks made of cotton." We do not know whether other descriptions of the elaborate attire of kings referred to the Mani in particular or to the indigenous Sapi, but the precedents mentioned above would suggest Mani derivation, and we know that Mani royalty ruled over Sapi subjects. Álvares de Almada, around 1615, described a king wearing a heavily embroidered costume with a royal hat. In 1807, Corry described chiefs rather differently, covered with gris-gris and fetishes, a mixture of feathers and other preposterous materials, calculated to obliterate any trace of human appearance, and possessing the virtue, as they conceived, of shielding them from danger."

European textiles in this area of West Africa have a very long history, and, although the trade in textiles is recorded in snippets, it is impossible to tell how thoroughly pervasive it was. From the beginning of the European trade along the West African coast, traders brought European and Asian cloth as well as tailored clothing. Álvares de Almada said that "the women dress decently, wearing clothes of different kinds, some of which they had woven (locally), and others they have obtained from the Portuguese." Álvares de Almada mentioned "red caps, black cloaks for the chiefs, new and used hats." In 1625, a Dutch expedition reported that a king from the interior behind the Sierra Leone Estuary arrived wearing a long gown, a gray hat with an orange plume (probably an earlier gift from the Dutch), orange stockings, and shoes. In 1875, Pere Muller was astonished to see the king of Boffa wearing a "grand royal costume, dressed in a long mantle of blue silk lace, with pieces of appliquéd velour, broad at the bottom, with a border of gold thread. A sword, a Panama hat and a pair of magnificent sandals completed his uniform."

We can get a vague idea of the dress of at least the ruling class prior to 1600 in the area of present-day Sierra Leone from the stone figures and ivory carvings of the time. The stone figures are principally from two separate areas—one on the coast near Sherbro Island and another area inland on the present Sierra Leone–Guinea border in the area of the Kissi people today. The accepted dating of the coastal production is roughly from the eleventh to the sixteenth centuries, but that of the inland group of carvings is more obscure, possibly of the same era but extending even into the nineteenth century. Most figures are completely nude, but a few indicate articles of clothing.

Temne women at a Bondo association coming-out of the initiates. Mabero, Sierra Leone, 1980. Photograph by Frederick John Lamp.

A large figure in the Metropolitan Museum of Art, New York (#1979.206.270) from the Kissi area shows elaborate costume: a sort of apron or ruff around the neck covering the chest; a wide belt placed high on the waist; a loincloth falling from the hips down to the knees; and a curious, seemingly stiff wrap tied around the waist in the back covering the buttocks and the thighs but exposing the front, perhaps tied to the loincloth. All of these garments are decorated with rows of circles or nodules separated by straight lines, suggesting perhaps a weave pattern, embroidery, stamped design, or tie-dye. The pattern is curiously close to that in an ivory carving from Sierra Leone representing Portuguese dress for both men and women (including Christ, the Virgin Mary, and soldiers) now in the collection of the Walters Art Museum. It may have simply been a standard schema adopted from the Portuguese to indicate textile.

Some figures, such as one found in Musée du Quai Branly, Paris, seem to show an elaborate gown tied at the waist with multiple, heavy ruffs around the neck, and one has a pleated or tufted conical cap. These heavily textiled figures seem to come from one style area or perhaps a single atelier, and they are rare. One completely idiosyncratic Kissi figure of undetermined sex appears with the head tied around with a denticulated ornament, perhaps a fringed laced trim, and a long panel falls from the back of the head to the ground. A long gown covering the large belly down to the feet with a fringe of triangular shapes bears vertical stripes that suggest strip-woven cloth. A band with crosshatching seems to indicate the collar of the dress or an ornamental choker.

Some of the stone figures and the wood figures found in the same style and presumably of the same dating indicate dress for women. One kneeling wood figure in the British Museum seems to show a cloth cape over the shoulders indicated by crosshatched lines, with a heavy beaded necklace, perhaps a ruff around the neck, and a short skirt over the thighs. The skirt resembles that found on female depictions on the ivory salt cellars of probably about the same period now in the British Museum.

Many stone figures depict some sort of headgear. One curious configuration on Kissi figures is an elaborate crown consisting of two thick crossed ribs forming a dome with a loop at the top and horizontal lines between the ribs. The crown resembles an English crown, but the makers, deep in the interior at the border of Guinea, would have had no knowledge of European royalty or of Europeans at all. One Kissi figure shows a type of skullcap with a border of denticulated design. Several figures from both the coast and the interior show a man wearing a conical hat much like those traditionally worn by the Fulbe of Guinea and Mali. One figure in the coastal style in the Musée du Quai Branly wears a huge bowl-shaped hat with a rim. Quite a few Kissi and coastal figures, such as one in the Pitt Rivers Museum, show a kind of wrapped turban or perhaps simply a coiled and twisted headband. The frequency of these turbans, hats, and caps seems to suggest already an influence from the north—the Manding, and ultimately the Arabic world.

Early European accounts of Sierra Leoneans describe and depict cicatrization on the human body, both male and female, which would have to be exposed to be seen. John Maddox left a drawing of a slave woman he saw at the Sierra Leone estuary in 1582 with elaborate markings from the neck to the buttocks. Alonso de Sandoval in 1627 described the markings of a Sapi man: "On the right side of his body he had four lines drawn down the whole flank. On the chest he had two castles depicted in blue paint, and the thicker parts of his limbs were covered with other markings. And so on for all his body." Álvares de Almada said probably of the Susu, "women wear nothing at all before they are circumcised [customarily today in the mid-teens, well after puberty]....Around their waists they wear a string of precious stones....The reason why the women wear nothing is so that the markings on their bodies, which they make in order to appear attractive and dignified, may be seen."

CONTEMPORARY DRESS

Dress of the current period is primarily European or American dress, even though indigenous dress still continues in the rural areas as well as in the cities, mostly for formal or ceremonial occasions but also in daily life. Some new Western dress is imported from England and the United States, and there are a few Western-style clothing shops patronized by the upper classes in which almost any current style can be found. Most imported new Western-style casual clothing, however, comes from China and is sold off the rack—more often off the heap—in the large open markets where most people shop. The most popular items are T-shirts, blue jeans, and casual shoes. For most Sierra Leoneans good Western-style clothing is tailor-made in little open sheds along the streets or throughout the open markets. The tailors are almost entirely from the Fula people (known as Fulbe, Peul, or Fulani elsewhere) who emigrated from Guinea heavily during the 1960s and 1970s. Most Western clothing is bought used, rummaged from a heap of clothes on the ground in the public markets. This secondhand clothing comes to the villages and towns through American entrepreneurs who buy up masses of used clothing from the surpluses of used clothing depots in the United States.

Dress tends to be modest for those who can afford it. Country boys may be found wearing scruffy shorts, but only by default, because every teenage and adult male who can afford it will choose long pants. A coat or jacket of any type is greatly coveted and is worn even in the hottest months of the year along with a knit cap. Women wear dresses, and, although women can occasionally be seen wearing slacks, this was, at the end of the twentieth century, still highly disdained as indecent by most people, even in the cities. Shorts for women were never seen. With the disruption of the 1990s, it remains to be seen whether a new aesthetic or moral code will emerge.

Snapshot: Sierra Leone—Dress and Undress

If the documented common and royal dress for men and women in Sierra Leone derives principally from Manding dress to the northeast, which owes something to Arabic and Egyptian dress, with some European influence in particular garments, the question arises: What did the people wear before that? The answer is: apparently nothing, essentially. Any discussion of dress in Sierra Leone and surrounding areas prior to the intervention of the European powers has to confront the question of nudity.

Sierra Leone is only seven degrees latitude above the equator. High levels of humidity and daytime temperatures in the 90s (Fahrenheit; in the 30s Celsius) are not uncommon, and there are generally only a couple of weeks during harmattan—the period of dusty breezes off the Sahara in January—when one would wish to cover up for the sake of comfort. Why anyone would want to wear clothes in this year-round virtual steam bath is hard to imagine, except that Christians (since the fifteenth century) and Muslims (for nearly a millennium) believed that bodies should be covered with textiles, and the desire for excess began to accompany the development of materialism. Most locally made garments are hot—unbearably so in the case of the heavier strip-woven cloths—and the

looseness and the open sides only help to ameliorate an already insufferable effect. It is fashion, not comfort, that keeps textile entrenched—a desire to escape what is seen as the "primitivism" of their past and to join the dominant cultures of the near and far North.

It is also the adoption of an alien concept of sexual impropriety. Through the late twentieth century, one could frequently find prepubescent boys and girls nude on the streets of any rural village. But children here are seen to be nonsexual, and they become sexual not simply through puberty but, more importantly, through the rituals of initiation into adulthood. It is only in adulthood that sexuality exists and therefore should be obscured. But it was not always thus.

It is the coastal Sierra Leoneans who have had contact with Europeans since the mid-fifteenth century and who are described in European records; until the mid-nineteenth century, Europeans knew nothing of the interior. To get an idea of the presence of textile in prehistory, it may help to look at the history of relatives of Sierra Leonean peoples living on the fringes who have had less impact from either the Europeans or the Manding.

Baga women of the village of K'fen, Guinea, from *Coffinières de Nordeck*, 1886. Courtesy of Frederick John Lamp.

The Temne and their relatives, the Baga across the Guinea border, are distinguished by their ethnonyms—essentially meaning, respectively, the elite ("the elders") and the marginalized ("the frontiersmen," also applied to less advanced Temne communities). Accounts of the Baga referring to the pre-Colonial and early Colonial period describe them as "entirely naked," "in all cases completely unencumbered by clothes," or the "naked Bagas"—as opposed to the clothed Bagas, or Temne. A Mr. Leroy reported around 1910 that young Baga women up to eighteen years of age wore only a simple corset of glass beads. Numerous drawings published in 1886 in *Coffinières de Nordeck* show the women of all ages, including mothers, wearing nothing but a string around the loins with a tiny triangle of cotton cloth hanging in front of the vulva, sometimes ornamented by tassels, glass beads, pins, locks and keys, and other household objects. These drawings are extremely accurate in every other detail and certainly were done on the site. A French administrator in 1907 described the Baga men as dressing in boubous, trousers, and caps and the women as almost nude, although wearing a cloth belt that obviously covered their genitals along with lots of beads on the arms, legs, and head. The images in *Coffinières de Nordeck* confirm that men wore long gowns and cylindrical caps, but one image shows a man in a hammock on his front veranda, presumably an elder (judging by the carved figurative stool underneath), without any clothes whatsoever.

Certain circumstances call for enhanced transparency. Temne female initiates of the Bondo association prior to the twentieth century were displayed in public at the end of their confinement completely nude except for a string of red beads around the waist in order to show their sexual desirability. Male initiates of the Bassari people of Guinea came out in a quite erotic costume that exposed the testicles and sheathed the penis in a permanently erect position for public display. It is not considered improper for either men or women to be exposed nude when they are bathing in the river or with a water pail beside the house; this involves a virtual privacy that is respected by passersby.

In Sierra Leone, as elsewhere in Africa historically, nudity has always been a choice that reflects not only practical considerations but also a philosophy about sexuality and access.

See also volume 10, Global Perspectives: Dress, Undress, Clothing, and Nudity.

References and Further Reading

Alldridge, Thomas Joshua. *The Sherbro and Its Hinterland*, London: Frank Cass, 1901.

Almada, André Álvares de. *Tratado Breve dos Rios de Guiné*. Translated by P.E.H. Hair. Issued personally for the use of scholars, Department of History, University of Liverpool, 1984.

Bulletin General 10 (1874–1877) to 12 (1879) (les Pères du Saint-Esprit, Paris) (or *Bulletin de la Congrégation* from o.s. 14 or n.s. 1 [1887–1888] to o.s. 28 or n.s. 25 [1915–1917]).

Coffinières de Nordeck, (Lieutenant) André. "Voyage au Pays des Bagas et du Rio Nuñez." *Le Tour du Monde* 1 (1886): 273–304.

Eberl, Rudolf. *Westafrikas letztes Rätsel: Erlebnisbericht über die Forschungsreise 1935 durch Sierra Leone*, Salzburg, Austria: Verlag das Berglandbuch, 1936.

Edwards, Joanna P. "The Sociological Significance and Uses of Mende Country Cloth." In *History, Design, and Craft in West African Strip-Woven Cloth*, 133–168. Washington, DC: National Museum of African Art, 1992.

Hair, Paul E.H. "Sources on Early Sierra Leone (3): Sandoval (1627)." *Africana Research Bulletin* 5, no. 2 (1975): 78–92.

Jones, Adam. "Sources on Early Sierra Leone (22): The Visit of a Dutch Fleet in 1625." *Africana Research Bulletin* 15, no. 2 (1986): 43–64.

Lamb, Venice, and Alastair Lamb. *Sierra Leone Weaving*. Hertingfordbury, Hertfordshire, UK: Roxford Books, 1984.

Lamp, Frederick John. "House of Stones: Memorial Art of Fifteenth Century Sierra Leone." *Art Bulletin* 65, no. 2 (1983): 219–237. [See revision in F. Lamp. *La Guinée et ses Heritages Culturels: Articles sur l'Histoire de l'Art de la Région*. Conakry, Guinea: United States Information Service, 1992].

Lamp, Frederick John. *Art of the Baga: A Drama of Cultural Reinvention*. New York: Museum for African Art; Munich: Prestel, 1996.

Prussin, Labelle. *Hatumere: Islamic Design in West Africa*. Berkeley: University of California Press, 1986.

Saint Pére, M., In *Bulletin du Comité d'Études Historiques et Scientifique* (1930): 26.

Taylor, Eva Germaine Rimington, ed. *The Troublesome Voyage of Captain Edward Fenton, 1582–1583*. Cambridge, UK: Hakluyt Society, 1959.

Wass, Betty M., and S. Modupe Broderick. "The Kaba Sloht." *African Arts* 12 no. 3 (1979).

Frederick John Lamp

See also Prehistory to Colonialism; Body Modification and Body Art; Headdresses and Hairdos; Guinea; Liberia.

Togo

Although dress in Togo is similar to that of its neighbors in West Africa, it has distinctive features that make it unique in the region. It is quite common for citizens of neighboring countries like Benin, Burkina Faso, and Ghana to identify a Togolese national by his or her clothes even though similar styles of dress might be present in these countries. Like most regions of the world, environment affects clothing choices, especially evident in practices distinguishing the north and the south of the country. The north is savanna grassland, and, toward the south, a plateau leads to the marshes and wetlands of the Atlantic coast. Dress is also, of course, influenced by political and religious affiliations as well as gender, ethnicity, class, and fashions of the day.

Togo does not have a single national dress, but it is telling to begin a discussion of its clothing practices with its national flag, of green and yellow horizontal stripes with a red square in the canton embedded with a white star. Red is the symbol for the blood that was shed during the struggle for independence, green for the hope for a better life, yellow for national unity and wealth of the nation, and the white star represents peace. Hence, on events that express national cohesiveness and pride, such as international soccer games, one is bound to see Togolese sports fans clad in green, yellow, red, and white, or they paint their faces and body in those colors. Naturally, the attire for the national soccer team is usually a combination of yellow, green, and white.

These colors extend to the political arena. There are several political parties in Togo, but the three major ones are Rassemblement du Peuple Togolais (RPT), Union des Forces de Changement (UFC), and Comité d'Action pour le Renouveau (CAR). RPT was founded in 1969 and, for a long time, was the only political party in the single-party dictatorship. Its primary color is green. UFC was the product of the democratic changes that were initiated in the 1990s through demonstrations and strikes. It is led by the son of the first prime minister of Togo and employs yellow as its color. CAR was also a product of the 1990s and features red as its dominant color. At political rallies, supporters of each party wear T-shirts or print cloth with their party's colors.

The main ethnic groups in the northern part of Togo are the Kotokoli, Bassari, Tchamba, Kokomba, Moba, Gourma, Tchokossi, Kabye, and Lamba. Some groups such as the Kotokoli, live around towns that embraced Islam in the nineteenth century. Muslims introduced circumcision, cavalry, spears, swords, muskets, looms, and some crafts. Islamic customs also influenced the dress of several peoples in the north. In addition, the influx of traders and migrant groups from the Sahel impacted the customs of the peoples of northern Togo.

The southern groups are dominated by the Ewe peoples, who trace their origins from Ketu in the southeastern part of the Republic of Benin. After successive wars with the Oyo (the Yoruba group in what is now southwestern Nigeria), the Ewe people migrated to Notse in south central Togo. From this position, they dispersed to populate much of the southern half of Togo and the Volta region of Ghana. The latter dispersal around the seventeenth century was attributed to the tyrannical rule of their king, who forced the people to build walls around Notse. They left in successive waves, establishing independent Ewe states throughout the region with their own chiefs but maintaining similar traditions.

Among the Peda people of southeastern Togo, a newborn baby cannot leave the house while the sun is up for a period of about six months, at which point he or she is given facial marks. These marks consist of two pairs of short parallel lines—one pair on the forehead and another pair on the cheek. A Peda citizen is easily identified by these marks.

Other facial marks are prevalent elsewhere in Togo. These may be ethnic, class, age, or religious identifiers. Some groups in the north such as the Moba, Kabye, Tchokossi, and Kotokoli also have facial marks. Among some Kotokoli, for example, ritual cicatrization usually consists of three long marks across the right jaw, another across the left jaw, and three parallel lines across the arms, buttocks, and stomach. There are also three smaller marks on the cheeks and necks of children to protect them from evil spirits. The Kabye and their immediate neighbors, Naoudemba and Lamba, have cicatrizations on the face, torso, abdomen, arms, and back. Women generally have these marks in the shape of herringbones. For these people, cicatrizations represent ethnicity, class, and age group, or they are symbols of beauty. Kokomba men and women have their body and face covered with skillfully and elaborately cut cicatrizations. Some of these represent subgroups of the Kokomba and are made on the cheek, making it possible to distinguish easily between the bi-Tchabob and the bi-Mankpimb or the bi-Kouomb. Cicatrizations considered to be aesthetic are found on the torso. Some ritual facial cicatrizations are dyed black with charcoal. All girls are marked before marriage, whereas boys receive their marks between the ages of sixteen and twenty. During festivals, both men and women use mascara around their eyes and trace black lines on the face, and most of the women make white spots on their face with flour. These practices are no longer as prevalent as they used to be; hence, one is likely to come across northerners with no marks.

In the south, one finds many converts to Vodoun with facial and body marks or tattoos on arms, chest, and back. These vary depending on the type of shrine or temple to which the convert belongs. Most visible are two sharp and short parallel marks on the forehead and cheeks, one short diagonal mark, or three on the cheek for men and two long diagonal herringbone marks crossing each other at the back or on the chest. It is common to see the same marks on sculptures that represent these gods.

Among the Ewe people, when a twin passes away, he or she is represented by a wooden figure that is usually treated as a living person and dressed as such. Depending on its gender, the twin figure is adorned with facial marks, black dyed head, cloths, beads on wrists and ankles, and necklaces. Ewe ritual cicatrizations are also very common features on clay or wooden shrine sculptures positioned at the entrances of towns (called *dulegba*) or at entrances of homes (*legba*). The shrine figures have marks on the cheeks and foreheads. Some of the dulegba are clothed in white calico or palm branches. The Ewe reserve unique facial marks for children whose parents have had several miscarriages, stillbirth, and high infant mortality. Since they believe in reincarnation, to prevent the dead child from returning to the mother only to die again, the child who survives is usually marked. The cicatrizations do not follow specific aesthetic or ritual rules but are made to make the child unappealing to death so that he or she will not be snatched away like the earlier siblings.

Gender, of course, plays a significant role in hairstyles. In the north, it was common for certain peoples such as the Kabye to shave their heads. Kokomba girls sometimes braided their hair and inserted copper rings; boys wore narrow copper wigs, and, during festivals, they added porcupine quills and some feathers. In modern times, Togolese men's hairstyles are rather uniform. Men either cut their hair short or shave it. Overgrown hair is discouraged among men. Dreadlocks in particular are not encouraged, except for religious specialists. Some converts of Vodoun may not cut their hair until the appropriate, rather expensive, religious ceremony is performed. It is not unusual, however, to find some young men with dreadlocks imitating Rastafarians. These men are usually called Rastas, whether they are adherents or not, and are thought to be associated with reggae artists or drug use.

Both men and women dye their hair black when white hair starts to show. A widow and widower are supposed to shave their heads during the period of mourning as determined by local custom. Women's hair is coiffed in a variety of styles. These include natural growth or Afro, cornrows, twists, braids of natural hair, or, if the hair is not long enough, they add extensions of artificial hair. Straightened hair has been around for a long time, but it has now become even more of a fashion statement with the introduction of African American hair fashions to several hair salons. Thus, curls, perms, and so on have all entered the repertoire of women's styles. Those whose hair cannot withstand the chemicals or those who have short hair resort to wigs. Kotokoli women and other northern women who converted to Islam wear head scarves but not veils. Large straw hats are popular in the north to protect the wearer from the sun. Fulani men are known for their hemispheric straw hats and the Lamba for their rice straw hats.

JEWELRY

The Fulani in the north were and are noted for extensive gold and silver jewelry with pendants and earrings in the shape of cones or disks. In earlier times, the Kabye used straw beads and bracelets in addition to ivory and elephant- or buffalo-hide bracelets. Necklaces of precious stones were reserved for the elite. Copper rings were also common among the northern peoples who acquired them through trade. The Kabye were also famous for their wooden noserings. Kokomba women used to wear lip plugs of clay or glass in the shape of cylinders or nails on the lower lip.

Togolese men do not wear earrings, but some wear necklaces with pendants and bracelets made of gold, silver, or iron. It is not uncommon to see some people wearing special twisted bracelets with two or three metals (iron, copper, and bronze). Watches are always worn on the left wrist. Married couples are not expected to wear wedding bands, so only a small percentage of Westernized couples wear them. All women in Togo are expected to pierce their ears. A girl's ears are pieced at infancy. An infant wears black thread in the newly pieced ears until they heal completely, at which time the thread is replaced with real earrings. Pierced ears are a major distinguishing factor between boy and girl babies. Earrings could be custom made by local goldsmiths—who are becoming increasingly rare as inexpensive imported jewelry from China, India, and Taiwan floods the market. Imported jewelry comes in different forms, shapes, and materials ranging from gold to gold-plated, silver, glass, aluminum, plastic, and copper. Popular motifs for jewelry include fish, animals, plants, and zodiac signs.

Jewelry forms an important part of royal regalia. Among the Ewe in the south, chiefs and other elites are noted for wearing gold and silver jewelry. These comprise gold-plated crowns and large and long gold or silver necklaces with varied pendants that could represent the symbol of the ruler or individual and convey powerful messages to observers. These are complemented with equally elaborate bracelets. It is important among the Ewe royalty that, on certain occasions, metal elements were not permitted; on such occasions, they wear glass or clay beads, necklaces, and bracelets, and the color(s) depend on the occasion.

Women also wear beads. Waist beads are required for Ewe women, partly to support their underwear and partly for aesthetic reasons. It is believed that a girl who does not wear waist beads beginning at infancy will not have a good body shape. Middle-aged women wear a wide variety of beads as necklaces, bracelets, anklets, and circlets below the knee. Many people know the value of these beads, and they often indicate one's social class within the community. Certain trade associations or groups order specific beads that members wear to identify each other. Some beads or combinations of beads identify the wearer with a particular religion and the rank of the individual in the group.

CLOTHING

A new baby born in Togo is supposed to be pure and is normally dressed in white. Many babies will have unisex white dresses, with silver earrings and bracelets distinguishing girls. The mother of the baby does not have to wear a pure white cloth; any cloth that has white as a dominant color is acceptable. A new mother also adopts jewelry made of silver.

In the north, the typically blue and white cotton smock or *batakari* is the casual attire for men. These are handwoven on a narrow strip loom and then sewn into tunics and pants, and they are often worn with a skullcap. On special occasions, a more elaborate version of the smock is worn, usually embroidered around the neck and lower edge of the pants. The skullcaps might also be embroidered on the edges. Women wear two pieces of the handwoven blue and white cloth as a wrapper set with a blouse and small scarf of the same material used as a head tie.

In earlier times among the Kotokoli, girls wore thin red belts holding a small cache-sex, but certain groups thought that the latter portend sterility and therefore preferred to wear small aprons. At puberty, girls wore triangular cache-sexes, and the men wore either cotton or goatskin aprons attached with a belt. Kabye girls wore only red or black belts made of plant fiber or a small piece of cloth (light blue or pink) on the waist. After marriage, women wore locally woven white or purple cloth tied around the waist. At puberty, Kokomba girls wore a rectangular piece of cloth twenty-five centimeters by thirty centimeters (ten by twelve inches) between their legs, whereas married women wore blue-and-white-striped wraparound cloth.

Men on festive occasions adopt a dance costume comprised of antelope skin worn on the back, a horse tail, and helmet mounted with antelope horns and hanging cowries as counterweight. The dancer represents the male antelope, which plays an important role in their beliefs. The dancer would hold a hunting stick and a bow in his hand.

In the south, traditionally, handwoven *kete* (kente) cloth is the norm. Cotton cloth has a long tradition among the Ewe; however, oral tradition supports the view that sisal, raffia, and bark cloth were used in the past. Because Notse was the last center of Ewe dispersal, it is also the ancestral center for the production of black and white locally handwoven cloth. Notse has all the prerequisites for the production of the cloth. Cotton, indigo dye, and other materials could still be found in abundance in the early twenty-first century. The heritage of this cloth is found in its use as shrouds, dowry, and at important ancestral festivals along with bark cloth or raffia cloth. Handwoven kente generally have names that may relate to philosophical ideas, social issues, or specific events rather than design elements. Thus, one finds names such as *atsusikpodzedzome* ("the second wife saw it on her rival and jumped into the fire"), *eduwodzi* ("you are the winner"), and *uagba* ("display of quality or wealth"). There are frequent disagreements on names of cloth designs between weavers and women cloth traders who commission these cloths.

Men drape the cloth like a roman toga, exposing the right shoulder and covering the left. Women wear wrappers of the same material. Married women would normally employ two wrappers and single women only one. With the introduction of cheap European wax-print cloth, many have adapted this material to traditional styles. This has made handwoven cloth more expensive, and it is reserved for special occasions such as weddings, community ethnic festivals, or royal regalia.

At weddings in the north, men and women wear the best imported cotton cloth known as *bazin*. These are elaborately embroidered locally; the wealthier the couple, the more intricate the embroidery. This dress of Muslim origin is now widespread in Togo, where the wealthy, regardless of ethnicity, wear the "grand boubou." The more appropriate traditional wedding attire in the south is expensive multicolored kente cloth worn in the toga fashion by the groom with a white, short-sleeved undershirt. The bride wears two identical kente cloth wrappers with a white blouse. The Western black tuxedo and long white dress are also common at weddings. Several festivals are celebrated in which participants put on their finest traditional clothes as a reenactment of ancestral dress. For example, the Ewe in the south perform the exodus of their ancestors from Notse by wearing handwoven kente cloth with more subdued colors (brown, green, blue, white).

A unique characteristic of handwoven kente among the Ewe is the weft-faced inlay figurative motifs such as stools, pineapples, lizards, chameleons, parrots, keys, open hands, birds, leaves, and even texts. Many of the same motifs are seen on linguist staffs of chiefs and convey specific messages. For example, the chameleon motif is associated with the saying that "the world is like a chameleon's skin, it changes," and a bird motif signifies, "a bird that grows feathers will always fly," meaning a child who survives infancy will always become somebody. The tortoise and the snail are symbols of peace, because they do not point guns at each other.

The same patterns of naming are extended to modern waxprint cloth for which Lome, the capital of Togo, is renowned as a major distribution center in Africa. A few wealthy women known as *nana-benz* (whose name originates from their favorite limousine, Mercedes Benz) have held a monopoly over the design and distribution of this cloth, which was originally manufactured in Holland and now has multiple sites of production. Individuals purchase this cloth and send it to their favorite tailor or seamstress to sew a specific style of blouse, skirt, shirt, shorts, or pants. Togolese who can afford it generally prefer custom-made clothes from their choice of dressmaker or tailor. Some popular styles are *jupe pagne* (a long or short skirt with an extra wrapper and a blouse in the same material, sewn in various styles) for women. They also wear *anago* (named after a Yoruba subgroup), a simple blouse with round neck, sleeves, and a wrapper. A version of these styles among men is *bomba*, a shirt made of print cloth with ample short or long sleeves and a round neck worn with drawstring pants of matching material. An elaborate version of bomba is *agbada*—basically the same style but with embroidery at the neck and the seams of the pants and sometimes worn with a third loose and long overdress with side slits but joined at the bottom.

In the north, one observes many ancient reproductions of dress with fiber skirts and rattles made from seeds tied around the feet that make distinctive sounds as the participants dance. Whereas traditional leaders in the north distinguish themselves by the intricacies and elaborate qualities of their smocks or tunics and skullcaps, in the south, the king or queen displays his or her position by wearing traditional kente cloth, with considerable gold or gold-plated jewelry (necklaces, rings, anklets, crowns, and so on). A northern chief's status is exemplified in his ample *batakari* or *fugu* in traditional blue and white stripes with accompanying pants. Again, the neck, sleeves, and seams of the outfit are elaborately embroidered. They wear either an embroidered skullcap or an elaborate straw hat and carry a walking stick. In the south, the chief wears a kente cloth toga style, which could be blue and white, muted earth tones and pastel colors, a combination of bright and vibrant colors, or plain white cloth with a white hat.

Some print cloths are purposely made for political or religious groups. In the era of a one-party state, party cadres wore clothing with political messages or the president's portrait. In addition, the visits of foreign dignitaries such as the president of France or Pope John Paul II were also marked with such cloth prints. Likewise, associations within the Christian churches usually have special print cloth to honor their leaders on special anniversaries or feasts of the saints, or the Virgin Mary. Finally, during funerals, families select a cloth that every member will sew for the event. Wealthy families often have the portrait of the deceased rollerprinted on the cloth.

RITUAL CLOTHES

Ritual clothing is linked to the traditions of the ancestors. In the performance of their duties, priests and priestesses, depending on the shrine, will wear specific colors or adopt prescribed conventions of dress. For example, many Vodoun converts wear white, blue, or red wrappers without a shirt or blouse when they enter their shrines or when performing rituals elsewhere. These colors are sometimes mixed in the attire, but most often one will see them clad entirely in white, blue, or red cloth. Many women clad in these colors also have temporary white symbols on their chest, back, and arms. Many also display visible ritual cicatrizations. Others shave theirs heads, and some wear bird feathers in the hair. Hunters' guild members also wear important ritual attire in the form of red to brownish smocks with amulets during the funerals of important people or during the festival processions of a chief. Completing the ensemble are caps, red kerchiefs, and traditional hunting guns that they fire into the air from time to time. While Muslims in Togo distinguish themselves by wearing a smock or grand boubou to the mosque on Fridays, Christians will wear their traditional kente cloth, modern wax prints, or Western clothing to church on Sundays.

WESTERN CLOTHING

Western dress has permeated the daily lives of the Togolese. Togo was a German colony until the end of the First World War, when the territory was divided between the British and the French. The latter took over what is now Togo, with the other part going to the British Gold Coast colony, now Ghana. The colonial and missionary impact is most obvious among men, for whom the wearing of shirts and pants is prescribed, especially for civil servants. Senior civil servants usually wear a long- or short-sleeved V-neck shirt with matching pants called *provisoire*, and professionals such as attorneys and bankers wear suits with ties. Affordable Western clothes are readily accessible to the average person because of the ever-present European and American used clothing market. In more casual contexts, it is not unusual to see individuals in blue jeans and T-shirts sporting American football or basketball team logos. A smaller percentage of women wear Western clothes as well. School uniforms also follow Western traditions. In public schools, boys in elementary schools wear white shirts and khaki shorts, whereas those in secondary schools wear white shirts and long pants. Girls in elementary schools wear long khaki dresses, and those in secondary schools wear a white blouse and khaki skirt. Most private schools determine their own uniform; however, the most common attire for the boys is khaki pants and checkered (blue or red) shirts, and the girls wear checkered long dresses. University students wear the dress of their choice, which is normally a Western type.

The security forces in Togo wear different uniforms depending on their units. The most common uniform for the army is green and camouflage-spotted clothing. One distinguishes the powerful presidential guard by their green berets, whereas the paracommandos wear red berets. The police wear light brown khaki shorts and shirts.

References and Further Reading

Agblemanyon, N. F. *Sociologie des sociétés orales d'Afrique noire: Les Eve du Sud-Togo*. Paris: Mouton, 1969.

Amenumey, D. *The Ewe in Pre-Colonial Times: A Political History with Special Emphasis on the Anlo, Ge, and the Krepi*. Accra, Ghana: Sedco, 1986.

Cornevin, R. *Histoire du Togo*. Paris: Berger Levreaut, 1987.

Curkeet, A. A. *Togo: Portrait of a West African Francophone Republic in the 1980s*. Jefferson, NC: McFarland & Co., 1993.

Decalo, S. *Historical Dictionary of Togo*. Metuchen, NJ: Scarecrow Press, 1976.

Froelich, J.-C., P. Alexandre, and R. Cornevin. *Les populations du Nord-Togo*. Paris: Presses Universitaires de France, 1963.

Manoukian, M. *The Ewe-Speaking People of Togoland and the Gold Coast*. London: IAI, 1952.

Posnansky, M. "Traditional Cloth from the Ewe Heartland." In *History, Design, and Craft in West African Strip-Woven Cloth*, 113–132. Washington, DC: National Museum of African Art, 1992.

Ross, Doran H., ed. *Wrapped in Pride: Ghanaian Kente and African American Identity*. Los Angeles: UCLA Fowler Museum of Cultural History, 1998.

"Togo Authentique." *Politique Africaine* (special issue on Togo) 27 (September/October 1987).

Agbenyega Adedze

See also The Kingdom of Benin.

Cameroon

Cameroon blends West and Central Africa, extending from the Atlantic coast to Lake Chad, bordering six countries. Geography ranges from savannas and highlands in the northwest to dense equatorial rain forests in the south. Among the many peoples in the country, dress and ways to manipulate the appearance of the body vary widely. Religion and history influenced choices to adopt, maintain, or discard forms of dress. Indigenous African religions with annual and life-cycle ceremonies, accompanied by masked rituals in some regions, demanded ritual dress and costumes. Islam came to the north when the Fulbe (Fulani) founded large kingdoms beginning in the early nineteenth century, and Christianity promulgated by European missionaries arrived in the southern and western parts after 1845. Both left their mark on dress, jewelry, and bodily practices, as did various colonial and postindependence initiatives. When the European imperial powers divided Africa during the 1884–1885 Berlin conference, Cameroon initially became a German colony. After World War I, it was put under French and British rule. Residents in the French part looked toward sister colonies and France for inspiration, while their neighbors, British subjects, oriented themselves toward Nigeria and the United Kingdom. Cameroon gained independence in 1961, neighboring British and French areas.

In the Islamic north, dress and jewelry of the Fulbe and Hausa share much with their kin in Nigeria and other West African countries. They are distinct from the clothing traditions of small non-Islamic peoples who had resisted Fulbe domination and partly retreated into mountainous areas, remaining fiercely independent. Among them are the Mafa (Matakam), Kapsiki, and others, who in older literature have been designated as *Kirdi*, a Kanuri term used by their Islamic neighbors that means "nonbelievers."

Peoples who live in the coastal regions of the Southwest and Littoral Provinces with Douala, the commercial hub and major harbor of the country, share many characteristics with their neighbors in adjacent southwestern Nigeria and the Niger Delta, while populations along the Cameroon coast to the south have had close ties to peoples in Gabon and Equatorial Guinea. In fact, these coastal residents have interacted with European sailors and merchants since at least the seventeenth century. From the nineteenth century onward, ships brought many Africans from other countries to Cameroonian shores—from Senegal, Sierra Leone, Ghana, Nigeria, Gabon, and the Congo. The cosmopolitan nature of the inhabitants of Cameroon's coast found its expression in dress and in a succession of clothing styles and fashions over time.

One region more than any other has become synonymous with Cameroonian dress: the Cameroon Grassfields. This mountainous area in the Northwest and West Provinces is home to many large and small kingdoms as well as egalitarian societies ruled by councils of elders on its western and northern peripheries. As a result of historical relationships, colonial impact, and scholarly traditions, the highlands are usually divided into three subsections: the English-speaking Northwest Province with the capital Bamenda; the mostly French-speaking realm of the Bamileke, a term that refers to related populations in the southern part of the Grassfields; and the large Bamum kingdom. The arts of the kingdoms of Kom, Bafut, and Nso to the north of Bamenda are famous. The Bamum kingdom and its capital, Foumban, have a long storied history, as do many of the kingdoms of the Bamileke peoples. In this article, the focus will be on dress, jewelry, and bodily practices of peoples in two Cameroonian regions: the small societies in the north that resisted Islamization and the inhabitants of the Grassfields. A third section examines trends in dress and adornment at the beginning of the twenty-first century.

NON-ISLAMIC PEOPLES

Well into the 1970s, visitors to the northern parts of Cameroon encountered men, women, and children in dispersed settlements dotting arid plains and hills who followed ancient practices of dressing and adorning the body so minimally that early travelers and ethnographers thought of them as "naked." However, the only major study devoted to material culture in this region, by the late German anthropologist Renate Wente-Lukas, includes chapters on dress and adornment and reveals a rich and symbolic array of genital coverings, belts, loin ornaments, coiffures, and head dresses that not only indicated gender, age, and status differences but also ethnic identity.

During much of the twentieth century, young girls and women wore cloth strips pulled between the legs or *cache-sexes* held by belts. The term comes from the French *cacher* (to hide) and *sexe* (gender). In many instances, the belts also supported a second small garment covering the buttocks called a back apron (sometimes referred to as *cache-fesse* from the French *cacher* [to hide] and *fesse* [buttocks]). The materials of the cache-sexes and back coverings ranged from leaves, plant fibers, and leather to beads, bronze, and iron. Especially in the case of bead and metal cache-sexes and back-aprons, the distinction between dress and adornment is fluid. The belts, too, appeared in different configurations, made from fiber or leather, covered with beads or metal strips, and created from materials such as threaded vertebrae of snakes. Among the many styles of cache-sexes, some of the most famous are triangular metal pieces that adorned Mafa (Matakam) women. They consist of narrow iron strips forged by local blacksmiths. Beaded strips and triangular or rectangular beaded aprons with different geometric patterns called *pukuram* or *pikuran* also enjoyed popularity and were displayed during dances. They became so fashionable that, by the 1970s, women of many different groups wore them during festivals—in a region where dress and adornment were usually markers of distinct ethnic

Dancing Koma women wearing back aprons made of leaves, Alantika Mountains, northern Cameroon, 1958. Photograph by Harald Widmer. Courtesy of Museum der Kulturen, Basel.

identities. Now major collector's items in Europe and the United States, most of the more recent multicolored pukuram and pikuran have been produced for the art market.

Among men of the region, Fulbe and Hausa attire took hold by the beginning of the twentieth century. Muslim-style short, sleeveless cotton garments (boubou) were common, often made from locally grown cotton, woven into strips and sewn together.

In addition, men also wore pointed cotton Phrygian-style caps with ear flaps. Leather footwear of Hausa manufacture completed the ensemble. Reconstructing pre-Islamic nineteenth-century men's dress proves difficult. When working in the fields or in the compounds, men wore no clothes, but on visits to neighboring residences and during feasts and funerary celebrations, they wrapped either locally woven cotton cloths or goat and cow hides around their loins. As with women, a great variety of genital covers in different materials and configurations defined ethnicity.

Men's and women's hairdos varied widely and went through changes in fashion. Some men and women shaved their heads. For women, this could also indicate widowhood. Others sported tufts of hair such as Gisiga men, who wore small tufts at the back of their heads and often adorned them with feathers. Young women and men used the opportunity of market days to look their best to attract future husbands and wives. Among some groups, the girls shaped their hair into small balls or braids with the help of a paste made from oil and ochre or red laterite soil. Bronze pins and rings, tin strips, and glass beads completed the coiffure, and woven cotton strips and beaded ribbons were draped around the head.

Necklaces from imported glass beads of various sizes and origins were common. Small brass beads were equally popular, and, by the 1960s, plastic beads and disks also made inroads. In some instances, particular types of jewelry were associated with the life cycle. Young men among the Bana gave their fiancées necklaces with four strands of yellow and white beads to indicate the engagement. Bana widows also donned special necklaces. Nose, ear, and lip plugs ranged from blades of grass and bone ornaments to aluminum disks and bronze rings. Iron or brass rings adorned arms and legs, and some had hollowed-out triangular extensions containing protective medicine. Brass bracelets, armlets, and leg ornaments came in a wide variety of styles, some in the form of wristbands or cuffs, others resembling manilas, which were copper ingots in the form of bracelets exported to Africa by Europeans as a standard of value.

With independence, the new government mandated that men and women in the region had to be fully clothed, beginning a slow process of change. By the beginning of the twenty-first century, with television and cell phones reaching more remote areas of Cameroon and people moving to larger towns to find employment, women—except for the very elderly—have adopted either Western-style dresses or the typical three-piece women's attire made from colorfully printed cotton cloth common in much of West and Central Africa: a wrapper, a blouse, and a head scarf or stole.

THE GRASSFIELDS

As in the north, dress, jewelry, and bodily practices in the Cameroon Grassfields underwent many changes traceable through early written and visual records to at least the nineteenth century. The picture emerging from these sources is one of constant innovation, appropriation, and modification of dress forms. In the nineteenth and early twentieth centuries, scarification was commonly practiced; for example, in Bamum, elite men and women had an elegant scar running down the center of their foreheads. Missionary teacher Anna Rein-Wuhrmann, who lived in Bamum from 1911 to 1915, reported that female specialists embellished Bamum women's bodies with designs such as frog/toad motifs on the upper arm, which were associated with royals and with fecundity and propagation in the Grassfields' iconic repertoire. Bamileke women also beautified their bodies with intricate patterns. Piercing ears and the nasal septum to accommodate plugs and jewelry was common, as was the careful chipping of teeth to a point. Body painting was associated with ritual occasions such as funerals, when widows covered themselves in white kaolin, the color of mourning. Red camwood, a powdery substance produced from the bark and core of the African sandalwood tree (*Baphia nitida*), was mixed with palm oil and used to anoint bodies and objects during ritual occasions. Applied in patterns to the body and face, red camwood indicated a woman's change in status or other ritual transitions. One such occasion is when a woman becomes a member of *kefab*, a powerful women's association common in the northern part of the Grassfields. Kefab members, who must have borne children and proven their ability to produce bountiful crops, share esoteric knowledge and keep strong medicines. While body painting still occurs in ritual contexts, scarification and the shaping of teeth had all but ceased by the mid-twentieth century.

Throughout the nineteenth century, local materials were used in the production of coverings, garments, and head dresses, most notably bark, fiber of the raffia palm, banana fiber, sisal, and cotton. In the Bali-Nyonga kingdom in the Northwest Province—as in the entire region—boys wore no clothes at all, while ordinary men covered their genitalia with cotton or bark cloth (from *Ficus mucosus*) strips pulled between their legs and held by belts, a type of attire that existed well into the 1940s in more remote areas of the kingdom. The bark cloth was of local manufacture, dyed red with camwood, and made pliable through the application of palm oil. In the Bamum kingdom, bark cloth was used for loincloths for ordinary men and women in the nineteenth century, but with the importation of European fabrics from the coast and superior woven cotton cloths from the Islamic north, its production and use declined. At the beginning of the twentieth century, only

Mabu masker from the Kwifo society, wearing a feathered gown and carrying spears at a death celebration in Mbesenaku, Oku, Cameroon, 1998. Photograph by Dr. Hans-Joachim Koloss.

slaves (two-thirds of the kingdom's population, who worked in the plantations of the nobility) still wore bark loincloths—their sole attire because they were not allowed to cover their heads. Bamum nobility dressed in fine garments of imported materials. During the First World War, when manufactured cotton cloth supplies from the coast dwindled, there was a revival of bark cloth production and use, spearheaded by King Ibrahim Njoya, who ruled from 1886/1887 to 1931, when he was deposed by the French administration and exiled to Yaoundé, where he died in 1933. This brilliant ruler, with the help of a group of creative young noblemen, implemented numerous changes in his kingdom, including innovative dress.

Raffia was another ancient material for clothing. Throughout the Grassfields, weavers produce cloth from the fibers of the raffia palm on vertical looms. Workshops in some chiefdoms, such as Nsei (Bamessing) and Meta, are famous for their excellent raffia weaves and products, among them bags in a myriad of colors—initially from natural and later from imported dyes. In the nineteenth and early twentieth centuries, weavers not only produced raffia cloth, they also tailored tuniclike robes by stitching together fifty-centimeter- (twenty-inch-) wide pieces, which served as costumes for maskers (see below). The weaving of cotton (*ndap*) into narrow strips for garments, in particular small loincloths for both men and women, has been documented for nineteenth-century Bali-Nyonga and Bamum, and it has been suggested that Hausa who arrived in the region as traders introduced their narrow-strip horizontal treadle loom, subsequently adopted by weavers in Bamum and elsewhere.

By the mid-nineteenth century, several kingdoms in the Grassfields had gained influence through territorial expansion and were involved in the long-distance trade linking them with the coastal area and the Islamic realm. According to a detailed study by the French anthropologist Jean-Pierre Warnier, complex transactions brought copper, glass beads, cowries, cloth, and garments to the region in exchange for ivory, kola nuts, and other products. New goods and materials for dress and adornment were the monopoly of the monarchs, and strict sumptuary laws regulated their circulation and use. Besides the king and the royals, male members of the elite had access only if the ruler granted them the right to wear and display certain materials and styles. How someone dressed signified rank and standing in the hierarchically organized Grassfields states.

Among the earliest nineteenth-century imports were indigo resist-dyed cloths from the Jukun area, particularly the town of Wukari, now in Nigeria, where members of the Abakwariga, thought to be of Hausa origin, specialized in their production. Weavers and dyers made the cloths from narrow cotton strips and reserved linear patterns produced by stitching them tightly with dye-resistant fibers. Called *ndop* (very likely derived from the word *ndab*, "cotton"), *doma*, Wukari cloth, and a number of other names, these stunning works became the cloths of kings. To this day, ndop serve as backdrops when rulers sit in state, appear in palace reception halls, and otherwise delineate ritual spaces. They also appear in royal attire—for instance, as billowing loincloths or as the center panels of royal robes. One of the most remarkable uses of ndop was captured in a 1908 photograph, showing the Bamum King Njoya with a retainer wearing a splendid beaded royal robe for the *nja* festival, an annual celebration of the riches of the kingdom assuring the country's well-being. Perhaps it once belonged to Njoya's father, Nsangu (died ca. 1886/1887).

Two gigantic pieces of ndop (called *ntieya* in Bamum) form wings supported by royal servants. The intricate patterns include circles and scrolls and differ from the sparse linear configurations of cloths imported from Wukari. Indeed, these pieces are of Bamum manufacture since Bamum textile artists and specialists in Bali-Nyonga and the Bamileke area started their own ndop production by the end of the nineteenth century.

Trade cloth from the coast—mostly of British manufacture—also entered the region in the nineteenth century. Initially, its use was reserved for the rulers and the male elite, who, in the second half of the nineteenth century, began to wear gowns called *yadala* unique to the Northwest Province and the Bamileke realm. According to detailed information by Swiss missionary Hans Knöpfli, who spent most of his life in the Bamenda region, the typical Grassfields robe for men combines three pieces of different fabric—a monochrome upper part, a midsection with a pattern, and a lower section in a solid color. Embroidery delineates the neckline, and appliqué and embroidery embellish the front and back. The entire ensemble, of which the yadala is just one part, consists of shorts and two rectangular cloth pieces or aprons (*su'ndzi*) tied around the waist and visible under the

robe. The yadala echoes the boubous of the Islamic peoples to the north. Based on the patterns of the embroidery, the Grassfields gowns may have been inspired by boubous from Bornu, as Swiss anthropologist Bernhard Gardi suggests. The similarities are no coincidence, because the first tailors and embroiderers in the Grassfields region were Hausa who settled permanently in many kingdoms, although they lived apart from the locals. In contrast to the Bornu boubous, however, the Grassfields gowns have no pockets, their embroidery and appliqué are symmetrical, and front and back are patterned in a matching manner.

In the nineteenth and well into the twentieth century, only rulers were allowed to have a round neckline and an upper circular embroidered section, while high-ranking men had gowns with rectangular sections arranged in a V pattern on the front and back. The embroidery of a royal robe was more ornate and included motifs reserved solely for the ruler, such as a circular pattern referred to as "moon." If men other than the king wore gowns with this motif, they had received the garment or the privilege to wear this style from the ruler in recognition of their services.

From the north and the coast came another precious commodity that indicated a man's status and wealth—leather footwear

Royal wives on their way to the site of the *nguon* festival in Foumban, Bamum kingdom, 2004. Their garments are made from woven cotton cloth resist-dyed with indigo. Photograph by Christraud M. Geary.

produced by specialized workers among the Hausa and imported from Europe. In the mid-nineteenth century, the only type of gear that protected a wearer's feet was wooden sandals commonly used during the rainy season when the ground was particularly slippery. At the beginning of the twentieth century, fine leather slippers and high boots with soft soles from the north indicated that a man was reasonably affluent, especially in the Bamum kingdom, where men adopted Islamic dress, while European-made laced shoes and boots were reserved for the wealthiest men, such as chiefs and those in the service of the mission or employed by the colonials. High-ranking women—queen mothers, royal wives, and princesses—had access to shoes as well, although mostly to men's styles. It was only from the 1930s onward that shoes became common, including fashionable styles for women and the ubiquitous sandals cut from tires worn by the less affluent members of the community. Footwear is thus a recent innovation, and some ancient rituals and ceremonies require that the participants walk barefoot, recalling older dress practices in these out-of-the-ordinary settings.

Head coverings are an essential element of male dress; typically, no free and self-respecting man will be seen in public without a head dress. The etiquette concerning when to wear a hat is complex. In some kingdoms, a man would face a fine if he appeared without a hat in public. In the presence of the ruler, however, most men must remove their head dresses, with the exception of grand officials, who may have the right to keep their heads covered—a privilege associated with important historical ties to the king or specific offices. Certain events, such as the death of the king, may require that all men and women of the kingdom remove their head coverings and shave their hair during the period of mourning, when life and the normal order are suspended and threatened. Head coverings thus are closely associated with civil behavior and well-being.

The styles and materials for head dresses range widely. Crocheted or stitched cotton caps with flat round top pieces and intricate patterns are the most common. In the nineteenth and early twentieth centuries, their predominant color scheme was white (i.e., natural) and indigo blue, while more recent caps from imported yarns are brightly colored. The patterns echo the motifs of the sculptural arts, ranging from stylized depictions of animals such as lizards, leopards, chameleons, and birds to geometric designs. Special hats are often associated with particular offices or roles their wearers occupy in society. Cotton caps with burls, for example, used to be the privilege of royalty and nobility. According to Knöpfli, shiny black caps crocheted from raffia fibers (tso'tu nkabnswi't) are the prerogative of the king makers entrusted to name a ruler's successor, high-ranking notables, and subchiefs in the Bali-Nyonga kingdom. Additional designs may indicate that a man is a member of a particular secret society, such as cowry shells for kwifo membership. The headdress may be specific to ritual occasions, as caps with a wrought brass or iron ornament worn by king makers in Bali-Nyonga during animal sacrifices. Headdresses with ear flaps embellished in appliqué are among the many prestigious coverings, as are feather caps reserved for the elite, which consist of a fiber mesh cap with long feathers anchored into it. Stored inside out, the cap and the feathers unfold into a stunning bouquet when worn on top of the head.

Beaded headdresses were particularly common in the Bamum kingdom, where nineteenth-century kings and court officials wore crescent-shaped prestige headdresses (mpelet) with bead and cowry embroidery as part of their ceremonial attire. They display many royal motifs such as frogs and toads, chameleons, spiders, and birds. The oldest such headdress, kept in the Bamum Palace Museum in Foumban, is that of the founder-king Nchare Yen, who ruled in the late eighteenth century. It consists of a leather backing and irregularly shaped tubular blue and large round white glass beads, which at the time were extremely rare and precious. Beaded caps distinguished officeholders in the kingdom and were also the prerogative of the queen mother, whose man's attire visualized her role as a statutory male.

Materials for jewelry range widely and indicate the status of the wearer. Ivory was the monopoly of rulers, and elegant bracelets from this material were their and their loyal followers' prerogative. Images of leopards, elephants, and pythons, considered to be the king's familiars, are commonly depicted on the bracelets. Until the first decades of the twentieth century, imported glass beads were reserved for necklaces, bracelets, belts, and headdresses of royalty and high-ranking men and women. Certain kinds of glass beads distinguished leaders throughout the region, most notably chevrons for necklaces, often strung with leopard teeth. Brass jewelry, with a few exceptions, was a male domain and ranged from solid and delicate openwork bracelets to finger and neck rings, hair pins, and hat ornaments. Brass casters in Bamum and Bagam, and later in Bamenda, continue to produce bronze jewelry in the lost-wax casting technique into the twenty-first century. Among the most remarkable emblems of status in the Bamum kingdom were bronze neck rings with delicately cast male heads displaying openwork high-status mpelet headdresses. They were reserved for the ruler and high-ranking officials. Similar rings display bird and buffalo heads. The buffalo was associated with royal servants, and the necklaces were thus a reminder of the servant corps' strength and endurance resembling that of the buffalo.

In the second half of the twentieth century, the typical Grassfields-style men's dress, headgear, and jewelry spread widely among many segments of the region's male population and even among Cameroonians from other parts of the country. Worn on special occasions such as family celebrations, festivals, and political events, the man's yadala is no longer reserved for the elite and the rulers. Dress thus allows upwardly mobile men to cross the boundaries of established hierarchies. Those who can afford it might buy a hat in the market or commission a tailor to make a gown. Hausa continue to work as expert tailors, but many others have also entered the profession, among them specialists from as far away as Senegal. When the gown is complete, the next step is to hire an expert to embellish it with embroidery or appliqué at great expense. Some embroiderers are known for the technical finesse and beauty of their work. Knöpfli mentions one such famous specialist. James Tawah, who lived in the Mutswa quarter of Bali-Nyonga, had learned his craft from another artist in nearby Bali-Kumbat as a young man in the first decades of the twentieth century. Women now embroider men's gowns as well, satisfying the great demand and making a living.

In the first half of the twentieth century, men's ensembles followed a restrained color scheme—the lower and upper part of the yadala were monochrome, usually dark blue or black, and only the cloth used for the midsection was patterned; the color of the embroidery yarns tended to be red, yellow, and white. More recent gowns are brilliant—they may be yellow or orange, for example, and display a rainbow of colors used in the rich embroidery and appliqué. Their designs repeat the repertoire of motifs, among them double gongs, lizards, and crosslike configurations.

MASKERS AND THEIR COSTUMES

Peoples in the Cameroon Grassfields are famous for vibrant masquerades associated with men's societies, lineages, and palaces that appear at funerals and during royal and village festivals. Much has been written about the symbolism of the maskers' wooden headpieces in anthropomorphic and zoomorphic form, but the garments and accoutrements that form an integral part of the mask have received little attention. The configuration and materials for the maskers' costumes reflect the hierarchy of masquerades, whether they belonged to the palace or a lineage, and may indicate the role particular masks play within a mask ensemble. Two examples from different parts of the region demonstrate the importance and symbolism of the mask costumes.

In several Bamileke kingdoms, the so-called elephant society (*kwo'si*) assembles wealthy men who gain prestige through membership and support of the king. Large fees allow them to attain certain grades in the society's hierarchical military-style organization and are reflected in the costumes, headdresses, and accoutrements the members display during flamboyant public dances and festivals. The most stunning parts of the costume are beaded fabric hoods with long cloth pieces (resembling elephant trunks) and large round ears topped by beaded or feather headdresses. Depending on the kingdom, the maskers wear a tuniclike garment over swaths of cloth or voluminous loincloths/skirts. In Bandjoun, these tunics are made from ndop associated with royalty and are trimmed with the fur of the colobus monkey. Leopard pelts cover the backs of some maskers, and beaded vests and belts complete the ensemble. Maskers hold staffs or horsetail fly whisks, and seed rattles encircle their ankles. The king, who participates in the spectacle, follows the long line of performers in the most extravagant of all costumes: a large headdress almost three meters (ten feet) wide and two meters (six and a half feet) high towers over him, not unlike the one in the splendid royal attire photographed in the Bamum kingdom in 1908. Royal wives are part of the performance as well and carry beaded leopard pelts on their backs as emblems of rank.

In kingdoms north of Bamenda, the masquerades of men's societies, lineages, and the palaces echo the strict hierarchical nature of the Grassfields kingdoms. According to the German anthropologist Hans-Joachim Koloss, maskers' costumes in the small kingdom of Oku consist of the *kefol kekum*, a wooden head piece in human or animal form worn on top of a netlike hood made by men. The configuration of the head piece identifies the wearer's character—such as male leader, woman, warrior, old man, buffalo, and bird—and places him in a hierarchy and sequence of maskers. The gown (*kebam*) may also indicate his role and the nature of the masquerade. Only performers in masquerades associated with the royal Mbele clan may wear gowns of the prestigious ndop cloth, called *kelanglang* in Oku, while raffia gowns adorned with small tufts of human hair have been reserved for the male leader masks (*kam*) in lineage performances. Maskers of the powerful secret society kwifo are the only ones who may wear red, a color considered to be ritually dangerous. Gowns with feathers are also kwifo maskers' prerogative and are most closely associated with *mabu*, a masker heralding the arrival of the masked persona *nko'*, who embodies the wild and threatening aspects of kwifo.

Maskers' costumes in the Grassfields have undergone many changes in the late twentieth and early twenty-first centuries. Colorful cotton tunics have replaced raffia fiber or ndop examples. Mask associations appear during the official visits of important politicians and dignitaries on national holidays and during special festivals, and their performances are documented in television news and specials. Grassfields masquerades have become increasingly folkloric—more entertainment centered and less ritually based. Collectively, they have become expressions of a modern Cameroonian identity.

WOMEN'S DRESS AND JEWELRY

Women's dress was less flamboyant than men's attire but nevertheless indicated rank, wealth, and marital status. Well into the 1950s, ordinary women in rural settings wore aprons or cachesexes held in place by a belt while doing daily chores in the compound and while farming in the fields. Belts made from small seed beads and beaded necklaces adorned them during ceremonial occasions. Queen mothers, royal wives, and the wives of important men had access to high-status materials, such as cowries and expensive trade beads. In Bafut and neighboring kingdoms, for instance, cowry headbands indicated that a woman was married to the ruler. During celebrations and rituals, high-ranking women would dress in precious materials, such as the wives of the King of Bali-Nyonga, who wore distinctive beaded aprons and jewelry on occasion of the annual Lela festival, which celebrated Bali military prowess and purified the country.

With the arrival of Protestant and Catholic missionaries in the Grassfields around 1900, women who converted and whose husbands worked in salaried positions in larger towns and administrative centers dressed in European-inspired styles. In photographs, one can see subtle changes in fashion indicative of upward mobility, because most converts initially belonged to the lower echelons of society. Their earliest dress patterns, supplied by missionaries, resembled children's frocks, to an extent infantilizing the missions' female charges. By the 1920s, more mature European fashions were found in the region, especially among women who had traveled to the coast. After the Second World War and independence, the three-piece dress—a wrapper, a blouse, and a head scarf—became the preferred attire of married women as elsewhere in Cameroon and other African countries. They shopped in the markets for Dutch wax prints and, from the 1970s onward, for the cheaper printed fabrics produced in Cameroon. They then commissioned a tailor or seamstress to create their ensemble. When men's robes (yadala) with embroidery and appliqué gained in popularity and became a signifier of upward mobility and of Grassfields—and, by extension, Cameroonian—identity, three-piece women's outfits for ceremonial and official occasions were modified to resemble the colorful garments of men. Vividly colored embroidery or intricate appliqué now also adorns wrappers, blouses, and head dresses tailored from black fabric. Elegant Western-style shoes and handbags are indispensable accessories.

DRESS AND POLITICS IN THE BAMUM KINGDOM

Change in dress over time occurs for many different reasons. Politics may play a major role in innovation and choices, and one of the most interesting examples in the African realm is the history of elite dress in the Bamum kingdom during the German Colonial period, which, in Bamum, lasted from 1902 to early 1915. Throughout most of the nineteenth century, high-ranking Bamum dressed similar to their counterparts in neighboring Grassfields kingdoms. Royal apparel consisted of a heavy beaded belt and loincloth of prestigious materials such as ndop or cherished trade cloth, a high-status beaded headdress (mpelet) with hat pins, various beaded necklaces, and ivory or bronze armlets. Elite Bamum dress and adornment, however, underwent changes in the late nineteenth century, when young King Njoya faced internal unrest as a result of efforts to usurp the throne. He enlisted the military support of the Fulbe *lamido* of Banyo and was able to defeat his adversaries. Subsequently, he and the court converted to Islam and adopted Fulbe and, by extension, Hausa dress and headgear such as turbans as a visual expression of the alliance and the newfound faith. Royal women wrapped themselves in cloths and began to wear wigs like their Fulbe counterparts. Hausa residing in Foumban not only worked for the court

as tailors, they also introduced northern-style embroidery, which soon became one of the major skills of Bamum artists. When the first Germans arrived in Bamum in 1902, they encountered a court that seemed thoroughly Muslim both in appearance and court etiquette.

Considering King Njoya's political acuity and emphasis on visualizing alliances and enhancing his power and influence, it comes as no surprise that he began experimenting with German imperial dress and uniforms soon after the arrival of the Germans. Just as he had modeled himself and the court after the Fulbe state of Banyo a few years earlier, he now integrated German elements into his own and the courtiers' attire. Some of the new accoutrements—among them elaborate armored helmets and breast plates—came directly from the Germans through gift exchanges and became part of the royal guards' uniforms. King Njoya's own German hats included a pith helmet, a helmet topped by an eagle, and various other military headwear. By 1908, he had outfitted himself and his military leaders with

Ta ngu (to the left), the head of Mutngu, the most important men's society of the Bamum kingdom, wearing a *mpelet* headdress during the *nguon* festival in Foumban, Cameroon, ca. 2000. Photograph by Christraud M. Geary.

hussar-style uniforms, boots, and leather shoes and gaiters, inspired by photographs he had seen of the emperor and other royals in popular illustrated German magazines and on postcards that circulated in the colony. Tailors working for the court became adept at recreating these uniforms and hats with indigenous embroidery, combining Bamum and German elements. They even produced bead-embroidered epaulets and medals.

The German colonial administration, however, became wary of what it considered the *Soldatenspielerei* (playing soldiers) of rulers in the colony and increasingly perceived it as a threat, especially when the indigenous troops in German-style uniforms began exercising with guns. It seems that King Njoya, who was deeply disappointed by the lack of support from the German administration, dropped the military attire around 1910. King Njoya and his courtiers, however, continued to experiment with dress—this time with German-style civilian attire, inventing, for example, dresses for the royal wives and princesses. The monarch's inspiration came from European aristocratic women's garments depicted in a fashion catalog that he had received from the missionaries. His tailors used locally available materials such as beads and excelled at embroidery, creating fascinating hybrid styles drawing on local and foreign ideas.

With the end of the German Colonial period, the king and the Bamum palace reverted back to Muslim dress, and the experimentation with German attire and self-invention modeled on German royalty ceased. Today, Bamum men of all backgrounds prefer Muslim-style attire, be they Muslim or Christian, members of the palace elite, or people in towns and in villages. Women wear wrappers, blouses, head ties, and, if they are fundamentalist Muslims, veils. Occasionally, a Bamum man may dress in an embroidered robe and don a crocheted hat, common in other parts of the Grassfields, attesting to the appeal of this style and a developing pan-Grassfields identity.

TWENTIETH AND TWENTY-FIRST CENTURY FASHIONS

The adoption, transformation, and rejection of new ideas and styles epitomize the complex histories of dress in Cameroon as elsewhere in Africa. By the 1960s and 1970s, young Cameroonians in the large cities and small towns appropriated Western fashions—ranging from miniskirts to bell-bottoms and platform shoes. Trendsetters were U.S. recording stars such as Marvin Gaye, James Brown, and the Supremes, whose pictures appeared on record covers and in magazines. At the same time, other developments impacted the dress of the emerging salaried middle class of teachers, nurses, bureaucrats, and successful businessmen. Depending on the area and religious orientation, men dressed Western style, in two-piece suits made popular by political figures such as Zairian president Mobutu Sese Seko or in Muslim attire, while women preferred Western-style dresses or the more conservative wrapper, blouse, and head-tie ensemble. Imported skirts, blouses, frocks, and men's suits and shirts sold in the markets satisfied the need for Western-style clothing as did local tailors and seamstresses, who created outfits based on Western patterns.

The development of Cameroonian cotton textile production, to compete with the more expensive imports of European companies such as Vlisco, the producer of Dutch wax prints in The Netherlands, was an important step in forging a national identity through dress. This was a particularly complicated task

for Cameroon, which—as mentioned at the beginning of this article—was an amalgam of many different peoples that had been under three different systems of colonial rule. In 1965, the Cotonnière Industrielle du Cameroun (CICAM) opened a mill in Douala, providing the market with reasonably priced printed cotton fabrics that resonated with Cameroonians. CICAM's commemorative cloths of Amadou Ahidjo and Paul Biya (the country's only two presidents after independence) and designs created for special occasions such as political party conventions and church festivals have been much in demand. Local tailors and seamstresses fashion the cloths into shirts or boubous for men and three-piece ensembles for women. CICAM designers also adopted and transformed cherished local cloth patterns, among them the ndop. Often men and women commission identical outfits to indicate solidarity and group or family identity—for instance, during funerals when the women of a savings association hold their assemblies or when notables of the Bamum palace and the wives of the current ruler of Bamum, King Mbombo Njoya, appear during grand festivals at the court. Similar to other textile mills in Africa, CICAM has fallen onto hard times because Chinese mills now copy its products and undercut its prices.

The rise of a contemporary Cameroonian fashion industry in the country's economic capital, Douala, at the end of the twentieth century shaped taste and consumption of the country's elites and those who aspire to higher status. In a posting on the *Infosud Belgique* press agency's Web site titled (in translation) "Fashion: The Triumph of the Local Label," Charles N. Forgang has commented on dress practices of his compatriots. He finds that well-to-do Cameroonians are abandoning European labels in favor of Cameroonian designers, many of whom worked in France and other European countries before coming home to open their own businesses. Abdel Aida, for example, returned from Paris to Douala in 1990 and participated in the development of the local fashion industry. His designs and those of his colleagues are colorful, extravagant creations combining African and Western styles. In 2005, a hall for fashion shows opened in Douala, and the first Grand Festival de la Mode took place. Two years later, fifteen houses from Cameroon and other African countries presented their latest fashions on the festival's runway. Private television stations broadcast the shows, and Internet sites provide the Cameroonian designers with an opportunity to stage their latest collections.

Besides Abdel Aida, other designers have become well known, among them Christalix and Anggy Haïf to name just two. Their inspirations come from many different local and global sources. Haïf, for example, tries to integrate natural materials such as raffia and bark cloth to bring African sensibilities to his national and international clientele. He has several collections—urban, ethnic, and trendy—to satisfy different tastes. Asked whether he considers himself an African designer, his answer is compelling: "I don't claim to be an African maker, nor an international maker, but simply a universal maker." It will be fascinating to see how this intersection of the local and the global will be received in the national and international fashion arenas of the twenty-first century.

References and Further Reading

Forgang, Charles. "Cameroun. Mode: le triomphe de la griffe locale." *Infosud Belgique Agence de Presse*, 4 October 2007. http://www.infosud belgique.info/article_pdf.php3?id_article=686 (accessed 7 December 2007).

Gardi, Bernhard. "Kamerun: Bamileke." In *Boubou—c'est chic. Gewänder aus Mali und anderen Ländern Westafrikas*, edited by Bernhard Gardi, 86–95. Basel, Switzerland: Museum der Kulturen and Christoph Merian Verlag, 2000.

Geary, Christraud M. *Things of the Palace. A Catalogue of the Bamum Palace Museum, Foumban (Cameroon)*. Studien zur Kulturkunde 60. Wiesbaden, Germany: Franz Steiner Verlag, 1983.

Geary, Christraud M. *Images from Bamun: German Colonial Photography at the Court of King Njoya, Cameroon, West Africa, 1902–1915*. Washington, DC: National Museum of African Art, 1988.

Geary, Christraud M. "Political Dress: German-Style Military Attire and Colonial Politics in Bamum Kingdom (Cameroon)." In *African Crossroads: Intersections between History and Anthropology in Cameroon*, edited by Ian Fowler and David Zeitlyn, 165–192. Oxford, UK: Berghahn Books, 1996.

Knöpfli, Hans. *Living in Style. Crafts and Technologies: Some Traditional Craftsmen of the Western Grasslands of Cameroon. Part 4: Handicrafts, Music and the Fabric of Social Life*. Basel, Switzerland: Basel Mission, 2002.

Koloss, Hans-Joachim. *World-view and Society in Oku (Cameroon)*. Berlin: Dietrich Reimer, 2000.

Lamb, Venice, and Alistair Lamb. *Au Cameroun. Weaving—Tissage*. Roxford, UK: Roxford Books, 1981.

Rein-Wuhrmann, Anna. *Mein Bamumvolk im Grasland von Kamerun*. Basel, Switzerland: Basler Missionsbuchhandlung, 1925.

Warnier, Jean-Pierre. *Échanges, développement et hiérarchies dans le Bamenda pré-colonial (Cameroun)*. Studien zur Kulturkunde 76. Wiesbaden, Germany: Franz Steiner Verlag, 1985.

Wente-Lukas, Renate. *Die materielle Kultur der nicht-islamischen Ethnien von Nortkamerun und Nordostnigeria*. Studien zur Kulturkunde 43. Wiesbaden, Germany: Franz Steiner Verlag, 1977.

Christraud M. Geary

See also Headdresses and Hairdos; Footwear; Masquerade, Theater, Dance Costumes.

PART 7

Central Africa

Central African Republic

A man cuts his brother's hair while wearing the latest soccer jersey and decorated blue jeans. Bangui, Central African Republic, August 2007. Photograph by Michelle Kisliuk.

As the name indicates, the Central African Republic (hereafter referred to as *Centrafrique*) is situated at the west-central heart of the continent. The capital, Bangui, sits on the shore of the Oubangui River, which flows along the southeastern border with Democratic Republic of Congo. To the south is Republic of Congo (Brazza), Chad to the north, Sudan to the northeast, and Cameroon to the west.

THE URBAN CONTEXT

Centrafrique proclaimed independence from the French in 1960. The goal of Barthelemy Boganda, the country's founder and first president-elect, was to raise the quality of life, which had deteriorated under colonial oppression. Boganda's vision for his government was to help support the population in five fundamental ways: "to dress, to house, to feed, to educate, and to heal." Independence celebrations (which took place after Boganda's death in an airplane crash) called for Centrafrican men to "put on your suit and tie" and for women to "put on your prettiest outfit, be proud, be dignified…night is over, day has dawned." This message was transmitted by politicians and echoed by popular musicians.

Men in Centrafrique, particularly those born around the time of independence, have a preference for imported clothing from Europe (especially from France and Italy). In Bangui, professional men or those who aspire to be such, dress as though each day were a holiday, even if they might not be able to afford other luxuries. They wear fine slacks and button-down shirts and ties, and sometimes suit jackets even when the weather is very hot. The key to attracting the most discerning women is a fine pair of imported leather shoes, though this is not necessarily the case for younger men in the twenty-first century, who might rather prize the brand-name athletic shoes trending from African American culture. Most Muslim men, from the northeast of Centrafrique or who have emigrated in moderate numbers from Chad or Sudan, wear the long (grand) boubous and leather sandals ubiquitous in African Muslim countries. Muslim women and girls wear synthetic cloth wraps, blouses, and head shawls—bright purple and gold solids being the most popular, sometimes with sequined borders.

Common among much of the female (non-Muslim) population is the traditional tailored outfit made from wax-print cotton cloth (*pagne*), the outfit consisting of a blouse with an embroidered collar and puffy sleeves matched with two wraps and a head scarf, or else as a full-length dress (preferably with an elaborate, machine-embroidered collar); also sometimes worn by men is the pagne tailored pant and matching collared shirt, comfortable in hot weather. As elsewhere in western and central Africa, married women usually wear double pagne wraps, the bottom layer straight to the ankles and the second wrap gathered and tucked around the waist, coming to just under the knees. When dressing up—whatever style the outfit—many women prefer fancy leather high-heel shoes or spike-heel sandals. By contrast, quotidian footwear affordable for most working and rural people is the simple rubber or plastic sandal or flip-flop.

Dress codes in the primary and secondary schools have emulated the French Colonial period. Girls are required to wear dresses or skirts with blouses to class. Not allowed at school is the single pagne wrap with tank top—quotidian wear for many unmarried girls when not in school. Boys are required to tuck button-down shirts into slacks or shorts and to have neat, short haircuts. Male instructors conventionally wear blue button-down shirts and black pants.

TWENTY-FIRST CENTURY TRENDS

During the early Independence period and until several decades later, it was rare for women to wear pants, with the exception of women in uniform or the occasional international traveler returned home. In the twenty-first century, however, with global travel and media commonplace, so too are the global trends in dress. Outside of school, many young people (both boys and girls) wear decorated jeans (embroidered with numbers, flowers, or other designs, some sequined, or decorated with areas faded or bleached into a design). These are often paired with soccer shirts (bright red, yellow, blue, or with black-and-red vertical stripes, along with the number and name of a famous African player)— as are popular around the world. These are sometimes worn with matching nylon shorts instead of jeans. Young women and girls also wore the diamond skirts and wispy Empire blouses that are simultaneously in fashion in the early twenty-first century in the United States.

Cosmopolitan Centrafricans encourage each other to "*se saper*," a verb borrowed from the popular culture of Kinshasa during the last half of the twentieth century and from the Congolese

Woman wearing a fashionable ready-to-wear African outfit that she bought at the open market in Bangui, Central African Republic, 2007. Photograph by Michelle Kisliuk.

musician Papa Wemba, who coined the term S.A.P.E. (*Société Anonyme des Personnes Elegantes*). At the entry of nightclubs in Bangui are signs noting that proper attire is required (for example, no flip-flops or work clothes), although, in the twenty-first century, what constitutes proper attire may depend on the perceived class and comportment of the client and on the pressed and bleached quality of the clothing rather than on the kind of clothing (jeans or T-shirts, for example).

ACCESSORIES

Accessories popular among women are imitation designer handbags; gold and silver earrings, necklaces, and bracelets; and sometimes sunglasses. In the twenty-first century, the pierced eyebrow, nose, and lip have also become popular among some young women aware of global trends in body piercing. Perfumes are also popular among both women and men; they are imported from Europe or from the United States for those who can afford them, otherwise from elsewhere in Africa. Another common "accessory" for women on the move is the baby on one's back, preferably tied on with a cloth that matches one's outfit. A sun umbrella or parasol that shades both woman and baby is a finishing touch. For the professional or aspiring man, a briefcase or leather portfolio is necessary when out and about on a weekday. Finally, the cell phone attached to one's belt (or in one's handbag), preferably Nokia brand, is a twenty-first-century accessory worn by the cosmopolitan Centrafrican. It is important to note that, with the exception of the small upper- and middle-class population, the financial situation for most of the population in Centrafrique at the beginning of the twenty-first century is under severe stress; therefore, those who have access to luxury accessories such as a cell phone may not always be able to purchase talk time.

SOURCES OF CLOTHING

In Bangui, there are several basic sources for clothing. To buy new cloth—Dutch or English prints with the "veritable wax" label, handmade indigo or batik cloth imported from West Africa, or the lower-cost industrial faux kente and other African-themed prints—one goes to the market at *Kilometre Cinq* (known colloquially as *cinq kilo*). Color choices are very important; bright designs (usually two-toned) are generally preferred. Other important features of pagne prints are the occasional special meanings or messages in the designs. Some are obvious, such as cell phones, computers, the Pope's face, or a political figure print. Others are more esoteric, like the bird flying out of its cage (called "if you go out, I'm going out"). Centrafrique used to have its own textile mill, Ucatex, which ceased to function in the early 1990s during political turmoil. Ucatex produced some locally themed pagnes such as "*Chemise/pantalon angba na cinq kilo*"—that is, "your shirt and pants are staying at cinq kilo," the hidden story being about a man who doesn't pay for visiting a prostitute and therefore must leave his clothing behind. The repeating imprinted design that accompanies the italicized phrase is of a young woman folding up a shirt and pants.

New casual clothes are for sale at the central market as well as at smaller markets and open-air kiosks around town and across the country: soccer shirts, children's dresses, jeans, shorts, sandals, and pagne print cloths. But by far the largest and most economical source for clothing at the market are the piles of *choisis* or used clothing imported mostly from the United States. Much of this is work attire and casual clothing, but there are also slacks, blouses, and dresses, as one might find in a good secondhand store in the United States. New ready-to-wear imported clothes of the finest quality are available at several boutiques in the downtown area (*ville*, which is the former colonial town center). There are also several haute couture European-style establishments, but these stores are very expensive and not frequented by many. A more common choice for fitted clothing is to visit the popular local tailors (usually men), who set up shop in small open-air kiosks, with a foot-driven sewing machine. One arrives with one's chosen pagne cloth in hand, stopping for measurements and to discuss the style one prefers and the timing and cost of the commissioned work. Alternately, one can also buy affordable, fashionable ready-to-wear African outfits at the market at cinq kilo (both men's and women's, in pagne print cloth or in cotton solids).

Another significant use of clothing in Centrafrique (as well as elsewhere in West Africa) is the funerary pagne and/or T-shirt. When someone of note dies, a family with significant means to memorialize the departed will purchase matching pagne prints for the relatives to wear at the funeral and afterward. Those in the funeral party may also invest in or sponsor a T-shirt imprinted with a photo and epitaph of the deceased.

HAIRSTYLES

During the first decade of the twenty-first century, women and girls' hairstyles have shifted from the more traditional cornrow braids (*pete*) to the striking spiked hairdos (*chicottes*) made by parting the hair into even squares of between three (for long hair)

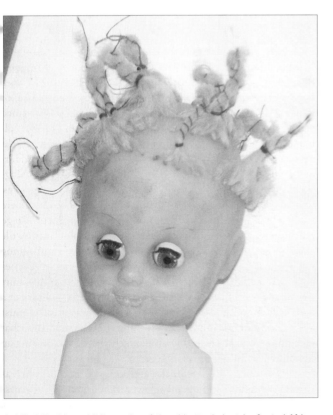

A doll clothed in a child's version of the *chicottes* hair style. Central African Republic, 2007. Photograph by Michelle Kisliuk.

and approximately twenty (for short hair) and tightly spiraling black thread around each portion to make it stick out straight from the head. Further fashionable styles are either chemically relaxed hairdos with splashes of fanciful color such as purple or red at the end of a twist, or microbraids with artificial extensions, or wigs that resemble relaxed or permed hair. Men's haircuts are usually simple fades or close-shaven all around the head with softened corners and shaped edges around the face. Some young men sport goatees; otherwise, beards and mustaches are uncommon.

ETHNIC TRADITIONAL DRESS

The descriptions offered so far in this article apply to the majority of the population. There are many ethnic groups in Centrafrique, however, each with its own traditional clothing that is displayed only rarely at festivals or dance exhibitions or worn by dancers at nightclub shows in the capital. These often consist of animal-skin loincloths, slippers, hats, and cowry shells or beads. In the far north (Bamingui Bangoran), dancers wear feathered hats. Traditional dance attire, such as that of the Gbaya, often includes ankle bells or rattles, and sometimes strings of rattles or bells cross the chest and go around the waist of a male dancer whose movements articulate a cross-rhythm between chest and feet. Traditional dancers in forested regions such as Isongo (Lobaye) create ankle shakers (*mangdzendze*) and waist rattles (*sengete*) from tree nuts drilled through, strung together, and then mounted on a leather anklet or belt. Another type of dancer's body rattle used widely across Centrafrique is made from the bark and nuts of the *kpo* tree; the rattle is attached to an animal-skin belt as a sonic and visual enhancement to the *motengene* (rib cage/shoulder rotating) dance and other traditional regional dance styles. Hard *sengete* nuts are sometimes strung into long ornamental necklaces worn by both men and women dancers, over the head and crossing the chest to the waist in an X.

Before the arrival of Europeans—and common across ethnic groups in the forested region of what is now Centrafrique—bark cloth was made from particular trees (which varied according to ecological region). The names of these trees are now synonymous in various languages with the word *clothing* (for example, *etobo* in Bagandou/Diaka and *toulou* in Mbati). This cloth was cut, decorated, and wrapped according to the current style of a particular ethnic group (such as Banda, Gbaya, Mbati) and according to gender: for men, it was cut to pass between the legs as a loincloth, and, for women, it was a bit larger so as to wrap around the waist as a skirt or to be attached across the chest to brace the breasts as a top (along with the separate skirt). The colors varied according to class and status; village chiefs and others of status would have special, larger cloths that were more carefully crafted and decorated with brighter colors (natural dyes made from tree barks and berries).

People across Centrafrique also wore animal skins and raffia. Skins such as panther, leopard, and monkey with bright and multicolored fur would be worn by those of higher status, while common people would wear antelope and other more commonplace animal skins. Healers would wear small multicolored skins sewn together, which would double as instruments of healing power: bright colored mongoose and squirrel, tree hyrax, and snake skins. Raffia skirts would also be worn by women, while men used raffia as belts. There were three kinds of women's raffia: daily raffia (not dyed or dyed with one color such as red/ochre),

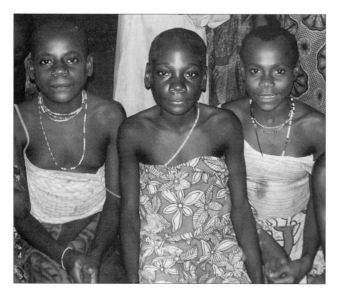

BaAka girls adorn themselves with bead necklaces, cotton cloths, and camisoles obtained from neighboring villagers. The camisoles are worn for style, not necessarily for covering. Bagandou, Central African Republic, July 2007. Photograph by Michelle Kisliuk.

festival raffia (red and white or red and black), and mourning raffia (dyed black and longer than the other skirts, reaching to the knees). BaAka women also wore raffia skirts or, alternately, would wear special sweet-smelling *mandudu* leaves as loin covers, which would be changed weekly. Young girls would wear different leaves than would the adult women.

BAAKA STYLE

The BaAka (the so-called pygmies, also known as Aka in the literature) are the one ethnic group in Centrafrique that, to this day, has for the most part its own distinct everyday way of dressing—although this style has also undergone changes. BaAka live in the forested regions of Centrafrique along the border with Congo (Brazza) and Cameroon (in the Lobaye and Sangha Mbaere prefectures, respectively). In the past, but beyond living memory, BaAka made loincloths out of bark cloth. In the twenty-first century, when BaAka go net hunting or foraging or are relaxing at home, both men and women often wear a loincloth only, now usually made from a piece of cotton pagne. When BaAka women wear a loin covering made from leaves, it is called *mandudu*; when it is made from a piece of pagne, it is called *maduka*. A man's regular short loincloth made of pagne, is called *kangbo*, but if it is from a full-length pagne and hanging far down in the front and back, it is called *solomu*.

In the twenty-first century, and especially when visiting a non-BaAka village, BaAka women prefer to wear a pagne cloth wrapped to the knees (instead of to the ankles as their neighbors would wear it). BaAka clothing is usually tattered and faded, evidence of both heavy use and the secondhand (or third- or fourth-hand) nature of the items, but clothing is worn with a distinctive casual elegance. BaAka men usually prefer shorts and shirts obtained from neighboring farmers with whom BaAka have a complex relationship of parallel clans, exchanging wild meat and labor for clothing and other items. BaAka move between forest and village-area encampments and tend to use more clothing when staying near the farmer's villages. They use this clothing in their own particular ways. A BaAka man might come into the village dressed in an old suit jacket, with shorts made from cut offs of the matching slacks. The size of an item is often not an important issue, and a boy might don an oversized T-shirt that hangs far off of a shoulder and reaches to the knees, or he might unself-consciously sport shorts with an enormous hole exposing a buttock.

The color of BaAka clothing is often distinguishable from that of other Centrafricans, because they have less access to laundry soap and use their clothing longer and more communally than do others; light-colored clothing becomes a uniform shade of earth tinted brownish red. Teen BaAka girls might use a cloth wrap as a dress, wrapped from above the breast, but might just as well unself-consciously pair a pagne skirt with a camisole that does not necessarily always cover one or both breasts. BaAka mothers carry their infants in side slings made of cloth or animal skin (not tied on the back like other Centrafrican babies), so that they can nurse or comfort the infant while they travel or work. Many BaAka also have tattoos, faint dark lines down the forehead to the bridge of the nose, or circles on the cheeks. Tooth filing (making the middle teeth come to a dainty point) is also still common among BaAka. Lip plugs for women have faded out of style in recent decades, while some girls are wearing nose studs. A single cord (made from vine) might be tied around the head or around the chest of a man or a woman as a medicinal amulet.

BaAka hairstyles and traditional accessories are also distinguishable from those of their Centrafrican neighbors. Both men and women keep their hair short, shaving it into creative shapes: a triangle with its point ending at the forehead is a favorite. Sometimes even eyebrows are styled into horizontal stripes or ellipses. Traditional BaAka accessories include the *sawala*, or animal-skin handbag, and the *djombi*, a hatchet that men hook over their shoulders when working or traveling to a place they may need to use it. Woven baskets with tump lines for carrying on the forehead are another common accessory also used by their farmer neighbors (although BaAka baskets have distinct, narrow bottoms, while farmer baskets have flat square bottoms) as well as the more ubiquitous *kako*, an elliptical woven backpack used by BaAka and others to transport meat and supplies into and out of the forest.

BAAKA DANCE ATTIRE

During a twenty-first-century dance event where many BaAka get together—some to court prospective spouses—people use clothing in particular and creative ways. Women and girls might roll up a pagne cloth that they had been wearing as a wrap while visiting the village and now tie it as a roll around the hips with a knot at the back to enhance their dancing. Women might also wear a dyed raffia skirt for a dance, but these are more common in areas where raffia is plentiful. An item that was originally a bra, now tattered, might be used by a young man as a headband, and a teenager might put on a single bright orange sock (the other is missing) or just the ankle part of the sock (the rest of it having already deteriorated). Some men layer on several pairs of cutoff shorts for a dance event or wear the long loincloth made from a large pagne print (solomu). BaAka rarely have access to new cloth and thus freely reinterpret the use of items that are now

A BaAka woman wears her baby in a cloth sling, along with a tank top hand-me-down from a Bagandou farmer. She has a medicinal cord around her head and filed teeth, a beauty practice still common among many BaAka. There is also a (now faded) line on her forehead made from a vegetable dye, for beauty. Bagandou, Central African Republic, July 2007. Photograph by Michelle Kisliuk.

the women's dance, Elamba, at the end of the twentieth century, consisted of layers of three or four raffia skirts sometimes hiding a bottom layer of rolled cloth that would help set the skirts swinging dramatically during the hip-swinging portion of the dance. In the early twenty-first century, the costume for this same dance has changed: the raffia skirts have been replaced with mandudu leaves (leaves tucked into the back of a G-string waistband), and, instead of dancing barefoot, the dancer is supposed to wear a pair of flip-flops (BaAka women usually go barefoot in everyday life). As in this instance, dance costume, and changes thereof, become contexts for symbolic negotiation, play, and reappropriation of identities (ethnic and gender identities, in particular). Another recent dance form, called Molimo, requires the male dancer to cover himself so that his identity is concealed in pagne cloths and a wooden face mask, and he is to dance with socks—this last item being particularly difficult for BaAka to obtain and which they rarely use otherwise. That one has scored a pair of socks to use for the dance displays a kind of status, cachet, and prestige that at once exhibits access to the material culture of BaAka neighbors and reappropriates it for a use rather different than the manufacturer's original intent.

THE INTERPLAY OF IDENTITIES

The sartorial choices that Centrafricans have made and continue to make reveal individual, familial, religious, urban or rural, gender, ethnic, and class identities while they embody, refashion, and sometimes playfully surmount the colonial and neocolonial legacies of their experience. This interplay of local, regional, and European elements instantiates the complex intermix of historical and cultural forces that are actively negotiated in the Central African Republic.

References and Further Reading

Bahuchet, Serge. *Les Pygmées Aka et la forêt centrafricaine: éthnologie écologique*. Paris: SELAF, 1985.

Bahuchet, Serge, and Robert Farris Thompson. *Pygmées?: peintures sur écorce battue des Mbuti (Haut-Zaïre)*. Paris: Musée Dapper, 1991.

Kisliuk, Michelle. *Seize the Dance! BaAka Musical Life and the Ethnography of Performance*. New York: Oxford University Press, 1998.

Michelle Kisliuk and Justin Serge Mongosso

several-generation hand-me-downs. BaAka have occasional access to newer items they might earn from certain kinds of work, and they may have long pants, sneakers, sunglasses, watches (that may or may not work, it does not matter), or baseball caps, all of which BaAka confidently wear with a physical comportment distinguishable from non-BaAka Centrafricans in its self-possessed and unassuming style.

Costumes for particular dance forms are another category of BaAka attire. The most widespread full-body mask is for the spirit known as Edjengi, who dances under a raffia canopy that swirls and dips as the dancer turns and ducks. The costume for

Chad

The Republic of Chad is a landlocked state in north-central Africa. Most of northern Chad is in the Sahara Desert with high daytime temperatures and cool nights, encouraging individuals to wear layered clothing styles. The central zone has a Sahelian climate and grassy steppes. Woodland savanna and a semitropical climate characterize the southern zone, where individuals prefer lightweight garments. The capital, N'Djamena, is south of Lake Chad, a dominant feature in the center of the country.

The Chadian population totals about ten million people, who live primarily in rural environments. The two official languages are French and Arabic (the local form of Arabic is called Tourkou), and Sara is spoken in the south. Islam was introduced fairly early in northern and eastern Chad; 52 percent of the population is Muslim and strongly supports conservative attitudes toward dress. Christianity spread during the Colonial era through the work of missionaries and represents 35 percent of the population. Varied forms of animism related to ancestors, spirits, and natural phenomena exist in the southern areas and result in distinctive ceremonial attire.

Dress ensembles worn by men and women in the Republic of Chad mirror the country's complex historical evolution and its peoples' adaptation to climatic and physical environments. Religious beliefs such as Islam and animism affect dress customs as well. For example, the Tubu in the north wear garments that differentiate them from their neighbors. The Sara in the south are also known for their distinctive dress at initiation ceremonies. The use of Westernized dress (such as dresses, shirts, T-shirts, and trousers) in the twenty-first century is common in urban centers and towns.

Cliff paintings in the Borkou, Ennedi, and Tibesti regions attest to early life in the eastern Sahara and depict cattle, camels, and individuals wearing wraps, stylized hairstyles, and jewelry. For centuries, Chad faced the continuous migration of Arab nomads from the north through the Tibesti Mountains and from the Nile Valley via Darfur. This encouraged the integration of Muslim peoples from the desert and the savanna with those in the central regions and the intermixing of their dress practices. From the sixteenth to the nineteenth centuries, a succession of Islamic states controlled the trans-Saharan trade routes, thus linking North Africa, the Nile Valley and sub-Saharan Africa. British explorations began in the early 1800s led by Denham and Clapperton, followed by German missions in the 1860s and French missions in the 1890s. Chad became a French colony in 1920 and gained independence in August 1960.

Chad's ethnic groups are commonly divided according to its three major climatic and vegetation zones that affect dress practices. The seminomadic Tubu and related groups inhabit the northern areas and the Kanem district. Thirteen percent of the population lives in the vast central Sahelian zone, along with neighboring seminomadic and nomadic Arab and Fulani communities. The Sara represent the largest group in the south. The proximity of these groups over time illustrates the complexity of Chad's ethnic tapestry and has contributed to cross-cultural assimilation and borrowing relating to dress. At independence, references to ethnicity were banned, and twenty-first-century Chadian dress and fashion practices emphasize the similarities between groups rather than their distinctive qualities.

OVERVIEW OF DRESS PRACTICES IN CHAD

Little boys and girls have shaven heads with only tufts of hair on the top. They wear amulets around their waists and necks. At a certain age, boys adopt shorts and girls a drawstring skirt, which become underskirts as they grow older.

Women dress in ensembles made of colorful batik or wax print cloth imported from other African countries or from The Netherlands, which have replaced traditional hand-loomed textiles. The ankle-length skirt or pagne (*pagne* refers to a multipurpose, two-yard [almost two-meter] length of cloth) is wrapped around and tucked into the waist and worn with a matching blouse with wide sleeves and an embroidered neckline. The types of fabrics used and the designs of sleeves set the latest trends: colors and patterns change constantly, and sleeves are embellished with ruffles and embroidery and are made in different shapes to emphasize new fashions. Married women are known to use another pagne as an overskirt. Head wraps and scarves complete these outfits; the more elegant and elaborate examples are reserved for festivities. Women in the central Sahelian zone prefer indigo pagnes that are wrapped around their chests and draped over the shoulder. Ensembles emphasize the length of the body and a woman's figure: corpulence is a sign of wealth and well-being. Muslim women don long veils over their ensembles and cover their faces in the presence of strangers.

Women from all groups dress their hair in elaborate braids, creating distinctive styles: some emphasize patterns, others include bangs, and others frame the face. These are often embellished with beads, shells, and metal ornaments, and all styles accentuate the forehead, the head, and the neck. Among certain groups, tattooed gums and lips are believed to enhance beauty, as is the use of kohl around the brows and eyes and henna for the feet and hands. Women use perfume or incense to enhance the way they smell, and all favor jewelry made by the artisans or *haddads*: head ornaments, nostril rings, earrings, necklaces, bracelets, and anklets.

In contrast, men's apparel is generally conservative, typically long-sleeved tunics over trousers that taper at the ankle. Arab men favor drawstring trousers. Muslim men are clad in long flowing robes or boubous with embroidered necklines over baggy trousers and turbans. Some shave their heads when they come of age and wear cotton caps covered with turbans.

French ethnographer Jean Chapelle notes that some groups, such as the Kanembou and the Kotoko in the Kanem district, use scarification patterns on their foreheads, cheeks, or chins to indicate group membership. Among the Kaba and other southern groups,

Nomadic herder, Sahara Desert, Chad, 2008. The Tubu people favor white ensembles such as the one worn in this photo, used as protection from the high daytime temperatures in the Sahara Desert. National Geographic/Getty Images.

women once wore wooden lip plates as a sign of beauty. In cities and towns, men often adopt Western-style clothing such as trousers, shirts, T-shirts, or *saharienne* jackets. The saharienne refers to the safari jackets worn by British officials in the colonies. These were popular in warm climates, because khaki is a lightweight fabric. Women, on the other hand, have adopted midcalf Western-style shirtwaist dresses fashioned from colorful print cloth.

THE TUBU

Tubu men (including the Teda and Daza subgroups) favor trousers, or *woono*, with thin tapered legs with a large white cotton shirt. These shirts, or *kobo*, have a chest pocket on the left side and decorative embroidered motifs on the right side. Men's turbans, or *debi*, are reserved for festivities. A turban is wound around the head, sometimes decorated with leather amulets, and one end rests on the shoulder. No social rules or taboos govern the use of turbans, although men cover their faces in front of strangers. In earlier times, men of the Aza group (artisans and hunters) wore a leather tunic, or *farto*, and a leather cap during hunting expeditions. Men wear leather or plastic sandals and adorn themselves with a silver or brass ring and stone bracelets. Men have scars on their foreheads and cheeks. Their heads are shaven when they come of age, and they wear a beard.

Today, little girls are covered by a cotton *cache sexe*, replacing the older leather belts with cowry-shell aprons. At the age of seven, a girl wears a white skirt at her waist, and, at puberty, it is worn above her breasts under a blue tunic as a symbol of her virginity. Tubu women, who are slender, wind a long piece of rectangular cloth around their chests and attach over the left shoulder. These dresses were once made with *guinées bleues* cloth, which refers to indigo-dyed cotton cloth once manufactured in India for trade. In the latter part of the eighteenth century, it was manufactured in England and in France for export to Africa, where it was used as currency. Dresses are also fashioned in black or white cloth (dyed light blue once it ages), emphasizing Tubu womens' preference for solid-colored fabrics. While working, traveling, or visiting, women wear a leather belt (*wurdu*) and a pagne as an underskirt. In the Tibesti areas, women once wore goatskin tunics (*delami*) as a protection against the cold. For feasts and holidays, they put on their finest jewelry and drape colorful silk scarves on their shoulders and heads. They do not veil their faces.

Girls start to dress their hair at the age of seven with the help of an older relative. They make ten to twelve plaits, braided close to the scalp and left free at the ears. A single braid frames the forehead. At the age of twelve, girls shave the top portion of the forehead to lengthen it. They add three median plaits from the forehead to the nape of the neck, holding them together with a pin. Upon marriage, women rebraid their hair into two median plaits. Women protect their hairstyles with a layer of grease and use coal or burnt clay to darken it.

Little girls are adorned with cowry, stone, or bead necklaces and a wooden peg in one nostril. When they are twelve, their upper lip is artificially swollen for the dyeing process and is colored blue, as are their gums. When they marry, women receive silver hoop earrings, silver and bead necklaces, anklets, and bracelets from their mothers. They also insert a silver hoop in their nostrils or a piece of coral and adorn their foreheads with striking metal spirals. All women wear amulets.

CEREMONIAL CLOTHING

Despite the prevalence of Islam and Christianity in Chad, traditional belief systems are still important. The significance of ancestors, divination and oracles, possession cults, and beliefs in spirits are a means people use to join the visible with the invisible aspects of their lives. Initiation ceremonies, agricultural festivals, and possession cults are all occasions for wearing extraordinary ensembles. They emphasize color, texture, surface, noise, layers, and movement, thus linking abstract and concrete worlds.

Sara children undergo initiation rites when they are ten or twelve years old. Girls participate in the Ndo Banan rites, and boys in the Yondo ceremonies. Both initiations symbolize the rebirth of children as members of their community. Girls shave their heads and wear long beaded veils. They adorn themselves with long bead necklaces and brass armlets and wear belts with iron bells, thus creating rhythm when they dance. Boys' bodies are embellished with ochre paint; they wear a leaf mask, short skirts, and beaded belts. The beaded veil and leaf mask represent the loss of their family identity.

Possession cults among the Moussei help individuals regain their health and social dignity; some join *fulina* groups, which intervene with nature spirits to invoke natural phenomena such as rain. People adorn themselves with necklaces, beaded headdresses, bracelets, and other items representing the spirits they are invoking. During initiations, young men wear feathered hats or straw helmets embellished with horns or bird beaks and cowry-shell belts. In a similar vein, the Dangaleat in the Korbo region believe in the *margaï*, a spirit guardian of the granaries.

During the harvest season, sacrifices are made to these spirits and men partake in dances. They wear long skirts made of strips of cloth and dress their hair in plaits decorated with ostrich feathers and metal headbands.

As noted earlier, Western-style dress is more common in urban centers; what were once distinctive elements of different peoples' dress are disappearing, especially as a result of new class structures and a sense of national identity.

References and Further Reading

Balfour-Paul, Jenny. *Indigo*. London: British Museum Press, 1998.

Chapelle, Jean. *Nomades Noirs du Sahara les Toubous*. Paris: Edition l'Harmattan, 1982.

Chapelle, Jean. *Le peuple tchadien. Ses racines, sa vie quotidienne et se combats*. Paris: Editions l'Harmattan, 1986.

Huet, Michel. *The Dance, Art and Ritual of Africa*. New York: Pantheon Books, 1978.

Lebeuf, Annie M.-D. *Les populations du Tchad (Nord du 10eme Parallele)*. Paris: Editions l'Harmattan 1959.

Le Cornec, Jacques. *Les mille et un Tchad*. Paris: Editions l'Harmattan 2002.

Kristyne Loughran

Republic of Congo and Democratic Republic of Congo

Before France and Belgium divided the area in the late nineteenth century, the Republic of Congo (capital Brazzaville) and the Democratic Republic of Congo (capital Kinshasa) were a continuous area that shared cultural traits, including fashion and body art. When the Portuguese arrived at the mouth of the Congo River in the late fifteenth century, they were amazed by the high quality of the raffia cloths produced in the Congo area. The Portuguese introduced European cloth and fashions, and two often-opposing fashion trends developed that continue into the twenty-first century: styles that reference Europe and styles that indicated ethnic identity, status, and beauty. With colonization in the late nineteenth and early twentieth centuries, European clothing flooded both Congos, and urban clubs developed that promoted particular looks. After independence in 1960, there was resistance to foreign styles in both Congos, but resistance reached a climax in the Democratic Republic of Congo in 1971, when President Mobutu Seke Seso banned foreign clothing and introduced the *abacost* for men. At the end of the twentieth century and into the twenty-first, dress was impacted by secondhand, tailor-made, and new inexpensive clothing shipped in from Asia that was available in both rural and urban areas.

GEOGRAPHY, CLIMATE, AND DRESS

The Congo River is the dominant feature in the geography of both of the Congos. Having its source in the southeastern region of the country, the river outlines a major basin bisected by the equator that was perhaps once a large inland sea and is bordered with high-altitude plateaus. It is the river and the basin that create a unity to the area, because the peoples are diverse in language and political, economic, social, and religious structures. As a result of the warm climate, clothing is rarely worn as protection from the elements; instead, dress demonstrates identity, status, and beauty. Dry season, which is December through February north of the equator and May through September south of the equator, is the time for special events and the wearing of clothing that marks ceremonial status. Fashions are not limited to clothing but also incorporate permanent body modifications, ephemeral body art, jewelry, makeup, and coiffure.

A seventeenth-century engraving from Olfert Dapper depicting lower-ranking Kongo officials. These men wore wraps that exposed their chests and went barefoot. The animal skins and elaborate textiles worn on top of the wraps demonstrated wealth and specific ranks. Courtesy of Elisabeth Cameron.

FIFTEENTH TO EARLY EIGHTEENTH CENTURIES

Western knowledge of dress and fashion in the Congo River basin before colonization varies across this broad and diverse area. The Portuguese documented the areas near the mouth of the Congo River, but written European documentation of the rest of the basin was extremely limited until the late eighteenth century and was sporadic in the nineteenth and early twentieth centuries.

The Portuguese arrived at the mouth of the Congo River in 1484 and interacted with the court of the Kongo, a kingdom that straddled the lower Congo River in what is now Democratic Republic of Congo, Republic of Congo, and Angola. The *manikongo* (king of the Kongo) became a Christian, took the name Alfonso I, and, in the early part of the sixteenth century, established diplomatic relationships with Portugal, Spain, the Low Countries, and the Holy See. The Portuguese documented life in the Kongo kingdom, including the dress of a continuum of peoples living in the lower Congo area.

Even though he never visited the Kongo kingdom himself and received his information from the Portuguese explorer Duarte Lopez, who visited the Kongo in 1578, the chronicler Filippo Pigafetta wrote the most-quoted description. After a century of Portuguese presence, Pigafetta and Lopez felt free to speculate about what had been worn "in ancient times." They describe the basic unit of clothing as raffia-cloth garments that hung from a belt in the front and the back. Royalty wore an additional circular netlike garment reaching to the knees and thrown back on the right shoulder to leave the right arm free. Aprons and capes of animal skins; a small, square yellow or red cap; and sandals made of palm fiber completed the royal look. Royal women chose from three lengths of aprons, the longest reaching the feet. They added a waist-length doublet, capes, and caps. Commoners and slaves wore the same basic raffia-cloth garments as nobility, although the fabrics used were not as fine, and nothing was worn above the waist or on the feet.

Whether commoner or noble, the Portuguese were greatly impressed by the variety and quality of Kongo textiles made of raffia and palm fiber. They described them as velvets with and without pile, brocades, satins, taffetas, and damasks. Cloth was woven primarily by men and in approximately one-meter (about one-yard) squares (the length of a palm frond). These squares were combined to make larger units that would be transformed into clothing or used singly as a form of currency, which continued in use along the coast until the seventeenth century.

After conversion to Catholicism, the king and the nobles adopted imported Portuguese dress of silks, velvets, and leathers. While fine raffia cloth made locally could be obtained as part of an existing economic system, imported clothing had to be purchased in a foreign economy based on the trade of slaves, ivory, and copper. Those who had credit with the Portuguese acquired the finest and richest European garments, rapiers, slippers, and (for the women) gowns, veils, jewels, and golden chains. Those who did not have good credit with the Portuguese either bought less-expensive dress or wore locally made garments.

European cloth soon replaced raffia cloth in both wear and meaning; as a result, the local raffia textile industry began to decline, and the skill to produce very high-quality textiles was lost in the coastal areas and slowly became compromised in inland areas.

An illustration of Ngaliema, a Tio ruler, wearing a special wrapper made of raffia cloth with a fringe. He is also wearing hairpins and copper armbands. From H. M. Stanley, *The Congo and the Founding of Its Free State*, vol. 1, London, 1885. Courtesy of Elisabeth Cameron.

Imported cloth was used in dress, furnishings, and as currency. It was exchanged as part of diplomatic proceedings, negotiations on marriages, and at funerals. As currency, cloth was valued against the cost of one slave. One piece of fabric was approximately six yards (five and a half meters) and originally was the price of one male adult. Around 1700, one slave sold for the amount of fabric needed to dress one noble: approximately six to eight pieces for a man and six to seven pieces for a woman. By 1770, the price had risen to thirty pieces for an adult male.

PRE-COLONIAL ERA (MID-EIGHTEENTH CENTURY TO LATE NINETEENTH CENTURY)

The Portuguese remained a close partner of the Kongo court and kingdom until, for better advantages in trade, they settled in what is now Angola. In the seventeenth century, the Kongo kingdom slipped into a civil war that lasted sixty years. By the end of the war, the proud, internationally known kingdom had been reduced to a decentralized and internationally impotent area. The French and Belgians began to evaluate the area for colonization and exploitation in the early nineteenth century. The Belgians followed the river and explored the larger river basin, eventually claiming an area demarcated by the river in the historic 1885 Berlin Conference. The French, on the other hand, led by Pierre Savorgnan de Brazza, negotiated directly with the head of the Tio kingdom (just to the north of the Kongo kingdom) and obtained a signed treaty in 1880, gaining control of what is now Republic of Congo.

European cloth continued to spread widely during this period. Explorers, missionaries, and other travelers used cloth as currency in both buying provisions and paying porters. The knowledge of and demand for European and Asian textiles became widespread and sophisticated. Several travelers commented that, even in areas where no European had been, people had a knowledge of types and qualities of European textiles.

During the late eighteenth and nineteenth centuries, the most information available on dress and adornment is from coastal areas where Europeans had lived for many generations. Europeans also began to explore the greater Congo basin—especially the southern savannas, where movement was fairly easy—and they left written accounts of their travels. In these documents, they often described the dress of the peoples they visited.

The Tio kingdom is well documented because it is near the coast. Raffia cloth, woven mainly by men, was still in use during this period. Designs were created through the inclusion of red, natural white, yellow, and black threads. Men and women wore a raffia-cloth wrapper brought under the arms and tied in front of the chest. Men attached a belt to secure the wrapper. Women wore an undergarment like a petticoat but did not belt the wrapper. Occasionally in dry season when the temperatures dropped somewhat, an additional length of cloth was worn over the shoulders. Although this basic dress was worn by people of all stations, the styles, lengths, and weave types of wrappers varied according to the wearer's wealth, status, and occupation. Knee-length wrappers that allowed freedom of movement were worn in work situations. For special events, holidays, or ceremonies, special wrappers were worn. Early chroniclers stated that men wore beautiful raffia cloth that was as soft as silk and bright with colored patterns. These wrappers sported fringes at the edges of each woven panel. Nobles and men of high status often wore great lengths of imported textiles and European blankets. By 1880, primarily European cloth and clothing was worn on a daily basis, and everyone owned one or two imported items.

Permanent body modifications and ephemeral body art were also an important part of appearance. Two types of scarifications were applied. Five to six shallow parallel lines reached from cheek to chin and signified ethnic and clan identity. Other scarifications, especially on women's torsos, were added for aesthetic purposes. Also to enhance beauty, the two upper front teeth were filed on a slant, and the eyebrows and a portion of the eyelashes were removed. The body was carefully bathed, and palm oil and camwood powder were applied to the skin. For special occasions, lines were painted on the face and arms with red, yellow, white, brown, and black pigments. Jewelry—including armlets, anklets, bead necklaces, and finger rings—was supplemented by gender-specific accessories such as knives, axes, or spears. Coiffures were gender and area specific. One man's style, compared to a rooster's crest, used a wicker frame to create a bun on the back of the head while the hair on the temples was shaped to point toward the eyes. Decorative iron pins were added to complete the look. Women's hairstyles were simpler; the hair was combed out, whitened with ash, and decorated with hair pins.

Dress styles would have specific names. Among the Bobangi—a less-stratified people who live to the northeast of the Tio in both Republic of Congo and Democratic Republic of Congo—dress names were recorded and give a glimpse what Bobangi wore. Some names correspond directly to size and construction of the textiles. *Enta* is a large cloth made of multiple raffia squares. *Mola* is a long, narrow cloth only one raffia square wide. Other names specify how the cloths are worn. *Limputa* is a large cloth draped over the shoulders. *Lingbanda* is a cloth tied at the waist and drawn between the legs. More specifically, *bongeke* is a long cloth tied at the waist and pulled very loosely through the legs, and *monkate* is a shorter cloth tied at waist but pulled tightly through the legs, allowing for freer range of movement. *Libenge* is a woman's wrapper fastened over the hip. *Lipepele* is a style where one side is worn higher over one hip than the other. *Mbendoli* is fastened high on the torso. Finally, *ntebele* is when the cloth is worn low on the hips.

COLONIAL ERA (LATE NINETEENTH CENTURY TO MID-TWENTIETH CENTURY)

During the Colonial era, European textiles and dress infiltrated both Congos, and, because of the colonial drive to research and chronicle and the academy's invention of anthropology, dress throughout the areas is documented in text, drawings, and photographs. Often anthropologists and colonial officials incorrectly assumed that what they documented in the early parts of the twentieth century was indicative of how people had dressed in previous centuries. On the contrary, as a result of far-reaching disruptions resulting from the fifteenth- to nineteenth-century slave trade and the repressive French and Belgian colonial policies that emphasized forced labor for colonial economic gain, change in political, economic, and social structures was widespread and affected dress and adornment throughout the area.

During the twentieth century, dress and adornment reflected ethnicity and identity within the colonial system and political, economic, social, and ceremonial status. Peoples who are linguistically related to the Kongo, for example, like the Yaka, Suku, and

Tio, also use the word *mpu* to refer to a hat that signifies political authority. The mpu type of headdress was worn widely as a symbol of political authority and continues as a political symbol into the twenty-first century. Among the Kongo, *mfumu* (chieftaincy) and mpu (hat) are equivalent in meaning. The mpu, made of pineapple fibers, was given to a leader during investiture, and a person wearing the hat was referred to as *mfumu a mpu*, or chief of the hat. Among the Yaka, the mpu was a cap that was originally made of raffia, but, as other materials became available, it was fabricated of woven cotton cloth and marked political authority.

Among the Yaka and Suku, other types of political leadership and authority were also signified by headdresses. The *bweni* was worn by the *kalamba* (land chiefs), who were leaders descendant from the founder of a family or community and considered to have a special spiritual connection with the land and ancestors. The bweni headdress was made of woven raffia fiber and, because of its protective functions, was worn by the kalamba at all times. The *tsala* headdress was a cluster of feathers that marked different types of leadership depending on the type of feathers used. These might be political but could also be worn by the leader of an initiation camp.

Headdresses and other dress could also be worn as markers of other types of social status in a community. Daniel Biebuyck, a Belgian anthropologist, documented the Bwami Society among the Lega in eastern Democratic Republic of Congo. Bwami is an association with multiple hierarchical levels that gives structure to the Lega society. When Biebuyck did his research in the 1950s, approximately 95 percent of all Lega men joined the lowest level of Bwami. A smaller percentage of women were members.

While what happened in the initiations into different levels was considered secret, the identity and level of members was common knowledge and marked through various insignia called "things that are pursued." The Bwami member who wore all of his or her insignia was called *kakenia* ("one who draws attention to him- or herself"). Insignia included hats, wrappers, animal pelts worn at the waist, necklaces, and fiber rattles. Each item was connected to Bwami or a specific level because of a specific meaning the object had. For example, the elephant, because it was a large, unstoppable animal that left marks wherever it went, became a metaphor for Bwami. Despite the identification of the elephant with all of Bwami, anything made of elephant by-products could only be worn by a member of the highest level of Bwami.

Not only was dress an important way Bwami members marked status, proper presentation of the body was also taught. The ideal body was oiled, covered lightly with red powder, and perfumed. Men's heads were cleanly shaven except a small patch at the back of the head used to anchor hats with pins. Women's hair was neatly coiffed in a variety of styles. In comportment, the body was held erect.

Dress with specific significance such as hats that show political authority or skins that have meaning within societies continued during the Colonial era to be worn on special or ceremonial occasions, but European garb and imported textiles quickly began to infiltrate both rural and urban areas in the two Congos; urbanites became fashion leaders because of the availability of European goods in the cities and towns.

Although European-style clothing was known and worn by the elite in coastal areas since the late fifteenth century, it became part of common wear for men in the late nineteenth century. Servants in the service of colonial officials became fashion leaders.

A group of *yananio* and *kindi* initiates taking part in a dance performance (*kamondo*) that preceded the initiation ceremonies of a male candidate to *yananio* grade, near Kalima, Democratic Republic of Congo, 1967. Each man in this photograph wears dress elements that identify him as being of *yananio* or *kindi* rank within the Lega's Bwami Society. Each element also is used in teaching ethics and morals within the society. Photograph by Eliot Elisofon, 1967. EEPA EECL 5423. Eliot Elisofon Photographic Archives, National Museum of African Art, Smithsonian Institution.

As each official, whether French or Belgium, prepared to depart for Africa, he received detailed instructions concerning appropriate clothing for the tropical climate in the colonies. Congolese servants were responsible for the care of these extensive wardrobes and became intimately familiar with European dress from underwear to outerwear. They also received, as gifts or pay, items that were no longer in style among the colonial officials or, as parting gifts, large quantities of clothing as an official returned to Europe.

Belgian and French wives who accompanied their husbands to the Congos were not given official lists, but several periodic publications such as *Le Monde Colonial Illustré* advised the wives on lifestyle and fashion, and clothing catalogs allowed European women to order clothing, hats, and other items from France and Belgium. House servants received not only cast-off clothing but also out-of-date copies of the women's clothing catalogs and fashion magazines.

While Congolese servants were at work, their uniform (shorts and shirt with short sleeves and no shoes) was strictly mandated and reinforced their inferior status. When the servant was not on duty, the colonial official often encouraged him to dress well, because it was seen as a reflection on the style and generosity of the European. Congolese men who held white-collar positions in

the colonial endeavor emphasized their privileged positions by adopting European outfits complete with socks and shoes. Clothing was obtained through colonial connections or by buying cloth and taking it to a tailor.

Urban women were slower than men to embrace European fashion and wore wrappers called *pagnes* (from the French word for loincloth) made originally of imported fabric. Women were judged more on the quality and pattern of cloth than on its style, with wax prints as the best and most expensive. Money was spent on head scarves and shoes, because only the poorest and worthless women went barefoot. The women who did introduce Western fashion were often wives of African traders or women who lived in colonial households casually or in temporary and often clandestine marriages arranged by their families. These women adopted short dresses, silk stockings, and high-heeled shoes and carried handbags. They styled their hair in European fashions and used rice flour as a face powder.

Prior to World War I, many European observers commented on the elaborate and smart dress worn by men and women on Sundays and holidays. In 1903, Bouteillier recorded colorful *pagnes* on women and secondhand trousers and frock coats on men. Other observers documented suits, canes, monocles, gloves, and pocket watches on chains. Baron Johan de Witte noted that men flaunted their wealth by wearing every item of clothing they owned, including, for example, layers of pants and multiple cardigans. To emphasize the number of garments worn, men often frustrated Europeans by wearing their shirttails out. Soon, however, it was not enough to own European clothing; it was also important to wear it correctly. The man who publicly wore surplus army pajamas became a long-standing joke that is still told in the twenty-first century.

Missionaries were also active in introducing, supplying, and promoting Western-style clothing. Mission schools had dress codes and often had to supply the clothing for the students to wear. The school uniform consisted of a shirt and loincloth or shorts for boys. Girls wore simply made ankle-length dresses or a loose blouse with a pagne. Additional clothing was also made available. The supply of clothing at missions became a major attraction, and advice given to new missionaries often suggested that clothing not be given out at the beginning of the school term for fear that, once the students received their clothing, they would return to their homes.

The 1950s saw changes in both colonization and dress. Urban areas had begun to form at the turn of the twentieth century, but urban growth escalated as the wage economy increased. Urbanites maintained and nurtured rural connections but also created new urban mutual aide societies. In a survey done by M. Soret in 1951, 20 percent of a man's income in Brazzaville was spent on clothing. In Poto-Poto, a suburb of Brazzaville, there was one tailor for every three hundred inhabitants, and in Bacongo, another suburb, there was one tailor for every ninety-five inhabitants.

The difference in the statistics cited above reflected the diversity of responses to urbanization and dress. The northern area of Republic of Congo, home of the Mbochi and Teke, was considered underdeveloped, while the south, where the Kongo lived, was thought of as progressive, and the Kongo were often called *mindele* ("white"). While the Kongo had adopted imported textiles, the Teke people were more conservative and maintained a raffia weaving tradition. Men wore these raffia cloths like togas, while women used them as wrappers. The Poto-Poto subdivision was a haven for immigrants from the north, while the fashion-conscious Kongo resided in Bacongo, perhaps explaining the greater number of tailors found there.

During the Colonial era, distinct differences existed between rural and urban areas in the presentation of the body. Whether in the country or city, men usually had physically demanding jobs resulting in a well-muscled body. In most rural areas, women were primarily farmers and had vigorous muscled bodies, but many women in urban areas no longer had to work as hard and what was expected of women's bodies changed to a slimmer shape. In rural areas, scarification marks were common as both identifying marks and for aesthetic and erotic reasons. In the cities, these marks were condemned by the colonial governments, and often people who had them were denied employment. As a result, people who anticipated movement into city life either refused scarification or made sure it was well covered by their clothing. In rural areas, a darker complexion was a mark of a hard worker and a desirable marriage partner, but, as urbanites no longer worked in the sun, a lighter complexion became sought after.

Urban clubs of various types had been known since the early part of the twentieth century, when members of one ethnic group, often close relatives, gravitated together to offer mutual support and comfort in the alien urban environment. New types of clubs developed in different parts of the countries, and, although their focus might be political, economic, or social, fashion often became a focus. After World War II in Brazzaville, urban clubs called *existos* grew up around fashion. Men had traveled during the war and came back to the Congo with a broader view of fashion and a feeling of connection to French institutions. These clubs took the name existos, short for existentialists, because it tied the clubs to Jean-Paul Sartre and contemporary French life. To reinforce French identity, the clubs adopted the colors red and black, which were thought to be Parisian colors.

The average age of the men in the existos was eighteen, and many of the members were married with families. The clubs became mutual aid societies that furthered the goal of the organizations to be the best-dressed club. Each club had one tailor who worked for the entire group and ensured a uniform appearance among the members. Clubs competed among themselves for status by appearing in the various urban night scenes in full dress. In the 1960s, the socialist movement in the newly independent Republic of Congo condemned the existos as conflicting with African identity and being antagonistic to the social revolution itself, resulting in a sharp decline in the number of and membership in the clubs.

Other cities also took prominence in fashion, including the mining town of Elisabethville (renamed Lubumbashi in 1966), where women's clubs evolved around fashions. While women in the western coastal area of Democratic Republic of Congo wore ensembles that were a variation on a blouse or camisole with a skirt or pagne, in the eastern areas, women in urban areas wore mainly European fashions. Following World War II, sewing machines became more available throughout the Congos, and there was an increase in the number of tailors, resulting in a florescence of women's fashions and a move to combine European fashions with the styles developed around the pagne.

One of the first women's fashion clubs, Diamant, was founded in 1933 by women merchants from Elisabethville who frequently traveled to Kinshasa, Brazzaville, and also south into Northern Rhodesia (now Zambia). Because of their travels, they were exposed to a variety of urban fashions and had access to materials that were not always available in Elisabethville. In time, membership was broadened to all women merchants whether married or single and regardless of whether they traveled. Because single women, especially ones who were active in business, were often assumed to be prostitutes, one goal of Diamant was to find a husband for all its single members. Within the club, older married women groomed younger women in appearance and deportment, and the club hosted a variety of social events to introduce the young single members to respectable men. These events not only resulted in new social connections but also expanded the club's economic networks.

Not long after Diamant was formed, other associations began to appear in Elisabethville that focused on particular groups of women such as single women, married women, and Christian women. Sami, for example, was a prosperous club limited to women who sold beer and alcohol, although one branch of Sami was sponsored by missionaries and Belgian administrators in order to deflect attention from alcohol. Sami's philosophy was that beautiful and well-groomed young women attracted a larger clientele who were willing to spend more money.

INDEPENDENT CONGOS
(MID-TWENTIETH CENTURY ONWARD)

Both Congos separately gained their independence in 1960. In 1946, the French colony of Congo, with Brazzaville as its capital, became an overseas territory of France with representatives in the French Parliament and an elected Territorial Assembly. In 1956, Congo had its own elected government and, in 1960, gained complete political independence. The country quickly became socialist and, in 1969, changed its name to People's Republic of Congo and, finally, in 1991, officially became Republic of Congo. Belgian Congo, with Kinshasa as its capital, on the other hand, was given its independence by Belgium in 1960. Its name and politics have changed repeatedly since. Originally Republic of Congo, the name was soon changed to the Democratic Republic of Congo. Joseph Desiré Mobutu took control of the government in 1965 and, in 1971, changed the name of the country to Zaire and his own to Mobutu Seke Seso. After his ouster in 1997, the name was changed back to Democratic Republic of Congo (DRC).

Independence in either country did not have an immediate effect on dress except in the sporadic availability of imported fabrics, garments, and fashion accessories that resulted from the political upheavals following independence in both Congos. Many urban trends continued: complexions became lighter, women became slimmer, and men tended to choose women based on beauty rather than on their ability to work hard in the fields.

Before independence, pagne was sold in four-meter (thirteen-foot) lengths, sufficient to make a simple bodice and one wrapper.

After independence, the six-meter (twenty-foot) length was introduced, and there was a florescence in the style and elaborateness of the camisole. In the DRC, each style had a name, which was generally in French or Lingala, the two languages of Kinshasa, making other areas of the DRC feel subordinate to Kinshasa in fashion. The names were references to the cultural heritage of the country or contemporary events. With the availability of new styles, women's associations ceased to be fashion leaders.

Hairstyles, whether simple or complex, had always been done primarily by family and friends. Groups of women would often gather to socialize, drink, and fix each other's hair. Sometimes, a woman known for her expertise was sought and paid for this work. In the early 1980s, formal hair salons began to spring up in urban areas. The first hair salon in Lubumbashi, for example, opened in 1980, and, by 1990, there were countless salons. By the twenty-first century, many salons, styles, and hair products were widely available in most urban and many rural areas.

While fashions were often shared between the two Congos, a great difference resulted from President Mobutu's call for authenticity on 27 October 1971. Mobutu attempted to rid Democratic Republic of Congo of foreign influences by outlawing, among many other things, European dress. Police could arrest any man who wore a business suit or woman who wore a dress or pantsuit, all of which had been declared decadent. People who refused to abandon these foreign styles were labeled as subversive, and there were incidents where men were surrounded by mobs who cut off their ties. Likewise, women were publicly

A family in Pompo, in the Democratic Republic of Congo, 1989, wearing clothing typical of the late twentieth century. The father wears an *abacost*, while the grandfather wears trousers and a short-sleeved shirt. The mother is wearing a double pagne with matching blouse, and the children are in an assortment of secondhand clothing. Photograph by Elisabeth L. Cameron.

stripped of offending Western dress. Both the importation and wearing of wigs was outlawed since most were European styles. These dress restrictions were enforced until Mobutu's departure in 1997.

Women and men were commanded to wear traditional dress. At the same time, emphasis was put on a national identity rather than an ethic one that most traditional styles enforced. The solution for women was to adopt the camisole and pagne, which came to be understood as a traditional African style. For formal occasions, women wore a tailored and elaborate camisole with two pagnes, one as a skirt and the other wrapped in elaborate folds that cascaded down the left side of the body. Similar styles were also worn in Brazzaville and Republic of Congo, but women from the DRC became known for their greater skill in wrapping their pagne. On a daily basis, women often wore a secondhand shirt, T-shirt, or simple tailored or older camisole and a single pagne or double one that was simply tied. The second pagne was also used for carrying a baby on the back, held over the head when walking in the rain, or as a shawl when it was chilly. For warmth, a woman draped it over her shoulders and then threw the right side over the left shoulder so that both hands were free.

President Mobutu introduced a new style for men called *abacost*, an abbreviation for *à bas le costume* ("down with the suit"). The original abacost was a Mao-style, short-sleeved tunic with patch pockets that was sometimes compared to a bush jacket, worn with trousers. The original ensemble was made from one solid and often somber color. Gradually the tunic's collars became more elaborate and print materials were used. To stress political associations and membership in Mouvement Populaire de la Révolution (Popular Revolutionary Movement or MPR), the only political party in the country, men ordered abacost made of textiles that commemorated Mobutu's presidency or the MPR. Mobutu himself became the prototype for the new style, adding cravats and brightly colored and patterned tunics. To stress that his leadership came from African sources and not compliancy with outside forces, he adopted a leopard-skin cap and carried a carved staff. He also wore the 1960s-style black or tortoiseshell glasses that reminded people of Patrice Lumumba, the first elected prime minister who was also one of the first state martyrs. After Mobutu's control over the country waned, opposition politicians showed their independence from the MPR by wearing European business suits. Once he left power, the abacost was immediately abandoned and men returned to Western-style business suits.

After 1997 in the Democratic Republic of Congo, men and women had greater choices in their garments. The influx of secondhand clothing in Western styles began in earnest in the 1980s. It was often less expensive to buy *mitumba* (secondhand clothing, word derives from Swahili for bale, the unit mitumba arrives in) than to purchase material and have an outfit tailor-made. The availability and economy of secondhand clothing has had a direct impact on what people wear. While urban fashions had always had some impact on rural style, secondhand clothing has become ubiquitous in even the most remote areas. Children who once would have worn very little, for example, now wore secondhand shorts, shirt, or dress. During Mobutu's regime, women who wore pants were widely considered to be prostitutes. Women's pants, however, are in the bales of secondhand clothing and, in the twenty-first century, are worn by younger fashionable women.

In the twenty-first century, the dress options in both Congos are multiple. Secondhand, tailor-made, and new inexpensive clothing shipped in from Asia allow each consumer to make individual choices. In contrast to Mobutu's regime of authenticity, many fashions are available in both rural and urban areas.

Snapshot: Le Sape

Le Sape, short for Société des Ambianceurs et des Personnes Elegantes, takes men's fashions to its most extreme. The man who becomes a *sapeur* dedicates his life to the acquisition of status by accumulating *le gamme*, a wardrobe of *le griffe* (clothing and accessories made by famous fashion designers). Le Sape originated in the existos found in Brazzaville following World War II and was fueled by Kinshasa's burgeoning music industry and the moneyed elite from both capitals. The twin cities of Kinshasa and Brazzaville became home for Le Sape as practitioners routinely use ferries to cross the Congo River and appear at clubs on either side of the river. The music star Papa Wembe has become known as the "Pope of Sape" and encourages young men and women to dress well and cleanly.

Many reasons have been given for the existence of Le Sape. Some think that it arose as a way of showing Europeans, who originally brought these types of clothing to the Congos, that the colonized had beat the colonizer at the fashion game by becoming better dressed and more elegant. Others assume it is a reaction to the unpopular authenticity movement begun in 1971 by President Mobutu. Either way, Le Sape is democratic; each member is judged based on accumulated wardrobe and the knowledge of how to wear it and not on whether he is a janitor or a white-collar worker.

The sapeur strives to look as wealthy and as immaculately dressed as the most accomplished businessman. The face is bleached to a shiny pale and slightly yellow complexion called "yellow papaya," affluence is shown in a small potbelly achieved through eating semolina, and the hips are curved and full but the waist is small. The hair is razor cut and occasionally the hairline is cut back from the forehead to give the appearance of an older, more accomplished person. The clothes carry expensive designer labels, and the body is held with elegance and in a way that shows off the clothing. Other accessories such as designer name watches, sunglasses, belts, and perfumes are also desired.

The young man who aspires to become sapeur begins by dressing in ready-to-wear clothing and copies of designer labels. The novice strives to become part of a network of sapeur by worshiping at the feet of a *parisien,* an accomplished sapeur who has returned from a ritual trip to Paris. Once in the circle, the younger man might be able to borrow less current designer labels owned by the great men. He also learns how to conduct himself and succeed on the ritual trip to Paris called *l'aventure.* When the *candidat à lémigration* (candidate for immigration) is ready, he departs for his time in Paris, where he will build le gamme, a large haute couture wardrobe. To achieve this goal, the sapeur can use both legal and illegal means. During l'aventure, the sapeur returns occasionally to Kinshasa and Brazzaville, trips called *descente* (descents), to show off the new wardrobe and begin to build a reputation. The final return to Kinshasa and Brazzaville occurs when the sapeur decides that his gamme and its display will gain him the proper reputation.

Upon his return, he participates in a ritual gala where several sapeur are presented. Immaculately dressed, groomed, and coiffed, the sapeur is announced by a master of ceremonies who lists all his qualities and each element of his wardrobe. His girlfriend, also elegantly dressed, embraces him and gives him a gift followed by others who also present small gifts. Finally, as music plays, the sapeur strikes various poses intended to show himself at his best. He then leaves the stage and the next sapeur is announced. When all sapeurs have been presented, *le dance des griffes* takes place. During this dance, each sapeur attempts by shifting or removing his clothing to display the label on each item he is wearing.

After the presentation, the community considers the sapeur as a parisien who will begin to instruct novices. In an effort to keep current, parisiens also might exchange clothing among themselves. For Le Sape to continue to exist and for parisiens to keep their status, there must be a continual movement of men back and forth from Kinshasa and Brazzaville to Paris.

Snapshot: Negotiating Identity

A pair of photographs taken in 1989 of a citizen of Democratic Republic of Congo graphically illustrates the constant negotiations of identities that occurred in the twentieth and twenty-first centuries. Colonialism created artificial boundaries that took no consideration of preexisting political, social, or ethnic identities. It expected people within those boundaries to take on a new Congolese identity that was more Belgian in dress. After independence, political difficulties arose as multiple ethnic groups strove to control the larger modern nation. To resolve these conflicts, personal identity became complicated as the new regime strove to move people's allegiances away from ethnicity to the modern nation state. Dress and fashion reflected these often-conflicting realities.

On one hand, the man in the photographs was a Kuba title holder and a high-level member of the community council. As a member of the council, this man paid homage to a dynasty that dates back to at least the seventeenth century and promised to uphold the ancient Kuba law. His ceremonial garments show his rank, and the ornateness demonstrates his clan's prosperity. His foundation garment is a fine *mapel* (men's ceremonial skirt) constructed of one-meter- (about one-yard-) square panels of woven raffia cloth. It is worn with the bulk of the skirt pleated in the front and tied with a belt so the top of the skirt falls forward, creating a two-tier effect. Tied to the belt is the pelt of a civet cat, again stressing the man's high status. The *laket* (hat) is decorated with feathers that associate him and his rank with the quality of specific birds such as eagles. Tied on the forehead is a section of a large snail shell that was imported from the Atlantic Ocean and marked both wealth and high status. The carved staff and fly whisk also designate his elevated rank.

On the other hand, the man was a citizen of the Congo and a local official in the Mouvement Populaire de la Révolution (Popular Revolutionary Movement or MPR), the only political party during the regime of Mobutu Sese Seko. To proclaim his loyalty to MPR, he wears an *abacost* made from a textile celebrating twenty years of Mobutu's presidency. The abacost was created to replace a man's business suit in 1971, when Mobutu attempted to remove outside influences from Zaire (now Democratic Republic of Congo). Two portraits of Mobutu are prominently placed on each side of the front of the abacost, creating a pyramid of leopard hats. Only MPR officials wear leopard-skin hats, so the man again reinforces his leadership in the political party. The man also holds a walking stick similar to one that Mobutu occasionally carries. The outfit is completed with trousers and black leather shoes.

In daily wear and away from the camera, the man wears secondhand trousers and a shirt similar to those of his assistants who are holding up the backdrop. This style of dress originated in urban areas during colonialism and has become ubiquitous in all urban and rural areas.

This pair of photographs taken in 1989 of a citizen of Bumbangi, Democratic Republic of the Congo, illustrates how he, like many, has to negotiate different identities. In the photograph on the left, he is dressed as a Kuba titleholder. His ceremonial skirt is constructed of roughly three-foot- (one-meter-) square panels of woven raffia cloth. The feathers in his hat, the carved staff, and the fly whisk also designate his elevated rank. In the photograph on the right, he proclaims his loyalty to the Mouvement Populaire de la Révolution (MPR) by wearing an *abacost* made from a textile celebrating twenty years of Mobutu's presidency. He also wears a leopard-skin hat that indicates he is an MPR official. Photograph by Elisabeth L. Cameron.

References and Further Reading

Biebuyck, Daniel. "Lega Dress as Cultural Artifact." *African Arts* 15, no. 3 (1982): 59–65, 92.

Bourgeois, Arthur. "Yaka and Suku Leadership Headgear." *African Arts* 15, no. 3 (1982): 30–35, 92.

Friedman, Jonathan. "The Political Economy of Elegance: An African Cult of Beauty." *Culture and History* 7 (1990): 101–125.

Gondola, Ch. Didier. "Dream and Drama: The Search for Elegance among Congolese Youth." *African Studies Review* 42, no. 1 (April 1999): 23–48.

Lopes, Duarte. "A Report of the Kingdom of Congo and of the Surrounding Countries, Drawn Out of the Writings and Discourses of the Portuguese Duarte Lopez," by Filippo Pigafetta. Translated from the Italian and edited, with explanatory notes, by Margarite Hutchinson. With facsimiles of the original maps and a preface by Thomas Fowell Buxton. *Cass Library of African Studies. Travels and Narratives,* no. 66. London: F. Cass, 1881/1970.

Martin, Phyllis. *The External Trade of the Loango Coast, 1576–1870: The Effects of Changing Commercial Values on the Vili Kingdom of the Loango.* Oxford, UK: Clarendon Press, 1972.

Martin, Phyllis. "Contesting Clothes in Colonial Brazzaville." *Journal of African History* 3, no. 3 (1994): 401–426.

Martin, Phyllis. *Leisure and Society in Colonial Brazzaville.* Cambridge, UK: Cambridge University Press, 1995.

Meurant, George, and Robert Farris Thompson. *Mbuti Design: Paintings by Pygmy Women of the Ituri Forest.* London: Thames and Hudson, 1995.

Sizaire, Violaine, Dibwe dia Mwembu, and Bogumil Jewsiewicki, eds. *Femmes-Modes-Musiques: Mémoires de Lubumbashi.* Paris: L'Harmattan, 2002.

Thomas, Dominic. "Fashion Matters: La Sape and Vestimentary Codes in Transnational Context s and Urban Diasporas." *Modern Language Notes* 118 (2003): 947–973.

Vansina, Jan. *The Tio Kingdom of the Middle Congo 1880–1892.* London: Oxford University Press, 1973.

Elisabeth L. Cameron

See also Mangbetu Dress; Kuba Dress and Textiles.

Mangbetu Dress

- Early History
- Personal Appearance and Significant Items of Dress

In the early twentieth century, the Mangbetu and related peoples who live in the northeastern part of Democratic Republic of Congo became iconic symbols in the West of African high fashion. Their practices of head elongation and body painting and their wearing of distinctive fiber and feather hats, bark cloth, and women's aprons were represented in their art works and in photographs and paintings by Western visitors. These images have persisted in the cultural iconography of the region until recent times, and traces of this fashionable dress can still be seen on ceremonial occasions or in staged performances into the twenty-first century.

Yet many of the styles that were current at the turn of the century and that were so widely depicted in sculpture and pottery have disappeared. Body decoration, clothing, and even ornaments have changed radically in the past century, and styles that were the height of fashion at the turn of the twentieth century have taken on new meanings. For example, eagle feathers were formerly restricted to chiefs, but nowadays are worn on dance hats and by any adult. Formerly, women rarely wore hats, but, in the twenty-first century, they wear them for dances. Dances and their costumes symbolize tradition and Mangbetu identity and are performed only on occasions that celebrate this identity—such as the installation of a chief, the visit of a government official, or the shooting of a film.

EARLY HISTORY

The Mangbetu were known for their striking treatment of the body, particularly head elongation, body painting, scarification, and, for women, the wearing of a decorative back apron, but these elements represented only one part of what was important to them. The art of adornment was often closely tied to notions of health and well-being. Many adornments were worn to protect the person, enhance some personal quality, or affect the outcome of an activity. Thus, protection and the idea of beauty could be closely intertwined, and a surfeit of beauty could indicate power. For example, the king's regalia were associated with the prowess of the animals reserved for him (eagles, okapi, leopard), but the beauty of the objects that the animals were made into was also important in demonstrating his power. Not only was the body treated with a concern for beauty, but protective objects, tools, useful household objects, and even houses (often covered with wall painting) were deliberately made to be beautiful. The objects, homes, and bodies of the most powerful people stood out for the care with which they were made.

Head elongation was a common practice among the Mangbetu at the beginning of the twentieth century. Children's heads are no longer bound, but elongated heads can still be seen on

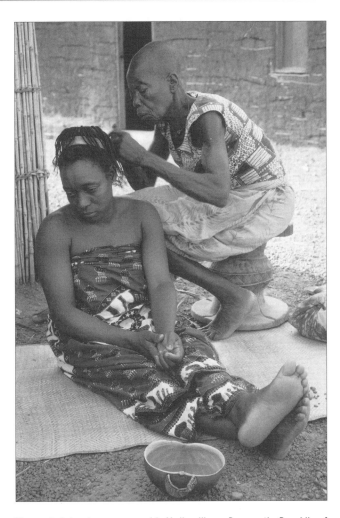

Woman hairdressing a young girl, Medje village, Democratic Republic of Congo, 1970. The Mangbetu take great pride in personal appearance, especially hairstyle. Head elongation was a common practice at the beginning of the twentieth century and can be seen on the older woman. Photograph by Eliot Elisofon, 1970. EEPA EECL 2950. Eliot Elisofon Photographic Archives, National Museum of African Art, Smithsonian Institution.

older people. Babies' heads were bound with braided cord made of human hair or plant fibers. The band was put on the very day of the child's birth after the first bath with lukewarm water had been given. It was taken off at irregular intervals. Popular Mangbetu belief credits Mangbetu kings with introducing head elongation. However, there is no clear history regarding the introduction of the practice. Various forms of head modification (like the removal of teeth or stretching of the ear lobes or lips) were common in central Africa, and the Mangbetu style may have predated the Mangbetu kingdoms that developed in the eighteenth and nineteenth centuries. Nevertheless, the fact that Mangbetu rulers commonly elongated their heads helped to popularize the practice among Mangbetu subjects and non-Mangbetu neighbors, and when Europeans first encountered the Mangbetu in the mid-nineteenth century, the practice was common—as was body scarification, done by both men and women.

PERSONAL APPEARANCE AND SIGNIFICANT ITEMS OF DRESS

In the past, if not still today, the Mangbetu spent a great deal of time on their personal appearance. The head was clearly the focus of Mangbetu personal aesthetics. The shape of the head, the hairstyle, and ornaments for the head—including hairpins, hat pins, hats, and combs—worn by both men and women were of paramount importance. Mangbetu hairstyles varied considerably according to the class of the wearer and the occasion. Wealthier people could afford the time to prepare elaborate coiffures. Georg Schweinfurth, the German botanist who first described the Mangbetu in 1871, noted that, at the court of King Mbunza, both men and women wove their hair over an arrangement of reeds and twisted the front hair into thin rows across the forehead. Hair taken from war victims or purchased from others was used to supplement a woman's hair and to make the arrangement larger. By 1910, when Herbert Lang visited on an expedition sponsored by the American Museum of Natural History, new hairstyles had developed. Men no longer dressed their hair to enhance the impression of head elongation, and women now added a halo-shaped basketry frame covered with hair. Lang wrote that this new style for women was very common and was considered especially pleasing by the Mangbetu. The hairstyle of upper-class women was widely depicted in the anthropomorphic art produced in the early part of the century. Lower-class women wore their hair more simply, as did women of the upper class when not preparing for public appearances. Lang's photographs show that variations on tightly braided rows and protruding spikes were common. Men's hair was arranged by women, and both men and women wore combs made of palm fiber, porcupine quills, wood, and metal.

In the third quarter of the nineteenth century, based on Schweinfurth's account, men wore hats fastened to the hair with pins, and women wore hairpins and combs made of metal, bone, or ivory. By the early twentieth century, women occasionally wore hats. The American Museum of Natural History's collection of nearly a hundred hats shows remarkable variety. Most of them were woven of palm fiber, and, as with sleeping mats and baskets, variety was created not only by the complex plaited patterning but also by the combination of natural and dyed colors. By utilizing the fibers with their glossy cuticle layer facing outward or inward, surfaces were created that reflected light differently. Strips of sorghum, which have a bright buff color, were sometimes woven into the hats as further adornment. Protruding wrapped loops and ribbonlike elements were exuberantly worked into the structure of the hats. Crossed sticks from the leafstalks of the raffia palm were often attached to the tops of the plaited hats by poking their ends through the corners. Bundles of many kinds of feathers, including those of the guinea fowl, owl, harpy eagle, touraco, the paradise flycatcher, chicken (sometimes from chickens that had been sacrificed to the ancestors), gray parrot, and others, were tied together and attached to the tops of the hats.

Another kind of hat was made from looped or knotted cordage and worn underneath basketry hats. Some looped hats were edged with cowries or dog's teeth or snail shells. Other hats were made from the loofah plant, often combined with ornamental shells and feathers. Animal skins, including leopard, okapi, colobus monkey, genet, and chimpanzee, were commonly used. The skins were untanned or tanned lightly by being manipulated with oil. Skin hats sometimes had basketry edgings and interiors, and they were often elaborately decorated with brightly colored feathers.

Most hats were made to be purely ornamental, but some had special meanings. For example, hunters wore special hats as a sign of mourning after they killed an okapi, while others were worn to mourn relatives. Mourning hats lacked the usual binding and were finished with a fringe.

Hat pins and hairpins were made in a great variety of materials, including wood, copper, iron, brass, silver, and, most spectacularly, ivory. Delicate ivory hat pins were prestige items and indicators of wealth. The entire end of a tusk was required to make a fine pin with a disklike top. Pins were worn by men and women—by men mostly in hats and by women in their hair.

In the past, Mangbetu women took great care in ornamenting their bodies with painting as well as scarification. For dances and special events, women painted geometric designs on their bodies with a black pigment made from the gardenia plant. Some designs were painted freehand, and some were applied with stamps or small carved cylinders of wood similar to those used on pottery. According to Schweinfurth, the variety of patterns was "unlimited" and included stars, Maltese crosses, bees, flowers, stripes, and irregular spots. He wrote that he saw "women streaked with veins like marble, and even covered with squares like a chess-board." The designs lasted for about two days and then were rubbed off and replaced by new designs. Mangbetu men and women rubbed their bodies with a mixture of pulverized redwood and oil from palm kernels to give the skin a coppery gloss.

Both men and women wore ornaments, both for adornment and for their protective or magical properties. Wooden ornaments were believed to have medicinal power; metal and ivory, on the other hand, were associated with wealth and political power. Women commonly wore multiple strands of brass-bead anklets made by Mangbetu smiths. Probably the oldest anklets were the spiral leg bands found throughout central and eastern Africa. Armbands of hide with twisted copper or brass wire were also common.

Teeth and tusks from a great variety of animals served as adornments and charms. Ornaments made from parts of forest animals were imbued with magical properties and could also serve as status symbols, particularly in the case of the leopard and the okapi. Canine teeth and claws were worn on belts or necklaces in great agglomerations or as single charms, sometimes encased in fiber covers made by men.

By the early twentieth century, important people wore great masses of glass beads, introduced by Europeans, especially when they posed for formal photographs. Brass wire, however, was much preferred to glass beads. On the rare occasions when glass beads were incorporated into ornaments, they were used in simple, single strings on which were suspended objects—such as animal claws and teeth—that had far more symbolic meaning than the beads themselves. Glass beads were never arranged in elaborate patterns as was done elsewhere in Africa.

Knives and daggers, tucked into a belt or held in the hand, were an important part of men's adornment. New ones were worn as ornaments before they were put to general use. The belt, made of rope or hide, fastened the main male garment: a piece of bark cloth wrapped between and around the legs. Chiefs and other important men displayed their status by wearing a large cloth that was new and stiff so that it would stand upright above the belt

Two women wearing *nogetwe*, a rectangular bark-cloth garment, worn as an apron, with a small plantain-leaf shield to cover the buttocks. Medje village, Democratic Republic of Congo. Photograph by Eliot Elisofon, 1970. EEPA EECL 5739. Eliot Elisofon Photographic Archives, National Museum of African Art, Smithsonian Institution.

and over the chest. Ordinary people wore older bark cloth, with the softened material drooping over the belt. Each man made his own cloth by removing a large piece of bark from either of two species of fig tree and pounding it with an ivory, wood, or elephant bone beater. In the 1880s, shades of bark cloth ranged from light brown to a deep red brown to gray; it could also be made black by burying it in mud. Three pieces sewn together side by side, the central one a natural color flanked by side panels of black, was a popular design. Bark cloth is still made today with alternate light and dark stripes, each about four inches (ten centimeters) wide being the most fashionable.

Women wore a rectangular bark-cloth garment, the *nogetwe*, as a short skirt or sometimes an apron. In the past, and still today for ceremonial displays, it was left open in the rear to reveal the *negbe*, or back apron, an oval fiber pad fastened around the waist with a string. Upper-class women's bark cloth was larger and of better quality than that of poorer women. Women fastened the nogetwe around the waist with a belt made from stem fibers of the oil palm. In front of the bark-cloth skirt, they often wore an arrangement of banana leaves formed into a small pouch and attached to the belt.

An upper-class woman almost always carried a small piece of decorated bark cloth on her right shoulder and laid it down on her stool before sitting down. Many of the pieces were painted with gardenia juice in a great variety of patterns resembling body painting. Such small bark-cloth pieces are today often associated with the Akka, Mbuti, and other Pygmy groups who lived near and among the Mangbetu. Westerners collect them as small paintings done by Pygmies, although, in the past, they clearly were used and made by the Mangbetu.

By the beginning of the twentieth century, upper-class Mangbetu women wore a small plantain leaf shield to cover their buttocks. Delicately cut and colored pieces of leaves were appliquéd onto an oval pad built up of layered plantain leaves. Color contrasts in the designs were achieved by blackening the leaves for the appliqué with mud or, occasionally, by adding lighter-colored corn fibers. Styles changed over time and the aprons collected in the 1930s and 1940s include raffia braids that are sewn as outer borders over the black-and-tan, banana-leaf patterns. Similar ones are still worn for dances.

By the early twentieth century, European clothing was available in the region and was worn by those who could afford it. Even now, the Mangbetu still make bark cloth and, basketry, feather hats, fiber and hide belts, and some ornaments, and they wear these for important ceremonial occasions such as the inauguration of a new chief or for greeting high officials of the government. Many changes in traditional dress have occurred, however, mainly in terms of democratizing certain objects that were formerly signs of status. Some former prestige items, such as leopard skins and okapi, can no longer be worn. The former was reserved for the president of the Congo after independence, and okapi hunting has been outlawed. The elaborate flared hairstyles have disappeared, as has the practice of head binding. Charms and amulets are not worn conspicuously because of the influence of colonial and state governments, Christian churches, and modern influences. Metal ornaments are disappearing, and it is rare to see a knife in a man's belt. For very special occasions, some women still wear the nogetwe and the negbe, and some men wear bark cloth or European cotton wrapped between the legs. Normally, women wear cotton skirts (wrappers) with blouses or shirts, and men wear cotton shorts, shirts, and pants. There is a brisk trade in secondhand Western clothing in local markets, which sell everything from baby clothes to bras and bathing suits.

References and Further Reading

Birnbaum, Martin. "The Long-Headed Mangbetus." *Natural History* 43, (1939): 73–83.

Schildkrout, Enid, and Curtis A. Keim. *African Reflections: Art from Northeastern Zaire*. New York: American Museum of Natural History; Seattle: University of Washington Press, 1990.

Schildkrout, Enid, and Curtis A. Keim, eds. *The Scramble for Art in Central Africa*. London: Cambridge University Press, 1998.

Schweinfurth, Georg A. *The Heart of Africa: Three Years' Travels and Adventures in the Unexplored Regions of Central Africa from 1868 to 1871.* Translated by Ellen E. Frewer. New York: Harper & Bros., 1874.

Van Overbergh, Cyrille, and Eduard De Jonghe. *Les Mangbetu*. Brussels: Institut international de bibliographie, Albert de Wit, 1909.

Enid Schildkrout and Curtis A. Keim

Kuba Dress and Textiles

- Daily Wear
- Ceremonial Dress
- Funerals and the Art Market

Dress in the Kuba kingdom (Democratic Republic of Congo), whether daily wear or ceremonial, marks both rank and prosperity. Men's and women's festive dress is an ensemble of skirt, hat, and other beaded and decorated accessories. Rank is indicated through the use of specific items such as eagle or owl feathers, the wearing of certain skirt styles, and restriction of some metals. The density and rarity of added materials demonstrates the resources a family or clan can control and thus their affluence. This special dress is worn at funerals, initiation events, and other more contemporary political, social, and religious events.

Located approximately five degrees south of the equator, the elevation of 1,500 feet (457 meters) makes the climate relatively temperate. While nighttime temperatures can be cooler, daytime highs average around 80 degrees Fahrenheit (27 degrees Celsius). The Kuba, then, wear clothing as visual statements of personal, family, and community identity rather than for protection from the elements.

To speak of the Kuba people as a cultural unity is deceptive. Made up of around eighteen different ethnic groups, many who speak their own distinct languages, each group is proud of its own unique heritage and history but has also been part of the Kuba kingdom since at least the seventeenth century. Each group pays tribute to the Kuba king (*nyim*) and participates in broader Kuba identity. The term *Kuba* was given them by their neighbors as the Kuba themselves have no name for the broader kingdom. Mutual proximity and allegiance over a span of more than three hundred years have produced a pan-Kuba approach to leadership and status. Throughout all Kuba ethnic groups, titles and status are well understood; dress is systematically used by both men and women to declare both position and prosperity. Kuba ceremonial dress clearly and immediately marks the wearer as being a holder of a specific title. Through its quality and the density of design, it also signals the wealth and prosperity of the clan to which the wearer belongs.

The highest rank is, of course, the nyim (an alternate term is *lukenga* in some southern areas of the kingdom)—that is, the king himself. With the administration of the Kuba kingdom located at Mushenge (alternate spelling Nsheeng), a group of titleholders located there assists the nyim in governing the kingdom. Beyond the center of the kingdom, leadership and the dress that mark each title vary only slightly between ethnic groups. In some areas, groups of communities share a council with ranked titleholders, while, in other areas, each community has their own council.

The Kuba's use of the dressed body to declare title and rank is and has been shaped by the availability of diverse natural materials found locally and accessed through trade to distant resources. The Kuba kingdom developed as early as the eighteenth century in a location ideal for natural resources and trade. Situated between the rain forest to the north and the savannas to the south,

Kuba family wearing contemporary dress for a family photograph, Pombo, Democratic Republic of Congo, 1989. The mother wears a double *pagne* with matching blouse. The father wears a modified *abacost* over his clerical collar while the children wear an assortment of secondhand clothing. Photograph by Elisabeth L. Cameron.

the kingdom had access to diverse natural resources ranging from natural plant fibers to animal and bird products. Major navigable rivers running on the northern and southeastern borders of the kingdom provided conduits for major short- and long-distance trade networks that the Kuba, from their privileged position, both accessed and partially controlled. This trade network brought in beads, cowries, and metal that was shaped and used in dress.

DAILY WEAR

On a daily basis, most Kuba wear mostly Western-style secondhand and tailor-made clothing. Clothing is cycled through uses, new clothing being worn for special or more formal occasions. As clothing becomes worn, it becomes work clothing and finally only appropriate for labor away from the community. Men commonly wear trousers and shirts within the community. For performing hard labor such as preparing a field, hunting, or fishing, older clothes that might have discernible wear are worn. Upon returning to the community, men quickly change into clothing that has less wear. Women wear *pagnes* (wrappers) and either a secondhand shirt or a blouse tailored to match their pagne. As with the men, older clothes are worn for daily work such as agriculture, child care, and other domestic tasks.

Kuba titleholders, including the king, who wears copper armbands, in ceremonial dress. Mushenge, Democratic Republic of Congo, 1989. Photograph by Elisabeth L. Cameron.

Before the introduction of Western-style clothing, men and women wore fairly simple garments made of woven raffia cloth. Men had roughly woven skirts called *mapel ma buaanya* (forest skirts) because they were only worn when the man went outside the community to work in the forest, savannah, or river. Once they returned to the community, the men would change into higher-quality garments. These skirts were worn wound around the waist and fastened with a belt made from a cord. Men would create simple pleats in the front to allow their legs more freedom of movement. When the first Westerners began to encroach on the kingdom, the king Kot aPey (r. 1902–1916) forbade anyone in the kingdom from wearing Western clothing. As the century passed and colonialism advanced, this decree was ignored until Kot aMbweeky (installed 1968), in a complete reversal, forbade the wearing of traditional dress except in ceremonial occasions such as funerals, initiation events, and royal dances. These ensembles might also be worn at major political, religious, and social events such as the opening of a public health clinic, political rally, or the welcoming of a new Catholic bishop.

CEREMONIAL DRESS

A complete man's or woman's ceremonial ensemble is made up of a gender-specific skirt, a hat (*laket*), and other accessories that might include anklets, armlets, bracelets, belts, necklaces, or a necklace worn over one shoulder and under the opposite arm. Ornamentation such as beads, cowries, metal pieces, and shells create colorful designs on each example. The rarity of the material and the density of the design designate the status of the wearer and his or her family. Copper can only be worn by the king and those to whom he gifts it; thus, wearing copper is a strong visual declaration of a person's connection to the king and the royal family. The king himself wears copper armbands. Other members of the royal family may wear a series of copper anklets that clink and jangle as they walk, alerting everyone within hearing that royalty approaches.

Men's ceremonial skirts (*mapel*) are up to twelve meters (thirteen yards) in length and worn only by initiated men. The long skirt is worn wound once around the body, then kilted in the front. A narrow belt is tied over the skirt and around the waist so that the top of the skirt falls over the belt creating a two-tiered effect. The body of the skirt is surrounded on three sides by large borders. There is no border on the inside edge. The borders on the long edges are attached in opposite directions so that, when the garment is worn with the top of the skirt folded down, the right side of both borders is displayed. The borders and main body or inside panels usually have contrasting colors and designs that make them visually distinct. The inside panel is made up of one-meter- (about one-yard-) square raffia cloth pieces sewn together to an appropriate length. This panel has one overall pattern that can be carried out with a variety of techniques such as tie-dye or patchwork creating a checkerboard or other shapes. Women will soften the fabric by beating it and will create specific embroidered or pile-work borders; otherwise, men weave and construct their own skirts.

Titled official with his wives wearing ceremonial dress, Mushenge, Kuba kingdom, Democratic Republic of Congo, 1989. Note the wives are wearing overskirts, which are wrapped around the body once and have borders that might differ sharply in technique or color from the center of the skirt. Photograph by Elisabeth L. Cameron.

Flowing layers of cascading raffia cloth echo and dramatize the dancing of Kuba men. As the men dance, the skirt extends each of the dancer's movements. Occasionally, the dancer will lift his knee as high as possible, move it from one side to the other, and then stamp his foot to the ground. This action is exaggerated in the multiple layers of cloth, and an excellent dancer can create a wavelike effect. Other dress accessories add delicate sounds to the sense of exaggerated movement produced by men's skirts. Belts covered with cowries and beads, strings of beads crisscrossing the chest, and necklaces of fur and metal softly whirr and clink as they move against the body and each other in the movement of the dancing. These are intimate sounds that guide the dancer in his movements but are not heard by many others over the sound of drums and singing.

A woman's ceremonial skirt (ncak) is shorter than a man's, averaging between six and nine meters (six and a half to ten yards) long. It is wound continually around the body and then tied around the waist with a cord. The top of the skirt does not fold over as does the man's skirt. Because of its length, the skirt will circle the woman's body a number of times, creating a subtle layered effect. The ncak is made of one-meter- (about one-yard-) square pieces of raffia cloth sewn end to end until the desired length is attained. The edges are finished in various ways to create a single finished and visually unified panel. Designs are applied to the body of the skirt with appliqué, embroidery, or a combination of both. Although made by many women in a clan, one will coordinate the effort so that there is a harmonious whole. Designs on the highest-quality skirts are evenly and densely applied to the entire length of the skirt, even though much of it will be hidden when worn. In lesser-quality skirts, parts of the skirt that will be visible when worn (the lower edge and end of the skirt) are thickly patterned, while the inside of the skirt might have little or no decoration. Men in the clan weave the fabric, but women complete all other work in constructing the garment.

Occasionally, a woman might add an overskirt, also called ncak. This overskirt is about one and a half meters (approximately one and a half yards) long and goes around the body once. While the women's skirts are usually limited to one overall decorative technique such as appliqué or embroidery, the overskirts have borders that might differ sharply in technique or color from the center of the skirt. Similar to the men's dress, other beaded and decorated elements are added. The enclosing shape of the skirt both limits and complements the women's more sedate dance style in which the shoulders and torso are held in an upright and straight position, while the feet and occasionally the arms carry the movement and rhythm of the music. The skirts do not move much with the dance, and sound produced by the ensemble is minimal.

The hat (laket) can be worn at special occasions by men and women but might also be worn on a daily basis by men. The hat visually signals the rank of the wearer. Feathers from specific birds placed on the hat and the position in which the feather is placed indicate the rank of the wearer. The highest-ranking title holders in a community, for example, are called eagle-feather chiefs (kum apoong) and wear eagle feathers in their hats. An eagle is considered to be the strongest and craftiest bird of the day skies, characteristics expected of the eagle-feather chief. The head of men's initiation camps, in contrast, wears an owl feather, a night bird that references unseen powers needed in the liminal initiation world. Additional decorations and materials on the hat connote the wearer's success and wealth.

FUNERALS AND THE ART MARKET

The final time a Kuba person wears complete formal dress is his or her own funeral. Many Kuba believe that, to be accept by their family in the afterlife, they must be appropriately dress according to their ethnic identity, their titles, and the status th have accumulated during their lifetime. Clan members exami the family's skirts and choose one in which to dress the body. T innermost skirt is usually a plain one, but more elaborate on are added, including one given by the spouse's family. Frien might also contribute textiles for the burial. A hat and other cessories are added, the body is rubbed in red tukula (similar camwood), and the body is displayed for several days.

The enduring nature and contemporary vibrant use of Ku textiles and dress can be attributed to the continued and consiste use of textiles in funerals and to the value of Kuba textiles on t international art market. Both older textiles and ones made for s appear in museum collections, private art collections, and as dec rative fabrics in interior design. Longer women's skirts are oft separated into individual panels and framed as modern works art. As long as the market demands Kuba textiles, they will co tinue to be produced for wear and for export.

Kuba textiles first came to the attention of the American fas ion world when, during the 1923 Brooklyn Museum exhibiti titled "Primitive Negro Art Chiefly from the Belgian Cong where Kuba textiles were on display, Bonwit Teller & Co. co missioned a line of women's clothing using Kuba textile patter Since that time, designs from both men's and women's textil have been used in both fashion and interior design in the Unit States and in Europe. Upscale furniture is upholstered with Ku cloth, cushions are constructed from Kuba pile-cloth, skirts a hung across the wall, and rugs reproduce Kuba patterns. Pieces Kuba textiles are incorporated into designer clothing, and Ku designs are printed and used in ready-to-wear clothing. Wh the appearance of Kuba textiles or designs in fashion or interi design creates connections, whether of heritage or the appeal the exotic, with Africa, the link to the Kuba people, their man facture of the dress, and how it is worn becomes lost.

References and Further Reading

Adams, Monni. "Kuba Embroidered Cloth." African Arts 12, no. 1 (197 24–39, 106–107.

Cameron, Elisabeth L., and Ann Svenson Perlman. "The Patterned Ku Cloth of Zaire." Piecework 5, no. 4 (1997): 29–33.

Darish, Patricia. "Dressing for Success: Ritual Occasions and Cerem nial Raffia Dress among the Kuba of South-Central Zaire." Ion Studies in African Art 3 (1990): 179–191.

Darish, Patricia. "Dressing for the Next Life." In Cloth and Human E perience, edited by Annette B. Weiner and Jane Schneider, 117–14 Washington, DC: Smithsonian Institution Press, 1991.

Darish, Patricia. "Kuba Dress and Adornment." In Sense, Style, Presen African Arts of Personal Adornment, edited by Susan Cooksey, 28–3 Gainesville, FL: Samuel P. Harn Museum of Art, 2004.

Vansina, Jan. The Children of Woot: A History of the Kuba Peoples. Mac son: University of Wisconsin Press, 1978.

Elisabeth L. Camero

See also Republic of Congo and Democratic Republic of Congo

Equatorial Guinea

The tiny central African country of Equatorial Guinea covers only 28,051 square kilometers (11,000 square miles). It is comprised of a few islands, of which Bioko—formerly known as Fernando Po—off the coast of Cameroon is the largest, and a 26,000-square-kilometer (10,000-square-mile) mainland territory known as Rio Muni nestled between Cameroon and Gabon. With European expansionism, these territories were ceded in 1778 from Portugal to Spain, but the Spaniards did not arrive until 1858. During this period, the indigenous Bubi increasingly came into contact with the British. The foundation of Malabo had special significance. Originally conceived as a temporary settlement for Africans rescued by the British Navy from slave ships, it eventually became a permanent haven for Africans of different origins, developing into a Creole community. Pidgin English, Christianity, and, very significantly, English clothing became the main markers of identity in Malabo. The antagonistic relationship between Creole and Bubi communities during the nineteenth century shaped, in many respects, future notions of civilization and savageness that were expressed through dress during the first half of the twentieth century.

By the late nineteenth century, Spain was trying to secure more territory on the neighboring mainland, where Britain, France, and Germany traded with the numerous coastal clans, later collectively known as Ndowe, and the Fang. Such commercial activities allowed the incorporation of imported items into local dress and fashion. Although in the European partition of Africa, Spain was awarded Rio Muni in 1901, dress continued to be dominated by internal dynamics until 1915, when Spain decided to occupy the interior. From then on, African culture came under attack from different elements of the colonial establishment.

Spanish contempt for African culture was emphatically expressed through their rejection of African dress—or rather, what they considered to be a lack thereof. Fang and Bubi dress came to epitomize their image of African barbarism, from which the Spanish, particularly the missionaries, sought to rescue them. Effective colonial domination profoundly changed local dress, for these Africans were now forced to adopt foreign styles to satisfy the values of the conservative and Catholic Spanish society. During the first half of the twentieth century, Equatorial Guineans lost interest in their local dress as they tried to come to terms with Western clothing and "civilization." By the late 1950s, Western-style dress was internalized, and Equatorial Guineans rediscovered the appeal of dress in their pursuit to be "modern."

The dynamics of the late Colonial period have continued to influence dress and fashion in Equatorial Guinea since its independence in 1968.

ENVIRONMENT AND DRESS

The influence of climate on dress in the area now occupied by Equatorial Guinea has always been important, given that the country, situated right above the equator on the western coast of central Africa, has warm temperatures all year, with oppressive humidity during the two annual rainy seasons. During the nineteenth century, the rain forest was the main source of cloth and apparel. Cloth was usually made of bark and other vegetable fibers. The absence of woven fabrics was due to the lack of soft fiber plants that could be spun into yarn. Contrary to common assumptions, the use of animal skins was not widespread, and they were mostly used as accessories. With the exception of elephants, gorillas, and chimpanzees, large mammals are not common in the rain forest; thus, animal skin never became an important material for clothing.

The small size of Equatorial Guinea facilitated Spanish campaigns to change African dress styles starting in the early twentieth century. Despite limited human and material resources, Spain was able to "dress" Africans relatively quickly. By 1950, it was no longer possible to see "undressed" Africans, with the exception of young children. For most of the twentieth century, important differences in dress and fashion existed between Malabo and Rio Muni. The former was perceived to have a much more cosmopolitan character thanks to the presence of Spanish settlers and the Creole community. Rio Muni remained relatively isolated from regional and international fashions until the late 1980s, when economic growth and especially the spread of television changed this situation.

CELEBRATING THE BODY (1850 TO 1915)

Traditional dress in Equatorial Guinea emphasized the body. By exposing the body, one could show how beautiful, attractive, and healthy one was. A clear sign of this is the enormous variety of enhancing or decorative items and techniques that existed in contrast with the limited repertoire of bark and fiber clothes. Hairstyles, tattoos, cicatrices, body paint, dental modification, jewelry, fragrances, and so forth were all used to enhance the body. By doing so, the peoples of Equatorial Guinea sought to stand out as individuals within societies characterized by their communitarian and egalitarian structures. Covering the body, on the other hand, sent the opposite message and raised suspicions as to why a person should wish to hide their beauty. Only the pelvic area, because of its explicit sexual connotations, was consciously covered out of decorum, although doing so simultaneously called attention to it.

The peoples of Equatorial Guinea considered dressing as an indicator of civilization. Among the Fang, for example, nudity was acceptable only in the case of young children, because they were not yet persons in the full sense of the word. As soon as children became aware of themselves, they also felt the need to dress

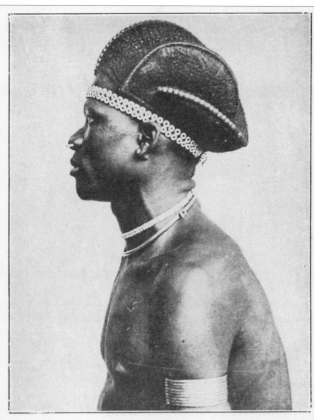

Fang du Haut-Ivindo (Gabon).
(Cliché Mission Cottes, communiqué par la maison Leroux).

A Fang man with helmet-style hair. Hairstyling and any kind of body augmentation, including facial accessories, were marks of individuality among the egalitarian Fang. This photograph was taken during the Cottes mission in southern Cameroon (1905–1908). General Research and Reference Division, Schomburg Center for Research in Black Culture, The New York Public Library, Astor, Lenox and Tilden Foundations.

and even experiment with fashion, imitating adults and decorating their bodies in various ways.

Nineteenth-century European descriptions of the Fang and the Bubi tended to objectify Africans, denying the great variety in dress that existed. In fact, the existence of fashion as such was denied, because fashion implies change and it was assumed that "primitive" Africans had not changed since time immemorial. Nonetheless, a comparison of different descriptions of the region's inhabitants from the late nineteenth and early twentieth centuries reveals that, indeed, they possessed an acute sense of fashion and a genuine concern about personal aesthetics. During this period, dress changed rapidly as a result of regional relations and European trade.

BUBI DRESS

The few detailed accounts of nineteenth-century Bubi dress are, by and large, very prejudicial. One of the first serious studies on the Bubi—*Die Bubi auf Fernando Poo*—was written by German ethnographer Günter Tessmann relatively late, in 1923. During most of the nineteenth century, the Bubi incorporated numerous European items, such as hats, beads, fabric, or blankets, into existing repertoires. Hats, for example, were profusely decorated with animal skins and feathers. The latter appears to have been a key dressing element that also carried implications regarding

social status. European blankets are also mentioned as having been incorporated by the Bubi and used by local chiefs as a sign of authority.

Undoubtedly, the most characteristic element of Bubi dress in the late nineteenth century was facial scarification. Both men and women enhanced their faces by drawing linear cicatrices on their cheeks using a sharp cutting object. In some cases, these cicatrices were extremely elaborate, suggesting that this technique had been around for quite some time. Likely, the Bubi brought this technique with them during the last wave of migrations from present-day Cameroon around the fourteenth century. Over time, both techniques and designs evolved, and by the turn of the twentieth century, the Bubi were masters of this type of facial enhancement.

The Spanish missionary Father Antonio Aymemí claimed that Bubi scarification was related to the slave trade: the cicatrices would help to identify members of the same family group in case they were captured by slave traders. This view is commonly accepted by Bubi elders in early-twenty-first-century Equatorial Guinea. Although they are unable to explain how this worked or whether certain designs were used by specific families, many consider facial cicatrices to be a distinctive element of Bubi culture. Despite Spanish aversion to and the ban on this practice imposed in 1925, Bubi parents continued to draw cicatrices on their children as late as the 1930s.

Fashion-conscious younger Equatorial Guineans in Bata, wearing Western-style clothing, ca. 2008. Photograph by Enrique Okenve.

Generally, the Bubi used plaited bamboo fibers to cover the pelvic area. In the case of women, bark cloth was used at the turn of the twentieth century to make a type of apron. The Bubi used body paint, which was one of the main techniques to enhance the body for special occasions. Pigments of different colors—yellow, white, brown, and especially red—were used for this purpose. Occasionally, different geometric shapes were painted on different parts of the body, especially on the face.

FANG DRESS

Tessmann's 1913 monograph on the Fang, *Die Pangwe*, is the most serious and detailed study of this culture prior to European colonization. Fang women and men cared much about their appearance, evidenced by the long hours, and sometimes pain, that they endured to decorate their bodies in the most intricate ways. Clearly, not all individuals shared the same concern about dressing the body. Individuals who did not pay attention to their appearance were often looked upon with disdain.

Late-nineteenth-century Fang clothing was not characterized by variety, but some regional differences existed. A man's loincloth (*ocan*) was made of bark and consisted of a strip some ninety centimeters (thirty-five inches) long by seventy centimeters (twenty-eight inches) wide that was worn between the legs and tied around the waist with a belt. The bark cloth could be left in its original color—from white to maroon—or it could be dyed with barwood. In most cases, the cloth was so finely beaten that people said it was difficult to distinguish it from woven fabric. Producing this cloth was so arduous that by the late nineteenth century, the Fang began to replace it with European cloth, which was worn in the same fashion as bark cloth. Women's dress resembled a short skirt made of two separate pieces that hung from the waist. The front piece consisted simply of a narrow and dried leaf from a banana tree or was made of bark or animal skin and tied to the body with a belt. The more elaborate back piece was made with different strips of bark cloth tied to form a fan

shape—some twenty-four centimeters (nine inches) long by thirteen to twenty-seven centimeters (five to eleven inches) wide and fastened to the belt by a peg. The back dress could also be made of raffia fibers that hung as a sort of ponytail.

Fang attention to dress is perhaps best represented by the numerous hairstyles that were popular at the turn of the twentieth century. Despite the stereotypical image of the Fang warrior in fine dreadlocks, it was possible to find multiple hairstyles even within the same village. No doubt, the most dramatic of these that one could find among the Fang at the turn of the twentieth century was the "helmet hairstyle," in which the hair was braided and decorated with shells, beads, buttons, and metal objects to resemble a helmet. This was typical of the interior of Rio Muni and Gabon and was known to be an extremely tedious process. A less laborious, but also less common, variation of this hairstyle was a hat (*adoban*) that imitated the shape and texture of the helmet style. Over a hood made of monkey skin or strips of palm leaves, the hat was elaborated in such a way that, once finished, it was difficult to distinguish from the real thing.

Feathers, flowers, sticks, bones, brass, leaves, ivory, beads, buttons, and so forth were used to enhance the nose, forehead, ears, neck, arms, wrists, fingers, legs, ankles, feet, and toes. Particularly striking were the brass accessories worn by both women and men and fashioned from imported brass. Heavy brass necklaces (*mvoat*) identified married women. Men's versions were often decorated with various patterns. The process of putting on and especially removing the necklace was difficult; therefore, it was worn permanently. Individuals also liked to enhance their forearms and calves with heavy brass bracelets and anklets. Also especially common among women was the use of spirals of brass wire that were wrapped around forearms, arms, thighs, and calves. Brass accessories were particularly uncomfortable, weighing up to three pounds, often making the skin sore, but such was their desire to look attractive that women endured the discomfort. Women in their full brass attire had a distinct gait due to the weight and scale of the accessories, which caught not only people's eyes but also their ears because of the clanking sound they made.

The Fang sought to stimulate all senses in their pursuit of beauty. Both women and men, for example, liked to rub their bodies and hair with oil (*mbon*) containing aromatic substances with appreciated scents. Body oil also stimulated the sense of touch, giving the skin a softer texture. Body and facial hair were generally disliked and were either shaved or plucked. Nevertheless, some men grew beards that were sometimes braided and adorned with beads.

Scarification was also practiced as a body enhancement technique by both women and men. The simplest and oldest technique was scarification by burning, in which a hot implement was applied to the skin. By the late nineteenth century, this technique was replaced by incision (*endon*), which was preferred because it allowed the drawing of more intricate designs. Unlike the Bubi, the Fang rarely used this technique on their faces. From the 1890s, tattooing (*kudeman*) began to replace scarification. At the beginning of the twentieth century, only young individuals, especially men, could be seen wearing tattoos, which were preferred over scarification because they were less painful.

Fang used paint to beautify the body, and, as with the Bubi, red was their favorite color. Women used to paint their bodies with barwood for special occasions such as weddings, after which brides could be seen painted for up to a month. Tessmann has noted that red, in addition to its aesthetic appeal, symbolized happiness. Perhaps because of this, women and babies were also painted with barwood after childbirth.

Dental modification was another form of body enhancement that consisted of chiseling, not filing, the incisor teeth to resemble canine teeth. This extremely painful technique shows, once again, the discomfort that both Fang men and women were willing to endure in order to look attractive. By the early twentieth century, this technique seemed to have gone out of fashion as a result of European influence—and, probably, the physical pain.

COVERING THE BODY (1915 TO 1959)

African dress was often misunderstood and misrepresented by European observers, and thus they imposed new dress codes on the native population. Spanish rhetoric and action during the early Colonial period implicitly reveal the illegitimacy of colonialism: it was necessary to denigrate African cultures to justify foreign domination. The Fang and the Bubi were suddenly considered "nude," illustrating how nudity and dress are historically and socially constructed concepts. Fang and Bubi dress, which once symbolized cultural sophistication, was now portrayed as culturally inferior, an idea reinforced by the loss of their sovereignty. Not surprisingly, men, women, and particularly youngsters sought to dissociate themselves from Fang and Bubi dress—and in the process, leaving themselves open for the Spanish to cover them with the cloth of "civilization." Furthermore, from a typical Catholic perspective, the human body was seen as impure. By growing ashamed of their bodies, Equatorial Guineans also became embarrassed by their heritage. The Spanish portrayed Bubi and Fang dress as symbols of African wickedness and depravity. African dress customs were both stigmatized and vilified by the Spanish, who saw all kinds of sexual connotations in nudity. Thus, the body had to be concealed, repressed. Fashion dictated that the body should be covered as much as possible by wearing long pants, jackets, shoes, hats, and so forth.

During the first half of the twentieth century, most Equatorial Guineans were concerned about covering the body in ways that would be acceptable to the Spanish. By and large, they continued to wear pieces of imported fabric, which were now worn as wrappers. Men began to wear imported cloth around the waist as a sort of skirt that reached below the knees. Women started using long pieces of fabric that covered their torso and legs. As part of evangelizing campaigns, missionaries gave away pieces of imported cloth, while teaching Africans to wear them "appropriately." In urban settings, where European presence and capitalist structures were significant, Equatorial Guineans mostly wore Western-style dress. Pictures from the 1940s, however, reveal that the use of shoes was rare.

One of the most significant changes of the first half of the twentieth century was the abandonment of permanent and semipermanent body enhancement techniques. Hairstyles became much simpler; men usually cut their hair short to have a neat appearance. Quite significantly, women were able to retain or recreate more African hairstyles, braiding their hair in multiple manners. Being largely ignored by colonialism, women were less susceptible to the sort of dress codes that men had to adopt to succeed within the colonial system.

During this period, Western-style dress represented social and economic success but was unaffordable for most people.

By the early twenty-first century, mature men, particularly in rural areas of Equatorial Guinea, such as Beayob (Mikomeseng District), were beginning to wear *popó* shirts (garments made from African-style fabric) on a more regular basis. Photograph by Enrique Okenve, 2008.

Appointed chiefs, however, rapidly adopted imported clothing to indicate their status and satisfy the colonial authorities who often removed them for not wearing appropriate—that is, Western—apparel. Access to Western-style dress required cash, so only Equatorial Guineans involved in the emerging capitalist system were able to purchase it. Most clothes worn locally were manufactured by local tailors and seamstresses. Western-style dress became so closely associated with civilization that Spanish missionaries, being the principal civilizing agents, made tailoring and sewing an essential part of the colonial curriculum.

Ndowe peoples and especially Creole communities, because of their close relationship with the Europeans, had adopted Western-style dress as far back as the second half of the nineteenth century. Western-style dress, which symbolized the new economic and social order, was the means by which one could express civilization and economic success. Not surprisingly, Creole fashion of the late nineteenth and early twentieth centuries tended to be elaborate, using all kinds of accessories, such as umbrellas or walking canes, in an effort both to look fancy and to distinguish itself from the look of "backward" Africans. Creole fashion became a model for many Equatorial Guineans who aspired to enjoy the same lifestyle as the Creole community.

Despite Spanish efforts to civilize—that is, Europeanize—Africans through clothing, many Spaniards reacted negatively to the re-creation of Western-style fashion by Africans. Equatorial Guinean re-elaboration of imported dress was often dismissed as imitation, a denial of African creativity. Such attitudes were symptomatic of the racism that characterized colonial interaction. Ironically, the Spanish preferred the idea of the "noble savage" in an exotic African world in which colonial settlers could feel at ease. In fact, during the 1930s and 1940s, African "nudity" was both accepted and encouraged during displays of native culture such as dances.

CHANGES IN DRESS AFTER 1960

By the late 1950s, most Equatorial Guineans had embraced Western-style dress, and since then it has been favored for most daily situations. Only during family events, such as weddings or funerals, is African-style dress considered acceptable for men and especially for women. As in other areas of colonial life, however, formal acceptance did not mean simple replication. Western-style dress was given local meaning, and, thus, Equatorial Guineans were able to reassess the significance of dress. Nonetheless, it is difficult to argue that an Equatorial Guinean fashion per se exists, as regional and international trends have been adopted by urban Equatorial Guineans since the 1960s. The development of dress and fashion trends requires a combination of freedom and creativity that, in many respects, have been repressed by the colonial and postcolonial administrations. In Equatorial Guinea, dress is yet to be used as a vehicle for cultural nationalism.

During the 1960s, economic growth made clothing relatively affordable, allowing the urban population to catch up with modern fashions. Especially in the shops of Malabo, people were able to buy fashionable clothes imported from Spain. The situation changed drastically in the 1970s, with the deterioration of political and economic conditions. A combination of government repression and mismanagement caused the collapse of the country's economy, restricting access to all kinds of imports, including cloth and clothing. So bad was the situation that, in some cases, people were forced to make pants out of sackcloth. The situation slightly improved after the signing of cooperation agreements with the People's Republic of China. Mao suits became relatively popular on the streets of Equatorial Guinea as a result. By the late 1980s and especially since the mid-1990s, economic growth again made it possible for Equatorial Guineans to express more fully their clothing preferences. Given that this prosperity is still restricted to Malabo and Bata, clothing issues are not perceived to be a

major concern in rural areas, where the levels of consumption remain very limited into the twenty-first century.

During this period, dress reflected a sort of cultural dualism created by colonialism, which divided reality into modern (Western) and traditional (African). Equatorial Guinean youngsters in the 1960s sought to affirm their modernity and cut ties with the past by adopting Western fashion. Youngsters in the twenty-first century do not share the same type of concern about the past, but they also seek to embrace modernity by following similar sartorial trends, reflecting their desire to enjoy the material well-being associated with Western societies. In the 1960s, access to Western media was limited to films and magazines, but since the early 1990s, urban dwellers have gained faster access to regional and international trends through the proliferation of local and satellite television. Music video clips serve as the main inspiration for dress and fashion. Artists from the Democratic Republic of Congo and Cameroon have the upper hand regarding regional trends. Nonetheless, African American trends, through hip-hop culture, have influenced dress and fashion since the 1990s. At this time, numerous small barbershops mushroomed on the streets of Bata and Malabo, advertising haircuts inspired by African American music stars. More recently, African American artists have popularized cornrows for men, a style that until recently only women used in Equatorial Guinea.

Afrocentric fashion from the African diaspora is commonly associated with modernity, whereas African-style fashion usually

In the early twenty-first century, many older women of Equatorial Guinea choose to wear *popós* (garments made from African-style fabric) on special occasions. Photograph by Enrique Okenve, 2008, in Niefang.

refers to tradition. African-style dress, as contemporary as it might be, is only worn for family events or informal situations. It is no coincidence that African-style dress is worn at home, during grocery shopping, or at family events. Colonialism did not directly interfere in all realms of African society, and somehow Equatorial Guineans feel that their African identity can be openly expressed in such intimate or personal situations. This is not the case at work or in other circumstances associated with modernity. Women, however, have been a very significant exception to this rule. They tend to wear African-style dress much more often than men, even in work environments. The same can be said about hairstyles, as women have continued using all types of braiding techniques in all social settings. Nonetheless, many women either straighten their hair or weave in synthetic hair.

Limited acceptance of African-style dress is also related to the absence of locally produced traditional textiles, making it difficult to formulate an indigenous style as a symbol of national cultural identity. African-style fabric, known as *popó*, has been used since the 1960s, but, at that time, only some of the economic and cultural elite wore it. During the 1970s, the communist-oriented government, despite its nationalistic character, banned the use of African-style dress. Commercial activities were controlled by the government, and, because there was no official commercial exchange with neighboring countries, the wearing of popó amounted to admitting involvement in smuggling activities. Since the 1980s, traders from Cameroon, Benin, Nigeria, Togo, Mali, and Senegal have been selling African-style clothing imported from their respective countries. At the turn of the twenty-first century, the material known as *wass* has become the most appreciated by women because of its quality and available colors. This material, imported from Benin and Senegal, is superior to the usual popó imported from Cameroon. Women either buy ready-made dresses or fabrics of this material for local manufacture. The most common styles are the *kaba* dress, which resembles a maternity dress because it has no waist, and two-piece suits consisting of a long skirt and a matching top. Many youngsters associate African-style dress with old people and complain about the lack of variety. Most of them prefer Western fashions, buying new and especially secondhand ready-made clothes imported from neighboring countries and Spain. In this respect, dress also reflects the kind of dependency that has characterized this country for the past hundred years.

Equatorial Guineans in the twenty-first century are generally reluctant to use many body enhancement techniques. Skin bleaching, however, is the main exception. This technique spread from neighboring countries in the 1980s and became popular in the 1990s. Since then, many urban women use skin-lightening solutions. In addition to its potential health side effects, the social and cultural connotations of this technique are certainly complex and controversial. Although many women argue that they do it simply to look more beautiful, it is difficult not to see a connection with notions of beauty created during the Colonial period. In recent years, a few men have also adopted this practice. At the beginning of the twenty-first century, other forms of body modification, such as body piercing and especially tattooing, have been gradually adopted by Equatorial Guineans, in particular by young men. Once again the influence of African American hip-hop has come to the fore.

References and Further Reading

Allman, Jean, ed. *Fashioning Africa: Power and the Politics of Dress.* Bloomington: Indiana University Press, 2004.

Aymemí, Antonio. *Los bubis en Fernando Póo: colección de los artículos publicados en la Revista Colonial La Guinea Española.* Madrid: Dirección General de Marruecos y Colonias, 1942.

Burton, R. "A Day amongst the Fans." In *Selected Papers on Anthropology, Travel and Exploration,* 94–108. London: Philpot, 1924.

Chamberlin, Christopher. "The Migration of the Fang into Central Gabon during the Nineteenth Century: A New Interpretation." *International Journal of African Historical Studies* 11, no. 3 (1978): 429–456.

Claretian Missionaries. *Cien años de evangelización en Guinea Ecuatorial (1883–1983).* Barcelona: Claret, 1983.

Nerín, Gustau. *Guinea Ecuatorial, historia en blanco y negro.* Barcelona: Ediciones Península, 1998.

Ortín, Pere, and Vic Pereiró, eds. *Mbini: cazadores de imágenes en la Guinea colonial.* Barcelona: Librería Altaïr, 2006.

Perani, Judith, and Norma H. Wolf. *Cloth, Dress and Art Patronage in Africa.* Oxford, UK: Berg, 1999.

Sundiata, Ibrahim. "Creolization on Fernando Po: The Nature of Society." In *The African Diaspora: Interpretative Essays,* edited by Martin L. Kilson and Robert I. Rotberg, 391–413. Cambridge, MA: Harvard University Press, 1976.

Tessmann, Günter. *Los Pamues (Los Fang): monografía etnológica de una rama de las tribus negras del África occidental.* Spanish translation by Erika Reuss Galindo. Madrid: Agencia Española de Cooperación, 2003.

Tessmann, Günter, and O. Reche. *Die Bubi auf Fernando Poo: Völkerkundliche Einzelbeschreibung eines westafrikanischen Negerstammes.* Darmstadt, Germany: Folkwang Verlag, 1923.

Trilles, Henri. *Chez les Fang, ou quinze années de séjour au Congo français.* Lille, France: Société Saint-Augustin, 1912.

Enrique Okenve

See also Fang of Equatorial Guinea and Gabon.

Gabon

HISTORICAL ACCOUNTS TO 1960

Gabon, a Central African country, is located on the Atlantic coast, bordered by Equatorial Guinea, Cameroon, and the Republic of Congo. Historically, Central African societies attach significance to a person's dress in indicating identity, societal standing, and specific events or moments of importance to individuals or communities. Many Central African peoples in the eighteenth to nineteenth centuries wore few clothes. However, the clothing, bodily adornment, and hairstyles and headdress that men and women displayed were strategic. In equatorial forest zones, clothing made from raffia, skins, or bark indicated social status. Headdress, jewelry, and bodily art would be distinctive for women and men in given societies. In Fang ethno-language communities of the nineteenth century, primary expectations for younger men included protecting their communities, hunting, and clearing away forest for women to farm. As such, men were to convey an appearance of strength. Fang men would file their teeth to a point and might wear a necklace made from leopard or other animal teeth, a belt made of bark from a tree, and animal skins tied around the hips. The leader of a Dan group might wear a headdress made of red feathers. Women might decorate their bodies with red or yellow inks derived from plants and cover their lower bodies with animal skins held by a belt of wooden pearls. In large-scale societies, the cultivation of trees, the

weaving of cloth from trees, and the distribution of cloth such as raffia was an important task that elder men controlled and could manipulate in order to attract followers. The types and quality of raffia, for example, could distinguish a wealthy person from a commoner.

Over the course of the late nineteenth century through the early few decades of the twentieth, Gabonese communities residing near Libreville and further in the interior acquired increasing amounts of imported cloth, clothing, and accessories. Americans and Europeans were interested in exporting Gabonese forest products, and Gabonese were interested in acquiring imported goods. The increased volume of trans-Atlantic trade and the mass production of cloth in Europe and Asia brought about greater availability. Although imported fashion displaced items such as raffia and animal skins and teeth, individuals and communities adapted these imported items to Gabonese cosmologies of fashion indicating status and identity. To sport a European item was an indication of elite status, and European observers commented that individuals sought secondhand European items that would distinguish them from others in their communities. In keeping with precolonial indicators of status, men in the Estuary region strategically deployed imported wares. In the late nineteenth century, a Mpongwé leader named Roi Denis was attempting to consolidate and expand his political rule. Images of him show him carrying a scepter and wearing a European military uniform and a king's crown—all of which were supposed to convey his attempt at greater political control. Although wearing a European crown and military uniform, the notion of clothing and headgear as conveying political power is grounded in Gabonese conceptions of strategically using fashion to convey political power. Furthermore, in early-twentieth-century Libreville, men wearing suits and women wearing long dresses would parade about the town in moments of leisure. Gabonese communities

Gabonese women wearing *pagnes* and headcloths, ca. 1912. General Research and Reference Division, Schomburg Center for Research in Black Culture, The New York Public Library, Astor, Lenox and Tilden Foundations.

also adapted imported fashions in consecrating marriages. Bride-wealth, a bundle of goods that a groom and his family remitted to the bride's male relatives, was a key exchange that made a marriage legitimate in Gabonese communities. Previously composed of the exchange of iron, bride-wealth by the mid-nineteenth century could also include European hats, cloth, silverware, and plateware.

Women's fashions also represented a stage around which individuals and communities determined social status. European observers, in particular, commented upon the deployment of European fashions by women of the Mpongwé ethno-language group. Yet more elite women—particularly women who were or had been involved in interracial unions with European men—wore heels, hosiery, and long dresses in more luxurious fabrics and hats resembling turn-of-the-century Parisian fashion. For European observers, the clothing styles of Gabonese women in urban areas were thought to be a marker of her morality, and, for missionaries, Gabonese women sporting such luxurious European clothes were equivalent to with prostitutes. Furthermore, as European ideas of female nakedness as immoral expanded within Gabon, women also covered their upper bodies. Women of varied ethnic groups whose societies had access to imported goods of trans-Atlantic trade wore *pagnes* (tied cotton cloth that might have originated from Europe and India) around their bodies. Older women tied matching head cloths or scarves around their heads, representing the regard with which society treated women in more advanced years.

By the end of World War II, the fashions of Libreville residents represented a myriad of styles—from cotton cloths printed with African-inspired designs to Muslim boubous of West African immigrants to European clothing. The types and quality of imported clothing and accessories that people chose to wear became increasingly important as less-wealthy people in Libreville began to be able to afford imported cloth and clothing. European observers noted that nearly all residents of Libreville—from those of varied ethno-language groups who newly migrated from rural areas to those who were indigenous to Libreville—wore imported clothing that looked like European clothing. Women might wear dresses and skirts, and men wore pants and shirts. Those with less access to cash might own only a few items of clothing, which they washed and pressed to look respectable. In urban homes, women would wrap cloth around their bodies, and, in rural areas, women continued to do so even outside of the home. Living in an urban region afforded more access to cash, and people who were less well off could afford lesser-quality cloth and secondhand goods.

Greater affordability of imported goods also represented a moment of fluidity in social hierarchy, class, and gender. Men who migrated to Libreville from rural areas commented that it was hard for them to distinguish whether a woman whom they met in a bar was a prostitute because every woman dressed the same. Women's clothing also became a battleground for the imagined nation of independent Gabon. In an oral interview, a Fang woman remembered an encounter that she had with the new president Leon Mba over what she was wearing. The woman was returning from working in the fields and was wearing a cotton wrapper. The president chastised her for wearing such a cloth instead of a proper dress because it demonstrated backwardness instead of the modern advancements that the nation should be making.

INDEPENDENCE AND THE EMERGENT GABONESE FASHION

After independence, Gabon retained close political, economic, and cultural ties with France. Gabonese wore smart Western dress and uniforms in public arenas, closely following Western trends such as the arrival of the miniskirt, Afro hairstyles, and *pattes d'elph* (elephant feet—the local term for flared trousers). High-class fashion was appropriated from Paris. Countrywide colonially initiated resettlement policies continued into the post-Independence period, bringing previously dispersed rural populations closer to roads to integrate them into the state system and appropriating further French dress codes and language. Tailoring existed as an occupation but was considered a lower-class women's trade that focused primarily on copies of Western uniforms and formal wear, such as the industrial tailoring company Soveman (later renamed MGV). Certain women members of the elite class, notably Rose Obame, received government support to study haute couture in Paris.

In 1970, Pierre Kassa became the first self-taught Gabonese designer to be recognized abroad in the Festival of Negro Arts in Lagos. As a result, he traveled to France to receive training and to work for Yves Saint-Laurent in Paris. Kassa's presentation in Lagos paved the way for future Gabonese designers in creating a collection that explored the relationship between contemporary dress and traditional Gabonese textiles. In particular, Kassa promoted the use of a local Myene pagne called *okoryel*. It is widely believed that, had this idea been adopted at the time, a uniquely Gabonese fashion might have been promoted. However, Kassa left for France, where he worked with European designers, and Gabon was overtaken by political and economic events heralding a new era that would shape and isolate Gabonese fashion in the years to come. These events, in particular, were the rise of single-party politics and the oil boom of the mid-1970s.

The newly appointed President Omar Bongo (1967–) announced a period of renovation involving lavish building projects, a taste for French baroque, military paraphernalia, and ostentatious spectacles mirroring those of other African leaders of the time. The Union des Femmes du Parti Democratique Gabonaise was established to support the reigning presidential party at all major functions and ceremonies through *groupes d'animation* (female dance troops). Nationwide street parades took place during key national holidays, such as 12 March, the foundation date of the ruling Partie Democratique du Gabon, and 17 August, Independence Day. Each female dance troop could be distinguished through its songs, dance, and identical dress: custom-printed T-shirts with pagnes wrapped around the waists, representing at once a sponsor and a geographical region. These events served as status displays for people of rank to parade their military uniforms and fine Western designer clothing. Men would also wear identical Western-cut shirts tailored from custom-printed pagnes. In 1976, the Gabonese industrial textile company Sotega was established, specializing in importing white cotton from China that would be custom printed in Gabon to meet these demands.

During the 1970s and 1980s, the oil boom coupled with Gabon's low population density intensified the phenomena of urban migration and immigration. The foreign community was predominantly French. Many West Africans came to find work in Gabon, leading to a degree of intermarriage and cultural fusion. African immigrants took over the service sector of Gabon,

men wearing specially printed *pagnes* for a street parade in Libreville, bon, in 2007. Photograph by Judith Knight.

abling many Gabonese to become higher-class civil servants in e metropolis distinguished by the wearing of quality Western ess and by their proficiency in cultured French language. Links ith France remained strong and mutually dependent. Many abonese were educated in France and traveled there frequently. ashion was characterized by foreign imports rather than local roduction. It was not unusual for a man of standing to spend normous amounts of money on Parisian designer clothing and cessories.

In the late 1980s, economic recession meant that previous lev-s of consumerism were no longer sustainable for many people. hus, Gabonese began to produce their own clothing. Influenced y trends in the Congo, many men adopted the Mobutu-style *aba-st* to express their African identity. Many styles of the time were fluenced by foreign African pop singers from West and Central frica. Women in particular wore tailored pagne and matching ead scarves made from traditional dyed or imported prints. Gab-nese women began to develop their own preference for pagne ilored into Western cuts.

It is during this period that the president's daughter, Lea-ono (Albertine Amissa Bongo), began to create new fashion esigns that continued the trend in exploring uniquely Gabonese shion through incorporating traditional Gabonese textiles into aute couture. Leamono had close links with American popular lture through her mother, Patience Dibany—first wife of the resident and a famous pop star. Leomono—meaning "come and e"—combined textiles made from raffia palm and leather with

a preference for sexy and chic and the colors white and black. She is credited with transforming the image of haute couture into a respected profession in Gabon. Leamono died prematurely in 1993. Ten years later, her mother reopened the boutique in her memory.

In 1990, democratic initiatives opened the country to new information technologies, markets, and popular trends. In 1994, Olga Odjele Ondjika opened her first boutique in Libreville, Christ Couture—in homage to the Malian designer, Chris Sey-dou Nourou for his contribution and commitment to African fashion. Ondjika, who had trained in manufacturing mechan-ics, was a self-taught designer whose goal was to give value to African dress in Gabon as a means to celebrate the female form and to add a distinct indigenous touch of class to it. She intro-duced raffia-based woven luxury products that were both tradi-tional and recognizably Gabonese. Her trade name, Olga ô, was established in 1996 as a brand of Christ Couture through which Ondjika launched the haute couture practice of combining raffia with pagne. This revolutionized Gabonese women's fashions and raised the image of Gabonese mode to the outside world, thus earning her the nickname The Queen of Raffia and numerous national and international prizes (e.g., Prix Yeye, Abidjan, 1999; Grand Prix du President Omar Bongo Ondimba, Libreville, 2001; D'Or Award Mondial, Paris, 2003). Ondjika initiated the national beauty competition in 2000, for which she is the presi-dent and head designer.

The advent of democracy allowed Gabonese fashion to con-tinue to evolve with a new sense of freedom of expression and creative exploration. In 1994, the School of Fashion in Nzion, Libreville, was established through Canadian funding in partner-ship with Notre Dame du Quebec. The school focused on giving unemployed women basic tailoring skills and later added fash-ion design to the curriculum. Tailoring and fashion design began to be included in the curriculum of other technical colleges, and model agencies and boutiques opened.

From 1998, the designer Alphadi visited Gabon as part of his pan-African caravan fashion tour. During his visits, Alphadi identified several young talented Gabonese designers and encour-aged them to unify and standardize Gabonese fashion in order to give it national identity within the international fashion forum. Consequently, the short-lived Association of Stylists, ASTYL Mod, was created with designer Vicky Muzadi in 1999. Despite challenges encountered, these influences motivated Gabonese to produce their own fashion shows and competitions and partici-pate in African and international fashion circles with professional competency.

Chouchou Lazare, a self-taught prodigy, received a French scholarship to travel to Niger to train with Alphadi and was the first Gabonese designer to gain a top prize in an international show outside of Africa: the Biennale International Design, St. Etienne, France (2002). President and founder of the Association du Designeres, Modelistes et Créateurs Gabonais, Lazare works in Libreville, where he has established an atelier for young tal-ented designers. He organizes an annual national fashion show appropriately named FashionShowchou. Lazare's designs and the themes of his collections (e.g., Paris and Me, Raffia from Here Raffia from Elsewhere, No to War Yes to Life) are eclectic and reflect his philosophy to embrace multiculturalism, tradition, modernity, and social activism—in particular AIDS awareness. His works incorporate local iconography, textiles, and natural

Detail of raffia bodice work by the Gabonese designer Chouchou Lazare, ca. 2000. The design incorporates diamanté stones and cowry shells. Photograph by Judith Knight.

products into Western cuts. Examples of his work include intricately embroidered bodices made of raffia (which he reworks himself to enhance its versatility); accessories such as diamanté stones and cowry shells; traditional color symbolism; Punu mask motifs; and the extensive use of feathers.

In 2003, Beitch Faro (Bernadette Mpaga Tchandi), who studied fashion in Italy, gained first prize in a fashion competition for young creators that was organized by Alphadi for the Festival International de Mode Africaine in Niger. She has been nicknamed "La femme Poisson" within the Gabonese fashion world because of her work with dyed fish scales as accessories on classic women's soiree cuts that look like mermaids—alluding to her cultural connection to the coast.

In the early twenty-first century, many up-and-coming designers are well known both within Gabon and internationally. The paths explored by the more famous Gabonese designers continue to be developed within the country. These include further refinement and embellishment of unique Gabonese textiles; the use of unusual accessories such as porcupine quills; the exploration of Western cuts and exposure of the body; and the transformation of traditional art (notably masks) into decorative motifs or as the inspiration for an outfit.

EVERYDAY DRESS IN THE TWENTY-FIRST CENTURY

The majority of the Gabonese population in the twenty-first century is concentrated in the metropolis, only returning to home regions during the dry season to attend ceremonies. In terms of fashion, strong links connect provincial capitals and smaller towns. Clothing and hairstyles in the urban context depend on nationality, age, social position, class, occasion, and season. Dress is fundamentally Western, although African fashions are common. Gabonese people are smartly dressed, earning them the

reputation in other parts of Africa as being epicures of taste and class closely influenced by French language and customs.

Government ministries have strict dress codes: men wear classic suits, ties, and quality leather shoes. These are designer (new or secondhand), locally tailored copies, or imitations from West Africa or Asia. Women wearing trousers are forbidden entry to ministries, and employees wear standard Western office dress or tailored African outfits (more common in middle-aged women). Many of the young women wear soiree cocktail dresses in an everyday context, which are often figure hugging and revealing. Shoes are invariably smart pumps or high heels from Europe or Asia, and color-coordinated designer (or counterfeit) handbags are popular. This code is mirrored by the middle class sector: managers, administrators, secretaries, and clerks, many of whom work for French-owned or established companies. Other workers wear pressed Western clothes or tailored pagnes. Uniforms are very common in all state and service sectors. During official dinners or formal receptions, Gabonese women wear a variety of the finest European or African haute couture (made of quality African materials). The combining of raffia with pagne in both men's and women's clothing is now common practice among local tailors. Men prefer designer suits and tuxedos.

Men's hairstyles tend to be short and simple, sometimes partly or totally shaven according to what styles are in fashion. Mustaches and beards are less common and tend to be light and subtle. Women emulate Western hairstyles by chemically straightening the hair for versatility. Older women cover their hair with a scarf or comb it back into a braided bun with a hairnet. Middle-aged women often have shoulder-length straightened hair, combed back off the face. Jewelry for men and women is mostly Western, high-quality, often designer or imitation, and relatively understated. Women also wear traditionally inspired accessories made of raffia and other natural products. These may be simple for daytime attire or more elaborate for more dressy occasions. The mobile phone has become an essential fashion accessory.

During the weekends and after work, more-relaxed, casual smart wear is adopted. Men wear shirts of a Western cut, often made with West African pagne or of mixed materials known as *mandela* (after the South African president who had a preference for this style) or casual designer-wear in upper circles (such as Olga ô Western-cut shirts with African pagne and raffia motifs). Shirts are invariably worn with tailored dark trousers and leather shoes. Some men also wear the West African boubou made of *bazin* (damask) or pagne or smart designer sports gear with sneakers (trainers) or sandals. Military prints, khaki trousers, and waistcoats with numerous pockets have become popular with recent environmental developments, notably the establishment of thirteen national parks. Baseball caps and a variety of Kangol hats are also common. At home women often relax in African dresses and pagnes.

Younger men's styles are heavily influenced by jeans, long shorts, baggy designer T-shirts, and brightly colored sports shoes (designer label or imitations) from Western and African American popular culture and music—in particular rap, hip-hop, and soul. There is currently a trend for younger men to have short dreadlocks or fine braids (close to the head or spiked), often with peroxide-dyed tips. A smaller sector of men have more substantial dreadlocks and associate themselves quite loosely with the Rastafarian movement as an expression of artistic liberalism. In 2000, the singer Luc Saga and his group Jet Set from Côte d'Ivoire visited Libreville, leaving in their wake the male fashion of the urban dandy (chic, flamboyant, and designer conscious). Typically, these "jet setters," as they are known locally, are characterized by sculpted and parted hairstyles, pin-striped suits, pointed squared-off shoes, and a preference for pastel colors. Displays of money, pens, phones, and fine cars are necessary accessories.

Women are highly influenced by fashion magazines from Europe, West Africa, and the United States. Young women typically adopt Western fashions such as tight T-shirts and jeans or fitted skirts and dresses. Hairstyles vary from very short Parisian chic and straight or curly bobs to long hair tied back or braided. Elaborate long hairstyles involving extensions, braids, twists, or dreadlocks are prolific in the dry season, which is the holiday period from June to September when people from Libreville visit their families in rural areas. It is widely believed that the hair should not be overhandled during this period, so such hairstyles are convenient because they can be left without alteration for up to three months. These hairstyles tend to follow contemporary fashion and individual whim. It is currently the fashion to wear wigs of all styles and colors. Girls tend to have braided hair decorated with colored beads.

Skin-enhancing products—including chemical depigmentation—are commonly used by both men and women. Makeup is Western and relatively understated. Women often shave and repencil their eyebrows. Many younger men have large modern tattoos on their forearms.

In rural villages, people wear Western clothes as soon as they can get them. Much depends on financial means, because most villagers live at subsistence level. Thus, access to Western clothes in good condition is associated with status and context. Local chiefs and government administrators tend to wear suits or abacost. Beards and hats are more common in rural areas, especially among older men of status. In forest contexts, such as Pygmy

Gabonese fashion in the early twenty-first century. In urban areas and for office work or social occasions, Gabonese men wear shirts and trousers, and women wear a boubou and wrapper. People are generally smartly dressed. Photograph by Judith Knight.

communities, men are often bare-chested or wear T-shirts or shirts where available. Trousers or pagne are wrapped around the waist or tied into a large loincloth or crossed over around the neck for local chiefs and elders. Likewise, women wear T-shirts where available and a pagne wrapped around their lower torso or covering their whole body. Villagers always save their best wear for a special event or photo. Election-logoed T-shirts and pagnes are fairly common in remote areas, because these are seasonally acquired community gifts. Shoes or flip-flops are worn if available. The same basic dress codes apply for children.

Babies are mostly naked, with the exception of simple bead or shell jewelry and metal earrings, if available; otherwise, liana thread or locally made tiny packages tied to a liana are worn frequently around the neck and waist (associated with traditional medicine). Young children wear underclothes or shorts.

In urban contexts and provincial capitals, Gabonese weddings display a range of styles from Western designer to locally tailored. This depends primarily on whether the ceremony is civil or traditional. The civil wedding is of Western origin and follows much of the occidental model. It is fashionable for the bride to wear a Western white dress and the groom a smart evening suit or military uniform. Close female relatives such as the mother and aunt dress in Western haute couture or fine African-fabric loose dresses, often with undertrousers and a matching scarf. Other female family members dress in same-colored outfits, often tailored specially from uniform pagne to differentiate the two sides of the family. In urban areas, some couples choose to dress in tailored raffia or traditional pagnes. Attire for customary weddings depends on ethnic group and region and may involve raffia, feathers, kaolin, and beauty-enhancing skin applications of palm oil. Among the Lumbu in the south, the bride wears a particular style of raffia associated with virginity. In traditional marriages in both urban and rural contexts, the clothes themselves form part of the marriage exchange.

In urban areas, symbolic clothing codes are adhered to within the rubric of modern industrial materials and factory-made objects in combination with more traditional elements such as kaolin and raffia. The widespread use of printed T-shirts and pagnes associated with parades has been extended to standard wear in funeral ceremonies and is considered a fashion. In rural areas, more traditional local products are used, such as leaves, bark cloth, raffia, cotton pagnes, fibers, lianas, gourds, seeds, and animal skins.

In the early twenty-first century, Gabonese societies continue to place a high emphasis on social distinction through dress. The way in which this dynamic has materialized through fashion is inextricably linked to the country's historical foreign relations, notably with France. The extensive adoption of the French language (and culture), as the language of domination, elitism, and nationhood has resulted in a paradox of widespread appropriation that is superimposed on, rather than assimilated to, the distinctive ethnic cultures. This paradox plays out in the work of emergent Gabonese designers who are unified by their desire to produce a typical Gabonese fashion characterized by the use of raffia, African pagne, and Western haute couture while retaining their unique individual styles that reflect their personal creative journeys and ethnic heritage.

References and Further Reading

Amina: Le Magazine de la Femme Africaine, no. 385 (2002); no. 38█ (2002); no. 438 (2006); no. 443 (2007).

Dupont, Victor Marquis de Compiègne. *L'Afrique équatoriale, gabonai█ pahouins-gallois*. Paris: E. Plon, 1875.

Grébert, Fernand. *Au Gabon: L'Afrique Équatoriale Française*. Paris, 1948█

Jean-Baptiste, Rachel. "'Une Ville Libre?' Marriage, Divorce, and Sexu█ ality in Libreville, Gabon; 1849–1960." Ph.D. dissertation, Stanfor█ University, 2005.

Largeau, Vincent. *Encyclopédie pahouine, Congo français, élements d█ grammaire et dictionnaire français-pahouin*. Paris: Ernst Laroux, 1901█

Lasserre, Guy. *Libreville: La ville et sa région*. Paris: Cahiers de la Fonda█ tion Nationale des Sciences Politiques, 1958.

Londres, Albert. *Terre d'ébène: La traite des noirs*. Paris: Michel, 1929.

Martin, Phyllis M. *Leisure and Society in Colonial Brazzaville*. Cambridg█ UK: Cambridge University Press, 1995.

M'Bokolo, Elikia. *Noirs et blancs en Afrique Équatoriale: Les sociét█ côtières et la pénétration française, vers 1820–1874*. Paris: L'École de█ Hautes Études en Sciences Sociales, 1981.

Mbot, Jean Émile. *Un Siècle d'histoire du Gabon raconté par l'iconographi█ Libreville, Gabon: Nkoussu Productions, 1984.

Mémorial du Gabon, Du Pétrol à l'atome 1980–1985, S. I. E, D.— Société Internationale d'Édition et de Diffusion. Case Postale 147 -12█ Genévève 3 et SYNER –B. P. 313 –MC 98000 Monaco (no date).

Merlot, Anne. *Le pays des trois estuaires: 1471–1900: Quatre siècles de rela█ tions extéreures dans les estuares du Muni, de la Mondah et du Gabo█ Libreville, Gabon: Centre culturel français Saint-Exupéry, 1990.

Ngolet, François, and David Gardinier. "Gabon." In *Encyclopedia of Afr█ can History, Vol. 1*, edited by Kevin Shillington, 543–549. New York█ Fitzroy Dearborn, 2005.

Perriman, Andrew. *Gabon*. New York: Chelsea House, 1988.

Rich, Jeremy. "'Une Babylone Noire': Interracial Unions in Colonial Li█ breville, c. 1870–1914." *French Colonial History* 4 (2003): 145–170.

Rich, Jeremy. "Civilized Attire: Dress, Cultural Change and Status i█ Libreville, Gabon, ca. 1860–1914." *Cultural and Social History* 2, no. █ (2005): 189–214.

Judith Knight and Rachel Jean-Baptist█

- Coiffure
- Scarification, Tattooing, and Dental Filing
- Clothing and Jewelry of Glass Beads and Metal
- Weapons as Badges of Social Status
- Care of Appearance

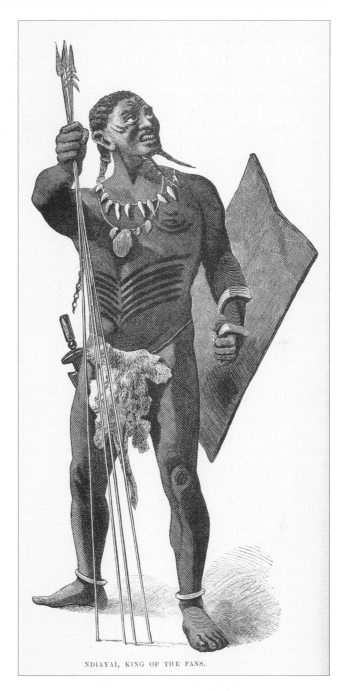

NDIAYAI, KING OF THE FANS.

A drawing of Fang "king" Ndiayi in equatorial Africa, by the French-American explorer Paul Du Chaillu, published in his book *Voyages et aventures*, 1861. According to Du Chaillu, Ndiayi had his hair styled in a thick braid forking "into two pointed ends weighted with copper rings, and embellished with white beads. His whole body was tattooed with fantastic designs." Courtesy of Louis Perrois.

The Fang of equatorial Africa dazzled all who crossed their path of east-to-west migration toward the Atlantic Ocean and Gulf of Guinea that ended in the early twentieth century. In 1843, U.S. pastor John Wilson noted, as quoted in Merlet's *Le pays des trois estuaires, 1471–1900*, that they were "naked except for a bark loincloth…. Their hair hangs in braids. They carry knives, spears, and many iron objects they make themselves." In 1847, French naval lieutenant Méquet, plying the Como River on the *Fulminante*, recounted with awe "their imposing presence, their athletic build of beautiful musculature unhidden by clothing." He noted that they wore just a *languti* (wraparound loincloth) made of *pitte* (bast) and commented on their iron neck rings, iron bracelets, braided hair, bodies painted with *rucu* (a red wood pigment), and teeth filed to a point. Méquet also described the white glass beads with which the Fang constructed coifs.

Descriptions from this period are consistently infused with such enthusiasm, sometimes with further elaboration. French-American explorer Paul Du Chaillu observed that the Make Fang of Muni Estuary and the Crystal Mountains, whom he visited on his first trip in 1856, had skin "lighter in color than any other coastal tribe." He said that the "king" of the area, Ndiayi, had his hair styled in a thick braid forking "into two pointed ends weighted with copper rings, and embellished with white beads. His whole body was tattooed with fantastic designs. His wife, Mashumba, was admired for her coiffed bonnet of white beads. But she was almost naked."

In 1876, Admiral Fleuriot de Langle cataloged several types of Fang coiffure: "The hairstyling is outstanding: Their hair is shaved above the ears, around the temples and on the neck; hair on top of the head is kept neat and braided into locks behind the ears; two braids hang down the back; two more wound with brass wire and studded with glass beads protrude like horns from the forehead; and completing the head's ornamentation a pouf of red feathers plucked from parrot tails."

Thirty years later, the accounts of Father Henri Trilles drawn from his observations from 1892 to 1901 during his pastoral journeys among the Fang of Gabon, then those from the 1905 to 1908 expedition of Captain Cottes along the borderlands, occasionally matched with invaluable photographs, provide realistic visualization of the richness and diversity of attire and coiffure of the Pahouin of Equatorial Guinea, Gabon, and neighboring southern Cameroon.

COIFFURE

The first Western travelers thus observed the variety and originality of Fang coiffure, *ésil* in Betsi dialect: hairstyling by shaving, braiding, and molding into hatlike structures; padded hairstyles; and wigs attached more or less to head hair. These hairstyles were not reserved for formal celebrations. Apparently, everyone felt compelled to wear an impressive coiffure, except women in mourning, who left their hair unkempt in cases of distant relation or who shaved their heads clean for a close relative.

Adult men, especially before 1914, and women as well, wore braids of varied thickness: thin braid strings, *étoghé* (pl. *bitoghé*), or ordinary, old-fashioned braids, *ékôma* (pl. *bikôma*). The latter could be either pulled back and cinched to sit on the nape of the neck or in locks tracing the temples, in front of the ears, or for women worked into a net encompassing the head (tight netting or light crisping) or arranged in a radiating geometric pattern swirling completely around the head from forehead to ears to the lengthening knot hanging very low on the nape of the neck.

Fang warriors had shaved coiffures as well. They preferred shaving all but a small tuft of hair on top of the head or at the temples or, more commonly, a circular coif called *asikh*; a hairstyle of one or two semicircular areas on the upper forehead called *asoma ésil*; a close-cropped and shaved spiral on top of the head called *mbom ésil*; a topmost square patch of hair called *ékoña*; a shaved spider design hairstyle with shorn interstices: *minten* (from the verb *ten*, "to burst"). German anthropologist Günter Tessmann illustrates additional hairstyles that are shaved and cropped into tiered crowns or tonsured (*ongoñ*) crescents. The small, fine razor with a handle (*ñgeñ*) for doing this was wrought in local villages by Fang blacksmiths, who were masters of the art of metalworking.

Children had a clean-shaven head until their coming-of-age initiation. Some, however, could keep their hair either cut very short for boys or in fine, flat, longitudinal braids on top of the head. All observers noticed that, compared to other peoples in the region, the Fang were very clean, most bathing often. Their hair stayed moisturized with a mixture of oil extracted from varieties of wild almonds gathered from the forest and an aromatic powder (*mbon ñkon*). This hairdressing was kept in a little pot for carrying and keeping close at hand.

These hairstyles attracted much unpleasant itching, so some Fang groups, notably the Ntumu of northern Gabon, perhaps for greater comfort created *nlo-o-ngo*, helmetlike wigs, literally meaning "head-coif with shell buttons." These wigs were made from a combination of braided cut human hair, plant fibers, bamboo strips, and filler of palm tree raffia pith. An assortment of ornaments was invariably sewn onto the wig's base: small rhinestone bead spheres or barrels in white and bright colors, cowries, imported mother-of-pearl buttons, round-headed upholstery tacks, brass ringlets, and fine chains. The wigs were lavishly constructed into myriad contours and volumes, flattened at the cranial summit or widely extended with ear flaps or an elegantly curled-in neck flap, visor, or headband, with or without a back knot, a wide, sagittal crest, or, more rarely, a transverse crest that could be angular or rounded. From the front, but more often on the sides, there could be long pendants encrusted with glass beads, cowries, and copper pieces sewn on a mat of finely woven plant fiber that cascaded onto the wearer's shoulders and chest.

These forms of ornamentation were in themselves minor masterpieces of craft, as much affirmations of sharp design sense as of nuance and confident execution. It appears that these wigs, made only by men, were highly prestigious ornaments gauging by their assemblage of cowries, brass, and shell buttons—commodity monies because they were scarce, precious luxury products. The body was thus a display of personal and family wealth and social standing.

A drawing of a Fang warrior in equatorial Africa, showing typical, partly shaved hairstyle, published in G. Tessman, *Die Pangwe*, 1913. Courtesy of Louis Perrois.

SCARIFICATION, TATTOOING, AND DENTAL FILING

Permanent ornamentation of the body by tattooing (*mvañ*) and scarification (*ndôl*) was practiced by all of the Fang. These incisions made with small stone-sharpened blades were operations of semiprofessional tattooers whom the Betsi and Make call *ñkwel minsoñ*, "craftsmen-decorators," contractors like house painters and later scribes. In olden days, some men and women tattooed or scarified their entire body or just the abdomen, chest, back, or face.

Most commonly, the *ñkwela asu* motif, a vertical line, was tattooed along the axis of the forehead. It also appears on wood masks called *ngil* and *ngontañ*. Most other motifs and iconography used by the Fang related to the natural environment (forest animals, waterways) but also, subtly, beliefs associated with eddies and rapids, particular plants (leaves, vines), and some animals (reptiles, toads and frogs, fishes, lizards, panthers, monkeys, a variety of insects, birds, chameleons). Motifs were rendered as either a silhouette of the animal or with characteristic details such as plumage, beak, skin, tail. Some designs featured natural and cosmological phenomena like rain, sun, and moon.

The tattooer used available space of skin surface with more attention to aesthetics and symbolism than to ritual. (Scarification marks on the nape of the neck were notable signs of initiation rituals.) Motifs were composed to conform to the shape of a particular body part, whether face, arms, or torso of a man or woman.

Early prints and photographs show Fang warriors with fierce faces baring pointed teeth. This was a custom reserved for men. An engraving after a sketch by naval officer Coffinières de Nordeck, published in 1878 by naturalist-explorer Alfred Marche, suggests how the "teeth cutter," called *nsañ*, proceeded: He cut the teeth, *mesôñ*, incisors and canines, with a knife, gradually chipping off the enamel in staged percussion by pressing the blade with a wood mallet, the teeth being protected from behind by a sort of wood bit, then filing with a sandpaper-like leaf. Surely, this operation was painful and the resulting smile of pointed teeth intimidating to neighboring enemies during the Fang's regular raids.

CLOTHING AND JEWELRY OF GLASS BEADS AND METAL

The Fang were adept blacksmiths who not only worked iron but also copper and brass. According to oral tradition, brass imported from Europe (*mvor* or *koñ*, words applied without distinction to copper, brass, and bronze) little by little replaced *éki* iron used earlier to make tools, weapons, and body ornaments, and even used for bride-wealth money, the small pieces of wrought iron shaped into spearheads called *kama*. This was due to the beautiful brilliance and easier processing of brass. Iron was considered precious, but copper and brass much more so; they were rare luxuries and conspicuous signs of wealth obtained from whites.

Brass pipes were cut and hammered into simple finger rings, decorative chains for pendant noserings and earrings, and fine-link chains coveted by all the villagers. The Fang wore a neck ring throughout adulthood. These cast and forged torques of copper or brass were extremely heavy. They could only be removed from the neck of the dead with a sledgehammer. After engraving motifs with a burin, primarily within a triangular section but not on those with two ridges, the torques were vigorously rubbed and polished to a beautiful red or yellow sheen. Judging from photographs of this period, engraved torques tended to be worn by women. (From time to time, women wore two, one on top of the other.) Men preferred simple, polished, double-ridged torques.

Motifs engraved on wrist and bicep bracelets, as on torques, recall the iconography of tattooing and scarification, weapons, and wood statuary: rectangles of concave line segments in the axis of the torque framed by additional rectangles and matte tinted grooves or cross-bars for the torques; parallel grooves banded into rectangles, circle of arches, and frieze of extended triangles for the bracelets. These motifs, according to Tessmann, the first European to stay for an extended period in Fang villages of Rio Muni (Equatorial Guinea), between 1904 and 1909, were in aesthetic terms stylized models of nature or more often interpretations of particular episodes of myths and the proverbs and folktales of oral tradition: bird tail feathers of kite, swallow, touraco, eagle, and parrot, monkey tail, spotted panther skin, hornbill beak, spider, scorpion, frog, fish, silhouettes and skin patterns of the monitor lizard; assorted plants; and evocations of the sun, moon, and stars. Stripes symbolize bands of plant cuttings; arrowheads stand for arms. These complex compositions are tours de force of engraving, and the motifs are applied according to strict rules

of geometry: symmetry, line straightness, perfect curves, finished framing, and clever choice of motifs relevant to the type of jewelry, even on the most diminutive objects.

WEAPONS AS BADGES OF SOCIAL STATUS

The Fang were primarily warriors, and, for this reason, their weapons were quasi-sartorial accessories. It was unthinkable for a man to put himself at risk by venturing outside his village without his personal weapons. Paul Du Chaillu and a few other explorers of the mid-nineteenth century noticed that Fang weapons were somewhat limited to short swords, throwing knives, fighting hatchets, and light spears.

Swords called *ñkawara* were at first pervasive but gradually replaced in the twentieth century by large cutlasses and machetes imported from Europe. These rather short swords resembling antique glaives were fitted with a narrow blade four to six centimeters (about two inches) in width and forty to forty-five centimeters (about seventeen inches) in length with two razor-sharp edges, a pointed or truncated tip, and, in some cases, embellished

Fan Warrior.

A drawing of a Fang warrior in equatorial Africa with a short sword and shield, published in Du Chaillu, *Voyages et aventures*, 1861. The Fang were primarily warriors, and their weapons were quasi-sartorial accessories, carried whenever they ventured outside the village. Courtesy of Louis Perrois.

with lateral barbed spikes below the hilt. These weapons were very effective and lethal in hand-to-hand combat. Bearing decorative patterns on both sides, but not on the sharp edges, these silken blades had thick butts to reinforce the solidity of the hafting. Brass wire was occasionally added too, not so much for embellishment as for keeping the blade firm in the wood hilt. Each sword had a sheath that was profusely decorated and hung with leather lashing that allowed it to be carried daily and conveniently over the shoulder. The scabbards were made of slender strips of bamboo and thin plaques of wood sheathed in snake, lizard, or monitor skin and further ornamented with brass wire and tacks. The contour of these scabbards could simply conform to the blade or more imaginatively to the accoutrements, for example, in scrolls.

The origin, Kota or Fang, of the *onzil* throwing knife with a blade shaped like a hornbill beak, typically with sober detailing, is difficult to pinpoint because it appears to be common to both cultures. It is one of those transcultural objects that harks back to very early contacts nearly impossible to determine today. With a curved spur at the hilt, the blade was curiously open-worked with a triangular center and was modestly, delicately burin engraved. The challenge for the blacksmith was finding the right balance of this distinctively formed weapon, so curved and counter curved. Approximating and used like a war hatchet but lighter than the hatchet-club, the onzil throwing knife was apparently not actually thrown. Its customized scabbard was a rectangle of wood and bamboo sheets, sometimes adorned with brass tacks or wire. The hilt or handle was carefully treated in decoration but also in form, which had to be perfectly functional. (The way that it was held in the hand relative to its expected usage and fighting position was evidently of utmost importance.)

The heavy iron war hatchet with a rounded blade engraved with the same symbols as those of tattooing and other body ornamentation completed the personal weaponry of Fang warriors. The handle of this hatchet was carved in the form of a club to reinforce its effectiveness in landing blows.

Weapons had the combined effect of being instruments for fighting and signs of social status, even ritual items, and quasi-personal attributes as important emblematically as coiffure and scarification.

CARE OF APPEARANCE

In the day-to-day reality of the Fang of Equatorial Guinea and Gabon, a people living nearly naked and rather pitifully in the eyes of the first Europeans who encountered them, appearance was absolutely essential to social and personal life: dressing up, styling the hair, displaying scarification marks, brandishing engraved weapons, finding refuge in dwellings with painted walls, dancing in rhythm, and singing the epics of the *mvet*—in short, showing off in the eyes of others who were central to the community and also neighboring peoples. Attention to appearance was far indeed from being a frivolous, useless behavior. It was a secular tradition that endured the worst of circumstances. This taste in body presentation became a century later what Central Africans called *sape*, or fashion. This sense of style in coiffure and clothing was seen as desirably extravagant in the urban neighborhoods of African capitals. This care for physical appearance was the motor of a veritable fountain of social dynamism for Fang peoples that has persisted to the present day.

References and Further Reading

Du Chaillu, Paul Belloni. *Explorations and Adventures in Equatorial Africa*. London: John Murray, 1861.

de Langle, Fleuriot. "Croisière à la côte d'Afrique, 1863." In *Le Tour du Monde*. Paris: Hachette, 1876.

Grébert, F. *Le Gabon de Fernand Grébert, 1913–1932*. Introduction and notes by C. de Savary and L. Perrois. Geneva: Éditions D and Musée d'Ethnographie de Genève, 2003.

Laburthe-Tolra, Ph. *Fang, Exhibition Catalogue*. Paris: Éditions Musée Dapper, 1991.

Méquet, Lt. "Nouvelle excursion dans le haut de la rivière Gabon: novembre–décembre 1846." *Revue Coloniale* 13 (1847).

Merlet, A. *Le pays des trois estuaires, 1471–1900*. Libreville, Gabon: Centre culturel français, 1990.

Perrois, L. *Arts du Gabon*. Arnouville, France: Éditions Arts d'Afrique Noire, 1979.

Perrois, L. *Ancestral Art of Gabon*. Translated by Francine Farr. Geneva: Éditions Barbier-Mueller Museum, 1985.

Perrois, L. *Fang*. Translated by Isabel Ollivier. Milan: 5 Continents Editions, 2006.

Perrois, L., and M. Sierra Delage. *The Art of Equatorial Guinea: The Fang Tribes*. Translated by Roger Marshall and Barry Kench. Barcelona: Ediciones Poligrafa, 1991.

Tessmann, G. *Die Pangwe*. Berlin: Wasmuth, 1913.

Louis P. Perrois
Translated by *Francine Farr*

PART 8

Horn of Africa

Ethiopia

- Religion and Dress
- Highland Dress
- Lowland Dress
- Urban Dress

Ethiopia, along with Eritrea, Djibouti, Somalia, and the Sudan, occupies a region in Africa known as the Horn. Among the Horn's striking contrasts is its diverse geography. Eritrea's capital of Asmara stands at more than 7,600 feet (2,316 meters) high, while the Danakil Depression in Djibouti, Eritrea, and Ethiopia is nearly 400 feet (122 meters) below sea level and is regarded as one of the hottest places on earth. Eritrea is one of the newest nations in Africa, achieving independence from Ethiopia in 1993, while Ethiopia is home to one of the earliest hominoids—the *Australopithecus afarensis* Lucy (known as Denkanesh in Ethiopia)—and one of the Africa's oldest civilizations. Ethiopia, the third most populous country in Africa, is also one of the few countries to have enjoyed continuous sovereignty.

Ethiopia has dry, hot plains; cool, mountainous terrain; and fertile valleys subject to flooding. This geographic range makes for distinct choices in dress. Coupled with many ethnic groups living within Christian, Islamic, and Judaic frameworks, the array of dress styles in Ethiopia is vast. The facts that half the population must receive food aid due to regular droughts and that the life expectancy ranges from forty to fifty-five suggest that most people do not have the financial means to devote time and resources to their dress styles. Yet we find remarkable creativity and ingenuity in the ensemble of things with which people dress themselves, including hairstyle, jewelry, clothing, tattooing, scarification, and body paint. Often dress is meaningful on several levels and may indicate age, status, political membership, religious belief, and ethnic affiliation. Each culture within Ethiopia has its own unique costume.

The abundance of dress styles in Ethiopia is largely due to the diversity of climate, geography, and culture. Ethiopian geography is divided into the highland and lowland regions. Temperatures in the eastern desert can hit over 140 degrees Fahrenheit (60 degrees Celsius), while evening temperatures in the highlands plummet to 32 degrees Fahrenheit (0 degree Celsius). Highland elevation can reach 16,000 feet (4,877 meters) at peak level and fall to 410 feet (125 meters) in the Danakil Depression. The Ethiopian population of seventy-five million is made up of some eighty ethnic groups, of which the Oromo, Amhara, Tigre, Sidamo, Somali, Afar, and Gurage are the largest. Muslims make up over half the Ethiopian population with Orthodox Christians closely behind in number.

RELIGION AND DRESS

One dress type worn throughout Ethiopia is the amulet. While children of the Orthodox Christian faith are given a baptismal cord as their first significant item of dress, the amulet necklace is one of the first types of adornment to universally appear around the neck of young Muslims, Christians, Jews, and traditional practitioners alike. Amulets consist of metal cases or, more commonly, square leather pieces stitched together to form a pouch. Depending on the belief system of the wearer, this pouch might be filled with a medicinal remedy or pieces of paper written with holy scripture. In places where paper is scarce, Islamic scribes dip the leather amulet in recycled ink once used by scribes to practice Qur'anic text on wooden writing tablets. The client wearing the amulet might also be made to drink this liquid. In this way, the amulet and the wearer imbibe the written prayer as an extra form of protection. Amulets can aid in or prevent physical and psychological illness or afflictions of the body as well as guard the wearer from attack by *buda*. Buda are individuals who are thought to have the evil eye or the ability to do harm to others through their gaze. Those with buda are often associated with the artisan classes of blacksmiths, potters, or tanners. Amulets worn at the neck are intended to draw the viewer's attention and harness the potentially harmful gaze of buda.

In Ethiopia, both Orthodox Christian and Muslim dress is influenced by thousands of years of trade across the Red Sea. The Orthodox Christian communities of the Amhara of the central highlands and the Tigre in the north are referred to historically as the Abyssinians, tracing their line of descent back to the mythical union of the Queen of Sheba and King Solomon. Christianity has existed in Ethiopia since the fourth century. While no textiles and artifacts exist from this period, early stone monuments depict figures draped in cloth and provide evidence to a long-standing textile trade in imported cotton as early as the first century in the Axumite Empire. These imported pieces were probably reserved for wear by the ruling classes. Cotton cultivation, spinning, and weaving on wooden pit-treadle looms were established in Ethiopia once cloth began to replace the dress of hide and fiber worn by commoners. While cotton cloth was imported from America, India, and Arabia, by the 1800s, locally produced cloth was of much higher quality and preferred by most of the population. Many people still prefer to wear handwoven cloth, though modern textile manufacturing of cotton and nylon fabrics is now an important industry in the country.

Sumptuous, imported textiles and elaborate costumes were historically restricted to the aristocracy and clergy in the Orthodox Church. During the time of Emperor Tewodros II (r. 1855–1868), for example, only those of royal blood could don silk shirts and dresses and capes of velvet and brocade, while palace soldiers were allowed silk shirts and the pelts of wild animals. In the early to mid-1900s, soldiers began adopting the modern khaki uniforms.

Dress is also used to indicate status in the liturgical ensembles of the clergy within the Orthodox Church and the Muslim faith. Priests conduct the Eucharist in distinctive shiny black hats that range in shape from a flat bowl to an upright cylinder. Priests may also carry fly whisks, bibles, hand crosses, and staffs that they use for support during funerals, baptisms, and long services. The attending male deacons who assist the priests may carry the church's large, processional crosses and wear crowns composed of a gold or silver frame and fine imported cloth. During special religious

Two monks (left) and a nun (far right), wearing locally spun white cotton garments, and a groundskeeper (center), at the Narga Selassie monastery on Dek Island in the middle of Lake Tana, Ethiopia, 2007. The nun wears a rosary made of imitation amber beads and her *shamma* is framed in red. Photograph by Laura Simmons.

ceremonies such as Timkat, the Epiphany, priests will parade with ornate, full-length brocade and embroidered robes and hold colorful umbrellas made from imported textiles. In contrast, nuns, who often enter their profession late in life, wear undecorated coarse dresses. On holy days, practitioners make pilgrimages to sacred sites in a sea of white cotton wraps. Muslim clerics do not differentiate their rank through clothing; rather, they wear simple clothing but allow their facial and head hair to grow and they carry prayer beads and a stick. Among the Afran Qallo Oromo, for example, sheikhs allow their hair to form dreadlocks and then dye it a brilliant orange red with henna. Borana Oromo Muslim clerics travel with a two-pronged metal stick.

The central form of jewelry for Orthodox men and women is the *matab*, a cotton cord given at baptism. As a child matures, he or she may add a silver cross to the matab. Neck crosses are worn by many Christian adults and usually are made through the lost-wax process. Older examples are directly cut from the Maria Theresa thaler, a form of currency bearing the portrait of the Austria-Hungarian queen that was in wide circulation by the mid-1800s. Cross shapes are distinct and may relate to a place name, epic individual, or proverb. Jewish men and women living near the town of Gondar wear a similarly constructed Star of David. Handheld crosses and processional crosses are carried by clergy and can also be seen as types of body supplements. When

a devotee approaches a priest, for example, he or she is offered the hand cross to kiss. In addition, a host of silver filigree ornaments made from the Maria Theresa thaler are worn on the body, including bracelets, beads, pendants, hairpins, earrings, and picks for cleaning the ears.

HIGHLAND DRESS

Highland dress has historically consisted of white or off-white hand-spun cloth made from long woven strips sewn together. Women wear a long gown of soft cotton called a *kemis*. Colorful decoration is reserved for the hem, sleeve, and neckline of the kemis, and embroidered crosses or abstract designs made with cotton or silk thread and beads may be added to the neckline design. Ethiopian Jewish women in the Beta Israel community also wear the kemis but with the embroidery of the Star of David. A long, cotton scarf called *shamma* or *netela* is worn over the head, shoulder, and/or torso of highland Christian and Jewish women. This dress, familiar to all highland women and to many outside Ethiopia as the official country dress, has recently been used by fashion designers like Gadol Ton and Elias Meshesha, who draw on indigenous styles and locally manufactured textiles for inspiration.

Highland men wear a white, cotton tunic with the full shawl (called netela) and jodhpurs. All Orthodox Christian men adopted

Four unmarried Arbore girls near Arbore, South Omo Valley, Ethiopia, 2007. Each girl wears an assortment of beaded necklaces with metal watch bands as the centerpiece. The white waist beads are often the first item of dress given to a child. These girls will allow their hair to grow after they marry. Photograph by Laura Simmons.

these pants during the reign of Menelik II in the late nineteenth century. For warmth, men and women wear a heavier shamma, called *kutta*. Highland infant and toddler boys wear their heads shaved with a tuft left in front. Boys, who often spend chilly mornings herding their family sheep, goats, or cattle, wear a wool blanket and wrap a sheepskin cape around their torso. They will keep their heads warm with a distinctive woven woolen hat tipped with a tassel of baboon or colobus monkey hair.

In all regions of Ethiopia, dress styles have evolved and changed over time due to shifting economic conditions, access to new materials, and outside demands. For example, in the Eastern Highlands near the ancient city of Harar, Muslim Oromo and Somali women once wore a leather skirt and leather torso wrap. During the Egyptian occupation of Harar (1875–1884), women were forced by Ismail Pasha's decree to adopt imported coarse canvas in order to enter the town to trade. By the early 1900s and after the Egyptian occupation, a single cotton sheet of Ethiopian-produced factory cloth became the dominant dress style among the agricultural communities near Harar. This dress is called *saddetta*, referring to the eight meters (twenty-six feet) of cloth used in its creation. Saddetta is a large, white imported textile worn toga style and tied at the left shoulder. Women often add a T-shirt over their saddetta to modestly cover their shoulders, and, in some regions, the saddetta becomes merely a skirt. The

saddetta is visually distinguished from the hand-spun highland shamma by the imported material and its skirt pleats that are created by storing the saddetta tied with accordion folds. A modern version of the saddetta called *mashiinii*, named after the sewing machine used in its creation, has became popular since the 1990s. The mashiinii dress has permanent pleats and is often made of the most fashionable and brightly colored imported textiles. These pleats and the dress style still visually reference the original leather skirt of the seventeenth and eighteenth centuries.

Before marriage, Eastern Highlands Muslim girls wear their hair in a variety of braided styles, but at marriage they adopt the *gufta*. The most crucial element of a married woman's costume is her gufta. A gufta is an imported black net hair covering used by women from both the Cushitic Oromo and Semitic Harari cultures. To wear gufta, the unbraided hair is pulled back to form two balls, tied at the nape of the neck and covered with the netting. This hairstyle is known as *hamasha*. Odiferous plants like myrrh, thyme, and garlic cloves may be inserted into the hairnet or tucked into the back of the hair. These plants give off a pungent smell that is designed to deflect harmful spiritual or human forces like buda that are particularly drawn to women during menses.

The Semitic Harari people, the original inhabitants of the walled city of Harar, which has been an important Red Sea trade center since antiquity, show their access to wealth and their

A Mursi woman in a village near Jinka, Ethiopia, 2007. The bracelets, the leather wrap, and the beaded hairstyle are commonly worn by Mursi women. The clay lip plate, however, is usually inserted only to pose for Western photographers, who will pay the women to be photographed. Photograph by Laura Simmons.

merchant status in their dress. Historically, Harari women wore an *atlas* (Arabic for "satin") and the *te eraz*, black clothing that is sewn with black cloth on one side and dark pink on the other. The te eraz is multifunctional. The dark pink side is available for daily use and can quickly be reversed if a death is announced or if a woman is rushing to a funeral. Underneath the Harari dress, women wear leggings called *ge ganafi*, meaning "trousers of the city." Ge ganafi are said to have been adopted to deter the advances of Egyptian male soldiers during the Egyptian occupation of Harar. These drawstring pants are tight fitting at the ankles and calf and made with ornate velvet, while the upper pant is loose fitting and composed of undyed cotton. This makes them both difficult to remove and less attractive from the knee up.

All Muslim city dwellers prefer colorful beads and bright imported head scarves, called *fohda*, which they casually pull over their hair when they enter public spaces. While Harari women can afford real amber and silver beads and medallions influenced by Indian, Persian, and Yemeni jewelry, Oromo and Somali women tend to wear imported plastic yellow beads and inexpensive coin substitutes. In the same manner, the locally made, gold mesh forehead jewelry called *qarma* that is worn on special occasions by Harari women is substituted for imported and inexpensive metal industrial link by Oromo women.

While Muslim women's dress in eastern Hararghe is visually identified by ethnicity, the dress for many Oromo, Somali, Harari, and Argobba men is almost indistinguishable. Men generally wear imported plaid wrappers from Indonesia with T-shirts or dress shirts, shawls, and jackets. Some unmarried Oromo men will wear a carved wooden comb or plastic hair pick in their hair, a practice that references a time when young men wore feathers in their hair to indicate brave feats. This tradition is still common among pastoral groups in southern Ethiopia and northern Kenya such as the Oromo subgroups of the Arsi and Borana, who still follow the indigenous Oromo governance system known as *gada*. In gada, as a man moves through a sequence of stages regulated by his age relation to his father, he ideally assumes a new social position every eight years and is enhanced by new body adornment, including a metal, phallic headpiece called *kallicha*, worn by men of the highest ranks. While women do not actively participate in gada grades, they do wear a range of hairpieces and jewelry and leather capes and dresses beaded with brass, copper, glass, and plastic beads to identify the position of their husbands and sons.

LOWLAND DRESS

The Sidamo region of lowland Ethiopia is known for its *ensete* culture. The ensete is a root tuber belonging to the banana family

A Dassanech girl near Omorate, South Omo Valley, Ethiopia, 2007. Her elaborate hairstyle is secured with mud and ochre. The beaded screen at the front is intended to accentuate the hairstyle and shield the eyes from the hot sun. Photograph by Laura Simmons.

and is the staple diet. The plant plays a dual role in dress and ritual as well. Ensete leaves were historically used to wrap and bury a corpse after death, and, after the birth of a child, ensete fibers are still used to tie off the umbilical cord. Ensete fibers were used to make clothing before the introduction of cotton to the region, and ensete leaves still fashion the umbrellas often used to protect sellers in the market from the midday sun.

Sidamo men wear colorful shirts and pants or shorts of woven striped cotton in red, white, yellow, and black. Sidamo women wear a dress of the same material and may add a leather cape around their shoulders, copper bracelets on the wrist and upper arm, and cowry shells on the ends of their hair braids. Men will use butter and mud to segment the hair into a cocoon shape. Older men will also don a tailored jacket, a Western-style hat, and a white wrap over their shoulders along with the traditional striped pants. Occasionally, older men will also carry an imported umbrella as a marker of status just as they once walked with ensete umbrellas.

The Gurage, Semitic-speaking agriculturalists in the southern region, have adopted neon green and pink material for men's tunics and pants in place of the more traditional white, hand-spun cotton tunic and tapered, three-quarter-length pants called *bombai suray*. While women continue to wear a white cotton dress called *hudjir* similar to a kemis, they have also adopted the green and pink prints favored in the marketplace. Young and married women tie back their hair with a black head scarf called *shash*.

The Nilotic groups who live along the Baro River in the Gambela region near the border of Sudan decorate their skin with fine keloid scars and call attention to the articulated parts of the body with strands of beads. Men in this region scar facial skin in raised patterns predominantly on the forehead and cheeks, while women's scars are centered on the torso in registers of raised dots. During initiation at puberty, for example, Nuer men have their forehead scarred in strong horizontal lines that extend into the hairline and get scarred with raised registers of dots on their upper arms. Nuer women wear asymmetrical hairstyles made of French braids set close to the scalp that run in creative curved patterns around the scalp. Clothing for both men and women is usually reserved to a waist wrap that covers the pubic region. Young women may wear a bark fiber apron studded with rows of beads that accentuate her scarification patterns. Anuak men will add white feathers to their coiffure on special occasions to contrast with their dark skin. In the past, the Anuak measured wealth through the ownership of beads and still refer to themselves as "bead people." They wear ivory, metal, and colorful glass beads strung on giraffe hair to adorn all jointed points of the body, including neck, elbow, wrist, knee, and ankle. Beads are also added to gourds and leather skirts.

In the Ethiopian southwest, near the Omo River in the Great Rift Valley, live several seminomadic cattle-herding and seasonal farming societies where men and women engage in a pastime of body adorning. Today, this region is referred to as the Southern Nations, Nationalities, and Peoples Region of Ethiopia with forty-five distinct ethnic groups. Women and men in this region wear a striking variety of beads. The most popular are strands of square aluminum beads, followed by flat ostrich-shell beads; red, white, and blue glass beads; and thin leather bands worn wrapped around the torso stitched with cowry shells.

Unmarried Surma men decorate their bodies and faces with paint on the occasion of stick dueling. White kaolin patterns in rhythmic swirls on black skin can signal group membership and indicate individual prowess. Some Surma women stretch their lower lips and earlobes to the extent that large, clay plates can be inserted. This practice of lip stretching had nearly ceased by the 1970s, but it has since resumed due to the financial compensation provided by Western photographers who have exoticized and popularized the practice through their images.

Karo men use white and ochre body and face paints and mud-packed hairstyles topped with plumes to look attractive, to indicate their age grade, and, more and more, to attract the attention of the tourist's gaze so as to collect payment for poses. Karo women scar the torso region at puberty in keloid patterns and wear a leather skirt with a long tail in the back that they flick when dancing.

Hamer women wear smooth and softened leather skirts embroidered with cowry shells and seed beads. The bottom edge of the skirt is sewn with metal ornaments like bent nails that jingle at the knee with each step. They use ochre to decorate their leather, their skin, and their hair so that the entire body takes on the appearance of a dark sienna shape from a distance. The

A married Hamer woman in a village near Turmi, Ethiopia, 2007. The metal rings around her neck symbolize that this Hamer woman is married but that she is not the first wife; her collar ring would be much larger and heavier if she were. The leather dress, ornamented with seed beads and cowry shells, is also typically worn by married women. Photograph by Laura Simmons.

distinctive hairstyle of Hamer women includes rows of straight, plaited strands, cut short at the top of the head to frame the forehead and the face. Younger women with shorter hair create a head full of buttered hair balls covered in ochre. These hairstyles may be topped with a headdress of leather and aluminum fashioned with oblong metal pieces that jut out over the forehead. In this polygamous society, the iron collar applied by a blacksmith at marriage to Hamer women indicates which number wife she is. This collar and the metal bracelets of the upper arms and wrists are never removed.

URBAN DRESS

Fashion has become very important in the lives of young people of the upper classes in Addis Ababa, the capital city. In Addis Ababa, billboards advertise the latest dress styles, and American and European fashion magazines are highly sought after and often referenced in tailor shops where most affluent women buy their clothes. In addition, Addis Ababa, Dire Dawa, and Harar offer exclusive clothing boutiques where imported Western and Middle Eastern fashions are readily available. And a few Ethiopian designers like Guenet Fresenbet, known as Gigi, have brought attention to clothes made with Ethiopian fabrics produced in local textile and leather factories through fashion shows of her clothing line. Although those raised in Addis Ababa have a cultivated fashion sense and may engage in current global trends that connect them to people and places beyond their immediate communities, most Ethiopians, wealthy or poor, make a conscious choice to wear what is culturally appropriate and socially relevant to their particular ethnicity, gender, age, and belief system.

References and Further Reading

Beckwith, Carol, Angela Fisher, and Graham Hancock. *African Ark: Peoples of the Horn*. London: Collins Harvill, 1990.

Cole, Barbie Campbell, and Peri Klemm. "Historical Threads. An Overview of Women's Dresses in Harar." *Archiv fur Volkerkunde* 53 (2003): 63–72.

Fisher, Angela. *Africa Adorned*. New York: Abrams, 1984.

Gibb, Camilla. "Religion, Politics and Gender in Harar, Ethiopia." Ph.D. dissertation, University of Oxford, 1996.

Klemm, Peri. "Fashioning History: Women's Costumes from Eastern Hararghe, 1850–1886." *Proceedings of the 14th International Conference of Ethiopian Studies*, Addis Ababa University, Ethiopia, November 2000.

Klemm, Peri. "Body Adornment and Clothing: Cosmetics and Body Painting." In *New Encyclopedia of Africa*, edited by John Middelton. Charles Scribner's Sons/Gale, 2007.

Klemm, Peri. "Leather Amulets in Ethiopia." In *Faith and Transformation: Votive Offerings and Amulets from the Alexander Girard Collection*, edited by Doris Francis, 98–100. Santa Fe, Museum of International Folk Art, New Mexico: 2007.

Klemm, Peri. "Oromo Fashion: Three Contemporary Body Art Practices among Afran Qallo Women." *African Arts* 42, no. 1 (2009): 54–63. Special issue on Expressive Culture in Ethiopia. Guest editors P. Klemm and L. Niederstadt.

Last, Jill. "Hairstyles Today." *Selamta* 12, no. 2 (1995): 14–18.

Last, Jill, and Nancy Donovan. *Ethiopian Costumes*. Addis Ababa, Ethiopia: Ethiopian Tourism Commission, 1980.

McKay, Roger. "Ethiopian Jewelry." *African Arts* 7, no. 4 (1974): 36–39.

Paulitschke, Philipp. *Beiträge Ethnographie und Anthropologie der Somâl, Galla und Harari*. Leipzig, Germany: Verlag von Eduard Baldamus, 1888.

Peri M. Klemm

Snapshot: Eritrea

Nine ethnic groups live in the mountain and lowland regions of Eritrea and identify equally as Orthodox Christian and Sunni Muslim. Eritrean inhabitants speak both Cushitic and Semitic languages. The Tigrinya and Tigre peoples of the Eritrean highlands make up 80 percent of the population. Women of the highlands traditionally wear the *zuria*, a long, white, handwoven, undyed cotton dress with long sleeves and thick bands of colorful embroidery at the chest, hem, and sleeves. When the zuria is elaborately embroidered with abstracted patterns in the shape of a cross, it is called a *tilfy*. Both the zuria and tilfy are worn with an imported scarf or a locally woven white shawl made of thin cotton with matching embroidery. On special occasions in the twenty-first century, this dress is accentuated with a beaded necklace of bright plastic beads joined in a triangular style from collar to breastbone and a matching beaded headband.

Urban highland women have adopted tailored dresses and skirts of pale floral prints. When they leave their homes, they add the white shawl, which, depending on its length, can cover the head and then wrap around the torso, extending down to the back of the knee. While many dresses are imported from Ethiopian textile factories, the finest are still woven locally on wooden looms. Women are responsible for the cleaning and spinning of the cotton, while men are the traditional weavers.

Women's hairstyle in the highlands, *shirruba*, consists of small braids that extend from the hairline just past the crown of the head, tightly fitted to the scalp. One popular stylistic variety is to French braid the hair back in such a way as to create ten or so billowing puffs on the head. Sometimes a thin piece of string or hair is plaited from the center part down to the ears, framing the hairline. The remaining hair is then freed and allowed to voluminously puff out to the shoulders. The finished style is rubbed with clarified butter. The butter conditions the hair and keeps it from breaking, discourages insects, and produces a distinct smell associated with the staple drink of coffee and particular meat dishes. Young girls, who do not cover their hair or wear shirruba until they are teenagers, wear a variety of hairstyles including loose styles and thick braids.

Rural Tigre women today, who also wear the shirruba, cover themselves in brightly colored full-length dresses made of imported materials with shawls made from the same material. Girls at seven or eight will be given the hairstyle of their mothers. Until then, their head is shaved, except for a circular ring at the hairline and a tuft of hair at the back of the head. As they mature, this hair will be finely braided. The forehead of young women is considered the most attractive area of the face. It will be emphasized with a headband made of gold—with the gold centerpiece resting on the forehead—and the forehead skin ornamented with a cross tattoo. Facial tattoos of crosses can appear on the forehead or chin to indicate devotion. Tattooed lines may also serve holistic purposes such as horizontal blue-black lines added to the neck to hinder goiter and marks around the eyes to protect from eye disease.

Tigre women, like all Orthodox Christian women, usually prefer to wear gold and wear round gold earrings and a gold cross on their baptismal cord, which is made of leather or yarn and given to Orthodox children as infants in Eritrea and Ethiopia.

Highland men of the Orthodox faith wear a long, white, three-quarter-sleeve shirt with loose-fitting drawstring pants called *jalabia;* a jacket; and a woven shawl, *gabbi,* around their shoulders or torso. Boys wear secondhand clothing, shawls, and wool hats to keep warm. To indicate gender, infant boys' heads are shaved except for a small patch at the crown.

The hot lowlands of northern Eritrea are also home to Muslim pastoral groups like the Kunama, who make up 40 percent of the population. Unlike Asmara, where Orthodox Christians wear mostly white, the lowlands abound with multihued garments. Both Bilen and Kunama women wear brightly colored clothing and a gold or silver nosering on the side of the nose. Traditional dress includes a locally made, full-length, sleeveless cotton dress of orange and black stripes with a fitted bodice. For Bilen and Kunama girls, material of striped yellow, orange, and red may be wrapped around the

Tigrinya women playing drums in Massawa, Eritrea, 2007. They wear the traditional *zuria*, a long, white, handwoven, undyed cotton dress with thick bands of colorful embroidery at the hem and along the edges of the matching shawl. Their hair is plaited in the hairstyle known as *shirruba*, and they wear round gold earrings made by local smiths. Peter Martell/AFP/Getty Images.

waist with breasts left bare. More and more, however, the pressure of Islam to keep breasts and shoulders concealed has resulted in a layering of girls' upper torsos with polyester T-shirts, silk wraps, or imported gauzes.

Everyday dress for the Kunama women includes brightly colored striped or plaid skirts wrapped tightly around the waist and hips worn with a T-shirt and a head cloth. Their hair is plaited in thin braids and finished with many colorful beads at ear level, a beaded choker, and beaded necklaces. Bilen women cover their hair entirely in fine imported shawls of the favored color orange and line their eyes and eyebrows in black kohl. Tattooed lines also may be added to the cheeks, and henna is used on the hands and face, particularly at wedding celebrations. The hair is braided in minute braids from a central part to the shoulders. The braids on the crown of the head are pulled back and secured with a band of flat beads. A few strands at the top of the part are pulled free and anchored with a gold medallion. The braids are then swept back and secured behind the ears. This creates a space between the top and bottom braids through which the forehead is visible. Bilen girls traditionally wear the tops of their hair shaved until four or five years of age, when the top is allowed to grow in but kept short. The unshaved sides of the hair are braided to the shoulders.

Unlike women, men generally do not distinguish themselves by ethnic affiliation. Muslim men, whether of the Bilen ethnic group or some other, predominantly wear white and cover their bodies in floor-length flowing white shirts with shorts or trousers beneath, with an accompanying white vest or tailored jacket and turban or cap called *taqiyah*. Their shirts are imported from India and Saudi Arabia or sewn by local male tailors. Rural men wear white, full-length waist wraps with a T-shirt. Traditionally, Kunama men wore leather amulet and bead necklaces with an incised wooden comb in the hair. Older men wear beards that they stain orange with henna on Muslim holidays to honor the Prophet.

Historically, Issa Muslim women wore a dark cloth over their mouth to conceal their emotions and an embroidered cloth over the head in proper Islamic prescription. Some still continue this practice. Because the eyes are then the only facial feature clearly visible, they are often accentuated with black kohl. Most married Muslim women wear a *shash,* a light cotton scarf that serves as a head covering when in public, a torso wrap if cold, and even as a handkerchief.

Bedouin Rashaida, who live as seminomadic camel herders, also call Eritrea home. The Rashaida live on both sides of the Red Sea in Saudi Arabia, Kuwait, Sudan, and Eritrea and speak Arabic. Out of respect for the Prophet Mohammed, women and men cover their bodies and hair. Due to their elaborate dress, girls in the lowlands of northern Eritrea adopt the lower nose and mouth covering prior to puberty but may keep their hair uncovered in their everyday chores. The wealthiest Rashaida women wear a heavily embroidered facial covering called a *burga* that extends from below the eyes to the waist. It may be decorated with metal beads, buttons, silver thread, and coins. The head scarf may also be embroidered with metal pendants that can extend down between the eyes. A more modest covering might include a black cloth embroidered with beads or gold thread and a colorful scarf over the head. Full skirts of red and black appliqué or any brightly colored materials will suffice. Married Rashaida men wear white, full-length, long-sleeved tunics called *djellabas* and wrap their head in turbans of white cotton cloth.

Peri M. Klemm

Somalia

GEOGRAPHY AND A BRIEF OVERVIEW

Somalia is located in the Horn of Africa. The northern coast is less than 100 miles (161 kilometers) from the Arabian Peninsula and shares a great deal of history and dress with that region. The southern coast has more in common with Swahili territory, an African-Arab region along the Indian Ocean coastline. Somalia is named after the Somali ethnic group, which makes up more than 90 percent of the population. Other citizens include the descendants of Arabs, Persians, South Asians, Ethiopians, Italian, and British expatriates and freed slaves from central Africa who are now referred to as the Somali Bantu. There are also millions of Somalis living in Djibouti, Ethiopia, and Kenya as well as refugees in Europe, North America, and the Middle East.

In terms of landscape, Somalia has four major regions: two desert zones, a fertile agricultural area, and the coastline, where most of the country's major cities—including the capital, Mogadishu—are located. In the cities, houses are built with thick walls to keep out the heat; in the deserts, nomadic people live in shelters constructed of branches covered with leather or plastic, and distinct differences in dress exist. In the cities, men and women were early adopters of fashions from the Middle East and Europe such as the caftan (a loose knee- or ankle-length shirt), *jilbab* (a modest ensemble for women that includes a two-piece head covering), *niqab* (a veil that covers the face), trousers, miniskirts, T-shirts, and three-piece suits. Nomadic dress has typically been more practical and flexible, consisting of leather, cotton wrappers, and loose garments made of thin cotton and synthetic fabrics.

For centuries, Somali dress has incorporated many imported garments and jewelry. The history of trade in the region goes back to the time of ancient Egypt and Rome. In exchange for luxuries such as frankincense (a resin from a tree native to Somali territory), tortoiseshell, and exotic animals, Somalis received items of dress from the Middle East and South Asia. These trade connections were reinforced as exiles from Persia and the Arabian Peninsula began settling along the coast of Somali territory as early as the eighth century C.E. When Ibn Battuta visited Mogadishu on his way from Spain to Mecca in the fourteenth century, he noted that the ruler was a non-Arab native who spoke Arabic and dressed in fine garments imported from Egypt and Jerusalem. For centuries, Somali culture has been profoundly influenced by these connections to the Middle East. Somalis were early converts to Islam, and, in 1974, Somalia was invited to join the League of Arab Nations.

In the nineteenth and early twentieth centuries, dress in Somalia was also affected by European colonization. By the

A red, black, and gold ensemble of *guuntina* (nomadic-style dress worn by knotting a long piece of cloth over the right shoulder and wrapping it around the torso), *shash* (headwrap) and *garbasaar* (shoulder cloth). This outfit would be worn in Somalia in the twenty-first century for weddings, folk dances, and other cultural events. Private Collection. Photograph by Heather Marie Akou.

mid-1800s, many Somalis were actively involved in trade; in exchange for products such as leather, tortoiseshell, ostrich feathers, and ivory (which were highly sought after in the European fashion industry) and slaves (who came from further inland and were traded to the Middle East and South Asia), Somalis received cotton cloth from Europe and the United States, beads, precious jewelry from the Middle East and South Asia, and foods such as dates, bananas, and spaghetti. This trade expanded rapidly after the Suez Canal opened in 1869. When present-day Somalia was colonized by Italy and Great Britain, however, Somalis were not quick to adopt these styles of dress. Many turned to religion for moral and political support, and Islamic dress became a visual symbol of resistance to colonization. Although some did experiment with mixing different styles of garments, European fashions were not widely accepted until nomads began migrating to urban areas in the 1940s. After World War II, a significant number of Italian expatriates decided to remain in Somalia, opening cafes and fashionable boutiques. When Somalia became an independent nation in 1960, delegates to the United Nations wore three-piece suits. Uniforms for the military were based on European styles of dress, and some young women in the cities experimented with dresses and miniskirts.

In 1969, the national government was taken over by a military dictator, Siad Barre. Although he did make some positive reforms, such as promoting literacy, his official socialist doctrine could not erase growing class differences. For people who benefited from the new regime, European-style villas, cars, and fashions were a sign of wealth and connections to the outside world; for people who did not benefit, these possessions became symbols of corruption and waste. In 1979, the Iranian Revolution unseated a similar government, and some Somalis viewed this as a positive model for change. Labor migrants, who traveled to the Middle East to support their families, were also exposed to new styles of thinking, eating, and dressing. For the first time, Somalis—not just the descendents of Arab and Persian settlers—were wearing *hijab* (veils). Essentially, Somalia was being torn between the West and the Islamic world. After two decades of civil unrest, imprisonments, executions, a brief war with Ethiopia, and a series of severe droughts, the government collapsed. As of 2010, Somalia is considered a "failed state."

THE FOUNDATIONS OF SOMALI DRESS

For centuries, Somalis have been wearing imported cloth and jewelry, but until at least the 1970s (when commercial products started to dominate), many items of dress were still constructed locally: leather clothing, shields made of leather and wood, metal weapons, amulets, simple pieces of jewelry, wooden combs, sandals, and headrests that were used to maintain elaborate hairstyles. Some pieces were made by nomads for their personal use; others were made by a caste of artisans known as the Saab, who forged objects out of iron and brass, hunted wild animals, made amulets, and performed circumcisions—activities that were considered too spiritually dangerous for people outside of the caste to perform. British explorer Ralph Drake-Brockman suggested that "as workers in leather their methods are crude"; however, shields, for example, were often decorated on the front with patterns of incised dots and painted on the reverse side with geometric designs. Although they were made for utilitarian purposes, nomadic men often carried shields and spears or tucked a dagger into the folds of their clothing. These pieces were meant to be visible and could easily be considered as part of their dress. Leather sandals were constructed from layers of leather that were pierced with an awl and sewn together in a stack up to one inch (two and a half centimeters) thick. The Smithsonian National

Museum of Natural History has an especially elaborate pair made for a wedding where the layers of leather were notched with tiny points (as if the sandals had been cut out with pinking shears).

Until the mid-1800s, nomadic men and women also wore clothing made of leather from their own herds of livestock. By the time European explorers reached Somali territory, however, this type of clothing was rapidly disappearing, being replaced by imported cotton cloth sold in lengths of seven cubits (one cubit was measured from the elbow to the tip of the middle finger). This was the standard length for a nomadic-style garment. For a man, the long rectangle of cloth would be cut in half and sewn together in a large square. An individual would often just wrap this around his waist, but for formal occasions or cold weather, it was possible to drape an edge over one or both shoulders. This was referred to as a *tobe*, an Arabic word for "garment," or *maro*, a Somali word meaning "cloth." A woman, on the other hand, would keep the rectangle of cloth in its original form, tying one corner in a knot over her right shoulder and wrapping the rest of the material around her torso. This was called *guuntina*. A longer version, called *saddexqayd*, was made from up to twenty yards (eighteen meters) of cloth wrapped around the body multiple times and secured with a belt of handmade rope. Although some ensembles were made of plaid or striped cloth, especially for leaders or ritual events, much of it was simply undyed white cotton called *merikani* ("American" cloth, reflecting one typical source in the late 1800s).

Body modifications were also very common and depended a great deal on gender, age, and social rank. Women used henna, for example, to dye the tips of their fingers and create designs on their hands, especially for occasions such as weddings. Men used it to change the color of their hair and beards (a practice considered *sunna*, something advocated by the Prophet Mohammed). Frankincense was often gathered for trade, but local women chewed the resin as a breath freshener and dissolved it in water as a form of laundry detergent. Women also burned frankincense and stood over the smoke to change the scent of their bodies and clothing. Unlike many groups in other parts of Africa, Somalis did not practice scarification; instead, hairstyles were used to mark gender and status. A young girl, for example, could expect to have her hair shaved in patterns. As she grew older and her hair grew longer, it would be styled in hundreds of tiny braids; this signified that she was old enough to be married. After her wedding, a woman would pull her hair back in two bundles at the nape of her neck, covering her hair with a black or indigo-blue headwrap called a *shash*. This was not hijab worn for religious purposes, but an item of dress that symbolized her elevated status in the community as a married adult woman. A young boy would also have his hair shaved. As he grew older, he would shape it into elaborate hairstyles using clay, camel butter, and a wooden comb. To keep his hair from being flattened or tangled at night, he would sleep on a wooden headrest called a *barkin*. This also had a practical function: It was thought to keep the user from entering a deep sleep—alert to any danger such as an ambush or a lion attacking the herds.

Amulets and jewelry were also an important part of Somali dress during the nineteenth and early twentieth centuries. For nomads—who faced dangers such as poisonous snakes, scorpions, drought, raids, and injuries—it was common for both men and women to wear some kind of amulet, usually a packet of

Dirac (dress) and *gorgorad* (petticoat) worn in twentieth-century Somalia with a *garbasaar* (shoulder cloth). In this case, the garments are thought to match from a Somali perspective but were made in different countries (India and Japan) and have different designs. The *garbasaar* has a gold and grey floral pattern, the *dirac* is a printed tie-dye, and the *gorgorad* is finished on the bottom with a fancy band of red and white lace. Private Collection. Photograph by Heather Marie Akou.

leather containing a verse from the Qur'an or a magical substance. These were made by the Yebir, a subclan of the Saab, who combined elements of Islamic and pre-Islamic rituals. A young child might wear an amulet with no additional clothing; women, on the other hand, often kept amulets hidden beneath their clothing. These were highly personal objects meant to offer protection during events like childbirth. Men also wore hidden amulets, but another common style was a rectangular packet strung on a thick band of leather worn closely around the neck (called *hardas*). Some men also carried or wore a strand of Islamic prayer beads (*tusbah*), which were used to recite the ninety-nine names of Allah or as "worry beads" (something to finger during times of boredom or stress). For women, jewelry also served as a portable bank account. In many cases, brides were given jewelry as part of their dowry; this might include precious materials such as carnelian, silver beads from the Arabian Peninsula decorated with filigree and granulation, glass beads from Venice and Bohemia, chunks of amber from the Baltic Sea, copal from South Asia, and coral beads from the Mediterranean (all obtained through trade). This jewelry belonged to her; in difficult times, she could sell it at her own discretion. Women also made simple pieces of decorative jewelry for themselves out of readily available objects such as shells, stones, hooves, bones, and palm kernels.

In the cities, Arab-style dress was much more common. Scholars and judges—men in positions of power—wore turbans along with garments such as the *qamis* (an ankle-length tunic), *bisht* (cloak), and *sirwal* (loose-fitting trousers that taper in at the calves; *sirwal qamis* is an ensemble that pairs the two garments). Women who were descended from Arab and Persian settlers wore hijab, covering everything but their hands and face (and sometimes even their face with niqab). A *garbasaar*, or shoulder cloth, served as a covering for the upper body and could also be draped over the head. For a nomadic woman who needed to perform constant physical labor, this kind of garment would have been impractical. In the cities, men shaved their heads and wore a *kufi*, a close-fitting cap that symbolizes devotion to God. Wearing a dagger was acceptable (a practice that Somalis and Arabs had in common), but elaborate hairstyles were left to the nomads.

INFLUENCE OF COLONIZATION

Although Somalis had been trading with the outside world for centuries, in the 1800s, the pace of trade dramatically increased. This was fueled in part by the Arab slave trade, but also to a great degree by the invention of the steamship, opening of the Suez Canal, European exploration, and eventually the colonization of present-day Somalia by Italy and Great Britain. In the north, trade was regulated by geography; nomads needed to feed their camels and sheep in the rich interior grasslands of present-day Ethiopia, but the coastal towns offered opportunities to sell products such as leather, livestock, frankincense, tortoiseshell, gum arabic, and ostrich feathers. Because of this, Somalis traveled between the interior and the coast on a regular basis. Ivory was also a sought-after commodity; because Somalis controlled all caravan trade in that region, they were the ones who profited by transporting it from the interior to the coastal towns. In southern Somali territory, there was also a history of using slaves from present-day Ethiopia as weavers, herdsmen, domestic servants, and concubines. During the Arab slave trade, which peaked in the mid-1800s, towns along the Benadir coast like Mogadishu and Brava served as transit centers for slaves coming from Central Africa, paying taxes to the Sultan of Oman. Although the British navy ended this trade in the 1890s, slavery continued on plantations where Somalis grew commodities such as orchella weed (a dye stuff), sesame seeds, and cotton for sale to the European market. Explorers like Richard Burton, Georges Révoil, and Luigi Bricchetti were keenly interested in these commercial activities.

It was probably during this time period that a very large and unique piece of jewelry known as an *audullis* became part of the dress for Somali women. The central feature of this necklace is a silver, crescent-shaped pendant that covers most of the chest. Along its base, the pendant has a row of tiny silver bells and sometimes a *xersi* (*hirz* in Arabic, meaning a silver or gold cylinder or box designed to hold a verse from the Qur'an; this is a common feature on silver jewelry from Yemen and Oman). Along the top of the pendant, three or four silver diamond-shaped elements conceal where the chain is attached; to make the necklace even more valuable, the chain would be strung with large beads of silver, glass, and chunks of coral or amber. The exact origin of the audullis is somewhat of a mystery. Allessandra Antinori has argued that it came from India; the crescent-shaped pendant is similar to (albeit larger than) a style of jewelry worn in Afghanistan. The silver beads, on the other hand, are more typical of work done by Jewish artisans on the Arabian Peninsula. In any event, the audullis is unique in terms of its sheer size as well as the fact that in the Horn of Africa it was worn only by Somali women (whereas the shash, for example, was also a common item of dress for Oromo and Afar nomads). In his travelogue, *First Footsteps in East Africa*, Richard Burton commented that the audullis was an especially "elaborate affair" and that "every matron who can afford it possesses at least one of these ornaments."

As the British navy curtailed the Arab slave trade in the late 1800s, power along the coast shifted from the sultan of Oman to the imperial governments of Europe. In 1889, the southern half of present-day Somalia was declared to be Italian Somaliland; in 1891, the northern half became British Somaliland. In the Berlin Treaty of 1897, all remaining parts of Somali territory were divided between Ethiopia, France (present-day Djibouti), and Great Britain (present-day Kenya). Compared to many other parts of Africa, European colonization was brief (just sixty years) and fairly restricted; unlike South Africa, for example, Somalis were not forced to live in "homelands," and, in many cases, nomadic life was allowed to continue.

At the same time, the end of the slave trade left tens of thousands of freed slaves from Central Africa stranded in Somali territory. This, along with the beginning of European colonization, led to changes in how Somalis viewed themselves as a group of people. In the British colonies of East Africa, for example, access to hospitals, housing, jobs, public education, and the court system was affected by one's classification as European, Asian, or African. Although Somalis were obviously native-born, some campaigned for non-native (Asian) status. Centuries of intermarriage with Arab and Persian settlers had given many Somalis a more Asian than African appearance. Compared to the freed slaves, who were derisively called *tiin jareer* ("hard hair"), Somalis had "soft hair" that could easily be braided or combed into elaborate shapes. Writing at the beginning of the Colonial period, Ralph Drake-Brockman observed that "the Somali is a great dandy, and is always admired by and is the envy of his friends if he possesses a well-kept chevelure [hairstyle]." Reading hair as a marker of age, gender, and status was already well established in Somali culture, but colonization fostered new meanings. During fascist rule in Italian Somaliland, the descendents of slaves were among the

first people conscripted into forced labor, so having "soft hair" was more than just a matter of personal vanity.

European explorers and colonial officials also brought new styles of dress such as boots, button-down shirts, neckties, walking sticks, and helmets. In British and Italian Somaliland, men who had direct experience with Europeans (for example, as hunting guides) did sometimes experiment with these garments. Harald Swayne's book *Seventeen Trips through Somaliland* includes a picture of Swayne with his Somali companions. In the front row, two men were dressed like Swayne in button-down shirts and trousers (minus the pith helmet and glasses). In the back row, each man was dressed in a wrapped garment (maro) but holding a rifle instead of a dagger or spear, as might be expected for a nomad. (Interestingly, two of them also had shields, which would have been unnecessary with the rifles). For women, however, European-style dress seems to have been off limits until after World War II. Somali women did not have as many opportunities to interact with Europeans (even if they had, most European explorers and colonial officials were men). In many cases, women were also viewed as safeguards against European influence, serving as guardians of their families and cultural traditions.

Postcard of Somali traders from the early 1900s. The man on the left wears an Islamic-style tunic and trousers (*sirwal*) along with a nomadic-style wrapper (*maro*) draped around his upper torso. He has on combat boots and carries a walking stick. The man on the right wears combat boots, turban, long tunic (*qamis*), and what appears to be a vest. He also carries a walking stick. Courtesy of Heather Marie Akou.

During the Colonial period, Islam and Islamic dress also became more important in Somali culture—not just in urban areas, but for nomads and freed slaves as well. As colonization disrupted the existing economic and political structures, many Somalis turned to Islam for guidance. Sufism (Islamic mysticism) became very popular, and sheikhs (scholars who led the Sufi brotherhoods) took advantage of leniency from the colonial governments to build new settlements complete with schools and mosques. In Italian Somaliland, members of the brotherhoods were even allowed to be judged by Islamic courts instead of the colonial court system. Ex-slaves and lower-class Somalis were especially attracted to these settlements, which offered some measure of peace and stability in very uncertain times.

In addition, faster and more reliable transportation made it possible for Somalis to foster increasing connections with the Islamic world. This was largely (but not intentionally) made possible by the British government, which built a network of steamship lines to connect its colonies in Egypt, East Africa, India, and the Arabian Peninsula. This created new opportunities for Somalis to make the pilgrimage to Mecca; study at universities in Europe, Egypt, and the Middle East; and serve as laborers on British ships. By the early 1900s, some sailors had married British women and established a small expatriate community in London.

Between these travelers, word of resistance to colonization in the form of *Mahdism* in the Sudan and *Wahabbism* in present-day Saudi Arabia spread quickly. In the early years of colonial rule, Mohammed Abdulle Hassan—who led an armed resistance against the British at the turn of the century and was nicknamed the "Mad Mullah"—was in his early thirties and made the hajj (pilgrimage) to Mecca. For three years, he stayed there as a student, learning primarily from a Sudanese scholar. This profoundly shaped his view of Islam and how it could be used to unite Somalis against colonization. Sheik-Abdi reports that when he returned to British Somaliland, Hassan's goal was to revive "the religious spirit in his people" by urging Somalis to reject what he saw as "excessive materialism and consumerism" expressed through practices such as "wearing infidel clothing, sporting foreign hair styles, walking like an unbeliever, or exhibiting outlandish manners of any sort." Considering that Somalis had been reaping the benefits of trade with outsiders for hundreds of years, Hassan's message was not entirely welcome. Within a few years, however, he had convinced more than six thousand men to join his militia. Uniforms for Hassan's "dervishes" were very similar to clothing worn by Mahdist rebels in Sudan, consisting of a wrapper (maro), prayer beads, and a white turban. For nomadic men, the turban was a new garment, called *imamad* after the word for an educated person who leads communal prayers (*imam*). Often, it was not worn as a head covering but simply draped over one shoulder.

Hassan's rebellion did not lead to any significant changes in the political structure of Somali territory; however, colonization was not destined to last for long. After World War II, the two halves of present-day Somalia (British and Italian Somaliland) were handed over to the newly formed United Nations to administer as a protectorate—no longer under colonial authority but not recognized as an independent nation. Instead of returning to their own devastated countries, thousands of British and Italian expatriates decided to stay in East Africa. To support their families, many turned to entrepreneurship, opening cafés and fashionable boutiques. Increasingly, expatriates in Somali territory were also joined by nomads attracted to the opportunities of urban life and by young, educated men and women looking for professional jobs. This represented a major shift in Somali society away from nomadic life and caravan trade to the acceptance of urbanization and Westernization.

THE NATION OF SOMALIA

From 1969 to 1990, the population of Somalia's new capital, Mogadishu, went from less than half a million to more than two million people. Although the country was recognized as an independent nation in 1960, European influence continued and in some cases even accelerated as Somalis took over positions in the new government. Foreign corporations were given rights to exploit Somalia's natural resources such as oil and uranium. In 1963, the national airline of Italy, Alitalia, partnered with the newly formed Somali Airlines; like their Italian counterparts, Somali stewardesses wore uniforms with jackets, skirts, and pillbox hats. Uniforms for the new police force and military were modeled after European dress: trousers, button-down shirts, belts, helmets, and combat boots (one exception was the border patrol, where soldiers were allowed to wear turbans). Somali women serving as secretaries and nurses in the auxiliary divisions wore miniskirts, calf-length socks, jackets, gloves, berets, and even neckties.

By the 1960s, European fashions were becoming much more popular and accepted as part of everyday dress, especially for men working as laborers. The back of the five-shilin banknote, for example, shows three men picking bananas while wearing shorts and sleeveless shirts—a practical choice for the climate and conditions but definitely a departure from nomadic or Arab-style garments. Men (and sometimes women) employed in the urban centers as doctors, lawyers, teachers, and politicians also adopted European fashions. While the first African head of state to address the United Nations, Kwame Nkrumah, wore kente cloth as his national dress, Somali delegates wore three-piece suits. Perhaps due to this more "civilized" image, in the 1960s, Somalia was awarded more foreign aid per capita than any other country in Africa. Much of the money, however, was diverted into the hands of an increasing number of bureaucrats, who used it to build lavish villas, send their grown children to universities, and purchase fashionable clothing and cars from Europe. For many citizens who did not benefit from the change in authority, European fashions were not viewed as a sign of progress but of extreme corruption.

Alternatives to this style of dress included Islamic dress, existing garments made from new fabrics, and a popular new style of clothing for women called *dirac* (dress) and *gorgorad* (petticoat). By the 1940s, many women in rural areas were still wearing wrapped dresses, but updating them with new fabrics—no longer just white merikani cloth, but colorful floral and geometric patterns imported from India and Japan. In southern Somalia, women also wore *kanga* prints (colorful two-yard [about two-meter] lengths of fabric) with slogans written in Swahili and sometimes Somali; much of the cloth came from India or other parts of East Africa.

Matching sets of dirac and gorgorad were also made from imported cloth, but the style of the garments was completely different. The dirac, a loose-fitting dress, was made by taking a long rectangle of cloth (at least three meters [about three yards]), folding it in half, cutting a small hole at the folded edge for the neckline, and sewing the selvages of the cloth together until there were just two small openings for the arms. The gorgorad was also presewn and designed to be worn under the dirac as a petticoat. Although a short wrapper (*futa*) could be worn instead, the gorgorad was more practical because wrappers often slip and need readjustment (which would be difficult with a long dress). Even for women who did not adopt European-style dress, aesthetics of the body were being questioned. Should a long, lean body be viewed as a symbol of youth (a Western value) or a sign of physical deprivation and hardship (a common understanding in many parts of Africa)? In contrast to the guuntina, which bares the shoulders and emphasizes the hips (giving a look of maturity and well-being), the dirac and gorgorad give the wearer an elongated silhouette.

As the result of a coup in 1969, Siad Barre (commander-in-chief of the army) became the president. For at least the first few years, the new government had popular support. In 1972, Barre commissioned scholars to create a written language for Somali (which had always been an oral language) and started an ambitious public literacy campaign. To gain control over the country's natural resources and economy, the government also seized many banks, factories, and other businesses from European expatriates.

Viewing himself as a modern-day Mohammed Abdulle Hassan, Barre commissioned a large equestrian statue in Hassan's honor. Currency and stamps were often designed with imagery that honored nomadic life as the foundation of Somalia's national culture. A series of stamps from the mid-1970s shows Hassan riding horses and leading his troops into battle, complete with spears, turbans, prayer beads, and wrapped clothing. Even though nomadic-style dress was rapidly disappearing by the 1970s (especially for men), another series of eight stamps contained images of men and women of various ages wearing guuntina, saddexqayd, and maro. An elderly man was depicted with a wrapped garment covering his torso and shoulders and a strand of prayer beads in his hand. One of the women, dressed in a guuntina, was shown holding a basket made to carry milk. Until the advent of aluminum and plastic vessels, basket making was a vital skill for nomadic women. The front of the one-thousand-shilin banknote also shows two women in wrapped garments weaving baskets by hand.

In 1976—in the middle of the Cold War—Somalia became a one-party socialist state. As Barre's popularity slipped, military symbolism became more and more prominent. Barre was always photographed in his military uniform and required all public buildings to display his portrait. He also created a new militia called Guulwadayaal (Pioneers of the Revolution) to spy on citizens suspected of disloyalty to the government. Because members wore distinctive green fatigues, they quickly became known to ordinary Somalis as the "green dogs," a derisive term that could land a person in jail if overheard by a member of the militia. In 1977, Somalia declared war on Ethiopia to take control over the Ogaden (an area largely populated by Somalis). Although the war ended a year later with the army's retreat, it severely destabilized the country's economic and political climate.

As tensions grew, another possibility—not Westernization, but also not socialism or a military dictatorship—started to emerge. In 1974, Somalia joined the League of Arab States. Although Somalis are not Arabs and Arabic had never been the primary language of Somalia, the Horn of Africa has been connected to the Islamic world for centuries—even longer than

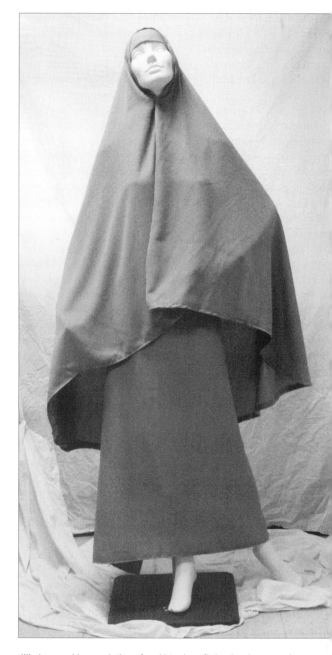

Jilbab ensemble, consisting of a skirt, close-fitting headwrap, and a second head covering that frames the face and drapes down over the torso. In the 1970s, this kind of Islamic dress was accepted by Somali women for the first time. Prior to that, the only women who veiled themselves were the descendants of Arab or Persian settlers. Private collection. Photograph by Heather Marie Akou.

North Africa. Membership in the Arab League gave thousands of young men and women opportunities to attend Islamic universities in Egypt and the Middle East and to travel back and forth as migrant laborers. This large-scale exchange was made possible by the discovery of oil in Iran, Saudi Arabia, and the United Arab Emirates and the increasing wealth and prominence of OPEC countries. To meet the demands of these rapidly growing economies, Muslims from all over the world were hired to teach classes, run banks, construct buildings, and serve as domestic workers. Somali men working alongside migrant laborers from Indonesia and Malaysia learned to wear a saronglike garment that Somalis called *macawis*. This offered a middle ground between wearing pants (a Western influence) and traditional nomadic wrappers.

Around the time of the Iranian Revolution in 1979, hijab or veiling also became part of ordinary dress for some Somali women. This was a new and controversial step; until the 1970s, the only women in the Horn of Africa who wore hijab were the descendants of Arab and Persian settlers—not nomads and certainly not the majority of Somalis. The miniskirt—a Western fashion—was increasingly viewed as something that only prostitutes would wear. To counter this influence, a special division of the police called the *buona costuma* ("good costume") was created to monitor nightclubs and bars. Although expatriates were exempt, a Somali woman caught wearing a miniskirt could be arrested and put in jail.

Inspired by the Iranian Revolution, some Somalis ultimately advocated for a new national government based on Islamic law. Barre saw this as a threat to his power and ordered the execution of ten prominent Islamic religious leaders. Barred from demonstrating in public or even going on strike—which was punishable by death—Islamist groups like Al-Itixaad al-Islamiya had to look for indirect methods of creating change. In addition to establishing Qur'anic schools and orphanages, Al-Itixaad insisted that women should wear more modest clothing (in line with Islamic law, covering everything but the hands and face) and that men and women should sit separately at both religious and secular gatherings. In the early 1900s, Mohammed Abdulle Hassan's "dervishes" had worn distinctive uniforms with turbans and prayer beads as a sign of their resistance to colonization, but this only affected dress for men. In the 1970s and 1980s, however, women's dress became the primary visual symbol of resistance to Siad Barre's regime—an effective tool, since individuals could claim that they were simply fulfilling their religious duties.

New styles of dress for Somali women included the *shuka*, an ankle-length, button-down overcoat, worn with a *khimar*, a triangular head scarf pinned under the chin so it covers the hair, neck, and upper chest. In Turkey and Palestine, where the shuka originated, this garment is called *jilbab*. For Somalis, however, the word *jilbab* refers to a three-piece set of garments that resembles the habit of Catholic nuns—a skirt, a scarf that covers the hair, and a second head covering that drapes down over the chest (sometimes down to the waist or even knees). In a few cases, Somali women also adopted niqab, a veil that covers the face. Although the niqab is common in Saudi Arabia, where veiling is compulsory, this very conservative head covering has always been controversial in Somalia. In general, Islamic dress is designed not to reveal the shape of the body. To be even more modest, the shuka, khimar, jilbab, and niqab are all made from solid-colored opaque fabrics—a significant contrast to both the guuntina and dirac, which reveal bare arms and are made from colorful fabrics with prints or stripes.

THE BREAKDOWN OF SOMALI SOCIETY

By the late 1970s, Somalia was in crisis. As the Horn of Africa went through a severe drought, the country's economic and political atmosphere continued to decline. Serious opposition started to form, and, in 1988, a group of armed rebels captured several cities in northern Somalia. The government retaliated by sending troops to destroy wells; burn grazing areas; rape women; and randomly detain, torture, and execute men. In 1990, rebels entered the capital city of Mogadishu; Barre's army retreated and the national government collapsed. As of 2007, the United Nations estimates that there are nearly 400,000 Somali refugees living in other parts of the world. Some are still in refugee camps in Kenya, but others have settled in the Middle East or in the West (including the United Kingdom, Italy, the United States, Australia, Canada, The Netherlands, and Finland).

For many of these refugees, dress has taken on new dimensions. At first, many were simply grateful to survive with the clothes on their backs. Early photographs taken in the refugee camps (see, for example, Fazal Sheikh's *A Camel for the Son*) show women in simple wrapped garments and children wearing ragged T-shirts. Many were haunted by their memories of fleeing from Somalia—seeing bodies in the streets, being forced to watch as neighbors and family members were raped and killed, or even being assaulted themselves. Clothing was just a way to cover the body; there was no time or money to play with fashion or think about the symbolic meaning of dress.

As time wore on, however, dress became an integral part of many struggles to find new ways of being in the world. Some Somalis saw the loss of their country as a sign from God; Islamic dress became a visible symbol of renewed commitment to Islam, whether for personal devotion or in hopes of restoring order to Somalia by reuniting Somalis through Islam. In northern Somalia, this goal became somewhat of a reality when the unrecognized state of Somaliland adopted Islamic law. In the more chaotic southern regions, efforts have been made to establish a similar government. Instead of skirts and blouses, many girls attending school in the early twenty-first century wear the jilbab as a uniform. For Somalis who resettled in the Middle East, Islamic dress is simply what ordinary people wear. In a country like Saudi Arabia, women are required to wear hijab regardless of their ethnic or religious background.

In countries like the United States and the United Kingdom, however—where Somalis and Muslims are in the minority—Islamic dress stands out. For many men, wearing pants and button-down shirts is a simple choice; for decades, this kind of clothing was common for men in Somalia, so why change? Considering that many are also struggling with employment barriers (language, race, religious duties, and lack of education and credentials), dress is at least one area where Somalis can look and behave like everyone else. For women, on the other hand, this is a more complicated issue. In Somalia, Western-style dress for women was never really accepted and, in some cases (e.g., the miniskirt), openly condemned. Any other style of dress—whether the jilbab, or shuka and khimar, or dirac and gorgorad—can be read as a symbol of a woman's commitment to Somali culture. Conversely, adopting mainstream fashion (especially something like pants or a sleeveless top) could signal a lack of commitment to her culture and family. At least in the West, a good Somali woman wears "Somali" dress. In this context, the guuntina has taken on new meanings. Although it has nearly disappeared as part of everyday dress, it is now worn as a kind of local costume for cultural events such as dances and ethnic festivals. Brides also wear the guuntina in red, gold, and black stripes. Even though the cloth is now imported from India, this kind of clothing has become a precious reminder of home—a sign of hope that Somali refugees and their families will someday return to a more peaceful Somalia.

Snapshot: Cultural Crosscurrents in Somalia

Over a century of exploration and colonization, Somalis were exposed to European forms of dress such as boots, button-down shirts, neckties, walking sticks, and helmets. In some cases, men with direct contacts to Europeans (such as traders, hunting guides, and appointed officials) were able to experiment with these new garments. Postcards of Somali traders from the early 1900s show men wearing a mixture of European, Islamic, and nomadic garments. These included Islamic-style tunics and trousers (sirwal), nomadic wrappers (maro) draped around the upper torso, and turbans, combined with combat boots and a walking sticks.

At the same time, some Europeans also experimented with the styles of dress they encountered in Somali territory. Abolitionist and explorer Luigi Bricchetti photographed an "Italian sheikh" wearing a turban, qamis, and cloak (bisht) with a Somali dagger (*bilawi*) tucked in at his waist. In the late nineteenth and early twentieth centuries, this kind of portraiture was a common souvenir for travelers and colonial officials. Richard Burton's translations of the *Kama Sutra* and *1,001 Tales of the Arabian Nights*, as well as his travelogue on northern Somali territory, *First Footsteps in East Africa*, were very popular in Europe. Photographs like this were fuel for the colonial imagination.

The guuntina has existed as part of Somali women's dress since at least the mid-1800s, when the pace of trade with Europe and the Middle East dramatically increased and nomads started to replace their leather clothing with imported cotton cloth. This dress is made by knotting a piece of fabric at least three meters (about three yards) long at the right shoulder, wrapping it around the torso (pleating as necessary to take up any slack), and then tucking the edge in at the waistline. At first, this was just a common, practical garment for nomadic women—comfortable in extremely hot weather but adjustable to fit different body sizes and various daily activities (sleeping, cooking, hauling water, and so on). By the time Somalia gained its independence in 1960, however, the guuntina was becoming a romantic symbol of nomadic life and the new national culture. Guuntinas might be colorful—luscious red, green, yellow, and blue dresses with equally colorful backgrounds. Even as the guuntina started to disappear from ordinary dress in the 1970s, it was gaining new value as a type of folk dress or national costume. In the 1990s, as tens of thousands of Somalis settled in other countries as refugees, the guuntina became another kind of symbol—something from home that could be treasured and worn for weddings, folk dances, and other cultural events. In most cases, however, the guuntina of the early twenty-first century does not come from Somalia (which has continued to be plagued by civil war); instead, the cloth is made in India specifically for export to Somalis around the world.

References and Further Reading

Abdullahi, Mohamed Diriye. *Culture and Customs of Somalia*. Westport, CT: Greenwood Press, 2001.

Akou, Heather Marie. "Nationalism without a Nation: Understanding the Dress of Somali Women in Minnesota." In *Fashioning Africa: Power and the Politics of Dress*, edited by Jean Allman, 77–97. Bloomington: Indiana University Press, 2004.

Akou, Heather Marie. "Macrocultures, Migration, and Somali Malls: A Social History of Somali Dress and Aesthetics." Ph.D. dissertation, University of Minnesota, 2005.

Ali, Ismail Mohamed. *Beautiful Somalia*. Paris: Somali Ministry of Information and National Guidance, 1971.

Antinori, Alessandra Cardelli. "Ornamenti della Persona." In *Aspetti dell'Espressione Artistica in Somalia*, edited by Annarita Pulielli, 91–109. Rome: Bagatto Libri, 1988.

Barnes, Virginia Lee, and Janice Boddy. *Aman: The Story of a Somali Girl*. New York: Vintage, 1994.

Berns McGown, Rima. *Muslims in the Diaspora: The Somali Communities of London and Toronto*. Toronto: University of Toronto Press, 1999.

Besteman, Catherine. *Unraveling Somalia: Race, Violence and the Legacy of Slavery*. Philadelphia: University of Pennsylvania Press, 1999.

Bricchetti, Luigi Robecchi. *Somalia e Benadir: Viaggio di Esplorazione nell'Africa Orientale*. Milan: Societa Editrice La Poligrafica, 1902.

Burton, Richard F. *First Footsteps in East Africa or, An Exploration of Harar*. London: Tylston and Edwards, 1856. Reprint Mineola, NY: Dover Publications, 1987.

Drake-Brockman, Ralph E. *British Somaliland*. London: Hurst & Blackett, 1912.

Hersi, Ali Abdirahman. "The Arab Factor in Somali History: The Origins and the Development of Arab Enterprise and Cultural Influences in the Somali Peninsula." Ph.D. dissertation, University of California, Los Angeles, 1977.

Loughran, Katheryne S., John L. Loughran, John William Johnson, and Said Sheikh Samatar. *Somalia in Word and Image*. Washington, DC: Foundation for Cross Cultural Understanding, 1986.

Révoil, Georges. *Voyage aux Pays Çomalis: Dix Mois a la Côte Orientale d'Afrique* [Voyage to Somali Land: Six Months on the East Coast of Africa]. Paris: Challamel et Cie, Éditeurs, 1889.

Sheik-Abdi, Abdi. *Divine Madness: Mohammed Abdulle Hassan (1856–1920)*. London: Zed Books, 1993.

Sheikh, Fazal. *A Camel for the Son*. Winterthur, Switzerland: Volkart Foundation, 2001.

Swayne, Harald G.C. *Seventeen Trips through Somaliland and a Visit to Abyssinia*. 3rd ed. London: Rowland Ward, 1899, 1903.

Heather Marie Akou

See also Ethiopia; Snapshot: Djibouti; Kenya.

Snapshot: Djibouti

The country of Djibouti, formerly French Somaliland and, in 1967, the French Territory of the Afars and Issas, achieved independence in 1977. It has around half a million inhabitants. Djibouti is made up of the Issa, a Somali clan, and the Afar, who also reside in Ethiopia. Both groups are Muslim and speak Cushitic tongues, but they have a history of civil conflict. The Djiboutian landscape of coastal plains and central plateau is mostly desert and very dry. Because this climate makes agricultural production difficult, most food is imported from Djibouti's ports that link the Gulf of Aden and the Red Sea to the Arabian Peninsula. Two-thirds of the population live in the capital city and wear Muslim dress or Western-style secondhand clothing. City women wear a variety of casual dress styles, including a floor-length tunic of bright print with a slip skirt beneath, a T-shirt with a long full skirt, or a tailored dress. In public, each dress is worn with a shawl of colorful rayon or gauze covering the head, shoulders, and arms. Afar and Issa men wear urban Muslim dress, including long white shirts with trousers beneath and a turban or Muslim cap, called *taqiyah*. In addition, men wear a cloth wrap at the waist on which they belt a curved knife in a decorated sheath of wood or horn.

Those who reside outside the city engage in nomadic pastoralism and are visually distinct in their attire. The Afar (also referred to as Danakil) live in the Danakil Desert located in Ethiopia, Eritrea, and Djibouti. In Djibouti, they make up one-third of the population. As nomadic herders of goats, sheep, cattle, and camels, they travel a great deal and have only one or two changes of clothes. Everyday dress for men includes a plaid cloth wrapper, usually imported from Indonesia, a secondhand T-shirt or button-down shirt, jacket, and heavy shawl around the shoulders. They protect their feet with sandals made from camel, giraffe, or, more rarely, hippopotamus hide. While working, all men carry sticks that are incorporated into dances and mock fights. Traditional dress for men, worn today on ritual occasions, includes a white shirt and white skirt with an embroidered hem and a sheathed knife at the waist front. Both pastoral men and women tie a cloth around their waist called *sanafil*, undyed for men and colorful for women. At marriage, women adopt a black cotton head scarf called

63. - DJIBOUTI. - La Coiffure d'une élégante

J.-G. Mody, photographe

Two married Somali women comb and plait the hair of an unmarried girl (center) in Djibouti, 1915. Unmarried girls wore their hair uncovered in long thin braids anchored to their scalp. The girl at center is in a striped waistcloth, while the woman on the left wears the typical contemporary dress of upper-class Issa and the oldest woman on the right wears a traditional white cotton dress. Both hairdressers wear a headscarf to indicate their status as married Muslim women with a silver bracelet (left), beaded armbands (left), and beaded necklaces. Photograph by J.-G. Mody. EEPA Postcard Collection, FT-5-2. Eliot Elisofon Photographic Archives, National Museum of African Art, Smithsonian Institution.

shash or *mushal*. Unmarried girls, who do not need to cover their head, may wear their hair in long thin braids anchored to the scalp with beaded jewelry, including the recent seed-bead necklaces made by the girls themselves.

Afar dress of the ruling classes, particularly the Sultanate clan, consists of sumptuous textiles. Traditionally, women wore red and black striped cotton cloth embroidered with gold thread and secured at the shoulder with a wealth of imported gold jewelry from the Middle East. Today, the upper classes select rayon, silk, or taffeta for their dresses. The hair of women of the upper class is braided from part to shoulder, and three projecting pieces of colored reed or wood are fastened to the back of the headpiece, creating a distinctive silhouette. Gold headpieces with gold embellishments that dangle freely on the forehead and loop down under the eyes and gold chains that connect the headpiece to the wearer's nosering complement the gold necklaces of large round hollow balls, dangling earrings, bracelets, and rings. During special social occasions, all Djiboutian women who can afford it wear imported gold in abundance.

Peri M. Klemm

See also Somalia.

Sudan

- Women's Dress
- Men's Dress
- Body Alterations
- Cosmetics
- Jewelry
- Hair Treatments

The public dress of five women in Sennar, central Sudan, 2001. The *tob*, a decorative length of fine, often brightly colored cloth, roughly thirty feet (nine meters) in length, is wrapped in a highly standardized manner around the body, with a fold to cover the head but leaving the face largely uncovered. Photograph by Susan Kenyon.

The Republic of the Sudan, popularly known as Sudan, is the largest country in Africa, encompassing nearly a million square miles (two and a half million square kilometers), with great diversity of both environment and population. Its landscapes range from desert in the north to rain forests in the south, and, although rainfall varies, temperatures are uniformly high—a significant factor in considering what people there wear. Sudan's approximately thirty million people include more than fifty ethnic groups, with differing identities reflected in their appearance. Another significant factor is the history of outside invasion and conquest, which has left various imprints on the way people of the region dress.

Linguistically, there is also great diversity. Today, the local or colloquial form of Arabic is the language of government, schools, and of most northern Sudanese, which includes those identified as Arab (almost 50 percent of the total population). Sudan is also divided by religion. Almost 70 percent (mainly in the north) are Muslim; 5 to 10 percent (mainly in the south) identify as Christian; and a large number follow so-called traditional beliefs. Among Muslims, tolerant Sufi beliefs and practices remain widespread, although in recent years a more orthodox form of political Islam has gained ascendancy, reinforcing tensions between north and south, Muslims and non-Muslims, so-called Arabs and Black Africans (a division that grossly oversimplifies both similarities and differences). A consequence of the rise of Islamism has been greater uniformity, even in non-Muslim communities, of styles of dress associated with the larger Muslim world. These are reinforced today through popular global culture, particularly television and cinema.

Sudan is also one of the poorest countries in the world. In the last two centuries, it has experienced successive colonial occupation by Ottomans/Egyptians (1821–1882) and by joint Egyptian-British Condominium rule (1898–1956), civil wars, political instability, famines, and drought, which have all adversely affected the region's economy and security. Sudan remains predominantly rural, but, since it became independent in 1956, there has been rapid expansion of the towns. Conditions of poverty affect not just the quality of dress but also the choice of styles.

As in the past, Sudanese fashions continue to reflect the diverse and broad cultural and political links this part of the world has long experienced. Historically, the main trade route with Sudan has followed the Nile River, with influence from the north—especially Egypt—being particularly strong. Reports from early European travelers in the region, such as Swiss explorer

J.L. Burckhardt, who visited northern Sudan in 1814, describe the fabrics and jewelry brought there from Egypt. Trade from the East, from India and beyond, has also been significant for several centuries at least, as Burckhardt also noted, bringing silks, perfumes (especially sandalwood), and fine jewelry to the Red Sea coast, from where it was traded inland. In recent years, this has intensified as cheaply produced fabrics, dresses, and robes are imported alongside luxurious silks and perfumes from South and East Asia. Influences from other parts of Africa are also old; travelers from West Africa, for example, en route to Mecca, brought beads and cosmetics to trade. In recent years, as Sudan positions itself within the African Union, these pan-African links continue to be reflected in both men's and women's dress. Influence from Europe came relatively recently, but, during the Condominium period, European fashions were adopted to a limited degree and continue to influence, for example, work clothes (including school uniforms) and underwear. European fashions are familiar throughout Sudan because of the global media, but many contemporary styles are rejected as inconsistent with Islamic values. Finally, increasing contact with the Arabian Peninsula, through employment and pilgrimage, has raised awareness of the fashions as well as the ideologies of the rest of the Muslim world.

It is surprising, therefore, given this diversity, that there are forms of dress and appearance that are distinctive to the region and signify a distinctive Sudanese identity, both internally and internationally. This has been due in part to government pressure, as with the recent promotion of Islamist dress for women; but there is also an attachment to certain items of Sudanese attire that cannot be detached from larger issues of nationalism. Alongside this unity, however, remains a range of differing ethnic attire that serve as visible reminders of the great diversity of peoples in Sudan.

WOMEN'S DRESS

In northern and central Sudan, the basic items of dress were consolidated in the nineteenth century under Ottoman rule, when concern for Islamic identity and women's modesty became an issue. Before that time, both men and women in northern Sudan wore a simple wraparound skirt that covered the lower body. The Bavarian missionary Theodore Krump visited the town of Sennar in 1701 and described a piece of cotton cloth "twenty-four arms long and two spans wide." The Arabs, in their language, called this *tob dammur*. Both men's and women's garments were made of this cloth, which was first folded and then wrapped twice about the hips and tucked in the end at the side, covering the lower part of the body.

This was the earliest known mention of the *tob* (also transliterated as *thawb*; it rhymes with *robe*), which has become *the* distinguishing item of clothing for women throughout the country. There was no full description specifically of women's dress, however, before the early nineteenth century, when Burckhardt, in *Travels in Nubia*, left an account of the women from Berber town:

> The women of Berber, even those of the highest rank, always go unveiled, and young girls are often seen without any covering whatever, except a girdle of short leathern tassels about their waists.... The women of the higher classes, and the most elegant of the public women, throw over their skirts white cloaks with red linings of Egyptian manufacture.

The girdle of short leather tassels, known by its Arabic name *al-rahatt*, was formerly worn by young unmarried girls in much of Sudan and has a long history. Traditionally, it was made at home by women from the skins of animals killed for domestic consumption and left its natural color. Although it is no longer seen in everyday life, it is still important in northern Sudanese wedding ritual. Toward the end of the marriage ceremony, the bride appears wearing over her wedding dress an ornamental rahatt dyed red or purple. In a ritual known simply as "cutting the

rahatt" (*gutt al-rahatt*), the groom ceremonially cuts and removes the girdle, thus marking the end of her girlhood.

During the Mahdiyya (1885–1898), the nationalist period that followed Ottoman rule, women were ordered by government decree to veil their faces in public. Traditionally, the only Sudanese women to wear face veils were the Rushaida in eastern Sudan. D. El-Tayib has suggested that it was at this time that the tob, an old Arabic word meaning both cloth and clothes, was adopted by women in the rising middle classes to wrap their whole body, including the head. Drawing the tob tightly across the face, they then tucked in by the cheek the remaining yard or two (about one or two meters) hanging heavily over the head, a style known as the *bullama*, which remained the correct outdoor style of wearing the tob until the 1950s and is still sometimes seen. In the last century, the tob has been adopted by women throughout the country, regardless of religion and (to some extent) class when they are in public. A decorative length of fine, often brightly colored cloth nine meters (ten yards) in length, it is wrapped in a highly standardized manner around the body, with a fold to cover the head but leaving the face largely uncovered. Wearing the tob—a strikingly beautiful garment but awkward to carry— has modified the movements of Sudanese women, who walk and act in it with particular style and grace. The tob covers up the body discretely and flatters all shapes and sizes. It is also a social leveler. Although to the discriminating eye it is evident whether a woman is wearing an expensive or cheap tob, the outward appearance is similar. However, wearing the tob makes it impossible to carry out any form of physical labor, and it is thus a statement about class and status as well as grace.

Women's fashions in Sudan traditionally have referred to fashions in the tob: the color, type of material, sort of decoration, embroidery, place of origin, and so on. Tobs are grouped by name, depending sometimes on the type of fabric, sometimes on the use to which the tob is put. For example, less-expensive *al-jiraan* are neighborhood tobs worn just for visiting locally. Sometimes the names refer to the place of origin or an event that occurred when the tob first appeared. El-Tayib has gathered some of the more common and descriptive terms.

There are a range of other wraps similar to the tob but different in size, fabric, and purpose. The *farda* is smaller and lighter in weight and historically preceded the tob; it was probably what Burckhardt saw in Berber. It is considered suitable for older women or for use around the house. Generally, it is found in plainer colors and fabrics, though characterized by its colored borders. Very common is the black farda with red and yellow borders, traditionally made in the town of Shendi.

The *tarha* is a much shorter length of cloth worn as a head covering, especially by young girls who are not used to wearing the tob. It is commonly used by school girls, although adult Muslim women might also use a tarha for praying. The *firka*, on the other hand, is a larger and more specialized length of cloth in strong colors and special fabrics. There are two distinct firka: the first, *firka garmasis*, is used on the three major ritual occasions for women: circumcision, marriage, and childbirth. It is made of silk or silk-like fabric and is woven in brightly colored stripes and checks of red, orange, and purple across a yellow warp. The second type is *firka um-safiyan*; it is heavier and coarser, made from black, purple, and dark red cotton, and is used as a night garment or wrap.

Underneath these garments women wear simple dresses, *fustan*, often locally made and designed for hot weather: sleeveless,

Formal attire for men in el Obeid, northern Sudan, 2001. Men wear the *jalabiya*, a full-length white shirt with long flowing sleeves. The head is covered by a turban (*'imma*), a length of fine white cloth that is wrapped round the head in a distinctive fashion. In cooler weather a striped cotton shawl is draped over one shoulder. Photograph by Simon J. Kenyon.

ow necked, and loose fitting. Shoes are equally important in Sudan's heat. In the past, flat shoes with pointed toes and heels, made from local hides, were a symbol of elegance. In the early twenty-first century, the preferred footwear is the simple *shibshib*, flat sandals with a single strap between the toes, the name representing the scraping sound they make as they drag along the ground.

With the most recent rise of political Islam in Sudan since the 1980s, Muslim women have been under increasing pressure (both political and cultural) to conform to the fashions of the greater Muslim world. Long skirts, loose long-sleeved overshirts, and head coverings have become commonplace in professional settings, sometimes worn underneath the tob. It is also increasingly common to see Muslim women wearing black or dark colored *abayah*, overcoats, traded from elsewhere in the Middle East or sent as gifts by expatriate relatives.

Southern women in urban areas also now wear the tob in public. In rural areas, women work unencumbered by any wrap, simply wearing the traditional wraparound skirt and sometimes a head scarf to protect their head. In cattle-herding societies such as the Nuer or Dinka, people traditionally wore very little clothing. Women wore simple goatskin skirts or aprons and, in public, might tie a blanket over one shoulder. Today, they usually prefer colorful cotton dresses.

MEN'S DRESS

So-called traditional men's dress in northern Sudan reflects the dominant Muslim religion and was also consolidated during the nineteenth century. Similar to that found elsewhere in the Middle East, it is well suited to the extremely hot weather Sudan experiences for much of the year. In the past, clothes were handmade by local tailors from local cotton, a fabric renowned worldwide for its softness and density. This has now become too expensive for local consumption, and machine-made fabrics are commonplace as well as mass-produced clothes imported cheaply from Asia.

The main men's robe is the *jalabiya*, a full-length white or pastel-colored shirt that slips over the head with long flowing sleeves. The Sudanese jalabiya is distinctive for its rounded neckline, although styles from elsewhere in the Muslim world are also common. The jalabiya is worn with several accessories. The *tagia*, a snug-fitting skullcap, is still sometimes handmade, crocheted employing fine white threads. West African immigrants introduced orange caps, and cheap imports have now become available from South Asia that modify the original Sudanese design into a more rigid pillbox form. For formal occasions, this is covered with the turban, *'imma*, a length of fine white cloth that is bound around the head in distinctive fashion. In cooler weather, a striped shawl also made from fine cotton is draped over one shoulder.

Nomadic herders sometimes wear sleeveless waistcoats over their jalabiya, and, in recent years, religious men are copying the fashion from elsewhere in the Muslim world of wearing a dark robe or overcoat over the jalabiya. Fundamentalist Muslims, known locally as *Ansar Sunna*, are recognizable by their shorter midcalf jalabiya as well as beards covering their whole chin, which contrast with the other clean-shaven Sudanese. The preferred footwear with this outfit remains handmade leather slippers, dyed orange in the process of softening. Less formal than the jalabiya are the *raggi* and *sirwal*, baggy pants and long, loose overshirt made from a lighter fabric than the jalabiya. These are often preferred around the house and are the working clothes of many rural laborers, being cool and loose in the hot sun.

Among the best known items of Sudanese dress in Western collections are the jalabiya captured as trophies of war during the Anglo-Egyptian reconquest of Khartoum in 1898. The Muslim holy man Mohammed Ahmed, called the Mahdi or "chosen one," had taken the capital in 1885 leading a force wearing distinctive tunics with rectangular appliqué in brown, blue, and red. The officers wore elegant garments sewn from new cloth with often symmetrical appliqué, but the rank and file were clad in tattered tunics with irregular patchwork reflecting a religious fervor born from a life of poverty. Some of the Mahdist forces were protected by chain mail body and head armor, the latter adorned with amulets, and carried multibladed throwing knives with Qur'anic inscriptions.

Men from many southern tribes wore minimal dress in everyday life. Cattle-herding Nuer or Dinka traditionally went naked or wore a simple loincloth. In some tribes, social differentiation was made through dress. Shilluk men were traditionally naked, but the chief (*reth*) and his noblemen could wear a wrap that was knotted like a toga on one shoulder. Certain Nuer prophets, known as "leopard-skin chiefs," wore a leopard-skin cape as their traditional mark of office, a form of royal insignia formerly worn also by the Funj and Shygiya kings. In tribes with a strong military ethos, like the Shilluk, all young men served as warriors, and their public dress included narrow hide shields, clubs, spears, drums, and leopard skins.

Today, most workmen prefer loose-fitting cotton shirts worn with shorts or long pants. Office workers also wear Western-style dress to work, long trousers and shirt; in recent years, pan-African-style safari suits of matching pants and loose shirt have become popular, particularly with middle-class southerners.

BODY ALTERATIONS

Throughout Sudan, appearance is enhanced by a range of decorative traditions. Body alterations were formerly commonplace, although many traditional forms of scarification are disappearing. Facial scarifications were widespread; they were a means of ethnic affiliation as well as an expression of particular styles of body aesthetics. In northern Sudan, many older people bear facial scars (*shelukh*) that were routinely adopted a generation ago. Today, shelukh are found only in some rural areas, although other types of facial markings—small cuts near eyes or mouth—are still performed for medicinal purposes to relieve eye or teeth complaints.

In southern Sudan, Nilotic peoples focused attention on the forehead, which was adorned with distinguishing marks as part of initiation rites for adolescents. Among the Shilluk, both boys and girls ritually had a series of pearl-sized lacerations inscribed across the forehead from ear to ear just above the eyebrows. This was done with a small fishing hook, which was pried under the skin and then severed by a sharp knife. Dinka, Nuer, and Atot had equally distinctive patterns, though these were inscribed only on young men's heads. To become a Nuer man, for example, in an excruciating ritual in which he had to show courage and indifference to the pain, a youth had a series of six horizontal lines known as *gar* cut across the entire forehead, right down to the bone.

In the past, lower-lip dyeing or tattooing (*shelufa*) was performed for young northern women at the time of their wedding and was considered the true mark of a married woman. This is not found among peoples of the south or the Nuba Mountains, where, some employ lip piercings decorated with metal ornaments instead. Others, notably the Nilotic tribes, remove the four lower incisors of both boys and girls around the age of eight and force outward their upper teeth to enhance their smiles. Nuba boys traditionally had two of their lower incisors broken off, supposedly for medical reasons. Kakwa girls had their front teeth filed, also for reasons of hygiene.

Many southern peoples, including the Ingessana Hills, Nuba Mountains, and Nilotic tribes, cover the upper torso with decorative scars in dotted designs. Although most people know how to do this, the artistry of tribal experts is especially admired. Nuba personal art, which combined body and facial scarification with colored paints and oils, results in some of the most visibly elaborate, complex, and unusual designs. Such art has been described by James C. Faris as expressing the "celebration of the strong and healthy body."

Circumcision remains widespread in Muslim Sudan for boys and excision for girls. It is generally performed on young children between the ages of six and ten, with much celebration. There are signs that the practice of female excision is slowly being dropped, or at least modified. Campaigns to eliminate this have gone on for almost a century, but only since the mid-1990s has it become less common, at least in urban areas. In the past, two forms of female excision were found: *pharaonic*, which involved infibulation (stitching) as well as cutting (excision) of the genital area, and *sunni*, which involved only cutting. In recent years, a modified form involving less alteration of the girl's genitals has become widespread. Non-Muslim tribes, for the most part, do not engage in these practices.

COSMETICS

Cosmetics have long been very important throughout Sudan. In the north, kohl (antimony) is widely used for both decoration and health, in the past by both men and women (as noted by Burckhardt) though today only by women, who line their eyes carefully with commercially or locally produced kohl. This seems to be an ancient tradition, and artistically elaborated kohl sticks and tubes have been excavated from the Meroitic Period (100 B.C.E. to 300 C.E.). Perfumes are particularly distinctive and include *dilka*, a strongly scented paste used for skin massage by both men and women; *karkar*, a highly perfumed oil used by women to anoint the body at night; *khumra*, a strongly scented women's deodorant applied generously to the body and head; and *bikhur*, perfumed incense wood, variously used as a room freshener, medication, and smoke bath. Adult women, particularly in the north, enjoy taking smoke baths in the privacy of the home, both as a means of relaxation and also for the much-admired tanned hue and scent it gives to their skin. *Henna*, a reddish brown dye obtained from the leaf of the plant *Lawsonia alba*, is also widely employed to stain women's hands and feet in elaborate patterns and is applied with scented oils such as sandalwood or surat wood. The *hanana*, the henna painter, has become an important local beautician, although many women continue to do henna themselves or for their friends. Men traditionally only have henna applied to their hand for their wedding ceremony. These traditional cosmetics are now available for sale alongside imported lipsticks, nail varnishes, and bottled foreign scents.

A Sudanese woman with facial scarification (*shelukh*), between 1890 and 1923. Library of Congress Prints and Photographs Division, LC-USZ62-88177.

JEWELRY

Jewelry is popular throughout the country, although again, there are distinctions between north and south. Shell bracelets have been recovered from archaeological sites dating from as early as 3400 to 3000 B.C.E. and necklaces with faience, shell, and carnelian beads from 2000 to 1600 B.C.E. Elaborate strings of beads in a variety of materials were relatively common grave goods during the Meroitic Period, as were iron and bronze finger rings with low-relief bezels with a variety of representational motifs. Gold jewelry has been valued since Meroitic times, a symbol of the woman's (and her family's) wealth. In the twenty-first century, young girls continue to have their ears pierced as young babies and plugged with gold studs. Wealthy adult women like to wear an armful of gold bangles as well as earrings and rings on several fingers, and imitation gold coins (especially British sovereigns) continue to be popular as rings or necklaces. The most elaborate display of gold is reserved for weddings, when the bride is loaned much of the family wealth and wears gold on her head and face as well as her body. This was part of the *jirtig*, a term used for the ritual ornaments reserved for the bride.

Beads are a popular form of decoration throughout Sudan—particularly black, white, and red colors. In the north, beads are largely imported, part of a very old trade. In the south, beads may be locally produced. Nuer women, for example, make white beads from broken ostrich eggshells, creating beautiful necklaces and waistbands. Ivory bracelets were worn on the wrist and upper arm by Nilotic men and women, though as ivory becomes scarce, bone, cowry shells, plastic, and glass ornaments have become more common. Armlets, breastplates, and bells were all used as bodily decoration. Some of the most spectacular forms of beadwork in East Africa are the so-called corsets worn by young men from wealthy Dinka families. From fifty to seventy strands of beads are secured in back and are stacked from the waist up covering most of the rib cage. Young women of marriageable age from prosperous families would wear comparable beaded yokes or bodices of up to eighty strands draped from the shoulders. Ivory finger rings, earrings, bracelets, armlets, and pectorals were worn by the wealthy of both sexes. Earrings are also popular in the south, with men as well as women, and multiple ear piercings are commonplace; sometimes the holes are stretched by progressively larger plugs. A popular Nuer fashion loops stiff black giraffe hairs through the piercings to make macramé-like decorations. Nuba girls spend long hours decorating their bodies with piercings through their nostrils and sometimes the entire rim of the ears, which are then decorated with red beads.

HAIR TREATMENTS

Many peoples in the Sudan remove all superfluous bodily hair. In the north, for example, women remove all their bodily hair except from the head, a depilation done with a sticky mixture of lime and sugar, used in combination with oils and smoke baths.

Hairstyles in Sudan vary. Northern women's hairstyle was traditionally based on braiding, but this now varies, reflecting global influences. The style and symbols of traditional Sudanese braids (mushat) differed from that found elsewhere in Africa. In mushat, the front of the hair, the masira, is parted and pulled forward. The rest of the head is plaited and called either kufat (large plaits), mahlab (the regular mushat), or simsim (the smallest plaits, often braided with silk, and used for the bridal hair style). This type of braiding was common from the mid-twentieth century, though it too had evolved from an earlier, less tightly plaited style that utilized a strong-smelling oil to prevent the hair from drying. Nowadays, many young Muslim women, particularly in the towns, cover their heads with a head scarf whenever they are in public, and this negates the need for the old elaborate braided hairstyles. Only older women continue to use mushat.

Many southern women, such as the Shilluk, shave their whole heads and cover them only when in Muslim areas or to protect their head from the sun. By contrast, Shilluk men enjoyed hair sculpture, especially in a flared helmet shape. Nuba peoples also like to shave their head but leave a slight growth of hair into which they can cut decorative patterns; these hairstyles they call manga.

References and Further Reading

Burckhardt, J. L. Travels in Nubia. 2nd ed. London: J. Murray, 1818.

El-Tayib, D. "Griselda Women's Dress in the Northern Sudan." In The Sudanese Woman, edited by Susan Kenyon, 40–66. London: Ithaca Press, 1987.

Faris, James C. Nuba Personal Art. Toronto: University of Toronto Press, 1972.

Gruenbaum, Ellen. "Nuer." In Worldmark Encyclopedia of Culture and Daily Life, edited by Timothy L. Gall. Vol. 1, 341–346. Florence, KY: Gale Group, 1997.

Gruenbaum, Ellen. The Female Circumcision Controversy: An Anthropological Perspective. Philadelphia: University of Pennsylvania Press, 2001.

Hochsfield, F. E., and Elizabeth Riefstaht, eds. Africa in Antiquity: The Arts of Ancient Nubia and the Sudan. 2 vols. Brooklyn, NY: Brooklyn Museum, 1978.

Hutchinson, Sharon. Nuer Dilemmas: Coping with Money, War and the State. Berkeley: University of California Press, 1996.

Kenyon, Susan, ed. The Sudanese Woman. London: Ithaca Press, 1987.

Kenyon, Susan M. Five Women of Sennar: Culture and Change in Central Sudan. 2nd ed. Long Grove, IL: Waveland Press, 2004.

Krump, Theodor. Hoher und fruchtbahrer Palm-Baum dess Heiligen Evangelii das ist: Tieff-eingepflantzter Glaubens-Lehr, in das Hertz dess Hohen Abyssiner Monarchen erwisen. Augsburg, Germany: In Verlegung G. Schlüter und M. Happach. Gedruckt bey J. Gruber, 1710.

Lesch, Ann. "Sudan." In Encyclopedia of the Modern Middle East and North Africa, edited by Philip Mattar et al., Vol. 4, 2098–2105. 2nd ed. Detroit, MI: Thomson Gale Publishers, 2004.

Lobban, Richard A. Jr. Historical Dictionary of Ancient and Medieval Nubia. Lanham, MD: Scarecrow Press, 2004.

O'Connor, David. Ancient Nubia: Egypt's Rival in Africa. Philadelphia: University Museum, University of Pennsylvania, 1993.

Picton, John, and John Mack. African Textiles. London: British Museum, 1979.

Spring, Christopher, and Julie Hudson. North African Textiles. London: British Museum, 1995.

Susan M. Kenyon

PART 9

East Africa

Madagascar

Madagascar is by far the largest of the islands lying off the coast of Africa, yet its traditions of dress and personal decoration are distinctively different from what is found even on adjacent parts of the continent. They also show considerable differentiation within the island itself. These two general characteristics can be related to Madagascar's particular history and its diversity of environments.

The island is vast: it is 587,000 square kilometers (227,000 square miles) in area and 1,600 kilometers (994 miles) in length, making it the fourth largest of the world's islands (after Greenland, New Guinea, and Borneo). It is located from twelve degrees south of the equator to just beyond the tropic of Capricorn (forty-three degrees south), which transects its southern belt, and it lies 400 kilometers (249 miles) off the continental coastline. Being oriented broadly north-to-south, it enjoys a rich variety of environments with hot arid semidesert in the south, tropical rain forests in the east, and temperate high plateau lands in the center. Clothing is adapted to extremes of both heat and, in the center of the island, cold—especially at night. Banana tree fiber, bark, hemp, and indigenous silk worms have all been exploited in making textiles, and, more recently, cotton and wool and Chinese silk have also been used. The island is renowned for its distinctive biodiversity, which, although there have been losses and predations, has largely survived due to a lack of population pressure. Even with recent rapid rises in population, the latest World Bank estimates (from 2007) give only 19.7 million people, distributed among the eighteen ethnic groups conventionally identified within the island. The largest ethnic groupings are the Merina and Betsileo in the central highlands, the Betsimisaraka along the eastern seaboard, the Sakalava in the west and northwest, and the Tandroy in the south.

Madagascar was occupied very late in human history. Although there are some traces of human activity from the third century B.C.E. and further evidence of people visiting the island from the early to mid-first millennium C.E., it is only from the eighth century that significant occupation began and several centuries after that before substantive and sustainable populations were established. The island lies at the southern end of the Indian Ocean wind and current system that links the East African littoral to the Arabian Gulf and to northwestern India. These early populations were probably culturally diverse, with Arab, Swahili, and Indonesian elements—all of which are still evident in the composition of the island's population today and in different styles of adornment. The language spoken with various dialects throughout Madagascar is Malagasy, which is also the generic name of the people as a whole; it is classed as Austronesian, with the nearest cognate languages so far analyzed being from the area

A portrait of the nineteenth-century governor of the coastal fort of Foule Points. He wears the hat, striped *lamba*, and jewelry of a high-ranking Merina aristocrat in central Madagascar. From the frontispiece to William Ellis, *History of Madagascar*, 1838. Courtesy of John Mack.

of Borneo. In addition to language and the physical appearance of some of the people, the material culture of the island also betrays this wider Indian Ocean background. For instance, *ikat* textiles reminiscent of those from Indonesia have been produced in living memory among groups of Sakalava on the west of the island, Indian imported textiles and dress have been important since at least the sixteenth century, and Swahili styles are still prominent in northwestern parts of the island. Direct evidence of continental African presence is more difficult to identify but was clearly significant in historical times, including people brought to the island by Malagasy slavers in the eighteenth century.

CLOTHING THE LIVING

The classic Malagasy dress consists of a long rectangular shawl typically worn round the shoulders and covering the upper body. This is known as a *lamba*, the primary word in the Malagasy vocabulary of dress. Other terms may refine its description—such as *lamba mena* (a burial cloth), *lamba akotyfahana* (an elaborately patterned colored textile) or *lamba hoany* (a modern printed cloth usually worn wrapped around the lower body); however, the basic reference is to an untailored rectangular wrapper that may be plain or patterned with warp stripes, in natural colors or dyed, and in any of the many fibers exploited by Malagasy weavers or imported from abroad. It is the basis of a series of sayings that emphasize its ubiquity: to be without a lamba is to have forgone the social world, to throw it off is a metaphor for madness, and to be unable to keep a lamba is to be unable to control your emotions. It is a mark of maturity to wear the lamba; children, by contrast, often go around naked. The dress style is so characteristic as to have national and nationalistic implications. Thus, although European styles of clothing began to be widely imitated in the nineteenth and into the twentieth centuries, this could be contextualized as Malagasy by the simple expedient of wearing a lamba over the shoulders. After the unpopular attempts at Westernization under the Merina ruler Radama II, which led to his assassination in 1863, the aristocracy (often referred to by the name Hova) and the populace at large in that part of the island all dressed ostentatiously in lamba. Furthermore, the anticolonial movement in Imerina in the late 1890s was known as the rising of the *mena lamba* (usually translated as "red shawls"), while a similar rebellion in the south of the island also adopted cloth imagery and was known as the *sadiavahe* (or the rising of the "loincloths of vines"). Although the everyday wearing of lamba is now largely restricted to rural areas and to occasions in towns such as church services, lamba may still be worn over Western-style suits by, for instance, government ministers or ambassadors, in which context it is a mark of postindependence Madagascar and national sovereignty. The lamba is mostly described in terms of it being a shawl, but in practice, it is a multifunctional piece of cloth, hooding the head in the cold, cradling a baby tightly to its mother's back, and acting as a blanket if required. In the highlands, a thin white scarf worn by women is known as a *lamba fitafy*.

Along the east coast, the area of the peoples known as the Betsimisaraka, the predominant fiber used in weaving (a female preoccupation, as in most of Madagascar) is raffia. This is produced in rectangular lengths usually with warp striping. Two garments are typically produced from these cloths. One is a wraparound tubular garment (*sadiaka*) that is worn by women around the waist or secured above the breasts. The other common type of raffia garment is a kind of smock for men tailored with openings for the arm and at the neck. This is known as an *akanjobe* (from *akanjo*, a shirt or blouse). It has been suggested that the term *raffia* entered the English language from the Malagasy *rofia*, *raofia*, or *raffia* through the practice of sewing up the slits in akanjobe and using them as sacks to export rice, cloves, and other products of the tropical eastern seaboard. If so, a complete reversal of this practice has taken place, because today, the plastic sacking used to *import* products (including nowadays lesser-quality rice) are often cut to create openings so they can be worn as smocks in agricultural work. Similar styles of dress, though often using retted bark fiber (*hafotra*), are found among other forest peoples slightly further inland, such as the Tanala and the Zafimaniry. Here also, even today, vests made of matting are still worn in some more remote parts of the forests where their water-resistant and robust qualities remain valued. Likewise in the southeast, matted tubular garments were once traditional wear.

Throughout Madagascar, a loincloth (*sikina*, *simbo*, or, sometimes, sadiaka) is used as underwear or, in the warm southern parts of the island among the Tandroy and the Bara, the sole garment. This is a length of cloth of similar dimensions to a scarf

that usually has a beaded panel at the end of colored plastic beads or silver. The decoration is usually geometric, but representations of the typical humped cattle of Madagascar are sometimes found along the length of the loincloth among the pastoralist peoples of the south. As worn, the cloth passes between the legs and around the waist so that the decorative panel hangs down at the front and likewise falls down to cover the back.

In terms of personal adornment, coiffure is everywhere a major concern. Hair is never long and unkempt unless the wearer is in a particular ritual state. A properly tressed coiffure, like the wearing of lamba, is part of the physical definition of someone whose exterior and interior condition is well attuned. Women's hair is always tightly plaited and either pulled back around the head (the style of the highlands) or arranged in a series of circles (as in parts of the south). Men's styles in the south, notably among the Bara, are similar to those of women, with tight circular tressing across the head. However, elsewhere hair is often worn short by men. Hats, usually locally made straw hats, are also familiar and are worn by both men and women. These range from the wide-brimmed hats of the highlands to conical hats with rolled brims among the Bara to squared bonnets among the peoples of the southeast, those of the Taimoro distinguished by a red blaze. The use of perfume is not well recorded in Madagascar, with the exception of the northwest, where, on the island of Nosy Be, the blossom of ylang-ylang from the *Cananga odorota* tree produces a heady scent. It is processed locally, but much is exported to France, where it is used in the Western perfume industry.

CEREMONIAL AND STATUS DRESS

A set of dynastic portraits of the various kings and queens of Imerina includes a retrospective picture of the founder of the Merina kingdom, Andrianampoinimerina (ruled from 1780 at the princedom of Ambohimanga and at Antananarivo, which became the capital of the kingdom and is the capital of the modern state of Madagascar, from 1795/1796 to 1810). The distinction between his attire and that of his successors is very marked. Andrianampoinimerina is pictured wearing a simple lamba or shawl over his shoulders and holding a spear. His successor, however, his son Radama I (ruled 1810 to 1828), is portrayed in a painting by André Coppalle toward the end of his reign in full Napoleonic military attire and carrying a sword. Indeed, at his death his grave goods were said to have included some eighty military uniforms accompanied by hats and feathers. In the interim, European travelers, missionaries, slave traders, and others had begun to make their way from the coast to the capital. From the French Radama had learned about the exploits of his near-contemporary Napoleon Bonaparte. Thereafter, European monarchic or imperial practice became the model of Merina painted (and eventually photographic) portraiture with successive queens and one further king, Radama II, all being portrayed in nineteenth-century royal attire. The queens also wore imported—usually French—jewelry, including crowns. This was kept in the palace complex (Rova) in Antananarivo until a disastrous fire destroyed much of the site in 1995. Only some of the royal wardrobe was salvaged, including a tiny pair of European leather shoes that belonged to Radama I.

In the same period, the Merina aristocratic class retained the distinctive attire of the upper echelons of the state. A painting dating to 1822 and reproduced in William Ellis's *History of*

Madagascar (1838) shows Rafaralahy, the Merina governor of Foule Point, a coastal fort on the island's east coast. He wears a multicolored silk lamba with a detailed pattern in its border. The use of silk is an indication of wealth and status, but it also represents the deployment of a sacred and pure substance. The term *andriamanitra* (literally, "perfumed lord," another word for God) is associated with royal paraphernalia, the ancestors, and with silk; the word for silk, *landy*, is also a popular child's name. Thus, silk wrappers were used on ceremonial occasions to dress participants, whether children at the first cutting of their hair, at circumcision (notably, by those officiating), at marriage where the bridal couple should always wear silk shawls, at the annual New Year celebration of the Royal Bath, and especially at funerals. Silk cloth was even used to strangle the modernizing King Radama II in 1863, an appropriate gesture to the ancestors whose lore Radama stood accused of impairing and a method of avoiding the spilling of royal blood.

The other prominent feature of Rafaralahy's attire is the use of distinctive jewelry. Around his waist is a large beaded boxlike ornament with domed silver tops and silver representations of crocodile teeth at the bottom. He also wears two similar ornaments on his chest and attached to the lower rim of his hat, which has representations of crocodile teeth around the lower edge. In addition to the silver ornaments of the aristocracy, versions in gold gilt are also known and were possibly the reserve of royalty. The use of crocodile teeth, whether in representation or the real thing, has powerful overtones. The crocodile is the only major predator on the island of Madagascar; thus, it acts uniquely to visualize powerful forces, with its teeth as the main material expression of this symbolizing role. Displayed on the body, it is a personal protective talisman (*ody*) and, as such, was worn by the Merina soldiery on military expeditions. Royal talismans (*sampy*)—like royal, aristocratic, or ritually significant persons—were similarly swathed in lengths of silk, which was regarded as their apparel. One case is recorded where cloth offered to a sampy is said to have rolled itself up and fitted itself into one of the compartments of the talisman. An equivalent practice of pulling actual crocodile teeth, or representing them, is also found in western Madagascar, where the Sakalava likewise wrap up royal sampy in cloth and use them to protect the community.

The wearing of silver jewelry—whether in the form of chains, coins, or images of cattle—was also a sign of the prosperity of the aristocracy. This was not just ostentation, however. The silver was derived from melted-down coins, usually Maria Theresa thalers that were imported into Madagascar in an attempt to create a trading currency, but initially were cut down into smaller pieces and used instead as weights. Complete coins were part of a sacred economy rather than a domestic one, for they would be given to headmen and to royalty in return for ancestral blessings, particularly at New Year ceremonies. Reformed into jewelry, therefore, they carried the consolation of the benediction of the lineage.

In the highlands also, the Betsileo, who weave a striped cloth known as *arindrano* that is traded widely particularly into southern Madagascar, also make a special silk cloth that is preserved in families and used only on rare occasions. This is a *lambabe* (or "great cloth"), a striped silk textile with a decorative border at the two warp ends. The textile is acquired at marriage, the groom supplying the silk and the bride's family the labor to weave it. Subsequently, a man may wear it carefully folded over his shoulder when representing the family on formal occasions, and it will be worn by any sons and daughters of the group when they, in their turn, become betrothed.

Photographs from the early years of the Colonial period show chiefs and rulers in several dispersed parts of the country in formal European military dress reminiscent of that used earlier in Imerina by Radama I. Among the Bara in the south and the Antankarana in the far north, for instance, these include white colonial-style attire with pith helmets, feathered admiral's hats complete with jackets furnished with fancy epaulettes and brass buttons.

Among the Sakalava in the west of the island, sustained external influence also led to rank and status being signaled by the acquisition of costly foreign dress, again usually silks, in the nineteenth century. These were mostly obtained from Arab, and more specifically Zanzibari, sources, who traded in particular with the Boina Sakalava at the ports along the northwestern coastline. The ultimate sources were Oman and India. A local tradition of weaving ikat cloth (*laimasaka*) seems to have been reserved for textiles used in ceremonial contexts to dress ritual space, as a form of mosquito netting, or, among local Muslims, as prayer mats. Clothing from early times seems to have depended largely on imports, and museum collections have very few examples of Sakalava clothing or cloth—presumably because it was judged less important, not having a local origin. Early descriptions already affirm that rank carried with it exclusive rights in the wearing of expensive imported silks. By the nineteenth century, there are descriptions of chiefs wearing red bonnets or large turbans, white tunics with multicolored belts holding curved knives, and with embroidered sandals. The characterization, supported by a number of extant photographs from the area, suggests a link to the ruling Omani dynasty, which, in 1837, moved its capital from Muscat to Zanzibar. Indeed, a wider influence in Madagascar is

A group of Antaimoro *katibo* (astrologers) wearing the red hats and Arabized dress of their profession. Ivato, southeastern Madagascar, 1980. Photograph by John Mack.

suggested by the accounts of missionaries returning to the Merina capital in the reign of Radama II in 1861 subsequent to a period of expulsion for fifteen years during the rule of Queen Ranavalona I. They found turbans and flowing colored garments to be much in evidence (even the royal prince wore an orange and green silk turban with a gold crescent in the center), suggesting an influence from the west and northwest otherwise undocumented by Europeans, who mostly entered Madagascar from the east coast port of Tamatave (modern Toamasina), often arriving from Europe by way of Mauritius.

Ritual specialists and those primarily involved in ritual events typically wear red prominently as part of their attire. The significance of red in Madagascar is also prominent in the context of burial. The associations of the color red are with ancestral vitality, mystical power, and political authority. White, by contrast, is linked with cooling, protection, and equanimity. Thus, in Imerina, for instance, the dress of those charged with circumcising boys consisted of a distinctive tall red felt hat, falling down at the back like a Western Santa Claus hat. Likewise, the *katibo*, or astrologers, among the Antaimoro in the southeast wear a distinctive red Ottoman-style hat. For ceremonial wear, however, they wear a red skullcap with white markings and an imported Betsileo striped cloth, while women wear a red cloth cap, red shirt, and striped textile secured around the upper body. *Ombiasy* (healer-diviners) are also usually separately identifiable, although their attire is not in any way uniform. One feature many share is the wearing of a necklace composed of beads and small lengths of wood. Their profession involves the dispensing of traditional medicines, many of which are derived from the unique flora of Madagascar (and many have been shown to have genuine pharmacological properties). These compounds are made from shavings taken from a necklace composed of sections of wood, perhaps mixed with water or rum, and with the indispensable ancestral invocation to ensure efficacy. Ombiasy (and, in the past, warriors) may also carry a beaded horn or a wooden carving in the form of a horn that is hung around the neck and often contains soil from ancestral graves, which offers powerful protection. People going on journeys may also carry small packets of such soil concealed in their dress.

Dress is also important in spirit possession ceremonies (*tromba*), which are an aspect of practices of healing. In the course of such events, spirit mediums attire themselves in styles appropriate to the possessing spirit, whose vehicle they become as the invasive personality takes up its human abode. Possessing tromba have their own distinctive and vigorous character; the dress adopted and their often aggressive gestures and behavior reflect this. Among some migrant groups in Sakalava country, for instance, possession by the spirits of boxers is familiar, and even possessed women will clench their fists and paint marks on their arms and hands. Among the Sakalava, royal possession is more commonly reported: Royalty live on by possessing commoners who go to live in the royal compound. However, the possessing spirits are more often of exotic origin. In southwestern Madagascar, possession by Merina royalty—notably, Andrianampoinimerina—from the central parts of the island is familiar, and, in some western seaports, possession by visiting sailors may be marked by adopting white sailors' uniforms. Europeans may be characterized by simpler expedients—for instance, the smoking of cigarettes or the wearing of sunglasses. African spirits may be characterized by a woman arranging her hair in a mass rather than the typical plaited coiffure of Malagasy women. In each case, the dress is matched by speech, which can be rapid and indistinct but with a mix of appropriate words—whether French, Kiswahili, or Arabic. The words need to be translated by an assistant.

CLOTHING THE DEAD

Clothing then is not just about the dress of the living—talismanic objects are also conceived of as dressed and are wrapped in textiles to clothe them. Likewise, the dead are also thought of as attired, and it is of fundamental importance to ensure that their wrappings are not neglected. Throughout Madagascar, the concept of the ancestors (*razana*) provides a fundamental underpinning for an understanding of life and its vicissitudes. Attention to the physical circumstances of the dead is a significant aspect of this. The best known example is the second-burial ceremonies in which the dead are reshrouded (*famadihana*), particularly associated with the peoples of the plateau, the Merina and the Betsileo. Reference to dress and clothing is a strong part of the ceremony. Not only do living participants dress up smartly for the event, but the decision to hold it, usually four or five years after someone has died, is generally triggered when one of the descendants has a dream in which a deceased relative complains of being cold and in need of rewrapping. Ancestors can be vengeful, and it is vital that the living ensure they are properly attired—not just that they are comfortable but also that their potential for cursing the living is limited by being literally contained in bundles of shrouds. Before the event, the cloths to be used are paraded before the large crowds of invitees who gather for the occasion; indeed, contact with the shroud is believed to increase human fertility. The event involves taking the deceased's remains from a communal tomb, rewrapping them in sometimes as many as fifty burial cloths, and binding them in a basketry mat before taking them in riotous and joyous procession around the tomb or sometimes around the nearby village. Usually when the tomb is opened to honor one individual, the opportunity is taken to rewrap a series of bodies.

The textiles used as burial shrouds are known as lamba mena and are typically made from indigenous silk, the most exploited of which belong to the species *Borocera madacascariensis*, which produces a thicker fiber than imported Chinese silk (*Bombyx mori*); Chinese silk is known in Malagasy as *landikely* (or "little silk") as opposed to the local silk, which is *landibe* ("big silk"). The name *lamba mena* translates literally as "red cloth." However, shrouds are not of necessity red in color; rather, red is a reference to their association with the empowered and empowering attributes of the ancestors. Many lamba mena, indeed, are plain and unpatterned, although individuals may specify to relatives the cloth that they want to be used for their own shrouds. In addition to rolling up the remains, various objects may be placed in association with the body. These are typically things that the deceased would have liked in life and can include items such as bottles of rum or local alcohol. A silver coin, the traditional offering in anticipation of receiving ancestral blessings, might be placed in the mouth of the skull. Radios have sometimes been incorporated, tuned to the deceased's favorite station.

The two days of the famadihana often include an open-air performance by a *hira gasy* troupe. These are families of musicians and singers who may be commissioned to perform at different kinds of events, often competitively. Their performances will contain ribald political comment. For famadihana, their style is more formal. Dress typically makes reference to late nineteenth-century European fashions with women wearing long gowns and men often wearing locally made red tunics and boater-style hats with black bands. Their instruments also make reference to military bands with large drums, trumpets, and sometimes violins. However, this is not straightforwardly an aping of colonial styles. The origins of the hira gasy would seem to lie rather in the traditions of the Merina royalty, who, from the early nineteenth century under Radama I, had adopted European dress and drilled their armies in a European manner. With the advent of French colonial rule in 1895 and the subsequent exile in 1897 of the then queen of the Merina (Ranovalona III) to Réunion and then Algiers, this came to an end. However, funerals—with their emphasis on the connection between the living and the blessings to be derived from the ancestors—became a focus of anticolonial, pro-restoration, politics.

Hira gasy harks back in its styles of dress to the nineteenth-century royalist tradition of Imerina. Indeed, at the performance, the family of the deceased in whose honor the event takes place is seated in the ancestral northeast corner of the performance space, the women with tightly tressed hair and wearing flowing gowns. Often their corporate identity as *zana-drazana* ("children of the ancestors") is expressed in the wearing of identical clothes (often suits) but always with an appropriate lamba draped over the shoulders. The tressing of hair is also significant. When a death first occurs, female relatives traditionally untress their hair as a mark of mourning. Second burial, however, implies the reincorporation of the dead into the world of the ancestors, something to be celebrated rather than grieved over. The content of the performance is strongly moralistic in tone and delivered in a sermonizing manner. It is as if the performers take the role of the ancestors issuing moral direction to the living. As performers (*mpira gasy*), however, the troupe will also incorporate other lighter and more contemporary elements from their repertoire, changing clothes as appropriate. A recent documentary film, *The Left-Handed Man of Madagascar*, follows a troupe in the famadihana season (May to October) and includes, among other performances, an acrobatic version of the music video that accompanied Michael Jackson's hit single "Thriller," with appropriate clothing copied from the video.

Second burial, in the sense of taking the body from the tomb and rewrapping it, is specific to the highlands. However, dressing the dead in some way and marking the end of mourning is common throughout Madagascar. Thus, in the south—for instance, among the Tandroy and Mahafaly—at death, the deceased are thoroughly wrapped, preferably in silk, and placed in a coffin. They are not buried immediately, but burial is still a double event because, although the body is not subsequently disturbed, several months later, the coffin is carefully and tightly bound in cloth with a large number of lamba mena carefully interwoven around the coffin in a plaited design before being buried.

For those in mourning, distinctive comportment is prescribed. For women, this includes untressing the hair, which stands out in an ungroomed mass, a marked contrast to the tight carefully combed and woven tresses that otherwise constitute traditional coiffure. In some places, hair may also be cut. Indeed, the name of one of the northern ethnic groups, the Tsumihety ("those who do not cut their hair"), comes from their refusal to show appropriate mourning practice at the death of a Sakalava sovereign. A special kind of cloth, *lamba maitso* (or "green cloth"—although, as with

Two Betsimisaraka *ombiasy* (diviner-healers) wearing raffia smocks, in a village near Mananara, eastern Madagascar, 1979. Photograph by John Mack.

so-called red shrouds, the color may not be strictly followed), is found in some areas. In effect, however, the wearing of white lamba involves the most usual color of mourning (rather than the black that is familiar in the Western world), and the contrast of its cooling associations with the energetic symbolic associations of the red cloth of the dead is evident. The practice is for those mourning to wrap their lamba in a distinctive manner around the body under the arms.

DRESS IN THE EARLY TWENTY-FIRST CENTURY

Today, European-style dress of shirts, trousers, skirts, T-shirts, and jeans is found throughout the island, particularly in urban areas. However, much of the wearing of such globalized clothing is given a distinctive Malagasy touch. Thus, an inexpensive, colorful, factory-produced cotton or rayon cloth, lamba hoany, is also used throughout Madagascar as clothing, as a wrapper to carry a baby on the back, or to carry belongings. Originally imported from India, they are now increasingly produced in Madagascar, notably by the firms Cotona and Sotima. In terms of design, they respond to strong local preferences. Typically, the body of the cloth is characterized by a repeat design, perhaps with a central medallion and image, and completed by a decorative border. Like the *khanga* of the Swahili coast of eastern Africa, lamba hoany also incorporate a short panel of text on the long border of the rectangular cloth. Malagasy is a language replete with proverbs, sayings, and ancestral invocations that, since the introduction of writing in the Roman script, have taken on the authority of astrological texts written in Arabic and the biblical texts introduced by the missionaries in the early decades of the nineteenth century.

Writing down or saying a proverb is not just an expression of a sentimental wish; it is also conceived as contributing to making something happen, as does an ancestral invocation.

Lamba hoany is worn in a number of ways by both men and women and shows considerable local variation. Thus, in some places, it may be tied as a short skirt; yet, among Sakalava women on the northwest of the island, cloth is draped over the head and is worn as a long skirt secured above the bosom so it completely covers the body in the manner of the older Islamized styles of attire in the region. It may be worn as a shawl, draped over shirts or trousers, or sewn at the ends to form a tubular skirt. However, the incorporation of texts with personal and local significance, together with the link to older styles of attire and methods of draping cloth, gives a distinctively Malagasy character to the usage of lamba hoany. This is most evident in contexts where common identity is expressed, such as anniversaries or particular ritual events and celebrations, some of which may be occasions for the production of special commemorative cloths. In the central highlands, the family hosting a hira gasy may all dress in the same color and pattern of lamba hoany, which acts as a marker of common identity.

Madagascar has a thriving contemporary fashion industry focused on an annual fashion review, Manja. In addition to producing clothing for urban Malagasy, a number of successful designers, such as Eric Raisina, have gone on to design for haute couture enterprises in Europe. Often their creations embrace both natural fibers and the distinctive striped patterning of locally produced Malagasy cloth, and their products include waistcoats, ties, and Western-style accessories. However, perhaps the most noticeable recent development has been a return to the wearing of lamba as a shawl, particularly among the Merina in the island's capital, where specialist outlets have begun to appear. Named designers have emerged: Mariana Andriamananantena, Nicole Rabetafika, and Suzanne Ramananantoandro among them. Their contemporary silk scarves and shawls inspired by the tradition of lamba akotyfahana are used on occasions such as weddings, when the bridal couple may drape a single cloth around their shoulders to symbolize their union.

Finally, this development may be contrasted with a slightly earlier venture that reproduces rather than innovates and whose market is largely outside Madagascar rather than local. This is the revival after nearly a century of the practice of producing full colored lamba akotyfahana with its complex patterning. This proved possible partly because the techniques had to some extent been retained through the production of patterned white lamba in Imerina and partly through the initiative of a British art historian and long-term resident in Madagascar, Simon Peers, and a group of weavers from the traditional weaving center at Arivonimamo to the west of the capital. Together, they formed the group Lamba SARL in 1989, which subsequently moved to an atelier near the queen's palace in Antananarivo, where they faithfully reproduce examples of the complex cloths from museum collections outside Madagascar and those formerly housed in the collection of the neighboring palace and largely destroyed in the fire of 1995. Exhibitions of their work have taken place in London, starting at the Museum of Mankind in 1994, and subsequently in the United States. In the past decade, their textiles have been acquired for museum collections in both Europe and the United States, and a number are also in private collections outside Madagascar. A similar attempt to revive traditional applied arts by a Frenchman, Pierre Heidmann, led to the display of silks at the Exposition Coloniale in Vincennes, France, in 1931, but his atelier subsequently closed. Lamba SARL has diversified and is now reproducing textile designs from south and southeastern Asia among other sources of inspiration.

References and Further Reading

Fee, Sarah. "Cloth in Motion, Madagascar's Textiles through History." In *Objects as Envoys: Cloth, Imagery and Diplomacy in Madagascar*, edited by Christine Mullen Kraemer and Sarah Fee, 32–93. Washington, DC: Smithsonian Institution Press, 2002.

Feeley-Harnik, Gillian. "Cloth and the Creation of Ancestors in Madagascar." In *Cloth and Human Experience*, edited by Annette B. Weiner and Jane Schneider, 73–126. Washington, DC: Smithsonian Institution Press, 1989.

Green, Rebecca. *Once Is Never Enough: Textiles, Ancestors, and Reburial in Highland Madagascar*. Bloomington: Indiana University Art Museum, 1998.

Green, Rebecca. "Lamba Hoany, Proverb Cloths from Madagascar." *African Arts* 36, no. 2 (2003): 30–43.

Kusimba, Chapurukha M., J. Claire Odland, and Bennet Bronson, eds. *Unwrapping the Textile Traditions of Madagascar*. Los Angeles: Fowler Museum Textile Series, University of California, 2004.

Mack, John. *Madagascar, Island of the Ancestors*. London: British Museum Publications, 1986.

Mack, John. *Malagasy Textiles*. Shire Ethnography Series, No. 14. Oxford, UK: Shire Publications, 1989.

Peers, Simon. "Weaving in Madagascar." In *The Art of African Textiles*, edited by John Picton, 46–47. San Francisco: Lund Humphries, 1995.

Picton, John, and John Mack. *African Textiles*. 2nd ed. London: British Museum Publications, 1989.

John Mack

Tanzania

There are more than one hundred twenty ethnic groups in modern-day Tanzania, which borders on eight other African countries: Burundi, Rwanda, Democratic Republic of Congo, Kenya, Uganda, Malawi, Mozambique, and Zambia. Originally, this East African region was inhabited by people who were related to southern Africa's San communities, but these early hunter-gatherers were gradually displaced by iron-using agriculturalists from the west and south and pastoralist Nilotes from the north. In coastal areas, Arab, Persian, and Chinese traders played an important role as early as the eighth century. They were subsequently joined by Indian traders before the Portuguese gained control of the entire coastline in 1506. Forced southward by indigenous coastal people in collaboration with the Oman Arabs, the Portuguese continued to conduct trade with communities in the southern regions of modern-day Tanzania, including the Yao. For a time, Yao porters traveled as far south as the Portuguese stronghold in present-day Mozambique to exchange ivory for beads and cloth. The Yao also cooperated closely with Arab slave traders, through whom they gained access to firearms, which gave them an advantage in their confrontations with neighboring groups such as the Ngoni and the Chewa.

Further north, Oman Arab influence remained intact well into the nineteenth century. There were almost four hundred Arab merchants on the island of Zanzibar by the mid-eighteenth century, and, as late as 1840, the Omani sultan Seyyid Said decided to move his capital to Zanzibar, the so-called spice island close to Dar es Salaam, which was first developed in 1865 and which eventually became Tanzania's coastal capital. Zanzibar's clove industry, which flourished after the introduction of this lucrative spice to the island in the early nineteenth century, was so labor intensive that it fueled a demand for slaves, many of whom were obtained further south from traders at Kilwa, who provided local communities with increasingly large quantities of cloth and beads in exchange for these captives.

Kilwa's regional importance first began in the thirteenth century, due partly to the fact that its off-shore location proved invaluable in providing protection against attacks from the mainland. Initially, its wealth was built on exchanging textiles, jewelry, porcelain, and spices from the East for gold and iron from Great Zimbabwe and other part of southern Africa, and ivory and slaves from mainland Tanzania. Sixteenth-century Portuguese records indicate that the traders at Kilwa, laden with commodities such as hoes, cloth, and beads, had by then extended their influence as far as the north end of Lake Malawi (formerly Lake Nyasa). By the early nineteenth century, other communities living in the interior of present-day Tanzania, such as the Nyamwezi, had also begun to develop trade links with the coast. Arab traders keen to capture this growing market for beads and imported cloth from the United States and India established Tabora, a settlement in the heart of Nyamwezi country, in 1852. By 1905, Indian merchants had set up shops throughout the region occupied by the Nyamwezi and their close neighbors, the Sukuma, exchanging cloth for groundnuts and animal products.

SKINS, BEADS, AND IMPORTED CLOTH

Early trade relations had a significant impact on the dress and different forms of adornment worn by communities living in present-day Tanzania. Yao chiefdoms in southern Tanzania and neighboring areas in present-day Malawi made richly patterned beaded girdles that were probably produced with the aid of looms. Beadwork garments and various other forms of adornment were also commonly used in rites of passage throughout Tanzania, notably among communities to the north, like the Barbeig, Iraqw, Maasai, and Mgubwe. Thus, for example, Maasai girls had their ears pierced before they underwent initiation, a practice that is still common to this day. Over a period of time, wads of rolled leaves (*engulaleti/engulale*) were pushed into the opening to stretch the hole. The lobes were then decorated with beaded strands, leather straps, or metal earrings.

In the past, women from these communities wore skin garments. Among the Mbugwe, these garments were decorated with circular beadwork patterns called *ntoto*. These skins were also decorated with *nyenje*, a loose fringe at the garment's end. Although commonly made from either sheep- or goatskin, they were sometimes sewn from the hides of antelope or zebra if the skins of domesticated animals were not available. Iraqiw women also wore garments made from animal skins. Their wedding skirts, which were pieced together from several skins, were richly decorated with glass beads, sinew thread, and metal bells. Although the practice of wearing garments like these has become increasingly uncommon, among the Barbeig, goatskin garments are worn to this day on special occasions associated with various rites of passage such as the initiation of young girls.

Elsewhere, the garments commonly worn during initiation rites were made from a variety of local materials such as bark cloth and leaves. Together with the rudimentarily fashioned fiber masks that were sometimes worn on these occasions, all initiation costumes were discarded before the initiates returned to their village homes. The still widespread tendency to burn garments worn during these initiation rites signals the break between childhood and adult status. The use of locally available natural materials in the production of these garments has survived even among groups such as the Yao, who still practice initiation despite the fact that they are self-declared Muslims who were converted through their long history of contact with Arab traders.

In most rural areas, the use of skin clothing was abandoned in the early twentieth century in response to the efforts of Christian missionaries to encourage people to wear "civilized" garments made from cloth. By 1885, five missionary societies were working in Tanzania. Although initially they focused their attention primarily on settlements of freed slaves, mission societies gradually began to build schools and churches in rural communities throughout Tanzania. By insisting that congregants and pupils wear European forms of dress, they played a major role in the gradual transformation of indigenous dress codes among large sections of the Tanzanian population.

Rural attitudes regarding skin garments were also influenced by the development of national game parks, which led to the introduction of punitive fines for poaching game. After the Arusha Declaration of 1967, in which Tanzania's first postcolonial president, Julius Nyrere, affirmed his commitment to game conservation, families living in the vicinity of game parks went so far as to bury heirloom cloaks and skirts made from wild animal skins for fear of being accused of illegal hunting. The introduction of hunting restrictions had the further effect of encouraging the use of copper and other metals for the production of various forms of adornment previously fashioned from the horns of giraffes or from ivory.

Earlier on, the growth of trade relations with coastal merchants had a similarly far-reaching impact on the use of skin and bark-cloth garments among communities like the Nyamwezi. Imported cloth supplied by the Arab traders who settled at Tabora in the mid-nineteenth century had become so common by the late nineteenth century that there is no evidence of the use of skin garments in photographs taken in the early twentieth century by German missionaries working in this area. Instead, both men and women wore draped and wrapped *kanga* and *vitenge*, some of which were undecorated, while others, worn mainly by women, were either striped or decorated with bold floral or geometric motifs.

Contact with Arab and Indian merchants also encouraged the adoption of *kanzu*, Arab-style long shifts, which became increasingly popular over the course of the twentieth century. Yet as late as the 1960s, relatively few men could afford to wear these shifts regularly. Together with fezzes, garments like these, therefore, tended to be reserved for dignitaries like chiefs. The importance some chiefs ascribed to these voluminous kanzus in signaling their status and authority is clearly evidenced by a photograph of the Nyamwezi chiefs of Kahama and Karitu taken at a public function in Kahama town in 1959. In many cases, dignitaries like these further underlined their wealth and status by draping additional pieces of cloth over the kanzu, which they tied across the shoulder of one of their arms.

RESISTANCE AND REVIVAL

The varied responses of Tanzania's rural communities to colonial—and postcolonial—rule is probably best illustrated by the example of the Maasai, who have repeatedly resisted the efforts of successive governments to abandon their cultural institutions, including long-established forms of dress and adornment. Over the course of the twentieth century, they lost much of their land to colonial farmers and to the creation of game reserves and were repeatedly pressured into supplying labor to the estate farms that gradually sprung up in northern Tanzania. As early as the 1920s, efforts were also made to convert them to Christianity, while in the 1960s, Tanzania's newly independent government tried to interfere in a number of their customs. Decrees were passed to prevent the Maasai from covering themselves with blankets during the daytime and from wearing cloth treated with red ochre

(*e'lukaria*). Maasai women were also informed that they had to abandon their leather garments, while young men were told to cut off their pigtails and to refrain from treating their hair with red ochre. Bus operators were directed not to accept passengers who failed to comply with these regulations. In 1978, Maasai dance groups were also prevented from performing at a national festival in Arusha because they had decorated themselves with red soil. There was no comparable harassment of participants from other communities who chose to wear customary forms of dress for the festival.

Following a nationwide outcry, the Tanzanian government eventually abandoned its attempts to curb what it characterized as the backward and unsanitary practices of the Maasai. To this day, therefore, young Maasai women continue publicly to display their beauty to male warriors (*morani*) when they are ready to take on the role of adult women. In preparation for these displays, which the Maasai use to proclaim their sense of moral superiority to communities that have failed to maintain their traditions, mothers clothe their daughters in special dresses (*engila*) and belts (*enalijanga*) made from the skins of domestic animals and decorated with beads of various colors. Girls also wear beaded necklaces, hair ribbons, and earrings similar to those once worn by their grandmothers to signify their social status and life accomplishments.

Despite negative attitudes to Maasai traditionalism in post-colonial Tanzania, President Nyrere also played an active role in

Maasai men wearing traditional red cloths, with their distinctive beads and hairstyles. Tanzania, 2002. Photograph by Lyle Owerko.

promoting indigenous values and non-Western forms of dress as part of his efforts to Africanize the country. Newspapers owned by the state were consequently furnished with a set of criteria regarding nationally acceptable dress codes, the use of cosmetics, and appropriate moral behavior. They were encouraged never to comment negatively on traditional makeup and body decorations—for example, henna and perfume made from natural materials—while people in public office, including politicians and television news readers, were encouraged to wear garments fashioned from locally produced cloth.

Partly in response to these postcolonial efforts to encourage Tanzanians to take pride in indigenous practices, many communities now celebrate local cultural traditions and have adopted local forms of dress on special occasions. Thus, for example, among the Sukuma, where there has been a growing interest in reviving traditions (*utamuduni*), increasing attention is being paid to clothing styles, the activities of chiefs and healers, and the role of artists and dancers in the community. But here, as elsewhere in Tanzania, a return to the past often goes hand in hand with a tendency to celebrate innovation and change, resulting in the production of richly inventive, hybrid garments. Famous throughout Tanzania for their creative dance styles, Sukuma dance groups fashion new costumes to compete in annual competitions that probably originated when cooperative farming groups first began to travel from farm to farm to assist one another in tilling the land. Initially, the songs associated with these cooperative groups were composed to underline the rhythmic activity of lifting and dropping their hoes. Today, cooperative groups like these still exist. By the mid-nineteenth century, Sukuma dancing had become competitive, leading to the formation of two dance societies, the Bagika and Bagalu.

Despite government efforts to suppress Maasai cultural practices, perhaps more than any other indigenous community, this group has benefited from the country's burgeoning postindependence tourist industry, which actively supports the ongoing production of Maasai beadwork and other forms of adornment through marketing strategies that seek to link the adventure of visiting game lodges in northern Tanzania with opportunities to study the Maasai and climb Mount Kilimanjaro. In recent years, Maasai beadwork and hairstyles have also become popular among Tanzanians living in urban areas, where these migrants now play an integral role in the local beauty industry. In Dar es Salaam and elsewhere, they find a ready clientele for their impromptu sidewalk hair salons and beaded jewelry, with styles adapted for urban tastes. As a result, the hair-plaiting business, which was previously dominated by women specialists, has gradually been cornered by migrant Maasai men, many of whom also work as night watchmen.

URBANIZATION

The emergence of densely populated settlements, which brought together people from different cultural backgrounds, played a major role in the gradual transformation of dress codes in modern-day Tanzania. This pattern of urbanization can be traced back to the pre-Colonial period, when communities first began to spring up around marketplaces and tariff collection points. But it was only in the early twentieth century, after manufacturing and other industries had been introduced to most parts of the country, that people began to flock to Tanzania's newly proclaimed towns and to already established urban centers like Dar es Salaam. Earning wages in the colonial economy, they used at least some of

their disposable income to purchase custom-made clothing from skilled seamstresses and tailors or to purchase ready-made garments similar to those worn in European cities. Urban communities consequently began to wear both cosmopolitan and ethnic forms of dress, with the result that styles became increasingly unstable and impermanent.

In the 1960s, the Tanzanian government banned some fashion trends, like the miniskirt and Afro hairstyles, which were first adopted after local newspapers published features on Angela Davis and other African American activists. Despite these state interventions, the shift toward greater cosmopolitanism became increasingly common in the 1970s, when wealthier Tanzanians began to spend their annual holidays in neighboring countries like Kenya and Uganda, where they were exposed to new values and ideas. By the 1980s, when Tanzania finally abandoned its efforts to curtail the importation of garments from the West, the practice of wearing international fashions had become increasingly popular, and the already growing trade in secondhand clothing began to dominate urban markets throughout the country.

In recent years, this importation of secondhand clothes and other materials, known as *mitumba*, has included not only dresses and skirts but also belts, underwear, brassieres, shoes, handbags, body sprays, shavers, and dryers, which have become increasingly popular in both urban centers and rural communities. In urban areas like Dar es Salaam, the spread of mitumba has been facilitated by waves of *machinga*, street vendors who carry imported items through the city, thus affording women the opportunity to buy unique garments. This interest in wearing one-off secondhand garments has fostered a growing conviction among Tanzanian women that they form part of a sophisticated international community of fashionable women. Simultaneously, mitumba has also encouraged wearers to develop a more local feeling of belonging through the equality that this consumption of secondhand fashion has afforded them.

EARLY TWENTY-FIRST-CENTURY DRESS STYLES

In keeping with the spirit of empowering women economically in terms of the Structural Adjustment Policies introduced in the late 1980s, the Tanzanian government has recently been providing funding for women to start small cooperative businesses. While this has enabled poorer women to set up independent food vending and other stalls, some wealthier, more educated entrepreneurs have used the opportunities afforded by these policies to open up hair salons and organize fashion shows that were officially sanctioned for the first time in 1986. The latter development was spearheaded by two designer firms, Farida along with Gwao and Baby Baruti, the latter owning boutiques in Dar es Salaam, where they sell clothing and perfumes imported from Paris, Germany, England, and the United States.

When these local designers first introduced fashion shows in Dar es Salaam, the government adopted a wait-and-see attitude. But once fashion models, viewed on TV by thousands of people, began to appear in one-piece swimsuits—incorrectly referred to as bikinis in Tanzania—there was such an outcry that the shows were briefly banned in 1990. Following intense lobbying from the organizers, who claimed that fashion shows enhanced the economic power of women, official attitudes quickly softened, however. In 1992, they were consequently reintroduced on condition that there would be no swimsuits on the catwalk. By then, they had become like beauty pageants, promoting both designer clothing and the glamorous models who wore their garments. The late twentieth-century transformation in the Tanzanian clothing industry can therefore be ascribed in part to the impact of beauty contests on this sector of the economy. First introduced in 1968 and initially restricted to urban centers, today these contests owe their widespread popularity, on the one hand, to Tanzania's consumption of global media images and, on the other, to the emergence and validation in the global fashion arena of black models such as Alek Wek, Iman, Naomi Campbell, and Oluchi Onweagba, the first winner of the M-Net Face of Africa competition, who secured contracts with Gap clothing and Ralph Lauren.

Complex contradictions have nevertheless accompanied the history of these contests. Opponents argue that they are questionable manifestations of the growing transnational fashion industry centered on the consumer values of industrialized nations. According to them, these contests ultimately serve the interests of the globalized entertainment industry, which promotes a very limited idea of culture in the international media. Defendants of Tanzania's beauty contests include some nongovernmental organizations and a number of women activists, who argue that they generally lead to lucrative employment opportunities and ultimately empower young women who are trying to negotiate life in a contemporary, cosmopolitan world.

The government has also come to accept that these beauty contests encourage economic growth. Because beauty contestants need clothes, cosmetics, and training, the competitions stimulate domestic investments in the textile industries and in pharmaceutical and cosmetics factories and open up employment opportunities in advertising and other industries. The establishment of local factories associated with the burgeoning cosmopolitan beauty industry has reduced the cost of importing clothing and other beauty products manufactured in foreign countries.

While Tanzania's increasingly cosmopolitan musical scene has had a similarly significant impact on the country's clothing industry, local genres, notably the *taarab* tradition, continue to exert a measure of influence among older, married women. In contrast to the shifting values reflected in contemporary popular musical genres, taarab musicians wear colorfully decorated long dresses influenced by Tanzania's coastal Islamic culture. At the same time, they constantly adapt and integrate new dress codes, thus affording a model of flexibility coupled with modesty that appeals to the large number of older women who remain ambivalent about embracing cosmopolitan forms of dress. Their openness to change, which is reflected in, for example, the facts that they never wear veils on stage and always appear in high-heeled, open shoes that afford opportunities to display painted toenails, is always balanced by the fact that they dress in voluminous, unrevealing garments.

CONCLUSION

It has become increasingly common for competing dress codes to exist side by side in contemporary Tanzania. Although some of these codes are restricted to particular social or economic groups, more commonly, people choose to wear different forms of clothing on different occasions. At official state functions and in some industries, people are either encouraged or required to wear garments made from locally manufactured vitenge—thereby projecting a very specific image of traditionalism and local pride, usually aimed at impressing foreign dignitaries and other visitors. But in their day-to-day lives, individuals and communities are free to choose from a variety of clothing styles, including international styles that have been adapted for local climatic conditions.

Whether the local textile industry will continue to capture a section of the market remains to be seen, however. Already transforming in an effort to accommodate the growing interest in cosmopolitan styles, since 2000, this industry has also been affected by the influx of commodities from South Africa, which spearheaded the emergence of downtown department stores and franchised fast food establishments in urban centers like Dar es Salaam. Albeit gradually, the demonstrable transformation of the urban landscape through this influx is shifting the balance in the Tanzanian clothing industry between local traders and transnational corporations. While the former continues to rely on the loyalty of its local customers, the latter are engaged in aggressive marketing strategies aimed at securing the support of the country's increasingly affluent middle class.

References and Further Reading

Abrahams, R. G. *The Political Organization of UnYamwezi*. Cambridge UK: Cambridge University Press, 1967.

Allman, J., ed. *Fashioning Africa: Power and the Politics of Dress*. Bloomington and Indianapolis: Indiana University Press, 2004.

Blom, Wilhelm. *Die Nyamwezi. Gesellschaft und Weltbilt*. Hamburg Germany: Friederichsen, De Gruyeter, 1933.

Cohen, C. B., et al., eds. *Beauty Queens on the Global Stage: Gender, Contests and Power*. London: Routledge, 1996.

Fair, L. "Remaking Fashion in the Paris of the Indian Ocean: Dress, Performance and the Cultural Construction of a Cosmopolitan Zanzibari Identity." In *Fashioning Africa: Power and the Politics of Dress*, edited by J. Allman, 13–30. Bloomington and Indianapolis: Indiana University Press, 2004.

Hodgson, D. L. *Once Intrepid Warriors: Gender, Ethnicity and the Cultural Politics of Maasai Development*. Indianapolis: Indiana University Press, 2004.

Ivanska, A. M. "Anti-Mini Militants Meet Modern Misses: Urban Style, Gender and the Politics of 'National Culture' in 1960s Dar es Salaam, Tanzania." In *Fashioning Africa: Power and the Politics of Dress*, edited by J. Allman, 104–124. Bloomington and Indianapolis: Indiana University Press, 2004.

Legum, C., and G. Mmari, eds. *Mwalimu: The Influence of Nyerere*. London: Africa World Press, 1995.

Lihamba, A. "The Role of Culture." In *Rethinking the Arusha Declaration*, edited by J. Hartman, Copenhagen: Centre for Development Research, 1991.

Roberts, A. D. "The Pre-colonial History of Tanzania." In *Self Reliant Tanzania*, edited by K. E. Svenden and M. Teisen, Dar es Salaam: Tanzania Publishing House Ltd, 1969.

Sandra Klopper and Rehema Nchimbi

See also: East Africa; Snapshot: Kanga; Kenya; Mozambique.

Snapshot: Kanga

A popular textile development of the late nineteenth century that spread relatively quickly to the hinterland of the East African coast is the *kanga* (also written as *khanga*), known and used by people from all walks of life—rich and poor, urban and rural, Muslims and Christians, and even lawyers, engineers, and doctors. Worn by men but most often by women, it serves as both a garment and as a nonverbal, often literate, means of communication. A kanga is a rectangular piece of cotton cloth approximately three feet by four and a half feet (about one meter by one and a half meters), fully bordered. It is commercially manufactured in an enormous variety of designs and colors and is sold in pairs (each pair is called a *doti*). The size of one kanga is usually described as equal to the span of outstretched arms, wide enough to cover an average person from neck to knee or from breast to toe.

Kanga designs have three parts. The first is the wide border on all sides called *pindo*. The border has an outer margin, usually black, and an inner double-bordered band with a plain, textured, or patterned background. The inner band frames the central part of the kanga and provides a clear distinction between the outer and inner sections. The border's colors usually match those in the second part, called *mji*, which is a central motif. This motif usually portrays an image such as a fruit, a tree, an animal, or a portrait and serves to convey a message (for example, a fruit indicates appreciation of beauty; a dove indicates love; a lion or a crocodile gives a message to beware). The mji can also portray pictures of religious or political leaders, church buildings, or even maps. Sometimes a kanga derives its name from the mji, especially if it is a distinguishable figure. The motif is printed on both sides with identical images. Printed inscriptions, usually a coded message, comprise the third part, called *jina* or *ujumbe*. The message can be a proverb, warning, or political slogan and is printed in uppercase letters in colors to match the central motif against a white background to allow easy reading. The message can be informational, educational, or teasing. The writing on the kanga must be understood in a social and cultural context, because it can convey a message of envy, flirtation, hatred, insult, jealousy, sympathy, advice, appreciation, or warning, among many other possibilities.

At home, women wear kanga for family and household chores, usually a pair with one wrapped over the breasts and the other overlapping the first around the waist, perhaps with only underwear to stay cool in the hot, humid climate.

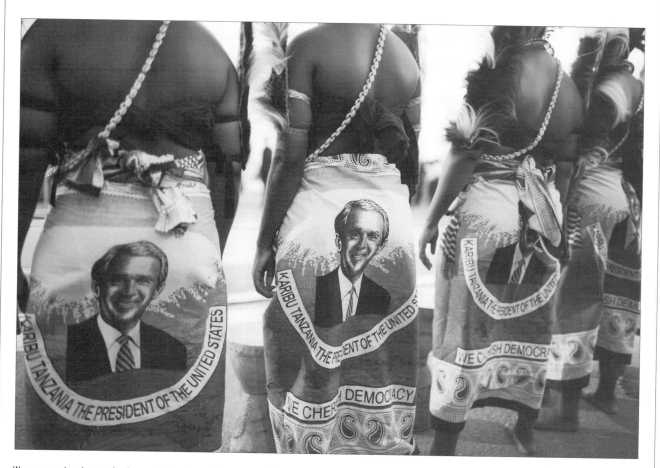

Women wearing *kangas* for George W. Bush's arrival ceremony in Dar es Salaam, Tanzania, 2008. The *kanga* is a rectangular length of cotton cloth worn as a wrapper and can be printed with a wide variety of motifs and slogans. Charles Ommanney/Getty Images.

Although the common style for all ages, ethnic groups, and classes, kanga may be worn in other ways. For example, one kanga wrapped around the body and another covering the head and shoulders indicates attending a funeral or, for Muslim women, prayers. For sleeping, a woman wraps one kanga around her body and dresses in the same style when in intimate company. Women also use kanga on their way to bathe and as a towel.

Kanga are also worn as head shawls, either covering the head and shoulders or wrapped around the head. Some women make dresses, skirts, and blouses from kanga, and some men wear shirts made from them. At home, men often wear them as a lower wrapper. A newborn is laid on a kanga or wrapped in it because of the warmth and softness of the fabric, thus starting a life in which kanga continue in importance throughout. Girls receive them as gifts to mark their passage to womanhood. In some ethnic groups, a husband and wife traditionally wear one of a paired set perfumed with heavy scent or incense on their wedding night. A large or small wardrobe of these cloths can indicate affluence or poverty, because a woman who possesses many pairs with every "issue" is seen as financially well off. It is not uncommon to find a relatively wealthy woman owning more than twenty pairs. In contrast, a woman wearing the same pair of kanga continuously is seen as impoverished. To some, kanga are regarded as the official or appropriate women's dress for a funeral, covering most of the body and showing only the face. Kanga may also be used to wrap and bury the dead, leaving life as they entered it. Some kanga are bought as souvenirs or kept as a memory of a loved one.

Kanga fabrics can be used for other purposes as well: for example, baby carriers, luggage, tablecloths, curtains, wall decoration, dance costumes, and bedspreads. Older and worn examples might be used as seat covers, windscreens, diapers, mops, rugs, aprons, and belts.

Some call kanga "cloth that speaks" because of significant meanings to wearers and observers. Its cultural and symbolic meanings go beyond the obvious when linked to social rituals or political and economic histories. Slogans and designs are said to depict changing moods and lifestyles and are even employed to mobilize people in public health campaigns, such as HIV/AIDS awareness. For example, in efforts to sensitize people to the problem, the words *naishi kidaktari* ("I'm living like a doctor/I'm being careful") or *fikiri sana maradhi* ("always be careful about diseases") utilize the cloth inscriptions to articulate thoughts that seem difficult to express verbally. In other instances, they have been worn to promote particular development projects such as tree planting, environmental conservation, and eradication of illiteracy. Indeed, people wearing them tend to serve as mobile human billboards, and, recognizing this potential, governments and organizations capture their propaganda value to support education and communication efforts. In the 2008 tour of Africa by then President George W. Bush, his portrait was displayed with an inscription on kanga produced for his trip. These textiles also featured images of both the Tanzanian and U.S. flags and the inscription *Udumu Urafikiki Kati Ya Marekani Tanzania*, which roughly translates as "Long live Tanzanian and American friendship."

Thadeus Shio

See also East Africa; Tanzania; Kenya.

Kenya

- Creating and Showing Identity, Status, Power, and Style
- Making and Marking Time and Occasion
- Contestation and Conflict over Dress
- Early Twenty-First Century Fashion: Urban, Rural, and International

K enya is a country of vast ecological variety in eastern Africa, with a coast on the Indian Ocean and bordered by Tanzania on the south, Uganda on the west, Sudan and Ethiopia on the north, and Somalia on the east. Kenya's complex histories of social interaction, migration, immigration, and trade have been the foundation of great diversity in dress and bodily practices. Archaeological evidence attests to the deep history of personal ornament in the region, including one of the oldest known ostrich eggshell bead workshops, dating to 40,000 years ago. During the pastoral Neolithic period over three thousand years ago, individuals were buried with necklaces of stone and seed beads at the Njoro River Cave site in the central Rift Valley, while the Jarigole Pillar site documents the variety of beads then in use near Lake Turkana (including beads or ornaments of ivory, ostrich eggshell, bone, amazonite, carnelian, agate, calcite, soft stone, and snail shell). These suggest enduring interior trade networks predating long-distance trade that brought new sources of cloth, clothing, and beads along the coast by the ninth century C.E.

The population of contemporary Kenya includes over forty African ethnic groups as well as people of Indian, Arab, and European descent. African language families spoken today reflect the millennia-long history of population movements and interchange and the range of dress traditions found there. Most indigenous hunting and gathering peoples were displaced or assimilated during these population shifts, despite long periods of symbiotic coexistence. Ancestors of Cushitic-language speakers came from what is now Ethiopia and Sudan four to five thousand years ago. Other population movements followed. Southern Nilotic speakers expanded from a Middle Nile Basin homeland in the north into the Kenya highlands almost three thousand years ago, where they may have assimilated many earlier speakers of southern Cushitic languages. Meanwhile, the first speakers of Bantu languages had reached western Kenya approximately two thousand years ago and were present on the Indian Ocean coast shortly afterward. By the thirteenth century C.E., many of the Bantu language groups found today had emerged, especially in the coastal area and central highlands. Western Nilotic speakers came from present-day Uganda into the Lake Victoria region during the fifteenth to seventeenth centuries, while eastern Nilotic speakers spread into northern and western Kenya and the Rift Valley in the seventeenth century.

Arab traders were visiting the coast two thousand years ago and later created settlements. Portuguese explorer Vasco da Gama reached the coast in 1498. Early in the sixteenth century, Portuguese established power at Mombasa, displaced two

Ndurururu Laboo, an Okiek elder, at a ceremony in Sapoitit, Kenya, 1989, wears a coat over a cotton cloth worn toga-style. His buffalo-horn tobacco container hangs from a long chain, and he has extended earlobes that once held earspools. Photograph by Corinne A. Kratz.

hundred years later by Arab rulers based in Oman and Zanzibar. Other European explorers and missionaries began traveling through the interior in the mid-1800s, and, in 1885, present-day Kenya became part of Britain's East African Protectorate. In 1895, Britain began building a railroad from Mombasa to Uganda, bringing indentured laborers from the Indian subcontinent. Some six thousand stayed, joining Indian traders already on the coast; other independent immigrants came from India later as shopkeepers, professionals, and artisans. In the early 1900s, European settlers (mostly British) began farming the fertile central highlands, displacing African farmers and pastoralists. Kenya became a British colony in 1920. After protests, armed struggle, and political negotiation, the country became an independent republic in 1963, with Jomo Kenyatta as Kenya's first president.

In the twenty-first century, all these linguistic-cultural currents are still present in Kenya's patterns of dress, along with additional international influences. Cushitic-language speakers (including Rendille and Somali) in northern and northeastern Kenya constitute a relatively small portion of the population. Southern Nilotic speakers in the west-central highlands and plains include Okiek and Pokot. Eastern Nilotic speakers in Kenya include Maasai, Samburu, and Turkana, while Luo near Lake Victoria and Uganda speak a western Nilotic language. Bantu-language speakers are the largest proportion of the population and include the Gikuyu Meru, Kamba, Swahili, and the Mijikenda groups. Asian communities (as people of Indian origin are called) are differentiated by religion, language, and regional origin, with associated distinctions in attire. Together with European residents, they comprised 1 percent of the population in 2006.

These historical crosscurrents entailed both a range of local and regional interactions over time as well as connections within wider systems of trade and interchange spanning the globe, creating a correspondingly rich array of contrasts and interactions in dress styles and bodily aesthetics. While the twenty-first century is often characterized as an era of globalization, far-reaching networks of commerce and communication are not new in eastern Africa. Even styles of dress that might be taken as traditional could include materials or stylistic elements from diverse international sources. New varieties of cloth and beads made available through trade, for instance, were incorporated into dress and personal ornament throughout the region, including cloth from India and China in the fifteenth century and glass beads of European manufacture brought inland by explorers and trade caravans in the nineteenth century.

Through Kenya's entwined social histories, some forms of dress and ornament became associated with particular ethnic-linguistic groups, while others define regional patterns crossing such divisions or attire associated with religious affiliations, social statuses, or particular occasions. Because colonial and national boundaries created in the late 1800s did not coincide with other social and historical patterns and divisions, ethnic groups and associated dress forms cross each of Kenya's national borders. While ethnic and regional dress patterns might cross Kenya's national borders, national differences in economic or political policies have also affected dress trends by altering materials available, regulating forms of attire, or promoting particular values in personal comportment. In the 1960s to 1970s, for instance, women in Western Province near the border bought *gomesi* dresses in Uganda, where its floor-length, sashed style originated and was widely worn on festive occasions. In the same period, Tanzanian Maasai were subject to Operation Dress-up, a government campaign that political scientist Leander Schneider describes as intended in part to persuade or coerce Maasai men to wear trousers instead of their togalike cotton *shuka* and to stop smearing their bodies with red ochre. As a final example, regulations about import licenses and tariffs have periodically interrupted Kenya's supply of colored glass beads from the Czech Republic, widely used in jewelry.

Throughout these historical shifts, dress, fashion, and body care have been resources through which people in Kenya have created and shown many social identities and distinctions, marked time and occasion, developed and displayed personal style, and contested moral values and political relations. The result has been a changing panoply of design in such materials as cloth, beads,

Young unmarried Samburu in Kenya, 1959. Samburu men's ornaments became more numerous and elaborate in the second half of the twentieth century. Photograph by Paul Spencer.

seeds, shell, leather, plastic, metal, mud, ochre, feather, and fur as well as body modifications that together tell elaborate stories of social and historical differentiation, interaction, and personal expression.

CREATING AND SHOWING IDENTITY, STATUS, POWER, AND STYLE

In the late nineteenth and early twentieth centuries, many people living in what is now Kenya wore a composition of clothing and jewelry first described by anthropologist Donna Klumpp Pido as the "East African silhouette," a visual form of similar shape with accepted areas for emphasis through ornamentation, providing a common basis upon which people developed distinctive dress codes. The general ensemble included decoration extending from the top of the head, top and bottom earrings (perhaps with extended earlobes), an array of necklaces, and ornaments on upper and lower arms, waist, calves, and ankles. The shape and density of necklaces usually distinguished men's and women's ensembles, as did the number and placement of hide or cloth wraps or aprons. Ethnic affiliation, gender, age, status, region, occasion, and personal preference might all be marked by distinctions that included color choices, patterns and combinations, motifs, manufacturing techniques, and ornament types and ensembles. The bodily forms and outfits created combined notions of aesthetics and social power. Headdresses, for instance, might amplify body morphology and project the wearer's fame and deeds, as Vigdis Broch-Due's extensive research about Turkana bodily aesthetics has shown. The East African silhouette identifies a broadly shared sense of body and attire, though this general type has had many variations.

For instance, historian Margaret Jean Hay has reported that Luo women in the early twentieth century wore a short apron of sisal fiber, beaded necklaces, and waist beads, with wire coils on their legs or arms. If married, they also wore a fiber tassel (*chieno*) from their waist in the back. Young Luo men had elaborate headdresses of ostrich feather or horn, iron wire around their arms and legs, red and white paint on their faces, and carried shields and swords. In the same period, Maasai women wore ankle-length leather or cloth wraps at their waist, another hide or cloth over their shoulders, wire around their calves and/or arms, bracelets, a layering of necklaces that included platelike wire and bead ornaments extending toward the shoulders and chest, and earrings in upper and lower ears. Young Maasai warriors then might also wear ostrich feathers in a face-framing head ruff, necklaces and bracelets, fringed fur strips on their calves and ankles, and a toga-like hide or cloth, decorating their bodies with vivid red ochre paste. Joseph Thomson, one of the earliest European explorers in the area, sketched Maasai and Luo dress in the 1880s along with attire worn by others he encountered. Thomson noted changing fashions and demands for beads of different colors and sizes and for different kinds of cotton cloth.

At the turn of the twentieth century, color patterns in personal ornament were in a state of change. Multicolored beads introduced by trade caravans in the late 1800s allowed people to create new color palettes and combinations, elaborating the basic red-black-white scheme common in the region. Those basic colors were expanded in various ways. Creative innovations in beadwork were taking place at the same time cotton cloth was becoming more widely available inland and spreading across the region, again made available by expanding commerce. For the entire nineteenth century, cloth was at the center of East Africa's global exchanges. East African demand for cloth would shape most of the region's trade relationships and draw economies around the world into dynamic relation with African consumers. American-made unbleached cotton (known as *merikani*) dominated the market until the U.S. Civil War disrupted cotton supplies and Indian textiles increased their market share. After cloth and beads, coils of American brass wire were the third most common import to Zanzibar in the mid-1800s. In demand throughout the region for making jewelry, quantities of brass and copper wire ornament indicated relative wealth and prestige in some settings.

Ethnic affiliations and identities were in formation and flux at the same time. The 1890s saw widespread drought, famine, cattle diseases, and human epidemics that required adaptations and shifts in the regional communities and economic interactions then prominent. As social identities and interactions were refashioned in these difficult circumstances, British colonial governance was also taking root and contributing to these redefinitions and ethnic formations. Modes of dress and personal ornament that recast and combined older styles and newer materials became more prominent as markers of ethnicity as designs became more elaborate. Many distinctive color patterns in beaded ornaments

associated with particular ethnic identities took shape before the First World War; those who have continued to wear ethnic-based attire have incorporated new elements, styles, and designs through the present.

Swahili people were a significant exception to this pattern of dress and the East African silhouette. Missionary Charles New lived and traveled along the coast in the 1860s, shortly before Thomson's inland journey; New's account describes Swahili dress in detail, with drawings based on photographs. There are also earlier descriptions of attire and cloth production throughout the Swahili area. Fine cloth and jewelry helped establish social hierarchies in Swahili society, with a major distinction between *waungwana* (elite) and those of lower social and economic status, once including slaves.

Swahili are often described as following Arab dress styles. In the 1500s, waungwana men wore floor-length cotton or silk cloths (*kikoi* or *shuka*) around their waist and across the torso and one shoulder. This style was largely replaced in the last hundred and fifty years by the loose full-length white shirt known as *kanzu*, although some men still wear kikoi alone or under the kanzu. The change to kanzu was related to rising Omani power in Zanzibar and stylistic influences from that country. In addition to cloth wraps or kanzu, men wore embroidered caps (*kofia*) and sandals. The embroidery quality and thread on the kofia also marked taste, refinement, and distinction. Some political elite wore turbans instead, while those of lower social class wore a kind of skullcap. Charles New reported red fez in the headwear repertoire of the late nineteenth century and also noted that men were heavily perfumed.

Wealthy waungwana women in the sixteenth century wore silk or cotton cloths around their waist and over their shoulders, with elaborate gold and silver necklaces and bangles. When Charles New wrote, middle-class Swahili women also wore matched trouser and tunic outfits, but most wore a pair of *leso* (also known as *kanga*)—cotton cloths with a colorful central motif and printed border patterns that later acquired a proverblike saying printed in Swahili above the lower border. Leso originated in Zanzibar in the 1870s; the name is said to derive from the Portuguese word for handkerchief. Depending on their social status and religious piety, many Swahili women wore a light black mantle (*buibui*) over their clothing as a form of modest veiling in public. Late-nineteenth-century women had elaborate hairstyles and wore kohl around their eyes, and their jewelry included nose studs, upper ear studs, bead and silver necklaces, rings, and bracelets.

These coastal Swahili dress styles were incorporated into colonial and missionary efforts to change how Africans dressed elsewhere in Kenya, taken as models of modesty and refinement. The kanzu and fez, for instance, were adopted as a uniform for Africans working as domestic servants in many colonial homes. Similarly, early-twentieth-century African colonial officials in western Kenya were given white kanzu, dark embroidered cloaks, waistcoats, fez, and ceremonial batons for official occasions, with specific clothing combinations indicating rank. By 1920, this coastal style was no longer used there, and European-style khaki clothing was officers' norm. The fez was also a fashion in the early 1900s for young Kamba men, who bought them at local bazaars. Kanga cloths also spread far beyond the coast during the twentieth century, adding to or replacing plain cotton wraps for many Kenyan women.

The twentieth century saw many developments and adaptations in attire as local, regional, and global interconnections

Sepita Lenteiye, a young unmarried Samburu, wears men's ornaments, including beaded collars, which became more elaborate and flamboyant in the second half of the twentieth century. Naiborkeju, Kenya, 1999. Photograph by Kyoko Nakamura.

altered in varied ways. In some cases, people worked with changing materials, options, and constraints to elaborate or create innovations in specific versions of the East African silhouette. In other cases, people abandoned dress and ornament related to the silhouette relatively rapidly. In many settings, additional differentiation and specialization in modes of dress developed, incorporating European attire into an expanded clothing and ornament repertoire. Young adults (particularly those who attended school), men, Christians, and those who identified with various "modern" values were often more likely to wear trousers, shirts, shoes, and coats regularly (if men) or long dresses and head scarves (if women). For special occasions or cultural ceremonies, however, people might still don outfits and ornaments regarded as traditional markers of identity and occasion.

The opposite pattern could be found in other areas. Okiek and Maasai men in Narok District in the 1980s, for instance, typically wore a cotton shuka; necklaces, bracelets, and earrings made of beads and metal; a carved and decorated tobacco or snuff container of buffalo horn or ivory on a chain; and a sheathed sword on a belt and carried a *rungu* (knobkerrie) or stick. Many wore a raincoat or jacket over this ensemble. When attending a ceremony, the same men might dress in long trousers and shirt, retaining personal ornaments and accoutrements. Okiek women

at the time wore either a pair of cotton cloths or a dress for daily wear but usually donned newer dresses with a kanga cape for special occasions. They, too, wore beaded necklaces, top and bottom earrings, bracelets, and bangles with both outfits. Nonetheless, younger Okiek, especially those who attended school, were likely to wear European-style clothing more often.

While the repertoires and combinations available for personal and aesthetic expression through bodily adornment expanded and shifted in Kenya over the last century, the precise form of such changes depended on local histories and social relations as well as particular modes of engagement with larger political and economic systems via trade and markets, missionization, labor migration, education, and various forms of government and administration. Some social movements, for instance, have supported a return to dress features seen as traditional to emphasize commitment to particular community values. In the 1920s, young men in western Kenya formed groups that organized riotous parties and opposed schooling, European clothing, and mission affiliation, including one group calling themselves "The Fornicators." Independent churches such as Dini ya Msambwa, Legio Maria, and Akorino often combine flowing white robes, dresses, scarves, or turbans with nativist elements of dress or ritual.

The Maasai and Gikuyu peoples provide one example of the different ways such processes have played out. Centuries of interaction between the two have included hostilities, intermarriage, trade, and many other relations. In the early 1900s, both wore variations of the East African silhouette. Married Gikuyu women wore long leather skirts of goat or sheepskin sewn with beaded line patterns and belted with multiple rows of beads, wire coils on their wrists or arms, an array of beaded necklaces, and distinctive earrings, *hang'i*, made of fifteen to thirty wire hoops per ear strung with small pink or red beads. Worn through a woman's extended ear lobes with the hoops' weight supported by a leather headband, hang'i indicated that her oldest child had been initiated; pink beads were distinctive of Gikuyu beadwork. Maasai women of the same status then typically wore similar leather clothing and wire coils. Their beaded collars tended to be wider than those of Gikuyu, with different color patterns. Instead of hang'i, the Maasai woman would wear an elongated beaded wire hoop at the top of each ear and intricately beaded leather earflaps or flat brass wire spirals in her extended earlobes. The latter earrings showed her married status.

Young Gikuyu and Maasai men of the warrior age grade wore similar garb, beginning with a soft leather toga. Both might have had coiled wire ornaments on their necks, arms, or legs, and a stiff ostrich-feather headdress decorated with beads was a sign of courage (*thitai* in Gikuyu; *esidai* in Maa). Maasai who showed bravery by killing a lion could wear a tall lion's mane headdress instead. Maasai warriors might also have fringed anklets of colobus monkey skin. Young Gikuyu and Maasai alike applied red ochre to their bodies and heads, and both wore their hair long, although Maasai grew theirs much longer and sometimes arranged a knot of braids on the forehead.

Similar detailed descriptions might be provided for each social identity in Maasai and Gikuyu societies. Particular ornaments, types of clothing, hairstyles, and ensembles marked a range of social distinctions, though the quality of work on particular pieces, the specific materials, patterns, size, and combinations of ornaments might be matters of personal style, skill, and available resources. In general, the Maasai silhouette has been more exaggerated than other Kenyan peoples, with greater height and volume of ornaments. Like several pastoralists in Kenya, Maasai also adorn animals in their herds with bells or bone or ivory neck ornaments.

As the Colonial period progressed, Gikuyu and Maasai dress diverged. Gikuyu lived on the path of trade caravans, the British established an administrative center in their midst, and they were subject to early evangelism by Christian missionaries. As they embraced schooling and Christianity in the following decades, more Gikuyu began wearing European clothing styles more often. Most abandoned the beauty practice of elongating earlobes by about the 1950s; American missionaries used to sew up earlobes at baptism. In the twenty-first century, Gikuyu associate extended earlobes with their grandmothers or great-grandmothers, and, in the rural areas, women wear loose-fitting dresses and skirts while men wear trousers and shirts.

While some Maasai also embraced schooling in the mid-twentieth century, they were a minority until the 1970s or later. For their part, Maasai continued elaborating the East African silhouette with new styles and patterns of ornament, with innovations and fashions changing with each age set (a time period and social group defined by initiation into adulthood during a common period of about seven years). In the context of tourism, Maasai attire became a sign of exotic culture and a putative native

Luyha leader Chief Mumia (seated) wears the "suitable robes" and fez issued by the British along with purchased leather boots, while the young man to his left is dressed entirely in Western-style khaki clothes, shoes, and cap. The other men wear a combination of Swahili-style and indigenous dress. Kenya, early 1900s. Hobley photograph Hob IV 40 19, copyright The British Museum.

nobility and closeness to nature; Maasai were increasingly part of expanding tourist displays and performances. Maasai women made beadwork to sell to tourists, and some young men also participated in long-distance cattle trade or labor migration to become night watchmen or security guards in urban centers. Even though young Maasai men commonly wore watches and similar items in the 1980s to 1990s, in tourist settings, such signs of contemporary life were removed to create an aura of tradition and authenticity.

Maa-speaking Samburu men from northern Kenya were also incorporated into the tourist economy and labor migration. In her extensive inventory of Samburu personal ornament, Kyoko Nakamura has noted that young unmarried men's adornments in particular had proliferated, becoming more elaborate and flamboyant in the past twenty years. In the 1990s and 2000s, Maasai and Samburu politicians and activists began wearing a version of traditional attire for women made of brown cotton decorated with beads like a leather skirt, then sewn with dangles (small chains with circular tin or aluminum disks) that provide a gentle ringing rustle as they walk. Accessorized with beaded collars, bracelets, and headdresses, this modern redesign of traditional dress emphasizes Maasai identity at nongovernmental-organization workshops, United Nations forums, and similar events.

This example illustrates the range of social and political processes that Kenyan societies have engaged during the last century—including colonialism, missionary evangelism, extensive socioeconomic transformations, development initiatives, tourism, and relations with national and transnational government and organizations—and the divergent ways they play out through dress and fashion. Sometimes these engagements heightened internal social divisions, divisions partially articulated in debates about how to dress. These disagreements signaled changing social expectations and power dynamics, particularly between generations and between men and women. Young Luo men in the 1910s to 1920s, for instance, took part in labor migration and schooling, forging new life paths that altered authority structures and access to resources; preferences for European clothing differentiated them from their elders. Similarly, when rural Luo wives and daughters wanted dresses and other European clothing, it was often seen as challenging the control and authority of their husbands and fathers. Some men saw such attire as a sign of sexual independence and assertiveness, too.

A photograph from the early 1900s of Luyha leader Chief Mumia with four other men shows styles and combinations ranging from the chief's government-issued robe and fez with heavy boots, to a smartly dressed young man in trousers, shirt, jacket, belt, shoes, and cap, to elders in white robes or wrapped in cloth or blanket with bangles, ear ornaments, upper arm ornaments, and long staffs. Such stylistic diversity and mixture of elements to create striking outfits remained characteristic of many Kenyan settings throughout the twentieth century. In the mid-1990s, researcher Johanna Schoss described different fashionable ensembles among young men at the Malindi coast, putting together a look that would "shine" and show their cosmopolitan values through either a professional style emphasizing European clothing, safari wear, or kanzu, or through inventive combinations of garments from kikoi cloth with jeans and T-shirts.

Just as debates about attire provided idioms for struggles and disagreements over social values and authority within Kenyan societies, they also concretized hierarchies and value differences in Kenyans' dealings with institutions of colonial and post-colonial governance. In some mission settings in the first half of the twentieth century, for instance, Africans were urged to adopt European apparel yet not allowed to wear shoes; at other mission stations, African converts were discouraged or forbidden from donning such clothing at all. Similarly, after independence, pastoralists in northern Kenya who continued to wear styles related to the East African silhouette have been forced on occasion to remove their ornaments or shamed because of their dress styles by members of the paramilitary General Service Unit police. In such situations, attire associated with ethnic traditions was seen as evidence of a lack of modernity or resistance to national government programs.

When most peoples in Kenya subscribed to the basic look of the East African silhouette early in the twentieth century, the range of social differentiation encoded in dress was a prominent feature for Kenyans and others alike, marking distinctions such as gender, age, ritual status, and special offices and occasions through what has been called the "social skin." With over a century of transformation in styles and dress since then and wide adoption of European modes of clothing, the kinds of social differentiation and values associated with ethnically based dress also shifted. At times, some people—both Kenyan and European—have seen the ornaments, garments, and bodily practices associated with the silhouette's look as a sign of backwardness, as in the missionary and police examples. In other contexts, such dress has been valued positively as a sign of heritage and associated with diverse cultural meanings and occasions. This positive valorization sometimes combines oral traditions about previous generations' attire with nostalgia for an imagined past ideal community and a concern for authenticity that fails to recognize the dynamic nature of ethnically based dress and its scope for personal style and innovation. Whatever the values ascribed, particular modes of dress are always also signs of personhood, identity, and personal style.

A collection of drawings by Austrian-born naturalist Joy Adamson has provided an invaluable snapshot of the compass of ethnically defined attire in Kenya between the Second World War and the Mau Mau guerrilla rebellion in the 1950s. Adamson was commissioned by the colonial government to produce portraits representing Kenya's major ethnic groups and traveled the country on the project from roughly 1948 to the mid-1950s. Concerned about authenticity, she relied on local elders to confirm the so-called traditional nature of her models' attire; this suggests that some innovations and dress combinations worn at the time were rejected as inappropriate for documentation. Despite a conservative emphasis on elder-authenticated modes of dress, Adamson did several portraits during her travels that depicted other kinds of clothing. These included an oil painting commissioned for a memorial hall in Kapsabet showing a Nandi man in what Adamson called "Burma kit" (army uniform with a wide-brimmed hat, medals, and rifle worn during the Burma campaign of World War II, where Kenyans distinguished themselves in the King's African Rifles regiment) as well as a portrait of a captured Mau Mau prisoner. Neither of these became part of the original collection, but this remarkable project resulted in nearly six hundred watercolor portraits for the Coryndon Museum's collection (later the National Museums of Kenya).

Adamson's portraits show distinctive variations in particular features of dress and body arts that signal ethnic differences among neighboring peoples. Just as Gikuyu had a particular

Ebey Kore, a Turkana man, from a watercolor portrait (Kenya, 1940–1950) by Joy Adamson (1910–1980). The Turkana hairstyle extends down the back of the neck from a clay mudcap. Hair is woven on the back of the head, using blue coloring on the base, building in ornament holders for ostrich feathers, tassels, or other items. Courtesy of National Museums of Kenya.

preference for pink beads, and Kamba ornaments have a recognizable design placing motifs against a white field, men's hair and spear styles in northern Kenya provided other visual and material languages of social distinction. Like beaded ornaments, spears of different shapes and styles were associated with different age grades, areas, and ethnicities in the past (rifles were also important in the 1960s to 1970s, with military assault rifles increasingly widespread since then). Hairstyles worn by Pokot and Turkana men have often been distinguished by different angles, colors, and extensions. Both create hard mudcaps of clay and hair woven onto the back of the head using blue coloring on the base and building in ornament holders for ostrich feathers, tassels, or other items. The Turkana mudcap extends back and down the neck; in the late nineteenth century, it might have reached almost to the waist as an extended chignon. A Pokot man's mudcap (siolip) is more horizontally oriented and may vary in color, shape, and ornament according to status or affiliation with a particular clan or age set. Only senior men, for instance, wear a small rectangular mini-mudpack on the forehead with large black feather pom-poms. Ugandan Karamojong and Daasenach men have worn other variations on these hairstyles. In the same region, coiffures for young

Samburu men—like Maasai—have focused instead on different styles for tying and arranging long thin braids and twists, perhaps colored with red ochre and accented with beaded headbands, earrings, and small designs painted on the cheekbones. Hairstyles for women and children in each group were distinctive as well, though less elaborate.

Hairstyles are just one body art through which Kenyans enhance their beauty and augment signs of identity and social status in dress. Pigmented ointments of red, blue-black, or white have been applied to the body in various ways depending on ethnicity, gender, social status, and occasion. Similarly, Swahili women have long celebrated special occasions, particularly weddings, by applying intricate floral designs of red-brown henna to their hands and feet, sometimes stretching up the legs and arms. Henna is used by some of Kenya's Asian communities, too, marking auspicious beginnings. Henna painting has also been adopted in tourism as a local experience for visitors who might have their hands decorated; it has also become part of the Lamu museum's annual cultural festival for the Maulidi holiday and, in 2007, was featured in a fashion article on designer shoes in a national newspaper.

Other bodily modifications practiced during the last century and in contemporary Kenya sometimes combine visual aesthetics with other sensory appeals. Patterns of scarification, for instance, hold both visual and tactile appeal as elements in Pokot and Turkana ensembles described above. Striped shoulder scarifications identify Pokot and Turkana men as successful raiders and warriors, while elaborate dotted lines of scarification on the abdomen, lower back, and groin were part of young women's beautification. Like several other Kenyan societies, Pokot also pierced their upper and lower ears for decoration with earplugs and earrings. Pokot and Turkana also wore nose plates and lip plugs; piercings were less common elsewhere in the country. Another widely practiced body modification included removal of the middle lower incisors, while Kamba people were noted for filing their front teeth in the nineteenth and early twentieth centuries.

Several such body modifications were done during ceremonies marking stages of social maturation, joining aesthetic and moral values to define qualities of a good person as one grew in stature and age. Circumcision is perhaps the most widespread such operation, usually practiced in Kenya for men and women alike as part of initiation into adulthood (though that social transition happens at different ages in different societies). Noncircumcising societies such as the Luo and Turkana might be seen by their neighbors as contravening notions of adult personhood, even as female circumcision became the subject of controversy during the Colonial era and again in the late twentieth century as a practice that contravened missionary and European understandings of the body and sexuality. In the late 1990s to 2000s, Luo have been debating the desirability of male circumcision as defense against HIV/AIDS.

Fragrance, sound, and movement are also aesthetic features of dress and body arts in Kenya. People might note the pleasing rustle and jingle of massed beadwork and metal ornaments, for instance, or create ceremonial outfits with feathery fringes of black and white colobus monkey skins that extend and draw attention to dance movements. Young Okiek and Maasai incorporate fragrance into personal ornaments with choker necklaces for men and women that contain sweet-smelling leaves (*sogomek* in Okiek, *esonkoyo* in Maa). For their part, Gabra women chew and burn frankincense for perfuming, while myrrh incense (*qumbi*)

is prized for its scent in addition to being powdered, mixed with clarified butter, and used as hair ointment. During rituals, Gabra use myrrh in blessings and affix bits in their eyebrows. Scent has also been important during Swahili weddings and special occasions, including rosewater baths and perfuming with aloe wood and gum for the bride.

Twenty-first-century Kenya includes a diverse mosaic of daily attire, with many styles and cosmopolitan combinations. European and Arabic dress styles are common throughout the country, including multicolored dresses, skirts, and blouses with scarves and a kanga or similar cloth worn as a cape, shawl, wrapped skirt, or carrier for a child as common women's attire in rural areas and trousers and shirts for men with a variety of hats and jackets. Kanga cloths have declined in popularity, however. The textile mills that manufactured them locally had closed by 2000, leaving that market to imports from India and Tanzania. Garments and ornaments that compose various versions of the East African silhouette are also widely known and still worn in many parts of the country. Shukas are labeled "warrior wear" in some shops and called a "fabric with a culture." The most common dress in Asian communities consists of sari for women and white cotton pants

Tshukune Kabrolim, a Pokot man, from a watercolor portrait (Kenya, 1940–1950) by Joy Adamson (1910–1980). The Pokot hairstyle extends horizontally from a clay mudcap. Hair is woven on the back of the head, building in ornament holders for ostrich feathers, tassels, or other items. Courtesy of National Museums of Kenya.

and shirts for men. Throughout the country, schoolchildren wear uniforms; members of the military and other occupation groups also have distinctive uniforms.

Each of Kenya's dress traditions includes various fashion trends and influences and particular outfits and styles for special occasions, depending on specific regional aesthetics and conventions. This stylistic range also occurs on the national political stage. For instance, when a delegation of Okiek leaders visited the president in the 1990s and 2000s about land tenure problems, they wore hyrax fur capes as emblematic of their identity, heritage, and rights. Leaders at government rallies might wear some traditional ornaments or carry such signs of political office as a beaded fly whisk or decorated knobkerrie (rungu). Jomo Kenyatta, Kenya's first president, sometimes wore a leopard-skin cap, a beaded belt, or leopard-trimmed cape over a well-tailored suit and always carried a fly whisk or elegantly carved walking stick in public. The very name Kenyatta came from the Maasai beaded belt (*kinyatta*) that he began wearing as a young man. His successor, Daniel Arap Moi, carried a handsome gold- or silver-tipped ivory rungu and sported a rosebud in the buttonhole of his suit (as did Kenyatta). Dance groups performing at rallies or national holiday celebrations might wear color-coordinated, modernized versions of traditional ensembles as a group uniform or performance costume.

MAKING AND MARKING TIME AND OCCASION

In addition to being resources for creating and showing social and personal identities and for aesthetic expression and pleasure, these last examples show that clothing and body arts also provide means through which time and occasion are marked and given social and personal meaning. While national holidays and political rallies include accoutrements of heritage and office and performances enhanced with arresting dance outfits and uniforms, other community and family ceremonies are replete with special garments, ornaments, ensembles, and body practices that help define these special occasions. As individuals progress through culturally defined age grades and life stages, rituals can include significant changes of outfit and shifts in daily grooming and adornment. Some body modifications already described are also part of life-cycle rituals and progressions through age grades.

In many Kenyan societies, initiation into adulthood is a high point for individuals and among the most elaborate community ceremonies. Shifts in initiates' attire are one means through which the transformation from child to adult is effected, and they are often coordinated with ceremonial speech, song, and spatial movements. Initiates' relatives might also wear special clothing or ornaments marking their ritual roles and connections with initiates. When Okiek girls are initiated, for instance, the entire process includes five complete changes in their mode of dress and ornaments; parents and ritual leaders wear ritual capes or hold particular objects during the ceremonies. In other societies, weddings or funerals might have particularly elaborated ceremonies and modes of dress.

Dress and body arts that mark particular life stages might simultaneously indicate changes in ritual power or political role and draw meaning from contrasts with other social categories and symbols. Among Gabra in northern Kenya, for instance, *d'abella* are ritual elders, the most senior male age grade, with particular religious and juridical roles. Considered female in this life stage,

An Okiek girl dances during her first initiation ceremony. Her rented nighttim dance outfit includes fringed black and white colobus monkey skins that ex tend her movements, leg bells, kneesocks, headdress, and a short *kanga* wra skirt. Sapoitit, Kenya, 1989. Photograph by Corinne A. Kratz.

d'abella dress entirely in white, a color associated with peace, life and fertility.

Absence of jewelry can also show ritual status, occasion, o stages of change just as hairstyle can contribute to outfits defining an event or period of time. In some situations, for instance, relatives might shave their heads or cut their hair short while mourning a death and forgo self-adornment for a specified period People in other societies, however, might show the same statu by refraining from cutting their hair during mourning. Such hai growth, trimmed at the hairline, shows ritual pollution for Maa sai and Okiek during periods including initiation and mourning

Ornaments and hairstyles associated with particular age grades or life-cycle ceremonies might also have changing fashions marking the passage of time and defining particular historica periods. Such generational styles are well recognized and fondly remembered by those whose youthful adventures included out fits with particular beadwork styles. At the same time, exchange of personal ornaments has been one currency of social relation among young people in many settings, demonstrating affection and affiliation with friends and lovers. Other changes in clothing styles and combinations can also distinguish particular historica periods, as with the brief period when African colonial officers in western Kenya wore kanzu and fez. In towns and cities, fashion changes in other dress traditions might also evoke distinctive as sociations and provide ways to trace historical change.

CONTESTATION AND CONFLICT OVER DRESS

The prominent role of clothing, body modification, and persona adornment in defining ceremonial occasions and ritual transfor mations draws attention again to how dress might contribute to cultural understandings of personhood, aesthetics, and morality Such connections make clothing and ornaments potent signs wher conflicts arise over politics, power, and meaning, offering visually compelling means to convey disagreement or disapproval. Such contests have erupted in multiple arenas and times, from personal and family relations to national and international politics, with attire as means of expression or as the very topic of dispute.

Women's clothing and cosmetics have often been the target of criticism when their self-presentation is interpreted as indicating moral degeneration or changes in authority, role, and status not welcomed by those complaining. Debates in western Kenya about women adopting European-style clothing in the 1910s to 1920s were described earlier, but periodic denunciations of women's wear followed throughout the twentieth century. For instance, 1950s Mau Mau songs complained of indecent women's dress, and letters and articles in national newspapers in the 1960s and 1970s decried miniskirts and hot pants as un-African. Several decades later, male members of Mungiki—a nativist religious cum vigilante group that gained national prominence in the 1990s to 2000s—took it upon themselves to police women's attire. Newspapers reported attacks where they stripped and whipped women wearing trousers, again denouncing the garb as un-African. In 2002, Mungiki also threatened to forcibly circumcise women in central Kenya as a return to traditional values. In unrelated cases between the 1980s and 2000s, Kenyan men from noncircumcising communities were also seized and forcibly circumcised to "make them men." Proper attire for African men became subject to national debate in 2003 when the speaker of Parliament evicted several members for wearing flowing Nigerian robes, violating a dress code requiring suit and tie. Within days, a coalition of parliamentarians came to the National Assembly in African attire; the speaker reversed himself, and a committee was formed to devise a new dress code.

Numerous conflicts over clothing during the Colonial period were situated in missionary encounters, as clergy associated different ways of dressing with moral and cultural values and sought to change both, and Kenyans claimed the right to wear shoes or other garments discouraged as inappropriate for Africans. Similar campaigns and prohibitions against ethnically based ornaments or garments have occurred in postcolonial Kenya, as already noted. Individuals register personal protests through attire, too, as one Okiek bride did in the 1980s by refusing to wear beaded ornaments for her wedding because she did not want the marriage her family had arranged for her.

Stripping in public has been a powerful means of protest for adult women in Kenya in several circumstances. Perhaps most famously, Gikuyu women stripped during the 1922 Harry Thuku Disturbances to protest the arrest of Thuku, a prominent labor activist. This anticolonial gesture, also used during the Mau Mau uprising, was based on a potent form of curse practiced by Gikuyu and several other Kenyan peoples. Deliberately violating intergenerational proprieties so that mothers were naked before their sons, such exposure was seen as cursing fertility and well-being and the strongest possible censure. The Pokot version of such cursing, *kilipat*, was a collective "shaming party" whereby a group of women punished an abusive husband by exposing themselves. Seventy years after the Thuku Disturbances, in 1992, a group of mothers whose sons were political prisoners again mobilized their nakedness during a hunger strike, this time to object and draw attention to police abuse in Kenya under President Moi. The participation of Wangari Maathai, a prominent activist who later won the Nobel Peace Prize, helped assure international media coverage. Since then, the gesture has been used in other local and regional protests throughout Kenya.

As Kenyan women used their nakedness to protest abuses of power and forge joint action with a shared vision of the nation, since independence, Kenyans have periodically debated whether there should be a national dress to emphasize Kenyan unity and identity and what such an outfit might look like. Efforts from the 1960s through the 1980s to devise a national ensemble by drawing on elements of the country's different ethnic traditions failed to produce designs that became widely accepted. In the absence of such a recognized outfit, many prominent Kenyan women wear voluminous robes and head ties of West African style and fabrics as a kind of pan-African national dress. Soon after the 2003 parliamentary contretemps over appropriate men's garb, the government launched another design competition in cooperation with Unilever, manufacturer of beauty and food products. Seeking commonalities across Kenya's modes of dress, a design team proposed a long robe, cloak, and head piece for women; men would wear a cape over a shirt with a slashed collar. Both outfits were red, green, and black—colors of the national flag. Despite a celebratory launch by national politicians, the outfits did not catch on. Others have suggested that the kanga or Maasai beadwork have become an unofficial national dress, widely used in contemporary fashion design and internationally recognized.

EARLY TWENTY-FIRST CENTURY FASHION: URBAN, RURAL, AND INTERNATIONAL

Changes in fashion and differences of personal style and panache are common across many modes of dress in every period of Kenyan history, whether the revolution in beadwork colors and designs in the early twentieth century, a vogue for the fez among young Kamba men in the 1920s, changing age set styles in Maasai or Samburu beaded ornaments, incorporation of plastic sunglasses and woolen hats into Turkana men's outfits in the 1990s, or the regular release of new designs in kanga cloths. At the same time, particular garments, styles, and features show considerable continuity over long periods despite elaborations and incorporation of new materials; the East African silhouette is one such enduring visual and stylistic framework. For each clothing tradition, one might ask which dress forms, which occasions, and which people were involved in fashion changes in different periods and how changing fashions were understood by different members of society. The descriptions already presented provide examples and hints about how analyses of fashion and style in Kenyan dress might proceed.

Fashion design has also developed in Kenya as a specialized industry with particular modes of production and display similar to those in other countries, with professional designers, formal training, fashion shows, and advertising layouts and style magazines promoting new fashions. Emphasizing dramatic individual style, most Kenyan designers draw on pan-African materials and combinations as well as European and American sources. International designers from elsewhere on the continent also participate in Kenyan fashion events, representing one contemporary articulation with global systems of fashion and production. An annual event called Kenya Fashion Week promoting the country's fashion and textile industry launched in 2001 with corporate sponsors and a student fashion award. The African Heritage boutique and gallery, cofounded in Nairobi in 1973 by

These outfits won a competition for a new Kenyan national dress design sponsored by the government of Kenya and Unilever Kenya. The men's and women's versions are modeled here by Elijah Kwasa and Joyce Ambasa at a launch ceremony held in Nairobi on 14 September 2004. Both outfits use red, green and black—the colors of the national flag—but they failed to gain popularity. Reuters/Thomas Mukoya.

Alan Donovan and Joseph Murumbi, was, for thirty years, a source of pan-African design and promotion. African Heritage trained jewelry designers; created stylish jewelry and outfits that combined a wealth of African aesthetic resources; staged festivals and fashion shows that showcased African jewelry, crafts, art, and fashion; and promoted and marketed Kenyan artistry and these pan-African styles in the United States and Europe. African Heritage was also involved in research and design of costumes for *Out of Africa* (1985), one of a series of Hollywood films set in Kenya that reanimated colonial-safari chic in popular imaginations internationally with their depictions of Kenyan dress and history. Other films about colonial Kenya included *Kitchen Toto* (1987), *Mountains of the Moon* (1989), *The Ghost and the Darkness* (1996), and later the postcolonial thriller *The Constant Gardener* (2005).

Kenyan styles have also been a regular source of design ideas in the world of international fashion. For instance, when actress Diane Keaton appeared in the 1977 film *Annie Hall* using a Kikuyu or Kamba basket (*ciondo*) as a purse, that became a must-have fashion accessory in the United States, where it became known as a "Kenya bag." Originally woven by women from sisal fiber in earth tones, bright plastics were incorporated as the market grew and the style was widely copied by manufacturers in Korea, the Philippines, and Taiwan. In the 1980s, the Smithsonian National Museum of Natural History made a collection showing the stylistic evolution and range of these baskets. Similarly, international designers in Europe and the United States periodically cite Maasai beadwork, color palettes, and overall style as inspiration for their creations, ranging from Calvin Klein's 1981 runway collection, Ralph Lauren's 1997 collection, John Galliano's jewelry for Dior and others, and Maasai-influenced collar necklaces by John Rocha in 2005 and in several spring 2007 collections, all the way to bed linens and houseware collections. In the 1990s, Swiss engineer Karl Müller was even inspired to develop a line of footwear called "Maasai Barefoot Technology."

For many Kenyans, the elite world of high fashion and couture is either unknown or distant from their own clothing practices and concerns. The explosion of imported *mitumba* (secondhand clothing) in the 1990s, however, touched virtually every corner of

with heavy metal neck rings. Women's necklaces were made out of brown seeds collected from the wilderness.

The Bagisu chiefs donned a cowry-covered helmet surmounted by the fur of a colobus monkey. This was secured with a band of cowries around the head. They also held the tail of the monkey as a wand to signify their authority. Body modification, painting, scarification, and piercing were established traditions of the Bagisu. Scarification of the face was a measure of beauty among Bagisu women. Two rows of marks on the forehead and around the cheekbone and a number of intricate incisions were made down the chest and stomach. The women also pierced the lower lip, where a white lip stone was inserted; but, since the late twentieth century, this practice has almost stopped.

The Bagisu practice male circumcision (*imbalu*) every even year, and the ritual is characterized by a distinct dress style for the initiates. In preparation for the ceremony, the initiates are splashed with fermented millet flour to psychologically prepare them. Until the end of the twentieth century, initiates wore six to eight large copper bells attached to the thigh by a leather band decorated with strings of cowry shells. They held two hand bells, each fastened on a supporting strap and lined with cowry shells. Several layers of multicolored beads crossed the chest along with several kerchiefs. Each initiate was crowned with a headgear sewn from colobus monkey skin lined with cowry shells, over which was placed a hippopotamus bone that was carved in a semicircular form. After circumcision, the newly initiated men were qualified to wear a goat- or sheepskin decorated with beads of various colors that were fastened around the neck, hanging down long enough to cover the front part of the body. The Bagisu have continued to observe the circumcision ritual, but the dress code has been modified and the animal skins are gradually being replaced with industrially manufactured textiles, especially with animal prints.

THE ACHOLI

The Acholi in northern Uganda are a collection of small groups brought together by the Luo migration, which is presumed to have taken place around the fifteenth century C.E. They are organized under a decentralized system of chieftaincy; thus, each clan had its own chief who donned leopard skins and a cape of ostrich feathers. The cape was attached to a wicker frame fitted to the crown of the head onto which colorful ostrich feathers were arranged in black, white, or orange.

Ordinary men wore a cheetah or baboon skin draped around the shoulders and a small apron of white kid skin about twenty centimeters (eight inches) square to cover the buttocks. The apron was cut into two tails at the bottom. Women's wear consisted of a small front apron and a large back apron made of fiber fringe, a hide girdle embellished with metal, as well as a strip of hide ending in three tails. Adolescent girls also wore two fiber aprons, a small one at the front, and a slightly larger one at the back. Fringe was fastened on a strip of hide embellished with small rolls of tin or with fiber stitching. When tied around the waist, the two ends of the strip of hide hang down on the right thigh. The back apron had a short belt tied on the left. Little girls wore a fiber girdle decorated with metal beads and metal decorations suspended at the front and back. The front part, around the pubic area, was embellished with a tuft of three or four fiber strings bound with narrow strips of tin, while a similar tassel of two strings was fastened at

A Karimojong girl blends indigenous and modern dress style in Kotido District, Uganda, 2002. Her beaded goatskin skirt drapes to the back of the knees with plenty of beads covering the front. Until the latter half of the twentieth century, young girls used to remain bare-chested, but from that time on, industrially manufactured garments have been adopted. Photograph by Gwoktcho Stephen.

the back. Acholi men, women, and children wore necklaces and anklets and adorned their chests with strings of beads. Nonetheless, this practice was more common among women. Rows of beads were often fastened together to form wider belts or were worn in single strands.

Historically, the Acholi, like most in northern Uganda, left their hair long and dressed it in an elaborate style. To maintain it, they plastered it with chalk and clay and gave it an ornamental finish using red ochre, seeds, beads, shells, ivory, and metal. This solid mass of stylized hair could be shaved off close to the head, to form a detachable headdress. However, by the mid-1950s, the most popular hairstyle among the Acholi men was a felted pad with a high cone-shaped ornament, slanting forward from the top of the head, embellished with strings of red and white beads, the upper part secured with copper, brass, or fiber strings. The old men wore a closely fitting round skullcap, plain or embellished with beadwork in a circular pattern.

The Acholi commemorate different events with dances requiring special attire to enhance movement. For example, for the *bwola*, a courtly dance performed on the orders of the chief, male dancers holding drums wore animal skin and a headgear made of ostrich feathers. Young boys wore a circlet of raffia with a bunch of cock's feathers behind. The lead singer and dancer were clad in a leopard skin and a headgear made of colorful feathers, typically a reserve of the chief. He also held a shield and a spear as part of his attire. Women dancers wore skin wrappers and multiple beaded strings across the chest and around the waist. In the twenty-first century, the traditional dance attire of the Acholi, as with that of most Ugandans, has been combined or replaced with modern clothing. The Acholi women have adopted the *lesu/kanga*, a printed textile of Swahili-Arab origin with border designs, to replace the skin wrappers and sleeveless tops to cover the bust.

THE LUGBARA

The Lugbara, the largest group of the West Nilotic peoples, are organized according to clans headed by a clan leader. They carefully aligned and sewed fresh leaves to make grass skirts for women and children. Both men and women wore a labret up to ten centimeters (four inches) long through a hole pierced immediately below the center of the lower lip. Regardless of age or gender, the Lugbara encircle their waist with strings of beads of various types, especially for dancing. Upon reaching the age of marriage, girls would wear a small beaded hood draping on the back. Men wore animal skins and detachable headdresses of colorful feathers as well as heavy metal anklets and upper and lower arm ornaments fashioned from coiled brass or iron wire.

During puberty, both girls and boys underwent two important rituals of tribal identification: scarification and the extraction of the lower incisors. Both girls and boys between the age of ten and fourteen had their four lower incisors extracted as a marker of membership to the clan and as a ritual of transition from childhood to adulthood. In addition, piercing the edge and lobes of the ears of both men and women and inserting grass or brass rings was a means of beautification and a marker of identity among the Lugbara. Women wore bands of colored beads around their necks and waists. Originally, necklaces were made from small disks of ostrich eggshell. Women wore as many as fifteen rows of stringed ostrich eggshell disks in varying lengths, forming a tightly fitting gorget from just below the chin to the breasts. Both

men and women cut different patterns over the face and around the arms and, for women, also around the waist.

THE KARIMOJONG

The Karimojong are a conglomeration of seminomadic groups found in northeastern Uganda whose livelihood is dependent on cattle. Cowhide provided clothing for the Karimojong; it was used to make shoulder capes, skirts, bell collars, armlets, and anklets. Due to the harsh tropical climate, they wore minimal clothing yet paid close attention to body adornment. Ear piercing, body painting, and scarification were common traditions. Both men and women pierced their earlobes and adorned them with brass rings; wooden plugs were also common among both sexes. Men wore noserings and aluminum ornaments over the brow and kept their hair long, styled up into a chignon, and worked into a felt mass using clay, grease, and cow dung. They accentuated their hairstyle with tufts of fluffy ostrich feathers in yellow and black and a diamond-shaped peak worn at the top of the head. Karimojong women braided their hair and often ornamented it with beads.

Women wore flared cowhide skirts with an apron decorated with cowry shells, seeds, or imported beads. Young girls wore a skirt of finely dressed cowhide and a beaded apron ornamented with rows of cowry shells and a stiff fringe of trade beads in various colors.

Both men and women adorned their neck with as many as fifteen strings of ostrich eggshell disks, iron beads, and larger tin cylinders threaded onto fiber string, although imported beads in various colors are more common than the tin. The Karimojong displayed boat-shaped ivory or wood bangles on their upper arms when dancing. A small horn with a leather cap fastened by a thong around the upper arm served a more functional purpose of storing tobacco mixed with ash for chewing. Women wore more bracelets and necklaces than men, and some of the body adornments differentiated married and unmarried women. For instance, among the Pokot, a Karimojong subgroup, married women wore iron or brass necklaces and bangles, and the wearing of a small strip of cowhide on top of the bangles signified that the husband paid dowry and thus no other man would seek a relationship with her. During annual initiation ceremonies, mothers of initiates were identified by an animal skin headband and waistband embellished with cowries.

The Karimojong scarified their bodies in different patterns as a symbol of group identification according to clans. For women, scarification also symbolized a stage of human development from childhood to adulthood, as was the case with the ritual of circumcision for men.

EXTERNAL IMPACT ON DRESS TRADITIONS

Since the mid-nineteenth century, styles of dress in Uganda have gradually become more homogeneous because of increasingly enhanced communication and the increased flow of textiles, garments, and accessories from Europe, America, Asia, and the Middle East. As such, a new dress aesthetic has emerged that represents a convenient yet unique marriage between indigenous and foreign styles of dress. For example, *gomesi* (alternatively referred to as *boodingi* or *busuuti*), a dress style that combines attributes from the Baganda, India, and British, was first adopted in Uganda in the early twentieth century. It has become a national dress for women since the late twentieth century. Made from six yards (five and a half meters) of fabric, the gomesi has a yoke, sleeves, and two big buttons. Ordinarily, a woman wraps the gomesi around her body and secures it with a sash, usually made of a shiny satin or jacquard-woven material. On special occasions, more attention is given to arranging part of the fabric into neat pleats on the left side, secured with a sash. Beneath the gomesi are several layers of kikooyi (Indian-made fabric) that serve as undergarments and to ensure a well-rounded bottom for the wearer. Among the Bantu, big bottoms articulate women's beauty.

The 1970s and 1980s were marked by political unrest, military coups, general decay of the economy, closure of textile and garment industries, and the advent of secondhand clothing (emivumba) in Uganda, initially as donations from Christian charitable organizations from the United States and Europe. Nonetheless, secondhand clothes became a popular form of dress among several communities in the mid-1980s after the civil war that brought Yoweri Kaguta Museveni, the current president, into power. As the demand and supply for secondhand clothes increased, it became a lucrative business that has actually surpassed trade in new textiles and garments.

Owino market in Kampala is the center of secondhand products ranging from used undergarments, shoes, shirts, trousers, jackets, skirts, and dresses to gowns, hats, and kerchiefs of varying quality. Owino market has not only sustained those who cannot afford the high prices of new clothes but also provides a repertoire of resources for fashion-conscious Ugandans to mix and match different items from the West with indigenous accessories. With a variety of choices in terms of color, fashion, and uniqueness, even those who can afford to buy new clothes but desire to be unique prefer to buy their clothes from Owino market. Many youths in urban centers have acquired hip-hop dress styles, tight trousers, short tops, and designer wear no different from what one would see in any city in the United States and Europe. Some women dress in tight trousers and short tops that expose the stomach, turning away from a culture that covered the entire body, especially among the Bantu-speaking peoples.

Garments from Dubai have also become popular, and many Ugandans have appropriated kitenge, printed cotton textiles made in the Democratic Republic of Congo or West Africa. Cut from a six-yard (five-and-a-half-meter) length of fabric, kitenge attire for women is comprised of a wrapper (two among the Nilotics) secured tightly at the waist, a wide-neck stylized top, and one yard (about one meter) or less of similar fabric for a turban. The men's kitenge is a two-piece pantalon and a collarless tunic (long- or short-sleeved) that drapes down to the knees or reaches the calves. Many Ugandans from different social, cultural, economic, and political backgrounds including politicians, feminists, popular artists, and religious leaders (in Pentecostal churches) tend to wear kitenge styles at important gatherings. These and other elites have become patrons of a fashion industry that has become more dynamic in the past decade. However, on a day-to-day basis, dresses, blouses, and skirts or shirts and pants are current choices. When it comes to ritual functions, however, etiquette demands that Ugandans wear traditional forms of dress. For example, on occasions marking his coronation anniversaries, the king of Buganda reverts to bark cloth and a leopard skin.

A few designers trained abroad have had an influence on fashion, and, with the introduction of formal courses in textile and fashion design in several art schools, new forms have emerged that

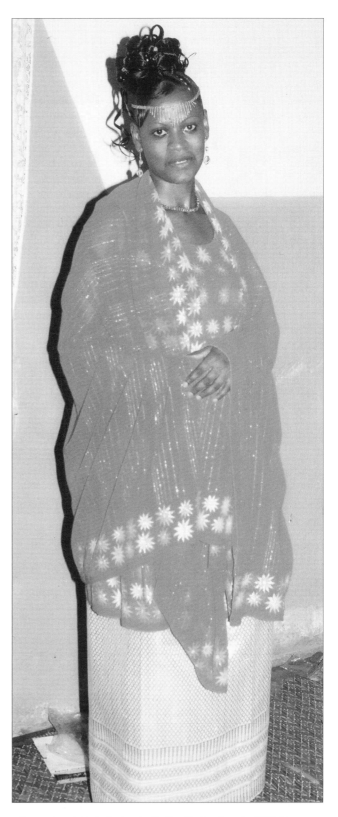

A Munyankore bride in Nnaluvule, Wakiso District, Uganda, 2006. She wears industrially manufactured fabrics but maintains the traditional dress style, which is composed of a short dress, a three-yard (roughly three-meter) fabric draping from over the shoulders to the knees, and another fabric of contrasting color, serving as a wrapper. Photograph by Kizito Fred Kakinda.

celebrate Uganda's diverse culture yet in a modern style. Popular designers in the early twenty-first century include Sylvia Owori of Sylvia Owori Ltd, Santa Anzo of Arapapa, Natasha Kainembabazi of House of Kaine, and Elly Tumwine of Creations Ltd.

Dress in Uganda has changed dramatically in the past two centuries. Access to international trends of fashion through trade, travel for education and leisure, the Internet, and printed and audiovisual media have impacted choices of dress, especially among youth and working-class women. Free-trade policies that have allowed free importation of goods have also influenced trends of dress and fashion in Uganda. Mobile phones and dangling flash drives have, since the dawn of the twenty-first century, become another addition to the dress of many Ugandans.

References and Further Reading

Burt, Eugene C. "Bark Cloth in East Africa." *Textile History* 26, no. 1 (1995): 75–88.

Lugira, Muzzanganda A. *Ganda Art: A Study of the Ganda Mentality with Respect to Possibilities of Acculturation in Christian Art*. Kampala, Uganda: Osasa Publications, 1970.

Nakazibwe, Venny. "Bark-Cloth of the Baganda People of Southern Uganda: A Record of Continuity and Change from the Late Eighteenth Century to the Early Twenty-First Century." Ph.D. dissertation, Middlesex University-London, 2005.

Nannyonga-Tamusuza, Sylvia. *Baakisimba: Gender in Music and Dance among the Baganda People of Uganda*. New York and London: Routledge, 2005.

Nzita, Richard, and Niwampa Mbaga. *Peoples and Cultures of Uganda*. Kampala, Uganda: Fountain Publishers, 1998 (1993).

Perani, Judith, and Norma H. Wolff. *Cloth, Dress and Art Patronage in Africa*. Oxford, UK: Berg, 1999.

Roscoe, John. "The Bahima: A Cow Tribe of Ankole in the Uganda Protectorate." *Journal of the Anthropological Institute of Great Britain and Ireland* 37 (1907): 93–118.

Roscoe, John. "Brief Notes on the Bakene." *Man* 9 (1909): 116–121.

Roscoe, John. *The Baganda: An Account of Their Native Customs and Beliefs*. London: Macmillan, 1911.

Thieme, O. C., and J. Eicher. "The Study of African Dress." In *African Dress II: A Selected and Annotated Bibliography*, edited by I. M. Pokomowski, J. B Eicher, M. F. Hans, and O.C. Thieme, 1–16. East Lansing: African Studies Center, Michigan State University, 1985.

Trowell, Margaret, and K. P. Wachsmann. *Tribal Crafts of Uganda*. London: Oxford University Press, 1953.

Venny Nakazibwe and
Sylvia Nannyonga-Tamusuza

See also Kenya.

Rwanda and Burundi

E xternal appearance has played an important role in the modern history of Rwanda and Burundi, and within this history, by a twist of fate, fashion has been surprisingly well recorded for more than a century. This record of clothing, ornaments, charms, and hairstyles shows that, although the material basis of dress has changed a great deal—especially with the shift away from bark cloth and animal skins—certain forms, such as the togalike *umwitero*, have persisted over time.

Rwanda and Burundi are adjacent highland countries, located along the mountainous ridgeline of the Congo-Nile divide and bordered by Democratic Republic of Congo, Uganda, and Tanzania. Rwanda is often called the "land of a thousand hills," and Burundi has been nicknamed the "Switzerland of Africa" because both are primarily comprised of grassy undulating hillsides.

Sociopolitically, precolonial Rwanda and Burundi were characterized by kingdoms. Although the territorial ranges of these two precolonial kingdoms did not extend throughout the entire zone that would later become Ruanda-Urundi, Colonial era assistance from Germany (which governed the region from the 1890s to about 1916) and Belgium (which controlled the region from 1919 until independence in 1962) would augment the reach of both royal dynasties. Colonialism would also heighten social, economic, and political distinctions between aristocrats and commoners in the two kingdoms. Colonial era clothing styles, particularly from the 1920s onward, would express this ever-increasing differentiation. Yet clothing, like many other aspects of political life in these colonies, would maintain a veneer of "tradition." Thus, royal regalia and the clothing of aristocrats as a class would continuously transform to mark the power differences between the rulers and the ruled, while maintaining a broad stylistic connection to clothing systems of the past.

NINETEENTH-CENTURY CLOTHING STYLES

Documentation of the clothing and ornaments of the people of Rwanda and Burundi began in the late nineteenth century, when European explorers, missionaries, and military units first arrived in the region. These foreigners brought with them two tools—photography and notions of ethnography—that inclined them toward recording the fashions of the region. They also brought

several more inducements—an attraction to royalty, an obsession with racial classification through phenotypes, and a biblical oral tradition about the grandsons of Noah lost in Africa—that stirred their interest in the aristocrats of the region. This motivated Europeans of the late nineteenth and early twentieth centuries to generate a substantial corpus of photographic and ethnographic documentation of the royals in Rwanda and Burundi, as well as of commoners to illustrate the contrast.

Early documentation establishes that Rwandans made their garments from softened hides and pelts, and Burundians made many of their garments from the bark of ficus trees. Ordinary Rwandans tended to wear two-piece outfits comprised of a broad belt or wrapper at the waist and an overpiece tied at the shoulder like a toga. Burundians also wore two-piece sets made from hide but, more often, bark cloth. Burundian elites tended to wear long, finely crafted bark-cloth robes, while their Rwandan

The mother of Mutara III Rudahigwa, the queen mother of Rwanda. Dress at the Rwandan royal court was more complex and stylized than that of the Burundian court. Photograph by Casimir Zagourski, between 1927 and 1937. L'Afrique qui disparaît! Series 2, no. 100, ca. 1937, silver gelatin print on postcard stock. EEPA 1987-242100. Zagourski Collection, Eliot Elisofon Photographic Archives, National Museum of African Art, Smithsonian Institution.

counterparts had taken to wearing cotton cloths procured from long-distance trade. These two-piece outfits kept people warm and dry in the chilly evenings, yet gave them the flexibility to take off one piece in the sun-baked heat of midday. The key to their warmth was the fact that they were made from animal skin.

RWANDAN CLOTHING IN THE NINETEENTH CENTURY

Among the clothing of ordinary Rwandans, the garments of married women were the most difficult and costly to produce. They were the only garments made of the skin of cows, which were the domestic animals of the greatest value in Rwanda. Women's clothing consisted of three pieces: the basic underskirt, an upper-body piece, and a belt, *umweko*, that had enormous social and spiritual significance to the wearer and her family.

The underskirt, *inkanda*, made from softened cowhide, was the garment that marked its wearer's status as a married woman. Until she was married, a young woman wore a fringed belt. This changed to an inkanda at a ceremony following nuptial seclusion that marked her public presentation as a married woman. The skirt was tied and knotted at the waist with a belt, umweko, ornamented with a tassel made from softened tree-bark fibers. The belt and its ornaments were politely referred to as *impumbya za umugabo*, the "husband's good luck charm." Also attached to the belt, particularly when its wearer became a mother, was a small gourd (*ubunure*) containing amulets and charms. The number and kinds of charms were augmented throughout the wearer's life. Some were personal. Others ensured the well-being of her family. All of them were secret: this set of charms was highly personal and powerful for the wearer. She guarded her small gourd with great care, believing that if it broke, her life would be endangered. She kept these charms on her belt until she was widowed or died. At her death, her daughter-in-law received the charm set and was charged with depositing it at the *umurinzi* tree that marked her mother-in-law's grave.

The third element of a woman's basic clothing was a wrap thrown over the shoulders or tied at one shoulder. This piece could be made from a variety of materials, including simple or bead-embroidered skin, bark cloth, or imported cotton. In the warm afternoons, women often removed this piece until the evening chill set in. Small children snuggled warmly against their mother's backs in sheepskins. The sheepskin was tied around the mother by its legs, which were knotted at the mother's chest.

Rwandan men's garments were made from other skins—commonly, goat, sheep, or antelope. Men's ensembles consisted of a belt or wrapper and an upper-body toga. The belt, or *ishabure*, was made from the skin of a male calf. The piece was worked in various ways, often with long, thin leather strips that descended to midcalf. It was held in place at the waist by a cord belt to which many wearers attached a small carryall sack, or *uruhago*. The second piece of the ensemble was a large skin tied at the shoulder by leather strips that had been the animal's legs.

Young adults, adolescents, and older children wore ishabure belt wrappers decorated with long fringes. Young men, when herding, replaced the ishabure with a belt called *uruyonga* made of banana fibers. These fibers descended in long fringes that the herders rolled and twisted. Many Rwandans of all ages, when engaging in tasks that might soil their clothing, wore protective aprons of banana leaves. They took off and folded up their togalike upper garment to protect it from harm, including heavy rain. To protect themselves from heavy rain, outdoor workers—notably herders—made small shelters of banana leaves shaped like a canoe end that they wore on the head and shoulders to keep their hands free when they were on the move.

BURUNDIAN CLOTHING IN THE NINETEENTH CENTURY

Bark cloth is the material most strongly associated with traditional Burundian garments. Burundians wore bark-cloth garments until Belgian colonial pressure pushed them to adopt cotton textiles. By the mid-1930s, bark cloth had virtually disappeared from daily life in Burundi. But this change occurred rapidly, because photographs show that, even in the 1920s, bark cloth was the preferred textile for Burundians of various regions, backgrounds, and social classes. Aristocrat and commoner alike wore garments made from this relatively warm, attractive, locally produced, and renewable material.

Bark cloth, called *impuzu*, was made from the bark of the ficus tree. Several species were used for producing impuzu. The preferred species were *umuvumu* (*Ficus ovata*), *umumanda* (*Ficus ovata*), and *umuhoro* or *umuhororo* (*Ficus congensis*). These species, regarded by Burundians as strong, sturdy, and well rooted, had the distinction of playing a major role in domestic architecture as the posts that anchored the protective fence surrounding the family homestead (*urugo*). These trees, therefore, were integrated into the majority of farming households. For many families, bark cloth was just one more element of a family's system of subsistence production.

For ordinary Burundians, making the bark textile itself was not considered specialized work—although it was a task for men—so the cloth was made locally, usually by a male family member or a neighbor. The next step—working the cloth into a garment—was considered specialized work. For this, people sought out a tailor who could fashion it into a well-fitting, personalized outfit.

The cloth maker pounded the bark with smooth, even strokes across its surface: flattening it, spreading it out further, and expanding its size. Impuzu is naturally reddish brown, but Burundians preferred darker colors. Sometimes people stenciled designs like triangles, crescents, and lines onto their cloth. To do this, they made the stencils from green banana leaves into which they cut designs. Once colored, the textile was ready to be made into a garment. At this point, people sought out a specialized tailor called *umupfunditsi*. The tailor cut the bark cloth by knife or spearpoint. The pieces were sewn together with thread made from thin, twisted leather strips or banana and other plant fibers.

The outfit for a man was composed of two pieces. The base was a tunic: the togalike *ipfundo*, which was tied at the shoulder. The other piece was a large cloth called the *umutamana* that hung capelike from a strap. The toga was an approximately knee-length cloth that passed under the left shoulder and was knotted on the right shoulder. This left the garment completely open on the right side with the right arm free and uncovered for maximum movement. Left-handed wearers dressed in the inverse.

The cape tended to cover the wearer's chest and right side and was of a length that went down below the wearer's knees. It was held in place at the left shoulder by a little strap that passed around the neck and was fixed in back. The cape's upper edge was neatly cut. Its bottom edge was frayed in a manner that resembled long fringes of bark fibers. Each of these garments was decorated at the shoulder with a tassel of long raffia fibers, essentially front-facing epaulettes. On the right shoulder, the tassel was affixed to the knot of the toga. On the left shoulder, the tassel hung from the strap of the cape. These and other ornaments were signs of the wearer's status. Social prominence and wealth were represented by more numerous and more prominent ornaments and by the length, suppleness, and condition of the garment. Ordinary men tended to wear their above-the-knee togas alone with few ornaments and without the outer cape. Poorer men wore shorter, rougher, shredding togas that emphasized (or at least exposed) their dusty, chapped legs.

The outfit for an adult (married) woman consisted of three pieces: a bark-cloth or skin wrapper (*umukenyero* or *umukesha*), a large cloak (umutamana or *umushanana*), and a wrapping piece for carrying an infant (*ipetso* or *ingovyi*). During daily activities, a woman normally just wore the wrapper, which she tied at the waist, leaving her upper body unencumbered by clothing. In the chilly evenings and in certain contexts, the woman might adjust her wrapper, pulling it upward to wrap around her chest. She might also pull her cloak over her shoulders. Mothers of small children wore an additional piece of clothing for carrying a child on the back. This piece was normally made of animal skin, such as antelope, goat, or gazelle. To protect the child from the midday sun or the evening chill, the mother draped the umutamana over the child.

Burundian women sought to soften and enhance their clothing by rubbing it with creams, often milk based, into which they crushed fragrant plants. Creams also improved the garment's impermeability to rain. To decorate their garments, both women and men twisted and braided in plant-fiber fringes. For special occasions, a woman added a special fringed belt and wore various ornaments (to be described in the next section).

In general, ordinary Burundian adults had two sets of clothing: everyday work clothes (*impuzu z'inkoranwa*) and dress clothes (*impuzu z'inkesha*) that they wore when they went to pay formal visits or attended ceremonies and occasions. Men's work clothes varied, depending on their particular livelihood. Some specialists, such as blacksmiths and certain hunters, used to work in the nude for a variety of reasons, both practical and spiritual. Generally, men and women protected their apparel, wearing fewer and older garments when they worked and leaving their newer, larger, and meticulously conditioned garments for nicer occasions. Wives tended to take charge of maintaining and storing the family's garments. They conditioned, perfumed, and then laid out the garments on clean woven mats, then rolled them up carefully to maintain their freshness and shape. Conserved like this, formal garments, which constituted a form of wealth, were expected to last for several years.

Burundian children of ordinary families, both boys and girls, wore a variety of charms and ornaments. Smaller children were not considered to be responsible enough for, or in need of, specially made clothing. Occasionally, children wore the remnants of adult garments, particularly skins. But an outfit constituted an investment of labor and resources that a child was not seen to require. It took a ficus tree about fifteen years to grow to a size sufficient to be used in textile production, and there was a rule of thumb that if a tree were planted when a child was quite small, then both the person and the tree would grow into readiness together. Youths usually received their own personal clothing at about adolescence. Boys old enough to remain away from the home for days at a time herding cattle were seen to be in need of their own cloak to cover them for the long hours spent in chilly pastures. Girls old enough to catch the attention of prospective suitors required their own wrapper (*igikwemu*), which they knotted just about the breast, and a decorative belt (*inyonga*).

AMULETS AND ORNAMENTS

In Rwanda as well as Burundi, nineteenth- and early-twentieth-century people wore a variety of amulets and ornaments. From early childhood, when individuals struggled with their initial, and often most dangerous, bouts of endemic illnesses, charms became a regular element of a person's apparel. Protective amulets or talismans, called *ibiheko* as a general category, were worn by Rwandans and Burundians throughout their lives around the waist, neck, wrists, arms, and even the top of the head. Amulets in the form of claws, teeth, medicine-filled horns, roots, seeds, and small metallic medicine-filled cones were tied to the body with strings of fiber, leather, and sometimes wire. In Burundi, children from large families, beginning with the sixth child, wore special amulets (*ibimazi*) linked to their birth order in the family.

Although they could be seen readily on young people, amulets were not just the domain of children; adults also wore them. Women, whose ability to bear children was a source of social leverage and power but also a source of constant anxiety, wore charms to protect their bodies against spiritual and terrestrial dangers. These ranged from accidental encounters with nature spirits—into whose territory a woman ventured regularly in the course of farming, water and firewood gathering, and other daily work—to magical assaults from jealous in-laws, co-wives, and neighbors. Women wore talismans to protect their children as well. Men also wore amulets. For men such as iron smelters and blacksmiths, hunters and lake navigators, amulets mitigated the hazards of their occupation. For prominent men such as sorcerers and princes, talismans reinforced and enhanced their considerable power. On adults, amulets were often more numerous but less visible than on children, tucked discretely into one's clothing.

In contrast to amulets, which sometimes conveyed magical strength and were meant to be seen but other times revealed fear and were meant to be hidden, ornaments were nearly always intended to be seen. Ornaments were statements about the social position and individuality of the wearer. Some ornaments, like the band of motherhood (*urugori*) attested to the social position or achievement of the wearer. This band, worn around a woman's head and passing across her forehead, was woven from stalks of sorghum, a plant strongly associated with fertility. The band was worn by women of both kingdoms, although it was more widespread in Rwanda. There, regional variations included single bands woven from maize plant fibers and thin, double bands of banana fiber. In some regions, all mothers of infants still young enough to be breast-fed were honored with this band (*akabubu*). In other regions, it was the mother who had given birth to her seventh child who wore the distinctive headdress (*urugori rw'ingara*). While the urugori band was imbued with slightly different meanings in various subregions and time periods, in all cases, it declared the wearer's position as a mother and hence an adult in the fullest sense.

The man's hunting bracelet was another ornament that conveyed the position and achievement of its wearer. This was a very large, thick, wooden wristlet, functionally meant to guide the bow-string and protect the arm from its recoil. The most lovely examples were decorated with inlaid copper or iron pieces. The bracelet was associated especially with Burundian men, although it was worn by residents of the southern reaches of Rwanda as well.

Some ornaments had intensely personal and even spiritual meaning, like a woman's belt. Other ornaments were primarily functional but had an idiosyncratic element, like the wooden or cane-nose pincers used to hold snuff in the nostrils, which Burundian men suspended from leather lace or a string tied to the shoulder of their clothes.

Ornaments and styles differed significantly between Rwanda and Burundi, at least in the late nineteenth century, when outside observers arrived and made written descriptions. Rwanda was more engaged in international trade. This was particularly true at the level of the royal court, which had an impact on styles of regional elites and ordinary people. Burundi was resistant to international trade at the level of the royal court, although it was engaged in regional long-distance trade. Commoners in both kingdoms decorated themselves with ornaments such as the polished teeth of hippos and wild pigs and metallic cones hanging from fiber threads around the neck or on the upper arm. But in Rwanda, trade beads appeared at the throats and on the arms of ordinary people. In Burundi, people wore primarily locally or regionally produced ornaments. In both Rwanda and Burundi, ordinary people wore woven fiber and iron or copper wire rings on their upper arms, wrists, and ankles. But in Rwanda, an especially wealthy commoner might enhance her outfit with a light cotton trade cloth (*merikani*), while her Burundian counterpart might be inclined to demonstrate her wealth with a carved shell necklace (*ikirezi*), which Rwandans did not wear, or a heavy iron bracelet instead.

In both Rwanda and Burundi, commerce moved because of the heavy use of commodity currencies—commodities such as beads were used as a medium in exchanges. The demand for these commodities was so regular and widespread that they held a widely accepted value. They were also standard enough in form, size, and weight that they could be regarded as interchangeable, like coins. Beads were commodity currencies in international long-distance trade. Wire anklets called *inyerere* were commodity currencies in regional long-distance trade. Both of these items were widely used personal ornaments among ordinary people in Rwanda, while in Burundi, anklets were more popular and beads were rather rare.

Nineteenth-century Rwandans and Burundians styled their hair and decorated their bodies in different ways as well. In Rwanda, elaborate hairstyles (*amasunzu*) won the admiration of turn-of-the-century visitors. Rwandan adults of both genders combed out their hair into high swirling ridges, which they emphasized by shaving the rest of the head. The ridges took various shapes, including halolike half-circles, geometric shapes, and intertwined crescents. Burundian adults tended to shave their heads entirely or, at most, leave a small tuft of hair (*isunzu*) on top of the head. Children of both kingdoms sometimes wore their hair in long braids or carefully twisted and matted dreadlocks dressed with hair cream. In Burundi, it was especially the wealthy children who wore such hairstyles. Most often, the children of commoners had their head shaved, except for a small tuft on top.

Skin care for the residents of both kingdoms was a small luxury sought by everyone but was carried out differently depending on social class. Wealthier people rubbed their skin with semiliquid, milk-based skin cream to which they added ground red minerals (*agahama*) and aromatic plants. This gave the skin of those who could afford such pampering a stylish reddish sheen. People of more modest means rubbed their head and body with a concoction of a very light gray color made from minerals, ashes, or a certain animal excrement. This made the skin smooth and also protected the skin from common parasites.

Tattoos or decorative scarification (*urusago*) were more prevalent in Rwanda than in Burundi. Wearers tended to have these patterns on the upper arm or down the two sides of the chest or the back from the shoulder to the waist (like suspender straps). A popular pattern was two aligned rows of half-moon crescents, each about the size of a finger. Another pattern featured a chain of crescents in sets of three, with two crescents open and facing a third. These patterns were produced with small parallel incisions made with a blade with a formula of crushed plant and ashes rubbed into the incision to make it raise up above the surface of the skin. Both men and women decorated themselves with these tattoos. There were special patterns (*imanzi*) for elite warriors.

Material differences between commoners and aristocrats existed in both Rwanda and Burundi, but the differences were far more marked in Rwanda. In part, this was because social distance between commoner and royal was greater in Rwanda than in Burundi. It was also because Rwandan aristocrats availed themselves of the opportunities of international trade prior to colonialism. They developed a set of styles that drew on non-Rwandan materials such as cotton cloth and beads but incorporated them into distinctively Rwandan fashions. Burundi, as a kingdom, initially resisted international trade and the political challenges that came with it. In addition, Burundian aristocrats, as the arbiters of taste and style, preferred their bark-cloth clothing, which they regarded as warmer, more modest, and more elegant. They saw the cotton textiles coming into Rwanda from English-dominated territories as flimsy and immodestly transparent. They, therefore, continued to wear bark cloth until well into the 1920s, when Belgian colonial pressure forced Burundians to relinquish their impuzu and to adopt Western modes of dress and fashion.

CLOTHING AT THE RWANDAN ROYAL COURT

Consistent with the fact that the ideology of royalty was more elaborated, and the social distance between royals and commoners was much greater in Rwanda than in Burundi, dress at the Rwandan royal court was more complex and stylized than that at the Burundian court. Most striking were the elaborate headdresses worn by the court's central figures: the queen mother, the king, and the king's wives. As replete as they were with ideological symbolism, the headdresses also incorporated glass beads, a material that was foreign to Rwanda and relatively rare.

Glass beads have been found in archaeological sites in the broader Great Lakes region dating from well before 1500, but up until the mid-nineteenth century, when trade with the Indian Ocean coast became firmly established, glass beads, cowries, and conus shells were regarded as fabulous and exotic pieces of jewelry. In the first half of the eighteenth century, Rwandan king Mazimpaka, a man remembered for his elegance and style, acquired a red bead from the Indian Ocean coast that created a sensation, according to historian Jan Vansina, who notes that, in the mid-eighteenth century, glass beads were so special that the word used to designate such a bead meant a "coveted thing." At the end of the eighteenth century, glass beads were still so rare and valuable that Rwandan king Ndabarasa was known as "the one who is wealthy in glass bead collars."

As it became available, the royals also incorporated foreign-manufactured trade cloth into their regalia. The exceptionalness that early-eighteenth-century Rwandans attributed to imported cloth is illustrated by the fact that a large red cotton trade cloth was kept in King Mazimpaka's royal treasury. A century later, foreign-manufactured cloth was still prestigious, although less unique. Members of the Rwandan royal dynasty used it, developing a syncretistic, as well as somewhat idiosyncratic, style that visually represented their claim to authority.

In an 1894 unplanned encounter with a German visitor, King Kigeri IV Rwabugiri of Rwanda wore a garland of green leaves on his head that dipped downward at his forehead. During the nearly two years of subsequent interaction between King Kigeri and various Germans, before his death in 1897, the king wore elaborate headdresses: crownlike beaded and woven-fiber bands from which fur or fibers rose up and encircled his head. A consistent element of the king's headdresses was the vertical strings of beads attached to the band that partially obscured his face almost like a veil. The obscuring of the face with a veil of beads was adopted and elaborated by Kigeri's successor, King Yuhi V Musinga. In his first

year of rule, the young king wore a beautifully worked bovine skin wrapper rolled around his waist that exposed his upper body and a beaded crown that partially hid his face.

By 1898, a German military administrator of Rwanda noted that the wealthy wore trade cloth, the ordinary wore skin and occasionally bark cloth. The king wore unique combinations of the two. Photographed in 1907, King Musinga wore an ankle-length white cloth wrapper edged at the bottom with fringe and accessorized with an apparently imported belt. He wore a dark cloth cloak tied at one shoulder and slung over the other shoulder, obscuring one arm. On the visible arm, he wore several bracelets to which were affixed various ornaments and possibly charms. On his head, he wore two bands in the style of hairbands extending from the top of his head to behind his neck and a third band horizontally around his forehead that sloped downward, touching the tops of his eyebrows. Affixed to the bands were two wires that stood up on each side of his head like antennas or horns. On the top of his head, he wore stars. Later that year, a Musinga seated on a litter received an ethnographic expedition. For this occasion, he was adorned in beads and ornaments and wore a leather apron decorated with strings of beads and an impressive beaded headdress. In later meetings, he wore flowing robes of cotton trade cloth.

Men wearing a contemporary interpretation of warrior dress during dance presentations at the royal court, Burundi, ca. 2000. Photograph by Bruno De Hogues.

King Musinga and the royal family, Rwanda, ca. 1910. The king (front row center) and queen mother (front left) wear elaborate headdresses, while the lesser members of the court wear headdresses that resemble cow horns. Photographer unknown, ca. 1910, silver gelatin print. EEPA White Fathers (Pères Blancs) Mission Collection. EEPA 1987-110092. Eliot Elisofon Photographic Archives National Museum of African Art, Smithsonian Institution.

Photographs from 1910 show headdresses that became more elaborate, larger, higher, and with more complex beadwork on the band and the "veil." The queen mother's headdress became even more elaborate than the king's, while lesser members of the royal court also wore headdresses designed with vertical wires resembling cow horns.

CLOTHING AT THE BURUNDIAN ROYAL COURT

The outfits of aristocrats—important regional families and the people at the royal court—were made by specialists. This specialty was not an ethnic specialty; rather, it was a family specialty, with particular branches of well-known clans having a recognized link to the royal court as vestment makers to the kings. They were also called *abapfunditsi b'umwami*. They lived in royal domains that belonged to the king and lands bestowed upon them for their service to the royal family. In addition, there were famous garment makers recognized for their skill who were sought after as private clothiers to the powerful, wealthy, and royal.

It was said that members of the royal family wore garments made of the cloth of the umuhororo tree only. So a royal clothier and his team produced large quantities of impuzu made especially from this tree, which they cultivated in abundance at their domain. When they had produced bark cloth sufficient to outfit the royals served and their key courtiers, the craftsmen rolled up their bark-cloth sheets by the dozen, a quantity known as *umutita*, and set off for the palace. At court, the craftsmen received lodging where they could set up an atelier, unroll the cloth, and set to work making outfits on measure. When the court's needs were

satisfied, the queen sometimes ordered extra outfits to give to her friends. It was an honor to receive a garment from the queen.

The craftsmen's journey to the palace usually took place in the season of *Umuganuro*, the annual first fruits festival. For that occasion, the king wore a vestment called *indaba*, made by a family designated by custom. At Umuganuro, female royal ritualists wore two-piece garments comprised of a skirtlike umukenyero and an umutamana cloak, tinted sometimes in black, sometimes in yellow, especially for the ceremony. The royal drummers and the royal warriors, all men, wore their performance garments. The warriors dressed in leopard-skin kilts; dramatic fur and fiber headdresses; numerous amulets, including medicine-filled horns; and ornaments, including sets of iron bells attached to leather cuffs worn around their ankles with which they stamped out complex rhythms when they danced at court.

The king, the queen, and other aristocrats wore bark-cloth clothing conceptually similar to that of commoners, but their garments were made from larger, finer bark sheets and much more elaborately decorated in delicate fringes. At their shoulders they wore large thick tassels of twisted and braided raffia fibers (*imihivu*), similar to enormous front-facing epaulettes. The magnificent tassels, scented with aromatic plants, descended from the wearer's shoulders to the chest to just above the knee. They exuded wealth and power.

The king of Burundi was himself a dynamic amulet whose existence ensured the prosperity of his people. His body, a conduit of sacredness, was covered in charms, quite literally from head to toe. By contrast, the queen and other royal women were covered in wealth, with arms so laden in heavy copper and iron bracelets

and legs so encumbered in nearly knee-high stacks of wire inyerere anklets that physical movement was significantly impeded.

Another highly expensive ornament that was characteristically
Burundian and often worn by aristocrats was a large crescent-
shaped shell necklace (*igihete*) imported from the Indian Ocean.

COLONIAL INFLUENCES

With Germany's defeat in the First World War came the loss of
its colonies. Rwanda and Burundi were ceded to Belgium, which
regarded the two kingdoms as needing extensive intervention
to "civilize" and modernize their administrations. In Burundi, where
these changes started taking effect in 1925, elites came under tremendous pressure to demonstrate or "prove" their commitment to
"civilization" by adopting Western dress. For example, aristocrats
and the successful commoners who worked with them as "subchiefs" found that they received better job evaluations from the
Belgian administrators who could promote them if they Westernized their dress. The example of Baranyanka, a young Burundian
"chief," made the situation clear: He wore three-piece suits, sports
jackets and nice shoes and drove around in an American automo-
bile, and he was regarded as the model of success. By the late 1920s,
this "dress-for-success" approach on the part of the Belgian administration had influenced elite male fashion and was beginning to
have a trickle-down effect on ambitious younger men. After 1934,
older men, who did not particularly appreciate the concept of
Western clothing, nevertheless shifted from bark cloth to cotton
cloth, even if they still preferred to wear it knotted at the shoulder.
This was because the colonial administration took advantage of
a 1934 typhus epidemic to prohibit bark cloth under the guise of
health and hygiene regulations. Meanwhile, formal and informal
work regulations encouraged the wearing of shorts and pants.

Colonial regulations tended to focus on men, leaving Burundian women somewhat more latitude to choose their clothing
trends, but the hygiene regulations were clear: no bark cloth.
Therefore, women shifted to cotton cloth wrappers, which their
fathers or husbands purchased from traders or the shops of regional commercial centers. Strings of beads, particularly the pinkish *ubudede*, inyerere anklets, and, increasingly, Christian medals
and rosaries worn as necklaces dominated the fashion of ordinary
women in the later 1930s through the 1940s. Westernized blouses
and skirts sewn by tailors were the domain of wealthier women.

In Rwanda, a quite different aesthetic developed. There, although Western clothing styles became one source of reference for
fashion, Rwandan traditional styles were at least equally influential, if not more so. The Rwandan royal court, for whom the myth
of Hamitic origins—that is, ancestry that traced from the biblical
tale of the sons of Noah—served as an important ideological underpinning of its colonial political power, emphasized its mythic
character visually with fashions that referenced the imaginary
Hamitic homeland in the Horn of Africa. These garments, worn
by both men and women, featured a two pieces of light-colored,
lightweight cotton cloth. The largest cloth wrapped around the
waist and extended to the ankles, while a second cloth was draped
across the torso, extended down to the knees or below, and tied
atop the right shoulder, toga style.

The men's version of this garment was worn over a Western-
style long- or short-sleeved tailored shirt and trousers, either
long or short, the latter being entirely covered by the long cotton
wrapper. In most cases, the two cloths were of a similar light-

A crowded market in Bujumbura, Burundi, ca. 2000. Vivid colors and patterns,
in cotton or in polyester, are a favorite choice of contemporary Rwandan and
Burundian women. Photograph by Bruno De Hogues.

colored fabric, creating an overall shape that resembled a tall, narrow column. This garment, in combination with a high amasunzu
hairstyle—that is, hair combed to stand up straight, forming high
vertical ridges—and a thin-pointed beard combed out to extend
four inches (about ten centimeters) downward and outward from
the chin gave an overall impression of height, slenderness, and a
long, narrow face and high forehead—not unlike a tomb engraving of an Egyptian king. The particulars of the fabric, especially
the wrapper, shifted with style changes. In general, the greater the
means of the wearer and the formality of the situation, the lighter
and more solid-colored the cloth. Less wealthy men wore more
colorful and decorative premeasured cloth pieces such as the East
African *kitenge*. A wealthier man in an everyday context would
have been likely to wear a wrapper of colorful, patterned cloth
purchased by measure from a cloth bolt, which tended to be more
expensive than premeasured cloth bought by the piece. His toga-
tied overgarment, however, was often solid, light-colored cotton
sheeting. Jewelry and other ornaments—including head ornaments like wreaths, furs, beads, and crown; neck ornaments like
beads and amulets; and wrist and ankle rings—varied according
to the wearer's age, position, region, wealth, and personal style.

Rwandan women of the Colonial era elite set—for example,
the wives of chiefs—preferred that their version of this garment
be made of very thin lightweight material, particularly the overpiece that they tied or fixed with a brooch at the right shoulder and

draped elegantly over the left arm to expose the left shoulder. Underneath, these upper-class women wore very feminine blouses, often delicately trimmed with lace or scalloping at the neckline or on the short sleeves. Beneath the skirt, which, according to mode, might be full, gathered at the waist, and held in place by a cord or slightly less full, women wore underskirts for modesty made of more opaque cloth. Jewelry, including multiple necklaces made exclusively of beads, special beads hung on cords, or Western-style pendants hung on delicate chains, adorned the women's necks, and bracelets, particularly on the exposed right arm, adorned their wrists. On special occasions, royal women wore complex headdresses made of two thick white bands. One band encircled the head at the hairline, from the forehead to the nape of the neck. To this was attached a second band, forward of each ear. This second band also encircled the head, but it did so more vertically, rising from the lower forehead, where it rested delicately at the bridge of the nose, to the lofty summit of the wearer's piled-high, dome-shaped hair. On the left side of this headdress, at the point just forward of the ear where the two bands met, a pair of vertically oriented, drumstick-shaped ornaments of approximately one foot (thirty centimeters) in length were affixed to and tucked into the headdress. These headdresses, which appeared at formal occasions well into the 1950s, recalled the cow horns that had risen from royal headdresses in the opening decade of the century.

While these distinctly stylized traditional garments appeared on adults of different generations at important occasions and on more conservative or elderly men and women in more quotidian circumstances, from the mid-1930s onward, wealthy urban dwellers tended to wear Western fashions. Men of the political class, following the example of King Mutara, wore business suits, often in a chic French or Italian cut, with crisp well-pressed shirts, stylish shoes, and watches. Their business-oriented counterparts wore suits cut in the more conservative Belgian style. All of these suits could be made to order at the tailors in urban Usumbura (Bujumbura), Burundi. Rwanda's elite women of the later Colonial era, particularly those who were educated, had dresses cut in the European style, as did young women who had the privilege of attending school. But the Rwandan sense of aesthetic weighed on the side of traditional garments for most social occasions until well into the era of independence.

In both Rwanda and Burundi, middle-level professionals such as clerks wore shirts, usually short-sleeved, and short trousers made from khaki-colored cotton drill imported from East Africa. Middle-class women wore blouses and wrappers made of cheerfully decorated cotton cloth, as well as East African kitenge and khanga. For daily work, women wore sturdy cotton cloth in dark colors or kitenge that was no longer their newest and best. Rural dwellers in Rwanda and Burundi wore various combinations of cotton drill, kitenge, bark cloth, and skin, depending on their age, region, and means.

POSTINDEPENDENCE STYLES IN RWANDA AND BURUNDI

The coming of independence in 1962 saw Rwanda and Burundi in political circumstances that differed greatly from each other and that oriented each country somewhat differently in terms of stylistic reference. Independent Burundi saw the coming of a new elite that was Tutsi but not royal. Its stylistic reference, especially at the highest echelons, soon became Paris, and Brussels

secondarily. Male members of the political class shopped at international capitals while visiting for professional matters, picking up suits, watches, shoes, jogging suits, and sports footwear for themselves, and cosmetics, perfumes, jewelry, accessories, dresses, and cloth for their wives. Less-well-traveled professionals sought goods of similar Western style from neighboring Kenya and from urban shops that brought in goods from West African capitals such as Dakar and Abidjan and Gulf emporia such as Dubai.

By the 1970s and 1980s, clothing and textiles from India, Pakistan, Dubai, Kenya, and Zaire as well as textiles produced by the Burundian manufacturer COTEBU fed into middle-class material culture whose styles clustered into the loose categories of *Senegalais* (West African fashion styles, featuring boubous with *pantalons* for both men and women, hats, and headwraps), *Zairois* (Central African fashions that for women were characterized by creatively shaped tailored blouses and matching wrappers made from lovely and expensive cloths like *Wax Hollandaise* and *Super Java*), Swahili (styles featuring East African khanga and kitenge), European, and *Burundais* (for women, styles that referenced the traditional togalike overgarment and wrapper).

Independence era Rwanda saw the reversal of the colonial order and the entrance into power of Hutus, first a political group that was strongly comprised of people from the same general region as the earlier kingdom and later a political group that explicitly defined itself as *not* coming from the region of the kingdom. Materially, Rwandans referenced Paris, but to a lesser degree than did Burundians. They embraced Zairois styles and Rwandan traditional styles for women, but, overall, Rwandans seemed to place less emphasis on clothing as a means of expressing class difference than did their Burundian neighbors.

In Rwanda, as in Burundi, a very brisk used-clothing market fostered a fashion mix at the middle-class level, even as people sought to reproduce the fashion that was in style at the time. In both countries, styles for poorer rural people referenced what was available in the region's shops, because clothing purchased in a shop had greater prestige than the used clothing for sale in the market.

In the 1990s, civil wars and civilian and military massacres on a catastrophic scale caused profound social rupture in both countries. Rwandans and Burundians experienced death and displacement on an enormous scale, and this has had a strong impact on all aspects of social life, including material culture. A visible consequence of this in postwar Rwanda was the adoption of military and militant styles, including the widespread wearing of military clothing by both soldiers and civilians, the ubiquitous presence of olive green, a much wider acceptance of the wearing of trousers by young women, a perceptible shift away from highly feminized hair and clothing styles among younger women, a proliferation of Chicago Bulls sportswear, and a general trend toward the adoption of American sportswear and styles. New and surprising shifts in style references will undoubtedly occur as transforming political and economic trends bring new goods and new images into the lives of the citizens of Rwanda and Burundi.

References and Further Reading

Bourgeois, R. *Banyarwanda et Barundi, Tome I : Ethnographie 8˚ des Mémoires de l'Académie royale des sciences coloniales.* Séries 2, no. 15. Brussels, Belgium: Académie royale des sciences colonials, 1957.

Celis, G. "La confection des tissus en écorce de focus." *Afrika-Tervuren* 3–4 (1970): 66–73.

Friedrich, Adolf. *Ins innerste Afrika*. Leipzig, Germany: Klinkhard and Biermann, 1909.

Gahama, Joseph. "Les vêtements en ficus au Burundi ancien." *Culture et Société* 5 (1982): 28–41.

Geary, Christraud M. *In and Out of Focus: Images from Central Africa, 1885–1960*. Washington, DC: Smithsonian National Museum of African Art; London: Philip Wilson Publishers, 2002.

Graf von Götzen, Gustav Adolf. *Durch Afrika von Ost nach West*. Berlin: Dietrich Reimer, 1899.

Lestrade, Arthur. *Notes d'ethnographie du Rwanda*. Archives d'Anthropologie, no. 17. Tervuren, Belgium: Musée royal de l'Afrique Centrale, 1972.

Maquet, Jacques J., and Denyse Hiernaux-l'Hoest. *Ruanda: Essai photographique sur une société africaine en transition*. Brussels: Elsevier, 1957.

Meyer, Hans. *Les Barundi*. Translated by Françoise Willamann. Paris: Société française d'histoire d'outre-mer, 1984.

Nsanze, Augustin. *Le Burundi Ancien: l'économie du pouvoir de 1877 à 1920*. Paris: Éditions L'Harmattan, 2001.

Ntahonkiriye, Melchior, and Richard Ndayizigamiye. *Regards sur le Burundi Ancien: Quelques scènes de la vie quotidienne à la fin du XIXème Siècle*. Bujumbura, Burundi: Ministère de la Jeunesse, des Sports et de la Culture, 1990.

Van der Burgt, J. *Un grand peuple de l'afrique equatoriale*. Bois-le-Duc, 1903.

Vansina, Jan. *Antecedents to Modern Rwanda: The Nyiginya Kingdom* Madison: University of Wisconsin Press, 2004.

Michele D. Wagner

See also Republic of Congo and Democratic Republic of Congo.

PART 10

Southern Africa

Angola

Angola is on the Atlantic Ocean and neighbored by Democratic Republic of Congo, Zambia, and Namibia. Angola was originally inhabited by Khoisan-speaking people (Bushmen, San, ¡Kung, or Khwe), most of them displaced by migrations of Bantu believed to have started around three thousand years ago. Today, small Khoisan populations remain spread through southern Angola with their territories extending to Namibia and Botswana, where some may continue their hunter-gatherer mode of livelihood or pursue trade and labor for pastoral (now mostly settled) Bantu peoples such as the Herero in farms and cattle stations. In southern Angola, Bantu pastoralist groups include the Herero, the Nyaneka-Humbe, the Ambo, and the Mbukushu.

Traditional dress in southern Angola reflects a shared taste for natural materials modified in a myriad of fashions to suit different lifestyles. Khoisan peoples' approach to clothing is suitable for those who pursue hunting and gathering in semiarid lands. Cache-sex aprons, belts, capes, and other clothing items are made from leather and may be decorated with beadwork manufactured from ostrich eggshell or from imported glass beads. Ostrich eggshell beads are an item of value for the Khoisan who continue to produce and trade long strands with their Bantu neighbors for use in their own dress.

DRESS IN PASTORAL SOCIETIES

Dress among the Bantu of southern Angola similarly draws from available material resources. Body ornamentation and dress become a true means of artistic expression with great material elaboration and attention to detail in stylization, decoration, and accessorizing. The styles are numerous, each meant to indicate ethnic affiliation as well as gender, age, and social status.

The dress of the Himba of southwestern Angola is considered one of the most elegant in type and style. Being pastoralists, the Himba have ready access to goat- and sheepskins to process into soft leather and wear as part of their traditional dress. Himba women wrap long leather skirts around the waist that are held in place with belts made from the same material. Some have numerous straps of leather that form free-flowing front aprons and others numerous metal and/or shell beads.

Especially dramatic is the traditional Himba *ekori* headdress constructed of leather with a thick fold arching over the wearer's forehead and extending back to cover the head. At the back, it is built upward to create three extensions rounded at the bottom and pointed at the ends. Some are proportionally quite large and suggest leaves or animal ears protruding several inches (about eight to thirteen centimeters) above the head. The ekori is decorated with bands of metal beads, and a strand of beads may be

A Himba woman wearing the *ekori* headdress, Angola, late twentieth century. The headdress is constructed of leather, with a thick fold arching over the wearer's forehead and extending back to cover the head. The *ekori* is decorated with bands of metal beads, and a strand of beads may be wrapped around the head a few times to hold the headdress in place. A long necklace with a large conical shell pendant usually accentuates a Himba woman's upper torso. The body and all items of dress are covered with a mixture of red pigment and animal fat. Photograph by Carol Beckwith/Angela Fisher.

wrapped around the head a few times, below the "ears," to hold the headdress and/or the superstructure in place. The ekori is worn over a wig made of numerous thin fiber braids. Additional strands of beads or beaded belts may hang down the sides or back of a Himba woman's head, with some ending in triangular or curved pendants also fully beaded. Multiple beaded necklaces (some bound together) may fully cover a woman's neck. A longer necklace with a large conical shell pendant usually accentuates a Himba woman's upper torso. Solid metal or beaded armlets, bracelets, and anklets (in multiples) are also displayed by women. The body and all items of dress are covered with a mixture of red pigment and animal fat used to condition and protect the skin from the sun and insects and to maintain the articles of dress. Aromatic herbs are kept by women inside small tortoiseshells (sometimes decorated with beads) to be used as deodorant or perfume. The smell of the red pigment and fat lotion and natural perfumes, plus the sounds of dangling beadwork and leather flaps in the wind and when the body is in motion, all add to the visual and aural richness of this and other forms of Himba traditional dress. These qualities in varying degrees are also found in the dress of other southern Angolan peoples, all creating independent styles and fashions using similar materials.

The most dramatic and artistically rich element of dress seems to be the hairstyles, coiffures, and headdresses of the region. These become extraordinarily sculptural and vary not only between groups but also within to indicate age grade and social status. Nyaneka-Humbe women create tightly packed coiffures held together with red ochre and fat or sometimes mud or dung. They cover their whole head with slightly raised bands arching over their foreheads and slightly protruding rows projecting front to back. The coiffure features flaring arches, perpendicular on the sides of the head. Beads are embedded in the coiffure to add texture, color, and decorative patterns. A beaded headband with geometric motifs is worn on the forehead, below the front arch of the coiffure.

Another coiffure worn by the same peoples features hair tightly held together and following the contours of the head toward the back, extending flat behind the neck, and splitting into two points that are decorated with beads. About a fourth of the head at the front is defined with thin braids arching flat on the head and highlighted by beaded color diadems with abstract designs. Thick beaded neck pieces extend to cover the lower chin; the neck piece and coiffure frame the face away from the torso. Facial painting may be added on ceremonial occasions, and painted motifs include graphic elements (like a cross dividing the face) with dotted highlights. Yet another example of many coiffure variations within one group features a low and broad arch front to back on the head that may extend several inches (about eight to thirteen centimeters) toward the front/sides of the head in a manner resembling ram's horns. The extensions end flat with squared tips and include beaded decorations or details made with other accessories such as pins and metal pendants.

Dress among the Mbukushu of southeastern Angola includes a type of beaded back apron shared with peoples further south in northeastern Namibia and in parts of the Okavango in Botswana. The apron is made of antelope skin decorated with strands of imported glass beads and long strips of leather. It may include strands of ostrich eggshell beads as well as locally manufactured brass beads for detailing. The apron is held together with a fully beaded (glass or ostrich-shell) belt with additional long rectangular beaded panels hanging the length of the apron. Like the belt, the beaded panels include intricate geometric designs such as repetitive triangles, lozenges, diamond shapes, and zigzags. These patterns are explained as deriving from nature with specific names such as "face of the zebra" or "tortoise legs." A front apron takes the form of a smaller square panel with similar patterns in beadwork. In ceremonial dances, the apron's flaps, panels, strings, and beadwork create a very particular sound and add motion and dynamism to the occasion. In motion, the beaded patterns reflect light, also adding a three-dimensional quality to the dance.

The Mbukushu also wear a wig (chikeka) made from natural fibers to create braided strings down to the shoulders. A raised arch above the forehead is made from bunched fibers packed with a mix of red ochre and fat or dung. Perpendicular to that, over the contour of the head, an additional raised element creates a "spine" for the wig structure; it may also be fully beaded with abstract patterns. The described wig and apron also fall within the realm of women's dress.

Throughout southern Angola, traditional men's dress generally benefits from the same choice of materials but is more austere than women's and often limited to a fiber or leather skirt and comparatively simpler hairstyles. Beaded necklaces and accessories such as bracelets, anklets, and armbands may also be displayed by men. It is in the context of ritual in southern Angola where men use a more elaborate dress with materials particular to the religious context.

An Mbukushu diviner may don a specific type of wig with relatively short braided strings and a front-to-back crowning element from the mane of a zebra. An ox or zebra tail normally protrudes from the top of the wig toward the front in a manner resembling an elephant trunk. The wig may include beads, bells, animal claws, and small horns placed throughout. Shoulder rings from zebra mane are also part of the ensemble. The diviner wears a skirt made either from animal furs or with long and numerous strings of cut and hollowed reeds and porcupine quills. A shoulder/chest piece made from similar materials is also part of a diviner's dress. These make a rattling sound in performance that demarcates the ritual space helped by the diviner's hand and leg rattles and the wig's bells.

The peoples of southern Angola (like elsewhere in the country) have endured conflicts with the Portuguese since colonial times and decades of a civil war that saw some of its major battles in these territories. The southern Angolan landscape is today still littered with the remains of military tanks and trucks, landmines, and other weapons. The people, however, remain, and culture continues to flourish in the face of ominous developments. Military dress, and other Western-style clothes such as imported textiles and sports' team jerseys have long been assimilated into dress in the area, both casually and in ceremonial contexts. Choice of imported textile print, wraparound skirt type, sweater, and shawl suit local tastes for pattern and decoration. Appropriating imported materials and styles and making them one's own through combination with particular hairstyles and modes of accessorizing falls within a proper definition of the traditional.

ROYAL DRESS: KONGO KINGDOM

Nowhere is the assimilation of imported traits (cultural, social, and other) turned into local tradition more evident than in the colonial history of the country and the documented exchanges between the Portuguese and the king of the Kongo, the mani Kongo, since the late fifteenth century. The Portuguese engaged in a mission of both Christianization and commercial trade; from the beginning, large quantities of cloth and other goods from Portugal were traded for ivory, wood, and other items, including very finely made and decorated raffia textiles. The history of the Kongo-Portuguese colonial relationship is quite complex, taking numerous twists and turns as entrepreneurs got involved in the trade affecting the political and economic environment throughout the country. The trade eventually included slaves and later rubber from Africa, with arms and diverse material goods reaching inner Angola. Trade routes were established from several ports on the country's Atlantic coast to the interior. The trade sprouted inward to reach most regions of the country.

Before the arrival of the Portuguese, the Kongo kingdom was well established with political influence over other polities in northern Angola and control of a territory that extended north to present-day Gabon, governed from the Kongo capital in Mbanza Kongo (in northern Angola). The material culture of the kingdom was highly sophisticated, and the royal courts had specific types of woven raffia hats decorated with intricate abstract motifs for different members of the court and for other dignitaries. Wood, copper, and ivory scepters and swords, bracelets, and lavish necklaces accessorized the elite, who dressed in fine garments, including bunch-piled raffia cloth with the feel of velvet. Early illustrations of Kongo court scenes include court attendants in long skirts and the king in garments with large and flowing skirts, long-sleeved blouse-type tops, and either a headdress resembling a turban or European-style royal crowns. Other depictions show the king wearing a military helmet. Most depictions illustrate the mani Kongo's (and dignitaries') assimilation of European dress with the court quickly turning into a European-style royal setting in Angola.

An 1880s photo of the Kongo king shows the paramount seated, wearing an embroidered military-type jacket over a thickly layered royal skirt. The dress is dark in color but accentuated by a large royal cape (European in style) with a broad white trim with dark dots and a shoulder cape in what seems to be faux fur. The king wears a military-style European hat as a crown and holds a scepter. A different photo, taken in 1930, shows another mani Kongo seated with the queen at his side. Five people stand behind them; three are apparently European clergymen in related attire, the other two individuals wear Western suits. What is most significant about this photo is that the king is probably wearing the exact same jacket, body and shoulder capes, and hat that are shown in the 1880s photo. He seems to hold the same or a similar scepter, and the only differentiating element of dress is evident in the fact that he is now wearing trousers instead of a layered skirt. It is also telling to see the Kongo queen wearing a formal white dress and a royal crown in a style reminiscent of another crown worn by Nzinga Mbande, queen of Ndongo and Matamba kingdoms of the Mbundu (southern allies of the Kongo) in the

Diviner from the Mbukushu people of Angola in ritual dress, Botswana, 2004. The outfit features a wig and skirt with animal parts and other elements. Photograph by Manuel Jordán Pérez, 2004.

seventeenth century, as portrayed in a contemporary illustration. Significantly, items of royal dress are kept in royal treasuries and may be inherited by royal successors and reused with relatively little change.

Outside the close political sphere of Mbanza Kongo, royal dress perhaps retains more of the native form blended with outside influences. South of Mbanza Kongo, the Ndembu still make chiefs' crowns that resemble those appearing in seventeenth-century illustrations. One type resembles a beret with tubular elements hanging to the sides of the wearer's face. The crown is made with loosely knitted fibers dyed in parts to create ring and diamond patterns. Large body capes are also worn by these chiefs, but these are at least partially woven or embroidered with geometric designs that recall those found on early Kongo weavings. These chiefs also bear scepters but made in a typically Ndembu fashion—in metal-plated wood with low-relief symbols, some of which are anthropomorphic. This type of scepter, an important item of royal dress, is exclusive to the Ndembu.

Further inland, in an area historically influenced by the Kongo kingdom on the west and the Lunda Empire to the east, the Suku represent another people with centralized political systems but with the majority of their populations within the borders of Democratic Republic of Congo. They may, however, have chiefs in Angola, and, at least until the 1930s, a more elaborate version of the Ndembu crown was documented among them. The type is fully woven very tightly with fine raffia fibers. The crown has a crescent moon shape, sitting horizontally on the chief's head, with points arching downward at the sides. Large diamond-shaped motifs are embroidered with dark cotton above the forehead and at the top toward the back of the three-dimensional crown. Smaller diamonds decorate the two ends of the crown above its tips. The patterns recall woven designs of Kongo-related people, although culturally the Suku have more in common with their neighbors to the east. Later crowns of the Suku and Yaka take on the Lunda model and become fully beaded with chevrons, triangles, and circular motifs. They also appear in different styles; a beaded crown with forward-projecting horns is the most common nowadays.

LUNDA-CHOKWE DRESS

The eastern part of Angola, particularly the northeast and center, is mostly populated by people who trace their roots to the Lunda Empire (seventeenth to nineteenth centuries) with a political center in the courts of the Mwata Yamvo paramount in Muzumba, in southern Democratic Republic of Congo. In Angola, these peoples include the dominant Chokwe or Lunda-Chokwe (mixed royalty) and others. These populations extend into Zambia beyond Angola's eastern border, where many related chiefs, including senior chiefs, still reside. This border is particularly fluid as, for example, southern Lunda chiefs are invested in the court of Lunda paramount Mwanta Ishindi in Zambia on the east bank of the Zambezi River. This is also where the royal crowns of the Lunda Empire (modeled after those of the Mwata Yamvo) are made and distributed into Angola, particularly for chiefs of direct Lunda ancestry. Within Angola, the Chokwe are the most populous ethnicity of the related groups.

In the nineteenth century, the Chokwe gained great wealth and power in the trade with the coast, acquiring weapons that facilitated their defeat of Lunda overlords. This allowed them to gain control over vast territories and to establish their own rulers. The Chokwe land of origin is in Muzamba in central Angola (with Songo and Ovimbundu traders to the west); their territory expanded to cover central and eastern Angola north to south. Benefiting from the trade and taking on the Lunda political model of rulership, several Chokwe chiefs spread through their territory to establish their courts. The Chokwe remain the dominant cultural group in northeastern Angola. Related groups maintain similar cultural traits throughout the eastern part of the country.

Nineteenth-century depictions of Chokwe chiefs include an engraved portrait of Chief Ndumba Tembo wearing what appears to be a metal crown composed of an embossed headband from which four narrow bands extend upward to meet at a central point several inches (about eight to thirteen centimeters) above the head. The openwork crown resembles the head superstructures of Chokwe masks representing powerful ancestors with symbolic royal associations. The demarcated four points on the crown and the mask headpieces refer to the cardinal points and (physical and spiritual) power in all directions.

A 1903 portrait photo of Chokwe chief Chauto shows the ruler wearing a different type of crown apparently constructed from sheet metal and cloth. The crown has a large arching element rising above the chief's forehead with four independent tablets held together with cloth or wire. The crown features backward-curving "wings." Tubular hairpins further decorate the crown and secure it. The surface is textured by ridges and metal bands alternating with another material, probably cloth. This type of crown, called *chipenya mutwe*, is one of two commonly found on carved wooden figures depicting Chokwe royals. The other crown type features a cap from which large crescent arches protrude upward, normally around a tall tubular element that is interpreted as a center point and receptacle for universal forces at the disposal of the chief. The surrounding arches project those (supernatural) powers three-dimensionally.

Today, the most common type of crown in the region follows the Lunda model; it features a beaded headband and diadems or consecutive arched elements (also beaded) one behind the other to cover the head. The crown may be attached to the chief's hair or over a piece of leather or cloth. A bunch of red tail feathers of the African gray parrot projects from the top-back, serving the same purpose as the tall tubular element in Chokwe crowns. Several variations indicate rank or are for use during formal or less-formal occasions. Beaded patterns are diamonds and rows of triangles, all with symbolic meaning. The crown itself places the chief at the center of the universe (physical and spiritual), and the patterns define the forces at play. Small diamond shapes with central dots in a row may refer to the "eyes of the stars"; a band of contrasting dots to the "Milky Way"; other patterns may be metaphorically related to the power and regenerative abilities attributed to some snakes; "mirrored" triangles relate semantically to the scales of the pangolin (scaly anteater) and to its protective skin and ability to dig holes (transit between the world of humans above ground and the world of ancestors below). All this symbolism reflects the meaningful associations imbued in items of dress and prestige such as chiefs' crowns.

As in the case of Kongo kings, Chokwe-related royals also took on European military clothing to symbolize status. The advent of civil war in Angola resulted in a profusion of military clothing reaching inner Angola, and, as a result, it is very common to see Chokwe, Lunda, or Lwena chiefs in ceremonies wearing military uniforms with a profusion of medals. In more casual occasions, a chief may wear a captain's cap in lieu of his crown. Lesser chiefs who are not entitled to beaded crowns may wear military hats to indicate their status. The more formal dress for a chief today may be a finely tailored top and dress set with a layered skirt featuring a white or light-colored band of cloth at the bottom. Others may wear a suit jacket and tie over the skirt.

Nonroyal traditional Chokwe dress includes wraparound skirts for both men and women. Today, these take the form of imported printed cloth (*chitenge*; pl. *vitenge*) that is worn mostly by women and by men in ceremonial occasions. Originally, animal pelts, woven raffia, or textiles made from beaten and processed tree bark were worn for the same purpose. Chokwe-related people have a variety of hairstyles and coiffures, including wigs that are manufactured from fibers, and are braided and plaited in different fashions. These and some of the hairstyles may be conditioned with oils and red ochre or camwood dyes. Today, imported wigs made from synthetic materials and hair extensions may be bought at any market along with Western-style clothes, either new or secondhand.

Lunda senior chief wearing a royal crown, Western-style jacket, and printed cloth, with images of the Virgin Mary, for Paramount Chief Ishindi's investiture ceremony in Zambia, 2006, at his palace, Mukundankunda. Subchiefs in similar dress but with Western-style hats sit behind him. Photograph by Manuel Jordán Pérez, 2006.

Accessorizing is also important in this area, and anklets, bracelets, armbands, and diadems are part of the dress as elsewhere in Angola. The Chokwe, in particular, have a taste for metal earrings and pendants. Many take the form of Portuguese/Christian-style crosses, although evidence shows that crosses were part of the graphic vocabulary of Angolan peoples well before the arrival of the Portuguese. The cross, called *chiengelyengelye* in Chokwe, similar to the European Maltese cross, is a quintessential Chokwe symbol of identity found in facial and body scarification marks, particularly on foreheads and on face masks.

BODY ARTS

Body scarification in Angola is another elaborate form of traditional dress. Covering or accenting the body with a graphic language indicates identity and class or rank. It is an art form that also reflects the maturity and elegance of the bearer. As in the case of abstract patterns on chiefs' crowns, particular designs also place the wearer within the universe (physical and spiritual) in which all humans and things coexist (a Kongo philosophical precept). Body scarification marks start at youth and become more and more elaborate according to male and female initiation requirements. Some marks develop as people may join particular societies (religious, political, or other). Scarification, simple cuts or incisions on the skin to which ash or other substances are applied, adds color and contrast against the color of the skin. Raised scarification marks may be the result of cuts treated to become keloids or of incisions made to insert pebbles or beads under the skin to create texture. The process is painful, and it often marks accomplishment within initiation or a ritual transition that changes the social status of an individual. Scarification designs and patterns are extremely rich throughout most of the upper two-thirds of Angola among most Bantu groups—with the exception of southern Angola, where pastoralists generally choose other forms of body ornamentation.

Some of the elaborate scarification patterns of Kongo-related peoples resemble those found in their early textiles. An artistic dialogue between the textile and bodily art form is quite evident, and traditional dress thus combines the decoration of the body with that of the materials worn. This is true in other parts of Angola. The earliest reference to the repertoire of designs and symbols utilized in traditional dress is found in the archaeological record. Numerous Angolan rock sites feature petroglyphs and pictographs—some relatively recent, others made hundreds of years ago—showing most of the symbols found in scarification, hairstyles, and crowns, and in the beaded ornaments of different Angolan peoples. This all suggests a continuity of thought and an ability to adapt to change while maintaining essential elements of culture, kept in a state of flux and continuity.

References and Further Reading

Arnoldi, Mary Jo, and Christine Mullen Kreamer, eds. *Crowning Achievements: African Art of Dressing the Head*. Los Angeles: UCLA of Cultural History, Fowler Museum 1995.

Estermann, Carlos. *Etnografia de Angola*. Vols. 1, 2. Lisbon: Junta de Investigação Científica Tropical, 1983.

Felix, Marc Leo. *Kongo Kingdom Art: From Ritual to Cutting Edge*. Hong Kong: Ethnic Art and Culture, 2003.

Hambly, Wilfrid. *The Ovimbundu of Angola*. Chicago: Field Museum of Natural History, 1934.

Jordán, Manuel, ed. *CHOKWE! Art and Initiation among Chokwe and Related Peoples*. Munich: Prestel, 1998.

Kerkham Simbao, Ruth. "A Crown on the Move: Stylistic Integration of the Luba-Lunda Complex in Lunda-Kazembe Performance." *African Arts* 39, no. 3 (Autumn, 2006): 26–41, 93.

Martínez Ruiz, Barbaro. "Kongo Machinery: Graphic Writing and Other Narratives of the Sign." Ph.D. dissertation, Yale University, 2004.

Palmeirim, Manuela. *Of Alien Kings and Perpetual Kin: Contradiction and Ambiguity in Ruwund (Lunda) Symbolic Thought*. Wantage, UK: Sean Kingston, 2006.

Redinha, José. *Etnias e culturas de Angola*. Luanda: Instituto de Investigação Científica de Angola, 1974.

Roberts, Allen F. *Animals in African Art: From the Familiar to the Marvelous*. Munich: Prestel, 1995.

Scherz, Anneliese, Ernts Scherz, et al. *Hair-Styles, Head-Dresses & Ornaments in Namibia and Southern Angola*. Windhoek, Namibia: Gamsberg Macmillan, 1992.

Sieber, Roy, and Frank Herreman, eds. *Hair in African Art and Culture*. New York: Museum for African Art, 2000.

Manuel Jordán Pérez

Botswana

B otswana is a landlocked country situated just to the north of South Africa with geography dominated by the Kalahari Desert spanning much of the country and the Okavango swamps and Chobe River area in the north.

HISTORICAL DRESS

Most evidence concerning dress worn in Botswana before the twentieth century comes from accounts of European explorers, adventurers, and missionaries in the nineteenth century. Prehistoric rock art in the northwest of the country focuses on animals and does not depict clothing. Figurines from the thirteenth to sixteenth centuries found in the eastern part of the country depict women with a length of what is possibly cloth wrapped around their waists and tucked between their legs. (Spindle whorls have also been found in archaeological sites to the north, although European travelers did not note woven cloth.) Explorers and missionaries entered Botswana from what is now Namibia and South Africa, but these borders, when they were eventually demarcated, did not (and do not in the twenty-first century) separate ethnic or cultural populations—Tswana lived in areas now divided into South Africa, Botswana, and Namibia; Herero lived in Namibia and Botswana; Kalanga in Zimbabwe and Botswana; Mbukushu in Angola, Namibia, and Botswana; Bushmen in Angola, Namibia, Botswana, and South Africa. This means that precolonial clothing styles associated with populations in today's Botswana may have been described in a range of adjacent territories. The territorial association of precolonial clothing styles is further attenuated by the fact that people were very mobile: They moved grazing and farming areas in response to climate change and land degradation; they engaged in far-flung trading journeys; and they joined and left political groups (or "tribes") through coercion, for protection, or for other reasons. People sometimes adopted clothing styles of those they lived with, regardless of ethnic background, so that a Bushman who lived in a Tswana chief's village was described by Thomas Baines in the finery of a Tswana chief's attendant. Other people, however, seem to have stuck to ethnic clothing traditions, so that Herero women would not be seen without their head covering no matter where they lived. The variety of dress styles and their changes over time and place were enhanced by creativity and inclination on the part of individuals or small groups.

Although the young Bushman sketched by Baines wore a fine, long leather cloak and a skin headdress with long hairs sticking

A sketch from 1861 by Thomas Baines, a South African artist who toured the area that is now Botswana, showing a man he described as a Bushman wearing his finery as an attendant of Leshulatebe, a Tswana chief. From Baines, *Explorations in South-West Africa*, London, 1864. Courtesy of Deborah Durham.

up in a sort of crown, along with thonged sandals, most Bushmen were described as wearing very little. Men typically wore a thin piece of leather covering their genitalia and pulled up as a thong between their buttocks to tuck into a belt. Some women wore a leather skirt reaching the knees and a leather cape or cloak tied around the shoulders or tied under the armpits above the breasts. In other groups, women wore a short leather breechcloth and cape. Travelers reported a variety of hairstyles, from hair simply kept short to shaved hairlines with the remaining hair treated with red earth and animal fats to look like a helmet or teased into long strands that hung three or so inches (about eight centimeters) behind. Hair was often ornamented with beadwork of ostrich eggshell, iron, or glass beads. One group of men was reported to sport a bird's head attached to the front of their hair. Women and men wore strings of ostrich eggshell beads, often interspersed with polished reed, bits of tortoiseshell, iron or glass beads, bits of metal from European artifacts, and other elements such as short and long necklaces, armlets, bracelets, anklets, and knee-lets. They also used the eggshell beads to create headbands and belts and to ornament leather bags. Like other peoples in the region, they made dance rattles from the cocoon of a moth sewn up around small stones or seeds and strung into lengths that were wrapped around their legs. The impression one gets from travelers' accounts is of dress practices that reflected small-group and individual creativity with a range of materials to make hair ornaments, necklaces, and other decorations.

Some Bushmen, especially those in remote parts of the central or northwestern Kalahari Desert, continued to wear skin clothing and ostrich eggshell beadwork well into the second half of the twentieth century. Facial tattoos were also practiced in some places. Many others, working and squatting on farms or cattle posts owned by Europeans or other Africans, wore tattered old Western clothing or a mix. Even the more remote Bushmen, however, supplemented skin dress with Western shirts, pants, dresses, hats, blankets and shawls, and industrially manufactured earrings or other jewelry. Knitted caps are very popular, and Bushmen often unravel and reknit them for themselves or as part of extensive gift-exchange networks known as *xharo*.

Herero, called *Damara* in some literature, lived mostly in today's Namibia after the seventeenth century and up to the twentieth, but some trekked frequently into territory that is now part of Botswana, and some may have lived there. Precolonial Herero dress styles were distinctive. As did most other inhabitants of southern Africa, they applied fat and red ochre and other reddish minerals to their skins to make them bright and light, a practice that Europeans deplored and tried to correct with soap. Herero men used fat and clay to mat their hair into strands; some tied a shell or other ornament into their hair over their foreheads. They wore several long strips of leather thong wrapped around their waists with a small loincloth tucked between their legs and sometimes the leather cloak seen across the subcontinent. Women wore a leather skirt and cloak and a leather cap ornamented with shells, which had three tall leather "ears" stitched onto it standing upright over the woman's head. Long strips of leather on which were strung iron beads dangled a couple of feet or more (up to a meter) from the back of the cap, and a veil or curtain of soft leather was attached to the front, which was usually rolled up to frame the face and drape down on either side. It was considered a most shameful thing for a mature woman to be seen in public without the headdress. Women also wore around their ankles heavy strings of iron beads acquired from Ovambo in the north. At age fifteen or older, Herero filed an inverted V out of their upper front incisors and later knocked out the bottom two teeth. (Herero today say that the practice, now abandoned, allowed good pronunciation of their language. The V and missing lower teeth also distinguished Herero from other peoples who did not modify their teeth or who modified them in other distinctive patterns.) Herero children wore a string of leather around their waist with a short flap or fringe dangling in front.

Although many Africans adopted Western-style clothing to the extent they could afford by the late nineteenth century, most Herero, apart from some elites and chiefs, continued to wear their traditional dress into the twentieth century. After losing a devastating war against German colonialists in Namibia in 1904,

Herero women began to wear a European dress style that was quite outmoded at the time of its widespread adoption in the 1910s and 1920s. The cloth dress was ground-length, with a tight waist that moved up over time to just below the breasts and had skirts supported by petticoats to be very full. Over time, the skirts became fuller, and a mutton-leg sleeve became favored on a tight bodice. A tall scarf headdress developed by the 1950s into a more complicated affair, with two "horns" projecting widely to the sides. Women favored colorful fabrics for the dress, and patchwork was especially popular for decades. Some Herero women continue to wear the long dress and headdress in the twenty-first century; seamstresses skillfully introduce innovations into neckline and sleeves but keep the high tight waist, bodice, and full skirts intact. Polyester fabrics are increasingly popular.

A Herero woman in Mahalapye, Botswana, 1996, wearing a Victorian-style dress and horn-shaped headdress. Herero women began to wear a European dress style that was quite outmoded at the time of its widespread adoption in the 1910s and 1920s in Botswana. The cloth dress was ground-length, with a tight waistline that moved up over time to just below the breasts and had full skirts supported by petticoats. A tall scarf headdress developed by the 1950s into a more complicated affair, with two "horns" projecting from the sides. Photograph by Deborah Durham.

Hambukushu people in the northwest of Botswana also had very distinctive headgear, which is popular with museums and collectors of African artifacts. These spectacular headdresses were large, full wigs of long strands of dark plant fibers that hung like hair, often pulled together at the back of the head to hang heavily down the back. Some were quite long, and people decorated them with various kinds of beads, cowry shells, and iron, copper, and other ornaments. Women wore a leather knee-length skirt heavily embroidered with beads and, along with necklaces, wore many bands of copper around their ankles and bands of skin with hair on it on their legs. Men, who engaged heavily in migrant labor in South Africa, adopted Western clothing by the 1950s, while many women continued to wear the skirt and headdress; by the 1970s, however, only Mbukushu refugees from Angola continued to do so.

If not numerically the majority, Tswana people dominated the territory of today's Botswana from the eighteenth century on, and many subject peoples, such as Yei in the north or Kgalagadi in the south, adopted or shared Tswana styles of dress. As for others in the area, while a stereotypical outfit has been described for Tswana, travelers' accounts make clear that there was a great deal of variety and individuation in dress, especially among young men. Tswana, like others, anointed their skin with animal fat and colored earth, which may have protected their skin from the dry winds and harsh sun, but also produced a much-admired glow. Some Tswana also used fat and iron specularite in their hair, producing a silvery helmetlike appearance. Tswana men, who manufactured clothing until missionaries "domesticated" women's activity, typically wore a loin-skin, and perhaps a skin or furred cloak (or *kaross*) of varying length. Tswana society was hierarchical, and certain forms of clothing were restricted to the upper classes. Only members of the dominant clan and other elites wore the furs of certain animals—such as genets, spotted cats, jackals, or bat-eared foxes—which they wore in small capelets around their shoulders or neatly sewn into long cloaks. Men also often wore caps and headdresses of animal skin or sometimes hats of woven grasses and sandals; their clothing could be ornamented with animal tails and other materials. Women wore a skin skirt, sometimes with a leather apron in front, and a skin kaross around their shoulders. A piece of skin served as a sling to carry babies on women's or children's backs. Necklaces, armlets, and anklets were also common among Tswana; they were made of the array of beads used across the region, shells, reeds and woven grass, bits of metal, and copper wire.

By the mid-nineteenth century, pieces of Western clothing were found in all the Tswana chiefdoms. Westerners wrote with amusement and scorn about Africans who mixed Western and local dress, as if the integrity of both were undone. It is likely, however, that Africans, whose dress had always incorporated trade goods from different local groups as well as items from as far as India, did not view Western and African dress items as incommensurate. Shirts and blankets, especially red ones, were particularly desired. Missionaries taught women to sew Western clothes, favoring dark colors, sturdy fabrics, and outdated European styles. While some people into the twentieth century signaled their rejection of growing Western domination by wearing only traditional skin clothing, and many others wore skin clothing for reasons of poverty into the 1970s, Western dress was well established for some by the end of the nineteenth century. Photographs of elites in the 1880s and 1890s show them in fashionable, elegantly tailored Western outfits. Outside the elite, however, Tswana developed a style of clothing that later became strongly associated with a national identity. The use of wool and later synthetic blankets as shawls (tied above the breasts or around the waist while working) became a traditional feature of local dress. The wearing of scarves or headdresses, too, came to distinguish Tswana dress from European styles. At the turn of the twenty-first century, these elements remain characteristic of traditional Tswana dress and are often worn at funerals or other ceremonies.

DRESS IN THE EARLY TWENTY-FIRST CENTURY

Most people in Botswana today wear some form of Western-style dress or forms of a generic African style associated with West and Central Africa. To Herero, and perhaps to other minorities, seemingly Western dress style is called *Setswana*, or Tswana-style, and is sometimes viewed as less dynamic than their own forms of dress, which look traditional to foreigners. This surprising contrast—a static Western/Tswana style versus a dynamic traditional style—reflects a sense by minorities of a Tswana hegemony that contrasts with forms of self-invention anchored in minority cultures. To Tswana people, *Setswana dress* refers to the use of specific cotton print styles and skirt designs (see below) along with blanket shawls and scarves and does not refer to general Western-style clothing. Most items of clothing are purchased from people with licenses to buy commodities at large wholesalers and sell them from their homes or in midsized shops; from chain stores like the cheaper Pep Stores or pricier Guys and Gals, which are based in South Africa; from catalogs like Ebony, also circulated from South Africa; from secondhand clothing dealers; or from small sewing enterprises that predominantly make school and other uniforms, German-cloth (a brown or blue cotton with a small repeating white print that is seen as traditional) skirts, and simply cut clothes. Wealthier people may also purchase clothes at more exclusive boutiques and while traveling abroad. Many people in very rural areas receive much of their clothing from relatives, employers, or patrons, often as hand-me-downs.

WOMEN'S DRESS

As one would expect, the widest range of styles occurs in the cities. Professional and working women wear suits (with skirts), dresses, and skirts and blouses or uniforms. Some elite women wear dress styles associated with West or Central Africa. These include one- and two-piece outfits, often with a matching scarf or head dress, made from an African cotton print. Some are loose constructions; others, especially the two-piece ones, have a top with a fitted bodice that flares out skirtlike briefly over the hips, under which is a tighter skirt. Women tend to wear high-heeled shoes in professional contexts; they are kept scrupulously polished and are repeatedly cleaned of the dust and dirt of the streets throughout the day. Professional women in the 1990s typically had long hair straightened and curled or extensions (small braids of hair that are braided into one's own hair) that they pulled back into elaborate coiffures or loose ponytails. In the 2000s, some powerful women were wearing their hair cropped very short, a style always common in villages and among young girls. During leisure time, these women often wear jeans, both in the city and when visiting home and other villages. Some people complain in newspapers or public speech that the "African body" does not look good in jeans or in the popular spandex pants. Others are unhappy that such clothes show the upper thighs and buttocks, which, when well developed, are admired as an important aspect of a woman's beauty but are also considered erogenous. By 2000, many women also wore track suits in their leisure time or while traveling long distances. In the twenty-first century, as well, some elites were beginning to indulge in locally designed fashion that was modern but alluded to traditional patterns from basketry, designs painted on rondavels, and skin clothing.

Some professional women, cosmopolitan students, and fashion lovers have flirted with short skirts following international trends. Others, especially women in the villages and those of the middle and lower classes, stick to skirts below the knee and relate their stylistic choices to propriety and to fashion trends within the country and neighboring countries rather than to fashions associated with Europe and North America. Although young girls generally wear shorter skirts, mature women who wear shorter skirts to venues associated with traditional authority, such as a chief's court (kgotla), or to a village funeral or church, are likely to be scolded. Village women traditionally sit on the ground in the chiefs' courts, with their legs extended directly in front of them, and are chided if their skirts are not tucked tightly around their legs and pulled down below the knee.

Women who live in villages, women in cities who are connected more extensively with home village life, poorer women, and more traditional women typically wear a skirt and a T-shirt or blouse. Many also wear a sweater, jacket, or a small blanket or shawl thrown over the shoulders. The blanket or shawl conveys a village identity. Older women, in particular, who are thought to suffer from the cold, wear such shawls; so, too, do women with infants or girls and young women caring for infants, who use the shawls to tie the children into a sling on their backs. During the day, while doing household work, women will wear old tattered clothes and worn sandals or flat shoes, and the dirt and dust of their work clings to them. Their T-shirts, which circulate widely, often bear faded logos of government health campaigns, liquor or condom marketing efforts, or messages from American culture that no one seems to bother to read. Housework skirts may be old, worn skirts originally purchased at one of the shops or very often a locally tailored skirt made from sturdy German cloth. Skirts made from this cloth are fashioned with a tight yoke extending down over the hips with gathered fabric sewn at the bottom of the yoke, making the skirt flare out gently. Skirts or dresses that are held to be traditional Setswana dress typically are wrapped even when part of a full dress, in which case the front of the skirt is sewn to the bodice, but the back of the skirt is wrapped and tied. Many women wear scarves over their hair. Some are required to do so by the churches to which they belong. (All women don a scarf and a jacket, sweater, or shawl when visiting mourners at the home where a death has occurred, a space also known as a "church.") Others wear scarves when sweeping dusty yards and doing other dirty work but go without them when visiting or downtown.

While shawls and scarves distinguish rural from urban styles, the difference between tattered clothing (makatana) and newer clothes may be more significant to citizens of Botswana, because these clothes distinguish status by wealth. Wealth differences are possibly more significant than the type of settlement (i.e., being a rural or urban person) to many citizens, because most people have associations with both city and village throughout their lives.

A village headman in Mahalapye, Botswana, listens to a complaint in 1996. The complainant is wearing a long coat and has a sock cap on his knee, which he has taken off in deference to the chief's court (kgotla). The long coat and the cap indicate his status as an older man. Photograph by Keith W. Adams.

When going downtown or to a city or to a funeral or celebration, most men and women will bathe and dress up in their better clothes. Bathing is very important to people in Botswana, and villagers ideally bathe at least twice a day and before dressing up. The baths, which are laborious to prepare without indoor running water, can be seen as part of bodily self-fashioning rather than simple avoidance of dirt. One cattle herder was praised highly for bathing each morning before going to do very dirty work, showing his interest in developing himself through his social interactions. Baths and clothes are important because one's bodily condition is seen to have direct physical and emotional effect on the well-being of others, both positive and negative. Dressing well also involves wearing clean, carefully ironed clothing, even for those whose clothes are old and marked with holes or burn marks. Although such practices may have originally been pressed upon Africans by missionaries and colonial figures, ironically today many *Batswana* find Europeans and Americans to be slovenly or dirty.

MEN'S DRESS

Men's dress in cities is generally Western in style, with differences in wealth marked strongly in the newness and condition of the clothes and in access to items such as two- and three-piece suits or to fashionable jeans and leather jackets. Men typically wear suits, or slacks and shirts with ties, or uniforms at work. Many men wear an outfit of pants and a short-sleeved shirt jacket made of polyester—typically khaki or pale blue or green—sometimes called a "safari suit" but understood as a modern African instead of foreign style. Some men wear jeans at work, but these are typically either men in very elite, nongovernmental positions or lower-level self-employed people. Jeans are often worn by young men during leisure times in the city, as are slacks. Few men wear

West African–styled shirts; more typically, in leisure, they wear T-shirts, buttoned shirts, and sweaters. Very poor men in the cities, including some of the homeless youths who roam the streets, wear very tattered clothing, including shorts. Men generally wear their hair cut fairly short; some men keep a neatly trimmed mustache and occasionally a beard. In the 1990s, men and women who let their hair grow long (without straightening) were often said laughingly to have Afro-American hair.

In villages, only people who fell into the status of "boys," apart from Afrikaner or European/American men, wore shorts at the end of the twentieth century. This is not to say older men didn't wear shorts—they often did. But when doing so, they appeared in the role of manual laborer or working for someone else, a status not quite that of full adulthood (such as fifty-year-old "herdboys"). One village chief in his thirties was chided by his constituents for wearing shorts around his yard while doing yard work. Youths in villages had rapidly passing and very local fads, including wearing neckties tied so that one end was extremely long and the other very short, or wearing shirttails tucked in only on one side in front. Other youth fads were of longer duration and wider spread—such as carrying a cell phone, working or not. Old men donned heavy outer coats; as with older women and their shawls, these coats were said to be needed to keep the aging body warm. But more so than the blankets, men's overcoats were associated specifically with the status of age, as were walking sticks and hats. Younger men in their late thirties and forties often tried tentative claims at full adulthood by putting on a coat or hat or carrying a walking stick when joining the men's circle at a funeral or wedding—where they were typically teased but welcomed.

Comportment is as important as clothing. As they attained adulthood—a status tied less to years than to an increasing self-mastery and the ability to command the labor of others—men and women adopted a slower, more measured demeanor in their

Women dressed in one of the uniforms of the Zion Christian Church at a ceremony in Mahalapye, Botswana, 1990. Many churches, associations, and groups in Botswana have their own uniforms. Photograph by Keith W. Adams.

walk and other movements. Sometimes respected adults jumped to herd cattle and run after goats; women worked swiftly and efficiently around their households during the day; and people bounced and ran in fundraising concert antics. In these cases, they were highlighting their youthfulness. By and large, jumping and running about was associated with children, and when asserting full maturity, people walked and moved slowly, implying that others did the fast moving. Demeanor, along with the cleanliness, neatness, and perhaps newness of dress, were the most important criterion for judging the numerous village-based beauty pageants at the end of the twentieth century. Those who served as judges and members of the audience said that they looked less at the facial beauty of the women in the pageants and more at the way they dressed and the way they held their bodies. It is likely that after Mpule Kwelagobe won the Miss Universe contest in 1999 (and in urban areas before then) facial beauty, slenderness, and different measures of style were used in urban beauty pageants; newspaper reports certainly suggest that this was the case.

UNIFORMS

Uniforms are an important part of dress in Botswana. Schoolchildren are required to wear uniforms to attend school. Poor families may find it difficult to afford school uniforms and will share uniforms among siblings and cousins or not send children to school. School uniforms and the sweaters that students wear over them largely support the small cottage clothing industry in Botswana. Some jobs involve uniforms—such as bank clerk or, more obviously, nurse, police officer, or soldier—and these occupations and their uniforms give prestige. People working in some government departments, including veterinary services and transportation, often wear a rough cotton coat on the job with "BGP" (Botswana Government Property) stamped on the back. Like other uniforms, this coat circulates beyond its assigned space, and one sees BGP coats worn by women working in their homesteads, cattle herders out at cattle posts, and old men sitting in the sun on cold days. School uniforms, too, as they get old, are worn by younger siblings playing in the streets.

Some uniforms, however, are treated with great care. Many of the churches have a uniform, and these uniforms, and uniforms adopted by burial societies, are often subject to special restrictions or respect in washing, storage, and wear. Voluntary associations, including burial societies, political parties, cultural associations, youth groups, or other community groups, will usually develop a uniform for their members. For the Herero Youth Association, based in Mahalapye, the uniform was both one of the first formal elements that members devised and was subject to continuous debate in association meetings. Women and men discussed over and over the precise shade of blue of women's skirts and how many gores the skirt should have for over a decade (the men's uniform was long settled). Choirs, whether associated with a church, school, local police station or other workplace, branch of a political party, voluntary association, or simply organized by a group of young people in a city or village, always devise uniforms. While church uniforms and cultural association uniforms may be very distinctive, with elaborate collars on blouses and jackets and intricate piping or trim, most uniforms consist of a simple skirt and blouse or logoed T-shirt for women, and slacks, shirt or T-shirt, and occasionally a suit coat for men. Some groups will have their uniforms made by a chosen seamstress from identical fabric; members of other groups cobble together items of clothing that are similar but not identical. For some burial societies or other associations, the uniform may consist only of a pin, or women may wear a colored beret or scarf of a particular fabric, while men wear hats with a colored cloth band. Wearing of such uniforms at times of associational unity—on the death of a member, at a wedding or celebration where the association does service, at a concert—is important, and many societies levy fines on members who do not wear uniforms at those times or who are caught in prohibited behaviors.

CHILDREN'S CLOTHING AND TRADITIONAL DRESS

As in many parts of Africa, in villages, very small children often wear little clothing at all, perhaps a small T-shirt with nothing else or a small leather apron or string of beads around the neck or waist. The leather aprons are special items, significant to the child and to the grandparent who may have provided it. Although dirt on adults is often seen as evidence of hard work, dirt on children is typically blamed on play, reflecting their foolishness and lack of self-development in forging positive interconnections with others. Adults often complain about how dirty children are. Children before school age are subjected to vigorous baths during the day, against which they protest noisily, and are rubbed all over with petroleum jelly or a glycerin-enriched lotion to make their skin soft and lustrous—important aspects of beauty for people of all ages but especially appreciated in the young. Botswana is rapidly developing a pronounced class system, and middle-class urban parents and those aspiring to a class position dress their small children more fully in store-bought children's outfits and use diapers in city settings.

Many schools in Botswana have choirs that compete against each other, and the competitions culminate in a national eisteddfod each year. Choirs singing Western choral music wear Western-style dress, but traditional choirs wear versions of precolonial African dress. Their outfits are varied and, since the 1990s, increasingly reflect interest in different (minority) groups' traditions in the country. They typically refer to initiation ceremonial clothing, especially when they include long strings of ostrich eggshell beads worn slung crosswise over girls' chests or animal skins worn by young men (cut like a bathing suit or underwear) with tails left hanging behind. Most outfits, but not all, are of leather, and the singer-dancers often wear strings of rattles wrapped around their legs below the knee. In some choirs, boys wear leather wrapped several times around their calves and smack their legs together resoundingly as part of the dance. While some girls in choirs leave their breasts uncovered, others wear leather bras or, rarely, T-shirts. The most polished costumes were made and bought in South Africa.

Only some Herero women wear markedly different traditional dress on a daily basis—the Victorian-style dress and horned headdress described above. Many Herero women, and most younger ones, don the dress only for special ceremonies. Although only children wear versions of traditional Tswana clothing, the state has used such dress on postage stamps issued in 1990. A growing movement to assert minority rights in the twenty-first century has been accompanied by research conducted by faculty and students at the University of Botswana and by museums. Such research on oral histories and different ethnic practices of non-Tswana groups may result in more extensive use of traditional dress in exhibitions, choral performances, and domestic ceremonies in coming years.

References and Further Reading

Andersson, Charles J. *Lake Ngami*. London: Hurst and Blackett, 1856; reprint Cape Town: C. Struik, 1967.

Baines, Thomas. *Explorations in South-West Africa*. London: Longman, Green, Longman, Roberts, and Green, 1864.

Comaroff, Jean. *Body of Power, Spirit of Resistance: The Culture and History of a South African People*. Chicago: University of Chicago Press, 1985.

Comaroff, John L., and Jean Comaroff. *Of Revelation and Revolution*. Vol. 2, *The Dialectics of Modernity on a South African Frontier*. Chicago: University of Chicago Press, 1997.

Denbow, James, and Phenyo C. Thebe. *Culture and Customs of Botswana*. Westport, CT: Greenwood Press, 2006.

Durham, Deborah. "The Predicament of Dress: Polyvalency and the Ironies of a Cultural Identity." *American Ethnologist* 26, no. 2 (1999): 349–411.

Durham, Deborah. "Did You Bathe This Morning? Baths and Morality in Botswana." In *Dirt, Undress, and Difference: Critical Perspectives on the Body's Surface*, edited by Adeline Masquelier, 122–148. Bloomington: Indiana University Press, 2005.

Larson, Thomas J. "The Hambukushu of Ngamiland from 1950 to 1994: A Study of Social Change." *Botswana Notes and Records* 32 (2000): 59–72.

Lee, Richard. *The Dobe Ju/'hoansi*. 3rd ed. Windhoek, Namibia: Wadsworth Publishing, 2002.

Livingstone, David. *Missionary Travels and Researches in South Africa*. New York: Harper and Brothers, 1858.

Ngwenya, Barbara Ntombi. "Gender, Dress and Self-Empowerment: Women and Burial Societies in Botswana." *African Sociological Review* 6, no. 2 (2002): 1–27.

van Binsbergen, Wim. "La Chambre de Mary: Ou comment devenir consommatrice à Francistown, Botswana." In *Changements au Féminin en Afrique Noire*. Vol. 1: *Anthropologie*, edited by Danielle de Lame and Chantal Zabus, 37–86. Paris: Éditions L'Harmattan, 1999.

Deborah Durham

Lesotho

- Nineteenth Century
- Dress and Symbolism
- Basotho Blankets
- Diviners

Lesotho, a kingdom named after its primary ethnic group, the Basotho, is surrounded by South Africa, where many of its citizens reside, remitting wages and bringing home sophisticated urban fashions and clothing, including, for those who can afford them, such global labels as Levi's and Diesel.

Contemporary dress in urban Lesotho is almost indistinguishable from other participants in the global economy, especially within the offices of Maseru, the capital. The shrewd observer, though, might notice, particularly in poorer areas, such third-world features as tattered hand-me-downs; incongruities of choice such as T-shirts with names and logos of first-world sports teams, which are mysteries to the new wearers; and the occasional confusion of category-specific items—as where a teenage boy might swank in a gossamer pajama top or blouse with a riotous floral print whose target market was middle-aged women.

Telling reflections of local notions of propriety include the rarity of grown men wearing shorts, even in sweltering heat, and the large frequency of middle-aged or older women with their heads covered, which once was considered necessary for married women but has been increasingly ignored in recent decades.

A local, or at least African, flavor is discernible occasionally in the motif or pattern of a fabric, more rarely in the cut of certain women's dresses, and in the persistent custom of binding infants to their mother's backs with a bolt of fabric or a blanket. Saturated colors and shiny fabrics worn in the bright African sunlight lend the streets a somewhat brighter sparkle than in much of the first world.

Distinctive Basotho dress still features at ceremonial occasions considered *sesotho*, meaning "rooted in tradition," particularly the coming-of-age ceremonies of young men and women and at public gatherings that honor the hereditary king, who traces his lineage back to the founding ruler, Moshoeshoe I (ca. 1786–1870).

NINETEENTH CENTURY

Moshoeshoe I solidified the Basotho nation by accepting refugees of various ethnic backgrounds who sought shelter during the regional upheavals of the 1820s, known as the *Lifaqane* (pronounced di-fa-KAH-nee), meaning "time of troubles." These diverse origins of modern Basotho are still sometimes marked in dress—for example, during women's initiation, when girls from different southern Sotho subgroups wear different types of skirts. In general, however, what is understood today as Basotho tradition is a relatively recent codification that Moshoeshoe carefully coalesced around the core values of his own lineage, the Koena, which are but one branch of the many Sotho peoples in southern Africa.

On the other hand, Moshoeshoe strategically accepted resident missionaries in 1833 and was extraordinarily open to their influence in many respects, including the adoption of Western clothing. This opened his people, particularly men, to European dress.

In 1833, Basotho wore little clothing during clement weather. Men wore a triangular leather loincloth (*tseha*), with one point drawn between the legs and joined to the others at the waist. The wearing of this garment distinguished the southern Sotho peoples from their Nguni neighbors along the coast, who coined the name *Basotho* in derisive reference to it. Basotho women wore a leather skirt, opening at the front, sometimes with an overapron. Men might also wear a fuller kiltlike sheepskin skirt, called *setsiba*, held up by a fiber belt.

Tanning was an important male communal activity. A dozen or so men would squat around an animal hide. In perfect time, producing a chorus of grunts, clucks, and shrill cries, they would seize, twist, rub, toss, and tease the animal skin until it was supple. This softening process was likened to the hardening that boys must undergo during circumcision and initiation in order to become pliant useful men.

Both sexes wore leather cloaks for warmth. The animal-skin or fur cloak (*kaross*) might be edged with, or fashioned from, fine fur if the owner could afford it. Among the pelts noted by the first missionaries were leopard, otter, jackal, and wildcat—all important regional commodities. Elders and chiefs deliberated over precious pelts before cutting them into numerous strips, which they limned with meticulous stitches into the most elaborate cloaks.

Basotho regiments were differentiated by the colors of the warriors' uniquely shaped shield, made from the thickest, untanned ox hide and topped with a vaunting spike of trimmed ostrich feathers (*mokhele*). Distinguished warriors wore a V-shaped brass collar called a *khau* and body scars in the form of inverted Vs. A hide breastplate, leather leggings (*likholo*), and wrist guards enhanced protection. Their elaborate headdresses were constructed from grasses, feathers, porcupine quills, or other natural materials.

Men often wore on their person practical objects such as a small knife suspended around the neck from its wooden sheath; awls for sewing hides and pelts; a *lebeko*, which was a multipurpose instrument of toilette for scraping the skin, nostrils, and fingernails; and sometimes whistles or various types of containers for powdered tobacco, which was both smoked and taken as snuff.

Women wore suspended from their skirts a tortoiseshell filled with powdered scent, also found among the San and Xhosa to the south. Additional embellishments for both genders included bracelets of ivory; grass, brass, and copper necklaces, earrings, and bangles; rattling hair ornaments made from the hooves of tiny antelopes; and various small amulets, including some with finely carved buffalo heads, a symbol of strength. A woman's cloak, earrings, and necklaces were key gifts from her husband upon marriage, when her girlhood clothes were burned. During mourning, coiffures were shorn, ornaments were replaced with small iron chains, and widows and children wore cords around their foreheads.

Little girls wore just a tiny fiber apron in front, sometimes embellished with beads. Young boys, until around age eight, wore nothing.

European glass beads made rapid inroads from the 1820s onward, supplanting beads of brass, iron, wood, and other materials. Leather garments then were often ornamented with distinctive circular beadwork motifs. Other features of nineteenth-century Basotho beadwork, rarely observed in that of neighboring people, include distinctive tan beads, faceted "fancy" beads, and certain types of seeds. Black, white, pink, and green provide a palette frequently combined in early Basotho beadwork, and a favored motif is that of stacked lozenges or truncated triangles. No recorded meanings exist for particular beadwork designs or motifs. Larger items of Basotho beadwork include beaded public aprons worn by women with children, blanket pins, and belts.

The first missionaries recorded early clothing adaptations made after contact with Europeans. Basotho men, adept at fashioning warrior headgear, simulated European formal felt hats by placing a downy material over a grass framework. They reinterpreted European straw hats, inventing both solid ones suitable for repelling rain and openwork sun hats. These conical hats became markers of Basotho identity. The elaborate boss at the apex was said to refer to Mount Qilane, a pointed mountain visible from Thaba Bosiu, the mountain fortress that was the original Basotho capital.

The missionary Thomas Arbousset, who accompanied Moshoeshoe I on an exploratory excursion in 1840, noted how the king appeared for Sabbath service dressed in white trousers and a nice frock coat of blue cloth. To impress a vassal, he wore fine white socks under "course carter's shoes," velvet trousers, a green striped waistcoat, and a long homespun jacket like those worn by sailors. He had a tricolored woolen band tied around his neck and a red one tied as a sash and belt. On his head, he wore a cotton hat and a blue cloth cap with the initials S. H., from a soldier garrisoned at Saint Helena (where the imprisoned Napoleon died in 1821). Arbousset has remarked that it took the king and his two valets considerable time and trouble to get the king dressed every morning, not so much because of his "love of finery as lack of know-how." This getup contrasts with the ceremonial clothing the king chose for his initial meeting with the missionaries just seven years before, appearing in a leopard kaross, a beaded headband with a tuft of feathers attached at his nape, a bracelet of ivory on his upper arm, and brass bracelets on his wrists.

DRESS AND SYMBOLISM

Of particular interest in the twenty-first century are the ways that clothing relates to the symbolism of the initiation schools, compulsory for young men and women. In the past, the schools lasted several months; today, they generally last a few weeks, during which the young people are taught traditions, customs, sayings, and songs that constitute the "way of the ancestors." Schools for both sexes involve genital modification: the men are circumcised, while women undergo labial stretching. Male initiation is harsh and sometimes fatal. The young men are beaten frequently, "tanned" to make them supple and ready for adulthood. Women's dress during initiation underscores their symbolic association with creation, the house, and vegetal fertility.

The shape of the traditional Basotho house (now almost extinct) was like an igloo with an elongated entrance tunnel called

a *mathule*. One crawled through the mathule toward the opening, which faced the rising sun in the east and emerged into the outdoor domestic courtyard called a *lapa*, which was fenced with reeds.

The orientation, form, and the construction materials of the dwelling refer to the site of genesis, called *Ntsoana Tsatsi*, which means "where the light comes from," and exists in the Free State province of South Africa. The creation myth states that the Basotho nation emerged there from an underground cave, or "womb" in the body of the earth, emerging into the light at the earth's surface through a muddy bed of reeds. The Basotho house, made of mud-plastered reeds (on a sapling framework) is symbolically a womb of earth. The mathule was like a birth canal. The doorway was—and still is, even in modern houses—a symbolic vagina, always singled out for symbolic decoration. Many other symbolic parallels and practices underscore the notion of the house—even one of modern, Western design—as a symbolic womb. One reinforcing parallel, for example, is that the igloo dwelling is also symbolic of an inverted pot, because pots are also metaphoric wombs—even the word for pot is a euphemism for womb. At the apex of the interior vault, the sapling arches were held together by a fiber ring, termed the *kgaratsa*, which echoed the *kgare* ring that women wore on their heads in order to carry pots.

Despite the symbolic overtones of the mathule entrance tunnel as a birth canal, the terms applied to its components refer instead to the ribs and backbone of cattle. These apparently divergent references are nonetheless consonant with feminine symbolism, because a wife is regarded as the "backbone of the family." Furthermore, the legality of a proper marriage, the foundation of a house, and the legitimacy of children all depend on the payment of cattle as a bride-price. Children are thus "born through cattle." From this point of view, the mathule is a passage through the body of a cow; its exterior is the animal's hide.

Before the introduction of Western clothing, Basotho wore cloaks of cattle hide. Born through the cow, Basotho remained clothed by cattle throughout their lives. The stripe formed by the ridge of hairs along the animal's backbone was always worn hanging down the wearer's own spine, reinforcing the conflation of person with beast. White traders quickly discovered that Basotho shunned blankets that lacked a stripe that could be positioned the traditional way.

During women's initiation, their body decoration and dress reinforce their connection to fertility and domestic architecture. Their bodies are painted with the three most important symbolic colors—black, white, and red. Black is the color of the ancestors and the dark rain clouds they bring. White is the color of liminality, purity, light, and enlightenment. Black and white form a duality of paired opposites and are used to highlight the mural paintings of doorways, windows, and the edges of buildings, where one surface meets another. Red is the color of earth, particularly red ochre, *letsoku*, called "blood of the earth." Red also signifies the blood of menstruation that indicates fertility and the blood of sacrifice that links the living to the dead, who in turn bring the rain that guarantees the fertility of the earth and everything that lives on it.

Initiation begins when women are painted with white ochre, *phepa*. White symbolizes the calm and purity that are associated with enlightenment and that the novices require for their liminal period. After undergoing sex education, their childhood "dies," and they are painted black to signify this. They then spend several weeks lodged in a special initiation hut made of reeds, learning such traditional feminine skills as weaving grass mats, making pots, and housekeeping.

In the third phase of their initiation, the young women initiates, called *bale*, don ensembles that parallel domestic architecture. They wear reed masks, just as the lapa courtyard is screened from public view by the reed fence, *seotloana*. The mask is called a *lesira*, which means windbreak, and also implies a screen that stands between someone and light or fire. When they emerge from these masks, the girls will be "born" as women. Often the lesira were ornamented with tiny clay beads, which embodied the element of earth vital to creation, architecture, vegetal fertility, and survival on earth.

Around their waists, bale wear thick, elaborate grass coils. They are reminiscent of the horizontal rails that hold up the seotloana fence and underscore woman's link with the vegetal realm. These belts are said to have no beginning and no end. Their name, *likholokoane*, provides another echo of eternal cycles, because it means "arranged order," suggesting that ideas of order, even cosmic order, are linked with the belts.

Into the white ochre on the legs of the bale are inscribed patterns similar to those that decorate the edges of the doorway, drawing attention to women's reproductive capacity. This completes the set of associations that link body decoration and dress to architecture and its cosmic metaphors of creation and birth.

Initiation culminates with women's graduation as women, ready to marry and establish their own houses. After midnight, the *Thojane* ceremony begins. Guests wait outdoors, huddled in blankets against the winter, until the leaders signal that the bonfire may be kindled. As the flames leap to life, the graduating women emerge from their hut into the light. Avoiding eye contact with friends and relatives, they walk as stiffly and silently as wooden puppets, without bending their limbs or swiveling their hips, and then lean on wooden staves. This choreography signals that they are not yet "supple," not yet fully women. Bare-breasted, they wear cowhide skirts or fringed pubic aprons (depending on their lineage, or subgroup).

The graduates' bodies are smeared with letsoku, which links menstruation, sacrifice, and rain. Rain is earth's blood, coursing through its "veins," its rivers, to ensure the cycle of life. Therefore, rain is red.

Around dawn, they retreat to dress for the graduation ceremony, hosted in a lapa. They emerge carrying grass marriage mats they have woven during the school. Onto these their relatives and friends carefully arrange practical, symbolic, and decorative gifts, creating vibrant montages anchored with patterned face cloths, kerchiefs, and shawls and highlighted with many smaller gifts related to toilette (mirrors and combs, often beaded, soap, toothpaste) and the idea of sweetness, conveyed by candy and chocolate bars. Mixed in are such hip signals as badges of Vogue models or Mickey Mouse and tinsel and other decorations. Bright balloons enhance the festive air and recall the symbolism of inflated goat gallbladders, which are attached to the heads of the initiates after goats have been sacrificed to their ancestors. Filled with human breath, a gallbladder or balloon also captures and renders visible the intangible air that epitomizes life and makes it possible. Also, they symbolize a womb filled with spirit and new life.

The graduates' hair is painted with white dots, symbolic of seeds, and they wear many strands of seed or bead necklaces. Some wear long strands of white beads anchored below the nose,

circling the head and trailing down the neck and spine, underscoring their calm breathing and poise. The women's shoulders and faces might be highlighted with even richer and brighter applications of red ochre. Relatives, friends, and admirers might pin money into their hair; abundance and fertility are aligned.

Finally, the women are marshaled into a column. Two abreast, they parade through the lapa holding their decorated mats and, in some cases, a rattle or doll. Traditional fertility dolls representing mature women were conical beaded objects with barely discernible heads. Today, the doll can be replaced by a Barbie, carried shirtless as the epitome of a beautiful and pure young woman of marriageable age. (Girls who have borne children before graduation must wear red shirts.) Despite the antipathy some in the West feel about Barbie as a symbol of the ideal woman, among Basotho, Barbie dolls epitomize the moral and physical beauty that Basotho women should reflect on their graduation and throughout their lives.

The graduation of male initiates, by contrast, is visually dominated by blankets and sticks. After their grueling sojourn in the bush for the initiation school, the boys burn their circumcision lodge, together with all their boyhood clothing, and return to the village naked (today, they come home in old blankets). At dawn the following morning, ranked by the seniority established during the school, they greet the rising sun naked and spit toward it a mouthful of beer, which, by virtue of fermentation, is a symbol of transformation intimately linked with human sexuality and which is also a primary medium for honoring and contacting the ancestors.

Then, the men's relatives approach with new blankets and gifts to attach to them, like those pinned to the women's mats. Some anoint their sons with red ochre mixed into petroleum jelly. Each is given a beaded headband, and some receive beaded belts. The finishing touch is a pair of sunglasses, useful as the young men face the rising sun. In turn, each young man holds aloft his personal knobkerrie and delivers the praise song he has composed during the circumcision camp. Impressive performances are rewarded with money or other small gifts pinned to the body or blanket of the young man.

The male graduates' use of blankets and sticks prominently distinguishes their appearance from the women's. A man's knobkerrie is a symbol of his manhood, and, in the past, it was never allowed inside the house. Before traders sold blankets, a male graduate wore a cloak hide advertising his family's ability to provide him with cattle for a bride-price (later bride-price negotiations included mention that the groom owned many fine blankets). The graduate's hide demonstrated his readiness to marry, establish his house, and have legitimate children "born through the cow"—an idea also evoked by the bovine and vaginal symbolism of the mathule tunnel. Furthermore, the word for "blanket," *koba*, also means "vagina," because it is said to clothe a person just as the vagina encloses the penis. Koba is a symbol of the elongated labia, while the verb *ho sarolla* is applied to stretching both the labia and preparing a wet animal skin.

Although blankets are associated with women's sexuality, they are not used in women's graduations. In male graduation, however, they provide a symbolic foil through which the man's body penetrates, an idea echoed in an interesting past practice: If a man discovered that his bride was not a virgin, he would pierce his blanket with a spear. The image of body and blanket is a reminder that man is born through the "blanket" of women and cattle, and this idea holds out the promise of marriage and building a family. Women, however, are most closely associated with the earth, the house, and creation, and their dress underscores this vegetal primacy.

BASOTHO BLANKETS

In the past, hide cloaks worn by a Basotho subgroup and that group's cattle both carried the same brand marks, emphasizing that the members were linked through cattle. People belonging to the same group—such as a chiefdom—are said to be covered by the same blanket. This was the political concept behind King Moshoeshoe I's famous request to Queen Victoria to protect his nation from the Boers by allowing Basotho to become the "lice in her blanket."

The development of a market economy during the diamond rush of the 1870s made blanket trading viable, and Basotho demand for blankets increased because of livestock epidemics and the increasing scarcity of wild game in their diminished territory. Bayer blankets made in Germany, consisting of columns of color, were early entries into the market. The monopolistic Frasers Trading Company of Basotholand sent designs of Basotho murals and a sample leopard kaross to an English blanket mill in 1885. The ready adoption by Basotho of British soldiers' woolen regimental blankets with heraldic motifs provided another avenue for design. A Queen Victoria blanket, celebrating her diamond jubilee, was produced for the Basotho market in 1887.

For a century, Frasers played the leading role in the design and supply of what became known as "Basotho blankets," sold in trading stores wherever Basotho lived, both in Lesotho and in South Africa.

Basotho blankets functioned as a cultural unifier—the Basotho nation as a whole was figuratively "covered in the same blanket"—but individuals selected different weights, colors, and patterns of blanket depending on their status and the occasion. After the 1980s, however, trade sanctions against South Africa and an unfavorable exchange rate opened the way for cheaper blankets woven with less or no wool and simpler designs. These increasingly dominate the market and have obscured the earlier social codes.

Until recent decades, mural-like designs, stripes, feline dapples, and British heraldry dominated Basotho blanket motifs. Numerous designs based on plants and flowers, echoing murals, are strongly linked with women and their relationship to vegetal fecundity. Several *sefate* (meaning "tree") designs were exclusively for women, such as *Sefate Ea Famahadi* (Tree of Senior Woman), which shows bulbs in bloom. Some sefate designs featured playing card spades and clubs, because these were logos on sacks of cornmeal, the staple diet of most southern African peoples. Similarly, blanket designs featured corn or were named after it; the *kotulo* (harvest) design celebrated agricultural abundance.

More manly and political were the *pitso* blanket, named after the national convocation. Basotho soldiers fought for the British Empire during both world wars, and military motifs included Spitfire airplanes, bombs, propellers, the Victoria Cross, and the V sign for victory. The *boipuso* (which means "independence, reign, sovereign, administration") blanket juxtaposed the British imperial crown and the Basotho hat to evoke their closeness. When Basotholand became the independent country of Lesotho in 1966, the Sesotho shield and axe and the crocodile totem of Moshoeshoe's Koena lineage were popular.

DIVINERS

Diviners are another social category recognizable by its dress, which is dominated by the sacred colors of blood red and pure white. Today, most Basotho diviners are women, and they embrace an African Christian church or sect that addresses the ancestors as spiritual messengers. The main features of a diviner's costume are conventional, but specific details are determined in dreams sent by her ancestors and guiding spirits. Most diviners wear beaded red skirts and red tunics and distinctive beaded headdresses, usually with loops or fringes of white beads and sometimes with a small silver disk suspended over the forehead to symbolize *lesedi*, light and enlightenment.

Diviners are always barefoot when practicing to be directly in contact with the sacred earth where the ancestors reside. They invariably carry an ox-tail whisk, made from the particular ox slaughtered at their inauguration—the animal they must envision in dreams and then locate on the occasion of their graduation in order to prove their genuine guidance by the spirits. In addition, diviners might carry a whip, stick, or ceremonial spear. Often, they wear beaded bandoliers strung across their shoulders. For those who embrace Christian elements, crosses might appear in their beadwork designs or cloaks.

References and Further Reading

Arbousset, Thomas. *Missionary Excursion into the Blue Mountains: King Moshoeshoe's Expedition from Thaba-Bosiu to the Sources of the Malibamatso River in the Year 1840*. Edited and translated by David Ambrose and Albert Brutsch. Morija, Lesotho: Morija Archives, 1991.

Bosco, Dan. "Why Basotho Wear Blankets." *African Studies* 40, no. 1 (1981): 23–32.

Morris, Jean, and Ben Levitas. *Tribal Life Today*. Cape Town: College Press, 1984.

Morris, Jean, and Martin West. *Abantu: An Introduction to the Black People of South Africa*. Cape Town: Struik, 1976.

Tyrrell, Barbara. *Tribal Peoples of Southern Africa*. Cape Town: Books of Africa, 1968.

Van Wyk, Gary N. *African Painted Houses: Basotho Dwellings of Southern Africa*. New York: Harry N. Abrams, 1998.

Gary van Wyk

See also Southern Africa.

Malawi

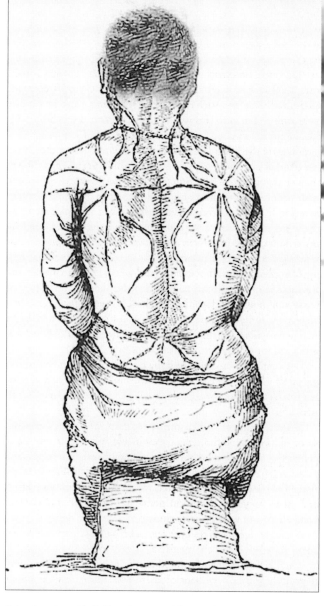

A drawing of an elderly Maravi woman with extensive cicatrization marks on her back. Adapted from David Livingstone's *Narrative of an Expedition to the Zambezi*, London, 1865. Courtesy of Barbara W. Blackmun.

The Republic of Malawi (*Dziko la Malawi*) was known as Nyasaland from 1907 to 1964. It is a scenic country of 45,747 square miles (118,484 square kilometers), bordered by Tanzania and Zambia in the north and northwest and surrounded by Mozambique on the east, south, and southwest. Until the late nineteenth century, the personal appearance of each individual in Malawi reflected ethnic and status distinctions within each region, modified by response to the varied topography and climate. The clothing of Malawi's diverse population has been influenced by external contacts for centuries through migrations from the Congo and southern Africa and through trade routes that link Malawi's large, navigable lake with kingdoms to the west and with ports along the coast. In the 1850s, farming populations near the lake were conquered by invasions of Nguni warriors from Natal, who were known in Malawi as *Ngoni*. Later incursions by Arab and Yao slave traders devastated the country before the arrival of British gunboats on the lake. In 1890, Malawi became a British protectorate, followed by incorporation as a crown colony. Indian Sikhs assisted in establishing colonial government, and many of them chose to remain in the country. Although each foreign group has left signs of its presence, most Malawians who have completed primary education have adopted European clothing.

Lake Malawi fills a deep trough in East Africa's Rift Valley. This vast and scenic lake covers 20 percent of the narrow country, including part of its eastern border with Mozambique. At the southern end of the lake, the Shire River flows into the Zambezi River, which empties its waters into the Indian Ocean. To the east and west of the lake are high plateaus that rise between 3,000 feet (914 meters) and 8,500 feet (2,591 meters) above sea level, the climate changing with each elevation. Seasonal differences vary by 40 degrees Fahrenheit (22 degrees Celsius) or more during the course of the year, adding diversity to the clothing appropriate to each region.

Malawi's population of over twelve million includes regional concentrations that remain linguistically distinct. Among the largest groups are Tumbuka and Tonga in the north, Jere Ngoni and Maseko Ngoni in separate enclaves of the central region, Yao in the southeast, and Maravi (including Chewa, Chipeta, Nyanja, Mang'anja, and smaller related groups) in the central and southern part of the country. Most of the expatriates reside in urban areas, and, although regional and foreign languages are in daily use, the primary tongues are ChiChewa and English. Between 1875 and 1961, almost all of the schools were provided by Christian missions, although about 20 percent of the population is Muslim. Lilongwe is the capital, with a population of 400,000, and 500,000 people live in the combined commercial centers of Blantyre and Limbe. Almost all of the rural population practice subsistence farming, although cotton, rice, peanuts, cassava, and maize are grown for local markets, and tobacco, tea, sugar, and coffee are exported internationally.

CLOTHING AND APPEARANCE PRIOR TO THE NINETEENTH CENTURY: THE MARAVI

By the 1400s, the Maravi had settled around the lake and along the Shire River. This population is related to Luba and Lunda kingdoms in the southeastern Congo. The Maravi are also related to the Tumbuka in northern Malawi, and blacksmiths from both areas smelted iron and forged superior tools. Maravi craftsmen also fashioned bracelets, finger rings, and anklets of copper, brass, iron, and ivory. Cotton was grown along the Shire River then spun into thread and woven into fixed lengths of cloth by Maravi men of the Mang'anja group. These products were traded along the Zambezi River.

Mang'anja weavers worked while seated on a mat placed on the ground. Each man wove on a broad horizontal loom about ten inches (twenty-five centimeters) high and seventy-two inches (one hundred eighty-three centimeters) long, the legs of which were firmly fixed into four holes in the earth. Two woven lengths of the resulting *machira* were sewn together for a Maravi woman's long wrapper, known as a *chirundu*. The versatile chirundu, which remains a popular garment, is wrapped around the body either at the waist or above the breasts and tucked in tightly. Babies were (and are) carried on their mothers' backs, secured by an additional length of cloth. Locally procured red and black dyes were used to create stripes on some Mang'anja textiles. A more thickly woven Mang'anja cloth was used during the cold season as a blanket or a cape, and nineteenth-century observers considered these textiles superior to imported calico. Nevertheless, the appeal of calico's brilliant patterns destroyed economic incentives to grow cotton, and Mang'anja weaving was abandoned in the early 1900s.

In warm weather, the customary men's Maravi costume consisted of a simple kilt called a *tewera* fashioned from a rectangular length of cloth passed through the legs and held in front and back by a belt. Fringed robes and the feathers of certain birds distinguished the clothing of Maravi chiefs. Mang'anja men carried staves or spears, and skin pouches containing snuff boxes, iron scrapers, or tobacco were slung over one shoulder.

Although early sources offer few descriptions of the hairstyles worn by Maravi women, men's hairstyles were endlessly varied. In 1874, David Livingstone noted that "the men take a good deal of pride in the arrangement of their hair...one trains his long locks till they take the admired form of the buffalo's horns; others prefer to let the hair hang in a thick coil down their backs... while another wears it in twisted cords, which, stiffened by fillets of the inner bark of a tree wound spirally around each curl, radiate from the head in all directions. Many shave their hair into ornamental figures."

By the end of the nineteenth century, simpler styles were in vogue, and men and women allowed their hair to grow only a few inches (about eight to thirteen centimeters) long. Sometimes it was shaved into patterns. In the twentieth and twenty-first centuries, some women have separated their short hair into sections, twisting and tying it into geometric designs, which might reflect styles in the past. Jewelry was customarily worn in all areas, and both men and women displayed finger rings and thin bracelets of copper, brass, ivory, or iron on their arms and legs.

For many centuries, colored beads have been a highly valued form of currency. Necklaces and hair ornaments of beads and cowry shells were common, and women wore strands of waist beads under their clothing. Sometimes elephant hair and charms were incorporated into Maravi beadwork, which was intricately woven by women using complicated patterns of colors. There are over twenty-five words in Maravi languages referring to beads of different sizes, shapes, styles, and colors In the early 1500s, the Portuguese drove the coastal Arabs from their trading outposts along the Zambezi River. The loss of markets on the Zambezi caused the Maravi to establish trade routes eastward, and their cotton machiras, carved ivory, and iron tools were sent overland to coastal trading centers.

Although the Maravi reached the height of their influence during the 1600s, Europeans who interacted with them paid little attention to their appearance. In 1798, the first descriptions were supplied by Lacerda e Almeida, who wrote that the Maravi were a handsome people with extensively patterned cicatrizations on their faces and bodies, similar to those in Congo kingdoms. Each Maravi subgroup displayed a characteristic design acquired by adolescents during preparation for adulthood. The most remarkable were large star-shaped patterns all over the face and body, which Lacerda described as "not without their own peculiar beauty." Cicatrization marks were rarely seen after the 1950s, but they appear on a few of the wooden masks used by the Mang'anja *ZiNyau* association.

In the 1800s, some Maravi women also wore an upper lip plug called a *pelele*. The explorer David Livingstone wrote in 1865 that "all the highland women wear the *pelele*, and it is common on the upper and lower Shire River. The poorer classes make them of hollow or solid bamboo, but the wealthier of ivory or tin. The tin *pelele* is in the form of a small dish. The ivory one is not unlike a napkin ring. No woman ever appears in public without the *pelele*, except in times of mourning for the dead." Use of the pelele died out in most areas of Malawi during the first decade of the twentieth century.

CLOTHING AND APPEARANCE IN THE NINETEENTH CENTURY: THE NGONI

In the 1820s, two contingents of Nguni warriors from Natal fled northward separately with their families to avoid the repression of Shaka, the Zulu king. They swept across the Limpopo River, raiding the populations of Zimbabwe, Mutapa, and other Shona-Karanga centers and became known as the Ngoni. Following the pattern of Zulu invasions, both the Maseko Ngoni and the Jere Ngoni contingents killed their male opponents, took conquered women as wives, and adopted the children as Ngoni. By the 1850s, the two groups swept through farming populations around Lake Malawi. The Maseko Ngoni conquered Chewa territories southwest of the lake, while the Jere Ngoni entered from the northwest, seizing Tumbuka and Tonga lands. When Yao communities on the eastern side of Lake Malawi were also invaded, they fled toward the southwest. As a result, Yao clans became dispersed among the Maravi throughout the southern lakeshore and highland regions.

The Ngoni differed from the Maravi, Tumbuka, Tonga, and Yao in appearance. In the late twentieth century, art historian Michael Conner obtained statements from Ngoni leaders describing the customary clothing of their fathers and grandfathers. They reported that each Ngoni man had always worn a short kilt or loin covering (called *ibetchu* by the Jere, *chitewe* by the Maseko). This was made of small animal pelts or of twisted bark cloth

A painting of a Ngoni warrior (Malawi) wearing a short kilt or loin covering. These coverings were commonly made of small animal pelts or of twisted bark cloth. The painting is by Sir Harry Johnston, published as a frontispiece in *British Central Africa*, London, 1897. Courtesy of Barbara W. Blackmun.

supported by a belt around the waist. It was essential to wear this garment, even beneath the long, togalike cloth *virundu*, which was wrapped around the body with one end thrown over a shoulder. The virundu could be plain black, striped, checked, or red and usually had a white border on the bottom edge.

A penis cover (*ncwado*) under any type of clothing was even more essential (and remained so for some time, even after European trousers were adopted by the Ngoni men). In contrast to the local groups, the Ngoni had no facial or body cicatrization. Until interethnic warfare was abolished by the British in the 1890s, a head-ring (*vidhlokhio*) was worn as a sign of manhood by each Ngoni warrior who had won distinction in combat. During the era of pacification, this head-ring was replaced by a brightly colored cloth worn around the forehead, sometimes accompanied by ornamental feathers. An exterior pocket (*himba*),

often of civet cat fur, was tied on the side of one hip and used for carrying snuff—an obligatory substance for polite interaction between men. Earrings (*izicazo* or *mitobvu*) were also essential and many Ngoni wore thick anklets made from the heel of an elephant.

Possibly because the Jere Ngoni and Maseko Ngoni arrived separately, some aspects of their regalia are distinct. A few of these seem to counter the claim that the Ngoni have never borrowed elements of culture. For example, Maseko Ngoni women make a wide bead-patterned belt for their husbands (*chihata*) that is laced tightly in front. Instead of the decorative Maseko belt, Jere Ngoni men wear narrow beaded bandoliers that cross the chest forming an X. The origin of these disparate beadwork traditions is unclear, as neither the Zulu nor the Ndebele in South Africa began to use beadwork of this type until after the Ngoni migrated northward. Conner has suggested that early coastal traders introduced small glass beads to the Chewa in Malawi and that Chewa women who were forcibly incorporated into Ngoni households might have brought beadwork skills with them. Alternatively, contacts with southeastern Africa might have continued after the Ngoni arrived in Malawi. For example, in the nineteenth century, a beaded apron called *nkhwindi* was worn by small Maseko Ngoni children and also by some unmarried Ngoni girls. In addition, the nkhwindi was associated with the bridal costumes of royal Ngoni women. These functions of the nkhwindi echo customs that developed in Natal some time later than the Ngoni migration north.

Ngoni men in full warrior regalia often perform at national festivals and on other ceremonial occasions. In public performances, men of both Ngoni groups wear a knee-length kilt of prestigious wild animal pelts with a long and flattened monkey tail attached to it in the back. Their arms and legs are decorated with long-haired fur, and rattles or bells are worn on their ankles. The flexible feathers worn in the impressive Ngoni headdress are selected for supple movement when a warrior imperiously tosses his head in the wind. Certain plumes, such as the crimson *uluvi* feathers of the *queda* bird, are reserved for Ngoni paramount chiefs. The oval black and white oxhide shields that they carry in these dances are smaller versions of celebrated Ngoni war shields.

Conner has found that Ngoni women take pride in creating a regal appearance that elicits the compliment, "Awoneni inthombi iyaphetgeza" (Here comes a lady walking with dignity and comportment). Although formerly women's clothing was often cut from the soft, tanned skin of domestic cattle, nineteenth-century Ngoni women soon adopted fashionably tied, uncut lengths of plain red or black trade cloth. Waist beads were worn underneath an ankle-length and multilayered cotton wrapper that was tucked up over the breasts, similar to the Maravi woman's chirundu. Sometimes a *chiyaga* shoulder cloth was tied to cover one shoulder, extending in a diagonal to the lower hip on the opposite side so that it covered the upper body and waist. Their art in tying layers of cloth, especially red, with each draped over another was dignified and fashionable. This aristocratic effect was enhanced by large earrings of ivory, stone, wood, or metal, along with several beaded necklaces.

Before the 1920s, the hair of married Ngoni women was customarily plaited and flared in shape, with small threads tied between the plaits to separate each section. Hair ornaments consisted of beads and ivory combs as well as small, decoratively

A labor supervisor near Lake Malawi, 1968. After Malawi's independence in 1964, Western clothing became more accessible to the general population. Photograph by Barbara W. Blackmun.

carved ivory pins, and a brightly colored cotton scarf was sometimes tied around the head at forehead level. The *isongo*, a continuous coil of brightly polished copper wire, was custom-wrapped around each woman's neck, and distinguished men and women wore multiple bracelets and leg ornaments of ivory.

The paramount chief of the Jere Ngoni had gained control of ivory used by Tumbuka craftsmen, whose carved bracelets (*makhoza*) were sent to Ngoni leaders as tribute. An Ngoni bride was sometimes honored with an ivory *khoza* by her new father-in-law, and, in the 1990s, Ngoni fathers presented makhoza to their sons as university graduation gifts.

CLOTHING AND APPEARANCE
IN THE NINETEENTH CENTURY:
THE YAO AND THE ARABS

In addition to the Ngoni, other ethnic groups also arrived in Malawi in the 1800s. As early as the fifteenth century, men from Yao communities had worked with Swahili traders near Kilwa. Yao blacksmiths, like the Maravi, were known for smelting and forging excellent tools. Selling these on the coast, they brought back calico, salt, cowries, and beads, which they bartered with Maravi traders in exchange for ivory, cattle, and cotton machiras. During the 1600s, the Yao carried Swahili merchandise farther west into Central Africa. On their return, their caravans brought elephant tusks from the interior, carried by slaves whom the Yao had purchased along the way.

In 1840, when British sea patrols suppressed the slave trade in West Africa, the search for slaves intensified in the Indian Ocean. Considering East Africa an alternate source of captives to use in this profitable trade, an Arab from Kilwa settled with a retinue on the western shore of Lake Malawi. This outpost soon became a major caravan base for the export of slaves from Central Africa. The Chewa and Tonga chiefs regarded the Swahilis and their soldiers as a defense against Ngoni invaders, and extensive trade in cloth and other luxuries developed between them. The resident Arabs also introduced Islam to Malawi. In the 1870s, another outpost and Islamic center was established on the northern lakeshore. Malawi's population includes the Muslim descendents of these Arab settlers, and mosques are maintained throughout the countryside. Muslim women cover their heads loosely (and stylishly) with thin, patterned cloth in colors that enhance their long wrappers, but face veils are unknown in Malawi. The influence of Arab culture is reflected in the close-fitting white caps and long unbelted tunics of many men near the lake, including some who are actively Christian.

CLOTHING AND APPEARANCE
IN THE NINETEENTH CENTURY:
THE BRITISH MISSIONARIES

In 1858, David Livingstone visited Mang'anja territory and realized that Lake Malawi had become the center of new slave routes to the Swahili coast. To stop this development, Livingstone sent for an armed vessel that could be used on the lake and wrote urgent letters asking British universities to send protective Christian missions to this area. By the time the missionaries arrived, Yao and Arab traders were sacking and burning Maravi villages and sending the inhabitants in chains to the Swahili coast. Livingstone estimated that nineteen thousand slaves from all the local populations were passing through customs at Zanzibar every year.

By 1875, missionaries had established residential schools for refugees. A British protectorate was established in the areas around Lake Malawi, and British gunboats ended the slave trade in 1895.

Boarding schools taught arithmetic and basic English literacy, along with carpentry, sewing, and other practical skills. At these schools, the sons of Tumbuka, Tonga, Maravi, and Ngoni chiefs mixed freely with the sons of militant Yao warriors and boys and girls from all of Malawi's ethnic groups. The desired result was pacification and widespread interethnic marriage among educated Malawians, who soon adopted European clothing and customs. Those who completed their training moved to the towns and served in the commercial, educational, and government sectors of the emerging economy. Prominent Malawian women wore Victorian gowns with long puffed sleeves, high collars, and sweeping skirts but retained their close-cropped hairstyles. Men in leading positions could be recognized by their dark suits, immaculate white shirts, and sober ties. Most urban women preferred a simple blouse with short, puffed sleeves combined with a patterned chirundu and head scarf, while urban men adopted a neat short-sleeved shirt with light-colored slacks and added a warmer shirt or jacket in cold weather. These clothing choices have persisted into the twenty-first century.

CLOTHING AND APPEARANCE IN THE TWENTIETH CENTURY: EXPATRIATES AND INDEPENDENCE

Foreign ethnic groups also joined Malawi's mixture of populations. Forty Sikhs who came as volunteers to keep law and order in the country soon increased to two hundred. Some stayed in the country, sent for their families, and became active merchants. Women wearing colorful silk saris and cool patterned cottons woven in India can often be seen in the Indian markets of Limbe, near Blantyre. Settlers from England and South Africa established

plantations that exported tea, coffee, and tobacco. When the nation became independent in 1964, additional expatriates staffed international educational, medical, agricultural, industrial, and other development projects. These people brought foreign clothing and customs with them that were not always welcomed by the conservative population.

In the 1960s, men and women of expatriate development staffs wore the European-based clothing that had become accepted throughout much of the country. Male African professionals continued to dress more formally than their European counterparts, with dark suits and sober ties. Some government messengers and minor officials still wore the fez and a belted tunic derived from East African military models, resembling uniforms of the Queen's African Rifles. The British governor general, in his last public appearances before formally ceding leadership of Malawi's government to its African president, wore a white-plumed colonial helmet and dress uniform, reminiscent of the height of Britain's imperial power. On ordinary duty, colonial officials preferred

Malawi women pounding dried maize into flour in Blantyre, Malawi, 1965. They are wearing traditional dress mixed with clothing typical of the 1960s. Photograph by Barbara W. Blackmun.

neat khaki safari shirts with short sleeves and matching trousers. In hot weather, trousers were short, and the ensemble included knee-length tan stockings, leather shoes, and a broad-brimmed hat. Expatriate men often followed their example. Informally, women wore imported sandals of colored plastic, and men preferred the thick black sandals fashioned locally from discarded rubber tires.

Ethnic mixing and Westernization have not completely eroded the indigenous cultures, even in the twenty-first century. Malawian urbanites retain links with the rural communities from which their families came, and most preserve the ability to speak their ancestral languages. During national or local holidays, these loyalties are encouraged. The paramount chiefs appear with fly whisks, headgear, or robes to mark their rank and ethnic identity, and troupes of Ngoni warriors perform for the public, wearing military regalia and carrying dance staffs and ox-hide shields. Maravi masqueraders offer fleeting glimpses of their ancient and secret *Gulu Wankulu*, which thrives in rural communities.

The first president of the independent Republic of Malawi was a Chewa, Hastings Kamuzu Banda. Although he held advanced medical degrees, he startled expatriates and urban populations by honoring conservative values. Customarily, rural women uncovered their breasts in hot weather or when caring for an infant. However, women's thighs were considered erotic by traditional villagers, and tight clothing that revealed the contours of a woman's buttocks in public was viewed as obscene. President Banda proclaimed strict rules of attire for women and girls, forbidding slacks, shorts, culottes, and any skirt that did not modestly conceal the hips and knees. This ban was applied not only to residents but also to female foreign tourists, who were supplied with chirundu cloth when they arrived at the airport and were subject to immediate deportation if they did not comply with Malawi's restrictions.

Banda also stopped the importation of used garments to Malawi, revived the cotton-growing industry, and opened a textile mill in Blantyre that produced attractive cloth from home-grown cotton. This colorfast, nonwrinkling cloth was dyed in rich hues, and imaginative patterns were designed by local artists. As part of the campaign to support the new mill, women from Malawi University sponsored a National Fashion and Fabric Exhibition in the late 1960s. Expatriates joined prominent Malawian women in modeling the blouse and chirundu in new colors and in displaying combinations of sophisticated prints. Colored short-sleeved shirts for men were also modeled at the exhibition, and the khaki uniforms of school children soon appeared in blue, turquoise, deep red, or gold. When Malawians throughout the countryside adopted the new fabrics, the appearance of rural communities dramatically improved.

Near the end of the twentieth century, the authority of the elderly President Banda waned, and restrictions were lifted on the importation of inexpensive clothing from abroad. Television was introduced, along with videos that had been available only in neighboring countries. Local publications assisted the population in gaining an awareness of global culture. In the twenty-first century, the chirundu remains popular for Malawi's women, especially when combined with a matching blouse. However, the enthusiasm for imports has crippled Malawi's revival of the textile industry. The youth of Malawi have adopted the fashions of their contemporaries throughout the world, and their urban elders are influenced more than ever by the conventions of international clothing.

References and Further Reading

Aguilar, Laurel Birch de. *Inscribing the Mask: Interpretation of Nyau Masks and Ritual Performance among the Chewa of Central Malawi.* Studia Instituti Anthropos, 47. Fribourg, Switzerland: University Press, 1998.

Alpers, Edward A. "The Mutapa and Malawi Political Systems." In *Aspects of Central African History*, edited by T.O. Ranger, 1–28. Evanston, IL: Northwestern University Press, 1968.

Blackmun, Barbara Winston, and M. Schoffeleers. "Masks of Malawi." *African Arts* 5, no. 4 (1972): 36–41, 69.

Chimombo, Steven, ed. *WASI, The Magazine for the Arts.* Balaka, Malawi: Montfort Missionary Press.

Conner, Michael. *The Art of the Jere and Masiko Ngoni of Malawi.* Woodmere, NY: Man's Heritage Press, 1993.

Cutter, Charles A. *Africa: The World Today Series.* Harper's Ferry, WV: Stryker-Post, 2005.

Debenham, Frank. *Nyasaland, Land of the Lake.* London: Her Majesty's Stationery Office, 1955.

Faulkner, Laurel Birch. "Basketry Masks of the Chewa." *African Arts* 21, no. 3 (1988): 28–31, 86.

Johnston, Sir Harry H. *British Central Africa.* London: Methuen, 1897.

Lacerda e Almeida, E.J. de. "Lacerda's Journey, 1798." In *The Lands of Kazembe*, edited and translated by Richard Burton, 1–103. Reprinted New York: Negro Universities Press, 1969.

Livingstone, David, and Charles Livingstone. *Narrative of an Expedition to the Zambezi … and of the Discovery of the Lakes Shirwa and Nyassa.* London: John Murray, 1865.

Livingstone, David, and Horace Waller. *David Livingstone's Last Journals.* Vols. 1 and 2. London: John Murray, 1874.

Macdonald, Duff. *Africana.* Vols. 1 and 2. London: Simpkin Marshall, 1882.

Pachai, Bridglal. *Malawi: The History of the Nation.* London: Longman Group, 1973.

Ransford, Oliver. *Livingstone's Lake.* London: John Murray, 1966.

Barbara W. Blackmun

See also Tanzania; Mozambique; South Africa Overview; Zambia; Zimbabwe.

Mozambique

- First Impressions
- Dress as Ethnic Marker
- Colonial Influences
- Liberation Movement and Independence
- Snapshot: Capulanas

Descriptions of dress and adornment in Mozambique were observed and discussed by visitors and Mozambicans beginning with the first written documents in the fifteenth century C.E. Mozambique—located in southeastern Africa with a long Indian Ocean coastline, also bounded by Tanzania, Zimbabwe, and South Africa—is home to several ethnic groups with a variety of styles of dress, which changed over the years as the arrival of European Christian missionaries and the spread of Islam made an impact. The earliest descriptions portray people wearing animal skins and metal rings and bracelets, but they increasingly mentioned cotton cloth and Western-style dress over the centuries. In more recent years, Mozambique fought a war of liberation from Portuguese colonial rule in the 1960s and 1970s, developed a socialist program of development, and fought a bitter internal war in the 1980s; in the 1990s, the country found a peaceful end to war and a way forward in the modern global marketplace. Throughout those events, most Mozambican women continued to wear a length of cotton cloth called a *capulana* wrapped around their bodies, while men and urban women adopted Western styles of dress. In traditional and modern communities, people wore clothing and jewelry that indicated their status as religious leaders or adherents or otherwise displayed their status.

FIRST IMPRESSIONS

Much of the knowledge of how people dressed and adorned themselves in early periods of Mozambican history comes from accounts written by explorers, missionaries, and Portuguese anthropologists, who were closely tied to the colonial regime. The earliest references from the fifteenth and sixteenth centuries mention Mozambican preferences in clothing as a part of trade concerns. People along the central coast preferred imported colored cotton cloth from India, which they would unravel and reweave into distinctive stripes. There was also a thriving business of weaving cloth from locally grown cotton, which the Portuguese traders bought along with straw hats, beads, and other goods. Imported cloth was noted as a trade item for gold, which was mined in the interior, and for ivory, which was collected throughout the region. Any Portuguese man who wished to vie for a leadership position needed to distribute Indian cloth to assert his status. Cloth and beads were also an important component in bride-wealth exchanges in central and southern Mozambique. The lengths of cloth were wrapped around the body, either at the waist or under the arms, and were generally not sewn into specific clothing styles.

A seventeenth-century description of a Makua community in northern Mozambique, where neither imported nor locally grown cotton was common, illustrates a very different style of dress. The Makua were barely covered at all, with only a few inches (about eight to thirteen centimeters) of cloth around the waist to cover the genitals. They were also noted for filing their front teeth to points, for having many tattoos or scars on their faces, and for wearing lip rings. When it was time to wed, men would wear animal horns on their heads, arranged front and back and over each ear with the points curving up and out like a crown. Children wore nothing. The Makonde, also in the north, were also known for the elaborate tattoos on their faces and bodies, as well as the lip plugs worn by women and the practice of filing their teeth to points.

Body coverings made from animal skins or material made from pounded tree bark were more common in the interior, where people had less access to international trade commodities. Throughout the region, both men and women would wear rings, bracelets, necklaces, and pendants made from metal or wood. Nineteenth- and early-twentieth-century photographs show Ngoni men described as warriors who wore animal skins as a kind of kilt, bracelets on their upper arms, and tall headdresses with animal horns.

Fisherwomen from Ibo Island, Mozambique, 1983. Their faces are thickly coated in *msiro*, a white paste that gives them smooth and clear skin and protection from the sun. Photograph by Ragnar Hansen.

Anthropologists, in particular, often recorded their observations of African physical attributes, and many publications amount to little more than a series of photographs of "typical" women and men from various ethnic groups posed to show off their body type and decorations. While the photos present some idea of how people dressed and decorated their bodies with scarification and lip plugs, the underlying and perhaps unconscious intent was to document how different and exotic Africans were from Europeans.

Observers particularly noted the presence of class markers, such as the Yao leaders in northern Mozambique who wore serval cat skins and ivory bracelets in an unspecified past, and the later observation that certain kinds of calico were reserved for chiefs and nobles. Yao chiefs' wives wore brass wire called *sapuli* that was acknowledged in a song: "To the wearer of *Sapuli*, We pay due fealty, For well we know that she must be, The wife of Royalty." Women wearing brass wire were treated with great respect and obedience; they were seen as "conspicuous and above all others." By the early twentieth century, Sena women in central Mozambique were noted as owning brass rings that were worn on their arms and legs, though wearing such rings did not necessarily indicate elite status.

DRESS AS ETHNIC MARKER

Islam spread throughout northern and central Mozambique from the sixteenth century, and there is much evidence of Yao adoption of Swahili style of dress and architecture, as well as religious beliefs. General attributes of "Swahiliness" included Arab-African descent, Islamic religious beliefs and practices, use of the Swahili language, urban living often related to trading activities, and material characteristics such as style of dress, architecture, and food. Men, in particular, dressed in Swahili-style long white robes and often wore a small round cloth cap. Yao women, however, did not cover their faces with a veil and did not wear any distinctive dress. As one observer noted, "There is, therefore, nothing to make them recognizable as Muslim."

The most common item worn by women throughout Mozambique was a piece of colorful printed cotton cloth called a capulana, usually about two meters (about two yards) in length. Photos and drawings sometimes show women wearing a single length of cloth wrapped above their breasts and reaching past their knees, although, by the late twentieth century, this was more often seen worn wrapped around the woman's waist with a blouse, a shirt, or a second capulana worn above the waist. The cloth was wrapped around the body with the opening in the front, and the top edge was rolled and tucked into itself to hold it in place. Capulanas were also used as slings to carry babies on women's backs. For special events, women wore a designated cloth. For instance, women in dance groups wore matching capulanas, often with appropriate designs printed on them, and women who march in May Day parades or participate in other political events may wear coordinated capulanas and head scarves. Although capulanas might illustrate a political leader or important event, they did not generally have the kinds of proverbial sayings often seen on similar cloths elsewhere in East Africa known as *kangas*.

An unusual and often noted custom among the Makua people along the northern coast of Mozambique, especially on the islands of Moçambique and Ibo, is women's use of white paste on their faces. Although usually restricted to young women, it can be seen on women of all ages. The material is known as *msiro* (sometimes spelled *mussiro* or *muciro*), and it is made by rubbing the bark or root of the small sour plum tree (*Olax dissitiflora*) and mixing the shreds with water. Various sources describe the paste as including sand or being based on ground coral. Women apply a thick coating that is worn throughout the day. The goal is to make the skin smooth and clear, though it also provides protection from the sun when the women are collecting shellfish on the ocean or beaches. Although these women are a small minority of the female population of the nation, their photos are frequently used in tourist advertisements to demonstrate an exotic aspect of Mozambique.

Women and men who were active in religious activities—for instance, as seers and healers with exceptional spiritual powers—wore particular kinds of adornment that often accompanied such activities. Dora Earthy, writing in the early twentieth century, mentioned that women who were mediums specializing in "smelling out" witches in criminal cases often wore a thong around their necks with a red bead with a white spiral inside; the bead was chipped at the end to display the white spiral. Other mediums and seers wore ochre wigs and cowry-shell headbands and used particular baskets and stools in the course of their work. Certain spirits would require the use of axes, drums, and rattles, and Earthy mentioned in particular that women who were commanded to dance by the spirit often used an ax as part of the dance. Such emblems marked women's noteworthy accomplishments and also demonstrated how some women administered to the spiritual life of their communities.

The use of wigs by the seers was part of a range of hairstyles that represented one's social position. For instance, in many Mozambican communities, men and women shaved their heads to indicate that they were in mourning, and girls in some areas shaved their heads as part of the initiation ceremony. Young married women often had very elaborate hairstyles, while older women who were widows wore a pattern that incorporated broader sections of braids than younger married women. Other hair design elements marked the wearers' age group, life status, social rank, and clan affiliation. Chopi women and women of other ethnicities would spend many hours braiding and oiling each other's hair in designs that were replicated in patterns on wooden serving bowls carved by men.

Chopi and Valenge men and women also marked their bodies with elaborate scars, often referred to as tattoos, which were cuts that were made dark by rubbing ground charcoal in the incisions. The various cuts had specific names according to their placement, style, and meaning. By the 1920s, many forms of body decoration were becoming less common. Few people any longer filed their teeth to points, a practice of earlier generations. Partly influenced by missionaries, women were less likely than previous generations to undergo a series of procedures that resulted in "the story of their lives on their own flesh" but were still more likely to undergo the procedure than men. Girls often had their first scars done before their initiation rites at puberty, in part to prepare them for that event. Many of the scars on women's thighs, buttocks, and outer genital area were done for heightened beauty and eroticism, while the design reflected items of symbolic import such as baskets or a rooster's comb. Some of the facial marks represented tears or saliva, bodily fluids that were considered sacred. Observers have speculated that the tattoos indicated ethnic affiliation, possibly as a way to differentiate people of different backgrounds; in other cases, people would adopt the markings associated with a group who conquered or otherwise came to dominate them, indicating their new affiliation and the fluid nature of ethnic identity.

Both men and women did the work of scarification, and usually men performed the incisions on men while women did it on women. Other work related to tattooing included preparing certain oils from the *mafurra* tree and caring for the fresh incisions to ensure that they healed properly. Those who did the scarification were sometimes paid and sometimes could claim labor time from those being adorned. Women in Chopi communities also removed their eyelashes and plucked their eyebrows for beautification; although it possibly had the added desire of avoiding witchcraft, because certain spells required obtaining an eyelash from the proposed victim. In the 1990s, Heidi Gengenbach found that, while tattooing was declining, older Shangaan women were pleased to discuss the community of purpose they had as young girls, when they would go as a group to have the tattoos cut. They remembered the experience as one of female interaction, and the scar designs were chosen for reasons of beauty and personal enhancement.

Although tattoos were sometimes described as part of initiation ceremonies that marked arrival at adulthood, women were more likely to obtain tattoos as an individual and somewhat secret project. Mozambicans also did not include genital cutting as part of their initiation rites, although many communities—especially in northern Mozambique—practiced a manipulation of the labia that resulted in their elongation. Such extended labia were found throughout southern and central Africa and indicated attention to women's sexuality and possibly were a visual way to mark the difference between girls and women.

COLONIAL INFLUENCES

As the Portuguese colonial presence increased after the mid-nineteenth century, more people adopted Western-style clothing. Men, in particular, were more often seen wearing shorts or pants and shirts that buttoned in the front. Men who were recruited to local police forces were called *cypais*, and photos from the 1920s show them standing barefoot and wearing shorts, long-sleeved military-style shirts, and fezlike hats as a mark of their office. Women were influenced by their contact with Christian missionaries. One missionary woman, Mrs. W. C. Terril, recounted in 1909 that she offered a class in "plain sewing," though the irregular sessions devoted to cutting and making "their own dresses have been of the most benefit to both teacher and scholar." Reports on sewing classes often appeared in missionary newsletters, such as the brief note written by Mrs. Terril in 1913, describing how "most of the girls know how to sew and they are making their own dresses…. Some of the girls have learned to sew on the sewing machine"; when they were good enough on the old machine, they sometimes had a chance to work on a new Singer machine that had been sent from Sweden.

The concern of the missionaries with what was viewed as improper dress emerges in many anecdotes and descriptions of the women attending the mission schools. A government decree in the early twentieth century that women should wear European attire led to a revolt by African market women near the southern coastal town of Inhambane, who refused to come to town unless they could dress in their usual capulana. The strike by the market vendors caused a shortage of vegetables and other food supplies in the markets. Indian shopkeepers were also opposed to the new law, which would have led to a decline in their own sales of capulanas. The decree was rescinded, with the addendum in the missionary account that conversion to Christianity was the solution for having women wear skirts, as "our Christian women are never immodestly attired and European dress is the usual style with them." Clothing styles were among the most obvious signs of conversion and represented the overt efforts of the missionaries to control both the bodies and souls of their African converts. It is difficult to retrieve the voices of African women from that time period, making the report of a concerted refusal by the market women to wear Western dress an intriguing glimpse of African resistance to colonial culture.

The dress that people wore was also a factor in determining their legal status under colonialism. The Portuguese permitted Africans who attained literacy in Portuguese, lived in Western-style urban houses, and otherwise demonstrated that they were following a European lifestyle to be legally considered assimilated (*assimilado*), a status that exempted them from forced labor demands. Wearing Western-style clothing—trousers and shirts for men and dresses for women—was an essential component in establishing legal status.

LIBERATION MOVEMENT AND INDEPENDENCE

In the 1960s, Mozambicans from three anticolonial movements came together to form the Mozambique Liberation Front, commonly known as *Frelimo* (Frente de Libertação de Moçambique). Photos from the liberation struggle show both men and women wearing camouflage uniforms. In the early years of independence, President Samora Machel called for Mozambicans to have greater pride in their African appearance, and, in several public speeches, he addressed issues of proper attire for school and workplaces. While he couched his comments in a broader discussion about respectful behavior in public social spaces, in a speech on 7 February 1980, he said that "Going to work in shirt-sleeves, sandals, T-shirts with slogans and advertisements, or jeans shows a lack of respect for the place of work, for colleagues, for superiors and above all for the public…. As regards women, we must urge decency and good taste. It is unacceptable to come to work in a headscarf." There was apparently never any actual law concerning wearing head coverings, but there was social pressure on girls and women to stop wearing head scarves, and, in at least one instance around 1980, women in Maputo who were wearing trousers were attacked on the street. In the end, many urban women did grow modified Afro-style hairdos or had elaborate braids and extensions added to their hair, while most Mozambican women continued on a daily basis to tie a scarf or small piece of cloth over their heads, knotted simply at the back of their necks.

After independence, women and men found work in garment factories, and the women's organization established sewing cooperatives where women could learn to sew. A newspaper article in 1983 included photographs of women modeling a variety of dress styles developed at the cooperative, showcasing the advances possible for women. Workers in the factories commonly wore *batas*, or long jackets of heavy cotton, at their workplaces. Young children in child care centers wore a kind of smock also called a bata, while children were usually attired in matching uniforms of shorts or skirts and shirts to school.

Throughout the 1980s and the early 1990s, Mozambique experienced an internal war that disrupted wide areas of both rural and urban life. It became very difficult to find clothing in the stores, and people were often seen wearing ragged clothing. Refugees in rural areas were described as covering themselves with rudimentary bark cloth in the absence of lengths of cloth. But after the ceasefire was signed in 1992, the shops began to fill again. Capulanas had been scarce and rationed in the 1980s, but, by the late 1990s, women could find piles of the brightly colored lengths of cloth, some from local textile factories and some imported from India in locally desirable designs such as cashew nuts. The sale of used clothing increased, as elsewhere in Africa, and had a negative impact on the local clothing manufacturing industry. In Mozambique, secondhand clothing was referred to as *calamidade* (calamity or crisis clothing), and it was a large part of the informal markets in the cities.

By the late 1990s, it was common to see young men and women wearing blue jeans and T-shirts, and there was no longer any social condemnation for wearing such casual Western clothing. Men often wore tropical-style cotton shirts with guayabera-style tucks and stitching on the front, worn with the squared-off shirttails outside the slacks. In the 1990s, the spread of evangelical churches usually referred to as Zionist saw women church members wearing white outfits to Sunday services. Such churches often introduced dietary rules and dress codes as part of their emphasis on a particular morality. The dress code allowed capulanas but required a white head scarf in the church and frowned on wearing jewelry and lipstick.

A local fashion industry has been slow to develop. In 2005, the first Mozambique Fashion Week was held, followed in 2006 with a show on the steps of Maputo's City Hall. Local designers were constrained by a lack of materials, though Marinela Rodriguez's use of capulana prints to make trouser suits and dresses for women garnered some attention. Paola Rolletta also encouraged local production of clothing made from capulana material and presented some design possibilities in a pamphlet that was itself covered with printed cotton cloth.

Snapshot: Capulanas

Some of the capulanas sold in the 1980s and 1990s commemorated events such as the one hundred and second anniversary of the founding of Beira (Mozambique's second-largest city); honored the main bank, the Banco de Moçambique; or paid tribute to the importance of cashew nuts in the local economy. Simpler geometric designs that suggested aspects of Mozambican culture were also popular, such as one that was widely sold in various color combinations in the mid-1980s; in one version, it had an abstract border in purple, orange, black, and beige and central panels of a musical instrument made from a gourd strung with beads. The yellow and black cloth recognizing the bank had a border of multi-colored banknotes interspersed with the seal of the bank; the central panel was a map of the country showing the different provinces, and the main background was more multicolored banknotes dispersed across a field of bright yellow with small black polka dots. A cloth that showed electoral support for the ruling party, Frelimo, did not mention the name of the party but had a midpoint design of a yellow and green ear of maize or corn across a drum in white, red, and black, with a corner diagonal design with Frelimo's colors, also green, black, yellow, and red. The background was a deep green and included doves with olive branches and the words "o futuro melhor" (a better future). A cloth manufactured for the National Conference on Culture in June 1993 focused on ancient rock art found in Manica Province; the border had a series of designs of masks, drums, thumb pianos, and pots in white and black; there was a narrow red and black border, and the central section was a repeated image of some of the rock paintings showing black human figures on a pale yellow background.

Many designs honor women, including Olympic track star Lourdes Maria Matola and revolutionary hero Josina Machel, and various cloths are sold for the women's organization. One that said "*7 de Abril/Viva a Mulher Moçambicana*" (7th of April

Dancing women in Mozambique, 1983. They wear *capulanas* (lengths of cotton cloth wrapped around the waist) of varying designs. Photograph by Ragnar Hansen.

[Mozambican Women's Day]/Long Live the Mozambican Woman) was illustrated with a central panel based on a photograph of a woman from the north with a characteristic white paste on her face. The photo was multicolored, while the background was black with a repeating pattern of small black, white, and yellow yin and yang symbols. Maize on an orange border and cashew nuts in repetitive designs formed the blue and orange background for a capulana that honored women's work. The central illustration within an oval frame showed a woman pounding nuts in a large mortar; she was also wearing a capulana with the same cashew-nut design on a smaller scale.

One elaborate capulana was printed for the Fifth Congress of the Frelimo Party in 1989. The oval central panels have then-president Joaquim Chissano rendered in a drawing speaking into a microphone; he is in black and white against a bright blue sky, with "Viva o Presidente Chissano" in a banner over each oval. The ovals are flanked by the Mozambican flag, and all are on a background of bright yellow with black squiggles, yellow stars, and the official seal of the party in red, yellow, black, and white. A narrow running banner in black and white along the top reads "*Republica Popular de Moçambique*," while a parallel banner along the bottom proclaims "Viva a unidade nacional força invencível do povo" (Long live national unity, the invincible strength of the people). An additional series of smaller horizontal oval panels under the president's illustration show scenes of Maputo, the capital city of tall modern buildings seen from boats in the bay, alternating with a depiction of the Heroes Monument, all rendered in vivid blue, green, yellow, and red. And, finally, there is a three-inch (eight-centimeter) design along the top and bottom edges that shows the official Frelimo seal of a yellow star with a book, a gun, and a hoe, all on a red background.

References and Further Reading

Abdallah, Yohanna B. *The Yaos: Chiikala cha Wayao.* Edited and translated by Edward A. Alpers. London: Frank Cass, 1973 (1919).

Cabral, António Augusto Pereira. *Raças, Usos e Costumes do Indígenas da Província de Moçambique* [Races, Practices, and Customs of the Natives of the Province of Mozambique]. Lourenço Marques, Mozambique: Imprensa Nacional, 1952.

de Lima, Américo Pires. *Notas Etnográficas do Norte de Moçambique* [Ethnographic Notes from Northern Mozambique]. Sep. dos. Anais Scientíficos da Faculdade de Medicina do Porto 4, no. 2 (1918).

Dias, Jorge, and Margot Dias. *Os Macondes de Moçambique.* Vol. 2, *Cultura Material* [The Makondes of Mozambique. Vol. 2, Material Culture]. Lisbon: Junta de Investigações do Ultramar, 1964.

Earthy, E. Dora. "On the Significance of the Body Markings of Some Natives of Portuguese East Africa." *South African Journal of Science* 21 (1924): 573–587.

Earthy, E. Dora. "On Some Ritual Objects of the Vandau in South Chopiland Gaza, Portuguese East Africa." *Annals of the Transvaal Museum* 11, no. 2 (1925): 125–128, with illustrations following.

Gengenbach, Heidi, "Boundaries of Beauty: Tattooed Secrets of Women's History in Magude District, Southern Mozambique." *Journal of Women's History* 14, no. 4 (Winter 2003): 106–141.

Machel, Samora. *Samora Machel: An African Revolutionary, Selected Speeches and Writings.* Edited by Barry Munslow. Translated by Michael Wolfers. London: Zed, 1985.

Monteiro Lopes, Manoel. "Usages and Customs of the Natives of Sena." *Journal of the African Society* 6, no. 24 (July 1907): 350–366.

"Must Wear Skirts: Order to Maidens." *Inhambane Christian Advocate* 39 (December 1919): 5.

Newitt, Malyn. *A History of Mozambique.* Bloomington: Indiana University Press, 1995.

Peirone, Frederico José. *A Tribo Ajaua do Alto Niassa (Moçambique) e Alguns Aspectos da sua Problemática Neo-Islâmica* [The Yao Tribe of Upper Niassa (Mozambique) and Some Aspects of the Neo-Islamic Problem]. Lisbon: Junta de Investigações do Ultramar, 1967.

"Report of Mrs. W. C. Terril." *Inhambane Christian Advocate* 31 (September 1909): 11.

Rolletta, Paola, ed. *Capulanas and Lenços/Capulanas and Kerchiefs.* Maputo, Mozambique: Missanga, 2004.

Sheldon, Kathleen. *Pounders of Grain: A History of Women, Work, and Politics in Mozambique.* Portsmouth, NH: Heinemann, 2002.

"Snap Shots." *Inhambane Christian Advocate* 40 (March 1913): 9.

Kathleen Sheldon

Namibia

In Namibia, the oldest indigenous forms of dress were made from the leather hides of wild and domesticated animals decorated with shell and locally made metal beads. Before the Colonial period, different cultural groups and social subgroups distinguished themselves through formalized yet highly inventive hairstyles, headgear, and tooth modification. Cloth dress was slowly introduced via Europeans and was adopted in uneven ways. Some indigenous people began wearing cloth early in the Colonial period, while others continue to wear leather today. For most, cloth dress has followed European trends.

Environment, culture, and history all affect the development of dress in a particular region. With about two million people in an area of about three hundred thousand square miles (a little under eight hundred thousand square kilometers), Namibia is one of the least-densely populated countries in the world. Its western boundary is formed by the Atlantic Ocean, and to the north, east, and south, it shares borders with Angola, Botswana, and South Africa. The land is mostly arid and semiarid desert and scrub land that is subject to regular droughts. Nonetheless, the environment has successfully sustained foraging, fishing, hunting, herding, trading, agriculture, wage labor, and combinations thereof. The mining of diamonds, uranium, and metals over the last century has constituted the major industry in the country.

INDIGENOUS PEOPLE

Historical differences among indigenous peoples have been both blurred and heightened by the political struggle for power during the Colonial period. Terms such as *Damara, Bushmen, Himba, Basters, whites, coloreds, Caprivians,* and *Oorlams* have been used to classify people into what appear to be distinct sociocultural entities. But these labels unevenly privilege such factors as economic practice, skin color, leadership, and relative wealth in making group distinctions. In fact, the cohesiveness, composition, way of life, and self-consciousness of social and cultural groups in the country have complex histories.

For this discussion of dress, key cultural groups will be distinguished along broad cultural and linguistic lines as San, Nama, Herero, Owambo, Kavango, and European. The San-speaking foragers are descended from people who first occupied the region many thousands of years ago. Nama herders, who speak Khoi languages closely related to those of the San, probably first entered the region about two thousand years ago. Bantu-speaking cattle herders with subgroups later called Herero, Himba, and Mbanderu are thought to have come into the region three hundred to four hundred years ago. At about the same time, the Ovambo—including the Kwanyama, Ndonga, Kwambi, Mbalantu, Ngandjera, Kwaluudhi, Kolonkadhi, and Eunda—began creating centralized agricultural societies in the better-watered land along the current Angolan border. Speaking a Bantu language very similar to Otjiherero, descendants of these people currently make up about half of the nation's population. The Kavango in the extreme northeast also worked ore and practiced farming and fishing mixed with some hunting and gathering. These Bantu speakers include the Kwangari, Mbundza, Sambyu, Gciriku, and Mbukushu.

German, English, and Finnish missionaries and traders arrived in the early nineteenth century. The Germans formalized their military presence in the country in 1884. They crushed local resistance to their control but lost the territory to South Africa during World War I. Defying the international community, South Africa governed until the late twentieth century, exporting apartheid into the region. Namibia finally gained independence and held its first democratic elections in 1990.

EARLIEST CLOTHING

The accounts of European missionaries, soldiers, and traders augmented by nineteenth-century photographs allow us to characterize precolonial adornment. Softened wild animal and livestock hides were used to make the earliest clothing. All men and women in the region covered their genitals with leather garments of varying size and shape. The chest was generally uncovered, though leather cloaks were worn. Hats and hairstyles were important everywhere. These denoted age and gender differences and, among some cultures, marked one's passage through puberty, marriage, and childbearing. Most groups occasionally made large antelope- or cowhide sandals for travel in rough country. Uniformly in the region, men prepared the leather, while women applied beadwork and, among some groups, pieced skins together with sinew thread.

Both clothing and the body were ornamented with shell, metal, ivory, and glass beads. Ostrich eggshell was the most common early material used, and salt-water shells were obtained from long distances. Metal jewelry was made by local ore-working cultures, and European glass beads were traded in from at least the eighteenth century on. Every group also used other naturally occurring substances such as ochre, specularite, plant fibers, bark, roots, wood pulp, ash, animal and vegetal fats, feathers, berries, and seeds to soften, shape, scent, color, and augment skin, hair, and clothing. Every group also made opportunistic use of found objects such as metal buttons, rifle cartridges, safety pins, and factory-made metal chains, rings, and clips in ornamenting their attire.

In varying ways, dress distinguished cultural groups from one another—women from men, the initiated from the uninitiated,

A man wearing United Nations (UN) buttons in 1989, just before the first democratic elections in Windhoek, Namibia. The UN had a long history in Namibia, and such buttons have become collectors' items. Photograph by Hildi Hendrickson.

the married from the unmarried, the richer from the poorer, the healer or the chief from ordinary people. Bead necklaces and ornaments were used in gift exchanges that reinforced kin relations, helped to effect marriages, and facilitated the circulation of other resources such as livestock. Body treatments were thought to affect spiritual and physical health in addition to proclaiming identities or changing social statuses. Clothing was sometimes burned to signal a change in social status and often inherited after death, corpses being buried mostly in simple hides.

EARLY DRESS AMONG SAN-SPEAKING GROUPS

Rock paintings from southern Namibia constitute the oldest images of the ornamented human body found thus far in the country. In a scene that may be as much as six thousand years old, for example, the mislabeled *White Lady of the Brandberg* shows a human figure with male genitalia who is painted white from feet to waist and wears bands around its knees and upper arms. While such images should not be assumed to be realistic, it seems significant that San-speaking foragers, among others, are known historically to have worn such bands. A San man's leather armbands were said to aid his ability to run, an essential hunting skill. Boys and men wore ornaments of leather and beads as well as twisted antelope tendon, eland hide, wood, braided grass, antelope tail hairs, feathers, and even the rolled-together strands of tree spider web.

Women and girls wore leather bands and strings of ostrich eggshell beads around their ankles, knees, necks, arms, and foreheads. Married women looped strings of beads under each arm so that the strands crisscrossed their chests. In later periods, women wore glass, copper, brass, and iron beads and bracelets and earrings.

San men wore caps made of jackal, spring hare, mongoose, caracal, fox, and aardwolf fur. Women and men wore three-cornered skin loincloths, which women augmented with one or two fringed, beaded leather aprons. Adults wore cloaks made of duiker, hartebeest, or steenbok skin that doubled as gathering bags and in which women carried small children. Hair was sprinkled with crushed plant fibers, and skin was rubbed with ochre and fat. Some San men shaved their hair, and women sometimes used a hair cream of pounded plant fibers mixed with fat from the feet of antelopes. Women carried their aromatic powders and skin creams in a decorated tortoiseshell, a wild orange shell, or a small animal horn. Butterfly cocoon rattles were worn around the ankles for dancing. Everyone wore more ornaments at dances, and women and men shamans wore the most ornaments of all.

NAMA-SPEAKING GROUPS

In precolonial times, front and back skin aprons were worn by Nama men and women. Women also wore a leather cloak/carrying bag tied over one shoulder. An array of caps made of jackal or other skins were worn, and leather bands decorated with eggshell and, later, metal beads were worn on the ankles, upper arms, and wrists. Like the San, the Nama are said to have oiled their skin with fat mixed with iron-bearing soil and powdered themselves with crushed wood, root, and other plant materials. Even after converting to Christianity, the Nama continued to wear amulets made of animal teeth, beads, plant fibers, and reptile skin around their necks. Some of these objects were tied onto parts of the body that needed healing. The value placed on clothing is suggested in the fact that it was considered part of a Nama family's communal property and could be inherited after a person's death.

HERERO-SPEAKING GROUPS

In the nineteenth century, both Herero women and men are said to have worn front and back leather aprons that were made of sheep, goat, or wild animal skin and secured to leather belts. Men hung leather strips from bands near their knees and wore a cloak made of sheep- or goatskin. Women's aprons were longer than men's, and married women helped each other make tall, multi-piece leather caps with three leaf-shaped points standing up at the back of the head. Decorated leather strips hung down from this headdress on top of the leather cloaks women wore. Some women wore an ostrich eggshell bead overskirt. Both men and women decorated their clothing with heavy metal beads made by metal workers in the region. Herero women also wore brass and copper bracelets on their arms and ankles that were so heavy they impeded movement. However, this was viewed by women and men alike as appropriate for the wealthy. Everyone applied a sparkly red cream of ochre and/or specularite mixed with animal fat to their skin, hair, ornaments, and leather clothing. Girls signaled their marriageability by lengthening their hair with tendon or bark after their first menstruation. During some marriage ceremonies, a web of fat from around the intestines of one of the bride-wealth cattle was worn over a girl's head like a veil. The esteem accorded to women in this society recognizing both male and female descent lines is glimpsed in the fact that men sometimes wore women's clothes when supplicating at their ancestors' graves. An Angolan mussel shell worn on the forehead marked a man as the inheritor of this religious practice from his father.

Into the late twentieth century, young Himba girls and boys wore one or two thick braids that reflected patrilineal descent group membership. For ceremonies, prepubescent girls wore wigs of many thin braids inherited from their mothers. A girl's own braids were lengthened just before puberty and pulled back from her face after initiation. Next, she was given a three-pointed headdress of sheep- or goatskin to mark her marriageable status. After a year of marriage or after giving birth, another headdress made from the skin of a goat's head was worn. An adult woman's braids were gradually lengthened, and beads and pendants added to the array of ornaments down her back. Women wore coiled copper bracelets, thick ropes of metal-bead necklaces, and laterally cut conus shell disks on their chests. Boys' hairstyles and ornaments also marked their passage through life stages. A particular thick beaded necklace showed that a boy had been circumcised. Young men wore one long braid down their back after puberty and two when marriageable. Beads and shells were tied into these braids. A married man wore a leather covering over his hair that was removed only for mourning and a white conus shell on his chest.

A Herero woman in a typical long patchwork dress and headscarf. Okakarara, Namibia, 1988. Photograph by Hildi Hendrickson.

KAVANGO-SPEAKING GROUPS

Kwangari men's dress consisted of front or both front and back panels of cow's stomach, duiker, wildcat, or leopard skin secured with an ox-hide belt. Women wore leather skirts front and back made of cow's stomach, goat, or duiker skin that fell to their knees and cloaks made of skins laced together with sinew. Women's skirts were held in place with two ox-hide belts, and they also draped a net of ostrich eggshell strings over their hips. Wearing giraffe or eland skins is said to have marked a wealthy person, as did the amount of jewelry worn. In addition to shell and glass beaded necklaces, men's ornaments included grass and metal armbands, brass bands below the knees, and leather bracelets of large antelope skin with the mane hair attached. A high-status item for both men and women was a white china medallion made to resemble the conus shell disks that the highest-status people wore. Each of these shell medallions was said to be equal in value to an ox in the nineteenth century.

All Kavango women's hairstyles included long, thin braids lengthened with plant fibers and smeared with powdered wood salve. Everyone treated their skin with this salve as well. Men shaved their hair, leaving only a patch on top of their heads, while boys left one band of hair laterally across their scalp. A very high-status woman might wear a net of ox fat around her neck, which oiled her skin. Amulets associated with warding off illness and misfortune were made of aromatic wood or root worn on a string around the neck. For women, these were also made of aardwolf entrails that were valued for their pungent smell.

The Sambyu used goatskin and antelope skin to make men's loinskins. Women wore front and back aprons decorated with black and white beads. Jewelry was similar to that of the Kwangari. Children wore grass bracelets, and a girl who had been betrothed put a notched stick in her hair. At marriage, she received beads from her husband that were worn on bands below her knees. Animal fat and bean and nut oils were used on the hair, skin, and leather. Plant roots were used to lengthen women's braids. Aromatic root nodules were strung around the neck and were appreciated for their scent. A cream made with pleasant-smelling plants was given to a young married woman by her mother or mother-in-law. The Gciriku wore leather clothes like the Sambyu, but, as metal workers, they produced the bracelets and brass wire coils worn by women. Girls' hairstyles were complex assemblages of coiled hair extending from the crown of the head, thin braids at the back that often fell below the waist, and curled or plastered hair on the forehead. Wood and fat mixtures were used to cover hair and skin.

Among Mbukushu, carnivore skins were used to make cloaks, hats, and bags. Twisted root fibers from a shrub were used by this basket-making culture to augment women's braids. Married women wore black leather loincloths with an intricately beaded skin in back that hung to the knees. Black and white were the early bead colors. Upon entering puberty, a girl's grandmothers gave her a leather apron to which beaded bands were attached by other female relatives. Both sexes wore copper anklets and armbands of copper and twisted animal tail hairs. Women especially wore belts, necklaces, and hair ornaments of ostrich egg and cowry shell. Carnivore claws were worn around the neck, as were inherited conus-shell ornaments. A girl was not initiated until she had the multiple necklaces and other jewelry required to adorn her postritually. Shamans wore root fibers and feathers in their headdresses; porcupine quill and reed skirts; seedpod, wildebeest, and zebra mane hair necklaces; genet cat skins; and insect cocoon or seedpod leg rattles. Many Kavango made wigs to wear for ceremonial purposes.

OVAMBO-SPEAKING GROUPS

Clothing helped mark gradations in political status among Ovambo chiefly lineages, land-owning families, and ordinary people. Ovambo smiths worked Angolan iron and copper ore into beads and bracelets as well as tools and weapons. Newborn babies' hair was shaved shortly after birth; if their mother had lost children, however, berries were attached to children's hair instead to ensure good health. Month-old children were given bark necklaces and belts by a friend of their father's at their naming ceremonies. In wealthy families, boys in their late teens spent several weeks away from home undergoing circumcision. An initiate's old leather clothing was burned, and when he rejoined the village, he wore new clothes.

Ordinary daily wear consisted of a front leather panel for men and front and back aprons for women. Women wore black ox-skin cloaks and an overskirt of ostrich eggshell bead strands. Longer skirts were worn by wealthier women. These skirts, as well as copper anklets and bracelets, were gifts from their husbands and were considered his property. The symbolic power of clothing in

the status hierarchy is suggested in the fact that no one was allowed to enter the chief's homestead wearing sandals or else it was thought a member of his family would die.

Women's hairstyles among the matrilineal Ovambo were particularly detailed. There were different styles worn by very young girls; by girls before, during, and after puberty; and by adult women. Kwanyama girls at about age twelve, for instance, wore fat and crushed teak roots smeared into ridges on the back and sides of the head. Slightly older girls added thick braids of leaf fiber and loose, shaved hair. Cowry shells were attached with sinew to the hair of women, and girls at this stage also wore a band of cut porcupine quills on their foreheads.

During initiation, a Kwanyama girl's hairdo was unwoven and further mixed with fiber to make multiple loose strands tipped with beads or berries. All girls had to be initiated to be marriageable, and after several weeks of physical ordeals, the girls' hair was shaped into the married woman's five-pointed headdress. The three front points represented a bull and the back two a cow. Next, a girl's body and face were covered in white ash, and she donned a many-stranded skirt and collar of tubular palm and aloe fibers. As the initiation period came to an end, groups of girls roamed the countryside with weapons and had license to harass any man they came upon. When they returned, they were cleansed of the ash and married in a ceremony that involved the couple rubbing fat and ochre on each other's chests.

With eggshell-string skirts, leather panels front and back, wide ox-hide belts, metal bracelets, ivory and shell medallions, and multiple necklaces, Mbalantu girls' preinitiate status was flamboyantly displayed. A married woman's thick braids were looped over the head so that they ringed the face. Many thick white beads were attached in rows to the sides of this coiffure. Sometimes a tuft of ground squirrel tail hair was attached at either cheek. Preinitiation, Kwaluudhi and Ngandjera girls wrapped bunches of their braids with reddened palm leaves, creating five or six curved hornlike appendages that curved across their shoulders and back. During initiation, their thin braids were again separated and tipped with palm leaves, and loose hair at the back of the head was bunched into a bun. Married Kwaluudhi and Ngandjera women wore the bun gathered by a leather band, and their braids were again wrapped into two hornlike appendages. Early-twentieth-century photographs show wealthy Ndonga girls dressed for marriage with whole tanned cheetah and leopard skins hanging down their backs.

BODY MODIFICATIONS: TEETH, TATTOOS, AND CIRCUMCISION

Tooth modification and extraction distinguished some Namibian Bantu-speaking groups from one another into the second half of the twentieth century. All Kavango chipped and filed the top two front incisors into an inverted V shape, and the Kwangari and Mbundza additionally knocked out the two center front lower incisors. Many Owambo speakers and all the Herero groups created the V shape on top and removed all four lower incisors. The Nama and San are not thought to have practiced tooth modification on any significant scale.

Tattooing was systematically practiced only among Kavango. Some Kwangari created geometric-shaped tattoos especially on men and keloids on women. Mbukushu adults believed that

V-shaped incisions on the forehead into which green dye was rubbed brought good luck. Early in the twentieth century, some Gciriku were tattooed, and some Sambyu women had special substances rubbed into incisions on their foreheads that would help them attract men. Some San had a line or lines tattooed on their foreheads with a green dye rubbed into them, and lines were incised onto men's legs after success in hunting large animals. However, all these marks seem to have been associated with hunting and health magic rather than group identities. Earlobe perforation was common among all early Namibian societies. Men were circumcised among the Herero-speaking groups and among some Ovambo.

CLOTH DRESS AND URBAN STYLES

Most people in urban Namibia today wear store-bought clothes made in factories in South Africa and Europe. Hairstyles and jewelry vary from individual to individual. School children wear uniforms, as do employees of banks and other companies. Church groups devise distinctively colored costumes, and T-shirts proclaim political affiliations. Karakul sheep pelts and other furs are

Herero military-style uniforms at a celebration in Okahandja, Namibia, 1989. Photograph by Hildi Hendrickson.

fashioned into women's coats for sale internationally. Gemstone jewelry is made in the country, and ostrich eggshell beads, feathers, and porcupine quills are now appearing on urban clothing.

The process involved in the shift from leather to cloth dress has not been systematically studied, but it seems to have taken about one hundred years. Several factors may have been critical: proximity to mission settlements, degree of participation in regional trade, local leadership, and relative economic autonomy. Nineteenth-century Europeans, believing that new Christians should cover the body more fully, encouraged women to wear long dresses with a fitted bodice and sleeves, while men were to wear trousers and jackets. Although conversion to the new religion was slow until the early twentieth century, new goods such as felt hats were sported by African men decades earlier to augment their personal reputations. It is unclear when the old body creams, hairstyles, and associated rituals were abandoned, but new ideas about hygiene eventually took hold.

Within groups, status, gender, and age affected one's style of dress. While politically powerful men often affected the new styles first, women and children in many groups wore the old clothing the longest. In many places, old and new were mixed for many years. For instance, while whole Nama groups came into the region from the south as cloth-wearing Christians, some Nama women continued to paint their faces with blackish red fat while menstruating or in early pregnancy. Most Ovambo had adopted cloth and Christianity by the twentieth century, but photographs show at least some of their leading families substituting cloth for leather in some aspects of dress before abandoning the old ways completely. The Kavango and later the San seem to have adopted cloth dress only in the twentieth century, being distant from mission, trading, and administrative centers and, for the San at least, politically marginalized as well. Meanwhile, European cloth dress developed some substyles such as the khaki shirt and shorts of Afrikaans-speaking men.

The dress of Herero-speakers is remarkable for its lack of change. Key Herero families adopted cloth dress in the mid-nineteenth century, and adult Herero and Mbanderu women have sewn and worn full-length cloth dresses and head dresses ever since. The fact that twenty-first-century Herero wives still wear Victorian styles has become a powerful part of their public identity, making them the primary articulators of their society's conservatism. Some of the cloth used is handmade patchwork. These dresses have changed in style, becoming more voluminous over the last several generations. Meanwhile, since the 1920s, Herero and Mbanderu men have worn military-style uniforms during annual neotraditional ceremonies at ancestors' graves. And among the twenty-first-century Himba, many continue to wear the old leather clothes, even when visiting urban areas.

Relative economic stability through successful cattle herding seems to have permitted this cultural and sartorial independence among Herero speakers. Although many urban workers wear garments for daily work that are similar to those worn in many urban places around the world, clothing production of such styles is largely carried out by tailors and dressmakers. One contemporary designer, Melanie Harteveld-Becker, is worthy of mention as having designed gowns for participants in the Miss Namibia contest, an event that connects modern Namibia with the rest of the world. Namibians also take pride, however, in the fact that the old cloth and leather styles of dress attract national and international attention from journalists, tourists, travelers, and politicians. Tourists seeking to experience "traditional" Africa journey to the north to visit the Himba and flock to Herero ceremonies to take photographs. In fact, the image of the Herero woman in a brightly colored head scarf and long dress has been a central component in the representation of Namibian identity over the last century nationally and internationally and now adds to their cultural cachet. There is no doubt that dress and adornment will continue to have complex symbolic value as a twenty-first-century Namibia takes shape.

References and Further Reading

Gibson, Gordon, Thomas Larson, and Cecilia McGurk. *The Kavango Peoples*. Wiesbaden, Germany: Franz Steiner, 1981.

Guenther, Mathias. *Kalahari Bushmen in German South West Africa*. Köln, Germany: Rüdiger Köppe, 2005.

Hahn, C.H.L., H. Vedder, and L. Fourie. *The Native Tribes of South West Africa*. London: Frank Cass & Co., 1966 (1928).

Hendrickson, Hildi. "A Symbolic History of the 'Traditional' Herero Dress in Namibia and Botswana." *African Studies* 53, no. 2 (1994): 25–54.

Hendrickson, Hildi. "Bodies and Flags: The Representation of Herero Identity in Colonial Namibia." In *Clothing and Difference: Embodied Identities in Colonial and Post-colonial Africa*, edited by Hildi Hendrickson, 213–244. Durham, NC: Duke University Press, 1996.

Kinahan, Jill. "Cattle for Beads: The Archaeology of Historical Contact and Trade on the Namib Coast." *Studies in African Archaeology* 17. Uppsala, Sweden: University of Uppsala, 2000.

Mertens, Alice. *South West Africa and Its Indigenous Peoples*. New York: Taplinger, 1966.

Scherz, A., E. R. Scherz, G. Taapopi, and A. Otto. *Hairstyles, Head-Dresses and Ornaments in South West Africa/Namibia and Southern Angola*. Windhoek, Namibia: Gamsberg Uitgewers, 1981.

Van Reenen, J. F. "Tooth Mutilating and Extraction Practices amongst the Peoples of South West Africa (Namibia)." In *Variation, Culture and Evolution in African Populations*, edited by Ronald Singer and John K. Lundy, 159–169. Johannesburg: Witwatersrand University Press, 1986.

Vedder, Heinrich. *South West Africa in Early Times*. Translated from German by Cyril Hall. New York: Barnes and Noble, 1966 (1938).

Hildi Hendrickson

See also Angola; Botswana.

South Africa Overview

- Landscape and People
- Precolonial Dress
- Material Signs of Distinction
- Colonial Encounters
- Ethnicity and Dress
- Ethnicity and Apartheid
- Fashioning South Africans

A watercolor painting by E.F. Steeb, 1812, of a Khoekhoe woman and child in Cape Colony (now part of South Africa), showing ostrich-eggshell bead ornaments and facial decoration. Copyright: William Fehr Collection, Iziko Museums of Cape Town.

S outh Africa offers a rich field for exploring the symbolic language of dress in the varied contexts of everyday life. It is a country of many cultural layers, with eleven official languages and a relatively recent history of racial segregation and imposed ethnically based "homelands." After 1994, however, when South Africa became a multiparty democracy, the new nation aspired to be united in its diversity, even though the inequalities of the past remained embedded in many social institutions and structures—most notably the economy. The motto on the national coat of arms proclaims, "People who are different join together," while the constitution of South Africa adopted in 1996 enshrines the right to freedom of association and expression among cultural, religious, and linguistic communities. The creative tension between unity and diversity—social cohesion on the one hand and cultural difference on the other—is a defining feature of post-apartheid South Africa. Dress—as a medium for expressing individuality, group affiliation, and respect for tradition—plays an active role in defining social distinctions, status, and identity and forms a material interface between personal and public realms. What people choose to wear is always telling, but the message is seldom unambiguous. The meaning of dress can only be understood in relation to context and the dynamic of social interaction. In South Africa, as elsewhere, dress is a complex cultural resource that people use in mediating their multiple roles in society. Using dress to negotiate the terrain of cultural difference and similarity in changing social contexts is part of the everyday experience of being South African.

LANDSCAPE AND PEOPLE

South Africa is a large country of over 1.2 million square kilometers (470,000 square miles) that can be divided into two major topographical regions: the interior plateau, edged by the mountains of the Great Escarpment, and the land between the mountains and the sea. The wide plains of the inland plateau become increasingly arid toward the west, but extremes of temperature occur in relatively few parts of the country and, in general, do not have a major impact on dress.

In 2005, the population of South Africa was estimated to be about forty-seven million people, of whom almost 80 percent were black South Africans, the rest being of European descent, Asian (mainly Indian), or of mixed ancestry. The latter include

descendants of slaves brought to Cape Colony, especially Cape Town, by the Dutch East India Company from the late seventeenth to the early nineteenth centuries, as well as the Creole population that resulted from relationships between Europeans, the indigenous people, and slaves. The latter came largely from the areas of present Indonesia, India, Sri Lanka, Madagascar, and Mozambique and brought with them elements of the clothing traditions of these countries, as did the Dutch, English, Scottish, French, German, and other European settlers.

In the late nineteenth century, the work of missionaries and others in codifying the languages of the indigenous people reduced the many oral dialects to standardized written versions that resulted in an ethnographic classification of the African people based largely on language. The main language groupings are Nguni (Zulu, Xhosa, Swazi, and Ndebele), spoken by about half of the population, with Zulu being the largest language group and Ndebele the smallest; Sotho-Tswana (Southern Sotho, Pedi, and Tswana), spoken by about a quarter of the population; Tsonga (4 percent); Venda (2 percent); Afrikaans (13 percent); and English (8 percent). Most speakers of African languages and

Afrikaans use English in addition to their home languages. A very small minority of the population traces its roots to the original San hunter-gatherer and Khoekhoe herder populations of the country (collectively referred to as *Khoe-San*), and only a few of their languages survive.

PRECOLONIAL DRESS

The earliest inhabitants of the African subcontinent were nomadic hunters and gatherers whose technology was based on the use of stone and organic materials. About seventy-five thousand years ago, hunter-gatherers living in a cave in the southern cape, now known as Blombos Cave, adorned their bodies with small perforated *Nessarius* shells. Traces of red ochre on the shell beads suggest that they were colored intentionally or that they absorbed the color from the skin of the wearer. Pieces of engraved ochre also from the site indicate that it was a highly valued pigment and that the owners were using color to distinguish themselves visually. These remarkable shell beads and engraved ochre from the southern coast of Africa are very early examples of modern cultural behavior that affirm the time depth of the human impulse to adorn the body.

By about two thousand years ago, herders with domestic livestock were living in the southwest, and African agriculturalists had moved into the northeastern parts of the country, bringing with them the knowledge of iron working.

Prior to the introduction of imported garments and cloth, all clothing was fashioned from the skins of game and domestic animals and, less frequently, from plants and ostrich eggshells. Traditionally, however, the softened skins of small antelope such as steenbok, duiker, and springbok, hunted with slender bows and stone-tipped arrows, were used to make clothing and accessories for both men and women. San men wore skin loincloths and cloaks in cold weather as well as hide sandals and, at times, caps made of jackal or fox fur. Women wore two skin front aprons decorated at the edge with ostrich-eggshell beads and a plain back apron. Skin cloaks were multipurpose garments used both for warmth and for carrying food and firewood from the veldt. Three ends of a cloak tied in front of the shoulder formed a bag that could carry a large quantity of melons, roots, nuts, or dried meat. The multifunctionality of a hide cloak was regarded as one of its main advantages over fitted garments. By the late nineteenth century in most parts of southern Africa, the indigenous hunter-gatherers and herders had been decimated and dispossessed of their hunting and grazing grounds as colonial settlers had moved into their territories, and the use of firearms had vastly reduced the herds of game and affected the supply of skins.

Ostrich-eggshell beads, made laboriously by San women, were worked into necklaces, headbands, bracelets, and girdles and were exchanged to affirm social ties. Women added pieces of aromatic wood to their necklaces and carried fragrant *buchu* powder in a small tortoiseshell container fitted with a puff of soft fur; charms and amulets were made of reed, wood, horn, roots, and claws. Fat mixed with red ochre (hematite or bloodstone) or charcoal was used as a cosmetic to accentuate the cheekbones and forehead. Red ochre, symbolically linked with the earth, blood, and life force, was an important element of dress and ritual, not only among Khoe-San people but also among Xhosa and Sotho speakers. Specularite, a metallic form of hematite, was widely traded and used as a cosmetic for the body and hair by Tswana-speaking people as well as their Khoekhoe neighbors. By the twentieth century, clothing dyed with red ochre had become the most overt sign of distinction between Xhosa traditionalists and their school-educated counterparts. Redness came to stand for a cluster of attributes signifying active adherence to tradition but also resistance to imposed systems of administration.

Although the dress of hunter-gatherers reveals an economy of form and function well suited to a nomadic way of life, outsiders regarded them as undressed, closer to the realm of nature than culture. By the late nineteenth century, remnant San groups wore mainly Westernized clothing—trousers, vests, shirts, dresses, and shoes—but, since the early 1990s, there has been a revival of cultural identity among people of Khoe-San descent who are proud to claim recognition as the indigenous people of South Africa. Traditional skin clothing and other material symbols of identity have been mobilized in relation to their political claims for indigenous rights and land restitution.

MATERIAL SIGNS OF DISTINCTION

Metal implements gave African chiefdoms advantages both in hunting and in fashioning garments from the hides of game animals and cattle. The fur, claws, and teeth of predators had prestige value, as did the feathers of certain birds. Leopard skin was widely associated with the authority of chiefs; the skin and tails of wild cats and monkeys were valued for men's apparel, as were rare sable antelope and otter skins. Hand-wrought metal ornaments were highly esteemed—notable historical examples being the *ingxotha* armbands bestowed as an honor on Zulu warriors and the heavy brass *indondo* beads worn by the Zulu elite. Ivory, associated with the power of elephants and prowess in the hunt, was the prerogative of chiefs. By 1100 C.E. at Mapungubwe on the Limpopo River, social stratification was well established; local gold and ivory were traded for imported cloth, glass beads, and Chinese porcelain, and the rulers were buried with precious gold objects and hundreds of rolled gold-wire bracelets. A similar rolling technique is still found among Venda and related people who make large quantities of leg rings from aluminum and other metal wire to adorn the wrists and ankles.

The striped *salempore* cloth that forms part of traditional Tsonga and Venda dress has its origins in the Indian Ocean trade from the east coast of Africa to the interior. Glass beads were similarly first introduced through Arab traders and later, from the sixteenth century onward, by Portuguese traders from Delagoa Bay. Glass beads were highly valued for their rarity as well as their luminosity and color. For Venda and related people, pale blue ancestral beads known as "beads of the water" are still kept as sacred amulets, and the insignia of Pedi chiefs included a necklace of sacred beads that was handed down in the royal line. At first, beads were highly valued as a form of currency and their circulation was controlled by chiefs, but, from the 1830s onward, the supply of beads increased through traders from the cape, and, by the late nineteenth century, there was a proliferation of bead varieties and colors, which allowed distinctive regional styles of beadwork to develop.

Among the most distinctive aspects of dress were hairstyle and headwear. From the blue crane feathers of Xhosa warriors, the wax head rings of Zulu men, the distinctive hairstyles of married and unmarried women, and the grass hats of young men, to the bonnets worn by settler women and the veils of brides, the head was an important signifier of identity. It follows that choice of headwear was a conspicuous way of expressing aspirations and social mobility. This was explicit when freed slaves at the cape, who had been required to go barefoot and without hats, acquired shoes and extravagant hats to mark their emancipation.

COLONIAL ENCOUNTERS

Travelers, traders, missionaries, soldiers, settlers, and industrialists contributed in different ways, and at different times and places, to changing styles of dress, new consumer patterns, and the formation of new social groupings. From the earliest contact between Europeans and the aboriginal inhabitants of southern Africa, perceptions of dress were starkly contrasted. To the Eurocentric gaze, the indigenous people were naked, whereas, by their own standards, they were fully dressed when smeared with fat and clothed in animal skins. The perceived nakedness of the indigenous people presented a moral challenge to missionaries and Victorian notions of respectability as well as a commercial opportunity to enterprising colonists and traders.

The body became a stage for the enactment of contested value systems. Missionary values of conformity, modesty, and cleanliness encouraged the adoption of Westernized garments and imported cloth, but the styles of dress that emerged were shaped as much by African people themselves as by missionary endeavor. If missionaries regarded Western clothing as a sign of civility, this view was not accepted unconditionally nor without modification by their converts. Traditional aprons made of animal skin, plants, ostrich eggshells, and combinations thereof were often worn by women under skirts made from imported cotton fabric, and men wore an animal skin cloak called a *kaross* over Westernized shirts and trousers. The blue print smocks introduced by missionaries were soon made their own by Pedi women and worn in combination with the traditional goatskin skirts of married women The semiflared Xhosa skirts, based on a Victorian pattern, were Africanized with braiding, stitching, and buttons, and contemporary designers of the Sun Goddess label have transformed this style for the catwalks of international fashion.

By the turn of the twentieth century, there were over one thousand trading stores in the Cape Colony, carrying, inter alia, a miscellany of beads, buttons, cloth, synthetic ochre, metal ware, and trinkets that were specifically targeted at rural communities. By this time, over two centuries of colonial expansion had undermined the autonomy of even the most powerful African chiefdoms, and white minority rule was on the rise. Regimental uniforms, with their brass buttons and epaulets, as well as Edwardian top coats and top hats had made an impact on men's dress, the latter especially among the educated classes. At the same time, the mining industry was growing and with it the demand for migrant labor. Men working in towns soon adopted and adapted Western-style clothing both to conform and to express their new status. Storekeepers in towns offered migrants a wide range of merchandise, including boots, coats, tweed jackets, waistcoats, shirts, braces, belts, hats, handkerchiefs, and pocket watches. The eclectic dress of migrants returning from the mines to their rural homes with an array of possessions served to affirm their newly earned status among their own communities.

ETHNICITY AND DRESS

The heartland of Nguni-speaking people is in the fertile southeastern areas between the mountains and the sea, but they live throughout the country. They can be grouped ethnographically into the northern Nguni (including the Swazi and Zulu kingdoms and the Ndebele) and the southern Nguni (including the Xhosa, Mpondo, and Thembu chiefdoms, the smaller Mpondomise and Bomvana groups, as well as the immigrant Mfengu, Hlubi, Xesibe, and Bhaca). In patriarchal Nguni families, a man could marry more than one wife, and seniority, kinship, and status were clearly expressed in dress and behavior. A junior wife who had not yet given birth dressed modestly and wore a head dress that restricted her gaze to show respect for her husband's family. Young Xhosa wives also wore necklaces made of the tail hairs of a cow from their father's herd to give them ancestral protection. Cattle were the preferred form of bride-wealth, and they were invested with deep spiritual significance. Their hide was used for shields and drums as well as certain items of dress—notably, the heavy pleated skirt, *isidwaba*, worn by married Zulu women in combination with beadwork girdles and ornaments, which varied regionally in color and design.

Early Sotho- and Tswana-speaking groups settled on the interior plateau across the Drakensberg mountains and toward the west, where the rainfall was lower, grazing was limited, and

A portrait of Mnyango Sandile, of the royal Ngqika line of the Xhosa, Eastern Cape, South Africa, 1930s. The ivory armband is a sign of nobility, the necklace is of rare *Nerita plexa* shells, and the longer necklace, known as *isidanga*, is worn on ceremonial occasions. Photograph by A. M. Duggan-Cronin. Duggan-Cronin Collection, McGregor Museum, Kimberley.

settlements tended to be more concentrated in villages near water sources. The nineteenth-century introduction by missionaries of indigo blue print fabric made a lasting impact on the dress of Sotho women, as did the woolen blankets that replaced the skin cloaks worn by both men and women. Like cloaks, blankets were fastened on the shoulder by men and across the chest by women, and beaded safety pins were used to keep the blanket in place.

Significantly, some of the most striking and distinctive forms of beadwork and dress are found among the least populous ethnic groups, the Ndebele. In the late nineteenth century, the Ndzundza Ndebele people had resisted incorporation into the Transvaal Republic, and, after their defeat in 1882, they were dispersed and forced to live as indentured laborers on white-owned farms. In response to being divided socially and geographically, they developed stronger expressions of identity through their clothing and mural painting. The wearing of characteristic boldly striped blankets as well as beaded aprons and ornaments—not only on special occasions but as part of their everyday dress—was an affirmation of their identity in alien surroundings. Colors and patterns of beadwork varied with clan association, and specific styles of dress denoted differences of status correlating with stages in the life cycle from childhood through adolescence to adulthood and old age. A particular leather apron, *itshogolo*, with broad flaps on the lower edge was worn only by a married woman who would have received it from the family of her husband when she was a young bride. At first, out of respect and modesty, it was worn unadorned; later, it was covered ornately with beadwork and worn on ceremonial occasions.

Among all Nguni-speaking people, including the Ndebele, wearing beadwork that communicated clan membership was of particular social importance, because it was customary to marry outside of their own clan, and wearing their clan colors communicated eligibility at a glance. The converse of this principle applied in relation to Sotho-speaking groups, who married within their own clans. In this case, there was less need to communicate clan membership through elaboration of dress, because marriage partners came from the same extended family group. This significant difference in marriage pattern between Nguni- and Sotho-speaking people accounts in part for the notable differences in courtship-related beadwork production and exchange among these two groups. In general, the coded language of beadwork is far less developed among Sotho speakers than it is among Nguni speakers.

Distinctive elements of ethnic dress continue to be worn on ceremonial occasions, in both urban and rural areas, to honor social values and religious beliefs, to display cultural pride or group affiliation, and to mark the transition from adolescence to adulthood. The traditions associated with initiation—involving a period of seclusion, discipline, and instruction (and, for young men, circumcision), followed by coming-out ceremonies and reincorporation—have proved remarkably resilient in changing social conditions. With the exception of the Zulu, most Nguni and Sotho groups conduct initiation schools for boys to mark the transition to adulthood, and Sotho groups also have initiation schools for girls. On entering initiation school, novices are stripped of their clothes and given white blankets, their heads are shaved, and their bodies are smeared with white clay that is

Venda married women, Sibasa district, Limpopo, South Africa, 1978. The woman on the left is wearing a *salempore* wrap with rows of braiding stitched on the lower edge, as well as an abundance of rolled-wire anklets. Photograph by Patricia Davison. Copyright: Iziko Museums of Cape Town.

believed to bring them ancestral protection and indicates their liminal status to outsiders. In the last stages of the school, the white clay is washed away, their white blankets are burned, and their bodies are smeared with fat and red ochre, representing social rebirth. The coming-out phase may involve the production of elaborate dance costumes of grass and reed, materials often associated with fertility. Fashionable new clothes are among the gifts presented to the initiates by their families; at the homecoming celebrations, mothers wear their finest beaded clothing and accessories to display their pride as mothers and as upholders of tradition. In this and other contexts from the early twentieth century onward, when migrant labor drew men increasingly to the cities, village women became the primary keepers of clothing traditions as well as being innovators of variations on these traditions.

ETHNICITY AND APARTHEID

During over forty years of formal apartheid (1948 to 1994), ethnicity was exploited by the minority Afrikaner-Nationalist government to divide the majority African population into separate "nations" and deny them South African citizenship. Traditional dress forms, as visible signs of difference, were implicated in giving credibility to the ideology of separate development. It was expedient for white politicians to emphasize cultural differences; thus, for example, Zulu ear plugs, women's *isicholo* headdresses, and animal skin regalia of chiefs became clichés of Zulu ethnicity; similarly, Ndebele beadwork was promoted for its picturesque otherness, while turbaned, pipe-smoking women in red blankets became the stereotype of Xhosa traditionalists.

For African people themselves, the situation was more complex—wearing ethnic dress could be a form of resistance to external ideological forces. This was highlighted dramatically in 1962 when Nelson Mandela, on trial for attempting to overthrow the government, appeared in court on the day of his sentencing wearing the traditional dress of his royal Thembu lineage in defiance of an imposed legal system. At the time, this sparked a lively debate in the press on whether African leaders should wear "tribal" dress, because this could play into the hands of their white oppressors. The dilemma was not resolved but drew attention to the ambiguity inherent in the symbolic role of dress. In the 1962 court case, Mandela's traditional dress was a clear statement of resistance. By contrast, in 1994, when Mandela was installed as president of South Africa, he wore an elegant tailored suit of international style—a sign of statesmanship and determination to build a nation that was not divided along racial or ethnic lines. Subsequently, he adopted what has become known as the *Madiba* shirt, based on a patterned Indonesian-style silk shirt that he had received as a gift. This has become his signature garment, worn with variation of design and color of fabric, on both informal and formal occasions. Mandela's stature, both physical and political, has elevated this garment to iconic status. It reflects his personal style but is also a skillful choice of attire that underplays ethnicity in favor of inclusiveness. At the installation in 2007 of Nelson Mandela's grandson, Mandla Mandela, to the Mveso chieftaincy, the newly inaugurated chief wore traditional royal Thembu dress and an impressive lion-skin cloak of office, while his grandfather chose to wear a version of his trademark shirt made in a black and white print.

Expressions of ethnicity in dress are never static reflections of tradition but must be understood in action. Among the Tsonga in the 1970s and 1980s, dress became a powerful symbol in the contestation of cultural boundaries and the construction of identity. In postapartheid South Africa, aspects of ethnic dress have been reclaimed and reshaped in both rural and urban settings.

FASHIONING SOUTH AFRICANS

By the late twentieth century, over half the population of South Africa was urbanized, and even rural villages were in touch with national and international fashion trends through the media. Imported and globalized commodities are widely available. Not surprisingly, South African dress embodies an ongoing conversation with the rest of Africa and the world. This conversation, however, gets translated into many local idioms of dress. American brand-name garments and accessories are widely desired as indices of wealth and status, but they are incorporated into local dress styles in unpredictable and innovative ways. Cell phones, for example, combine the functional value of connecting people with being contemporary material symbols that can evoke multiple meanings. A young traditional healer (*sangoma*), wearing a cell phone with red, white, and black beadwork bandoliers, suggests a stylish bridging of communication realms; at one level, transnational

Married Pedi women wearing blue print smocks over their goatskin skirts. Limpopo, South Africa, 1974. Photograph by John Kramer. Copyright: Iziko Museums of Cape Town.

technology is evoked, while, at another, the sangoma's power to heal depends on spiritual contact with the ancestral realm, mediated in part by the color and style of his beadwork.

South African dress is a fusion of styles—hybrid in appearance, multilayered in cultural references, and responsive to social circumstance. Members of the many independent African churches in South Africa often wear distinctive attire for church gatherings. The dress of politicians such as the Zulu chief Mangosuthu Buthelezi ranges from full tribal regalia of animal skins on ceremonial occasions to Indian Nehru-style jackets, West African shirts, or three-piece suits. No single dress form is recognized as formal attire or as national dress. On the contrary, many styles of dress are worn on both formal and state occasions, such as the opening of Parliament. These styles include variations on customary dress as well as international styles. Innovative responses to ethnic traditions and vintage styles have found their way into fashion collections—modern interpretations of Dutch or English settler styles intermingle with reimagined ethnic dress and Indian saris made of African-print fabric. In a totally different setting, the khaki shirts and trousers and *velskoene* (locally made leather, lace-up shoes) worn by farmers and game rangers are also essentially part of South African dress, associated with an outdoor lifestyle and rugged masculinity.

In considering dress in South Africa, economic and class differences loom large and should not be overlooked, but it is also important to recognize the resourcefulness of people within their material limitations. Quite unwittingly, the makeshift attire of street people has provided an inspiration to designers. The diversity of cultures in South Africa, freedom of expression, and the complex history of this country are manifested in everyday dress and in emerging fashion trends. As South African couturier Amanda Laird Cherry noted at the 2006 SA Fashion Week, "Of course clothes are political. If you understand the innuendos of fabric and cut, or even the way a belt is worn, then you'll notice them, and you'll understand their connection to the history of this country."

References and Further Reading

Beinart, William. *Twentieth-Century South Africa*. Oxford, UK: Oxford University Press, 2001.

Comaroff, John, and Jean Comaroff. "Fashioning the Colonial Subject." In *Of Revelation and Revolution: The Dialectics of Modernity on a South African Frontier*. Vol. 2, 218–273. Chicago: University of Chicago Press, 1997.

James, Deborah. "'I Dress in This Fashion': Transformations in Sotho Dress and Women's Lives in a Sekhukhuneland Village, South Africa." In *Clothing and Difference*, edited by Hildi Hendrickson, 34–65. Durham, NC: Duke University Press, 1996.

Magubane, Peter (photographs), and Sandra Klopper (text). *African Renaissance*. Cape Town: Struik Publishers, 2000.

Mayer, Philip. *Townsmen or Tribesmen: Conservatism and the Process of Urbanization in a South African City*. Cape Town: Oxford University Press. 1971.

Morris, Jean (photographs), and Eleanor Preston-Whyte (text). *Speaking with Beads: Zulu Arts from Southern Africa*. London: Thames and Hudson, 1994.

Shaw, E. M., and N. J. Van Warmelo. "The Material Culture of the Cape Nguni. Part 4, Personal and General." *Annals of the South African Museum* 58, no. 4 (1988): 447–949.

Strutt, Daphne. *Clothing Fashions in South Africa 1652–1900*. Cape Town: Balkema, 1975.

Tischhauser, Anthony. *10X SA Fashion Week: Voices & Images from Ten Years of South African Fashion Week*. Johannesburg: Channel F Publishing, 2006.

Patricia Davison

See also Beads and Beadwork; Nguni, Zulu, and Xhosa Dress and Beadwork; Pedi, Ndebele, and Ntwane Dress and Beadwork; Tsonga Dress and Fashion; Migrant Workers, Production, and Fashion; Women's Cooperatives and Self-Help Artists.

Nguni, Zulu, and Xhosa Dress and Beadwork

The Nguni peoples of South Africa include the Xhosa- and Zulu-speaking peoples of the southeast and northeast coast. Despite shared distant Nguni origins, they are differentiated today by language, culture, tradition, history, and other factors. They have in common remarkable traditions of beadwork, which, together with those of the Ndebele (a Nguni people of the interior), are outstanding among African beadwork.

The Xhosa peoples, also known as the South Nguni or Cape Nguni, share Xhosa dialects and other cultural features but comprise several distinct peoples. The Xhosa groups to the west, who had earlier and more frequent contact with the European colonists at the cape, include the Xhosa proper, who held seniority over the nearby Thembu and Bomvana, and the Mfengu, who were refugees from the upheavals in Zulu-speaking territories to the north. The Mpondo, settled far to the east, were largely beyond Xhosa control and reflected greater cultural differentiation, as did the Mpondomise, Xesibe, and Bhaca.

Among Zulu speakers, the identity question is more complex. The rise of the Zulu kingdom under Shaka in the 1790s and early 1800s catapulted his minor Zulu chiefdom into the dominant regional power among hundreds of others. Shaka incorporated or dispersed neighboring North Nguni chiefdoms, which, though they had a broadly similar culture, were descended from distinct Nguni branches. Cultural difference was both effaced and preserved within the Zulu kingdom—and asserted on its borders by those who resisted its power.

After the British defeated the Zulu kingdom in 1879, they installed to prominence chiefs who had been subordinates within the kingdom, further altering the distribution of power among regional chiefs. By then the label "Zulu" had seized hold as colonial shorthand for the diverse North Nguni peoples of the region, including those who had never been amalgamated into the kingdom. Subsequent administrations further standardized the Zulu language and entrenched the label, which continues to overarch differences today.

North Nguni societies followed a historical pattern of settlement, aggregating in clans or chiefdoms that could be widely dispersed and interspersed, so their identities cannot be as neatly mapped as among Xhosa speakers. Despite this territorial complexity, clan and/or regional identity are flagged in several distinct mid-twentieth-century (about 1920 to 1970) Zulu styles of beadwork and dress, including from the regions of Nongoma, Msinga, Maphumulo, Ndwedwe, Drakensberg foothills, and the most southerly and northerly portions of the KwaZulu-Natal coast.

Among both Zulu and Xhosa speakers, each regional and subethnic style is identifiable by the conventional form and/or texture of the beaded object, by its palette, and often by distinctive motifs. These features combine within a gestalt that seldom leaves any question of origin and frequently can be dated, because the constituent elements changed historically with fashion.

HISTORY OF BEADWORK

Because detailed accounts survive from the establishment of Cape Town in 1652 onward, Xhosa dress is more familiar than that of other groups. Almost every aspect of the dress of Xhosa peoples is chronologically recorded in the *Annals of the South African Museum*. The records reveal dynamic fashions and dramatic influences on dress through the new materials introduced by Europeans, particularly beads and cotton fabrics—especially after 1825, as rules governing frontier trade with the Xhosa were relaxed. This also broke chiefs' control over prestige imported goods. Zulu speakers gained access to colonial trade later, and only after the defeat of the Zulu kingdom were its controls lifted.

The supply of European cloth and beads—mainly Venetian—increased steadily from the early 1800s and fueled the invention of these distinctive traditions of dress, displacing costumes of leather and natural decorations. During the first half of the twentieth century, South Africa was the world's greatest beadwork producer. Between 1932 and 1955, the leading bead manufacturer, which then had a virtual monopoly, exported to South Africa about half of all the beads sold to Africa, which consumed more beads than any other continent. Beadwork became a remarkably democratic vehicle for aesthetic expression, available to all rather than just to leaders, and wearing beadwork on ceremonial occasions became an essential aspect of both identity and tradition for both Xhosa and Zulu speakers.

Although global economic lulls slowed bead imports during the Great Depression and World War II, local traditions peaked in the 1950s and 1960s. During the 1970s and 1980s, traditional dress declined, because it became associated with the apartheid government's agenda of dividing the black population into ethnic "homelands." Trade sanctions also shrank bead supply. With the arrival of political freedom in the 1990s, traditional dress rebounded, often ignoring earlier codes governing costume.

BEADWORK AND IDENTITY

Beadwork traditions fulfilled manifold functions. First, they signaled a sense of belonging to a people, a place, and to a chain

Xhosa boys fighting during an initiation ceremony. During liminal stages, it is traditional for boys to cover parts of their body in white clay (*ingceke*). Tshatshu, South Africa, 2000. Photograph by Per-Anders Pettersson.

of tradition. The category of clothing worn and the patterns and colors of beadwork indexed ethnic and regional differences, much like the tartan kilts of Scottish clans. These identities were not fixed or rigid, and people often were uprooted. However, several synchronic surveys illustrate how finely costume styles proclaimed origin and identity, including artist and illustrator Barbara Tyrrell's (1968), undertaken from the late 1940s onward, and the photographs of Jean Morris (1959 to 1990s) and Alice Mertens (working with Joan Broster in the 1970s).

Second, dress indexed social types: a person's gender, age grade, marital status, and sometimes social rank and role and spiritual state. For example, pleated black ox-hide skirts and columnar or flared coiffures or wigs colored with red ochre instantly identified married Zulu women. In the Zulu kingdom, a warrior's regiment was indicated by the feathers, pelts, or other items in his head-dress and the colors of his ox-hide shield.

Similarly, the essential item of dress for Xhosa-speaking men until around 1950 was a penis sheath made of animal skin, woven grass, calabash, or the large cocoon of a type of moth, varying according to ethnic group, region, and status. Joan Broster illustrates how Thembu boys' age grades were indexed according to sheath. Boys aged thirteen wore calabash sheaths; at age fifteen, their sheaths were of civet or wild cat fur, which they could decorate with the tail from the pelt when they were seventeen. At age eighteen or nineteen, they wore fluffy angora sheaths. At around twenty, before circumcision, a young man was entitled to a goat-skin sheath. He was also allowed a beaded pipe, a beaded can for tobacco, and a jackal-tail headdress, indicative of some of the many keys to gender, age, and status conveyed by his costume. Even types of clothing or beadwork shared by people of different status would be differentiated by color. So, at this stage of life, his broad, navy-and-white choker necklace contrasted with the dark

turquoise beadwork highlighted with cerise wool that was worn by slightly younger men and women. His costume now included around 135 items. After circumcision, he could don skirts and a beaded collar within a magnificent beadwork costume of 150 to 200 items and was deemed suitable for courting.

Third, beadwork was, and still is, a vehicle of self-expression. Women made virtually all beadwork, so it reflects their labor, skill, and creativity, but the way men and women selected and combined their items of costume within local codes of dress showed personal style.

A fourth key function of beadwork was spiritual. Because tradition linked the living to their ancestors and honored them, beadwork was spiritual art. The cultures of Xhosa and Zulu speakers were essentially iconoclastic. The Xhosa peoples produced virtually no figurative sculpture. Among the Zulu, even as late as the 1920s, making an image of any living thing was improper. Visual art for these peoples, therefore, was located mainly in abstract forms. Absent the ancestor figures and masks that focused belief in other African cultures, beadwork connected the living to the dead. Beadwork often served as sacred signs, a function reinforced by the predominance of spiritually symbolic colors and the use of beadwork in religious and ceremonial contexts.

For ordinary people, contact with the ancestors was closest during ceremonial occasions—when dances were held and animal sacrifices were made or beer was drunk—because these activities summoned the ancestors and were closely associated with them. On these occasions, a profusion of beads was worn, the heaviness of the glass impressing upon the wearer the weight of symbolism contained in the beads. The beaded costumes thus functioned as dance costumes, and, like many masquerade costumes, they served as mediums for connecting with ancestral spirits.

Early Xhosa speakers apparently regarded glass beads and shell and brass buttons as immanent media. They believed that glass beads washed up on the shore came from ancestors in the sea. Mother-of-pearl buttons probably carried similar associations; certainly, they were seen as extraordinary. Anything made of metal manifests the magical transformation of ore from the earth into a new shiny substance. The awesome power of these materials probably obviated pattern creation in the earliest dress and beadwork. Rather, each gleaming iteration added power within an additive aesthetic. Also, because these materials were currency, each addition was value added, pronouncing the sacrifice of wealth in the service of personal presentation, which in turn saluted the ancestors from whom abundance flowed.

Last but not least, many aspects of dress, including beadwork colors, patterns, and motifs, conveyed symbolic references, many but not all religious.

XHOSA SYMBOLISM OF RED AND WHITE

The basic ingredient of Xhosa peoples' dress was ochre, which tied them to the traditions of their ancestors. Different shades of red body paint that were made of ochre mixed with fat or butter differentiated Xhosa-speaking subgroups and age grades. White was applied during liminal states. Yellow or black were decorative additions.

Red ochre was closely associated with the ancestors and fertility, which the ancestors underwrite if they are properly appeased through blood sacrifice and other means. Xhosa speakers who rejected Christianity symbolized their traditionalism by wearing red ochre and consequently were termed *amaQaba*, the Red People. Similarly, their ochred clothing signified religious and cultural continuity.

Xhosa customs, such as the welcome of a newborn, demonstrate that red and white were primary symbolic colors. The Thembu, for example, welcomed a newborn by reddening it with ochre and then conducted a thanksgiving ceremony for the ancestors that was marked by the sacrifice of a goat. The baby's father then gave each guest two white beads, which they returned to him; he passed them to the child's mother, who strung them into a necklace she placed on the child. Joan Broster, an amateur ethnographer who lived in a Thembu community between 1952 and 1966, wrote about this custom in *The Tembu: Their Beadwork, Songs, and Dances*, comparing the ceremony to Christian baptism. She commented that the red ochre and beads are a Xhosa's first symbols of the Qaba faith (song and dance as forms of worship would come later in life). For this reason, Christian Africans do not wear red ochre beads; in the absence of written law, beads and ochre strongly convey ideas of custom and practice. Thus, bead symbolism has been developed through variations of pattern and color between age groups and communities.

Xhosa peoples regarded white as the primary color of purity, calm, and mediation—and traditionalists still do. White clothing accented with beads and black braid was also worn for important ceremonial occasions. Only white beads were used as offerings to spirits and, on very rare occasions, to the creator. White clay (*ingceke*) was, and is still, used to indicate such liminal states as male circumcision, female initiation, and nursing at the breast. Equally persistent is the use of predominantly white beads among diviners, *amagqirha*, known as "white people" who must be pure to receive illumination from the spirits. Important items in a diviner's

costume include a beaded spear that symbolizes the ancestral spirits who inspire the diviner; beaded horns and calabashes for holding medicinal fats and powders; a beaded cow-horn trumpet; and a white-beaded veil known as *amageza* ("beads of madness"), which induces trance when swaying before the eyes.

OTHER SYMBOLIC COLORS AMONG XHOSA SPEAKERS

Broster states that every color was symbolic among the Thembu with whom she lived, but she specifies only that yellow beads symbolized fertility and green represented new life. This also applied to other Xhosa peoples and accounts for the inclusion of these colors in fertility dolls and adult costumes. Most Xhosa beadwork contains black; although its symbolism is unknown, throughout much of southern Africa, black carries ancestral associations within the sacred triad of black, red, and white. Similarly, although shades of turquoise and blue dominate the beadwork of Xhosa speakers, no symbolical associations are recorded except that royal blue, called *ulwandle*, means "ocean," and turquoise, called *ihobe*, means "dove"—the same association turquoise conveys among the Zulu but without their symbolic meaning of fidelity.

THEMBU BEADWORK SYMBOLS

Among Thembu symbols described by Broster was a zigzag motif that represented a local river and was named after it. Combinations of zigzags suggested multiple rivers in rugged terrain. Trees were denoted by chevrons of various orientations and by diagonal or serrated vertical lines; diamonds often connoted stars. Behind such environmental symbols may lie concepts related to the ancestors underwriting fertility and the health of the land, but this cannot be corroborated. Locally intelligible messages could be conveyed in Thembu beadwork panels on pins or necklaces by combining motifs and bead colors particular to age grades. Compositions could indicate states of relationships and pregnancy, the number of cattle paid in bride-price, number of children, and such personal qualities as a woman's diligence or dancing ability.

ZULU COLOR SYMBOLISM

In Zulu symbolism, red, white, and black are the main sacred colors. In combination—particularly in the clothing of diviners, who also code medicines as white, black, or red—these colors suggest an understanding of the universe and the cycle of life within it. White is associated with the ancestors; concepts of purity, calm, and good intentions; and light and divine enlightenment. In some contexts, black represents darkness, evil, death, and defilement. In other contexts, black is associated with the ancestors and carries positive connotations—it is associated with the dark rain clouds necessary for the sustenance of life, for example, and Zulu pots, some sculptural objects, and the leather skirt of marriage are blackened to please the ancestors. Red is the color of blood, menstruation, and fertility, and red ochre is strongly associated with the earth and women and their fertility; white clay is associated with the ancestors.

A Zulu girl wearing a traditional bead skirt for the annual Reed Dance. Nongoma, South Africa, 2004. Photograph by Per-Anders Pettersson.

ZULU BEADWORK AS LANGUAGE

In the Zulu kingdom in the late 1800s, an elaborate bead language was used mainly to communicate messages about courtship in love tokens—the "Zulu love letters" of colonial lore. Princess Magogo, a daughter of King Dinizulu (1868 to 1913) and the mother of Chief Gatsha Buthelezi, provided a window into this semiotic system in 1963. Raised among the wives of King Cetshwayo (1826 to 1884), she had a detailed knowledge of Zulu history and customs at the royal court. She interpreted the meaning of an elaborate message conveyed by a string of sixty beads consisting of twenty-five different types. In her reading, for example, translucent red beads implied a heart inflamed with love and pink implied poverty. The meaning of each bead, however, depended on its syntactical placement between neighboring beads. In one grammatical arrangement, a white bead could imply a heart calm and full of love, but, in another, it questioned why the lover was laughing. The princess pointed out that the reading of such messages depended on in-depth knowledge of Zulu customs, proverbs, and associations related to flora and fauna. She criticized contemporary women who deviated from these conventional rules in their beadwork for disrespecting Zulu custom. Apparently, by this time, the courtly language of love conveyed in beads had atrophied. The dissolution probably proceeded from about the 1920s onward, as regional beadwork styles developed, because their flaglike palettes contained few colors compared to the twenty-five types of beads that Princess Magogo interpreted.

This courtly language evidently was legible in the early 1900s far beyond the borders of the Zulu kingdom. The missionary Franz Mayr, who was stationed close to Pietermaritzburg, recorded the following reading of the color sequence white-yellow-blue-black-pink-black-yellow-red-white-red-white. "Here is my letter to you; I know you have two oxen (= two neighboring beads) for my father [to pay the bride-price to marry me]; if I were a dove (blue), I would fly to you; but darkness (black) prevents me; you are still poor (pink); and the dark night (black) disturbs me; your cattle are only two, work to get more; my eyes are red looking out for you in vain; but my heart is white as the long days go on; I have looked out for you, my eyes are red." In this message, for example, the signification of pink (poverty) and white (symbolizing a pure heart) corroborates Princess Magogo's reading.

MSINGA BEADWORK

Remarkably consistent meanings survived among the Mchunu, a clan settled in the Msinga region, despite their adoption between about 1920 to 1960 of a beadwork style known as *isishunka*, which had a restrictive seven-color palette and applied to most beadwork items, not just love tokens. As late as the 1980s, elders stated that white represented all that is good (love, spiritual purity, happiness, truth). Black was the opposite (evil, misfortune, sorrow) but could also refer to the black skirt of marriage. Translucent red represented hot-blooded passion (the name for this bead, sometimes incorrectly called "carnelian," is *umgazi*, meaning "blood"). Yellow represented gossip; pink symbolized poverty, particularly inability to pay the bride-price for marriage; turquoise represented fidelity; deep green represented youthfulness or pining away like a withering reed.

Green is the dominant color in isishunka-style beadwork, followed by black. When combined, the two colors suggest readiness for marriage; in this context, green means new growth and young life, while black stands for the black skirt of marriage.

Isishunka's seven colors often were arranged in a fixed sequence of seventeen bars, which included several stable triads: translucent red–black–translucent red; green; pink-turquoise-pink; black; green-yellow-green; turquoise-black-turquoise, green-white-green. The central color in a triad was called *isiqaba* (pl. *iziqaba*) meaning "field," with those on the sides called "boundaries" (*iminqamulo*, sing. *umnqamulo*). These terms link the beadwork to agriculture, which, together with ideas about fertility, is otherwise absent from the symbolism described for the isishunka palette.

Though isishunka rules of composition limit the color symbolism possible in earlier times, omitting or repeating colors or triads changed the symbolic weight of beadwork items.

VARIATIONS ON ISISHUNKA

Deviations from isishunka rules served to differentiate neighbors and changes in fashion and social composition. The neighbors of the Mchunu in the Msinga region initially differentiated themselves through slightly different palettes. Instead of the color fields in Mchunu beadwork, they used patterns formed from graphic shapes. By the 1930s, as distinctions between neighbors were becoming less relevant, they adopted the Mchunu field pattern but maintained different colors.

In the late 1950s, some Msinga people moved southeast into lowland areas, where they applied a new palette called *unzansi* (sap green, white, opaque red, and navy) to the Mchunu field pattern. *Umzansi* means "people from the lowlands," and this style reflected both territorial and generational shifts. By about 1960, the umzansi palette formed the basis of a modern style, *isimodeni*, which dropped the field pattern for a wide variety of graphic patterns. Later, isimodeni abandoned the umzansi palette by substituting black for navy and/or orange for red. Although elders such as Princess Magogo disparaged isimodeni, it was a fashion, *imfeshini*, that became a convention, because it symbolically united the regional clans when their shared experience eclipsed their original differences.

NONGOMA BEADWORK

The Nongoma region surrounds the Zulu royal court and its attendant founding clans. In Nongoma beadwork, the sap green color added to the primary Zulu symbolic colors (white, red, and black) is associated both with the food of cattle, which were the core of Zulu traditional life and a physical link with their ancestors, and the gall of animals sacrificed to honor the ancestors. A Nongoma variant that adds or substitutes blue and/or yellow

is associated with the region between Ceza and Mahlabatini, which is the territorial base of the Buthelezi chiefdom, long allied with the Zulu. Chief Gatsha Buthelezi is the cousin of King Zwelethini and the leader of Inkatha, the Zulu nationalist party, whose colors are black, green, yellow, and red, also frequently seen in patterns set on white backgrounds from this area.

These related Nongoma palettes are used to create dazzling geometric designs that vary from simple patterns such as alternating checks, triangles, or diamonds to complex combined motifs. The diamond shape represents a shield, symbolizing protection. The triangle is associated with the heart because they share the same word in Zulu, *inhliziyo*; and, when combined with the diamond-shaped shield, may imply protection for a loved one. Researchers record that a profusion of small diamonds, triangles, and other motifs celebrate fruitfulness; an upward-pointed triangle connotes the male principle; a downward-pointed triangle or V represents the female pudenda; two triangles joined in an hourglass shape represent a married man; two diamonds joined top to bottom represent a mature woman.

Some Nongoma patterns echo stepped-diamond motifs in Asian weaving. It is possible that Zulu beadworkers adopted these from members of the Muslim community in colonial Natal, particularly Gujarati immigrants from Pakistan and India whose fabrics employed identical motifs, and grafted onto them their own symbolism. Gujarati fabrics adopted this motif from kilim rugs, where the motif is widely used from Turkey to western China but most consistently in neighboring Afghanistan.

BEADWORK FROM THE MAPHUMULO AND DRAKENSBERG REGIONS

Married women's capes and aprons beaded onto cloth and men's leather back skirts are the largest Zulu beadwork items. Among the most elaborate are those produced in the Maphumulo region, especially around 1940 to 1960; they are distinguished by their lacy technique and regional palette, with motifs of green, black, navy, and deep turquoise set on white grounds, occasionally with red, orange, yellow, or pink highlights. The women's pieces are on black cotton cloth, whereas the men's, which are beaded onto thick hide, must be commissioned from specialists. Women's marriage capes from the Drakensberg region—where Ngwane, Ngweni, and Hlubi peoples who were scattered by the rise of the Zulu kingdom are settled today—are constructed of several beaded strips of differing ages, each contributed by the bride's female relatives. The older versions of these capes have a predominance of white and turquoise beads; strips that are predominantly black probably date to the 1970s or later. Many such capes were produced specifically for the curio market.

WESTERN SYMBOLS AND LETTERS IN ZULU BEADWORK

Zulu beadwork also incorporates Christian and Western motifs. Members of the Shembe Church, a Zulu Christian sect founded in about 1910, wear a remarkably consistent beadwork style featuring stylized crosses. The meaning of crosses and other motifs can vary regionally, however. A cross motif from the Estcourt region, for example, was identified as *isiambolosi*, meaning "ambulance."

From at least the 1950s onward, some Zulu beadwork included literal messages spelled out in Western letters, but the meanings of the written statements were often unclear, even within the territory of their creation. For example, the message *isakuhle* can be interpreted either as "it is going fine" or "she comes willingly." Similarly, a Zulu woman reads the necklace message *ngiLikHU ningObA AnginAKi* to mean: *ngilikhuni* = hold everything inside; *ngoba* = because; *anginaki* = I do not care—implying that a girl knows that her boyfriend is having affairs with other girls. Another observer, however, translated this from a man's point of view: "I am very strong because I am careless," like a bull in a china shop.

Today, the way people dress in South Africa is more a reflection of global marketing and mall culture than tradition. However, the ceremonial functions of beadwork do continue in traditional settings and for such formal occasions as the opening of Parliament or gala events. Nguni beadwork and dress traditions have influenced both local and international couture designers, and large department stores in South Africa carry contemporary dresses in traditional styles and colors, such as Xhosa skirts.

References and Further Reading

Bedford, Emma, ed. *Ezakwantu: Beadwork from the Eastern Cape*. Cape Town: South African National Gallery, 1993.

Broster, Joan A. *Red Blanket Valley*. Johannesburg: Hugh Keartland, 1967.

Broster, Joan A. *The Tembu: Their Beadwork, Songs, and Dances*. Cape Town: Purnell, 1976.

Broster, Joan A., and Alice Mertens. *African Elegance*. Cape Town: Purnell, 1973.

Jolles, Frank. "Traditional Zulu Beadwork of the Msinga Area." *African Arts* 26, no. 1 (1993): 42–53.

Klopper, Sandra. "From Adornment to Artefact to Art: Historical Perspectives on South-East African Beadwork." In *South East African Beadwork 1850–1910: From Adornment to Artefact to Art*, edited by M. Stevenson and M. Graham-Stewart. Vlaeberg, South Africa: Fernwood Press, 2000.

Mayr, Franz. *"Good Bye, Dear Blacks," Collected Writings of the Tyrolian Missionary Franz Mayr (1865–1914) Edited and Annotated by Clemens Gütl*. Vienna: Böhlau Verlag, 2004.

Morris, Jean, and Eleanor Preston-Whyte. *Speaking with Beads: Zulu Arts from Southern Africa*. London: Thames & Hudson, 1994.

Shaw, E. M., and N. J. Van Warmelo. "The Material Culture of the Cape Nguni: Part 4 Personal and General." *Annals of the South African Museum* 58, no. 4 (1988): 1–101.

Tyrrell, Barbara. *Tribal Peoples of Southern Africa*. Cape Town: Books of Africa, 1968.

Van Wyk, Gary N. "Illuminated Signs: Style and Meaning in the Beadwork of the Xhosa- and Zulu-Speaking Peoples." *African Arts* 36, no. 3 (Autumn 2003): 12–33.

Gary van Wyk

See also Body and Beauty; Beads and Beadwork; Southern Africa; South Africa Overview.

Pedi, Ndebele, and Ntwane Dress and Beadwork

D espite their surprisingly diverse histories, the Pedi, Ndebele, and Ntwane communities developed increasingly close links, including dress practices, in the course of the nineteenth and early twentieth centuries in what is now South Africa's Mpumalanga Province, south of the Zimbabwe border. In some cases, the ritual practices and ceremonial clothing and beadwork styles of these three peoples are virtually identical. Oral tradition indicates that the Pedi migrated to their present location as early as the seventeenth century. The Ndebele moved from the KwaZulu Natal region either before or during the seventeenth century and split into two groups, one settling in present-day Zimbabwe and the other in Mpumalanga province. The Ntwane migrated to this area after a series of relocations that probably began toward the end of the eighteenth century in Botswana.

By the early nineteenth century, regional power was consolidated under the Pedi and subsequently challenged by the arrival of European colonists, who developed increasingly centralized structures of authority throughout present-day South Africa in the course of the second half of the nineteenth century. Claiming rights to land that historically had belonged to African communities, they ultimately excluded these African communities from rights of citizenship following the formation of the Union of South Africa in 1910.

FROM CULTURAL COHESION TO REGIONAL FUSION

In the twenty-first century, there are two distinct Ndebele communities: the Manala and the Ndzundza. Descendents of the former group still live on farms north of Pretoria in the Rust de Winter district, where they gradually lost touch with traditional forms of dress and beadwork production through the influence of missionaries. In contrast to this group, the Ndzundza were forcibly indentured to white farmers in the 1880s. Probably because of this experience of radical dislocation, they actively worked to maintain a sense of cultural cohesion, which they gradually regained through the revival of male initiation practices, the development of a distinctive mural art tradition, and the adoption of common forms of dress, including beadwork styles associated with various rites of passage.

Most other groups living in Mpumalanga province have also continued to uphold traditional practices and the different forms of dress associated with various rites of passage. In recent decades, however, historically important traditional leaders have, in many cases, lost the sway they formerly had over minor chiefs.

The centralized control they once had over male initiation practices has therefore given way to an increasingly entrepreneurial approach to these rites. Thus, although boys are still encouraged to undergo initiation, they often attend initiation schools held by chiefs from neighboring communities at initiation lodges located in the veldt or bush. This helps to explain why the current dress codes of Pedi, Ndebele, and Ntwane initiates have become increasingly similar since the mid-twentieth century.

Among all these peoples, male initiates usually wear leather loincloths during their seclusion away from home. Forced to endure extraordinary hardships, including exposure to the elements, their scanty clothing is in marked contrast to the dress worn by the masters of their initiation lodges, who normally wear leather cloaks and a richly decorated leather breastplate (iporiyana). Historically, both of these garments were made from the skins of wild cats, but because it has become prohibitively expensive to purchase these skins from licensed merchants, they are now commonly made from commercially produced imitation leopard skin available in a variety of materials, including nylon and corduroy.

On their return to the village, these youths wear richly beaded garments made by their mothers, including headbands, necklaces, and bandoliers. Their reintegration into the village is marked not only by celebratory feasts but also by additional gifts of clothing that affirm their newly attained status as adult men. This wardrobe (isogana), which is pinned onto grass mats and displayed for all to see, usually includes a three-piece suit, a hat, some shirts and underpants, a pair of shoes, and several pairs of socks. Before the initiates discard the richly beaded garments and blankets given to them by their mothers in favor of these suits, they sing the praises of their ancestors, thereby acknowledging their gratitude for the protection they received from their deceased forebears during their period of seclusion in the initiation lodge.

In contrast to the suits and other symbols of urban sophistication that have come to mark these celebrations, the initiates' proud mothers wear clothing that harks back to the past. Among the Ndebele, this includes heavily beaded blankets and a fully beaded leather front apron (ijogolo). When it was still common for married women to wear beadwork on a daily basis, this five-panel apron was worn to celebrate a woman's success in bearing a child. This explains why the central panel, which is sometimes longer than the other four, is described as the "mother" (umama), while those on either side are referred to as her "children." The mothers of returning Ndebele initiates also wear long beadwork panels attached to beaded headbands. Draped down the front of their bodies, these linga koba, literally "long tears," are said to signal both the relief mothers experience when their sons return from the circumcision lodge and the sense of loss they feel at losing their boys to adult status.

Both male and female initiates also wear beaded grass waist hoops at the end of the initiation period, while Pedi and Ntwane girls wear short stringed front aprons and distinctive, partially embellished swallow-tail back aprons that, to this day, are made from tanned cowhides. The beaded hoops and bangles worn by Ndebele girls are combined with very stiff rectangular front aprons (isiphephetu) distinctively decorated with geometric beadwork patterns, bulky beaded leg hoops, and semicircular leather back aprons that are normally either beaded or covered with closely linked brass hoops and colorfully striped towels.

The initiation rites observed by young women focus primarily on preparing postpubescent girls for their future roles as wives and mothers. These normally take place either in the homes of the initiates or at the homesteads of local chiefs. At their coming-out ceremonies, young women from the Mpumalanga region commonly wear carefully chosen accessories to complement their beadwork garments, including stylish berets, hair extensions, and sunglasses. Pedi girls also carry vanity cases filled with cosmetics, combs, and hairpins. In recent years, these ceremonies have consequently been transformed into something more akin to contemporary beauty pageants than celebrations aimed at underlining notions of ideal motherhood.

MARRIED WOMEN AS CUSTODIANS OF TRADITION

Because of the migrant labor system upheld by successive white governments in twentieth-century South Africa, most married women remained in their rural homes tending the family's fields and livestock and raising their children, while their husbands worked in the mines and in large cities such as Johannesburg and Pretoria.

Partly for this reason, women living in rural communities became the custodians of indigenous cultural practices, which they helped to sustain through the production of household murals and by making pottery and other items from locally available materials, including grass mats and various types of baskets. Like women living elsewhere in South Africa, the wives of Pedi, Ntwane, and Ndebele migrants also contributed to the survival of a flourishing beadwork tradition. They not only sewed beads onto leather capes and commercially manufactured blankets purchased from local traders, but also made other labor-intensive beadwork items for themselves and their families. Until quite recently, the artistry of these garments, which sometimes took months to complete, was seldom acknowledged by outsiders. But the dedicated commitment of these women to upholding traditions that date back at least to the mid-nineteenth century, when beads first became both readily available and comparatively affordable, was deeply valued by their own communities.

Historically, women wore beautifully beaded garments as part of their wedding ceremonies. Among the Ndebele, this included a long beadwork train (*nyoga*, literally "snake") and a beaded goatskin cape signaling the bride's respect for her husband's ancestors. Pedi and Ntwane women also wore capes and beaded leather front aprons (*lebole*) and back aprons (*nthepa*), but, over the course of the nineteenth century, the former adopted long shirts

Young Ndebele female initiates, Gauteng province, South Africa, 1996. They wear colorful beaded hoops around the legs and waist with semicircular leather back aprons. Photograph by Carol Beckwith/Angela Fisher.

decorated with smocking, while the latter began to wear ankle-length dresses of the same type. Inspired by the Victorian dress styles of British and European missionaries, married women still wear these garments over their beaded leather aprons when they get married and on other ceremonial occasions.

Although at this stage it is difficult to provide a clear account of the historical factors that may have contributed to appropriation of nonindigenous dress styles by Pedi and Ntwane women, there is a widespread misconception that the European missionaries who first came to southern Africa in the late eighteenth and early nineteenth centuries tried to "civilize" local communities through dress. On the contrary, many of these missionaries were so dependent on bartering beads in exchange for meat and other essentials that it was not until major trade routes had been firmly established—thereby lessening their dependence on this barter system for their own survival—that they began to condemn the use of beads and other African forms of dress as barbaric and un-Christian.

Understanding the adoption of smocked Victorian garments by Pedi and Ntwane women is further complicated by the fact that, contrary to the conviction of missionaries and their wives, indigenous communities did not necessarily aspire to so-called civilized Christian values through their appropriation of these European forms. Initially, this clothing appears to have been favored, quite simply, because of the comparatively easy protection it afforded against certain climatic conditions or because it offered novel ways of giving material expression to local political rivalries. In the case of married women, cotton clothing also came to play a significant role in underlining the wealth and status of homestead heads, often replacing earlier signifiers of social attainment such as beads and brass. In many cases, the adoption of European dress thus served to reinforce indigenous values and concerns. This is confirmed by the fact that, on one occasion in the late nineteenth century, incensed German missionaries working among the Pedi went so far as to force women wearing crinolines to burn their richly braided dresses.

The smocked pinafores contemporary Pedi and Ntwane women wear over their front and back leather aprons are decorated with braiding and are worn in conjunction with beaded necklaces and head scarves that emulate the style of the clay and graphite headdresses formerly adopted by married women from these communities. Despite their vociferous commitment to tradition, as these shifts in the clothing and other styles of rural women demonstrate, their sartorial choices are ultimately shaped as much by an interest in fashion and comfort as by a concern to honor the past. This confident manipulation of long-established indigenous forms and traditions is reflected in virtually all aspects of the dress worn by these contemporary women on festive and ritual occasions. One obvious example is provided by the brass or copper neck rings (*idzila*) Ndebele women formerly wore as a sign of marriage. Believing that the removal of these rings would incur the wrath of the ancestors, possibly leading to illness or death in the family, they suffered irreversible deformation of their collar bones. Although, in the past, a husband's wealth and status was signaled in part by the number of neck rings these women wore, today it is more usual for married women to wear clip-on plastic neck rings, which they reserve for special occasions such as the celebrations following the return of their sons from initiation lodges.

For a relatively short period during the 1960s and 1970s, many Ndebele women used plastic in the production of their marriage aprons. Stitched onto canvas or a thick plastic base, these aprons were decorated with colorful plastic trim rather than beads, leading to the development of a stylish, contemporary aesthetic. Commonly referred to as *plastici*, these aprons appear to have been made in response to a sudden market interest in Ndebele beadwork, which encouraged women to sell their beadwork garments to urban-based dealers. It was also at this time that household murals and various beadwork items began to be decorated with symbols of consumer wealth and material attainment such as aircraft, houses lit with electric light bulbs, two-story houses with internal staircases, and cars. In reality, most of the women who employed this vocabulary of forms relied on donkey carts for transportation, and, although the electrification of rural homes was prioritized following the election of South Africa's first democratic government in 1994, to this day, many remote communities rely on candles, wood, and paraffin to light their homes and cook their food.

The use of other new materials has also become increasingly common in recent decades. Among most southern African communities, the tendency to purchase comparatively large, locally produced plastic beads is especially widespread today, in part because it is much less time-consuming to string these large beads into colorful necklaces and onto other items of adornment like the blankets most women continue to wear as capes. This growing interest in plastic beads can probably also be ascribed to the fact that they are much cheaper than glass beads and to the greater comfort afforded by garments made from comparatively light materials.

Not surprisingly, the use of consumer goods in the production of traditional garments often involves a radical redefinition of function. Notable in this regard is the fact that Ntwane women now incorporate elaborate Christmas decorations into the head dresses they make for use on ceremonial occasions. In some cases, ornaments like these are worn in combination with colonial coins; pieces of candy in shiny foil wrappers; whistles; bird mirrors; white gloves similar to those used by traffic officers; and leather belts with large, flashy metal buckles. Other popular accessories include peaked caps, safety pins, keys, plastic medicine spoons, individually decorated umbrellas, and brightly colored tennis shoes. This integration of richly varied materials has led to the emergence of a complex aesthetic that is at once traditional and insistently modern.

The inventive integration of forms and materials by Pedi, Ndebele, and Ntwane women notwithstanding, the beaded and other garments worn by Pedi and neighboring communities living in contemporary Mpumalanga province are unlikely to survive beyond the present generation. Since the 1970s, when large numbers of young girls began to attend school, the habit among women of wearing beads on a daily basis has declined so rapidly that many younger women are reluctant to learn beadworking skills, which they regard as embarrassingly outdated. In contrast to former generations, when these skills were almost invariably passed on from mother to daughter and young girls took pride in their ability to make beadwork garments, it has become unusual to find beadworkers who are prepared to devote long hours to making the capes and aprons that once formed an indispensable part of the wardrobes of married women.

RURAL VALUES, URBAN LIFESTYLES

Although families living and working in cities like Pretoria and Johannesburg tend to retain close links with their rural relatives, often participating in initiation ceremonies and other rites of passage such as traditional weddings, most people residing in outlying villages in Mpumalanga province have come to regard the loss of traditional values and forms of dress as inevitable. In the increasingly cosmopolitan world that has come to dominate their day-to-day experiences, the only exception to this gradual erosion of past practices is provided by healers and diviners, who continue to play a meaningful role in the lives of most South Africans. Although in urban centers, these ritual specialists sometimes modify their dress, in Mpumalanga and other outlying areas, they still wear very distinctive garments and materials.

Unlike healers, who are generally men and whose ritual garments are made by their wives, many contemporary diviners continue to make beadwork garments, even if they are men, and many male diviners cross-dress. The garments worn by these diviners include necklaces with magical properties, beaded gourds and bottles containing medical potions, strips of skin and inflated gallbladders obtained from ritually slaughtered goats, and, in most cases, commemorative cloths similar to the *kanga* of East Africa. The latter, which were first adopted in the mid-twentieth century, are invariably decorated with white, black, and red motifs—the three colors associated with divination across large parts of southern Africa. Some of these cloths also include images of long-established symbols of power such as lions.

Healers, who study herbal medicine under experienced practitioners, commonly wear necklaces made from the vertebrae of snakes. Often decorated with the claws of wild animals, these necklaces signal the powers vested in these herbalists, who claim to rely on their ancestors to locate rare herbs and other substances used in the production of their medicines. Like diviners, they still wear beadwork items to the present day in the belief that beads facilitate their communication with the ancestors and therefore with the spiritual forces that sustain their lives and activities.

CLOTHING AS CULTURAL HERITAGE

As early as the 1940s, Ndebele tourist villages were established north of present-day Pretoria, thus providing outside visitors easy access to exotic displays of colorful beaded garments and mural decorations that promoted the idea of Africa as a place of timeless primitive beauty. This practice of presenting the twentieth-century dress and other art forms of not only the Ndebele but also other South African groups as dying remnants of a static past has become increasingly common since the country's first democratic election in 1994, primarily because of the growing number of foreign tourists who visit ethnic cultural sites located on the outskirts of big game destinations like the Kruger National Park.

The multicolored geometric forms characteristic of Ndebele beadwork and mural designs have also influenced other South African fashion designers. Notable among the designers is Peter Soldatos, who came up with the idea of producing textiles based on Ndebele motifs when he attended the inauguration of South Africa's first black president, Nelson Mandela, in May 1994 and saw textiles produced by the Dutch textile company Vlisco

printed with African National Congress (ANC) patterns. Convinced that there would be a renewed interest in South Africa's rural art traditions in postapartheid South Africa, Soldatos felt that the stark, clean-cut, geometric simplicity of Ndebele designs offered an opportunity to create something distinctly South African. He approached Vlisco with a view to developing a fabric based on Ndebele design principles.

Soldatos's decision to approach Vlisco was based on the company's entering the South African market in 1992, initially by renting a stall at the annual Rand Easter Show in Johannesburg. Vlisco's Dutch predecessor and other European cloth manufacturers had produced textiles for West and Central African consumers since the mid-nineteenth century. Vlisco's entry was done against the advice of local clothing chains, whose marketing managers claimed that South African tastes were too Western for these textiles and argued that the company therefore would find it difficult to market its fabrics to South African buyers. At first, their advice proved to be correct: local consumers resisted buying Vlisco's brightly colored, richly patterned, and sometimes textured cotton fabrics in part because South Africa's traditions of cotton clothing production—like the smocked missionary-inspired dresses worn to this day on festive occasions in Mpumalanga province—are generally made from solid, brightly colored fabrics, which are then decorated with bias trim and other forms of braiding.

Vlisco's South African operation, however, has since developed a ready market for fabrics that have a local resonance, such as a green, yellow, and black striped cloth that South Africans call the ANC or Mandela print because this color combination echoes the colors associated with the country's ruling African National Congress. The company's unexpected commercial success was also fueled by Soldatos's intervention, which, in 1995, led Vlisco to introduce a new fabric for the South African market based on Ndebele design principles. This textile, which is now printed in fourteen colors, has since become extremely popular. Used to make handbags, hats, dresses, and umbrellas, it has attained an extraordinary status among South African consumers keen to affirm their pride in their African roots. In the late 1990s, Soldatos, who developed some of his own designs in Vlisco's Ndebele cloth, traveled to Prague with several models who were photographed against a backdrop of stately old buildings wearing garments that he described as European in cut, but African in volume. Among these garments was a 1950s-style swing jacket that he produced in several color ways.

CONCLUSION

Although it is unlikely that time-consuming beadwork traditions and the production of garments from leather will survive into the future, South Africa's rural traditionalists continue to find new ways of expressing their commitment to making garments associated with long-established customs such as weddings and initiation ceremonies. In response to the increasingly cosmopolitan world they live in, they constantly adapt and transform the styles, forms, and materials they inherited from earlier generations. In this regard, they differ little from their nineteenth-century forebears who adopted mission-style clothing and distinctively patterned red and black blankets that have since become part of the dress codes of many traditionalists living in present-day Mpumalanga province.

References and Further Reading

James, D. *Mmino wa setso: Songs of Town and Country and the Experience of Migrancy by Men and Women from the Northern Transvaal.* Johannesburg: University of the Witwatersrand Press, 1994.

Klopper, S. "Re-Dressing the Past: The Africanization of Sartorial Style in Contemporary South Africa." In *Hybridity and Its Discontents. Politics, Science, Culture,* edited by A. Brah and A. E. Coombes. London: Routledge, 2000: 216–232.

Magubane, P. *The Bantwane. Africa's Unknown People.* Text by Sandra Klopper. Cape Town: Struik Publishers, 2000.

Magubane, P. *Amandebele.* Text by Sandra Klopper. Cape Town: Jonathan Ball, 2005.

Reuther, Kirsten. "Heated Debates over Crinolines: European Clothing on Nineteenth-Century Lutheran Mission Stations in the Transvaal." *Journal of Southern African Studies* 28, no. 2 (June 2002): 359–378.

Sandra Klopper

See also Southern Africa; South Africa Overview; Nguni, Zulu, and Xhosa Dress and Beadwork.

Tsonga Dress and Fashion

- Place, Dress, and Public Display
- A Side Step
- State of the Nation
- Beadwork
- Body Markings
- Changes in Male Dress

Since 1994 and the new democratic government in South Africa, the word *Tsonga* has been used primarily to describe a language. It is a conscious shift to use *Tsonga* to describe a language, group, or people rather than an ethnicity or tribe because of the latter terms' association with the policies of apartheid. Tsonga is now one of the eleven official languages protected in the new constitution and was offered as one of the mother tongue options in the 2001 census, when 2.3 million people out of 44 million chose Tsonga as one of the ways to define themselves. The census showed that the Tsonga are one of the smallest groups in South Africa. The unquestioned acceptance of Tsonga, even as a language, denies a contested history during which the making of the modern Tsonga emerged. Part of the problem lies in the fact that the history of the Tsonga is clouded in issues of migration and many different names. All Tsonga in South Africa originally came from Mozambique. Small groups of peoples from the eastern seaboard had settled in the northeast of South Africa before the major migrations during the nineteenth century. From the 1820s, large numbers of refugees fled from the invasions of various Nguni groups who moved through Mozambique from the Zulu kingdom further south, particularly that led by Soshangane, who established the Gaza kingdom.

PLACE, DRESS, AND PUBLIC DISPLAY

The role that dress played at this time is of note. By the 1970s, Tsonga women had an identifiable style of dress that is singular and that arguably became bolder and brighter in the face of competing interests but that had deep roots in the past and in the region where the refugees and migrants had first settled. Over an approximately one-hundred-year period, ending in 2004, the development of a Tsonga iconic dress style can be viewed. In the early 1900s, women and girls wore skirts called *xibelani* (the X in the Tsongan language is pronounced as \sh\ in English), which were made from striped cotton fabric called *salempore* in blue tones, reaching to below the knees and gathered and folded over at the waist. At that time, females of all ages wore this type of skirt, denoting that, from inception, it was not a ritual garment bound to maturation or marriage. In addition, all wore beaded ornaments around their waists and necks and twisted wire circles around their ankles. Over time, the skirt became shorter and fuller. By the 1930s, it was enhanced with white beads that define the top edge of the skirt where it folded over with circles and horizontal lines sewn onto the lower section. The skirt was heavy because it was made from eighteen yards (sixteen and a half meters) of fabric, and, although it was placed at the waist, it tended to slip down to the hips, thus encouraging the wearer to swing and sway her hips following a rhythm set by the combination of the weight and movement. It is not surprising that the skirt was used for dancing, during which the upper fold often flipped and swung in the opposite direction to the lower. To enhance this effect, a *xigejo*, a shorter skirt, was worn on top of the fold. The back of the skirt was also important, because a red piece of salempore sometimes was inserted into the center back and called the menstrual stripe. In the twenty-first century, alterations to the skirt include the substitution of white braid for beads and wool for the salempore, giving the wearer an even more generous, rounded figure.

The main changes over the last hundred years involve the upper body. In the 1930s, many more beaded ornaments were used to decorate the exposed upper torso, arms, and head. Later in the century, women adopted blouses and T-shirts. More coverage of the body was provided by the *minceka*—two rectangular pieces of fabric approximately two yards (one and a half meters) in length tied on the opposite shoulders and crossing front and back to form a loose cover for the body and skirt. Unlike the large skirt, minceka cloths changed regularly, with bright colors and bold patterns in contrasting colors. For example, lime greens might be favored one year and purples the next, making for frequent fashion changes. Even in the nineteenth century, Tsonga women showed a preference for bright colors. The only standards have been the white and black cloths. The white with delicate pink or blue floral patterns have been used for initiation ceremonies but also for other occasions. Dark minceka—either flat black or self-patterned navy toned fabrics—have been favored at times of mourning but developed into another kind of style (see below). By the early twenty-first century, women's garb typified the contemporary, local, fashionable image of Tsonga womanhood. The style is created in the combination of skirt, crossed-over cloths, beaded ornaments, many colored head scarves, and white *takkies* (sneakers, tennis shoes) or no shoes at all. Going barefoot has been an option. Some groups of women such as choral groups, care groups, or the two wives of one man will wear identical printed cloths, like a uniform acknowledging a relationship.

This style was developed in northern Limpopo, where refugees and migrants settled in the nineteenth century. It has no connections with Tsonga origins in Mozambique, except perhaps in the broadest sense of showing a preference for imported machine-manufactured fabrics. Photographs of women in Mozambique show them wearing cloth tightly wrapped around their bodies. Nor is this dress style worn by Shangaan women further south. A version used to be worn in Zimbabwe. Nothing like this is worn by their neighbors in the Transvaal: the Venda and Sotho. Although Venda women use salempore, they use it differently and prefer a different color range. The Tsonga did not adopt the skin and beads of the Sotho possibly for economic reasons. Nothing is written about the emergence of this style, but it is possible to see it reflecting a migrant community living in a space between being what they were and what they had to become to survive. What is mentioned in the literature is that the migrants maintained some

Two Tsonga girls wearing many-beaded ornaments over their torso and head. Thabina, South Africa (then Northern Transvaal), 1933. Photograph by A. M. Duggan-Cronin. Duggan-Cronin Collection, McGregor Museum, Kimberley.

of their culture—such as the food they ate and the way they prepared it—and, because the migrants did maintain the dress style, they arrived preferring to create one to mark themselves as different and that was suitable for the weather conditions. The Tropic of Capricorn runs across Limpopo, so the region is generally hot. It rains often in summer, though the region is also prone to drought. When it is very hot, a woman will often not wear her skirt; when it is cold, she will wear a sweater under or over her draped cloths or a blanket or towel over her shoulders like a cape.

All the cloth used for the Tsonga outfit was made from imported fabric and beads. Initially the cloth was imported, but it is now produced locally. Every piece of fabric and every glass bead then and now is the result of some form of exchange. The Tsonga were among the first in the region to wear imported cloth. To obtain this fabric, the women were reliant on outside suppliers for their materials. An interdependent network was created between customer and dealer, who often played an active role in finding and even designing the right fashionable fabric, and the migrant laborer, who supplied the cash to clothe his wife.

This style is not only about imported cloth and beads—which touches on questions of indigenous meaning through indigenous materials—but it is also about how the imported items were used to make them their own. The Tsonga dress style developed within the boundaries of ready-made lengths of cloths—eighteen yards (sixteen and a half meters) for the skirt and two yards (one and a half meters) for each shoulder cloth. Fabric was purchased in these dimensions and was not cut and shaped nor tailored into garments. These ready-made lengths were fit around the body and were shaped by it rather than the other way around. Later, when sewing machines were readily available, the way in which the cloth was manipulated did not change. Theirs is not the art of tailoring. This does not mean that Tsonga women did not work with the cloth, but when they used needle and thread, they did something else with it and enhanced the fabric with embroidery and beadwork as already seen on the large skirt.

A SIDE STEP

No precise date is available for when embroidered minceka first appeared or why, but as flat pieces of fabric, they were ideal picture formats with the dark ground acting as a contrast for glass beads and embroidery threads. A great variety of images were created, ranging from the recognizable such as fish, birds, suns, and stars to arcane signs such as the tattoo marks received at initiation. Often the makers "signed" their works in large letters with their names and birth dates from Identity Documents, an affecting claim from women who frequently could not read. Short embroidered stripes at the bottom of the fabric are sometimes identified as sticks and suggest that these works are either fantasy landscapes or about home, because many homesteads are surrounded by roughly hewn stick fences. Inventions extend to additions such as small gold safety pins, small round mirrors, plastic ornaments, hair clips, and bits of wool. After the democratic elections in 1994, a number of minceka became narrative spaces and began to reflect contemporary history and showed the leaders of the African National Congress or people voting. They became pictures in the more conventional sense, although the method was unconventional. Many elaborate and pictorial minceka have become desirable commercial commodities and are made solely for sale. These minceka provided a starting point for a number of embroidery groups, not all of whom are Tsonga.

STATE OF THE NATION

Images of Tsonga women wearing their trademark skirts, bright cloths, and head scarves are frequently published on the covers of tourist guidebooks and DVDs. They are one of the signs for Limpopo, and the DVD images provide a shorthand to the language and origin of the performer. Perhaps the most public display for identity in post-apartheid South Africa is Parliament's main annual social event: the state of the nation address held in February each year. While it is not the ramp of high fashion, it is certainly a site that talks to another kind of fashioning of self and modernity. Visiting Tsonga women from Limpopo often wear their large skirts and beaded items or some contemporary version of Tsonga style. Other visitors also wear modern versions of their own traditional ethnic dress. The emergence of these styles in this context suggests that an alternative to Western formal dress is developing in South Africa. Invitations to special events now offer a choice between formal or traditional dress. Obviously, these new styles, while dependent on inherited ideas about tradition, are

Two Tsonga women at Mamitwa, Limpopo, in 2004, at the Provincial Department of Sports, Arts and Culture's district competition for the best dance groups and craft makers. The woman on the right wears many-beaded anklets, bracelets, and necklace, and both women display modern versions of the traditional dress in their outfits. Photograph by Petra Terblanche.

adapted to reflect modern South Africa. These styles, of which Tsonga is one, offer something different from Western dress to define a contemporary African identity.

BEADWORK

Tsonga beadwork covers a range of purposes from secular to ritual. The use of beads as trade items dates back to the sixteenth century, when they were exchanged for ivory and food. Travelers' accounts record that local people knew exactly what colors and sizes they wanted. Over time, beads were incorporated into the local economy and were sometimes included in bride-wealth transactions.

Although beadwork is seen in photographs taken in Mozambique in the late nineteenth century, it is different from that which developed among the Tsonga who settled in the Transvaal—a development attributed to the influence of the neighboring Ndebele, who have a rich tradition of beadwork. Despite this influence, Tsonga beadwork is distinctive, and a vocabulary of forms was established by the mid-twentieth century. Characteristic features are colored geometric shapes on a white ground, as in the *xipereta*, small beaded panels that are attached to a large safety pin, which allows for many different placements. These small detachable panels were often added to the top of the large skirt but could be attached to other garments, such as wraparound loincloths. Most of these panels have names that refer to the real world, although the patterns themselves are abstract or geometric. The six-pointed image is a star; the chevron is a sledge, because it looks like the marks a sledge leaves on the ground when it is pulled; and the diamond shape with regularly placed white dots is *rhimangela* (Guinea fowl), because the pattern looks like the flecks on the feathers of that bird. It is made from bright yellow and red beads widely spaced on a modern equivalent for horsehair and is named firefly, because the beads are like sparks of light in the dark.

Decorative Tsonga beadwork is worn primarily by women, although some items are made specifically for men for particular occasions. A new form is a waistcoat made entirely of beads. Some items of beadwork are intimately linked to ritual, such as that worn and used by *tin'anga* (healers), and special items are made for particular age groups and ceremonies. The continuing use of white beads for ritual items would seem to have some residual significance. White is generally associated with liminal states of transition or mediation between childhood and adulthood, between this world and that of the ancestors. The wraparound loincloths worn by healers have white beads organized in horizontal registers with repeating linear patterns or abstract designs. These too have a direct association with the healers, because they are either red, black, or dark blue fabric. These garments, like many other items of Tsonga beadwork, have become more colorful. Turquoise and orange cloths are used with red, black, and yellow beads sewn alongside the white. Two overlapping cloths are usually worn. The whole outfit is more colorful and flamboyant than earlier styles. Many more elements have been added, such as rattles around her ankles and a whistle in her mouth, making for a splendid and noisy presence.

Another item, the *nxanga*, is a ritual belt associated with female maturation and menstruation and is specific to the Tsonga. It is one of a few items linked into the life cycle of women and that occupies the private spaces of women as opposed to the public space of the dress. It is a long, wide belt made entirely of beads with ties on either end. Although patterns and colors vary, they are inevitably placed on a white bead ground. The whole belt is enhanced with fringes and metal ornaments such as silver or brass beads, circular disks, and brass curtain rings, and many have small bells. The effect is colorful, and the belt jingles when it moves. The beaded ground is the decorative support for the significant element on the nxanga: a small metal piece (tubing or squashed bracelet) covered with beads and attached to the top center of the beaded support.

The belt is used in fertility rites around the time of a girl's first menstruation. Later, when the girl becomes engaged, it is taken to her future husband's family as a sign of her purity, and the husband must pay to see it. When the girl gives birth to her first child, the metal piece is removed and placed in boiling water, which is subsequently used as medicine for the child. The beads can then be unpicked and reused for items for the child, which reflects ideas of accumulating value with further use and supports the idea inherent in the nxanga that it is a means of linking generations.

Other pieces associated with initiation are shared with the Sotho. Female initiates wear a front apron, *titho*, which is the same name as that used by the Sotho for the same item. It is an item that extends into the rituals themselves, as both Tsonga and Sotho boys and girls could attend the same ceremonies. At the end of initiation, though, young Tsonga boys are dressed differently and wear bright red pieces of cloth over their ochred bodies.

BODY MARKINGS

The Tsonga also marked their identity on their skin. In earlier times, both men and women had used cicatrization and tattooing. Today, cicatrization is no longer used, and tattooing is practiced by some women but rarely. Tattooing leaves blue marks on the skin, and only marks on the faces and arms are visible to outsiders. Rows of dots, double triangles touching at one of the points, and other geometric signs are used. Some are similar to the cicatrization marks in photographs from the nineteenth century.

The markings most frequently referred to in the literature are the pronounced cicatrices that are associated with the migrant

A group of Tsonga women and children wearing their distinctive skirts from Pretoria, South Africa, 1927, as featured in Henri Junod's *The Life of a South African Tribe.* Courtesy of Rayda Becker.

Tsonga in the Transvaal during the nineteenth century. These facial marks led to the nickname *knobneusen* (literally, "knob nose"). Men had one line of bumps down the center of their faces, and women had two additional horizontal lines on their foreheads and three on each cheek.

Aspects of a woman's public and private life were cut into her flesh. The lines on the face were the overt, visible signs of identity and maturity, and those on the abdomen were individual and private. One set of marks connected a woman to her bridewealth and were located below the waist in a position associated with fertility and where only her husband could see them. These marks imply the use of a coded female language with marks and signs about women's labor, cosmology, value, and status. This was a language transmitted from woman to woman because those who did the cutting were female—although now much of that knowledge has been lost.

CHANGES IN MALE DRESS

Tsonga men in the early twenty-first century show no outward signs of who they are in how they dress. With few exceptions, all wear Western dress for ceremonial, formal, and leisure events. Nevertheless, versions of or references to past styles are worn by some chiefs at select ceremonial occasions. The explanation for men's adoption of Western styles of dress lies in the fact that men have had more direct and continuous contact over a longer period of time with the urban areas and started to wear Western dress early in the twentieth century.

Henri A. Junod, the famous missionary and anthropologist who wrote the seminal text on the Tsonga at the beginning of the twentieth century, described men wearing kiltlike skirts made from animal tails as the main item of dress. He also found a few similarities between the Tsonga and Zulu and suggested that the piercing of the earlobes was an influence from the Zulu. The Tsonga began to pierce their earlobes when they stopped tattooing their noses. Because none of their neighbors in the Transvaal adopted this habit, the earplug that fitted into the lobe functioned as an external identifying feature. It is of note that both men and women among the Tsonga pierced their ears.

The adoption of the head ring was another possible Zulu influence. A circle of beeswax was placed on the head, and the hair was encouraged to grow around it. It was not removable and was replaced only when the hair grew too long to support the ring. In the transfer from Zulu to Tsonga, however, the use and associated meaning of the ring shifted. Among the Zulu, the head ring was associated with men who had achieved military success and, as a result, were eligible for marriage. Among the Tsonga, the application of the head ring was less prescribed, and it could be worn by all older men irrespective of their military status; thus, it became associated with maturity and wisdom. Modern versions of head rings are occasionally found, but they are removable and are made from plastic, rubber tubing, or the tire from a child's toy.

References and Further Reading

Becker, Rayda, and Anitra Nettleton. "Tsonga-Shangana Beadwork and Figures." In *Ten Years of Collecting (1979–1989)*, edited by David Hammond-Took and Anitra Nettleton, 9–15. Johannesburg: University of the Witwatersrand Art Galleries, 1989.

Duggan-Cronin, Arthur M. *The Bantu Tribes of South Africa: The Vathonga*. Vol. 4, Section 1. With introduction and notes by H. P. Junod. Cambridge, UK: Deighton-Bell, 1935.

Earthy, Dora E. *Valenge Women: The Social and Economic Life of the Valenge Women of Portuguese East Africa*. London: Frank Cass, 1968. (Originally published in 1933.)

Eicher, Joanne B., ed. *Dress and Ethnicity: Change across Space and Time*. Oxford, UK: Berg, 1999.

Harries, Patrick. "Exclusion, Classification and Internal Colonialism: The Emergence of Ethnicity among the Tsonga-Speakers of South Africa." In *The Creation of Tribalism in Southern Africa*, edited by L. Vail, 82–117. London: James Currey, 1989.

Harries, Patrick. *Work, Culture, and Identity: Migrant Laborers in Mozambique and South Africa, c. 1860–1910*. Johannesburg: Ravan, 1994.

Junod, Henri A. *The Life of a South African Tribe*. 2 vols. New York: University Books, 1962. (Originally published in 1927.)

Rayda Becker

Migrant Workers, Production, and Fashion

ORIGINS AND HISTORY

South Africa's migrant labor system first began in the 1850s when African men from rural communities flocked to the newly discovered diamond and gold fields on the Witwatersrand in search of work. Originally miners brought their own clothing to work in the mines, primarily shorts. Eventually the mining companies, to protect their human resources, decided it was in their best interest to provide rubber boots, coveralls, and hard hats to protect miners working in a very dangerous occupation. By the 1930s, the expansion of new industries afforded these migrants expanded opportunities to secure more lucrative employment in the service sector or as messengers or factory workers in the cities. Following the introduction of increasingly strict influx control laws also in that decade, it became gradually more difficult for these migrants to secure permanent access to residential rights in South Africa's towns and cities. Initially it was men who found domestic work in cities like Pretoria and Johannesburg, but, in some cases, women also moved to urban centers, usually against the wishes of elders and chiefs, who encouraged and even forced them to remain behind. Confined to their rural homes, the wives of men migrants tended fields and livestock and looked after both their children and the elderly members of their communities. To this day, these women produce beadwork and other items such as clay pots, long-established traditions that have, in many cases, been transformed through their own intermittent contact with South Africa's urban centers.

MINING COMPOUNDS AND THE NOSTALGIA FOR HOME

When rural migrants first began to work in South Africa's diamond and gold mines in the second half of the nineteenth century, they usually took with them treasured artifacts such as fighting sticks and headrests. In the mining compounds, to which these men were confined during their prolonged absence from their families, they rapidly developed a nostalgia for home that found expression in a fierce attachment to rural forms of dress and adornment, carved artifacts, and the rituals and songs associated with life in the communities they had left in search of wage labor. Numerous early photographs record these migrants laden with their rural treasures, including blankets, which had gradually replaced the use of leather karosses over the course of the nineteenth century. Although initially these blankets were introduced through trade relations with early European settlers, to this day, they form an integral part of the traditional clothing worn by various southern African communities.

As late as 1947, the acclaimed documentary photographer Leon Levson recorded rural migrants striding through the streets of South Africa's largest city, Johannesburg, wearing thick blankets stylishly draped across their shoulders. Here and in other urban centers across South Africa, some storekeepers still specialize in selling expensive, highly valued pure wool blankets to rural migrants from Lesotho and elsewhere. Likewise, rural traders continue to travel to the cities, where there is always a ready market for meat plates and items of dress such as beadwork at the taxi ranks surrounding the single-sex hostels that were reserved for men migrants until the apartheid state's influx control regulations began to break down in the late 1980s. Like the carved meat plates rural communities use to this day, this clothing plays an important role on occasions such as weddings and funerals, where the roasted meat of ritually slaughtered goats and cattle is served in celebration of the ancestors. Since the cost of traveling to their rural homes is prohibitive given the generally meager wages these migrants earn, they usually return briefly over the Easter weekend and for a more extended period over the Christmas to New Year period.

BETWEEN TWO WORLDS

The introduction of influx control regulations transformed what initially was a voluntary system of migration into a carefully policed institution. This enforced way of life had far-reaching implications for rural communities, whose lives and experiences were shaped by the movement of men to and from South Africa's mines and large urban centers. Unable to settle permanently in the country's cities, migrants maintained strong links to their rural homes and lifestyles, often contrasting the sense of belonging afforded by institutions like initiation and chieftainship with the immorality and cultural poverty of life in urban South Africa. To make sense of their journeys back and forth between these two worlds—one characterized by the harsh realities of poverty and economic depravation, the other by obvious signs of wealth and the apparent rewards of economic success—these migrants not only idealized their memories of home but also developed "home-boy" networks through which they maintained contact with men from their own communities.

But while the notion of home is a source of social and emotional comfort, it also plays an ambivalent role in the lives of these migrants. Describing the meaning this concept has for Sesotho men seeking work on the mines, ethnomusicologist D. B. Coplan has noted that "home is familiar and secure; to stay there is ruinous and cowardly. Work on the mines destroys body and soul but to go there is not only necessary but manly." These concerns are also evidenced in migrant songs, many of which include themes like initiation, in which the experience of leaving home for the initiation lodge after a carefree youth of herding cattle is equated with the frightening but economically and socially empowering experience of working long hours in the dark, hot depths of the mines. For many migrants, it is through this experience that boys finally become men, a belief that is captured very poetically in the Sesotho proverb, which (in translation) reads: "To know the world, one must walk the country."

HYBRID FORMS OF DRESS AND ADORNMENT

Migrants either made or purchased clothing and other items that served to affirm their ongoing connection to the rural communities from which they came. At the same time, however, they soon began to take an interest in cultural forms and ideas encountered in the cities and on the mines. As a result, many of the items of dress and adornment they brought with them from their rural homes were gradually transformed through the incorporation and adoption of new techniques and materials associated with the very different worlds they encountered on the mines and in the cities. Early paintings and sketches by European artists provide telling evidence of this practice. Even before the discovery of gold and diamonds, when migrant labor first became widespread, artist-explorer Thomas Baines repeatedly recorded migrants leaving the Cape Colony carrying blankets, cotton cloth, iron pots, guns, and other manufactured items of European origin. An 1854 painting by the same artist depicts one of the Mfengu warriors who fought with the British against the Xhosa in the Eighth Frontier War (1850 to 1853) wearing aspects of European dress such as trousers, a shirt, and closed leather shoes with a stylish feathered hat and fur pelts. This hybrid collaging of imported (European) and indigenous (African) forms of dress became increasingly common in subsequent decades, when large numbers of men began to seek work in the newly established gold mines along the Witwatersrand and in the Kimberley diamond fields. Various artists and early photographers recorded some of these men returning home from the mines wearing cast-off military jackets and cartridge belts with blankets and beads. As these images suggest, once appropriated, the function of European items was often transformed.

When, toward the end of the nineteenth century, the system of migrant labor had clearly become entrenched, migrants gradually began to form associations to protect themselves from the hostile gangs that by then had become a common feature in South Africa's urban centers. These associations included groups like the Maliaita, who gathered on Sundays before marching together to venues where they held boxing contests. South African writer Ezekiel Mpahlele has remembered how these migrants arrived at their Sunday gatherings "dressed in shorts, tennis shoes and caps and handkerchiefs dangled from their pockets. They crouched, shook their fists in the air so that the bangles round their waists clanged." By combining rural beadwork with symbols of urban leisure and sophistication like shorts and tennis shoes, these migrant associations literally enacted their increasingly complex sense of identity through their choice of dress.

The vibrant integration of traditionalist forms of clothing with styles encountered in urban contexts is also evidenced in the practice among Zulu-speaking groups of sewing beadwork panels onto secondhand tailored jackets and waistcoats (*intolibhantshi*). Reserved for special occasions such as weddings, items like these are worn in combination with leather loin-coverings (*amabeshu*). These hybrid forms of dress attest to the inventive ways in which migrants negotiate their experiences of the very different worlds and value systems they encounter. Beaded secondhand jackets are a reminder that, while more traditional art forms such as beadwork are still valued today, it has also become common to

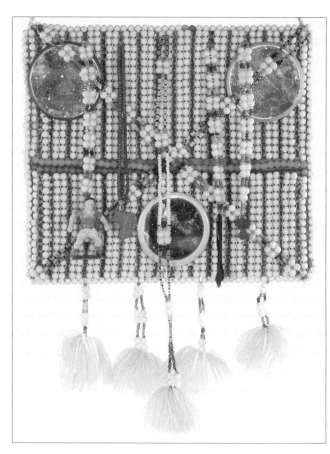

A Lovedu girl's apron made from plastic beads and recycled objects, late twentieth century. This kind of apron is associated with female initiation practices in Limpopo province, South Africa. The use of commonplace objects is at once highly inventive and playful. Photograph by Adrienne van Eeden.

give expression to the idea of dignity and manly sophistication through forms of dress associated with the urban middle-class establishment. The powerful impact this has had on the perceptions of migrants is further reflected in the fact that there is now a common conviction that, as an expression of respect, men must wear tailored jackets when they engage their ancestors.

The preoccupation among migrants with the idea of manliness and worldly sophistication is further underlined by twentieth-century studio photographs. Surrounded by the trappings of another world, such as houseplants, the migrants who commissioned these photographs commonly wear crisply ironed and tailored pants. At the same time, however, many of them display with obvious pride beadwork items made for them by women from their rural homesteads. Half urban, half rural, they divide their bodies quite literally into two distinct spheres—two separate but connected worlds—thus clearly revealing what it takes—or means—to be at once worldly and sophisticated and rooted in the values of one's past.

TAILORS AND THE EMERGENCE OF URBAN MARKETS

Initially, migrants working in the mines made almost all of the garments they wore on special occasions, using their very limited leisure time to do so. Old photographs of mining compounds attest to the prominent presence in these compounds of part-time tailors who sewed the uniforms these migrants designed for their boxing and dancing associations. In the absence of a ready supply of the beadwork panels made by rural wives and mothers, these tailored uniforms often simulated the colorful patterns associated with beadwork items through the addition of braid trim and carefully arranged patchwork patterns.

Later, garments of this kind were bought at urban markets like the Dalton Market in Durban, situated next to the city's largest minibus taxi rank, and the Mai Mai market in Johannesburg, which, in the 1940s, was initially established as a hostel for men migrants. Over time, the Mai Mai and other hostel complexes became flourishing markets where traders sold artifacts like meat plates, headrests, and beadwork obtained from rural producers, as well as objects and clothing produced at the markets. Many of the artisans who set up shop in these markets became specialists who worked with particular materials. Those who produced traditional items made from leather began to decorate these forms with metal studs, brass buckles, and other factory-manufactured goods. Discarded urban waste items such as machine gaskets have also been incorporated into the beadwork pieces rural women make for their migrant men. Notable in this regard is the *ugcazimbana*, a version of a traditional collar necklace worn by the Xhosa speakers from the Eastern Cape.

In contrast to these leather workers, tailors sewed hybrid garments from cheap cottons, while others fashioned cotton clothing with leopard-skin trimmings. Originally a sign of status and authority, the addition of strips of leopard skin increasingly signaled the wealth of the wearer. But because leopard skin—used to add details to the cuffs and collars of garments—has become prohibitively expensive in recent years, most tailors now use imitation leopard-skin trim printed on velvetlike corduroy that, at a distance, simulates the texture of fur. Since the 1980s, T-shirt manufacturers have supplemented this growing market for the leopard-skin look—in some cases, augmenting the dramatic impact of these sleeveless garments by including images of growling leopards embedded in a dense field of leopard-skin spots.

Always innovative, the inventions and interventions of migrants and their suppliers suggest an extraordinary freedom of expression that extends to the production of mundane functional items such as sandals made from discarded car tires. Variations include *mbadada*, which have both cross-straps and soles made from car tires, and *odabuluzwane*, dancing sandals with diagonal thongs secured between the big and second toes of the wearer's foot. Likewise, migrants now either decorate their highly valued fighting and dance sticks, often made in rural areas from comparatively rare hardwoods, with plastic wire and plastic rings or paint them with intricate patterns similar to those associated with regional beadwork styles.

In the twenty-first century, other forms of plastic are recycled in equally inventive ways—for example, in the production of crocheted hats. Soccer fans also transform plastic construction-site safety helmets into dramatic headgear emblazoned with the colors and advertising logos of their favorite soccer teams such as the Kaizer Chiefs or Orlando Pirates. Likewise, from about the 1950s onward, colorful pieces of plastic were cut into geometric shapes before being nailed with fine metal shafts (apparently modified used gramophone record needles) onto circular disks of wood to form *iziqhaza* (earplugs). Inserted into stretched holes in the wearer's earlobes, these earplugs are still fashionable to this day. Sold regularly at the Mai Mai market in Johannesburg, contemporary examples of these earplugs have elasticized loops so that people without holes in their earlobes can attach them around their ears. Another version clips on to the lobes of both ears and features two disks bound together with elastic bands. This willingness to embrace cultural forms that are both foreign and modern attests to the fact that South Africa's migrant communities are concerned not so much with the idea of authenticity as with finding appropriate ways to articulate and negotiate complex realities and identities.

Not surprisingly, this highly inventive layering of styles and materials extends beyond forms of dress and other types of adornment. Thus, for example, an artist who appears to have worked at the Mai Mai market in the 1970s produced a series of headrests that are entirely unlike any traditional examples in that they are covered in colorful Plexiglas panels. Some of these headrests have words like *snuff*, also cut from plastic, attached to them, while others incorporate newspaper cuttings from Johannesburg's daily newspaper, *The Star*. The horizontal lintels of at least one of these headrests are covered in off-cuts taken from carpet tiles. Yet despite their radical departure from the traditional materials used to make items like these, they are unmistakably similar in style to headrests from the Thukela Ferry region of present-day KwaZulu-Natal. Thus, although they shatter established artistic cannons, they suggest a concern to retain a relationship not only through style but also through function to long-entrenched rural practices like the commissioning of headrests, which formed an important part of the dowries of most brides living both south and north of the Thukela River. In rural communities like these, some women still fashioned their hair into elaborate semipermanent styles that require them to use headrests when they lie down to sleep.

RURAL TRANSFORMATIONS

These vibrant and increasingly hybrid artistic traditions have had a significant impact on the production of various art forms associated with rural ceremonies such as weddings, divination rites, and the initiation of young men and women. An obvious example is provided by the cheap plastic trinkets and plastic medicine spoons women from various communities add to the necklaces they make for themselves and their migrant husbands. Many of these trinkets are believed to have protective qualities. In the past, Zulu speakers from the Msinga area wore magical bands (*umam 'langeni*) around the arm just under the shoulder on top of the biceps. Normally hidden from sight, these bands now have bicycle reflectors and rivets applied to them. When exposed to the light, their reflective qualities provide ancestral protection for wearers against the dangers they encounter in the cities.

Over the past few decades, it has become fairly common to transform South Africa's urban waste into powerful aesthetic statements. An obvious example of this practice is afforded by beadwork items associated with female initiation practices in Limpopo province. Made from cheap plastic beads, these aprons and breastplates are decorated with watches, bird mirrors, medicine spoons, and small plastic toys. These transformations of the commonplace are at once highly inventive and playful. But in their tendency to excess, they also raise interesting questions regarding both symbolic and commercial notions of value.

This tendency to excess in the incorporation of discarded consumer items is evidenced elsewhere in South Africa in the production of diviners' skirts from the Debe Nek and King Williamstown area in the Eastern Cape. In contrast to earlier skirts of this kind, which were made from sparsely decorated strips of leather, these recent examples are covered in reflective metal bottle tops, colorful pieces of cloth, medicine spoons, and the open-weave plastic webbing that grocers use to package fruit and vegetables. Covered in discarded objects and materials, these diviners' skirts are transformed into opulent, shimmering, percussive instruments. The use of recycled materials in the production of these costumes, which diviners wear when they attend political rallies or to welcome young male initiates returning from initiation lodges, contributes to a sense of festivity—a feeling of celebration—that is actively reinforced through song and dance.

Elsewhere, among the Kopa living the in the Moutse district of Mpumalanga, the clothing of married women has become quite literally festive through the addition of Christmas decorations to the elaborately styled headdresses they wear on special occasions like events organized to celebrate the return to the community of young male and female initiates. Shimmering symbols of the glitzy world of consumer capitalism, they are a comparatively cheap way of suggesting a sense of opulence and excess. Because items like these are not readily available in this outlying rural area, they are brought back from the cities by migrant husbands.

As early as the 1960s, rural beadworkers also began to allude to life in South Africa's urban centers. One example of this phenomenon is provided by a beaded marriage cloak from the Bergville district of present-day KwaZulu-Natal, some of which includes images of cars and the letters TJ, formerly the registration tag for vehicles from Johannesburg. Although garments like these evoke the alluring material gains those who work in the city generally aspire to, wealth of this kind eludes most migrants, who have little formal education and who therefore normally find work as menial laborers. The inclusion of letters and words on beadwork garments and clay pots has also become common among other communities in KwaZulu-Natal, notably those living in the Msinga area. Like the images of consumer goods found on beadwork items from the Bergville area and on some of the mural decorations produced by communities elsewhere in South Africa, the inclusion of these letters and words provides demonstrable evidence of the various ways in which migrants and their families negotiate the complex experience of moving between two radically different worlds.

CONCLUSION

Like consumers elsewhere in the world, the producers of beadwork and other items among Africa's migrant workers are caught up in the global circulation of cheap commodities. But because their responses to these commodities are often highly inventive rather than merely predictable, their creativity bears close comparison with the new and unusual ways in which Punk and other youth groups have plundered and recontextualized the everyday objects and artifacts that surround them.

Despite the abject conditions faced by many migrants living in urban hostels and mining and other compounds, their artistic production is, and has been, characterized by a vibrant and challenging creativity. Thus, although the migrant labor system has undoubtedly had a devastating impact on the lives of countless South Africans, migrants have nevertheless managed to find ways of shaping and making sense of their experiences through music, dance, dress, and other household and personal items. Although, in many cases, this creativity seems to break with traditional forms by using new materials and by drawing on new values and ideas, more often than not, the artifacts migrants have either used or produced tend to affirm a sense of continuity between the past and the present, the rural and the urban, the homesteads where these migrants grew up and the hostels and compounds to which they were, and still are, confined during their long absences from home.

References and Further Reading

Coplan, D.B. *In the Time of Cannibals. The Word Music of South Africa's Basotho Migrants.* Johannesburg: Witwatersrand University Press, 1994.

Delius, P. *A Lion amongst the Cattle: Reconstruction and Resistance in the Northern Transvaal.* Oxford, UK: James Currey, 1997.

Hindson, D. *Pass Controls and the Urban African Proletariat.* Johannesburg: Ravan Press, 1987.

Klopper, S. "The Postmodern Context of Rural Craft Production in Contemporary South Africa." In *The Future Is Handmade. The Survival and Innovation of Crafts, Prince Claus Fund Journal* 10a (2005): 84–99.

Mpahlele, E. *Down Second Avenue.* London, 1959.

Nettleton, A., J. Charlton, and F. Rankin-Smith. *Engaging Modernities. Transforming the Commonplace.* Johannesburg: University of the Witwatersrand Art Galleries, 2003.

Sandra Klopper and Fiona Rankin-Smith

See also Footwear; volume 10, Global Perspectives: Conventional Work Dress.

Women's Cooperatives and Self-Help Artists

- Minceka and Household Linen
- Minceka as Wall Hangings
- Embroidered Tops, Designer Jackets, and Conference Carry Bags
- Painted and Silk-Screened Fabrics
- Protest Art

During the 1980s and 1990s, a number of art-making cooperatives were set up to address the dire poverty of communities in South Africa as well as so-called homelands such as Gazankulu and Bophuthatswana. Some catered to men and women, coupling an imperative to generate income for members with an agenda to protest against apartheid through the creation of art. The majority, however, catered specifically to women who, in addition to being denied human rights and economic opportunities through apartheid, were victims of gender discrimination. Neglected or abused by fathers, husbands, and male partners as well as by the apartheid state, numerous black women in South Africa found in cooperatives the opportunity and agency to support themselves and their children. In postapartheid South Africa, women's art-making cooperatives continue to play an important role in redressing the gender inequities that were perpetuated during apartheid. Twenty-first-century women-led cooperatives allow women to collaborate with each other and achieve greater economic security through the creation and sale of apparel.

The *nceka* (pl. *minceka*), a rectangular-shaped cloth worn by many Tsonga-speaking women in the former homeland of Gazankulu, has had an important influence on cooperative embroidery projects. Two minceka are worn at once, one over each shoulder and slung over the opposite hip in the manner of a sarong. Accompanied by a blouse that is often brightly colored and popularly known as a "skipper," minceka are also usually slung over a gathered or bustle-like underskirt called a *xibelani*. Two embroidery projects established in the 1980s, Xihoko and Chivirika, adapted the nceka to produce household linen and wall hangings marketed to non-Tsonga buyers.

Apart from producing household linen influenced by design elements in an item of clothing, self-help projects have made garments. Chivirika has produced minceka for sale to non-Tsonga buyers, and other cooperatives have made more conventionally Westernized garments such as blouses, jackets, tote bags, and T-shirts with imagery rendered through needlework, paint, and silkscreen. Although often intended to generate an income for economically disadvantaged women, garments made by cooperatives have also been used to express political viewpoints or to mobilize people to deal with social issues. A use of clothing to articulate sociopolitical viewpoints had its genesis in projects that sought ways of resisting an oppressive apartheid regime, but this strategy is also used by cooperatives such as Philani and Wola Nani, which were established after the first democratic election in 1994.

MINCEKA AND HOUSEHOLD LINEN

Daina Mabunda, a Tsonga speaker from the Xihoko region of Gazankulu (a former homeland that became part of the Northern province of South Africa in 1994), was wearing minceka she had embroidered with birds and animals when, in 1981 or 1982, she was spotted by Jane Arthur, a medical doctor working in a hospital in nearby Tzaneen. Arthur, fascinated by minceka that local women were wearing, commissioned Mabunda to produce a couple of embroidered cloths. Recognizing that embroidered minceka might provide prototypes for needlework that could be marketed via craft outlets and art exhibitions in cities such as Johannesburg, Arthur worked with Mabunda and her husband, Reckson, to establish the Rural Development Project (better known as Xihoko) in 1982. Including no more than twenty-five women at any one point in its history, Xihoko produced bedcovers, tablecloths, and pillowcases that, as clothing scholar Bronwen Findlay has noted, were often based on designs in cloths used by Tsonga people that Jane Arthur and her husband, David, collected from Gazankulu, Venda, and downtown Johannesburg but were adapted by Daina or Reckson Mabunda when devising templates for embroidery.

Motifs frequently had their genesis in imagery included in embroidered or beaded minceka. Not only were many of the animal and bird motifs that feature in Xihoko cloths gleaned from these kinds of garments, but, as scholar of South African creative expression Rayda Becker has observed, so, too, were "some abstract images—such as the circles constructed from lines tipped in a different colored dots, variations on Maltese crosses or geometric shapes." And while most items made by the project were embroideries on white cotton cloth, in the late 1980s, its members also began to produce some others in brightly hued thread on black cotton. The latter relate to embroidered and beaded minceka that are made out of dark material—either black or very deep blue with a muted floral pattern. Embroidered minceka may also include the names and birth dates of their makers, and this was a further influence on Xihoko cloths that, similarly, often incorporate the signatures of the embroiderers who produced them or the dates when they were made. There is, however, a crucial difference between Xihoko embroideries and minceka of this type. As Becker has noted, the motifs in embroidered minceka are frequently randomly organized, while those in Xihoko cloths "were carefully selected and more ordered and composed within their formats." This difference undoubtedly had much to do with Arthur's taste as well as preferences of non-Tsonga buyers. Presumably, however, it was also bound up with a sense that a bedcover or tablecloth, displayed on a flat surface, may call for a very different aesthetic than a cloth intended to be draped over a xibelani.

Minceka do not necessarily contain handwork. They may also be constituted entirely from brightly patterned and commercially printed fabrics with designs that, as Findlay has noted in her research, are specified by local Indian dealers but printed in Japan. Purchased ready-made by Tsonga-speaking women, they are items that dealers design to accord with their conceptions (or misconceptions) about Tsonga preferences but that are also ultimately influenced by their own tastes. These minceka, like embroidered ones, include motifs that feature in Xihoko cloths—ones that are

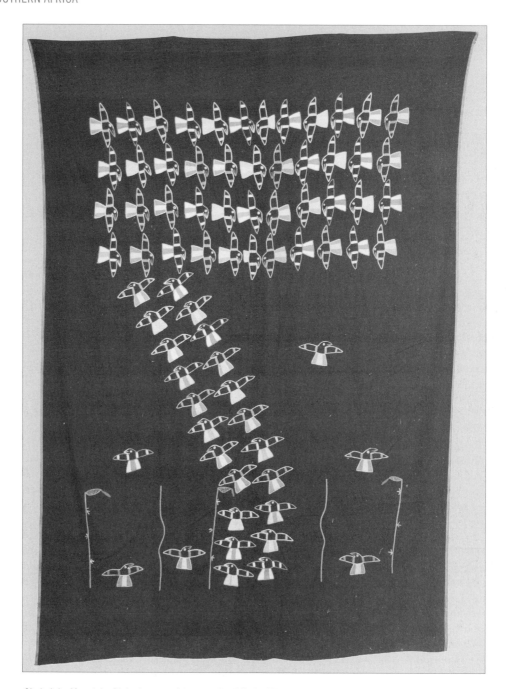

Chabalala Mountain Birds, by an unknown artist (of the Xihoko project, South Africa), late 1980s. Although this design was taken from an embroidered curtain, the use of brightly hued thread on black cotton is typical of embroidered *minceka* (cloth worn over the shoulder or hip in pairs). Embroidery thread on black cotton cloth, approximately 8 x 5.5 feet (238 x 170 cm), private collection. Photograph by Paul Mills.

imbued with cross-cultural influences. A favorite Xihoko motif such as the peacock, for example, "is used extensively in Indian iconography and appears on many goods such as trays, mats, plastic tablecloths, headscarves, amongst others" marketed in South Africa but is also associated with commercially printed minceka. Arvind Gokal, a dealer, has indicated that he once sold minceka made of fabric with a peacock design that proved enormously popular with Tsonga buyers, and Aubrey Blecher, a mathematics lecturer at the University of South Africa (UNISA) who handled fundraising for the project, "remembers seeing a label depicting a peacock attached to minceka sold in a shop."

In 1993, Jane Arthur and her husband decided to emigrate from South Africa, and the project was taken over and renamed Shangaan Motifs. Xihoko did not prove an enduring enterprise, however, and, while Daina Mabunda continued to make embroideries in her personal capacity, the cooperative had ceased operation by the mid-1990s. The nceka would nevertheless also be the primary inspiration for works made by another self-help project in Gazankulu that continues to operate in the twenty-first century. Mbhanyele Jameson Maluleke, employed by UNISA as a security guard, learned about Xihoko from Aubrey Blecher and decided to establish a similar cooperative at his home in the Mphambo Village.

Two Peacocks, by an unknown artist (of the Xihoko project, South Africa), 1990. The peacock motif is associated with commercially printed *minceka* (cloth worn over the shoulder or hip in pairs). In an adaptation of embroidered *minceka* (which traditionally include the birth dates of their makers), this Xihoko cloth includes the date when it was made. Embroidery thread on white cotton cloth, approximately 8 x 8 feet (230 x 225 cm), private collection. Photograph by Paul Mills.

MINCEKA AS WALL HANGINGS

Initiated in September 1986, Chivirika (meaning "toil and sweat" in Tsonga) was, as Maluleke has indicated, intended to "improve the quality of life in a rural community." But coupled with its aim to generate an income for women who faced little prospect of finding employment in Gazankulu, Maluleke also intended that it assert the Tsonga identity of its members: "We wanted [to express] something about our identity, something that can tell us more about our tradition as a people," he indicated in an interview on 4 April 2002. A use of minceka was intricately bound up with this vision: "The *nceka* is the only traditional cloth that is left to our people. You can identify our people by that cloth…. We took is as a symbol of our people." While promoting discreet identities among the people of South Africa was often viewed as the marker of collaboration with an apartheid government that sought to locate each ethnic group in its own distinct region, Maluleke was instead proposing that the celebration of a garment specific to Tsonga speakers could affirm a group who had been marginalized and oppressed under colonial and apartheid rule. For Maluleke, the establishment of a project that focused on a marker of Tsonga identity, the nceka, would enable him to "contribute towards the liberation of our people" rather than to support an apartheid concept of tribalism.

The earliest works made by the project were minceka, albeit examples that their non-Tsonga buyers would use as wall hangings rather than clothing. In the 1980s, women sometimes made embroidered minceka not only from dark-colored cloth but also from the cotton bags in which maize meal was packaged. In the latter case, the manufacturer logos printed on a bag serve as a pattern for its design. Maluleke discovered that minceka such as these, which were normally made by Tsonga-speaking women in Gazankulu for use on special occasions, could be marketed successfully in Pretoria. "I was in Pretoria at the time and I thought that I would bring them there," he commented in the interview on 4 April 2002. "And we were surprised that white people liked these things." While exposure to works by Andy Warhol and pop art has long encouraged recognition of the aesthetic possibilities of brand names and product design, buyers of these minceka (who might well have included tourists from Europe and the United States or temporary residents associated with embassies) doubtless also appreciated the care and attention that Tsonga-speaking women lavish on materials that are normally viewed as throwaway as well as the technical excellence of their stitching.

The maize industry's replacement of cotton with plastic packaging meant that these works ceased being produced during the 1990s. Women in the Chivirika group would continue to make minceka, however, focusing on an equally attractive variant in which dark blue cloth, often with a muted floral design, is embellished with motifs such as Maltese crosses or diamonds produced through beadwork or embroidery, large numbers of safety pins arranged in various geometric formations, and items such as small bells or mirrors designed for bird cages. Such garments have the most impact when they are worn. "Legible, static, flat and disembodied," the nceka displayed as a wall hanging is, as Elizabeth Delmont has noted, markedly "different from the effect of a worn *nceka* swathed around a three-dimensional figure, with light catching the pins, glass and beads and the motifs shifting in and out of full legibility as the body sways and moves." For non-Tsonga buyers who might encounter them in craft stores in Pretoria or Johannesburg and perhaps not even realize they were garments, minceka of this type could nevertheless be enjoyed for their geometry and vibrant patterning and, like the versions made from maize meal bags, their transformation of cheap brand products into aesthetically pleasing handmade objects.

Chivirika would ultimately become best known for cloths that were not minceka but were indebted to these garments. Janétje van der Merwe, a fine art graduate employed in the marketing and corporate communication department at UNISA, volunteered assistance to Chivirika in 1988. The typical Chivirika cloth that she helped develop has a black linen ground, animals and foliage embroidered in bright colors at its center, and a geometrically patterned border—always toward its top and bottom edges and sometimes on its sides as well. Like some Xihoko examples, Chivirika works occasionally incorporate the embroidered signatures of needlework artists and are thus reminiscent of minceka that, likewise, include the names (and dates of birth) of their makers. But if a use of brightly colored thread on black cloth is reminiscent of many embroidered minceka, motifs included here are much more systematically ordered than in the garments that were their primary influence, while animals, birds, and foliage are on a considerably enlarged scale. Van der Merwe was quite evidently seeking to create a type of work that might appeal to a tourist market attracted to South Africa because of its game viewing possibilities and scenic beauty, and she may well have borne in mind the proximity of Gazankulu to the Kruger National Park.

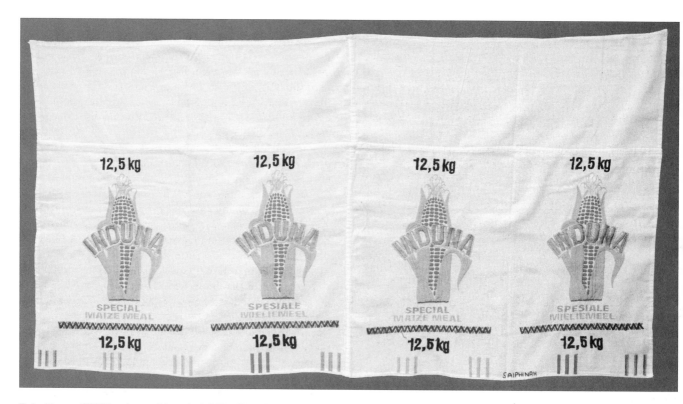

Embroidery on INDUNA maize meal bags by Salphina Maluleke (of Chivirika Embroidery Project, South Africa). In the 1980s, Tsonga-speaking women sometimes made embroidered *minceka* (cloth worn over the shoulder or hip in pairs) from the cotton bags in which maize meal was packaged. Embroidery thread on maize meal bags, approximately 3.25 x 4.5 feet (100 x 143 cm), private collection. Photograph by Paul Mills.

EMBROIDERED TOPS, DESIGNER JACKETS, AND CONFERENCE CARRY BAGS

Van der Merwe, along with other staff at UNISA, the Sisters of Mercy, and the international women's organization Soroptomists International, would play a key role in the formation of another cooperative in 1991. Located in the Winterveld, a periurban area about twenty-eight miles (forty-five kilometers) northwest of Pretoria that was part of the so-called independent homeland of Bophuthatswana but is now in the Gauteng province, the Mapula Embroidery Project was initially a small cooperative including about ten or twenty women. In contrast to Chivirika, which has always included between fifteen and thirty members, Mapula (meaning "mother of rain" in Tsonga) grew dramatically in the postapartheid period and, by late 2005, was supporting about 150 women. Its members, who speak different languages, do not make embroideries that assert an ethnic identity, and, in that respect also, the project is very different from Xihoko and Chivirika. Furthermore, subject matter in works by Mapula is considerably more diverse than in the two projects from the former homeland of Gazankulu. While initially producing embroideries focusing primarily on flora, fauna, and biblical stories, many Mapula works made since the first democratic election in 1994 represent scenes of contemporary life or topical issues and news stories.

Mapula's primary output is cushion covers and cloths that are used as wall hangings. These have some affinities with embroidered or beaded minceka, although the Winterveld is a considerable distance away from the region in which such garments are worn. Motifs are normally worked in brightly colored thread on a black cotton ground, and Mapula works commonly include embroidered wording, although not normally the names of their makers.

Mapula also produced clothing. When Mapula was initiated, members learned stitches and techniques by working on very small scraps of cloth. To adapt these into finished items, a UNISA art history lecturer, Antoinette du Plessis, devised a design for a blouse or top with an inset panel of embroidery. These garments disappeared from the Mapula repertoire by about 1994, however. Cushion covers were proving more saleable than blouses, and, as van der Merwe notes, it seemed counterproductive for the project to attempt to compete with the "rag trade," particularly because the shops Mapula supplied were South African craft shops or craft fairs rather than clothing stores. Yet Mapula continued to make embroidered garments from time to time, although not normally for craft shops.

In 1998, the project was commissioned to embroider some panels for waistcoats that a small home industry was producing for dissemination to clothing boutiques in South Africa. Six years later, South African fashion designer Francois Rall incorporated embroideries by project members in up-market couturier garments to be sold through exclusive clothing boutiques. A photograph of a young model posed in a jacket that was included in the winter 2004 fashion supplement of the South African women's magazine *Rooi Rose* (Red Rose) reveals an adaptation of the characteristic Mapula style of embroidery—brightly colored thread on a black cotton ground—into a dazzling and glamorous sartorial statement. The imagery used here is one in which the Mapula embroiderer celebrates customs and norms of subsistence-level South African life. Somewhat ironically, representations of rural

Two Giraffes, by Salphina Maluleke (of Chivirika Embroidery Project, South Africa), early 1990s. A use of brightly colored thread on black cloth in typical Chivirika wall hangings from the late 1980s and early 1990s is reminiscent of many embroidered *minceka*. Embroidery thread on black cotton cloth, approximately 3.8 x 3.6 feet (118 x 112 cm), private collection. Photograph by Paul Mills.

homesteads and livestock have been located in a garment designed for a fashionable urbanite able to afford its price tag of 7,800 South African rand (approximately US$1,000).

Mapula has also been making large numbers of carry bags since 2005. Conference organizers often seek innovative ways of packaging printed matter for delegates, and an embroidered bag is not only a practical way of carrying documents but also doubles as a memento of the event. Examples by Mapula are similar in scale to their cushion covers, include the same kind of imagery, and are produced by using brightly colored embroidery thread on black cotton cloth. By adapting a standard item in the project's repertoire, the project has been able to cater to a burgeoning conference market and thus generate additional income for its members Bags such as these are almost always made to meet an order by conference conveners and only very rarely are sold via craft shops.

This type of initiative is by no means unique to Mapula, however, and conference bags have also been made by, for example, the approximately thirty members of the Intuthuko sewing project in the township of Etwatwa near Benoni in Gauteng, a project run by Celia de Villiers and Sonja Barac and initiated in 2002. As in Mapula, examples made by Inthuthuko are embroidered in brightly colored thread on a black ground. But this coloration had become so popular by the time Intuthuko was initiated that its use here may well be the outcome of the project organizers' familiarity with embroideries by other South African community projects rather than necessarily the embroidered and beaded minceka where it originated.

Community projects have produced clothing through techniques besides embroidery. The Bethesda Arts Center, begun in 1999 in Nieu Bethesda in the Eastern Cape, is an empowerment and income-generating program including a women's textile workshop where sixteen artists create, along with household linen, bags and clothing embellished with appliqué. These artists have found a good measure of financial success since the launching of their designer label, Pomegranate, in 2004, and garments from this line are sold in galleries and shops in Johannesburg as well as ordered via the project's Web site.

PAINTED AND SILK-SCREENED FABRICS

Although artists in the Bethesda Textile Workshop create appliquéd designs that are gleaned from their personal experiences, these are not as politically overt or informative as works by some projects that produce clothing with painted or printed imagery. The Philani Printing Project in the Western Cape is especially notable in this regard. Artists in Philani (meaning "to get well" in Xhosa) create fabric works by silk-screening and then hand-painting designs onto cotton surfaces. Sometimes using purely decorative patterns, such as those influenced by Xhosa women's ceremonial dress, Philani fabrics often also showcase more complicated visual narratives. Both of these iconographical styles also appear on a wide range of clothing and household items including bags, aprons, and T-shirts. These garments are at once practical items intended for everyday use and aesthetically compelling visual narratives that hold profound personal meaning for the artists.

Similar to other women's art-making cooperatives in South Africa and throughout other regions of the world, Philani was created as a women's self-help project intended to empower impoverished women through economic advancement and artistic self-expression. Initiated in 1997 by the Philani Nutrition Project and the Western Cape Department of Social Services, the Philani Printing Project was founded as part of an ambitious nationwide antipoverty initiative. The project provides skills training and printing facilities to unemployed mothers with children under the age of five. The women participate in a three-month course where they are trained in textile design, silk-screening, and painting, after which they are granted unlimited access to a generous workshop space, printmaking equipment and art-making materials. From the sale of these items, most of the artists employed at Philani earn an income that helps to clothe, feed, and pay school fees for their families.

The cooperative's artistic production and image development began under the skilled guidance and dedicated leadership of Cape Town artist Jane Solomon. The other forty-five artists who have worked at the project are residents from Crossroads and the surrounding township communities. The initial image design and creation of products was done on a collaborative basis through creative workshops run by Solomon, which entailed discussions of important issues affecting the artists. Several sets of designs and aesthetic preferences evolved from these discussions. For example, the design called Amaproduct, Xhosa for "products," depicts a variety of commercial products such as laundry detergent, cola, and marmite, which are commonly used in the households of Crossroads women. Amaproduct consists of thick, black outlines that roughly delineate the objects in the image, colored in with a wide range of bright, vibrant colors—both features are part of Philani's signature style. The Amaproduct design celebrates the fact that the salaries the women earn from their art making at

A bag designed by Stella Mnisi (of the Mapula Embroidery Project, South Africa), 2007. Conference organizers often seek innovative ways of "packaging" printed matter for delegates, and an embroidered bag not only is a practical way of carrying documents but also doubles as a memento of the event. Embroidery thread on black cotton cloth, approximately 13 x 11 inches (35 x 28 cm), private collection. Photograph by Paul Mills.

Philani make these commercial items more readily affordable to them. By 2000, the Philani Printing Project had become an economically independent venture managed and run entirely by Xhosa-speaking women from the Crossroads area.

An important facet of the Philani Printing Project is the artists' desire to employ art making as a form of activism in order to promote social justice. They do this partly through a collection of designs that overtly address political and social issues, including labor exploitation, violence, health care, employment, and HIV/AIDS, and partly through depicting themselves or other women as activists in these images. For example, in Stop AIDS and Stop Crime designs, the artists identify specific women's issues that require immediate attention in South Africa's transformation and visually demonstrate how one might take action on these issues. Similarly, *Umanyano Ngamandla* (Xhosa for "unity is power"), a work that celebrates women's agency and achievement, depicts the artists as a group of women actively engaged in community-based political action. In addition, in 1998, five Philani artists responded to the high rates of violence against women by creating a series of T-shirts carrying designs that testify to their individual experiences with violence. The T-shirts depict scenes of domestic violence, rape, and sexual harassment in the workplace, among other, often violent or abusive experiences. Kim Miller has reported that, because these stories are printed on T-shirts—and then worn and circulated in the public sphere (often in the very communities where the acts of violence took place)—the artists engage with a tradition of visual resistance that has historical significance in South Africa's anti-apartheid movement.

PROTEST ART

Artists in other community-based arts projects have created and worn T-shirts as cultural tools to resist oppression and demand social justice. The Community Arts Project (CAP) is perhaps the most historic and well known of these protest art projects. Founded in 1975 in Cape Town, CAP formed to train black South Africans (both men and women) as artists in response to the segregationist Bantu Education Act, which excluded most people of color from art schools and higher education. CAP ran politically oriented printing workshops on site and at other locations in the surrounding townships. Many of the individuals who sought training at the project were anti-apartheid activists who effectively utilized visual culture as a means of resistance. Renowned for their protest posters, banners, and T-shirts, CAP artists knew how to use visual arts to quickly communicate political messages and to mobilize people. The T-shirts, especially useful in this regard, became common at political rallies and funerals. The power of these T-shirts was recognized by government officials, who responded by censoring them along with all other subversive statements. As artist/activist Sue Williamson (who was once arrested for creating and wearing a women's rights T-shirt) has recalled, "the humble T-shirt has become a potent way of making a personal political statement." A body wearing such a shirt was a vulnerable body and a likely target for government violence. Like other self-help projects, CAP provided disadvantaged South Africans with a unique and effective opportunity to express themselves politically through political apparel. CAP continues to function as a training program for unemployed artists, although its original mission of using arts to oppose the government necessarily changed with the end of apartheid.

In 2003, CAP merged with Mediaworks, another local organization that aimed to empower disadvantaged peoples and communities through the creation of activist arts and media. Like CAP, Mediaworks ran various education and training programs tailored specifically to media and communications issues. Many Mediaworks projects focus exclusively on women, such as the Gender and Communications project, which trains community-based activists on gender issues. In the years since their merger, the new CAP/Mediaworks project has formed a prison rehabilitation program where women prisoners participate in a T-shirt workshop, producing garments that express their personal and political views.

More recently, the self-help project Wola Nani (Xhosa for "we embrace and develop one another") created a series of politically oriented T-shirts in the tradition of the protest shirts donned

Say No to Domestic Abuse, T-shirt, by Nontsikelelo (Ntsiki) Stuurman (of the Philani Printing Project), 1998. When sociopolitical imagery is printed on T-shirts—and then worn and circulated in the public sphere—Philani artists engage with a tradition of visual resistance that has historical significance in South Africa's anti-apartheid movement. Acrylic paint on cotton, 31 x 22 inches (79 cm x 56 cm), private collection. Photograph by Kurt Gohde.

by anti-apartheid activists of the past. Founded in 1994 in the Western Cape and specifically geared toward women and children (but not exclusive to their needs), Wola Nani seeks to bring relief to individuals and communities who have been affected by HIV/AIDS. The project takes a multifaceted approach in its efforts, offering programs that help people cope with financial and emotional stress, health care, and other everyday needs. Wola Nani also runs empowerment programs through various craft-making workshops that are also aimed to raise awareness and educate the public about HIV/AIDS. In 1998, Wola Nani devised a well-publicized T-shirt campaign entitled "Calling All Freedom Fighters." Each shirt featured a black-and-white portrait of a recognizable hero—including Steve Biko, Nelson Mandela, Miriam Makeba, Bob Marley, and Jesus Christ—wearing a bright red and equally recognizable AIDS awareness ribbon. Together, Wola Nani and the Philani Printing Project extend the work of the Community Arts Project by utilizing the protest T-shirt to express and transmit political messages, although their demands for justice are no longer directed toward an apartheid state.

References and Further Reading

Becker, Rayda. "A Stitch in Time: The Xihoko Project." In *Material Matters: Appliqués by the Weya Women of Zimbabwe and Needlework by South African Collectives*, edited by Brenda Schmahmann, 108–115. Johannesburg: Wits University Press, 2000.

Delmont, Elizabeth. Untitled discussion of an nceka in the Wits Art Galleries. In *Voice Overs: Wits Writings Exploring African Artworks*, edited by Anitra Nettleton, Julia Charlton, and Fiona Rankin-Smith, 52–53. Johannesburg: Wits Art Galleries, 2004.

Findlay, Bronwen. "Aspects of Cloth Usage and Adaptation among the Tsonga-Shangana Women of the Northern Transvaal." Master's thesis, University of Natal, 1995.

Maluleke, Mbhanyele Jameson. "Toil for Your Survival: Chivirika Self-Help Project." In *Material Matters: Appliqués by the Weya Women of Zimbabwe and Needlework by South African Collectives*, edited by Brenda Schmahmann, 116–118. Johannesburg: Wits University Press, 2000.

Miller, Kim. "The Philani Printing Project: Women's Art and Activism in Crossroads, South Africa." *Feminist Studies* 29, no. 3 (Fall 2003): 619–637.

Miller, Kim. "T-shirts, Testimony and Truth: Memories of Violence Made Visible." *Textile: The Journal of Cloth and Culture* 3, no. 3 (2005): 250–273.

Schmahmann, Brenda. "On Pins and Needles: Gender Politics and Embroidery Projects before the First Democratic Election." In *Between Union and Liberation: Women Artists in South Africa 1910–1994*, edited by Marion Arnold and Brenda Schmahmann, 152–173. Aldershot, UK: Ashgate Publishing, 2005.

Schmahmann, Brenda. *Mapula: Embroidery and Empowerment in the Winterveld*. Johannesburg: David Krut Publishing, 2006.

Williamson, Sue. *Resistance Art in South Africa*. New York: St. Martin's Press, 1989.

Younge, Gavin. *Art of the South African Townships*. London: Thames and Hudson, 1988.

Kimberly Miller and Brenda Schmahmann

See also Nguni, Zulu, and Xhosa Dress and Beadwork; Tsonga Dress and Fashion.

Swaziland

The kingdom of Swaziland is located in southern Africa and is landlocked between South Africa and Mozambique. It has a largely homogeneous population of just over one million and is ruled by a monarchy. The Swazis share a culture, language, and loyalty to the monarch. After the South African War of 1899 to 1902, Swaziland became a British protectorate and was granted independence in 1968. King Mswati III ascended to the throne in 1986 after the death of his father, King Sobhuza II. The Swazis regard their king as someone who helps them to maintain their traditional culture and values. The country is viewed as following a traditional, conservative path while combining its customs with modern Western initiatives and technologies. Tradition and modernity are, for the most part, peacefully juxtaposed. Different social classes exist in Swaziland, and the divisions between the classes are seen in the elaborateness of traditional attire.

In the 1840s, European settlers arrived in Swaziland, bringing trade goods such as cloth and beads, which soon appeared in Swazi traditional dress. These things were used as additions to rather than replacements for traditional items. Through unique combinations of Western goods, the Swazis created their own fashions in ways that were original rather than imitative.

Men wear woven textiles with geometric prints that cover the lower body, and women wear similar textiles that cover both the upper and lower body. Knots hold the woven textiles together. Other items include beaded necklaces, earrings, goatskin bracelets and anklets, goatskin aprons, scarves, and loin skins. Donning traditional Swazi dress makes a strong visual statement about the strength and resilience of Swazi culture in the face of the influence of the West.

Dress continues to be one way in which Swazis maintain their traditional cultural heritage. Swazis may be observed in both rural and urban areas in wholly traditional attire or in a combination of traditional and modern dress. Traditional dress is worn for national celebrations such as the king's birthday, annual cultural events such as *umhlanga* (the Reed Dance to celebrate feminine beauty) and *incwala* (an annual male ceremony acknowledging the kingship and first fruits), and traditional wedding ceremonies. Overall, traditional attire plays an important role in maintaining cultural ties.

Documenting changes in traditional Swazi attire in response to Western fashion influences is not a straightforward matter because of Swazis' more fluid approach to time and the absence, in the past, of clocks, calendars, and written records. The history and customs of the culture, including dress, are mostly based on oral traditions. Oral transmission of cultural history and traditions has, along the way, been tweaked and customized to accommodate

Swazi male regiment at Incwala near the king's royal residence (Ludzidzini), Swaziland, in 2006. The men are wearing *sigeja* (shredded cow tails) and carrying a shield called a *lihawu*. Photograph by Phephisa Khoza. *The Times of Swaziland.*

social changes. Accordingly, the absence of written records of correct attire has resulted in modifications by each generation, which are incorporated into traditional ways of dressing.

TRADITIONAL SWAZI DRESS

Culture may be described as a context for shared meaning. It provides a perspective that allows people to make sense of the world around them. It also determines a society's way of life, whether through politics, economics, or dress. Clothing itself serves to express meanings associated with cultural categories (for example, gender and age) and is a valuable source of information. Linguistically and ritually, Swazis distinguish eight periods of individual growth from birth to death. The age-class system of the nation defines the stages of childhood, maturity, and old age for both genders.

Traditionally, Swazi infants are dressed in a string of beads until the third year of life. Between three and six years of age, gender differentiation becomes culturally conspicuous. In this patriarchal society, once a child is able, he or she is expected to fulfill certain roles in society. In contemporary Swaziland, major gender role differences still apply.

TRADITIONAL MALE DRESS

Between the ages of three and eight, little boys wear a loin skin (*lijobo*) made of goatskin. From age eight to seventeen, males continue to wear the loin skin and begin to wear a penis cap that is made of a pumpkin gourd. After age seventeen, males wear the loin skin over a woven textile (*sidvwashi*) that is rectangular and reaches from the waist to the calves. It is knotted at the side. This textile is usually dark brown or navy blue with small geometric prints. Decorative accessories include a beaded necklace (*ligcebesha*) or a strand of beads and bracelets; anklets (*siphandla*) made of goatskin, cowhide, or oxhide; and a scarf around the upper arm. Sashes (*umgaco*) made of cow or ox tails (when they are called *inkhonyane*) or beads, are worn diagonally across the upper body. The head may be adorned with a colorful feather.

Men may carry a shield whose hide denotes their age-group regiment. The regiments, usually named by the king, do not participate in military exercises, although members may learn to mock fight. As well as a shield, men can also carry a stick and/or a short wooden club with a knobbed head (knobkerrie). Such clubs were once used as weapons but are employed as accessories today.

Married men continue to wear the loin skin over the calf-length cloth and may occasionally drape over the upper torso a brightly colored rectangular length of fabric (*umhelwane*) decorated with large geometric designs. Men tend to favor dark purple, dark red, or dark orange. Older men continue to dress in this way, and elderly men may also wear a head ring (*umbhodze*) made of clay.

Royalty tend to be distinguished by their manner of dress. The king wears a headdress that resembles a lion's mane, as his title *ingwenyama* denotes. It is made of long black feathers, with a conspicuous and lengthy white tail that trails behind the feathers in imitation of a lion's tail. The crown is shaped from short

Swazi male regiment at Incwala near the king's royal residence (Ludzidzini), Swaziland, 2006. The adult male wears a *sidvwashi* (a flat printed textile) under a *lijobo* (a loin skin made of goatskin) and is adorned with neck and chest accessories made of beads and leather (*simohlwane*). Photograph by Phephisa Khoza. *The Times of Swaziland*.

black feathers with three distinct long white feathers tucked into it and several red lourie bird feathers nestled in between. His loin skin (*umdada*), worn over the calf-length fabric, is made of leopard skin. On his upper torso, a capelike garment (*sigeja*) made of shredded cow tails is worn. He carries a traditional shield supported by a stick and a battle-ax (*sizeze*). When he is not wearing the mane of black feathers, he wears the red feathers fanned across the back of his head like a crown. Depending on how directly related they are to the king, princes and chiefs will wear red feathers as well, although fewer of them.

TRADITIONAL FEMALE DRESS

From the age of three months to three years, girls wear a string of beads around their hips. Between the ages of three and eight, girls wear the string of beads and also a skirt (*luvadla*) formed of grass or strips of fabric. Girls aged eight to seventeen continue to wear the skirt, but, as they mature, a rectangular length of fabric (*sidvwashi*) reaching from the waist to the knees replaces the skirt; the fabric is knotted on either side of the waist. An even longer rectangular length of fabric (*lihiya*) covers the upper torso. It drapes diagonally over the left shoulder, around the body and under the right arm, and ties just above the left breast in an intricate knot. The knot has various traditional names such as "monkey knot" and "dog knot." The tying method of this knot is complicated, because all the ends must be hidden.

From the age of eighteen until they are married, young women wear two rectangular lengths of fabric (*sidvwashi*) that overlap each other and are knotted on either side of the waist. When it comes to the longer rectangular fabric, women tend to favor bright orange and celebratory fabrics (for example, for the king's birthday or Independence Day) bearing the king's image and the Swazi flag colors of blue, yellow, red, and white. They may wear bracelets and a beaded necklace (*ligcebesha*) or a simple strand of beads.

Newly married women wear an apron (*sidziya*) made of goatskin and a skirt (*sidvwaba*) made of tanned cowhide. To protect against chafing, an underskirt (*sidvwashi*) is worn beneath the sidvwaba. The apron is worn under the armpits and, after the birth of the first child, is raised over one shoulder. The hair of a married woman is molded into a beehive shape (*sicholo*) using a traditional mixture of animal fat and clay and then dusted with colored soil. A thin white strip woven from tree bark is worn around the hairline. When a married woman is nursing, she traditionally wears a necklace formed of short wooden beads. Older married women continue to dress in this way.

The quality and lavishness of the accessories worn convey social distinctions, although the basic elements of a married woman's traditional attire remain consistent across classes. Traditional accessories include the beaded necklace, bead or seed bracelets, and the goatskin bracelet (*siphandla*). Both single and married women may wear an anklet (*lifahlawane*) made of pupa that contains pebbles. In Swazi culture, this attire is worn not only for weddings but other cultural events and on visits to the bride's in-laws as a sign of respect for them and the community at large.

Although the basic bridal garments are the same for all social classes, their quality reflects the bride's social and economic status. If the bride is marrying the king, a prince, or a chief, she is attired in additional lavish ensembles. If the bride is of royal descent, she adds elements to her basic attire, no matter what social class she is marrying into. In addition to the basic garments, the

king's bride or a princess wears long black feathers in her hair that radiate around her beehive. Such brides also wear a sigeja.

The queen mother plays a major role in ruling the country by assisting the king. Her appearance is marked by a single red feather positioned centrally at the front of her head and supported by a row of short reeds that encircle the hairline. She dresses like a married woman but also wears a long cape made of oxhide over her traditional attire. Her appearance is consistent and hardly changes.

One major ceremony is the Reed Dance (*umhlanga*), which celebrates feminine beauty and virtue and is held annually in the spring. It lasts for a week. Swazi young women of marriageable age congregate at the queen mother's residence and set out in parties, grouped according to their age, to gather reeds at designated locations. The reeds are used to repair the fencing around the queen mother's residence. The girls wear short beaded skirts (*indlamu*) decorated with fringes and buttons, together with anklets, bracelets, necklaces, and colorful sashes and pom-poms. Each sash is formed using different-colored wool streamers; these denote whether the maiden is betrothed. A royal maiden's indlamu is longer than that worn by a nonroyal. The beading and accompanying appendages are usually more ornate as well due to her status.

To understand the basis for contemporary Swazi life, it is important to examine the practice of acculturation, or the process whereby individuals of a minority culture adopt the norms and values of a majority culture. Acculturation has been linked to colonization and religion. It is a process of continuity and change that has occurred historically and persists into modern times. The arrival of missionaries in Swaziland created ambiguities concerning Western and traditional dress. Missionaries tried to impose their own ideas of acceptable appearance. Although no specific regulations were passed prohibiting Swazis from appearing in public in traditional dress, European employers insisted upon clothes that accorded with their own dress norms.

Acculturation has not been a linear process. Swazis continue to express pride in their history and cultural traditions. Part of this pride stems from the ability of the late King Sobhuza II to hold onto his traditions while embracing social change. He was able to engage in a meticulous form of appearance management, delicately balancing cultural traditions with Western modernity. King Mswati III continues to employ this mode of dress today. When he wears a Western-style suit, he does not combine it with traditional attire; the only traditional symbol he will carry is his wooden stick. Sometimes, however, he dresses traditionally but with the addition of Western rings, a watch, and leather sandals. This type of balance is precisely the sort of interplay between cultural continuity and change, social relations, and everyday acts of dressing that needs to be understood in the context of the process of change.

Because change is intimately connected to both the past and the future, it has been noted that social change generally involves deliberate selection, which is always influenced by past experience. Some traditional customs and institutions have adjusted readily, while others have shown a resistance that is difficult to explain in terms of Western rationale. Changes in the usage of the infant string and married women's attire have occurred over the years. Dressing infants in a string is still practiced by some, even though yarn is often used in preference to beads. The wearing of traditional dress has remained for married women, albeit with modern updates.

chemically straightened hair or braids and beehive-shaped wigs of human or synthetic hair, which are easier to maintain than the traditional molded beehive. The white headband continues to be worn but is now braided of white acrylic yarns instead of tree bark. Women may add hat pins and barrettes to decorate the beehive hairstyle.

Changes in the skirt (sidvwaba) and underskirt (sidvwashi) have also occurred. The skirt is now often made of black terry cloth, and women may wear modern petticoats or half-slips under the terry cloth skirt.

The word for the goatskin apron (sidziya) is also used for another garment worn by married Swazi women. At some point in the late twentieth century, the word sidziya began to be used to describe a cut-and-sewn garment made from a woven textile (sishweshwe) that resembles a Western-style jumper or wraparound dress. In the twenty-first century, many married women wear these types of sidziya over their Western clothing during visits to in-laws as a sign of respect. The fashionable sidziya garment has style characteristics such as pockets, decorative piping, appliqué, embroidery, and other creative sewing applications. The Western-style clothing worn underneath could be a dress, blouse and skirt, or T-shirt and skirt. Any form of pants, short or long, would not be worn by married women at their in-laws' residence, because some elders discourage women from donning what they view as men's clothing and would consider pants disrespectful. The dress or skirt should reach below the knee.

The textile known as sishweshwe has a design of small repeat geometric shapes. In the last few years, it has become a fashionable item regionally, its profile having been heightened by local and other southern African designers. It is now somewhat trendy, yet still considered "traditional attire."

The rectangular upper body drape (lihiya) has become the most fashionable part of traditional Swazi women's attire. The modern lihiya is made of polyester fabric woven in floral or geometric designs, a style attributed to one of the present king's wives. These rectangular cloths come in various distinct motifs that are commonly seen on the continent at national events. In 1982, the former king celebrated his jubilee, and his image was printed on the fabric with a message commemorating the day. Similarly, the present king's image was printed on the fabric for his coronation. Other such fabrics have been produced for his twenty-first and thirtieth birthdays and for Independence Day celebrations.

The accessories worn by brides have undergone changes that may also be attributed to the impact of Western fashion. Designer fashion accessories in Swaziland, as in the West, indicate wealth and social status. Modern brides wear Western fashion accessories such as jewelry, wristwatches, and designer sunglasses with traditional bridal attire. In addition, they wear fashionable Western shoes or sandals, whereas traditionally they would not have worn any footwear.

Accessories also maintain and identify social class distinctions. Brides who marry into the royal family wear accessories indicative of their family's high social and/or economic status. As in the West, they use accessories as a sign of conspicuous consumption and to demonstrate the wealth of their families.

The changes occurring in traditional bridal dress create dilemmas for many Swazis. The use of brooches or pins instead of the traditional knot to tie the lihiya is one such example. Many elders fear the absence of the traditional knot indicates that the bride has never been taught, or simply could not master, the correct tying method. The position of the knot also concerns many

A young Swazi girl wearing a short skirt made of strips of knit fabric (luvadla), Swaziland, 2006. Traditionally, this would have been made of grass. She also is wearing a head scarf across the chest instead of a sash (umgaco). Photograph by Phephisa Khoza. *The Times of Swaziland.*

The basic married woman's attire symbolizes a shared meaning for the Swazi, bridging the past and the present. When a Swazi woman chooses to wear traditional bridal attire, she provides a degree of continuity and structure from one context to another, as well as some variety and change. In adapting non-Swazi customs and molding them to the traditions of her culture, the Swazi married woman is faced with choices and consequences that must balance the new with the maintenance of sociocultural traditions.

CHANGES IN DRESS

The changes in Swazi attire for married women reflect the influence of Western material culture. Modern married women typically wear their hair in fashionable Western styles, preferring elders. The knot traditionally resided on the right side above the breast for men and on the left side for women so that they had the freedom of movement to perform work tasks. Today, however, this distinction has become blurred; for example, men might well tie a knot on the customary women's side.

The adoption of the married woman's beehive hairstyle by unmarried women is another visual change that has occurred since the mid-1990s. Some unmarried women with children wear the beehive-shaped hairstyle with no white yarn strip. The presence or absence of the narrow white strip in the traditional hairstyle is today an important visual clue to a woman's marital status.

Overall, it would be fair to say that purely traditional attire is becoming less common for married Swazi women. Items borrowed from the West, such as synthetic print cloth and brooches, are often creatively used and juxtaposed with traditional elements, resulting in a style that is still readily identifiable as that of a married woman.

For Swazi men, there has not been much change except for the updated designs of the sidvwashi and umhelwane and the fact that more men are wearing sandals and athletic shoes that may or may not be designer brands or fashionable. Accessories include watches, bracelets, and rings.

In the twenty-first century, dress in southern Africa still includes items fashioned from local resources such as grass and animal skins. Dress often combines local materials and imported materials—for example, imported West African fabrics and designs. Fashionable Swazi dress includes imported items from Europe, Asia, Australia, and the United States. Designer garments are made locally from both imported and locally produced textiles. Some Swazi designers, such as Bongi Grey, have had clothes featured at New York Fashion Week, and others have showcased their designs nationally and regionally. In Swaziland, dress traditions from regional cultures have been reworked into high-fashion clothing and marketed across the region, the continent, and the globe.

The year 1994 enabled all South Africans to freely participate in elections. Thereafter came a transformation that impacted the country's socioeconomic structure and produced exposure to the outside world. Domestic immigration from rural to urban areas resulted in globalization and economic empowerment and transformed South Africans' culture, lifestyle, and social trends. Dramatic changes in people's wardrobes, attitudes, and appearance occurred.

Swaziland has not been immune from the trends affecting neighboring South Africa, especially the social impact on lifestyles. Fashionable Swazis have been able to keep up with new trends in dress, music, and all manner of contemporary life. Being a large, homogeneous ethnic group and having good economic ties with South Africa, Swaziland's fashionable youth is affected when trends spill across borders. Young men and women have followed these trends and reconstructed their identities in response to the world of popular culture. They are the primary consumers and producers of popular culture.

SWAZI YOUTH FASHIONS

Changes in dress may be analyzed historically or viewed through the contemporary lens of fashion. Swazi youth show evidence of changes in standards of dress; both fashion leaders and followers are aware of keeping up with accepted fashion norms. In many places, young men and women have adopted jeans and T-shirts as a staple fashion item.

Other common looks incorporate brand-name athletic shoes and fashionable accessories such as hats, caps, sunglasses, necklaces, bracelets, and rings. Body tattoos have also become common. Imitation brand-name handbags are popular with women.

Young unmarried Swazi girls at the Reed Dance (*umhlanga*) on the grounds of the king's royal residence (Ludzidzini), Swaziland, 2006. The girls wear different colored sashes (*umgaco*) to signify the region or area to which they belong. Photograph by Phephisa Khoza. *The Times of Swaziland.*

Ethnic-inspired fashions such as those common in neighboring South Africa have gained popularity among the youth, especially if the designer has high status because he or she is known to have created exclusive clothing for celebrities, including members of the royal family. Hairstyles are not immune from trends. Dreadlocks and short twists are worn by both sexes. Traditional healers have typically worn these styles and accessorized them with beads or shells. The short twists have been observed on the king and his sons during the incwala ceremony as well as on some young women at umhlanga. This look was once achieved by placing the head under a rushing waterfall as opposed to visiting a hairstylist at a salon.

By functioning as both fashion and ethnic dress, African fashion systems complicate the thorny problem of authenticity. Through a process of cultural authentication, the fashions come to symbolize ethnic identity. African fashion participates in all these modes of producing the authentic and complicates them as well, because fashion so intimately blends with and so powerfully influences bodies, selves, and identities. The notion of the authentic entangles African fashion in endless plays of paradox.

CREATING NEW IDENTITIES

The wives, known as queens (*emakhosikati*), of King Mswati III, by wearing both traditional dress and Western fashion, represent for some the national goal of reconciling the conflicting forces of change and the existing structures of power. When a queen travels outside Swaziland, she is dressed in what is considered fashionable clothing. The queens will engage a designer to construct their traveling wardrobe. Uniquely designed hats purchased from South Africa are worn during trips abroad. Lately, at royal receptions for important visitors, the queens have been observed in high-fashion, Western-style evening wear, with their hair styled in the latest manner.

When the queens are performing royal duties in their own country, they wear fashionable materials made of Asian silk and other synthetics in bright colors with floral or printed designs, as opposed to the traditional print cloth (lihiya). In recent years, the queen mother has been observed in modified Westernized ball gowns and matching capes made of modern fashion fabrics. Like her daughters-in-law, she wears jewelry, handbags, and fashionable shoes. Her hairstyle remains traditional, whereas her daughters-in-law will wear large hats or manipulate their hair into modern styles.

Traditional rites, rituals, and customs prescribe codes of social behavior through every stage of a Swazi's life and remain an integral part of life despite increasing modernization. The Swazis preserve and practice traditional customs as a reflection of their great pride in their culture, and they seek to continue to balance living in a modern society and maintaining strong ties to the past. Because change is intimately connected to both the past and the future, some traditional dress codes have adjusted readily, while others—such as the married Swazi woman's traditional attire—have not. The quality and lavishness of traditional attire, including hairstyles, headgear, and accessories, convey social distinctions and often determine the ways in which Western fashions are used. At the same time, the apparent worldwide trend toward a homogeneous style of dress is evident in regional fashions and popular culture, and its influence is especially apparent in the dress of Swazi urban youth. Continuity and change combine to create a dynamic process for Swazi traditions and culture.

References and Further Reading

Aris, Giselle. "The Power and Politics of Dress in Africa." *Undergraduate Interdisciplinary Journal of History* 4, no. 1 (2006): 1–18.

Behrman, Carolyn. "The 'Fairest of Them All': Gender, Ethnicity and a Beauty Pageant in the Kingdom of Swaziland." In *Dress and Ethnicity*, edited by J. B. Eicher, 195–206. Oxford, UK: Berg Publishers, 1999.

Diouf, M. "Engaging Postcolonial Cultures: African Youth and Public Space." *African Studies Review* 46, no. 1 (2003): 1–12.

Dolby, Nadine. "Popular Culture and Public Space in Africa: The Possibilities of Cultural Citizenship." *African Studies Review* 49, no. 3 (2007): 31–47.

Eicher, Joanne B. "Africa, Sub-Saharan: History of Dress." In *Encyclopedia of Clothing and Fashion*, edited by V. Steele, 19–27. Detroit, MI: Thomson Gale, 2005.

Forney, Judith. "Missionaries and Colonialism: How Ideologies Change in Native Dress." *ACPTC Proceedings* (1987): 129.

Khoza, Lombuso, and Laura Kidd. "Swazi Bridal Attire: Culture, Traditions and Customs." In *Wedding Dress across Cultures*, edited by Helen Foster and Donald Johnson, 93–100. Oxford, UK: Berg Publishers, 2003.

Kuper, Hilda. *An African Aristocracy: Rank among Swazi*. London: Oxford University Press, 1947.

Kuper, Hilda. *The Swazi: A South African Kingdom*. New York: Holt, Rinehart, and Winston, 1982.

Rabine, Leslie W. "Global Suitcase: The Informal African Fashion Network." In *The Global Circulation of African Fashion*, edited by Leslie W. Rabine, 1–26. Oxford, UK: Berg Publishers, 2002.

Ribane, Nakedi. *Beauty: A Black Perspective*. Scottsville, South Africa: University of KwaZulu-Natal Press, 2006.

Lombuso Khoza

Zambia

- Migration and Trade
- Royal Regalia and Ceremonial Dress
- Body Modifications and Accessories
- Rites of Passage

Zambia (previously Northern Rhodesia) has a complex history of dress that reflects past migrations, vibrant interactions with international peoples, and a creative desire to register style and social status. The significance of dress has been incorporated into language, and a Bemba person might greet a female friend by saying, "*Mwafwalukeni!*" which on one level means "Hello" but at the same time acknowledges that the friend is wearing a new dress.

Zambia is a landlocked country surrounded by Botswana, Zimbabwe, Mozambique, Malawi, Tanzania, Democratic Republic of Congo, and Angola. There are over seventy sociolinguistic groups in Zambia. Due to continued cross-border interactions with these countries, as well as historical migration and trade, there are numerous different styles of dress in Zambia that have creatively incorporated desirable designs and materials from elsewhere. As such, there is no single national Zambian dress but rather a rich array of styles that reflects Zambia's history of movement. Further, while people might talk of traditional or ceremonial dress, it is important to realize that even "traditional" Zambian dress consists of an assemblage of both local and foreign styles. In fact, many materials or designs that might once have been considered to be foreign have, indeed, become Zambian.

MIGRATION AND TRADE

Zambia's history is marked by migration, and naturally the movement of people results in the spreading of many types of dress. Numerous Zambian peoples are believed to have migrated from the Lunda and Luba chiefdoms in what is now Democratic Republic of Congo, and similarities can therefore be seen in some of their traditions of dress. Others, such as the Ngoni, traveled northward from South Africa, and today, they maintain the symbol of the Zulu warrior's shield, spear, and knobkerrie (stick with a round knob). During the first fruits festival, the Ngoni paramount chief, Mpezeni, wears a lion-skin robe. His warriors wear an array of animal skins hanging from their waists and attach bells to their ankles that make a loud, rhythmic noise as they perform the Ngoma dance.

Those who migrated to and settled in Zambia were further exposed to outside styles of dress through trade that reached even the most remote areas of the country. During the eighteenth and nineteenth centuries, the Portuguese attempted to join their west and east coast trading posts by providing the inland Lunda-Kazembe people and their leader, Mwata Kazembe, with cloth and beads. The Portuguese were surprised by the cosmopolitan flair displayed by the Lunda-Kazembe, whose keen interest in

Mwata Kazembe XIX wears a large cotton skirt when he performs the Mutomboko dance in Mwansabombwe, Luapula province, Zambia, 2004. The skirt is made from roughly eighty-two feet (twenty-five meters) of cotton cloth that bunches up at the front in a red rosette. As he waves a sword and axe, his performance alludes to the migration of the Lunda-Kazembe people from what is now Democratic Republic of Congo. Photograph by Ruth Kerkham Simbao.

cloth resulted in the investiture of chiefs being referred to as *ukufwika*, meaning "to dress." Even today, the importance of cloth is registered in the ceremonial dress of Mwata Kazembe, which consists of an enormous skirt made from twenty-five meters (eighty-two feet) of cotton cloth that bunches up at the front in a large, red rosette. Less senior Lunda chiefs may wear similar skirts, but the length of cotton is necessarily less, because abundance suggests status and power and is reserved for high-ranking chiefs.

Trade cloth quickly became very popular in central Africa, including parts of Zambia, as it replaced previously worn bark-cloth garments that were laborious to make. The Bemba have a saying that emphasizes the long process of making bark cloth (*ciombo*): "It is not the bark cloth being beaten that gets tired; it is the one beating the bark who gets tired." The thick bark cloth that was used in winter was called *cikungu*, which is why the coldest time of the year is known as *cikungu lupepo*. Imported cloth was not only worn but also acted as cash, and, in 1880, the Portuguese trader Silva Pinto claimed that cloth had become the "gold" of central Africa.

Besides cloth, beads and *impande* (round disks made from the spiraled end of seashells) were brought to Zambia by Portuguese and Swahili traders. The impande disks that came from the Indian Ocean became very valuable, particularly among the Ila, Tonga, Soli, Tabwa, and Mambwe, and were mostly worn by chiefs, rainmakers, and traditional healers. They were hung around the neck, strapped to the forehead, or worn just above the temples. Some Tonga mothers would wear them suspended at the back of their necks as a form of protection for carrying their babies on their backs, and today, Soli *moye* (girl initiates) sometimes wear impande at the back of their necks when they dress up for their coming-out ceremony. These impande are attached to brightly colored beaded neckbands (*nsabi*) or are worn on top of the head attached to a beaded veil (*myompwe*), signifying the fertility of the newly trained initiates.

When the nineteenth-century Portuguese traders realized how popular impande shells were, they produced ceramic and porcelain disks in India, The Netherlands, and Czechoslovakia as substitutes. However, the British colonial government discouraged their use because they were believed to have certain ritual powers, and instead they issued chiefs with their own badges of authority.

When the British introduced taxes, people were forced into labor migration. The Copperbelt became a vibrant urban hub, and migrant laborers brought with them various styles of both dance and dress. In the 1930s, the *mbeni* dance from Tanzania was being performed on the Copperbelt. Based on the notion of military drill, smart dressing, cleanliness, and discipline were key characteristics of this dance. Similarly, the *kalela* dance, which spread to the Copperbelt with the movement of Bisa people from Luapula province, expressed the necessity of meticulous dress in an urban setting, where people worked as clerks, doctors, and nurses. Male dancers would dress in well-pressed slacks and polished shoes and would carry white handkerchiefs in their hands. (This seems to anticipate the trademark white handkerchief that Zambia's first president, Kenneth Kaunda, always had in his breast pocket or in his hand.) A female nurse character would also dance with a handkerchief, using it to wipe the sweaty brows of the male dancers. As theater historian Albert Matongo has suggested, the Western style of dress worn by kalela dancers did not indicate an attempt to be European, but rather reflected the urban situation of the Copperbelt, where people dressed appropriately for their jobs.

ROYAL REGALIA AND CEREMONIAL DRESS

Certain forms of European dress became so integrated into Zambian styles that they ceased to be viewed as foreign. An example of this is the British admiral's uniform worn by the Lozi king (*litunga*). In 1902, Lewanika attended the coronation of Edward VII in England, where he acquired a royal coach, an admiral's uniform, and scarlet coats for his servants. Rather than seen as a foreign import, the uniform is viewed as Lozi royal regalia and has become a signifier of the Lozi chiefdom. Similarly, Lozi women's "traditional" outfits (*misisi*), which consist of many layers of brightly colored skirts and a blouse, is based on the style worn by Victorian missionaries. Interestingly, the Leya people who live near Victoria Falls have also adopted this outfit and claim that it is traditional Leya dress that was worn before the Lozi people came to this region.

Some royal dress in Zambia consists merely of red or black cotton robes in the style of graduation gowns that were provided by the British colonialists. Such dress was usually accompanied by a brass scepter, a medal, and a fly whisk. The colonialists failed to understand that certain societies were not organized as chiefdoms with hierarchical structures of chiefs and subchiefs, but rather were led by clusters of headmen and headwomen. Due to this misunderstanding, colonial officials invented the notion of chiefs and royal regalia for people such as the Tonga. In the early twenty-first century the ceremonial garb of the Gwembe-Tonga leader, Chief Simamba, simply consists of a black cotton gown, a colonial-style pith helmet, and a fly whisk.

Other people in Zambia, such as the Lunda and the Luvale, have long histories of regalia that can be traced back to Democratic Republic of Congo and Angola. The Lunda-Kazembe, for example, have various beaded royal crowns that reflect their historical relationship to the Luba-Lunda complex. Incorporated in these crowns are various protective substances related to powerful animals such as the elephant and the striped weasel. Lunda and Luvale chiefs often cover their thrones with leopard skins,

An *impande* disk on a headdress, worn by Joseph Chooka, Zambia, 2004, at the Tonga Lwiindi ceremony at Gonde, Southern province. *Impande* disks are made from the spiraled end of seashells and are worn by chiefs, headmen, ritual specialists, and traditional healers. Photograph by Ruth Kerkham Simbao.

and, when Mwata Kazembe sits on his throne, he rests his feet on a lion skin. Although many traditional leaders such as the Lunda, Luvale, Chewa, Ngoni, and Leya chiefs consider leopards and lions to be incredibly powerful signifiers of royalty, the Lozi litunga disassociates himself from predatory animals with claws, because he believes that he is protected by his people and does not need symbols of weaponry. Instead, he associates himself with the nonpredatory elephant and carries a fly whisk made from rhino horn. His warriors, however, wear berets topped with tufts of lion mane and hang the pelts of various cats around their waists in a gesture of willingness to protect their chief.

Certain royal associations with animals reflect not only the particular characteristics of animals, such as speed and power, but also royal clan names. For example, the related Lenje and Soli leaders, Chief Mukuni and Chieftainess Nkomeshya, belong to the clan of the cow (*Bena Ngombe*). Nkomeshya's ceremonial cotton robe is printed with the black and white marks of a cow, and Mukuni wears a beaded crown with actual cow horns attached to it. The Leya chief Mukuni is related to the Lenje Mukuni, but historically, this ruler migrated further south from where the Lenje settled and ended up near Victoria Falls. There he met the woman ruler, Bedyango, who was originally from the Rozwi chiefdom in what is today Zimbabwe. Although the Leya Mukuni, like the Lenje Mukuni, used to be associated with the symbol of the cow, he adopted the symbol of the lion of the Rozwi chiefdom when he and Bedyango decided to co-rule the Leya people. Today, the

Leya reenact the original meeting of Mukuni and Bedyango during the annual Lwiindi ceremony. In this ceremony, Bedyango cloaks Mukuni with a lion skin, announcing that, "Now your roar will be loud like the roar of the Victoria Falls."

Although the adornment of the human body is not restricted to royalty, great quantities of cloth, beads, and other forms of adornment are usually associated with wealth and chiefs. However, there are two sides to such abundance: not only does it indicate power, but it can also be viewed as a burden. For example, in the nineteenth century, Bemba chiefs wore heavy rings on their legs and heavy strings of beads across their chests, and their wives wore metal leg rings that affected their stride. Although these rings might have looked extravagantly beautiful, it is also believed that their weight prevented people from running away. While restrictions placed on chiefs are often reflected in dress and regalia, today, chiefs reserve their grand and often encumbering dress for ceremonial functions.

In contemporary Zambia, many people participate in annual ceremonies that recall, revise, and celebrate their histories of migration, as well as their inherited and adopted customs and cultural practices. During these ceremonies, which amount to over sixty, chiefs parade before their people in ceremonial dress, and dancers, musicians, and ritual specialists don traditional outfits and body adornment. Organizing committees run fundraisers in Lusaka and the Copperbelt, where urban professionals enjoy the opportunity to wear the traditional dress of their specific ethnic groups. Of course, some attendees, such as spouses and friends, might not belong to that particular ethnic group but still dress up accordingly. Similarly, politicians who travel to annual ceremonies as a gesture of political diplomacy sometimes wear the attire of an ethnic group to which they do not belong. For example, in 2004, President Mwanawasa, who is Ila, danced at the Ngoni *Nc'wala* ceremony with an Ngoni shield and knobkerrie, and former vice president Nevers Mumba, who is Bemba, attended the Lozi *Kuomboka* ceremony in traditional Lozi dress. As such, the wearing of traditional dress today in Zambia can be seen as a strategy rather than a straightforward symbol of heritage. This fluidity of style reflects the fact that, even historically, fashions would come and go according to the tastes of not only chiefs, but also everyday people in both urban and rural areas.

BODY MODIFICATIONS AND ACCESSORIES

Ordinary people in Zambia express interest in decorating their bodies with beads, shells, and body paint or altering their bodies through the sculpting of hair, the filing of teeth, and the decorative scarring of skin. At times, such adornment is done simply for aesthetic pleasure, but it can also serve various practical, social, ritual, or spiritual functions. Many of these examples are no longer common today and are seen only during ceremonial occasions such as annual festivals, inaugurations, weddings, or initiations.

Beads have been worn by both males and females—sometimes from a very young age. As soon as an infant's navel cord had dropped off, the nineteenth-century Lamba would support the baby's neck with a bark-cloth collar (*iciponje*). In the early twentieth century, the collar was made from fabric and would sometimes be decorated with beads. When a baby was able to sit, beads would be placed around his or her waist. Young Tonga children would also wear strings of beads around their waists or wrists, and older women would drape their hips with many

On ceremonial occasions, Senior Chief Mukuni of the Lenje people wears a beaded cow-horn crown as well as an *impande* disk around his neck. Lenje Kulamba ku Bwalo ceremony at Chibombo, Central province, Zambia, 2004. Photograph by Ruth Kerkham Simbao.

strings of small beads beneath their skirts. They would also wear round carrying pads made from cowry shells on their heads, tied into their hair.

Today, most women use small plastic beads, but in the past, beads were often made from seeds. Bemba women used to wear seed beads around their necks, foreheads, and hips or in the form of a girdle. Even in urban areas today, some women wear strings of beads around their waists, but strict codes of modesty deem it inappropriate for anyone except one's husband to see them.

At times, bells are worn to attract attention through sound. On festive occasions, Ila women used to wear a palm leaf belt that was decorated with white and blue beads and little iron bells. They would also wear bracelets around their arms, which were usually made from brass or copper or from ivory if the woman were married to a chief. Completing the ceremonial outfit would be a beaded neck collar (*inkonde*), a row of beads around her head, an impande shell hanging around her neck, and a ceremonial hoe carried in her hands. At times, a small medicinal horn would hang around a woman's body for protection. The Ila draw a distinction between *kusama* (to clothe) and *kusakila* (to adorn themselves). Objects that are entirely ornamental are called *inkwela*, while *misamo* are objects used for medicine, *shabwami* are objects of regalia indicating authority, and *shalumamba* are objects used for war.

Ila men were famous for their distinct, elaborate hairstyles. To mark a boy's emergence from childhood, he would grow his hair, gather it into a cone shape held together with wax and clay, and the rest of his head would be shaved. In the late nineteenth and early twentieth centuries, this cone (*impumbe*) was decorated with brass furniture tacks purchased from traders. Adult men sometimes wore the impumbe, but, when work in the fields was finished and there was a break before the harvest, they would turn the impumbe into the elaborate *isusu*, which reached an astounding three feet and ten inches (over one meter) high. The process was long and painful and could take a month to complete. The man would have to collect lots of hair, which would be stitched into a very tall, narrow cone on top of his head. Halfway up, the hairdresser would introduce a slender strip of delicately pared sable antelope horn that was tapered to a very fine point. The isusu had to be supported by a wooden pillow at night, and the tip was attached to the roof of the house so that the man could turn his head. Obviously, such a hairstyle could only be worn during times of leisure, and, after two or three months, the man would either go back to the shorter impumbe or would clip diamond, square, or triangular patterns into short hair. Lamba men also used to wear elaborate hairstyles. Sometimes a visor shape would be sculpted above the forehead, or two horns of hair would stand on top of the head, one in front of the other.

At times, more permanent modifications were made to the body. In the past, the Lamba and Chokwe considered it fashionable to file their teeth into "crocodile teeth." The Lamba believed that at night whole teeth would go out and eat dung, whereas filed teeth would eat mealie (cornmeal). Similarly, many people including the Bemba, Tonga, and Ila would knock out some of their top teeth. For the Bemba, a gap between the front upper teeth was considered to be beautiful, and, if an Ila youngster maintained his teeth, his friends would mock him saying, "Beware, the zebra bites." Some people suggest that the Tonga knocked out their front teeth to resemble their cattle, and others say it was to prevent the teeth from running away at night and eating offal, which created bad breath.

A man with an Ila hairstyle (*isusu*) that was worn in Zambia until the early twentieth century. A slender strip of sable antelope horn is woven into the top part of the nearly four-foot- (just over one-meter-) high cone. This man also wears *impande* disks around his neck and on top of his head. From Edwin W. Smith and Andrew Murray Dale, *The Ila-Speaking Peoples of Northern Rhodesia*, 1920. Courtesy of Ruth Kerkham Simbao.

Another Tonga form of facial modification was the nose plug (*cisita*), which consisted of a thin thorn pushed through the middle nasal cartilage that was later replaced by larger reeds. Bisa women would also pierce this cartilage, and sometimes, they would hang little strings of beads from their noses. Nsenga women would pierce the nostril and plug it with a tiny disk of wood or tin. They would also wear wooden disks in their upper lips and tattoo an inverted crescent between their eyebrows.

The Lamba have three categories of scarification: hunting medicine placed in incisions on a hunter's hand, general medicine inserted into cuts on various parts of the body, and incisions made for personal adornment. Some were produced for visual or tactile pleasure by rubbing charcoal and soot into incisions, and others served medicinal or ritual functions. Lamba men would scarify their chests, upper arms, and backs, and women would create lines between their breasts and navels.

Some Tabwa women had scarification patterns known as *kondenge* around their navels. The term for this pattern comes from the word *kulenga*, "to create," suggesting a concern with fertility and reproduction. Similarly, the Tabwa sometimes created keloids on their backs that formed circles, representing the impande disk. For the Tabwa, the impande was a lunar symbol, and the spiral on the inside of the disk represented kinship and the mythological origins of humans.

Often it was not the individual patterns that had meanings but rather the areas of the body being tattooed that suggested certain ideas. Particular parts of the body are kept very private due to their erotic associations, and Luvale female initiates were tattooed over the pubic area, around the waist, and just above the buttocks for erotic pleasure. Ila women would also have their highly private pubic areas and inner thighs tattooed.

RITES OF PASSAGE

Various forms of body art and dress are used to mark rites of passage such as initiation, marriage, the passing into the spirit world, or the temporary return of ancestral spirits. Youngsters who are initiated are often covered with body paint. When Bemba girls go through the *cisungu* initiation ceremony, they are covered with white powder (*impemba*) that is ground from white clay, whereas Tonga girls are adorned with a reddish brown ochre. In the past, when a young Tonga girl was to be married, a relative would daub ochre on her shoulder, announcing the girl's impending marriage. Soli initiates are covered with red clay, and today, red floor polish is used. The bodies of Luvale girl initiates are painted with the patterns of the knitted body suits that are worn by the *makishi* masquerade figures believed to be spirits of the ancestors. Interestingly, the masked makishi are strictly performed by men only,

Masked *makishi* figures in the Luvale Likumbi lya Mize ceremony, Zambezi district, Northwestern province, Zambia, 2004. *Makishi* are believed to be ancestral spirits that emerge from the graveyard during the ceremony. They are associated with boys' circumcision. The figures are performed by Mbunda, Chokwe, and other related peoples. Photograph by Ruth Kerkham Simbao.

but, during initiation, the girls are sometimes referred to as makishi even though they are not masked and only wear body paint alluding to the masquerade costumes.

Initiations always end with a coming-out ceremony, where the initiates are presented to the community as young adults. Dress is a very significant aspect of this ceremony, and new clothes symbolize the new phase of life that initiates enter. When a Soli initiate is presented to the community, she is neatly dressed in a new *citenge* (cloth wrap with bright printed patterns) and a newly acquired wristwatch. Over her citenge, she wears a skirt made from pieces of bamboo and bottle tops that make an incredibly loud sound when she performs her energetic dances. Ankle rattles (*nsense*) made from seed pods filled with little pebbles add to the noise that the initiate makes. The emphasis on noisy attire that is animated through vigorous, celebratory dance is particularly interesting, because, throughout her initiation, the *moye* is taught that it is well mannered to be quiet in terms of both one's voice and one's actions. She is taught never to make eye contact with an elder and wears a beaded veil (*myompwe*) that covers her eyes. However, when she dances at the coming-out ceremony, her movements are so vibrant that the veil swings away from her face.

Another transition that is marked by dress is death. While Lamba relatives in mourning shave their heads, other people such as the Bemba and Ila might leave their hair uncut for a certain period of time after a funeral. Chiefs who die are often buried with certain objects of regalia such as crowns or thrones. Similarly, certain makishi performers are buried with their masquerade costumes unless these objects had already been burned at the end of a performance. The strange sounds that makishi often make indicate that these creatures are not just humans, but are ancestral spirits. Similarly, the Chewa *nyau* masqueraders also make strange noises and wear masks and costumes that identify them as spirits of animals, humans, or mythological figures. The antelope masks only come out at night and are usually associated with the death of a chief. Other animal costumes represent elephants, tortoises, giraffes, zebras, and dogs.

The masks and costumes that represent humans reflect the interaction that the Zambian Chewa have had with many other people, such as Arabs, Portuguese, and white South African farmers. The masquerade figure Maria, also referred to as Dona (from the Portuguese word for lady), reveals an interesting combination of past customs and new innovations. Her wooden face piece combines both traditional scarification that is no longer used and modern, bright red lipstick. Many other nyau masquerade figures reveal this fluid incorporation of the old and the new. Although many face masks are handcrafted from wood, fabric, or sponge, some recent ones simply consist of plastic or rubber Halloween-type masks that are bought in shops. Other full body masks represent modern amenities such as cars, motorbikes, or helicopters.

The incorporation of modern styles into traditional masquerade is significant, because it reflects the ease with which Zambians have always created innovative fashions to suit new tastes and creative expressions. Today, Zambians might proudly talk of traditional dress in the context of cultural ceremonies, but, on a daily basis, they wear Western-styled clothes either found at *salaula* (secondhand clothing) stores or the South African–styled malls in Lusaka. The term *salaula* refers to the action of picking clothes from a pile and has been in use since the mid-1980s.

Soli initiates (*moye*) in Nkomeshya village, Lusaka province, Zambia, 2005, wear beaded veils when they dance at the coming-out ceremony after their confinement. Sometimes an *impande* is attached to the top of the head or to the back of the beaded neckband, as seen here. Photograph by Ruth Kerkham Simbao.

Anthropologist Karen Tranberg Hansen has discussed the incorporation of imported secondhand clothing into the Zambian market and argued that, even though many of these clothes come from Western countries, Zambians are not simply mimicking Western styles, because "clothes are not worn passively but require people's active collaboration." Today, items of salaula can be mixed with new clothes and can even be incorporated into traditional dress.

Although young women wear jeans and slacks, older women still consider pants to be inappropriate and expect girls to wrap a citenge cloth over their pants or skirts. In many ways, the citenge has become the one style that could be considered national, because it is not associated with one particular ethnic group. Although the citenge cloth is often manufactured in China, it is bought by tourists as a symbol of authentic Zambian dress, and even Zambians view it as traditional dress, wearing it to weddings and kitchen parties. Dress in Zambia, used for both ceremonial and practical purposes, is fluid in its meaning and persists in creatively reflecting desires for new fashions and styles.

References and Further Reading

Cameron, Elisabeth, L. "Women = Masks: Initiation Arts in Northwestern Province, Zambia." *African Arts* 31, no. 2 (1998): 50–61.

Colson, Elizabeth. *Social Organization of the Gwembe Tonga.* Manchester, UK: Manchester University Press, published on behalf of the Rhodes-Livingstone Institute of Northern Rhodesia, 1960.

Cunnison, Ian. *The Luapula Peoples of Northern Rhodesia.* Manchester, UK: Rhodes-Livingstone Institute and Manchester University Press, 1959.

Doke, Clement M. *The Lambas of Northern Rhodesia: A Study of Their Customs and Beliefs.* London: George G. Harrap, 1931.

Felix, Marc Leo, and Manuel Jordán. *Makishi lya Zambia: Mask Characters of the Upper Zambezi Peoples.* Munich: Fred Jahn, 1998.

Hansen, Karen Tranberg. *Salaula: The World of Secondhand Clothing and Zambia.* Chicago: University of Chicago Press, 2000.

Kalaluka, Likando. *Kuomboka: A Living Traditional Culture among the Malozi People of Zambia.* Lusaka: National Educational Company of Zambia, 1979.

Matongo, Albert B. K. "Popular Culture in a Colonial Society: Another Look at Mbeni and Kalela Dances on the Copperbelt, 1930–1963." In *Guardians in Their Time: Experiences of Zambians under Colonial Rule, 1890–1964,* edited by Samuel N. Chipungu, 180–217. London: Macmillan Press, 1992.

Roberts, Allen F. *Animals in African Art: From the Familiar to the Marvelous.* Munich: Prestel, 1995.

Roberts, Andrew. *A History of Zambia.* New York: Africana Publishing Company, 1976.

Simbao, Ruth Kerkham. "A Crown on the Move: Stylistic Integration of the Luba-Lunda Complex in Lunda-Kazembe Performance." *African Arts* 39, no. 3 (2006): 26–41.

Smith, Edwin W., and Andrew Murray Dale. *The Ila-Speaking Peoples of Northern Rhodesia.* Vols. 1 and 2. London: Macmillan, 1920.

Ruth Kerkham Simbao

See also Republic of Congo and Democratic Republic of Congo; Angola; Malawi; South Africa Overview; Nguni, Zulu, and Xhosa Dress and Beadwork.

Zimbabwe

Ndau (Shona) diviner/herbalist Dr. Mabvongere in Mabvongere village, wearing a twisted bark-fiber hat in Garwe Chieftaincy area, Zimbabwe, 1994. Photograph by William J. Dewey.

Zimbabwe (formerly Southern Rhodesia) has an ethnic mix composed of the Shona-speaking peoples, with about 80 percent of the population; the Ndebele, with approximately 12 percent; and the Tonga people, with perhaps another 2 percent. Each group has variations in dress. Smaller communities found around the periphery of Zimbabwe are related to much larger ethnic groups in neighboring countries. These include the Venda, Sotho, and Kalanga in the south and southwest; the Barwe Tonga, Tavara, and Chikunda in the northeast; and the Hlengwe of the southeast, who are related to the Tsonga of Mozambique and South Africa. Some of the subgroups of the Shona, such as the Manyika and Ndau, extend into Mozambique, and many Tonga also live north of the Zambezi River in Zambia.

ANCIENT FORMS OF DRESS

San peoples once occupied much of Zimbabwe and left paintings on many of the rock shelters and outcroppings that can be seen around the countryside. Direct dating of the rock paintings is very difficult, but archaeological excavations of late Stone Age deposits suggest that some of the paintings could have been painted as many as thirteen thousand years ago. There is no evidence of any depictions of the Iron Age practices such as agriculture, metalwork, or pottery, which came to the area approximately two thousand years ago, and so most scholars feel this is the latest date these rock paintings could have been done. Unlike the case in neighboring Botswana, there are no living populations of San people in Zimbabwe, and so their paintings provide the main evidence of what these ancient people wore and how they ornamented themselves.

Men (the hunters) are usually depicted nude and carrying bows and arrows and narrow shoulder bags. Women (the gatherers) are depicted with animal-skin aprons over their buttocks and fronts. Their digging sticks, capes, and large collecting bags are also frequently depicted. Ornamentation of the body and hair is indicated, and archaeologist Peter Garlake has proposed that some images with body painting and wearing of tufts of hair and

tails depict men performing dances to imitate antelopes such as the sable to tap into their supernatural potency. Other objects attached to, or emanating from, the peoples' bodies are more ambiguous. Lines across men's penises and leaf, disk, comb, and tusk shapes emerging from various parts of men's bodies have been interpreted by Garlake as not depicting real ornaments but instead representing the supernatural potency that at times was associated with trance and healing ceremonies.

EARLY BANTU-SPEAKING PEOPLE AND THE KINGDOMS OF ZIMBABWE

Early forms of dress by the Bantu-speaking people who came into the Zimbabwe region approximately two thousand years ago are, unfortunately, difficult to visualize. Some small anthropomorphic terra-cotta figurines with dates ranging from the third to the fifteenth centuries C.E. have been found, especially in the southern half of the country, but they usually consist of very rudimentary heads or female torsos. What appear to be cicatrization patterns on the head and various parts of the body are often depicted on women's torsos, and so it is assumed that this was an ancient practice.

Aside from these small figures, there was almost no figurative art made in Zimbabwe until relatively recent times, and so we must rely on archaeological excavations and the observations of Europeans (beginning with the Portuguese in the sixteenth century) to reconstruct early Zimbabwean forms of dress. The archaeological sites of Mapungubwe, Great Zimbabwe, and Kame, dating from the twelfth through seventeenth centuries, and their many related smaller sites scattered throughout Zimbabwe, all have produced extensive finds of copper and copper alloy necklaces, bracelets, rings, bangles, and beads. Necklaces made of strips of copper wound over an organic core are prominent in much of the archaeological remains. Beads were made of local materials such as ostrich eggshell and mussel shells, and glass beads of foreign origin were also found. These latter came through the external trade conducted with the Swahili traders of the east coast of Africa (directly or through intermediaries), and recent chemical analysis of the beads has shown that eighth- and ninth-century beads probably originated in Iran; from the thirteenth century on, the most likely origin of imported beads was Rajasthan, India.

The Portuguese who observed Zimbabwean people in the sixteenth and seventeenth centuries noted that people wore both animal skins and locally woven cloth. They also observed that the rulers (such as those of the Mutapa kingdom) wore wrappers extending from their waist to their feet, with another cloth draped over their shoulders as a cloak. This mode of dress was similar to that worn by the coastal Muslim Swahili, and the material was often of expensive imported silks, damasks, and satins. Sometimes the clothes were so long that they dragged along the ground and quickly wore away in an overt display of conspicuous consumption. Locally made copper, gold, and shell beads and necklaces were observed being worn along with conus-shell spiral disks (soon copied in porcelain by the Portuguese for sale) and imported glass beads.

The history of cloth production and usage is not well known in the Zimbabwe area. Cloth does not often survive in the archaeological contexts of southern Africa, with the exception of small fragments that are preserved when they are in contact with iron or copper. A few such samples exist for sites in the Zimbabwe area, and, although some of these may have been of imported cloth, there is strong evidence that other pieces were locally woven. No such cloth fragments have been recovered from Great Zimbabwe, but indirect evidence of the making of cloth here is provided by the numerous ceramic spindle whorls that have been found at this site and many others throughout Zimbabwe. The Portuguese noted that local weaving with cotton was done on a low, horizontal, fixed-heddle loom, but the process was so time-consuming that probably only the wealthiest of patrons could afford it. A few photographs from the around the turn of the twentieth century show men weaving in areas of northeastern Zimbabwe, and historian Aviton Ruwitah has reported that some cloth was woven in this area for ritual use as late as the 1970s. For the most part, however, weaving is a long-forgotten craft in Zimbabwe.

NINETEENTH- AND TWENTIETH-CENTURY DRESS IN ZIMBABWE

Casual observers of Zimbabwean culture would be hard pressed to identify anything that can be called typically Zimbabwean dress. Western clothes, and occasionally East or West African outfits (especially for ceremonial or government functions), are now the norm. But there are some vestiges of what were once quite common forms of dress.

A Shona woman, Musodzi Mucheka, with the *gudza* (finger-woven bark cloth) blanket she made as a young woman. Photographed in Zimunya, Zimbabwe, 1984. Photograph by William J. Dewey.

The Zimbabwe Ndebele (a different people from the Ndebele of South Africa) established themselves in the southwestern part of the country in the 1840s after migrating earlier in that century from the Zululand area of South Africa. This, and many other such migrations, was the result of considerable intergroup clashes (with other Nguni-speaking groups) and external conflict (such as with the Dutch descendant Afrikaners) that started at the beginning of the nineteenth century. Several militaristic states such as the Ndebele came into being at this time. As the Ndebele moved north, they defeated and incorporated many other peoples such as the Sotho, Tswana, Nyai, and Kalanga, and then on arrival, some of the southwestern Shona peoples. The class structure of the Ndebele state reflected this history, with those descending from the original Nguni people having the highest status and holding the important offices in the nation. Those peoples incorporated on the journey north were second in status, and the conquered Shona peoples were considered subordinate to the others. These differences were important during the nineteenth century and were certainly reflected in patterns of dress. With the defeat of the Ndebele by the occupying British South Africa Company forces, however, and the flight of King Lobengula at the close of the century, the Ndebele state came to an end, and these status differences diminished.

Ndebele dress (especially the military outfits of the warriors) was very similar to that of the Zulu of South Africa when Westerners first observed the Ndebele in the 1870s. The minimum acceptable amount of clothing for men was a woven fiber penis sheath, but most boys and men also wore aprons made of animal skins. Military dress consisted of kilts made of monkey and wildcat tails and headdresses, capes, and elbow and knee ornaments, all of ostrich and guinea fowl feathers. A large distinctive leather shield and assegai or stabbing spear completed the ensemble. Mature and distinguished men were given permission by the king to wear head rings interwoven into their hair. Women wore front and back aprons of leather, and, for married women, a piece of leather covered the breasts. Glass beads, seeds, brass buttons, and bead-covered rope ornaments embellished the ankles, waist, arms, neck, and head.

Western dress was making inroads even in the time of the last king, Lobengula, as illustrated in an 1870 drawing by artist Thomas Baines in which the king is wearing a fur-strip kilt and a European shirt and hat. Traditional dress is rarely seen today, but some are trying to revive it. The controversial singer and dancer Sandra Ndebele, of the Amakhosi Arts Centre in Bulawayo, wears the traditional short beaded skirt of unmarried Ndebele women while performing her provocative dances. She feels she has a positive role to play in the fight against HIV and AIDS and has told Steve Vickers of the BBC, "Our culture is going down the drain, and I'm trying to revitalize it."

While there are larger populations of Tonga people living in Zambia, the Gwembe or Valley Tonga who live along the northwestern portion of the Zambezi River form an important minority group of Zimbabwe. A matrilineal people with no system of chiefs (until imposed upon them by colonial forces), they have long participated over the centuries in trade with their more powerful neighbors but, because of their remote location, have largely been outside their control or influence. The construction of the Kariba Dam and subsequent creation of Lake Kariba in the 1950s and 1960s have had a devastating effect on the Tonga. Whereas before they were self-sufficient with fishing and farming activities in the rich alluvial soils beside the Zambezi, the dam construction forced them to be relocated to higher unfertile, desolate land, and they are now among the most impoverished of all Zimbabwean populations.

Cicatrization on the face, torso, and limbs used to be common, especially on women, and was usually done at puberty. Formerly, the upper six front teeth of both men and women were knocked out at puberty, but this practice has mostly been abandoned. A nose plug was also inserted through the pierced septum of both men and women, but, again, this practice has mostly been discontinued. The nineteenth century missionary, Dr. David Livingstone, described the Tonga as the *Baenda Pezi* (or "Go Nakeds") and thought that all they wore was a coating of red ochre and oil. Men long ago abandoned this custom in favor of Western garb, and women don the ochre nowadays only for rituals such as first menstruation. Female initiates also put a circle of cowry shells on their hair, a special beaded cord is worn across their chests, and veils of strings of beads (formerly ochred fibers) cover their faces.

Both men and women formerly wore a variety of beaded ornaments, but men only wear them in the twenty-first century for dance rituals. An antelope tail affixed to a wire frame that projects vertically above the man's head is also worn on these occasions. Women once wore short fiber aprons and skirts, but,

more recently, black or dark blue cloth equivalents became more popular. These outfits are still worn for dances (such as funerals), but Western wear has largely taken over. Red, white, and blue are the favorite colors for beadwork ornamentation, with common designs including checkerboards and zigzags. The most distinctively Tongan beadwork decoration is the fan shape.

BARK CLOTH

In addition to the locally woven cotton cloth previously described, the Shona peoples made a unique type of bark cloth. This bark cloth is not of beaten manufacture (as, for example, is still commonly made by the Ganda people of Uganda); instead, it is made of twisted bark fibers that are finger woven into the desired form. A few elderly Shona women still remember how to make the bark cloth, and some craft cooperatives (especially in the Nyanga area) make the cloth into rugs and hats for the tourist market. Aside from this, however, the tradition seems to be dying out and now has few uses by the Shona apart from a few spirit mediums among the eastern Shona who still wear fringed bark-cloth hats.

Such bark-cloth objects are known as *gudza* among most of the Shona-speaking peoples. While previously finger-woven gudza was apparently made in all Shona-speaking areas, since the 1950s, it has continued to be made primarily in the Manyika- and Ndau-speaking areas. Finger-woven bark cloth is probably a much more ancient technique than cotton weaving, but no remains have been found archaeologically, undoubtedly because it disintegrates even more quickly than cotton. The first written descriptions of this type of bark cloth are by British prospectors, hunters, explorers, and missionaries who started coming to the area at the end of the nineteenth century. Theodore Bent, an archaeologist for example, has described how "it was the season just then [probably July] in which they frequent the forests—the 'barking season,' when they go forth to collect large quantities of the bark of certain trees.... They weave textiles out of bark, they make bags and string out of bark."

Women's skirts or aprons were also made of bark fiber. Bent collected an example in "Kunzi's country" that he described as "a dexterously wrought garment for a young lady, about half the size of a freemason's apron; it is made of bark fibre, with geometrical patterns of excellent design worked into it." A type of hat that was made of bark fiber continues to be made. It is close fitting, almost like a wig or stocking cap, and is covered with long twisted bark-fiber strands, often colored with red ochre. This type of ritual headwear was said to be very old, but the earliest photograph seems to be one taken by Leo Frobenius an ethnologist, during his 1928–1930 expedition to Zimbabwe. He labeled the man wearing such a hat an "Inyanga rain priest." This multistranded type of hat for diviners and spirit mediums (the most powerful of whom could be "rain priests") seems to have been common only among the eastern Shona speakers, because elsewhere fur and feathered hats are the norm for such religious officials.

Previously, the most important use of the gudza seems to have been as a blanket, and often people related that gudza-type blankets were used as burial shrouds. Earlier blankets and skirts often had raised designs woven into them. The usual decorations are geometric embellishments such as lines, zigzags, triangles, and chevrons—as are seen on a number of other Shona artifacts. None of the women still making objects of bark fiber in the 1980s and 1990s knew how to create this type of decoration.

Chief Dotito (Fourpence Majidza) in government-issued regalia, with chief's guard in khaki uniform, Muchanza Goto village, Zimbabwe, 1984. Photograph by William J. Dewey.

Mrs. Makamba is probably the most skilled bark fiber artist still practicing in the early twenty-first century. The fibers she uses are always very fine and uniform, her products are consistently well shaped, and she utilizes a range of colors to dye the fibers. Her working procedure involves taking inner bark fiber of the *mapfuti* (*Brachstegia boehmii*) tree and boiling it in a pot of water to which various types of ash are added to make the different colors. She then pounds the fiber in a mortar or chews it with her teeth to soften it. After she splits the bark fiber to the desired size, she rolls it on her leg to twist it before weaving. The weaving is done entirely by hand with no other tools. She starts with only two strands and adds more as she goes along, so in essence the technique is more like basket making or what is known as finger weaving. She says it would sometimes take up to a year to make a large blanket, because she only performs the activity part-time.

BEADWORK

While many people wore animal skins as loincloths and aprons in the nineteenth and early twentieth centuries, there also was, in the case of women's aprons, a good deal of beadwork decoration applied to the skins. A few examples of this type of beadwork on leather aprons can be seen in museums, and Thomas Baines, describing the dress of women in 1871, noted that "all have fore and after aprons of skins, either of sheep or goat or of the smaller antelopes, or sometimes of leopard or panther, the hair in the latter case being left on, while from the unornamental skins it is removed, and beads in triangles, vandykes or circles stitched on instead."

Another type of beaded ornament worn on top of women's heads is decorated with red, white, and black beads and is sometimes attached to a circular or oval leather backing. It is known to some as *shampopuri* and is made for use in *shave* (nature or foreigner) spirit dances. Others, however, said it was called *chamugo* and was not necessarily for shave spirits and sometimes just functioned as a head ornament. Black, white, and red are a common color triad throughout much of southern and central Africa and often are described as exhibiting a particularly Bantu set of symbolic associations. For the Shona, there are many different associations with the colors that depend on the contexts in which they are used. Red was frequently associated with blood, hunters, and menstruation; black and white are associated with good, evil, life, death, souls, and ancestors—with the meanings often switching depending on the context. In the context of objects and art forms, black was frequently described as a desirable quality, because it is the color associated with the ancestors.

These practices of using bead-ornamented skins and circular bead hair ornaments now, however, seem to be obsolete in the twenty-first century. Beadwork seems to be mostly restricted to necklaces and headgear primarily worn by diviners and spirit mediums. The favored color combinations for necklaces are red, white, and black or black and white. The hats used by diviners and spirit mediums are composed of either furry skins or ostrich feathers with a band of black and white beads arranged into triangular motifs and added to the forehead area.

COMMERCIAL CLOTH

Commercial cloth in distinctive colored patterns is more prominent in the twenty-first century than beadwork. There is archival evidence that cloth was imported for many centuries into the area through Portuguese and Swahili traders and their local intermediaries. What this cloth looked like and how widely it was distributed is unknown. In the twentieth century, there was a huge increase in the amount of cloth and clothing being imported into the area from a variety of European, Indian, and Asian sources. Later in the twentieth century, cloth and clothing also began to be manufactured locally by such well-known companies as David Whitehead.

Designs on printed cloth now include local flora and fauna, famous sites such as Great Zimbabwe Ruins and Victoria Falls, and political party logos and politicians. Of particular interest is *retso*, a commercially manufactured cotton cloth with a distinctive red, white, and black printed design on it that is in quite common usage throughout Shona-speaking areas. Many seemingly simple utilitarian tools have largely left the realm of utility and function as ceremonial emblems of the presence of ancestral spirits. Personal objects such as ceremonial knives and axes as well as snuff containers and headrests are distributed when a person dies in an important part of the inheritance ceremony. They not only are tangible objects once owned by the ancestors but serve as a conduit to them in prayers. People often bring such objects out and then address the ancestors by saying something like, "Grandfather, here is your headrest, this is what we are doing, and here are our problems." The commercially produced retso cloth serves the same function, declaring that the wearer acknowledges the presence and involvement of ancestral spirits in his or her life.

COLONIALISM AND WESTERN INFLUENCES

Clearly, colonialism and mission work had a great impact on the Shona, just as these forces did elsewhere around the world. Colonialism started relatively late in Zimbabwe, but with the defeat of Ndebele and Shona forces by Cecil Rhodes's British South Africa Company in the 1890s, colonial rule was imposed extremely quickly. Likewise, missions made quick progress in establishing stations and schools after the 1890s. Rhodes gave generous tracts of land to more than a dozen mission societies in the 1890s, and the country was neatly divided into areas of jurisdiction for the various Protestant and Catholic denominations. The colonial government did not want the responsibility of establishing an educational system for Africans and so encouraged the missions to do this. Another important development was the relatively large immigration of whites into what was then called Rhodesia—278,000 settlers at the peak of white population in 1975.

The quick transformation is depicted clearly in a 1924 hand-colored lantern slide used for mission fundraising in the United States by the Methodist World Service Commission. It shows Shona young women engaged in a "Course in Laundry Work," and all wear Western dresses. Even so-called traditional chiefs have been issued Western symbols of their positions of authority, including robes, medallions, pendants, and pith helmets. Western-style uniforms are commonly seen being worn by military, police, school children, and church women's organizations. Military-type khaki uniforms have also been adopted by African Independent Churches such as Guta re Jehovah (City of God). Weddings are often events in many cultures where traditional dress is worn. Among the Shona, however, although there are traditional wedding ceremonies, there are no types of dress associated with them. It is at the church or "white" wedding ceremonies (also seen in many other African countries) where there are huge outlays of money for Western-style suits and bridal gowns.

RITUAL WEAR

The exception to this almost total switch to Western dress is primarily in the religious realm. Spirit mediums always wear traditional-type hats such as those made of black ostrich feathers. Although Western-type clothing is worn underneath, these religious leaders insist that the manufactured textile capes or robes (usually black or black and white) they wear are traditional. The other categories of religious figures who wear traditional outfits are those affected or possessed by shave spirits. They are usually defined as wandering or outsider spirits such as animal or foreigner spirits and are associated with particular types of skills or behaviors. The accoutrements of a baboon shave spirit, for example, include a black and white skirt, and the possessed person will climb a tree like a baboon. There are many different kinds of shave spirits, but most wear accoutrements (beads, skirts, and capes) of various combinations of red, white, and black.

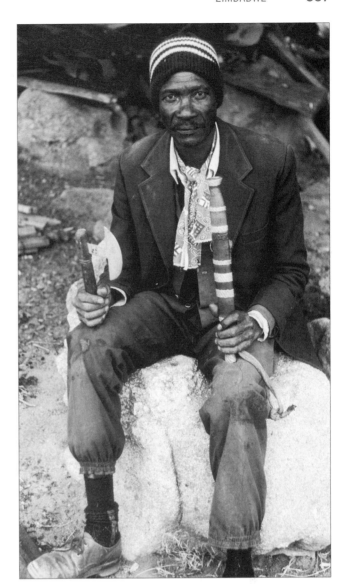

Shona blacksmith/carver Munyikwa Titiya, with ceremonial knife and axe in his hands and *retso* cloth around his neck, Makoni district, Zimbabwe, 1984. Photograph by William J. Dewey.

Diviners/healers and herbalists known as *n'angas* among the Shona also wear traditional headgear and skirts and capes of manufactured cloth in various combinations of red, black, and white. A red, white, and black cloth that n'angas favor features a lion as the central motif. The other type of cloth favored by spirit mediums and diviner/healers is the retso-type cloth already discussed. It is not only healers and diviners who use the retso cloth; family members wear it at spirit possession ceremonies known as *bira*. Artists also make use of the cloth. A blacksmith/carver named Munyikwa Titiya, for example, related how he became very ill when he was younger and no cure could be found for him. The spirit of his grandfather (who had been a blacksmith/carver) came to him in a dream and instructed him to take up this ancestral profession. He did that, put on the retso cloth, and was cured. In postindependence Zimbabwe, there is a renaissance of things related to the ancestors, and the popularity of retso cloth is part of this. *Retso* was defined in a 1959 dictionary as a "shave spirit cloth (black joined to another color)." But in the 1980s and 1990s, most people associated retso with the red, white, and black printed cloth and, more often than not, associated it with the ancestors rather than shave spirits.

FASHION DESIGN IN THE EARLY TWENTY-FIRST CENTURY

Zimbabwe has a relatively small fashion industry, being largely overshadowed by South Africa, its neighbor to the south. Some interesting developments, however, include the recent inauguration of the Miss Rural Zimbabwe Pageant, with one of its goals being to foster local fashion incorporating natural products and using locally manufactured cotton textiles. Also of interest is the Zimbabwe Council of Chiefs' expressed intention to redesign the uniform of chiefs and abandon the colonial-style pith helmets and capes that have been the norm for more than half a century. Fashion designers in Zimbabwe include such groups as Black Scissors, the Zuva Ecowear of Joyce Chimanye, Brighton Benhura's labels, Faithware, and African Designs. Currently, however, the future of Zimbabwean fashion design looks bleak; as the government-controlled newspaper, *The Herald*, reported on 7 February 2007, "Designers and other players in the fashion industry have described the fashion industry as moribund and operating at its lowest ebb as a result of insufficient funds, lack of support from the corporate world and the general public."

References and Further Reading

Baines, Thomas. *The Northern Goldfields Diaries of Thomas Baines. Second Journey 1871–72*, edited by P. R. Wallis. London: Chatto and Windus, 1946.

Beach, David N. *The Shona and Zimbabwe 900–1850: An Outline of Shona History*. London: Heineman, 1980.

Bent, James Theodore. *The Ruined Cities of Mashonaland*. 3rd ed. London: Longmans, Green, 1896.

Bhebe, Ngwabi, and Pathisa Nyathi. "Material Culture and Visual Traditions of the Ndebele." In *Legacies of Stone: Zimbabwe Past and Present*, vol. 1, edited by William J. Dewey and Els De Palmenaer, 147–160. Tervuren, Belgium: Royal Museum for Central Africa, 1997.

Bourdillon, Michael F.C. *The Shona Peoples*. Revised ed. Harare, Zimbabwe: Mambo Press, 1987.

Davidson, Patricia, and Patrick Harries. "Cotton Weaving in South-east Africa: Its History and Technology." In *Textiles of Africa*, edited by Dale Idiens and K.G. Ponting, 175–192. Bath, UK: Pasold Research Fund, 1980.

Dewey, William J., and Els De Palmenaer, eds. *Legacies of Stone: Zimbabwe Past and Present*. Vol. 1. Tervuren, Belgium: Royal Museum for Central Africa, 1997.

Garlake, Peter S. *Great Zimbabwe*. New York: Stein and Day, 1973.

Garlake, Peter S. *The Hunter's Vision: Prehistoric Art of Zimbabwe*. Harare, Zimbabwe: Zimbabwe Publishing House, 1995.

Hannan, Michael. *Standard Shona Dictionary*. Salisbury, Rhodesia: Literature Bureau, 1981.

Pikirayi, Innocent. *The Zimbabwe Culture: Origins and Decline in Southern Zimbabwean States*. Walnut Creek, CA: Altamira Press, 2001.

Reynolds, Barrie. *The Material Culture of the Peoples of the Gwembe Valley*. Manchester, UK: University Press, 1968.

Ruwitah, Aviton. *Pre-Colonial Cotton Production and Trade in the Zambezi and Save Valleys*. Harare, Zimbabwe: National Museums and Monuments of Zimbabwe, 1999.

Vickers, Steve. "Raunchy Dance to Sell Zimbabwe Culture." *BBC News*, 24 January 2007. http://news.bbc.co.uk/go/pr/fr/-/2/hi/africa/6248529.stm. (accessed 15 April 2009).

William J. Dewey

Index

Italic numbers denote reference to illustrations.